MICROELECTRONIC DEVICES AND CIRCUITS

McGraw-Hill Series in Electrical and Computer Engineering

Senior Consulting Editor

Stephen W. Director, *Carnegie Mellon University*

Circuits and Systems
Communications and Signal Processing
Computer Engineering
Control Theory
Electromagnetics
Electronics and VLSI Circuits
Introductory
Power and Energy
Radar and Antennas

Previous Consulting Editors

Ronald N. Bracewell, Colin Cherry, James F. Gibbons, Willis W. Harman, Hubert Heffner, Edward W. Herold, John G. Linvill, Simon Ramo, Ronald A. Rohrer, Anthony E. Siegman, Charles Susskind, Frederick E. Terman, John G. Truxal, Ernst Weber, and John R. Whinnery

Electronics and VLSI Circuits

Senior Consulting Editor
Stephen W. Director, *Carnegie Mellon University*

Consulting Editor
Richard C. Jaeger, *Auburn University*

Colclaser and Diehl-Nagle: *Materials and Devices for Electrical Engineers and Physicists*
Elliott: *Microlithography: Process Technology for IC Fabrication*
Fabricius: *Introduction to VLSI Design*
Ferendeci: *Physical Foundations of Solid State and Electron Devices*
Fonstad: *Microelectronic Devices and Circuits*
Franco: *Design with Operational Amplifiers and Analog Integrated Circuits*
Geiger, Allen, and Strader: *VLSI Design Techniques for Analog and Digital Circuits*
Grinich and Jackson: *Introduction to Integrated Circuits*
Hodges and Jackson: *Analysis and Design of Digital Integrated Circuits*
Huelsman: *Active and Passive Analog Filter Design: An Introduction*
Ismail and Fiez: *Analog VLSI: Signal and Information Processing*
Laker and Sansen: *Analog Integrated Circuits*
Long and Butner: *Gallium Arsenide Digital Integrated Circuit Design*
Millman and Grabel: *Microelectronics*
Millman and Halkias: *Integrated Electronics: Analog, Digital Circuits, and Systems*
Millman and Taub: *Pulse, Digital, and Switching Waveforms*
Offen: *VLSI Image Processing*
Roulston: *Bipolar Semiconductor Devices*
Ruska: *Microelectronic Processing: An Introduction to the Manufacture of Integrated Circuits*
Schilling and Belove: *Electronic Circuits: Discrete and Integrated*
Seraphim: *Principles of Electronic Packaging*
Singh: *Physics of Semiconductors and Their Heterostructures*
Singh: *Semiconductor Devices: An Introduction*
Smith: *Modern Communication Circuits*
Sze: *VLSI Technology*
Taub: *Digital Circuits and Microprocessors*
Taub and Schilling: *Digital Integrated Electronics*
Tsividis: *Operation and Modeling of the MOS Transistor*
Wait, Huelsman, and Korn: *Introduction to Operational and Amplifier Theory Applications*
Yang: *Microelectronic Devices*
Zambuto: *Semiconductor Devices*

MICROELECTRONIC DEVICES AND CIRCUITS

Clifton G. Fonstad
Department of Electrical Engineering and Computer Science
Massachusetts Institute of Technology

McGraw-Hill, Inc.

New York St. Louis San Francisco Auckland Bogotá
Caracas Lisbon London Madrid Mexico City Milan
Montreal New Delhi San Juan Singapore Sydney Tokyo Toronto

Dedicated to the memory of my father, Clifton G. Fonstad, Sr.

This book was set in Times Roman by Publication Services.
The editors were Anne T. Brown and John M. Morriss;
the production supervisor was Denise L. Puryear.
The cover was designed by John Hite.
Project supervision was done by Publication Services.
R. R. Donnelley & Sons Company was printer and binder.

MICROELECTRONIC DEVICES AND CIRCUITS

This book is printed on recycled, acid-free paper containing a minimum of 50% total recycled fiber with 10% postconsumer de-inked fiber.

1 2 3 4 5 6 7 8 9 0 DOC DOC 9 0 9 8 7 6 5 4 3

ISBN 0-07-021496-4

Library of Congress Cataloging-in-Publication Data

Fonstad, Clifton G.
Microelectronic devices and circuits / Clifton G. Fonstad.
p. cm. — (McGraw-Hill series in electrical and computer engineering. Electronics and VLSI circuits)
Includes index.
ISBN 0-07-021496-4
1. Microelectronics. 2. Electric circuit analysis. 3. Electric circuits, Nonlinear. I. Title. II. Series.
TK7874.F645 1994
621.381—dc20 93-32500

ABOUT THE AUTHOR

Clifton G. Fonstad is a full professor in the Department of Electrical Engineering and Computer Science at the Massachusetts Institute of Technology (MIT). He received his BS degree in 1965 from the University of Wisconsin, Madison, and his MS and Ph.D. degrees in 1966 and 1970, respectively, from MIT. He conducts a large and active graduate student research program concerned with the application of InGaAlAs heterostructures grown by molecular beam epitaxy in a variety of advanced electronic and optoelectronic devices. With his students he has authored or coauthored over 100 technical publications on such topics as heterojunction bipolar transistors, resonant tunneling diodes and three-terminal quantum-well-base tunnel-barrier devices, quantum well intersubband transitions, and semiconductor laser diodes. Professor Fonstad has taught the basic physics, modeling, and application of semiconductor devices for over 20 years at MIT, and for many years was responsible for the microelectronics teaching laboratory. He is currently in charge of Electronic Devices and Circuits, the header course of the Devices, Circuits, and Systems concentration in the Department's new 5-year Masters of Engineering curriculum. He is faculty supervisor of the MIT Center for Materials Science and Engineering Microelectronics Technologies Central Facility and serves as chairman of the MIT Microsystems Technology Laboratory Policy Board. He is also the project leader of a directed project on Very Large Scale Optoelectronic Integrated Circuits in the National Center for Integrated Photonics Technology. He is a member of the Institute of Electrical and Electronics Engineers and of the American Physical Society. Professor Fonstad enjoys woodworking and such outdoor activities as running, hiking, camping, and canoeing; he regularly commutes to and from MIT by bicycle.

CONTENTS

PREFACE

Most books exist because the authors felt that there were no other books that said what they felt needed to be said in the way they wanted to say it. I felt that a different book was needed, too, and this book is my attempt to fill that need. This text is "different" for what it does not include as well as for what it does include, and this uniqueness merits some discussion.

First, this text *does* span a range of topics from semiconductor physics to device function and modeling to circuit analysis and design. It is a basic premise of this text that it is important in a first course on semiconductor electronics to address this broad range of topics. Only in this way can we adequately emphasize from the beginning the interactions between physics, devices, and circuits in modern integrated system design.

Second, this text *does not* include, except as an appendix, semiconductor band theory or any of the associated theoretical baggage that implies (e.g., Fermi statistics, effective mass theory, etc.). It is another basic premise of this text that such material is best left for later, specialized courses and is in fact not necessary for a first, thorough treatment; you do not need to understand energy bands to understand *p-n* junctions, bipolar transistors, and FETs. As a consequence this text can be used by college sophomores who have had only a basic introduction to physics and circuits. More importantly, by teaching no more semiconductor physics than is necessary to understand the devices, this text can place more emphasis on actually developing this understanding.

Third, this text *does* take as its mission to teach the broader topic of modeling using semiconductor electronics as a vehicle. Therefore it is a text that should be of value to all engineering students. If you learn something about semiconductor electronics, so much the better, but you will certainly gain an appreciation of the issues inherent in developing and applying physical models.

At the same time, this text *does not* emphasize the use of sophisticated computer models. The focus here is instead on understanding and choosing between various approximate models to select one that might be suitable, for example, for a back-of-the-envelope calculation, estimation, and/or evaluation of a design concept. Computer models have their place and are extremely important for engineers, but in a text at this level they are more dangerous than anything else since they tend to work against developing the insight we seek.

Fifth, this text *does* include design, as well as analysis. Design is admittedly not a main focus, nor is much time devoted specifically to it, but some design excercises are included, and a design experience is recommended as a complement to any course based on this text. Only through the exercise of design—of, for example, choosing a circuit topology and, given a topology, selecting component values to achieve certain performance goals—can the lessons of this text be truly learned.

Sixth, this text *does not* attempt to be the final word on any of the topics it addresses. It presents a correct first treatment and imparts a functional level of knowledge, but it is also only preparation for a second tier of specialization, be it in physics, devices, circuits, and/or systems, that surely must follow.

Seventh, this text *does* contain much more material than can be covered in any one course; yet, eighth, an instructor using this text *does not* have to use all of this material, nor, in fact, does he or she have to use it in the order it appears in the table of contents. I have attempted to write this text in such a way that it is possible to use many different subsets and orderings of the material, and in such a way that discussions of more advanced modeling and of more specialized and less pervasive devices can be skipped over without loss of continuity. (Please see "Comments on Using This Text" below for more on these points.)

Also, this text *does* have its roots in a long legacy of semiconductor electronics education at MIT, and none of the preceding litany of do's and don'ts are claimed to be original to this text. In 1960 the Semiconductor Electronics Education Committee (SEEC) was formed under the leadership of MIT faculty members to address the question of undergraduate electrical engineering education in light of the dramatic changes that were then taking place in the field of electronics with the advent of the silicon transistor and integrated-circuit technology. An important product of that effort was an appreciation for the close coupling between semiconductor physics, device modeling, and circuit analysis and for the value of teaching these topics in a coherent unit. The SEEC produced an excellent, very carefully written series of seven paperback volumes and led indirectly to the publication of a textbook: *Electronic Principles—Physics, Models, and Circuits* by Paul E. Gray and Campbell L. Searle (Wiley, New York, 1969). The present text unashamedly builds upon these SEEC foundations. It addresses a similarly broad range of topics at a similarly accessible level, differing primarily only in that it does so in a way that reflects the field of semiconductor electronics as it exists now over 30 years after SEEC (i.e., in the 1990s).

COMMENTS ON USING THIS TEXT

As stated earlier, I have attempted to write this text in such a way that it is possible to use many different subsets and orderings of the material, and I have used it to teach the subject 6.012—Electronic Devices and Circuits at MIT following several topic sequences. The order in which the material appears in this text is a relatively traditional one and it works well. It does, however, mean that circuits are discussed only after a considerable amount of time has been spent on physics and devices. A convenient, timely way to get circuits in sooner is to present the MOSFET before the BJT, and to discuss MOS logic circuits right after finishing the MOSFET. When doing this, I have found that it is useful to follow the text through the reverse biased *p-n* diode (Section 7.2) so the depletion approximation has been introduced, and to then go to Chapters 9, 10, and 15 before returning to Chapter 7 and continuing with Section 7.3.

Chapters 14 and 16 contain material that can also be presented earlier with good effect. One can easily argue that all of the material in these chapters could have been integrated into the earlier device and circuits chapters, but I resisted doing this because I feel it is useful to have the discussions of frequency response collected in one place; the same is true of the switching transients discussions. Having said this, however, I do usually include the discussion of switching times of MOSFET inverters with the discussion of their other characteristics. Another example is the switching transient of a *p-n* diode, which is a good issue to discuss soon after teaching diode current flow. The fact that there are plenty of carriers to sustain a reverse current immediately after a diode has been switched from forward to reverse bias is easy to see, and it reinforces the students' understanding of current flow in a diode.

Finally, it is important to realize that we are unable to cover all of the material in this text in our one-semester course at MIT. Typically, we wait until a senior-level device elective to cover the more advanced device models; to discuss JFETs and MESFETs, optoelectronic devices, memory, and bipolar logic; and to cover much of the discussion of large signal switching transients. I recommend considering the following topics and sections (section numbers in parentheses) when you are looking for material to delete or de-emphasize: physics issues such as high-level injection solutions (3.2.3) and certain boundary conditions (5.2.3 c–e); advanced models for diodes (7.4.1b), BJTs (8.2.1b), and MOSFETs (10.1.1b); and certain more specialized or less pervasive devices such as photoconductors (3.3), photodiodes (7.5), LEDs (7.6), phototransistors (8.3), JFETs (10.2), MESFETs (10.3), memory cells (15.4), and charge-coupled devices (16.2.2b). If, on the other hand, you are looking to expand upon, or add to, any of the material in the main text, there is ample material in the appendices presented at much the same level on energy bands, Fermi statistics, and the effective mass picture (Appendix C), on metal-semiconductor junctions (Appendix E), and on processing (Appendix G).

ACKNOWLEDGMENTS

First and foremost, I thank my wife, Carmenza, and my sons, Nils and Diego, for their support, tolerance, and love throughout this project.

The present text reflects very much the philosophy of the late Professor Richard B. Adler, who had a great influence on me since the day I first set foot on the MIT campus. Many others, including Professors A. C. Smith, R. F. Morgenthaler, D. J. Epstein, and R. H. Kyhl, have also taught me a great deal about this material and how to teach it over the years, and I gratefully acknowledge their influence and impact on me and this text.

I also thank my colleagues at MIT, especially Jesus del Alamo, Dimitri Antoniadis, Jim Chung, Martha Gray, Leslie Kolodziejski, Harry Lee, Marty Schlecht, and Charlie Sodini, who have taught from these notes and/or who have set me straight on various issues, for their many constructive comments and suggestions. Thanks are also due to the many students who have used these notes in classes for their numerous helpful student's-eye-view comments. A particular thank you to Tracy Adams for the many hours she spent going through much of the near-final version. My thanks also to Angela Odoardi, Charmaine Cudjoe-Flanders, Karen Chenausky, and Kelley Donovan for their enormous help translating my scrawl into a presentable manuscript.

In addition, McGraw-Hill and I would like to thank the following reviewers for their many helpful comments and suggestions: Scott E. Beck, formerly of University of Arizona; currently at Air Products in Allentown, PA; Dorthea E. Burke, University of Florida; John D. Cressler, Auburn University; Robert B. Darling, University of Washington; William Eisenstadt, University of Florida; Eugene Fabricus, California Polytechnic Institute; Mohammed Ismail, Ohio State University; J. B. Kreer, Michigan State University; M. A. Littlejohn, North Carolina State University; Gerald Neudeck, Purdue University; and Andrew Robinson, formerly of University of Michigan; currently with Advanced Technology Laboratories in Bothell, WA.

Finally, I welcome further comments, suggestions, or corrections from users of this text; I invite you to communicate with me by electronic mail (fonstad@mtl.mit.edu).

Clifton G. Fonstad

CHAPTER 1

MODELING

The title of this text is *Microelectronic Devices and Circuits*, but it is really a book about modeling. Inevitably, this focus will tend to be neglected as we concentrate on learning how semiconductor diodes and transistors work and how they are used in analog and digital circuits. Thus, it is important that we start with a few comments on models and on our hidden agenda.

1.1 GENERAL COMMENTS

You are familiar with models for circuit components—resistors, capacitors, inductors, wires—and you have learned that, for example, the terminal current-voltage relationship of a real resistor that you might get from a stockroom or buy at an electronics store may be represented, or modeled, by an "ideal" resistor for which $v_{RR'} = i_R R$, where $v_{RR'}$ is the voltage difference between the two terminals of the resistor, i_R is the current into the positive reference terminal (and out the negative terminal), and R is the resistance of the resistor, in units of ohms (Ω). We tend to think of this model when we encounter an actual resistor, and the distinction between a real resistor and the model becomes blurred. This is all right as long as we do not lose sight of the fact that $v = iR$ is just a model, and that as such it has limitations. For example, if we change the temperature of a resistor, its R value will change, and at very high current levels, the variation of voltage with current is no longer linear, in part because of internal heating. An important part of learning a model is learning its limitations, and an important part of using a model is remembering that it has limitations and knowing what they are.

In this text, one of our objectives is to develop accurate models with as few limitations as possible. We also want models that are useful. By "useful" we mean models that are analytical and, often, that are easy to use in hand calculations. We also mean models that are conceptual and through which we can gain insight into problems. Not surprisingly, the two objectives of utility and accuracy are not always consistent, and compromises usually must be made. This often leads to a hierarchy of models for a device, ranging from the very simple and approximate to the very precise and complex. An important part of modeling and analysis is knowing which model to use when.

The real value of a good model is that it lets us predict performance. It lets us improve, modify, and apply; it lets us design new things, not just analyze old ones; and it provides a high degree of confidence that what we design will work. The most successful models are founded on an understanding of the physical processes at work in what is being modeled. Such models are conducive to the development of physical insight, and they are essential for predicting the unknown.

To illustrate the importance of understanding the physics of a process in order to develop useful models for it, we can look at two examples where the physics is not yet understood, and thus for which models capable of predicting performance do not exist: high-temperature superconductivity and cold fusion. In the first instance, people ask, "Can we make a room-temperature superconductor? If not room temperature, how high?" We cannot even pretend to answer these questions without understanding the basic mechanism behind the lack of resistance in the new "high-temperature" superconductors. The same is true for cold fusion. We cannot predict whether test-tube fusion will be a useful source of energy, nor can we begin to improve upon the minuscule amounts of energy produced thus far without understanding the physics of the phenomenon, that is, without a model for it.

As a final example, let us look at models for our planet and at how those models evolved. Hundreds of years ago, many fairly isolated civilizations existed, all of which had developed models for the universe. In the Western European civilization there were two competing models: the flat-earth model and the round-earth model. There was also a great deal of interest among businessmen in developing trade with the Chinese, Indian, and other Far Eastern civilizations; and depending on which model of the earth you believed in, you saw different possibilities for getting to the Far East. According to both models, you could go directly east over land, but that was known to be both dangerous and difficult. Both models also indicated that you might be able to sail along the coast of Africa, but this journey was also very dangerous. The round-earth model suggested a third route, namely, west. According to the model subscribed to by Columbus, sailing due west would be a long, but practical, way of getting to the Far East.

On the one hand, the model Columbus used, which was based on a better physical understanding of the solar system, was the more correct; it gave him the confidence to sail west from Spain without fear of sailing off the edge of the earth into an abyss. On the other hand, the model had some serious flaws and needed to be modified. For one thing, the model didn't include North and South America, but that was not a fatal flaw. More important for Columbus, his model didn't use the right diameter for the earth, so he thought the Far East would be a lot closer than it was. At that time many scientists thought the earth was bigger than Columbus did; and, ironically, if Columbus had believed the big-earth advocates (who were right, after all), he might not have even tried to sail west, since he could not have carried all of the provisions needed on the ships then available. The colonization of America might have been delayed a few years, but bigger boats and a belief in the round-earth model would eventually have led someone to sail west.

Today we know that the earth is round and we know how big it is, but how often do we use the round-earth model in daily life? For most of what we do, a flat-earth model is perfectly adequate and much easier to work with. Mathematically, we recognize that the flat-earth model is a linear approximation to the round-earth model, valid for motion in our immediate vicinity. In circuit jargon, we would call it a small-signal, or incremental, linear equivalent model for the earth.

There are many different models for the earth, ranging from a flat slab to an infinitesimal point, and each has utility in the right situation. One of the important things to learn about modeling is how to trade off complexity and accuracy, and how to choose the appropriate model for the task at hand.

1.2 EMPIRICAL DEVICE MODELS

Consider the bipolar transistor. You are familiar with its terminal characteristics, shown in Fig 1.1, and with the large-signal and incremental models for the bipolar transistor, shown in Fig 1.2. You might legitimately ask, "Don't I know enough? Why do I need to bother with a lot of physics and spend an entire semester learning more about transistor models?"

The problem is that so far these models are only empirical. We got the large-signal model by measuring a device's characteristics and then mathematically fitting those measured characteristics to an ad hoc collection of ideal circuit components—model building blocks, if you will—that give the same behavior of terminal currents and voltages. In general, more than one combination of components will give the same terminal characteristics, but experience with several devices and a little common sense helps us select a model topology that doesn't

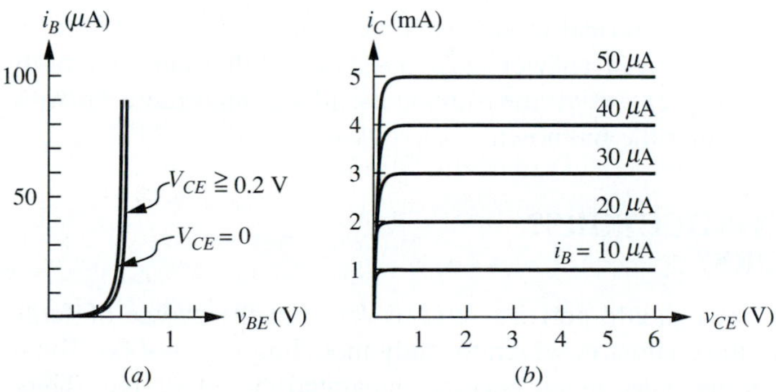

FIGURE 1.1
Input (*a*) and output (*b*) families of terminal characteristics for an *npn* bipolar junction transistor (BJT).

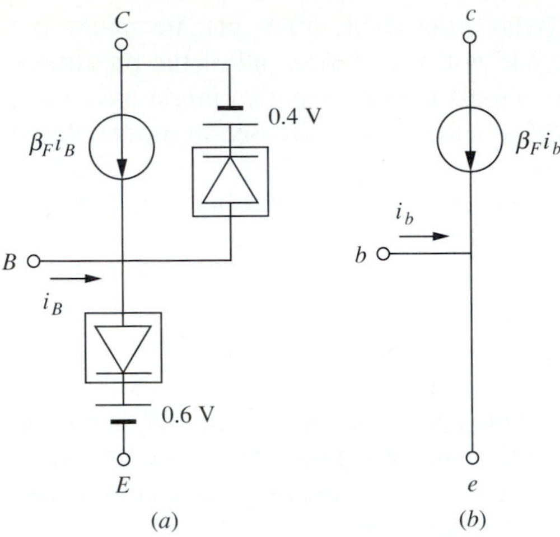

FIGURE 1.2
Large-signal (*a*) and incremental (*b*) circuit models for the terminal characteristics of an *npn* bipolar junction transistor.

change dramatically from device to device, a topology that somehow "fits" the bipolar transistor. We may develop confidence that our model is "right" for the bipolar transistor, but it is purely empirical, with only a fortuitous connection at best to the internal workings of the device. Based on this model, we have no way of knowing if, for example, there is any way of changing the diode breakpoint values of 0.6 V and 0.4 V. We don't know what determines β and how it can be changed, what happens if the temperature is raised or lowered, or whether the device will work at 1 GHz or with 100 A of collector current. We don't even know whether we have to ask such questions or if there are other, more important questions we should be asking. With empirical modeling, what you've seen is what you've got, and if you want to try something new, you have to take some new measurements.

We want to go beyond empirical modeling to develop models based on the physics of devices so that we can answer such questions with some generality and confidence, before doing extensive measurements. More important, we want models that will let us predict the unknown.

1.3 WHY SEMICONDUCTORS? WHY TRANSISTORS?

The need to learn modeling should now be clear to you, but the choice of semiconductor transistors as the context in which to study modeling may not be. Today electronic system design has very much become integrated circuit design. Thus, whereas at one time an engineer could specialize either in devices or in circuits or in systems, it is now impossible to separate systems from the semiconductors used to realize them. Now more than ever it is essential that engineers dealing with electronic devices, circuits, or systems at any level have the basic familiarity with semiconductors and transistors that this text provides.

In addition, there is an elegance in the modeling of semiconductor transistors and in the hierarchy of models that exists for them that makes this a very satisfying subject to learn. Many students actually end up enjoying this material.

CHAPTER 2

UNIFORM SEMICONDUCTORS IN EQUILIBRIUM

We begin our exploration of semiconductors with a discussion of thermal equilibrium, a concept that is very important to understand and very powerful to use. We will then look at semiconductors in thermal equilibrium and discuss how to modify their charge carrier populations in useful ways.

2.1 THERMAL EQUILIBRIUM

Thermal equilibrium is not easy to define in precise language, and a course in thermodynamics is really needed to quantify the concept, but our purposes require no more than basic understanding. The following description should help you develop an intuitive feel for the concept of thermal equilibrium.

When we speak of an object being "in thermal equilibrium with its surroundings," we mean that it has the same temperature as its surroundings (which must, in turn, all be at one temperature) and, furthermore, that it is completely free of external stimulation. It is not being heated or cooled, it is not being illuminated, it is not being influenced by an electric or magnetic field, and it is not being pushed by the wind. It gives as much energy to every object with which it interacts as it receives from that object, and there is no net change in its condition over time. It just is.

Example

Question. Consider a bucket of water sitting with you on the floor in a closed room. Assume the room is at a comfortable 291 K (18°C or 65°F), and the water and bucket are also at 291 K. Is the water in thermal equilibrium?

Discussion. If the lights are on or if there is light coming in through an open window, the bucket is not in thermal equilibrium because the light source is at a much higher temperature than 18°C, and the water is being warmed by that light. The water may well be losing heat to the room, which is in turn losing heat to the outside, and the temperature of the whole ensemble may remain essentially constant, but the water is not in thermal equilibrium.

What if you cover the windows and turn out the lights? That is a big improvement but you are still in the room. You are hotter than 18°C, and you are a source of energy that is heating the water.

What if you leave the room? Can we now assume that the bucket is in thermal equilibrium? Probably, but be careful. It sounds like nothing is happening, but in fact the water, bucket, and surroundings are all seething with activity. The atoms and molecules that make up these materials are all vibrating rapidly. Still, that is no reason to say that the bucket of water is not in thermal equilibrium. This motion is, after all, what is involved in being at a finite temperature. An object in thermal equilibrium with its surroundings is not changing with time in a global or average sense, but that is not inconsistent with motion of individual, indistinguishable atoms, electrons, or bonds. There must simply be no *net* motion of any of these particles.

If you were to check on the bucket of water a month later, you would find that most of the water had evaporated from the bucket. Some would be in the air (i.e., it would be more humid in the room), some would be adsorbed on surfaces of the room or absorbed in them (depending on what they were made of), and some might be on the floor. Clearly, the water and bucket were not in thermal equilibrium in an absolute sense when you left the room a month earlier. Are they now? The answer really depends on the room and, more important, on how strictly thermal equilibrium is defined. It will never be in absolute thermal equilibrium—not in your lifetime, anyway—but it may be close enough.

The important lesson to be learned here about modeling is that every model has limitations, and none is perfect, but all you really need is one that is close enough for the task at hand. For the example of the bucket of water, we should have been asking not "Is it in thermal equilibrium?" but rather "Can it be modeled as being in thermal equilibrium?" And to answer that question, we have to know why we are modeling the bucket of water in the first place. For some applications, the fact that the bucket was illuminated and someone was in the room with it would be insignificant, and treating it as if it were in thermal equilibrium would be entirely satisfactory. In others—say, an experiment that took two years—it may never be possible to assume that it is in thermal equilibrium.

To summarize, we say that an object is in thermal equilibrium if it is "free" of all external stimulation. Recognizing that an object will always have surroundings and that its having a finite temperature means that its constituent atoms are in constant random motion, we understand that no practical object can ever be in strict thermal equilibrium, yet we also understand that in many instances an object will be close enough.

To progress further, we need to understand more about the reason for having a concept of thermal equilibrium. The answer is that thermal equilibrium is useful as a reference point, a baseline. It represents a condition we can define and use as a starting point for modeling what happens to semiconductors when we apply external stimulations. That is what we really care about, of course: semiconductors that have been shaped into devices and that have voltages applied, currents flowing, heat and light exciting them—and that are doing something useful. They certainly are not in thermal equilibrium, but to understand them we first have to understand semiconductors in thermal equilibrium.

2.2 INTRINSIC SILICON

One of the simplest semiconductors, and by far the most important, is single-crystal silicon, Si. Silicon is element 14 in the periodic table and has four outer bonding electrons. It forms a covalent crystal in which each atom shares its four outer electrons with its four nearest neighbors. Physically, each silicon atom in a silicon crystal is at the center of a tetrahedron of four other silicon atoms; this arrangement is illustrated in Fig. 2.1. The extended crystal structure arising from this local arrangement is illustrated in Fig. 2.2. It consists of two interwoven face-centered cubic lattices, or crystal structures, one of which is shifted a quarter of the way along the cube diagonal with respect to the other lattice. To help you see this, a single face-centered cubic lattice is illustrated in Fig. 2.3*a*, and in Fig. 2.3*b* the two sublattices forming the silicon lattice are shown. The arrows in Fig. 2.3*b* are provided to help you visualize the quarter shift; notice that although the arrows show a shift along one particular body diagonal, the structure can just as well be viewed as having been formed by a shift along either of the two other body diagonals. The crystal in Fig. 2.2 is called the diamond lattice, because this structure was originally identified as the form of crystalline carbon called diamond.

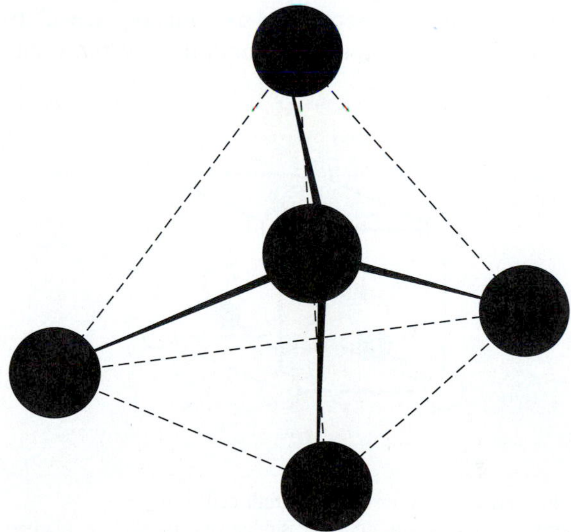

FIGURE 2.1
Representative silicon atom with its four nearest neighbors. The circles represent the atoms, the solid lines indicate covalent bonds, and the dashed lines outline the tetrahedral shape.

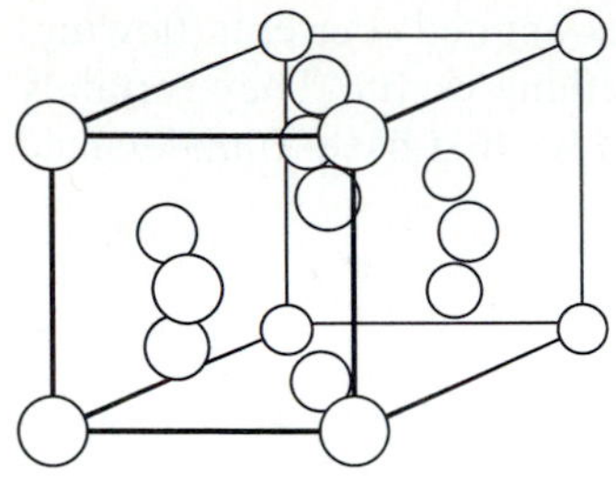

FIGURE 2.2
The unit cell of the diamond lattice. This cell repeated in all directions forms the extended silicon crystal. The unit cell is approximately 5.43 Å on a side in silicon (see App. A for data on other semiconductors), and there are roughly 5×10^{22} Si atoms per cubic centimeter.

Drawing three-dimensional pictures of a silicon lattice can be difficult, tedious, and confusing, so we often use a flat representation, as illustrated in Fig. 2.4, realizing full well that this model does not display the spatial arrangement of the atoms. It is, however, perfectly adequate for counting and locating the electrons. In the flat model of the silicon lattice in Fig. 2.4, the circles represent the Si nucleus and the inner two shells of 10 electrons (the "ion core"). It thus has a net charge of $+4q$, where q is 1.6×10^{-19} C. The lines in Fig. 2.4 each represent one bonding electron in a covalent bond between two Si atoms. These electrons each have a charge of $-q$, and the entire structure is electrically neutral. In a perfect silicon crystal in thermal equilibrium at 0 K (i.e., at absolute zero temperature), all of the electrons either are in one of the inner atomic energy levels or are participating in the bonding. No electrons are free to move about the crystal, and the material is insulating.

An important property of semiconductors is that electrons can be removed from the covalent bonds by supplying sufficient energy and can thus be "freed" to move about within the crystal. Once an electron can move about the crystal, it can

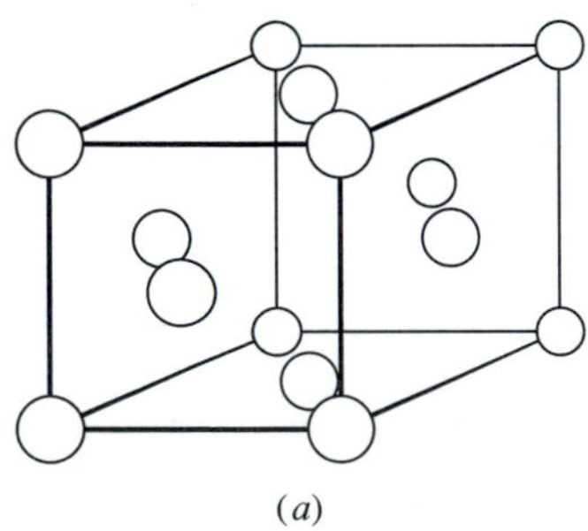

(*a*)

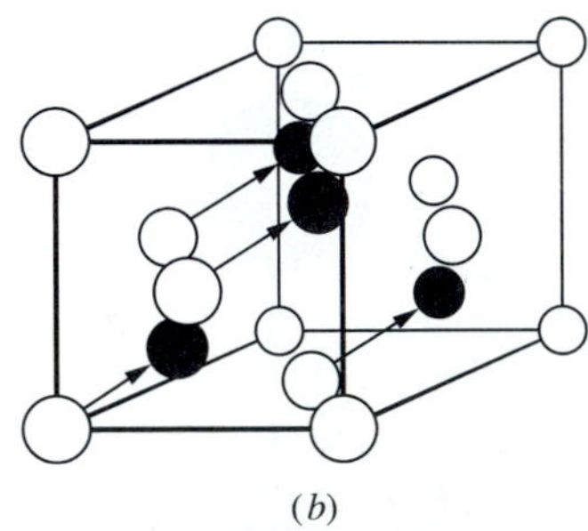

(*b*)

FIGURE 2.3
(*a*) The unit cell of the face-centered cubic crystal structure. (*b*) The unit cell of the diamond structure, showing the two interwoven face-centered cubic sublattices. In the diamond structure both sublattices are composed of the same atomic species; if the sublattices are composed of different elements, this is called the zinc-blend structure. Note that only the atoms of the second sublattice (black atoms) falling within the unit cell of the first sublattice (white atoms) are shown.

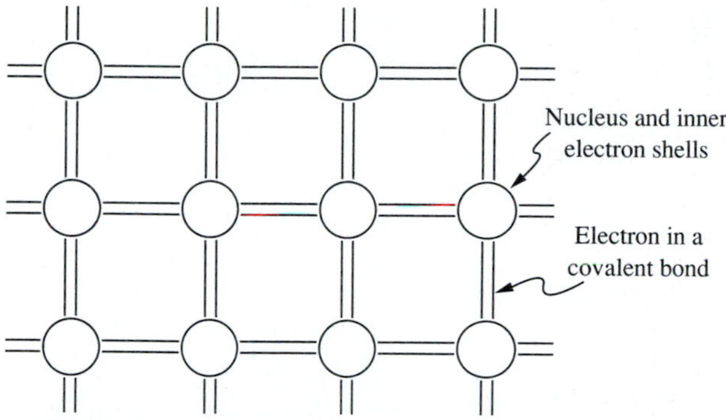

FIGURE 2.4
A two-dimensional representation of the diamond lattice. Each line represents a shared electron in a covalent bond. Each circle represents a nucleus with its inner two shells of electrons.

carry electric charge from one place to another—that is, it can produce current—and this is very much of interest to electrical engineers, as well as others.

In a useful semiconductor, it takes a substantial amount of energy to free an electron from a bond. By "substantial" we mean much more energy than is available from the normal thermal motion of the ion cores in the crystal. This latter energy is on the order of kT, where k is Boltzmann's constant, 8.62×10^{-5} eV/K, and T is temperature. At room temperature, kT is approximately 0.025 eV or, 1/40 eV. (This is an important number to remember, as you will use it repeatedly when working with semiconductor devices.)

In silicon it takes a minimum of 1.124 eV of energy to "free" an electron from a bond so that it can move about the crystal and conduct (i.e., carry current). To visualize this, refer to Fig. 2.5, where the number of allowed energy locations or levels for electrons is plotted as a function of the energy of the electrons occupying them. The electrons in the covalent bonds are in a set of energies called the *valence band*. The inner-core-level electrons are at still lower energies (not shown in the figure). Electrons free to conduct are in a set of energy levels called the *conduction band*. They are at a higher energy and separated from the valence band by 1.124 eV in Si. This separation is called the *energy gap*, or *bandgap*, and designated ΔE_g. (For a more thorough, quantitative discussion of the band model, refer to App. C, Sec. C.1.)

At a temperature greater than absolute zero, the electrons in bonds continually exchange energy with the ion cores (nuclei and their inner electron shells) of the crystal lattice, which are vibrating with their thermal energy. That is, after all, what it means for the crystal to be at a temperature greater than absolute zero; it means that we have put energy, thermal energy, into the crystal. The energy of an average ion or electron in the crystal is on the order of kT, but some have much less energy and some much more. In fact, a small fraction of the electrons acquire enough energy through collisions with other electrons and ions to move from the valence band to the conduction band.

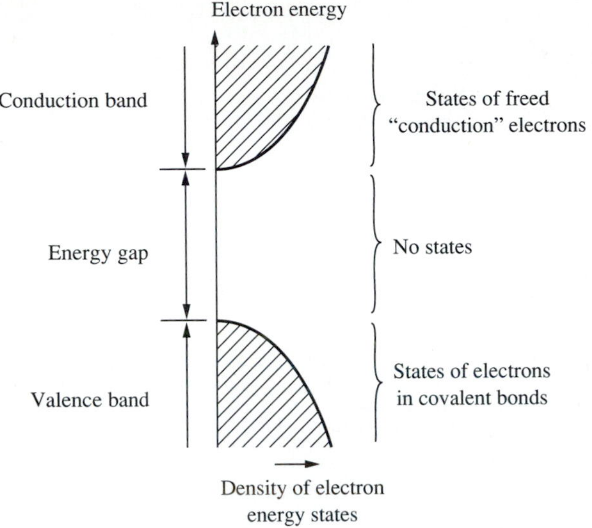

FIGURE 2.5
Schematic plot of the density of states available to electrons about the energy gap of a semiconductor as a function of electron energy.

At the same time that some electrons are getting enough energy to be freed from their bonds, other electrons already in the conduction band suffer collisions, giving up their extra energy and falling back into an empty bond. The process is a very dynamic one, with bonds continually being broken and reformed, even though the crystal is in thermal equilibrium. Over a period of time the average number of electrons in the conduction band depends on the temperature and on the size of the energy gap. In intrinsic silicon at room temperature an average of 1.08×10^{10} electrons per cubic centimeter are in the conduction band. This sounds like a large number, until one realizes that there are over 10^{22} electrons per cubic centimeter in bonds. Thus, only one in a trillion (10^{12}) of the outer electrons have gotten enough energy to move from the valence to conduction band. Electrically, as we shall see in Chap. 3, the crystal is still effectively an insulator.

Thus far we have focused on the electrons, but in semiconductors it is equally important to look at the empty bonds left when an electron is excited up to the conduction band. The electron has a negative charge of $-q$, where q is 1.6×10^{-19} C, so that removing an electron from a previously neutral bond leaves an empty bond that has associated with it a positive charge of $+q$. The interesting thing is that the empty bond can also move about the crystal and transport electricity. An electron in a neighboring bond can move over into the empty bond with little or no additional energy, as illustrated in Fig. 2.6. The empty bond is thus effectively "moved" over to the position of the neighboring bond. It is an electron that has moved, but it is much easier to keep track of the empty bond, since there are so few of them, than to keep track of the

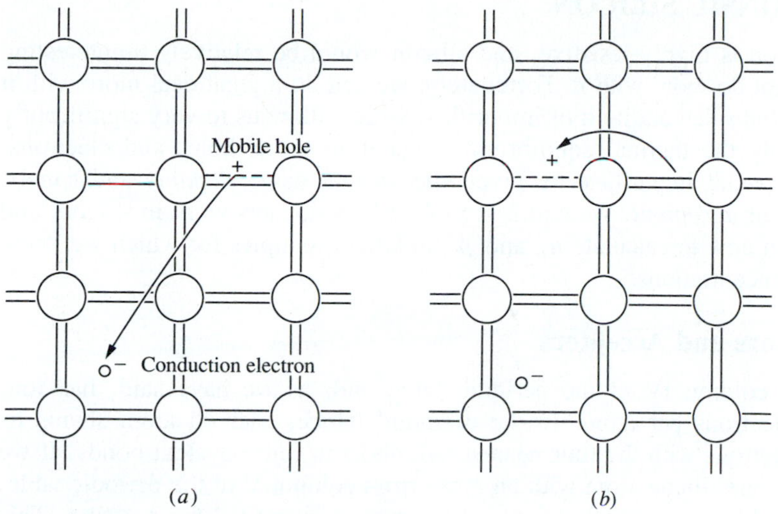

FIGURE 2.6
(*a*) The formation of a hole-electron pair through excitation of an electron from a valence bond to a conducting state. (*b*) The motion of a hole through the change in location of an unfilled valence bond.

bonding electrons. As the empty bond moves, the net positive charge associated with it also moves. Amazingly, this empty bond, which we call a *hole*, can be modeled very nicely as a particle itself, a particle similar to an electron but with a positive mass and a positive charge, $+q$ (see App. C, Sec. C.2).

Thus, when an electron is excited from the valence band to the conduction band, two particles that can carry electrical current are "created." One is a conduction electron, which we will generally call just an electron, and the other is a hole. We will denote the concentration of electrons per cubic centimeter as n and the concentration of holes as p. We will add the subscript o to these symbols to denote their values in thermal equilibrium. Thus, n_o and p_o are the thermal equilibrium concentrations of electrons and holes, respectively. The unit we will use for concentrations is cm^{-3}.

In a perfect crystal of pure silicon, electrons and holes can only be created in pairs, since for every electron freed there is an empty bond left behind, and their concentrations are equal (i.e., $n_o = p_o$). Such a perfect, pure crystal is called *intrinsic*, and the carrier concentrations in an intrinsic semiconductor are equal to what is called the intrinsic carrier concentration, denoted by n_i. As already indicated, n_i in silicon at room temperature is 1.08×10^{10} cm^{-3}. The intrinsic carrier concentration is a very sensitive, exponential function of temperature, and thus it is very important to state the temperature. Unless otherwise specified, we will be concerned with operation at room temperature, or roughly 300 K.

To summarize, in an intrinsic semiconductor,

$$n_o = p_o = n_i(T) \tag{2.1}$$

2.3 EXTRINSIC SILICON

Intrinsic silicon is highly resistive, and silicon would be relatively uninteresting if we could not do more with it. Fortunately, we can do a great deal more with it through the controlled addition of impurities, which allow us to vary significantly and predictably the thermal equilibrium concentrations of holes and electrons. These very special impurities are given the special name *dopants* and can be either *donors* or *acceptors*. We will first look at how dopants work in silicon, and then will learn how to calculate n_o and p_o in silicon samples for which we know the dopant concentrations.

2.3.1 Donors and Acceptors

Silicon is in column IV of the periodic table and, as we have said, has four outer-shell electrons per atom. In the diamond lattice, each Si atom shares its four outer electrons with the four nearest neighbors in four covalent bonds. If we could replace one silicon atom with an atom from column V of the periodic table, that atom would have one more outer electron than is needed for bonding. This situation is illustrated schematically in Fig. 2.7*a*. This atom also has one more positive charge on its nucleus than does Si, so the dopant atom is electrically neutral overall, but it is the presure of the "extra" outer electron that is important to us. It is not a priori obvious that an arbitrary atom from column V can be put into the silicon lattice in this manner, but it turns out that phosphorous (P),

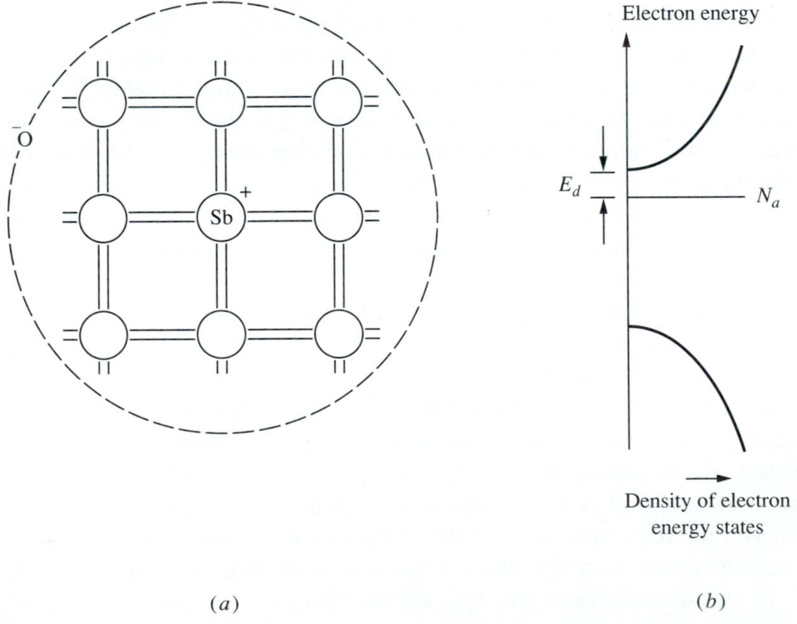

FIGURE 2.7
(*a*) An antimony donor atom substitutionally located in a silicon lattice electron. (*b*) The location on an electron energy scale of the fifth electron on a donor atom.

arsenic (As), and antimony (Sb) atoms can be substituted for silicon atoms in a Si crystal; nitrogen (N) atoms, on the other hand, cannot.

The next question is where on the energy scale the extra electron associated with a substitutional column V dopant lies. It turns out for P, As, and Sb dopant atoms that the electron's energy is approximately 50 meV below the bottom edge of the conduction band. This is illustrated in Fig. 2.7*b*. If this electron gets just 50 meV of additional energy, perhaps from vibrations of the crystal lattice, it can be excited to the conduction band and freed to move about the crystal; it is then indistinguishable from any other conduction electron. Notice an important difference, however, from the situation where a conduction electron is created by breaking a covalent bond. In that situation a mobile electron and a mobile hole are created. Now a mobile electron is created, but the positive charge associated with the column V ion is fixed in place; it cannot move.

Elements that can be put substitutionally into a semiconductor lattice and that then have electrons at energies where they can be easily excited into the conduction band are called *donors*. The energy needed is called the *donor ionization energy* E_d, and a donor whose electron has been excited into the conduction band is said to be *ionized*. It has a net charge of $+q$. Donors of practical interest in silicon, such as P, As, and Sb, are termed *shallow* donors. They have ionization energies sufficiently low that, at concentrations of interest in devices, they will be ionized at room temperature. That is to say, if a silicon crystal contains N_d shallow donor atoms per cubic centimeter, then almost all will be ionized at room temperature, and the density of ionized donor ions, N_d^+, will be essentially N_d:

$$N_d^+ \approx N_d \tag{2.2}$$

Logically, the next question is what are n_o and p_o, the thermal equilibrium hole and electron concentrations, in a silicon crystal doped with a known concentration of donors, N_d. We cannot answer this question yet, but because each conduction electron came either from a donor or from a valence bond, we can say that the concentration of mobile electrons, n_o, must equal the concentration of holes, p_o, plus the concentration of ionized donors:

$$n_o = p_o + N_d^+ \tag{2.3}$$

Using Eq. (2.2), we also know that

$$n_o \approx p_o + N_d \tag{2.4}$$

Before proceeding with the determination of n_o and p_o, let us consider what would happen if instead of putting impurities from column V into the Si crystal, we put in impurities from column III. A column III atom—boron, for instance—has only three outer electrons; thus, although it will be electrically neutral if put substitutionally into a silicon lattice, it will not be able to fill one of the four covalent bonds it is expected to make with its four nearest neighbors (see Fig. 2.8*a*). What happens is perhaps more difficult to visualize than the case for a donor, but the situation is analogous, and in this case it is a mobile hole that can be readily created. The column III dopant introduces a new energy level for electrons just above the valence band, as pictured in Fig. 2.8*b*. An electron in a covalent bond that gets enough energy, about 50 meV in the case of boron in silicon, can form the missing bond of the dopant. That electron is now located spatially in the vicinity of the dopant atom, and a hole is created that can move about the crystal. In this case the dopant is called an *acceptor*, and it is said to be ionized. The energy the electron had to acquire is the *acceptor ionization energy*, E_a, and the ionized acceptor has a net charge of $-q$ associated with it.

Useful acceptors are shallow and have ionization energies small enough that at room temperature all of them will be ionized. Thus, if the shallow acceptor concentration is N_a, we have

$$N_a^- \approx N_a \tag{2.5}$$

In silicon, the most useful acceptor dopant is boron (B). Of the other possibilities, indium (In) is not good because its ionization energy is too large, aluminum (Al) is not good because it oxidizes too readily and is difficult to work with as a dopant, and gallium (Ga) is too hard to introduce into silicon in a controlled way.

As was the case with donors, we cannot yet say what n_o and p_o are given N_a, but we can get one equation relating these two unknowns:

$$n_o + N_a^- = p_o \tag{2.6}$$

Using Eq. (2.5), we have

$$n_o + N_a \approx p_o \tag{2.7}$$

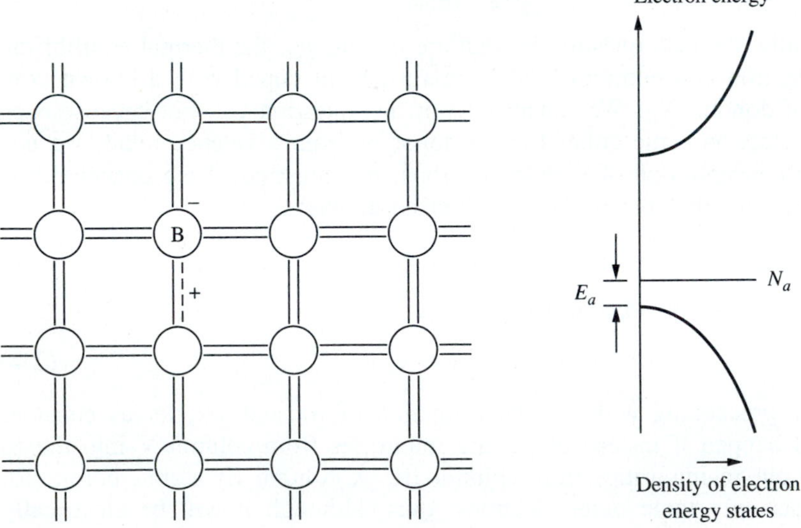

FIGURE 2.8
(*a*) A boron acceptor atom substitutionally located in a silicon lattice with its unfilled bond, or hole. (*b*) The location on the electron energy scale of the unfilled bonding electron sites.

In a crystal with both donor and acceptor atoms present, we can do the same bookkeeping or charge concentration accounting. The total number of electrons in the conduction band, n_o, and on ionized acceptors, N_a^-, must equal the number of empty bonds (i.e., holes), p_o plus the number of ionized donors, N_d^+:

$$n_o + N_a^- = p_o + N_d^+ \tag{2.8}$$

Unless otherwise specified, we can assume that the donors and acceptors are shallow and completely ionized. Thus, using Eqs. (2.2) and (2.5),

$$n_o + N_a \approx p_o + N_d \tag{2.9}$$

This can also be written as

$$n_o - p_o \approx N_d - N_a \tag{2.10}$$

We define $N_d - N_a$ as the net donor concentration N_D. At times it is convenient to also define a net acceptor concentration N_A, as $N_a - N_d$. Thus,

$$N_D \equiv N_d - N_a \tag{2.11}$$

and

$$N_A \equiv N_a - N_d \tag{2.12}$$

2.3.2 Detailed Balance

We are trying to find n_o and p_o in a crystal of silicon for which we know N_d and N_a, and thus far we have one equation, Eq. (2.10). We need another equation. To get it, we need to understand the principle of detailed balance and what this principle means for holes and electrons in semiconductors.

To proceed we will look in even more detail at what is happening inside a doped, or "extrinsic," silicon crystal in thermal equilibrium. We have mentioned several times that a crystal in thermal equilibrium is seething with activity. The constituent atoms are vibrating about their nominal locations within the crystal; pairs of holes and electrons are continually being created as bonds are being broken and simultaneously electrons and holes are combining to reform covalent bonds; and the conduction electrons and holes are moving randomly about the crystal. There is no net motion of charge, and there is no net change in n_o or p_o, but microscopically there is continual motion and continual change. A very dynamic equilibrium exists.

Look for a moment at the carrier generation processes. We can think of three processes that might be occurring, and we can represent them using a notation familiar from chemistry:

$$\text{Completed bond} \leftrightarrows \text{Hole} + \text{Electron}$$

$$\text{Neutral donor} \leftrightarrows \text{Ionized donor} + \text{Electron}$$

$$\text{Neutral acceptor} \leftrightarrows \text{Ionized acceptor} + \text{Hole}$$

Focus now on the first process, hole-electron pair generation and recombination, and consider what more we might be able to say about it. Begin with the generation process,

$$\text{Covalent bond} \rightarrow \text{Hole} + \text{Electron}$$

and define a generation rate $G(T)$, which is the rate, in number per cubic centimeter per second ($\text{cm}^{-3} \cdot \text{s}^{-1}$), at which electrons are being excited from covalent bonds to the conduction band, that is, the rate at which hole-electron pairs are being created. We expect G to be a function of temperature.

Although we have mentioned only energy from lattice vibrations as the source of the approximately 1.1 eV needed in Si to create a hole-electron pair, there are many other ways this energy can be acquired. Some are intrinsic, involving just the silicon lattice; some are extrinsic and involve impurities or defects in the crystal; and some are external, involving external stimulation. (Clearly, these external processes must not be present in thermal equilibrium.)

Consider some possible intrinsic processes. One is generation due solely to thermal energy in the lattice (i.e., vibrations), and we can denote this as $G_{\text{th}}(T)$. Another involves absorption of optical energy, $G_{\text{op}}(T)$. You may not be used to thinking of objects at room temperature as emitting light, but just as a red-hot object glows visibly, objects at room temperature are glowing—that is, radiating—albeit very weakly and primarily too far into the infrared region for us to see their radiation. Still, there are some quanta of light (photons) that are energetic enough to excite electrons from the valence band to the conduction band.

Still other generation paths might involve a combination of lattice vibrations (we call them phonons) and light quanta (photons). Generation might be caused by one phonon and one photon, $G_{c1}(T)$; by two phonons and one photon, $G_{c2}(T)$; or by i phonons and one photon, $G_{ci}(T)$.

The total generation rate $G(T)$ is the sum of all of these and any other intrinsic generation rates, the extrinsic generation rates, and the external generation rates:

$$\begin{aligned} G(T) &= G_{\text{th}}(T) + G_{\text{op}}(T) + \sum_i G_{ci}(T) + \sum G_{\text{other intrinsic}} \\ &\quad + \sum G_{\text{extrinsic}} + \sum G_{\text{external}} \end{aligned} \tag{2.13}$$

For each of these generation mechanisms there is a corresponding recombination mechanism. Defining $R(T)$ as the recombination rate ($\text{cm}^{-3} \cdot \text{s}^{-1}$), we can immediately write

$$\begin{aligned} R(T) &= R_{\text{th}}(T) + R_{\text{op}}(T) + \sum_i R_{ci}(T) + \sum R_{\text{other intrinsic}} \\ &\quad + \sum R_{\text{extrinsic}} + \sum R_{\text{external}} \end{aligned} \tag{2.14}$$

For example, $R_{\text{th}}(T)$ is the rate of recombination with all of the energy involved being given to the lattice as thermal energy, (i.e., phonons), $R_{\text{op}}(T)$ is recombination where the energy is released as a quantum of light (i.e., a photon), and so on.

Next we want to consider how we can relate G and R to the carrier populations, n and p.

For generation we argue that G will be independent of n and p as long as there are plenty of covalent bonds left to break and lots of room in the conduction band for electrons to go. That is, we restrict ourselves to situations where the density of broken bonds, p, is much smaller than the total density of bonds, roughly 10^{22} cm^{-3}, and where the density of conduction electrons, n, is much smaller than the total number of conduction sites, again roughly 10^{22} cm^{-3}. In this case $G(T)$ is not a function of n and p.

R, on the other hand, must depend on n and p because, clearly, we must have at least one hole and one electron for recombination to occur. Thus, we must have at least $R(T, n, p)$. But we can say more. For n and p small, we must have

$$R(T, n, p) = r(T)np \tag{2.15}$$

One way to understand this is to think of forming a Taylor's series expansion of $R(T, n, p)$ in terms of n and p. We would have

$$\begin{aligned} R(T, n, p) = &A + Bn + Cp + Dn^2 + Ep^2 + Fnp + Gn^3 \\ &+ Hp^3 + In^2p + Jnp^2 + \text{still higher-order terms} \end{aligned} \tag{2.16}$$

All of the coefficients of terms not involving both n and p (i.e., A, B, C, D, E, G, H, etc.) must be zero because R must be zero if either n or p is zero. The first nonzero term is the second-order term, Fnp. If n and p are sufficiently small, we can stop the expansion there and ignore In^2p, Jnp^2, and all higher-order terms. This gives us Eq. (2.15).

Next we restrict ourselves to thermal equilibrium and to finding n_o and p_o. In thermal equilibrium there will be no net change in p_o and n_o with time, so generation must equal recombination, that is,

$$G_o(T) = R_o(T) = n_o p_o r(T) \tag{2.17}$$

Note that we have added a subscript o to denote thermal equilibrium.

Equation (2.17) says that the total generation equals the total recombination, but by the *principle of detailed balance* we can say even more. This principle states that each individual recombination and generation process must balance. That is,

$$\begin{aligned} G_{\text{th}} &= R_{\text{th}} = n_o p_o r_{\text{th}} \\ G_{\text{op}} &= R_{\text{op}} = n_o p_o r_{\text{op}} \\ G_{ci} &= R_{ci} = n_o p_o r_{ci} \end{aligned} \tag{2.18}$$

and so on. If this were not true, some pretty nonsensical things might happen. Suppose, for example, that we had a sample in which every process was balanced except for the intrinsic optical process and the intrinsic thermal process:

$$G_{\text{th}} + G_{\text{op}} + \sum_{\text{other}} G = R_{\text{th}} + R_{\text{op}} + \sum_{\text{other}} R \tag{2.19}$$

with $\sum_{\text{other}} G = \sum_{\text{other}} R$, but $G_{\text{th}} \neq R_{\text{th}}$ and $G_{\text{op}} \neq R_{\text{op}}$. We are left with

$$G_{\text{th}} + G_{\text{op}} = R_{\text{th}} + R_{\text{op}} \tag{2.20}$$

Suppose for the sake of discussion that $G_{\text{op}} > R_{\text{op}}$, and that, as must then also be true, $G_{\text{th}} < R_{\text{th}}$. This implies that more optical energy is being absorbed by the sample than is being emitted, while more thermal energy is being given to the crystal lattice than is being absorbed from it. Thus, the sample absorbs optical energy from its surroundings and heats up. This is nonsense if the sample is supposed to be in thermal equilibrium with its surroundings. We conclude that the only way we can avoid inconsistencies such as this is to insist on detailed balance of all of the processes. Clearly, we must have $G_{\text{th}} = R_{\text{th}}$, $G_{\text{op}} = R_{\text{op}}$, $G_{ci} = R_{ci}$, and so forth in thermal equilibrium.

This is the result we need to find n_o and p_o. There are many generation-recombination processes that do not involve donors and acceptors and thus do not change with the addition of dopants. For such processes, $G_j(T)$ and $r_j(T)$ are unchanged by the addition of dopants, and we will have

$$G_j(T) = n_o p_o r_j(T) \tag{2.21}$$

We argued earlier, however, that adding dopants changed n_o and p_o. What we see now is that they may change, but their product must not. At a given temperature, the product $n_o p_o$ must be independent of N_a and N_d.

Another way to see that the product $n_o p_o$ must be independent of doping is to think of the process of hole-electron pair generation and recombination as a chemical reaction:

$$\text{Complete bond} \rightleftarrows \text{Hole} + \text{Electron}$$

and use the law of mass action, which says that in equilibrium

$$\frac{[\text{Hole}][\text{Electron}]}{[\text{Completed bond}]} = K(T)$$

where the brackets indicate concentration and $K(T)$ is the mass action constant. The hole concentration is p_o, and the electron concentration is n_o. Thus, we have

$$p_o n_o = K(T)[\text{Completed bond}]$$

and we see again that the product $n_o p_o$ is independent of doping (i.e., of the individual values of n_o and p_o), as long as the concentration of completed covalent bonds is not reduced noticeably.

To evaluate $n_o p_o$, recall that we know what n_o and p_o are in one special case, namely, in intrinsic silicon. In intrinsic silicon, $n_o = p_o = n_i$. Clearly, then, in this case and in general,

$$n_o p_o = n_i^2(T) \tag{2.22}$$

This is our second equation relating n_o and p_o. It is valid as long as n_o and p_o are much smaller than 10^{22} cm^{-3}. A safe limit is 10^{19} cm^{-3} in silicon.

2.3.3 Equilibrium Carrier Concentration

By combining Eqs. (2.10) and (2.22) we obtain a quadratic equation. Assuming for the moment that N_d is greater than N_a, so that we have $(N_d - N_a) \equiv N_D > 0$, we find that solving the quadratic equation yields

$$n_o = \frac{N_D}{2} + \frac{N_D}{2}\sqrt{1 + \frac{4n_i^2}{N_D^2}} \tag{2.23}$$

and

$$p_o = -\frac{N_D}{2} + \frac{N_D}{2}\sqrt{1 + \frac{4n_i^2}{N_D^2}} \tag{2.24}$$

As a practical matter, it will almost always be the case that $N_D \gg n_i$, in which case these expressions can be simplified to

$$n_o \approx N_D + \frac{n_i^2}{N_D} \approx N_D \tag{2.25}$$

and

$$p_o = \frac{n_i^2}{n_o} \approx \frac{n_i^2}{N_D} \tag{2.26}$$

Looking at this result we see that n_o is indeed greatly increased over its value in intrinsic material, whereas p_o is suppressed correspondingly. The mobile carriers are thus predominantly electrons, and we say that the sample is an *extrinsic n-type* semiconductor. The electrons are called the *majority carriers*, and the holes are called the *minority carriers* in an *n*-type semiconductor.

If, on the other hand, N_a is greater than N_d and $N_A \gg n_i$, then

$$p_o \approx N_A \tag{2.27}$$

$$n_o = \frac{n_i^2}{p_o} \approx \frac{n_i^2}{N_A} \tag{2.28}$$

In this case the hole population is greatly increased over n_i, and the electron population is suppressed. The predominant mobile charge carriers are holes, and the semiconductor is said to be an *extrinsic p-type*. In a *p*-type semiconductor, holes are the majority carrier and electrons are the minority carrier.

Example

Question. Consider a sample of silicon that contains 5×10^{17} cm^{-3} boron atoms and 8×10^{16} cm^{-3} arsenic atoms. What are the equilibrium hole and electron concentrations in this sample at room temperature?

Discussion. Boron is in column III of the periodic table and is thus an acceptor, and arsenic is in column V and is a donor. Thus N_a is 5×10^{17} cm^{-3} and N_d is 8×10^{16} cm^{-3}; since N_a is greater than N_d, we see that we have a net acceptor concentration N_A, of 4.2×10^{17} cm^{-3}. Thus the sample is *p*-type, holes are the majority carrier, and the equilibrium hole concentration p_o is approximately N_A. That is,

$$p_o = 4.2 \times 10^{17} \text{ cm}^{-3}$$

The equilibrium minority carrier (i.e., electron) concentration n_o, is given by Eq. (2.28). In silicon at room temperature, the intrinsic carrier concentration n_i is 10^{10} cm^{-3}, and n_i^2 is roughly 10^{20} cm^{-3}. We thus find that

$$n_o = 2.4 \times 10^2 \text{ cm}^{-3}$$

Notice that p_o is much greater than n_i in this extrinsic, *p*-type sample, whereas n_o is much, much less than n_i.

2.4 ADDITIONAL SEMICONDUCTORS

Although silicon is by far the most widely used semiconductor, there are many other materials, both elements and compounds, that are semiconductors. Many are widely used in applications where silicon is not suitable, and we will have the opportunity to mention some of these applications as we study various devices.

2.4.1 Elemental Semiconductors

The column IV elements, carbon, silicon, germanium and tin, can all form diamond structure crystals, and all except tin are semiconductors. After Si, germanium is the most important. The energy gap of Ge is 0.7 eV. Much of the early research and development of semiconductor devices was done using Ge because it was initially easier to grow single crystals of Ge than of Si. Eventually, however, the lower sensitivity to temperature of Si and, more importantly, its advantageous processing features made it the material of choice.

Today germanium is used primarily in infrared optical detectors and in power diodes and transistors. Ge is used for infrared detectors because it has a much smaller bandgap than silicon, which makes it sensitive to lower-energy, longer-wavelength light. In power device applications, Ge's smaller bandgap is also useful because it leads to a lower *p-n* diode forward turn-on voltage than the usual 0.6 or 0.7 V seen in Si diodes. The charge carriers in Ge are also more mobile than in Si, which is also an advantage, especially in high power devices. You will be in a much better position to appreciate these facts after we discuss diodes and transistors in later chapters.

2.4.2 Compound Semiconductors

Many compounds are semiconductors, but the most important are those formed of elements from columns III and V of the periodic table and, to a lesser extent, from columns II and VI. We speak of these as III-V ("three-five") and II-VI ("two-six") semiconductors, respectively. We will concentrate here on the III-V's, but much of what we will say extends in very obvious ways to the II-VI's; key properties of many members of both families of materials are listed in Table A.2 of App. A.

The III-V's are of practical interest in part because the conduction electrons are in general more mobile in them than in silicon, so the III-V's offer the possibility of producing faster devices. Furthermore, they tend to be more useful than silicon for many optical device applications. When holes and electrons recombine in many III-V compounds, the energy that is released is given up primarily as light, rather than thermal energy as with silicon. This makes these III-V's useful for making light-emitting diodes and laser diodes. It then becomes desirable to make other devices (i.e., transistors, detectors, modulators, etc.) from these same materials so that all the devices in an integrated system can be made of a common material or family of materials.

The III-V's and most of the II-VI's crystallize into a zinc-blend structure, named after the II-VI compound zinc sulfide, ZnS. We have already seen this structure in Fig. 2.3*b*. In a zinc-blend lattice, each of the face-centered cubic sublattices in the diamond structure is composed of a different element. For example, in the III-V compound gallium arsenide, GaAs, one of the sublattices is made of gallium atoms and the other is made of arsenic atoms.

Any of the elements in the middle part of column III of the periodic table [i.e., aluminum (Al), gallium (Ga), and indium (In)] can be combined with an element from column V [i.e., phosphorus (P), arsenic (As), and antimony (Sb)] to form a useful III-V compound semiconductor. Since they involve two elements, these III-V's are also called *binary compounds*, or simply *binaries*. Of the nine possible binaries that can be formed from the elements just listed, the most important is gallium arsenide. It is widely used in high-frequency transistors for high-speed logic and communications, and in infrared laser diodes for compact disc players and fiber optics systems.

The spectrum of possible III-V compounds is greatly enlarged by the fact that binary compounds can be mixed to form ternary and quaternary compounds with properties intermediary between those of the constituent binaries. A common example is the ternary aluminum gallium arsenide, $(AlAs)_x(GaAs)_{1-x}$, or, as it is more usually written, $Al_xGa_{1-x}As$, where x is between 0 and 1. The energy gap of $Al_xGa_{1-x}As$ falls between that of GaAs and AlAs, and, in a fortuitous twist of fate, all of these compounds have the same crystal size, that is, the same lattice constant. This makes it possible to fabricate $Al_xGa_{1-x}As$ layered structures on GaAs without worrying whether the crystals fit well together. The resulting structures, termed *heterostructures*, can be used to great advantage in designing advanced device structures with significantly higher performance than achievable with a single semiconductor.

Other ternary compounds, however, do not in general have a lattice constant that is invariant with composition, and in order to produce lattice-matched heterostructures a fourth element must be added, yielding a quaternary. One example is indium gallium arsenide phosphide, $In_xGa_{1-x}As_yP_{1-y}$, which can be used to produce heterostructures on indium phosphide, InP. This material system is of interest because it has band-gaps with lower energies than those of $Al_xGa_{1-x}As$.

It can thus be used in laser diodes emitting at longer wavelengths, where glass fibers are the most transparent and have their minimum dispersion. Materials in this quaternary system also have highly mobile conduction electrons and have been used to produce devices that operate even faster than do gallium arsenide-based devices.

We will only occasionally mention III-V compounds from now on in this text, and we will not deal at all with heterostructure devices—not because these topics are so complicated, but simply because there is only so much that a first electronic devices and circuits text should attempt to cover. Once you master the material and concepts presented here, their extension to new materials, and even to heterostructures, will be easy.

2.5 THE EFFECTS OF CHANGING TEMPERATURE

The semiconductors used in most modern electronic devices and integrated circuits (primarily silicon, but also germanium, gallium arsenide, and others) have been chosen and engineered for use at room temperature. This means, as we have discussed with respect to extrinsic silicon, that they have energy gaps that are large enough for the intrinsic carrier concentration at room temperature to be sufficiently small that, without dopants, the semiconductor is effectively an insulator. It also means that the ionization energies of the chosen dopants are small enough that the dopants are totally ionized at room temperature. Thus, for example, boron is used in silicon when an acceptor is desired, whereas indium, another column III element, is not. The ionization energy of indium in Si is too large, and only a small fraction of the indium atoms in a Si crystal are ionized at room temperature. The semiconductors we use in room-temperature applications tend to have energy gaps greater than roughly 0.5 eV. If the energy gap is much smaller, the intrinsic carrier concentration will be too high and will dominate over any impurities we might introduce, making it impossible to make the material either strongly *n*- or *p*-type rather than simply intrinsic.

Now that we understand that semiconductors must be chosen and engineered (i.e., designed) for use in specific temperature ranges, we need to understand what happens to these materials as we change the temperature significantly from the "design" value. We will continue to focus on room temperature in most of our discussions without quantifying the effects of temperature change, but we do want to have at least a qualitative understanding of what happens. We will consider an extrinsic silicon sample and look first at decreasing, and then increasing, its temperature.

As the temperature is decreased, our assumption that all of the donors and acceptors are ionized eventually becomes invalid, and Eqs. (2.2) and (2.5) can no longer be used. They must be replaced by more accurate relationships derived from statistical mechanics (see App. C, Sec. C.1). But this is the only change that must be made. It remains true that the product $n_o \cdot p_o$ is n_i^2. (Note, however, that n_i is much lower at lower T, as the next paragraph shows.) Furthermore, our expressions for the equilibrium carrier concentrations, Eqs. (2.25) and (2.26) for n-type material and Eqs. (2.27) and (2.28) for p-type, remain valid if the net donor and acceptor concentrations, respectively, are replaced by the net ionized donor and net ionized acceptor concentrations, and if the proper value of the intrinsic carrier concentration is used. Reexamination of these equations will show you that if the donors and acceptors are not fully ionized, the equilibrium carrier concentrations will be lower than if the dopants were fully ionized. This loss of mobile carriers to un-ionized dopant atoms as temperature is lowered is termed *freeze-out*.

As the temperature is increased above the extrinsic temperature region (room temperature in the present example), we must be concerned about the intrinsic carrier concentration n_i. This concentration is a very sensitive function of temperature, which statistical mechanics teaches us can be written approximately as

$$n_i(T) = AT^{3/2} \exp\left(\frac{-E_g}{2kT}\right) \tag{2.29a}$$

where A is some constant and E_g is the energy gap. It is sometimes convenient to write this in terms of n_i at room temperature (300 K):

$$n_i(T) = n_i(300 \text{ K})\left(\frac{T}{300}\right)^{3/2} \exp\left\{-\left[E_g\left(\frac{1}{2kT} - \frac{1}{600k}\right)\right]\right\} \tag{2.29b}$$

In either form, we see that as temperature increases, the intrinsic carrier concentration increases exponentially and will eventually exceed the net doping concentration (donor or acceptor) and the sample will no longer appear extrinsic. Both the equilibrium hole and electron concentrations again approach n_i, and the material becomes intrinsic, and, as we shall see, useless for devices. In silicon this situation does not occur until very high temperatures, but in germanium, for example, which has a much smaller energy gap ΔE_g, this may occur at several hundred degrees centigrade.

The variation of the equilibrium majority carrier concentration as function of temperature in a generic semiconductor can be summarized by the graph in Fig. 2.9. The asymptotic dependences of the concentration on temperature in each of the three regions, freeze-out, extrinsic, and intrinsic, are indicated. Our objective in designing devices is to choose materials that operate in their extrinsic regime for the intended device applications.

2.6 SUMMARY

We have seen in this chapter that there are two types of mobile charge carriers in semiconductors, holes and electrons, and that we can engineer the dominant carrier type and its concentration by adding specific impurities, called dopants, to semiconductor crystals. An important conclusion we reached was that the product of the hole and electron concentrations, p_o and n_o, respectively, in thermal equilibrium is n_i^2, where n_i is the intrinsic carrier concentration. That is,

$$n_o \cdot p_o = n_i^2(T)$$

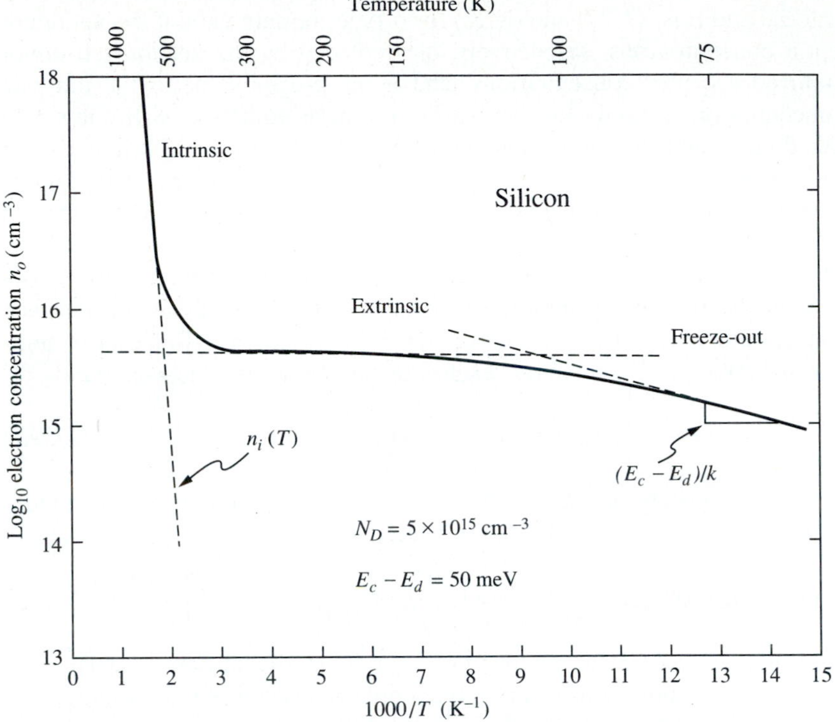

FIGURE 2.9
Variation of the equilibrium electron concentration over a wide temperature range for a representative n-doped semiconductor sample. The vertical axis is a logarithmic scale; the horizontal axis is inverse temperature, $1/T$. With this choice of axes the asymptotic behavior of the carrier concentration is linear in each of the three regions: freeze-out, extrinsic, and intrinsic.

This result, combined with the requirement of charge conservation,

$$n_o + N_a^- = p_o + N_d^+$$

allows us to determine n_o and p_o given the donor and acceptor concentrations. Assuming full ionization, we have

$$n\text{-type}: \qquad n_o \approx N_D, \qquad p_o = \frac{n_i^2}{n_o}, \qquad \text{with } N_D \equiv N_d - N_a$$

$$p\text{-type}: \qquad p_o \approx N_A, \qquad n_o = \frac{n_i^2}{p_o}, \qquad \text{with } N_A \equiv N_a - N_d$$

Our focus has been on silicon at room temperature, but we have also seen that there are numerous other semiconductors, many of which are of great practical interest and importance. Some of these are single elements from column IV of the periodic table (e.g., Ge) but the largest number are based on binary compounds formed of elements from columns III and V or from columns II and VI. Binary compounds can be used alone (e.g., GaAs and CdTe) or alloyed with other binaries to form ternary and quaternary semiconductors (e.g., $Al_xGa_{1-x}As$ and $In_xGa_{1-x}As_yP_{1-y}$).

Finally, we have seen the features of silicon and its dopants that make it attractive for use around room temperature, and we have discussed qualitatively what to expect as the temperature is increased above or decreased below room temperature.

PROBLEMS

2.1 A sample of silicon is uniformly doped with 10^{16} arsenic atoms per cm^3 and 5×10^{15} boron atoms per cm^3. Using this information and assuming n_i is 10^{10} cm^{-3} at 300 K determine the following items for this sample at $T \approx 300$ K:

(a) The type (n or p)

(b) The majority carrier concentration

(c) The minority carrier concentration

Repeat parts (a) and (b) when

(d) The sample instead contains 10^{17} cm^{-3} Al and 10^{16} cm^{-3} Sb

(e) The sample instead contains 10^{15} cm^{-3} Ga and 5×10^{15} cm^{-3} B

2.2 *(a)* A germanium ($n_i = 2.4 \times 10^{13}$ cm^{-3} at 300 K) sample is doped with 6×10^{16} cm^{-3} arsenic atoms (donors).

(i) What are n_o and p_o at 300 K in this sample?

(ii) An additional 10^{18} cm^{-3} gallium atoms (acceptors) are added to this specimen. What are the new n_o and p_o? (*Note*: Assume full ionization.)

(b) Determine the carrier type of a sample of the covalent semiconductor indium phosphide, InP, containing the following substitutional impurities:

(i) Te substituting for P

(ii) Be substituting for In

(iii) Si substituting for P

(iv) Si substituting for In

2.3 *(a)* An intrinsic semiconductor has the following characteristics: intrinsic carrier concentration n_i, electron mobility μ_e, and hole mobility μ_h; where $\mu_e > \mu_h$. When this semiconductor is doped with a certain impurity, it is found that its conductivity initially *decreases* as the doping concentration is increased. It eventually increases, however, as still more dopant is added.

(i) What type of impurity is being added: donor or acceptor?

(ii) Find an expression for the initial rate of change of conductivity with dopant concentration (i.e., find the initial value of $d\sigma/dN$). You will find that the answer depends in a simple way on the difference between the two mobilities.

(b) The intrinsic carrier concentration n_i varies with temperature as

$$T^{3/2}\exp(-E_g/2kT)$$

where $k = 8.62 \times 10^{-5}$ eV/K.

(i) Calculate n_i for Ge at the following temperatures given that $n_i = 2.4 \times 10^{13}$ cm^{-3} at 300 K. Neglect any change of E_g with T, and assume $E_g = 0.67$ eV.

(a) $-23°$ C (250 K)

(b) $127°$ C (400 K)

(c) $327°$ C (600 K)

(ii) At which of the temperatures in part (i) would a Ge sample with $N_D = 1 \times 10^{16}$ cm^{-3} be considered "extrinsic"?

(iii) Which of the factors in the expression for n_i dominates its temperature dependence?

2.4 How large must $|N|/n_i$ be in order for the minority carrier concentration to be less than 10 percent of the majority density? Less than 1 percent?

2.5 Consider an n-type silicon sample at room temperature. It is known that n_o in this sample is 5×10^{16} cm^{-3}. It is also known that this sample contains arsenic in a concentration of 6×10^{16} cm^{-3}.

(a) This sample is known to also contain one other impurity, either phosphorus or boron.

(i) Which impurity is it and why?

(ii) What is the concentration of this impurity?

(b) What is the room-temperature thermal-equilibrium hole concentration in this sample? Assume $n_i = 1.0 \times 10^{10}$ cm^{-3}.

2.6 One important model for a substitutional donor atom (P, As, or Sb) in silicon is the *hydrogenic donor* model. In this model it is assumed that the "extra" fifth electron and the positively charged donor ion can be modeled much like the electron and positively charged ion (proton) of a hydrogen atom. The only necessary modifications are that the dielectric constant must be changed from that of free space to that of the semiconductor, and the mass of the electron must be changed from that of a free electron to that of an electron in the semiconductor.

The binding energy and orbital radius of the electron in a hydrogen atom are given by

$$E_o = \frac{q^4 m_o}{8h^2 \varepsilon_o^2} = 13.6 \text{ eV}$$

$$r_o = \frac{h^2 \varepsilon_o}{\pi q m_o} = 0.53 \text{ Å}$$

(a) Use this information to calculate the binding energy and the orbital radius of the electron associated with a hydrogenic donor (i.e., a donor that can be described by the hydrogenic model). In silicon, $m_e/m_o = 0.26$ and $\varepsilon/\varepsilon_o = 11.7$.

(b) How does the orbital radius compare with the space between Si atoms in the lattice, which is approximately 2.5 Å? How many silicon atoms would be encompassed by the sphere defined by the orbital radius? The unit cube (cell) of the Si lattice is 5.43 Å on a side, and there are eight atoms per unit cell.

(c) At what density of donor atoms would the orbital spheres of their electrons begin to overlap?

2.7 Silicon is an interesting dopant for gallium arsenide, an important compound semiconductor. If Si replaces Ga in the crystal, it acts like a donor; if it replaces As it is an acceptor. Which site it occupies depends on how the dopant was introduced and the thermal history of the sample. Heat-treating the sample can also cause some of the Si to move from As to Ga sites, or vice versa, depending on the temperature.

(a) A certain sample of gallium arsenide, GaAs, is known to contain 5×10^{17} cm^{-3} Si atoms and to be n-type with a net donor concentration of 3×10^{17} cm^{-3}. What is the concentration of Si atoms on Ga sites (i.e., N_d), and what is the concentration on As sites (i.e., N_a)?

(b) Suppose that after a particular heat cycle, the net donor concentration is reduced by a factor of two. What type of dopant redistribution has occurred, and what are the values of N_d and N_a now?

2.8 Four different compound semiconductors and their bandgap energies are listed below. For each semiconductor calculate the longest wavelength of light that will pass through it, without being absorbed, to create hole-electron pairs. Indicate also whether each will appear opaque, like silicon, or will transmit visible light; and if it does, what color will it appear? Note that wavelength in microns and energy in electron volts are related as λ (μm) = $1.237/E_g$ (eV), and that visible light falls between 0.4 μm and 0.7 μm.

a. AlSb, aluminum antomonide: $E_g = 1.63$ eV
b. GaP, gallium phosphide: $E_g = 2.24$ eV
c. ZnS, zinc sulfide: $E_g = 3.6$ eV
d. InAs, indium arsenide: $E_g = 0.33$ eV

CHAPTER 3

UNIFORM EXCITATION OF SEMICONDUCTORS

Now that we have a model describing a uniformly doped semiconductor in thermal equilibrium, we are ready to disturb this thermal equilibrium and watch how the semiconductor responds. We hope that something will happen that we can exploit to perform some useful function. We will start modeling nonequilibrium conditions by restricting ourselves to uniformly doped semiconductors and by applying uniform excitations. We will look at two types of excitation: (1) a uniform electric field, and (2) uniform optical carrier generation.

3.1 UNIFORM ELECTRIC FIELD: DRIFT

One of the first devices about which an electrical engineer learns is a linear resistor, and one of the first laws he or she learns is Ohm's law. So, too, will the microscopic formulation of resistance and Ohm's law arise first as we begin our look at semiconductors in nonequilibrium situations. We first introduce the concept of drift motion and mobility and then turn to drift currents and conductivity.

3.1.1 Drift Motion and Mobility

A charged particle, which we will identify with the index I, in a uniform electric field $\mathscr{E}$ experiences a force **F** given by

$$\mathbf{F} = q_I \mathscr{E} \tag{3.1}$$

where q_I is the electric charge on the particle. For sake of convenience and simplicity in this text we will assume that the field is directed in the x-direction and that we are dealing with isotropic materials. Thus we do not need to use vector notation, and deal only with scalars. We will have

$$F_x = q_I \mathscr{E}_x \tag{3.2}$$

If the charged particle in question is in free space, the force F_x will cause the particle to accelerate as

$$a_x = \frac{F_x}{m_I} = \frac{q_I \mathscr{E}_x}{m_I} \tag{3.3}$$

where m_I is the mass of the particle. The particle will accelerate until it hits something, that is, has an interaction with its surroundings.

If the charged particle is inside a solid, as is the case with a conduction electron or a mobile hole in a semiconductor, it will typically hit something very quickly (e.g., a dopant ion in the lattice, the vibrating atoms in the crystal lattice, defects in the crystal structure, etc.) and it will do so after traveling only a relatively short distance. At this point it exchanges energy and momentum with whatever obstacle it encounters, rebounds or is deflected, and starts being accelerated again due to the force of the field. The net motion is quite different than the constant acceleration of a free charged particle and instead is very viscous. The particle attains a net average velocity proportional to the field given by

$$\bar{s}_x = \pm \mu_I \mathscr{E}_x \tag{3.4}$$

where the proportionality factor μ_I is called the *mobility* of the particle I and the sign (+ or −) is the same as the sign of the charge of the particle, q_I. The mobility is in general a function of the electric field, but in many situations encountered in devices it can be assumed to be a constant independent of $\mathscr{E}_x$ (see below).

Notice that above we speak of an average net velocity. We do so because even in the absence of an electric field the particles are in constant motion with large, yet random, velocities due to their thermal energy. Recall that we earlier stated that at a finite temperature the atoms in a crystal are constantly vibrating due to their thermal energy. The conduction electrons and mobile holes also have thermal energy; they move about, deflecting off obstacles, exchanging energy and momentum, and literally bouncing back and forth. The average magnitude of the thermal velocity of electrons and holes in a semiconductor is in fact quite large at room temperature—on the order of 10^6 to 10^7 cm/s—yet the net average velocity is zero. Thus in the absence of an electric field there is no net motion of the holes or electrons. This situation is illustrated for a conduction electron in Fig. 3.1*a*.

When a uniform electric field is applied, the carriers are accelerated slightly by the field between collisions; averaged over many collisions they acquire a net average velocity. This is illustrated in Fig. 3.1*b*. The collisions occur at a high rate, on the order of 10^{12} a second, or once every picosecond. Unless we are studying things that happen this fast, we "see" only the net average velocity of the particles.

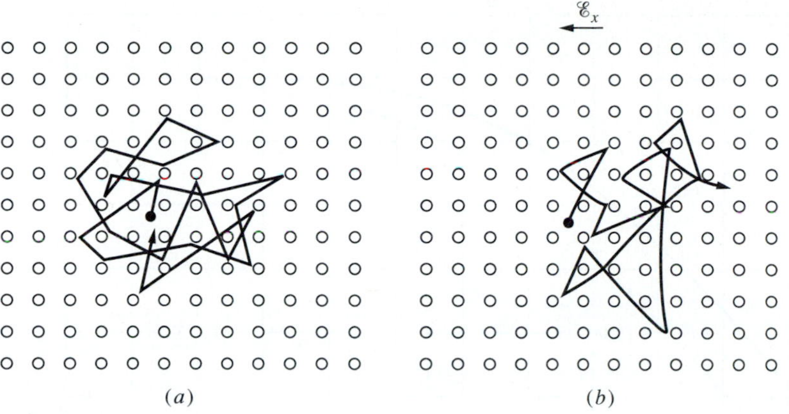

FIGURE 3.1
(*a*) Pictorial illustration of the continuous random thermal motion of a conduction electron in a semiconductor lattice. (*b*) The same electron with an electric field applied from right to left, exhibiting net motion superimposed on the random thermal motion.

The motion of charged particles in an electric field and with a net average velocity proportional to the field is called *drift*. In semiconductors, where the particles of interest are electrons and holes, we write for electrons

$$\bar{s}_{ex} = -\mu_e \mathscr{E}_x \tag{3.5}$$

and for holes

$$\bar{s}_{hx} = \mu_h \mathscr{E}_x \tag{3.6}$$

Notice that the net motion of the holes is in the direction of the field, whereas the electrons move in the opposite direction. These directions are, of course, the same as those in which positively and negatively charged particles accelerate in free space.

For low to moderate electric fields the mobility is constant and not a function of the electric field. Thus in low and moderate electric fields the drift velocity is linearly proportional to the electric field.

At very high electric fields, as the drift velocity begins to approach the thermal velocity (i.e., 10^6 to 10^7 cm/s) we find that the velocity saturates in the vicinity of 10^6 cm/s. The carriers suffer collisions so rapidly and transfer energy to the lattice so quickly that increasing the electric field no longer increases the kinetic energy of the carriers.

To illustrate this the overall variation of the drift velocity with electric field strength in silicon is presented in Fig. 3.2. Most carrier drift motion in devices occurs in the linear part of this curve, but increasingly there are key regions in modern devices in which carriers are moving at their saturation velocity. Examples of this are especially prevalent in field effect devices.

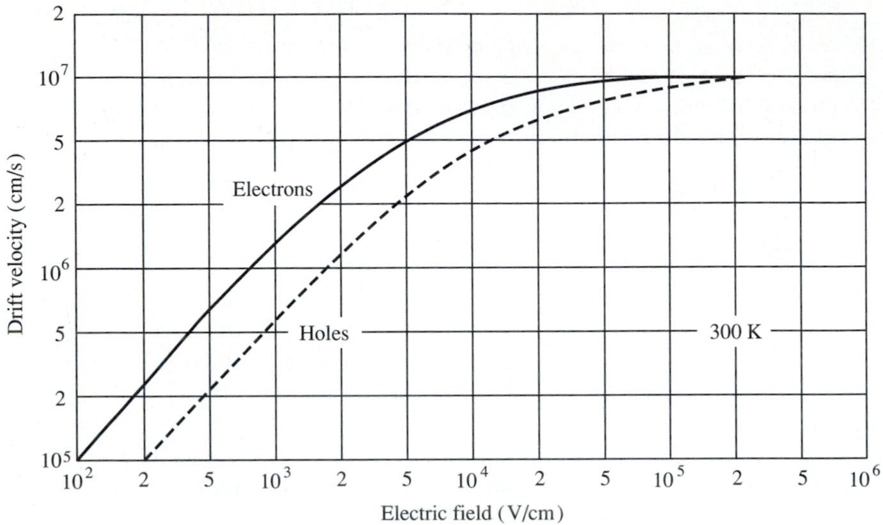

FIGURE 3.2
Log-log plot of the net drift velocity of electrons and holes as a function of the electric field in high-purity silicon at 300 K. (Reproduced from Yang, E., *Microelectronic Devices*, 1988, with permission from McGraw-Hill, Inc.)

It is possible to model the motion and collisions of charge carriers in a solid in more detail than we have shown here. It is from such models that the numbers stated earlier for the rate of collisions and the distances traveled between collisions were obtained, but we will not go further in this text. This means, however, that we should not expect our model of viscous flow and drift to be able to successfully model events happening on a time scale comparable to or less than the mean time between collisions, or on a distance scale comparable to or less than the mean collision length. This is not a severe restriction for most present-day devices, but we should know that it exists and that it places bounds on our modeling. It begins to become important in extremely small devices wherein carriers can transit all or most of the device before suffering a collision. In this case their motion is described by Eq. (3.3) and their motion is said to be *ballistic*.

3.1.2 Drift Current and Conductivity

Moving charged particles make up an electric current. This is the macroscopic consequence of applying an electric field to a solid. To explore this further, consider a semiconductor sample with thermal-equilibrium hole and electron concentrations p_o and n_o, respectively, and imagine applying a uniform electric field $\mathcal{E}_x$ in the x-direction. If the field is not too large, the electron and hole populations remain at p_o and n_o, respectively. The net flux density of electrons crossing any plane normal to the x-direction, F_{ex}, will in general be

$$F_{ex} = n_o \bar{s}_{ex} \tag{3.7a}$$

and, at low to moderate electric fields where Eq. (3.5) holds,

$$F_{ex} = -n_o\mu_e\mathscr{E}_x \tag{3.7b}$$

Since each electron carries a charge $-q$, the net electron current density J_{ex}, due to the electric field will be

$$J_{ex} = qn_o\mu_e\mathscr{E}_x \tag{3.8}$$

Similarly for holes, the hole flux density F_{hx} will be

$$F_{hx} = p_o\mu_h\mathscr{E}_x \tag{3.9}$$

and the hole current density due to the electric field will be

$$J_{hx} = q\,p_o\mu_h\mathscr{E}_x \tag{3.10}$$

The total current density J_x is the sum of the hole and electron current densities;

$$J_x = J_{ex} + J_{hx} \tag{3.11}$$

or, substituting from Eqs (3.8) and (3.10),

$$J_x = q(n_o\mu_e + p_o\mu_h)\mathscr{E}_x \tag{3.12}$$

This current is called the *drift current density*. The quantity $q(n_o\mu_e + p_o\mu_h)$ is called the *conductivity* and is given the symbol σ. The units of conductivity are siemens per centimeter, S/cm. Thus we can write

$$J_x = \sigma\mathscr{E}_x \tag{3.13}$$

The inverse of the conductivity is called the *resistivity* ρ:

$$\rho = \frac{1}{\sigma} \tag{3.14}$$

The units of resistivity are ohm-centimeters, $\Omega \cdot$ cm.

Equation (3.13) is the microscopic statement of Ohm's law, $v = iR$. The resistance R of a sample depends on its dimensions and its conductivity. Suppose a sample of length l, width w, and thickness t has electrical contacts A and B on either end with a voltage difference v_{AB} between them. We will discuss contacts at length later, but for now assume they are "ideal ohmic" contacts and that all of the voltage difference is across the sample, so that it has in it a uniform electric field

$$\mathscr{E}_x = \frac{v_{AB}}{l} \tag{3.15}$$

The current density at any point in the bar will then be

$$J_x = \frac{\sigma v_{AB}}{l} \tag{3.16}$$

and the total current will be the current density multiplied by the cross-sectional area of the sample, wt. That is,

$$i = J_x wt = \frac{\sigma wt}{l} v_{AB} \tag{3.17}$$

We can now easily identify the resistance of the sample as

$$R = \frac{l}{\sigma wt} = \rho \frac{l}{wt} \tag{3.18}$$

In semiconductors the equilibrium carrier concentrations can be varied over many orders of magnitude, as we saw in Chap. 2. Moreover, it is possible to dope a sample so that either holes or electrons are in the majority by a vast amount. Looking back at our expression that introduced conductivity, Eq. (3.12), we see that the conductivity can similarly vary over wide ranges, and that the drift current can be carried predominantly by either holes or electrons. In an n-type semiconductor, the drift current due to electrons is far greater than that due to holes (assuming that the electron and hole mobilities are of the same order of magnitude, which they typically are). Similarly, in a p-type semiconductor the drift current is predominantly carried by holes.

The electron and hole mobilities in a semiconductor in general depend on the concentrations of dopants present as well as on the temperature and the number of structural defects in the crystal. Generally, the higher the doping level, the higher the temperature; and the larger the number of defects, the lower the mobility. In this text, we will assume that mobilities of the carriers in a given sample have been measured experimentally; a method for doing this for the majority carriers, the Hall effect measurement technique, is described in App. B. Representative values of the electron and hole mobilities in high-quality silicon at room temperature are 1500 $cm^2/V \cdot s$ for μ_e, and 600 $cm^2/V \cdot s$ for μ_h.

Example

Question. What is the conductivity at room temperature of (a) intrinsic silicon, (b) Si doped n-type with $N_D = 10^{16}$ cm^{-3}, and (c) Si doped p-type with $N_A = 10^{16}$ cm^{-3}? Use $n_i = 10^{10}$ cm^{-3}; use the carrier mobilities stated just above.

Discussion.

(a) In intrinsic Si, n_o and p_o are equal to n_i and we find that the conductivity is 3.5×10^{-6} S/cm. To put this in perspective, the conductivity of a typical metal is on the order of 10^6 S/cm and that of a good insulator is 10^{-12} S/cm. Intrinsic Si is thus closer to being an insulator than a metal.

(b) For Si doped n-type with $N_D = 10^{16}$ cm^{-3}, our calculations give $n_o = 10^{16}$ cm^{-3} and $p_o = 10^4$ cm^{-3}. Thus the conductivity σ is 2.4 S/cm and, equivalently, the resistivity ρ is approximately 0.4 $\Omega \cdot$cm. This conductivity is essentially all due to electrons (i.e., the majority carriers).

(c) A p-type sample doped with the same magnitude of net acceptors (i.e., $N_A = 10^{16}$ cm^{-3}) has a lower conductivity than the n-type sample because the hole mobility is less than that of electrons. With $N_A = 10^{16}$ cm^{-3}, we find that $p_o = 10^{16}$ cm^{-3}; $n_o = 10^4$ cm^{-3}; and $\sigma \approx 1$ S/cm, or $\rho \approx 1$ $\Omega \cdot$ cm.

In both of the doped semiconductors considered in the example above, the conductivity is much less than that of a good metal, but it is high enough to be useful. In most semiconductor devices the doping levels range from 10^{15} cm^{-3} to 10^{18} cm^{-3}. Correspondingly, the conductivity ranges from 0.1 S/cm to over 200 S/cm.

3.1.3 Temperature Variation of Mobility and Conductivity

Before leaving uniform electrical excitation and the concept of drift, we would do well to ask how temperature affects mobility and conductivity. By developing detailed models for carrier motion in a solid and for the various collision, or "scattering," processes that the carriers experience, it is possible to show that in general the mobility decreases as the temperature increases. This result, which we will not attempt to quantify in this text, should seem feasible to you; at higher temperatures there is more random motion of the crystal lattice, so it is reasonable that the carriers suffer more collisions and that their motion is impeded. In silicon the mobility decreases as $T^{-1/2}$ above room temperature, whereas for most compound semiconductors the mobility falls as $e^{-\theta/T}$, where θ is a characteristic phonon temperature. As the temperature is lowered below room temperature, the mobility increases, at least initially. As the temperature becomes very low, however, collisions with impurities and defects in the crystal lattice become more important than the thermal motion of the lattice (i.e., the phonons). Thus the mobility eventually saturates and does not increase more. At even lower temperatures it may even decrease as the temperature is lowered further because the defects and impurities are actually more effective scattering centers at low temperature.

The conductivity involves both the mobility and the carrier concentration and thus can have a more complicated dependence on temperature. We discussed the temperature dependence of the carrier concentration in Sec. 2.5. In extrinsic semiconductors around room temperature, the carrier concentration is largely temperature-independent, so the conductivity will decrease along with the mobility as the temperature is increased. At high enough temperature, when the sample becomes intrinsic, the carrier concentration increases very rapidly with temperature and the conductivity also increases. At low temperature, where freeze-out occurs, the conductivity may either increase or decrease depending on whether freeze-out or the increase in mobility dominates. Typically the conductivity will at first increase as the temperature is lowered below room temperature because the mobility increases, but ultimately the conductivity will decrease with temperature at very low temperatures, say below 70 to 80 K, because of the freeze-out and the eventual decrease of mobility.

3.2 UNIFORM OPTICAL EXCITATION

A second important way that semiconductors can be forced out of thermal equilibrium is by illuminating them with light of energy greater than the energy gap.

In Si, where $E_g = 1.1$ eV, this corresponds to light in the visible and ultraviolet regions of the spectrum as well as very near-infrared radiation. In this section we will consider optical excitation of semiconductors with such light.

3.2.1 Minority Carrier Lifetime

We discussed hole-electron pair generation and recombination mechanisms in Chap. 2 when we discussed detailed balance. We defined the generation rate as G and the recombination rate as R. Clearly the time rate of change of the hole and electron populations in a uniform sample with uniform excitation will be the excess of generation over recombination:

$$\frac{dn}{dt} = \frac{dp}{dt} = G - R$$

If we write R as npr, this becomes

$$\frac{dn}{dt} = \frac{dp}{dt} = G - npr \tag{3.19}$$

In thermal equilibrium, $n = n_o$, $p = p_o$, and $dn/dt = dp/dt = 0$. Thus we must have

$$G_o = n_o p_o r \tag{3.20}$$

Now we will consider adding an external generation term in the form of light, which generates hole electron pairs uniformly throughout the sample at a rate $g_L(t)$. The total generation rate becomes

$$G = G_o + g_L(t) \tag{3.21}$$

and we want to calculate the new carrier concentrations. We have

$$\frac{dn}{dt} = \frac{dp}{dt} = G_o + g_L(t) - npr \tag{3.22}$$

Substituting Eq. (3.20) in this equation yields

$$\frac{dn}{dt} = \frac{dp}{dt} = g_L(t) - (np - n_o p_o)r \tag{3.23}$$

This is a nonlinear differential equation because of the product term, np. It is, in general, difficult to solve. To proceed further, we can get solutions in some important special cases if we first define the excess populations of holes and electrons, p' and n', respectively, as follows:

$$n' \equiv n - n_o \tag{3.24a}$$

$$p' \equiv p - p_o \tag{3.24b}$$

Using these definitions we can write n and p as

$$n = n_o + n' \tag{3.25a}$$

$$p = p_o + p' \tag{3.25b}$$

Next, notice that any carriers created in excess of the thermal equilibrium populations are always created in pairs; that is, for every excess hole there is an excess electron. Thus we must have

$$n' = p' \tag{3.26}$$

The thermal equilibrium populations do not change with time, so we can also write

$$\frac{dn}{dt} = \frac{dn'}{dt} \quad \text{and} \quad \frac{dp}{dt} = \frac{dp'}{dt} \tag{3.27}$$

Using the definitions of n' and p' and the observations we just made, we can now write Eq. (3.23) as

$$\frac{dn'}{dt} = g_L(t) - [(n_o + n')(p_o + n') - n_o p_o]r$$

or

$$\frac{dn'}{dt} = g_L(t) - n'(p_o + n_o + n')r \tag{3.28}$$

This now is one equation in one unknown, n', but it is still nonlinear because of the $(n')^2$ term, and it is in general difficult to solve. If the squared term is relatively small, however, we might be able to neglect it, in which case we have a simple first-order linear differential equation.

The situation where n' is small is called the *low-level injection* condition. By small we mean that n'(which equals p') is much smaller than the majority carrier population; that is,

$$n' = p' \ll p_o + n_o \tag{3.29}$$

In this case we have

$$n'(p_o + n_o + n') \approx n'(p_o + n_o) \tag{3.30}$$

and our equation is

$$\frac{dn'}{dt} \approx g_L(t) - n'(p_o + n_o)r \tag{3.31}$$

Defining $(p_o + n_o)r$ to be $\tau_{min^{-1}}$, we write

$$\frac{dn'}{dt} + \frac{n'}{\tau_{min}} = g_L(t) \tag{3.32}$$

which is an equation that we can solve given $g_L(t)$ and information on the initial state of the sample.

We should point out that although τ_{min} is written as $1/(p_o + n_o)r$, it is wrong to assume that τ_{min} varies inversely with the total carrier concentration because r may, and in general does, depend on the carrier concentrations as well. It is better to think simply in terms of a certain $\tau_{\min}$ for a given sample. This $\tau_{\min}$ is the consequence of the sample's purity, quality, composition, etc.—anything that might contribute a term to Eq. (2.14). However, developing a specific model relating $\tau_{\min}$ to p_o, n_o, and/or r is beyond the scope of this text. In practice $\tau_{\min}$ is usually determined experimentally, rather than theoretically, by measuring population transients such as those discussed below in Sec. 3.2.2.

Before discussing solutions to Eq. (3.32), we make a final note that we could solve for either n' or p' but that we choose to solve for the excess minority carrier concentration. When we discuss nonuniform excitations, we will see that the minority carriers are the most important to us; we focus on minority carriers here in anticipation of that result. Furthermore, the quantity $\tau_{\min}$ is called the *minority carrier lifetime*, again in anticipation of this result.

3.2.2 Population Transients

For the sake of this discussion, let's assume that we are dealing with a uniformly doped, p-type sample of silicon. The equilibrium hole population p_o is then N_A, and the equilibrium electron population is n_i^2/N_A. Suppose that $g_L(t)$ hole-electron pairs are being generated optically throughout the sample and we want to know what the excess hole and electron populations are. The equations we must solve are

$$\frac{dn'}{dt} + \frac{n'}{\tau_e} = g_L(t) \tag{3.33}$$

where τ_e is $\tau_{\min}$ in this p-type sample, and

$$p' = n' \tag{3.34}$$

Equation (3.33) is a first-order linear differential equation. To solve it we need to find its homogeneous solution and a particular solution, which depends on $g_L(t)$. We then need to determine the relevant initial (boundary) condition and combine the homogeneous and particular solutions so as to satisfy it. The result is the total solution.

The homogeneous solution to Eq. (3.33) is

$$n' = Ae^{-t/\tau_e} \tag{3.35}$$

where A is a constant that will ultimately be determined by fitting the sum of the homogeneous and particular solutions to the boundary condition. We see that the minority carrier lifetime τ_e is the characteristic response time of the homogeneous solution.

The particular solution depends on the particular $g_L(t)$ imposed.

Example

Question. What are the excess electron populations with the following types of low-level optical excitation: a) constant illumination; b) step-on, step-off illumination, c) square wave illumination; and d) steady sinusoidal illumination?

Discussion.

(a) *Constant illumination.* If $g_L(t)$ is a constant,

$$g_L(t) = G \tag{3.36}$$

then the particular solution for $n'(t)$ is also a constant,

$$n'(t) = G\tau_e \tag{3.37}$$

The total solution is then $n'(t) = G\tau_e + Ae^{-t/\tau_e}$, where we still need to find A. In this case, if we assume that the illumination has been on for a very long time, we know that all transients (i.e., all remnants of the homogeneous solution) must have died out and thus A must be zero. In terms of an initial condition, we are saying that the excess population must remain finite, and unless A is zero, $n'(t)$ would become infinite in the limit of $t \to -\infty$.

We have found that $n'(t)$ is $G\tau_e$ in a uniform sample under steady illumination generating G hole-electron pairs uniformly throughout its bulk, but we are not done yet. We got our solution under the assumption of low-level injection, and we must check that that assumption was valid. Thus we must confirm that $G\tau_e \ll p_o$. If it is, we are done. If it is not, we must go back and solve Eq. (3.28), rather than using Eq. (3.33).

(b) *Step-on, step-off illumination.* Now imagine that our p-type sample is in thermal equilibrium for $t < 0$; at $t = 0$ a steady illumination creating $g_L(t) = G$ is turned on, and then at $t = T$, where $T > 0$, the illumination is turned off. This is illustrated in Fig. 3.3*a*.

For $t < 0$, $n'(t) = p'(t) = 0$. This is our initial condition on $n'(t)$ at $t = 0$. To reach this conclusion it is important to realize that we have implicitly used the constraint that according to Eq. (3.33), $n'(t)$ must be continuous and cannot change instantaneously—that is, dn'/dt must be finite—unless $g_L(t)$ is infinite. Since $g_L(t)$ is not infinite in this example, we must have $n'(0) = 0$.

For $0 \leq t \leq T$, the particular solution is again $G\tau_e$ and we have

$$n'(t) = G\tau_e + Ae^{-t/\tau_e} \qquad \text{for } 0 \leq t \leq T \tag{3.38}$$

subject to the initial condition $n'(0) = 0$. Imposing this condition, we see that A is $-G\tau_e$ and thus

$$n'(t) = G\tau_e\left(1 - e^{-t/\tau_e}\right) \qquad \text{for } 0 \leq t \leq T \tag{3.39}$$

For $T \leq t$, $g_L(t)$ is again zero, and thus the particular solution is also zero. Then the total solution is just the homogeneous solution, Eq. (3.35), with A chosen to satisfy the initial condition. The initial condition is

$$n'(T) = G\tau_e\left(1 - e^{-T/\tau_e}\right) \tag{3.40}$$

We find

$$n'(t) = G\tau_e\left(1 - e^{-T/\tau_e}\right)e^{-(t-T)/\tau_e} \qquad \text{for } T \leq t \tag{3.41}$$

This solution is illustrated in Fig. 3.3*b* for a situation where T and τ_e are comparable.

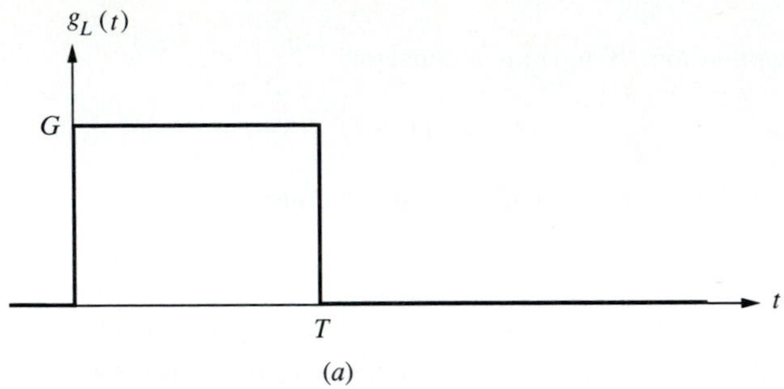

(a)

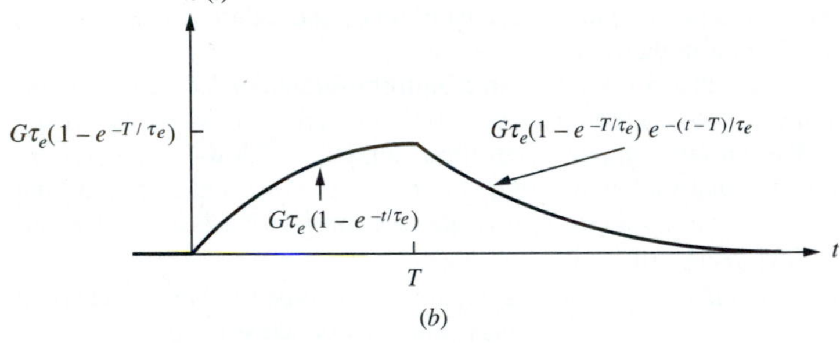

(b)

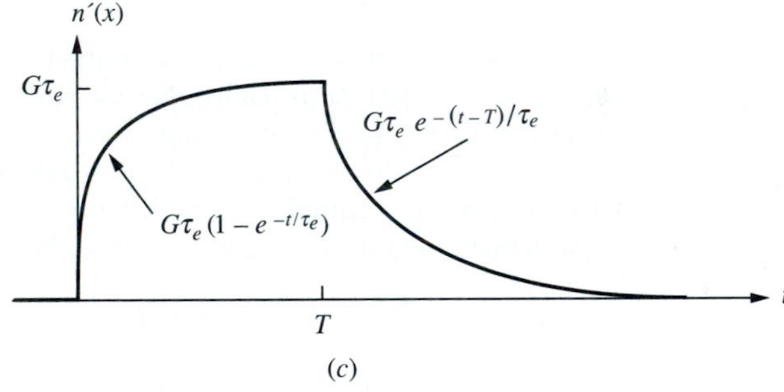

(c)

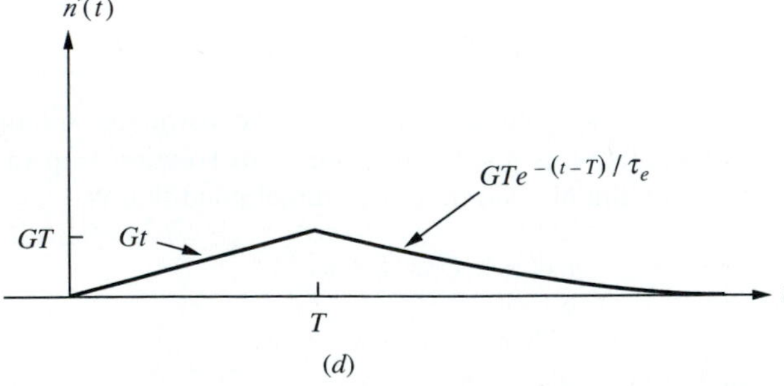

(d)

FIGURE 3.3
Step-on, step-off illumination: (a) the generation term $g_L(t)$; (b) the excess minority carrier concentration $n'(t)$ for $\tau_e \approx T$; (c) $n't$ for $\tau_e \ll T$; and (d) $n'(t)$ for $\tau_e \gg T$.

It is worthwhile to consider two other extremes of T: when $T \gg \tau_e$ and when $T \ll \tau_e$. In the first case, the transient will have died out by the time the illumination is turned off, and for $t \geq T$ we will find

$$n'(t) \approx G\tau_e e^{-(t-T)/\tau_e} \qquad \text{for } T \leq t \tag{3.42}$$

This is illustrated in Fig. 3.3c.

When $T \ll \tau_e$, the exponential factor in the solution for $0 < t < T$, that is, Eq. (3.35), will always be small and we can approximate the term using $(1 - e^{-x}) \approx x$ when $x \ll 1$. Thus

$$n'(t) \approx Gt \qquad \text{for } 0 \leq t \leq T \tag{3.43}$$

and

$$n'(t) \approx GTe^{-(t-T)/\tau_e} \qquad \text{for } T \leq t \tag{3.44}$$

This solution is illustrated in Fig. 3.3d.

In all of these cases, we would of course have to verify that low-level injection was not violated before we could say that we were truly done solving the problem.

(c) *Square wave illumination.* Next consider that the illumination is turned on and off regularly for equal amounts of time, $T/2$, and that this process has been continuing for a very long time, so that a steady state has been reached. The corresponding $g_L(t)$ is illustrated in Fig. 3.4a. The boundary condition in this case is that $n'(t)$ must be repetitive, that is, that $n'(t + T) = n'(t)$. We can also simplify the task of finding $n'(t)$ if we use the fact that we have a linear system. We know then that the average of the response will be the same as the response to the average input. The average of the excitation is $G/2$ so the average of the excess population should be $G\tau_e/2$. Also, since the excitation is symmetrical about its average value, the response should also be symmetrical about its average value. With these suggestions you should be able to complete the solution yourself; the results for $T \approx \tau_e$, $T \gg \tau_e$, and $T \ll \tau_e$ are illustrated in Figs. 3.4b, c, and d, respectively.

(d) *Steady sinusoidal illumination.* If $g_L(t)$ is varying sinusoidally with frequent ω, and the illumination has been on for a very long time before $t = 0$, we have

$$g_L(t) = G(1 + \cos\, \omega t) \tag{3.45}$$

Notice we must always have $g_L \geq 0$, so we must add a steady illumination G, to the sinusoidal term. Nonetheless, we can mathematically solve for $n'(t)$ using a $g_L(t)$ that becomes negative; that is, we can use superposition and solve for $n'(t)$ due to G and for $n'(t)$ due to $G \cos \omega t$ and combine these results to obtain $n'(t)$ due to $G + G \cos \omega t$, which is our actual $g_L(t)$.

We know that the excess population due to G is $G\tau_e$. We thus need to find only $n'(t)$ due to $G \cos \omega t$. There are two ways we might proceed. The first is to realize that the solution will be of the form $B \cos(\omega t + \theta)$, substitute this form into Eq. (3.33), and solve for B and θ. The second is to recognize $G \cos \omega t$ as the real part of $Ge^{j\omega t}$. The particular solution for this later excitation is of the form $Be^{j(\omega t+\theta)}$, and the solution we seek is $Re[Be^{j(wt+\theta)}]$.

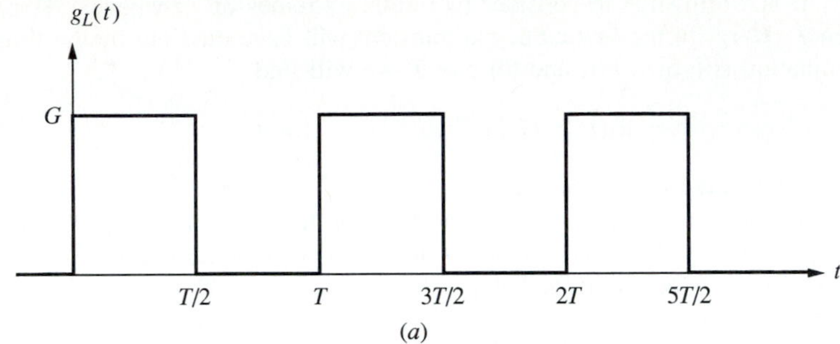

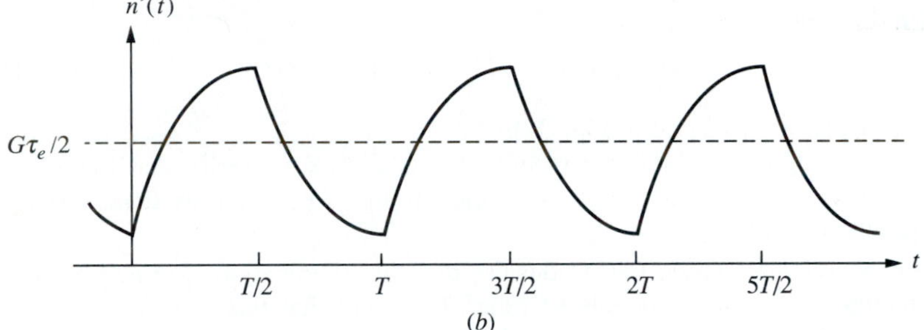

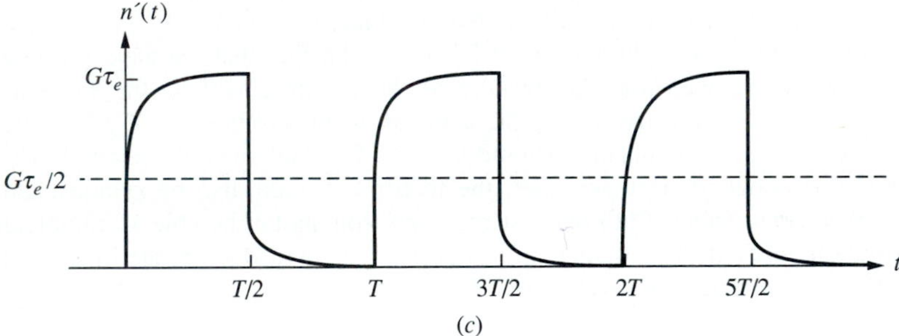

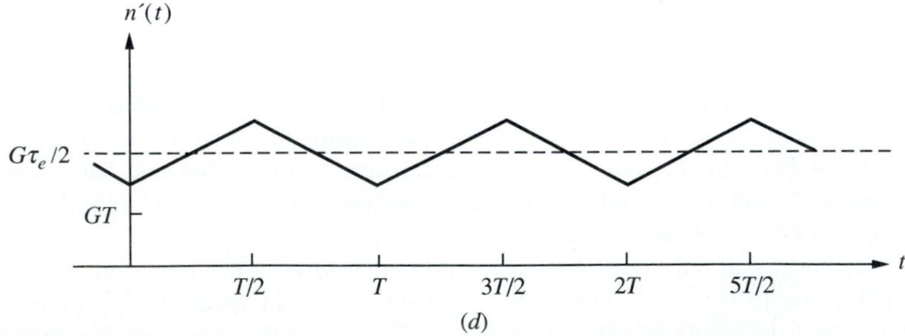

FIGURE 3.4
Square wave illumination: (*a*) the generation term $g_L(t)$; (*b*) the excess minority carrier concentration $n'(t)$ for $\tau_e \approx T$; (*c*) $n'(t)$ for $\tau_e \ll T$; and (*d*) $n'(t)$ for $\tau_e \gg T$.

Proceeding by either of these routes, the details of which are left as an exercise, we obtain

$$B = \frac{G\tau_e}{\sqrt{1 + \omega^2\tau_e^2}} \qquad \text{and} \qquad \theta = \tan^{-1}(\omega\tau_e) \tag{3.46}$$

Clearly, when $\omega\tau_e \ll 1$, the response "tracks" the excitation, and when $\omega\tau_e \gg 1$, the response is a small variation about the average value 90° out of phase with, and behind, the excitation. These results are summarized in Fig. 3.5. You may wish to compare these results with what we found for a square wave excitation, Fig. 3.4.

3.2.3 High-Level Injection Populations and Transients

When low-level injection conditions are no longer met we must deal with the nonlinear differential equation, Eq. (3.28), which we rewrite here using our definition of τ_{min} to replace r:

$$\frac{dn'}{dt} = g_L(t) - \frac{n'}{\tau_{min}} - \frac{(n')^2}{(p_o + n_o)\tau_{min}} \tag{3.28$'$}$$

As we noted earlier, this equation is in general difficult to solve, but there are two important special problems for which we can get solutions: (1) the steady-state population under constant illumination, $g_L(t) = G$; and (2) the initial population transient after extinction of intense illumination.

a) Constant illumination. With steady illumination, $g_L(t) = G$, the time derivative of the population is zero in the steady state and the excess population, which we will label N', satisfies

$$\frac{N'^2}{(p_o + n_o)\tau_{min}} + \frac{N'}{\tau_{min}} - G = 0 \tag{3.47a}$$

or, rearranging factors,

$$N'^2 + (p_o + n_o)N' - G(p_o + n_o)\tau_{min} = 0 \tag{3.47b}$$

Solving this quadratic, we find

$$N' = \frac{(p_o + n_o)}{2}\left[\sqrt{1 + \frac{4G\tau_{min}}{(p_o + n_o)}} - 1\right] \tag{3.48a}$$

You can easily confirm that this result reduces to Eq. (3.37) when $G\tau_{min}$ is much less than $(p_o + n_o)$, which corresponds to low-level injection. You should also note that N' is always less than $G\tau_{min}$, a fact you can see by rearranging Eq. (3.47a). You may want to think about the significance of this observation—does it make intuitive sense?

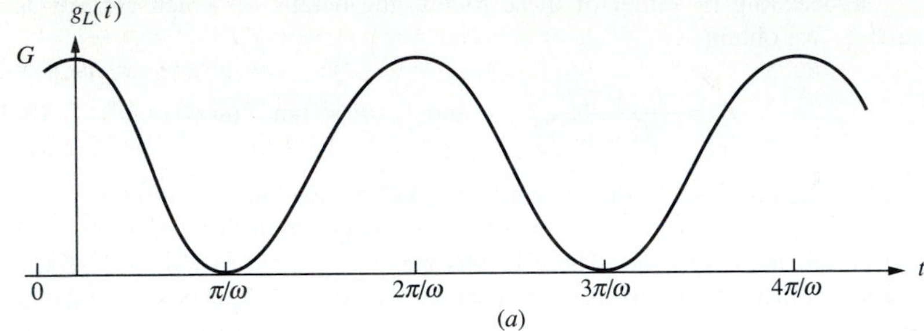

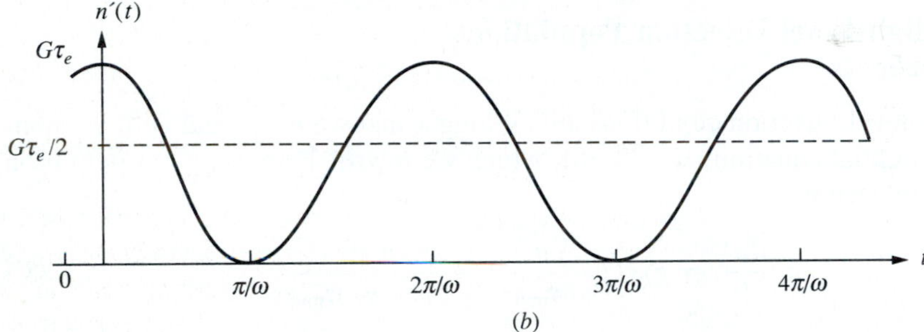

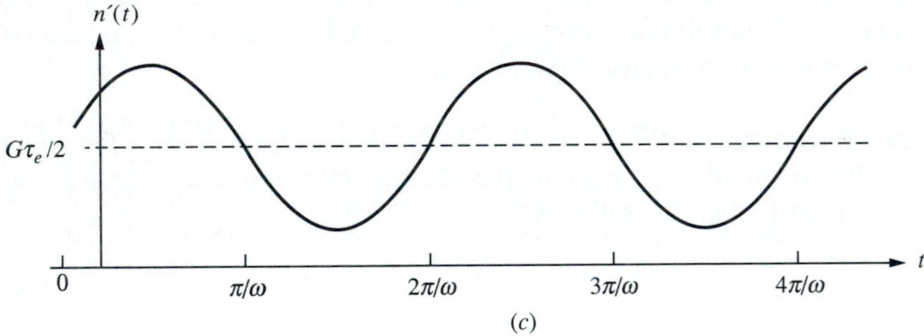

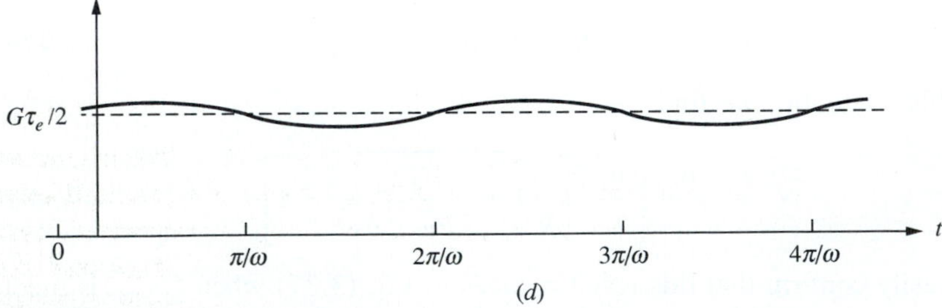

FIGURE 3.5
Sinusoidal illumination: (*a*) the generation term $g_L(t)$; (*b*) the excess minority carrier concentration $n'(t)$ for $\omega t_e \ll 1$; $n'(t)$ for (*c*) $\omega\tau_e \approx 1$; and $n'(t)$ for (*d*) $\omega\tau_e \gg 1$.

Finally, you should notice that in the limit of G being much greater than $(p_o + n_o)/\tau_{\min}$, N' is given by

$$N' \approx \sqrt{G\tau_{\min}(p_o + n_o)} \tag{3.48b}$$

Note that N' increases only as $\sqrt{G}$ in this extreme, rather than as G, as it does in low-level injection.

b) Initial decay transient. In the preceding section we found the steady-state carrier population under constant intense illumination. In this section we address the question of how rapidly this population decays (i.e., decreases) when this intense illumination is extinguished. To answer this question we can find the homogeneous solution to Eq. (3.28′) when the $(n')^2$ term is dominant, that is, when $n' \gg (p_o + n_o)$. Thus we want the solution to

$$\frac{dn'}{dt} + \frac{(n')^2}{(p_o + n_o)\tau_{\min}} = 0 \tag{3.49}$$

subject to the initial condition that $n'(0)$ is given by Eq. (3.48b). This solution is

$$n'(t) = \frac{n'(0)}{1 + [n'(0)t/(p_o + n_o)\tau_{\min}]} \tag{3.50a}$$

For $t \gg (p_o + n_o)\tau_{\min}/n'(0)$, the 1 in the above denominator can be neglected and we have essentially

$$n'(t) \approx \frac{(p_o + n_o)\tau_{\min}}{t} \tag{3.50b}$$

that is, $n'(t)$ varies inversely with t.

These expressions are valid as long as $n'(t)$ is much greater than $(p_o + n_o)$, that is, as long as t is much less than $\tau_{\min}$.

An interesting question to ask is whether the rate of decay of the excess population is faster or slower after excitation to high-level injection (HLI) conditions than it is after low-level injection (LLI) excitation. To examine this question we turn to Eqs. (3.33) and (3.49), and use them to evaluate the rate of change of n' at $t = 0^+$. Upon doing this we find that the initial rates of decay in LLI, $n' \ll (p_o + n_o)$, are

$$\left.\frac{dn'}{dt}\right|_{t=0^+} = -\frac{n'(0)}{\tau_{\min}} \tag{3.51a}$$

and in HLI, $n' \gg (p_o + n_o)$, they are

$$\left.\frac{dn'}{dt}\right|_{t=0^+} = -\frac{n'(0)^2}{(p_o + n_o)\tau_{\min}} \tag{3.51b}$$

Not surprisingly, in both cases increasing the initial population $n'(0)$, increases the absolute rate of decay, and the HLI case indeed decays more rapidly. A more meaningful quantity to consider, however, is the rate of decay normalized to the initial population, rather than the absolute rate; that is, dn'/dt divided by n', rather than just dn'/dt. Upon dividing the above expressions by $n'(0)$ we find that the normalized rates in LLI are

$$\left.\frac{dn'/dt}{n'}\right|_{t=0^+} = -\frac{1}{\tau_{\min}} \tag{3.52a}$$

and in HLI they are

$$\left.\frac{dn'/dt}{n'}\right|_{t=0^+} = -\frac{n'(0)}{(p_o + n_o)\tau_{\min}} \tag{3.52b}$$

When the equations are written in this way we see clearly that the normalized decay rate is independent of the pumping level as long as LLI conditions are maintained, whereas when a sample is pumped to HLI the normalized decay rate is much larger and varies in direct proportion to the excess population.

3.3 PHOTOCONDUCTIVITY AND PHOTOCONDUCTORS

Thus far in this chapter we have considered the individual effects of a uniform electric field and uniform optical excitation on a uniformly doped semiconductor. If we now consider applying a uniform electric field to a uniform semiconductor that is uniformly excited optically, we discover a phenomenon called *photoconductivity*; we also have the essential ingredients of a device called the *photoconductor*, which can electrically detect, or "sense," the presence of light. As we shall see, photoconductors are extremely simple devices, and historically they were some of the first successful semiconductor devices. Cadmium sulfide (CdS) photoconductors, for example, have for years been used in light meters for photography. In spite of the long history of photoconductor design, innovations still continue. Some of the fastest semiconductor switches ever made use gallium arsenide (GaAs) photoconductors fabricated using state-of-the-art processing technologies.

In this section we will look first at the basic phenomenon of photoconductivity and then we will turn to specific issues relevant to the design of photoconductors for particular applications.

3.3.1 Basic Concepts

The idea of photoconductivity is that simply illuminating a semiconductor sample increases the carrier concentration in that sample and this, in turn, increases its conductivity. This optically induced conductivity is called photoconductivity.

Quantitatively, we know that the conductivity is in general given by

$$\sigma = q\,[\mu_e n + \mu_h p] \tag{3.53a}$$

Writing this specifically in terms of the equilibrium and excess populations, we have

$$\sigma = q\left[\mu_e(n_o + n') + \mu_h(p_o + p')\right] \tag{3.53b}$$

From this expression we can identify the thermal equilibrium conductivity σ_o as

$$\sigma_o = q\,[\mu_e n_o + \mu_h p_o] \tag{3.54}$$

and the excess conductivity, or photoconductivity, σ' as

$$\sigma' = q\left[\mu_e n' + \mu_h p'\right] \tag{3.55a}$$

Since holes and electrons are generated in pairs, $n' = p$ and we have

$$\sigma' = q(\mu_e + \mu_h)n' \tag{3.55b}$$

We already know how to calculate n' for a semiconductor sample given the generation function, so we can easily calculate the change in conductivity, σ', corresponding to particular illumination conditions.

We next consider the design of devices that are optimized to use the phenomenon of photoconductivity to detect light.

3.3.2 Specific Device Issues

As a practical matter the fractional change in conductivity represented by Eq. (3.55b) is in general small if the hole and electron mobilities are comparable and if the excitation is low-level injection. If one wants simply to detect the presence or absence of light, one solution to this problem is to use a very lightly doped piece of semiconductor and excite it to high-level injection conditions. The unilluminated device will then have a very high resistance, and the illumination will make the resistance much smaller. This change will be easily detectable, and such a device will make a good light-activated switch.

In many situations, however, it is desirable to have a sensor with a response that is linearly proportional to the intensity of the illumination. For such applications we must restrict ourselves to semiconductors operating under low-level injection conditions (to see this, refer to Eqs. (3.37) and (3.48) for n' as a function of G with constant LLI and HLI excitation, respectively). The type of device described in the previous paragraph is not particularly useful for this type of application.

An interesting solution to the dilemma of achieving a large fractional change in conductivity while still retaining LLI conditions, has been to develop materials for use in photoconductors for which the majority carriers have effectively zero mobility and the minority carriers have a normally high mobility. In such a photoconductor (i.e., one in which, for example, $\mu_h \approx 0$) we have no conductivity in the absence of light (i.e., $\sigma_o \approx 0$) whereas under illumination we find $\sigma \approx q\mu_e n'$, assuming the majority carriers are holes.

The situation we have just described can be achieved by having a concentration, N_a of shallow acceptors and a larger concentration N_t of relatively deep donors, where "relatively deep" means that the donor energy E_t is such that $(E_c - E_t)$ is many times kT/q. This situation is illustrated in Fig. 3.6 in terms of our energy pictures of Chap. 2.

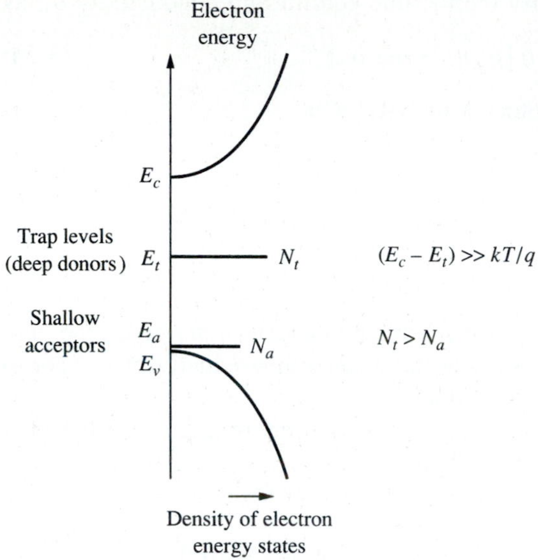

FIGURE 3.6
Relative positions on an electron energy scale of the possible sites for electrons in a photoconductor containing deep donors and shallow acceptors.

Because the donors have been selected so that $(E_c - E_t)$ is much greater than kT/q, it is unlikely that electrons will be thermally excited from these deep donors, which we call *traps*, into conduction states and so n_o will be very small. However, even though these deep donors do not become thermally ionized with the creation of conduction electrons, N_a of them are nonetheless ionized because they provide electrons to fill the N_a acceptor states. Denoting the equilibrium density of ionized traps as N_{to}^+, we thus have

$$N_{to}^+ = N_a \tag{3.56}$$

These N_a ionized trap states play the role of the majority hole carriers in our discussion and clearly have zero mobility because they can't move.

When electrons are optically excited from the bonding states to the conduction states in such a sample (i.e., when a mobile electron and a mobile hole are created) an electron from a trap level very quickly recombines with the hole, leaving behind an additional ionized trap. The net effect of the light is then to create excess mobile, negatively charged conduction electrons and excess fixed, positively charged ionized traps, rather than excess mobile, positively charged holes. If we denote the excess density of ionized traps as N_t^+, we have

$$n' = N_t^+$$

The equivalent of the low-level injection restriction is now that these excesses be much less than N_{to}^+. Since we have said that N_{to}^+ is equal to N_a, we thus want to have $n' \ll N_a$. When this is the case, n' is a linear function of g and it satisfies Eq. (3.33), which we repeat here:

$$\frac{dn'}{dt} + \frac{n'}{\tau_{\min}} = g_L(t) \tag{3.33}$$

The value of $\tau_{\min}$ appropriate to the sample in question must, of course, be used. Physically this lifetime corresponds to the rate at which the conduction electrons reoccupy the ionized trap levels.

A second issue that arises in photoconductor design concerns the fact that it is desirable to have the light absorbed completely in the device so as to generate the largest possible number of carriers and make the largest possible change in conductivity. However, if all of the light is to be absorbed, the generation function cannot simultaneously be constant (i.e., uniform) throughout the thickness of the device. Instead, g_L must decrease moving in from the surface as the illuminating radiation is absorbed and its intensity decreases. We can model the interaction of light with an absorbing solid in terms of an absorption coefficient. We say that the rate at which absorption occurs and thus at which the intensity decreases is proportional to the intensity; the constant of proportionality is the absorption coefficient α. Assuming the light is propagating in the x-direction and denoting the intensity as L, which has the units photons/cm$^2 \cdot$ s, we have

$$\frac{dL}{dx} = \alpha L \tag{3.57}$$

where α has the units cm^{-1}. Solving this equation yields

$$L(x) = L_0 e^{-\alpha x} \tag{3.58}$$

where we have assumed that the absorbing solid occupies the region $x > 0$ and that the light is incident from the left with an intensity L_0 at $x = 0$. This situation is illustrated in Fig. 3.7.

If each photon that is absorbed creates one hole-electron pair, the generation function g will be αL, which is clearly a function of x. This violates our basic assumption in this chapter that we have uniform excitation. Interestingly, however, in a situation like that illustrated in Fig. 3.7, in which the electric field and conduction are normal to the direction of incidence of the light and thus normal to the nonuniformity, we can still get a solution. The key is that the sample can be thought of as an infinite number of infinitesimally thin slabs, each with thickness dx and each with a mobile carrier concentration $n'(x)$. The conductance of each slab W wide, D long, and dx thick is $q\mu_e n'(x)W\,dx/D$; and the total conductance of the sample is the sum of all these slab conductances because they are connected electrically in parallel. Thus

$$G' = q\frac{\mu_e W}{D}\int_0^T n'(x)\,dx \tag{3.59}$$

From this result we see that what matters is the total number of excess carriers per unit area normal to the surface, not their detailed distribution. Thus even if

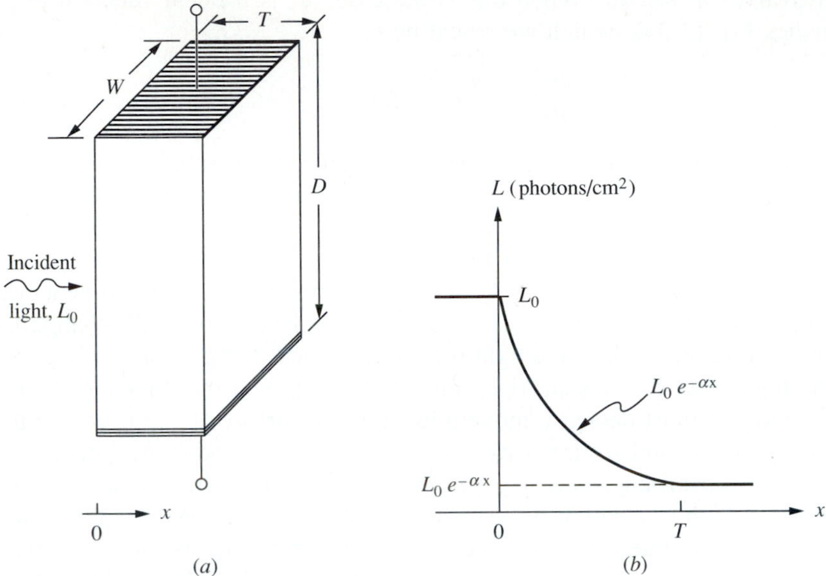

FIGURE 3.7
(*a*) Representative photoconductor; (*b*) variation of the light intensity with position into the structure. It has been assumed in this plot that there is negligible reflection at the interfaces in the structure, and that the absorption coefficient α is comparable to $1/T$.

the excess carriers move in the x-direction away from the point where they are created (as the next chapter shows they will), the sample's conductance is not changed.

If we restrict ourselves to low-level injection conditions, the rate at which the excess carriers recombine in the sample is similarly independent of their position in the x-direction. To see this we recall that the recombination per unit volume in any plane is $n'/\tau_{\min}$. Thus the total recombination rate in the sample is $WD\int_0^T n'(x)\,dx/\tau_{\min}$. Because this result depends only on the integral of n', not on the detailed distribution, the total recombination and hence the total excess population will not be changed if the carriers move around.

Because the final answer is not affected by where the carriers are normal to the surface, we can proceed by again imagining the sample to be divided into thin slabs that are isolated so that the carriers cannot move up or down from one slab to the next. In such a situation, n' in each slab is $\tau_{\min} g$. If we then have a constant low-level illumination L_0 incident on the top surface of the sample, g is $\alpha L(x)$, where $L(x)$ is given by Eq. (3.58), and thus $n'(x)$ is $\tau_{\min}\alpha L_0 e^{-\alpha L}$. Substituting this in Eq. (3.59) we have

$$G' = q\frac{\mu_e W}{D}\tau_{\min}\alpha L_0 \int_0^T e^{-\alpha(x)}\,dx \tag{3.60a}$$

which gives us

$$G' = q\frac{\mu_e W \tau_{\min} L_0}{D}\left(1 - e^{-T\alpha}\right) \tag{3.60b}$$

This result teaches us that it is advantageous to have $T \gg 1/\alpha$ so that the factor $e^{-T\alpha}$ is essentially zero and G' is as large as possible.

This completes our discussion of photoconductors.

3.4 SUMMARY

In this chapter we have looked at two important ways of exciting a semiconductor: electrically and optically.

Applying a uniform electric field led us to consider a form of carrier motion we call drift, which we model with the concepts of mobility and conductivity. Charge carriers in a solid under the influence of a moderate uniform static electric field attain a net average velocity proportional to that field:

$$\bar{s}_x = \pm \mu_I \mathscr{E}_x$$

where the sign assumed is the same as that of the charge on the carriers. This net velocity results in a net motion of charge (i.e., a current density) proportional to the electric field. In a semiconductor with two carrier types, holes and electrons, the drift current density is

$$J_x = q(n_o \mu_e + p_o \mu_h)\mathscr{E}_x$$

The factor of proportionality between the electric field and drift current density is called the conductivity, which in a semiconductor is given by

$$\sigma = q(n_o \mu_e + p_o \mu_h)$$

Applying uniform optical excitation to a semiconductor led us to a nonlinear differential equation for the carrier concentrations, but we found that restricting the excitation to low levels of injection allowed us to linearize the problem. We introduced the concepts of excess carriers, low-level injection, and minority carrier lifetime to model this problem, and showed that under low-level conditions (i.e., $n' \ll p_o$) the excess minority carrier concentration obeyed the following equation (we assume p-type here):

$$\frac{dn'}{dt} + \frac{n'}{\tau_{\min}} = g_L(t)$$

The homogeneous solution of this equation has the form $e^{-t/\tau_{\min}}$, from which we saw that the minority carrier lifetime is the natural response time of the system. The particular solution depends on the form of the optical excitation. Several common forms were considered as examples, and we saw that, as expected, the excess minority carrier concentration will follow, or "track," changes in $g_L(t)$ occurring slowly (on a time scale of τ_{min}) but will lag behind more rapid changes.

Finally, we considered the simultaneous application of optical and electric field excitation to a semiconductor and introduced the concept of photoconductivity, which is the change of the conductivity of a semiconductor sample under the influence of light. This modulation forms the basis of an important class of optical sensors called photoconductors. Photoconductors can be designed and used either as optically activated switches or as linear sensors of light intensity. In the latter case, we saw how, by the introduction of deep donors, semiconductor materials can be engineered to have a large conductivity change even under low-level injection conditions.

PROBLEMS

3.1 What is the conductivity of the following semiconductor samples at room temperature, assuming $\mu_e = 1500$ cm^2/V · s and $\mu_h = 600$ cm^2/V · s?

(a) $n_o = 4 \times 10^{16}$ cm^{-3}, $p_o = 5 \times 10^3$ cm^{-3}
(b) $n_o = 2 \times 10^3$ cm^{-3}, $p_o = 1 \times 10^{17}$ cm^{-3}
(c) $n_o = p_o = 1 \times 10^{10}$ cm^{-3}

3.2 Consider a sample of germanium with 3×10^{15} cm^{-3} gallium atoms. Determine the following quantities at room temperature for this sample.

(a) Majority carrier type
(b) Majority carrier concentration
(c) Minority carrier concentration
(d) Conductivity

3.3 *(a)* Calculate the root-mean-square velocity of an electron in silicon at room temperature, assuming it has a thermal kinetic energy $m^*v^2/2$ equal to $3kT/2$, where kT is 0.025 eV. The effective mass m^* of an electron in silicon is about 26 percent that of an electron in free space and can be taken to be 2×10^{-31} kg. (Be careful with your units.)

(b) Calculate the average net velocity of an electron in silicon moving under the influence of an electric field of 10^3 V/cm.

(c) Repeat part a, assuming that, in addition to the 3×10^{15} cm^{-3} gallium atoms, there are also 1×10^{16} cm^{-3} arsenic atoms in this sample.

3.4 *(a)* Consider a sample of n-type silicon L cm long, W cm wide, and T cm thick that is nonuniformly doped in such a manner that the equilibrium majority carrier population varies throughout its thickness as $n_o(x)$ (see Fig. P3.4*a*). Show that if the mobility μ_e is constant, independent of the doping level, then the end-to-end resistance of this sample depends only on the integral of $n_o(x)$ over the thickness of the sample (i.e., from $x = 0$ at the top surface to $x = T$ at the bottom surface) and not on the actual shape of $n_o(x)$. (*Hint:* Mentally divide the sample into thin slabs of material *dx* wide, and add the conductances of these slabs connected in parallel.)

(b) In an integrated circuit, dopants are introduced to the top surface of a silicon wafer (slab) to produce nonuniformly doped regions like the sample described in (a) and resistors are formed by putting contacts at the ends of rectangularly

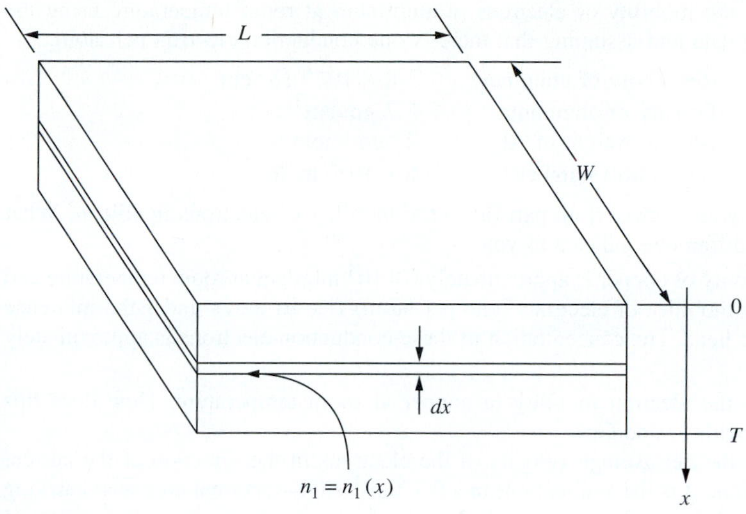

FIGURE P3.4*a*

shaped regions doped in this manner. Suppose that the doping profile of such a resistive region is such that

$$n_o(0) = 10^{18} e^{-x/X} \text{ cm}^{-3}$$

where X is 2 μm. (Note: 1 μm = 10^{-4} cm.) What resistance would a square region with this profile, L units by L units in size, have? This resistance is called the sheet resistance R_s of the region.

(c) The dopant profile in part (b) is introduced in a pattern like that illustrated in Fig. P3.4*c*. What is the approximate resistance between points A and B of this resistor?

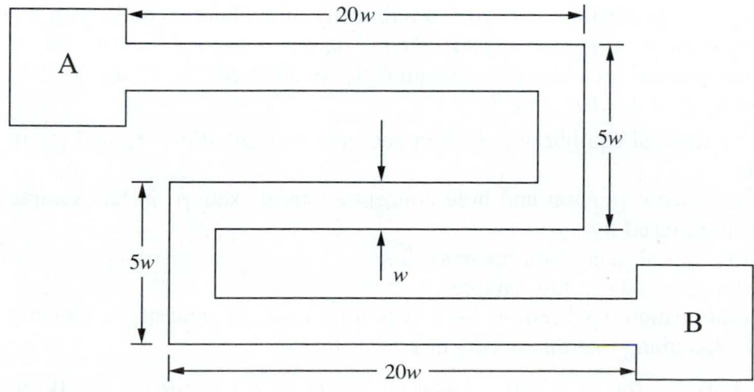

FIGURE P3.4*c*

3.5 *(a)* Calculate the mobility of electrons in aluminum at room temperature using the following data and assuming that there is one conduction electron per atom.

Resistivity of aluminum	$2.8 \times 10^{-6}\ \Omega \cdot \text{cm}$
Density of aluminum	2.7 gm/cm^3
Atomic weight of Al	27 gm/mole
Avogadro's number	6×10^{23} mole^{-1}

(b) Compare your answer from part (a) to the mobility of electrons in silicon. What does the difference indicate to you?

3.6 The conductivity of copper is approximately 6×10^5 mho/cm at room temperature and is due to the mobility of electrons (one per atom) free to move under the influence of an electric field. The concentration of these conduction electrons is approximately 10^{23} cm^{-3}.

(a) Calculate the electron mobility in copper at room temperature. How does this compare with Si and Ge?

(b) Calculate the net average velocity of the electrons in the direction of the current flow (assume it is the x-direction) in a 0.1-mm^2 cross-sectional area wire carrying a current of 1 A. [Assume that the current is due to the cooperative motion of the electrons ("drift") superimposed on their random thermal velocity (which by itself does not lead to any net current).]

3.7 A sample of silicon uniformly doped with 2×10^{16} cm^{-3} donors is illuminated by penetrating light that generates 10^{20} hole-electron pairs per second per cm^3 uniformly throughout its bulk. The conductivity of the sample is found to increase by 1 percent (i.e., from σ_o to $1.01\ \sigma_o$) when it is illuminated. You may use $\mu_e = 1500$ cm^2/V·s, $\mu_h = 600$ cm^2/V · s, and $n_i(300\text{ K}) = 1.0 \times 10^{10}$ cm^{-3}.

(a) Calculate n_o, p_o, and s_o.

(b) What are n' and p'?

(c) Do low-level injection conditions hold? Why?

(d) What is the minority carrier lifetime τ_h?

(e) How does the conductivity vary with time if, after being on for a long time, the illumination is extinguished at $t = 0$?

3.8 Consider a uniformly doped germanium sample with reflecting boundaries in which the minority carrier lifetime τ_m is 10^{-3} s. The sample is illuminated by steady-state light generating G hole-electron pairs/cm^3 · s uniformly throughout its bulk, with the result that everywhere $n = n_o + n' = 5 \times 10^{16}$ cm^{-3} and $p = p_o + p' = 10^{13}$ cm^{-3}. Assume that for germanium at room temperature $\mu_e = 3900$ cm^2/V · s, $\mu_h = 1900$ cm^2/V · s, and $n_i = 2.4 \times 10^{13}$ cm^{-3}.

(a) Calculate the thermal equilibrium electron and hole concentrations n_o and p_o in this sample.

(b) Calculate the excess electron and hole concentrations n' and p' in this sample when it is illuminated by $g_L = G$.

(c) Calculate the optical generation intensity G.

(d) Calculate the resistivity of this sample.

(e) After the illumination has been on for a very long time, its intensity is abruptly cut in half. Assuming that this occurs at $t = 0$, that is,

$$g_L(t) = G \quad \text{for} \quad t < 0 \quad \text{and} \quad g_L(t) = \frac{G}{2} \quad \text{for} \quad t \geq 0$$

find an expression for $p'(t)$ valid for $t \geq 0$.

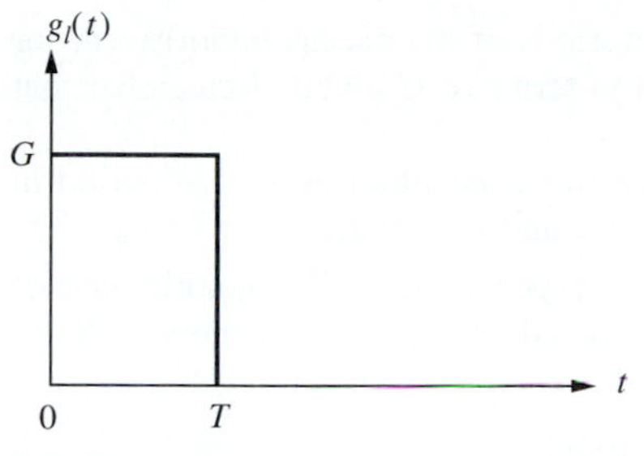

FIGURE P3.9

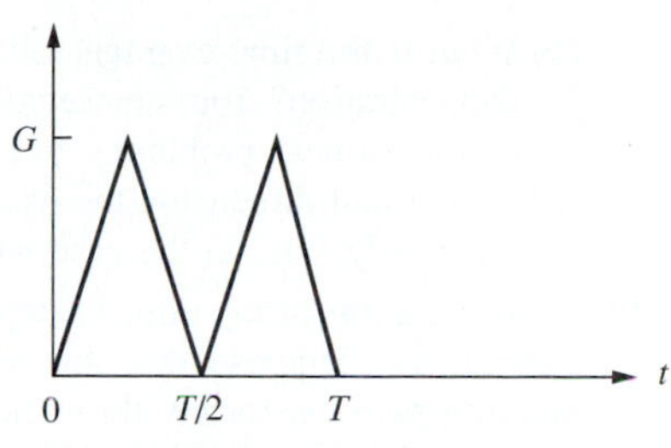

FIGURE P3.9e

3.9 A uniformly doped p-type germanium sample, $p_o = 10^{17}$ cm^{-3}, is illuminated such that the generation function, $g_l(t)$, varies with time as illustrated in Fig. P3.9.

The minority carrier lifetime in this sample is τ_e. You may assume that low-level injection is maintained.

(a) What is $n'(t)$ for $0 \leq t \leq T$?

(b) If the excess minority carrier population at $t = T$ is $n'(T)$, what is the population as a function of time for $t \geq T$?

(c) Find a linear expression for $n'(t)$ in the range $0 \leq t \leq T$ valid when $T \ll \tau_e$.

(d) What is $n'(T)$ in the limit $T \ll \tau_e$?

(e) The generation function is changed to that indicated in Fig. P3.9*e*. In the limit $T \ll \tau_e$, what is $n'(T)$ for this excitation. What is $n'(t)$ for $t > T$?

3.10 A sample of germanium which is uniformly doped with 5×10^{16} cm^{-3} boron atoms and in which the minority carrier lifetime is 10^{-4} s is illuminated with light, generating hole-electron pairs uniformly throughout it with a repetitive time variation illustrated in Fig. P3.10. Assume that the illumination has been on for a long time and that the quantity a is a constant between 0 and 0.5, that is, $0 < a < 0.5$.

(a) Sketch and dimension the excess minority carrier concentration for one period in the steady state in the case where the product aT is much greater than the minority carrier lifetime, that is, when $T \gg 10^{-4}$ s.

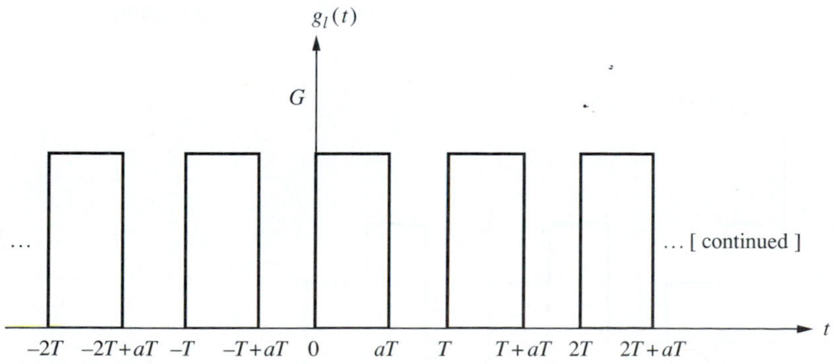

FIGURE P3.10

(b) What is the time-average value over many periods of the excess minority carrier concentration? Your answer should be given in terms of G and a. Remember that this is a linear problem.

(c) Sketch and dimension the excess minority carrier concentration for one period in the steady state in the case where $T \ll 10^{-4}$ s and $a = 0.25$.

3.11 Consider a uniformly doped sample of extrinsic p-type silicon with a minority carrier lifetime τ_e. Suppose that this sample is illuminated by light that generates hole-electron pairs uniformly throughout its bulk as

$$g_L(t) = G_L + g_l(t)$$

G_L is not a function of time and is of sufficient magnitude that it violates low-level injection conditions, and $g_l(t)$ is time-dependent and does not alone violate low-level injection. When G_L alone is illuminating the sample, call the excess electron population n_1'; when $g_l(t)$ alone is illuminating the sample, call it n_2'; and when g_L $(= G_L + g_l)$ is illuminating the sample, call it n_3'.

(a) Find the quadratic equation that must be solved to find n_1' in terms of τ_e, G_L, and p_o. (This was done in the text, but go through it yourself.)

(b) Show that n_3 can be written as $n_3 = n_1 + n_4$ where n_4 satisfies the differential equation

$$\frac{dn_4'}{dt} = g_l(t) - \frac{n_4'}{t'}$$

(c) Find an expression for τ', argue that it is reasonable physically (i.e., that it looks "right"), and explain why.

(d) Is $n_2' = n_4'$? Explain your answer.

3.12 Consider an n-type sample of gallium arsenide with $N_D = 5 \times 10^{16}$ cm^{-3} and $\tau_{min} = 10^{-8}$ s, which is illuminated in such a way that $g_L(t)$ hole-electron pairs/cm$^2 \cdot$ s are generated uniformly throughout it. The waveform of $g_L(t)$ is periodic and is illustrated in Fig. P3.12.

(a) Show that $g_L(t)$ can be written as

$$g_L(t) = G + g_l'(t)$$

where G is the average value of $g_L(t)$ and $g_l'(t)$ has zero average value, by sketching G and $g_l(t)$. [Note that $g_l'(t)$ becomes negative, which is not possible physically but is perfectly fine mathematically.]

(b) What is the average value of excess hole concentration p' in this sample?

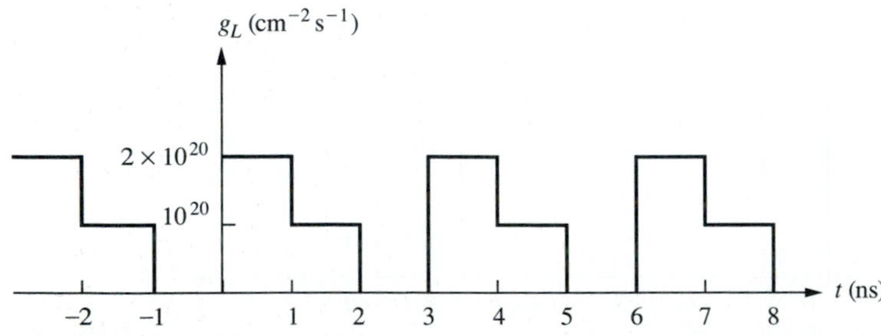

FIGURE P3.12

(c) Sketch the solution for $p'(t)$ corresponding to the excitation $g_l(t)$ you found in a, assuming $\tau_{\min} \gg 1$ ns.

(d) Your solution in (c) should look a lot like the integral of $g_l(t)$.

(i) Explain why this is the case.

(ii) Explain why a similar integration approach can't be used on $g_L(t)$ directly.

3.13 You are asked to design a light detector like that illustrated Fig. P3.13, in which the photoconductivity of a thin semiconductor film is used to sense the light. You are to choose the semiconductor from the choices listed below, select its carrier type and doping level, and specify the lateral dimensions of the device. Your design objective is to produce a detector that

(i) Has a conductivity G in the dark ($g_L = 0$) of under 10^{-4} mho

(ii) Displays a change in conductivity that is linearly proportional (with 10 percent to the incident light intensity for g_L up to 10^{20} cm$^{-3}\cdot$ s)

(iii) Has a high sensitivity, defined as dG/dg_L, in its linear region

(iv) Has a high ratio of photocurrent to dark current

No lateral dimension in your device should be less than 2 microns or greater than 100 microns. The film is one micron thick, and the light generates carriers uniformly throughout it.

Choose the semiconductor from the following list. It can be either n- or p-type and can have any doping level you want. The intrinsic carrier concentration at room temperature in both materials is less than 10^{10} cm^{-3}.

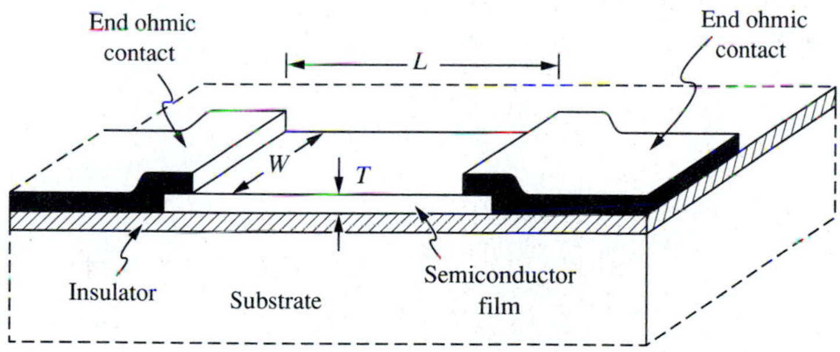

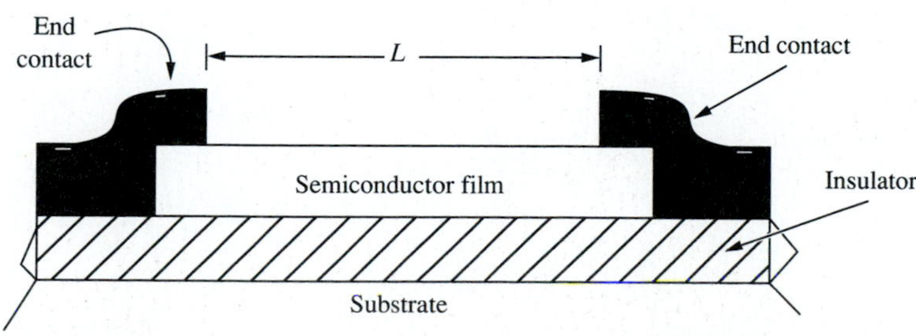

FIGURE P3.13

(i) Semiconductor #1: $\mu_e = 2000\ \text{cm}^2/\text{V}\cdot\text{s}$; $\mu_h = 0.1\ \text{cm}^2/\text{V}\cdot\text{s}$; $\tau_{\text{min}} = 10^{-4}$ s
(ii) Semiconductor #2: $\mu_e = 3500\ \text{cm}^2/\text{V}\cdot\text{s}$; $\mu_h = 500\ \text{cm}^2/\text{V}\cdot\text{s}$; $\tau_{\text{min}} = 10^{-4}$ s

List the following items together on your solution in a clear manner:

(i) Which semiconductor you chose, its carrier type, and the doping level
(ii) Length L and width W of the device
(iii) Dark conductivity G_o
(iv) Sensitivitiy in the linear region and the bound on g_L for this region
(v) Ratio of the photocurrent to the dark current

CHAPTER 4

NONUNIFORM SITUATIONS: THE FIVE BASIC EQUATIONS

We have looked at the carrier concentrations in a uniformly doped semiconductor in thermal equilibrium and also when uniformly excited by light. We have also looked at charge carrier motion under the influence of a uniform electric field (i.e., drift). Now we will consider nonuniform situations. We will consider both nonuniformly doped semiconductors, and uniformly doped semiconductors that are excited nonuniformly, for example, by light or at a contact or junction in a device. We want to learn how to find the carrier distributions, the electric fields, and the currents that in general will exist in such cases. The solutions to these types of problems play a central role in our models for diodes and bipolar transistors, as we shall see in Chaps. 7 and 8. We begin our treatment of nonuniform conditions by discussing diffusion and diffusion currents. We then discuss the formulation of five basic equations describing nonuniform situations in semiconductors.

4.1 DIFFUSION

We have already discussed the drift motion of charged particles under the influence of gradient in electrostatic potential (i.e., an electric field). Another "force" that can lead to a net movement of particles is a gradient in their concentration. This type of movement is called *diffusion*. Diffusion is a very widespread phenomenon that is encountered in many situations and has been applied in many useful ways. One important thing to realize about diffusion is that diffusing particles need not be electrically charged, as they must be in order to drift. Diffusion has nothing to do with the electrical charge of the particles. If the particles do carry charge, however, then a diffusing flux of those particles will carry an electrical charge flux, or current. We will see this in detail later. For now we simply consider uncharged particles and look at the general process of diffusion.

4.1.1 A Model for Diffusion

Diffusion is the net motion of carriers in a concentration gradient. This motion results from the continual random thermal motion of the carriers. To see how this occurs and how we can express it mathematically, imagine that we have a concentration of particles of species m, C_m, that varies with position in the x-direction; that is, $C_m(x)$. These particles are at a finite temperature T and have random thermal motion. We assume that the motion of any one particle is independent of the other particles and thus that the motion of the particles is random and independent of their concentration.

Now consider mentally dividing the sample into slabs, normal to the x-direction, that are Δx thick. The slab centered about $x = x_1$ will contain approximately $\Delta x C_m(x_1)$ particles per unit area in the slab; per unit time a fraction a of those particles will move (due to their random thermal motion) over to the slab at $x = x_1 + \Delta x$, yielding a flow of particles to the right equal to $a(\Delta x)C_m(x_1)$ per unit area. This concept is illustrated in Fig. 4.1. Similarly, the slab centered at $x = x_1 + \Delta x$ contains $\Delta x C_m(x_1 + \Delta x)$ particles per unit area, the same fraction a of which will move per unit time over to the slab at $x = x_1$. (The fractions a are the same because we are assuming random, independent motion.) The net flow to the right across the plane between $x = x_1$ and $x = x_1 + \Delta x$ is the difference of these two terms. This net flux density is

$$F_m = a\Delta x[C_m(x_1) - C_m(x_1 + \Delta x)] \tag{4.1}$$

We next use a Taylor's series expansion to relate $C_m(x_1)$ and $C_m(x_1 + \Delta x)$ to the gradient of $C_m(x)$ at $x = x_1$

$$C_m(x_1 + \Delta x) \approx C_m(x_1) + \Delta x \frac{\partial C_m}{\partial x}\Big|_{x=x_1} \tag{4.2}$$

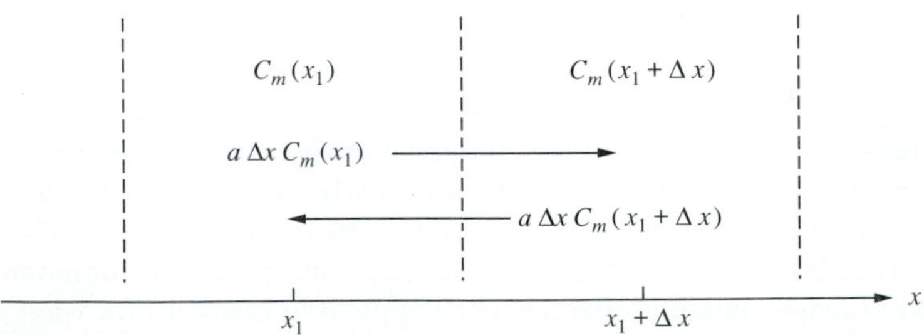

FIGURE 4.1
Illustration of the setup of the diffusion model of Sec. 4.1.1.

Using this expression in Eq. (4.1) yields

$$F_m = -a(\Delta x)^2 \frac{\partial C_m}{\partial x} \tag{4.3a}$$

Thus we find that a net flux exists because of the gradient in the concentration and is proportional to it; we call this flux the *diffusion flux*. We define the product $a(\Delta x)^2$ to be the diffusion coefficient D_m of the species m and write Eq. (4.3a) as

$$F_m = -D_m \frac{\partial C_m}{\partial x} \tag{4.3b}$$

The diffusion coefficient D_m has the units cm^2/s. The units of flux are particles/$cm^2 \cdot s$, or simply $cm^{-2} \cdot s^{-1}$. Equation (4.3) is the general diffusion relation; it is often called Fick's First Law.

In this model D_m appears to depend on Δx, but one must remember that a will also depend on Δx. The net result is that D_m does not depend on Δx; that is, it is independent of the details of the model, as we know it must be. D_m does, however, depend on temperature (exponentially, in fact), on the type of particles diffusing, and on the environment in which the particles are diffusing.

4.1.2 Diffusion Current Density

If the diffusing particles are charged we have a net charge flux, or current density, given by

$$J_m = q_m F_m \tag{4.4}$$

where q_m represents the charge on each particle. Focusing our discussion on holes and electrons in a semiconductor, we have the following:

$$\text{Hole diffusion current:} \quad J_h^{\text{diff}} = -qD_h \frac{\partial p}{\partial x} \tag{4.5a}$$

$$\text{Electron diffusion current:} \quad J_e^{\text{diff}} = qD_e \frac{\partial n}{\partial x} \tag{4.5b}$$

Notice that for electrons we had to use $q_m = -q$, so the original minus sign has disappeared.

4.1.3 Other Diffusion Important in Devices

Diffusion is a very common phenomenon that has important applications in the fabrication of semiconductor devices as well as in their operation. One important means of introducing n- and p-type dopants into a semiconductor is through diffusion. A high concentration of the dopant is established on the outside surface of the semiconductor, and it is allowed to diffuse into the surface. Negligible dopant diffusion occurs at room temperature, but when silicon is heated to 1000°C, for example, a dopant like boron will diffuse several microns into the surface in an hour or two. (See App. G for more discussion of this.)

4.2 MODELING NONUNIFORM SITUATIONS

With nonuniform excitation or doping, we anticipate that the excess carrier populations will be nonuniform, and since there will be gradients in the charge carrier concentrations, there will be diffusion currents. Furthermore, since the carriers will in general diffuse at different rates, we can anticipate that there will be charge imbalances from which an electric field will arise. An electric field implies that there will be drift currents as well as diffusion currents. All told, we will have a total of five unknown quantities to determine: the excess electron and hole concentrations, $n'(x, t)$ and $p'(x, t)$; the electron and hole currents, $J_{\text{ex}}(x, t)$ and $J_{\text{hx}}(x, t)$; and the electric field, $\mathscr{E}_x(x, t)$. As this notation indicates, these quantities will in general all be functions of position and time. Also, recall that we are restricting ourselves to variations in the x-direction only.

4.2.1 Total Current Densities

We have discussed drift currents and diffusion currents. In any general situation, the *total* electron and hole current densities are the sum of the respective drift and diffusion current densities:

$$J_h = J_h^{\text{drift}} + J_h^{\text{diff}}$$

and

$$J_e = J_e^{\text{drift}} + J_e^{\text{diff}}$$

Using Eqs. (3.8), (3.10), and (4.5), we can write

$$J_h = q p \mu_h \mathscr{E}_x - q D_h \frac{\partial p}{\partial x} \tag{4.6}$$

and

$$J_e = q n \mu_e \mathscr{E}_x + q D_e \frac{\partial n}{\partial x} \tag{4.7}$$

The total current density is, of course, the sum of the electron and hole current densities:

$$J_{\text{tot}} = J_h + J_e \tag{4.8}$$

These expressions for the electron and hole currents give us two of the equations we need relating to our five unknowns.

4.2.2 The Continuity Equations

When we discussed generation and recombination in uniformly excited uniformly doped material, we had the following equations relating the hole or electron concentration at a point to the net generation or recombination occurring at that point:

$$\frac{dn}{dt} = \frac{dp}{dt} = g_L - r(np - n_o p_o) \tag{3.23}$$

In nonuniformly excited or doped material we must modify these equations to account for the fact that there is now another mechanism by which the carrier concentrations can change; namely, through nonuniform flow of particles. Before proceeding to do this, however, it is also worth noting that the product $n_o p_o$ is still n_i^2, even if n_o and p_o are functions of position, and n_i^2 is, of course, not a function of position.

Consider a given region in a sample. If the particle flux into that region is the same as the flux out, there will be no net increase or decrease in the particle concentration in that region. If, however, the flux out is larger than the flux in, the concentration must be decreasing with time. If the flux out is smaller, then the opposite is true. We can state this mathematically (in one dimension) as

$$\frac{\partial C_m}{\partial t} = \frac{-\partial F_m}{\partial x} \tag{4.9}$$

where C_m is the particle concentration and F_m is the flux (cm^{-2}-s^{-1}). This expression is another basic diffusion equation known as Fick's Second Law. To see where this result comes from, consider a region located between $x = x_1$ and $x = x_1 + \Delta x$ that is Δx long in the x-direction and has a cross-sectional area (normal to x) of A. For simplicity we will consider only a one-dimensional problem, so we restrict the flux to the x-direction and allow it to vary only with x; that is, we have $F_m(x)$. The number of particles entering the region from the left per unit time is $AF_m(x)$, and the number leaving to the right at $x = x_1 + \Delta x$ is $AF_m(x_1 + \Delta x)$. The rate of increase in the number of particles M in the region is given by

$$\frac{\partial M}{\partial t} = A[F_m(x_1) - F_m(x_1 + \Delta x)] \tag{4.10}$$

Expanding about x_1 we obtain

$$F_m(x_1 + \Delta x) \approx F_m(x_1) + \frac{\partial F_m(x_1)}{\partial x}\Delta x$$

which, when substituted into Eq. (4.10), gives us

$$\frac{\partial M}{\partial t} = -A\Delta x \frac{\partial F_m}{\partial x} \tag{4.11}$$

Dividing by the volume of the region to get the particle density, we have

$$\frac{\partial C_m}{\partial t} = -\frac{\partial F_m}{\partial x} \tag{4.12}$$

Returning now to our original problem, we want to generalize Eq. (3.23) to nonuniform situations by adding the change in the carrier concentration due to the gradient in the particle fluxes or, in this case, currents. We divide the currents by the charge on the carriers and add these components to the previous equations:

$$\frac{\partial n}{\partial t} = g_L - r(np - n^2{}_i) - \frac{1}{-q}\frac{\partial J_e}{\partial x} \tag{4.13a}$$

and

$$\frac{\partial p}{\partial t} = g_L - r(np - n^2{}_i) - \frac{1}{+q}\frac{\partial J_h}{\partial x} \tag{4.13b}$$

Note that we write the derivatives as partials because now n, p, and J can all be functions of both x and t. We have also replaced $n_o p_o$ with n_i^2.

Note that the g_L and $r(np - n^2{}_i)$ terms are common to both equations, so we often write these equations as

$$\frac{\partial n}{\partial t} - \frac{1}{q}\frac{\partial J_e}{\partial x} = \frac{\partial p}{\partial t} + \frac{1}{q}\frac{\partial J_h}{\partial x} = g_L - r(np - n_i{}^2) \tag{4.13c}$$

These *continuity equations,* as they are termed, give us two additional relationships between the carrier concentrations and fluxes, bringing our total number of equations to four.

4.2.3 Gauss's Law

The fifth equation we need to begin solving for our five unknowns is Gauss's law, which relates the net charge at any point to the gradient in the electric field. In one dimension this is

$$\frac{\partial[\varepsilon(x)\mathcal{E}(x,t)]}{\partial x} = \rho(x,t) \tag{4.14}$$

where $\varepsilon(x)$ is the dielectric constant. Writing out $\rho(x,t)$ we have

$$\frac{\partial[\varepsilon(x)\mathcal{E}(x,t)]}{\partial x} = q[p(x,t) - n(x,t) + N_d(x) - N_a(x)] \tag{4.14$'$}$$

This is the final relationship we need relating our five unknowns.

4.2.4 The Five Basic Equations

We collect the five equations together below:

$$J_e(x,t) = qn(x,t)\mu_e(x)\mathcal{E}(x,t) + qD_e(x)\frac{\partial n(x,t)}{\partial x} \tag{4.15}$$

$$J_h(x,t) = q\,p(x,t)\mu_h(x)\mathscr{E}(x,t) - qD_h(x)\frac{\partial p(x,t)}{\partial x} \quad (4.16)$$

$$-\frac{1}{q}\frac{\partial J_e(x,t)}{\partial x} + \frac{\partial n(x,t)}{\partial t} = g_L(x,t) - r(T)[p(x,t)n(x,t) - n_i^2(T)] \quad (4.17)$$

$$\frac{1}{q}\frac{\partial J_h(x,t)}{\partial x} + \frac{\partial p(x,t)}{\partial t} = g_L(x,t) - r(T)[p(x,t)n(x,t) - n_i^2(T)] \quad (4.18)$$

$$\frac{\partial[\varepsilon(x)\mathscr{E}(x,t)]}{\partial x} = q[p(x,t) - n(x,t) + N_d(x) - N_a(x)] \quad (4.19)$$

This set of equations forms the starting point for our analysis of semiconductor devices. These differential equations are, however, coupled and nonlinear and are in general very difficult to solve, even with the aid of a large computer. Fortunately there is a broad class of problems, flow problems, that form an important subset in which significant simplifications can be made and the five equations can be linearized and largely decoupled. We address this subset in the next chapter. There is yet another broad class of problems, *p-n* junctions, for which a second set of approximations and simplifications can be made, leading again to analytical models. We will discuss these problems in Chap. 6.

4.3 SUMMARY

In this chapter, we began our consideration of nonuniform situations and introduced the very important concept of diffusion, the second mechanism—along with drift—by which charge carriers move, and thus current flows, in semiconductors. We saw, however, that diffusion does not depend on charge or electric fields; it occurs simply because a concentration gradient exists. Nonetheless, if the diffusing particles are charged, their diffusion leads to a diffusion current density.

Having defined diffusion, we then looked at defining the scope of the problem we face under nonuniform situations and at the equations at our disposal to model them. We identified five "unknowns": the two carrier concentrations, the two corresponding carrier fluxes (currents), and the electric field; and we developed five equations, collected above as Eqs. (4.15) through (4.19), which can be solved for the five unknowns. Their solutions in two special sets of circumstances will be the topics of Chaps. 5 and 6.

PROBLEMS

4.1 *(a)* The diffusion coefficient for boron in silicon is 2×10^{-14} cm^2/s at 1000°C. Use this fact and the definition of D in terms of a and Δx that precedes Eq. (4.3b) to estimate the rate at which boron atoms move from lattice site to lattice site ($\Delta x \approx 2.5$ Å) in Si at 1000°C.

(b) As a function of temperature, the diffusion coefficient of silicon can be written as $D_o e^{-Ea/kT}$ where D_o is 2 cm^2/s, E_a is 3.5 eV and k is 8.62×10^{-5} eV/K. Using this information, verify the value for D given in a.

(c) Calculate the diffusion coefficient of boron in Si at room temperature, and again estimate the rate at which boron atoms move to a new lattice site.

(d) Repeat *c* at 1150°C.

4.2 Simplify the five equations in the special case of uniform material under uniform time-varying low-level optical excitation, and show that they reduce to Eqs. (3.33) and (3.34).

4.3 Simplify the five equations in the special case of uniform material with no optical excitation and with a uniform, constant electric field within the sample, and show that they reduce to Eq. (3.12).

4.4 Basic models for solid-state diffusion, that is, the diffusion of dopant atoms in a semiconductor, assume that the diffusing atoms are uncharged and that there is thus no drift component to their flux. The only flux is that due to diffusion and is given by Fick's First Law, Eq. (4.3). Furthermore, there is no generation or recombination of atoms, so the only way the concentration of atoms at a point can change with time is if there is a divergence in the flux, as shown by Fick's Second Law, Eq. (4.9). These two equations give us the two relationships we need between the two unknowns in this problem, the concentration $C_m(x,t)$ and flux $F_m(x,t)$.

(a) Combine Eqs. (4.3b) and (4.9) to get a differential equation for $C_m(x,t)$.

(b) Show that the expression

$$C_M(x,t) = \frac{A}{\sqrt{\pi D m t}} \exp\left[\frac{-(x-x_o)}{4D_m t}\right]$$

satisfies the equation you found in (a). A curve with this shape is called a Gaussian.

(c) When a fixed number of dopant atoms is introduced in a shallow layer on a semiconductor surface and they diffuse into the surface over time, their profile is Gaussian (see App. G, Fig. G.3b).

(i) Show that a Gaussian fits the boundary constraints of this type of a problem by showing that

$$\int_{-\infty}^{\infty} C_m(x,t)dx = \text{Constant independent of } t$$

and

$$\lim_{t\to 0} C_m(x,t) = \begin{Bmatrix} 0 \text{ if } x \neq x_o \\ \infty \text{ if } x = x_o \end{Bmatrix}$$

(ii) Explain the significance of each of these relationships.

(d) If a Gaussian satisfies the differential equation you found in (a), so too will an infinite sum of Gaussians. An important sum is the error function erf(y), defined as

$$\text{erf}(y) \equiv \frac{2}{\sqrt{\pi}} \int_0^y e^{-\alpha^2} d\alpha$$

and another is the complementary error function erfc (y), defined as

$$\text{erfc}(y) \equiv 1 - \text{erf}(y)$$

Look up the properties of the complementary error function in a mathematics reference, and show that it fits the boundary conditions of a diffusion into a semiconductor surface in which the concentration at the surface is held fixed, that is, $C_m(0, t) =$ constant. (See App. G, Fig. G.3a.)

4.5 Our equations for current density, Eqs. (4.15) and (4.16), can be viewed as composed of a diffusion current density due to a gradient in the concentration and a drift current density due to a gradient in the electrostatic potential (because $\mathscr{E} = -\partial\phi/\partial x$). If we remove our requirement of constant temperature, we must add another term to the current density, namely, one due to a gradient in the temperature.

(a) Add electron and hole flux current density terms to Eqs. (4.15) and (4.16) that are proportional to the gradient in the temperature, $\partial/\partial T$.

(b) What are the signs on the terms you added in (a)? Explain your reasoning.

(c) How do the terms you added depend on the carrier concentrations? Rewrite them, if necessary, to show this dependence explicitly.

CHAPTER

5

NONUNIFORM CARRIER INJECTION: FLOW PROBLEMS

An important set of problems for which we can get analytical solutions to the five basic equations developed in Chap. 4 [Eqs. (4.15) through (4.19)] are those involving nonuniform, low-level, essentially static injection of carriers into a uniform extrinsic semiconductor. Although you have no reason a priori to suspect that such problems are of interest to anybody, these problems, which we will call *flow problems*, are at the heart of *p-n* diode and bipolar transistor operation. Understanding flow problems is essential to our modeling of these devices, and developing that understanding is our goal in this chapter.

5.1 DEVELOPING THE DIFFUSION EQUATION

To proceed with a solution of the five basic equations relating the carrier populations, currents, and electric field, we restrict ourselves to situations in which the following five assumptions are valid:

1. The material is extrinsic and uniformly doped.
2. There is only low-level injection.
3. There is very little net charge density; that is, the material is *quasineutral*.
4. The minority carrier drift current is negligible.
5. There is very little variation with time; that is, the excitation is *quasistatic*.

We will look in turn at each of these assumptions before arriving at our ultimate goal, the diffusion equation.

5.1.1 Uniformly Doped Extrinsic Material

If the material we are considering is extrinsic and is uniformly doped, then we know the equilibrium electron and hole concentrations, n_o and p_o, already and just have to find the excess electron and hole populations, $n'(x, t)$ and $p'(x, t)$, respectively. Furthermore, any spatial or temporal derivatives of the populations, $n(x, t)$ and $p(x, t)$, reduce to derivatives of the excess populations, $n'(x, t)$ and $p'(x, t)$, because the equilibrium concentrations are functions of neither time nor position. Thus we have

$$\frac{\partial n}{\partial x} = \frac{\partial n'}{\partial x}, \qquad \frac{\partial p}{\partial x} = \frac{\partial p'}{\partial x}$$

and (5.1)

$$\frac{\partial n}{\partial t} = \frac{\partial n'}{\partial t}, \qquad \frac{\partial p}{\partial t} = \frac{\partial p'}{\partial t}$$

Finally, we know that $N_d(x) - N_a(x)$ can be related to $p_o - n_o$ as

$$p_o - n_o + N_d(x) - N_a(x) = 0 \tag{5.2}$$

so that the last of our five basic equations, Eq. (4.19), reduces to

$$\varepsilon \frac{\partial \mathscr{E}(x, t)}{\partial x} = q[p'(x, t) - n'(x, t)] \tag{5.3}$$

Notice that in writing Eq. (5.3) we have used the fact that our material is uniform to conclude that the dielectric constant ε is not a function of x, so it can be pulled out of the derivative.

5.1.2 Low-Level Injection

Recall that by low-level injection we mean that the excess carrier concentrations must be much less than the majority carrier concentration. A general way of writing the low-level injection condition is

$$n', p' \ll p_o + n_o \tag{5.4}$$

The sum on the right is essentially just the majority carrier concentration because in extrinsic material the equilibrium population of majority carriers is many orders of magnitude larger than the minority carrier population.

If low-level injection conditions exist, we can remove the nonlinearity in the continuity equations, Eqs. (4.17) and (4.18), as we have seen in Chap. 3. To review, we begin with

$$G - R = G_o + g_L(x, t) - n\,p\,r \tag{5.5a}$$

Replacing G_o with $n_o p_o r$ yields

$$G - R = g_L(x, t) - (np - n_o p_o)r \tag{5.5b}$$

Next, replacing n and p with $(n_o + n')$ and $(p_o + p')$, respectively, neglecting the term involving the product $n'p'$, and assuming $n' \simeq p'$ (which we will justify in the following subsection) we have

$$G - R \approx g_L(x, t) - n'(n_o + p_o)r \tag{5.5c}$$

We may write

$$G - R \approx g_L(x, t) - \frac{n'}{\tau_{\min}} \tag{5.5d}$$

if we define the minority carrier lifetime $\tau_{\min}$ as

$$\tau_{\min} \equiv \frac{1}{(n_o + p_o)r} \tag{5.6}$$

Thus, under low-level injection conditions, Eqs. (4.17) and (4.18) become

$$\frac{\partial n'}{\partial t} - \frac{1}{q}\frac{\partial J_e}{\partial x} = g_L(x, t) - \frac{n'}{\tau_{\min}} \tag{5.7a}$$

and

$$\frac{\partial p'}{\partial t} + \frac{1}{q}\frac{\partial J_h}{\partial x} = g_L(x, t) - \frac{n'}{\tau_{\min}} \tag{5.7b}$$

When we are dealing with extrinsic material, as we are here, either p_o or n_o will dominate the sum $p_o + n_o$ in the definition of the minority carrier lifetime, so it is more common to write Eq. (5.6) as

$$\tau_{\min} \equiv \tau_e \approx \frac{1}{p_o r}$$

in p-type material, and as

$$\tau_{\min} \equiv \tau_h \approx \frac{1}{n_o r}$$

in n-type material.

5.1.3 Quasineutrality

By quasineutrality we mean that any charge imbalances are small, that is, that

$$n'(x, t) \approx p'(x, t) \tag{5.8}$$

and

$$\frac{\partial n'(x, t)}{\partial x} \approx \frac{\partial p'(x, t)}{\partial x} \tag{5.9}$$

We don't mean that these quantities are equal; rather, their differences are much smaller than their sums:

$$|n' - p'| \ll n' + p' \tag{5.10}$$

and

$$\left|\frac{\partial n'}{\partial x} - \frac{\partial p'}{\partial x}\right| \ll \left|\frac{\partial n'}{\partial x} + \frac{\partial p'}{\partial x}\right| \tag{5.11}$$

Quasineutrality is a very important concept. It is also a very rugged assumption in most semiconductors because the mobile majority charge carriers readily move so as to reduce and essentially eliminate any deviations from neutrality. Simplistically, the negative and positive charge distributions attract each other and, if possible, move together to balance each other out.

We can quantify our argument that quasineutrality is a widely applicable assumption by examining the spatial and temporal characteristics of $(p' - n')$. We find (see App. D) that temporal deviations from quasineutrality dissipate on a time scale on the order of the dielectric relaxation time τ_D, given by

$$\tau_D \equiv \frac{\varepsilon}{\sigma_o} \tag{5.12}$$

where ε is the dielectric constant and σ_o is the thermal equilibrium conductivity. We also find (again see App. D) that spatial deviations from quasineutrality dissipate within a few extrinsic Debye lengths, L_{De}, given by

$$L_{\text{De}} \equiv \sqrt{D_{\text{maj}}\tau_D} \tag{5.13}$$

where D_{maj} is the majority carrier diffusion coefficient.

Example

Question. A moderately low conductivity semiconductor might have a conductivity σ_o, of 1 S/cm. What are the dielectric relaxation time and extrinsic Debye length in such a sample? Assume that the majority carrier diffusion constant D_{maj} has a value typical of n-type silicon, 16 cm^2/s. The permittivity ε of silicon is approximately 10^{-12} C/V · cm.

Discussion. Using Eq. (5.12), we find that the dielectric relaxation time τ_D is one picosecond, (i.e., 10^{-12} s). This result tells us that it is hard to maintain an appreciable difference between p' and n' for more than a few picoseconds in such a sample.

Next, using Eq. (5.13) and this value for the dielectric relaxation time, we calculate that the extrinsic Debye length L_{De}, is 4×10^{-6} cm, or 400 Å. Again this result tells us that any deviations from charge neutrality will exist only over very short distances.

All told, the tendency to quasineutrality is very strong in a typical semiconductor. We have already used it to linearize the continuity equations in Sec. 5.1.2, and we will use it again in the next section.

It is important to note that we are not saying that n' equals p', for that would mean that there is no gradient in the electric field [see Eq. (5.3)]. We *are* saying, however, that n' and p' are similar, and in many cases one can be substituted for the other. On the other hand, when the difference between n' and p' is important, as in Eq. (5.3), we must be more careful.

5.1.4 Minority Carriers Flow by Diffusion

A traditional assumption is given by the statement "Minority carriers flow only by diffusion." What this really means is that under low-level injection conditions the minority carrier drift current is always a very small fraction of the total current. Thus if we have to worry about the minority carrier current at all in flow problems, the minority carrier diffusion current will be what matters.

The conclusion that minority carrier *drift* current is unimportant in extrinsic material should not be surprising to you because you already know that the majority carrier population is significantly greater than the minority carrier population as long as low-level injection conditions hold. Thus the minority drift current will be much, much less than the majority carrier drift current.

The minority and majority carrier *diffusion* currents, on the other hand, depend not on the total number of carriers but rather on their gradients; and their gradients are comparable [Eq. (5.9)]. The diffusion coefficients for holes and electrons, D_h and D_e, are also of the same order of magnitude, so the diffusion currents of holes and electrons tend to be of comparable magnitude (but, of course, of opposite sign).

We can make no general statement with respect to the relative sizes of the majority carrier drift current and the two diffusion currents other than to say that there are no restrictions. Sometimes the current is essentially all majority carrier drift, other times it is all majority and minority carrier diffusion; still other times it comprises comparable magnitudes of majority carrier drift and diffusion and minority carrier diffusion components.

However, we can in general say that it is probably correct to assume that the minority carrier drift current is negligibly small in flow problems. We can say this because we realize that the minority carrier diffusion current is the only component of the minority carrier current that has a chance of being comparable to, or larger than, the majority carrier drift current. Thus, if there is any appreciable minority carrier current, it must be the minority carrier diffusion current and we can therefore approximate the total minority carrier current density as simply

$$J_{\min} = -q_{\min} D_{\min} \frac{\partial C_{\min}}{\partial x} \tag{5.14}$$

This single observation has an enormous simplifying impact on our set of equations. It removes the nonlinear product term of the minority carrier concentration and the electric field from the equation for the minority carrier current, and in fact eliminates the electric field from that equation altogether.

5.1.5 Time-Dependent Diffusion Equation

Before considering the fifth assumption—that our excitation is quasistatic—we should rewrite our five equations in light of our assumptions thus far. Since we know that it matters which are the minority and majority carriers, let us assume for the sake of discussion that we are considering a p-type sample. We then use our assumptions to write

$$J_e(x,t) \approx qD_e \frac{\partial n'(x,t)}{\partial x} \tag{5.15}$$

$$J_h(x,t) \approx q\mu_h p_o \mathscr{E}(x,t) - qD_h \frac{\partial p'(x,t)}{\partial x} \tag{5.16}$$

$$-\frac{1}{q}\frac{\partial J_e(x,t)}{\partial x} + \frac{\partial n'(x,t)}{\partial t} + \frac{n'}{\tau_e} = g_L(t) \tag{5.17}$$

$$\frac{1}{q}\frac{\partial J_h(x,t)}{\partial x} + \frac{\partial p'(x,t)}{\partial t} + \frac{n'}{\tau_e} = g_L(t) \tag{5.18}$$

$$\varepsilon \frac{\partial \mathscr{E}(x,t)}{\partial x} = q\left[p'(x,t) - n'(x,t)\right] \tag{5.19}$$

Our set of five equations is now completely linear, and some of the coupling has been eliminated. In fact, we see that Eqs. (5.15) and (5.17) now each involve only the excess minority carrier concentration $n'(x,t)$ and the minority carrier current $J_e(x,t)$; they form a set of two equations in two unknowns. Eliminating $J_e(x,t)$ from them by inserting Eq. (5.15) into Eq. (5.17) results in a single linear differential equation for $n'(x,t)$:

$$\frac{\partial n'(x,t)}{dt} - D_e \frac{\partial^2 n'(x,t)}{dx^2} + \frac{n'(x,t)}{\tau_e} = g_L(x,t) \tag{5.20}$$

This equation describes the diffusion of minority carriers under low-level injection conditions in a uniformly doped, extrinsic semiconductor, but it turns out to be even more general than that. It describes the motion of any particles moving primarily only by diffusion. It describes, for example, the diffusion of dopant atoms into silicon.

We have already seen Eq. (5.20) in the special case of uniform excitation. In this situation there is no dependence on x, and the $\partial^2/\partial x^2$ term is zero. In this case, Eq. (5.20) reduces to Eq. (3.32).

We will not at this point consider solutions to Eq. (5.20) when we have both space and time variations. Rather, we next restrict ourselves to situations where the time variations are negligible.

5.1.6 Quasistatic Diffusion: Flow Problems

If the variation of $g_L(x,t)$ with time is slow enough that the time derivatives of the carrier concentrations are small relative to the other terms in the equation, we say we have a quasistatic excitation and that we can make the quasistatic approximation. For convenience, we will tend to concentrate on problems where there is no time variation of g_L, but this is, strictly speaking, unnecessarily restrictive. We can have time variation if all of the time derivatives are negligibly small and things look essentially static (i.e., quasistatic).

With the quasistatic approximation, our equation for n' (Eq. 5.20) becomes, after dividing by $-D_e$,

$$\frac{d^2n'}{dx^2} - \frac{n'}{D_e\tau_e} = -\frac{g_L(x)}{D_e} \tag{5.21a}$$

Note that the derivative is now a total, rather than a partial, derivative. The quantity $D_e\tau_e$ has units of length squared, so we may write

$$\frac{d^2n'}{dx^2} - \frac{n'}{L_e^2} = -\frac{g_L(x)}{D_e} \tag{5.21b}$$

where L_e, a minority carrier diffusion length, is given by

$$L_e \equiv \sqrt{D_e\tau_e} \tag{5.22}$$

Equation (5.21b) is a second-order linear differential equation that we will call the *quasistatic diffusion equation*. We will discuss solving it for the minority carrier concentration in the next section. Before doing that, however, we want to show that once we have solved Eq. (5.21b), we can solve for our other unknowns in short order.

Once we know the minority carrier concentration, in this case $n'(x)$, and have verified our assumption of low-level injection, we can immediately get the minority carrier current density $J_e(x)$ using the quasistatic approximation to Eq. (5.15):

$$J_e(x) = q\,D_e\frac{dn'}{dx} \tag{5.23}$$

Assuming we know the total current density J_{TOT}, we next calculate the majority carrier current density as

$$J_h(x) = J_{\text{TOT}} - J_e(x) \tag{5.24}$$

This may seem unreasonable because we have said nothing thus far about J_{TOT}, but the problem being solved will often be defined in such a way that the total current density J_{TOT} is known at at least one point. This is sufficient to tell us J_{TOT} at all x because we can show that J_{TOT} will not change with position if the excitation is quasistatic. To see that this is true, we first subtract Eq. (5.17) from Eq. (5.18) to yield

$$\frac{1}{q}\frac{dJ_h(x)}{dx} + \frac{1}{q}\frac{dJ_e(x)}{dx} = 0 \tag{5.25a}$$

which we can also write as

$$\frac{d}{dx}\left[J_h(x) + J_e(x)\right] = 0 \tag{5.25b}$$

Identifying J_{TOT} as $J_h(x) + J_e(x)$ we have

$$\frac{dJ_{\text{TOT}}}{dx} = 0 \tag{5.25c}$$

This last result tells us that J_{TOT} is not a function of position. Thus if we know J_{TOT} anywhere (even at only one position x), we know it everywhere. Fortunately, as we will discuss at greater length in Section 5.2.4, we will in general be able to find J_{TOT} in any given problem with little difficulty.

From $J_h(x)$ we calculate the electric field $\mathscr{E}(x)$ using Eq. (5.16) and quasineutrality (i.e., $dn'/dx \approx dp'/dx$). We have

$$\mathscr{E}(x) \approx \frac{J_h(x) + qD_h(dn'/dx)}{q\mu_h p_o} \tag{5.26}$$

Next, we calculate $p'(x)$ using Eq. (5.19), which gives us

$$p'(x) = n'(x) + \frac{\varepsilon}{q}\left(\frac{d\mathscr{E}}{dx}\right) \tag{5.27}$$

Finally, we compare our result for p' to our n' in order to verify our assumption of quasineutrality. As with any solution involving assumptions, our last step must be to check that all of our assumptions are valid.

Clearly, our first and most involved problem is to find the excess minority carrier population. After we have done that, everything else follows rather directly and readily. Thus we turn next to solving the quasistatic diffusion equation.

5.2 FLOW PROBLEMS

We will refer to problems involving the solution of Eq. (5.21b) under various boundary conditions and with various excitations $g_L(x)$ as *flow problems*. Developing an understanding of the solutions of flow problems is a very important step in understanding semiconductor devices.

5.2.1 Homogeneous Solutions

The homogeneous solution to Eq. (5.21b), that is, the $n'(x)$ that satisfies this equation with the excitation $g_L(x)$ set to zero is

$$n'(x) = A\, e^{x/L_e} + Be^{-x/L_e} \tag{5.28}$$

where A and B are constants whose values we will determine later by requiring that the total solution, which is the sum of the homogeneous and particular solutions, satisfies the boundary conditions.

Equation (5.28) can also be written in terms of hyperbolic sine and cosine functions as

$$n'(x) = C\cosh\left(\frac{x}{L_e}\right) + D\sinh\left(\frac{x}{L_e}\right) \tag{5.29}$$

The two constants C and D are related to the constants A and B in Eq. (5.28) as $C = A + B$ and $D = A - B$.

Looking at either Eq. (5.28) or (5.29), we see that the minority carrier diffusion length L_e is an index by which dimensions can be judged. That is, in any particular problem, saying that a length w is "very small" would mean w is small relative to L_e (i.e., $w \ll L_e$); whereas saying that w is "very large" would correspond to $w \gg L_e$. Conversely, saying that the minority carrier diffusion length is very long in a given sample implies that $L_e \gg w$, and saying it is short implies the opposite.

We will see later during our discussion of junction devices that it is often advantageous to make the dimensions of devices very small relative to the minority carrier diffusion length. In such situations, the parameter x will also always be much less than the minority carrier diffusion length and we can then simplify the homogeneous solution by using the approximation

$$e^{\pm x/L_e} \approx 1 \pm \frac{x}{L_e} \tag{5.30}$$

when $x \ll L_e$. With this substitution, the homogeneous solution for $n'(x)$, Eq. (5.28), can be approximated as

$$n'(x) \approx (A + B) + (A - B)\frac{x}{L_e} \tag{5.31a}$$

Thus we see that in the special case of a small device, or equivalently, a large minority carrier diffusion length $w \ll L_e$, the value of $n'(x)$ varies approximately linearly with position:

$$n'(x) \approx Ex + F \tag{5.31b}$$

where E and F are related to our earlier A and B as $E = (A - B)/L_e$ and $F = A + B$.

The minority carrier lifetime is a material parameter that is affected by the purity and crystalline quality as well as by the sample's processing history, whereas the diffusion coefficient (which plays an equal role in determining the minority carrier diffusion length) varies much less from sample to sample. Thus differences in the minority carrier lifetime are the primary reason that the minority carrier diffusion length might vary from sample to sample of a given material. We often speak of cases for which $w \ll L_e$ and for which $n'(x)$ can be approximated by a linear equation [i.e., Eq. (5.31b)] as corresponding to an *infinite lifetime*. In this regard, it is a useful exercise to look at Eq. (5.21a) in the limit $\tau_e \to \infty$. In this limit Eq. (5.21a) becomes

$$\frac{d^2 n'}{dx^2} \approx \frac{-g_L(x)}{D_e} \tag{5.32}$$

Clearly Eq. (5.31b) is the homogeneous solution to this second-order linear differential equation.

5.2.2 Particular Solutions

Determining the particular solution requires knowledge of the excitation function $g_L(x)$, and we will present several specific examples in Section 5.2.4. For now, we will simply make a general comment about obtaining a particular solution.

Often an excitation function $g_L(x)$ will have different functional forms in different sections of the sample. A simple, very common example involves having only a portion of the sample illuminated, that is, when $g_L(x)$ is nonzero only between $x = x_1$ and $x = x_2$ and is zero elsewhere. In such cases, it is advisable to divide the problem of finding particular and total solutions accordingly. Particular, and then total, solutions can be found in each region and matched at the boundaries. In the situation just described, for example, one would find solutions for $x \leq x_1$, for $x_1 \leq x \leq x_2$, and for $x_2 \leq x$ and would then match them at $x = x_1$ and $x = x_2$. Furthermore, the solutions for $x \leq x_1$ and $x_2 \leq x$ are just the homogeneous solutions; that is, the particular solutions are zero where the excitation is zero.

Finally, we should note that in many device situations there is no generation, and again the total solution is simply the homogeneous solution adjusted to match the boundary conditions.

5.2.3 Boundary Conditions

Equation 5.21b is a second-order differential equation, and thus our homogeneous solution has two unknown constants. This in turn requires that we have two, and only two, independent boundary conditions in order to determine these two constants. These boundary conditions may be constraints on the excess minority carrier population or on its derivative.

There are a few standard boundary conditions that we will encounter in the course of our work with flow problems in semiconductors.

a) Reflecting boundary. Consider first the boundary condition at the surface of a semiconductor sample in which the minority carrier lifetime is unchanged right up to the surface. Such a boundary is called a *reflecting boundary.* Electrons and holes cannot normally flow out of a surface, so the boundary condition at a reflecting boundary must be that the carrier fluxes, and currents, there are zero. In particular, the minority carrier current is zero, and consequently the gradient of the excess minority carrier concentration must also be zero at this boundary; that is,

$$\left.\frac{dn'}{dx}\right|_{x=x_3} = 0 \tag{5.33a}$$

where for the sake of discussion we have assumed a p-type sample with a reflecting boundary at $x = x_3$. The boundary condition at a reflecting boundary is thus a condition on the excess minority carrier concentration gradient. The excess minority carrier concentration in a sample with a reflecting boundary at $x = w$ is illustrated in Fig. 5.1.

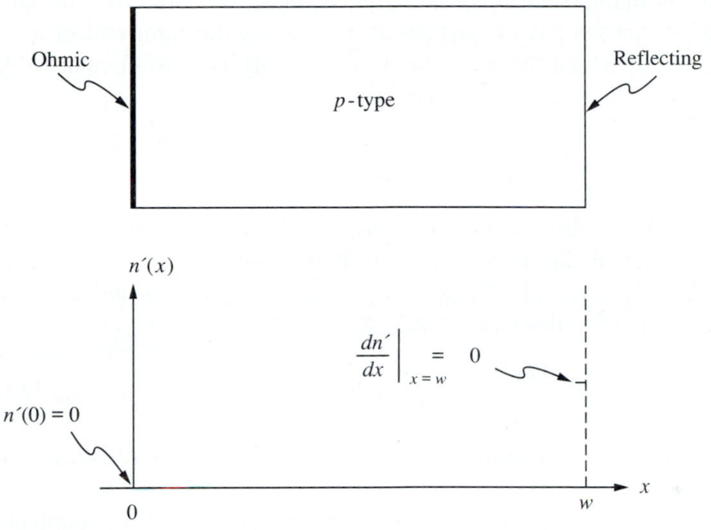

FIGURE 5.1
A p-type semiconductor sample with an ohmic contact on the end at $x = 0$ and a reflecting boundary on the end at $x = w$.

b) Ohmic contact. At the other extreme from a reflecting boundary (where the minority carrier lifetime is unchanged up to the surface) is an *ohmic contact,* which is defined as a surface at which the minority carrier lifetime is identically zero.

Assume for the sake of discussion that we have a p-type sample with an ohmic contact at $x = x_4$. If the minority carrier lifetime at $x = x_4$ is zero, then the only way that the term $n'(x_4)\tau_e$ can be finite is if $n'(x_4)$ is also zero, that is, $n'(x_4) = 0$. Thus at an ideal ohmic contact, the boundary condition on the excess minority carrier concentration is that it is zero:

$$n'(x_4) = 0 \tag{5.33b}$$

The excess minority carrier concentration in a sample with an ohmic contact at $x = 0$ is illustrated in Fig. 5.1.

Physically the minority carrier lifetime at and/or near a surface can be made very small, and the ideal ohmic contact boundary condition can be approached, either by putting certain metals on the surface (see App. E) or by introducing additional recombination sites in a thin surface layer by adding certain impurities or by damaging the crystal at the surface.

c) Surface recombination velocity. The ohmic contact and reflecting boundary represent two extremes of a general situation in which some extra recombination may occur at a boundary, but some excess minority carrier population may exist at the same boundary as well. This situation may be described by saying that there is a finite recombination velocity at the surface in question. The amount of recombination occurring at this surface depends on the excess minority carrier population there and is manifested as a finite flux of carriers "into" the surface. Imagine, for example, that we have a surface at $x = w$ on the right end of a p-type semiconductor bar at which the recombination velocity is s. Mathematically the boundary condition at $x = w$ in this case is

$$-D_e \left.\frac{dn'}{dx}\right|_{x=w} = sn'(w) \tag{5.33c}$$

The general rule is that the flux is into the surface. Thus at the left end of a sample, the negative sign in the above expression becomes a positive sign. To illustrate, suppose that the left end of a p-type sample is at $x = 0$ and that the surface recombination velocity there is s; then, at $x = 0$,

$$D_e \left.\frac{dn'}{dx}\right|_{x=0} = sn'(0) \tag{5.33d}$$

A sample with two surfaces with finite recombination velocities is illustrated in Fig. 5.2.

Notice that the first two boundary conditions we discussed, ohmic contacts and reflecting boundaries, can be viewed as special cases of surfaces with recombination velocities. At an ohmic contact the recombination velocity is infinite, whereas at a reflecting boundary the recombination velocity is zero.

d) Internal boundaries. When we discussed particular solutions in Sec. 5.2.2 we suggested that, when the excitation is not continuous over the length of a sample, it is often desirable mathematically to divide the sample into separate

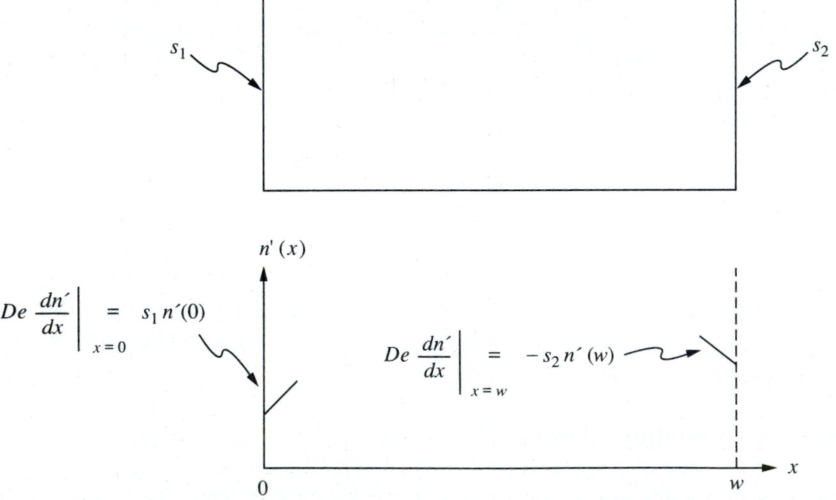

FIGURE 5.2
A p-type semiconductor sample with surface recombination velocities of s_1 and s_2 on the end surfaces at $x = 0$ and $x = w$, respectively.

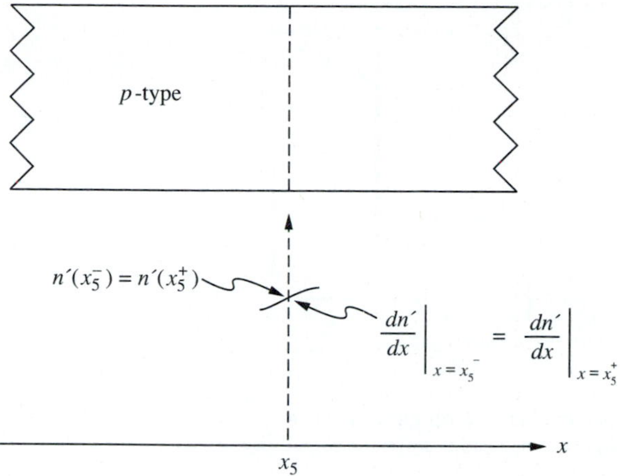

FIGURE 5.3
Internal boundary at $x = x_5$ in a p-type semiconductor sample, illustrating the continuity of the excess minority carrier concentration and its derivative.

regions and to obtain solutions in each individual region. Boundary conditions then need to be found to relate the various solutions across the boundaries between these regions. Upon examination of Eqs. (5.21b) and (5.23) we see that the minority carrier concentration and its derivative must be continuous across any boundary. A discontinuity in the gradient would imply infinite generation or recombination, whereas a discontinuity in the concentration would imply an infinite current density.

The internal boundary conditions on the excess minority carrier concentration and its derivative are illustrated for a p-type sample in Fig. 5.3.

e) Injecting contacts. A final boundary condition that we will encounter in semiconductor devices is one where either the excess minority carrier population or the minority carrier current is set by conditions external to the sample. It is usually the excess minority carrier population that is constrained, but in either case the boundary condition on the excess minority carrier population or its derivative (i.e., the minority carrier current density) will be obvious.

A word of caution is in order at this point. In order to maintain quasineutrality and to have a quasistatic situation, we must remove at least as much charge as we inject. Thus a sample with an injecting contact at one end must have an ohmic contact at the other, and the two contacts must be connected in some manner through an external circuit, as Fig. 5.4 illustrates. If they are not, the problem will not fit within the class of flow problems.

5.2.4 The Total Current

In Sec. 5.1.6 a procedure was outlined for obtaining the majority carrier current, the electric field, and the excess majority carrier concentration once the excess

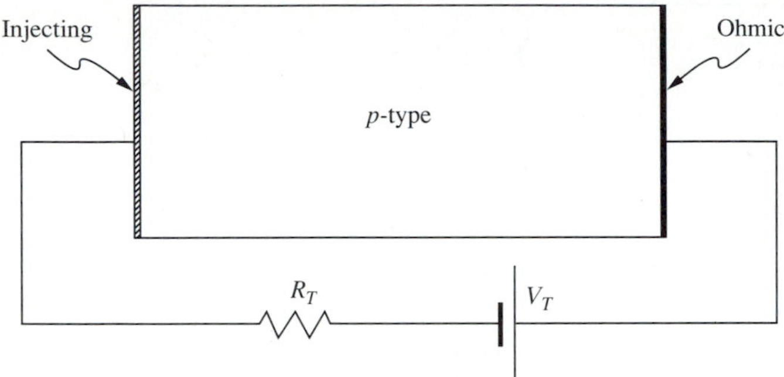

FIGURE 5.4
Sample with an injecting contact on one end and an ohmic contact on the other. The current will be determined by the characteristics of the specific injecting contact and the external circuit.

minority carrier concentration and the total current are known. At this point we should make a few additional comments concerning the total current, particularly how we can determine its value.

When ohmic and/or injecting contacts are not on both ends of a sample, or when ohmic contacts are not part of a complete circuit, then the total current is trivially zero.

When there is an injecting contact at one end of a sample and an ohmic contact at the other, the sample must be part of an external circuit; to have a well-specified problem either the total current or the majority carrier current will have to be set by this circuit.

When there are ohmic contacts on both ends of a sample and they are connected through an external circuit, the total current density will simply be related to the voltage difference between the two ohmic contacts by the conductivity of the sample, σ_o (i.e., by Ohm's law). To obtain this result we begin by adding Eqs. (5.15) and (5.16) to get an equation for J_{TOT}:

$$J_{\text{TOT}} = \sigma_o \mathcal{E} - qD_h \frac{dp'}{dx} + qD_e \frac{dn'}{dx} \tag{5.34}$$

Assume that the sample extends from $x = x_A$ to $x = x_B$, and integrate J_{TOT} from one end of the sample to the other:

$$\int_{x_A}^{x_B} J_{\text{TOT}}\, dx = \sigma_o \int_{x_A}^{x_B} \mathcal{E}(x)\, dx - qD_h \int_{x_A}^{x_B} \frac{dp'}{dx}\, dx + qD_e \int_{x_A}^{x_B} \frac{dn'}{dx}\, dx \tag{5.35}$$

Looking at each term we have

$$\int_{x_A}^{x_B} J_{\text{TOT}}\, dx = J_{\text{TOT}}\,(x_B - x_A) \tag{5.36a}$$

$$\sigma_o \int_{x_A}^{x_B} \mathcal{E}(x)\, dx = \sigma_o v_{\text{BA}} \tag{5.36b}$$

$$qD_h \int_{x_A}^{x_B} \frac{dp'}{dx}\,dx = qD_h\left[p'(x_B) - p'(x_A)\right] = 0 \tag{5.36c}$$

$$qD_e \int_{x_A}^{x_B} \frac{dn'}{dx}\,dx = qD_e\left[n'(x_B) - n'(x_A)\right] = 0 \tag{5.36d}$$

The last two integrals are zero because the excess carrier populations must be zero at the two ohmic contacts. Combining these results, we then have our final result:

$$J_{\text{TOT}} = \sigma_o \frac{v_{\text{BA}}}{(x_B - x_A)} \tag{5.37}$$

5.2.5 Specific Situations

We now have the mathematical models and tools we need to solve flow problems, but our task is still formidable. There is an infinite variety of possible generation functions $g_L(x)$, and finding solutions for them is in general very difficult. Fortunately, most of the flow problem situations that are of interest to us in devices—in, for example, p-n diodes and bipolar transistors—can be solved analytically. These situations correspond to cases in which there is (1) uniform injection over all or part of a sample, (2) there is injection only from an injecting contact or boundary, and/or (3) the minority carrier lifetime is infinite (i.e., the minority carrier diffusion length is very long). We will discuss each of these situations and present examples of each, in the following several subsections.

In still other situations, in which it is in general difficult or impossible to get analytical solutions, there are steps we can take to get approximate solutions and thereby gain insight into the full solution. Of course, as well-trained electrical engineers with a full arsenal of analytical techniques for treating linear differential equations and quasi-infinite computational power at our disposal, we can certainly grind out a solution in any complex situation, but we would like to do better. We need methods of getting quick, engineering solutions. We will discuss approximate techniques to do just that after we consider those cases in which we can find analytical solutions.

We are first going to solve for the excess minority carrier population from the quasistatic diffusion equation, which, assuming a p-type sample, is

$$\frac{d^2n'}{dx^2} - \frac{n'}{L_e^2} = -\frac{g_L(x)}{D_e} \tag{5.38}$$

Then, we can proceed to calculate $J_e(x)$, $J_h(x)$, $\mathscr{E}(x)$, and $p'(x)$.

a) Partially illuminated bar. One situation for which an analytical solution can be obtained is when the generation function has a constant value throughout various regions of the sample. The particular solutions in those regions are then constants. They are equal to the strength of the generation function, say G, multiplied by the minority carrier lifetime τ_{min}. That is, if $g_L(x)$ is G_L between x_1 and x_2, the particular solution between x_1 and x_2 is $G_L\tau_{min}$. The solution for the entire bar is obtained by matching the solutions at the boundaries between the various regions.

Example

Question. Consider the p-type silicon sample of length w illustrated in Fig. 5.5a. The sample end at $x = 0$ is a reflecting surface, and there is an ohmic contact at $x = w$. The excitation $g_L(x)$ is G_L for $0 \le x \le x_1$ and zero for $x_1 \le x \le w$. Assume that N_A, μ_h, μ_e, D_h, D_e, τ_e, τ_h, and the sample dimensions are all specified. What are the excess minority carrier population and minority carrier current in this sample?

Discussion. To find $n'(x)$ we first divide the problem into two sections: from $x = 0$ to $x = x_1$ and from $x = x_1$ to $x = w$. We have the following homogeneous solution:

$$n'_{hs}(x) = \begin{cases} Ae^{x/L_e} + Be^{-x/L_e} & \text{for } 0 \le x \le x_1 \\ Ce^{x/L_e} + De^{-x/L_e} & \text{for } x_1 \le x \le w \end{cases}$$

The particular solution is

$$n'_{ps}(x) = \begin{cases} G_L\tau_e & \text{for } 0 \le x \le x_1 \\ 0 & \text{for } x_1 \le x \le w \end{cases}$$

The total solution is

$$n'(x) = \begin{cases} Ae^{x/L_e} + Be^{-x/L_e} + G_L\tau_e & \text{for } 0 \le x \le x_1 \\ Ce^{x/L_e} + De^{-x/L_e} & \text{for } x_1 \le x \le w \end{cases}$$

The boundary conditions are as follows:

At $x = 0$: $$\left.\frac{dn'}{dx}\right|_{x=0} = 0$$

At $x = x_1$: $$n'\left(x_1^-\right) = n'\left(x_1^+\right)$$

$$\left.\frac{dn'}{dx}\right|_{x=x_1^-} = \left.\frac{dn'}{dx}\right|_{x=x_1^+}$$

At $x = w$: $$n'(w) = 0$$

The only item in this list that we have not discussed already is the particular solution for x between 0 and x_1. There are several points to keep in mind about particular solutions. The first is that they are unique. Thus we can be confident that if we find a solution that works, it will be the only one. The second point is that particular solutions in general take the same shape, or functional form, as the excitation. Thus a good first guess is a function that looks like the excitation. In

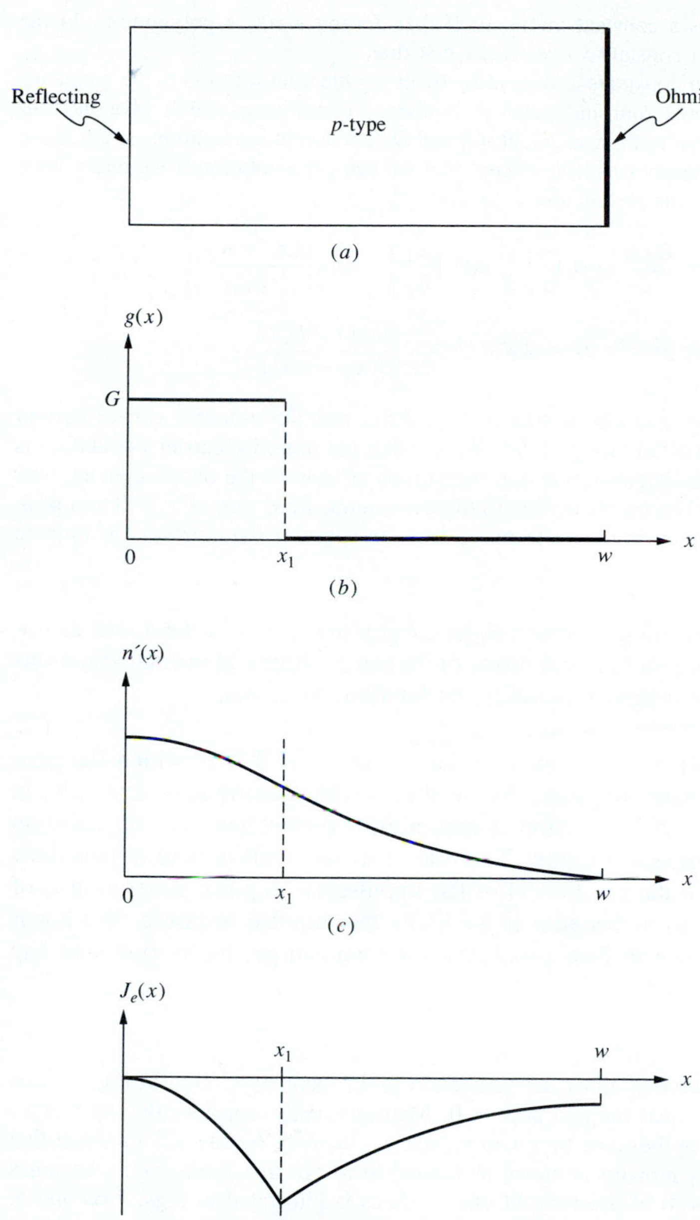

FIGURE 5.5
(*a*) A uniformly doped, p-type silicon bar with a reflecting boundary on one end and an ohmic contact on the other; (*b*) uniform illumination between $x = 0$ and $x = x_1$ and zero illumination elsewhere; (*c*) solution for $n'(x)$; (*d*) solution for $J_e(x)$.

this case we guess a constant value, or if that doesn't work, a polynomial. In the present problem, a constant value works just fine.

We have four constants to determine by fitting the total solution to the boundary conditions. We have four independent boundary conditions, which give us four equations in our four unknowns, A, B, C, and D. Their solution requires an algebraic tour de force and teaches us little except that we can get a solution if we really have to. For the record, the results are

$$A = B = \frac{G_L \tau_e}{2} \cosh\left(\frac{x_1}{L_e}\right)\left\{\tanh\left(\frac{x_1}{L_e}\right) - \tanh\left[\frac{(x_1 - w)}{L_e}\right]\right\}$$

$$C = e^{2w/L_e}\, D = Ae^{-w/L_e} \frac{\sinh(x_1/L_e)}{\cosh\left[(x_1 - w)/L_e\right]}$$

The corresponding $n'(x)$ is plotted in Fig. 5.5c, and the minority carrier current density $J_e(x)$ is plotted in Fig. 5.5d. We see that the minority carrier population is highest where there is generation and then drops off toward the ohmic contact. The electron flux $J_e(x)/q$ builds up due to the generation, from zero at $x = 0$ to a peak at $x = x_1$, and then decreases from x_1 to w as some of the electrons recombine with holes.

Rather than proceeding to obtain $J_h(x)$, $\mathscr{E}(x)$, and $p'(x)$ in the above example, we will leave this problem and move on to some additional special situations that will give us more insight into solutions for flow problems.

b) Impulse illumination. Another important situation is that in which the generation function is a spatial impulse. As we shall see by looking at an example, in this situation the generation function is zero almost everywhere and the solution is simply the homogeneous solution. The role of the generation is to impose new boundary conditions at the position(s) of the impulse(s). Impulse generation is of particular importance to us because if we know the impulse response of a linear system, such as we have in flow problems, then we can get the response to any arbitrary generation function.

Example

Question. Imagine that all of the generation in the sample pictured in Fig. 5.5a is concentrated very near the end at $x = 0$. Mathematically, consider the limit as x_1 goes to zero, but at the same time you reduce x_1, increase G_L in such a manner that the product $G_L x_1$ remains constant and equal to M. In this limit, $g_L(x)$ becomes an impulse at $x = 0$ of intensity M cm^{-2}s^{-1}, as is illustrated in Figs. 5.6a and b. What are $n'(x)$ and $J_e(x)$ in this situation?

Discussion. We could get a solution by taking the appropriate limit of the solution we just obtained for a bar with illumination from 0 to x_1, but we will instead take another approach. We recognize that as x_1 becomes very small we will inevitably be in the limit $x_1 \ll L_e$, and thus in the region $0 \leq x \leq x_1$, L_e will always be much larger than x. Thus on the size scale with which

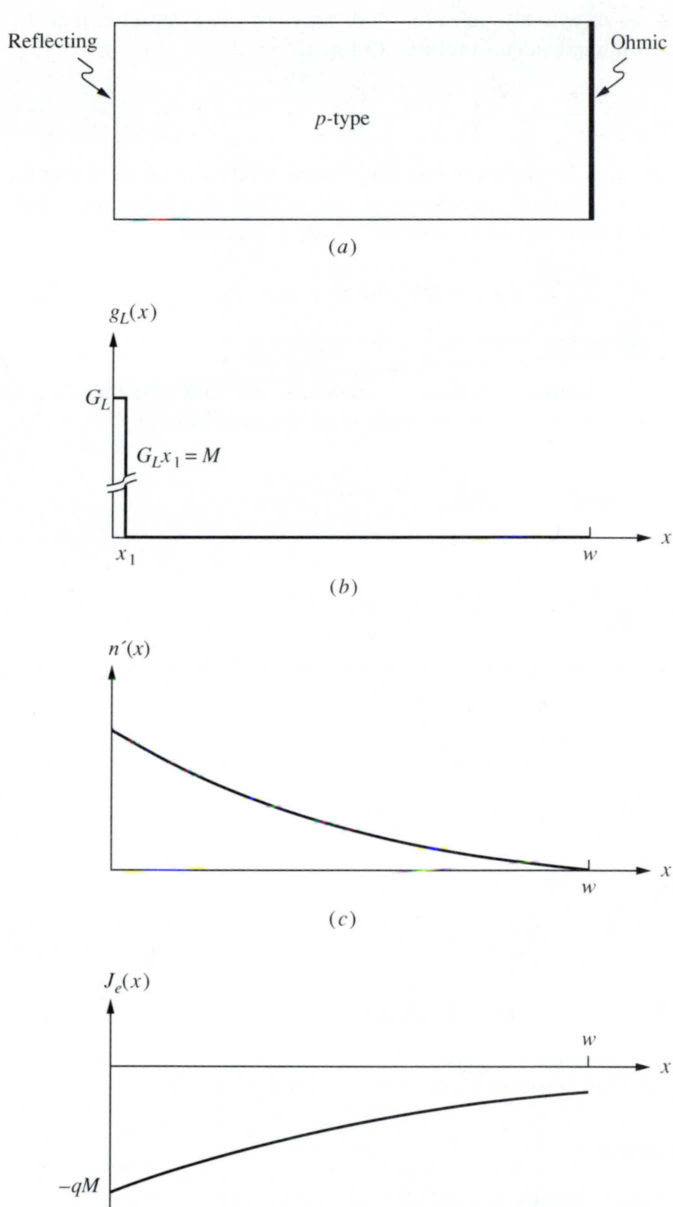

FIGURE 5.6
(*a*) A p-type semiconductor bar; (*b*) impulse illumination at $x = 0$; (*c*) solution for $n'(x)$: and (*d*) solution for $J_e(x)$.

we are dealing, L_e is effectively infinite, and once we can assume that L_e is infinite, Eq. (5.21b) immediately simplifies to Eq. (5.32b):

$$\frac{d^2n'}{dx^2} = -\frac{g_L(x)}{D_e} = -\frac{G_L}{D_e}$$

for $0 \leq x \leq x_1$. Integrating twice, we obtain directly the total solution for $n'(x)$ for $0 \leq x \leq x_1$. (For a more thorough discussion of this method of solving for $n'(x)$, see subsection d below.) Thus our total solution for all x becomes

$$n'(x) = \begin{cases} -\dfrac{G_L x^2}{D_e} + Ax + B & \text{for } 0 \leq x \leq x_1 \\ Ce^{x/L_e} + De^{-x/L_e} & \text{for } x_1 \leq x \leq w \end{cases}$$

Applying our boundary conditions to these expressions, we find first that $A = 0$ from the boundary condition at $x = 0$. Second, from the condition at $x = w$, we find that

$$Ce^{w/L_e} + De^{-w/L_e} = 0$$

Next, by matching n' at $x = x_1$, we obtain

$$-\frac{G_L x_1^2}{D_e} + B = Ce^{x_1/L_e} + De^{-x_1/L_e}$$

which, in the limit $x_1 \to 0$ and $G \to \infty$ such that $G_L x_1 = M$, is

$$B = C + D$$

Finally, by matching dn'/dx at x_1 we obtain

$$-\frac{2G_L x_1}{D_e} = \frac{Ce^{x_1/L_e} - De^{-x_1/L_e}}{L_e}$$

which in our limit is

$$-\frac{2M}{D_e} = \frac{(C - D)}{L_e}$$

Solving for C and D we obtain our total solution

$$n'(x) = \frac{ML_e}{D_e} \frac{e^{(w-x)/L_e} - e^{-(w-x)/L_e}}{e^{w/L_e} + e^{-w/L_e}} \qquad \text{for } 0 \leq x \leq w$$

This can also be written as

$$n'(x) = \frac{ML_e}{D_e} \frac{\sinh[(w - x)/L_e]}{\cosh(w/L_e)} \qquad \text{for } 0 \leq x \leq w$$

(Note that since we have let x_1 go to zero, the region $0 \leq x \leq x_1$ no longer exists.)

The electron current density is

$$J_e(x) = -qM \frac{\cosh[(w - x)/L_e]}{\cosh(w/L_e)} \qquad \text{for } 0 \leq x \leq w$$

You will note that $J_e(0) = -qM$. This result might at first seem to be inconsistent with having a reflecting surface at $x = 0$, but everything is proper because with our impulse illumination we are injecting M hole-electron pairs right at the surface at $x = 0$. These carriers diffuse away, giving an electron flux at $x = 0$ of M, or a current density of $-qM$.

The expressions we have found for $n'(x)$ and $-J_e(x)$ are plotted in Figs. 5.6*c* and *d*, respectively.

In the above example, the impulse occurred at the end of the sample. If it were to occur within the bulk of the sample, the injected carriers would in general diffuse both to the left and to the right. The boundary conditions at the position of the impulse are then (1) that the excess minority carrier population will be continuous and (2) that there will be a discontinuity in the minority carrier current density equal to the strength of the impulse multiplied by the minority carrier charge (which is $-q$ for electrons, $+q$ for holes).

c) Injecting contacts. The above example in which there was impulse generation at one end of a sample corresponds to the situation that arises when there is an injecting contact at one end of a sample. This situation is extremely important to us because it is what occurs in junction devices (e.g., *p-n* diodes and bipolar transistors).

Refer to Fig. 5.6*a*. If instead of an impulse of light at $x = 0$ we had an injecting contact at the same point that was injecting M electrons/cm$^2 \cdot$ s, the solutions for $n'(x)$ and $J_e(x)$ would be unchanged. The injecting contact, as we have specified it, imposes exactly the same boundary condition as did the impulse generation function.

Another way of specifying an injecting contact is to say that it fixes the excess minority carrier population at the contact. That is, in our example, we might have specified that the injecting contact at $x = 0$ maintains $n'(0)$ at some value, say N'. The shapes of the $n'(x)$ and $J_e(x)$ profiles would be the same as they were previously, but the magnitudes would be different, depending now on the value of N'.

Example

Question. Consider a sample identical to that pictured in Fig. 5.6*a* except that it has an injecting contact at $x = 0$; $g_L(x)$ is identically zero. The injecting contact establishes $n'(0) = N'$. What are $n'(x)$ and $J_e(x)$?

Discussion. The total solution for $n'(x)$ is just the homogeneous solution with the two constants chosen to fit the boundary conditions, namely $n'(0) = N'$ and $n'(w) = 0$. Thus we have

$$n'(x) = Ae^{x/L_e} + Be^{-x/L_e}$$

Applying the boundary condition constraints tells us that

$$A + B = N'$$

and

$$Ae^{w/L_e} + Be^{-w/L_e} = 0$$

from which we can easily solve for A and B.

By now, however, we should start being more clever in our solutions. Specifically, we know that the homogeneous solutions can be written as combinations of sinh and cosh functions, and we know certain properties of sinh and cosh. We know, for instance, that a sinh function can have a zero value and thus could be chosen to solve the boundary conditions. A little thought should convince you that the solution we seek for $n'(x)$ is

$$n'(x) = N' \frac{\sinh[(w - x)/L_e]}{\sinh(w/L_e)}$$

If this is not "obvious" to you, and it may well not be, you should be able to solve for A and B above and arrive at the same result. Having $n'(x)$, we can immediately find $J_e(x)$:

$$J_e(x) = -\frac{qD_eN'}{L_e} \frac{\cosh[(w - x)/L_e]}{\sinh(w/L_e)}$$

Comparing these results with those we obtained for impulse excitation will show you that the shapes are identical and that only the magnitudes are different. [The magnitudes differ only because the boundary condition in this case was on $n'(x)$, whereas in the earlier case it was on $J_e(x)$.]

Two special cases of samples with one injecting contact are those in which the sample is either very long or very short. By very long we mean that the ohmic contact on the other end of the sample is many minority carrier diffusion lengths away from the injecting contact (i.e., $w \gg L_e$, where w is the length of the sample). By very short we mean the opposite (i.e., $w \ll L_e$).

In the case of a very long device, which we will refer to as the *long-base limit*, the profiles are single decaying exponentials falling away from the injecting contact. All of the excess minority carriers injected at the contact recombine well before they reach the ohmic contact, and the minority carrier current drops to zero well before the ohmic contact.

Example

Question. Consider a p-type sample like that discussed above with an injecting contact at $x = 0$ injecting M electrons/cm$^2 \cdot$ s, with an ohmic contact at $x = w$, and in which L_e is much smaller than w (i.e., $L_e \ll w$). What are $n'(x)$ and $J_e(x)$ in this sample?

Discussion. In the limit $w \gg L_e$, our solutions for impulse injection at $x = 0$ are

$$n'(x) \approx \frac{ML_e}{D_e} e^{-x/L_e}$$

and

$$J_e(x) \approx -qMe^{-x/L_e}$$

These results are plotted in Figs. 5.7*a* and *b*. We see that the excess holes and electrons generated at $x = 0$ all recombine well before they reach the ohmic contact. Consequently the electron current has also gone to zero well before $x = w$.

In the other extreme, that of very short devices, which we will refer to as the *short-base limit*, we have the situation we discussed in Sec. 5.2.1 that corresponds to an essentially infinite minority carrier lifetime. The solution for $n'(x)$ in a sample with an injecting contact on one end and an ohmic contact on the other is a straight line that decreases from a finite value at the injecting contact to zero at the ohmic contact. The minority carrier current is constant throughout the sample because there is essentially no recombination in the sample and almost every excess minority carrier injected at the contact flows through the sample to the ohmic contact, where it recombines.

Example

Question. Consider a p-type sample like that discussed above with an injecting contact at $x = 0$ injecting M electrons/cm$^2 \cdot$ s, with an ohmic contact at $x = w$, and in which L_e is much greater than w (i.e., $L_e \gg w$). What are $n'(x)$ and $J_e(x)$ in this sample?

Discussion. In the limit $w \ll L_e$, our solutions are

$$n'(x) \approx \frac{M}{D_e}(w - x)$$

and

$$J_e(x) = -qM$$

These results are plotted in Figs. 5.7*c* and *d*. Note that now $n'(x)$ decreases linearly to zero at $x = w$, as we said it would, and note that $J_e(x)$ is constant between 0 and w. This is because having $L_e \gg w$ is equivalent to an extremely long minority carrier lifetime. This in turn implies that very little recombination occurs in the sample (except, of course, at the ohmic contact, where essentially all of the excess hole-electron pairs recombine).

We say that "essentially none" of the carriers injected at the contact recombine in a sample in the short-base/infinite lifetime limit because very little recombination occurs and for purposes of calculating $n'(x)$ and $J_e(x)$ we can ignore it. At the same time, it is important to realize that if we ever really need to know how much recombination occurs we can readily estimate it. To do so we simply notice that the recombination occurring at any point x is $n'(x)/\tau_e$. Thus,

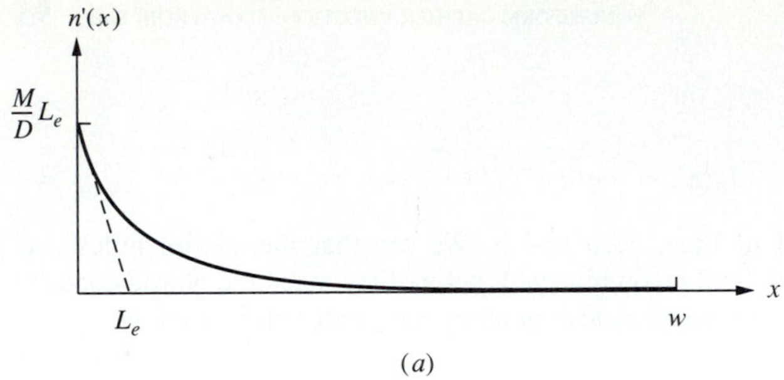

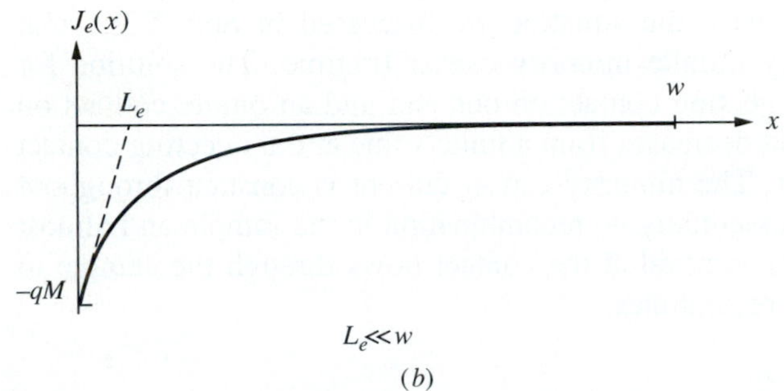

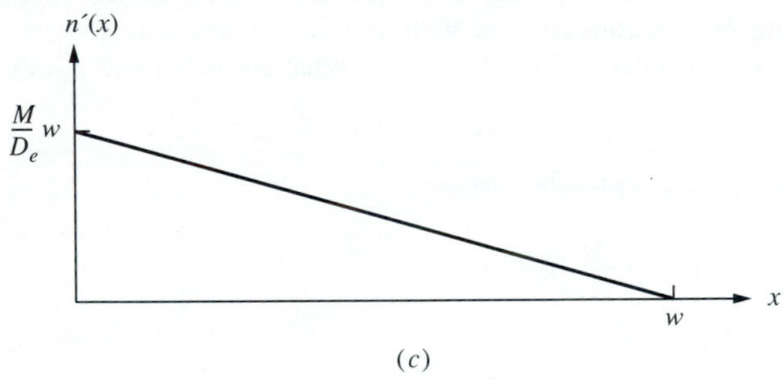

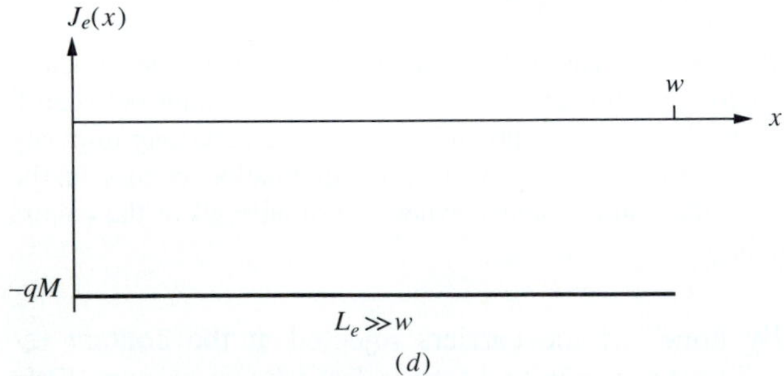

FIGURE 5.7
Minority carrier concentration and current density, respectively, as functions of position in a p-type silicon bar with a contact injecting M electrons/$\text{cm}^2 \cdot \text{s}$ at $x = 0$: (a and b) for $L_e \ll w$; (c and d) for $L_e \gg w$.

the total recombination per unit area occurring between 0 and w is

$$F_R = \int_0^w \frac{n'(x)}{\tau_e}\, dx \tag{5.39}$$

which in the case considered in the last example is

$$F_R = \frac{Mw^2}{2D_e\tau_e} = M\frac{w^2}{2L_e^2} \tag{5.40}$$

Of the total number M of hole-electron pairs unit area that were generated at $x = 0$, a fraction equal to $w^2/2L_e^2$ recombine between 0 and w; the rest recombine at the contact. Clearly, when $L_e \gg w$, a very small fraction recombine because w^2/L_e^2 is a very small number.

Repeating this exercise for the case $L_e \ll w$, we find that

$$F_R = \int_0^w \frac{n'(x)}{\tau_e}\, dx = M \tag{5.41}$$

Now all of the hole-electron pairs generated at $x = 0$ recombine in the sample, and none recombine at the ohmic contact, which is just what we had concluded earlier by looking at the electron current.

d) Infinite lifetime solutions. We have mentioned that in short samples, where "short" implies small relative to the minority carrier diffusion length, the quasistatic diffusion equation reduces to

$$\frac{d^2n'}{dx^2} = -\frac{g_L(x)}{D_e} \tag{5.32}$$

This situation is often referred to as the infinite lifetime approximation because the same result is obtained in the limit $\tau_e \to \infty$ and, more physically, because the term that has dropped out of the equation is the recombination term n'/τ_e (actually, n'/L_e^2). No recombination implies infinite lifetime.

It is not necessary to find homogeneous and particular solutions to solve Eq. (5.32). Doing so works, but it is far easier to simply integrate twice; the boundary conditions are then used to determine the two constants of integration.

Example

Question. Consider a p-type sample of length w with ohmic contacts on each end (i.e., at $x = 0$ and at $x = w$). The minority carrier lifetime in this sample is sufficiently long that $L_e \gg w$, and it is illuminated by light generating $g_L(x)$ carriers/cm$^3 \cdot$ s. What are $n'(x)$ and $J_e(x)$?

Discussion. Integrating Eq. (5.32) yields

$$\frac{dn'}{dx} = -\frac{1}{D_e}\int_0^x g_L(x')\, dx' + A$$

and integrating again yields

$$n'(x) = -\frac{1}{D_e}\int_0^x \int_0^{x'} g_L(x'')\,dx''\,dx' + Ax + B$$

We now must use the boundary conditions to evaluate the two constants of integration, A and B. In this example the sample has ohmic contacts on both ends, so the boundary conditions are that $n'(0)$ and $n'(w)$ are zero. Imposing these conditions, we find from the condition at $x = 0$ that B is zero; from the condition at $x = w$ we find that A is given as

$$A = \frac{1}{D_e w}\int_0^w \int_0^{x'} g_L(x'')\,dx''\,dx'$$

If the boundary conditions had been on the current, that is, if we had had injecting contacts and/or reflecting boundaries, then we would have had to use our solution for the gradient of n' to evaluate one or more of the constants.

e) Finite lifetime solutions. The observation that it is relatively easy to find $n'(x)$ when the lifetime is infinite leads us to suggest a convenient method of estimating the solution in situations where the assumption of an infinite lifetime is not valid and where finding the particular solution proves difficult or impossible. In such cases we can first assume that the lifetime is infinite and get the solution by integrating $g_L(x)$ twice as we have shown. We can then "adjust" this solution for the fact that the lifetime is finite by letting the infinite lifetime solution "sag" appropriately. To appreciate what this means, compare Figs. 5.7*a* (short lifetime), 5.6*c* (moderate lifetime), and 5.7*c* (infinite lifetime). The increasing "sag" in the profile with decreasing lifetime is quite graphic. Fig. 5.8 summarizes these observations.

f) Superposition. The diffusion equation is a linear differential equation, so the response to a sum of excitations is equal to the sum of the responses to the individual excitations. We can thus use superposition to solve flow problems. An example is illustrated in Fig. 5.9.

Keep in mind, however, that the total solution must satisfy our assumptions: it is not enough that the individual parts alone each satisfy the assumptions. Thus, for example, the total n' must be much less than p_o for low-level injection to be a valid assumption. It is not enough for n' due to each individual excitation to satisfy this condition.

5.2.6 The Currents, Electric Field, and Net Charge

Thus far we have concentrated on the problem of finding the excess minority carrier concentration, and rightly so, because that is the difficult part. Once this concentration is known, finding the currents, electric field, and net charge is more

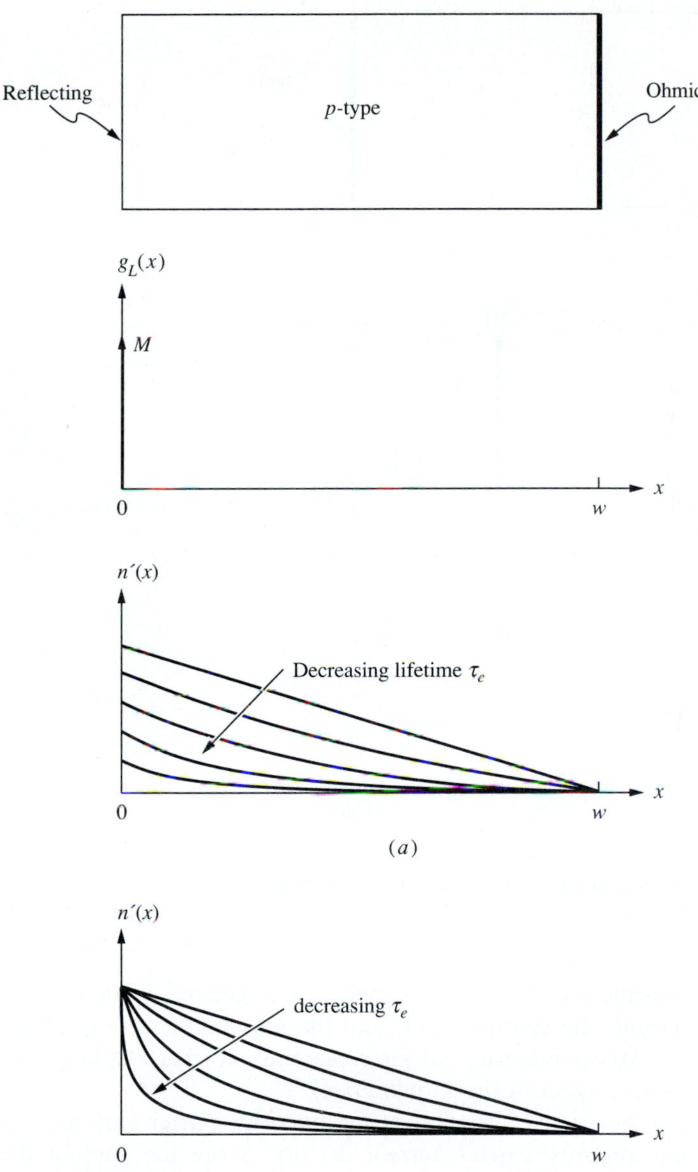

FIGURE 5.8
Illustration of the "sag" in $n'(x)$ as the lifetime is decreased: (*a*) assuming constant injected flux; (*b*) assuming constant $n'(0)$.

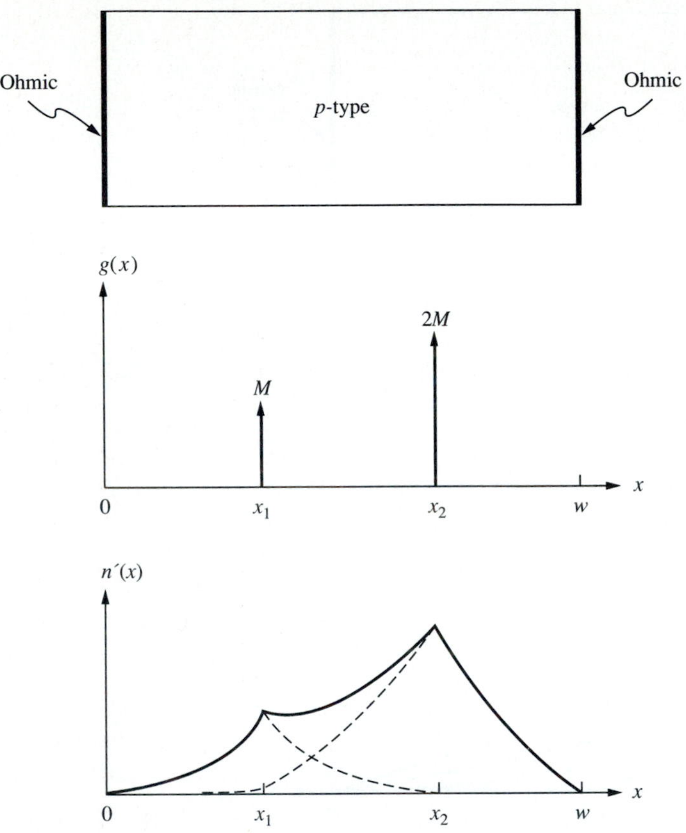

FIGURE 5.9
Illustration of superposition. Note that $n'(x)$ need not consist of straight lines for superposition to be valid.

or less mechanical. Nonetheless, we can still make some general comments on the majority carrier current, the electric field, and the net charge density (from which we determine the excess majority carrier concentration) that can help you develop some insight with respect to these quantities.

First, we note that the spatial variation of the majority carrier current density mirrors that of the minority carrier current density. Since the sum of the two currents is a constant, J_{TOT}, when one increases the other must decrease and vice versa. Physically, when the magnitude of the current changes, there is hole-electron pair generation or recombination. If, for example, the hole current density increases going from left to right, holes are being added to the flux stream, so there must be net generation in that region. Correspondingly, the electron current density will decrease going from left to right because more negative charge is simultaneously being added to the stream. If, on the other hand, the hole current is decreasing, holes are disappearing (i.e., recombining) in that region. At the same time the electron flux must also be decreasing, implying an increase in the electron current. The two fluxes must change in concert.

Second, we note that the shape of the electric field reflects that of the currents. This can easily be seen by referring to Eq. (5.26), but we can go further with the help of a bit of algebraic manipulation. Assuming that we have a p-type sample, we can show that the electric field can be written as either

$$\mathscr{E}(x) = \frac{J_{\text{TOT}} - [1 - (D_h/D_e)]J_e(x)}{q\mu_h p_o} \tag{5.42}$$

or

$$\mathscr{E}(x) = \frac{D_h}{D_e}\frac{J_{\text{TOT}} + [1 - (D_h/D_e)]J_h(x)}{q\mu_h p_o} \tag{5.43}$$

Realizing that $D_h < D_e$ in the typical semiconductor, we see that the shape of the electric field is the same as that of the hole current (offset by a constant amount proportional to J_{TOT}). Physically this results from the fact that the electrons diffuse more quickly than the holes, so the electric field that develops to maintain charge neutrality must be such that it pushes holes in the direction of any concentration gradients. Thus the hole drift and diffusion currents are codirectional.

The same conclusion is reached even if the sample is n-type. A bit of algebra tells us that in an n-type sample the field is

$$\mathscr{E}(x) = \frac{J_{\text{TOT}} + [1 - (D_h/D_e)]\,J_h(x)}{q\mu_e n_o} \tag{5.44}$$

Comparing this result with that for the p-type sample above reveals that the forms are identical. The two results do differ in magnitude, however. If we compare samples with identical doping levels (i.e., majority carrier concentrations), the field in the p-type sample is larger by a factor of D_e/D_h (or, equivalently, μ_e/μ_h). This simply reflects the fact that less field is needed to adjust the majority carrier population in an n-type sample than in a p-type sample because electrons drift more readily than holes.

Finally, we note that we can show that the net charge is directly proportional to the net generation of hole-electron pairs. Assuming a p-type sample, we use our expression above for $\mathscr{E}(x)$, Eq. (5.42), in Poisson's equation, Eq. (5.19), to write the net charge density $\rho(x)$, which equals $q[p'(x) - n'(x)]$, as

$$\rho(x) = \varepsilon\frac{d\mathscr{E}(x)}{dx} = \frac{\varepsilon}{q\mu_h p_o}\frac{d}{dx}\left[J_{\text{TOT}} - \left(1 - \frac{D_h}{D_e}\right)J_e(x)\right] \tag{5.45}$$

Using the fact that J_{TOT} is not a function of x and that $J_e(x)$ can be written as $qD_e(dn'/dx)$, we arrive at

$$\rho(x) = -\varepsilon\frac{(D_e - D_h)}{\mu_h p_o}\frac{d^2n'}{dx_2} \tag{5.46}$$

Note that d^2n'/dx^2 is proportional to the negative of the net generation, that is, $-[g_L(x) - n'/\tau_e]$ [see Eq. (5.21a)], so we have

$$\rho(x) = \varepsilon \frac{(D_e - D_h)}{\mu_h p_o D_e} \left[g_L(x) - \frac{n'}{\tau_e} \right] \tag{5.47}$$

We could pursue this line of discussion further and reach additional conclusions on quasineutrality, but that would be too much detail for now. It is important to realize that $\rho(x)$ should look like the net generation, particularly when τ_e is very large, and that you can use this fact as a check on your answer when you are calculating $\rho(x)$.

One last point to make is that if we differentiate the electric field and solve Poisson's equation for $\rho(x)$, we find an impulse of negative charge at an ohmic contact (assuming that excess carriers diffuse that far and recombine there) because the electric field drops immediately to zero at the contact. This is totally consistent with Eq. (5.47) because there is infinite recombination at an ohmic contact, but it is hard to reconcile with the assumption of quasineutrality. The problem stems from our modeling of the ohmic contact and the fact that things are happening very quickly (spatially) there. Our model for an ohmic contact is itself an approximation in which we assume that the recombination becomes infinite at the contact. If we use a more physically realistic model that had the recombination occur over a small but finite distance, we can avoid having infinite recombination, but our model needlessly becomes much more complex. We probably still could not apply our quasineutrality assumption in such a thin region because the region would be small relative to an extrinsic Debye length. However, we do not need to know in detail what goes on in the contact. The situation is very much like the case of impulse injection. Furthermore, if we intend to simplify our modeling task by ignoring what goes on in detail in the contact and assume infinite recombination, then we should not be disturbed if our model seems to predict other nonphysical results. One of the lessons of modeling is learning when to worry about nonphysical results (i.e., when they indicate serious problems with the model) and when not to worry about them (i.e., when they are artifacts that are harmless and can be ignored).

5.3 SUMMARY

In this chapter we have considered situations in which one particular set of assumptions concerning a semiconductor is valid, and we have learned how to determine the excess carrier concentrations, the various current densities, and the electric field in such situations. We have seen that when we can assume that we are dealing with uniformly doped, extrinsic material under low-level quasistatic excitation, and when quasineutrality is valid and the minority carrier drift current is negligible, then the five coupled nonlinear differential equations we developed in Chap. 4 to describe semiconductors in general can be simplified to one second-order linear differential equation for the excess minority carrier concentration (we assume a p-type sample for the purposes of our discussion):

$$\frac{d^2n'}{dx^2} - \frac{n'}{L_e^2} = -\frac{g_L(x)}{D_e}$$

where L_e is the minority carrier diffusion length given by $\sqrt{D_e \tau_e}$. Since this is a second-order differential equation, there are two unknown parameters in the solution and two boundary conditions are needed to determine them. We have discussed several common boundaries we might encounter, including ohmic contacts, reflecting boundaries, and injecting contacts, as well as internal boundaries. We have labeled this special class of problems as flow problems, and we have discussed their solution in a variety of situations.

A particularly important situation for device analysis occurs when the minority carrier diffusion length L_e is very large compared to the size of the sample. In this situation, which is referred to either as the infinite lifetime case or the short-base limit, the factor n'/L_e^2 is negligible and our equation becomes

$$\frac{d^2n'}{dx^2} = -\frac{g_L(x)}{D_e}$$

This equation can be solved by integrating twice; again two boundary conditions are needed, this time to evaluate the two constants of integration.

Once the excess minority carrier concentration is known, we have seen that it is relatively easy to determine the currents, the electric field, and the net charge density, from which we calculate the excess majority carrier concentration. One other factor that we do need to determine, however, is the total current density J_{TOT}, but we have seen that this is just a constant and that it is in general possible to determine its value from the problem specifications.

As a practical matter, we will find when we discuss devices that 90 percent of the flow problems in devices are one of two types: low-level injection at one end of a bar, and arbitrary low-level excitation of a bar with infinite lifetime (or minority carrier diffusion length). In the first instance the excess minority carrier distributions look like those in Fig. 5.8, and are given by

$$n'(x) = \frac{ML_e}{D_e} \frac{\sinh[(w - x)/L_e]}{\cosh(w/L_e)}$$

where we have assumed that we have a p-type sample with an injecting contact at $x = 0$ injecting M electrons/cm$^2 \cdot$ s and an ohmic contact at $x = w$. In the second instance the excess minority carrier concentration is found by integrating the generation function:

$$n'(x) = \int_0^x \int_0^{x'} g_L(x'')\, dx''\, dx' + Ax + B$$

The constants A and B are determined by fitting the boundary conditions.

PROBLEMS

5.1 Consider the p-type silicon sample ($p_o = 10^{17}$ cm^{-3}) shown in Fig. P5.1 in which the minority carrier lifetime is zero in the portion $x < 0$ and is 10^{-4} s elsewhere.

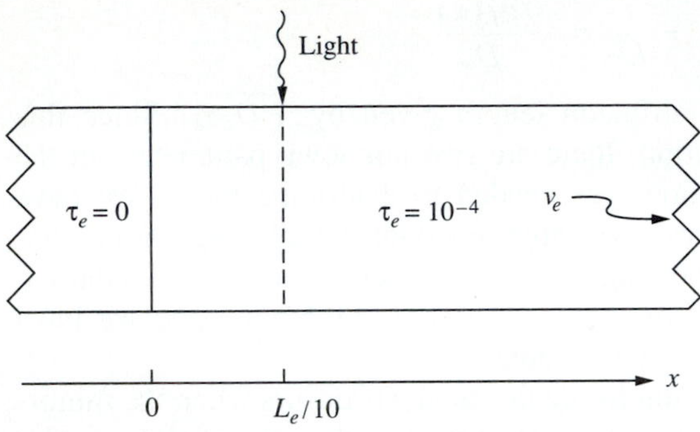

FIGURE P5.1

The sample is illuminated with light, creating an excess minority carrier population of 10^{15} cm^{-3} across the plane at $x = L_e/10$, where L_e is the minority carrier diffusion length.

(*a*) What is $n'(x)$? Give three expressions valid in each of the regions $x \le 0$, $0 \le x \le L_e/10$, and $L_e/10 \le x$. Sketch your answer.

(*b*) What is the optical hole-electron pair generation rate in the plane $x = L_e/10$?

5.2 This problem concerns the p-type silicon bar of length w illustrated in Fig. P5.2*a*. There are ohmic contacts on each end of the bar. $N_p = 5 \times 10^{17}$ cm^{-3}, $\mu_e = 1500$ cm^2/V · s, $\mu_h = 600$ cm^2/V · s, and the minority carrier lifetime is 6×10^{-5} s. You may assume that the minority carrier diffusion length is much greater than w (i.e., $L_e >> w$).

The bar is illuminated by a constant light (i.e., $dg_L/dt = 0$) in such a way that the electron current density is as illustrated in Fig. P5.2*b*.

Assume that low-level injection and quasineutrality are both valid assumptions.

(*a*) Sketch and dimension the hole current $J_h(x)$ for $0 \le x \le w$, being careful to indicate its values at $x = 0$, $w/2$, and w.

(*b*) (i) What is the ratio of the electron diffusion current density at $x = w/4$ to the hole diffusion current density at $x = w/4$?

(ii) What is the ratio of the electron drift current density at $x = w/4$ to the hole drift current density at $x = w/4$?

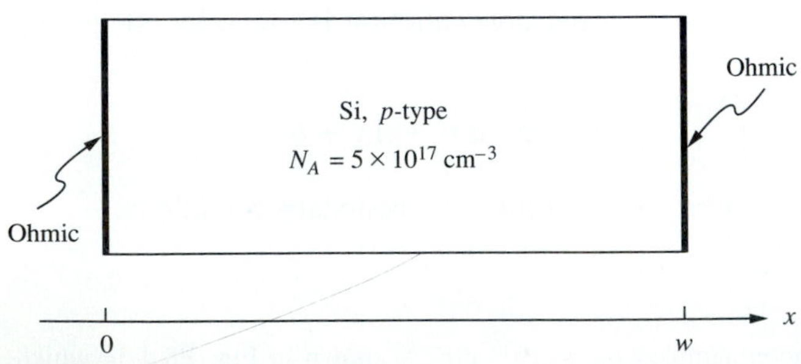

FIGURE P5.2a

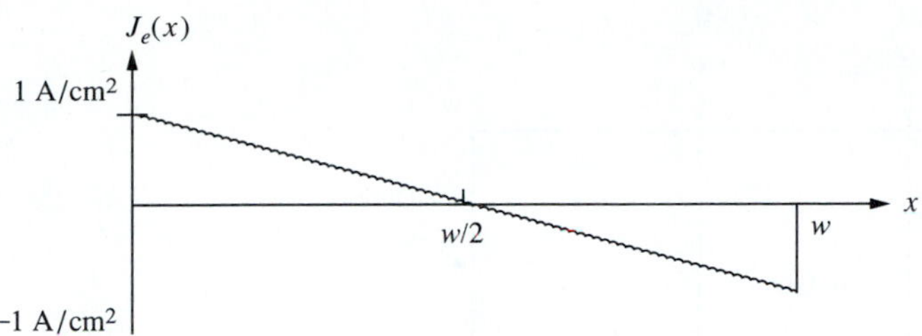

FIGURE P5.2b

(*c*) Sketch and dimension (i) the electric field and (ii) the net charge density for $0 \leq x \leq w$.

(*d*) Sketch and dimension the excess electron concentration $n'(x)$, for $0 \leq x \leq w$, being careful to indicate its values at $x = 0$ and w, and the shape of $n'(x)$.

(*e*) Sketch and dimension the optical generation rate $g_L(x)$ for $0 \leq x \leq w$. Specify the peak value of $g_L(x)$.

5.3 Consider the uniform p-type sample illustrated in Fig. P5.3 for which $L_e >> L$. It is uniformly illuminated for $L/3 \leq x \leq 2L/3$ with light that generates G_L hole-electron pairs/cm$^3 \cdot$ s in the bulk. One end of the sample has an ohmic contact, the other has a reflecting boundary.

Assume that low-level injection, quasineutrality, and minority carrier flow by diffusion are valid assumptions. Assume room temperature also.

Sketch and dimension the following quantities:

(*a*) $n'(x)$
(*b*) $J_e(x)$
(*c*) $J_h(x)$
(*d*) $\mathscr{E}(x)$
(*e*) $p'(x) - n'(x)$

5.4 Consider the uniform n-type ($N_d = 10^{17}$ cm^{-3}) silicon sample illustrated in Fig. P5.4. The two light sources at $x = L/3$ and $x = 2L/3$ are identical and each generate 10^{15} hole-electron pairs/cm$^2 \cdot$ s. $L = 10^{-4}$ cm.

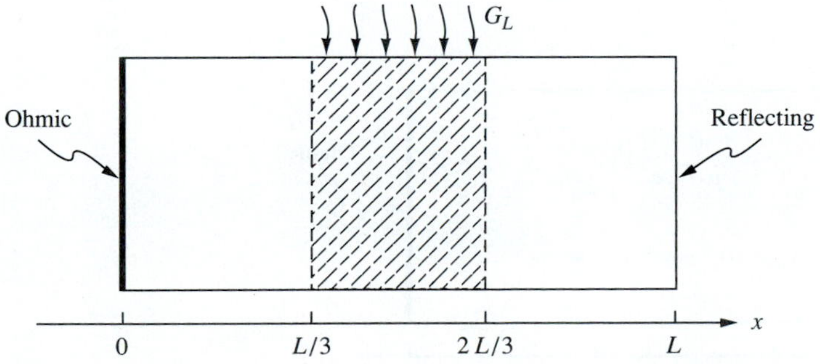

FIGURE P5.3

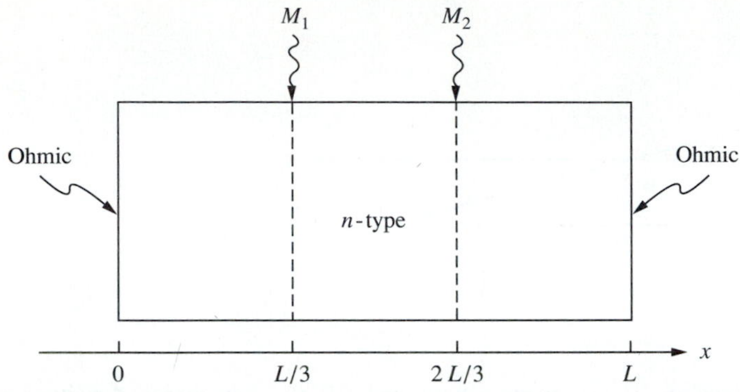

FIGURE P5.4

(*a*) (i) Assume that $L_h >> L$, and find $p'(x)$.
(ii) Sketch and dimension your result.
(iii) On your sketch indicate $p'(x)$ due to M_1 alone illuminating the sample and $p'(x)$ due to M_2 alone illuminating the sample.
(iv) Indicate whether superposition is valid.

(*b*) Assume that L_h is no longer much greater than L, but rather that the two are comparable. Make a *rough* sketch of $p'(x)$ now, indicating how the shapes and peak values change relative to those corresponding to part a.

5.5 Consider the uniformly doped p-type sample illustrated in Fig. P5.5*a*, which has ohmic contacts on both ends and is open-circuited. The doping level is 10^{16} cm^{-3}, $D_e = 40$ cm^2/s, $D_h = 10$ cm^2/s, and the minority carrier diffusion length is much greater than L (i.e., $L_e >> L$).

The sample is illuminated nonuniformly in such a manner that the electron current density is as plotted in Fig. P5.5*b*.

Sketch and label the following quantities for $0 \leq x \leq L$:

(*a*) Hole current density $J_h(x)$
(*b*) Excess electron density $n'(x)$
(*c*) Electric field, $\mathscr{E}(x)$
(*d*) Generation function $g_L(x)$.
(*e*) Net charge density $\sigma(x)$.

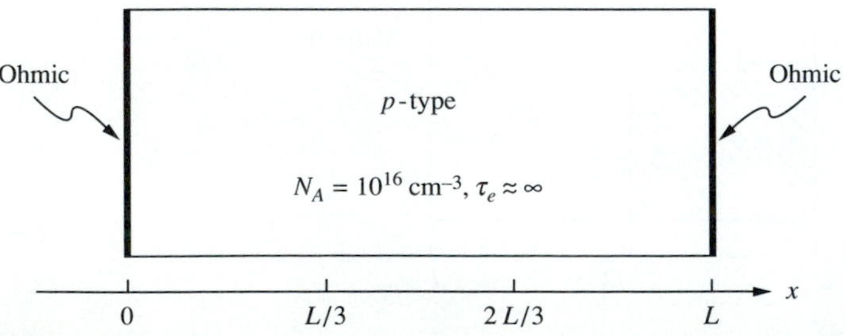

FIGURE P5.5a

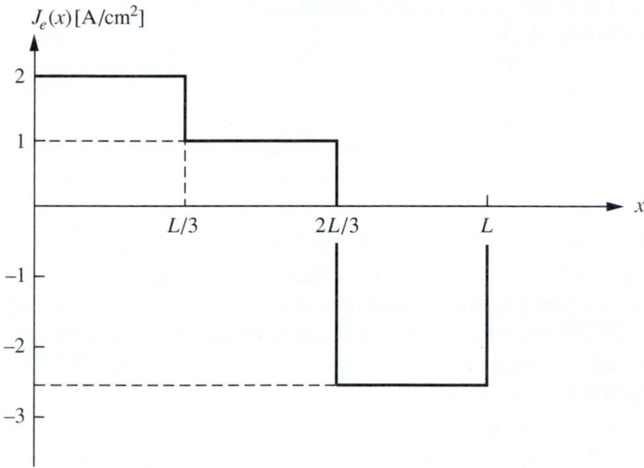

FIGURE P5.5b

5.6 The uniformly doped p-type ($N_a - N_d = 10^{17}$ cm^{-3}) Si sample of length $L = 6\ \mu$m and cross section 0.1 cm^2 with ohmic contacts on each end illustrated in Fig. P5.6 is illuminated by light, with the resultant excess electron population also shown.

Assume the following for silicon at room temperature: $\mu_e = 1500$ cm^2/V · s, $\mu_h = 600$ cm^2/V · s, $n_i = 1.0 \times 10^{10}$ cm^{-3}. Assume also that $L_e >> 6\ \mu$m.

(a) What are the diffusion coefficients D_e and D_h in this sample?

(b) If it is known that the minority carrier diffusion length in this sample is 60 μm, what is the minority carrier lifetime?

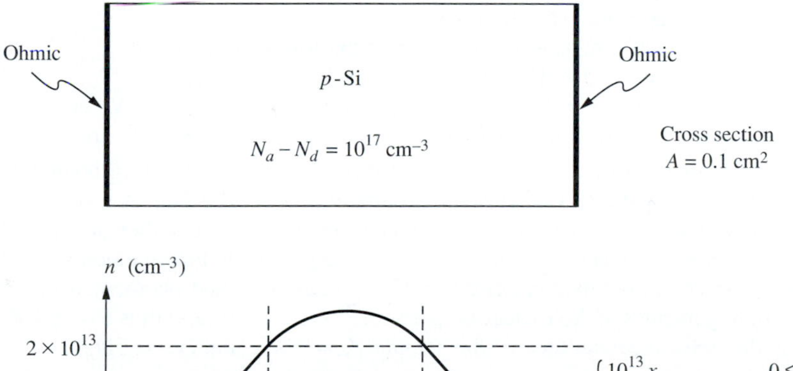

FIGURE P5.6

(*c*) Sketch and dimension the following quantities assuming $L_e >> 6\ \mu$m.
  (i) Electron current density $J_e(x)$.
  (ii) Total current density $J_{TOT}(x)$.
  (iii) Hole current density $J_h(x)$.
  (iv) Optical generation function $g_L(x)$.

(*d*) The sample is now changed to one in which the minority carrier lifetime τ_e is 10 μs ($= 10^{-5}$ s); all other parameters are unchanged. Using this value for τ_e, calculate the total recombination occurring within this sample between $x = 0^+$ and $x = 2$. (*Note:* The units of your answer should be hole-electron pairs/s.)

5.7 We argue that it is very difficult to maintain charge imbalances for long times or over long distances in an extrinsic semiconductor, and thus that the material tends to stay electrically neutral (we call it quasineutral). The relevant time factor is the *dielectric relaxation time*; the relevant distance factor is the *Debye length* (see App. D). This problem deals with dielectric relaxation time.

(*a*) A macroscopic example of dielectric relaxation is the decay of charge stored on a "leaky capacitor." Such a capacitor might be a parallel plate capacitor having a conducting dielectric (i.e., one with a dielectric constant ε and a nonzero conductivity σ). A "leaky capacitor" can be modeled as an ideal capacitor in parallel with an ideal resistor.
  (i) Show that the charge stored on a capacitor of capacitance C in parallel with a resistor of resistance R will delay as

$$Q(t) = Q_o e^{-t/RC}$$

  if the charge at $t = 0$ is Q_o.
  (ii) Find an expression for the resistance R of a leaky capacitor with plate area A and plate separation d.
  (iii) Find an expression for the capacitance C of the same leaky capacitor as in part ii.
  (iv) Find an expression for the RC time constant of the above leaky capacitor. This is the dielectric relaxation time.

(*b*) Calculate the dielectric relaxation time ε/σ of the following materials:
  (i) A metal with $\sigma = 10^6\ (\Omega \cdot \text{cm})^{-1}$ and $\varepsilon = 10^{-13}$ C/V · cm
  (ii) An insulator with $\sigma = 10^{-16}\ (\Omega \cdot \text{cm})^{-1}$ and $\varepsilon = 3 \times 10^{-13}$ C/V · cm
  (iii) A semiconductor with $\sigma = 10^0\ (\Omega \cdot \text{cm})^{-1}$ and $\varepsilon = 10^{-12}$ C/V · cm

5.8 The sample illustrated in Fig. P5.8 is illuminated on one end, a reflecting boundary, with light generating a sheet of electron-hole pairs at $x \approx 0$. The light has sufficient energy that all of the generated electrons are given so much energy that they are ejected from the semiconductor, where they are attracted to the positively biased electrode and appear as a current i in the external circuit. (This process is called photoemission.)

The light generates M hole-electron pairs/cm^2 · s at $x = 0$, and thus $i = qAM$, where A is the cross-sectional area of the sample. $L = 10L_h$ and $D_e = 3D_h$.

(*a*) Sketch $p'(x)$ for $0 \le x \le L$. Indicate the values of $p'(x)$ at $x = 0$ and at $x = L$.

(*b*) (i) Sketch the total current density $J_{TOT}(x)$ for $0 < x < L$.
  (ii) Sketch the hole current density $J_h(x)$ for $0 < x < L$. Indicate the values of $J_h(x)$ at $x = 0^+$, that is, just to the right of the surface at $x = 0$, and of $J_h(x)$ at $x = L^-$, that is, just before the ohmic contact at $x = L$.
  (iii) Sketch the electron current density $J_e(x)$. Indicate the values of $J_e(0^+)$ and $J_e(L^-)$.

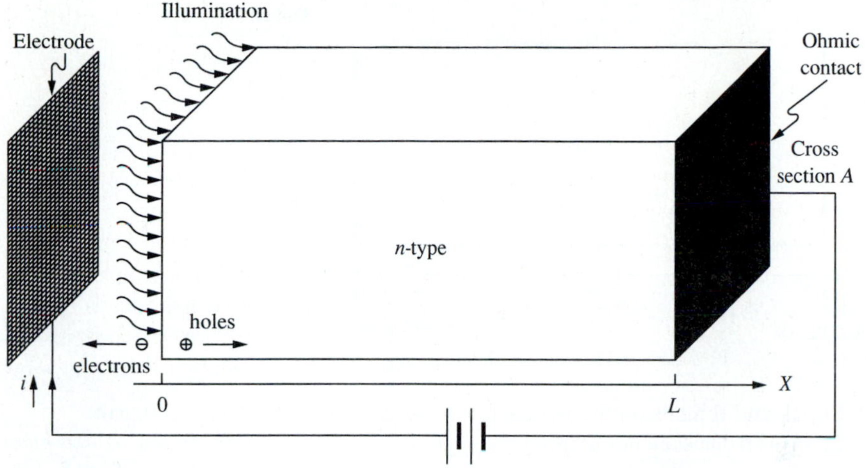

FIGURE P5.8

5.9 Consider an open-circuited silicon bar 100 mm long with ohmic contacts on each end. The bar is p-type with $N_A = 5 \times 10^{16}\ \mathrm{cm}^{-3}$; the electron mobility μ_e is 1600 cm²/V·s; the hole mobility μ_h is 600 cm²/V · s; and the minority carrier lifetime τ_e is 10^{-3} s. The bar is illuminated with constant illumination generating $g_L(x)$ hole-electron pairs/cm³ · s in its bulk so that the resulting excess minority carrier concentration is as illustrated in Fig. P5.9.

(*a*) Calculate the minority carrier diffusion length for this sample, and justify the assumption of infinite lifetime. (See the discussion in Sec. 5.25*d*.)

(*b*) Sketch and dimension the minority carrier current $J_e(x)$ for $0 \le x \le 100\ \mu$m.

(*c*) Sketch and dimension the majority carrier current $J_h(x)$ for $0 \le x \le 100\ \mu$m.

(*d*) Sketch and dimension the electric field $\mathscr{E}(x)$ for $0 \le x \le 100\ \mu$m.

(*e*) What is the generation function $g_L(x)$? Sketch and dimension $g_L(x)$ for $0 \le x \le 100\ \mu$m.

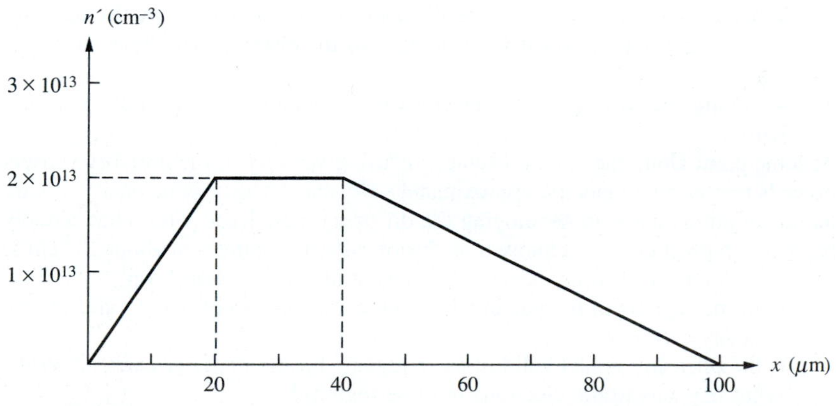

FIGURE P5.9

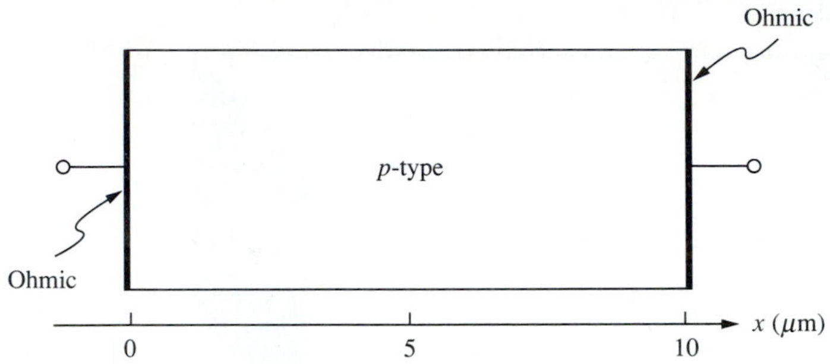

FIGURE P5.10

(*f*) Sketch and dimension the net charge density $\rho(x)$ for $0 \leq x \leq 100$ μm. Compare your sketches of $\rho(x)$ and $g_L(x)$. They should look similar, which gives you a check on the consistency of your solution. (This is discussed in Sec. 5.2.6.)

(*g*) Thus far in this problem you have assumed no recombination in the bulk of this sample (i.e., infinite lifetime), but τ_h is not infinite, and recombination does occur.

(i) What is the total recombination flux density in the bulk of this sample in hole-electron pairs/cm^2 · s? [See Eq. (5.35) and the discussion preceding it.]

(ii) Compare this with the total rate at which hole-electron pairs are being generated (injected) in this sample by $g_L(x)$.

(iii) Where do the other hole-electron pairs go?

5.10 In this problem we want to compare the average velocities of drifting and diffusing charge carriers in the p-type silicon sample illustrated in Fig. P5.10. In this sample $N_A = 1 \times 10^{17}$ cm^{-3}, $\mu_e = 1600$ cm^2/V · s, $\mu_h = 600$ cm^2/V · s, $D_e = 40$ cm^2/s, $D_h = 15$ cm^2/s, and $\tau_e = 10^{-6}$s.

(*a*) If we apply a voltage of 2 V to this sample, what are the electron and hole drift current densities and what are the average drift velocities of the electrons and holes?

b) Assume that the sample is illuminated with a narrow beam of light that generates hole-electron pairs in the plane at $x = 5$ μm and produces an excess electron population n' at $x = 5$ μm of 5×10^{15} cm^{-3}.

(i) What are the electron and hole diffusion current densities in the bar, and what are the average diffusion velocities of the electrons and holes at $x = 1$ μm?

(ii) What are the average drift velocities of the holes and electrons at $x = 1$ μm?

(*c*) At some point along the bar the average diffusing velocity of the minority carriers exceeds the thermal velocity, approximately 10^7 cm/s, which is inconsistent with the assumptions made in developing the diffusing model and with what actually happens. In practice, the velocity of diffusion carriers saturates at about 10^7 cm/s, and the velocity of drifting carriers saturates at about the same level.

(i) Find the regions in the bar in which the diffusion model is not valid for the minority carriers.

(ii) Is the diffusion model valid in these regions for the majority carriers? Why?

(iii) What happens to the electrons in these regions?

CHAPTER 6

NONUNIFORMLY DOPED SEMICONDUCTORS IN THERMAL EQUILIBRIUM

Thus far we have considered only uniformly doped, homogeneous samples. We now want to consider samples in which the doping is a function of position. We restrict ourselves to one-dimensional variations, that is, $N_d(x)$ and $N_a(x)$, and begin by considering samples in thermal equilibrium. The question we will ask is, "Given $N_d(x)$ and $N_a(x)$, what are the thermal equilibrium hole and electron concentrations, $p_o(x)$ and $n_o(x)$, respectively, and what is the electric field $\mathcal{E}(x)$?" We do not ask about the electron and hole currents, J_e and J_h, because in thermal equilibrium these currents are identically equal to zero and we need not be concerned any further with calculating them. In addition, we will show that it is still true in thermal equilibrium that $n_o(x)p_o(x) = n_i^2$ even if n_o and p_o are functions of position. Thus if we know $n_o(x)$, we know $p_o(x)$, and vice versa.

Before proceeding with answering the above question, we should consider why we even have a problem. Imagine that we have an n-type sample with $N_D(x)$ as illustrated in the Fig. 6.1. If we assume that $n_o(x) \approx N_D(x)$, then $n_o(x)$ would increase going from left to right and $p_o(x)$ would decrease. However, these gradients in n_o and p_o will cause the diffusion of electrons to the left and holes to the right, which in turn will lead to a charge imbalance and a negative electric field. This field will oppose the diffusion by tending to drift the holes to the left and electrons to the right (i.e., back to their original positions). A balance, or

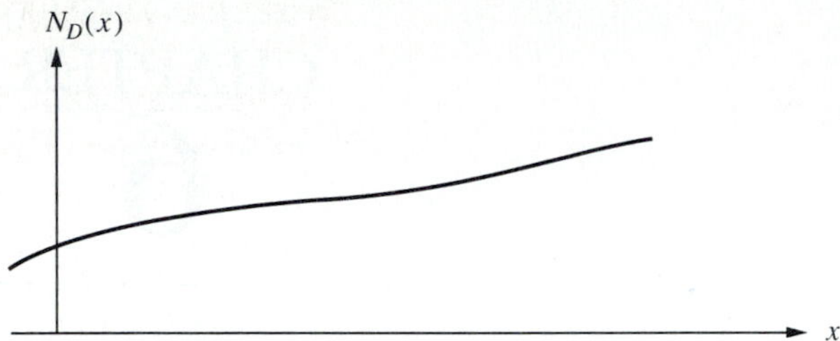

FIGURE 6.1
Example of a net donor concentration $N_D(x)$, which varies with position.

equilibrium, is established in which the drift and diffusion fluxes just cancel each other. Clearly, however, we must anticipate that $n_o(x)$ will not equal $N_D(x)$, and that there will be an electric field.

6.1 GENERAL DESCRIPTION: THE POISSON-BOLTZMANN EQUATION

We begin by rewriting our five basic equations from Chap. 4:

$$J_e(x,t) = qn(x,t)\mu_e(x)\mathscr{E}(x,t) + qD_e(x)\frac{\partial n(x,t)}{\partial x} \tag{4.15}$$

$$J_h(x,t) = q\,p(x,t)\mu_h(x)\mathscr{E}(x,t) - qD_h(x)\frac{\partial p(x,t)}{\partial x} \tag{4.16}$$

$$-\frac{1}{q}\frac{\partial J_e(x,t)}{\partial x} + \frac{\partial n(x,t)}{\partial t} = g_L(x,t) - r(T)[p(x,t)n(x,t) - n_i^2(T)] \tag{4.17}$$

$$\frac{1}{q}\frac{\partial J_h(x,t)}{\partial x} + \frac{\partial p(x,t)}{\partial t} = g_L(x,t) - r(T)[p(x,t)n(x,t) - n_i^2(T)] \tag{4.18}$$

$$\frac{\partial[\varepsilon(x)\mathscr{E}(x,t)]}{\partial x} = q[p(x,t) - n(x,t) + N_d(x) - N_a(x)] \tag{4.19}$$

In the special circumstances that we are dealing with now (i.e., nonuniform doping and thermal equilibrium), there is no generation [i.e., $g_L(x,t)$ is zero]; the currents J_e and J_h are identically zero; and the carrier populations have their thermal equilibrium values. Furthermore, there is no time variation, so the time derivatives [in Eqs. (4.17) and (4.18)] are zero and all of the partial derivatives become total derivatives. In this case, Eqs. (4.17) and (4.18) reduce to $0 = 0$ and our five equations become three:

$$0 = qn_o(x)\mu_e(x)\mathscr{E}(x) + qD_e(x)\frac{dn_o(x)}{dx} \tag{6.1a}$$

$$0 = q p_o(x)\mu_h(x)\mathcal{E}(x) - qD_h(x)\frac{dp_o(x)}{dx} \tag{6.1b}$$

$$\frac{d[\varepsilon(x)\mathcal{E}(x)]}{dx} = q[p_o(x) - n_o(x) + N_d(x) - N_a(x)] \tag{6.1c}$$

In spite of the enormous simplifications that these three equations represent compared to our initial five equations, they still form a set of coupled, nonlinear differential equations, and their solution is still difficult.

In order to proceed toward finding $p_o(x)$, $n_o(x)$, and $\mathcal{E}(x)$ given $N_d(x)$ and $N_a(x)$ we start with Eq. (6.1a). Writing the electric field $\mathcal{E}(x)$, as $-d\phi/dx$, where $\phi(x)$ is the electrostatic potential, and rearranging terms yields

$$\frac{1}{n_o(x)}\frac{dn_o(x)}{dx} = \frac{\mu_e}{D_e}\frac{d\phi(x)}{dx} \tag{6.2}$$

This equation can be integrated from a reference point to the position x of interest. We obtain

$$\ln n_o(x) - \ln n_{\text{ref}} = \frac{\mu_e[\phi(x) - \phi_{\text{ref}}]}{D_e} \tag{6.3a}$$

or, equivalently,

$$n_o(x) = n_{\text{ref}} e^{\mu_e[\phi(x)-\phi_{\text{ref}}]/D_e} \tag{6.3b}$$

where ϕ_{ref} is the electrostatic potential at some point that we will take as our reference position and n_{ref} is the electron concentration at that same position.

It can be shown that the mobility μ and diffusion coefficient D of a carrier are related through what is called the Einstein relation:

$$\frac{\mu_e}{D_e} = \frac{\mu_h}{D_h} = \frac{q}{kT} \tag{6.4}$$

This relation occurs because both drift and diffusion involve carrier motion in gradients (of electrostatic potential energy and of concentration, respectively) and are dominated by the random thermal motion of carriers and collisions with the crystal lattice and defects. The Einstein relationship is easy to remember because it rhymes: "Mu over dee, is cue over kay tee." In fact, inverted it still rhymes: "Dee over mu, is kay tee over cue."

Using the Einstein relation, Eq. (6.3b) becomes

$$n_o(x) = n_{\text{ref}} e^{q[\phi(x)-\phi_{\text{ref}}]/kT} \tag{6.5}$$

From the hole current equation we can obtain a similar expression for holes:

$$p_o(x) = p_{\text{ref}} e^{-q[\phi(x)-\phi_{\text{ref}}]/kT} \tag{6.6}$$

We will take as our reference point intrinsic material. Thus $n_{\text{ref}} = n_i$ and $p_{\text{ref}} = n_i$. We will also take the zero reference for our potential to be intrinsic material (i.e., $\phi_{\text{ref}} = 0$). We can do this as long as we are consistent and measure all potentials relative to this zero reference. With this reference convention Eqs. (6.5) and (6.6) become

$$n_o(x) = n_i e^{q\phi(x)/kT} \tag{6.7}$$

and

$$p_o(x) = n_i e^{-q\phi(x)/kT} \tag{6.8}$$

The exponential factors in these equations are called Boltzmann factors. We can see that they take the form

$$e^{-\text{PE}/\text{TE}} \tag{6.9}$$

where PE is the potential energy of the particle and TE is the thermal energy kT. The equations for $n_o(x)$ and $p_o(x)$ state that the ratio of the density, n_1 or p_1, of carriers with potential energy PE_1, to the density, n_2 or p_2, of carriers with potential energy PE_2 is a Boltzmann factor dependent on the difference between PE_1 and PE_2:

$$\frac{n_1}{n_2} = \frac{p_1}{p_2} = e^{-(\text{PE}_1 - \text{PE}_2)/kT} = e^{-\Delta\text{PE}/kT} \tag{6.10}$$

This type of behavior of a particle population at thermal equilibrium is found in a large number of physical systems. It is a feature we will make use of in a number of different device contexts.

Equations (6.7) and (6.8) give us two equations in three unknowns, $p_o(x)$, $n_o(x)$, and $\phi(x)$. Equation (6.1c), which is Poisson's equation, is the third equation. Assuming that the dielectric constant ε does not vary with position and writing $\mathscr{E}(x)$ as $-d\phi/dx$, we have

$$\frac{d^2\phi(x)}{dx^2} = -\frac{q}{\varepsilon}[p_o(x) - n_o x) + N_D(x)] \tag{6.11}$$

where we have also used $N_D(x) \equiv N_d(x) - N_a(x)$ to denote the net donor concentration. Using Eqs. (6.7) and (6.8) in Eq. 6.11 gives us one equation in one unknown, $\phi(x)$:

$$\frac{d^2\phi(x)}{dx^2} = -\frac{q}{\varepsilon}[n_i(e^{-q\phi(x)/kT} - e^{q\phi(x)/kT}) + N_D(x)] \tag{6.12a}$$

or, equivalently,

$$\frac{d^2\phi(x)}{dx^2} = -\frac{q}{\varepsilon}[2n_i \sinh\frac{q\phi(x)}{kT} - N_D(x)] \tag{6.12b}$$

This equation is called the Poisson-Boltzmann equation. It is a nonlinear, second-order differential equation that is in general difficult to solve analytically. It can be readily solved by iteration using numerical methods, but it is still a solution best left for a computer. There are two special cases, however, in which approximate solutions can be found analytically: the first is when the doping varies gradually with position, and the second is an abrupt *p-n* junction. We will discuss both of these in turn next.

6.2 GRADUAL SPATIAL VARIATION OF DOPING

If $N_D(x)$ [which is defined as $N_d(x) - N_a(x)$] is sufficiently slowly varying, then we can show that quasineutrality holds and that

$$n_o(x) - p_o(x) \approx N_D(x) \tag{6.13}$$

If the material is extrinsic, $|N_D(x)| \gg n_i$, then for n-type materials we have

$$n_{no}(x) \approx N_D(x) \tag{6.14a}$$

$$p_{no}(x) \approx \frac{n_i{}^2}{N_D(x)} \tag{6.14b}$$

and

$$\phi_{no}(x) \approx \frac{kT}{q} \ln \frac{N_D(x)}{n_i} \tag{6.14c}$$

For p-type material, we have $N_a(x)$ greater than $N_d(x)$ and use $N_A(x)$ [defined as $N_a(x) - N_d(x)$] rather than $N_D(x)$. We find

$$p_{po}(x) \approx N_A(x) \tag{6.15a}$$

$$n_{po}(x) \approx \frac{n_i^2}{N_A(x)} \tag{6.15b}$$

and

$$\phi_{po}(x) \approx \frac{kT}{q} \ln \frac{N_A(x)}{n_i} \tag{6.15c}$$

Notice that in writing Eqs. (6.14) and (6.15) we have introduced subscripts to indicate the net doping type (i.e., n or p) of the regions in question.

When $N_D(x)$ is sufficiently slowly varying we thus know all of the answers; that is, we know $n_o(x)$, $p_o(x)$, and $\phi_o(x)$. Quantitatively we can show that a "slow" variation of $N_D(x)$ means

$$\left|\frac{d\phi}{dx}\right| \ll \sqrt{\frac{kT\,|N_D|}{\varepsilon}} \tag{6.16}$$

To see what this means physically, it is first useful to notice that the quantity on the right-hand side of this equation can be written in terms of the extrinsic Debye length, which we have defined [see Eq. (5.13) and App. D] as

$$L_D = \sqrt{D_{\text{maj}}\tau_D} \tag{6.17}$$

For the sake of discussion let us assume that we have a p-type sample so that $\tau_D = \varepsilon/q\mu_h p_{po}$ and $D_{\text{maj}} = D_h = \mu_h kT/q$. Using these we can rewrite L_D as

$$L_D = \sqrt{\frac{\varepsilon kT}{q^2 p_{po}}} \tag{6.18}$$

Writing L_D this way we see that Eq. (6.16) can also be stated as

$$\left|\frac{d\phi}{dx}\right| \ll \frac{kT}{qL_D} \tag{6.19}$$

Now we can interpret this constraint more easily. It says that any change in the electrostatic potential of kT/q must occur over many extrinsic Debye lengths L_D; alternatively, it says that over a distance of one extrinsic Debye length, the change in electrostatic potential must be much less than kT/q for the quasineutrality condition to hold.

To cast these statements in terms of a variation in the doping concentration directly, assume that we have an n-type sample for which $N_D(x)$ is sufficiently slowly varying that $n_{no}(x) \approx N_D(x)$. In this case we also have

$$\phi(x) \approx \frac{kT}{q} \ln \frac{N_D(x)}{n_i} \tag{6.20}$$

and thus

$$\frac{d\phi}{dx} \approx \frac{kT}{qN_D(x)} \frac{dN_D}{dx} \tag{6.21}$$

Inserting this into Eq. (6.19), we see that for our assumption of quasineutrality to hold, we must have

$$\left|\frac{dN_D}{dx}\right| \ll \frac{|N_D|}{L_D} \tag{6.22}$$

where we have added absolute value signs to handle positive and negative doping gradients and net acceptor, as well as net donor, concentrations.

Thus far in this section, we have simply stated Eq. (6.16) and its other forms, Eqs. (6.19) and (6.22). To develop a feel for where these results come from we now look at an example in which we can obtain an approximate analytical solution. Consider a doping profile in which $N_D(x) = N_o$ for $x > 0$ and $N_D(x) = N_o + \Delta N$ for $x < 0$, where $\Delta N/N_o$ is small. This situation is illustrated in Fig. 6.2*a*.

For large x, that is, $x \gg 0$, we have $\phi(x) = \phi_o(kT/q)\ln(N_o/n_i)$. For any position we can write $\phi(x)$ as

$$\phi(x) = \phi_o + \Delta\phi(x) \tag{6.23}$$

and we can write the Poisson-Boltzmann equation for $x > 0$ as

$$\frac{d^2\phi}{dx^2} = \frac{d^2\Delta\phi}{dx^2} = \frac{q}{\varepsilon}\{n_i[e^{-q(\phi_o+\Delta\phi)/kT} - e^{q(\phi_o+\Delta\phi)/kT}] - N_o\}$$

Assuming that $|\Delta\phi| \ll kT/q$ and $N_o \gg n_i$, we find that this can be simplified to

$$\frac{d^2\Delta\phi}{dx^2} \approx \frac{q^2 N_o \Delta\phi}{\varepsilon kT} \tag{6.24}$$

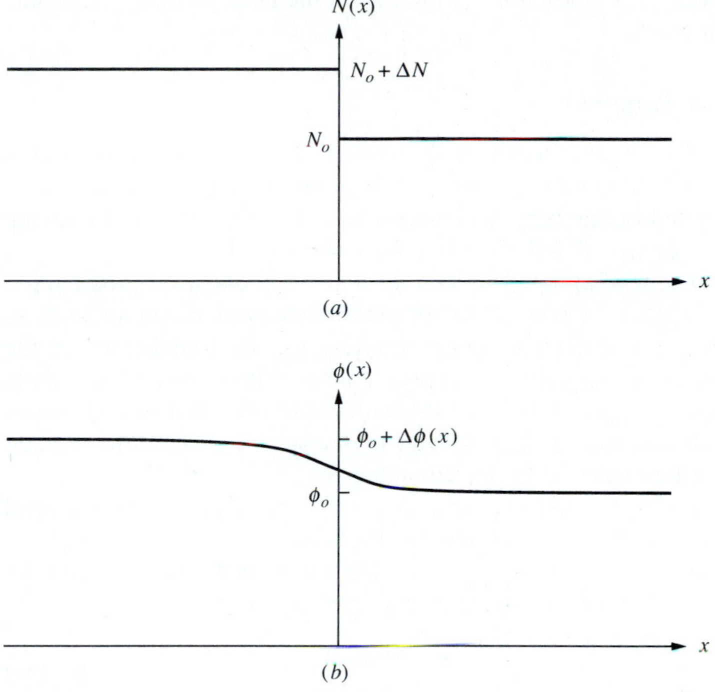

FIGURE 6.2
(a) Doping profile with a step decrease in concentration at $x = 0$; (b) the corresponding $\phi(x)$.

From this we obtain the result that, for $x > 0$,

$$\Delta\phi(x) = Ae^{-x/L_D} \tag{6.25}$$

with $L_D \equiv (\varepsilon kT/q^2N_o)^{1/2}$. Figure 6.2$b$ illustrates this function, which tells us that the carrier concentration will track the doping profile with a natural reaction distance of L_D. Our restriction, Eq. (6.19), follows directly.

We could continue with this solution, solving for $x < 0$ and (by matching the two solutions at $x = 0$) determining A, but the significance of the extrinsic Debye length should already be clear, and there is little to be gained by going further.

To summarize: if the variation in the doping profile $N(x)$ is gradual, then the equilibrium majority carrier population will be approximately $|\, N(x)\, |$. A "gradual" variation in doping implies a change in doping of no more than roughly 10 to 20 percent in one extrinsic Debye length L_D.

6.3 *p-n* JUNCTION: THE DEPLETION APPROXIMATION

A doping variation with tremendous practical importance is one in which the semiconductor type changes from n-type to p-type over a relatively short distance.

Such structures are called *p-n* junctions, which form the heart of many electronic devices, as we shall learn.

6.3.1 Abrupt *p-n* Junction

An abrupt *p-n* junction is one in which the change from *n*- to *p*-type occurs abruptly and in which the doping levels on either side of the junction are constant. This situation, illustrated in Fig. 6.3, can be represented mathematically by saying that $N_D(x) = -N_{Ap}$ for $x < 0$ and $N_D(x) = N_{Dn}$ for $x \geq 0$.

To treat the problem of abrupt *p-n* junctions we will use an approximation called the *depletion approximation*. This approximation, which can be used to treat junctions with many different doping profiles, has its foundations in the exponential variation of the equilibrium carrier concentrations with electrostatic potential, that is, Eqs. (6.7) and (6.8). This dependence implies that small changes in the potential ϕ will lead to very large changes in carrier concentrations, n_o and p_o, and this fact can be exploited to our advantage.

In the *n*-type region, far from the junction, $n_o = N_{Dn}$, $p_o = n_i^2/N_{Dn}$, and $\phi = (kT/q)\ln(N_{Dn}/n_i)$. In the *p*-type region, far from the junction, $p_o = N_{Ap}$, $n_o = n_1^2/N_{Ap}$ and $\phi = -(kT/q)\ln(N_{Ap}/n_i)$. The electrostatic potential on the *n*-side is written as ϕ_n and on the *p*-side as ϕ_p, and we have

$$\phi_n = \left(\frac{kT}{q}\right)\ln\frac{N_{Dn}}{n_i} \tag{6.26a}$$

and

$$\phi_p = -\left(\frac{kT}{q}\right)\ln\frac{N_{Ap}}{n_i} \tag{6.26b}$$

Example

Question. What is the value of the electrostatic potential, referenced to intrinsic material, in each of the following silicon samples at room temperature: a) N_{Dn} =

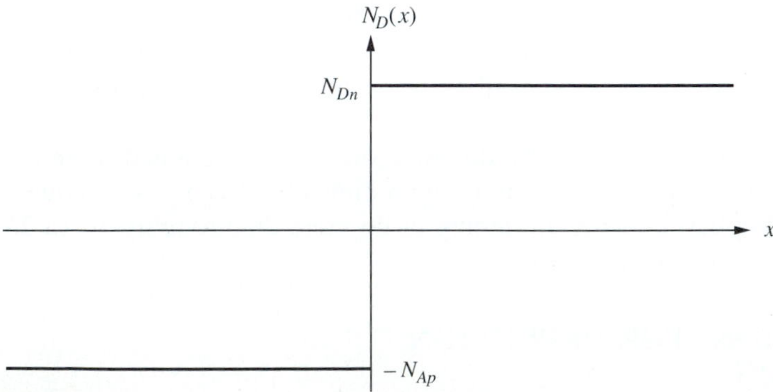

FIGURE 6.3
Doping profile at an abrupt *p-n* junction.

2.5×10^{15} cm^{-3}; b) $N_{Dn} = 2 \times 10^{17}$ cm^{-3}; and c) $N_{Ap} = 4 \times 10^{16}$ cm^{-3}? Assume that n_i is 1×10^{10} cm^{-3} and kT/q is 0.025 V.

Discussion. Using Eqs. (6.26) we find that ϕ is 0.31 V in sample a, and 0.42 V in sample b, and −0.38 V in sample c. We see that although the doping levels differ by almost two orders of magnitude, the magnitudes of the electrostatic potentials are all very comparable; this reflects the fact that the electrostatic potential depends only logarithmically on the doping level.

Crossing from the n-region to the p-region, n_o changes many orders of magnitude and the associated gradient in concentration leads to a diffusion flux of electrons from the n-side to the p-side of the junction. The complementary change in p_o leads to an oppositely directed diffusion of holes. These diffusion currents will be counterbalanced by drift currents because the motion of negatively charged electrons in one direction and positively charged holes in the other causes a polarization, or charge imbalance, that creates an electric drift field that opposes further motion. An equilibrium situation develops in which the drift and diffusion currents exactly cancel and the net hole and electron currents are identically zero, as we have discussed before.

The electric field, of course, reflects the fact that ϕ changes from ϕ_n to ϕ_p going across the junction. As $\phi(x)$ decreases from ϕ_n as the junction is approached, it must be true that $n_o(x)$ decreases even more quickly from N_{Dn} (because it depends exponentially on ϕ). This is illustrated in Fig. 6.4. Any decrease in $N_0(x)$ below N_{Dn}, leaves a net, fixed positive charge density $\rho(x) \approx q[N_{Dn} - n_o(x)]$ at that position. This is illustrated in Fig. 6.4. The hole population $p_o(x)$ is increasing exponentially at the same time that $n_o(x)$ is decreasing, but until $\phi(x)$ becomes very negative (approximately $-\phi_n$) the amount of charge due to the mobile holes is negligible. Thus when the change in ϕ is

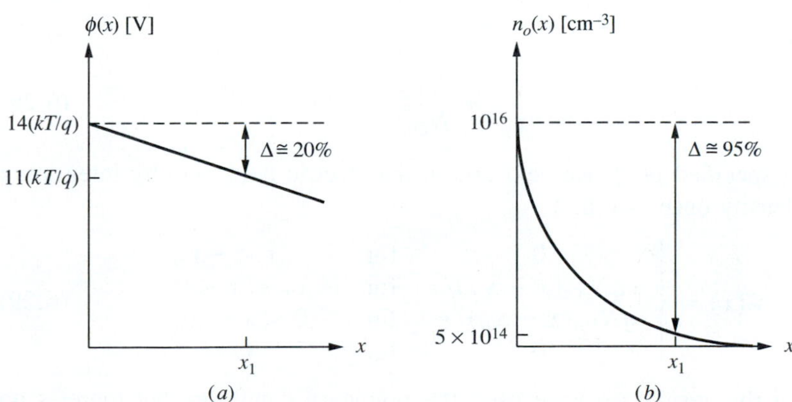

FIGURE 6.4
Comparison of changes in (*a*) electrostatic potential, versus (*b*) equilibrium electron population. (The values at $x = 0$ correspond to silicon at room temperature with $N_{Dn} = 10^{16}$ cm^{-3}.)

more than a few kT/q, $n_o(x)$ will be much smaller than N_{Dn} and the net charge density $\rho(x)$ will be essentially qN_{Dn}.

Similarly, on the p-side, as $\phi(x)$ increases from ϕ_p, $p_o(x)$ decreases quickly, and after an increase of only a few kT/q in ϕ, $p_o(x)$ is much less than N_{Ap} and we have $\rho(x) \approx -qN_{Ap}$.

The total change in potential, $\phi_n - \phi_p$, is many kT/q, so we might anticipate that these initial changes of only a few kT/q will occur over only a small fraction of the total distance over which the total change in ϕ occurs. In the *depletion approximation* we assume that the changes illustrated in Fig. 6.4 occur over negligibly short distances and thus that the change from $\rho(x) = 0$ to $\rho(x) = qN_{Dn}$ on the n-side occurs abruptly at some $x \equiv x_n$. Similarly we say that $\rho(x)$ changes abruptly from 0 to $-qN_{Ap}$ at $x \equiv -x_p$ on the p-side. Between $x = -x_p$ and $x = x_n$, both $n_o(x)$ and $p_o(x)$ are assumed to be negligibly small compared to the fixed donor and acceptor densities, N_{Ap} and N_{Dn}. This is illustrated in Fig. 6.5*a*. Having an estimate of the net charge density $\rho(x)$, we can proceed to solve Eq. (6.11) for the electrostatic potential.

Formally, in the depletion approximation we assume that the charge density has the following positional dependence:

$$\rho(x) = \begin{cases} 0 & \text{for} \quad x < -x_p \\ -qN_{Ap} & \text{for} \quad -x_p < x < 0 \\ +qN_{Dn} & \text{for} \quad 0 < x < x_n \\ 0 & \text{for} \quad x_n < x \end{cases} \tag{6.27}$$

The positions x_p and x_n are unknown at this point in our discussion, but we will obtain expressions for them shortly. We will get one relationship between x_p and x_n by insisting that the total change in the potential must be equal to $\phi_n - \phi_p$. We can get another relationship by noticing that the total charge in the system must be conserved and that the net charge must be zero. Thus it must be true that

$$qN_{Ap}x_p = qN_{Dn}x_n$$

so we can write

$$\frac{x_n}{x_p} = \frac{N_{Ap}}{N_{Dn}} \tag{6.28}$$

Having specified $\rho(x)$, we next obtain the electric field $\mathscr{E}(x)$ by integrating the charge density once. We find

$$\mathscr{E}(x) = \begin{cases} 0 & \text{for} \quad x < -x_p \\ -qN_{Ap}(x + x_p)/\varepsilon & \text{for} \quad -x_p < x < 0 \\ qN_{Dn}(x - x_n)/\varepsilon & \text{for} \quad 0 < x < x_n \\ 0 & \text{for} \quad x_n < x \end{cases} \tag{6.29}$$

In arriving at this result, we have used the boundary condition that there is no electric field far away from the junction on either side of the space charge region. This electric field is plotted in Fig. 6.5*b*.

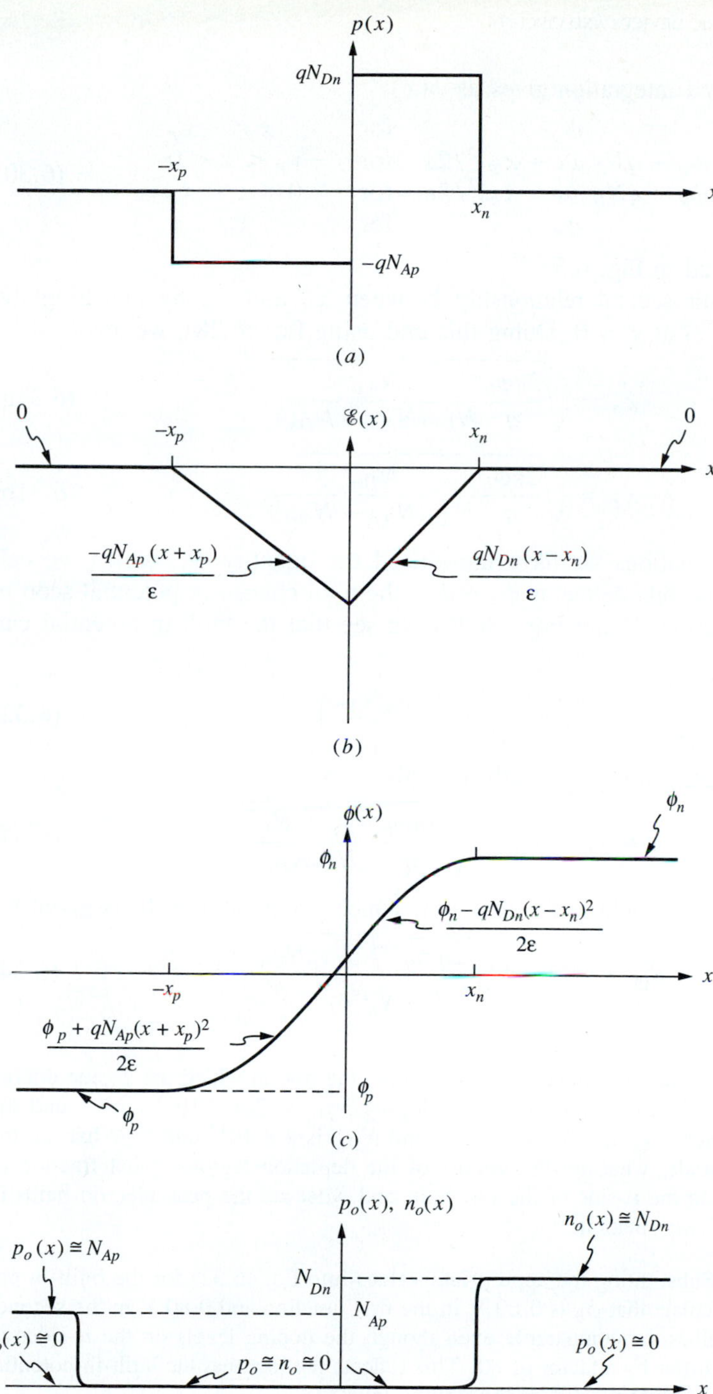

FIGURE 6.5
Depletion approximation solution in the vicinity of an abrupt p-n junction for: (a) the net charge density; (b) the electric field; (c) the electrostatic potential; and (d) the mobile charge populations.

Next, a second integration gives us $\phi(x)$:

$$\phi(x) = \begin{cases} \phi_p & \text{for} \quad x < -x_p \\ \phi_p + qN_{Ap}(x + x_p)^2/2\varepsilon & \text{for} \quad -x_p < x < 0 \\ \phi_n - qN_{Dn}(x - x_n)^2/2\varepsilon & \text{for} \quad 0 < x < x_n \\ \phi_n & \text{for} \quad x_n < x \end{cases} \tag{6.30}$$

This result is plotted in Fig. 6.5*c*.

We obtain our second relationship between x_n and x_p by matching the expressions for $\phi(x)$ at $x = 0$. Doing this and using Eq. (6.28), we arrive at

$$x_n = \sqrt{\frac{2\varepsilon\phi_b}{q}\frac{N_{Ap}}{N_{Dn}(N_{Ap} + N_{Dn})}} \tag{6.31a}$$

$$x_p = \sqrt{\frac{2\varepsilon\phi_b}{q}\frac{N_{Dn}}{N_{Ap}(N_{Ap} + N_{Dn})}} \tag{6.31b}$$

In writing these equations we have introduced the quantity ϕ_b, which we call the *built-in potential* and define as $\phi_n - \phi_p$, the total change in potential seen in traversing the junction. Using Eqs. (6.26) we see that the built-in potential can be written as

$$\phi_b = \frac{kT}{q}\ln\left(\frac{N_{Dn}N_{Ap}}{n_i^2}\right) \tag{6.32}$$

The total depletion region width w is given by

$$w \equiv x_n + x_p = \sqrt{\frac{2\varepsilon\phi_b}{q}\frac{N_{Ap} + N_{Dn}}{N_{Ap}N_{Dn}}} \tag{6.33}$$

The peak electric field in the junction, which occurs at $x = 0$, is given by

$$\mathscr{E}_{\text{pk}} = \mathscr{E}(0) = \sqrt{\frac{2q\phi_b}{\varepsilon}}\sqrt{\frac{N_{Ap}N_{Dn}}{N_{Ap} + N_{Dn}}} \tag{6.34}$$

Example

Question. Consider two silicon *p-n* junctions, the first in which the *p*-side doping N_{Ap} is 4×10^{16} cm^{-3} and the *n*-side doping N_{Dn} is 2.5×10^{15} cm^{-3}, and the second in which N_{Ap} is 4×10^{16} cm^{-3} and N_{Dn} is 2×10^{17} cm^{-3}. What are the built-in potentials, what are the widths of the depletion regions, what fraction of this width is on the *n*-side of the junction, and what are the peak electric fields in each of these two junctions?

Discussion. Substituting the appropriate values into Eq. (6.32) for the built-in potential we calculate that ϕ_b is 0.69 V in the first junction and 0.80 V in the second. These two values are comparable even though the doping levels on the *n*-sides of the junctions differ by a factor of 80. This reflects the fact that the built-in potential depends only logarithmically on the doping levels.

Using Eq. (6.33) for the depletion region width we calculate that w is 0.6 μm (600 nm) in the first junction and 0.17 μm (170 nm) in the second. We see that the width is greater in the more lightly doped junction (i.e., the first junction). This is true in general and is an important observation.

In the first junction the depletion region on the n-side is 16 times as wide as that on the p-side, since, as we know from Eq. (6.28), the widths vary inversely with the doping levels. Thus 94 percent of the depletion occurs in the n-region, which is the more lightly doped side of this junction. In the second junction, in which the n-side of the junction is the more heavily doped, the depletion region on the n-side is the smaller of the two depletion regions, being one-fifth as large as that on the p-side. The observation that the depletion region extends primarily into the more lightly doped side of a junction has important implications and applications. We will encounter it in several device situations.

Finally, using Eq. (6.34) to calculate the peak electric field in each of the two junctions, we find that it is 2.2×10^4 V/cm in the first and 8.8×10^4 V/cm in the second. That the electric field is higher in the more heavily doped junction is another general observation that must be taken into consideration in device design.

The solution of the depletion approximation is now complete in that we have an expression for $\phi(x)$. This is only an approximate solution, however. Notice that it is not a self-consistent solution. If we use our approximate $\phi(x)$ to calculate $n_o(x)$ and $p_o(x)$ using the Boltzmann factor expressions, Eqs. (6.7) and (6.8), we get the results shown in Fig. 6.5d. If we then calculate $\rho(x)$, we find that it is not the same as we originally assumed, that is, according to Eq. (6.27). In particular, $\rho(x)$ does not change from 0 to qN_{Ap} abruptly at $x = -x_p$, nor does it change abruptly at $x = x_n$, as we of course know it must not. But it does change quickly, changing by a factor of 100 within about three extrinsic Debye lengths. If we wish to improve the solution (and the self-consistency) we could use the "new" $\rho(x)$ as the starting point for a second solution for $\phi(x)$, integrating $\rho(x)$ twice as we did with our first $\rho(x)$. This iteration process could be continued as long as we wished, that is, until the solution converged to within acceptable limits (set by us) to the "true" solution, as evidenced by how little it changed between successive iterations. Because of the exponential dependence of n_o and p_o on ϕ and because the two integrations have a strong smoothing effect, this iterative process converges very quickly. This is one common method of solving the Poisson-Boltzmann equation numerically.

In Fig. 6.6 more accurate solutions obtained by such an iterative technique are compared with the depletion approximation. Certainly in terms of the quantities of interest, the peak electric field and the depletion region width, the depletion approximation is very good and is an extremely useful model.

Example

Question. For the junctions considered in the previous example, what are the extrinsic Debye lengths on the n- and p-sides of the junctions and how do they compare with x_n and x_p, respectively?

Discussion. The extrinsic Debye lengths are 40 nm, 10 nm, and 4.5 nm, respectively, in the regions doped to 2.5×10^{15} cm^{-3}, 4×10^{16} cm^{-3}, and 2×10^{17} cm^{-3}. In the first diode the depletion width on the p-side of the junction is 35 nm and on the n-side is 565 nm. The corresponding extrinsic Debye lengths are 10 and 40 nm, respectively. We can see that the depletion region width is only 3.5 extrinsic Debye lengths on the p-side, whereas it is more than 10 on the n-side. Nonetheless, the

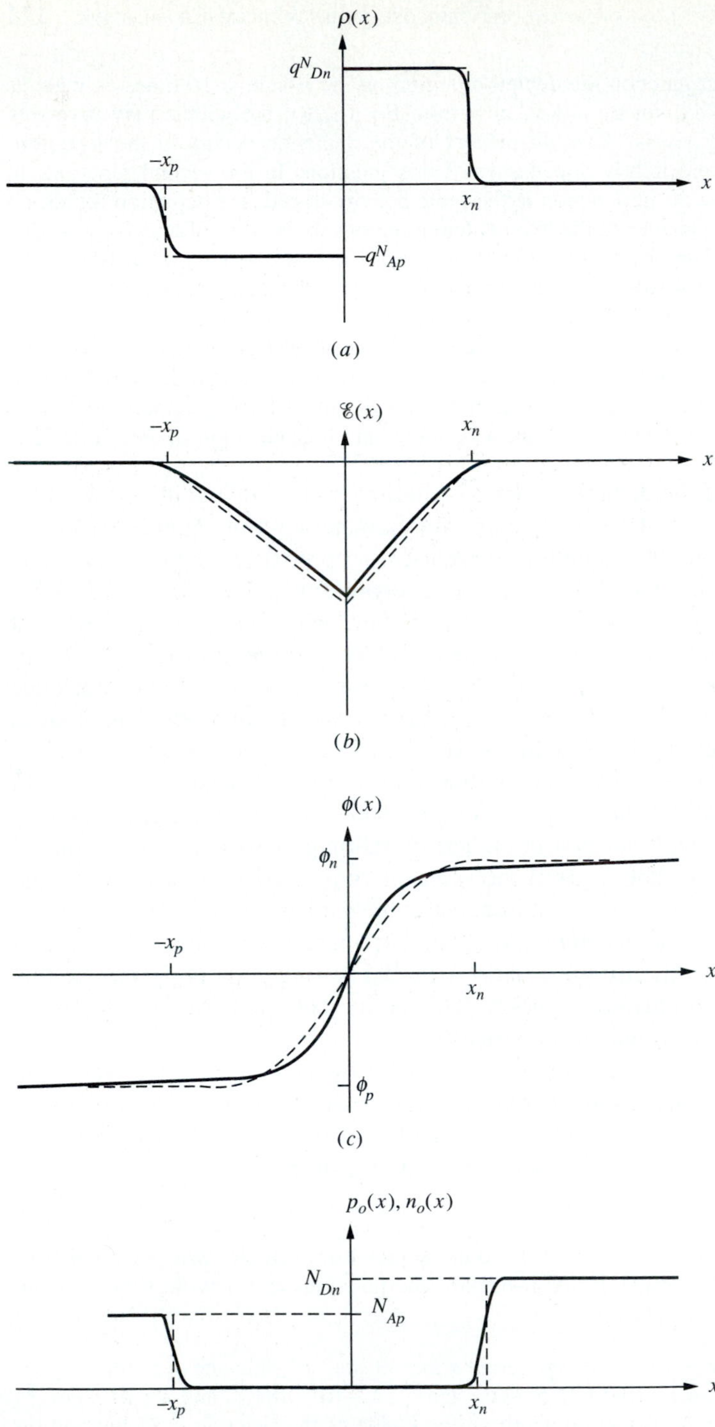

FIGURE 6.6
Comparison of accurate solutions in the vicinity of an abrupt *p-n* junction with the results of the depletion approximation: (*a*) $\rho(x)$; (*b*) $\mathscr{E}(x)$; (*c*) $\phi(x)$; (*d*) $n_o(x)$ and $p_o(x)$. (Dashed lines represent the approximation.)

depletion approximation is a good model even on the p-side. In the second diode the depletion width on the p-side of the junction is 140 nm, whereas the extrinsic Debye length is 10 nm; and on the n-side x_n is 28 nm and L_{De} is 2.5 nm. The depletion approximation can be expected to be very good for this junction.

6.3.2 Other *p-n* Junction Profiles

The abrupt p-n junction is only one of many possible doping profiles encountered in practical situations. Strictly speaking, a perfectly abrupt junction is never found in practice because the change from p- to n-type doping always occurs over a finite distance, depending on the fabrication technique used to produce the junction. If the distance is much less than the depletion region width w, however, and the regions outside the transition are uniformly doped, then the assumption that the junction is abrupt will still be a good one. If the change is somewhat more gradual but still narrower than w, the depletion approximation can still be applied, as long as the true $N_D(x)$ is used.

In fact, the depletion approximation can be applied to any junction profile for which $N_D(x)$ is "slowly varying" (as described earlier) at the edges of the depletion region. The only difficulty may be in obtaining a closed-form solution because the change in potential in crossing the junction will depend on the doping levels at the edges of the depletion region. A certain amount of additional iteration is required.

A useful nonabrupt doping profile is the linearly graded junction, that is, one in which $N_D(x)$ can be expressed as

$$N_D(x) = ax \tag{6.35}$$

where the grading constant a has units of cm^{-4}. This profile is illustrated in Fig. 6.7(a). Another common profile is the exponentially graded junction:

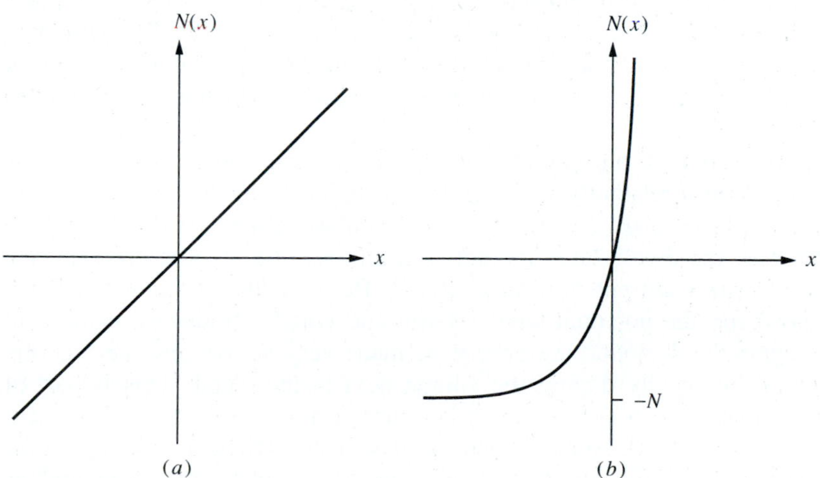

FIGURE 6.7
Two commonly encountered junction profiles: (a) linearly graded; (b) exponentially graded.

$$N_D(x) = N[e^{(x-x_j)/L} - 1] \tag{6.36}$$

where x_j is the position of the junction and L is the dimension describing the specific profile under study. This profile, with $x_j = 0$, is illustrated in Fig. 6.7*b*.

6.4 THE ELECTROSTATIC POTENTIAL AROUND A CIRCUIT

A reasonable question to ask upon looking at Fig. 6.5*c* is whether the potential change of ϕ_b going from the p-side to the n-side of a p-n junction can be measured with a voltmeter at the diode terminals and possibly even be used as a battery. The answer is no, but understanding why requires a bit of explanation and is worth considering before the next chapter, where we will be applying an external bias to such diodes.

To measure the voltage across a junction requires that we apply contacts to the end of the device. In the process, we form several other junctions including those between the contact metal or metals and the n- and p-type semiconductor, and possibly between several semiconductor regions with different doping levels. A possible example is illustrated in Fig. 6.8*a*. In this figure we assume that the contact metal and wires are all aluminum. We have also added heavily doped n- and p-regions on either end of the diode to facilitate making good ohmic contacts.

We can calculate the electrostatic potential relative to intrinsic silicon in each of the variously doped regions of the semiconductor bar in Fig. 6.8 using Eqs. (6.26). The electrostatic potential of aluminum relative to intrinsic silicon is approximately -0.3 V. If we now plot the potential, moving from one lead and contact into the heavily p-type region and on through the device to the other contact and lead, we find that the potential decreases at some junctions and increases at others, as is illustrated in Fig. 6.8*b*. The net change in potential, however, is zero. Thus no voltage is measured between the terminals and no current flows when the two leads are shorted together, as they are in Fig. 6.8*a*. We know this must be the case if we are in thermal equilibrium because a nonzero current would imply that there is a net flow of energy, which is clearly not an equilibrium situation.

At each junction in the circuit a dipole layer forms, just as it did at the p-n junction where a relatively wide depletion region formed. At points where the potential steps are small, and between two similarly doped regions (i.e., n to n^+ or p to p^+), the dipole layer is very thin and will be of little consequence to us when we study current flow in Chap. 7. Between the aluminum and the n-silicon, however, the potential step is large and could introduce a significant barrier, but again the depletion region can be made very narrow and the junction inconsequential by heavily doping the silicon next to the metal. This is part of the science of making good ohmic contacts; such technology is not our concern here, but it is discussed in Apps. E and G. It will be sufficient in Chap. 7 for us to say that we can build diodes in which the only junction that "matters" as far as the external bias and current flow are concerned is the main p-n junction. For purposes of our thermal equilibrium discussion in this chapter, however, it

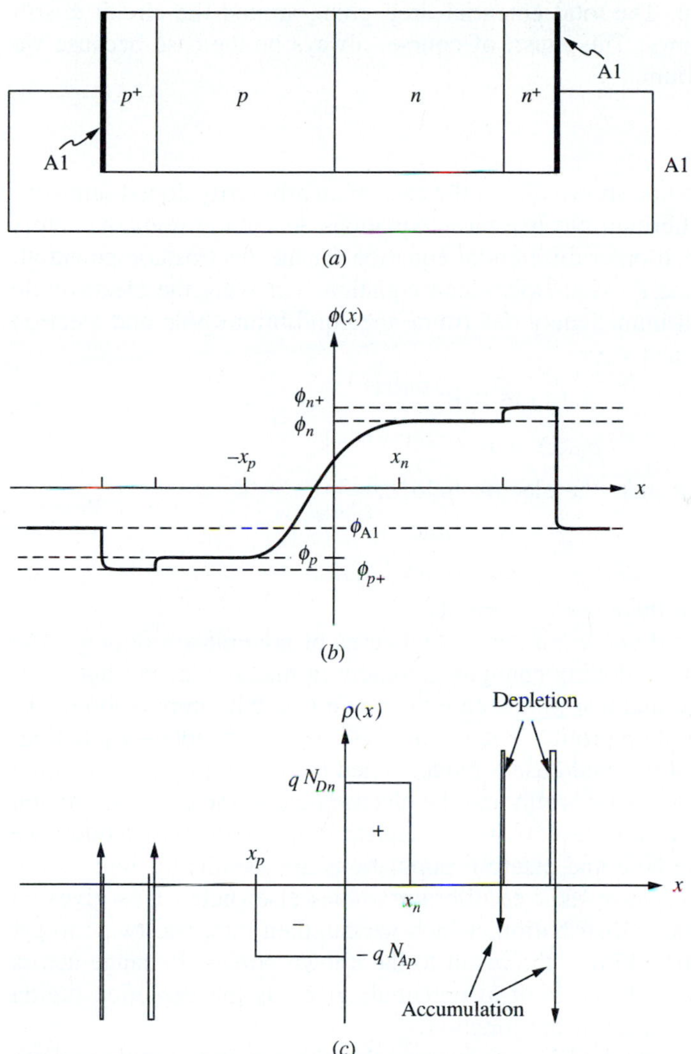

FIGURE 6.8
(*a*) Typical abrupt *p-n* diode with two aluminum ohmic contacts and an aluminum wire connecting them; (*b*) plot of the electrostatic potential through the structure in (*a*); (*c*) the corresponding net charge distribution.

does not even matter whether the dipole layers are thick or thin. In either event the total potential step crossing each junction is the difference in the electrostatic potentials on either side, and thus the total potential charge in going around a circuit is identically zero.

Consider what would happen if one of the leads on the device in Fig. 6.8*a* were copper. As soon as you complete the circuit—whether by touching the copper and aluminum leads or by shorting them together with yet a third metal, say silver—small dipole layers develop at each new junction and the appropriate potential steps develop. The total potential drop going around the circuit is still zero and no current flows. This must, of course, always be the case because we are in thermal equilibrium.

6.5 SUMMARY

In this chapter we have first shown that in the case of an arbitrarily doped semiconductor in thermal equilibrium, our five basic equations describing semiconductors reduce to a single second-order differential equation for the electrostatic potential; we call this equation the Poisson-Boltzmann equation. Knowing the electrostatic potential $\phi(x)$, we can immediately determine the equilibrium hole and electron concentrations, $p_o(x)$ and $n_o(x)$:

$$n_o(x) = n_i e^{q\phi(x)/kT}$$

$$p_o(x) = n_i e^{-q\phi(x)/kT}$$

We can also readily calculate the electric field $\mathscr{E}$:

$$\mathscr{E}(x) = -\frac{d\phi(x)}{dx}$$

(In thermal equilibrium there are no currents.)

We have considered two common special cases of nonuniform doping. The first was that in which the doping changes gradually in magnitude, but not type, with position, and we found that in this case the majority carrier population tracks the net doping concentration profile. The second case was an abrupt p-n junction, for which we found that we could use a model called the depletion approximation to estimate the depletion region width and the electric field in the depletion region (also called the space charge layer). In the depletion approximation model, we assume that the mobile hole and electron populations are identically zero within the depletion region and have their equilibrium values elsewhere. This gives an estimate for the net charge distribution, which we can then integrate twice to get the electrostatic potential. Fitting the result to the known potential change across the junction, which we call the built-in potential, gives us the depletion region widths on the n- and p-sides of the junction.

Having developed our model, we observed that the depletion region extends predominantly into the more lightly doped side of a junction and also that the depletion region is wider in more lightly doped junctions and relatively narrower in heavily doped junctions. We have also seen that the peak electric field in the depletion region is greater in more heavily doped junctions. These are all important observations that we will use when designing junction devices such as diodes and bipolar transistors.

Finally, we have discussed the electrostatic potential change experienced crossing a p-n junction and asked whether it represents a possible source of energy. We argued that as we add leads to our device and complete the circuit through which this energy would flow, we find that there are, in fact, potential steps, some up and some down, at each interface or junction between different materials in the circuit. We saw that the net result is that the change in potential going around a circuit in thermal equilibrium is zero and that a *p-n* junction in thermal equilibrium is not a battery.

PROBLEMS

6.1 This problem provides practice with basic relationships.

(a) Find the electrostatic potential ϕ in the following samples, assuming ϕ is zero in intrinsic material:

(i) n-type Si, $n_o = 5 \times 10^{17}$ cm^{-3}
(ii) p-type Si, $p_o = 1 \times 10^{18}$ cm^{-3}
(iii) p-type Si, $p_o = 1 \times 10^{16}$ cm^{-3}
(iv) p-type Ge, $p_o = 1 \times 10^{16}$ cm^{-3}

(b) Find the carrier diffusion coefficient or mobility as indicated in each of the following samples at room temperature (300 K, $kT/q \approx 0.025$ eV):

(i) Si: $\mu_e = 1500$ cm^2/V · s, $D_e = ?$
(ii) Si: $D_e = 30$ cm^2/s, $\mu_e = ?$
(iii) GaP: $D_e = 30$ cm^2/s, $\mu_e = ?$
(iv) Ge: $\mu_h = 2000$ cm^2/s, $D_e = ?$

(c) Repeat b at 125°C (approximately 400 K).

6.2 In this problem we will be concerned with three different silicon samples: an n-sample with $N_n = 5 \times 10^{15}$ cm^{-3}, an n^+-sample with $N_n = 10^{18}$ cm^{-3}, and a p-sample with $N_p = 10^{17}$ cm^{-3}. (Note: By writing n^+ we denote a heavily doped n-type sample.)

(a) Following our convention that $\phi = 0$ in intrinsic material, what is ϕ in each of these samples at room temperature?

(b) Calculate the built-in voltage ϕ_b of a junction (i) between the p- and n-samples and (ii) between the p- and n^+-samples.

(c) Derive an expression for the electrostatic potential difference between two uniformly doped n-type regions. Use this expression to calculate the potential difference (built-in potential) between the n- and n^+-samples.

(d) The electrostatic potential of a certain metal relative to intrinsic silicon is -0.05 V at room temperature. What is the contact potential between this metal and (i) the n^+-sample? (ii) the p-sample?

(e) Use your answers from parts a through d to show that the change in electrostatic potential going around the circuit shown in Fig. P6.2 is zero.

6.3 Calculate the depletion region width in the following junctions. In each case compare your answer to the extrinsic Debye length on the more lightly doped side of the

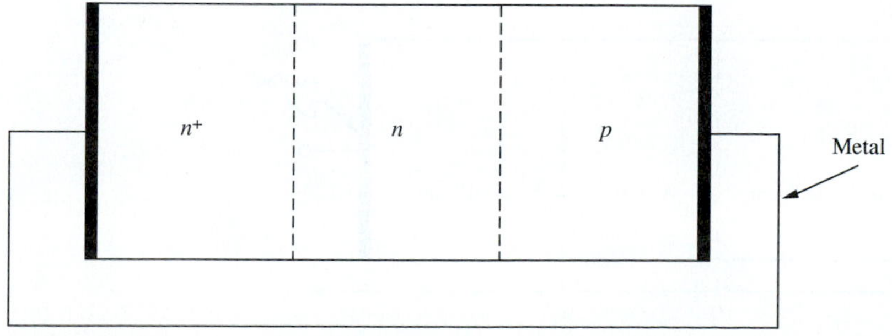

FIGURE P6.2

junction. Refer to Table A.1 of App. A as needed.

(*a*) Silicon: $N_{Dn} = 10^{17}$ cm^{-3}, $N_{Ap} = 5 \times 10^{15}$ cm^{-3}

(*b*) Silicon: $N_{Dn} = 10^{17}$ cm^{-3}, $N_{Ap} = 5 \times 10^{18}$ cm^{-3}

(*c*) Germanium: $N_{Dn} = 10^{15}$ cm^{-3}, $N_{Ap} = 5 \times 10^{16}$ cm^{-3}

(*d*) Gallium arsenide: $N_{Dn} = 10^{17}$ cm^{-3}, $N_{Ap} = 5 \times 10^{18}$ cm^{-3}

6.4 A linearly graded junction is an approximation to the doping profile created by the diffusion of impurities into a semiconductor to form a deep *p*-*n* junction. It is described by the relationship

$$N(x) = N_d(x) - N_a(x) = ax$$

where a has the units of cm^{-4} and is called the *grading constant*.

(*a*) Use the depletion approximation to calculate expressions for and make rough sketches of the following quantities when $v_A = 0$, assuming that the depletion region width w is known:

(i) Net charge density $\rho(x)$ for $-w < x < w$

(ii) Electric field $\mathscr{E}(x)$ for $-w < x < w$

(iii) Electrostatic potential $\phi(x)$ for $-w < x < w$

(*b*) Derive two expressions for the built-in potential $\phi_1 = \phi(w/2) - \phi(w/2)$ as follows:

(i) Based on your expression in part (iii) above

(ii) Based on knowing $p_1(-w/2)$ and $n_1(w/2)$ and using the Boltzmann relations ($n = n_i e^{q\phi/kT}$, etc.)

(*c*) Setting equal the two expressions you found in b for ϕ_o equal yields a transcendental equation that would have to be solved to find w. Write out this equation and find ϕ_o and w when a is 10^{20} cm^{-4}.

6.5 A useful variant on the abrupt *p*-*n* junction is the *p*-*i*-*n* diode, where *i* stands for intrinsic. An example is pictured in Fig. P6.5. The idea of this structure is that the largest electric fields and most of the voltage drop occurs across the intrinsic region. In this problem use $w_n = w_p = 2$ μm and $w_i = 1$ μm. Also assume that $T = 27$°C (300 K) and that $n_i = 10^{10}$ cm^{-3}.

(*a*) What is the electrostatic potential on the *n*- and *p*-sides of this diode far from the interfaces (i.e., in the quasineutral regions)?

(*b*) What are both n_o and p_o in each of the two quasineutral regions?

(*c*) Sketch and dimension $N(x)$, the net donor concentration as a function of x, for $-w_p < x < w_i + w_n$.

(*d*) Assuming depletion regions of width x_p and x_n on the *p*- and *n*-sides of the junction, respectively, what is the ratio of x_n to x_p?

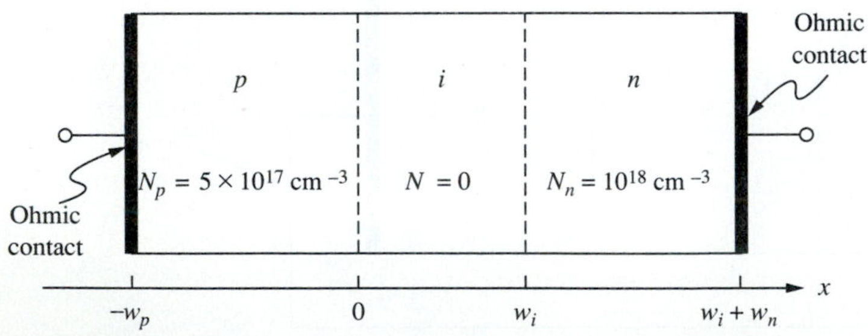

FIGURE P6.5

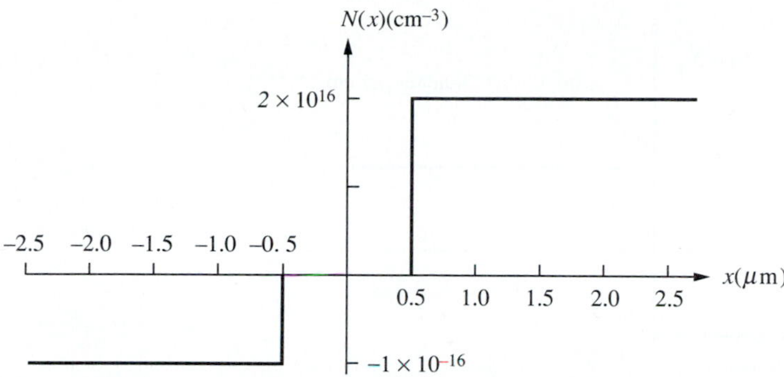

FIGURE P6.06

(e) Sketch and dimension the net charge distribution $\rho(x)$ as a function of x for $-w_p < x < w_i + w_n$, assuming that the depletion approximation is a good model. Do not solve for x_n and x_p, but assume that they are known and are smaller than w_i.

(f) Sketch and dimension the electric field profile $\mathscr{E}(x)$ for $-w_p < x < w_i + w_n$ using the depletion approximation. Assume that x_n and x_p are known and are smaller than w_i.

(g) Estimate a realistic lower bound for the approximate applied voltage that would result in a peak electric field of 10^5 V/cm in this device. Think about this question a bit; you should not have to solve for x_n and x_p in order to answer.

6.6 Consider a silicon diode with the doping profile illustrated in Fig. P6.6.

(a) Sketch and label the net charge distribution $\rho(x)$ in this structure, assuming that the depletion approximation is valid.

(b) Sketch and label the electric field profile $\mathscr{E}(x)$ throughout this structure.

(c) Sketch and label the electrostatic potential $\phi(x)$ in this structure.

(d) Calculate the zero bias depletion region width in this structure.

6.7 Use Gauss' law to find the electric field $\mathscr{E}(x)$ produced by the charge distribution shown in Fig. P6.7. Make labeled sketches of $\mathscr{E}(x)$ and the potential $\phi(x)$. In your potential plot take the reference potential to be $\phi = 0$ at $x = 0$.

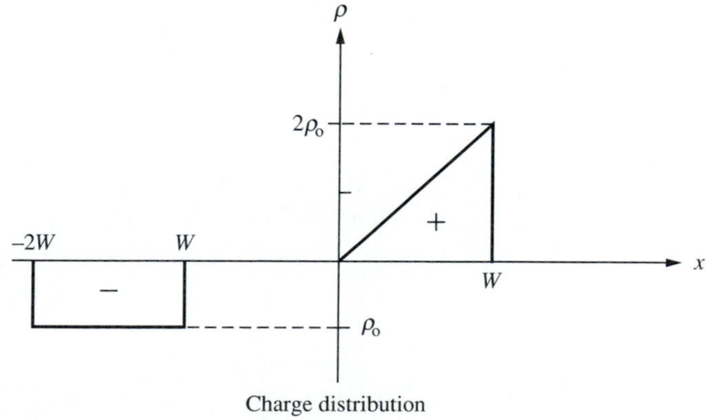

FIGURE P6.7

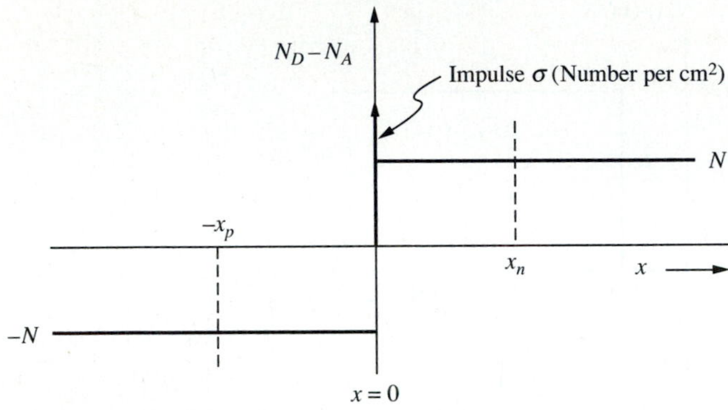

FIGURE P6.8

6.8 The p-n junction shown in Fig. P6.8 has an impulse of doping, σ, at the origin. The width of the space charge layer on the p-side is x_p and on the n-side is x_n.

(a) Find an expression that relates x_n to x_p.

(b) Make a labeled plot of $\mathscr{E}(x)$. Label in terms of N, σ, x_p and $\mathscr{E}$.

(c) Write an equation for x_p (in terms of q, N, σ, $\mathscr{E}$, and ϕ_o) that you can use to solve for the value of x_p.

CHAPTER 7

JUNCTION DIODES

The *p-n* junction diode is a very important device that we are now in a position to understand. We have just discussed modeling a *p-n* junction in thermal equilibrium, and the next logical step is to force our junction out of equilibrium. We will do this by applying a voltage, illumination, or both to it, and we will then see what happens. As we shall see shortly, some extremely useful things happen, and we will be able to do a great deal even with a single *p-n* junction.

7.1 APPLYING VOLTAGE TO A *p-n* JUNCTION

In Sec. 6.4 we considered the changes in the electrostatic potential as we went around a circuit through a short-circuited abrupt *p-n* diode and found that although there were steps up and down, the net change in potential was zero, as we knew it had to be. Now consider breaking the circuit by parting the wire connecting the two ohmic contacts, which we label A and B, and applying an external voltage source that will create a potential difference v_{AB} between the two contacts. This is illustrated in Fig. 7.1*a*.

In our model for a *p-n* diode, we will assume that the only effect of introducing v_{AB} on the electrostatic potential picture of Fig. 6.5*c* is to change the potential step in crossing the junction from ϕ_b to $\phi_b - v_{AB}$. None of the other potential steps change.

This assumption, in effect, says that none of the other parts of the diode structure present a significant impediment to current flow and equilibrium; only the abrupt *p-n* junction plays a major role, and it somehow (as we shall describe shortly) "absorbs" the deviation from equilibrium (i.e., the effects of the nonequilibrium external voltage source excitation).

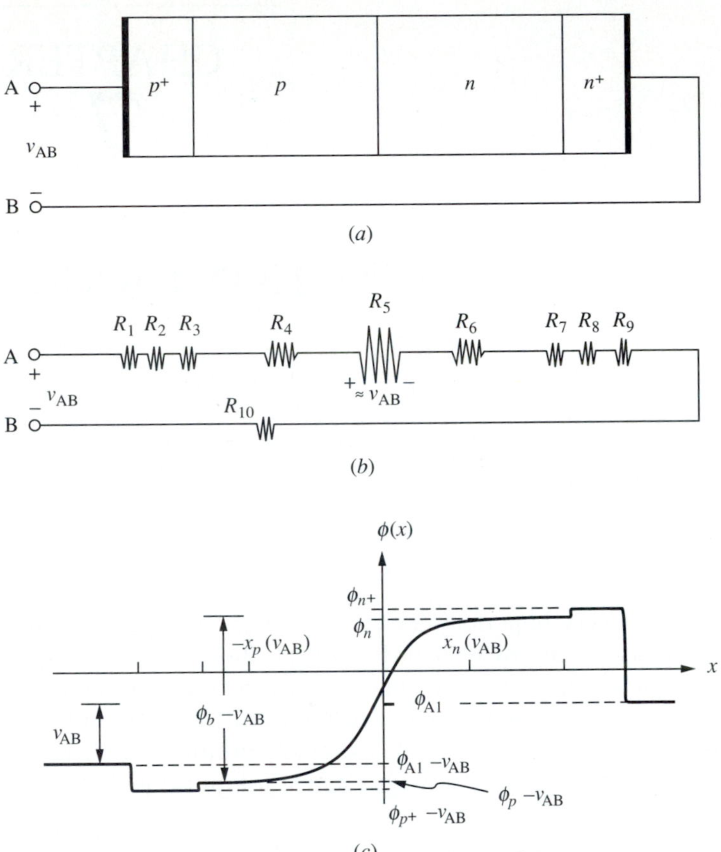

FIGURE 7.1
(*a*) The diode of Fig. 6.8*a* with an external voltage applied to the terminals; (*b*) the possible contributions to the effective nonlinear resistance of a *p*-*n* diode like that in Fig. 7.1*a*; (*c*) the variation in the electrostatic potential through the structure with a negative applied bias (i.e., $v_{AB} < 0$).

A simple picture may help you understand. Figure 7.1*b* shows schematically the various pieces in the diode circuit that might impede current flow and thus absorb some of the applied voltage. We picture these pieces as resistors, recognizing that this may be very crude given that there is no a priori reason to expect all of these regions to show ohmic behavior (i.e., a linear relationship between voltage and current). Beginning with the left-most contact, we have first the interface between the metal and the p^+-silicon (R_1), then the resistance of the p^+-region (R_2), the p^+-p junction (R_3), the resistance of the *p*-region up to the edge of the space charge region (R_4), the *p*-*n* junction proper (R_5), the resistance of the *n*-region (R_6), the *n*-n^+ junction (R_7), the resistance of the n^+-region (R_8), the n^+-region-to-metal contact (R_9), and finally the resistance of the wire (R_{10}). Some of these resistances (R_2, R_4, R_6, and R_8) can clearly be made low by suitably doping the semiconductor and others (R_{10}) by using good wire.

The contact resistances (R_1 and R_9) and the p^+-p and n-n^+ resistances (R_3 and R_7) are less familiar to you. Referring to Fig. 7.1*c* and looking first at the p-p^+ and n-n^+ interfaces, we know from Chapter 6 that the potential step height at each of these interfaces is simply kT/q times the natural logarithm of the ratio of the two doping levels. Thus if the doping changes by three orders of magnitude, a typical situation, then the step height is about $7kT/q$, or 0.17 V at room temperature. It turns out that this is a very ineffective barrier to current flow and that these resistances, R_3 and R_7, are negligible. The potential step at the contact to the p^+ region is similarly small, and R_1 is also negligible. The contact to the n^+ region is more troublesome because the potential step height is relatively large and because making a low-resistance contact to n-type silicon requires some effort. If aluminum is put on lightly n-doped silicon it does not form a low-resistance contact but rather looks like a diode itself; this is called a metal-semiconductor, or Schottky diode (see App. E). To make a low-resistance contact we need to use a heavily doped n-region (i.e., an n^+-region) under the metal, as we have here. Then the depletion region in the n^+-silicon is so narrow and the electric field at the interface so high that the carriers can readily penetrate right through the barrier. This "tunneling" through a very narrow barrier is a quantum mechanical effect. We will not attempt to model it further in this text. Suffice it to say, however, that it allows us to make low-resistance ohmic contacts to n-type silicon in spite of the large electrostatic potential step at the interface and, in this case, to make R_9 negligible. Thus in a well-designed p-n diode, the only significant impediment to current flow is the p-n junction itself (R_5 in Fig. 7.16).

Summarizing, we conclude that in a well-designed p-n junction diode, all of the voltage applied to the external terminals, v_{AB}, appears across the depletion region as a change in the potential step from ϕ_b to $\phi_b - v_{AB}$. There are two main consequences of this that we will treat in turn next. First, the width of the depletion region changes and, along with it, the net charge, electric field, and electrostatic potential profiles. Second, current flows.

7.2 DEPLETION REGION CHANGES

We can still use the depletion approximation model for the p-n junction depletion region unless there is a significant increase in the charge in the depletion region because a current is flowing. When a negative voltage is applied to the p-n diode we will see (as you may already know) that only a very small current flows. It is not difficult to accept that there is little additional charge associated with such a small current. When v_{AB} is positive, however, much larger currents flow, as we shall see, but even then the charge density of the carriers flowing through the depletion region is much less than the charge density of the ionized donors and acceptors. Thus to an excellent approximation, the net charge distribution $\rho(x)$ can still be assumed to be given by Eq. (6.27), as pictured in Fig. 6.5*a*. The only difference is that now x_n and x_p are changed because the potential step is $\phi_b - v_{AB}$ rather than ϕ_b. We will look first at this change and then at its practical implications.

7.2.1 Depletion Width Variation with Voltage

The derivation of the electric field and potential profiles through an abrupt *p-n* junction with an applied bias is identical to what was done in Chap. 6, except that ϕ_b is replaced everywhere with $\phi_b - v_{AB}$. Thus we can immediately write an expression for the total depletion region width, as well as x_n and x_p, by referring to Eqs. (6.31) and (6.32). The results are

$$w(v_{AB}) = \sqrt{\frac{2\varepsilon(\phi_b - \phi_{AB})}{q} \frac{N_{Ap} + N_{Dn}}{N_{Ap} N_{Dn}}} \tag{7.1}$$

and, as before,

$$x_n = w \frac{N_{Ap}}{(N_{Ap} + N_{Dn})} \tag{7.2a}$$

$$x_p = w \frac{N_{Dn}}{(N_{Ap} + N_{Dn})} \tag{7.2b}$$

We see that the depletion region increases with increasingly negative applied voltage and that the increase is roughly as the square root of the magnitude of the voltage. Incidentally, we often call the applied voltage a *bias* and speak of a negative bias as a *reverse* bias.

The peak electric field is also changed by the applied bias, similarly increasing with increasing reverse bias. With bias, Eq. (6.34) becomes

$$\mathscr{E}_{pk}(v_{AB}) = \sqrt{\frac{2q(\phi_b - v_{AB})}{\varepsilon} \frac{N_{Ap} N_{Dn}}{(N_{Ap} + N_{Dn})}} \tag{7.3}$$

The appearance in Eqs. (7.1) and (7.3) of the term $(\phi_b - v_{AB})^{1/2}$ raises the concern that there might be a problem if v_{AB} is greater than ϕ_b, at which point the term becomes imaginary. As we shall see, however, we will never encounter this situation because as v_{AB} is increased toward ϕ_b, the current increases exponentially. Long before v_{AB} equals ϕ_b, our assumptions of modest currents, negligible voltage drop elsewhere in the device, negligible charge density in the depletion region due to the charge carrier fluxes, and low-level injection are violated and our model will have to be modified. We will discuss this further in Sec. 7.3.3.

7.2.2 Depletion Capacitance

If the voltage bias on a *p-n* diode is changed, the depletion region width changes, as we have just seen, and some of the current that flows will be that which supplies or removes the charge associated with the change in the depletion region width. If v_{AB} is made more positive, the depletion region decreases and positive charge (i.e., holes) must flow into the *p*-terminal to neutralize some of the depleted acceptors and reduce x_p, whereas on the *n*-side of the junction, electrons must be supplied to reduce x_n. Similarly, if v_{AB} is made more negative, the depletion region widens, some holes must be removed from the *p*-side as x_p increases, and electrons must be removed from the n-side as x_n increases. This process is pictured in Fig. 7.2.

The depletion region of a p-n diode thus stores charge, a fact that must be included in our modeling of the current-voltage characteristics of a diode. We begin by considering how the charge on the p-side of the junction, $q_{DP}(v_{AB})$, depends on the voltage v_{AB}. The depletion region charge $q_{DP}(v_{AB})$ on the p-side of the junction is given by

$$q_{DP}(v_{AB}) = -AqN_{Ap}x_p \tag{7.4}$$

where A is the cross-sectional area of the junction. Using Eq. (6.31b) we have

$$q_{DP}(v_{AB}) = -A\sqrt{2\varepsilon q(\phi_b - v_{AB})\frac{N_{Ap}N_{Dn}}{(N_{Ap} + N_{Dn})}} \tag{7.5}$$

We see that the stored charge is a nonlinear function of the applied voltage, so we clearly cannot identify a conventional linear capacitor with the depletion region. However, if the change in voltage is small enough, the corresponding change in the stored charge will be linearly proportional to the change in the voltage. In this case we can define a linear depletion capacitance C_{dp}.

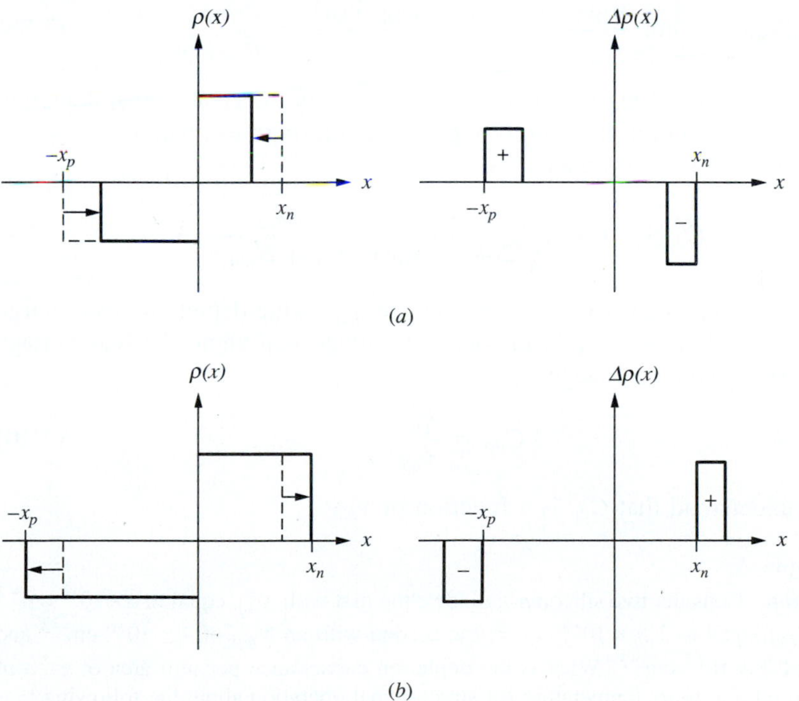

FIGURE 7.2
Changes in the charge distribution in the vicinity of an abrupt p-n junction: (a) as v_{AB} is increased; (b) as v_{AB} is decreased.

Imagine that the voltage on the diode, v_{AB}, changes from V_{AB} to $V_{AB} + v_{ab}$, where v_{ab} is "small." The charge q_{DP} will change from $q_{DP}(V_{AB})$, which we denote as Q_{DP}, to $q_{DP}(V_{AB} + v_{ab})$, which we denote as $Q_{DP} + q_{dp}$. We know (and will show below) that if v_{ab} is small enough, then q_{dp} will be linearly related to v_{ab} as

$$q_{dp} = C_{dp} v_{ab} \tag{7.6}$$

where C_{dp} will in general depend on V_{AB}.

There are several ways we might proceed to obtain an expression for C_{dp}. One is to consider approximating q_D about V_{AB} using a Taylor series expansion:

$$q_{DP}(V_{AB} + v_{ab}) = q_{DP}(V_{AB}) + \left.\frac{dq_{DP}}{dv_{AB}}\right|_{V_{AB}} v_{ab} + \text{Higher-order terms} \tag{7.7}$$

If v_{ab} is small enough we can neglect the higher-order terms. Doing this and then comparing Eq. (7.7) to Eq. (7.6), we find that

$$C_{dp}(V_{AB}) = \left.\frac{dq_{DP}}{dv_{AB}}\right|_{V_{AB}} \tag{7.8a}$$

Another way to get this same result is to take the limit:

$$C_{dp}(V_{AB}) = \lim_{v_{ab}\to 0} \frac{q_{DP}(V_{AB} + v_{ab}) - q_{DP}(V_{AB})}{v_{ab}} = \left.\frac{dq_{DP}}{dv_{AB}}\right|_{V_{AB}} \tag{7.8b}$$

We will use Eq. (7.8a) to define what we mean by the small signal depletion capacitance $C_{dp}(V_{AB})$ of a junction. Using this definition to evaluate $C_{dp}(V_{AB})$ for an abrupt *p-n* junction, we obtain

$$C_{dp}(V_{AB}) = A\sqrt{\frac{\varepsilon q}{2(\phi_b - V_{AB})} \frac{N_{Ap}N_{Dn}}{(N_{Ap} + N_{Dn})}} \tag{7.9}$$

Summarizing, $C_{dp}(V_{AB})$ relates the change q_{dp} in the depletion layer charge q_{DP} due to a small change v_{ab} in the applied voltage v_{AB} about the bias voltage V_{AB}, to the small voltage change v_{ab}:

$$C_{dp} = \frac{q_{dp}}{v_{ab}} \tag{7.10}$$

where it is understood that C_{dp} is a function of V_{AB}.

Example

Question. Consider two silicon *p-n* diodes: the first with N_{Ap} equal to 4×10^{16} cm^{-3} and N_{Dn} equal to 2.5×10^{15} cm^{-3}; the second with an N_{Ap} of 4×10^{16} cm^{-3} and N_{Dn} of 2×10^{17} cm^{-3}. What is the depletion capacitance per unit area of each of these diodes at room temperature for small-signal operation about the following bias points: a) $V_{AB} = 0$ V; b) $V_{AB} = -5$ V; and c) $V_{AB} = +0.4$ V?

Discussion. Notice that these diodes are the same as those considered in the examples of Chap. 6. We calculated ϕ_b for these junctions there; substituting those results and the other parameter values into Eq. (7.9), we find that C_{dp} at zero bias is approximately 1.7×10^{-8} F/cm^2 in the first diode and approximately 6×10^{-8} F/cm^2 in the second.

Because device areas are often measured in microns, a useful unit for area is microns squared, μm^2. In these terms, C_{dp} for these two devices is 0.17 fF/mμ^2 and 0.6 fF/mμ^2 for diodes one and two, respectively. The "f" here stands for "femto," the suffix implying a multiplier of 10^{-15}; that is, 1 fF is equal to 10^{-15} F.

The fact that C_{dp} is higher in the more heavily doped diode is a general result that reflects the fact that the depletion region is narrower in more heavily doped junctions.

At a reverse bias of -5 V, the depletion capacitances of the two junctions decrease to approximately 0.06 and 0.2 fF/μm^2, respectively. At a forward bias of 0.4 V, they increase to approximately 0.27 and 0.86 fF/μm^2, respectively.

If the voltage v_{ab} is a function of time, there will be a current equal to dq_{dp}/dt, into the diode due to this small-signal depletion capacitance. That is,

$$i = \frac{dq_{dp}}{dt} = C_{dp}\frac{dv_{ab}}{dt} \tag{7.11}$$

We will use this result when we develop circuit models for *p-n* diodes.

Before leaving our discussion of depletion capacitances, notice that C_{dp} can be expressed in terms of the depletion region width w when $v_{AB} = V_{AB}$. Using Eq. (7.1) in Eq. (7.9), we find that we can write

$$C_{dp}(V_{AB}) = \frac{\varepsilon A}{w} \tag{7.12}$$

where w is the depletion region width at $v_{AB} = V_{AB}$. This is simply the expression for the capacitance of a parallel-plate capacitance of width w. It may help to refer to Fig. 7.2 to see that this makes perfect sense. Clearly, any additional charge is added or removed from the outer edges of the depletion region.

7.2.3 Applications of the Depletion Capacitance

The linear small signal depletion capacitance associated with a *p-n* junction turns out to be an extremely useful "device" in its own right. It can, for example, be used in circuits as a voltage-variable capacitor; it can also be used as an analytical tool to characterize the doping profile in a diode. We will discuss each of these applications briefly below.

a) Voltage-variable capacitors. The depletion capacitance clearly depends on the bias voltage V_{AB}, as Eq. (7.9) shows. This fact can be useful in certain circuits as a way of obtaining frequency tunability. You know from other course work that the time constants and resonant frequencies of RC and LRC circuits depend on the sizes of the capacitors in them. If one of those capacitors is a junction depletion capacitance, its value can be changed by changing the reverse-bias voltage on it. Thus one can adjust, or "tune," the time constants and resonances of the circuit by changing the bias voltage on the relevant junction. A junction designed specifically for such an application is called a *varactor*.

A word of caution is in order here. You must remember that the charge stored in the depletion region is a nonlinear function of the voltage applied to the junction and that we cannot represent this large signal charge with a linear capacitance. We define a linear depletion capacitance only for small-signal variations about a bias level. The large signal dynamic behavior of RC and LRC circuits containing *p-n* junctions will in general be complicated to analyze and quite different from what you are familiar with from linear circuit theory. Analyzing the linear behavior for small-signal operation about a bias point, on the other hand, is something very familiar to you.

The bias voltage dependence of C_{dp} in an abrupt *p-n* junction is rather weak, and, as you might expect, circuit designers would like capacitors that vary more strongly with bias. The solution is to use diodes with doping profiles that are not abrupt but instead are graded, and furthermore are graded in such a manner that the doping level decreases as one moves away from the junction. This grading is the opposite of that found in a linearly graded or exponentially graded diode (see Sec. 6.3.2) and is much more difficult to obtain. It is, however, commonly used in commercial varactors.

b) Doping profile characterization. A measurement of the small-signal depletion capacitance of a *p-n* junction as a function of the bias voltage provides a great deal of information on the doping profile in that junction. To appreciate this, rewrite Eq. (7.9) by inverting and squaring it; the result is

$$\frac{1}{C_{\text{dp}}^2} = \frac{2}{\varepsilon q A^2} \frac{(N_{Ap} + N_{Dn})}{N_{Ap} N_{Dn}} (\phi_b - V_{\text{AB}}) \tag{7.9$'$}$$

Graphing $1/C_{\text{dp}}^2$ versus V_{AB} should thus yield a linear plot. If it does not, the junction doping profile is not abrupt and the assumption that Eq. (7.9) is valid is incorrect. (We will discuss this situation in the next paragraph.) If the plot is linear, the junction doping is abrupt and Eq. (7.9) is valid. If we fit a straight line to this plot, the intercept of this line on the voltage axis (i.e., $1/C_{\text{dp}}^2 = 0$) is the built-in voltage ϕ_b. The slope of this line contains information on the doping levels on either side of the junction, N_{Ap} and N_{Dn}. If the junction is asymmetrically doped, as is often the case, then the doping-dependent term in the slope, $N_{Ap}N_{Dn}/(N_{Ap} + N_{Dn})$, is approximately equal to the doping level on the more lightly doped side of the junction. For example, in a p^+-n junction, this term is approximately equal to N_{Dn}, and we have

$$\frac{1}{C_{\text{dp}}^2} \approx \frac{2}{\varepsilon q A^2 N_{Dn}} (\phi_b - V_{\text{AB}}) \tag{7.9b}$$

Thus in an asymmetrically doped junction, the slope of the graph of $1/C_{\text{dp}}^2$ versus V_{AB} tells us the doping level on the more lightly doped side of the junction.

The doping level on the more heavily doped side can then be calculated from ϕ_b (which, as we have said, we get from the intercept with the horizontal axis, that is, the extrapolation to $1/C_{\text{dp}}^2 = 0$) using Eq. (6.32):

$$\phi_b = \frac{kT}{q} \ln\left(\frac{N_{Dn}N_{Ap}}{n_i^2}\right) \tag{6.32}$$

Solving this equation for N_{Ap}, we have

$$N_{Ap} = \frac{n_i^2}{N_{Dn}} e^{q\phi_b/kT} \tag{7.13}$$

At this point you can check that the junction is indeed asymmetrical, as was assumed to obtain N_{Dn}.

If the graph of $1/C_{\text{dp}}^2$ versus V_{AB} is not a straight line, the doping profile is not abrupt but the data on the dependence of C_{dp} on V_{AB} may still be very useful. We can show, in fact, that in an asymmetrically doped junction it can give us detailed information on the doping profile on the more lightly doped side of the junction. Specifically, the slope of the C_{dp} versus V_{AB} curve at each bias point is proportional to the doping level at the edge of the depletion region on the more lightly doped side of this junction for that same bias level. By changing the bias level and moving the edge of the depletion region through the device, the doping level can be measured as a function of position through the device.

Measurements of this sort are commonly referred to as *C-V* profiles. They are a very important, widely used characterization technique.

7.3 CURRENT FLOW

We have just studied how the depletion region width of a *p-n* junction changes when we apply bias. The other thing that happens when we bias a *p-n* junction is that current flows. Our objective in this section is first to understand how this current comes about and then to develop a quantitative model relating the current i_{D} through a *p-n* junction diode to the applied voltage v_{AB}.

We argued in Chap. 6 that there can be no net current in thermal equilibrium, and we used this observation to show that in a *p-n* junction at equilibrium the tendency of the charge carriers to diffuse from the region in which they are in the majority to that in which they are in the minority is counterbalanced by an electric field that develops in the intervening depletion region. Drift (due to the field) and diffusion (due to the concentration gradient) exactly balance, and the current is zero.

When we apply a bias to a *p-n* junction we change the height of the electrostatic potential barrier at the junction and the magnitude of the electric field in the depletion region, and we disturb the balance between drift and diffusion. For example, consider applying a forward bias, $v_{\text{AB}} > 0$. This reduces the electric field and drift, and more carriers can diffuse across the junction. Alternatively, we can say that the barrier height is reduced and that more carriers can surmount it. In either case, a current flows and the magnitude of this current increases as we apply more forward bias, further lowering the barrier to diffusion and, equivalently, further reducing the drift field.

When we apply a reverse bias, the potential barrier height is increased along with the magnitude of the electric field and there will be a net current in the reverse (by convention "negative") direction. However, it will not be a very large current because there are very few electrons on the p-side of the junction and there are very few holes on the n-side of the junction to drift across. The few minority carriers that wander to the edge of depletion region and experience the large field are quickly swept across the junction, to be sure, but there are so few of these carriers that the current remains small even at very high reverse-bias levels.

To quantify the above discussion we will pursue a line of reasoning first presented by William Shockley in the late 1940s. Shockley pointed out that except at very high current levels—and we will be able to quantify what we mean by "very high" later—our p-n diode can be divided into three regions: the depletion region and two quasineutral regions (one on the p-side and one on the n-side of the junction). This is illustrated in Fig. 7.3. The quasineutral regions can be treated using the techniques we developed for solving flow problems in Chap. 5 as long as low-level injection conditions are satisfied. We simply need to know the boundary conditions on the excess minority carrier populations on either side of the depletion region, that is, $p'(x_n)$ and $n'(-x_p)$, and we can get these by extending the models introduced in Chap. 6. Given the boundary conditions, we can solve the flow problems in the two quasineutral regions to find the minority carrier currents there. Knowing the minority carrier currents on either side of the depletion region, we relate them across this region and in a straightforward manner obtain an expression for the total diode current.

We thus first turn our attention to a consideration of modeling the excess populations, n' and p', on either side of the depletion region, then to solving the relevant flow problems in the quasineutral regions, and finally to getting the current-voltage relationship. Once we obtain our result we will look back at what

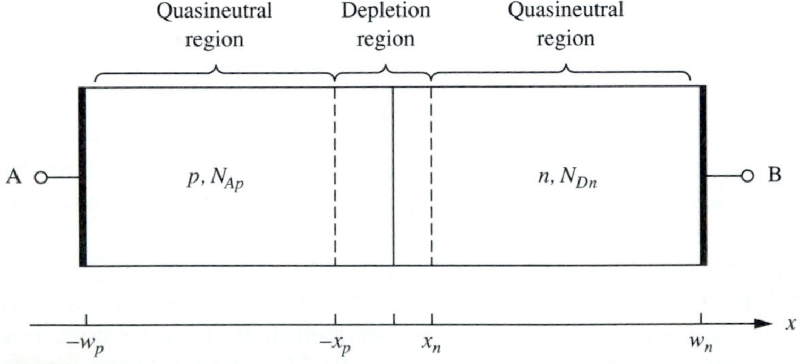

FIGURE 7.3
Identification of the depletion region and the two quasineutral regions in a general p-n junction diode.

assumptions and approximations we have made and will discuss the limitations of our model.

7.3.1 Excess Populations at the Depletion Region Edges

To understand how we can model the minority carrier populations at the edges of the depletion region, we begin by again considering the structure in thermal equilibrium. Looking first at the holes, we have $p_o(-x_p) = N_{Ap}$ and $p_o(x_n) = n_i^2/N_{Dn}$. Dividing these two expressions relates the hole population on one side of the depletion region to that on the other:

$$p_o(x_n) = \frac{p_o(-x_p)n_i^2}{N_{Dn}N_{Ap}}$$

Referring back to Eq. (6.32),

$$\phi_b = \frac{kT}{q}\ln\left(\frac{N_{Dn}N_{Ap}}{n_1^2}\right) \tag{6.32}$$

we can relate the factor $n_i^2/(N_{Dn}N_{Ap})$ to the potential barrier at the junction, that is,

$$\frac{n_i^2}{N_{Dn}N_{Ap}} = e^{-q\phi_b/kT}$$

and we see that $p_o(x_n)$ can be written as

$$p_o(x_n) = p_o(-x_p)e^{-q\phi_b/kT} \tag{7.14}$$

Equation (7.14) reflects a useful result from statistical thermodynamics that models the energy distribution of particles such as holes and electrons. Specifically it tells us that the particles in any population at thermal equilibrium have a distribution of thermal energies. Many have low thermal energy, and fewer have higher amounts of energy. Mathematically we say that if the concentration with energy E_1 or greater is c_1, then the concentration c_2 with energy E_2 or greater, where $E_2 > E_1$, is $c_1e^{-(E_2-E_1)/kT}$. In other words,

$$c_2(E \geq E_2) = c_1(E \geq E_1)e^{-(E_2-E_1)/kT} \tag{7.15}$$

Returning now to Eq. (7.14) and the holes, the variation in the electrostatic potential energy of holes $q\phi$ encountered in moving from one side of a junction to the other is illustrated in Fig. 7.4. At $x = -x_p$, ϕ is ϕ_p and the population of holes with energy greater than $q\phi_p$ is $p_o(-x_p)$. As we move to the right of $-x_p$, the potential energy increases and thus the population of holes should decrease because fewer and fewer have that much energy. We have a potential energy "hill" for holes that rises a total of $q\phi_b$ up to a height of $q\phi_n$ at $x = x_n$. The population of holes with sufficient energy to surmount the hill (i.e., with more

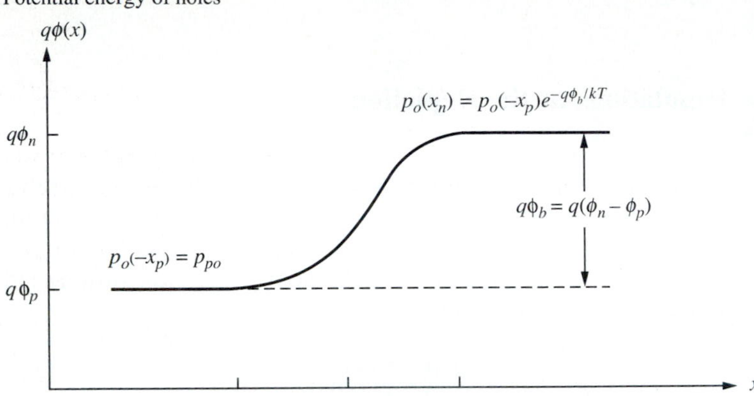

FIGURE 7.4
Potential energy hill for holes at an abrupt *p*-*n* junction in thermal equilibrium.

energy than $q\phi_n$) should be related to the total population at the bottom of the hill according to Eq. (7.15) as follows:

$$p_o(x_n) = p_o(-x_p)e^{-q\phi_b/kT} \tag{7.14}$$

This is just Eq. (7.14) again. Stating this in words, we say that the hole population is in thermal equilibrium with the potential barrier at the junction. The population to the right of the barrier is related to the population to the left of the barrier by the Boltzman factor, $e^{-q\phi_b/kT}$.

The electron population is also in thermal equilibrium with the potential barrier, but because the potential energy of electrons is $-q\phi$, the low side of the hill is to the right for *n*-type material and the "top" is to the left. You can easily show that the equivalent to Eq. (7.14) for electrons is

$$n_o(-x_p) = n_o(x_n)e^{-q\phi_b/kT} \tag{7.16}$$

Thus far we have been in thermal equilibrium, but now we want to apply a voltage v_{AB}. The potential barrier at the junction changes from ϕ_b to $\phi_b - v_{AB}$, but what happens to the carrier populations? We look first at the majority carrier populations, specifically the hole population on the *p*-side. Assume that we maintain low-level injection conditions in the *p*-side to the left of $-x_p$, so that the hole population at $-x_p$ remains unchanged at N_{Ap}. Further assume that the hole population can maintain itself in equilibrium with the potential barrier throughout the depletion region, that is, up to $x = x_n$. Past that point (i.e., for $x > x_n$), the holes are minority carriers in a quasineutral region and their motion is limited by their diffusion away from the edge of the depletion region into the *n*-side. Saying that the holes maintain themselves in equilibrium with the potential barrier in the depletion region means that the holes can move across this region rather freely. The depletion region does not represent a bottleneck, as it were, to their motion, whereas diffusion in the quasineutral region, which is in series with it, does.

If we can say that the holes are in equilibrium with the barrier, it must still be true that $p(-x_p)$ and $p(x_n)$ are related by a Boltzmann factor, which in this case is $e^{-q(\phi_b - v_{AB})/kT}$. That is,

$$p(x_n) = p(-x_p)e^{-q(\phi_b - v_{AB})/kT} \tag{7.17a}$$

Furthermore, as long as low-level injection conditions are maintained, we will have $p(-x_p) \approx p_o(-x_p)$. Thus

$$p(x_n) \approx p_o(-x_p)e^{-q(\phi_b - v_{AB})/kT} \tag{7.17b}$$

This situation is illustrated in Fig. 7.5.

Eq. (7.17b) can be written in terms of the equilibrium hole population at x_n using Eq. (7.14). We have

$$p(x_n) = p_o(x_n)e^{qv_{AB}/kT} \tag{7.17c}$$

and because we know that $p_o(x_n) = n_i^2/N_{Dn}$ we have

$$p(x_n) = \frac{n_i^2}{N_{Dn}} e^{qv_{AB}/kT} \tag{7.17d}$$

Finally, the excess hole population at x_n, $p'(x_n)$ [which is $p(x_n) - p_o(x_n)$] is given by

$$p'(x_n) = \frac{n_i^2}{N_{Dn}}(e^{qv_{AB}/kT} - 1) \tag{7.18}$$

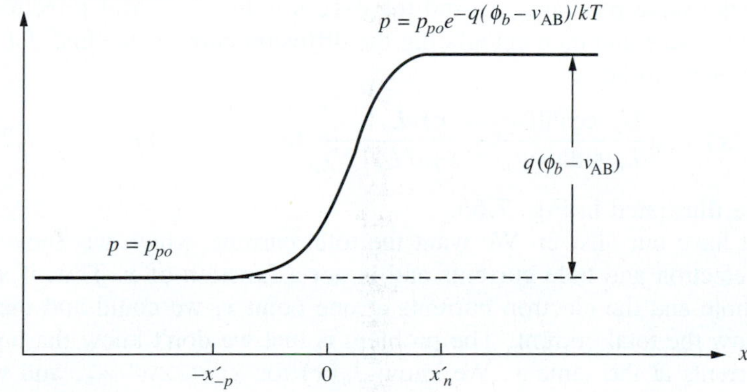

FIGURE 7.5
Potential energy barrier for holes and the hole populations on either side of a biased *p-n* junction.

Similarly we can argue that the electron population stays in equilibrium with the barrier, and we find that

$$n'(-x_p) = \frac{n_i^2}{N_{Ap}}(e^{qv_{AB}/kT} - 1) \tag{7.19}$$

These excess minority carrier populations are the boundary conditions we need to solve for the minority carrier currents in the *p*- and *n*-regions of the diode and to ultimately calculate the total diode current.

7.3.2 Current-Voltage Relationship for an Ideal Diode

Having established the boundary conditions at either side of the depletion region of a biased *p-n* junction, we are in a position to solve the flow problems in the two quasineutral regions. Looking first at the *n*-side of the junction, we have $p'(x_n)$ given by Eq. (7.18), $p'(w_n) = 0$, and $g_L(x) = 0$. The solution for $p'(x)$ for $x_n \leq x \leq w_n$ is

$$p'(x) = p'(x_n)\frac{\sinh[(w_n - x)/L_h]}{\sinh[(w_n - x_n)/L_h]} \tag{7.20}$$

This result is illustrated in Fig. 7.6a.

The hole current on the *n*-side for $x_n \leq x \leq w_n$ is therefore

$$J_h(x) = q\frac{D_h p'(x_n)}{L_h}\frac{\cosh[(w_n - x)/L_h]}{\sinh[(w_n - x_n)/L_h]} \tag{7.21}$$

Substituting Eq. (7.18) for $p'(x_n)$ into this result, we obtain

$$J_h(x) = q\frac{D_h}{L_h}\frac{\cosh[(w_n - x)/L_h]}{\sinh[(w_n - x_n)/L_h]}\frac{n_i^2}{N_{Dn}}(e^{qv_{AB}/kT} - 1) \tag{7.22}$$

Following the same reasoning to find the excess minority carrier (electron) population on the *p*-side and then calculating the diffusion current, we find $J_e(x)$ for $-w_p \leq x \leq -x_p$ to be

$$J_e(x) = q\frac{D_e}{L_e}\frac{\cosh[(w_p - x)/L_e]}{\sinh[(w_p - x_p)/L_e]}\frac{n_i^2}{N_{Ap}}(e^{qv_{AB}/kT} - 1) \tag{7.23}$$

These results are illustrated in Fig. 7.6*b*.

We almost have our answer. We want the total current, which we know is the sum of the electron and hole currents and is not a function of *x*. Thus if we knew both the hole and the electron currents at one point *x*, we could add them together and know the total current. The problem is that we don't know the hole and electron currents at the same *x*. We know $J_h(x)$ for $x_n < x < w_n$, and we know $J_e(x)$ for $-w_p < x < -x_p$, but these two spans do not overlap.

We proceed by assuming that there is negligible generation or recombination in the depletion region. That is, we say that the only holes that flow out of the depletion region at $x = x_n$ are the ones that entered at $x = -x_p$.

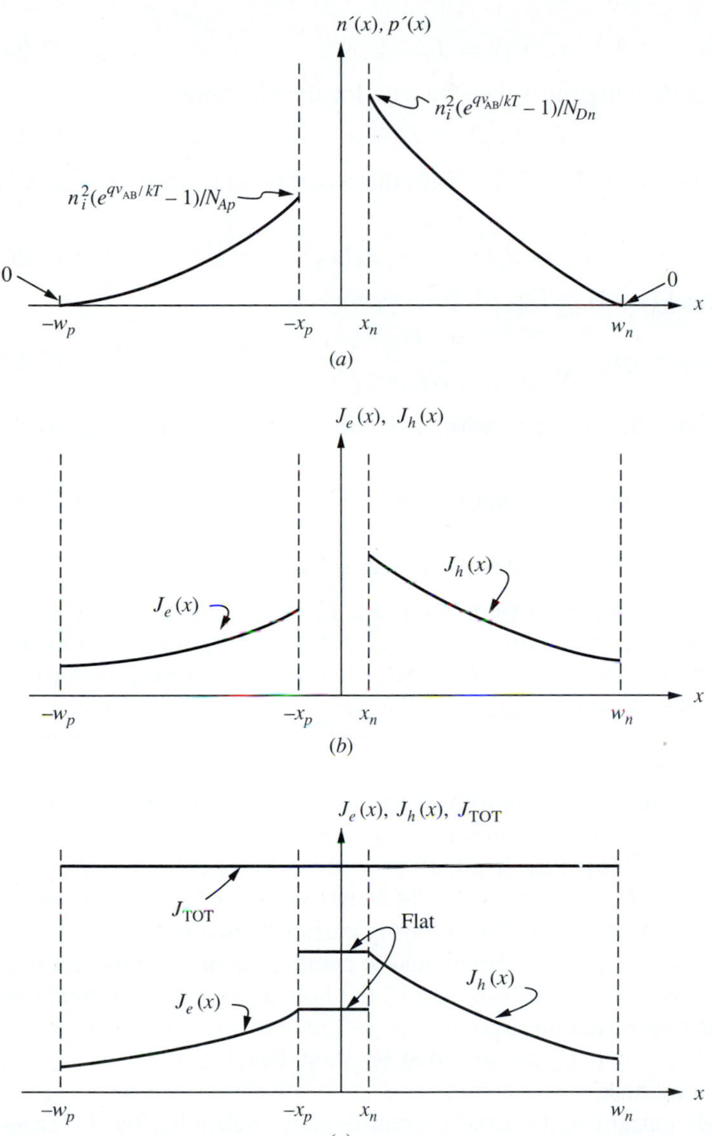

FIGURE 7.6
(*a*) Excess carrier populations in a forward-biased *p-n* junction diode; (*b*) the corresponding minority carrier diffusion current densities on either side of the junction; (*c*) the connection of the currents through the depletion region to obtain total current density.

Thus

$$J_h(x_n) = J_h(-x_p) \tag{7.24}$$

It follows that the same thing must then be true for the electrons:

$$J_e(-x_p) = J_e(x_n) \tag{7.25}$$

These results are illustrated in Fig. 7.6*c*. With this assumption we can immediately write

$$J_{\text{TOT}} = J_e(-x_p) + J_h(x_n) \tag{7.26}$$

Using Eqs. (7.22) and (7.23) in Eq. (7.26), we find

$$J_{\text{TOT}} = qn_i^2\left(\frac{D_e}{N_{Ap}w_p^*} + \frac{D_h}{N_{Dn}w_n^*}\right)(e^{qv_{\text{AB}}/kT} - 1) \tag{7.27}$$

where w_p^* and w_n^* are the effective widths of the *p*- and *n*-sides, respectively, defined as

$$w_p^* \equiv L_e \tanh[(w_p - x_p)/L_e] \tag{7.28a}$$

$$w_n^* \equiv L_h \tanh[(w_n - x_n)/L_h] \tag{7.28b}$$

Often we will be in either of two limits: the *short-base limit*, which corresponds to the situation when the minority carrier diffusion length is much greater than the width of the device, and the *long-base limit*, which corresponds to the situation when the minority carrier diffusion length is much smaller than the width of the device. Looking first at the short-base limit, if we assume, for example, that $L_e \gg w_p$, we find that Eq. (7.28a) reduces to $w_p^* \approx w_p - x_p$. In general, in the short-base limit the effective width of the relevant side of the device is the actual physical width of the corresponding quasineutral region.

Turning next to the long-base limit, if we assume that $L_e \gg w_p$, then Eq. (7.28a) reduces to $w_p^* \approx L_e$. In general, in the long-base limit the effective width of the relevant side of the device is the minority carrier diffusion length.

To illustrate these two limiting cases, and to compare them with the intermediate situation, refer to Fig. 7.7. In this figure, the hole and electron currents are plotted as a function of position throughout a $p-n$ diode for three cases: $L_e \approx w_p$ and $L_h \approx w_n$; $L_e \gg w_p$ and $L_h \gg w_n$ (that is, short base); and $L_e \ll w_p$ and $L_h \ll w_n$ (that is, long base).

The total diode current is the total current density multiplied by the cross-sectional area of the diode, *A*. Thus

$$i_D = AJ_{\text{TOT}}$$

We often write

$$i_D = I_S(e^{qv_{\text{AB}}/kT} - 1) \tag{7.29}$$

and we can now write the saturation current I_S as

$$I_S = Aqn_i^2\left(\frac{D_e}{N_{Ap}w_p^*} + \frac{D_h}{N_{Dn}w_n^*}\right) \tag{7.30}$$

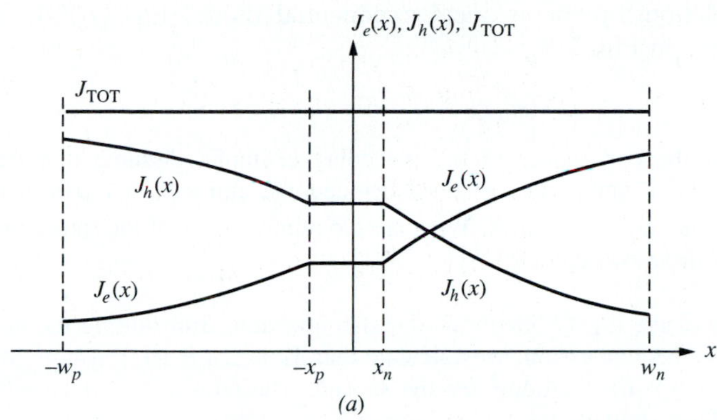

(a)

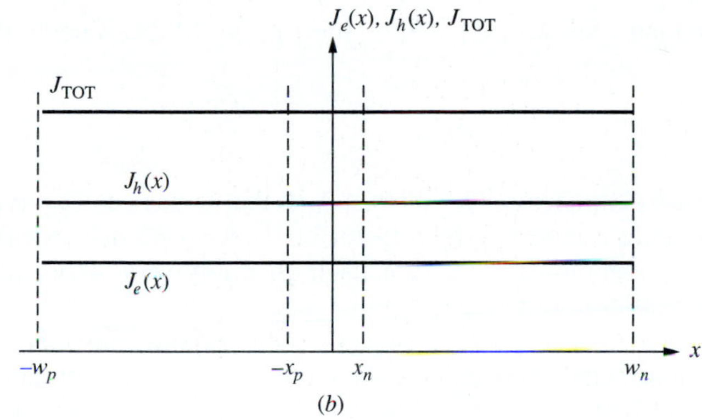

(b)

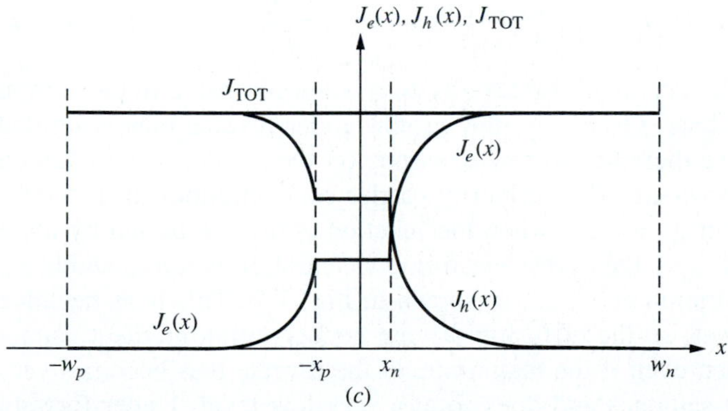

(c)

FIGURE 7.7
Current density profiles through a forward-biased abrupt *p-n* junction diode in three cases: (*a*) $L_{min} \approx w$; (*b*) $L_{min} >> w$; (*c*) $L_{min} << w$.

The current-voltage relationship for an ideal exponential diode, Eq. (7.29), is plotted as the solid curve in Fig. 7.8.

Example

Question. Consider the two diodes in the preceding example. Assume that the effective widths of the n- and p-sides of these devices, w_n^* and w_p^*, is 1 μm, and that D_e is 40 cm^2/s and D_h is 15 cm^2/s. What are the relative sizes of the saturation current densities of these two diodes?

Discussion. We must use Eq. (7.30) to answer this question. Substituting the appropriate values into this expression, we calculate that J_s is 2.4×10^{-9} A/cm^2 for the first diode and 3.6×10^{-10} A/cm^2 for the second. The ratio is 6.7 to 1, with the lightly doped diode showing the higher current.

When v_{AB} is more than a few kT/q positive, the 1 in Eq. (7.29) is negligible and we can write

$$i_D \approx I_S e^{qv_{AB}/kT} \qquad \text{when} \qquad v_{AB} >> \frac{kT}{q} \tag{7.31}$$

The diode current increases exponentially, which means that it does so relatively quickly. At room temperature it increases by a factor of 10 every 60 mV (roughly 2.3 kT/q at 300 K). The saturation current I_S is itself generally very, very small, but because of the exponential multiplier, i_D can be large.

When v_{AB} is more than a few kT/q negative, the exponential factor is negligible and the current remains fixed at $-I_S$. We refer to this as i_D "saturating" at $-I_S$ in reverse bias and write

$$i_D \approx -I_S \qquad \text{when} \qquad v_{AB} << \frac{-kT}{q} \tag{7.32}$$

This "reverse" current is very small, essentially zero when compared to the current flowing under forward bias. Physically, the current under reverse bias is limited to a small value because there are so few electrons on the p-side of the junction and so few holes on the n-side. The minority carrier concentrations at the edges of the space charge layer go to zero when the junction is reverse-biased by more than a few kT/q, so at $-x_p$ the excess electron concentration is $-n_{po}$ and at x_n the excess hole concentration is $-p_{no}$, as shown in Fig. 7.9. This is as negative as these excesses can get, so the diffusion-driving concentration gradient cannot become any larger either, even if the magnitude of the reverse bias becomes very large. Thus the current saturates and does so at a very low level. Under forward bias, by contrast, there is no limit to how large the excess populations and the concentration gradients can get; accordingly, the forward current can be very much larger than the reverse current.

Returning to our expression I_S [e.g., Eq. (7.30)]:

$$I_S = Aqn_i^2\left(\frac{D_e}{N_{Ap}w_p^*} + \frac{D_h}{N_{Dn}w_n^*}\right) \tag{7.30}$$

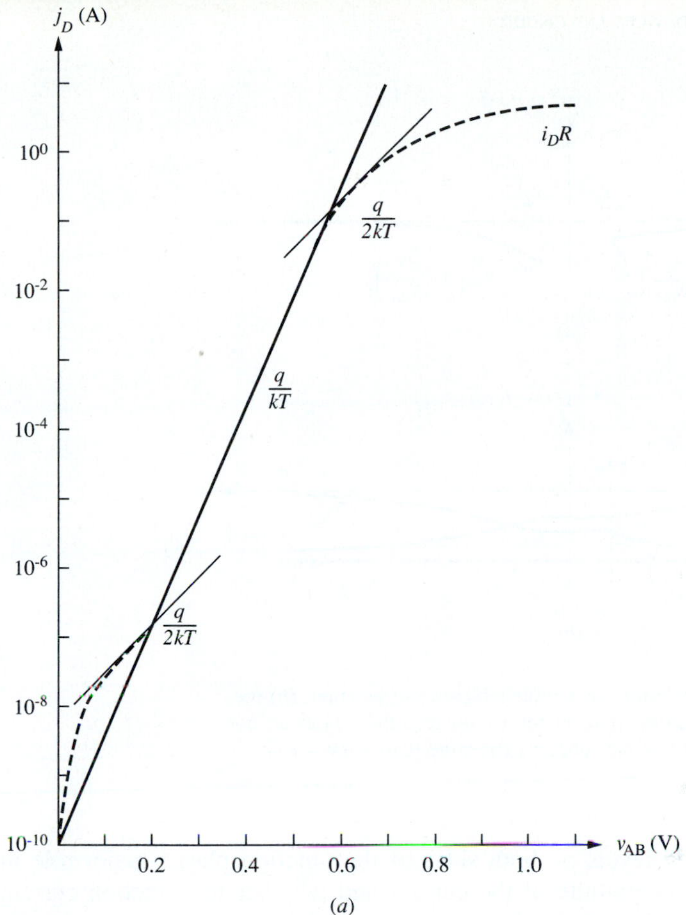

(*a*)

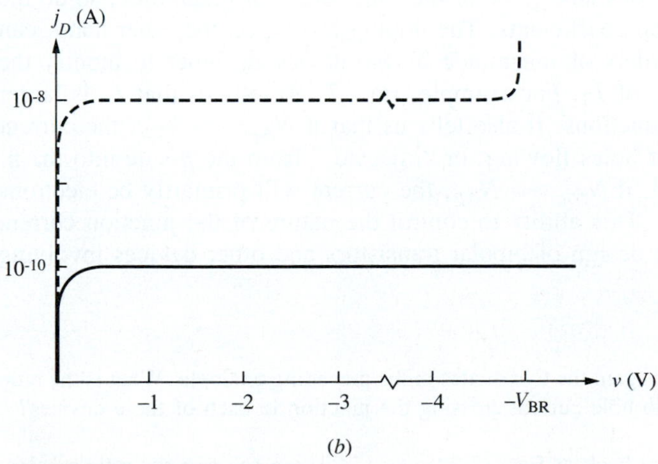

(*b*)

FIGURE 7.8
Current-voltage relationship for a *p-n* junction on a semilog scale: (*a*) forward bias; (*b*) reverse bias. [The solid curve is the ideal exponential diode expression, Eq (7.29), and the dashed curve is typical of what one would measure for a real diode (see Sec. 7.3.3).]

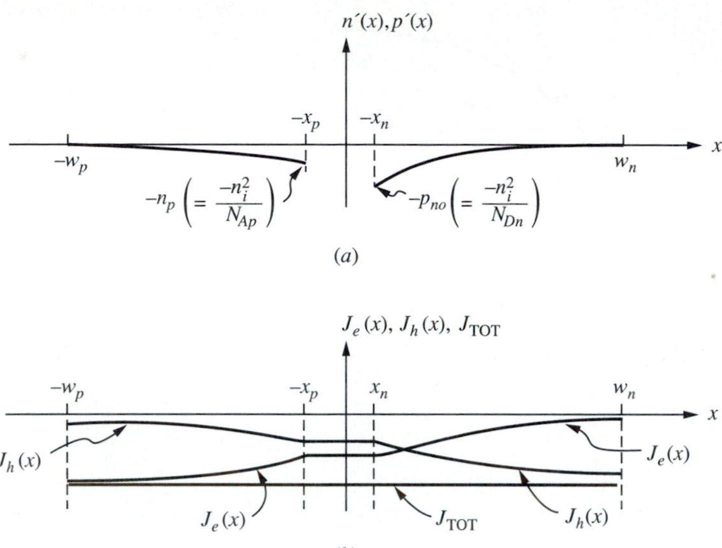

FIGURE 7.9
(*a*) The excess carrier populations in a reverse-biased *p-n* junction; (*b*) the corresponding current densities. (Except for x_n and x_p, these plots do not change with increasing reverse bias once v_{AB} is more than a few kT/q negative.)

we see that the doping levels on both sides of the junction play a major role in determining both the magnitude of the current and whether the junction current is carried primarily by holes or electrons. The device dimensions and carrier transport parameters also enter this expression, but in most diodes the effective widths of the *n*- and *p*-sides tend to be of the same order of magnitude; so do the minority carrier diffusion coefficients. The doping levels, on the other hand, can be varied over many orders of magnitude by the device designer to modify the magnitude and make-up of I_S. For example, Eq. (7.30) tells us that I_S is larger in more lightly doped junctions. It also tells us that if $N_{Ap} >> N_{Dn}$, the current will consist primarily of holes flowing, or "injected," from the *p*-side into the *n*-side. On the other hand, if $N_{Dn} >> N_{Ap}$, the current will primarily be electrons injected into the *p*-side. This ability to control the nature of the junction current is very important in the design of bipolar transistors and other devices involving *p-n* junctions.

Example

Question. Consider again the two diodes in the preceding example. What is the ratio of electron current to hole current crossing the junction in each of these devices?

Discussion. Looking back at Eqs. (7.22) and (7.23) we see that the ratio of electron to hole current across the junction is given by $D_e N_{Dn} w_n^* / D_h N_{Ap} w_p^*$. Upon evaluating this factor we find that it is 0.17, or 1/6, for the first diode and 13 for the second. We see that electrons dominate the current in the diode that has its n-side more heavily doped than its p-side (diode #2), whereas holes dominate when the p-type side is the more heavily doped (diode #1). We must be careful generalizing here because the diffusion coefficients and effective widths, as well as the doping levels, enter this relation, but the relative doping level is a very useful parameter to use to control injection across a junction.

7.3.3 Limitations to the Simple Model

If we plot the ideal diode current-voltage relationship, Eq. (7.29), on a semilog plot, we obtain the curve given by the solid line in Fig. 7.8. If we then measure a real p-n diode and plot its current-voltage relationship on the same graph, the data will typically look more like the dashed curve in Fig. 7.8. The general shapes of the curves are similar, and they agree quantitatively over a substantial range of forward biases, but there are important differences at low and high current levels. We want now to understand the reason for these differences and to decide whether they present serious problems. We begin by examining the region of low biases and then considering large forward and reverse biases.

a) Low current levels. At low forward-bias levels and low to moderate reverse-bias levels, where the magnitude of the current is ideally on the order of I_S or less, we find in actual diodes that the magnitude of the current is considerably higher than I_S. More extensive study of the "extra" current reveals that it is due to generation and recombination in the depletion region. In forward bias there are excess holes and electrons in the depletion region, and we should anticipate that there will be some recombination in the depletion region. In our ideal diode model we neglected this recombination and arrived at Eqs. (7.24) and (7.25). In order to include a depletion region recombination current, assume that the total recombination in the depletion region is $R(v_{AB})$ hole-electron pairs/cm^2·s, which, as we have indicated, will be a function of the applied voltage. The hole current due to this recombination is qR, and the electron current is $-qR$.

To relate the currents in and out of the depletion region we now note that if there is recombination in the depletion region more holes must flow in from the left than flow out to the right (assuming an orientation like that in Fig. 7.1). Defining J_R as qR, we thus write

$$J_h(-x_p) = J_h(x_n) + J_R \tag{7.33a}$$

For electrons, more electrons must flow in from the right than flow out to the left. The correct expression is

$$J_e(-x_p) + J_R = J_e(x_n) \tag{7.33b}$$

Thus, the total current is now

$$J_{TOT} = J_e(-x_p) + J_h(x_n) + J_R \tag{7.34}$$

which is the ideal diode current plus J_R.

J_R is itself a function of the applied voltage. It turns out that a good approximate model for J_R is that it varies exponentially with v_{AB} as $e^{qv_{AB}/nkT}$ for

$v_{AB} >> kT/q$, where n is approximately 2. The factor of two in the denominator of the exponential means that J_R does not increase as quickly with increasing bias v_{AB} as does the ideal diffusion current and that at sufficiently high forward bias the ideal relationship dominates. This variation is illustrated in Fig. 7.8*a*.

The factor of two in the denominator of the exponential in J_R arises because of the fact that the carriers halfway up the potential hill on either side of the junction barrier are the most active in the recombination process. The model that is used to describe this process is called the Shockley-Read-Hall model, but we will not study it specifically in this text. Our primary concern is to learn that if we go to very low currents our ideal model may be incomplete; beyond that we will simply try to avoid working at such low current levels.

For reverse biases, there is a deficiency rather than an excess of holes and electrons in the depletion region and generation rather than recombination. Additional holes and electrons are created in the depletion region, so more flow out than flow in. If the generation is G, then the hole generation current will be $-qG$ and the electron generation current will be qG. G will be only a weak function of v_{AB} because the depletion region width will increase slightly with increasingly negative v_{AB}. If we neglect this effect, to first order we can write a general depletion region generation-recombination current as

$$J_{GR} = J_{GRS}(e^{qv_{AB}/2kT} - 1) \tag{7.35}$$

and, writing AJ_{GRS} as I_{GRS}, we can write the total current as

$$i_D = I_S(e^{qv_{AB}/kT} - 1) + I_{GRS}(e^{qv_{AB}/2kT} - 1) \tag{7.36}$$

I_{GRS} is typically much greater than I_S.

You need not be concerned with learning Eq. (7.36). The important message is that depletion region generation and recombination have a weaker dependence on applied bias v_{AB} than the diffusion currents, so that at sufficiently high forward bias the ideal behavior will dominate. This is where we will want to operate *p*-*n* junctions used in bipolar transistor emitter-base junctions. It is also why we use high-purity single crystals to make *p*-*n* diodes; if we did not, J_{GRS} would be so large that the ideal behavior might never dominate the junction current. In building diodes we always want to minimize J_{GRS}.

b) Large forward bias. At large forward biases the current does not increase as quickly as the ideal diode expression indicates that it should. Two effects account for this. The first is that at high current levels we can no longer neglect resistive voltage drops in the bulk *n*- and *p*-regions of the diode (R_4 and R_6 in Fig. 7.1*b*). Thus the entire applied voltage v_{AB} does not appear across the junction but rather is reduced by $i_D(R_4 + R_6)$. Our current-voltage relation at high current levels becomes transcendental:

$$i_D = I_S e^{q(v_{AB} - i_D R)/kT} \tag{7.37}$$

where $R \equiv R_4 + R_6 +$ any other series resistances.

The second effect that becomes important at high current levels is high-level injection into the quasineutral regions. Our entire diffusive flow model becomes questionable then, and we have a much more difficult problem to treat analytically. Interestingly, if we include high-level injection in our boundary condition model, Eqs. (7.18) and (7.19), we find that the excesses increase only as $e^{qv_{AB}/2kT}$ at high injection levels. A factor of two now appears in the denominator, and again the rate of increase is less than the ideal diode equation would predict.

The onset of high-level injection is often taken to be the point at which the excess minority carrier population on either side of the junction equals some percentage of the equilibrium majority carrier population; in an asymmetric diode this occurs first on the more lightly doped side of the junction. Suppose, for example, that we have an n^+-p junction with a doping level on the p-side of N_{Ap} and that high-level injection occurs when $n'_p \geq N_{Ap}$. Using Eq. (7.19) we thus see that the junction voltage at the onset of high-level injection is given by

$$V_{AB} = \frac{2kT}{q} \ln \frac{N_{Ap}}{n_i} \tag{7.38}$$

As was the case at low current levels, our main concern in this text is to realize that there is a limit to ideal diode behavior at high current levels. In general, we want to operate below this limit.

c) Large reverse voltages. At large reverse biases the current in any real diode will suddenly increase abruptly. We call this phenomenon *reverse breakdown*, but it is not necessarily a destructive process. It is, in fact, used in several important devices, namely voltage reference diodes and avalanche photodiodes. The sharp increase in reverse current when a diode junction breaks down is due to a sharp increase in the depletion region generation current caused by one of two mechanisms. In most junctions, the few carriers flowing across the junction in reverse bias gain enough energy because of the large potential energy step that if they happen to collide with an electron in a bond they can knock it free. The carrier pair created and the original carrier can in turn accelerate, collide with more bonds, and create still more hole-electron pairs. An avalanche of carriers is suddenly created. This process is called *avalanche breakdown*.

In very heavily doped junctions, the depletion region is very narrow and the electric field is very large. The distances are too short for an avalanche to build up. Instead, breakdown occurs when the fields get so intense that electrons can actually be torn from the bonds; hole-electron pairs are generated in this fashion. This process is called *Zener breakdown*, after the man who first suggested it.

We often model breakdown by saying that it occurs when the electric field in a junction reaches a critical value $\mathscr{E}_{CRIT}$, which to first order we take to be constant for a given material. Using Eq. (7.3), we see that the breakdown voltage V_{BR} is

$$V_{BR} \approx -\frac{\varepsilon \mathscr{E}_{CRIT}^2}{2q} \frac{(N_{Ap} + N_{Dn})}{N_{Ap} N_{Dn}} \tag{7.39}$$

Looking at this expression, we see that the last term is dominated by the doping level of the more lightly doped side of the junction and that $|V_{BR}|$ varies inversely with that doping level (i.e., it is larger for a lightly doped junction than for a heavily doped junction).

Because reverse breakdown is so sharp and is not destructive, it is often used to provide a voltage reference. Both breakdown processes occur at very specific peak electric field intensities, and it is possible through suitable selections of N_{Ap} and N_{Dn} to design diodes to break down at specific applied voltages using Eq. (7.3) and knowledge of the breakdown field of the semiconductor being used.

7.3.4 Diffusion Capacitance

In Sec. 7.2.2 we pointed out that stored charge was associated with the depletion regions that varied with the applied voltage and looked from the device terminals like a nonlinear capacitor. There is also stored charge associated with the excess carrier populations on either side of a biased *p-n* junction. This charge also varies with the applied bias and also looks like a nonlinear capacitor. We call this the *diffusion capacitance*. We will define a linear, small-signal diffusion capacitance C_{df} in a manner similar to the one we used for the depletion capacitance.

To minimize confusion we will treat an asymmetrically doped junction, so that minority carriers are injected primarily into only one side of the junction, and we will treat a short-base diode. The model is easily generalized to arbitrary doping levels and diffusion lengths, but treating the general case is unnecessarily complex. Assume that we have an abrupt p^+-n junction, that $L_h >> w_n$, and that we have cross-sectional area A. The excess carrier profile through such a

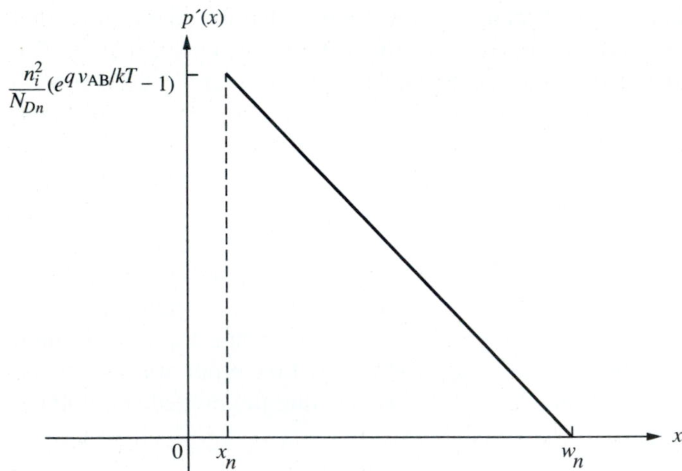

FIGURE 7.10
Excess hole and electron profile in a forward-biased asymmetric abrupt p^+-n junction.

device under forward bias is shown in Fig. 7.10. For a given applied bias v_{AB}, the total excess hole concentration on the n-side of the junction, $P_n'(v_{AB})$, is given by

$$P_n'(v_{AB}) = A\frac{(w_n - x)n_i^2}{2N_{Dn}}(e^{qv_{AB}/kT} - 1) \tag{7.40}$$

The total concentration of excess electrons is exactly the same because quasineutrality is a valid assumption, at least for low-level injection. The interesting thing about the stored positive and negative charge associated with these excess hole and electron populations is that they occupy the same physical space, $x_n < x < w_n$. This is in contrast to a standard capacitor, where the positive charge is on one of two capacitor plates and the negative charge is on the other. Nonetheless, the excess populations do represent stored charge, and when the applied voltage is increased (or decreased), additional positive and negative carriers have to be added to it (or removed), as Fig. 7.11 illustrates. The positive charge is supplied from (or removed through) the p-side of the junction and the electrons via the n-side.

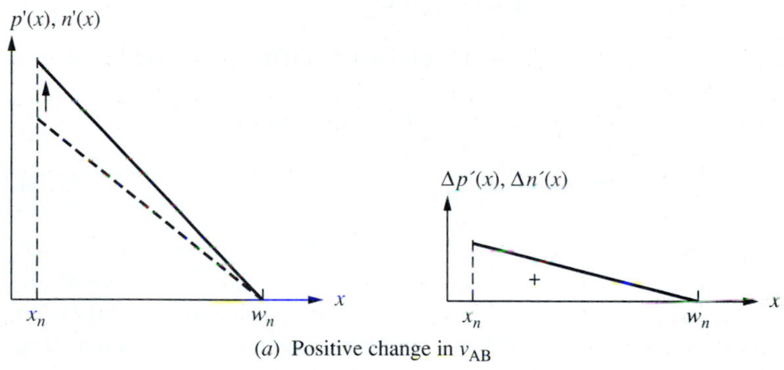

(a) Positive change in v_{AB}

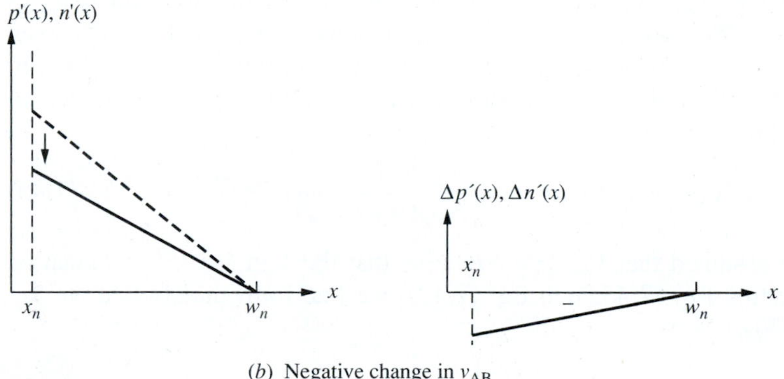

(b) Negative change in v_{AB}

FIGURE 7.11
Changes in excess hole and electron populations: (a) for an increase in applied voltage; (b) for a decrease in applied voltage.

Following the same process that we used with the depletion capacitance in Section 7.2.2, we first get an expression for the total excess positive charge q_{DF} (i.e., that due to excess holes). Using Eq. (7.40), we have

$$q_{DF}v_{AB} = qA\frac{(w_n - x_n)}{2}\frac{n_i^2}{N_{Dn}}(e^{qv_{AB}/kT} - 1) \tag{7.41}$$

Again we see that the charge is a nonlinear function of the applied voltage. For small changes in applied voltage, however, the change in q_{DF} will be linearly proportional to the change in the applied voltage. Again we assume that the applied voltage changes from V_{AB} to $V_{AB} + v_{ab}$ and find the change in q_{DF}, which we will denote as q_{df}. We will call the ratio of q_{df} to v_{ab} the diffusion capacitance C_{df} of the junction at this bias point. That is,

$$\frac{q_{df}}{v_{ab}} = C_{df} \tag{7.42}$$

Clearly this ratio must equal the derivative of q_{DF} with respect to v_{AB} at V_{AB}:

$$C_{df} \equiv \left.\frac{dq_{DF}}{dv_{AB}}\right|_{v_{AB}=V_{AB}} \tag{7.43}$$

We will take Eq. (7.43) as a general definition of the diffusion capacitance of a junction.

Using Eq. (7.41), we find for an abrupt p^+-n junction that

$$C_{df}(V_{AB}) = q^2A\frac{(w_n - x_n)}{2kT}\frac{n_i^2}{N_{Dn}}e^{qV_{AB}/kT} \tag{7.44}$$

Looking more carefully at this expression for the diffusion capacitance, we see first that when V_{AB} is negative (i.e., $V_{AB} << -kT/q$), C_{df} is essentially zero. This is not surprising because we know that the very little current and excess charge associated with a reverse-biased *p-n* junction doesn't change much with reverse bias.

For a positive V_{AB}, in contrast, q_{DF} increases exponentially with bias, as does the current. We can make the connection between C_{df} and current even clearer if we write C_{df} directly in terms of the diode current. The diode current in the asymmetrically doped $p^+ - n$ device we are discussing is essentially all hole current. Thus

$$i_D(V_{AB}) \approx I_D(V_{AB}) \cong Aq\frac{n_i^2D_h}{N_{Dn}(w_n - x_n)}e^{qV_{AB}/kT} \tag{7.45}$$

where we have assumed that $V_{AB} >> kT/q$ so that the 1 in $(e^{qv/kT} - 1)$ can be neglected. Inserting Eq. (7.45) into Eq. (7.42), we find immediately that we can also write $C_{df}(V_{AB})$ as

$$C_{df}(V_{AB}) = \frac{(w_n - x_n)^2}{2D_h}\frac{q}{kT}I_D(V_{AB}) \tag{7.44$'$}$$

The term $(w_n - x_n)^2/2D_h$ has units of time and can crudely be identified with the time that the average hole spends diffusing across the *n*-side of the diode. It is called the transit time t_{tr}. An important and perhaps startling observation is that C_{df} does not depend on the junction area, only on the total current through it!

If the voltage v_{ab} is a function of time, there will be a current into the diode equal to dq_{df}/dt due to the diffusion capacitance. That is,

$$i = \frac{dq_{df}}{dt} = C_{df}\frac{dv_{ab}}{dt} \tag{7.46}$$

We will use this result, along with our earlier result for the current into depletion capacitance (Eq. 7.10), when we develop circuit models for *p-n* diodes.

Example

Question. Consider a short-base p^+-n diode biased at a quiescent current level of 1 mA. Assume that D_h is 15 cm^2/s and that the effective width of the *n*-side of the junction, $w_n - x_n$, is 1 μm. What is the diffusion capacitance per unit area of this junction at room temperature for small-signal operation about this bias point?

Discussion. Using Eq. (7.4b) we calculate C_{df}/A to be 2.75×10^{-8} F/cm^2, or 0.27 fF/μm^2. Interestingly, the diffusion capacitance is of the same order of magnitude as the depletion capacitance of the p^+-n diode in our earlier example (diode #1). This is often the case.

7.4 CIRCUIT MODELS FOR JUNCTION DIODES

Equation (7.29) describes the current-voltage relationship of an ideal *p-n* junction diode based on our models for the depletion region and for current flow in the quasineutral regions. We now turn to the problem of developing models for *p-n* diodes that can be used to analyze circuits incorporating them. We begin with large-signal models and then develop small-signal linear models for *p-n* diodes.

7.4.1 Large-Signal Models

We call a diode with terminal characteristics described by Eq. (7.29) an *ideal exponential diode*. Specifying the reverse saturation current I_S of such a device specifies its terminal characteristics completely. We will use the circuit symbol of Fig. 7.12*a* for an ideal exponential diode with its current-voltage relationship shown in Fig. 7.12*b*.

In many situations we will want to use simplified approximations to the ideal exponential diode representation of a *p-n* diode; in others we will want to use more complicated models that include physical effects and terminal behavior not included in the ideal exponential model. In this section we will look at a variety of large-signal models evolving from this ideal model, beginning with simplified models and then moving to more complex models, including dynamic models.

a) Simplified diode models. In certain applications, even the use of a simple exponential expression like Eq. (7.29) is inconvenient and unnecessarily precise,

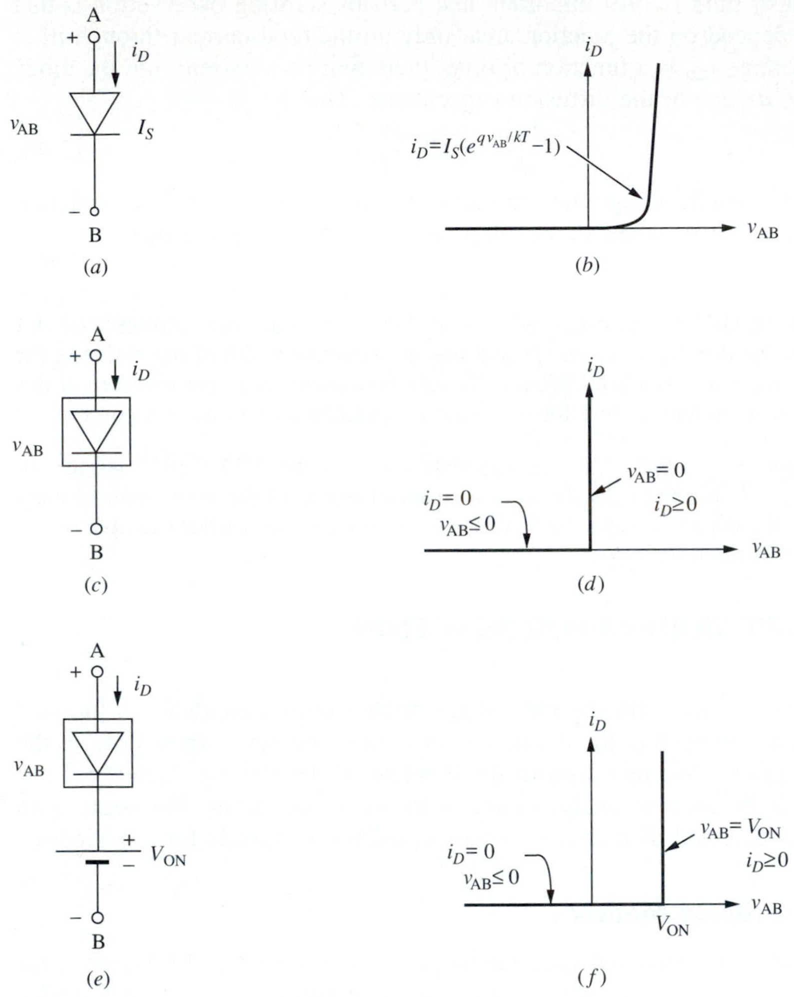

FIGURE 7.12
Circuit symbols and current-voltage relationships for three relatively simple large-signal *p-n* diode models: (*a* and *b*) the ideal exponential diode; (*c* and *d*) the ideal diode; (*e* and *f*) the break-point diode.

and it is desirable to use more approximate but also more readily analyzed models. The simplest is perhaps the ideal diode, which is shown in Fig. 7.12*c*. The current-voltage relationship for this device is shown in Fig. 7.12*d*. Mathematically, this relationship can be described by saying that $i_D = 0$ when $v_{AB} \leq 0$ and $v_{AB} = 0$ when $i_D \geq 0$.

The ideal diode model for a *p-n* junction diode ignores the fact that there is some voltage drop across the diode terminals when the diode is forward-biased. In the typical operating range of most silicon diodes, this drop ranges from 0.5 V to 0.7 V. We will tend to approximate it as 0.6 V in our discussions. This forward "offset" voltage can be incorporated into our model by adding an ideal voltage source to an ideal diode, as shown in Fig. 7.12*e*. We will call this a break-point diode. Its current-voltage characteristics are shown in Fig. 7.12*f*.

The decision to use forward offset voltage when approximating the large-signal behavior of a diode must be based on the application at hand. Because the actual diode current increases exponentially with the applied voltage, there is clearly no unambiguous turn-on voltage. At very low currents, a given silicon diode might appear to turn on much below 0.6 V, say at 0.4 V, for example, whereas at very high current levels the turn-on may appear to occur at 0.7 V or more. And if the diode is fabricated from a semiconductor other than silicon, a quite different turn-on voltage may be found. In general, the larger the bandgap of the semiconductor used, the larger the turn-on voltage.

An important feature of these simplified large-signal models for a diode are that they are piecewise linear. They are thus relatively simple to use, which in many instances more than makes up for the lack of precision.

b) Expanded diode models. In some situations, particularly in computer-aided modeling and analysis, the goal is not to use simplified models appropriate for hand calculations, but rather to model as much of the detail of the device performance as possible. We turn now to modeling diodes in this limit.

We saw in Sec. 7.3.3 and Fig. 7.8 that a typical *p-n* diode behaves like an ideal exponential diode over a part of its range but deviates at low and high current levels. At low current levels the characteristic is still exponential but with a dependence on qv_{AB}/nkT, where n is approximately 2. This behavior has led to the definition of a generalized exponential diode model, which we say has the following current-voltage relationship:

$$i_D = I_S(e^{qv_{\text{AB}}/nkT} - 1) \tag{7.29$'$}$$

The factor n is called the *ideality factor*; along with I_S, it fully specifies any exponential diode. The circuit model of an exponential diode is shown in Fig. 7.13*a*. Notice that the ideal exponential diode is a special case of the exponential diode model for which n is 1.

The low-current behavior of a real *p-n* diode can be modeled as the parallel combination of two exponential diodes, one with an ideality factor $n = 1$ and a certain value of saturation current I_S, and the other with $n = 2$ and a somewhat higher saturation current* I_{SR}. This is illustrated in Fig. 7.13*b*. The second diode (the one with $n = 2$) accounts for generation and recombination in the junc-

---

*The notation we are using here corresponds closely to that used in the popular circuit and device simulation program SPICE and its derivatives.

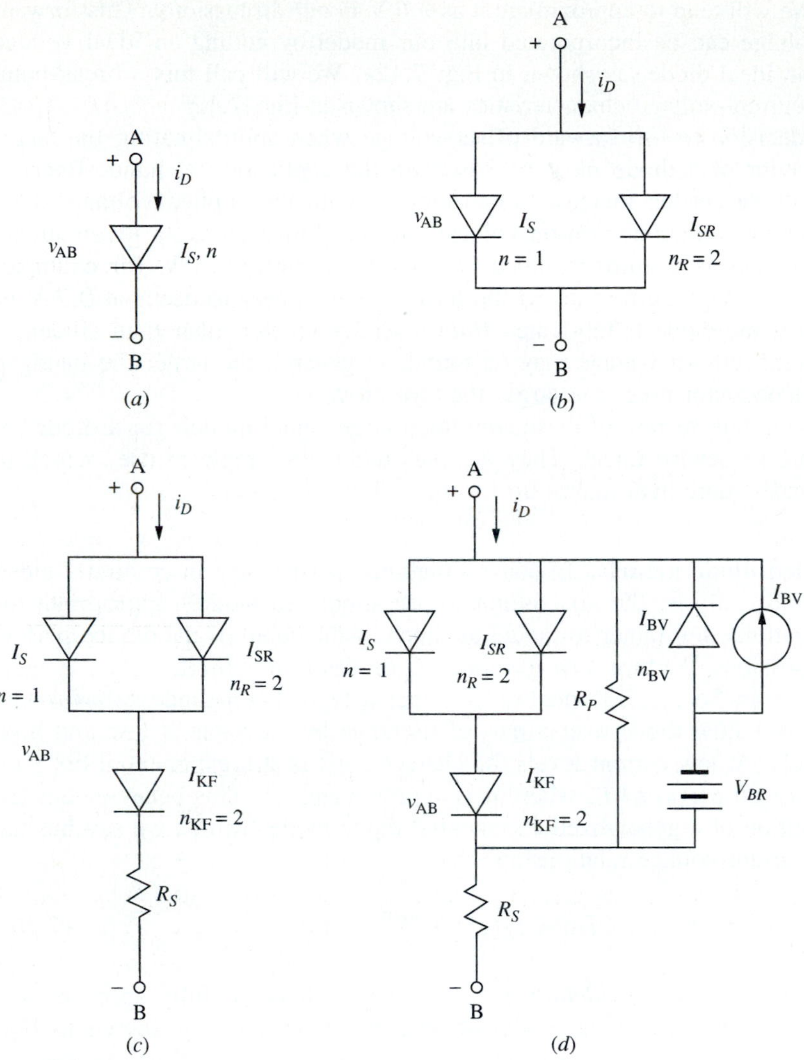

FIGURE 7.13
Circuit models for a *p-n* diode, including elements to model the effects not included in the ideal exponential diode model: (*a*) general exponential diode; (*b*) two general exponential diodes used in parallel to account for low-level space charge layer recombination; (*c*) elements included to model high-level injection and series resistance; (*d*) reverse-breakdown and reverse-bias leakage also included in the model.

tion depletion region. Because the depletion region width varies with the junction voltage, it is common, especially in computer simulation programs such as SPICE, to make I_{SR} vary in a similar fashion with voltage, that is, as $(\phi_b - v_J)^a$, where v_J is the voltage drop across the junction and, for an abrupt *p-n* junction, a is 0.5.

The high-current behavior can be accounted for by adding a resistor of resistance R_S and a second $n = 2$ diode with a much higher saturation current

I_{KF} in series with this parallel combination of diodes. This is illustrated in Fig. 7.13*c*.

To better model the reverse-bias behavior of a diode, several additional elements can be incorporated into the model. The reverse breakdown of the diode can be modeled by shunting the forward model with another exponential diode connected in opposite polarity relative to the other diodes and in series with a voltage source equal in magnitude to the breakdown voltage. When this is done, a current source I_{BV} has to be included in parallel with this new exponential diode so that i_D will be zero when v_{AB} is zero. This is shown in Fig. 7.13*d*. Finally, a resistor of resistance R_P can be added in parallel with the exponential diodes to allow for the possibility of parasitic current leakage paths shunting the junction. This element is also included in Fig. 7.13*d*.

c) Dynamic models with charge stores. The large-signal diode models we have developed thus far do not include any information on charge stores within the device. It is quite appropriate to ignore these charge stores when the terminal voltage on the diode is changing slowly enough that the currents that result from charging and/or discharging the charge stores are negligibly small. However, if the terminal voltages change more rapidly (as occurs during a switching transient or for a high-frequency sinusoidal input signal, for example), then the charging and discharging currents can be substantial and must be accounted for in our modeling. This is traditionally done by adding charge storage elements (i.e., capacitors) to the circuit model in the appropriate places. These capacitors are in general nonlinear; that is, the charge stored on them is a nonlinear function of the voltage difference between their terminals.

In the case of a *p-n* junction diode, we have two charge stores: the depletion region charge store and the diffusion charge store. The charge-voltage relationship for the depletion region charge store is given, in the case of an abrupt doping profile, by Eq. (7.5):

$$q_{DP}(v_{AB}) = -A\sqrt{2\varepsilon q(\phi_b - v_{AB})\frac{N_{Ap}N_{Dn}}{(N_{Ap} + N_{Dn})}} \tag{7.5}$$

The diffusion charge is described in the case of an abrupt $p^+ - n$ diode by Eq. (7.41):

$$q_{DF}(v_{AB}) = qAF\frac{(w_n - x_n)}{2}\frac{n_i^2}{N_{Dn}}(e^{qv_{AB}/kT} - 1) \tag{7.41}$$

A little thought will show you that these charge stores appear electrically in parallel, so they can be represented by a single nonlinear capacitor. This nonlinear capacitor is in turn parallel with the junction, which we represent by an exponential diode. The resulting circuit model is shown in Fig. 7.14*a*. Notice that the symbol we use for nonlinear capacitor is the usual symbol for a linear capacitor with a diagonal arrow across it. The arrow implies that the capacitance

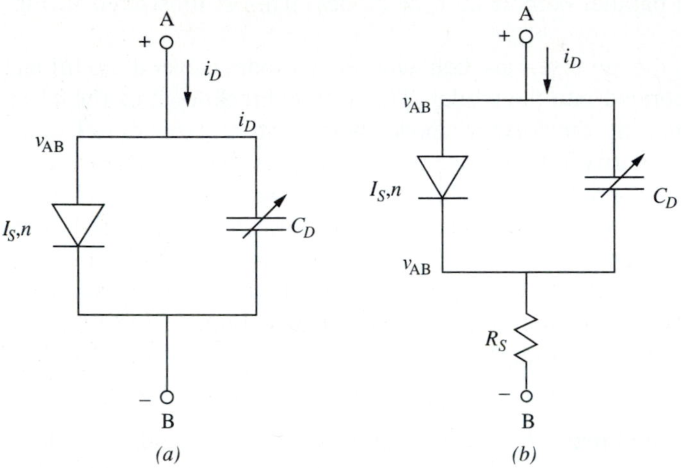

FIGURE 7.14
Addition of large-signal, nonlinear charge stores: (*a*) to a large-signal exponential diode model; (*b*) to an exponential diode model with series resistance (note that the charge store occurs in parallel with the junction but in series with the diode bulk and the contacts, which together are the source of R_S).

of this capacitor, which we define as dq/dv, varies with the voltage across the capacitor.*

The remarks we made in Sec. 7.4.1*b* about expanding the complexity of our model can be repeated here, and again our understanding of the device physics guides us in placing the additional elements. A common example is accounting for series resistance R_S. Clearly R_S can play an important role in any charging and discharging transients, and it is an obvious parasitic to want to consider. A little thought shows us that R_S enters in series with the junction and the charge stores, and thus should be added to the model as illustrated in Fig. 7.14*b*.

7.4.2 Static Small-Signal Linear Models

The large-signal models we developed in the preceding section are needed when analyzing circuit situations in which the terminal voltage and currents can assume

---

*It is important that you keep the distinction between a capacitor and its capacitance clear. We are using the term "capacitor" to represent any charge store $q(v)$ and the term "capacitance" to indicate the instantaneous rate of change of the charge store with terminal voltage (i.e., dq/dv). A linear capacitor has a constant capacitance; the capacitance of a nonlinear capacitor in general varies with the terminal voltage. To specify the nonlinear capacitor in this circuit we must specify its charge-voltage relationship. In the present example we would have

$$q_{AB} = q_{DF}(v_{AB}) + q_{DP}(v_{AB})$$

where $q_{DF}(v_{AB})$ and $q_{DP}(v_{AB})$ are given by Eqs. (7.41) and (7.5), respectively.

wide ranges of values. Another common type of analysis in which we will be interested concerns small variations in the terminal variables (i.e., the voltage and current) about some reference condition. In such cases it is often the details of the nonlinear characteristic in the vicinity of the reference values that are of primary interest. The reference condition values are termed the *quiescent operating point* or *bias point* values, and if the variations about them are small enough the changes in current and voltage will be linearly related.

To proceed, we first set up a notation convention to use in our discussion. We denote the total variable with a lowercase letter and uppercase subscripts. Thus the total diode voltage is v_{AB}, and the total diode current is i_D. We will denote the quiescent portion of these quantities with an uppercase letter with uppercase subscripts. Thus, the quiescent diode voltage is V_{AB}, and the quiescent diode current is I_D. Any change from the quiescent value is denoted by a lowercase letter with lowercase subscripts (i.e., v_{ab} and i_d) for the present examples. Thus we can write

$$v_{\mathrm{AB}} = V_{\mathrm{AB}} + v_{\mathrm{ab}} \tag{7.47}$$

and

$$i_D = I_D + i_d \tag{7.48}$$

We will in general have to determine V_{AB} and I_D using our large-signal models for the characteristics, but ideally, once they are known, we will be able to determine v_{ab} and i_d using linear circuit analysis techniques. Often we will not need to know V_{AB} and I_D with a high degree of accuracy and our simple piecewise linear model, possibly that of Fig. 7.12*e*, will be perfectly adequate. At the same time, we may want to know v_{ab} and i_d much more precisely, and having linear models relating them will make it relatively easy to achieve the necessary precision.

Returning now to the device at hand (i.e., the *p-n* diode), we will first develop a small-signal linear model based on our quasistatic exponential diode model. We will then extend our model for use with high-frequency signals by adding linear capacitors that account for the diffusion and depletion charge stores we identified earlier.

a) Low-frequency models. To relate v_{ab} and i_d for a diode, we perform a Taylor's series expansion of i_D about $v_{\mathrm{AB}} = V_{\mathrm{AB}}$. We write

$$i_D(v_{\mathrm{AB}}) = i_D(V_{\mathrm{AB}}) + a_1(v_{\mathrm{AB}} - V_{\mathrm{AB}}) + a_2(v_{\mathrm{AB}} - V_{\mathrm{AB}})^2 + \text{Higher-order terms} \tag{7.49a}$$

where a_1 is di_D/dv_{AB} evaluated at V_{AB} and a_2 is $(1/2)d^2i_D/dv_{\mathrm{AB}}^2$ evaluated at V_{AB}. The quantity $i_D(V_{\mathrm{AB}})$ is I_D, and using Eqs. (7.47) and (7.48) we have $(v_{\mathrm{AB}} - V_{\mathrm{AB}}) = v_{\mathrm{ab}}$ and $(i_D - I_D) = i_d$. Thus, Eq. (7.49a) can be written as

$$i_d = a_1 v_{\mathrm{ab}} + a_2 v_{\mathrm{ab}}^2 + \text{Higher-order terms} \tag{7.49b}$$

We are now in a position to put bounds on v_{ab} for linear operation. We want to be able to neglect the quadratic and higher-order terms, so we restrict $|v_{ab}|$ so that the quadratic term is no more than some fraction f of the linear term. Thus we require that

$$| a_2 v_{ab}^2 | \leq f \, | a_1 v_{ab} | \tag{7.50}$$

which thus means that

$$| v_{ab} | \leq f \frac{a_1}{a_2} \tag{7.51a}$$

If the diode is an ideal exponential diode, then i_D and v_{AB} will be related through Eq. (7.29) and a_1 and a_2 are given by

$$a_1 = \left. \frac{d i_D}{d v_{AB}} \right|_{v_{AB} = V_{AB}} = \frac{q}{kT} I_s e^{q V_{AB}/kT} \tag{7.52a}$$

$$a_2 = \left. \frac{d^2 i_D}{2 d v_{AB}^2} \right|_{v_{AB} = V_{AB}} = \frac{1}{2} \frac{q^2}{(kT)^2} I_s e^{q V_{AB}/kT} \tag{7.52b}$$

Thus we have

$$| v_{ab} | \leq f \frac{a1}{a2} = 2f \frac{kT}{q} \tag{7.51$'$}$$

Restricting v_{ab} to this range, we have our desired linear relationship

$$i_d \approx a_1 v_{ab} \tag{7.53}$$

The factor a_1 has the units of conductance. We usually use the symbol g_d for this factor and call it the incremental equivalent diode conductance about the quiescent operating point (I_D, V_{AB}). In general we have

$$g_d \equiv \left. \frac{d i_D}{d v_{AB}} \right|_{V_{AB}} \tag{7.54}$$

This result tells us that incrementally any diode looks like a simple linear conductance g_d, where the magnitude of this conductance is simply the slope of the diode current-voltage characteristic evaluated at the quiescent operating point. This conclusion is illustrated in Fig. 7.15.

In the special case of an ideal exponential diode, we have

$$g_d = \frac{q}{kT} I_s e^{q V_{AB}/kT} \tag{7.55a}$$

If V_{AB} is much greater than kT/q, then $I_s e^{q V_{AB}/kT}$ is approximately I_D and thus we can also write g_d as

$$g_d \approx \frac{q I_D}{kT} \tag{7.55b}$$

This is the expression that we will usually use to calculate g_d.

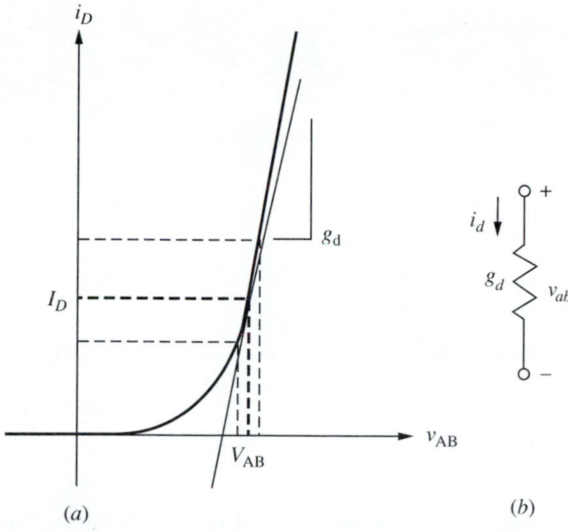

FIGURE 7.15
(*a*) Variation of the current and voltage of a *p-n* diode about a quiescent operation point (I_D, V_{AB}); (*b*) the corresponding static small-signal equivalent circuit.

Example

Question. What is the incremental conductance at room temperature of a diode biased at a quiescent current of 1 mA? If we want f to be 0.1, what is the restriction on $| v_{ab} |$?

Discussion. Using Eq. (7.55b) we calculate that g_d is 40 mS; the corresponding incremental resistance r_d (which is $1/g_d$) is 25 Ω. (Notice that these values do not depend on any of the diode dimensions, doping levels, etc.—only the bias level.)

From Eq. (7.51b), we find that the second-order term will be less than 10 percent of the linear term (i.e., $f = 0.1$) if $| v_{ab} |$ is less than $0.2kT/q$, which at room temperature is 5 mV. This doesn't seem like a very large voltage range, but then an exponential is not a very linear function. We will have to see whether this restriction is a problem when we look at applications of junction diodes.

Our notation does not identify the quiescent point explicitly; we simply write g_d, but it is very important to remember that the value of g_d depends directly on the quiescent point parameters.

To summarize our incremental model for the *p-n* diode, we find that for small variations about a quiescent operating point (I_D, V_{AB}), the changes in current and voltage, i_d and v_{ab}, respectively, are linearly related by the incremental equivalent diode conductance g_d, where g_d is defined as the slope of the diode characteristic at the quiescent operating point [i.e., Eq. (7.54)]. The fact that these small variations are linearly related is a purely mathematical result that stems from Taylor's

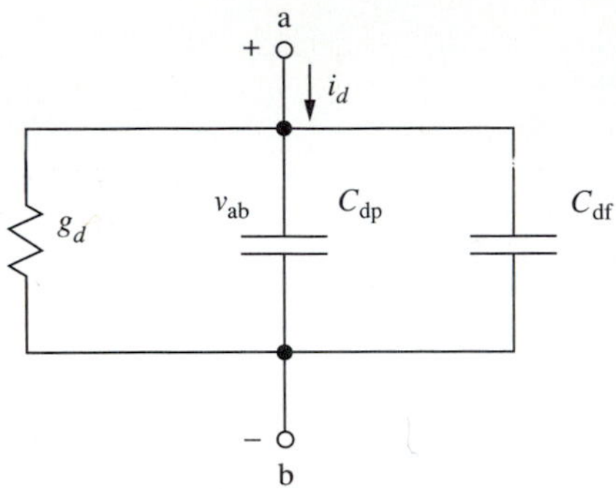

FIGURE 7.16
Small-signal equivalent circuit of a *p-n* diode, including the depletion and diffusion capacitances.

Theorem. The physics enters our analysis only when we evaluate the incremental diode conductance g_d, as we did in Eq. (7.55).

b) Small-signal models for time-varying signals. Our exponential diode expression, Eq. (7.29), and the small-signal equivalent circuit that we derived from it were developed assuming static conditions. This does not restrict us from having some variation of our currents and voltages with time, but it does mean such variations must be "slow." Mathematically, "slow" means that all time derivatives are negligible; physically it means that the carrier and current profiles must be able to respond essentially instantaneously, on the scale of the time variation, to any voltage changes and that any currents supplying or removing charge as the depletion and diffusion charge stores change are negligible. Strictly speaking, if we want to treat rapidly varying situations, we should return to our original equations and include the terms involving time derivatives, but this is a very difficult task. A more manageable and highly successful approach has been to incorporate the charge storage elements that we know must exist in the *p-n* diode (i.e., the depletion capacitance and diffusion capacitance) and use the resulting hybrid (in a theoretical or modeling sense) model.

Adding the capacitive currents to the exponential diode current, we have

$$i_d = g_d v_{ab} + (C_{df} + C_{dp})\frac{dv_{ab}}{dt} \tag{7.56}$$

A circuit representation of this relationship is illustrated in Fig. 7.16.

In Eq. (7.56) and Fig. 7.16, g_d is given by Eq. (7.55), C_{df} by Eq. (7.44), and C_{dp} by Eq. (7.9). All are clearly functions of the quiescent operating point (I_D, V_{AB}).

7.5 SOLAR CELLS AND PHOTODIODES

Thus far we have considered only voltage excitation of *p-n* junction diodes. Another important excitation form is light. We consider next optical excitation of *p-n* diodes and some useful applications of devices operated in this manner.

7.5.1 Optical Excitation of *p-n* Diodes

Consider the *p-n* diode illustrated in Fig. 7.17, which is illuminated with spatial impulse of light generating M hole-electron pairs/$\text{cm}^2 \cdot \text{s}$ in the plane at $x = x_L$. Our objective is to find the diode current as a function of the terminal voltage and the position and intensity of the illumination. For convenience, we denote the diode current as $i_D(v_{AB}, M)$ to remind us that we have two excitations.

You know enough about *p-n* junctions and flow problems to solve for $i_D(v_{AB}, M)$ directly, but it is far more instructive if we use superposition to obtain a solution. We will first calculate the diode current with only the light applied (i.e., with $v_{AB} = 0$), and then we will calculate the diode current with only the voltage v_{AB} applied (i.e., with no light). We can then add these two currents, $i_D(0, M)$ and $i_D(v_{AB}, 0)$, respectively, to obtain $i_D(v_{AB}, M)$. We of course, know the second of these current components already; it is just our ideal diode relationship, Eq. (7.29). The problem is to find $i_D(0, M)$.

Before proceeding, it is worthwhile to comment about our use of superposition. The flow problems in the quasineutral region are linear problems, and superposition is, of course, a valid technique with them. The boundary conditions at the edges of the depletion region, however, are not linear functions of the junction voltage v_{AB}. Thus we must be very careful when separating excitations to make certain that we don't run into problems. Specifically we must make certain that only one portion of our decomposition has a nonzero voltage applied to the junction. Clearly our formulation of the problem meets this requirement.

To calculate $i_D(0, M)$, we want to find $J_e(-x_p)$ and $J_h(x_n)$, add them to get J_{TOT}, and finally multiply by A to get i_D. We begin by identifying the boundary conditions on the excess carrier populations. Clearly, at the ohmic contacts and at the edges of the depletion region, the excess populations are zero. At $x = x_L$, the discontinuity in the slopes of $n'(x)$ on either side of x_L is M/D_h. This information is summarized in Fig. 7.18*a*, where for the sake of convenience we have assumed a very long minority carrier diffusion length. The corresponding minority currents

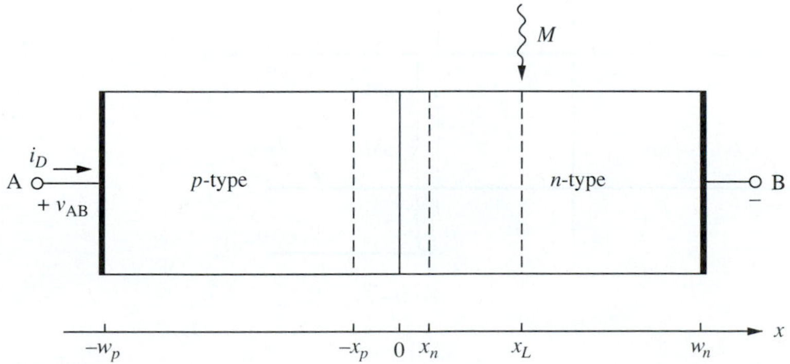

FIGURE 7.17
A *p-n* diode illuminated with a spatial impulse generating M hole-electron pairs/$\text{cm}^2 \cdot \text{s}$ uniformly across the plane at $x = x_L$.

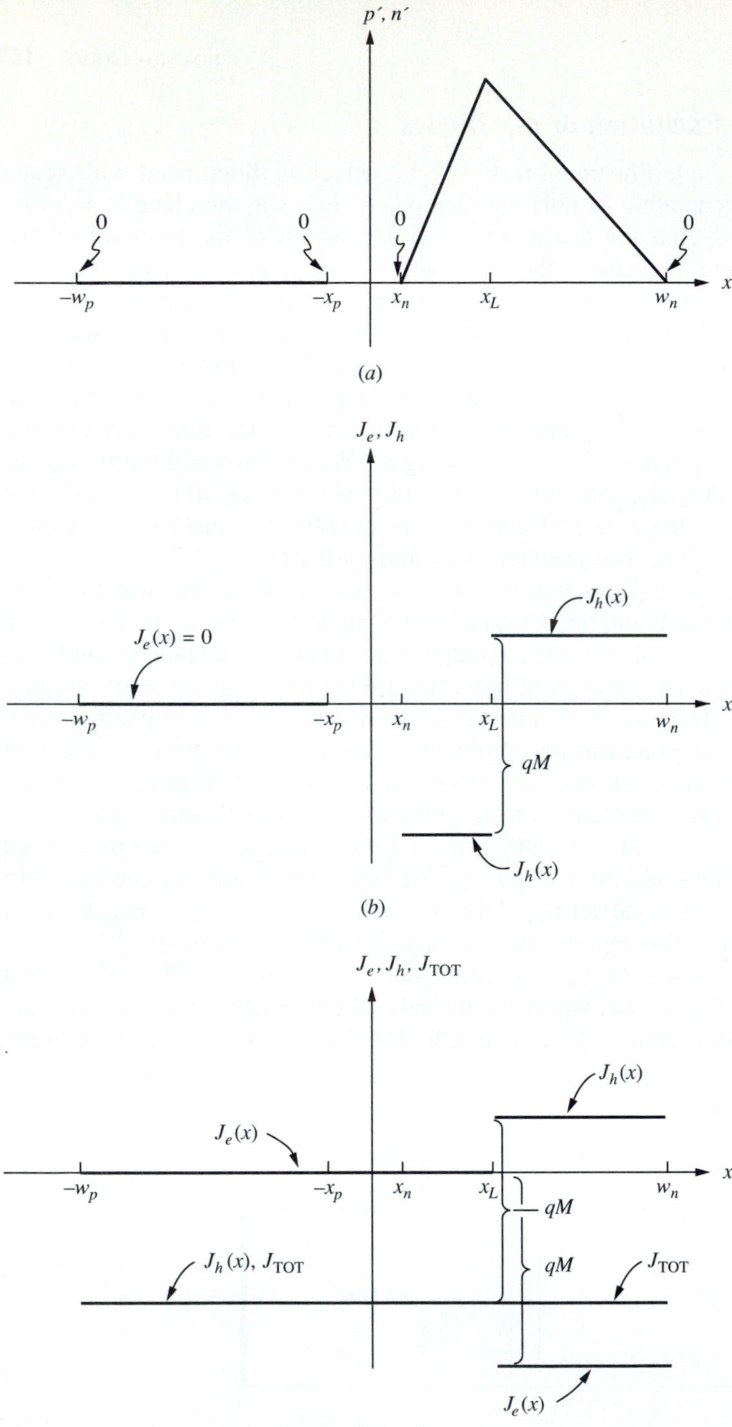

FIGURE 7.18
(*a*) Excess minority carrier distributions in the illuminated *p-n* diode of Fig. 7.17; (*b*) the corresponding minority carrier diffusion current densities on either side of the junction; (*c*) the complete current density variations throughout the device.

are shown in Fig. 7.18*b*. The complete current density variations are shown in Fig 7.18*c*.

A bit of algebra leads us to the result

$$J_h(x_n) = -qM\frac{(w_n - x_L)}{(w_n - x_n)} \tag{7.57}$$

The electron current $J_e(-x_p)$ is zero, so we have

$$i_D(0, M) = -qAM\frac{(w_n - x_L)}{(w_n - x_n)} \tag{7.58}$$

for $x_n \leq x_L \leq w_n$.

Looking at Fig. 7.18 and Eq. (7.58), we see that the fraction of the optically injected carriers that flow to the depletion region and across the junction result in a diode current. The sign of the current is negative, and its magnitude increases as the illumination moves nearer to the junction.

If the illumination had been on the *p*-side of the junction, we would have found

$$i_D(0, M) = -qAM\frac{(w_p - x_L)}{(w_p - x_p)} \tag{7.58a}$$

for $-w_p \leq x_L \leq -x_p$.

If the illumination is in the depletion region, all of the injected carriers cross the junction and

$$i_D(0, M) = -qAM \tag{7.58b}$$

for $-x_p \leq x_L \leq x_n$.

In general, then, we can write

$$i_D(0, M) = -qAMf \tag{7.59}$$

where f is a number between 0 and 1 that depends on the position x_L of the illumination.

With both light and voltage applied to the diode we have

$$i_D = I_s(e^{qv_{AB}/kT} - 1) - I_L \tag{7.60}$$

where we have defined I_L as the magnitude of the optically generated current $-qAMf$ in our example. This characteristic is plotted in Fig. 7.19.

7.5.2 Applications of Illuminated *p-n* Diodes

Referring to Fig. 7.19, we can identify two important features of the current-voltage characteristic of an illuminated *p-n* diode. First, there is a current in reverse bias that is directly proportional to the illumination and is independent of the applied voltage. This effect can be used to sense the presence of light and forms the basis for a device called the photodiode.

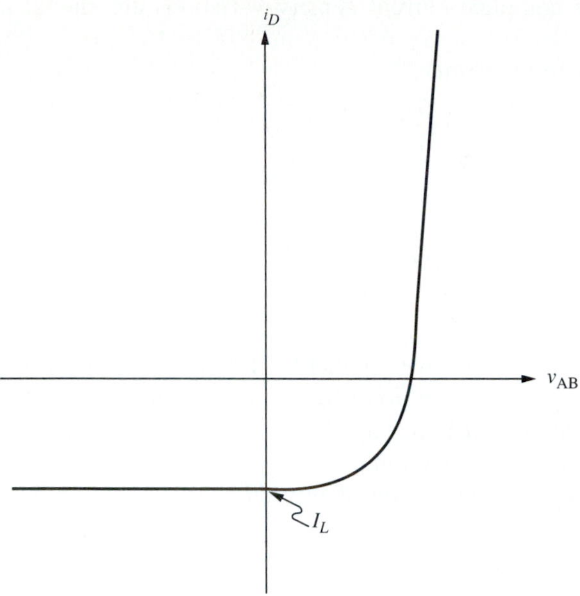

FIGURE 7.19
Current-voltage characteristic of an illuminated *p-n* junction diode.

The second feature is that the diode characteristic now extends into the lower right-hand quadrant of the *i-v* plane. In this quadrant the device is supplying power; that is, the product of the current into the device times the voltage across its terminals is negative. This observation forms the basis for a device called the solar cell.

We will consider each of these applications in turn below.

a) Photodiodes. The magnitude of the current through a reverse-biased *p-n* diode that is not illuminated is generally very small. The precise value will, of course, depend on the particular device under consideration, but it will typically be on the order of a few picoamperes or less. When the junction is illuminated this can easily be increased many orders of magnitude to a level well above the background noise. This phenomenon then provides an extremely useful method of sensing the presence of light.

Any *p-n* junction will be sensitive to light, but several straightforward things can be done with a diode's design to enhance its sensitivity to illumination. Most basically, one should make the junction area large and place the junction near the top surface of the device because, as we know from our discussion of illuminated *p-n* diodes in Sec. 7.5.1, it is only those photogenerated minority carriers that are able to diffuse to the edge of the space charge region that contribute to the photocurrent. In addition, we should make the top ohmic contact relatively small and place it off to one side, so that it does not block the light from reaching the junction and does not lead to an excessive amount of recombination. A typical device cross section is shown in Fig. 7.20. The top surface of the device will not in general be an ideal reflecting boundary; rather, it will have a finite surface recombination velocity (see Sec. 5.2.3*c*) and will thus be a source of some loss due to recombination. One way of reducing this is putting a thin, heavily doped region at the surface as illustrated in Fig. 7.20; referring to Fig. 6.8*b*, you should realize that this creates a potential barrier that tends to keep the minority carriers away from the surface and thereby increases the light sensitivity of the device (i.e., increases the magnitude of the photocurrent obtained for a given light input). Diodes designed in this way specifically to be sensitive to light are called photodiodes.

The amount of photocurrent generated by light depends not only on the intensity of the light but also on the energy of the incident photons. You know from our earlier discussion in Chap. 3 that the energy of the photons must at least exceed the energy gap. On the other hand, if the photons have too much energy they will be absorbed very quickly in the semiconductor and will generate hole-electron pairs very near the surface, where a disproportionately large fraction will recombine. This leads to a drop in the sensitivity of a photodiode at high energies. Thus a photodiode will in general respond only to photons within a limited range of energies; that is, it will respond only to light falling within a limited band of wavelengths. Light of too long a wavelength, or, equivalently, too low an energy, will not generate hole-electron pairs; whereas light of too short a wavelength, that is, of too high an energy, will be absorbed so close to the surface that most of the photogenerated minority carriers will recombine before reaching the space charge layer.

Silicon photodiodes typically respond best to light with a wavelength between 0.7 and 0.9 microns; by taking special care to shield the photogenerated carriers from the surface and by placing the junction very close to the surface, it is possible to extend the range of sensitivity of a Si photodiode to also cover the visible spectrum, 0.4 to 0.7 μm, and perhaps even the ultraviolet range of less than 0.4 μm. If you want to detect light of longer wavelength (lower en-

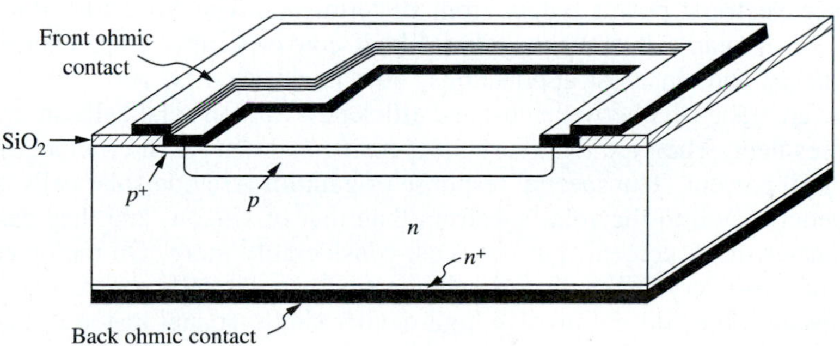

FIGURE 7.20
Cross-sectional drawing of a typical silicon photodiode.

ergy), however, silicon is not useful. A semiconductor with a smaller energy gap is needed. Germanium and indium gallium arsenide photodiodes, for example, are well suited for use in the near-infrared region around 1.5 μm, and mercury cadmium telluride photodiodes can be designed to respond to wavelengths of anywhere from 2 to 20 μm, depending on the relative amounts of mercury and cadmium in them.

Photodiodes are extensively used as light sensors in many different applications, and you very likely encounter them daily, often without realizing it. The sensor for the remote control on a television set or VCR is a photodiode, for example; so is the sensor for the laser scanner at the supermarket checkout counter. The light meter in a camera very likely also uses a photodiode, and when you call home for money, there is a good possibility that the signal carrying your conversation is sent as light over an optical fiber and converted back to an electrical signal by a photodiode.

For some applications a simple photodiode like that pictured in Fig. 7.20 is not fast enough or sensitive enough. In such situations more sophisticated device designs are required. One alternative design is to place an undoped (i.e., intrinsic) layer between the *p*- and *n*-type sides of the junction. The resulting *p-i-n* structure has a relatively wide, uniform electric field across the *i*-region. A large fraction of the light in a *p-i-n* photodiode is absorbed in the depletion region, and the photogenerated carriers are quickly swept (drifted) across the junction. The structure is both sensitive and fast. Yet another photodiode design is the avalanche photodiode. This device is designed to be operated with a reverse bias just at the edge of avalanche breakdown (see Sec. 7.3.3*c*). Photogenerated carriers crossing the junction then will create additional hole-electron pairs through the avalanche process. Each photon thus creates many carriers; that is, there is gain, whereas in the other photodiodes we have discussed each photon leads to at most one carrier crossing the junction. Avalanche photodiodes are particularly useful where very high sensitivity is required.

b) Solar cells. A solar cell is a simple *p-n* junction photodiode designed so that its spectral response is well suited to illumination by sunlight. It is operated so that there is net electrical power output from its terminals. The most important characteristics of a solar cell are how efficiently it converts input solar energy to electrical energy and, in most applications, how much it costs. As might be expected, there are trade-offs between cost and efficiency. Silicon solar cells are by far the most prevalent. They are relatively inexpensive and can reach efficiencies on the order of 10 percent. The spectral response of gallium arsenide solar cells is a somewhat better match to the solar spectrum than that of silicon, and they can achieve efficiencies of 25 percent, but they cost considerably more. On the other extreme, thin-film (polycrystalline or amorphous) silicon solar cells can be made very cheaply because they do not involve high-quality single-crystal material, but for the same reason they are relatively inefficient (only a few percent). Many light-powered pocket calculators rely on such thin-film silicon solar cells.

7.6 LIGHT-EMITTING DIODES

In a forward-biased long-base *p-n* diode, all of the excess minority carriers injected into either side of the junction recombine with majority carriers in the quasineutral regions (refer to Fig. 7.7*c*). In silicon diodes, each hole-electron pair that recombines releases an amount of energy equivalent to the energy gap (i.e., approximately 1.1 eV) and does so primarily in the form of thermal-energy phonons (i.e., heat). In other semiconductors such as gallium arsenide, an appreciable fraction of this recombination energy is released as optical-energy photons (i.e., light). A forward-biased long-base GaAs diode will thus generate an appreciable amount of light. If the diode is configured and packaged so that it forms a useful source of light, it is called a *light-emitting diode* (LED). Getting the light out is actually a rather difficult problem. The light is emitted in random directions, but because of the large index of refraction of GaAs ($n \approx 3.5$) it must intersect the surface of the device within 15° of the normal or it will suffer total internal reflection and never get out. (It will eventually be absorbed.) The usual solution is to keep the junction close to the top surface to minimize the absorption before the light reaches the top surface the first time, and to package the device in a hemisphere-shaped high-refractive-index plastic dome. The diode is typically a rectangular chip 250 to 300 microns on a side, with the junction near the top surface; the dome will be several millimeters in diameter, as pictured in Fig. 7.21*a*. The high refractive index of the plastic increases the critical angle at the semiconductor-plastic interface, considerably increasing the fraction of the light able to exit the semiconductor. Once the light enters the plastic it will intersect the surface of the dome at near normal incidence and most of it will exit.

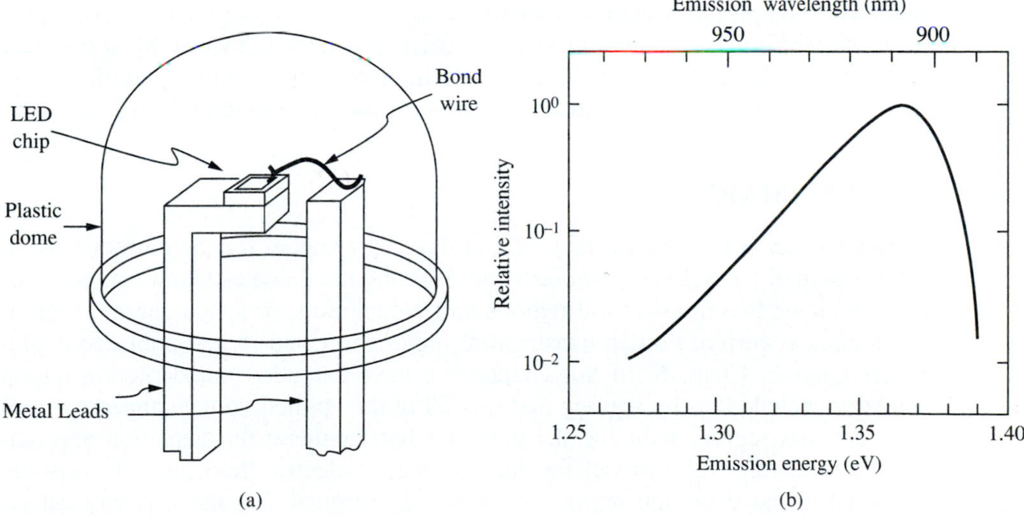

FIGURE 7.21
(*a*) Sketch of a typical light-emitting diode chip and its package; (*b*) the emission spectrum of a GaAs LED.

The energy gap of GaAs is about 1.4 eV, and GaAs LEDs emit in a narrow band at about 0.9 μm, as shown in Fig. 7.21*b*. Our eyes are not very sensitive at this wavelength, so we cannot see this emission, but it is very well matched to silicon photodiodes (see Sec. 7.5.2*a*). The light source in the remote control on a VCR is probably a GaAs LED.

The red, amber, and green light-emitting diodes in the dashboards of many cars are made from semiconductors with wider energy gaps than gallium arsenide. Many red and amber LEDs are made of gallium arsenide phosphide. The ratio of arsenic to phosphorus in the semiconductor crystal used to make the device determines the color. Green LEDs and some red LEDs are made of gallium phosphide. In this case it is the dopant that determines the color. Nitrogen doping yields green emission, whereas doping with zinc and oxygen yields red. The details of how this works are not difficult to understand but are beyond the scope of this text.

To date there are no efficient blue LEDs, but there is a great deal of research effort being expended in an effort to make them. In the infrared direction there are a variety of materials that can be used to make light-emitting diodes operating out as far as 30 microns, though most applications are much nearer to 1 micron.

Finally, it is significant that hole-electron recombination can be optically stimulated, that is, that a photon passing a conduction electron can catalyze the recombination of that electron with a hole, causing it to emit another photon traveling in the same direction as (and in phase with) the original photon. If there is a very large population of excess conduction electrons and a large population of excess holes, then this process can lead to a veritable avalanche of coherent photons, and with the addition of a suitable optical resonant cavity a laser can be formed. The excess populations can be created at a forward-biased *p-n* junction, and the cavity can be formed by suitably cutting the semiconductor crystal. The details are complex and again beyond the scope of this text, but the basic concept is quite straightforward, and laser diodes are extremely useful devices. Most compact disc players, for example, use laser diode light sources to interrogate the discs. Most optical fiber communication systems also use laser diode sources.

7.7 SUMMARY

In this chapter we have seen that we can develop a model for the current-voltage relationship of a *p-n* junction diode by envisioning the diode as being composed of three regions: two quasineutral regions and a depletion, or space charge, region. We looked at current flow in quasineutral regions in Chap. 5 and unbiased depletion regions in Chap. 6. In this chapter we have extended our depletion region model to include bias by arguing first that all of the applied voltage appears across the depletion region, reducing the potential barrier there; the depletion approximation remains a valid model for the net charge, electric field, and electrostatic potential in the depletion region. We have also argued that the majority carrier populations remain essentially in thermal equilibrium with the potential barrier at the junction; this gave us a way of determining boundary conditions on the excess minority carrier concentrations on either side of the junction. Finally, we have argued that except for a small amount of generation or recombination in the depletion region, the hole and electron currents are continuous across the depletion region; this gave us a way of determining the total diode current. With these assumptions we obtained

$$i_D = I_S(e^{qv_{AB}/(kT)} - 1)$$

with I_S given by

$$I_S = Aqn_i^2\left(\frac{D_e}{N_{Ap}w_p^*} + \frac{D_h}{N_{Dn}w_n^*}\right)$$

where w_p^* and w_n^* are given by

$$w_p^* \equiv L_e \tanh\left(\frac{w_p - x_p}{L_e}\right)$$

$$w_n^* \equiv L_h \tanh\left(\frac{w_n - x_n}{L_h}\right)$$

Looking at these expressions we have seen that the diode current can become very large in forward bias, whereas it saturates at a very small value in reverse bias. We have also seen that the current across an asymmetrically doped junction tends to be dominated by carriers from the more heavily doped side. Furthermore, for two otherwise similar diodes with the same voltages applied, the more lightly doped diode has more current.

We have seen that there are limitations in our model, particularly at very low and very high current levels as well as at very large reverse biases. We have shown how our ideal exponential diode model could be extended to incorporate effects not considered in our basic model, as well as how it could be simplified to obtain a model useful for hand calculations. One of the important things you will want to develop as you use these models to analyze circuits is an appreciation of when a simple model can be used and when it is necessary to use a more complicated model.

We have also shown that there is charge storage associated with a *p-n* junction and have introduced the concepts of depletion and diffusion capacitance. The amount of stored charge in each of these charge stores was seen to be a nonlinear function of the diode voltage.

We have discussed linear equivalent circuit models for *p-n* diodes valid for small-signal operation about a bias point. We have shown that at low frequencies a diode looks incrementally like a resistor whose value kT/qI_D depends on the bias current level I_D. To extend this model to higher frequencies, we have defined two small-signal capacitances, the depletion capacitance and the diffusion capacitance, to model the two junction charge stores in small-signal linear equivalent circuit analyses.

Finally, we have considered the interaction of light with *p-n* diodes. We have seen that an illuminated *p-n* diode can convert optical energy to electrical energy and can serve as a useful power source and light detector. We have also seen that *p-n* diodes fabricated in certain materials emit light when forward-biased because a large fraction of the accompanying hole-electron recombination occurs via radiative processes. These red, yellow, and green light emitters can be found in many modern electronic gadgets.

PROBLEMS

7.1 Consider an abrupt silicon *p-n* junction with $N_p = 5 \times 10^{17}$ cm^{-3} and $N_n = 10^{16}$ cm^{-3} at room temperature.

(*a*) Find the numerical value for the ratio of the depletion region width on the *n*-side, x_n, to the width on the *p*-side, x_p.

(*b*) Find the total width of the depletion layer (in microns).

(*c*) Find the maximum electric field $\mathscr{E}_{max}$ in this junction for applied biases of (i) $V_A = 0$ and (ii) $V_A = -12$ V.

(*d*) The breakdown electric field in moderately doped silicon is approximately 5×10^5 V/cm. At what reverse bias will $\mathscr{E}_{max} = 5 \times 10^5$ V/cm, and what will the depletion region width be at that bias?

7.2 A certain silicon *p-n* junction is known to have the doping profile illustrated in Fig. P7.2. Note: $N(x) \equiv N_d(x) - N_a(x)$. Assume that this device is at room temperature, $n_i = 1.45 \times 10^{10}$ cm^{-3}, $kT/q = 0.025$ V, and $\varepsilon_{si} = 10^{-12}$ f/cm. The cross-sectional area is 2.5 cm^2. Use the depletion approximation to arrive at your answers.

(*a*) What is the thermal equilibrium electrostatic potential relative to intrinsic silicon far to the left and right of the junction (i.e., for $x >> 0$ and for $x << 0$)?

(*b*) For a certain applied bias the width of the depletion region on the *n*-side, x_n, is 2 μm. What is the corresponding depletion region width on the *p*-side, x_p?

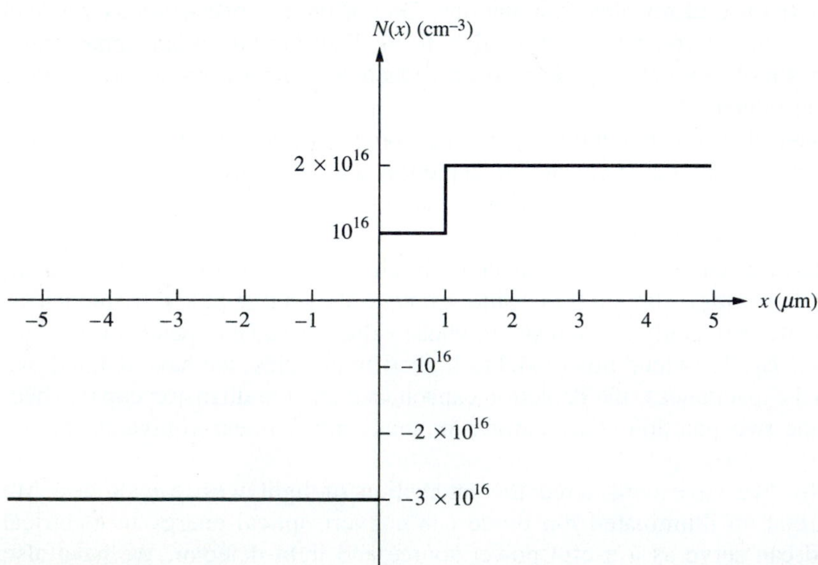

FIGURE P7.2

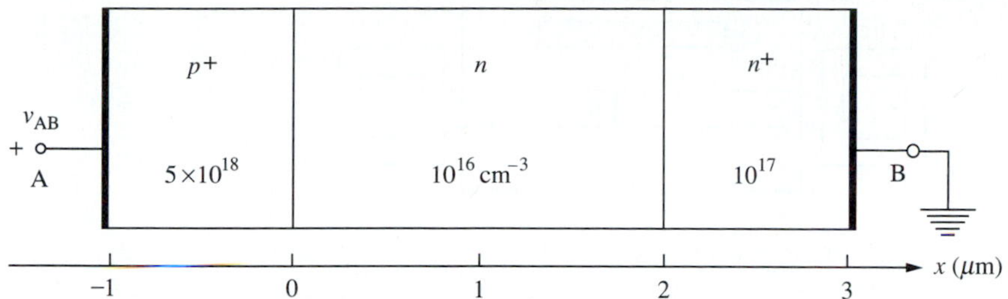

FIGURE P7.3

7.3 Consider the p^+-n-n^+ diode pictured in Fig. P7.3.
Use the depletion approximation to answer this question.

(*a*) At what bias level v_{AB} is the n-region fully depleted?

(*b*) (i) Find an expression for the depletion region width as a function of v_{AB} when v_{AB} is negative and $|\, v_{AB}\,|$ is greater than the value you found in part a (i.e., when the depletion region extends into the n^+region).

(ii) Find an expression for the peak electric field in the same bias range.

(*c*) If the critical electrical field for breakdown is 5×10^5 V/cm in Si with n_o = 10^{16} cm^{-3}, what is the maximum voltage that can be applied to this device before it breaks down?

(*d*) Compare your answer in part c to the breakdown voltage of a comparable p^+-n diode (i.e., one with a long n-region rather than the n^+-region). Does the presence of the n^+-region increase or decrease the breakdown voltage? Can you explain your answer?

7.4 This problem concerns the design of a voltage adjustable resistor like that pictured in Fig P7.4. This device is simply a diffused resistor like the one you designed in Problem 3.4 with a heavily doped p-region added over the conducting channel that thins it and increases its resistance. By varying the reverse bias between the p- and n-regions we vary the width of the conducting channel and thus adjust the resistance of the diffused resistor.

In your design you may assume that the n-region is uniformly doped. Also assume that the voltage drop in the resistor is small, so that it is essentially all at the same potential for purposes of calculating the junction depletion widths. Select the dimensions of the device and doping level of the n-region subject to the constraints that the minimum line width, W, is 2 μm; the final thickness of the n-region, T, must fall between 1 and 4 μm; and the doping of the n-region should be between 10^{15} cm^{-3} and 10^{18} cm^{-3}. You want to design a device that meets the specifications given in part a below that has the smallest possible capacitance between terminals 2 and 1.

(*a*) Design a device that will have a resistance of 1 kΩ with $v_{21} = -10$ V and a resistance of 2 kΩ with $v_{21} = -5$ V.

(*b*) Plot the resistance (at low v_{31}) versus v_{21} of the device you have designed over what you feel is the useful operating range. Explain why you have chosen this operating range.

(*c*) Discuss qualitatively how the resistance of your device changes as v_{31} becomes large (i.e., on the order of a volt or more). You should find looking ahead to the discussion in Sec. 10.2 useful in this regard.

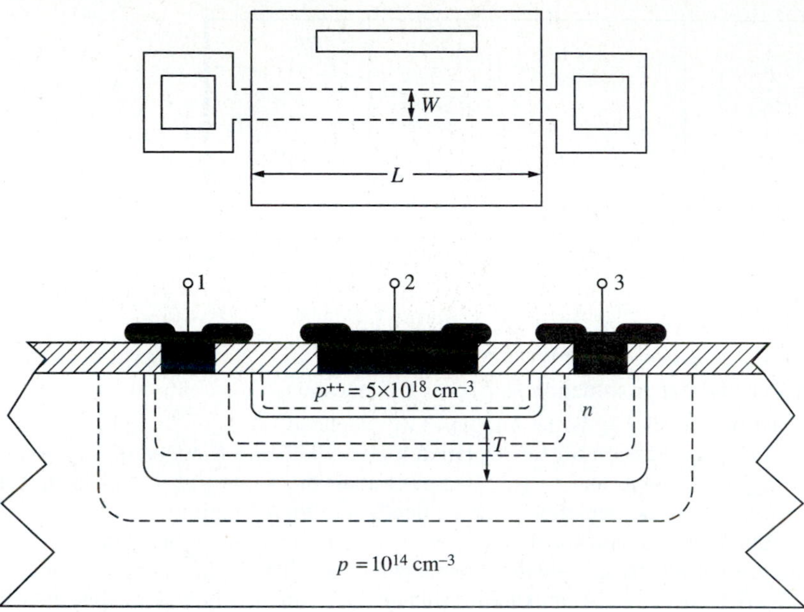

FIGURE P7.4

7.5 The data from a measurement of the small-signal capacitance of a silicon p^+-n diode structure as a function of bias voltage is plotted in the form $1/C_{\mathrm{dp}}^2$ versus V_{AB} in Fig. P7.5. The area of the junction is 10^{-5} cm^2. Use this data to answer the following questions about the device.

(*a*) What is the built-in potential of this junction?

(*b*) What is the doping level of the more lightly doped side (*n*-side) of this diode in the vicinity of the junction? Note that in a p^+-n junction, $N_{Ap} >> N_{Dn}$ and we can write $N_{Ap}N_{Dn}/(N_{Ap} + N_{Dn}) \cong N_{Dn}$, so Eq. (7.19a) can be simplified somewhat.

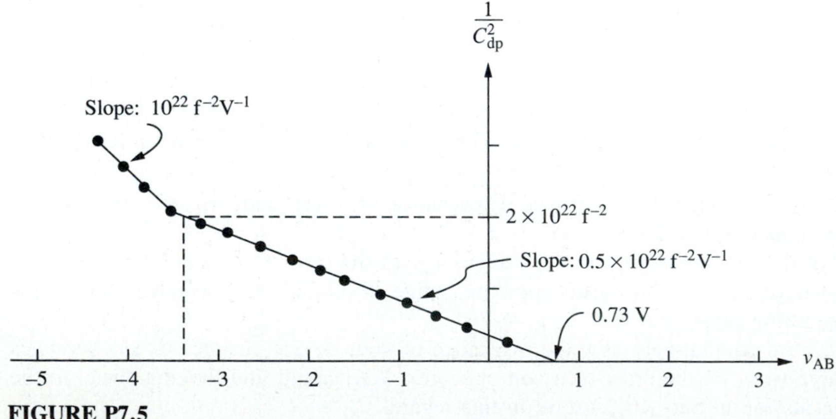

FIGURE P7.5

(*c*) What is the doping level of the more heavily doped side? *Hint*: Use your knowledge of ϕ_o and N_{Dn}.

(*d*) At some distance from the junction the doping level changes.

   (i) At what distance from the junction does the change occur?

   (ii) Does the doping level increase or decrease at this point, and what does it become?

(*e*) Suppose that in addition to the above structure there is a very heavily doped n^+-region 3 μm from junction. How would you expect the plot of $1/C_d^2$ versus V_{AB} to look in this case? Sketch and explain your answer.

7.6 Consider two abrupt silicon *p-n* diodes with identical dimensions, carrier mobilities, and minority carrier diffusion lengths that differ in terms of doping. In diode A, $N_n = 10^{16}$ cm^{-3} and $N_p = 10^{17}$ cm^{-3}; in diode B, $N_n = 10^{17}$ cm^{-3} and $N_p = 10^{18}$ cm^{-3}.

(*a*) With the same reverse bias applied to each diode, which of these diodes has the largest depletion capacitance and why?

(*b*) With the same forward current flowing in each diode, which of these diodes has the larger diffusion capacitance and why?

(*c*) With the same forward voltage bias applied to each diode, which of these diodes has the larger diffusion capacitance and why?

(*d*) Which of these diodes has the largest reverse breakdown voltage and why?

7.7 Consider a *p-n* diode with the following dimensions and doping levels:

$$
\begin{aligned}
n\text{-side}: \quad N_{Dn} &= 5 \times 10^{17}\ \text{cm}^{-3} \\
w_n &= 1\ \mu\text{m} \\
\tau_h &= 10^{-6}\ \text{s} \\
p\text{-side}: \quad N_{Ap} &= 10^{-16}\ \text{cm}^{-3} \\
w_p &= 4\ \mu\text{m} \\
\tau_e &= 10^{-5}\ \text{s}
\end{aligned}
$$

This diode is fabricated in silicon for which $\mu_e = 1600$ cm^2/V·s, $\mu_h = 600$ cm^2/V·s, and $n_i = 1.0 \times 10^{10}$ cm^{-3} at room temperature. The cross-sectional area of this device is 10^{-4} cm^2.

(*a*) Can this diode be modeled using either the long- or short-base approximation? Which one, if either, and why?

(*b*) What is I_S in the expression for the diode current, that is, in the relation $i_D = I_S(e^{qv_{AB}/kT} - 1)$?

(*c*) When this diode is forward-biased, what fraction of the total current is holes flowing from the *p*- to the *n*-side? Which fraction is electrons going from *n* to *p*?

(*d*) What is the built-in potential of this junction?

(*e*) At what bias level does the low-level injection assumption start to be violated, assuming that LLI is valid as long as n' and p' are less than 10 percent of the majority carrier population?

(*f*) Is LLI violated first on the *n*-side or on the *p*-side, or does violation occur simultaneously on both?

(*g*) (i) What is the diode current density at the bias point of part e?

   (ii) What are the resistive voltage drops in the quasineutral regions at this bias level?

(*h*) Plot the excess electron concentration on the *p*-side of this diode on a linear scale for the following bias conditions:

(i) 0.2 V forward bias, $v_{AB} = +0.2$ V

(ii) 1.0 V reverse bias, $v_{AB} = -1.0$ V

(*i*) How would your plots in (ii) of part h change if v_{AB} was -5.0 V?

7.8 Consider the three diodes shown in Fig. P7.8. All have the same cross-sectional area *A*, and all contacts are ohmic. Carrier mobilities are as follows:

$$N_A \text{ or } N_D = 10^{17}/\text{cm}^3 : \mu_e = 600 \text{ cm}^2/\text{V}\cdot\text{s}$$
$$\mu_h = 250 \text{ cm}^2/\text{V}\cdot\text{s}$$
$$N_D = 10^{15}/\text{cm}^3 : \mu_e = 1300 \text{ cm}^2/\text{V}\cdot\text{s}$$
$$\mu_h = 350 \text{ cm}^2/\text{V}\cdot\text{s}$$

The minority carrier lifetime in the *p*-type material is 10^{-8} s. In the *n*-type material the minority carrier lifetime is 4×10^{-7} s for $N_D = 10^{15}/\text{cm}^3$ and 5×10^{-8} s for $N_D = 10^{17}/\text{cm}^3$.

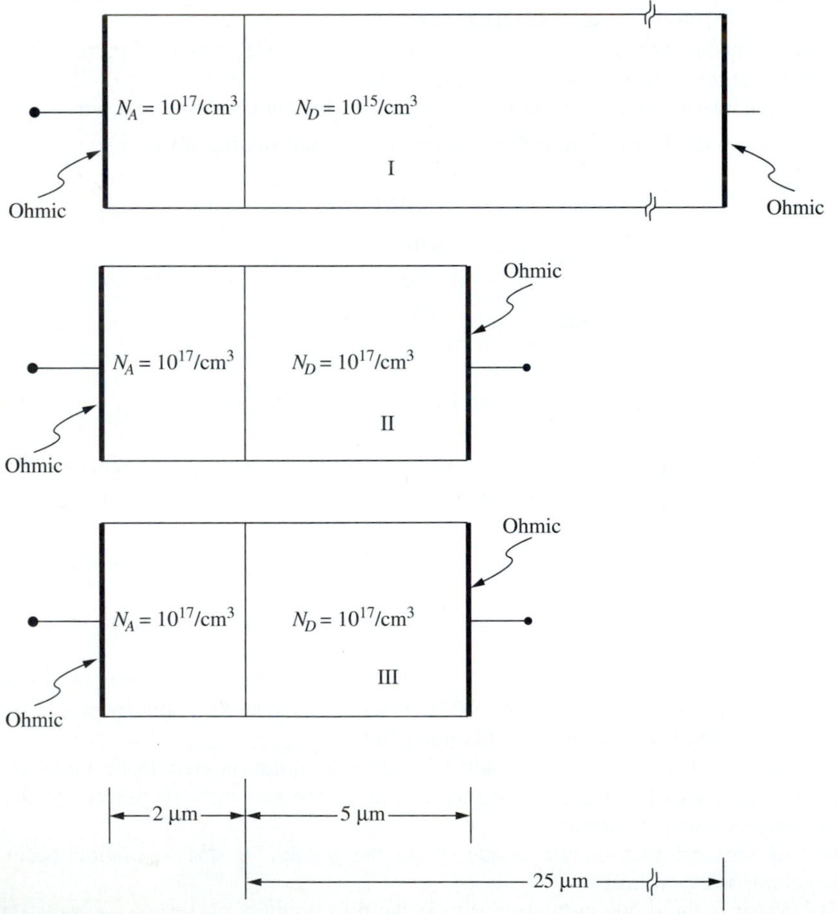

FIGURE P7.8

(*a*) For each diode find the numerical ratio of the hole current to the electron current at the junction.
(*b*) Find the numerical ratio of the total junction current in diode I to that in diode II, and find the numerical ratio of the current in II to that in III, assuming that the diodes are operated at the same voltage.
(*c*) Diodes I and II are connected in parallel across a forward-bias voltage source $v_D = 0.25$ V. What fraction of the total current goes through diode I?
(*d*) Diodes II and III are connected in series so that both conduct in forward bias when connected to a voltage source $v_D = 1$ V. What fraction of the total voltage appears across diode II?
(*e*) A forward-bias voltage $v_D = 0.36$ ($= kT/q \ln 10^6$) is applied to diode I. Make labeled sketches showing how the following quantities vary throughout the diode: $p'(x), n'(x), J_h(x), J_e(x)$.

7.9 In Problem 6.4 you analyzed a linearly graded junction. Now consider applying bias to this same junction. Assume that ϕ_o is known and that a reverse bias $v_A < 0$ is applied to the junction. From your expression in (i) of part b of that problem show that $w(v_A)$ varies as the cube root of $(\phi_b - v_A)$.

7.10 The short-circuited, symmetrically doped *p-n* diode shown in Fig. P7.10 is illuminated by a *distributed source* that generates $g_L = g_o \sin(\pi x/w)$ hole-electron pairs/cm$^3 \cdot$s in the region of $0 \le x \le w$. Assume the following: low-level injection: $w << L_h, w_R << L_e; \mu_e = 4\mu_h; N_a = N_d$.

Make labeled sketches of the following over the range $-w_p \le x \le w_n$.

(*a*) $n'(x)$
(*b*) $J_e(x)$
(*c*) $J_h(x)$
(*d*) Find the *total* short-circuit current of the diode.

7.11 Design an instrument that uses the semiconductor bar shown in Fig. P7.11, with two *p-n* junctions, as part of an accurate position sensor. Although the structure resembles

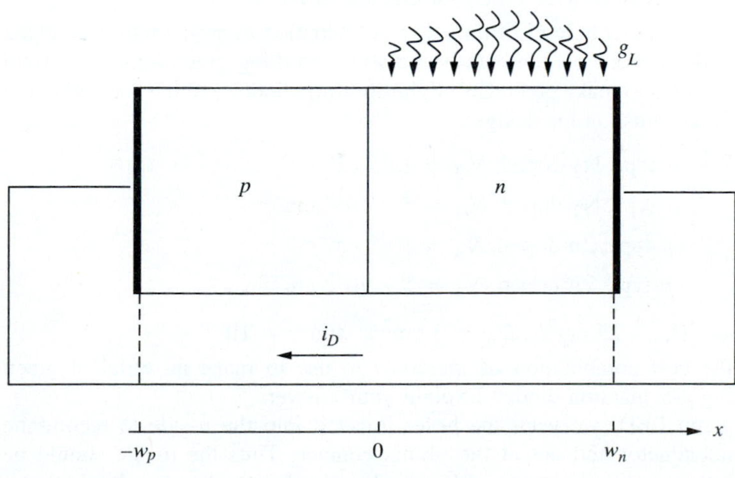

FIGURE P7.10

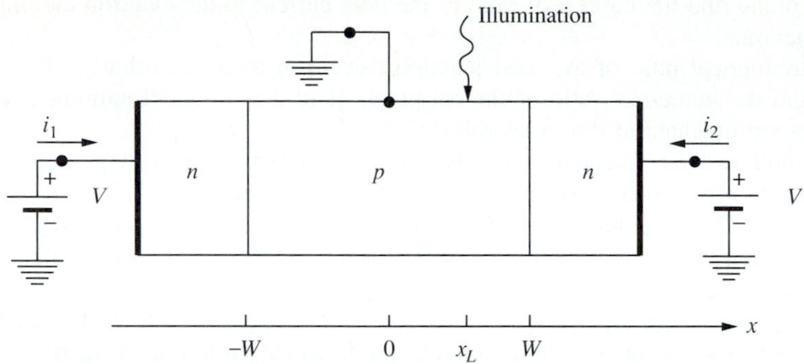

FIGURE P7.11

an *n-p-n* bipolar transistor, both junctions are reverse-biased during operation. The way it works is that a spot of light hits the *p*-region of the sample at position x_L and the two currents i_1 and i_2 are measured. From these two values, the instrument should calculate the value of x_L. The two junctions are a distance $2W$ apart, and for convenience the origin is taken to be midway between the two junctions. Consider only current flow in the *x*-direction.

(*a*) Neglect recombination in the *p*-region. Find i_1 and i_2 as functions of x_L and the number of electron-hole pairs generated per unit time, *M*. You may restrict x_L to be between $-W$ and W.

(*b*) Because the light source generating the illumination has an intensity that cannot be controlled accurately, you have to design the logic in the instrument to find x_L independent of *M*. What equation can you use? (Continue to neglect recombination in the *p*-region.)

(*c*) During production of the instrument, one shipment of semiconductor bars was suspected of having high recombination in the *p*-region. You have asked the quality control engineer to measure i_2 versus x_L; before he returns, you calculate the expected curve for a high-recombination case, where the electron diffusion length in the *p*-region is *W*/5. Plot your calculated curve.

7.12 It has been discovered that hole-electron pair recombination in *n*-type nitrogen-doped gallium phosphide, GaP, is predominantly radiative, emitting green light. A certain device designer wants to make green GaP light-emitting diodes and has the following materials available to use in his design:

$$\begin{aligned} n\text{-type, N}_2\text{-doped}, N_D &= 10^{18}\ \text{cm}^{-3} \\ n\text{-type, N}_2\text{-doped}, N_D &= 5 \times 10^{16}\ \text{cm}^{-3} \\ p\text{-type, Zn-doped}, N_A &= 10^{18}\ \text{cm}^{-3} \\ p\text{-type, Zn-doped}, N_A &= 5 \times 10^{16}\ \text{cm}^{-3} \end{aligned}$$

In each instance, $D_e = 25\ \text{cm}^2/\text{s}$, $D_h = 5\ \text{cm}^2/\text{s}$, and $\tau = 10^{-6}$ s.

(*a*) Which is the best combination of materials to use to make an efficient green light-emitting *p-n* junction diode? Explain your answer.

(*b*) In a GaP green LED, we want the holes injected into the *n*-side to recombine in the semiconductor and not at the ohmic contact. Thus the *n*-side should be much wider than a minority carrier diffusion length. How wide, w_n, should the *n*-

side be to ensure that less than 10 percent of the injected carriers recombine at the contact? GaP is costly, so find a lower limit for the width w_n. Use reasonable approximations.

(*c*) When designing this device, is it better to select the width of the *p*-side so that it operates in the long-base limit or short-base limit, or does it matter? Explain your answer.

(*d*) Consider for the sake of argument a GaP LED that is sufficiently thick that it operates in the long-base limit on both sides of the junction; that is, $|w_p| >> L_e, |w_n| >> L_h$. Assume also that the device is doped as you said it would be in part a above. When the diode is forward-biased, what fraction of the total current is carried by electrons at the following positions in the device and why:

(i) In the depletion region at the junction?
(ii) Inside the semiconductor close to the ohmic contact on the *p*-side?
(iii) Inside the semiconductor close to the ohmic contact on the *n*-side?

7.13 Consider the p^+-n diode illustrated in Fig. P7.13. The *n*-side of this diode is relatively lightly doped (10^{16} cm^{-3}) over the half of its thickness nearest the junction and is more heavily doped (10^{17} cm^{-3}) over the portion nearest the contact. Assume that the low-level injection assumption is valid for the purposes of this question and that the minority carrier diffusion lengths are much greater than w_p and w_n (i.e., that the infinite lifetime assumption is valid).

(*a*) (i) Find the electrostatic potential step $\Delta\phi$ between the lightly doped *n*-region ($0 < x < w_n/2$) and the more heavily doped n^+-region ($w_n/2 < x < w_n$).
(ii) Sketch the electrostatic potential in the vicinity of $x = w_n/2$.

(*b*) (i) Find the equilibrium minority carrier population in the *n*- and n^+-regions.
(ii) Find an expression for the ratio of the equilibrium minority carrier population in the *n*-region to that in the n^+-region in terms of $\Delta\phi$.

(*c*) Assume now that the diode is forward-biased and that excess minority carriers (holes) are injected into the *n*-side of the junction.

(i) Use your result in (ii) of part b above to relate the total population of holes just to the right of $w_n/2$ to that just to the left of $w_n/2$, assuming that the hole population stays in quasiequilibrium with the potential step at $w_n/2$, [i.e., maintains the ratio that you found in (ii) of part b].
(ii) Assuming that the excess minority carrier population $p'(x)$ substantially exceeds the equilibrium minority carrier population $p_o(x)$, find a relationship between the excess population of holes just to the right of $w_n/2$ and that just to the left of $w_n/2$.
(iii) Sketch the excess minority carrier population $p'(x)$ between the edge of the depletion region x_n and the ohmic contact at w_n. The excess minority

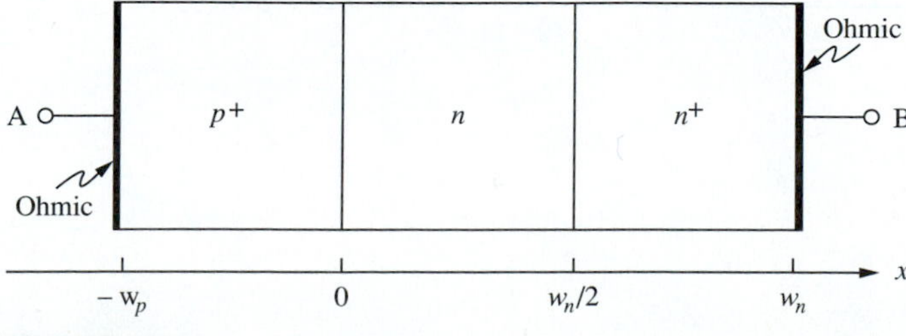

FIGURE P7.13

carrier population at the edge of the depletion region on the n-side of the junction is $n_i^2(e^{qv_{AB}/kT} - 1)/N_{Dn}$. Also remember that the minority carrier diffusion length is much greater than w_n. You should assume that x_n is much less than w_n.

(*d*) Find an expression for the current through this diode, i_D, as a function of the applied voltage v_{AB}.

(*e*) Compare your answer in part d to what you would have obtained if the n-side of this diode was uniformly doped. Use this comparison to find the "effective width" of the n-side of the original diode, where we define the effective width as the width the n-side would have to have in a diode with a uniformly doped n-side and the same hole current density. (Note: The effective width you find should be much greater than w_n.)

7.14 Consider the abrupt, symmetrically doped silicon p-n diode with a n^+-region next to the n-side contact as illustrated in Fig. P7.14. The net doping level on either side of the junction is 5×10^{16} cm^{-3}, and the doping level in the n^+-region is 10^{18} cm^{-3}. The electron and hole mobilities, μ_e and μ_h, are 1600 cm^2/V · s and 640 cm^2/V · s, respectively, and the minority carrier lifetime throughout the device is 10^{-6} s. The instrinsic carrier concentration n_i is 10^{10} cm^{-3}. Assume kT/q is 0.025 V.

(*a*) What is the built-in potential at the p-n junction in this device?

(*b*) Sketch and dimension the electrostatic potential as a function of position in this device for x between -5 μm and $+11$ μm. Do not calculate any depletion region widths.

(*c*) Assume now that the diode is illuminated by light that creates 10^{20} hole-electron pairs/cm^2 · s uniformly across the plane at $x = -5$ μm.

(i) Sketch the excess minority carrier concentration profile as a function of position throughout the device with this illumination.

(ii) What is the short-circuit current through the illuminated diode? Give an answer accurate to ±5%.

(*d*) Repeat (i) and (ii) of part c, assuming that the illumination is now across the plane at $x = +5$ μm rather than at -5 μm.

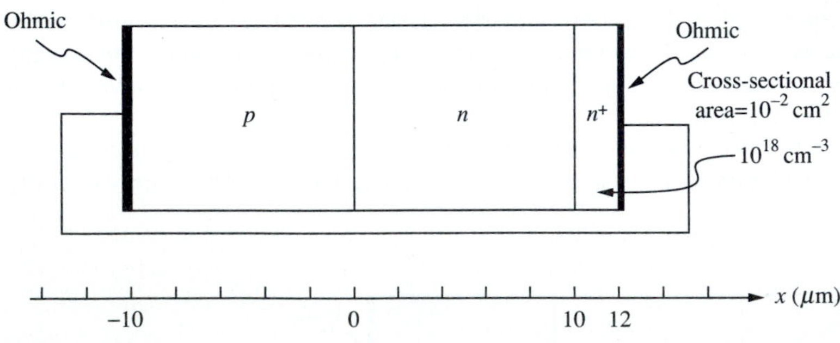

FIGURE P7.14

CHAPTER

8

BIPOLAR JUNCTION TRANSISTORS

Having completed our modeling of the *p-n* junction diode, we now turn our attention to the bipolar junction transistor, or BJT. There are two types of BJTs, *pnp* and *npn*, one structure being simply an *n*-for-*p* and *p*-for-*n* transformation of the other. We will initially focus our attention on the *npn* BJT. After that, treating the *pnp* BJT will be straightforward.

An example of what an *npn* bipolar junction transistor might look like is illustrated in Fig. 8.1. The working "heart" of the device is the portion directly beneath contact E, the *emitter* contact, and extending to the back contact C, the *collector* contact. Contact B represents the *base* contact. This portion of the device is illustrated in Fig. 8.2. This is the structure that we will analyze in this chapter to develop a model for the terminal characteristics of the BJT. Before doing so, however, we will first try to understand qualitatively how this device works.

The BJT can be thought of in several ways. One way is to regard it as two closely spaced and interacting *p-n* junctions which is basically how our model in this chapter will present it. One of these junctions, the *base-collector* junction, is reverse-biased, and its current (the collector current) would normally be negligibly small. In the BJT, however, this junction is very near the second junction, the *emitter-base* junction. If the emitter-base junction is forward-biased, electrons will be injected across it from the emitter *into* the base and *toward* the base-collector junction; the result will be a collector current because these electrons will readily flow across the reverse-biased base-collector junction. Furthermore, the size of this collector current will depend directly on the number of electrons emitted into the base (i.e., on the emitter current), which in turn depends directly on the emitter-base voltage. We thus view the collector current as being controlled by the emitter-base voltage and as being proportional to the emitter current or, equally

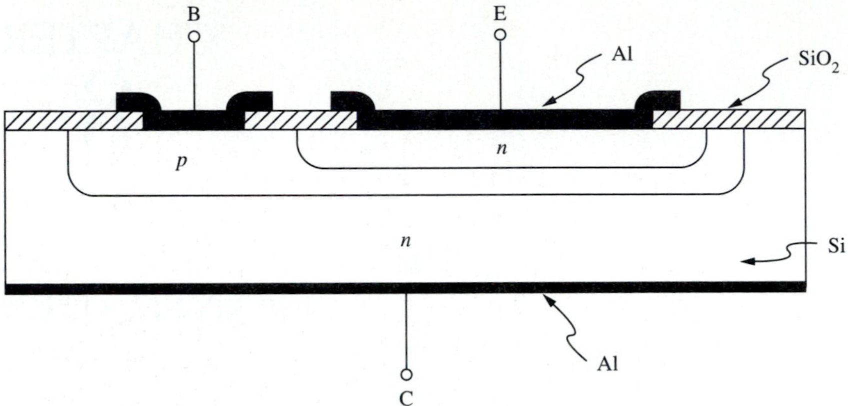

FIGURE 8.1
Cross section of a rudimentary *npn* bipolar transistor fabricated in silicon using a so-called planar process.

well, to the base current (which is the difference between the emitter and collector currents).

Another way to think about an *npn* BJT is as two *n*-type semiconductor regions separated by a *p*-type barrier. A positive bias is applied between one of the *n*-regions, the *emitter*, and the other, the *collector*, so that electrons in the emitter are attracted to the collector. No current flows, though, because the intervening *p*-region, the *base*, blocks the electrons. However, by applying a second bias between the first *n*-region (the emitter) and the *p*-region (the base), the potential barrier to electron flow presented by the base region can be reduced and a current will flow. If things are done correctly, a small change in the base-to-emitter voltage will lead to a large change in the current flowing from the emitter to the collector and the transistor will have appreciable gain. In the bipolar transistor we make electrical contact directly to the middle, current-blocking region of the device and we vary the potential of that region relative to the outer regions directly. Later

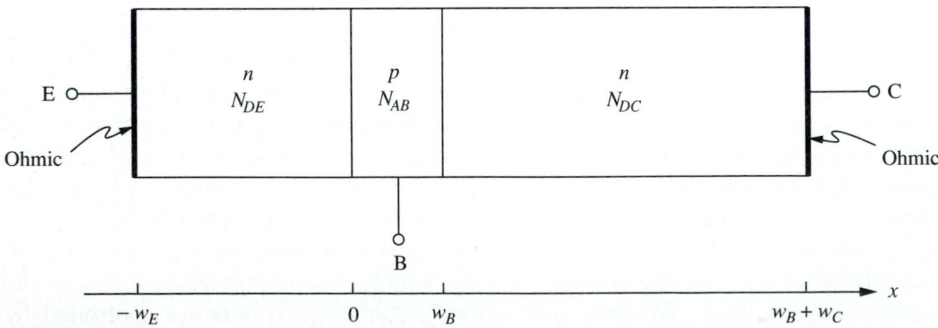

FIGURE 8.2
Quasi-one-dimensional bipolar transistor structure to be used in modeling the device in Fig. 8.1.

(in Chap. 10) we will see another type of device, the field effect transistor, in which we will make capacitive contact to the blocking region. After discussing that device it will be interesting to compare and contrast these two devices.

In this chapter we will begin with a quantitative model for the static relationships between the terminal voltages and currents in the bipolar junction transistor; the model we will develop is called the *Ebers–Moll model*. After discussing this model and its limitations, we will develop several large-signal circuit models for bipolar junction transistors, including models for time-varying signals. We will also develop a variety of linear circuit models for BJTs suitable for describing the response of this device to small-signal variations about a quiescent operating point. The models we develop will vary widely in their complexity and in the assumptions we make in deriving them; one of our goals will be to understand which model to use when. We will conclude this chapter with a look at optically excited BJTs, devices we call phototransistors.

8.1 THE EBERS–MOLL MODEL FOR UNIFORMLY DOPED ONE-DIMENSIONAL BJTS

The heart of the BJT illustrated in Fig. 8.1 is the region under the emitter contact, which can to a large extent be modeled as a quasi-one-dimensional transistor like that illustrated in Fig. 8.2.* The device is composed of three uniformly doped regions—the emitter, base, and collector—with, respectively, doping levels N_{DE}, N_{AB} and N_{DC} and widths w_E, w_B, and w_C, as illustrated in Fig. 8.2. Note that we have added a subscript E, B, or C to indicate that we are dealing with the emitter, base, or collector, respectively. We will also add such a subscript (an E, B, or C) to certain other parameters to denote to which region they pertain. For example, D_{eB} is the electron diffusion constant in the base. Finally, the minority carrier diffusion length in each region is assumed to be much greater than the effective width of that region (e.g., $L_{hE} >> w_E^*$).

We apply arbitrary voltages v_{BE} and v_{BC} to the terminals of the device and ask what the currents i_E and i_C are. That is, we want to determine $i_E(v_{BE}, v_{BC})$ and $i_C(v_{BE}, v_{BC})$. Note that the third current, i_B, is not independent of these two; that is, i_B is $-(i_E + i_C)$. Similarly, the third voltage, v_{CE}, is also not independent; that is, v_{CE} is $v_{BC} - v_{BE}$.

8.1.1 Superposition

It is possible, and not even particularly difficult, to solve this problem directly. Once v_{BE} and v_{BC} are specified, all of the boundary conditions are known and

*We call this device quasi-one-dimensional because the base current, the current into terminal B, must clearly flow in from the side, so the problem cannot be truly one-dimensional. Nonetheless, it is a good first approximation to neglect the lateral resistive voltage drop due to this current, arguing that it will be small over most of the operating range of most transistors.

the corresponding flow problems are all well defined and solvable. However, a much greater understanding of the BJT is obtained if we first break the problem into two pieces by applying one voltage at a time, solve for the resulting currents, and then use superposition to combine the two solutions into the total solution. We thus divide the problem into a "forward" portion in which v_{BE} is applied, with v_{BC} set to zero; and a "reverse" portion in which v_{BC} is applied and v_{BE} is zero.

You should be a bit uncomfortable at this point because we are talking of using superposition in a problem that contains various nonlinearities. To begin with, the boundary conditions are nonlinear functions (exponential) of the junction voltages. Each junction has only one nonzero voltage applied to it, however, so this nonlinearity never becomes an issue and superposition is applicable. A more serious nonlinearity is the dependence of the space charge layer widths and, consequently, the dependence of the quasineutral region widths on the junction voltages. We avoid this problem for now by assuming that we can neglect the space charge layer widths relative to w_E^*, w_B^*, and w_C^* and thus that the quasineutral region widths are unchanged with changing junction bias (i.e., are not functions of v_{BE} and v_{BC}). We will return to this point in Sec. 8.1.5 and discuss how to design a device to ensure that this is a good assumption. We also will see how the device characteristics are affected when this assumption begins to break down.

8.1.2 The Forward Portion ($v_{BC} = 0$)

In the forward problem, we have $v_{BC} = 0$ and want to obtain $i_E(v_{BE}, 0)$, which we label i_{EF}, and $i_C(v_{BE}, 0)$, which we label i_{CF}. The excess minority carrier populations on either side of the base-collector junction are zero because $v_{BC} = 0$. We denote this as $n'(w_B^-) = 0$ and $p'(w_B^+) = 0$, where the + and − superscripts indicate the space charge layer edges on either side of the junction. Furthermore, the excess populations at $x = -w_E$ and at $x = w_B + w_C$ are zero because of the ohmic contacts on the emitter and collector, respectively.

At the emitter-base junction the excess populations are set by v_{EB}. They are

$$p'(0^-) = \frac{n_i^2}{N_{DE}}(e^{qv_{BE}/kT} - 1) \tag{8.1}$$

$$n'(0^+) = \frac{n_i^2}{N_{AB}}(e^{qv_{BE}/kT} - 1) \tag{8.2}$$

Because $L_{hE} \gg w_E$, $L_{eB} \gg w_B$, and $L_{hC} \gg w_C$, we know that the excess minority carrier profiles in the transistor are linear and must look as shown in Fig. 8.3. We can immediately write an expression for the emitter current:

$$i_{EF} = -qA\left[\frac{D_h p'(0^-)}{w_E^*} + \frac{D_e n'(0^+)}{w_B^*}\right] \tag{8.3}$$

where A is the cross-sectional area of the junction. Using Eqs. (8.1) and (8.2), this becomes

$$i_{EF} = -qAn_i^2\left(\frac{D_h}{N_{DE}w_E^*} + \frac{D_e}{N_{AB}w_B^*}\right)(e^{qv_{BE}/kT} - 1) \tag{8.4}$$

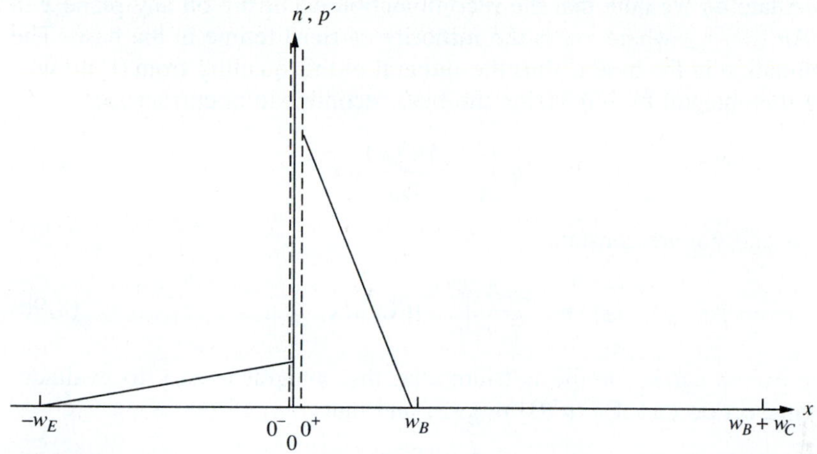

FIGURE 8.3
Excess minority carrier profiles for the device of Fig. 8.2 with $v_{BE} > 0$ and $v_{BC} = 0$.

This current consists of holes flowing from the base into the emitter (the first term in the first parentheses) and electrons flowing from the emitter into the base (the second term). That is,

$$i_{EF} = i_{Fh} + i_{Fe} \tag{8.5a}$$

The emitter electron current i_{Fe} is the most important component of the emitter current in *npn* transistors, and we will focus our attention on it. Referring to Eq. (8.4) we see that i_{Fe} can be written as

$$i_{Fe} = -qAn_i^2 \frac{D_e}{N_{AB} w_B^*} \left(e^{qv_{BE}/kT} - 1\right) \tag{8.6}$$

Using this we can write

$$i_{EF} = i_{Fe}(1 + \delta_E) \tag{8.5b}$$

where δ_E, defined as i_{Fh}/i_{Fe}, is called the *emitter defect*. From Eq. (8.4) we see that

$$\delta_E = \frac{D_h N_{AB} w_B^*}{D_e N_{DE} w_E^*} \tag{8.7}$$

Some of the electrons in i_{Fe} recombine with holes in the base, but the vast majority flow across the base and out the collector. Thus, the collector current can be written as

$$i_{CF} = -i_{Fe}(1 - \delta_B) \tag{8.8}$$

where δ_B represents the fraction of the electrons entering at the emitter that recombine in the base. The term δ_B is called the *base defect*. The product $\delta_B i_{Fe}$ is the *base recombination current*, which we will write as i_{Br}.

To calculate δ_B we note that the recombination occurring on any plane x in the base is $An'(x)/\tau_{eB}$ where τ_{eB} is the minority carrier lifetime in the base. The total recombination in the base is thus the integral of this quantity from 0^+ to w_B^-. Multiplying this integral by $-q$ yields the base recombination current i_{Br}:

$$i_{Br} = -q \int_{0^+}^{w_B^-} \frac{An'(x)}{\tau_{eB}} dx \tag{8.9a}$$

or, because A and τ_{eB} are constants,

$$i_{Br} = -\frac{qA}{\tau_{eB}} \int_{0^+}^{w_B^-} n'(x) dx \tag{8.9b}$$

Because the excess carrier profile is triangular, this integral is easy to evaluate. We find by inspection that it is $n'(0^+)w_B^*/2$, and that

$$i_{Br} \approx -\frac{qA\, n'(0^+)w_B^*}{2\tau_{eB}} \tag{8.9c}$$

Recognizing that $i_{Fe} = -qA\, D_{eB} n'(0^+)/w_B^*$ [see Eqs. (8.3) and (8.5a)] we can write

$$i_{Br} = \frac{w_B^{*2}}{2\, D_{eB}\tau_{eB}} i_{Fe} \tag{8.10}$$

Thus, because $i_{Br} = \delta_B i_{Fe}$, we immediately have

$$\delta_B = \frac{w_B^{*2}}{2\, D_{eB}\tau_{eB}} \tag{8.11a}$$

which can also be written as

$$\delta_B = \frac{w_B^{*2}}{2\, L_{eB}^2} \tag{8.11b}$$

Returning to the terminal currents, we first rewrite Eq. (8.4) as

$$i_{EF} = -I_{ES}\left(e^{qv'_{BE}/kT} - 1\right) \tag{8.12a}$$

where we have defined I_{ES}, the emitter-base diode saturation current, as

$$I_{ES} \equiv qAn_i^2(D_h/N_{DE}w_E^* + D_e/N_{AB}w_B^*) \tag{8.12b}$$

Using Eqs. (8.12) in Eq. (8.6), we find we can write i_{Fe} in terms of i_{EF} and I_{ES} as

$$i_{Fe} = \frac{i_{EF}}{(1+\delta_E)} = \frac{I_{ES}}{(1+\delta_E)}\left(e^{qv_{BE}/kT} - 1\right) \tag{8.6$'$}$$

Combining this result with Eq. (8.8) yields

$$i_{CF} = -\left(\frac{1-\delta_B}{1-\delta_E}\right) i_{EF} = \frac{(1-\delta_B)}{(1+\delta_E)} I_{ES}\left(e^{qv_{BE}/kT} - 1\right) \tag{8.13a}$$

We will write this as

$$i_{CF} = -\alpha_F i_{EF} = \alpha_F I_{ES}\left(e^{qv_{BE}/kT} - 1\right) \tag{8.13b}$$

where we have defined α_F, the forward alpha, as

$$\alpha_F \equiv \frac{(1-\delta_B)}{(1+\delta_E)} \tag{8.14}$$

Note that α_F will be very near to 1 if δ_E and δ_B are small, but it will always be less than 1.

The third current, the forward portion base current i_{BF}, is given by

$$i_{BF} = -i_{EF} - i_{CF} \tag{8.15a}$$

Using Eqs. (8.6) and (8.8), this can be written as

$$i_{BF} = -i_{Fe}(\delta_E + \delta_B) \tag{8.15b}$$

At this point we should consider what these results mean. The three equations we want to examine are Eqs. (8.6), (8.8), and (8.15b), which we collect here:

$$i_{EF} = i_{Fe}(1+\delta_E) \tag{8.6}$$

$$i_{CF} = -i_{Fe}(1-\delta_B) \tag{8.8}$$

$$i_{BF} = -i_{Fe}(\delta_E + \delta_B) \tag{8.15b}$$

The emitter current is made up of electrons flowing from the emitter into the base region, i_{Fe}, and holes flowing from base into the emitter. Equation (8.6) focuses our attention on the emitter electron current, because the electrons are what can lead to collector current. The hole current is "lost," so it is desirable to keep δ_E small. The collector current is the emitter electron current less the electrons that recombine in the base. Clearly we also want to keep δ_B small.

The base current is composed of the holes forming the hole portion of the emitter current, $i_{Fh} = -\delta_E i_{Fe}$, and the holes recombining with electrons in the base, $i_{Br} = -\delta_B i_{Fe}$. By making δ_E and δ_B small, we keep the magnitude of i_{BF} small relative to i_{CF} and i_{EF}.

All of the terminal currents and their various components are represented in Fig. 8.4. You may wish to refer to it and review the preceding discussion before proceeding.

We often write the collector current in terms of the base current and view the base current as the signal, or control, current. We see from Eqs. (8.8) and (8.15b) that i_{CF} and i_{BF} are proportional, and we call the factor of proportionality the forward beta, β_F. We write

$$\beta_F \equiv \frac{i_{CF}}{i_{BF}} \tag{8.16}$$

which we see from Eqs. (8.8) and (8.15b) can be written as

$$\beta_F = \frac{(1-\delta_B)}{(\delta_E + \delta_B)} \tag{8.17a}$$

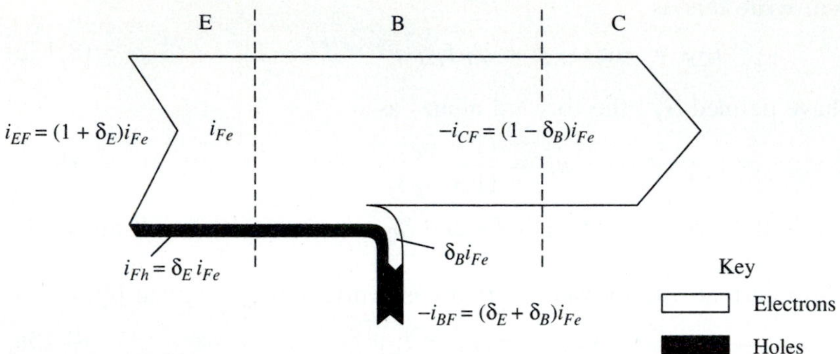

FIGURE 8.4
Schematic representation of the current flux components in an *npn* bipolar transistor with $v_{BE} > 0$ and $v_{BC} = 0$.

β_F is related to α_F as

$$\beta_F = \frac{\alpha_F}{(1 - \alpha_F)} \tag{8.17b}$$

Conversely,

$$\alpha_F = \frac{\beta_F}{(\beta_F + 1)} \tag{8.17c}$$

We note from Eq. (8.17a) that if δ_E and δ_B are small, β_F will be large. This is, of course, entirely consistent with Eq. (8.17b) and our earlier observation that α_F is very near 1 if δ_E and δ_B are small.

Summarizing, for the forward portion of the transistor characteristics, we have

$$i_{EF} = -I_{ES}(e^{qv_{BE}/kT} - 1) \equiv -i_F \tag{8.12'}$$

and

$$i_{CF} = -\alpha_F i_{EF} = a_F i_F \tag{8.13a'}$$

with

$$I_{ES} = qAn_i^2\left(\frac{D_h}{N_{DE}w_E^*} + \frac{D_e}{N_{AB}w_B^*}\right) \tag{8.18}$$

A circuit model that has the same terminal characteristics is illustrated in Fig. 8.5. The diode in this circuit is an ideal exponential diode.

8.1.3 The Reverse Portion ($v_{BE} = 0$)

In the reverse portion of our decomposition of the general terminal characteristics of the BJT, we have $v_{BE} = 0$ and are looking for $i_E(0, v_{BC}) \equiv i_{ER}$ and

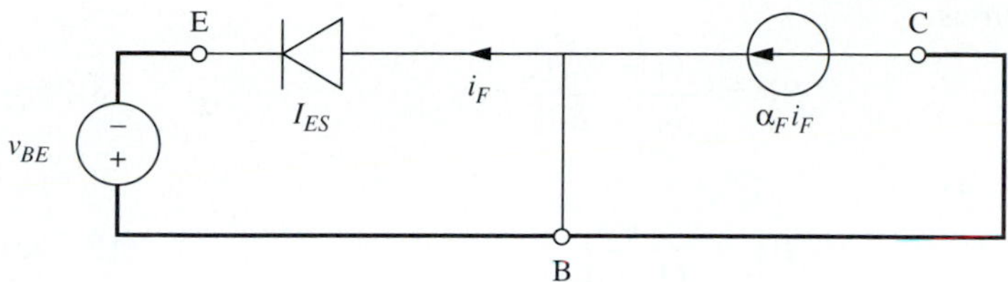

FIGURE 8.5
Circuit representation of the terminal characteristics of an *npn* bipolar transistor with v_{BE} applied and $v_{BC} = 0$.

$i_C(0, v_{BC}) \equiv i_{CR}$. The treatment is exactly analogous to that followed in the forward portion. We find that

$$i_{CR} = -qAn_i^2\left(\frac{D_h}{N_{DC}w_C^*} + \frac{D_e}{N_{AB}w_B^*}\right)(e^{qv_{BC}/kT} - 1) \tag{8.19a}$$

Writing this as

$$i_{CR} = i_{Rh} + i_{Re} \tag{8.19b}$$

we define a collector defect δ_C, as

$$\delta_C \equiv \frac{i_{Rh}}{i_{Re}} \tag{8.20a}$$

From Eq. (8.19a),

$$\delta_C = \frac{D_h N_{AB} w_B^*}{D_e N_{DC} w_C^*} \tag{8.20b}$$

Using Eq. (8.20a) we can write

$$i_{CR} = i_{Re}(1 + \delta_C) \tag{8.21}$$

Also, we find that

$$i_{ER} = -i_{Re}(1 - \delta_B) \tag{8.22}$$

where the base defect δ_B is the same as that defined in Eq. (8.11).

We define a reverse alpha α_R as

$$\alpha_R \equiv -\frac{i_{ER}}{i_{CR}} \tag{8.23}$$

which, using Eqs. (8.21) and (8.22), is

$$\alpha_R = \frac{(1 - \delta_B)}{(1 + \delta_C)} \tag{8.24}$$

We can also define a reverse beta β_R as

$$\beta_R \equiv \frac{i_{ER}}{i_{BR}} \tag{8.25a}$$

which can be written as

$$\beta_R = \frac{(1 - \delta_B)}{(\delta_C + \delta_B)} \tag{8.25b}$$

or, using Eq. (8.24), as

$$\beta_R = \frac{\alpha_R}{(1 - \alpha_R)} \tag{8.25c}$$

To summarize the reverse portion terminal currents, we have

$$i_{CR} = -I_{CS}(e^{qv_{BC}/kT} - 1) \tag{8.26}$$

with

$$I_{CS} = qAn_i^2[\frac{D_h}{N_{DC}w_C^*} + \frac{D_e}{N_{AB}w_B^*}] \tag{8.27}$$

and

$$i_{ER} = -\alpha_R i_{CR} = \alpha_R i_R = \alpha_R I_{CS}(e^{qv_{BC}/kT} - 1) \tag{8.28}$$

An equivalent circuit for the reverse portion is shown in Fig. 8.6. Notice in this figure that for convenience we have defined a new current i_R, which we have taken to be $-i_{CR}$.

8.1.4. Full Solution: The Ebers–Moll Model

Having solved for the current-voltage relationships at the terminals, first with only v_{BE} applied and then with only v_{BC} applied, we are now ready to use superposition to obtain the terminal characteristics when both v_{BE} and v_{BC} are implied. We simply add the currents to get

$$i_E = i_{EF} + i_{ER}$$

Using Eqs. (8.12) and (8.28) we arrive at

$$i_E(v_{BE}, v_{BC}) = -I_{ES}(e^{qv_{BE}/kT} - 1) + \alpha_R I_{CS}(e^{qv_{BC}/kT} - 1) \tag{8.29a}$$

Similarly,

$$i_C = i_{CF} + i_{CR}$$

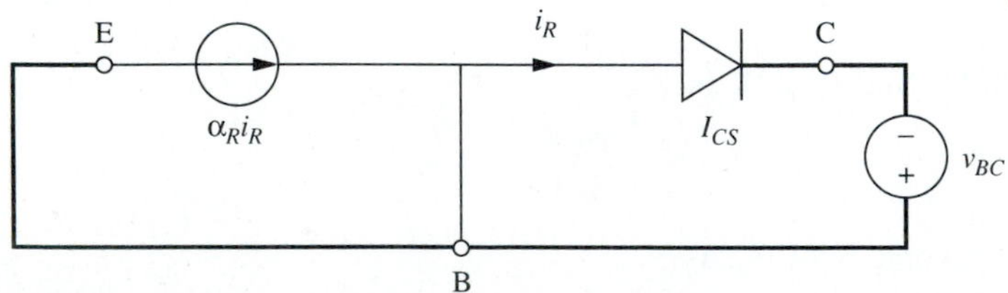

FIGURE 8.6
Circuit representation of the terminal characteristics of an *npn* bipolar transistor with v_{BC} applied and $v_{BE} = 0$.

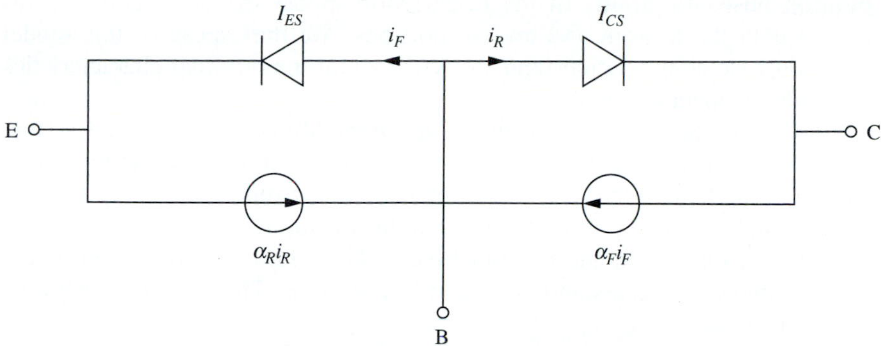

FIGURE 8.7
Circuit representation of the Ebers–Moll model equations for the *npn* bipolar transistor.

which, using Eqs. (8.13) and (8.26), is

$$i_C(v_{BE}, v_{BC}) = \alpha_F I_{ES}(e^{qv_{BE}/kT} - 1) - I_{CS}(e^{qv_{BC}/kT} - 1) \tag{8.29b}$$

Equations (8.29a) and (8.29b) represent the Ebers–Moll model for the bipolar junction transistor. The circuit representation is shown in Fig. 8.7. This circuit is often referred to as the Ebers–Moll model of the bipolar transistor, although, of course, the model also includes the assumptions and approximations that went into developing it.

The four parameters in the Ebers–Moll model are not all independent. Using our earlier expressions it is easy to show that

$$\alpha_F I_{ES} = \alpha_R I_{CS} \tag{8.30}$$

That this be true is required by reciprocity, one of the properties of realizable systems.

8.1.5 Characteristics and Operating Regions

Now that we have obtained expressions for the terminal characteristics of a BJT, we should see what these characteristics look like and consider what they can teach us about how best to use this device. The BJT is a three-terminal device. We usually view it as a two-port network that has one terminal in common with both the input and output ports. We did this when we derived the Ebers–Moll model, for example; we took the base to be the common terminal, but we also could have selected the emitter or collector, although the latter is of little interest. We will look in this section at characteristics for two modes of operation, *common-base* and *common-emitter*.

We also have choices to make with respect to the terminal variables (i.e., currents and voltages). We must choose which variables will be dependent and which will be independent. In the Ebers–Moll model, for example, we took the emitter and collector currents to be dependent on the base-emitter and base-collector voltages. We will consider other possibilities below.

a) Common-base operation. In the Ebers–Moll model the base terminal was common to both the forward and reverse portions. We thus speak of this model as a common-base configuration, and we will look at the terminal characteristics for this mode of operation first.

Consider first the collector current. The Ebers–Moll expressions tell us that it is composed of two components: the base-collector exponential diode current and a fraction of the emitter-base exponential diode current. These two components are plotted as a function of the base-collector voltage v_{BC} and for several values of v_{BE} in Figs. 8.8*a* and *b*, respectively. The total collector current is the sum of these two components and is plotted in Fig. 8.8*c*. This plot represents the

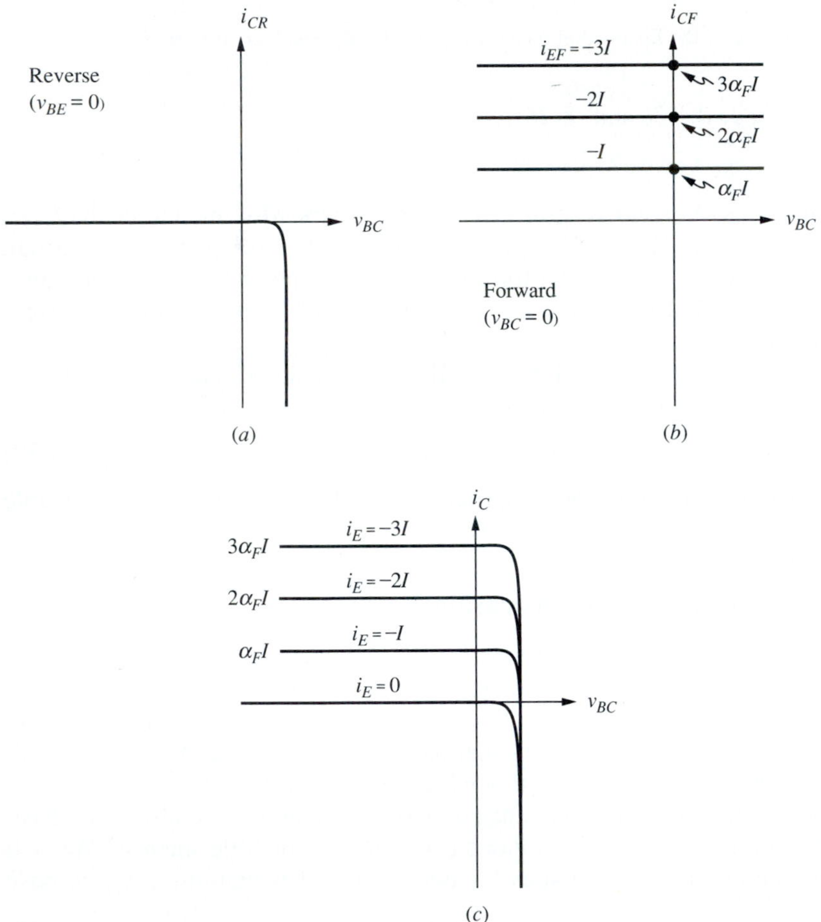

FIGURE 8.8
Common-base output characteristics of an *npn* BJT: (*a*) the base-collector exponential diode characteristic; (*b*) the collector current due to the base-emitter diode current for several values of v_{BE} chosen to give linear increments in i_E; (*c*) the total collector current.

common-base output characteristic because the base terminal is common to both of the voltage parameters, v_{BC} and v_{BE}, and because the collector terminal is commonly thought of as the output terminal, whereas in this case the emitter terminal is viewed as the input terminal.

We indicated above that the families of curves in Fig. 8.8 were created by varying v_{BE}, which strictly speaking is true. However, it makes much more sense to think of varying i_E to create a family because i_C depends linearly on i_E over a substantial range (i.e., $i_C \approx -\alpha_F i_E$ when $v_{BC} < 0$). In contrast, i_E, and thus i_C, depend exponentially on v_{BE}, and exponential dependences are awkward to work with; it is much easier to deal with linear variations. Thus families of curves such as those in Fig. 8.8*c* are presented with i_E rather than v_{BE} as the input parameter. Mathematically, we think in terms of $i_C(i_E, v_{BC})$, rather than $i_C(v_{BE}, v_{BC})$.

The common-base input characteristic (i.e., i_E versus v_{BE}, with i_C or v_{BC} as a parameter) is identical in shape to the output characteristic. It does, however, differ quantitatively to the extent that I_{ES} and I_{CS}, and α_F and α_R differ in magnitude. Examples of both characteristics are illustrated in Figs. 8.9*a* and *b*. (Notice that the horizontal axes are $-v_{BE}$ and $-v_{BC}$. This differs from Fig. 8.8 and is a more common way of plotting these curves.)

Although the common-base input and output characteristics look similar, it is important to realize that we normally operate BJTs using different regions on each characteristic. That is, we normally operate with the emitter-base junction forward-biased ($v_{BE} > 0$) in the present *npn* example and with the base-collector junction reverse-biased ($v_{BC} < 0$). Thus we operate in the first quadrant of the output characteristics, Fig. 8.9*b*, and in the third quadrant of the input characteristics, Fig. 8.9*a*. Notice that for input characteristics we do not change the independent variables from v_{BE} and v_{BC} to v_{BE} and i_C. Because we usually use the BJT with the base-collector junction reverse-biased, i_C is very small and has less meaning

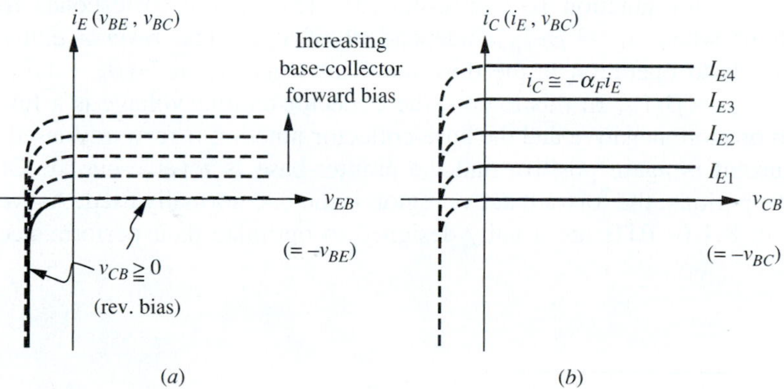

FIGURE 8.9
Input and output families of common-base characteristics for a BJT: (*a*) the input family; (*b*) the output family. (The normal operating region in each set of characteristics is indicated by the solid curves.)

than v_{BC}, which is useful for calculating the base-collector junction depletion capacitance.* In any event, the input characteristic of a good device is essentially independent of the output variable, whether i_C or v_{BC}.

In summary, to operate the BJT in the common-base mode, we first establish an emitter diode current i_E by adjusting the input voltage v_{BE}; the output current i_C will then essentially match this input current independent of the output voltage v_{BC} as long as the base-collector junction is kept reverse-biased. In this operating region, the output current tracks the input current.

Note that we could also consider operating this device with the emitter-base junction reverse-biased and the collector-base junction forward-biased, in which case the collector would be used as the input and the emitter as the output (i.e., $iE \approx -\alpha_R i_C$). However, as we shall see in Sec. 8.1.6, α_F is usually much closer to 1 than α_R is, so this alternative biasing arrangement is clearly less attractive.

b) Common-emitter operation. A second important mode of operating a BJT is common-emitter operation, for which the output is taken from the collector-emitter pair and the input is applied to the base. If we use the Ebers–Moll expressions to calculate the common-emitter characteristics, we obtain the plots shown in Fig. 8.10. The input family of characteristics is i_B as a function of v_{BE} and v_{CE}, and the output family is i_C as a function of i_B and v_{CE}. The voltage applied to the base can also be considered the input control signal, but the best choice for the output control parameter is the base current i_B. This is so because when v_{CE} is more than a few tenths of a volt positive, i_C is essentially $\beta_F i_B$, and when it is negative, i_C is $-(\beta_R + 1)i_B$. These dependences are indicated in Fig. 8.10.

There are several different regions for the output characteristics of Fig. 8.10*b*. First, there are the active regions, which are the regions where the output currents are proportional to i_B. The *forward active* region corresponds to operation with the base-emitter junction forward-biased so that the base current is positive and with the collector-emitter voltage a few tenths of a volt positive (in which case the base-collector junction is reverse-biased). This region corresponds to the first quadrant where $i_C \approx \beta_F i_B$, independent of v_{CE}. The *reverse active* region corresponds to operation in the third quadrant where i_C is $-(\beta_R + 1)i_B$, or equivalently, $i_E \approx \beta_R i_B$. In this region, the collector-emitter voltage is a few tenths of a volt or more negative and the base-collector junction is forward-biased, so the base current is again positive and the emitter-base is reverse-biased. Of these two active regions, the forward active region is the one normally used. As we shall see in Sec. 8.1.6, BJTs are usually designed to optimize their performance in this region.

---

*As a useful rule of thumb, when a *p-n* junction is forward-biased on we usually care most about the *current* through it because that is what varies over a wide range (i.e., the voltage stays within a tenth of a volt or so of 0.6 V). For a reverse-biased *p-n* junction, the *voltage* across it is of more interest because the current through a reverse-biased diode is largely independent of the junction voltage.

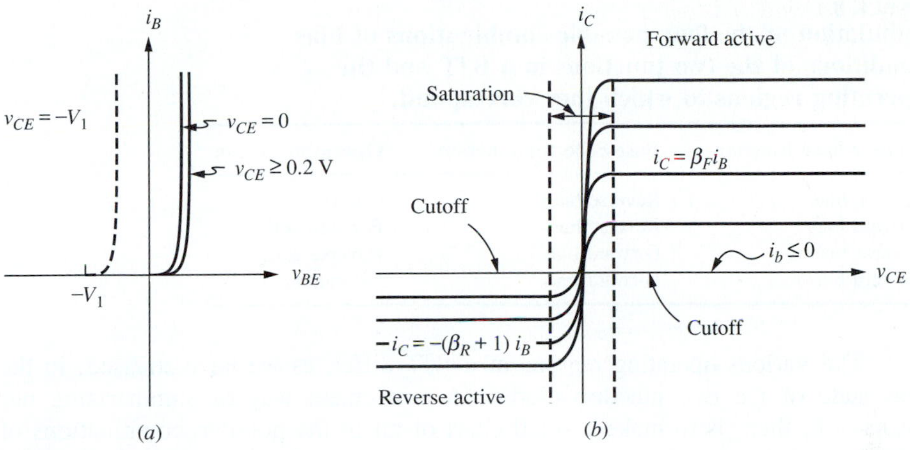

FIGURE 8.10
Common-emitter characteristics, with the various regions of operation indicated: (*a*) input family (the dashed curve shows a representative input curve for v_{CE} negative); (*b*) output family.

The input characteristics for a BJT biased in the forward active region (see Fig. 8.10*a*) are those of the base-emitter diode and are largely independent of v_{CE}, as long as v_{CE} is greater than a few tenths of a volt positive. This corresponds to having the base-collector junction either reverse-biased or at least not sufficiently forward-biased to be conducting. (Notice that the bias across the base-collector junction, v_{BC}, is the base-emitter voltage v_{BE} minus v_{CE}, so even a small positive v_{CE} is enough to ensure that the base-collector junction is off.)

Another important region on the BJT characteristics is where i_B is zero or negative (in an *npn* device). This region is called *cutoff* and corresponds to the portion of the characteristics in Fig. 8.10*b* along the horizontal axis where i_C and i_E are extremely small. In this region both junctions are either reverse-biased or not sufficiently forward-biased to be turned on.

Finally, the region on the BJT characteristics in the vicinity of the vertical axis where it is no longer true that the output current is proportional to i_B and independent of v_{CE} is called the *saturation* region. In this region both of the junctions in the BJT are forward biased. They need not be forward-biased to an extent that they strongly conduct, but they must be forward-biased enough that they conduct somewhat (e.g., 0.4 V in silicon devices).

The cutoff and saturation regions often represent the limits of operating a BJT as a switch (an application we will study in Chap. 15). A cutoff BJT looks at its output like an open switch; a saturated BJT looks like a closed switch. If, on the other hand, we want to use a BJT as a linear amplifier (the topic of Chaps. 11 through 14), we will operate it in the forward active region. We seldom operate in the reverse active region because β_R is typically much smaller than β_F in a well-designed BJT.

TABLE 8.1
Tabulation of the four possible combinations of bias conditions of the two junctions in a BJT and the operating regions to which they correspond.

Emitter-base junction	Base-collector junction	Operating region
Reverse bias	Reverse bias	Cutoff
Forward bias	Reverse bias	Forward active
Reverse bias	Forward bias	Reverse active
Forward bias	Forward bias	Saturation

The various operating regions of a BJT differ, as we have stressed, in the bias state of the two junction diodes. A convenient way of summarizing our discussion, then, is to make a small chart of all of the possible combinations of forward and reverse biases on the junctions and identify each combination with an operating region. This is illustrated in Table 8.1.

Another useful way to solidify our understanding of the operating regions is to sketch the excess minority carrier profiles through a BJT biased in each of the four regions. An example of such a set of plots is shown in Fig. 8.11. In addition to helping you visualize what is happening in the device in each of the four regions and developing your BJT intuition, these plots will also have practical significance when we discuss how quickly transistors can be switched from one operating region to another (as we shall do in Chap. 16). The excess charge distributions change a great deal in going from one region of operation to another, and the charge making up these excess distributions has to be supplied or removed in the process of switching. The amount of charge that has to be supplied or removed will determine how quickly the switching will occur.

8.1.6 Basic Transistor Design

We now turn our attention to what the Ebers–Moll model can teach about designing a better transistor. Consider first the defects we defined in developing that model. Judging from their names, one would guess that it is desirable to keep the defects, δ_E, δ_B, and δ_C, small when designing a bipolar transistor. We will see now that we can indeed structure a device to keep δ_E and δ_B small, but we will also see that we obtain better device characteristics if we don't insist on making δ_C small.

The base defect δ_B [Eq. (8.11a)] will be small if w_B is much less than L_{hB}, which was actually one of our initial assumptions. As a consequence of this requirement, BJTs are constructed with narrow base regions, that is, with w_B from 0.1 to 1.0 μm. One limit on making w_B small is the lateral resistance of this layer. Recall that we have neglected any voltage drop due to the base current flowing in from the side (see Fig. 8.1). In very thin-base devices, this voltage drop may no longer be negligible when the base current becomes large, which can severely limit the operation of the BJT at high current levels. Another limit on w_B is our assumption that the junction depletion widths and their variation with

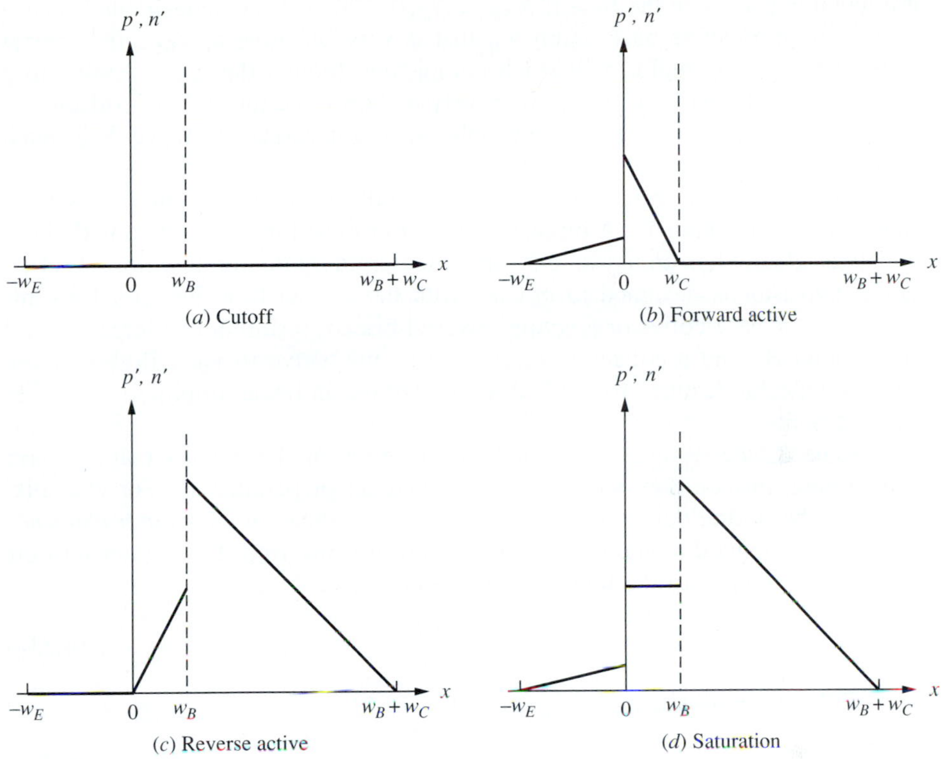

FIGURE 8.11
Minority carrier profiles through a BJT biased in (*a*) cutoff, (*b*) the forward active region, (*c*) the reverse active region, and (*d*) saturation. (It is assumed that the doping level in the base is one-fifth of that in the emitter and twice that in the collector. The same forward bias level is assumed in all cases.)

v_{EB} and v_{CB} are negligible with respect to w_B. The smaller the value of w_B, the weaker this assumption.

The emitter defect δ_E [Eq. (8.7)] depends on many parameters, but the most important are the emitter and base doping levels. Clearly it is desirable to have N_{DE} much greater than N_{AB}, so silicon BJTs are fabricated with the emitter much more heavily doped than the base. The device designer has less flexibility in the other factors that affect δ_E. The ratio of D_h to D_e is set by the material; in fact, in an *npn* it is less than 1, which is one reason to favor an *npn* over a *pnp*. The ratio of w_B^* to w_E^* is restricted to be in the range of 2 to 5, typically, because of the practical problems of fabricating a device with a thick w_E and of keeping L_h large in heavily doped material.

The collector defect δ_C [Eq. (8.20b)] is a function similar to δ_E. It can be made small by making N_{DC} much greater than N_{AB}, but this leads to a problem. BJTs normally operate with the base-collector junction reverse-biased, but the depletion region increases with reverse bias, primarily into the lightly doped side of a junction (i.e., into the base if $N_{AB} < N_{DC}$). This is very undesirable because it leads to an effective base width w_B^* that is very sensitive to v_{BC}. In extreme cases, the depletion region will reach completely through the base, leading to a condition called *punch-through*, effectively a short-circuiting of the collector to the emitter. In order to avoid these problems, it is necessary to make N_{AB} much greater than N_{DC}.

With N_{AB} much greater than N_{DC}, δ_C will be large and thus β_R will be small (in fact, less than 1). A bipolar transistor designed in accordance with these guidelines clearly has an asymmetry and a preferred operating direction. That is, such a transistor is designed to operate with the emitter-base junction forward-biased and the base-collector junction reversed-biased, resulting in a large forward current gain β_F and a collector current that is insensitive to v_{BC}. Both of these are very desirable features for BJTs designed for use in linear amplifiers and other analog circuits.

Some device designers do not think in terms of the defects that we have defined here; instead they use a closely related set of parameters. For example, instead of the emitter defect δ_E, we can equivalently speak of the *emitter efficiency* γ_E, which is defined as the ratio of the current flowing from the emitter into the base, i_{Fe} in an *npn*, to the total emitter current, i_{EF}:

$$\gamma_E \equiv \frac{i_{Fe}}{i_{EF}} \tag{8.31a}$$

This can be written in terms of δ_E using Eq. (8.6).

$$\gamma_E = \frac{1}{1 + \delta_E} \tag{8.31b}$$

Clearly if we want the emitter defect δ_E to be as small as possible, we also want the emitter efficiency γ_E to be as close to 1 as possible.

In a similar spirit, some designers also define a *base transport factor* γ_B as the fraction of the minority carriers injected from the emitter into the base, i_{Ee}, that flows into the collector, $-i_{CF}$:

$$\gamma_B \equiv -\frac{i_{CF}}{i_{Ee}} \tag{8.32a}$$

Using Eq. (8.8) we find that, in terms of δ_B, γ_B is

$$\gamma_B = 1 - \delta_B \tag{8.32b}$$

Again it is clear that this is a factor we want to design to be as close to 1 as possible.

When written in terms of γ_E and γ_B, the forward alpha α_F takes on a particularly simple form:

$$\alpha_F = \gamma_E \gamma_B \tag{8.33a}$$

whereas β_F is a bit more complicated:

$$\beta_F = \frac{\gamma_E \gamma_B}{1 - \gamma_E \gamma_B} \tag{8.33b}$$

From both expressions, the desirability of keeping γ_E and γ_B as close as possible to 1 is clear.

Example

Question. Consider a silicon *npn* transistor, similar in structure to the device pictured in Fig. 8.2, with the following dimensions and properties. The emitter, base, and collector dopings—N_{DE}, N_{AB}, and N_{DC}—are 5×10^{17} cm^{-3}, 1×10^{16} cm^{-3}, and $1x10^{15}$ cm^{-3}, respectively. The effective widths of the emitter, base, and collector—w_E^*, w_B^*, and w_C^*—are 1 μm, 0.25 μm, and 5 μm, respectively. The electron and hole diffusion coefficients are 40 cm^2/s and 15 cm^2/s, respectively. The minority carrier lifetime in the base is 1 μs. The device is at room temperature, and n_i = 1×10^{10} cm^{-3}. What are the defects, δ_E, δ_B, and δ_C; what are the emitter efficiency and base transport factor, γ_E and γ_B; and what are the forward and reverse alphas, α_F and α_R? Also, what are the forward and reverse betas, β_F and β_R? Finally, what are the emitter and collector saturation current densities, J_{ES} and J_{CS}?

Discussion. We calculate the defects first, using Eqs. (8.7), (8.11), and (8.20b), and find that δ_E is 2×10^{-3}, δ_B is 8×10^{-6}, and δ_C is 0.2. We find that γ_E is 0.998 and γ_B is 0.999992 (or, for all practical purposes, 1, because it is much closer to 1 than is γ_E). Notice that the base defect is very small; this is a very typical result in modern, narrow-base transistors.

Using the defects to calculate the forward and reverse alphas, we find that α_F is 0.998 and α_R is 0.83. The corresponding forward and reverse betas, β_F and β_R, are 500 and 5, respectively. As we anticipated because of the device asymmetry, the reverse gain is much lower than the forward gain. Notice also that the forward beta is dominated by the emitter defect, consistent with the very small base defect.

Finally, we calculate the emitter and collector saturation current densities, J_{ES} and J_{CS}, to be 1.25×10^{-9} A/cm^2, and 1.5×10^{-9} A/cm^2, respectively.

8.1.7 Beyond Ebers–Moll: Limitations of the Model

The model we have presented for the bipolar junction transistor is very simple. Therefore, although it does a remarkable job of describing the BJT and illuminates many of the basic issues in BJT design, it does neglect many effects. These effects tend to be important not so much in the normal forward active region of the device but rather in setting the limits on what the normal operating region of a given structure is. We will next look briefly at the following issues: (1) base width modulation, (2) punch-through, (3) base-collector junction breakdown, (4) space charge layer recombination, (5) high level injection, (6) emitter crowding, (7) series resistances, and (8) nonuniform doping profiles.

a) Base width modulation. In a transistor in which N_{AB} is greater than N_{DC}, operating in the forward active region, the depletion region width on the base side of the base-collector junction varies very little with v_{CB} (but it does vary some) and w_B^* decreases with increasing $|v_{CB}|$. Consequently, δ_B and δ_E also both decrease and β_F increases. This leads to a fanning out of the transistor output family of characteristics, as illustrated in Fig. 8.12. [The effect is severe in this

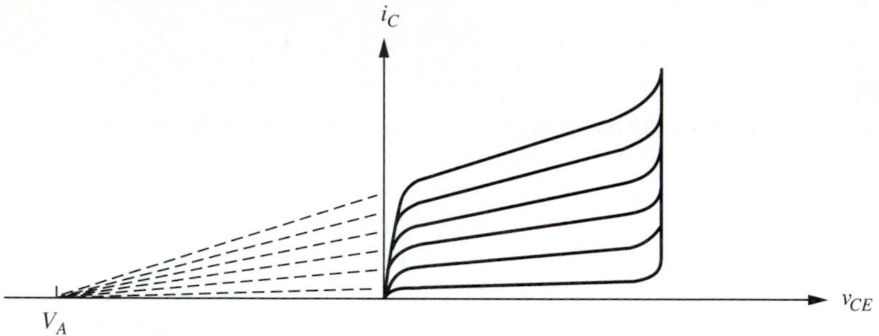

FIGURE 8.12
Output characteristics of a bipolar transistor with severe base width modulation, or Early effect. As indicated, the Early effect in a device is often characterized by extrapolating the curves back to a common voltage point on the voltage axis; this voltage V_A is called the Early voltage of the device.

figure; devices can be made (by heavily doping the base, for example) in which base width modulation is barely observable in the characteristics.]

b) Punch-through. Punch-through is the extreme case of base width modulation where the base-collector junction space charge layer reaches through to the emitter and w_B^* goes to zero. At this point the collector current increases uncontrollably and all transistor action is lost. This is in itself not a destructive process, but if the current is not limited by the circuit in which the transistor is being used, the device may be destroyed by excessive Joule (i^2R) heating.

c) Base-collector junction breakdown. The base-collector junction will eventually break down as its reverse bias is increased further and further. Once this happens, all control over the collector current is again lost and the transistor is no longer useful.

Both punch-through and base-collector junction breakdown appear in the transistor characteristics as a sharp, essentially i_B-independent increase in i_C at some critical v_{BC} (or v_{CE}); the characteristic of a device displaying base-collector junction break-down is shown in Fig. 8.13. Neither process is in and of itself destructive, but any resulting excessive device heating can be.

In most devices junction breakdown will be the determining factor in setting the maximum voltage rating of a transistor. Thus, in designing a transistor to have a certain voltage rating, the doping of the collector is chosen to be just low enough that the junction breakdown voltage exceeds the desired rating. Making the doping level any lower needlessly increases the resistance of the collector region. Similarly, the thickness of the collector is made only large enough to accommodate the depletion region at the maximum reverse bias. Making it any thicker again adds needless resistance, whereas making it thinner will reduce the breakdown voltage.

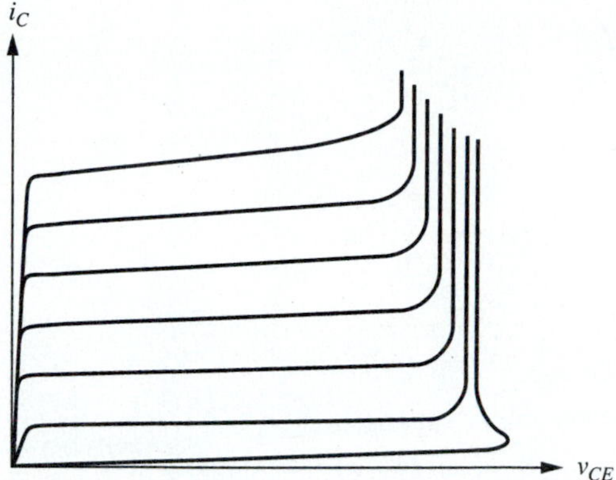

FIGURE 8.13
Output characteristics of a bipolar junction transistor showing base-collector junction breakdown at large v_{CE}.

d) Space-charge layer recombination. At low forward biases, the emitter-base junction current may have an appreciable component of space-charge layer recombination current and the emitter defect will appear to be much greater than it is in the region where the current is limited by diffusion. Thus α_F and β_F will be smaller at low current levels. If we plot β_F (obtained by measuring i_C and i_B and calculating i_C/i_B) as a function of i_C, a typical variation might look like that in Fig. 8.14 (we will discuss the high-current decrease in β_F in the next section).

Another type of plot that is often used to see this effect is called a *Gummel plot*. In a Gummel plot, the collector and base currents, i_C and i_B, on a log scale are graphed versus the base-emitter voltage v_{BE} on a linear scale. An example is shown in Fig. 8.15, where the dashed straight lines represent the ideal exponential behavior and the solid curve is the measured data. Since both i_C and i_B are plotted

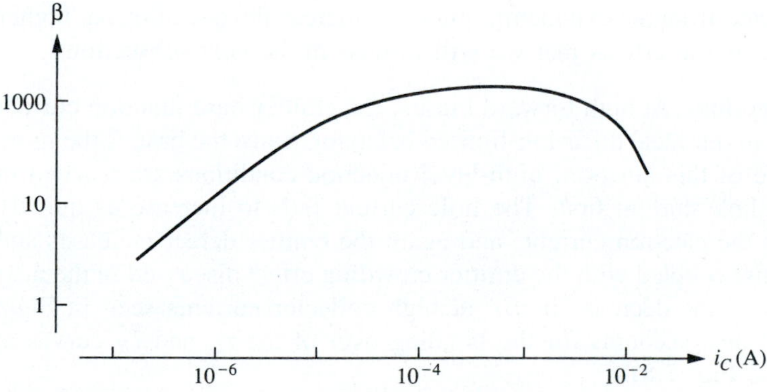

FIGURE 8.14
Typical variation of β_F with collector current level.

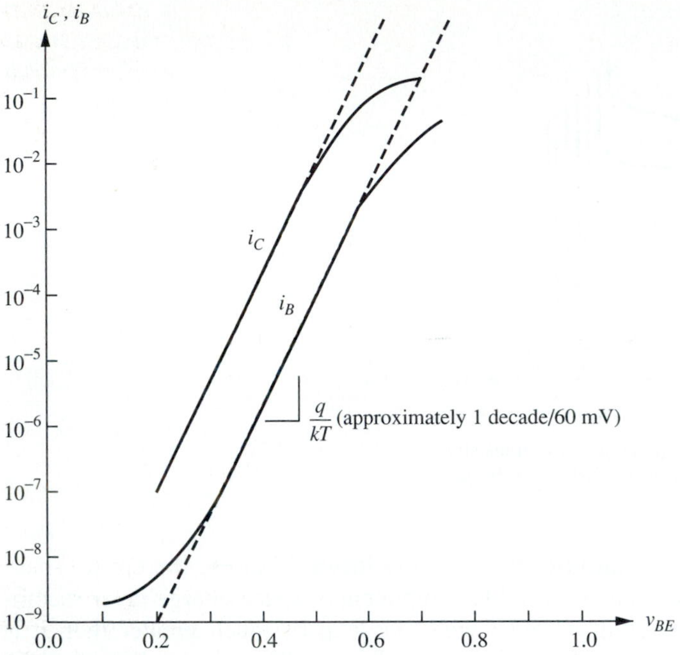

FIGURE 8.15
Gummel plot of the collector and base currents versus the base-emitter voltage on a log-linear scale. The effects of space-charge layer recombination at low current levels and of high-level injection and series resistance at high current levels are clearly seen as deviations from the ideal (dashed) curves.

on a log scale their ratio β_F is proportional to the vertical distance between these two curves. The curves move closer together at high and low values of i_C (and, equivalently, v_{BE}), showing the same β_F decrease as in Fig. 8.14. The effects of space-charge layer recombination are evident at low v_{BE}, where the base current is higher than expected from the exponential model; whereas the deviations at higher values of v_{BE} are due to effects that we will discuss in the next subsections.

e) High-level injection. At high forward biases, the emitter-base junction current again deviates from our ideal diffusion-limited behavior. Since the base is the more lightly doped side of this junction, high-level injection conditions are reached in the base and the hole current first. The hole current fails to increase as quickly with v_{EB} as does the electron current, and again the emitter defect increases and β_F decreases. This, coupled with the emitter crowding effect discussed in the next subsection, leads to the decrease in β_F at high collector currents seen in Figs. 8.14 and 8.15. It also accounts for the bending over of the i_C and i_B curves at high v_{BE} (see also Fig. 7.8).

f) Emitter crowding. Based on the above discussion, it might seem that to make a higher-current transistor we can simply make a device with a larger-area emitter-base junction, but simply increasing the junction area does not work. Rather, it is the perimeter that must be increased. The problem lies in the fact that at high current levels there will be appreciable lateral voltage drop in the base region because of the resistance of the base layer. Thus the amount of forward bias on the emitter-base junction will decrease as one moves under the base region away from the outer edge. Since the amount of bias is small to begin with (i.e., 0.6 to 0.7 V in a silicon transistor) and the current is an exponential function of the bias, the inner portions of the emitter-base junction will not even be turned on if there is more than 0.1 or 0.2 V of lateral resistive voltage drop. Only the edges will be active. This effect is called *emitter crowding*. The emitter current is essentially crowded to the outside edges, the periphery, of the junction at high levels, so the junction perimeter rather than the total junction area determines the high-current performance. For this reason power transistors are designed with an emitter composed of many thin fingers, each sufficiently narrow that no part of the junction is more than a few microns from the thicker base contact region.

g) Series resistances. In the Ebers–Moll model, resistive voltage drops in the quasineutral regions are neglected. At high current levels, particularly, the resistance of the quasineutral region in the collector, as well as the sheet resistance of the base, must be taken into account. We have already discussed the design of the collector region to minimize the collector resistance and the role of the base resistance in limiting the transistor current. We will do nothing further with these resistances in our large-signal modeling of the BJT, but we will have more to say about them when we discuss incremental transistor models.

h) Nonuniform doping profiles. Uniformly doped emitter and base regions are rarely encountered in bipolar transistors, and the assumption of uniform N_E and N_B made during the development of the Ebers–Moll model does not really apply to many actual devices. Fortunately, it turns out to be relatively simple to account quite accurately for the nonuniform doping and "fix" the model. Where the products $N_E w_E^*$ and $N_B w_B^*$ appear in the Ebers–Moll expressions, we replace them, respectively, with

$$\int_{-w_E}^{0^-} N_E(x)dx$$

and

$$\int_{0^+}^{w_B^*} N_B(x)dx$$

These are simply the total doping concentrations per unit area in the emitter and base layers, respectively.

Nonuniformly doped regions and many of the other limitations in the Ebers–Moll model that we have pointed out are incorporated into the Gummel–Poon model for the bipolar transistor, which is the next step in sophistication past Ebers–Moll in large-signal modeling.

8.2 CIRCUIT MODELS FOR BIPOLAR JUNCTION TRANSISTORS

The Ebers–Moll equations describe the large-signal terminal characteristics of an ideal, quasi-one-dimensional bipolar junction transistor. We have seen that they can be conveniently represented by a circuit composed of ideal exponential diodes and dependent current sources (i.e., Fig. 8.7). Using this representation as a starting point we now want to develop models we can use in circuit analysis.

8.2.1 Large-Signal Models

The Ebers–Moll equations will be our starting point in developing large-signal circuit models for bipolar junction transistors. We will also go beyond that model and introduce the basic elements of the Gummel–Poon model as well. We will also add nonlinear charge stores to the model as a first step in analyzing the responses of BJTs to rapidly time-varying inputs.

a) Static models based on Ebers–Moll. The circuit representation of the Ebers–Moll equations in Fig. 8.7, which we repeat here in Fig. 8.16*a*, is our basic model for the terminal characteristics of a bipolar junction transistor. It is particularly

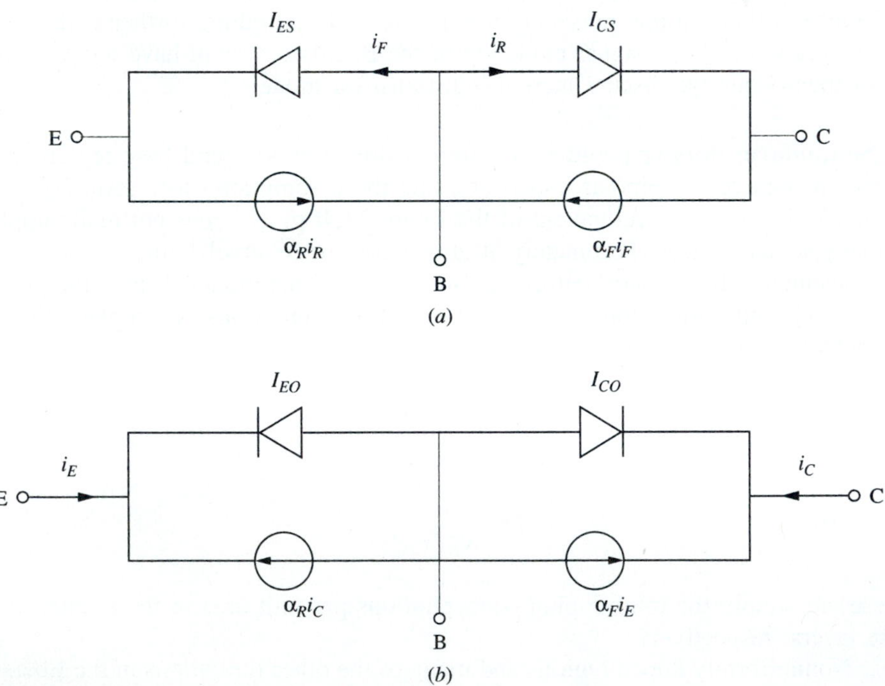

FIGURE 8.16
Circuit representations of the *npn* transistor Ebers–Moll model equations configured for use when (*a*) the terminal voltages are known; (*b*) the terminal currents are known.

useful when the terminal voltages, v_{EB} and v_{CB}, are known. If, however, the terminal currents, i_E and i_C, are known, then it is more convenient to use the equivalent circuit shown in Fig. 8.16*b*. In this figure the dependent sources depend on the terminal currents rather than the diode currents. A little algebra will show that the models in Figs. 8.16*a* and *b* are equivalent if

$$I_{EO} = I_{ES}(1 - \alpha_F \alpha_R) \tag{8.34a}$$

and

$$I_{CO} = I_{CS}(1 - \alpha_F \alpha_R) \tag{8.34b}$$

For a *pnp* transistor we simply reverse the diodes in the circuit representations to obtain the models in Figs. 8.17*a* and *b*. Note that the definitions of i_F and i_R and the polarities of the dependent current sources are, by convention, also changed. The Ebers–Moll equations for a *pnp* transistor become

$$i_E = I_{ES}(e^{qv_{EB}/kT} - 1) - \alpha_R I_{CS}(e^{qv_{CB}/kT} - 1) \tag{8.35a}$$

$$i_C = -\alpha_F I_{ES}(e^{qv_{EB}/kT} - 1) + I_{CS}(e^{qv_{CB}/kT} - 1) \tag{8.35b}$$

Example

Question. Consider a *pnp* transistor with the same emitter, base, and collector doping levels as the *npn* transistor in the preceding example. The two transistors are

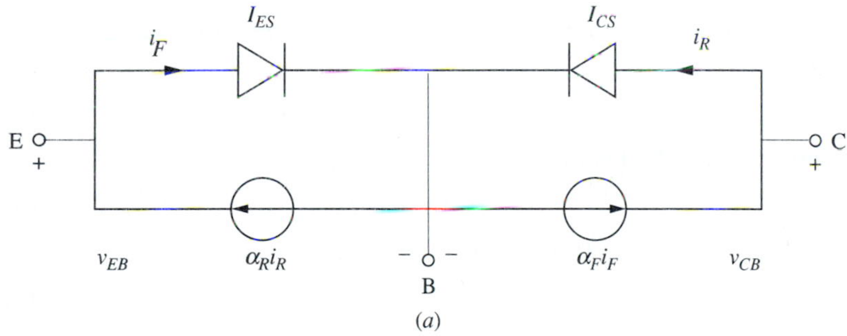

(*a*)

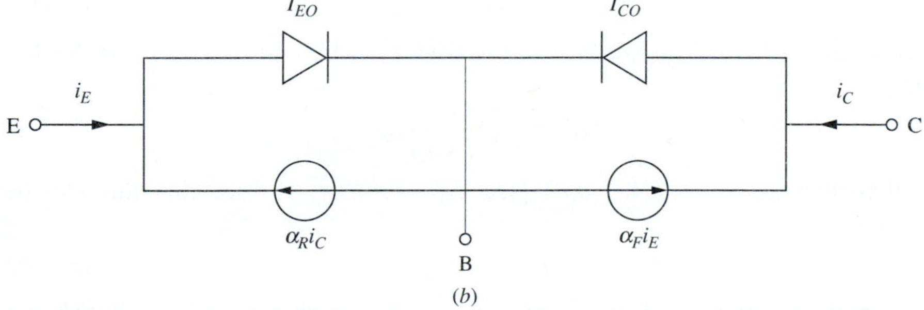

(*b*)

FIGURE 8.17
Circuit representations of a *pnp* BJT: (*a*) when the terminal voltages are known; (*b*) when the terminal currents are known.

identical in all other relevant ways as well. What are the emitter, base, and collector defects, δ_E, δ_B, and δ_C, in this device, and what are the forward and reverse alphas and betas?

Discussion. Our calculations proceed as before, except that the electron and hole diffusion coefficients switch roles, a change that reduces the gains and increases the defects. We now calculate that δ_E is 1.3×10^{-2}, δ_B is 2×10^{-5}, and δ_C is 6.7. Correspondingly, α_F is 0.987 and α_R is 0.13; β_F is now 76 and β_R is 0.15. The poorer characteristics of the *pnp* structure compared to the *npn* structure are one of the main reasons why *npn* is the preferred bipolar transistor type.

The full Ebers–Moll model is necessary if we are dealing with completely general terminal voltages, but we usually work in more restricted regions; in such cases it is often possible to simplify the model. For example, we are often interested in situations in which the base-collector junction is reverse-biased and the emitter-base junction is forward-biased. In this situation, the current i_R will be essentially $-I_{CS}$ and will be negligible relative to i_F and $\alpha_F i_F$. The Ebers–Moll model circuit can then be approximated as illustrated in Fig. 8.18*a*. We have, for a *pnp*,

$$i_E \approx I_{ES} e^{qv_{EB}/kT} \tag{8.36}$$

and

$$i_C \approx -\alpha_F i_E \tag{8.37}$$

It is also convenient to relate the collector current to the base current. We can write i_B as

$$i_B = -i_E - i_C \tag{8.38a}$$

which, using Eq. (8.37), becomes

$$i_B = -(1 - \alpha_F) i_E \tag{8.38b}$$

Substituting Eq. (8.36) into this yields

$$i_B = -(1 - \alpha_F) I_{ES} e^{qv_{EB}/kT} \tag{8.38c}$$

We write this as

$$i_B = -I_{BS} e^{qv_{EB}/kT} \tag{8.38d}$$

where in the last equation we have defined $(1 - \alpha_F) I_{ES}$ as I_{BS}. We can further write

$$i_C = \frac{\alpha_F}{(1 - \alpha_F)} i_B \tag{8.39a}$$

Recalling that $\beta_F = \alpha_F/(1 - \alpha_F)$ [see Eq. (8.17b)], we see that this can be written as

$$i_C = \beta_F i_B \tag{8.39b}$$

Circuit representations of Eqs. (8.38) and (8.39) are shown in Figs. 8.18*b* and *c*. All of these representations are equivalent, and each is more useful than the others in certain situations.

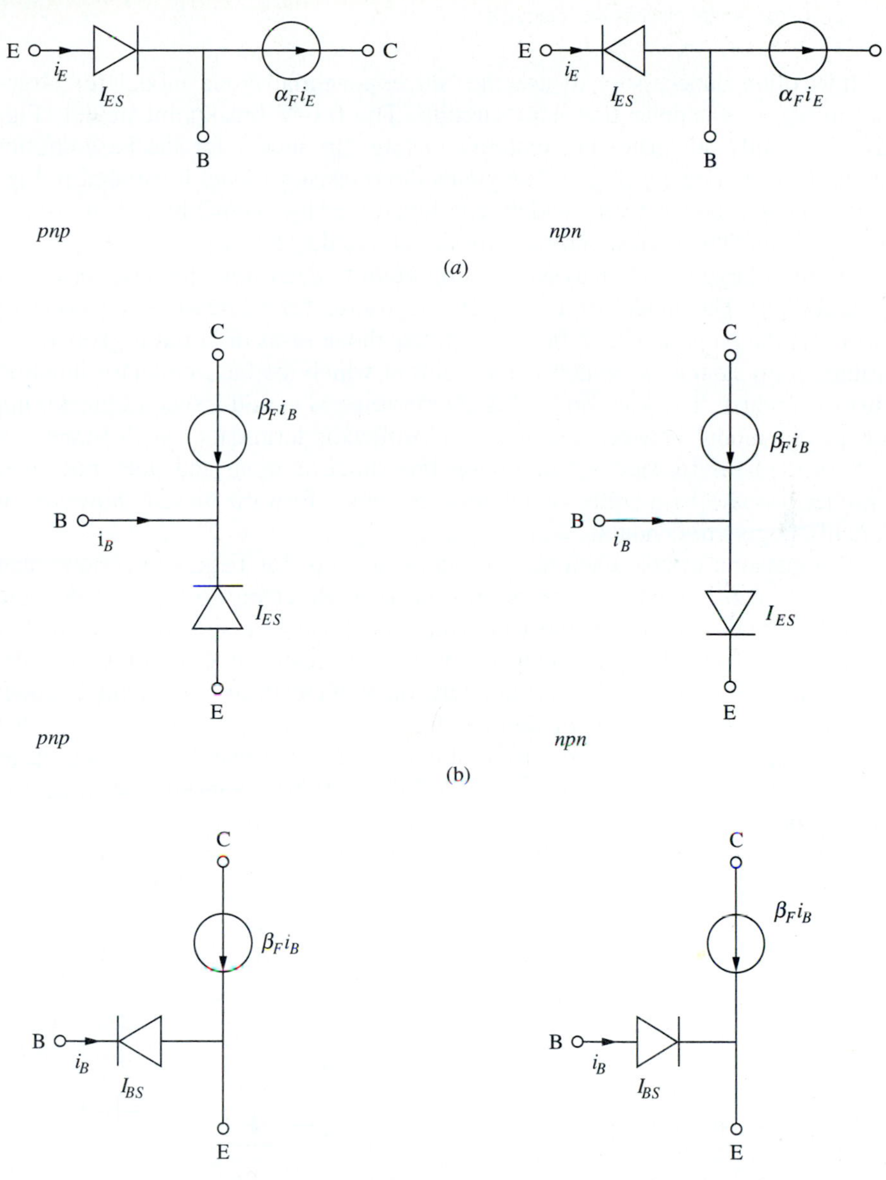

FIGURE 8.18
Approximate large-signal models for bipolar junction transistors based on the Ebers–Moll model, valid when the base-collector junction is reverse-biased and $|I_{CS}|$ is negligible. The figures to the right correspond to *npn* transistors, those on the left to *pnp* transistors. The models in (*a*) are common-base models derived directly from the Ebers–Moll models by setting I_{CS} equal to zero. The models in (*b*) are common-emitter models derived directly from those in (*a*) simply by writing i_C as $\beta_F i_B$ [Eq. (8.39b)] rather than as $-\alpha_F i_E$ [Eq. (8.37)]. The models in (*c*) extend those in (*b*) one step further by moving the diode from the emitter leg of the circuit to the base leg, which requires that we also change the saturation current of the diode from I_{ES} to I_{BS} [see the discussion following Eq. (8.38d)].

It is often unnecessary to use the full exponential diode model for large-signal analysis of bipolar transistor circuits. The 0.6-V breakpoint model, Fig. 7.12*e*, is usually adequate. For example, using this model for the base-emitter diode in the *npn* model of Fig. 8.18*c* yields the transistor model illustrated in Fig. 8.19*a*. This *npn* model is very widely employed for large-signal bipolar transistor circuit analysis. The corresponding *pnp* model should be obvious.

Often in large-signal analysis it is important to determine the onset of cutoff and saturation. The model of Fig. 8.19*a* is useful for addressing the issue of cutoff (i.e., the point at which the base-emitter diode turns off), but it gives us no information on saturation, which is the point at which the base-collector junction begins to conduct. The solution to this shortcoming is to add a second breakpoint diode to the model between the base and collector terminals, as illustrated in Fig. 8.19*b*. In the forward active region this diode is open and does not enter the model. As the base-collector junction becomes forward biased, however, it eventually begins to conduct.

The question of just when the base-collector junction begins to conduct and a transistor enters saturation is an interesting one. Referring to Fig. 8.19*b*, note that the breakpoint voltage of the base-collector diode of a silicon transistor has been taken to be 0.4 V rather than 0.6 V. If you recall our discussion near the end of Sec. 7.4.1, there is no abrupt turn-on voltage in an exponential diode; rather, the choice is a matter of degree. In this case then, we want to say that we are in saturation and that the transistor has left its forward active region as soon as the diode starts to conduct a "little bit." We don't want to wait until it is forward-biased by 0.6 V and is really "on"; rather, we say that 0.4 V is sufficiently "on" to be of concern. Recall also that I_{CS} is typically much larger than I_{ES},

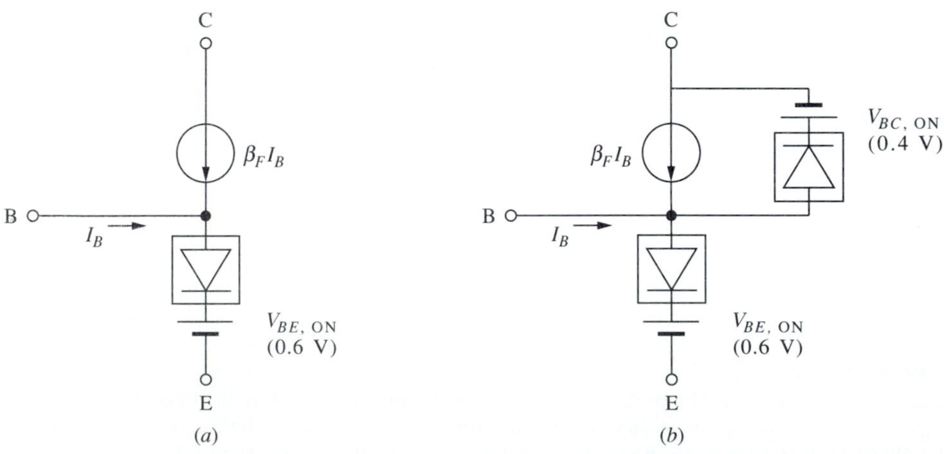

FIGURE 8.19
Large-signal *npn* transistor models incorporating breakpoint diode models: (*a*) the equivalent of the model in Fig. 8.18*c*; (*b*) the model modified to predict the onset of saturation. (The quiescent point notation is used for the base current in this figure to emphasize that these models are used primarily for bias point analysis. The numerical values given refer to silicon transistors.)

so the current through the base-collector diode biased to 0.4 V may very well be comparable to that through the emitter-base diode with 0.6 V bias.

b) Beyond Ebers–Moll, toward Gummel–Poon. We mentioned in the preceding discussion of limitations of the simple Ebers–Moll model that there is another model, called the Gummel–Poon model, in which effects such as nonuniform doping of the emitter, base, and collector regions, and space-charge layer recombination are taken into account. Although the development of this model is not beyond our ability, it is beyond our needs, so we will not do it. However, we can obtain the basic Gummel–Poon model from our Ebers–Moll model, which is worth the effort.

The basic Gummel–Poon model is shown in Fig. 8.20. It is developed using a formulation of the current flow problem that lets us treat nonuniformly doped regions, so it is more general than the approach used in the Ebers–Moll model. At the same time, however, the approaches are equivalent for transistors with uniformly doped emitters, bases, and collectors, and the basic Gummel–Poon for a uniformly doped transistor can easily be obtained from the Ebers–Moll model. The process is illustrated in Fig. 8.21 and is described in the following several paragraphs.

We first draw the Ebers–Moll model with the emitter down, as in Fig. 8.21*a*. Then we add two pairs of equal-magnitude, oppositely directed, dependent current

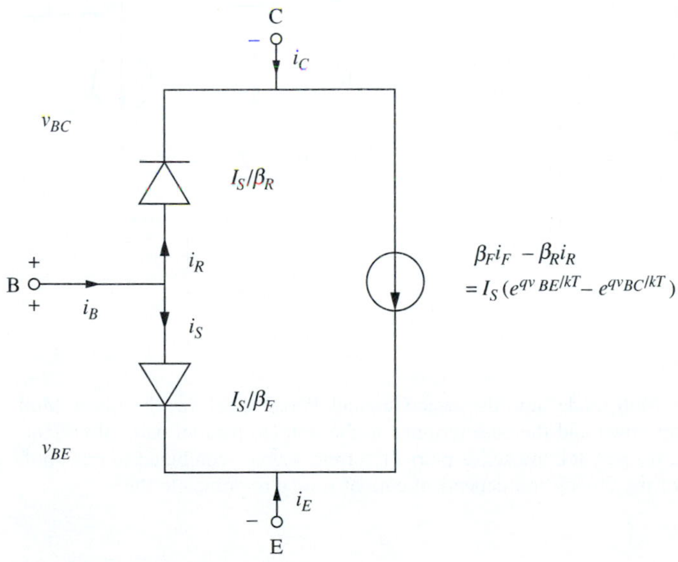

FIGURE 8.20
Basic Gummel–Poon model for the bipolar junction transistor. This model is also called the large-signal hybrid-pi model. It is commonly drawn with the emitter terminal down and the base terminal to the left, reflecting the most common connection of bipolar transistors in circuits.

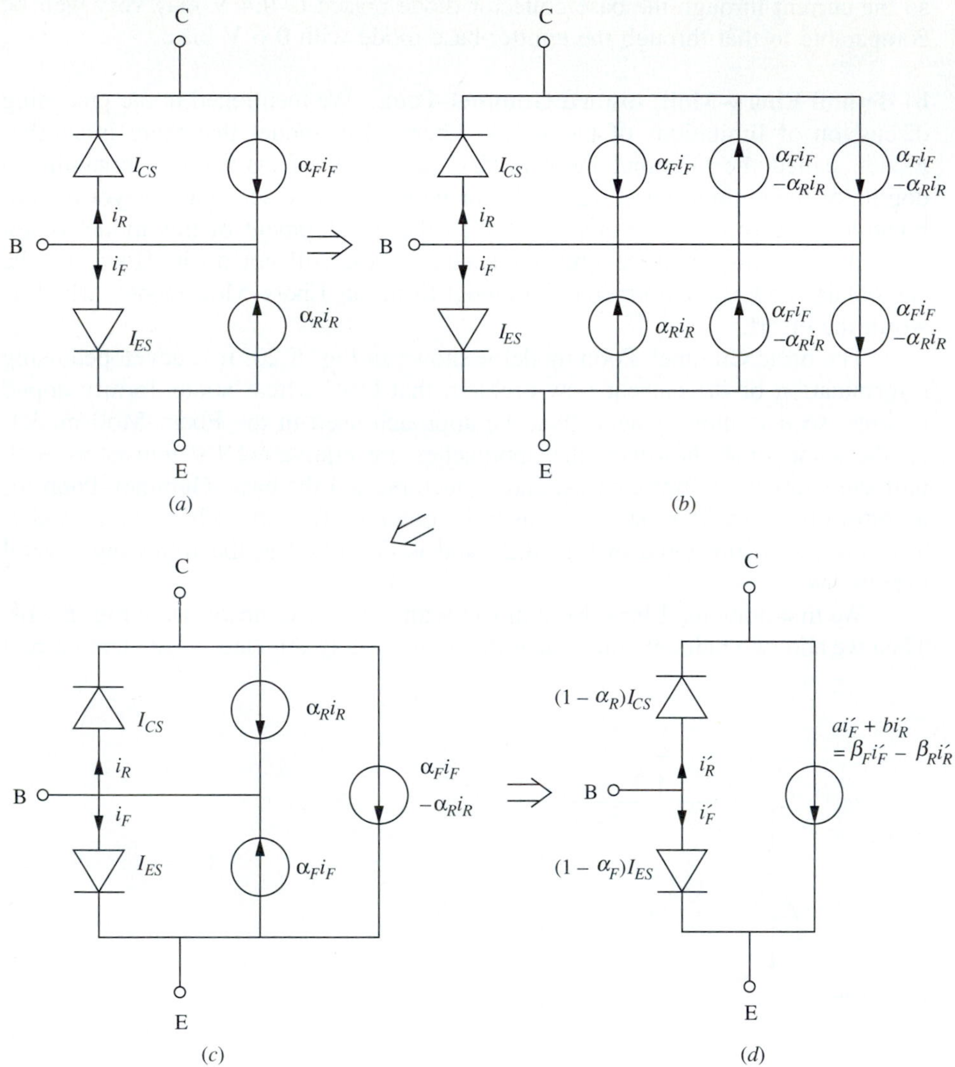

FIGURE 8.21
Transformation of the Ebers–Moll model into the basic Gummel–Poon model: (*a*) the Ebers–Moll model drawn with the emitter down and the base terminal to the left; (*b*) parallel pairs of current sources added to the circuit; (*c*) parallel and series pairs of current sources combined to resimplify the circuit; (*d*) redefinition of the diodes and dependent current source to complete the transformation.

sources in parallel with the original dependent sources, as shown in Fig. 8.21*b*. We next combine the left-most member of each of the two pairs of dependent current sources with the original generator. Having done this, we also recognize that since the right-most dependent sources are equal and connected in series, there must be no current flowing in the link connecting the midpoint of this pair of generators to the rest of the circuit. This link can therefore be broken without affecting the performance of the circuit. Breaking this link does simplify the circuit, however, because the right-most two generators, being identical and connected in series, can now clearly be combined into one source. The resulting circuit is shown in Fig. 8.21*c*.

The next step is to note that the dependent current sources in parallel with the diodes are each dependent only on the current through its companion diode. Thus they can be combined with the diodes, and each combination can again be modeled as another ideal exponential diode. The saturation current of the diode between the base and emitter is $(1 - \alpha_F)I_{ES}$; the saturation current of the diode between the base and collector is $(1 - \alpha_R)I_{CS}$. This is illustrated in Fig. 8.21*d*.

When we combine the current sources and diodes to simplify the circuit, we have to realize that the other dependent current source (i.e., the one between the collector and emitter) depends on the currents through the original diodes. If those diodes disappear, we must recalculate the dependence of the current sources in terms of some current that we can still clearly identify or in terms of the terminal voltages. To do this and proceed, we next define two currents, i'_F and i'_R, as shown in Fig. 8.21*d*. The current source between the collector and emitter will then clearly depend on both i'_F and i'_R; it can be written as $ai'_F + bi'_R$. To see what a and b are, refer to Fig. 8.21*c*, from which it is clear that ai'_F must be $\alpha_F i_F$, and bi'_R must be $-\alpha_R i_R$. Writing i'_F, i_F, i'_R, and i_R in terms of v_{BE}, v_{BC}, and the diode parameters, we have

$$a(1 - \alpha_F)I_{ES}(e^{qv_{BE}/kT} - 1) = \alpha_F I_{ES}(e^{qv_{BE}/kT} - 1) \tag{8.40}$$

and

$$b(1 - \alpha_R)I_{CS}(e^{qv_{BC}/kT} - 1) = -\alpha_R I_{CS}(e^{qv_{BC}/kT} - 1) \tag{8.41}$$

from which we see immediately that a is $\alpha_F/(1 - \alpha_F)$, which we see from Eq. 8.17b is just β_F; and b is $-\alpha_R/(1 - \alpha_R)$, which is just $-\beta_R$. This result is also shown in Fig. 8.21*d*.

The final step that we take is to define a new saturation current I_S, given by

$$I_S \equiv \alpha_F I_{ES} = \alpha_R I_{CS} \tag{8.42}$$

and to notice that in terms of I_S the saturation currents of the new diodes between the base and emitter and the base and collector are I_S/β_F and I_S/β_R, respectively. We can then write the dependent current source, $\beta_F i'_F - \beta_R i'_R$, as follows:

$$\beta_F i'_F - \beta_R i'_R = I_S(e^{qv_{BE}/kT} - 1) - I_S(e^{qv_{BC}/kT} - 1) \tag{8.43a}$$

which in turn simplifies to

$$\beta_F i'_F - \beta_R i'_R = I_S(e^{qv_{BE}/kT} - e^{qv_{BC}/kT}) \tag{8.43b}$$

This definition of I_S and these expressions for the diode saturation currents and dependent current source give us the basic Gummel–Poon model in Fig. 8.20.

We can now use our earlier expressions for I_{ES}, α_F, δ_E, and δ_B in terms of the device dimensions and other parameters, that is, Eqs. (8.12), (8.14), (8.7), and (8.11), respectively, to obtain a similar equation for I_S. We can write

$$I_S = qAn_i^2 \frac{D_e}{N_{AB} w_B^*}(1 - \delta_B) = qAn_i^2 \frac{D_e}{N_{AB} w_B^*}\left[1 - \frac{\left(w_B^*\right)^2}{2L_{eB}^2}\right] \tag{8.44}$$

Before continuing, look at Eq. (8.43a) and consider whether it makes sense in light of what you know about the physics of a bipolar transistor: the excess electron concentration at the edge of the base nearest the emitter is proportional to $(e^{qv_{BE}/kT} - 1)$, and that at the collector edge is proportional to $(e^{qv_{BC}/kT} - 1)$. The minority carrier diffusion current across the base from emitter to collector should therefore be proportional to their difference, which is just what Eq. (8.43a) says. A little thought will further show you that the proportionality factor should be $qAn_i^2 D_e/N_{AB} w_B^*$ multiplied by $(1 - \delta_B)$, which is the fraction of the minority carriers injected at the emitter that successfully transit the base. This, of course, is just what Eq. (8.44) says.

Efforts to add "nonideal" effects to models for the terminal characteristics of bipolar junction transistors usually begin with the basic Gummel–Poon model. We mentioned earlier that the effects of nonuniform doping in the various regions of the device can be included by replacing the doping-concentration/layer-width product that appears several places in the Ebers–Moll model with the integral of the doping profile over the layer. An obvious example is in the expression for I_S in Eq. (8.44). The effects of space-charge layer recombination are easily included by adding two $n = 2$ exponential diodes between the base and emitter and the base and collector, respectively, just as we did with the diode in Sec. 7.4.1*b*.

High-level injection effects can be added to the model as we did with the diode in Sec. 7.4.1*b*, but more commonly we handle them by expanding the model for β_F to include a dependence on the collector current because the main impact of high-level injection is on β_F anyway. In an ad hoc manner we say that β_F varies as

$$\beta_F = \frac{\beta_{F0}}{1 + I_C/I_{KF}} \tag{8.45}$$

where β_{F0} is the zero- (i.e. low-) current forward beta and I_{KF} is the current level at which β_F has fallen to half its low-current value. A similar model is used for the reverse beta β_R.

Another effect that is often included in the Ebers–Moll model for a bipolar transistor is series resistance in the device leads. Looking back at the cross section of a typical BJT in Fig. 8.1, it is not surprising that there may at times be significant resistances in series with at least the base and collector leads. The possibility of significant resistance in series with the emitter is less obvious; in fact, the emitter series resistance tends to be small, but it is not zero, and in certain instances even a small emitter resistance can have significant consequences. To model these resistances, suitable-value resistors can easily be added to the model in series with the emitter, base, and collector leads. A model including elements to account for all of these effects is shown in Fig. 8.22.

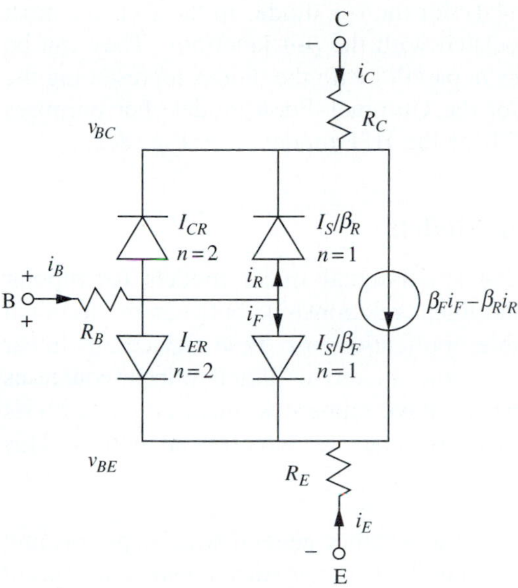

FIGURE 8.22
BJT model containing elements to account for space-charge layer recombination and series lead resistances.

Finally, base width modulation, or the Early effect*, is typically taken into account through the variation of I_S with w_B^* [see Eq. (8.44)]. The dependence of w_B^* on v_{BC} and v_{BE} is, as you can appreciate, messy mathematically, but experience has shown that a useful fit to device characteristics can be obtained by the following relatively simple expression:

$$w_B^*(v_{BE}, v_{BC}) = \frac{w_B^*(0,0)}{1 + (v_{BC}/V_A) + (v_{BE}/V_L)} \tag{8.46}$$

where V_A is called the Early voltage and V_L is called either the reverse Early voltage, or, believe it or not, the Late voltage.† V_L accounts for the Early effect in the reverse mode of operation. Equation (8.46) is used where w_B^* appears in the first factor in Eq. (8.44) for I_S, but where $(w_B^*)^2$ appears in δ_B its variation with voltage is neglected.

c) Dynamic models with charge stores. To extend our bipolar transistor models to dynamic situations it may be necessary to account for the charge stored in the

*The Early voltage is named after Dr. James Early, who first explained base width modulation.

†The Late voltage was named by someone with the same sense of humor as the folks who brought you the units "mho" for conductance and "daraf" for inverse capacitance.

device, just as we had to do in Sec. 7.4.1*c* for the *p-n* diode. In the BJT, the most important charge stores are those associated with the *p-n* junctions. They can be modeled by adding nonlinear capacitors in parallel with the diodes representing the two junctions in the Ebers–Moll and/or the Gummel–Poon model. For purposes of illustration, this is done in Fig. 8.23 for the BJT model from Fig. 8.22.

8.2.2 Static Small-Signal Linear Models

Our primary motivation for developing small-signal linear models for bipolar junction transistors is that if we can find linear relationships between the terminal variables, then there are many possible applications of these devices in linear circuits, such as audio amplifiers. It is also true, moreover, that nonlinear equations are difficult to treat analytically and that we have numerous linear circuit analysis techniques at our disposal, which we can use once we have linear models. This is also an important consideration.

a) Common-emitter models. We proceed in a rather general way by performing a linear expansion of the transistor terminal characteristics about a quiescent operating point. The most useful model for us will be one in which the emitter terminal is common to both the input and the output circuit, so we select our

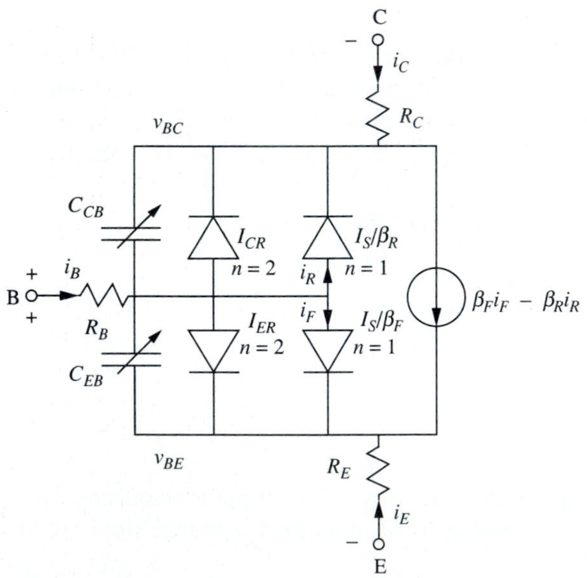

FIGURE 8.23
BJT model from Fig. 8.22 modified by adding two nonlinear capacitors to account for the nonlinear charge stores associated with the emitter-base and base-collector *p-n* junctions.

voltages as v_{BE} and v_{CE} and our currents as $i_B(v_{BE}, v_{CE})$ and $i_C(v_{BE}, v_{CE})$. We will discuss other choices of variables later.

Assume that our quiescent operating point Q is (V_{BE}, V_{CE}) and thus our expansions of i_B and i_C are

$$i_B(v_{BE}, v_{CE}) = i_B(V_{BE}, V_{CE}) + \left.\frac{\partial i_B}{\partial v_{BE}}\right|_Q (v_{BE} - V_{BE}) + \left.\frac{\partial i_B}{\partial v_{CE}}\right|_Q (v_{CE} - V_{CE}) + \text{Higher-order terms} \tag{8.47a}$$

and

$$i_C(v_{BE}, v_{CE}) = i_C(V_{BE}, V_{CE}) + \left.\frac{\partial i_C}{\partial v_{BE}}\right|_Q (v_{BE} - V_{BE}) + \left.\frac{\partial i_C}{\partial v_{CE}}\right|_Q (v_{CE} - V_{CE}) + \text{Higher-order terms} \tag{8.47b}$$

Recognizing that $i_B(V_{BE}, V_{CE})$ is I_B; $i_C(V_{BE}, V_{CE})$ is I_C; $(v_{BE} - V_{BE})$ is v_{be}; $(v_{CE} - V_{CE})$ is v_{ce}; $(i_B - I_B)$ is i_b; and $(i_C - I_C)$ is i_c; and assuming that v_{be} and v_{ce} are small enough that we can ignore the higher-order terms, we have

$$i_b = \left.\frac{\partial i_B}{\partial v_{BE}}\right|_Q v_{be} + \left.\frac{\partial i_B}{\partial v_{CE}}\right|_Q v_{ce} \tag{8.48a}$$

and

$$i_c = \left.\frac{\partial i_C}{\partial v_{BE}}\right|_Q v_{be} + \left.\frac{\partial i_C}{\partial v_{CE}}\right|_Q v_{ce} \tag{8.48b}$$

The partial derivatives have the units of conductance and are given the following names:

$$\left.\frac{\partial i_B}{\partial v_{BE}}\right|_Q \equiv g_\pi, \text{ input conductance} \tag{8.49}$$

$$\left.\frac{\partial i_B}{\partial v_{CE}}\right|_Q \equiv g_r, \text{ reverse transconductance} \tag{8.50}$$

$$\left.\frac{\partial i_C}{\partial v_{BE}}\right|_Q \equiv g_m, \text{ forward transconductance} \tag{8.51}$$

$$\left.\frac{\partial i_C}{\partial v_{CE}}\right|_Q \equiv g_o, \text{ output conductance} \tag{8.52}$$

The use of g_π and g_m for the input conductance and forward transconductance, respectively, rather than g_i and g_f, for example, is a matter of convention that we will respect.

Thus far our small-signal modeling has been, except for our choice of a common-emitter configuration, purely a mathematical exercise. The specific device physics enters only when we evaluate the various conductances and transconductances using our large signal model. We assume that the quiescent operating point Q is in the forward active region of the transistor characteristics. In that case, the large-signal model reduces essentially to that of Fig. 8.18*b*. We see immediately that there is no dependence of the terminal currents on v_{CE}, so g_r and g_o are both identically zero.

Turning next to g_m, we can use Eqs. (8.38) and (8.39) to obtain

$$g_m = \frac{q}{kT}\beta_F I_{BS} e^{qV_{BE}/kT} \tag{8.53a}$$

which can be conveniently written as

$$g_m = q\frac{|I_C|}{kT} \tag{8.53b}$$

Similarly we find that g_π is given by

$$g_\pi = \frac{q}{kT}I_{BS} e^{qV_{BE}/kT} \tag{8.54a}$$

We could write this as qI_B/kT, but it turns out that a more practical and more general way of writing this is in terms of g_m. Comparing this last equation to the first expression we obtained for g_m, we find that g_π and g_m are related as

$$g_\pi = \frac{g_m}{\beta_F} \tag{8.54b}$$

We will use Eqs. (8.53) and (8.54b) to evaluate g_m and g_π, respectively, in this text. It turns out that in situations where β varies with the collector current, Eq. (8.54b) is a valid expression for g_π as long as β_F is replaced with $\beta_f \equiv \partial i_C/\partial i_B|_Q$. This issue is discussed further in App. F.

A linear circuit representing the small-signal linear model we have developed for the bipolar junction transistor is shown in Fig. 8.24*a*. This model is valid for both *npn* and *pnp* transistors. You should take the time to convince yourself of this fact.

Example

Question. Consider an *npn* bipolar transistor with a forward beta β_F of 150, and an I_C of 1 mA. What are g_m and g_π for this device at this bias point? Assume room-temperature operation.

Discussion. Using Eqs. (8.53) and (8.54b), we find that the transconductance g_m is 40 mS and that the input conductance g_π is 0.267 mS. We often think in terms of resistance when we deal with the input of a device; inverting g_π, we see that the corresponding input resistance r_π is 3.75 kΩ. Notice that if β_F were larger, r_π would be larger (g_π smaller); and if β_F were smaller, r_π would be smaller (g_π larger). The value of g_m does not change with β_F, assuming that I_{CQ} remains unchanged.

We can modify our model slightly by changing the dependent current source from one that depends on v_{be}, the voltage across r_π, to one that depends on i_b, the current through r_π. Because i_b is $g_\pi v_{be}$ and g_π is g_m/β, the magnitude of the dependent current source, $g_m v_{be}$, is also βi_b; the model can thus be redrawn

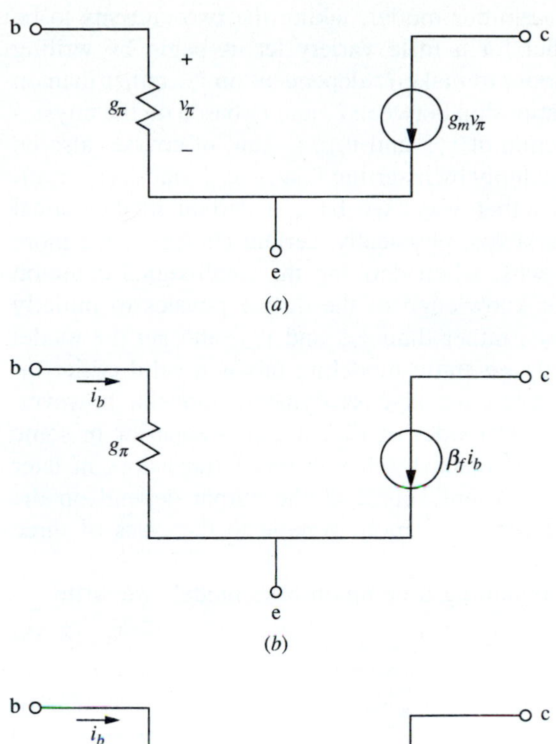

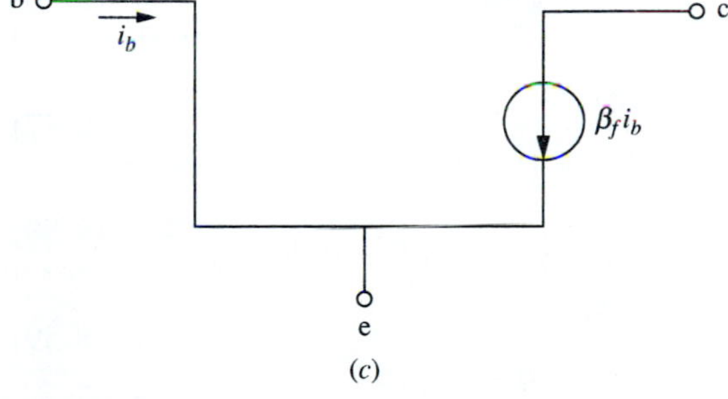

FIGURE 8.24
Static small-signal linear equivalent circuits for bipolar transistors in a common-emitter connection: (*a*) g_m (transconductance) model; (*b*) β_f (current gain) model; (*c*) β-model with zero base resistance.

equivalently as shown in Fig. 8.24*b*. This is a particularly useful configuration if g_π is large, that is, if r_π ($\equiv 1/g_\pi$) is small, which is frequently the case because a rough first approximation to the operation of a circuit can often be obtained by setting $r_\pi = 0$. This model is drawn in Fig. 8.24*c*.

b) Common-base model. Sometimes a bipolar transistor is connected in a circuit with its base terminal common to the input and output. To model this so-called common-base connection, it is convenient to choose v_{eb} and v_{cb} as the independent variables and i_c and i_e as the dependent variables. We could proceed exactly as we did for the common-emitter model, taking the two currents to be dependent on the two voltages, but for a little variety let us begin by writing $i_e(v_{eb}, v_{cb})$ and $i_c(i_e, v_{cb})$. We choose to make i_c dependent on i_e, rather than on v_{eb}, because we expect a linear relationship between i_c and i_e based on the physics of the device. Because i_e is a function of v_{eb} and v_{cb}, i_c can, of course, also be written as a function of v_{eb} and v_{cb} simply by inserting $i_e(v_{eb}, v_{cb})$ into $i_c(i_e, v_{cb})$.

Stating these observations another way, we have a certain mathematical flexibility in how we select our variables; physically, certain choices make more sense than others. You might ask why, when deriving the small-signal common emitter circuit, we did not use our knowledge of the device physics to initially write i_c as dependent on i_b and v_{ce}, rather than v_{be} and v_{ce}, and get the model of Fig. 8.24*b* directly. Based strictly on static modeling this is a valid criticism. We will see in the next section when we discuss dynamic models, however, that our original choice that led to the model of Fig. 8.24*a* is superior in some situations. We will also see when we discuss other types of transistors in later chapters that having the dependent current source at the output depend on the input voltage rather than on input current is more generic to the class of three terminal transistor-like devices.

Returning to the problem of obtaining a common-base model, we write

$$i_e = g_e v_{eb} + g_{rb} v_{cb} \tag{8.55}$$

and

$$i_c = \alpha_f i_e + g_{ob} v_{cb} \tag{8.56}$$

where we have

$$g_e \equiv \left.\frac{\partial i_E}{\partial v_{EB}}\right|_Q \tag{8.57}$$

$$g_{rb} \equiv \left.\frac{\partial i_E}{\partial v_{CB}}\right|_Q \tag{8.58}$$

$$\alpha_f \equiv \left.\frac{\partial i_C}{\partial i_E}\right|_Q \tag{8.59}$$

$$g_{ob} \equiv \left.\frac{\partial i_C}{\partial v_{CB}}\right|_Q \tag{8.60}$$

The subscript b has been added to distinguish some of these quantities from the common-emitter parameters. Referring to our large-signal common-base model, Fig. 8.18*a*, we see that g_{rb} and g_{ob} must be zero and that $\alpha_f = \alpha_F$. The small-signal emitter resistance g_e based on this same Ebers–Moll-based model is $q|I_E|/kT$. A more general expression, useful even when β varies with I_E, can be obtained by manipulating the common-emitter models in Fig. 8.24. Doing so, we find that we can write both α_f and g_e in terms of g_m and β_f as

$$\alpha_f = \frac{\beta_f}{(\beta_f + 1)} \tag{8.61}$$

and

$$g_e = \frac{g_m}{\alpha_f} \tag{8.62}$$

We will use these expressions to calculate α_f and g_e. This common-base small-signal model is illustrated in Fig. 8.25*a*.

If we were to use $i_C(v_{EB}, v_{CB})$ rather than $i_C(i_E, v_{CB})$, we would obtain the model of Fig. 8.25*b*, where g_m is the same as for the common-emitter model.

c) Parasitic elements. The small-signal models we have developed are satisfactory in most low-frequency applications, but in certain situations it is necessary to include small effects that we have thus far neglected. There are two such "parasitic" elements we will consider: the output conductance g_o and the base series resistance r_x.

In the Ebers–Moll model, the output conductance g_o is zero, but in Sec. 8.1.7 we saw that the Early effect, or base-width modulation, leads to a finite slope in the output characteristics. That is, $\partial i_C/\partial v_{CE}$ (i.e., g_o) is not identically zero. In such cases the Early voltage is an important device parameter to know because it enables us to calculate the incremental output conductance g_o at any bias point in the forward active region. This is illustrated in Fig. 8.26. Assuming that V_A is much greater than V_{CE}, we can approximate the slope of the characteristics (i.e., g_o) for a given quiescent output current I_C as

$$g_o \cong \frac{|I_C|}{V_A} \tag{8.63}$$

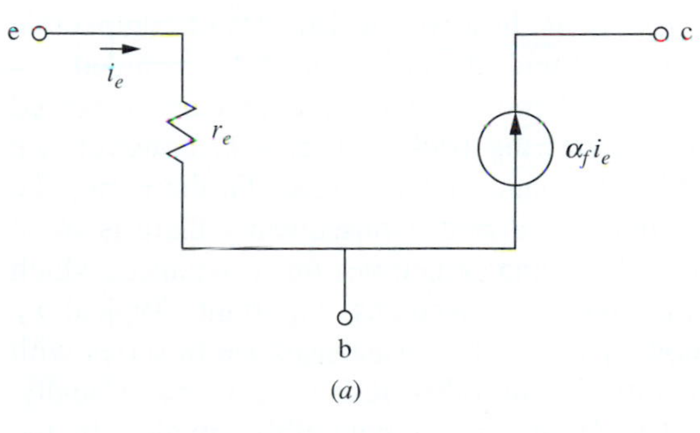

(*a*)

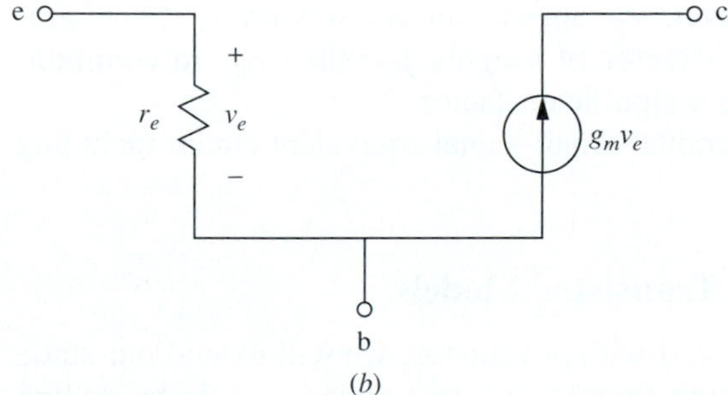

(*b*)

FIGURE 8.25
Common-base static small-signal linear equivalent circuits for a bipolar transistor: (*a*) α_f model; (*b*) g_m model.

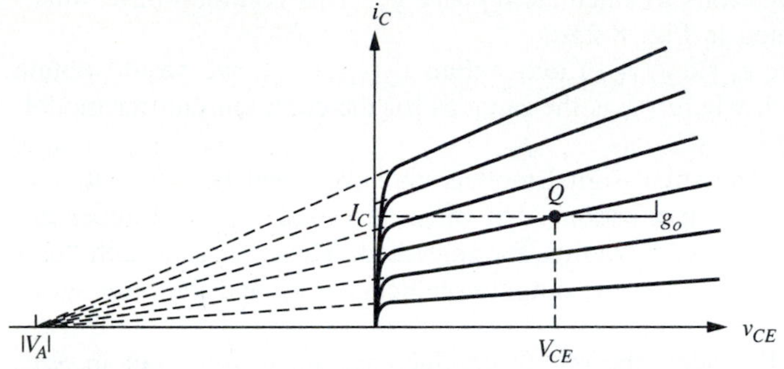

FIGURE 8.26
Output characteristics of an *npn* BJT illustrating the relationship between the Early voltage V_A, the quiescent collector current I_C, and the incremental output conductance g_o.

In a well-designed transistor, g_o will be very small and can usually be approximated as zero. However, in situations where the performance depends on g_o being zero, the fact that it is small but not exactly zero must be taken into account. Conceptually, it is often easier to think in terms of $1/g_o$, which we define as the output resistance r_o. Typical values of r_o are 10^5 to 10^6 Ω. When the circuit in which the transistor is found has resistances of 10^4 Ω or less in parallel with r_o, then r_o can be neglected. If, however, resistances of comparable or larger magnitude than r_o are in parallel with it, then r_o must be included.

We also assumed in the Ebers–Moll model that the base current flowed in from the base contact unimpeded. Referring back to Fig. 8.1, however, we see that this contact is often far off to the side of the device. Furthermore, the base itself is quite thin and only moderately doped. Consequently there is some resistance to lateral current flow in the base and sometimes this resistance, which we will call the *parasitic base resistance* r_x, becomes important. Typical r_x values are 25 to 50 Ω. The issue now is what other resistances are in series with r_x. In the common-emitter configuration, this other resistance is r_π. Usually, this resistance is on the order of 10^3 Ω and r_x is negligibly smaller. In the common-base configuration, however, r_x appears in series with r_e ($\approx 1/g_e$), which is considerably smaller (by a factor of roughly β_f) than r_π. In common-base applications, then, r_x may be a significant factor.

The low-frequency common-emitter small-signal equivalent circuit including g_o and r_x is shown in Fig. 8.27.

8.2.3 Dynamic Small-Signal Transistor Models

Following the same logic we employed with *p-n* diodes, we will extend our static small-signal transistor models to high-frequency time-varying signals by adding the appropriate junction capacitances. There are two *p-n* junctions in a bipolar transistor, the emitter-base junction and the base-collector junction.

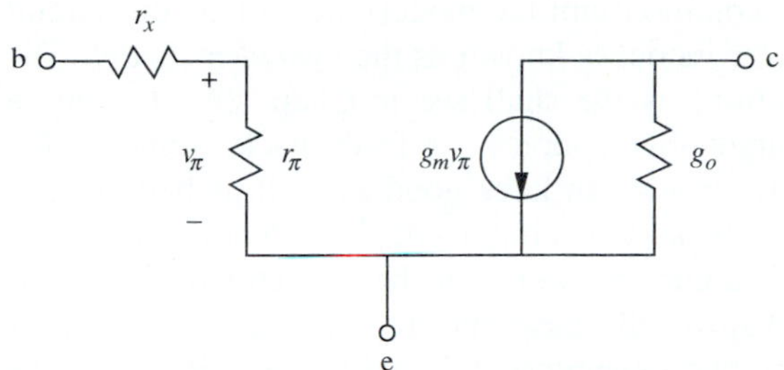

FIGURE 8.27
Common-emitter small-signal equivalent circuit including the parasitic base resistance r_x and the output conductance g_o.

In the forward active region the base-collector junction is reverse-biased, so there is negligible diffusion capacitance associated with this junction. The base-collector capacitance is thus exclusively depletion capacitance. By convention, we label this capacitor C_μ.

The emitter-base junction is forward-biased, and the emitter-base junction voltage determines the amount of excess carrier injection into the base, so at this junction there is both diffusion and depletion capacitance. The sum of these two capacitances forms the emitter-base capacitance, which we label C_π.

C_π and C_μ depend on the quiescent operating just as g_π and g_m do. The depletion capacitance contributions to them depend on the relevant junction voltage. The diffusion capacitance component of C_π is most conveniently written in terms of the quiescent collector current I_C. Referring to Eq. (7.44′), we find that it can be written as

$$C_{eb,df} = \frac{w_B^{*2}}{2D_{\min,B}} \frac{q}{kT} |I_c| \tag{8.64}$$

where we assume that β_f is large, so $I_C \approx I_E$ and there is negligible excess minority carrier injection into the emitter. Defining $(w_B^*)^2/2D_{\min,B}$ as the base transit time τ_b and recognizing $q|I_C|/kT$ as g_m, we can write this contribution to C_π as

$$C_{eb,df} = g_m \tau_b \tag{8.65}$$

Notice that the diffusion capacitance contribution to C_π increases with increasing I_C, which in turn increases exponentially with V_{BE}, whereas the depletion capacitance increases only slightly. Furthermore the diffusion capacitance does not depend on the diode area, whereas the depletion capacitance is directly proportional to this area. At high current levels, then, C_π will be dominated by $C_{eb,df}$ and it will dominate sooner in smaller devices. As we shall see in Chap. 14, it is advantageous for this reason to operate transistors at high current densities when high-speed operation is important.

Adding C_μ and C_π to the common-emitter model, we obtain the circuit shown in Fig. 8.28*a*. This particular model is known as the *hybrid-π model*. The capacitor C_μ is in a critical position, as we shall see in Chap. 14. It forms a bridge between the input and output that couples, or feeds back, some of the output signal to the input. Such feedback can have good as well as bad effects, but in this case it primarily tends to be an undesirable coupling. Notice, also, that it now becomes clear why we use a current source in the collector that depends on the voltage across r_π rather than on the base current. The base current now includes current that flows into the two capacitors, C_π and C_μ, but it is only the current through r_π that appears at the collector. It is much more convenient in practice, as we shall see, to keep track of v_π, the voltage across r_π, than it is to calculate the current through it.

In the common-base configuration, adding C_μ and C_π yields the circuit in Fig. 8.28*b*. Notice that in this case there is no feedback between output and input. As with the common-emitter model, because the emitter current now includes current into C_π, it is most convenient to use the version of the model in which the dependent current source is a function of the voltage across r_e rather than the current through it.

Finally, we should remind ourselves that we are still using a quasistatic model for the bipolar transistor, to which we have added junction capacitances in a rather ad hoc fashion. Strictly speaking, we still need to justify our assumption

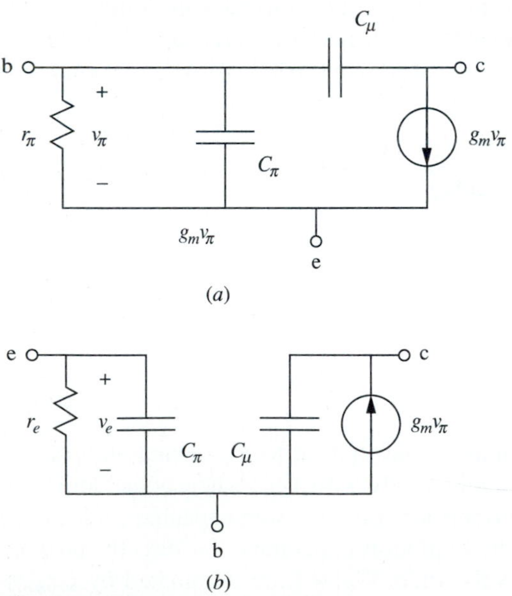

FIGURE 8.28
High-frequency small-signal transistor models: (*a*) the common-emitter, or hybrid-π, model; (*b*) the common-base model.

that this is a valid approach (i.e., that the quasistatic description of the intrinsic bipolar transistor physics is still valid). We will return to this issue in Chap. 14 and demonstrate that our modeling is indeed justifiable after we first discuss circuit analysis at low frequencies and look at high-frequency limits to circuit performance.

8.3 PHOTOTRANSISTORS

In Chap. 7 we saw that interesting and useful things happen when we shine light on a *p-n* diode. Interesting and useful things also happen when we illuminate a bipolar transistor. Bipolar transistors designed to respond to light are called *phototransistors*. We will discuss how they function and how they are constructed in this section.

To model the effect of illumination on a biased bipolar transistor, we will again use superposition. We already have a model, the Ebers–Moll model, for a bipolar transistor excited by externally applied voltages, so we will next develop a model for a bipolar transistor excited by light. The model we seek for a transistor disturbed from equilibrium by both applied voltages and light can be obtained by combining these two models.

Consider the one-dimensional *npn* transistor shown in Fig. 8.29*a*. Assume that the transistor's terminals are short-circuited so that the junction voltages, v_{EB} and v_{CB}, are zero. Assume further that the transistor is illuminated by light that generates M hole-electron pairs per $\text{cm}^2 \cdot \text{s}$ uniformly across the plane at $x = x_l$. If x_l is in the base region between 0^+ and w_B^-, then the excess minority carrier concentration profile is like that shown in Fig. 8.29*b* and the minority carrier current densities are as illustrated in Fig. 8.29*c*. If the cross-sectional area of the device is A, then the emitter current is $AqMf$ and the collector current is $AqMg$, where f is between 0 and 1 and is given by $(w_B^- - x_l)/(w_B^- - 0^+)$ and where g is $(1 - f)$.

You should be able to convince yourself that if x_l falls within the emitter-base junction depletion region (i.e., if $0^- \leq x_l \leq x^+$), then f is 1 and g is 0; and that if x_l falls within the base-collector junction depletion region (i.e., $w_B^- \leq x_l \leq w_B^+$), then f is 0 and g is 1. Furthermore, if the illumination falls in the emitter region (i.e., if $-w_E \leq x_l \leq 0^-$), then g is equal to 0 and f is $(-w_E - x_l)/(-w_E - 0^-)$; whereas if the light falls in the collector [i.e., if $w_{B+} \leq x_l \leq (w_B + w_C)$], then f is 0 and g is $(w_C + w_B - x_l)/(w_C + w_B - w_B^+)$.

To summarize, with a spatial impulse of illumination generating qM pairs/$\text{cm}^2 \cdot \text{s}$ uniformly across the plane at x_l, the short-circuit emitter and collector currents are, respectively,

$$i_E = AqMf \tag{8.66}$$

and

$$i_C = AqMg \tag{8.67}$$

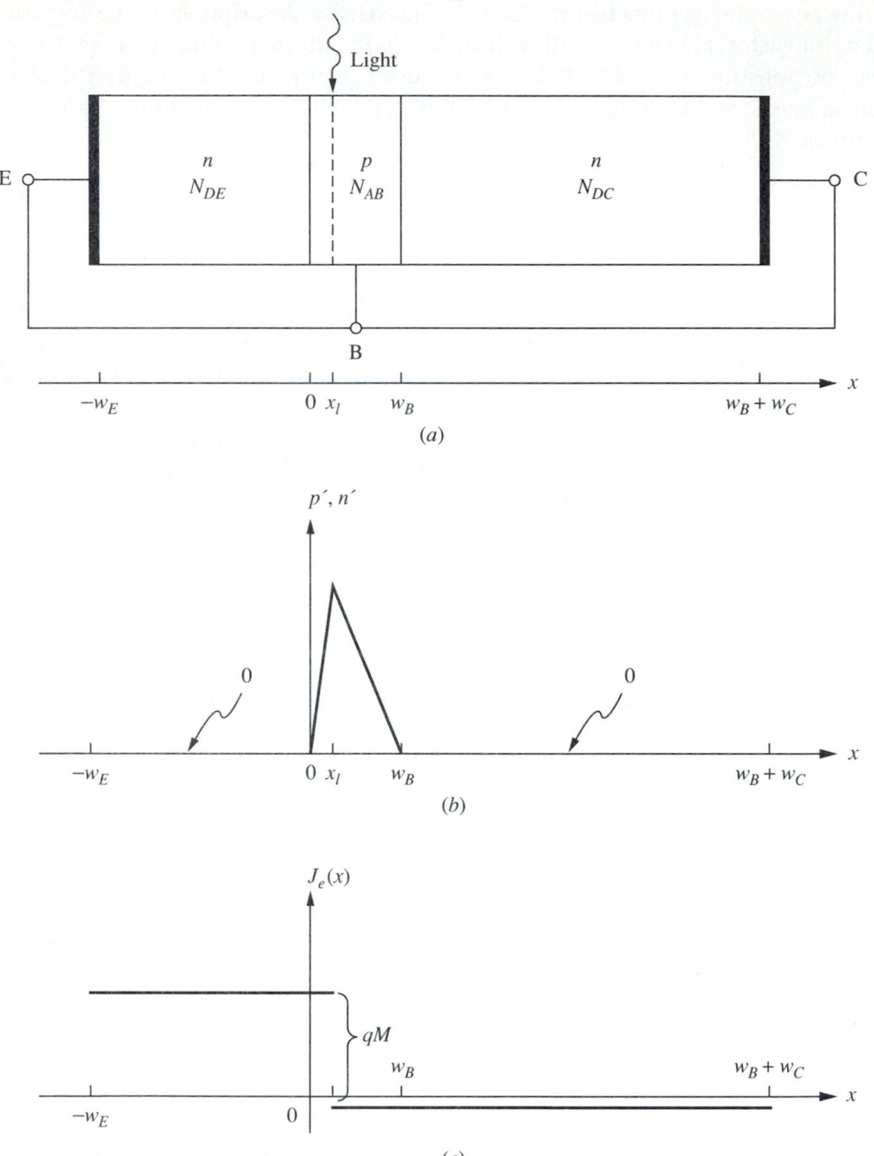

FIGURE 8.29
(*a*) Short-circuited one-dimensional *npn* bipolar transistor illuminated with light generating M hole-electron pairs/$\text{cm}^2 \cdot \text{s}$ uniformly across the plane at $x = x_l$; (*b*) excess minority carrier distribution assuming x_l is in the base region; (*c*) the corresponding minority carrier current distribution.

where the factors f and g take on the following values when x_l is in each of five regions:

$$f = \frac{(-w_E - x_l)}{(-w_E - 0^-)}, \quad g = 0 \qquad \text{for } -w_E \le x_l \le 0^- \tag{8.68a}$$

$$f = 1, \quad g = 0 \qquad \text{for } 0^- \le x_l \le 0^+ \tag{8.68b}$$

$$f = \frac{(w_B^- - x_l)}{(w_B^- - 0^+)}, \quad g = 1 - f \qquad \text{for } 0^+ \le x_l \le w_B^- \tag{8.68c}$$

$$f = 0, \quad g = 1 \qquad \text{for } w_{B^-} \le x_l \le w_B^+ \tag{8.68d}$$

$$f = 0, \quad g = \frac{(w_C + w_B - x_l)}{(w_C + w_B - w_B^+)} \qquad \text{for } w_{B^+} \le x_l \le (w_B^+ w_C) \tag{8.68e}$$

An equivalent circuit for these characteristics is shown in Fig. 8.30*a*. Combining the circuit of Fig. 8.30*a* with the Ebers–Moll model (Fig. 8.7) results in the complete large-signal phototransistor model shown in Fig. 8.30*b*.

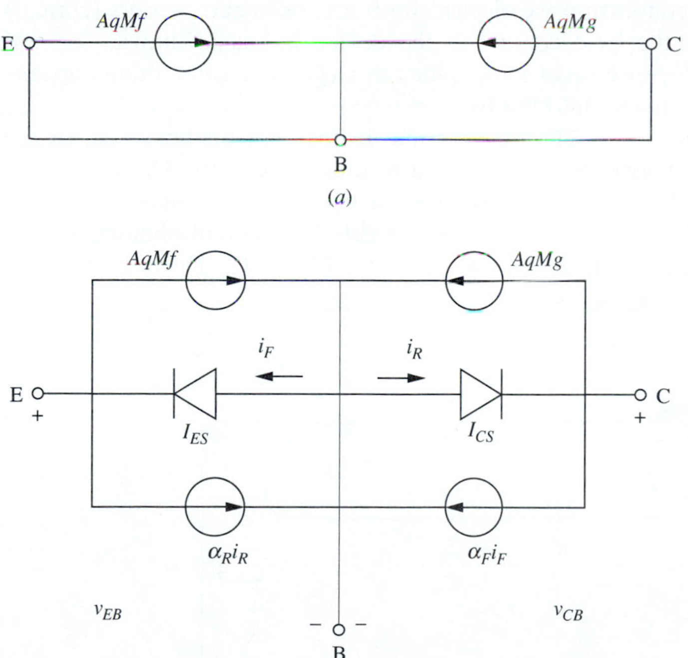

FIGURE 8.30
(*a*) Large-signal equivalent circuit for the terminal characteristics of an illuminated short-circuited *npn* transistor; (*b*) the circuit in (*a*) combined with the Ebers–Moll model to give a large-signal equivalent for an *npn* bipolar phototransistor.

To see how the phototransistor differs from a photodiode, consider an *npn* phototransistor biased into its forward active region with v_{CE} very positive (i.e., much greater than kT/q) and with the base terminal open-circuited (i.e., $i_B = 0$). The base-collector junction is clearly reverse-biased, and i_R is I_{CS}. We find after a little algebra that

$$i_C = -i_E = [\beta_F(f + g) + g]qMA + \frac{(1 - \alpha_F\alpha_R)}{(1 - \alpha_F)}I_{CS} \tag{8.69a}$$

In a well-designed device, I_{CS} will be much smaller than qMA and β_F will be much greater than 1, so we can approximate this result as

$$i_C = -i_E \approx \beta_F qMA(f + g) \tag{8.69b}$$

The thing to note about this result is that the photocurrent $qMA(f + g)$ is now amplified by β_F. In a photodiode there is no amplification and every photogenerated hole-electron pair results in at most only one q of charge flowing through the device. The current through a phototransistor is β_F times as large, so a phototransistor is β_F times more "sensitive" than a photodiode.

We can think of the optical illumination as injecting majority carriers into the base of a phototransistor and thereby playing the same role as the base contact. In a common emitter connection we electrically force, or inject, carriers (current) into the base through the base contact; if the device is biased into its forward active region, the collector current is β_F times as large. The same thing happens when we photoinject carriers into the base.

We can see from our results thus far that it does not matter which of the two junctions is illuminated. Nor do we need to illuminate both. These observations, combined with the physical reality of a practical bipolar transistor structure as illustrated in Fig. 8.1, (i.e., thin and spread out) lead to real phototransistors that look like the device illustrated in cross section in Fig. 8.31. The base-collector

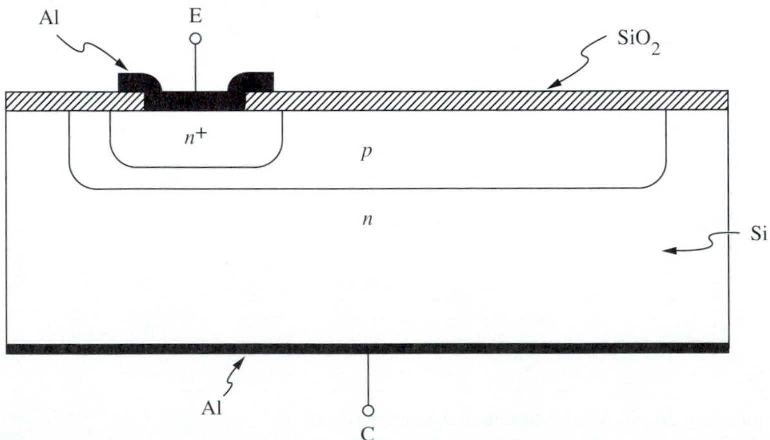

FIGURE 8.31
Cross-sectional drawing of an *npn* bipolar phototransistor fabricated in silicon using a planar process.

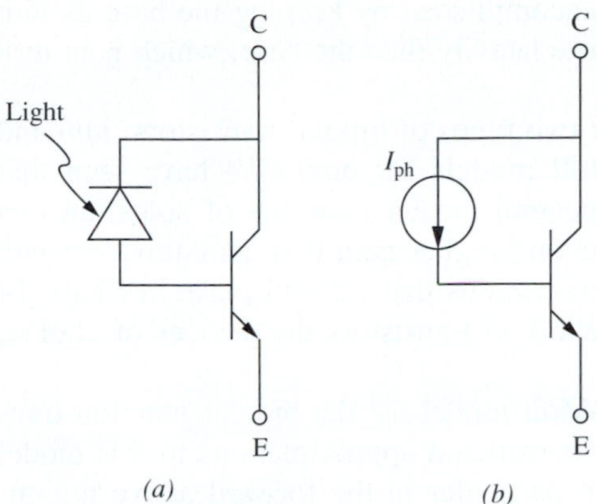

FIGURE 8.32
(*a*) Circuit schematic for a phototransistor like that of Fig. 8.31, in which the nature of the device as a photodiode merged with a transistor is highlighted; (*b*) circuit schematic for a phototransistor in which the photodiode in (*a*) is represented as an independent current source.

junction is made as large as necessary to collect the incident signal, and the emitter-base junction is kept small to block as little of the lower junction as practical. Built this way, of course, the device even physically looks very much like a photodiode merged with a bipolar transistor into a composite device like that illustrated in Fig. 8.32*a*. The photodiode looks like a current source whose output provides the base current of the transistor; Fig. 8.32*b* emphasizes this idea.

Phototransistors are used as sensors and detectors in many applications similar to those of photodiodes. It would also be tempting to think of using them in solar cell applications if we could get β_F times the solar-generated current from them, but a little thought should convince you that such an approach is unsound. To get the gain of β_F we needed to bias the transistor into its forward active region (i.e., add an external power source). The extra current and energy come from that source, not from the light, so the phototransistor is no better than a solar cell at converting optical energy to electrical energy.

8.4 SUMMARY

We began this chapter with a development of the Ebers–Moll model, a large-signal model for the terminal characteristics of a bipolar junction transistor. Although it is based upon a simplified one-dimensional approximation to a practical device structure, this model gives us excellent insight into the internal operation of bipolar transistors and provides important guidance in the design of these devices. We have introduced the concepts of the emitter, base, and collector defects and shown that the operation of the transistor is optimized by minimizing the emitter and base defects. We have seen that this can be accomplished by keeping the base as thin as possible and by doping the emitter more heavily than the base, which is in turn more heavily doped than the collector.

We have pointed out that there are two types of bipolar transistors, *npn* and *pnp*, and we have developed Ebers–Moll models for both. We have seen that because the mobility of electrons is in general greater than that of holes, an *npn* bipolar transistor will have lower defects and higher gain than an equivalent *pnp* device. This observation, along with observations that we will make in Chap. 14 concerning their higher speed, often make *npn* transistors the devices of choice, all else being equal.

After developing the basic Ebers–Moll model for the bipolar junction transistor and discussing its limitations, we considered approximations to this model in certain common operating regions, in particular in the forward active region. We have shown that the forward portion of the Ebers–Moll model dominates the transistor characteristics in the forward active region of operation and that in this region the model can be simplified considerably. We have also developed variants on this simplified model in which the base current is viewed as the signal that controls the collector current; the parameter of interest in this approach is the forward common-emitter current gain β_F, which we have shown can be made very large by minimizing the emitter and base defects.

We next developed linear equivalent circuit models for the terminal behavior of bipolar junction transistors. These models are useful for small-signal operation about fixed quiescent, or bias, points in the forward active region; we found that the parameter values in these models depend on the bias point chosen. We have developed models in both the common-emitter and common-base configurations and in which either the specific base current, the emitter current, or the base-emitter voltage was viewed as the input signal that controls the output signal, the collector current. We have seen that in all cases the small-signal models are the same for both *npn* and *pnp* transistors.

We have argued that we could extend our transistor models, which were derived under quasistatic conditions, to high frequencies by adding the energy storage elements associated with each junction in the device. We have done this for our incremental models by adding a capacitor in parallel with the base-emitter junction to represent the diffusion and depletions charge stores associated with this junction in the forward active region (i.e., when it is forward-biased); we added a second capacitor in parallel with the base-collector junction to represent the depletion charge store of this junction, which is reverse-biased in the forward active region. The common-emitter small-signal high frequency model is called the hybrid-π model and is used extensively in circuit analysis.

Finally, we have considered the optical excitation of a bipolar transistor. We have seen that the effect of light is to inject current into the base terminal and that this current will be amplified by the forward common-emitter current gain of the transistor, β_F, if it is biased in its forward active region. This process can be used very effectively as an optical light sensor, and bipolar transistors designed specifically to be sensitive to light are called phototransistors.

PROBLEMS

8.1 The *npn* silicon transistor shown in Fig. P8.1 is characterized by the following parameters:

$$N_{DE} = 5 \times 10^{17}/\text{cm}^3,\ w_E = 3\ \mu\text{m},\ \tau_{hE} = 0.1\ \mu\text{s},\ \mu_{hE} = 250\ \text{cm}^2/\text{V}\cdot\text{s}$$
$$N_{AB} = 5 \times 10^{16}/\text{cm}^3,\ w_B = 0.8\ \mu\text{m},\ \tau_{eB} = 0.1\ \mu\text{s},\ \mu_{eB} = 1000\ \text{cm}^2/\text{V}\cdot\text{s}$$
$$N_{DC} = 5 \times 10^{15}/\text{cm}^3,\ w_C = 6\ \mu\text{m},\ \tau_{hC} = 0.1\ \mu\text{s},\ \mu_{hC} = 500\ \text{cm}^2/\text{V}\cdot\text{s}$$

You must not assume that the lengths w are small compared to the diffusion lengths. Instead, you will have to check this point and proceed accordingly. The active cross-sectional area of the transistor is 5×10^4 cm^2. Use $kT/q = 0.025$ V and $n_i = 1.0 \times 10^{10}/\text{cm}^3$.

(*a*) The transistor is operated in the forward mode with $v_{BE} > 0$ and $v_{BC} = 0$. Obtain numerical values for the base and emitter defects, δ_{EF} and δ_{BF}.

(*b*) Obtain numerical values for the corresponding defects, δ_{CR} and δ_{BR}, when the transistor is operated in the reverse mode with $v_{BC} > 0$ and $v_{BE} = 0$.

(*c*) Obtain numerical values for β_F and β_R.

(*d*) Obtain numerical values for the Ebers–Moll parameters: $I_{ES}, I_{CS}, \alpha_F, \alpha_R$.

(*e*) Show that your numerical calculations give $\alpha_F I_{ES} = \alpha_R I_{CS}$.

8.2 Two *npn* transistors, Q_A and Q_B, are structurally identical in all respects except that the cross-sectional area of Q_B is four times that of Q_A. These transistors are both biased in their forward active regions with $I_C = 2$ mA and $V_{CE} = 6$ V.

The questions below concern the parameters in the Ebers–Moll and hybrid-π models for these two devices. Indicate how each quantity specified compares for the larger transistor Q_B and the smaller transistor Q_A. You may assume that space-charge layer recombination is negligible and that the transistors are biased to operate under low-level injection conditions.

(*a*) Ebers–Moll emitter-base diode saturation current I_{ES}

(*b*) Ebers–Moll reverse alpha, α_R

(*c*) Quiescent emitter-base voltage, V_{EB}

(*d*) Hybrid-π transconductance, g_m

(*e*) Diffusion capacitance component C_{eb}^{df} of the hybrid-π emitter-base capacitance C_π

(*f*) Hybrid-π base-collector capacitance, C_μ

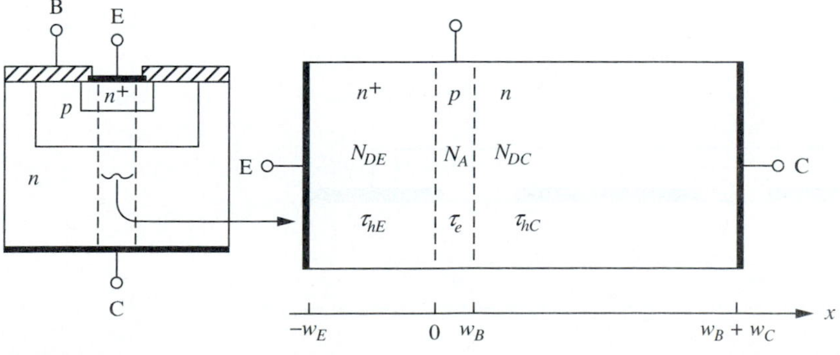

FIGURE P8.1

8.3 Two high-gain bipolar transistors have identical dimensions and identical emitter, base, and collector doping profiles, except that transistor A is *npn* and transistor B is *pnp*. Indicate which device, if either, has the property stated below and explain why.

(*a*) Largest forward current gain β_F
(*b*) Smallest transconductance g_m with $|I_c| = 1$ mA
(*c*) Largest base-collector diode saturation current I_{CS}
(*d*) Lowest parasitic base resistance r_x

8.4 Consider an *npn* bipolar junction transistor, like that pictured in Fig. 8.2, that is fabricated of silicon and has the following doping levels and dimensions:

$$N_{DE} = 5 \times 10^{18} \text{ cm}^{-3}, \qquad w_E^* = 0.5\ \mu\text{m}$$
$$N_{AB} = 2 \times 10^{17} \text{ cm}^{-3}, \qquad w_B^* = 0.2\ \mu\text{m}$$
$$N_{DC} = 5 \times 10^{15} \text{ cm}^{-3}, \qquad w_C^* = 10\ \mu\text{m}$$

Assume that $\mu_e = 1600$ cm^2/V · s, $\mu_h = 600$ cm^2/V · s, $n_i = 10^{10}$ cm^{-3}, and $\tau_{\text{min}} = 10^{-4}$ s. Assume also that the device is to be modeled using the Ebers–Moll formulation.

(*a*) What are the emitter, base, and collector defects in this device?
(*b*) What are α_F and α_R?
(*c*) What are J_{ES} and J_{CS}?
(*d*) Confirm that $\alpha_F J_{ES} = \alpha_R J_{ES}$.
(*e*) What is β_F?

8.5 (*a*) For the bipolar transistor in problem 8.1, calculate the emitter current density at the onset of high-level injection in the base, assuming that this corresponds to $n'(0^+) = 0.1 N_{AB}$.

(*b*) If the emitter, viewed from the top, is a rectangular stripe 3 μm wide and L μm long, how large must L be if this transistor is designed to operate at collector currents up to 2 mA without entering high-level injection?

(*c*) What is the incremental transconductance g_m of this transistor with a quiescent collector current of 1 mA?

(*d*) (i) Calculate the resistance of the base region (i.e., between 0^+ and w_B^- from long edge to long edge). Assume this region is $w_B^*(= 0.2\ \mu$m) thick.

(ii) This type of transistor would typically be constructed with two base contact stripes on either side of the emitter stripe; each contact will supply half of the base current, which in turn flows at most halfway under the emitter (see

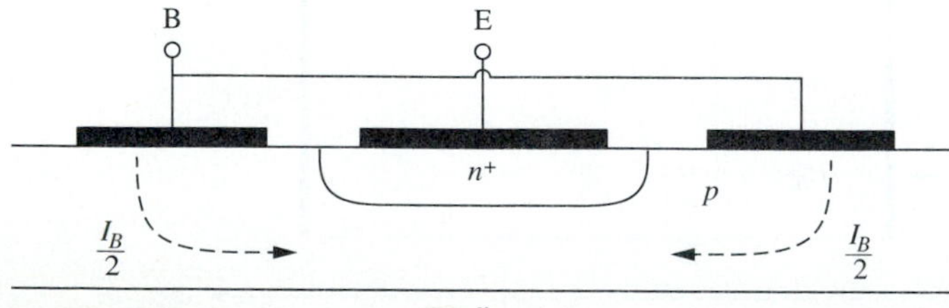

FIGURE P8.5

Fig. P8.5). Estimate the lateral voltage drop from the edge to the middle of the base region due to the base current when $I_C = 1$ mA.

8.6 A lateral transistor has the structure illustrated in Fig P8.6a (the drawing is idealized and not to scale). Electrically this device can be modeled as a high-β *pnp* transistor Q with diodes D_{S1} and D_{S2} shunting the emitter-base and base-collector junctions. This question concerns the Ebers–Moll model for such a lateral *pnp* transistor. In answering parts a through c, ignore the space-charge layer widths. Also assume that one-dimensional models can be used for all of the junctions. Make appropriate engineering approximations.

The device dimensions and parameters are as follows:

$$w_p = w_B = 1.0\ \mu\text{m}, \qquad L_{hB} = 10\ \mu\text{m}, \qquad D_e = 40\ \text{cm}^2/\text{s}$$
$$w_S = 100\ \mu\text{m}, \qquad w_C^* = w_E^* = 5\ \mu\text{m}, \qquad D_h = 15\ \text{cm}^2/\text{s}$$

Areas of emitter and collector bottoms: 5×10^{-2} cm^2 (each)
Areas of emitter and collector sides: 10^{-2} cm^2 (each)
p^+-regions: $p_o = 5 \times 10^{18}$ cm^{-3}
n-region: $n_o = 10^{16}$ cm^{-3}

Use $n_i^2 = 1 \times 10^{20}$ cm^{-3}.

(*a*) What are the numerical values of the saturation currents of the following diodes?
  (i) The shunting diodes (i.e., the vertical diodes). Call this saturation current I_{SS}.
  (ii) The Ebers–Moll model diodes of the high-β *pnp* transistor (i.e., the lateral diodes). These are I_{ES} and I_{CS}.

(*b*) Make an Ebers–Moll model valid for the composite transistor, that is, including the shunting vertical diodes (see Fig. P8.6b).
  (i) What are I'_{ES} and I'_{CS} in terms of $I_{ES}, I_{CS}, I_{SS}, \alpha_F$, and α_R?
  (ii) What are α'_F and α'_R?
  (iii) Is β'_F greater than, equal to, or less than β_F?

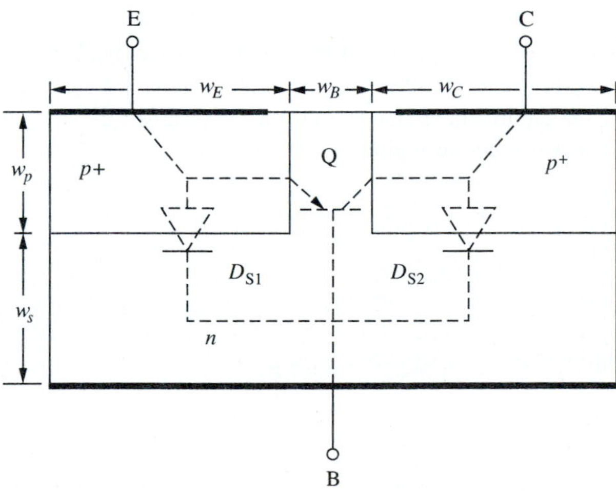

FIGURE P8.6a

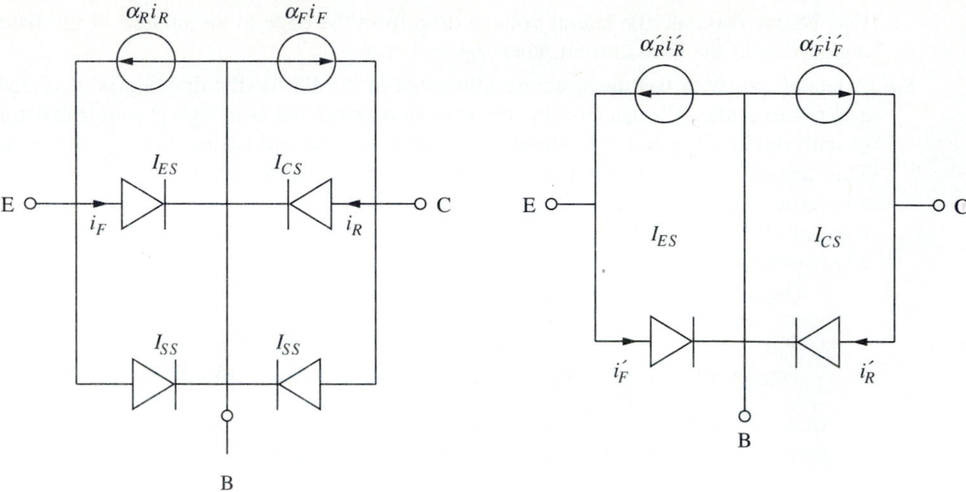

FIGURE P8.6b

(*c*) Lateral transistors have symmetrical doping profiles and thus have $N_{AE} = N_{AC} >> N_{DB}$. Discuss the consequences of each of the following situations for transistor characteristics, and state whether they are desirable or not:

(i) $N_{AE} >> N_{DB}$

(ii) $N_{AC} >> N_{DB}$

8.7 Consider two bipolar junction transistors, an *npn* transistor and a *pnp* transistor. Both transistors have values of $\beta_F = 200$ and $\beta_R = 20$ and have comparable values of I_{ES}.

(*a*) What is the numerical value of the ratio I_{CS}/I_{ES} for each transistor?

Assume that there is negligible recombination in the base regions of these devices. In both transistors, the current crossing the emitter-base junction consists of both electrons and holes.

(*b*) Find the numerical value for the fraction of the emitter current carried by electrons in the *npn* transistor and by holes in the *pnp*.

These transistors are used in the circuit illustrated in Fig. P8.7. Assume that the *npn* transistor is operating in the forward active region.

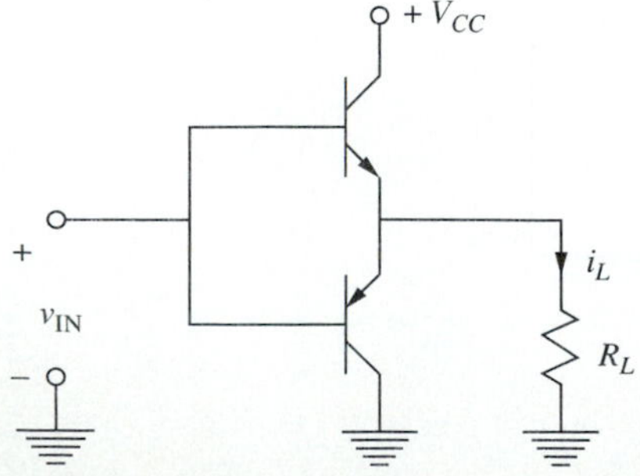

FIGURE P8.7

(a)

(b)

(c)

(d)

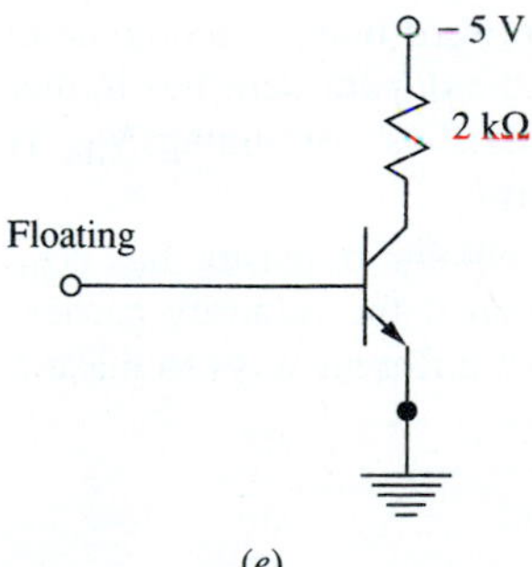

(e)

FIGURE P8.8

(c) Determine the region of operation of the *pnp* transistor, and briefly justify your choice. Your choice should be one of the following: forward active, reverse active, saturation, or cutoff.

8.8 For each of the transistor circuits shown in Fig. P8.8, sketch the excess minority carrier distribution through the device. For each transistor, $\beta_F = 100$, $V_{BE,\text{ON}} = 0.6$ V, and $N_{DE} > N_{AB} > N_{DC}$. Assume infinite minority carrier lifetimes and $W_E = W_B = 0.2W_C$.

8.9 Consider designing an integrated circuit according to the following simplified design rules:

Minimum oxide opening that can be etched:	1 μm by 1 μm
Minimum-width line (opening or feature) that can be defined:	1 μm wide
Minimum separation between metal lines:	2 μm
Minimum nesting allowance, i.e., contact opening within a diffusion, metal pattern overlap of a contact opening, etc.:	2 μm all around

(*a*) Lay out a bipolar transistor like that pictured in Fig. 8.1 with the smallest emitter possible under these design rules. Use a rectangular, rather than circular, geometry.

(*b*) Calculate the approximate ratio of the area of the base-collector junction to that of the emitter-base junction, and discuss the implications of this for C_π and C_μ. Assume a base-collector junction depth below the top wafer surface of 0.5 μm and an emitter-base junction depth of 0.3 μm; also assume that a diffusion through an oxide opening spreads laterally 80 percent of the junction depth.

(*b*) What fraction of the electrons flowing from the emitter into the base when the emitter-base junction is forward biased recombines in the base?

(*c*) Suppose you want to change the dopant densities in this transistor to improve its forward active region characteristics. Assuming that N_{AB} is fixed, what would you do to N_{DE} and N_{DC} and why?

8.10 This question concerns an *npn* bipolar transistor that has the following dimensions and properties:

$$N_{DE} = 2N_{AB} = 4N_{DC}, \qquad D_e = 2D_h$$

$$w_E^* = w_B^* = w_e^* = W, \qquad L_e = L_h = 10W$$

(*a*) Based on the emitter-base junction, what is the ratio of hole to electron current crossing this junction in forward bias?

(*b*) What fraction of the electrons flowing from from the emitter into the base when the base-emitter junction is forward biased recombine in the base?

(*c*) Suppose you want to change the dopant densities in this transistor to improve its forward active region characteristics. Assuming N_{AB} is fixed, what would you do to N_{DE} and N_{DC}, and why?

8.11 A certain one-dimensional *npn* bipolar transistor has $N_{DE} = 2N_{AB} = 4N_{DC}$ and $W_E = W_B = 0.25W_C$. Throughout it the minority carrier lifetime is infinite. This transistor can be connected in five different ways to make a *p-n* diode, as illustrated in Fig. P8.11.

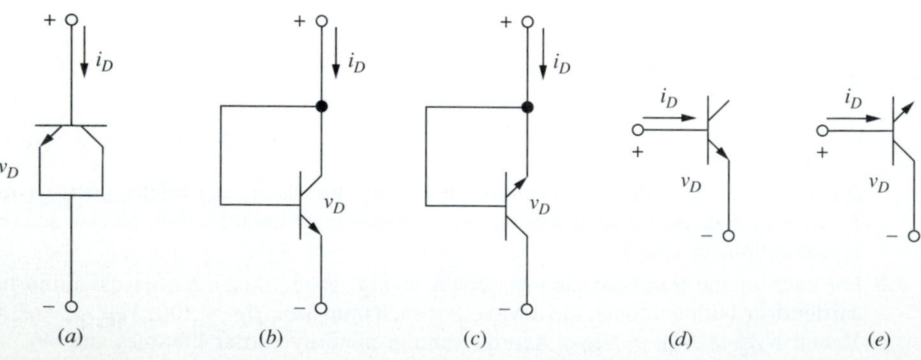

FIGURE P8.11

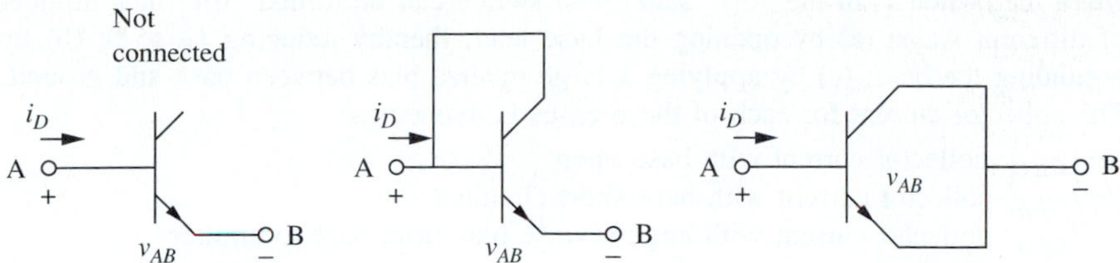

FIGURE P8.12

For the same value of V_D, given that $V_D >> kT/q$, sketch the excess minority carrier distribution in the device in each connection.

8.12 Consider using the emitter-base junction of an *npn* transistor as a diode. We want to compare the three possible connections illustrated in Fig. P8.12.

(*a*) (i) Find a relationship for i_D as a function of v_{AB} in terms of the Ebers–Moll parameters ($\alpha_F, \alpha_R, I_{ES}$, and I_{CS}) of the transistor.

(ii) For which of these "diodes" is "I_S" largest? Smallest?

(*b*) For each of these connections find expressions in terms of the Ebers–Moll parameters for the ratio of the collector current in the transistor to the emitter current.

(*c*) Indicate on sketches of each of the connections the main current path through the device from A to B.

(*d*) Sketch the excess hole and electron distributions through this transistor in each of the connections. Assume that $N_{DE} = 2N_{AB} - 4N_{DC}$, and $W_E = W_B = 0.5W_C$. Assume infinite lifetimes.

(*e*) (i) In which of these diode connections is the total density of excess minority carriers under forward bias the smallest, assuming the same applied voltage v_D, and why?

(ii) In which of these diode connections is the total density of excess minority carriers under forward bias the smallest, assuming the same total current i_D, and why?

(iii) In which connection is the diffusion capacitance largest, assuming the same voltage bias V_D, and why?

8.13 An *npn* transistor with $\beta_F = 200$ and $\beta_R = 1$ is used as a switch in the circuit shown in Fig. P8.13. For this application it is important to know the collector current

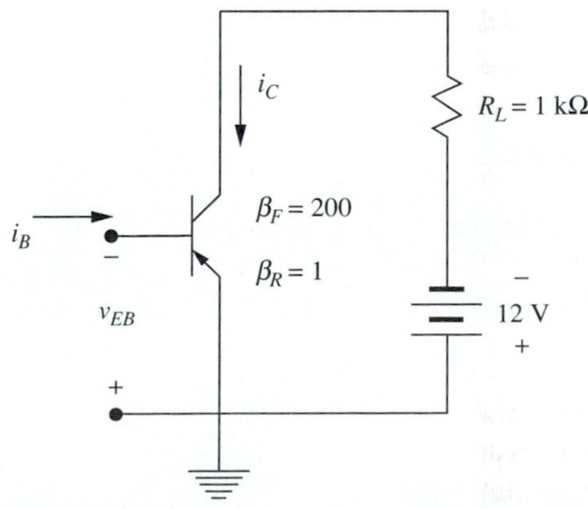

FIGURE P8.13

when the switch is in the "off" state. The switch can be turned "off" in a number of different ways: (a) by opening the base lead, thereby reducing i_B to 0; (b) by grounding the base; (c) by applying a large reverse bias between base and ground. The collector current for each of these cases is defined as

(*a*) I_{CEO}: collector current with base open
(*b*) I_{CES}: collector current with base short-circuited
(*c*) I_{CEX}: collector current with large reverse bias from base to emitter

Find numerical values for each of these currents when $I_{CS} = 10$ nA.

CHAPTER 9

THE MOS CAPACITOR

In modern semiconductor electronics there are a number of fundamental structures, including the *p-n* junction, the metal-semiconductor contact, and the metal-oxide-semiconductor capacitor. We discussed *p-n* junctions in Chaps. 6 and 7, and Appendix E deals with metal-semiconductor contacts. In this chapter we focus our attention on the metal-oxide-semiconductor (MOS) capacitor structure.

The MOS capacitor forms the heart of an important family of devices called *MOS field effect transistors*, or MOSFETs. In much the same way that understanding *p-n* junctions is central to understanding the operation of bipolar junction transistors, understanding the MOS capacitor is central to understanding the operation of MOSFETs. The MOS capacitor is also a useful device in its own right (i.e., as a capacitor), and the MOS capacitor structure is also useful as an optical sensor.

We will begin our study of the MOS capacitor in this chapter by looking at this structure in thermal equilibrium. We will then study what happens when we apply voltage to an MOS capacitor and look at the unique features that make the MOS capacitor so useful in devices.

9.1 THE MOS CAPACITOR IN THERMAL EQUILIBRIUM

To form an MOS capacitor we start with a sample of uniformly doped semiconductor, say *p*-type silicon, with an ohmic contact on one side. The other side is covered with a thin insulating layer; in the case of silicon this is usually silicon dioxide, SiO_2, or a combination of silicon dioxide and silicon nitride, Si_3N_4. A thin film of metal—aluminum is a common example—deposited on this insulator completes the metal-oxide-semiconductor capacitor structure. Such an MOS capacitor is illustrated in Fig. 9.1.

Now consider the electrostatic potential variation through this structure, assuming thermal equilibrium. Assume for simplicity that the ohmic contact is also made of aluminum, as in fact it often is. As we have done before, we will begin by considering variation only in one dimension, the x-direction, which in this case we will take to be normal to the silicon surface, as illustrated in Fig. 9.2a. The potential in the aluminum relative to intrinsic silicon is ϕ_{Al}, and that of p-type silicon is ϕ_p. The thickness of the silicon dioxide is t_o. If the silicon dioxide can be modeled as a perfect dielectric and if there are no ions in it or at any of the interfaces, the potential profile must look like the plot in Fig. 9.2b. The two aluminum contacts are assumed to be shorted together as shown in Fig. 9.2a, and the structure is assumed to be in thermal equilibrium, so the net change in potential going around the circuit is zero. Because the potential in the metal is higher than that in the semiconductor, there must be a slight depletion in the semiconductor at each surface (i.e., at $x = 0$ and at $x = w$) and an excess of positive charge in the metal. The potential profile and net charge distribution are illustrated in Figs. 9.2b and c, respectively.

Your attention should be focused on the metal-oxide-semiconductor structure on the left of Fig. 9.2a, rather than on the contact structure on the right. We will assume that the contact to the silicon on the right performs like an ideal ohmic contact. All of the "action" is on the left.

The structure, as you can see, is relatively simple. Although we have yet to quantify our description, you should be comfortable with these pictures after having studied p-n junctions in Chap. 7.

9.2 ISOLATED MOS CAPACITOR WITH APPLIED VOLTAGE

Given our qualitative picture of what an MOS capacitor looks like in thermal equilibrium, let us now open the circuit and apply an external voltage source between the two terminals. We will discuss what happens qualitatively as well as develop a quantitative model based on the depletion approximation.

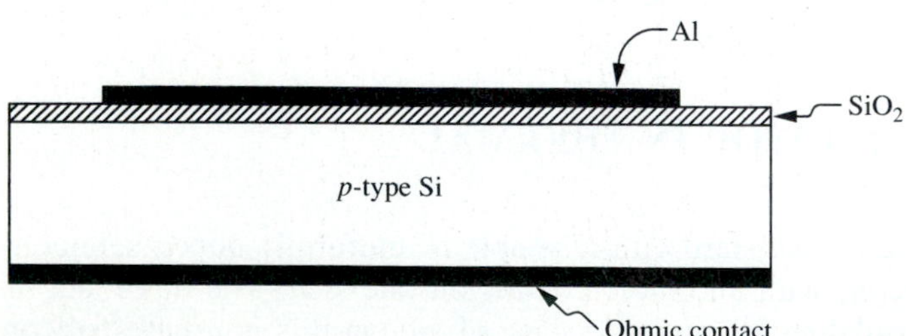

FIGURE 9.1
Typical MOS capacitor formed of aluminum, silicon dioxide, and p-type silicon.

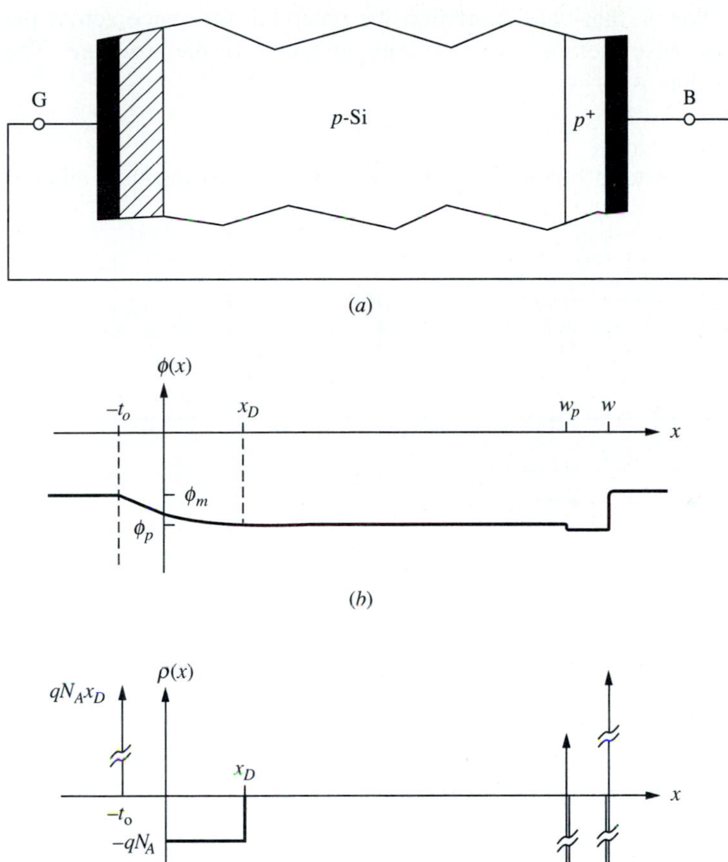

FIGURE 9.2
(*a*) One-dimensional MOS capacitor structure with its terminals shorted and in thermal equilibrium; (*b*) the variation in the electrostatic potential relative to intrinsic silicon through this structure; and (*c*) the corresponding net charge distribution.

9.2.1 Flat-band

Consider first applying a voltage v_{GB} to the left-hand capacitor electrode, which we label G for "gate," relative to the ohmic contact, which we label B for "back," that is negative. The potential at the interface between the oxide and the semiconductor, $\phi(0)$, decreases toward ϕ_p, and the depletion region width also decreases. At the same time the positive charge is removed from the capacitor electrode (i.e., at $x = -t_o$). For some particular applied voltage, there will be no depletion of the semiconductor and the potential at the surface of the semiconductor will equal that in its bulk [i.e., $\phi(0) = \phi_p$]. This situation, illustrated in Figs. 9.3*a* and *b*, is called the *flat-band* condition, and the corresponding applied voltage V_{FB} is an important point of reference. For the flat-band condition the potential difference across the oxide is also zero because there is no net charge anywhere in the structure. The flat-band voltage is thus

$$V_{FB} = -(\phi_m - \phi_p) \tag{9.1}$$

where ϕ_m is the electrostatic potential of the metal relative to intrinsic silicon. This is illustrated in Fig. 9.3*a*.

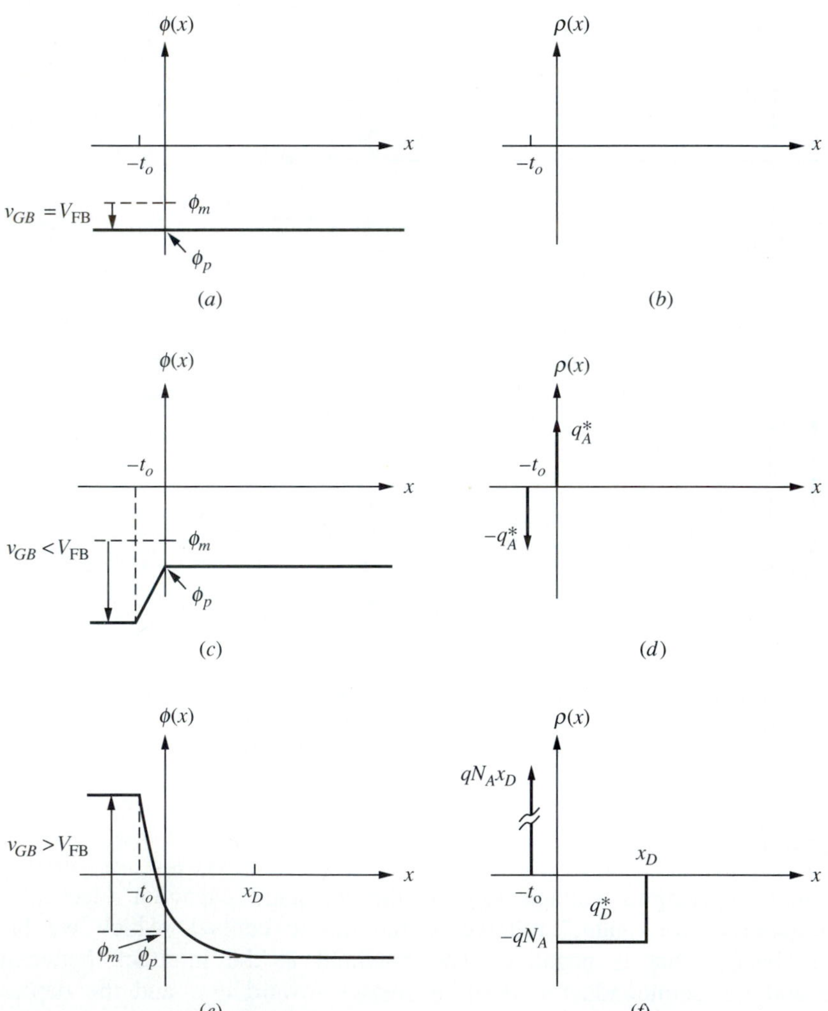

FIGURE 9.3(a-f)
Electrostatic potential and net charge distributions for an MOS structure on a p-type semiconductor under various bias conditions, assuming that the depletion approximation is valid: (*a* and *b*) flat-band, $v_{GB} = V_{FB}$; (*c* and *d*) accumulation, $v_{GB} < V_{FB}$; (*e* and *f*) depletion, $V_{FB} < v_{GB} < V_T$; (*g* and *h*) threshold, $v_{GB} = V_T$; (*i* and *j*) inversion, $v_{GB} > V_T$.

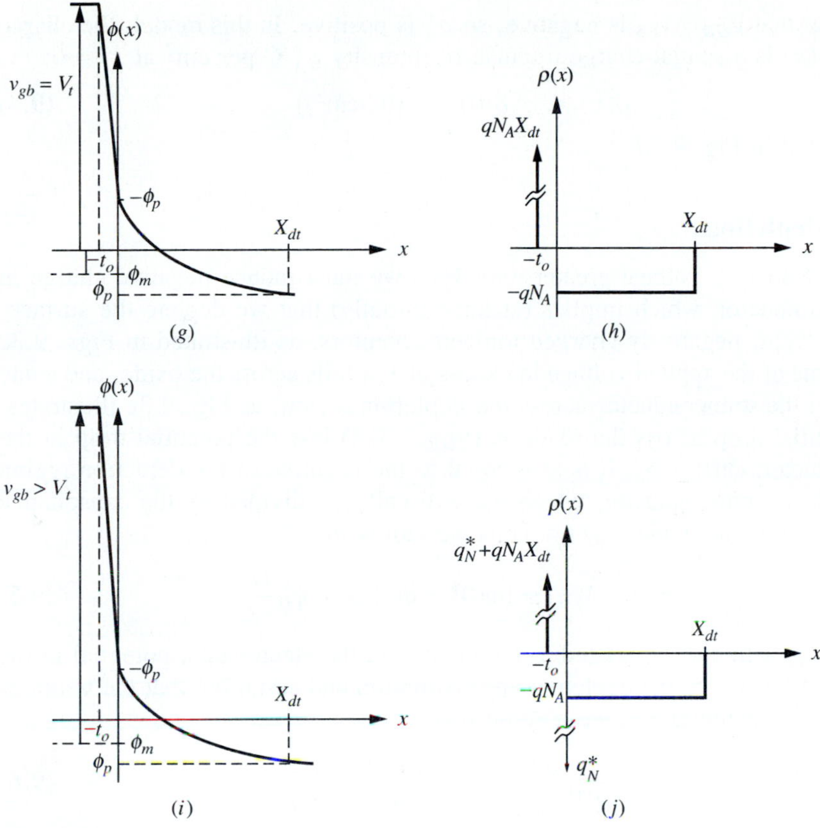

FIGURE 9.3(g-j)
(*continued*)

9.2.2 Accumulation

If we apply a voltage more negative than V_{FB}, the electrostatic potential in the semiconductor decreases, the hole density at the surface increases rapidly, and all of the additional field is terminated on a thin layer of holes that accumulates in the semiconductor within a few nanometers of the interface. This condition is called *accumulation* and is illustrated in Figs. 9.3*c* and *d*. Assuming that all of the accumulated holes are right at the interface, we can write the resulting charge density using

$$v_{GB} - V_{\text{FB}} = -\frac{q_A^* t_o}{\varepsilon_o} \tag{9.2}$$

so that we have

$$q_A^* = -(v_{GB} - V_{\text{FB}})\frac{\varepsilon_o}{t_o} \tag{9.3}$$

Remember that $v_{GB} - V_{\text{FB}}$ is negative, so q_A^* is positive. In this model, the charge density $\rho(x)$ is a spatial charge impulse of intensity q_A^* C per cm^2 at $x = 0$:

$$\rho(x) = q_A^* \delta(0) \qquad [(\text{C/cm}^2)] \tag{9.4}$$

as illustrated in Fig. 9.3*d*.

9.2.3 Depletion

If we next apply a voltage greater than V_{FB}, we must induce negative charge in the semiconductor, which implies (at least initially) that we deplete the surface, exposing fixed, negatively charged ionized acceptors, as illustrated in Figs. 9.3*e* and *f*. Some of the applied voltage in excess of V_{FB} falls across the oxide, and some appears in the semiconductor across the depletion region, as Fig. 9.3*e* illustrates. The potential drop across the oxide is $(v_{GB} - V_{\text{FB}})$ less the potential drop in the semiconductor, $\phi(0) - \phi_p$. It is also equal to the negative of the depletion region charge of the semiconductor, which we will call q_D^*, divided by the capacitance per unit area of the oxide, ε_o / t_o. Thus we can write

$$(v_{GB} - V_{\text{FB}}) - [\phi(0) - \phi_p] = -q_D^* \frac{t_o}{\varepsilon_o} \tag{9.5}$$

But q_D^* can also be related to the change in the electrostatic potential in the semiconductor. Using the depletion approximation and assuming that the width of the depletion region is x_D, we assume that

$$\rho(x) = \begin{cases} -qN_A & \text{for } 0 \le x \le x_D \\ 0 & \text{for } x \ge x_D \end{cases} \tag{9.6}$$

Thus

$$q_D^* = -qN_A x_D \tag{9.7}$$

The electric field must then be given by

$$\mathscr{E}(x) = \begin{cases} \dfrac{qN_A(x - x_D)}{\varepsilon_{\text{Si}}} & \text{for } 0 \le x \le x_D \\ 0 & \text{for } x \ge x_D \end{cases} \tag{9.8}$$

and the electrostatic potential must be

$$\phi(x) = \begin{cases} \dfrac{qN_A(x - x_D)^2}{2\varepsilon_{\text{Si}}} + \phi_p & \text{for } 0 \le x \le x_D \\ \phi_p & \text{for } x \ge x_D \end{cases} \tag{9.9}$$

Thus

$$\phi(0) = \frac{qN_A x_D^2}{2\varepsilon_{\text{Si}}} + \phi_p$$

or

$$x_D = \sqrt{\frac{2\varepsilon_{\text{Si}}[\phi(0) - \phi_p]}{qN_A}} \tag{9.10}$$

and

$$q_D^* = -\sqrt{2\varepsilon_{\text{Si}} q N_A [\phi(0) - \phi_p]} \tag{9.11}$$

Using Eqs. (9.5) and (9.11), we can solve for $\phi(0)$ in terms of v_{GB}, so we can find x_D and q_D^* if we so desire.

Clearly, as the applied voltage increases, the depletion width in the semiconductor increases and the electrostatic potential at the oxide-semiconductor interface, $\phi(0)$, increases.

As the electrostatic potential in the semiconductor changes, the hole and electron populations also change. We already used this fact without making note of it when we used the depletion approximation. That is, just as when we treated an abrupt *p-n* junction in Chap. 6, we implicitly argue above that as the potential increases above ϕ_p for $x \leq x_D$, the mobile hole population decreases rapidly and the net charge density increases rapidly with x to $-qN_A$. Before going further, we must question our assumption that the carrier populations are still related to the electrostatic potential as they are in thermal equilibrium. Specifically, is it still valid to use the thermal equilibrium expressions

$$n_o(x) = n_i e^{q\phi(x)/kT} \tag{6.7}$$

$$p_o(x) = n_i e^{-q\phi(x)/kT} \tag{6.8}$$

when we have voltage applied to an MOS capacitor?

The answer is yes in the present situation, because in the steady state there is no current flowing through the structure and the semiconductor remains in thermal equilibrium. In the steady state, the source providing the applied voltage v_{GB} supplies no energy to the system and both the electron and hole currents are zero. If that is the case we again arrive at Eqs. (6.1), which led to the expressions above.

Now we can see another important consequence of the increase in electrostatic potential in the semiconductor, in addition to the decrease in hole concentration $p(x)$, for $0 \leq x \leq x_D$; namely, that the electron population increases. The density stays low and the negative charge density due to electrons, $-qn(x)$, is negligible compared to that due to fixed ionized acceptors, $-qN_A$, until the electrostatic potential, ϕ, approaches $-\phi_p$. When $\phi(x) \approx -\phi_p$, however, $n(x) \approx N_A$ and the electrons can no longer be ignored. This occurs first at the oxide-semiconductor interface. We call the applied voltage for which $\phi(0) = -\phi_p$ the *threshold voltage* V_T.

9.2.4 Threshold and Inversion

The threshold voltage V_T is defined as v_{GB} such that $\phi(0) = -\phi_p$. Using Eqs. (9.10) and (9.11) we can thus write

$$X_{DT} = \sqrt{\frac{2\varepsilon_{\text{Si}} |2\phi_p|}{qN_A}} \tag{9.12}$$

and

$$Q^*_{DT} = -\sqrt{2\varepsilon_{\mathrm{Si}} q N_A |2\phi_p|} \tag{9.13}$$

where a subscript T has been added to denote threshold values and capital X and Q are used to emphasize that these are special values. The situation in the semiconductor when $v_{GB} = V_T$, a situation we describe as "being at threshold" is illustrated in Figs. 9.3*g* and *h*.

By using this last result in Eq. (9.5) we can obtain

$$V_T = V_{\mathrm{FB}} - 2\phi_p + \frac{t_o}{\varepsilon_o}\sqrt{2\varepsilon_{\mathrm{Si}} q N_A |2\phi_p|} \tag{9.14}$$

For $V_{\mathrm{FB}} \leq v_{GB} \leq V_T$ the depletion approximation model described in Sec. 9.2.3 is appropriate, but for $v_{GB} \geq V_T$ we use a different model. The electron density near the oxide-semiconductor interface increases exponentially with the electrostatic potential ϕ, so once it equals and surpasses N_A, the electrons will become the dominant source of new negative charge induced in the semiconductor by further increases in applied voltage. A slight increase in $\phi(0)$ above $-\phi_p$ increases $n(0)$ dramatically (i.e., exponentially).

Rather than try to calculate $n(x)$ for $x \geq 0$, we argue that all of these induced electrons will be in a very thin layer near the surface, which we treat spatially as an impulse of negative charge q_N^* at $x = 0$. Thus, above threshold (i.e., for $v_{GB} > V_T$) we approximate the net charge distribution in the semiconductor as

$$\rho(x) = \begin{cases} q_N^*\delta(x) - qN_A & \text{for } 0 \leq x \leq X_{DT} \\ 0 & \text{for } x \geq X_{DT} \end{cases} \tag{9.15}$$

Notice that we have assumed further that the depletion region width does not increase above threshold, neither does $|q_D^*|$. We know that the electrostatic potential must increase slightly over a shallow distance near the oxide-semiconductor interface, but we assume that this leads to a negligible increase in the depletion region width and thus in $|q_D^*|$. All of the action, if you will, above threshold is near the interface.

The situation at the interface above threshold is analogous to what it was for accumulation, except that now we have a high density of mobile electrons rather than mobile holes. A thin surface layer has been created in which the majority carriers are electrons. This pseudo-n-type layer is called a *channel*, or *inversion layer*. The surface is said to be inverted (from p-type to n-type), and this condition is called *inversion*. This situation is summarized in Figs. 9.3*i* and *j*.

The sheet charge density in the channel, q_N^*, is a very important quantity. We can calculate it because, as we have said, it is induced by the applied voltage in excess of threshold. Thus,

$$q_N^* = -(v_{GB} - V_T)\frac{\varepsilon_o}{t_o} \tag{9.16}$$

when $v_{GB} \geq V_T$.

Example

Question. Consider an MOS capacitor fabricated on a p-type silicon substrate that is doped with a net acceptor concentration N_A of 2×10^{16} cm^{-3}. The electrostatic potential in the gate metal relative to intrinsic silicon, ϕ_m, is +0.3 V; and the gate dielectric is silicon dioxide 25 nm thick. The relative dielectric constant of silicon dioxide is 3.9, and that of silicon is 11.7. What are the flat-band and threshold voltages, V_{FB} and V_T, respectively; what are the width of the depletion region above threshold, X_{DT}, and the sheet charge density in the depletion region above threshold, Q_{DT}^*; and what is the sheet charge density in the inversion layer, q_N^*, when the gate voltage v_{GB} is 2 V greater than the threshold voltage V_T? Assume room temperature, and take n_i to be 10^{10} cm^{-3} and kT/q to be 0.025 V.

Discussion. We first calculate the electrostatic potential ϕ_p in the bulk of the p-type silicon substrate. Using Eq. (6.26b), we find that ϕ_p is −0.35 V. Thus, from Eq. (9.1), we find that V_{FB} is −0.65 V.

To find the threshold voltage, we use Eq. (9.14) and find that V_T is approximately 0.9 V.

To calculate the maximum depletion region width, X_{DT}, we use Eq. (9.12) and calculate that it is approximately 0.2 μm. The corresponding sheet charge density in the depletion region, Q_{DT}^*, is -1.34×10^{-8} C/cm^2.

Finally, using Eq. (9.16) we calculate that with the gate biased in excess of threshold, the sheet charge density in the inversion layer, q_N^*, is -2.8×10^{-7} C/cm^2. This corresponds to a sheet electron density of 1.7×10^{12} cm^{-2}.

9.3 BIASED MOS CAPACITOR WITH CONTACT TO THE CHANNEL

The n-type inversion layer that forms under an MOS capacitor structure on a p-type semiconductor can be thought of as an n-type surface layer. Thinking this way we can see that we have effectively formed a p-n^+ junction at the surface. Thus far in our discussion, the semiconductor has been in thermal equilibrium throughout, including up to the oxide-semiconductor interface, and so this junction is also in equilibrium (i.e., zero-biased). Imagine, however, that we can make electrical contact to the n-side of this junction and reverse-bias it by increasing the potential on that side relative to the p-side. No appreciable current will flow, but the potential drop across the depletion region will increase and the depletion region width will increase above the value X_{DT} specified in Eq. (9.12). Clearly q_D^* will change, and as a consequence q_N^* will also change, assuming that the voltage on the top metal electrode, v_{GB}, is held fixed. These effects are very important in field effect transistors that use MOS capacitors, so we will consider them in more detail now. First we will assume that we somehow have direct electrical contact to the channel as we have just argued; then we will assume that we get access to the channel through a heavily doped n-region next to the MOS capacitor.

9.3.1 Direct Contact to the Channel

To model the changes that occur when we can apply a voltage on the channel relative to the semiconductor bulk, let us assume that we can have direct electrical contact to the n-type inversion-layer side of our induced p-n diode such that we can apply a voltage v_{CB} to the channel, relative to the back contact, where $v_{CB} \geq 0$. We assume that all of this applied reverse bias (remember that our positive reference is now the n-side of the diode) appears across the depletion region. The change in electrostatic potential across this region is now $-2\phi_p + v_{CB}$ rather than simply $-2\phi_p$, so the depletion region becomes

$$X_{DT}(v_{CB}) = \sqrt{\frac{2\varepsilon_{\text{Si}}(|2\phi_p| + v_{CB})}{qN_A}} \tag{9.17}$$

and the depletion layer charge is

$$Q^*_{DT}(v_{CB}) = -\sqrt{2\varepsilon_{\text{Si}}qN_A(|2\phi_p| + v_{CB})} \tag{9.18}$$

The sheet mobile charge density in the inversion layer, Q^*_n, is found by calculating the change in potential across the oxide and setting it equal to $(q^*_N + Q^*_{DT})t_o/\varepsilon_o$. Because we know Q^*_{DT} from Eq. (9.18), we can calculate q^*_N. The potential change across the oxide must be the total potential difference between the gate electrode and the quasineutral region ($x > X_{DT}$), which is $v_{GB} - V_{\text{FB}}$, less the potential change across the depletion region, which is $|2\phi_p| + v_{CB}$. Thus we must have

$$v_{GB} - V_{\text{FB}} - |2\phi_p| - v_{CB} = -\frac{t_o}{\varepsilon_o}\left[q^*_N(v_{CB}) + Q^*_{DT}(v_{CB})\right]$$

Solving this for q^*_N yields

$$q^*_N(v_{CB}) = -\frac{\varepsilon_o}{t_o}\left[v_{GB} - V_{\text{FB}} - |2\phi_p| - v_{CB}\right] + Q^*_{DT}(v_{CB}) \tag{9.19}$$

where Q^*_{DT} is given by Eq. (9.18), and we assume that $v_{GB} \geq V_{\text{FB}} + |2\phi_p| + v_{CB}$.

These results are summarized in Fig. 9.4, which compares the electrostatic potential and net charge density profiles through an MOS capacitor with $v_{CB} = 0$ and with $v_{CB} > 0$.

It is worth noticing that when $v_{CB} > 0$, the inversion layer charge q^*_N can be zero even though v_{GB} is greater than the V_T specified in Eq. (9.14). That is, the threshold voltage is now increased by the presence of v_{CB} to a value of

$$V_T(v_{CB}) = V_{\text{FB}} + |2\phi_p| + v_{CB} + \frac{t_o}{\varepsilon_o}Q^*_{DT}(v_{CB}) \tag{9.20}$$

This makes sense physically because the depletion region is wider, which in turn means that there is more voltage drop both across it and, because q^*_{DT} is larger, across the oxide. Clearly the voltage v_{GB} that must be applied to invert the surface and create or sustain the channel must be larger.

Finally, note that Eq. (9.16) for the channel charge density above threshold is still valid if the appropriate expression, Eq. (9.20), is used for the threshold voltage.

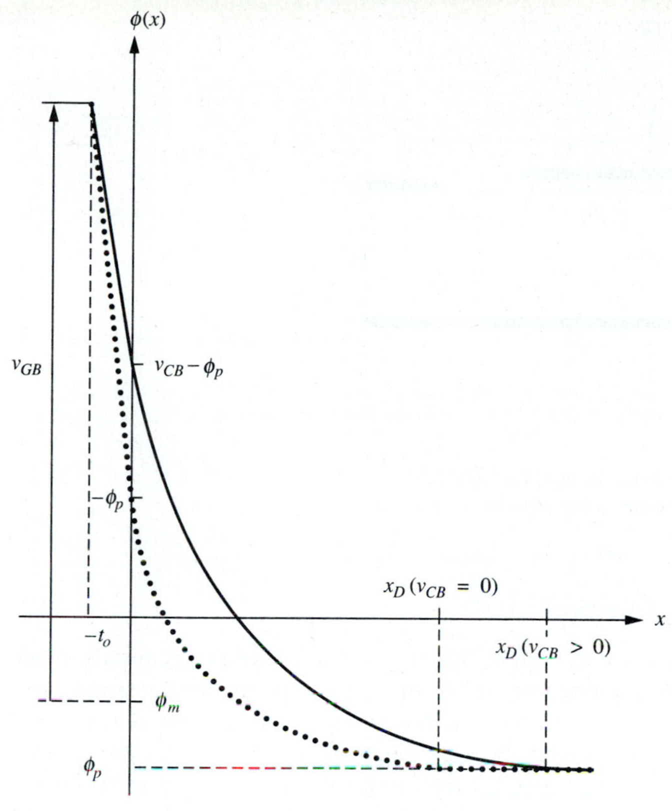

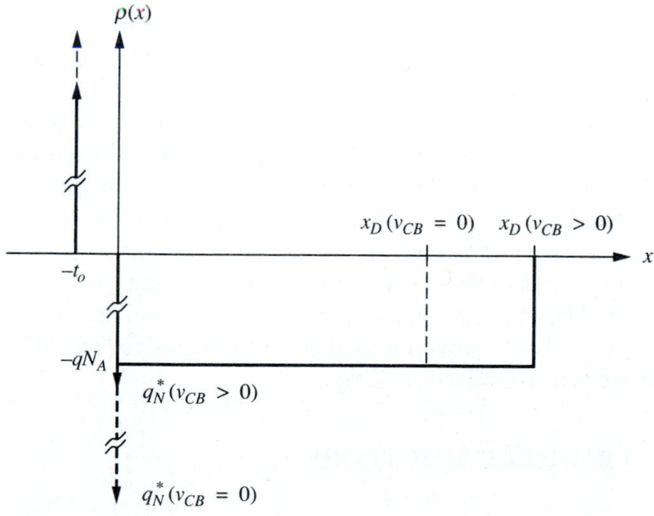

FIGURE 9.4
Profiles throughout an MOS capacitor above threshold for two different channel bias conditions: (*a*) the electrostatic potential; (*b*) the net charge density. (The dashed plots are for no voltage applied to the channel, $v_{CB} = 0$, and the solid plots are for reverse bias on the channel, $v_{CB} > 0$, relative to the *p*-region, or "substrate.")

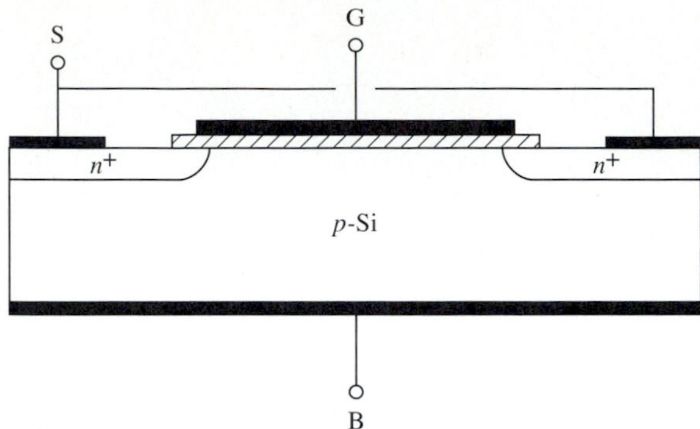

FIGURE 9.5
MOS capacitor on a p-type silicon sample, or "substrate" with heavily doped n-type regions adjacent to the ends of the channel.

9.3.2 Adjacent *p-n* Junction

As a practical matter, electrical contact to an inversion layer is generally made through an adjacent heavily doped region of the same type as the inversion layer (e.g., n-type in the structure we have been discussing). An example is illustrated in Fig. 9.5. When the region under the gate electrode G is inverted, we assume that there is little or no barrier to electron motion from the n^+-regions to the inversion layer and vice versa. Thus the channel and the n^+-regions are all at the same potential; therefore $v_{CB} = v_{SB}$. Notice that we label the contact on the n^+-regions with an S, which stands for "source." This name comes from the fact that in this structure the n^+-regions are the origin, or source, of the electrons that form the inversion layer.

In the next chapter we will consider what happens when the two n^+-regions on either side of the gate electrode are not at the same potential. We will see that there will be a gradient in potential in the channel, moving from left to right. A gradient in potential implies an electric field, which will in turn drift the carriers in the channel (electrons in this case) from one n^+-electrode to the other. Clearly the amount of motion (i.e., the drift current) will depend on the amount of charge and thus on the gate voltage. The gate can therefore be used to control the current between the two n^+-regions. This phenomenon will form the basis for the MOS field effect transistor that we will introduce in Chap. 10.

9.4 CAPACITANCE OF MOS CAPACITORS VERSUS BIAS

We call the metal-oxide-semiconductor "sandwich" that we have been discussing an MOS capacitor, but we have not yet looked explicitly at its capacitance, that is, at how the charge stored in this structure varies with the voltage applied to it. This issue is very interesting and provides us with an important tool for understanding and characterizing MOS capacitors.

We will take the charge stored on an MOS capacitor to be the charge on the gate electrode, which we call q_G. We envision a structure like that shown in Fig. 9.5, with $v_{BS} = 0$, and ask how q_G varies with v_{GS}. As you may already realize, and as we shall show shortly, q_G is a nonlinear function of v_{GS}, so we cannot model this charge store as a linear capacitor. We can, however, define a capacitance for the structure that relates incremental changes in the stored charge to incremental changes in the gate voltage. This capacitance will clearly be a function of the quiescent gate voltage. We define it as

$$C_{gs}(V_{GS}, 0) \equiv \left. \frac{\partial q_G}{\partial v_{GS}} \right|_{v_{GS} = V_{GS}, v_{BS} = 0} \tag{9.21}$$

Thus for small voltage deviations away from V_{GS} (i.e., if v_{GS} is $V_{GS} + v_{gs}$), the charge on the gate, q_G, will be given approximately by

$$q_G = Q_G + q_g \approx Q_G + C_{gs} v_{gs} \tag{9.22}$$

We next use our discussion from Secs. 9.2 and 9.3 to obtain expressions for q_G in each of the three bias regions of an MOS capacitor (accumulation, depletion, and inversion). We will calculate C_{gs} in each of these regions. We continue to assume that we have an MOS structure fabricated on a p-type semiconductor; assume further that the gate electrode is L units long and W units wide.

Beginning with accumulation, we see from Fig. 9.3d that q_G, the charge on the gate at $x = -t_o$, is simply $-q_A^* LW$, which, using Eq. (9.3) and recalling that $v_{GB} = v_{GS}$, gives us

$$q_G = LW \frac{\varepsilon_o}{t_o} (v_{GS} - V_{FB}) \tag{9.23a}$$

It is convenient at this point to define the factor ε_o / t_o as the oxide capacitance per unit area, C_{ox}^*, so that we write

$$q_G = LW\, C_{ox}^* (v_{GS} - V_{FB}) \tag{9.23b}$$

Applying the definition of gate capacitance, Eq. (9.21), we find that in accumulation (i.e., for $v_{GS} \leq V_{FB}$) we have

$$C_{gs}(V_{GS} \leq V_{FB}) = LW\, C_{ox}^* \tag{9.24}$$

This result makes perfect sense. In accumulation, charge is stored on either side of the oxide just as it is in a metal plate capacitor, and the capacitance of such a structure is its area LW multiplied by the dielectric constant of the insulator, ε_o, divided by the plate spacing t_o.

Moving next to biases in depletion, we can refer to Fig. 9.3f, where we see that q_G , the charge on the gate at $x = -t_o$, is $qN_A x_D LW$, which is also $-q_D^* LW$. We did not obtain an expression for either x_D or q_D^* as a function of the gate voltage in Sec. 9.2, so we need to do so now in order to see how q_G varies with v_{GS} and to calculate C_{gs}. To proceed we solve Eq. (9.5) for $[\phi(0) - \phi_p]$

and substitute it into Eq. (9.11). This yields a quadratic equation for q_D^* that we can solve. Doing so yields

$$q_D^* = -\frac{\varepsilon_{\text{Si}} q N_A}{C_{\text{ox}}^*}\left(\sqrt{1 + \frac{2C_{\text{ox}}^{*\,2}(v_{GS} - V_{\text{FB}})}{\varepsilon_{\text{Si}} q N_A}} - 1\right) \tag{9.25}$$

We have already pointed out that $q_G = -q_D^* LW$, so we arrive at

$$q_G = LW\frac{\varepsilon_{\text{Si}} q N_A}{C_{\text{ox}}^*}\left(\sqrt{1 + \frac{2C_{\text{ox}}^* 2(v_{GS} - V_{\text{FB}})}{\varepsilon_{\text{Si}} q N_A}} - 1\right) \tag{9.26}$$

This expression is not terribly instructive at this point, but it does show us that q_G varies as the square root of $(v_{GS} - V_{\text{FB}})$, which reflects the depletion region increase with v_{GS}. Note also that when v_{GS} equals V_{FB}, $q_G = 0$, as we know it must (see Fig. 9.3*b*).

Using Eq. (9.21) to calculate C_{gs}, we find that in depletion

$$C_{gs}(V_{\text{FB}} < V_{GS} < V_T) = \frac{LWC_{\text{ox}}^*}{\sqrt{1 + \dfrac{2C_{\text{ox}^2}^*(V_{GS} - V_{\text{FB}})}{\varepsilon_{\text{Si}} q N_A}}} \tag{9.27}$$

Looking at this expression, we see that C_{gs} has a value of $C_{\text{ox}}^* LW$ when $V_{GS} = V_{\text{FB}}$ and decreases for V_{GS} greater than the flat-band value. Physically, the depletion region width increases with increasing v_{GS} above V_{FB}. Since the increments in the charge store, q_g and $-q_g$, are added (and removed) from the gate and the edge of the depletion region, the capacitance of the structure decreases as the effective width of the capacitor (i.e., the separation between q_g and $-q_g$) increases.

Pursuing this line of reasoning further, we can view this structure as two capacitors—the oxide capacitance LWC_{ox}^* and the depletion region capacitance, $LW\varepsilon_{\text{Si}}/x_D$—in series. From this viewpoint, we must have

$$C_{gs} = \frac{LWC_{\text{ox}}^* LW\,(\varepsilon_{\text{Si}}/x_D)}{LWC_{\text{ox}}^* + LW\,(\varepsilon_{\text{Si}}/x_D)} \tag{9.28a}$$

or, simplifying a bit,

$$C_{gs} = \frac{LW}{(x_D/\varepsilon_{\text{Si}}) + (1/C_{\text{ox}}^*)} \tag{9.28b}$$

To see that this is equivalent to the expression in Eq. (9.27), we return to Eq. (9.25) for q_D^* and realize that $x_D = q_D^*/qN_A$. Thus we have

$$\frac{x_D}{\varepsilon_{\text{Si}}} = \frac{1}{C_{\text{ox}}^*}\left(\sqrt{1 + \frac{2C_{\text{ox}}^{*\,2}(v_{GS} - V_{\text{FB}})}{\varepsilon_{\text{Si}} q N_A}} - 1\right) \tag{9.29}$$

When this expression is substituted into Eq. (9.28b), we get Eq. (9.27).

We have said that when v_{GS} reaches V_T the depletion region width reaches its maximum and that the additional charge stored for any v_{GS} in excess of V_T appears in the inversion layer at the oxide-semiconductor interface. By now you should realize that this means that C_{gs} is just the oxide capacitance $WL\,C_{\text{ox}}^*$. To see formally that this is indeed the case, refer to Fig. 9.3*i*; where we see that q_G^* is now $-q_N^* + Q_{DT}^*$. Using Eq. (9.16) for q_N^*, we have

$$q_G^* = WL(v_{GS} - V_T)C_{\text{ox}}^* + Q_{DT}^* \tag{9.30}$$

and we immediately see that above threshold, C_{gs} is given by

$$C_{gs}(V_{GS} > V_T) = WLC_{\text{ox}}^* \tag{9.31}$$

A convenient way to summarize these results and to appreciate their significance is to plot C_{gs} as a function of V_{GS} over a range of voltages from below the flat-band value to above threshold. An example of such a plot for an MOS capacitor on p-type silicon is shown in Fig. 9.6*a*. (The numerical values in this plot correspond to those in the example earlier in this chapter.) As is consistent with our model, we see that for biases below V_{FB} and above V_T, C_{gs} is WLC_{ox}^*, which we call simply C_{ox} in the figure. For a bias between V_{FB} and V_T (i.e., when the structure is in depletion), C_{gs} is less than C_{ox} and decreases nonlinearly with V_{GS}.

You can see from Fig. 9.6*a* that a measurement of C_{gs} versus V_{GS} can yield a great deal of information about an MOS capacitor. First, it provides us with a measurement of V_{FB} and V_T. Second, from the value of C_{gs} in the horizontal regions (i.e., from C_{ox}), we can calculate the oxide thickness t_o (assuming we know ε_o, W, and L). Third, from the shape of the plot in depletion we can estimate N_A. Alternatively, we can also estimate N_A from the difference between V_T and V_{FB} [see Eq. (9.14)].

In practice, a plot of C_{gs} versus V_{GS} is neither as flat nor as sharp as our ideal curve in Fig. 9.6*a*. The problem is that the charge stores in accumulation and inversion are not ideal impulse, or delta, functions at the interface; instead they are distributed over a finite (albeit very thin) layer. Consequently C_{gs} in accumulation and inversion is a bit less than C_{ox}. Furthermore, the threshold does not correspond to a perfectly abrupt change in the state of the surface; rather, it is a specific point along a continuous (albeit sharp) transition, so the change in C_{gs} at V_T is not an abrupt step, but rather a more rounded step. Such a "real" C-V plot for an MOS capacitor is plotted as the solid line in Fig. 9.6*b*; the dashed curve in this figure is the ideal curve from Fig. 9.6*a*. Modeling and calculating the solid curve in Fig. 9.6*b* requires the use of the full Poisson-Boltzmann equation, Eq. (6.12b), just as is necessary if we want to go beyond the depletion approximation model when treating a p-n junction.

Finally, we should consider the effect on C_{gs} of applying a fixed reverse bias V_{BS} between the substrate and the n^+-regions. (Note that this V_{BS} will be a negative quantity.) Several things happen. First, the flat-band point on the plot is shifted left by $|V_{BS}|$ because we are now measuring the gate voltage relative to the source, not the substrate. The actual voltage between the gate G and substrate B at flat-band conditions is the same as before, but the corresponding v_{GS} is $|V_{BS}|$

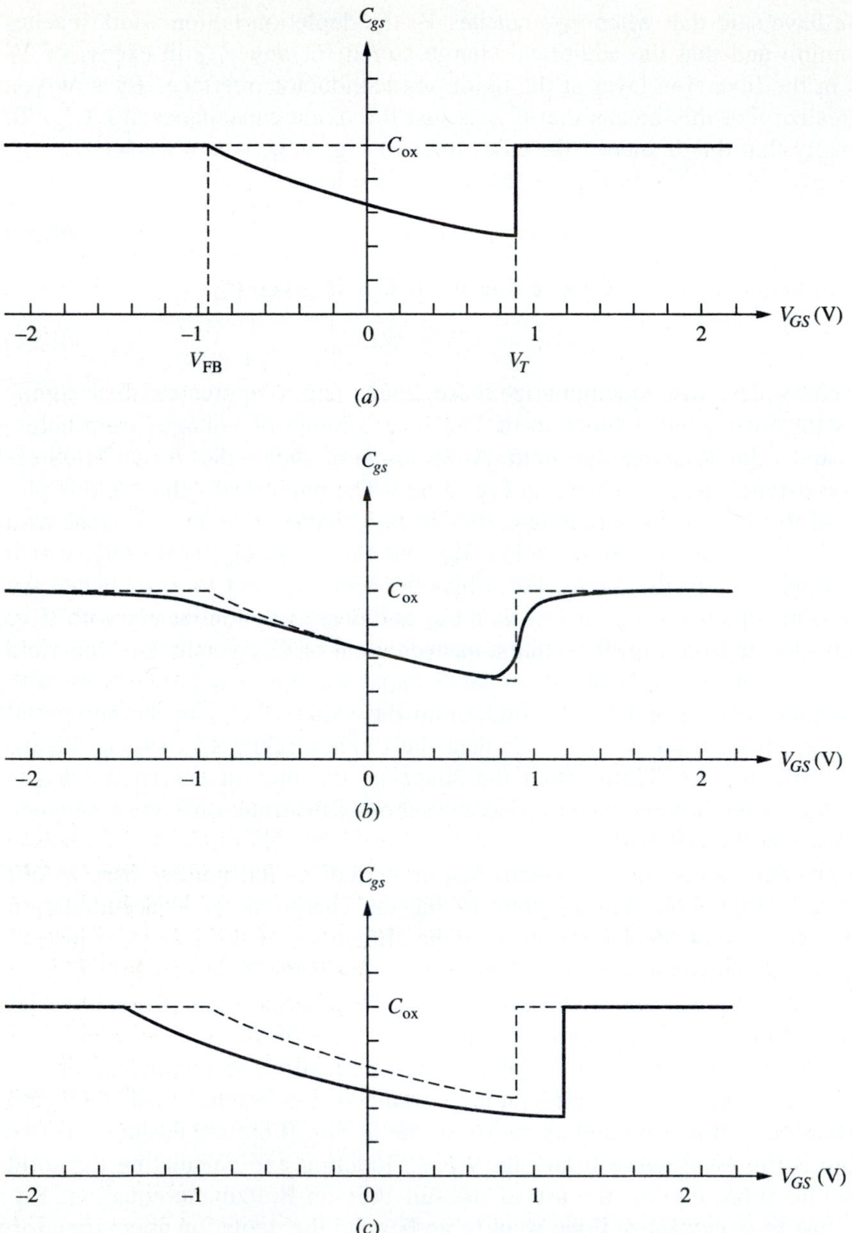

FIGURE 9.6
Capacitance-voltage (*C-V*) plots for an MOS capacitor structure like that illustrated in Fig. 9.5 and used in the example earlier in this chapter: (*a*) C_{gs} versus V_{GS} for $V_{BS} = 0$, assuming the depletion model and delta function inversion and accumulation layers; (*b*) a "real" *C-V* plot on the same structure, showing the softening of the curve that occurs in practice; (*c*) C_{gs} versus V_{GS} (depletion model) for the same structure, assuming $V_{BS} = -0.5$ V. [The dashed curves in (*b*) and (*c*) repeat the ideal, $V_{BS} = 0$ curve from (*a*).]

smaller (i.e., v_{GS} is $v_{GB} + V_{BS}$ and V_{BS} is negative). Second, the threshold point is shifted slightly to the right by an amount $[Q^*_{DT}(V_{BS}) - Q^*_{DT}(0)]/C^*_{ox}$, as you can see by referring to Eq. (9.20), which gives v_{GB} at threshold, the corresponding v_{GS} is $v_{GB} - vSB$, so we obtain

$$v_{GS} \text{ (at threshold conditions)} = V_{FB} + |2\phi_p| - \frac{t_o}{\varepsilon_o} Q^*_{DT}(V_{SB}) \tag{9.32}$$

The third change is that value of C_{gs} at this threshold value of v_{GS} is smaller than before because now the threshold depletion region width is larger. These changes are evident in Fig. 9.6*c*.

9.5 IONS AND INTERFACE CHARGES IN MOS STRUCTURES

Before proceeding to summarize our results and then move on to field effect transistors, we must modify our picture slightly to make it more general and to better represent reality. In practice we find that there are often fixed ions (i.e., fixed charges) at the oxide-silicon interface. If wafers become contaminated during processing, it is also possible for there to be ions in the oxide itself. We identify three different types of such nonideal, or extrinsic, charge: interface charge, and fixed and mobile oxide ions.

9.5.1 Interface Charge

The charge found at the oxide-silicon interface, which we call interface charge, is usually positive and is the result of a number of causes. A small number of interface charges appears to be intrinsic to (or inherent in) this interface; others arise from imperfections in the fabrication process; still others may be introduced intentionally to adjust certain device characteristics, as we shall see later. In any event, we should allow for the possibility of some fixed charged ions at this interface. We will call this charge Q^*_I, which has units of C/cm^2. Including this fixed interface charge in our plots of potential and net charge through an MOS capacitor in thermal equilibrium modifies these plots as shown in Fig. 9.7. Comparing Figs. 9.7*a* and *b* to Fig. 9.2, we see that there is now less potential drop across the oxide and less charge on the left-most electrode in equilibrium, but the depletion region is somewhat wider and the depletion region charge qN_Ax_D has increased.

When we bias the structure to flat-band, we have the situation illustrated in Figs. 9.7*c* and *d*. There is an additional potential drop $-Q^*_I t_o/\varepsilon_o$ across the oxide, and the flat-band voltage is modified to be

$$V_{FB} = -(\phi_{A1} - \phi_p) - Q^*_I \frac{t_o}{\varepsilon_o} \tag{9.33}$$

The convenient thing about Q^*_I is that it is fixed, so its effects are independent of v_{GB} and can simply be superimposed on all of the effects of our preceding

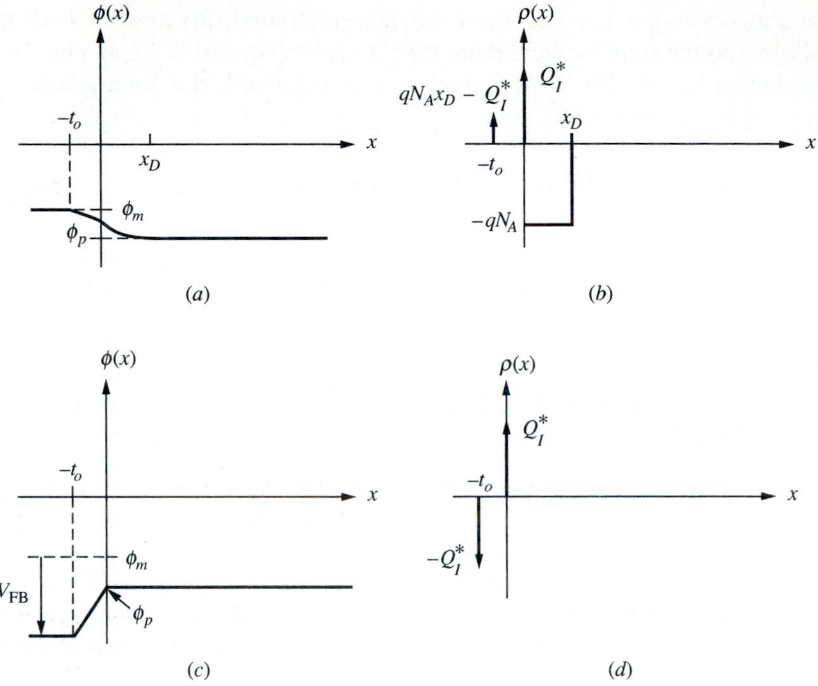

FIGURE 9.7
Net charge distribution and electrostatic potential profile through an MOS capacitor in thermal equilibrium with a fixed interface charge density Q_I, under two bias conditions: (*a* and *b*) $v_{GB} = 0$; (*c* and *d*) $v_{GB} = V_{FB}$.

discussions. Thus the presence of interface charge will be fully accounted for by using Eq. (9.33) to calculate the flat-band voltage V_{FB} and by using this value everywhere V_{FB} appears in our expressions. No other modification is required.

Example

Question. Suppose the interface sheet charge density Q_I^* is 10^{11} cm^{-2}, or 1.6×10^{-8} C/cm^2. In the MOS capacitor that we considered in the preceding example, how much would this interface charge shift the flat-band and threshold voltages?

Discussion. The amount of shift is $-Q_I^* t_o/\varepsilon_o$, or in this case approximately -0.12 V. Thus the flat-band voltage would become -0.53 V and the threshold voltage would be reduced to $+0.65$ V.

Notice in this example that if the interface charge density were another order of magnitude higher, the threshold voltage would become negative and the device would change from enhancement mode (see Sec. 9.6.1) to depletion mode.

9.5.2 Oxide Charge

If sufficient care is not taken during processing, it is possible for the oxide in an MOS structure to be contaminated with ions, usually positively charged ions.

The effect of these ions is very much like that of the interface charge. The only new element is that because they are not all in the same plane, their impact on V_{FB} depends on their distribution within the oxide. Suppose that their charge density profile is given by $\rho_O(x)$, in C/cm^3. At flat-band conditions, in addition to this negative oxide charge, there will be a positive charge on the gate electrode equal to the total amount of charge within the oxide. Integrating this charge distribution twice, we find that V_{FB} will be modified to

$$V_{FB} = -(\phi_m - \phi_p) - \frac{1}{\varepsilon}\int_0^{-t_o}\left[\int_0^x \rho_O(x)dx\right]dx \qquad (9.34)$$

In general, a distributed oxide charge like this cannot be experimentally distinguished from an interface charge Q_I^* because both are manifested as a shift in V_{FB}.

Any oxide charge is bad, but the situation is even worse if the ions in the oxide are mobile, which is the case under certain conditions for some common contaminant ions in silicon dioxide (in particular, sodium ions). The problem with such ions is not only that their presence causes a large flat-band and threshold voltage shift, but also that the shift is unstable because the profile $\rho_O(x)$ is unstable, so that V_{FB} and V_T wander with time and operating conditions.

The mobility of such ions as sodium can be used to our advantage to develop a diagnostic procedure to measure the total amount of such mobile charge in the following way. Sodium ions, which are the most common oxide contaminant, will move under the influence of an electric field, particularly if the sample is heated to several hundred degrees centigrade. A common measurement technique used to access the quality of an oxide (i.e., to measure the total density of mobile ions) is a voltage stress test. A positive bias is first applied to the gate of an MOS test structure held at high temperature, and the ions are drifted to the oxide-semiconductor interface; the resulting flat-band voltage is measured and labeled V_{FB+}. Then a negative bias is applied so that the ions are drifted to the metal-oxide interface, and the flat-band voltage is measured and called V_{FB-}.

In the first instance, when all of the mobile oxide ions are at the oxide-silicon interface, their contribution to V_{FB+} is $-Q_O^*/C_{ox}^*$, where Q_O^* is the total mobile ion sheet concentration in the oxide. In the second case, when all of the ions are at the metal-oxide interface, they make no contribution to V_{FB-}. Clearly, we can then calculate Q_O^* from the difference between V_{FB+} and V_{FB-}:

$$Q_O^* = (V_{FB-} - V_{FB+})C_{ox}^* \qquad (9.35)$$

The goal in processing is to have Q_O^* be zero, but when something goes wrong and the oxide becomes contaminated, a voltage stress measurement is a useful way to identify mobile ion contamination and assess the magnitude of the problem.

9.6 TYPES OF MOS CAPACITORS

We chose to consider an MOS capacitor made on p-type silicon, but we can construct an MOS capacitor on n-type silicon just as well. Suitable changes in sign and polarity have to be made to account for the fact that donors now replace acceptors and the roles of holes and electrons are reversed. When made on p-type silicon, MOS structures are referred to as n-channel devices, whereas when the bulk of the device is n-type, the structures are referred to as p-channel devices.

Before ending this chapter, we will collect here the expressions for the key parameters identified in this chapter and state them for devices made on both n-type and p-type silicon. The expressions of interest are those for the flat-band and threshold voltages, V_{FB} and $V_T(v_{CB})$, respectively, and for the inversion layer charge density $q_N^*(v_{CB})$.

9.6.1 *n*-channel, *p*-type Si

For MOS capacitors fabricated on p-type silicon, the flat-band voltage, threshold voltage, and inversion layer charge density are given by Eqs. (9.33), (9.20), and (9.19), respectively. Repeating those equations here, we have, after substituting Eq. (9.18) in Eq. (9.20) and using Eq. (9.20) to simplify Eq. (9.19),

$$V_{FB} = -(\phi_m - \phi_p) - Q_I^* \frac{t_o}{\varepsilon_o} \tag{9.36}$$

$$V_T(v_{CB}) = V_{FB} + |2\phi_p| + v_{CB} + \frac{t_o}{\varepsilon_o}\sqrt{2\varepsilon_{Si} q N_A(|2\phi_p| + v_{CB})} \tag{9.37}$$

$$q_N^*(v_{CB}) = \begin{cases} -[v_{GB} - V_T(v_{CB})]\dfrac{\varepsilon_o}{t_o} & \text{if } v_{GB} \geq V_T \\ 0 & \text{if } v_{GB} \leq V_T \end{cases} \tag{9.38}$$

We restrict v_{CB} to be greater than zero. Q_I^* is typically positive.

If the oxide-semiconductor interface is not inverted when $v_{GB} = 0$, the threshold voltage will be positive and the inversion layer, or channel, must be created by applying a larger positive gate voltage (i.e., $v_{GB} > V_T$). This type of device is called an *enhancement mode* device because an applied gate voltage is required to enhance the channel. If, however, V_T is negative, a channel will exist when the gate voltage is zero. This type of device is called a *depletion mode* device: a gate voltage must be applied to eliminate the channel (i.e., to deplete it of carriers). This latter gate voltage must, of course, be negative.

9.6.2 *p*-channel, *n*-type Si

For MOS capacitors fabricated on n-type silicon, these expressions change in several ways. N_A is replaced by N_D, ϕ_p is replaced by ϕ_n, and v_{CB} must be less than zero. The interface charge Q_I^* is still typically positive.

The expressions are now

$$V_{FB} = -(\phi_m - \phi_n) - Q_I^* \frac{t_o}{\varepsilon_o} \tag{9.39}$$

$$V_T(v_{CB}) = V_{FB} - 2\phi_n + v_{CB} - \frac{t_o}{\varepsilon_o}\sqrt{2\varepsilon_{Si} q N_D(2\phi_n - v_{CB})} \tag{9.40}$$

$$q_P^*(v_{CB}) = \begin{cases} -[v_{GB} - V_T(v_{CB})]\dfrac{\varepsilon_o}{t_o} & \text{if } v_{GB} \le V_T \\ 0 & \text{if } v_{GB} \ge V_T \end{cases} \tag{9.41}$$

Note that now the threshold voltage V_T is smaller than the flat-band voltage V_{FB}. Also, the gate voltage v_{GB} must be smaller than the threshold voltage for inversion. The entire sequence of states is, in fact, reversed: accumulation occurs when $v_{GB} > v_{FB}$, depletion when $v_{FB} > v_{GB} > V_T$, and inversion when $v_{GB} < V_T$.

There are depletion and enhancement mode p-channel devices as well. In a p-channel structure, however, an enhancement mode device has a negative threshold voltage and a depletion mode device has a positive threshold.

9.7 SUMMARY

In this chapter we have introduced our second basic semiconductor device structure, the metal-oxide-semiconductor (MOS) capacitor. We have described three distinct bias conditions of this structure—accumulation, depletion, and inversion—and we have identified the bias voltages defining the boundaries between these regions as the flat-band and threshold voltages, respectively. The fact that we can invert the surface of the semiconductor under the metal electrode in an MOS capacitor structure, inducing an n-type layer, or "channel," on a p-type substrate and a p-type channel on an n-type substrate; and that we can control the conductivity of this layer by the voltage that we apply to the metal electrode, is the key to the usefulness of this structure in field effect transistors, as we shall see in Chap. 10.

To quantify our description of the effects of an applied voltage on an MOS capacitor, we have developed the MOS-capacitor equivalent of our depletion approximation model for p-n junctions and have obtained expressions (summarized in Sec. 9.6) for the flat-band and threshold voltages; the depletion region width, charge, and electric field; and the inversion layer charge. We have also incorporated the effects of an interface charge on these parameters and have allowed for the application of a bias to the channel of an MOS capacitor that is biased into inversion.

Finally, we have noted that there are both n- and p-channel devices and have developed models (summarized in Sec. 9.6) for both.

PROBLEMS

9.1 You are given an MOS capacitor made on silicon, and you are told that its flat-band voltage V_{FB} is +1 V and that its threshold voltage V_T is +3 V. You are also told that the thickness t_o of the gate insulator is 800 Å (8×10^{-6} cm) with $\varepsilon_r = 3.9$ ($\varepsilon_o \approx 3.5 \times 10^{-11}$ f/cm).

(a) What is the carrier type of the silicon, n-type or p-type?

(b) What is the condition of the oxide-silicon interface when v_{GB} is 0 V?

(c) For what range of v_{GB} is the silicon surface in what is termed the depletion condition and is neither accumulated nor inverted?

(d) This capacitor is biased such that $|v_{GB} - V_T| = 3$ V and the oxide-silicon surface is inverted.
  (i) What is the sheet charge density in the inversion layer?
  (ii) What is the sheet resistance of this layer? Assume that the electron mobility is 100 $cm^2/V \cdot s$ and the hole mobility is 500 $cm^2/V \cdot s$. Recall that the sheet resistance is defined as side-to-side resistance of a square piece of material and that it has units of ohms per square.

(e) Another MOS capacitor is identical to the first except that its oxide is contaminated with 10^{16} cm^{-3} sodium ions, Na^+.
  (i) What is the total charge per cm^2 in the oxide?
  (ii) Sketch the net charge distribution $\rho(x)$ throughout the structure under flat-band conditions. Assume that there is no interface charge Q_I.
  (iii) How much is the flat-band voltage changed by the presence of this charge?

9.2 Consider an MOS capacitor structure like that in Fig. 9.2 but fabricated on an n-type Si substrate with $n_o = 5 \times 10^{16}$ cm^{-3} and an oxide thickness of 200 Å. Assume zero interface state density initially and an electrostatic potential difference between the gate metal and intrinsic silicon of 0.6 V.

(a) What is the flat-band voltage? (Take the gate to be the positive reference for voltage.)

(b) What is the threshold voltage?

(c) (i) What is the sheet charge density in the inversion layer when the gate voltage is 5 V in excess of the threshold?
  (ii) What is the sheet resistance of this charge layer assuming $\mu_h = 300$ $cm^2/V \cdot s$?

(d) If there is a positive interface state charge density of 1.6×10^{-9} C/cm^2, what will the flat-band and threshold voltages be?

9.3 Consider the MOS capacitor in Fig. 9.5 and assume that V_{NB} is +2 V. Assume also that the other dimensions and doping levels in the structure are the same as those in the example in Sec. 9.2.4.

(a) What is the change in electrostatic potential crossing the depletion region at and above threshold? How does this differ from the value when V_{BN} is zero? (See the example.)

(b) What is the depletion region width at and above threshold?

(c) What is the threshold voltage (i) relative to terminal B and (ii) relative to terminal N?

(d) What is the sheet charge density in the inversion layer when the gate voltage is 2 V in excess of threshold?

(e) What is the flat-band voltage?

9.4 Consider using the MOS structure of problem 9.2 in a device like that pictured in Fig. 9.5, and assume v_{BS} is zero. The gate electrode area is 0.1 cm^2.

(a) Find an expression for the total charge on the gate, q_G, as a function of V_{GS} for $-5 \text{ V} \le v_{GS} \le +5$ V. Sketch and label your result.

(b) Find expressions for the gate-to-source capacitance $\partial q_G / \partial v_{GS}$ as a function of V_{GS} over the same range. Sketch and label your result.

9.5 What would flat-band and threshold voltages be if the MOS structure in the example in Sec. 9.2.4 had been fabricated on an n-type substrate with $N_D = 2.5 \times 10^{17}$ cm^{-3} rather than on a p-type substrate?

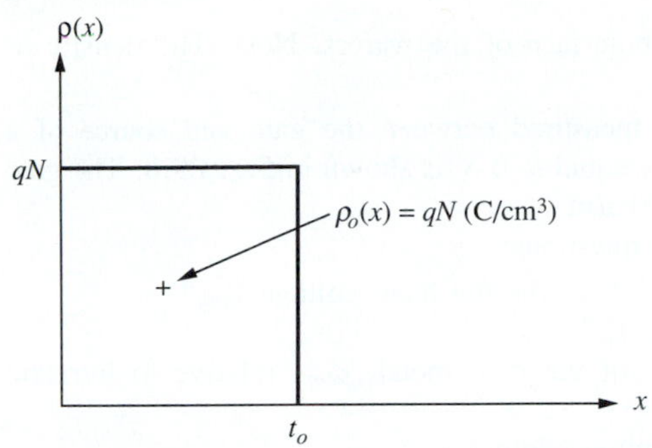

FIGURE P9.7

9.6 An n-channel MOS capacitor with a 600-Å (6×10^{-6} cm) thick gate oxide, $\varepsilon_r = 4$, becomes contaminated with 10^{10} cm^{-2} fixed positive ions at the silicon-oxide interface.

(a) By how much does the threshold voltage V_T change?

(b) Does V_T increase or decrease? Explain your answer physically.

9.7 Assume that there is a uniform density N of positive ions in the oxide of a MOSFET, as illustrated in Fig. P9.7.

(a) Show that the expression for the change in threshold voltage caused by this charge is

$$\Delta V_{\text{th}} = \frac{1}{\varepsilon_o} \int_0^{t_o} \left[\int_x^{x_o} \rho(x)\, dx \right] dx = -\frac{qNt_o^2}{2\varepsilon_o}$$

(b) What density N of sodium ions, Na$^+$, will cause a $\Delta V_{\text{th}} = -0.5$ V? Assume $t_o =$ 1000 Å. Use $\varepsilon_r = 3.9$.

(c) If a 0.5-V threshold shift is enough to ruin a certain MOS circuit, how many 3-in.-diameter wafers could a crystal of table salt (a cube 0.1 mm on a side) destroy? Assume that the Na$^+$ ions are uniformly distributed throughout a 1000-

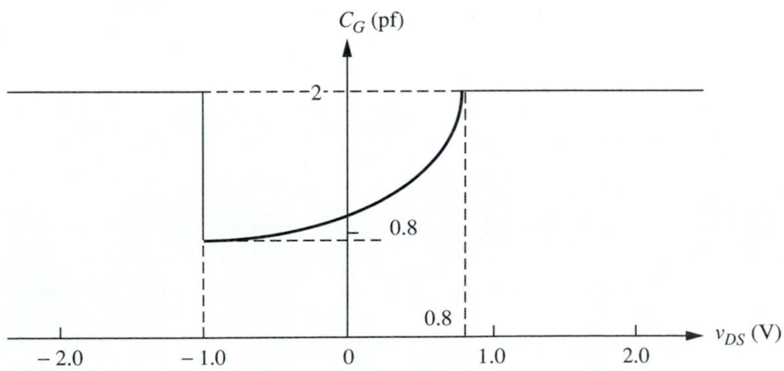

FIGURE P9.8

Å-thick oxide layer over the entire surface of the wafers. Note: The density of NaCl is 2×10^{22} molecules/cm^3.

9.8 The capacitance-voltage relationship measured between the gate and source of a particular MOSFET with v_{DS} and v_{BS} equal to 0 V is shown in Fig. P9.8. The gate of this device measures 20 μm by 100 μm.
Use this data to answer the following questions:

(a) What is (i) the threshold voltage V_T? (ii) the flat-band voltage V_{FB}?

(b) What is the thickness of the oxide, t_o?

(c) What is the electrostatic potential of the gate metal, ϕ_m, relative to intrinsic silicon?

(d) What is the maximum depletion region width X_{DT}?

(i) What is the carrier type of the substrate, n or p?

(ii) What is the net doping level of the substrate? Hint: Use Eqs. (9.12) and (9.14) (or their equivalents for an n-type substrate) to write $V_T - V_{\text{FB}}$ in terms of X_{DT} and the net doping of the substrate. You know X_{DT} from part c, so you can solve for the net doping.

CHAPTER
10

FIELD EFFECT TRANSISTORS

In Chap. 8 we studied the bipolar transistor and saw how the voltage between the base and emitter controlled the current through the device from emitter to collector. One way of visualizing this process is by plotting the potential energy of the majority carriers in the emitter and collector through a bipolar junction transistor; this is done in Fig. 10.1*a* for an unbiased structure. In Fig. 10.1*b* the same structure is shown biased in its forward active region. From these plots it is clear that forward-biasing the emitter-base junction in a bipolar junction transistor lowers the potential energy barrier between the emitter and collector presented by the base. When the barrier is reduced, more carriers can surmount it and current flows between the emitter and collector.

In the bipolar junction transistor, direct electrical contact is made to the base. The height of the potential barrier posed by the base is modulated directly by the base-emitter voltage. Another way to control this potential energy barrier is indirectly by means of a field plate; that is, to induce a change in the barrier via a sheet of charge on an adjacent electrode. This approach eliminates the annoyance of having to deal with a control electrode current (i.e., the base current in a bipolar junction transistor), but this advantage comes at the expense of lower transconductance; that is, the control electrode voltage in this approach has less effect on the current than it does when the contact is direct (as it is in a bipolar junction transistor).

Transistors that use a field plate to control current flow are called *field effect transistors*, or FETs. The control electrode is called the *gate* rather than the base; the terminal corresponding to the emitter is called the *source*; and the third terminal is called the *drain*. There are several types of field effect transistors that are important in modern electronics. We will look at three: the metal-oxide-semiconductor field effect transistor (MOSFET), the junction field effect transistor (JFET), and the metal-semiconductor field effect transistor (MESFET).

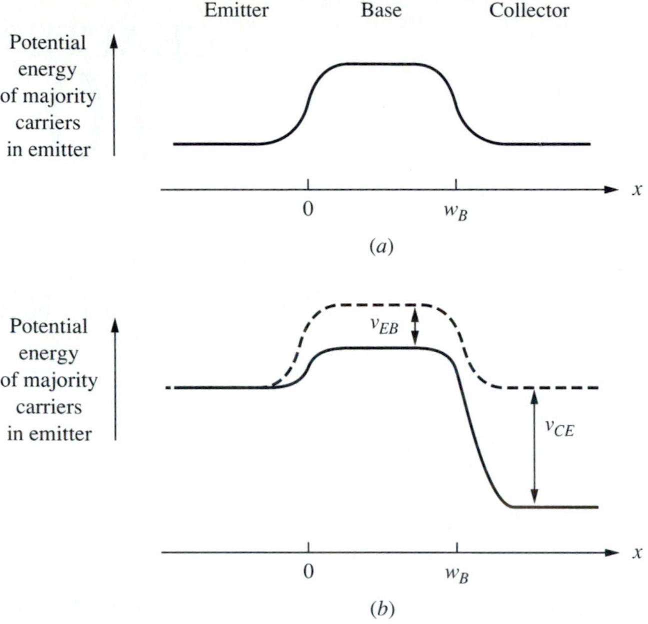

FIGURE 10.1
Potential energy of the majority carriers in the emitter of a bipolar junction transistor plotted as a function of position through the device: (*a*) no bias applied; (*b*) bias in forward active region.

In addition to the differences in how the barrier to current flow is controlled in BJTs and FETs, there are other important differences that you should watch for as we study FETs in this chapter. First, and by far most important, in an FET the carriers flow between the source and drain by means of drift, whereas the carriers in a BJT flow between the emitter and collector by diffusion. Second, the region between the emitter and collector in a BJT (i.e., the base) is quasineutral. In an FET, the region in which the current flows between the source and drain, which is called the *channel*, may have a net charge. And finally, an FET will frequently have four terminals, whereas a BJT always has only three.

10.1 METAL-OXIDE-SEMICONDUCTOR FIELD EFFECT TRANSISTORS

A metal-oxide-semiconductor field effect transistor, or MOSFET, uses an MOS capacitor structure as its control, or gate. A typical *n*-channel MOSFET structure is illustrated in Fig. 10.2. There are four terminals in this structure; but one, the back gate B, is biased so that negligible current flows through it. We can focus initially on the gate G, source S, and drain D. The basic operating principle is that a voltage is applied between the gate and the source so as to invert the region under the gate electrode to create a conducting channel between the source and drain regions. Thus, when a voltage is applied between the drain and the source, there will be a current from the drain to the source through this channel. The magnitude of this drain current i_D will depend on the drain-to-source voltage v_{DS} and, most importantly, on the gate-to-source voltage v_{GS} (i.e., on the amount of inversion charge in the channel). At low values of v_{DS}, the drain current varies linearly with v_{DS}, so that the MOSFET looks like a resistor whose value is controlled by v_{GS}. As v_{DS} increases, however, the resistive voltage drop along the channel causes the level of inversion to be less at the drain end of the channel than at the source end. The resistance of the channel thus increases as v_{DS} increases, and the drain current increases less rapidly (i.e., sublinearly with v_{DS}). At high enough drain-to-source voltage the inversion layer disappears completely at the drain end. This point is called *pinchoff*. Beyond this point, in what is called *saturation*, the current no longer increases with v_{DS} but stays constant at a level determined by v_{GS} (and, of course, the details of the specific device structure in question). This characteristic is illustrated in Fig. 10.3.

The MOSFET illustrated in Fig. 10.2 is called an *n-channel* MOSFET because the majority carriers in the channel inversion layer are electrons. It is also possible to fabricate *p-channel* MOSFETs in which the inversion layer is comprised of holes. Such a device is made on an *n*-type substrate and has *p*-type source and drain regions.

Our discussion thus far has implied that there is no channel in the absence of a gate-to-source bias (i.e., when $v_{GS} = 0$). This is indeed the most common situation; we call a device in this situation a *normally off*, or *enhancement mode*, MOSFET. In order to turn an enhancement mode MOSFET "on," a channel must be created by applying bias to the gate. It is also possible, however, to fabricate devices in which a channel exists even in the absence of any bias on the gate (i.e., with $v_{GS} = 0$). This is typically done, for example, by putting a suitable amount of interface charge Q_I^* under the gate. Such a device is called a *normally*

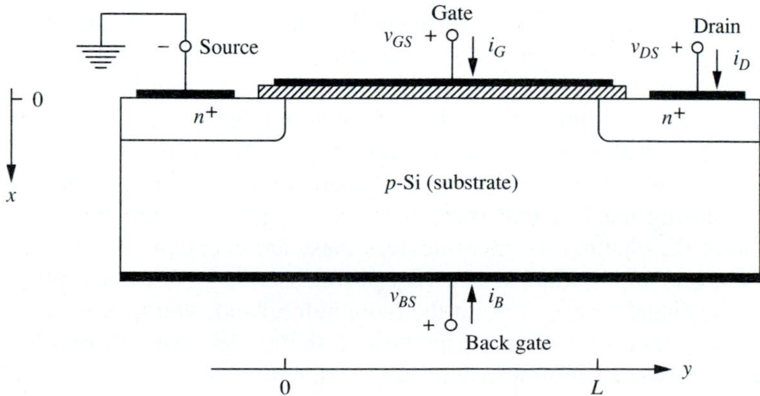

FIGURE 10.2
Typical *n*-channel MOSFET structure, which will be used in developing a large-signal model for the terminal characteristic.

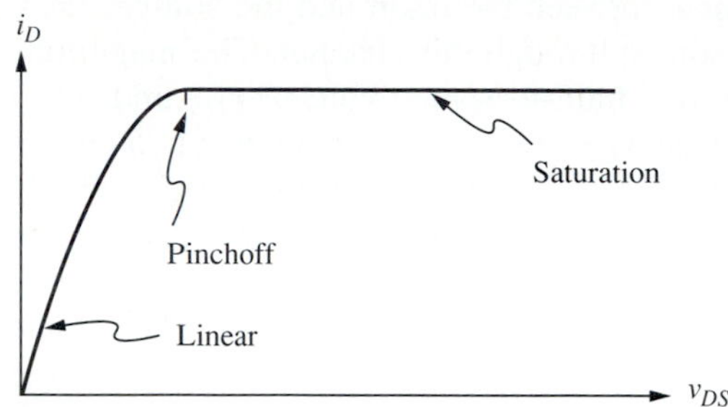

FIGURE 10.3
Drain current through a MOSFET as a function of v_{DS} when v_{GS} and v_{BS} are held fixed.

on, or *depletion mode*, MOSFET. To turn a depletion mode MOSFET "off," a bias must be applied that forces the surface out of inversion and into depletion.

We will now turn to developing a quantitative model describing the MOSFET operation just outlined. We will then develop a small-signal linear model based on our quasistatic large-signal model. Finally, we will extend this small-signal model to high-frequency operation.

10.1.1 Large-Signal Model: The Gradual Channel Approximation

To quantify the relationships between the gate, drain, and back contact currents (i_G, i_D, and i_B, respectively) and the gate-to-source, drain-to-source, and back-to-source voltages (v_{GS}, v_{DS}, and v_{BS}, respectively), we will develop a model called the *gradual channel approximation*. The MOSFET is intrinsically a two-dimensional device with the gate field acting approximately vertically, in what we will take to be the x-direction, to induce the channel; and with the drain-to-source voltage acting approximately horizontally, in what we will take to be the y-direction, to cause a drift current i_D in the channel. In the gradual channel approximation we assume that these two aspects of the problem can be treated as strictly one-dimensional problems. We will first solve the field problem in the x-direction to model the inversion layer charge, ignoring the fact that the "vertical" field must have a slight y-component. We will then solve the drift problem in the y-direction, ignoring the fact that there must be a slight x-component to the "horizontal" field in the channel. In most devices these are excellent assumptions and the gradual channel approximation is a very powerful model. The assumptions are so good, in fact, that if we didn't point them out beforehand, you may not even have noticed them, at least on the first time through the model. We will return to further discussion of these assumptions later, after we complete our discussion of large-signal FET models.

a) Basic parabolic model. We will treat an n-channel device like that pictured in Fig. 10.2; we begin by restricting our model to certain useful bias ranges.

Specifically we want the drain and source n^+-regions to always be reverse-biased with respect to the p-type silicon region, which we call the substrate, so that the substrate current i_B will be negligible. Thus for the device of Fig. 10.2 we insist that $v_{BS} \leq 0$ and $v_{DS} \geq 0$. With this restriction we can immediately conclude that $i_B \approx 0$. We can also conclude that another of our currents, the gate current i_G, is approximately zero as well because the gate is insulated from the substrate by the gate oxide.

To proceed with i_D we note that unless the gate-to-source voltage v_{GS} is above threshold there will be no path for conduction between the drain and the source; the drain current will be essentially zero (i.e., $i_D \approx 0$ if $v_{GS} \leq V_T$). Thus we conclude that we need only be concerned with modeling i_D when v_{GS} is above threshold and there is an inversion layer to form the channel.

Assume now that the gate-to-source voltage is sufficient to create a channel. Based on our introductory discussions we must anticipate that the channel sheet charge density is a function of position, $q_N^*(y)$. (Notice that we have taken the y-direction as being parallel to the semiconductor-oxide interface and normal to the drain and source, with $y = 0$ at the source and $y = L$ at the drain.) Because the source and drain will in general be biased with respect to the p-type silicon substrate, the channel is also at some potential $v_{CB}(y)$ relative to the substrate. Clearly this voltage is a function of position y along the channel if $v_{DS} \neq 0$, because at the source end we have $v_{CB}(0) = v_{SB}$ and at the drain end we have $v_{CB}(L) = v_{DB}$. If we reference the voltage in the channel to the source, which is the usual convention in modeling FETs, we can write

$$v_{CS}(0) = 0 \tag{10.1}$$

$$v_{CS}(L) = v_{DS} \tag{10.2}$$

Since the voltage in the channel varies with position, it must have a nonzero gradient, which in turn means that there is an electric field in the channel in the y-direction. This field is given by

$$\mathscr{E}_y = -\frac{dv_{CS}}{dy} \tag{10.3}$$

If there is an electric field, there must be drift of the inversion layer carriers (electrons in this case), so there must be an electric current in the channel. This current is the negative of the drain current, $-i_D$. This current must be given by the sheet charge density at any point y, $q_N^*(y)$, times the drift velocity of the charge carriers, s_y (which at low and moderate values of electric field is their mobility times the electric field at that point y), multiplied by the width of the device. Defining W as the device width normal to the xy-plane, we thus have

$$-i_D = +Wq_N^*(y)\,s_y(y) = -Wq_N^*(y)\mu_e\mathscr{E}_y \tag{10.4a}$$

which, using Eq. (10.3), is

$$i_D = -W\mu_e q_N^*(y)\frac{dv_{CS}}{dy} \tag{10.4b}$$

where μ_e is the drift mobility of the electrons in the channel. Notice that i_D itself is not a function of y; that is, the current in the channel does not change in going from the drain to the source.

We derived an expression for q_N^* in terms of v_{GB} and v_{CB} in Chap. 9, Eq. (9.19). Rewriting that expression here, but with the voltages referred to the source rather than to the back, we have

$$q_N^*[v_{CS}(y)] = -\frac{\varepsilon_o}{t_o}[v_{GS} - v_{CS}(y) - |2\phi_p| - V_{FB}] + \sqrt{2\varepsilon_{Si} q N_A[|2\phi_p| + v_{CS}(y) - v_{BS}]} \tag{10.5}$$

Combining Eqs. (10.4) and (10.5) gives us a single differential equation for $v_{CS}(y)$:

$$i_D = W\mu_e q_N^*[v_{CS}(y)]\frac{dv_{CS}(y)}{dy} \tag{10.6}$$

We don't care specifically about $v_{CS}(y)$, however; we are only trying to relate i_D to v_{DS}, which makes our task easier. If we multiply both sides of Eq. (10.6) by dy and integrate from 0 to L we can get our desired result:

$$\int_0^L i_D dy = -W\mu_e \int_0^L q_N^*[v_{CS}(y)]\frac{dv_{CS}(y)}{dy}dy \tag{10.7}$$

The left-hand integral is simply

$$\int_0^L i_D dy = i_D L \tag{10.8a}$$

The right-hand integral looks complex, but it can easily be changed from an integral performed with respect to position to one done with respect to voltage as follows:

$$\int_0^L q_N^*[v_{CS}(y)]\frac{dv_{CS}(y)}{dy}dy = \int_0^{v_{DS}} q_N^*(v_{CS})dv_{CS} \tag{10.8b}$$

where we have made use of Eqs. (10.1) and (10.2) to get the proper limits on the integral. This integral is now easily performed after substituting Eq. (10.5) for $q_N^*[v_{CS}(y)]$. The final result is

$$i_D(v_{DS}, v_{GS}, v_{BS}) = \frac{W}{L}\mu_e\frac{\varepsilon_o}{t_o}\left\{\left(v_{GS} - |2\phi_p| - V_{FB} - \frac{v_{DS}}{2}\right)v_{DS} + \frac{3}{2}\sqrt{2\varepsilon_{Si} q N_A}[(|2\phi_p| + v_{DS} - v_{BS})^{3/2} - (2\phi_p - v_{BS})^{3/2}]\right\} \tag{10.9}$$

This result is an expression for the drain current i_D in terms of v_{DS}, v_{GS}, and v_{BS}, to be sure, but it is far too complex to be easily used. To get a more useful expression, we should pause and consider the physics of the situation and the relative sizes of the terms before doing the integration in Eq. 10.8. Specifically we notice that the last term in Eq. (10.5) for q_N^*, which corresponds to the depletion region charge $q_D^*[v_{CS}(y), v_{BS}]$, is small and varies slowly with v_{CS}. If we assume that it can be approximated by a constant value, usually taken to be $Q_D^*(0, v_{BS})$, the channel charge can then be written as

$$q_N^*[v_{CS}(y)] \approx \frac{\varepsilon_o}{t_o}[v_{GS} - v_{CS}(y) - |2\phi_p| - V_{FB}] + Q_D^*(0, v_{BS}) \tag{10.5'}$$

Using this in Eq. (10.8b) we find that our expression for i_D is markedly simplified. Instead of Eq. (10.9), we obtain

$$i_D = \frac{W}{L}\mu_e\frac{\varepsilon_o}{t_o}\left[v_{GS} - |2\phi_p| - V_{FB} + \frac{t_o}{\varepsilon_o}Q_D^*(0, v_{BS}) - \frac{v_{DS}}{2}\right]v_{DS} \tag{10.10a}$$

This expression is much easier to work with than Eq. (10.9), and yet it has a remarkably similar shape because the assumption we made concerning Q_D^* is a very good one. In the field, making this assumption is known as "ignoring the body effect."

We will usually write Eq. (10.10*a*) as

$$i_D(v_{DS}, v_{GS}, v_{BS}) = K\left[v_{GS} - V_{TS} - \frac{v_{DS}}{2}\right]v_{DS} \tag{10.10b}$$

where K is defined as

$$K \equiv \frac{W}{L}\mu_e\frac{\varepsilon_o}{t_o} \tag{10.11}$$

and V_{TS} is the threshold voltage relative to the source, defined as

$$V_{TS}(v_{BS}) \equiv V_{FB} - |2\phi_p| - \frac{t_o}{\varepsilon_o}Q_D^*(0, v_{BS}) \tag{10.12a}$$

We write the dependence on v_{BS} explicitly to remind ourselves that V_T is a function of v_{BS} through Q_D^*:

$$Q_D^*(0, v_{BS}) = -\sqrt{2\varepsilon_{Si}qN_A(|2\phi_p| - v_{BS})} \tag{10.13}$$

Combining Eq. (10.13) with (10.12a) yields

$$V_{TS}(v_{BS}) = V_{FB} - |2\phi_p| + \frac{t_o}{\varepsilon_o}\sqrt{2\varepsilon_{Si}qN_A(|2\phi_p| - v_{BS})} \tag{10.12b}$$

which is a common way of writing $V_{TS}(v_{BS})$. Another common way of writing the threshold voltage is in terms of its value for $v_{BS} = 0$. A little algebra will show you that we can write

$$V_{TS}(v_{BS}) = V_{TS}(0) + \gamma\left[\sqrt{(|2\phi_p| - v_{BS})} - \sqrt{|2\phi_p|}\right] \tag{10.12c}$$

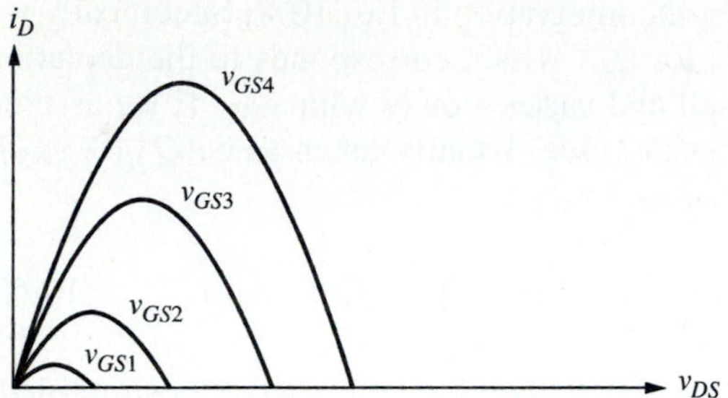

FIGURE 10.4
Equation (10.10b) plotted (solid lines) for four values of gate-to-source voltage v_{GS} greater than the threshold voltage V_T for a fixed value of back-to-source voltage v_{BS}.

where γ, which is called the *body effect coefficient*, is defined as

$$\gamma \equiv \frac{t_o}{\varepsilon_o} \sqrt{2\varepsilon_{\text{Si}} q N_A} \tag{10.14}$$

If we plot Eq. (10.10b) for i_D as a function of v_{DS} for fixed values of v_{GS} and v_{BS}, we find that we get inverted parabolas, as illustrated for four values of v_{GS} in Fig. 10.4. In a real device, however, we find that the current does not decrease after reaching its peak; instead, it stays constant at its peak value, as indicated by the horizontal lines in Fig. 10.5. What is going on? The answer is that as v_{DS} increases, the inversion layer charge decreases at the drain end of the channel. It drops all the way to zero when the voltage from the gate to the

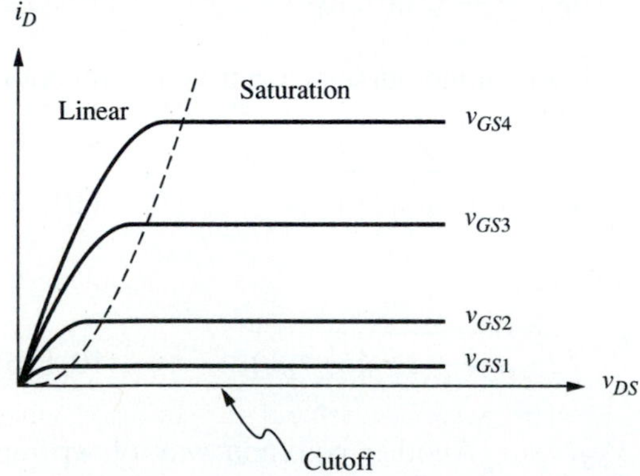

FIGURE 10.5
Characteristics for an *n*-channel MOSFET as described by Eq. (10.15) drawn for four values of gate-to-source voltage v_{GS} above threshold and for $v_{BS} \leq 0$.

drain, v_{GD}, decreases to the threshold voltage V_T. This occurs at a drain-to-source voltage of $v_{GS} - V_T$, which is precisely the value of v_{DS} at which i_D reaches its peak value, $K(v_{GS} - V_T)^2/2$. For larger v_{DS} the current does not decrease, because that would imply less voltage drop in the channel from source to drain. Instead the current stays constant at its peak value; that is,

$$i_D = \frac{K}{2}(v_{GS} - V_T)^2 \quad \text{when } v_{DS} \geq V_{GS} - V_T$$

The excess of v_{DS} over $v_{GS} - V_T$ appears as an ohmic voltage drop across the now very high-resistance short section of channel near the drain.

This completes our large-signal gradual channel approximation model for the MOSFET. In summary, when $v_{BS} \leq 0$ and $v_{DS} \geq 0$ the gate and substrate currents, i_G and i_B, respectively, are zero and the drain current is described by one of three expressions:

$$i_D = \begin{cases} 0 & \text{for } (v_{GS} - V_T) \leq 0 \leq v_{DS} \quad (10.15\text{a}) \\ \dfrac{K}{2}(v_{GS} - V_T)^2 & \text{for } 0 \leq (v_{GS} - V_T) \leq v_{DS} \quad (10.15\text{b}) \\ K\left(v_{GS} - V_T - \dfrac{v_{DS}}{2}\right)v_{DS} & \text{for } 0 \leq v_{DS} \leq (v_{GS} - V_T) \quad (10.15\text{c}) \end{cases}$$

The output characteristic (i.e., i_D versus v_{DS} for various values of v_{GS}) is presented in Fig. 10.5. The three regions in this characteristic corresponding to the three expressions for i_D in Eqs. (10.15) are called the cutoff, saturation, and linear (or triode) regions, respectively. Notice that the saturation region in a MOSFET is much different than saturation in a bipolar transistor. Also, the parameter defining the family of curves is a voltage, v_{GS}, rather than a current (as in a BJT), and the curves are not evenly spaced for equal increments of v_{GS} (as they were for equal increments of i_B in a BJT).

Example

Question. Consider an *n*-channel MOSFET that incorporates in the gate the MOS capacitor structure in the examples in Chap. 9. The channel length L is 1 μm, and the channel width W is 20 μm. The electron mobility in the channel is 750 $\text{cm}^2/\text{V} \cdot \text{s}$. What is the value of K for this device, and what will the drain current i_D be in saturation when the gate-to-source voltage v_{GS} is 2 V? Recall that V_T for this structure is 0.65 V.

Discussion. Using the expression for K, that is, $(W/L)\mu_e(\varepsilon_o/t_o)$, we calculate that K is approximately 1.0 mA/V^2. Thus we find that when v_{GS} is 2 V, $(v_{GS} - V_T)$ is 1.35 V. From Eq. (10.15b), the drain current in saturation is approximately 0.9 mA.

The magnitude of the drain current, about 1 mA, is a typical bias level that we often encounter in bipolar transistors. You will notice, however, that to achieve this current level with our MOSFET we had to apply substantially more input bias voltage than is needed with a BJT (i.e., 2 V versus roughly 0.6 V). This is in spite of the fact that this MOSFET is actually somewhat larger than a typical bipolar transistor. This is a common result, and in general FETs tend to be lower-current devices than BJTs.

You may have noticed that the mobility specified in this question is about half the value that we have been assuming for electrons in our previous discussions. The reason is that the electrons in the channel undergo more scattering than those in the "bulk" because of the strong normal electric field from the gate and because they are confined so closely to the semiconductor-oxide interface.

The characteristics described by Eqs. (10.15) and illustrated in Fig. 10.5 correspond to an *n*-channel MOSFET and hold for both enhancement and depletion mode devices. The only difference is that the threshold voltage is greater than zero for an enhancement mode *n*-channel MOSFET, whereas it is less than zero for a depletion mode *n*-channel MOSFET. This is illustrated in Figs. 10.6*a* and *b*, which show the output characteristics of an enhancement and a depletion mode *n*-channel MOSFET, respectively.

For *p*-channel MOSFETs, all of the voltages and currents change sign, but otherwise the characteristics are identical. The gate current i_G is, of course, zero, and we must now have $v_{BS} \geq 0$ and $v_{DS} \leq 0$ to ensure that $i_B = 0$. The expressions for the drain current i_D are

$$i_D = \begin{cases} 0 & \text{for } v_{DS} \leq 0 \leq (v_{GS} - V_T) \quad (10.16a) \\ -\dfrac{K}{2}(v_{GS} - V_T)^2 & \text{for } v_{DS} \leq (v_{GS} - V_T) \leq 0 \quad (10.16b) \\ -K\left(v_{GS} - V_T - \dfrac{v_{DS}}{2}\right)v_{DS} & \text{for } (v_{DS} - V_T) \leq v_{DS} \leq 0 \quad (10.16c) \end{cases}$$

where K is $(W/L)\mu_h(\varepsilon_o/t_o)$. V_T is negative for an enhancement mode *p*-channel device and positive for a depletion mode *p*-channel device. The characteristics of enhancement mode and depletion mode *p*-channel MOSFETs are illustrated in Figs. 10.6*c* and *d*. For the sake of illustration, the threshold voltage in this figure has been taken to be either plus or minus two volts. The threshold voltage can, of course, have any magnitude.

The circuit symbols used for the various types of MOSFETs are also illustrated in Fig. 10.6. Notice that the arrow indicates the direction of forward current flow through the substrate-to-channel diodes and that the heavy solid line symbolizes the existence of a channel with zero gate bias in the depletion mode devices. Alternatively, some people draw the arrow on the source terminal in such a way as to indicate the normal direction of current flow; others indicate enhancement mode devices with a broken line between drain and source (solid for depletion mode).

With the bipolar junction transistor and the Ebers–Moll model it was possible to find a very convenient circuit representation for the terminal characteristics using ideal exponential diodes and dependent current sources. To do something similar for the MOSFET, we would have to use a single dependent current source whose value depends on the voltages on the various terminals according to Eqs. (10.15) or Eqs. (10.16), as illustrated for an *n*-channel device in Fig. 10.7. Such a model is much less satisfying than the Ebers–Moll circuit, however, because

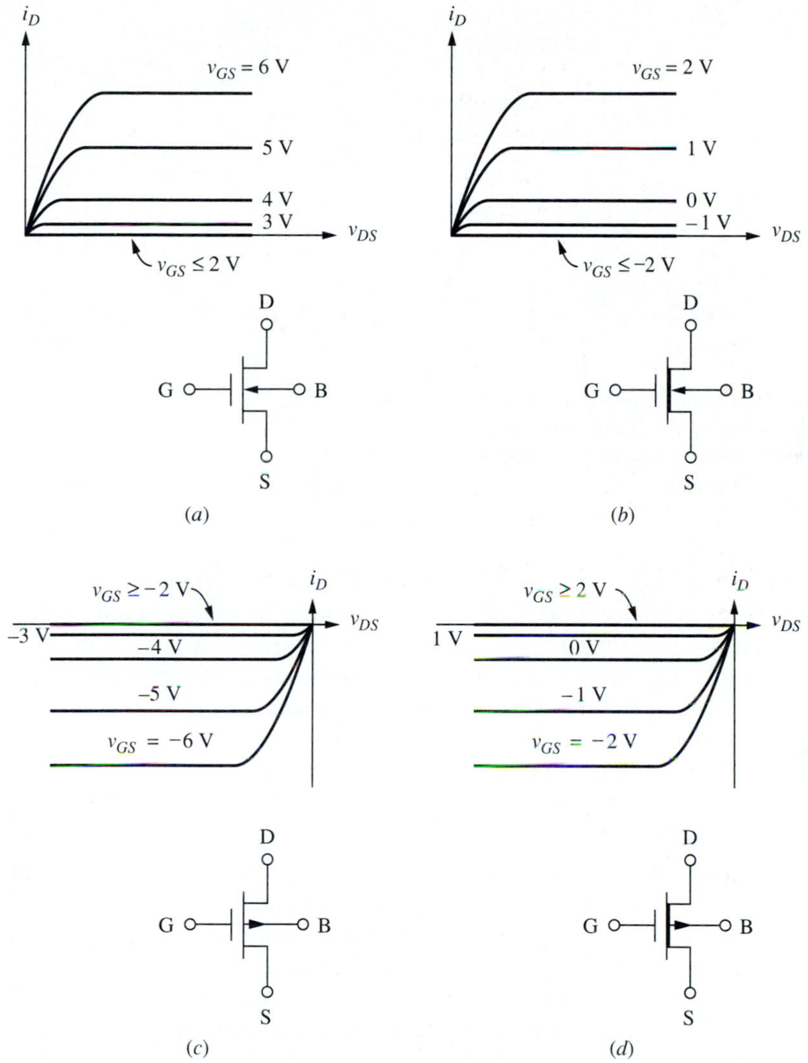

FIGURE 10.6
Output characteristics for the four types of MOSFETs: (*a*) *n*-channel enhancement mode, $V_T = 2$ V; (*b*) *n*-channel depletion mode, $V_T = -2$ V; (*c*) *p*-channel enhancement mode, $V_T = -2$ V; (*d*) *p*-channel depletion mode, $V_T = 2$ V. The corresponding circuit symbols are also shown.

little additional insight is gained by using it and it does not appreciably simplify the calculation of large-signal voltages and currents. In most solutions, Eqs. (10.15) or Eqs. (10.16) are used directly.

b) More advanced modeling. The basic parabolic MOSFET model is extremely useful and easy to use for hand calculations. However, when it is necessary or

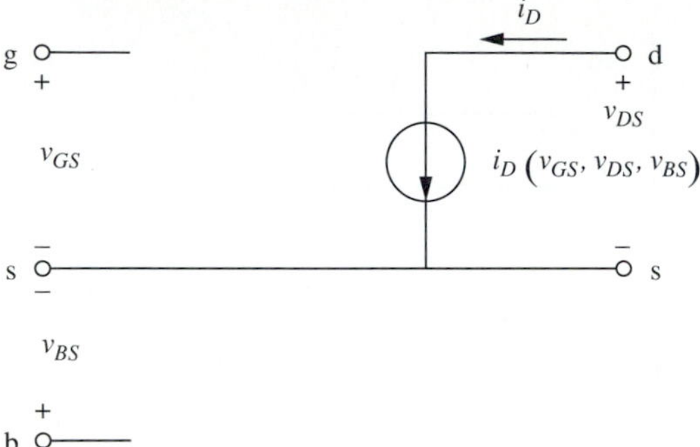

FIGURE 10.7
Circuit representation of the large-signal model for a MOSFET as described by the gradual channel approximation, Eq. (10.15). Use of this model is restricted to $v_{BS} \leq 0$ and $v_{DS} \geq 0$.

desirable to include effects not treated in the basic model, certain additions are commonly made to the basic model. We want to look at several common "fixes" now. The models we will develop should be viewed as more advanced in much the same way as the Gummel–Poon BJT model is more advanced than the Ebers–Moll model. We will not use these models in most of what we do, but it is worth your while to be aware of their existence and origin.

The first effect we will add to our basic model is *channel length modulation*, or the MOSFET equivalent of the Early effect in BJTs. In saturation, the effective length of the channel decreases with increasing v_{DS} because the width of the region near the drain where the channel has disappeared increases slightly as v_{DS} increases above its value at saturation, $v_{GS} - V_T$. This means that the K-factor, $(w/L)\mu_e(\varepsilon_o/t_o)$, increases with increasing v_{DS} and thus that the drain current does not truly saturate at a fixed value; instead, it increases slightly with increasing v_{DS}. A common way to model this effect is to assume that in saturation the effective channel length L_{eff} is given by

$$L_{\text{eff}} \approx \frac{L}{1 + [(V_{DS} - V_{DS\text{sat}})/|V_A|]} \tag{10.17}$$

where V_A is called the Early voltage, and $V_{DS_{\text{sat}}}$ is the voltage at which the device goes into saturation. (We will discuss $V_{DS_{\text{sat}}}$ at more length below.)* Our earlier expression for i_D is unchanged in the linear region of operation, but in saturation

*It is very common when modeling channel length modulation is MOSFETs to define a parameter λ as $1/|V_A|$, and to then write the equations in terms of λ, rather than $|V_A|$. We choose to use $|V_A|$ in this text because it is already familiar to us from our bipolar transistor models.

we replace L with L_{eff}. For example, our model for an n-channel MOSFET would become

$$
i_D = \begin{cases} 0 & \text{for } (v_{GS} - V_T) \leq 0 \leq v_{DS} \quad (10.18a) \\[2ex] \dfrac{K}{2}(v_{GS} - V_T)^2 \left[\dfrac{1 + v_{DS} - v_{DS_{\text{sat}}}}{|V_A|} - \dfrac{(v_{GS} - V_T)^2}{4|V_A|^2} \right] & \\ & \text{for } 0 \leq (v_{GS} - V_T),\ v_{DS_{\text{sat}}} \leq v_{DS} \quad (10.18b) \\ K\left(v_{GS} - V_T - \dfrac{v_{DS}}{2}\right) v_{DS} & \text{for } 0 \leq (v_{GS} - V_T),\ v_{DS} \leq v_{DS_{\text{sat}}} \quad (10.18c) \end{cases}
$$

with $v_{DS_{\text{sat}}}$ defined as $(v_{GS} - V_T) - (v_{GS} - V_T)^2/2|V_A|$. Only the expression for the drain current in saturation, Eq. 10.18b, has changed. Looking at it, you will recognize that it is our earlier expression multiplied by a factor (the term in square brackets). The bulk of this factor comes directly from substituting Eq. (10.17) in for L, but a small correction term is needed to make the curves continuous in going from the linear region into saturation. Eqs. (10.18) are plotted as solid curves in Fig. 10.8*a* for several values of $v_{GS} - V_T$, for a device in which K is 1.0 mA/V^2, V_T is 0.6 V, and V_A is -20 V. For comparison, the dashed curves show the characteristics for the same device assuming no channel length modulation, i.e., $|V_A| = \infty$.

At this point it is useful to spend a few lines discussing how $v_{DS_{\text{sat}}}$ is determined. When there is no channel length modulation, $v_{DS_{\text{sat}}}$ is $v_{GS} - V_T$, which is the value of v_{DS} that corresponds to the peak of the parabolic expression for i_D in the linear region (see Fig. 10.4). Notice that this is also the value of v_{DS} at which di_D/dv_{DS} is zero. Thus it is the value of v_{DS} where the incremental channel conductance becomes zero, which is its value in saturation when there is no channel length modulation. We use this observation to extend the concept of saturation to the case where channel length modulation is an issue. In particular, we say that saturation occurs when di_D/dv_{DS}, calculated using the expression for i_D in the linear region, equals the output conductance in the saturation region. A bit of algebra shows that this occurs when V_{DS} is $V(v_{GS} - V_T)^2/2|V_A|$, which was our definition of $v_{DS_{\text{sat}}}$ above.

There are a number of variants of Eqs. (10.18a) through (10.18c) that you may see used to treat channel length modulation in MOSFETs, and it is perhaps useful to say a few words about some of them now. A common approach is to approximate L_{eff} as

$$L_{\text{eff}} \approx \frac{L}{1 + \dfrac{v_{DS}}{|V_A|}} \tag{10.17$'$}$$

That is, $v_{DS_{\text{sat}}}$ is left out of the expression. Then this value is substituted for L in the expression for the drain current in the saturation region (just as we did before) and in the expression for the current in the linear region (this must be done so that i_D will be continuous when going from one region to the other). Our original definition of the boundary between the linear and saturation regions is retained

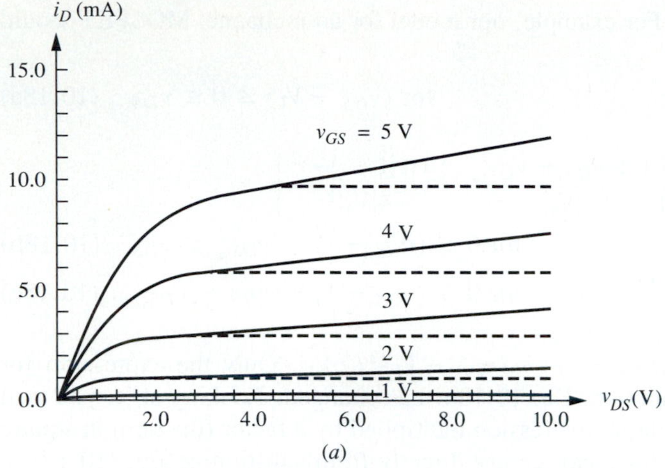

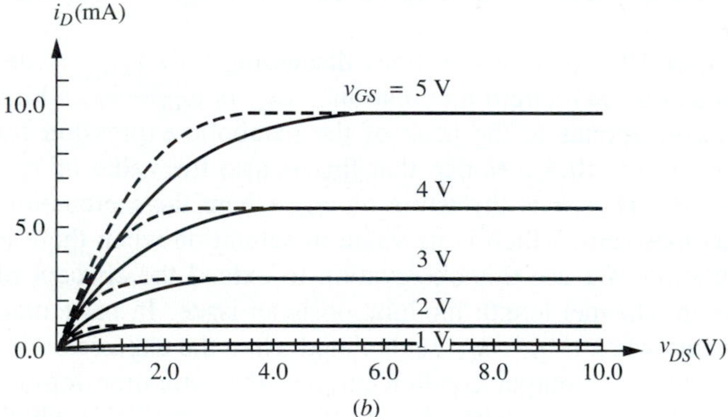

FIGURE 10.8
The output characteristics for an n-channel MOSFET showing the effect of channel length modulation. The solid curves are calculated using Eqs. (10.18) assuming a K-factor of 1.0 mA/V^2, a threshold voltage of 0.6 V, and an Early voltage of -20 V; the dashed curves were calculated assuming no channel length modulation, i.e., using Eqs. (10.15) or, equivalently, assuming $|V_A| = \infty$ in Eqs. (10.18). *(b)* The output characteristics for an n-channel MOSFET showing the impact of a body effect. The solid curves are calculated using Eqs. (10.18) assuming a K-factor of 0.7 mA/V^2, a threshold voltage of 0.6 V, an α of 0.3, and no channel length modulation. The dashed curves were calculated assuming a K-factor of 1.0 mA/V^2 and no body effect, i.e., using Eqs. (10.15) or, equivalently, assuming $\alpha = 0$ in Eqs (10.25).

(i.e., it is defined as when $v_{DS} = v_{GS} - V_T$), and the device characteristics become

$$i_D = \begin{cases} 0 & (v_{GS} - V_T) \le 0 \quad (10.18\text{d}) \\ \dfrac{K}{2}(v_{GS} - V_T)^2\left[1 + \dfrac{v_{DS}}{|V_A|}\right] & 0 \le (v_{GS} - V_T) \le v_{DS} \quad (10.18\text{e}) \\ K(v_{GS} - V_T - \dfrac{v_{DS}}{2})v_{DS}\left[1 + \dfrac{v_{DS}}{|V_A|}\right] & 0 \le v_{DS} \le (v_{GS} - V_T) \quad (10.18\text{f}) \end{cases}$$

Looking at these expressions and comparing them to our earlier equations, we see that we are simply ignoring higher order terms, and that by doing so we end up with expressions that are much more familiar to us, that look less formidable, and that are in general easier to work with. It is common to see that these expressions have been further simplified by leaving the term involving $|V_A|$ out of the expression for the linear region. (In effect, L_{eff} is substituted for L only in the expression for the saturation region, just as we did originally.) When this is done, both the characteristic and its slope are discontinuous in going from the linear region to the saturation region (as opposed to just the slope being discontinuous, as is the case when the expression for L_{eff} given by Eq. 10.17′ is substituted for L in the expressions for both regions). Nonetheless, the channel length modulation effect is really important only in saturation, so this makes some sense. Furthermore, such modest discontinuities are not troublesome when doing hand calculations; they are much more troublesome to computers, but computers can handle the more complex expressions, and there is no need to simplify things for them.

Another effect often dealt with differently when extending the basic model is the *body effect*. In deriving the basic parabolic model we said that the depletion region charge under the gate was approximately constant from one end of the channel to the other and that the channel charge q_N^* could be approximated using Eq. (10.5′). The body effect is then felt only in its effect on the threshold voltage, V_T. Another common approximation is to model q_N^* differently. Returning to Eq. (10.5), we do not neglect $v_{CS}(y)$ under the square root in the last term; instead, we expand the square root dependence. First, we write the last term as follows:

$$\sqrt{2\varepsilon_{\text{Si}}qN_A[|2\phi_p| + v_{CS}(y) - v_{BS}]} = \sqrt{2\varepsilon_{\text{Si}}qN_A[|2\phi_p| - v_{BS}]}\sqrt{1 + \frac{v_{CS}(y)}{|2\phi_p| - v_{BS}}} \tag{10.19}$$

Focusing on the last term on the right-hand side of this equation we make the following approximation:

$$\sqrt{1 + \frac{v_{CS}(y)}{|2\phi_p| - v_{BS}}} \approx 1 + \frac{v_{CS}(y)}{2(|2\phi_p| - v_{BS})} \tag{10.20}$$

This approximation is, strictly speaking, valid only if v_{CS} is much less than $2(|2\phi_p| - v_{BS})$; this will not always be true, but we make the approximation anyway.

With this approximation, we can write q_N^* as

$$q_N^*[v_{CS}(y)] \approx -\frac{\varepsilon_o}{t_o}\{v_{GS} - v_{CS}(y) - |2\phi_p| - V_{\text{FB}} + \frac{t_o}{\varepsilon_o}\sqrt{2\varepsilon_{\text{Si}} q N_A(|2\phi_p| - v_{BS})}\left[1 + \frac{v_{CS}(y)}{2(|2\phi_p| - v_{BS})}\right]\} \tag{10.21a}$$

which becomes, after a bit of algebra,

$$q_N^*[v_{CS}(y)] \approx -\frac{\varepsilon_o}{t_o}\left\{v_{GS} - |2\phi_p| - V_{\text{FB}} + \frac{t_o}{\varepsilon_o}\sqrt{(2\varepsilon_{\text{Si}} q N_A(|2\phi_p| - v_{BS})} - v_{CS}(y)\left[1 - \frac{t_o}{\varepsilon_o}\sqrt{\frac{\varepsilon_{\text{Si}} q N_A}{2(|2\phi_p| - v_{BS})}}\right]\right\} \tag{10.21b}$$

We now define the threshold voltage just as we did earlier:

$$V_{TS}(v_{BS}) \equiv V_{\text{FB}} - |2\phi_p| - \frac{t_o}{\varepsilon_o}\sqrt{2\varepsilon_{\text{Si}} q N_A(|2\phi_p| - v_{BS})} \tag{10.22}$$

which is identical to Eq. (10.12b). We also define a factor α as

$$\alpha \equiv \frac{t_o}{\varepsilon_o}\sqrt{\frac{\varepsilon_{\text{Si}} q N_A}{2(|2\phi_p| - v_{BS})}} \tag{10.23}$$

Using these definitions, we can write

$$q_N^*[v_{CS}(y)] \approx -\frac{\varepsilon_o}{t_o}[v_{GS} - V_T - v_{CS}(y)(1 - \alpha)] \tag{10.24}$$

Putting this into Eq. (10.7) and doing the integration yields the following model:

$$i_D = \begin{cases} 0 & \text{for } \dfrac{(v_{GS} - V_T)}{(1-\alpha)} \leq 0 \leq v_{DS} \quad (10.25\text{a}) \\[2ex] \dfrac{K}{2}\dfrac{(v_{GS} - V_T)^2}{(1-\alpha)}\left[1 + \dfrac{v_{DS} - v_{DS_{\text{sat}}}}{|V_A|} - \dfrac{(v_{GS} - V_T)^2}{4(1-\alpha)^2|V_A|^2}\right] & \\ & \text{for } 0 \leq (v_{GS} - V_T), \quad v_{DS_{\text{sat}}} \leq v_{DS} \quad (10.25\text{b}) \\[2ex] K\left[v_{GS} - V_T - \dfrac{v_{DS}}{2}(1-\alpha)\right]v_{DS} & \\ & \text{for } 0 \leq (v_{GS} - V_T), \quad v_{DS} \leq V_{DS_{\text{sat}}} \quad (10.25\text{c}) \end{cases}$$

with $V_{DS_{\text{sat}}}$ now defined as $(v_{GS} - V_T)/(1-\alpha) - (v_{GS} - V_T)^2/2|V_A|(1-\alpha)^2$. These expressions are very similar to our earlier results, Eqs. (10.15) and (10.18), but in this model saturation occurs at a somewhat higher voltage and somewhat higher current level than in our basic parabolic model. Figure 10.8*b* compares the predictions of this model with the basic parabolic model, without the Early effect (i.e., $|V_A| = \infty$), assuming a threshold voltage of 0.6 V, an α of 0.3, and a *K*-factor of

0.7 mA/V^2. This α corresponds to a structure similar to the one that we analyzed earlier (see page 273). For comparison, the dashed curves show the characteristics when the body effect is negligible, i.e., when α is zero. In calculating the dashed curves we take K to be 1.0 mA/V^2 so that both sets of characteristics saturate at the same current level. This makes the increase in saturation voltage due to the body effect more evident. It also corresponds to the situation we typically find in practice. That is to say, we are often comparing how well several different models fit measured data on a given device, and in such a case the meaningful thing to do is to adjust the K-factor in the models we are comparing to give the same saturation currents, as was done in Fig. 10.8*b*.

A common situation is one in which we are trying to fit data measured on a particular device. In such a case the meaningful thing to do is adjust the K-factor in our models to predict the same saturation currents. This is done in Fig. 10.8*b*. The curves calculated using the basic model, Eqs. (10.18), are calculated assuming that K is 1.0 mA/V^2 (as before), and the curves calculated using Eqs. (10.25) assume a K-factor of 1.4 mA/V^2.

Physically, α turns out to be the ratio of the depletion region capacitance (with $v_{DS} = 0$) to the gate oxide capacitance. It tends to be on the order of a few tenths and can be made smaller by increasing the reverse bias on the substrate. (In calculating the characteristics in Fig. 10.8 it has been assumed that v_{BS} is zero.)

The final additions that we can make to our basic model, which are also included in SPICE, are to add resistors in series with the gate, source, and drain (these are typically very small-value resistors); to add exponential diodes between the source and the substrate and between the drain and the substrate to represent the source-to-substrate and drain-to-substrate diode junctions, respec-tively; and to add a high-value resistor in parallel with the channel between the source and drain to represent any possible source-to-drain leakage path in parallel with the channel. A circuit schematic including all of these elements is presented in Fig. 10.9.

c) Velocity Saturation in Silicon MOSFETs. We mentioned in Sec. 3.1.1, and saw in Fig. 3.2, that the velocity/electric-field relationship for holes and electrons in silicon is linear at low fields (from which we define the mobility μ as $s/\mathcal{E}$), but at high fields the velocity no longer increases with increasing electric field. Thus we say that the velocity *saturates*.

In modern, short-channel MOSFETs it is possible that the channel electric field $\mathcal{E}_y$ can be high enough to result in velocity saturation. In such a case our replacement of s_y with $\mu_e \mathcal{E}_y$ in Eq. (10.4) is wrong and the current-voltage expressions we developed are similarly incorrect. Although this is not the case for most silicon MOSFETs, it may be true for so-called submicron MOSFETs (i.e., devices with gate lengths less than 1 μm). To model these devices we should use a different expression to relate s_y to $\mathcal{E}_y$. A commonly used model, especially in materials like silicon in which the saturation of s_y is rather gradual, is

$$s_y(\mathcal{E}_y) = \frac{\mu_e \mathcal{E}_y}{1 + (\mathcal{E}_y/\mathcal{E}_{\text{crit}})} \tag{10.26}$$

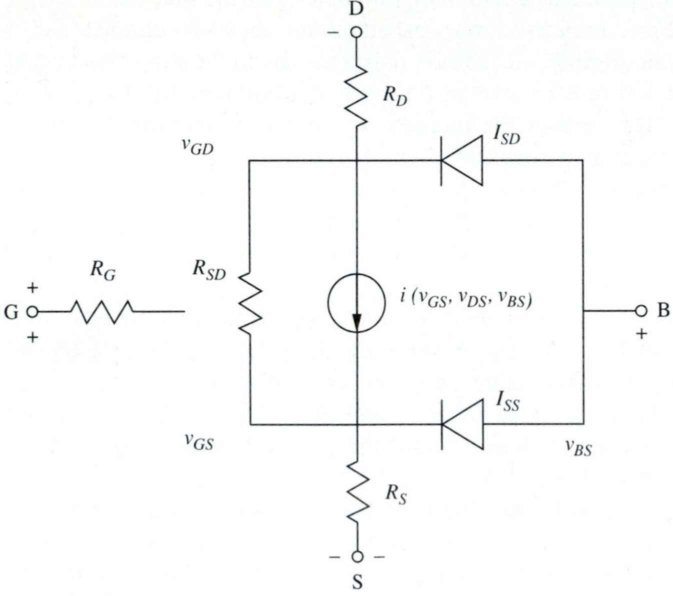

FIGURE 10.9
Circuit schematic representation of a model for an *n*-channel MOSFET including lead series resistances, the source-to-substrate and drain-to-substrate diodes, and a resistor representing source-to-drain leakage. The user must decide whether to represent the dependent current generator using Eqs. (10.15), (10.18), or (10.25).

where μ_e is the traditional low field mobility and $\mathscr{E}_{\text{crit}}$ is the field at which s_y is half its saturation value.* For the data in Fig. 3.2, $\mathscr{E}_{\text{crit}}$ is 5×10^3 V/cm and μ_e is 1300 cm^2/V·s. In a Si MOSFET channel the mobility is lower because the carriers are moving near the oxide-silicon interface; typical values are 200 to 300 cm^2/V·s for μ_e, and 5×10^4 V/cm for $\mathscr{E}_{\text{crit}}$.

If we use Eq. (10.26) in Eq. (10.4) we find

$$i_D = W q_N^* \frac{\mu_e \mathscr{E}_y}{1 + (\mathscr{E}_y / \mathscr{E}_{\text{crit}})} \tag{10.27}$$

Since we know that we are going to want to substitute $-dv_{CS}/dy$ for $\mathscr{E}_y$ and integrate, it is best to rearrange this equation a bit. Multiplying both sides by $(1 + \mathscr{E}_y/\mathscr{E}_{\text{crit}})$ and collecting terms involving $\mathscr{E}_y$ on the left, we have

$$i_D = \left(W q_N^* \mu_e - \frac{i_D}{\mathscr{E}_{\text{crit}}} \right) \mathscr{E}_y \tag{10.28}$$

*You will find this expression plotted in Fig. 10.27.

If we now make our substitution for $\mathscr{E}_y$ and use Eq. (10.5′) for q_N^* and Eq. (10.12a) for V_T, we have

$$i_D dy = \left[W \mu_e \frac{\varepsilon_o}{t_o}(v_{GS} - v_{CS} - V_T) - \frac{i_D}{\mathscr{E}_{\text{crit}}} \right] dv_{CS} \tag{10.29}$$

Integrating from one end of the channel to the other we have

$$i_D L = W \mu_e C_{\text{ox}}^* \left[(v_{GS} - V_T) v_{DS} - \frac{v_{DS}^2}{2} \right] - \frac{i_D v_{DS}}{\mathscr{E}_{\text{crit}}} \tag{10.30}$$

where we have also written ε_o / t_o as C_{ox}^*. Solving for i_D yields

$$i_D = \frac{W}{L + (v_{DS}/\mathscr{E}_{\text{crit}})} \mu_e C_{\text{ox}}^* \left(v_{GS} - V_T - \frac{v_{DS}}{2} \right) v_{DS} \tag{10.31a}$$

which can also be written as

$$i_D = \frac{1}{1 + (v_{DS}/L\mathscr{E}_{\text{crit}})} K \left(v_{GS} - V_T - \frac{v_{DS}}{2} \right) v_{DS} \tag{10.31b}$$

where K is $\mu_e C_{\text{ox}}^* W/L$ as before [see Eq. (10.11)]. This is the same as our earlier result except for the leading term. Again it is valid until i_D reaches its peak at some value of v_{DS} that we call $v_{DS,\text{sat}}$, at which point i_D saturates (i.e., stays constant as v_{DS} is increased further). We find this value of v_{DS} by determining when $\partial i_D / \partial v_{DS}$ is zero. Doing this yields

$$v_{DS,\text{sat}} = L\mathscr{E}_{\text{crit}} \left[\sqrt{1 + \frac{2(v_{GS} - V_T)}{L\mathscr{E}_{\text{crit}}}} - 1 \right] \tag{10.32}$$

The behavior predicted by this model is illustrated in Fig. 10.10, where we plot Eq. (10.31b) for a device for which K is 0.1 mA/V^2, $L\mathscr{E}_{\text{crit}}$ is 2 V, and V_T is 0.5 V. A family of curves is plotted for v_{GS} equal to 1, 2, 3, 4, and 5 V.

At first glance the characteristics in Fig. 10.10 look very similar to other MOSFET characteristics we have seen, but closer examination shows that there are important differences. First, the saturation voltage is less than $(v_{GS} - V_T)$, especially when $(v_{GS} - V_T)$ is large, as in the curves for $v_{GS} = 3$, 4, and 5 V. For example, when $(v_{GS} - V_T)$ is 0.5 V, $v_{DS,\text{sat}}$ is 0.45 V (i.e., they are similar). However when $(v_{GS} - V_T)$ is 1.5 V, $v_{DS,\text{sat}}$ is only 1.16 V, and the difference increases as $(v_{GS} - V_T)$ increases. We find that $v_{DS,\text{sat}}$ is approximately 1.75, 2.25, and 2.7 V when $(v_{GS} - V_T)$ is 2.5, 3.5, and 4.5 V, respectively.

Second, the saturation current is lower. In our model without velocity saturation, $i_{D,\text{sat}}$ is $K(v_{GS} - V_T)^2/2$. Thus when $(v_{GS} - V_T)$ is 4.5 V we would expect the saturation current to be 2 mA. In Fig. 10.10 it is less than 0.4 mA!

To explore these characteristics more, it is most instructive to consider two situations. The first is when L and/or $\mathscr{E}_{\text{crit}}$ is relatively large and the product $L\mathscr{E}_{\text{crit}}$ is appreciably larger (by a factor of 2 or more) than $(v_{GS} - V_T)$. In this case we have our earlier result; that is,

$$v_{DS,\text{sat}} \approx (v_{GS} - V_T) \tag{10.33}$$

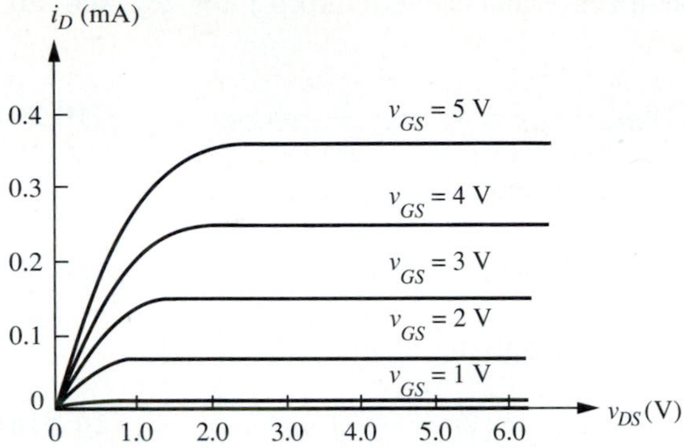

FIGURE 10.10
Output characteristic family for a MOSFET in which velocity saturation is a factor. Velocity saturation is not important for the $v_{GS} = 1$ V curve, it plays a modest role in the $v_{GS} = 2$ V curve, and it is a major factor in the $v_{GS} = 3$, 4, and 5 V curves.

and i_D saturates at

$$i_{D,\text{sat}} = \frac{1}{1 + (v_{GS} - V_T)/L\mathscr{E}_{\text{crit}}} \frac{K}{2}(v_{GS} - V_T)^2 \tag{10.34a}$$

From Eq. (10.34a), we see that the first impact of velocity saturation is to lower the current of a MOSFET in saturation. How much it is lowered depends on how large the factor $(v_{GS} - V_T)/L\mathscr{E}_{\text{crit}}$ is.

Another way of looking at this $i_{D,\text{sat}}$ result is obtained by substituting our expression for K into Eq. (10.34a). Doing this and writing $\mu_e\mathscr{E}_{\text{crit}}$ as s_{sat}, the velocity at which the electrons in the channel saturate when $\mathscr{E}_y$ is much greater than $\mathscr{E}_{\text{crit}}$, we obtain

$$i_{D,\text{sat}} = \frac{W s_{\text{sat}} C_{\text{ox}}^*}{2[(v_{GS} - V_T) + L\mathscr{E}_{\text{crit}}]}(v_{GS} - V_T)^2 \tag{10.34b}$$

Written this way, the reduced sensitivity of $i_{D,\text{sat}}$ to $(v_{GS} - V_T)$ is a bit clearer and the virtue of a large s_{sat} is certainly apparent.

When the channel length L is very short, and/or $\mathscr{E}_{\text{crit}}$ is small so that the product $L\mathscr{E}_{\text{crit}}$ is smaller than $(v_{GS} - V_T)$, then $V_{DS,\text{sat}}$ takes a much different value. Returning to Eq. (10.32), we find now that

$$v_{\text{DS,sat}} \approx \sqrt{2(v_{GS} - V_T)L\mathscr{E}_{\text{crit}} - L\mathscr{E}_{\text{crit}}} \tag{10.35}$$

and i_D saturates at

$$i_{D,\text{sat}} \approx KL\mathscr{E}_{\text{crit}}\left[v_{GS} - V_T - \sqrt{\frac{(v_{GS} - V_T)L\mathscr{E}_{\text{crit}}}{2}}\right] \tag{10.36}$$

This characteristic is much different than one that we find in a device in which velocity saturation is not significant. The family of curves of i_D versus v_{DS} for different values of v_{GS} saturate at a voltage that increases more nearly as $\sqrt{(v_{GS} - V_T)}$, rather than linearly with $(v_{GS} - V_T)$. The saturation current $i_{D,\text{sat}}$ increases at best linearly with $(v_{GS} - V_T)$, rather than as $(v_{GS} - V_T)^2$. These features are evident in Fig. 10.10, which corresponds to the present limit when v_{GS} is 4 and 5 V.

In summary, we have shown that both the saturation voltage and saturation current are lower than when velocity saturation is not considered. This is actually a good result as far as the saturation voltage is concerned; a low saturation voltage is desirable. The fact that the saturation current is lower is not so good, however, because we like to get as much current as we can from a device at a given voltage. Another important factor to note in Fig. 10.10 is that the weaker dependence of $i_{D,\text{sat}}$ on $(v_{GS} - V_T)$ means that the family of $(i_{D,\text{sat}} - v_{DS})$ curves for equal $(v_{GS} - V_T)$ increments are more closely and evenly spaced. This is equivalent to saying that the small-signal transconductance g_m is reduced and is less sensitive to bias points in the extreme of severe velocity saturation (i.e., when Eq. (10.36) holds).

Finally, before leaving this issue it makes sense to look at a few more numbers. For example, we said above that $\mathscr{E}_{\text{crit}}$ in the channel of a silicon MOSFET is on the order of 5×10^4 V/cm. If the channel length L is 2 μm, then the product $L\mathscr{E}_{\text{crit}}$ is 10 V and velocity saturation is not an issue, certainly not in most digital circuits where supply voltages are between 3 and 5 V (5 V in older circuits with longer gate lengths; down to 3 V or even 2 V in newer circuits with submicron gate lengths). If, however, L is reduced to 0.5 μm, the $L\mathscr{E}_{\text{crit}}$ product is 2.5 V and velocity saturation begins to be a factor. As L gets even smaller, velocity saturation can be a dominant factor.

d) Dynamic models with charge stores. To make our MOSFET model suitable for dynamic analyses we must examine the device structure and identify the energy storage elements (primarily capacitances) that we must add to our model. Two representative MOSFET device structures are shown in cross section in Fig. 10.11. The first structure, Fig. 10.11*a*, is a device built using what is called a metal-gate technology. This technology necessitates a considerable overlap of the gate metal and the diffused source and drain n^+-regions. The second structure, shown in Fig. 10.11*b*, is a self-aligned, silicon-gate structure, which uses heavily doped, polycrystalline silicon as the gate "metal" to eliminate this overlap. The use of silicon for the gate permits the source and drain region edges to be aligned with the edges of the gate during fabrication of the device.

Looking at the device structures of Fig. 10.11 to identify capacitances, we see that there are several. Clearly the gate electrode is a large capacitor plate, so there should be a capacitance between the gate and the channel and there should be additional capacitance because of the overlap of the gate metal and the n^+ source and drain diffusions. Finally, there must be capacitance associated with the source and drain n^+-regions.

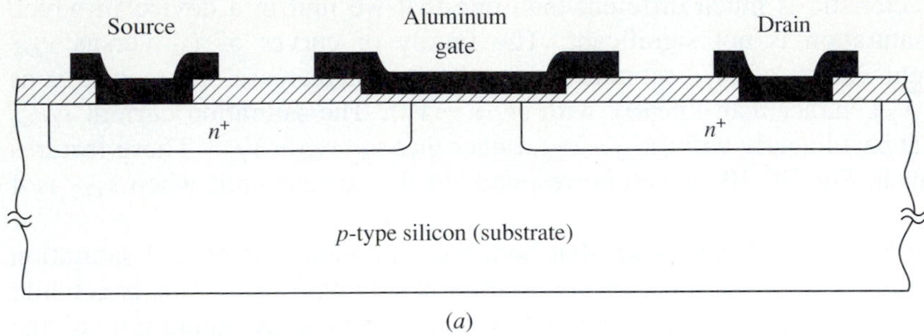

(a)

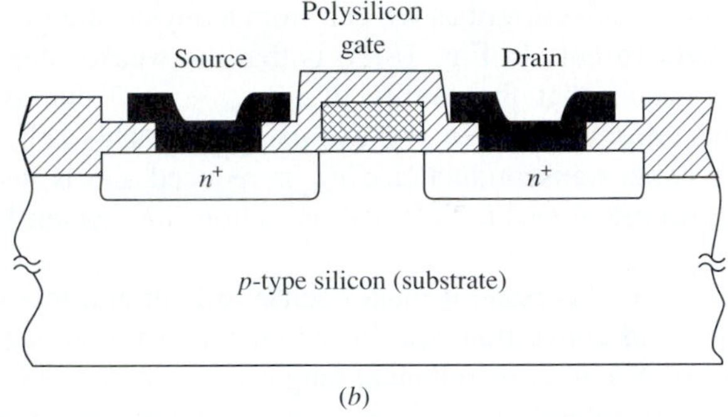

(b)

FIGURE 10.11
Cross-sectional drawings of two MOSFET structures: (a) metal-gate; and (b) self-aligned silicon-gate.

The gate-to-channel capacitance actually deserves very careful attention. Although it is clear that the charge on the gate enters through the gate electrode, it is less clear whether the charge in the inversion layer enters through the source or the drain electrode. In saturation the drain electrode is decoupled from the source and gate as far as the intrinsic device operation is concerned, so any change in the inversion layer charge can be supplied only by the source. Any gate-to-drain capacitance in saturation must therefore be only that due to any physical overlap of the gate metal and the drain n^+-region. In the linear, or triode, region, however, a significant fraction of the channel charge can come through the drain and a correspondingly larger fraction of the gate capacitance must appear between the gate and drain.

These arguments can be quantified by writing an expression for the total gate charge and examining its dependence on the gate-to-source and gate-to-drain voltages. Rather than take the time to do this now, however, we will defer the calculation of $q_G(v_{GS}, v_{GD})$ to Sec. 14.3.2* and simply note here that these

*You will find that you can easily follow the discussion in Sec. 14.3.2, beginning with the paragraph containing Eq. (14.31), and are encouraged to look ahead to that section if you are interested. However, it makes the most sense to wait until after you finish reading Sec. 10.1.

intrinsic contributions to the gate charge are, in general, nonlinear functions of the voltages involved; in addition, they are, in general, proportional to the gate area WL and the oxide capacitance per unit area, C_{ox}^*, $(= \varepsilon_o/t_o)$.

Returning now to our dynamic large-signal model, we can add nonlinear capacitors representing the four charge stores we have identified—one each between the gate and source and between the gate and drain, and one each associated with the source-to-substrate and the drain-to-substrate n^+-p junctions. With these additions our model becomes as illustrated in Fig. 10.12. For completeness, we used our most complex MOSFET model for this figure; you should be able to add these nonlinear capacitors to the simpler model of Fig. 10.7 yourself.

10.1.2 Static Small-Signal Linear Model

The development of a small-signal linear model for MOSFETs follows the same reasoning that we used for diodes and bipolar junction transistors. The only change is that now we have four terminals, so we must model three independent terminal currents in terms of three independent terminal voltages. We will look at two connections, common-source and common-gate.

a) Common-source. In the common-source connection, we want to find linear relationships for the small-signal gate, back gate, and drain currents (i_g, i_b, and i_d, respectively) in terms of the small-signal gate-to-source, back-to-source, and drain-to-source voltages (v_{gs}, v_{bs}, and v_{ds}, respectively). Since the gate and back currents are zero in our large-signal model, they remain zero for small-signal voltages:

$$i_g = 0 \tag{10.37a}$$

$$i_b = 0 \tag{10.37b}$$

assuming a bias point such that $V_{DS} \geq 0$ and $V_{BS} \leq 0$. The drain current, on the other hand, is in general not zero and may depend on all three terminal voltages. We can write

$$i_d = g_m v_{gs} + g_{mb} v_{bs} + g_o v_{ds} \tag{10.37c}$$

where we define the various conductances as follows:

$$\text{Forward transconductance, } g_m \equiv \left.\frac{\partial i_D}{\partial v_{GS}}\right|_Q \tag{10.38}$$

$$\text{Substrate transconductance, } g_{mb} \equiv \left.\frac{\partial i_D}{\partial v_{BS}}\right|_Q \tag{10.39}$$

$$\text{Output conductance, } g_o \equiv \left.\frac{\partial i_D}{\partial v_{DS}}\right|_Q \tag{10.40}$$

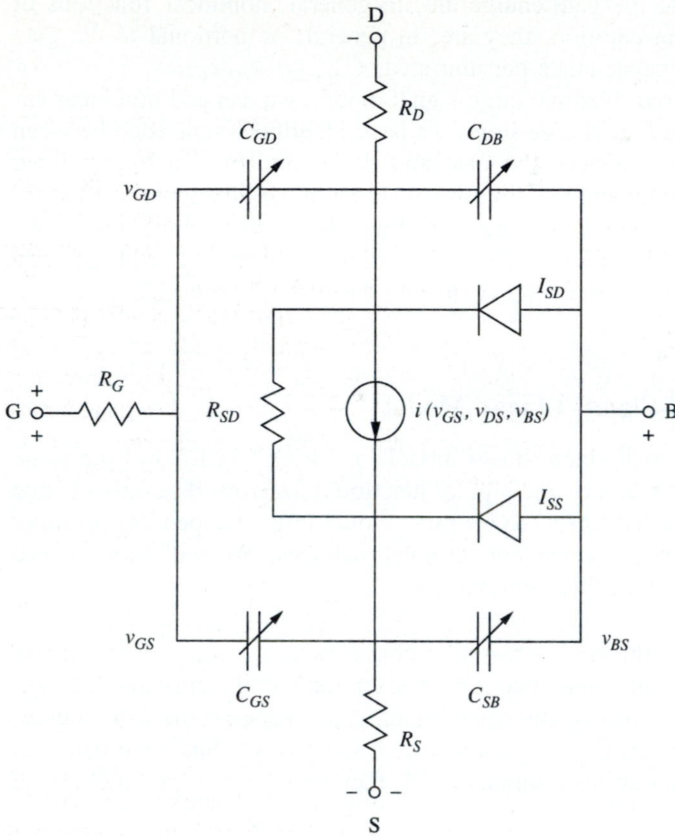

FIGURE 10.12
MOFSET circuit model from Fig. 10.9 with the addition of nonlinear charge stores to account for the gate charge and for the junctions between the source and drain n^+-regions and the substrate.

The corresponding small-signal model is illustrated in Fig. 10.13. This model is the same for both *n*- and *p*-channel MOSFETs.

We next use our large-signal model to evaluate the three parameters in the small-signal model. We will assume an *n*-channel device for purposes of discussion, but the results can be used for either type of device. The parameter values will depend on the bias point, and the expressions for them will depend upon the region in which the device is biased. In cutoff, $V_{GS} < V_T$, we find that all currents are zero, so $g_m = g_{mb} = g_o = 0$. In saturation, $0 \leq (V_{GS} - V_T) \leq V_{DS}$, we see from Eq. (10.15b) that

$$g_o = 0 \tag{10.41}$$

$$g_m = K(|V_{GS} - V_T|) \tag{10.42a}$$

or, equivalently,

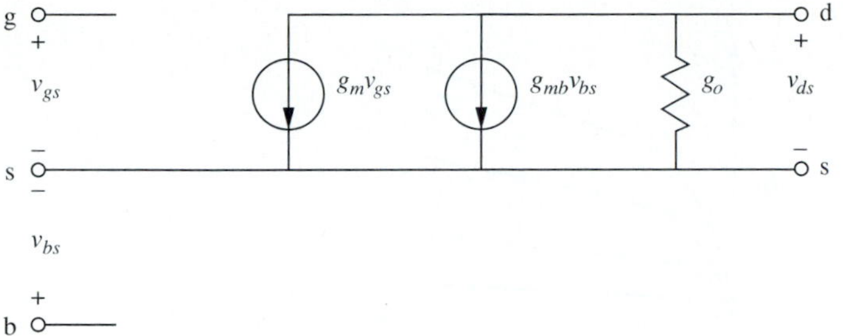

FIGURE 10.13
Small-signal equivalent circuit for the MOSFET. This model is restricted to operation about a bias point for which $V_{BS} \leq 0$ and $V_{DS} \geq 0$.

$$g_m = (2K|I_D|)^{1/2} \tag{10.42b}$$

and

$$g_{mb} = \eta g_m \tag{10.43}$$

where we have defined η as

$$\eta \equiv -\left.\frac{\partial V_T}{\partial v_{BS}}\right|_Q \tag{10.44}$$

In practice we find that η is a positive number whose magnitude is typically on the order of 0.03 to 0.1.

The conclusion that the output conductance g_o is zero in saturation is a consequence of our assumption that the current truly saturates above a drain-to-source voltage of $(v_{GS} - V_T)$. Often, however, the width of the region near the drain over which the channel has disappeared increases slightly as v_{DS} is increased above $(v_{GS} - V_T)$. This reduces the effective length of the channel slightly, leading to a small increase of drain current in saturation and thus to a very small, but finite, output conductance for bias points in the saturation region. This is illustrated in Fig. 10.14. The analogous effect with bipolar transistors was the Early effect, or base width modulation. For MOSFETs, too, we define an Early voltage and use it to calculate the output conductance at any bias point, as is also illustrated in Fig. 10.14. We have, assuming that $|V_A| >> V_{DS}$,

$$g_o = \left|\frac{I_D}{V_A}\right| \tag{10.45}$$

An important observation is that in MOSFETs, as a general rule, the Early voltage scales with the gate length L. That is, the Early voltages V_{A1} and V_{A2} of two otherwise identical devices with different gate lengths L_1 and L_2 will be related approximately as

$$\frac{V_{A1}}{V_{A2}} \approx \frac{L_1}{L_2} \tag{10.46}$$

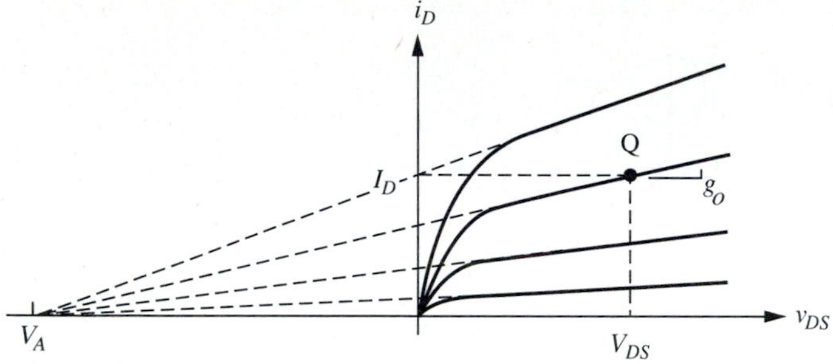

FIGURE 10.14
Output characteristics of a MOSFET in the forward active region extrapolated back to intersect the horizontal axis at the Early voltage V_A.

The Early voltage of a device does not scale with the device width; that is, two otherwise identical devices with different gate widths will have the same Early voltage.

Finally, in the linear region, $0 \leq V_{DS} \leq (V_{GS} - V_T)$, we find

$$g_o = K(|V_{GS} - V_T - V_{DS}|) \tag{10.47}$$

$$g_m = |K V_{DS}| \tag{10.48}$$

$$g_{mb} = \eta g_m \tag{10.49}$$

We can notice immediately that in the linear region the output conductance g_o is nonzero, even in the ideal device. Notice also that the transconductance g_m is lower than it was in the saturation region.

Example

Question. Find the small-signal equivalent circuit for the MOSFET in the preceding example for operation about the gate-to-source bias voltage specified there (i.e., $V_{GS} = 2$ V) and assuming (a) V_{DS} is 0.5 V, and (b) V_{DS} is 4 V.

Discussion. We first note that since $(V_{GS} - V_T)$ is 1.35 V, the transistor is biased in the linear, or triode, region in (a) and is saturated in (b).

With the MOSFET biased in the linear region with $V_{DS} = 0.5$ V, we find by using Eqs. (10.48) and (10.47) that g_m is 0.60 mS and that g_o is 0.55 mS. This latter value corresponds to an output resistance $r_o(= 1/g_o)$ of 1.8 kΩ.

With the MOSFET biased in saturation, g_o is identically zero according to our model and we find from either Eqs. (10.42a) or (10.42b) that g_m is 1.35 mS.

The transconductance g_m of the MOSFET is considerably smaller than that of a bipolar junction transistor (BJT) biased at the same output current level; that is, g_m(BJT), which equals qI_C/kT, is 36 mS if I_C is 0.9 mA. This is again a fairly typical result, and a large transconductance is not the reason circuit designers are attracted to MOSFETs. Often a far more significant feature is MOSFETs' extremely high input resistance.

Thus far we have ignored g_{mb}, which is related to g_m through the factor η. To calculate η we return to Eq. (10.12c) for $V_T(v_{BS})$ and calculate $-\partial V_T/\partial v_{BS}|_Q$.

Doing this we find

$$\eta = \frac{t_o}{\varepsilon_o}\sqrt{\frac{\varepsilon_{Si} q N_A}{2(|2\phi_p| - v_{BS})}} \tag{10.50}$$

which, for the particular MOSFET we are considering, turns out to be a relatively large 0.34. Notice that η is related to the body effect coefficient γ as

$$\eta = \frac{\gamma}{2\sqrt{|2\phi_p| - v_{BS}}} \tag{10.51}$$

Notice also that η is equivalent to the parameter α we introduced in Eq. (10.23).

Before leaving the quasistatic common-source small signal model, it is appropriate to make a few comments about the impact on circuit analysis problems of having to deal with the back-gate, or substrate, transconductance current source, $g_{mb}v_{bs}$. Having this additional dependent source at first appears to complicate our model and analysis enormously compared to what we had with a bipolar junction transistor. In practice, however, the situation is usually quite different. In many circuits the substrate is either connected directly to the source or is at a fixed bias relative to the source, so that v_{bs} is zero and the $g_{mb}v_{bs}$ generator does not enter the picture. The small-signal equivalent circuit is then as shown in Fig. 10.15*a*.

In many other circuits, the substrate is incrementally connected to the drain, so v_{bs} is equal to v_{ds}. In this case the $g_{mb}v_{bs}$ generator is equivalent to a transconductance in parallel with g_o and the equivalent circuit becomes that illustrated in Fig. 10.15*b*. Again the resulting circuit is no more complicated than that of a BJT.

b) Common-gate. Sometimes it is desirable to have a linear incremental circuit model for the MOSFET that has a common-gate topology, rather than a common-

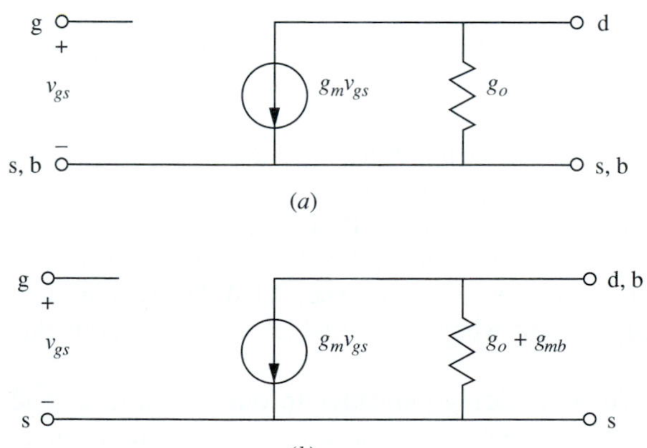

FIGURE 10.15
Small-signal linear equivalent circuit models for MOSFETs in two special common-source situations: (*a*) when $v_{bs} = 0$; (*b*) when $v_{bs} = v_{ds}$.

source topology like the model we just discussed (see Fig. 10.15). In this case we want a model in which i_s and i_d are viewed as the input and output currents, respectively, and are written as functions of v_{sg}, v_{dg}, and v_{bg}. One way to get this model is to begin with our low-frequency common-source model, Fig. 10.13, and write the current expressions

$$i_g = 0 \tag{10.52}$$

$$i_b = 0 \tag{10.53}$$

$$i_d = g_m v_{gs} + g_{mb} v_{bs} \tag{10.54}$$

Note that we have assumed a bias point in saturation and that $g_o \approx 0$ (we will consider later what happens when g_o cannot be neglected). We then solve for i_s, using the fact that i_g, i_d, i_b, and i_s must sum to zero. Since i_g and i_b are themselves zero, the result is very simple and powerful. We have simply

$$i_s = -i_d \tag{10.55a}$$

That is, what goes in the input comes out the output (while at the same time, as we shall see, what happens at the output does not affect the input). In terms of terminal voltages this is

$$i_s = -g_m v_{gs} - g_{mb} v_{bs} \tag{10.55b}$$

Our next step is to write this equation in terms of the terminal voltages referenced to the gate (i.e., v_{sg}, v_{bg}, and v_{dg}). Recognizing that v_{gs} is $-v_{sg}$, v_{bs} is $(v_{bg} - v_{sg})$, and v_{ds} is $(v_{dg} - v_{sg})$, and substituting these in Eq. (10.55b) we find

$$i_s = (g_m + g_{mb}) v_{sg} - g_{mb} v_{bs} \tag{10.55c}$$

$$i_d = -i_s = -(g_m + g_{mb}) v_{sg} + g_{mb} v_{bg} \tag{10.56}$$

A circuit model representing these expressions is illustrated in Fig. 10.16. Note that we have made use of the fact that $(g_m + g_{mb})$ can be written more conveniently as $g_m(1 + \eta)$.

You will notice that in Fig. 10.16*a* we have chosen to write i_d in terms of its dependence on the terminal voltages rather than simply saying that it is $-i_s$. This deserves a bit of discussion. First, it is very powerful to observe that i_d is $-i_s$ and thus that the common-gate topology operates with a unity current gain and as what could be termed a current-follower (analogous to the voltage-follower operation of the source-follower circuit discussed in Sec. 11.4.4). This is how you should view the common-gate circuit when you consider applications of this topology.

On the other hand, when we start adding parasitics to our model to extend the model to high frequencies, or g_o to account for a finite output conductance, the identity of i_s tends to get lost, just as the identity of i_b got lost in the high frequency hybrid-π model (see Sec. 8.2.3). In this case it becomes desirable to have a model dependent on quantities—the terminal voltages, in this case—whose identities remain unambiguous.

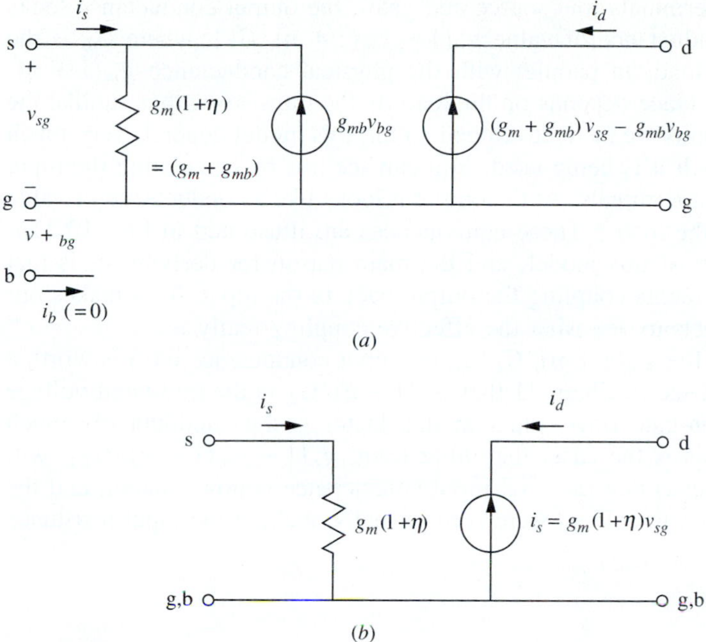

FIGURE 10.16
Linear incremental equivalent circuit models for the MOSFET in a common-gate configuration: (*a*) the full model with an arbitrary voltage signal on the substrate lead b; (*b*) the model relevant when, as is often the case, v_{bg} is zero. The latter model is much simpler than the first and is the one most commonly used in initial designs with the common-gate stage.

Having said all this, let us now return to the model of Fig. 10.16*a* and discuss it a bit more. First we note that in many common-gate applications both the gate and substrate are incrementally grounded so that v_{bg} is zero. In such cases the model of Fig. 10.16*b* results. For many applications, and certainly for a "first cut," this model is ideal for visualizing what the common-gate topology will do, which may be described as follows: First, as we said earlier, it has unity current gain. Second, it has very low input impedance. Conceptually, then, it can be used to sense a current in a lead without disturbing the circuit (i.e., it adds very little resistance), and it can transmit an identical current to an "arbitrary" load.* We will discuss the common-gate amplifier circuit at some length in Sec. 11.4.3.

Looking next at the issue of output conductance, we find that g_o appears between the drain and source, as shown in Fig. 10.17*a*. In this position, if we

*We put arbitrary in quotation marks because the load is not entirely arbitrary, of course. In particular, its conductance must at least be large relative to the output conductance g_o of the MOSFET.

look into the input terminals (the source and gate), the output conductance looks like an effective conductance of value $g_o[1 - g_m(1+\eta)/G_L]$, where G_L is the conductance of the load, in parallel with the physical conductance $g_m(1+\eta)$. The effective conductance depends on the load on the transistors; thus, unlike the other equivalent circuits we have developed so far, this model depends very much on the circuit in which it is being used. You can see this by calculating the input resistance at the input terminals. At the output it looks like a conductance of value g_o in parallel with the load.* These equivalences are illustrated in Fig. 10.17*b*. An important feature of this model, and the main reason for deriving it, is that there are now no elements coupling the output back to the input. This makes our analysis easier and lets us see what the effective coupling really is.

The factor $g_o[1 - g_m(1+\eta)/G_L]$ in the input conductance term is worth a few words. We shall see in Chap. 11 that $g_m(1+\eta)/G_L$ is the mid-band voltage gain of this common-gate stage and that this factor is thus undoubtedly much greater than 1. If this is the case, the entire term, $g_o[1 - g_m(1+\eta)/G_L]$, will be negative. This means that the total input conductance is now smaller, and the input resistance larger, than if g_o were zero. Usually, making the input resistance

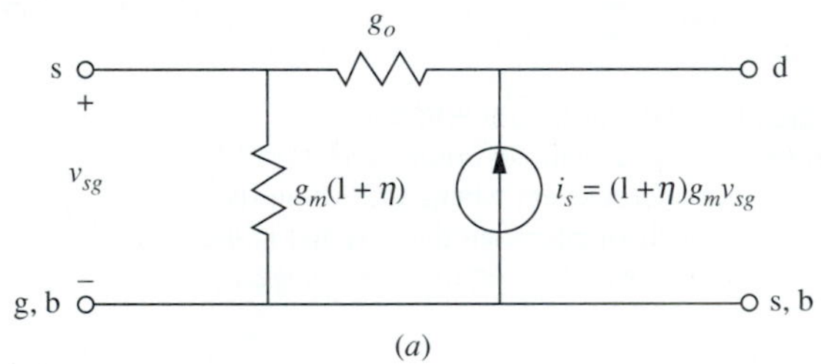

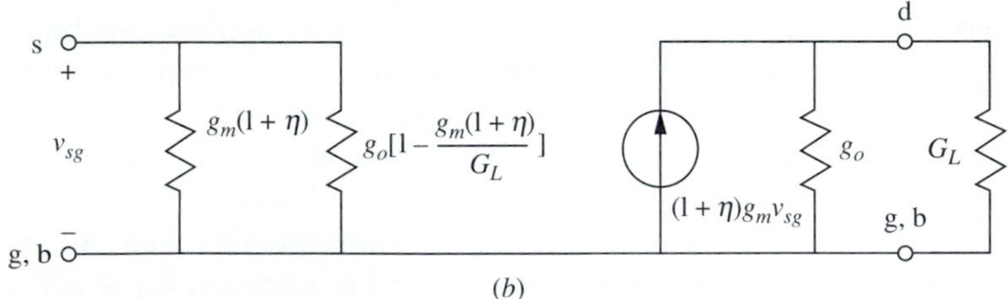

FIGURE 10.17
Effects of accounting for a nonzero output conductance on the common-gate linear incremental equivalent circuit: (*a*) a model for which the output conductance g_o is simply added between the drain and source, which is where it appears physically; (*b*) the equivalent conductances that bridge the input and output terminals incorporated in a model in which there is no longer an element that couples the output back to the input.

*The exact value is $g_o(g_m - G_L)/(g_m + g_o)$, which is essentially g_o.

larger is a very desirable result, but in this case it is not because a major reason for using the common-gate topology is to get a low input resistance. It is somehow reassuring to find that a parasitic element (i.e., g_o) can do no good; if it had turned out differently we would have had to be very suspicious that we had made a mistake.

The observation that the effective input conductance is related to the voltage gain of the stage is a general consequence of the fact that the element g_o is coupling, or feeding back, output signal to the input. This is termed the Miller effect. We will study this effect at length in Chap. 14 when we discuss the high-frequency performance of our circuits.

c) High-Frequency Small-Signal Model. To extend our small-signal MOSFET model to high frequencies we must examine the device structure shown in Fig. 10.11 and identify the energy storage elements (primarily capacitances) that we must add to our model, just as we did in Sec. 10.1.1*d* when we developed our dynamic large-signal model. Equivalently, we can look directly at the dynamic model in Fig. 10.12 and replace the nonlinear charge stores with their linear equivalent capacitors valid for the particular bias point in question. For either approach, we see immediately that there is significant capacitance between the gate and the source due primarily to the MOS gate electrode structure; we call this capacitor C_{gs}. There is also capacitance between the gate and the drain; that is, the gate charge depends on v_{GD} as well as on v_{GS}, at least when the device is not saturated. In saturation the channel is ideally decoupled from the drain, and the gate-to-drain capacitance, which we call C_{gd}, is ideally zero. In a real transistor, however, C_{gd} is not zero (although it can be very small) because of the inevitable physical coupling between the gate electrode and the drain n^+-region and contact.

This discussion can be quantified and C_{gs} and C_{gd} can be modeled by writing an expression for the gate charge q_G as a function of the terminal voltages and taking the appropriate derivatives. That is,

$$C_{gs} \equiv \left.\frac{\partial q_G}{\partial v_{GS}}\right|_Q \tag{10.57a}$$

and

$$C_{gd} \equiv \left.\frac{\partial q_G}{\partial v_{GD}}\right|_Q \tag{10.57b}$$

We will not do this here; rather, we defer the calculation of C_{gs} and C_{gd} until we need expressions for them in Chap. 14.*

There must also be capacitances between the source and substrate, between the gate and substrate, and between the drain and substrate, due in part to the

*See footnote in Sec. 10.1.1*d*.

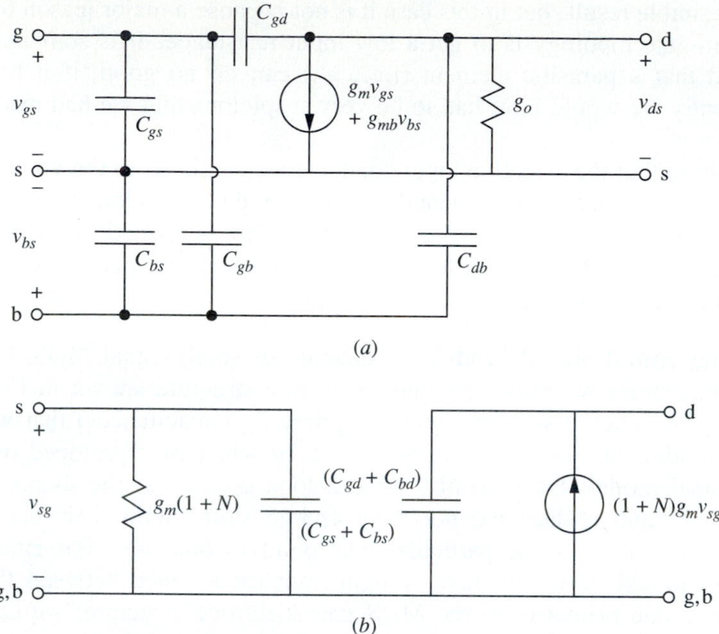

FIGURE 10.18
(*a*) Small-signal common-source equivalent circuit MOSFET model of Fig. 10.8 modified for high-frequency applications by the addition of small-signal parasitic capacitances; (*b*) the common-gate incremental circuit ($v_{bg} = 0$) with the parasitic gate-to-drain, gate-to-source, substrate-to-drain, and substrate-to-source capacitances added.

respective n^+-p junctions and in part to the depletion region charge under the channel. We denote these capacitors as C_{sb}, C_{gb}, and C_{db}, respectively. All of these capacitances are shown added to our small-signal common-source model in Fig. 10.18*a*. Similarly, the common-gate incremental circuit model with the parasitic capacitances added is shown in Fig. 10.18*b* (in drawing this circuit we have taken v_{bg} to be zero). Notice that in the common-gate circuit there are no capacitors connecting the input and output as there are in the common-source circuit; this is an important feature of this circuit, as we shall see in Chap. 14.

10.2 JUNCTION FIELD EFFECT TRANSISTORS

Another important field effect transistor is the junction field effect transistor, or JFET. A typical JFET device structure is illustrated in Fig. 10.19. This device uses the fact that by changing the bias voltage on the gate junction diode, one can change its depletion region width and thereby change the width of the conducting channel between the source and the drain. This in turn controls the amount of current flowing through the device. This is a very simple concept but an extremely powerful one.

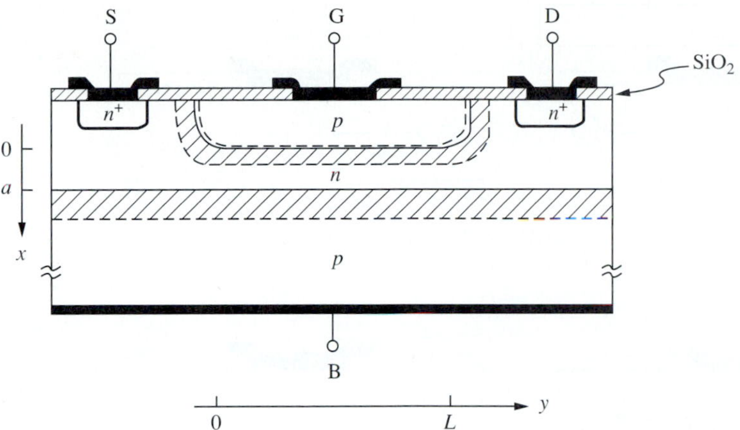

FIGURE 10.19
Cross-sectional drawing of a typical n-channel junction field effect transistor. This structure is used in the derivation of the large-signal JFET model in the text.

When the voltage difference between the drain and source is small and the drain-to-source current is small, the widths of the depletion region and of the conducting channel are essentially uniform, as illustrated in Fig. 10.20*a*, and the drain current i_D increases approximately linearly with v_{DS}. This is illustrated in Fig. 10.20*e*. As the drain-to-source voltage and current increase further, however, the reverse bias on the gate junction and the depletion region width increase appreciably moving from the source to drain, as illustrated in Fig. 10.20*b*, and the increase of i_D is sublinear with v_{DS}, as shown in Fig. 10.20*e*. Eventually the depletion region at the drain end of the channel will completely pinch off the conducting channel, as illustrated in Fig. 10.20*c*, and the current will saturate just as it does in a MOSFET, as shown in Fig. 10.20*e*. If the gate-to-source bias is too negative, the depletion region, even with no drain-to-source voltage, will extend throughout the channel and completely block conduction between the drain and source, as shown in Fig. 10.20*d*. In this condition, no current will flow for any drain bias, as illustrated in Fig. 10.20*e*. The terminal behavior and modes of operation are very much similar to those of a MOSFET.

We will begin our analysis of JFETs by developing a large-signal description for the terminal behavior of these devices. Then we will develop small-signal models based on this large-signal model.

10.2.1 Large-Signal Model

We now turn to the problem of modeling the drain, gate, and substrate (or back) currents (i_D, i_G, and i_B, respectively) for the JFET illustrated in Fig. 10.19 as functions of the drain-to-source, gate-to-source, and back-to-source voltages (v_{DS}, v_{GS}, and v_{BS}, respectively). As we did with the MOSFET, we will limit the terminal voltages to certain useful bias ranges rather than attempting to model

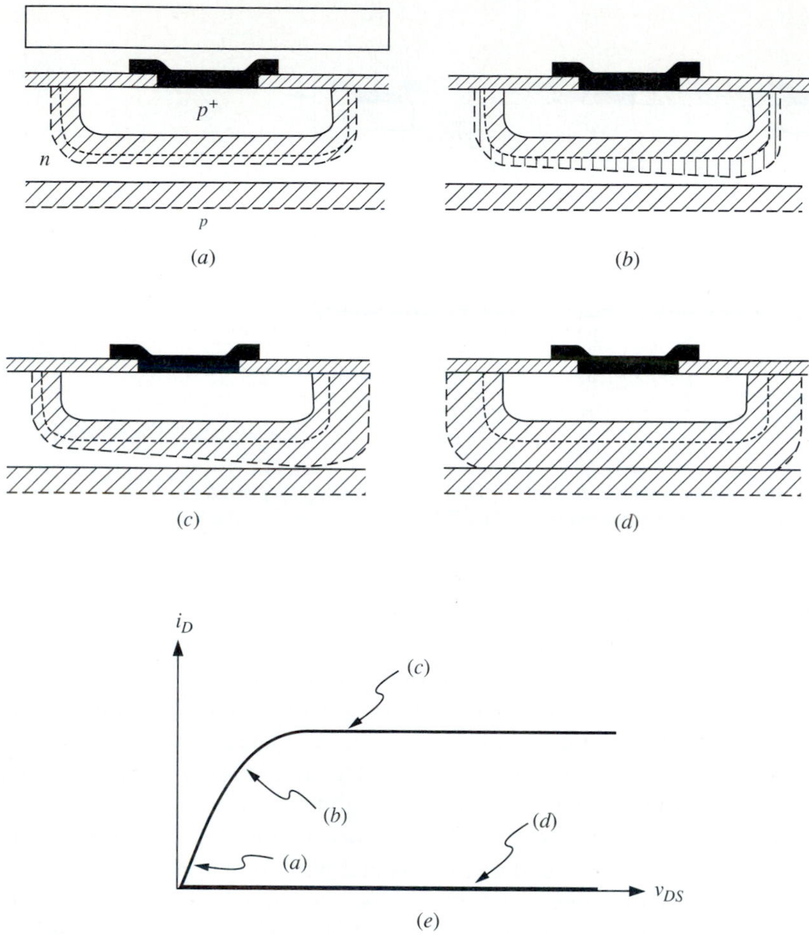

FIGURE 10.20
Illustrations of the depletion region shape in the channel region of a JFET under different bias conditions: (*a*) near the origin: $V_p < v_{GS} < 0$, v_{DS} very small, $v_{BS} = 0$; (*b*) in the linear region: $V_p < v_{GS} < 0$, v_{DS} appreciable; (*c*) saturation: $V_p < v_{GS} < 0$, $v_{DS} > (v_{GS} - V_p)$; (*d*) cutoff: $v_{GS} < V_p$; (*e*) current-voltage characteristics corresponding to the bias and depletion region conditions illusrated in (*a*) through (*d*).

the terminal currents for arbitrary terminal voltages. This makes our modeling task much easier, to be sure, but it is also all we really care about since the device is only useful when biased properly.

We first restrict ourselves to biases such that the lower *p-n* junction, the substrate-to-channel junction, is never forward-biased. Just as we did when modeling the *n*-channel MOSFET, we restrict our model to $v_{BS} \leq 0$ and $v_{DS} \geq 0$. With this restriction the substrate current is negligible (i.e., $i_B \approx 0$).

Next we restrict ourselves to operation where the gate current is negligible (i.e., $i_G \approx 0$) by requiring that $v_{GS} \leq V_{ON}$, where V_{ON} is the forward-bias voltage above which this junction conducts appreciably. We use the bound V_{ON} rather than zero in anticipation of the fact that it will in some instances be useful to slightly forward-bias the upper *p-n* junction, the gate-to-channel junction. As long as the forward bias is small, the junction current will still be negligible.

When i_B and i_G are negligible, we have only one current, the drain current i_D, to deal with. Our approach to relating i_D to v_{DS}, v_{GS}, and v_{BS} will be similar to the one we used with the MOSFET. We relate the current density at any point in the channel to the electric field at that point, $\mathscr{E}_y$; and to the number of charge carriers in the channel, their charge, and their mobility. Doing this we will obtain an expression that can be integrated from one end of the channel to the other to yield $i_D(v_{DS}, v_{GS}, v_{BS})$.

To proceed we first assume that the electric field and current flow in the channel are entirely horizontal (i.e., in the *y*-direction only). Clearly this is an approximation because if the channel becomes wider moving from the drain to the source (see Figs. 10.20*b* and *c*) there must be some component of the current (and field) in the *x*-direction. But if the rate at which the width of the channel increases is sufficiently small (i.e., if the channel is sufficiently gradual), the *x*-component will be negligible. This is the gradual channel approximation in the context of the JFET.

Using the gradual channel approximation, the voltage in the channel, v_{CS}, is a function only of y. At any position y along the channel, the voltage relative to the source is $v_{CS}(y)$ and the electric field $\mathscr{E}_y(y)$ is $-\partial v_{CS}/\partial y|_y$. We will further assume that there are negligible voltage drops between the source and the drain contacts and the ends of the channel at $y = 0$ and $y = L$. We thus have

$$v_{CS}(L) = v_{DS} \tag{10.58a}$$

$$v_{CS}(0) = 0 \tag{10.58b}$$

The current in the channel, i_D, is the drift current density in the channel, $-q\mu_e N_D \mathscr{E}_y$, multiplied by the cross-sectional area of the channel, $[a - x_D(y)]Z$, where a is the distance between the upper and lower *p-n* junctions and $x_D(y)$ is the sum at y of the depletion region widths on the *n*-sides (i.e., channel sides) of the upper and lower *p-n* junctions. Z is the extent of the device in the *z*-direction (i.e., normal to the cross section in Fig. 10.19). Thus

$$i_D = Z\mu_e q N_D[a - x_D(y)]\frac{dv_{CS}(y)}{dy} \tag{10.59}$$

You may want to compare this equation to Eq. (10.4) for the MOSFET; these results are analogous.

The next step is to relate the total depletion region width $x_D(y)$ to the voltage in the channel, $v_{CS}(y)$. Again we make use of the gradual channel approximation and say that at any point y we can assume that the electric field in the depletion region is entirely vertical (i.e., solely in the *x*-direction). We then use the depletion approximation to solve for the depletion region widths at each junction.

We will assume that the device we are modeling is built with the n-type channel region much more heavily doped than the substrate. Thus the width of the depletion region on the channel side (i.e., the n-side) of this junction is negligible. As a result, $x_D(y)$ is essentially just the n-side depletion region width of the upper p-n junction. At any point y, the bias applied to the junction, $v_{GC}(y)$, is $v_{GS} - v_{CS}(y)$. Using this we have

$$x_D(y) \approx \sqrt{\frac{2\varepsilon_{\text{Si}} N_{Ap}[\phi_b - v_{GS} + v_{CS}(y)]}{qN_{Dn}(N_{Dn} + N_{Ap})}} \tag{10.60a}$$

In a well-designed JFET, the p^+ gate region is more heavily doped than the channel region (i.e., $N_{Ap} >> N_{Dn}$), so that the depletion region at the upper junction extends primarily into the channel. In this case we can use the approximation

$$x_D(y) \approx \sqrt{\frac{2\varepsilon_{\text{Si}}[\phi_b - v_{GS} + v_{CS}(y)]}{qN_{Dn}}} \tag{10.60b}$$

We are now ready to complete our derivation. We insert Eq. (10.60b) into Eq. (10.59) and integrate from $y = 0$ to $y = L$, or equivalently from $v_{CS} = 0$ to $v_{CS} = v_{DS}$, just as we did for the MOSFET. The result is

$$i_D = a\frac{Z}{L}q\mu_e N_{Dn}\left\{v_{DS} - \frac{2}{3}\sqrt{\frac{2\varepsilon_{\text{Si}}}{qN_{Dn}a^2}}\left[(\phi_b - v_{GS} + v_{DS})^{3/2} - (\phi_b - v_{GS})^{3/2}\right]\right\} \tag{10.61}$$

This expression is plotted in Fig. 10.21 for a representative JFET.

Equation (10.61) is valid as long as the depletion region width $x_D(y)$ is less than a. If $x_D(y)$ is equal to or greater than a at some position between 0 and L, we must modify our expression. There are two circumstances where this occurs. The first is when the gate junction is sufficiently reverse-biased that the channel is fully depleted over all its length, as was illustrated in Fig. 10.20*d*. The gate voltage at which $x_D = a$ is called the pinchoff voltage V_P. Thus

$$V_P \equiv -\frac{qN_{Dn}a^2}{2\varepsilon_{\text{Si}}} + \phi_b \tag{10.62}$$

If $v_{GS} \leq V_P$, then the JFET channel is fully pinched off and the drain current is zero:

$$i_D = 0 \qquad \text{for } v_{GS} \leq V_P \tag{10.63}$$

The second circumstance in which the channel disappears occurs when the drain-to-source voltage is sufficiently large that the depletion region at the drain end of the channel is a or larger, as was illustrated in Fig. 10.20*c*. This occurs whenever v_{GD} is less than V_P, which in terms of v_{DS} is

$$v_{DS} \geq v_{GS} - V_P \tag{10.64}$$

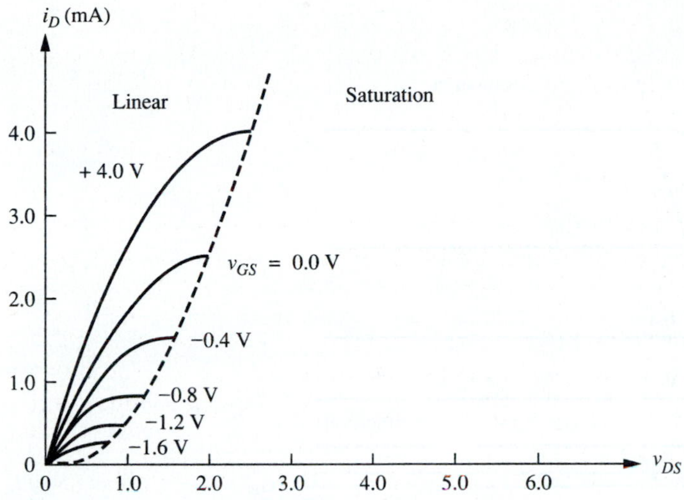

FIGURE 10.21
Drain current expression, Eq. (10.61), plotted for a Si device in which $\phi_b = 0.6$ V, $a = 0.8$ μm, $Z/L = 50$, $\mu_e = 1500$ cm^2/V·s, and $N_{Dn} = 5 \times 10^{15}$ cm^{-3}.

This condition is called saturation. In this region the drain current remains fixed (i.e., saturated) at its value just prior to pinchoff of the channel. We call this current the saturation value $i_{D,\text{sat}}$. Putting $v_{DS} = v_{GS} - V_P$ into Eq. (10.61) for i_D, we obtain

$$i_{D,\text{sat}} = a\frac{Z}{L}q\mu_e N_{Dn}\left\{(v_{GS} - V_P) - \frac{2}{3}\sqrt{\frac{2\varepsilon_{\text{Si}}}{qN_{Dn}a^2}} \times \left[(\phi_b - V_P)^{3/2} - (\phi_b - v_{GS})^{3/2}\right]\right\} \tag{10.65}$$

This equation is plotted along with Eq. (10.61) in Fig. 10.22 for the same device as in Fig. 10.21.

This completes the gradual channel model for the JFET. To summarize our model, when $v_{BS} \leq 0$, $v_{DS} \geq 0$, and $v_{GS} \leq V_{\text{ON}}$; the substrate and gate currents, i_B and i_G, are zero. The drain current i_D is also zero if $v_{GS} \leq V_P$. In this case, which we can also write as $(v_{GS} - V_P) \leq 0$, the device is said to be in pinchoff. If $0 \leq (v_{GS} - V_P)$, then i_D is given by Eq. (10.61) when $0 \leq v_{DS} \leq (v_{GS} - V_P)$ and by Eq. (10.65) when $0 \leq (v_{GS} - V_P) \leq v_{DS}$. The latter range of v_{DS} is called the saturation region, and the former is termed the linear region.

The drain current expressions are complicated in appearance, and it is difficult to do much about simplifying them in a meaningful way. One modification of their presentation is to use the definition for V_P [Eq. (10.62)] to simplify the factor $(2\varepsilon_{\text{Si}}/qN_{Dn}a^2)^{1/2}$ and to replace the factor $q\mu_e N_{Dn}$ with the channel conductivity σ_o. Going further, we can define G_o as the conductance of the undepleted channel.

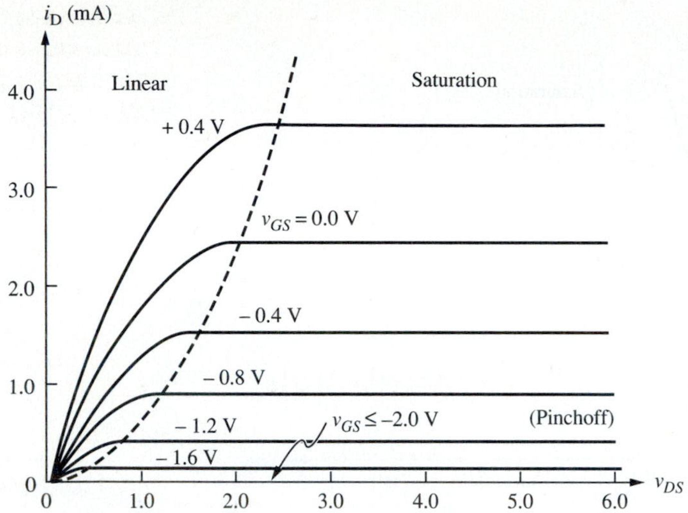

FIGURE 10.22
Plot from Fig. 10.21 extended into the saturation and pinchoff regions. Using the same device parameters as in Fig. 10.21, we obtain $V_p = -2$ V and $G_o = 4.8$ mS.

$$G_o \equiv a\frac{Z}{L}q\mu_e N_{Dn} = \sigma_o a\frac{Z}{L} \tag{10.66}$$

and then write

$$i_D = G_o\left\{v_{DS} - \frac{2}{3}\left[\frac{(\phi_b - v_{GS} + v_{DS})^{3/2} - (\phi_b - v_{GS})^{3/2}}{(\phi_b - V_P)^{1/2})}\right]\right\} \tag{10.67}$$

when $0 \leq v_{DS} \leq (v_{GS} - V_P)$, and

$$i_D = i_{D,\text{sat}} = G_o\left\{(v_{GS} - V_P) - \frac{2}{3}\left[\frac{(\phi_b - V_P)^{3/2} - (\phi_b - v_{GS})^{3/2}}{(\phi_b - V_P)^{1/2})}\right]\right\} \tag{10.68}$$

when $0 \leq (v_{GS} - V_P) \leq v_{DS}$.

Example

The characteristics in Figs. 10.21 and 10.22 have been plotted for a device with typical dimensions and doping levels. As stated in the captions for these figures, the characteristics correspond to a silicon device with $\phi_b = 0.6$ V, $a = 0.8$ μm, $Z/L = 50$, $\mu_e = 1500$ cm^2/V·s, and $N_{Dn} = 5 \times 10^{15}$ cm^{-3}; and thus for which $V_p = -2$ V and $G_o = 4.8$ mS.

As was the case with MOSFETs, there are also several types of JFETs. We have just developed a model for an *n*-channel JFET; there are also *p*-channel JFETs, which are modeled in the same way with identical results except, as you might expect, that all of the voltages and currents change sign. Also, the implication in our modeling discussion was that the channel was not pinched off when no voltage was applied to the gate. In terms of V_P, the implication was that the pinchoff voltage for an n-channel device was negative (i.e., $V_P < 0$). When this is the case, the device is said to be a depletion mode JFET. If V_P for an n-channel device is positive (i.e., $V_P \geq 0$), there will be no channel until the gate junction is forward-biased. Such a device is called an enhancement mode JFET. Clearly there is a limit to how far forward the gate junction of a JFET can be biased before it conducts heavily, so there is a limit to how strongly an enhancement mode JFET can be turned on. For this reason, enhancement mode JFETs are much less common than depletion mode JFETs. The circuit schematic symbols used for n- and p-channel JFETs are illustrated in Fig. 10.23.

10.2.2 Static Small-Signal Linear Model

The static small-signal linear model for the JFET is topologically the same as that for the MOSFET, which was illustrated in Fig. 10.13. The definitions for all of the parameters, g_m, g_{mb}, and g_o, are also identical and are given by Eqs. (10.38), (10.39), and (10.40). What is different is that we must use the JFET equations to evaluate these definitions. We will examine each in turn.

The forward transconductance g_m is found to have the following forms in the various operating regions:

$$g_m = \begin{cases} 0 & \text{for } (V_{GS} - V_P) \leq 0 \leq V_{DS} \quad (10.69) \\ G_o \dfrac{\sqrt{\phi_b - V_P} - \sqrt{\phi_b - V_{GS}}}{\sqrt{\phi_b - V_P}} & \text{for } 0 \leq (V_{GS} - V_P) \leq V_{DS} \quad (10.70) \\ G_o \dfrac{\sqrt{\phi_b - V_{GS} + V_{DS}} - \sqrt{\phi_b - V_{GS}}}{\sqrt{\phi_p - V_P}} & \text{for } 0 \leq V_{DS} \leq (V_{GS} - V_P) \quad (10.71) \end{cases}$$

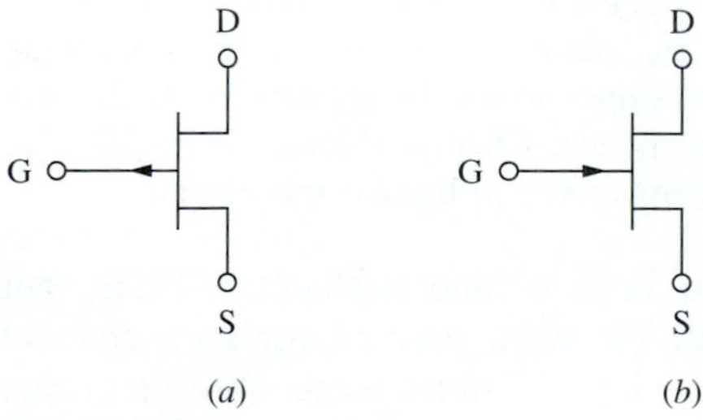

FIGURE 10.23
Symbols used for n- and p-channel JFETs in circuit schematic drawings: (a) n-channel JFET; (b) p-channel JFET.

Notice that g_m has its maximum values in saturation. Looking a bit more closely at g_m in saturation, Eq. (10.70), we see that we can also write this equation as

$$g_m = G_o\left[1 - \sqrt{\frac{(\phi_b - V_{GS})}{(\phi_b - V_p)}}\right] \tag{10.70$'$}$$

Written this way it is easy to see that g_m is a maximum when the gate junction is as forward-biased as possible, usually on the order of 0.3 or 0.4 V, and that G_o is a firm upper bound on g_m. It might seem desirable to make V_p as negative as possible to make the denominator of the fraction small, but this is usually not a wise design choice. A large V_p requires a large V_{DS} to put the device in saturation, and this leads to large power dissipation. We usually want to keep V_p on the order of a volt or two.

The substrate transconductance g_{mb} is zero in our model because we have said that the depletion region on the n-side of the lower p-n junction is negligible. We can thus eliminate the $g_{mb}v_{bs}$ current source from the small-signal incremental model and simplify it to that shown in Fig. 10.24.

Finally, the output conductance g_o is given by the following expressions in the various regions of operation:

$$g_o = \begin{cases} 0 & \text{for } (V_{GS} - V_P) \le 0 \le V_{DS} \quad (10.72) \\ 0 & \text{for } 0 \le (V_{GS} - V_P) \le V_{DS} \quad (10.73) \\ G_0\left[1 - \sqrt{\dfrac{(\phi_b - V_{GS} - V_{DS})}{(\phi_b - V_P)}}\right] & \text{for } 0 \le V_{DS} \le (V_{GS} - V_P) \quad (10.74) \end{cases}$$

Example

Question. Consider a device with the output characteristics shown in Fig. 10.22. What is the small-signal transconductance g_m of this device if it is biased in saturation with $v_{GS} = 0$ V?

Discussion. Using the fact that for this structure $\phi_b = 0.6$ V, $V_P = -2$ V, and $G_o = 4.8$ mS, we find using Eq. (10.70$'$) that g_m is 2.5 mS, or about half the value of G_o. By forward-biasing the gate 0.4 V, g_m can be increased to 3.5 mS. Looking at Fig. 10.22, we see that the drain current values would be approximately 2.4 mA and 3.7 mA, respectively, at these two bias points. Clearly, JFETs, like MOSFETs, have relatively low transconductances in comparison to bipolar transistors.

The model of Fig. 10.24 is valid for both n- and p-channel JFETs, but the expressions in Eqs. (10.69) through (10.74) were derived for an n-channel device. To modify them for a p-channel device we must write absolute value signs around all of the factors under the square root signs [e.g., $(\phi_b - V_P)^{1/2}$] and the various bias ranges must be defined properly. That is, for a p-channel device, cutoff corresponds to $V_{DS} \le 0 \le (V_{GS} - V_P)$; the saturation region corresponds to $V_{DS} \le (V_{GS} - V_P) \le 0$; and the linear region corresponds to $(V_{GS} - V_P) \le V_{DS} \le 0$.

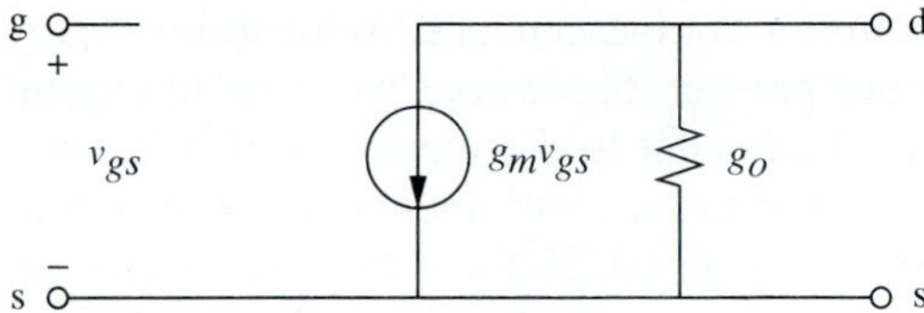

FIGURE 10.24
Linear small-signal equivalent circuit of a JFET biased in its forward operating region.

10.2.3 High-Frequency Small-Signal Model

The common-source small-signal high-frequency equivalent circuit for a JFET is the same as that of a MOSFET shown in Fig. 10.18 with $g_{mb} = 0$. We must retain the substrate terminal in this model because v_{bs} is not necessarily zero, although it often is, and current may flow through the capacitors C_{sb} and C_{db}.

10.3 METAL-SEMICONDUCTOR FIELD EFFECT TRANSISTORS

The final field effect transistor that we will study in this text is the metal-semiconductor field effect transistor, or MESFET. This device is very similar to a JFET, as we shall see in the next subsection, and we have already done much of its basic analysis. However, because MESFETs can be made with extremely short gate lengths and because they are typically fabricated of very high-mobility semiconductors, we must be very careful to include velocity saturation. We will do this in the final subsection after first introducing the basic MESFET structure and model.

10.3.1 Basic Concept and Modeling

In Chap. 6, when we first discussed making electrical contact to a semiconductor, we pointed out that there is a difference in electrostatic potential between a metal and a semiconductor. We also said that there in general will be a depletion region in the semiconductor adjacent to the metal-semiconductor interface. When forming electrical contacts, our objective is to make the depletion region at this interface as thin as possible and the barrier as low as possible (by heavily doping the semiconductor and by choosing a metal that yields a low barrier) so that this barrier does not form an impediment to current flow. In other situations, however, we can go the other way. If the semiconductor is lightly doped and the barrier is high, there will be a wide depletion region and an appreciable barrier for current flow. The metal-semiconductor interface will then behave very much like a p^+-n or p-n^+ junction diode, where the metal plays the role of the heavily doped semiconductor. Such structures are called metal-semiconductor diodes or Schottky diodes.

Schottky diodes have a number of important features and applications, many of which are discussed in App. E. For our present discussion, we want to exploit the fact that the semiconductor is depleted adjacent to the metal and that, as in a *p-n* diode, the width of this depletion region increases with increasing reverse bias on the diode. This situation is illustrated in Fig. 10.25 for a Schottky diode on *n*-type silicon. The device and the electrostatic potential and net charge profiles through it are shown for zero and reverse bias. As in an abrupt p^+-n junction, the change in electrostatic potential occurs entirely across the depletion region of

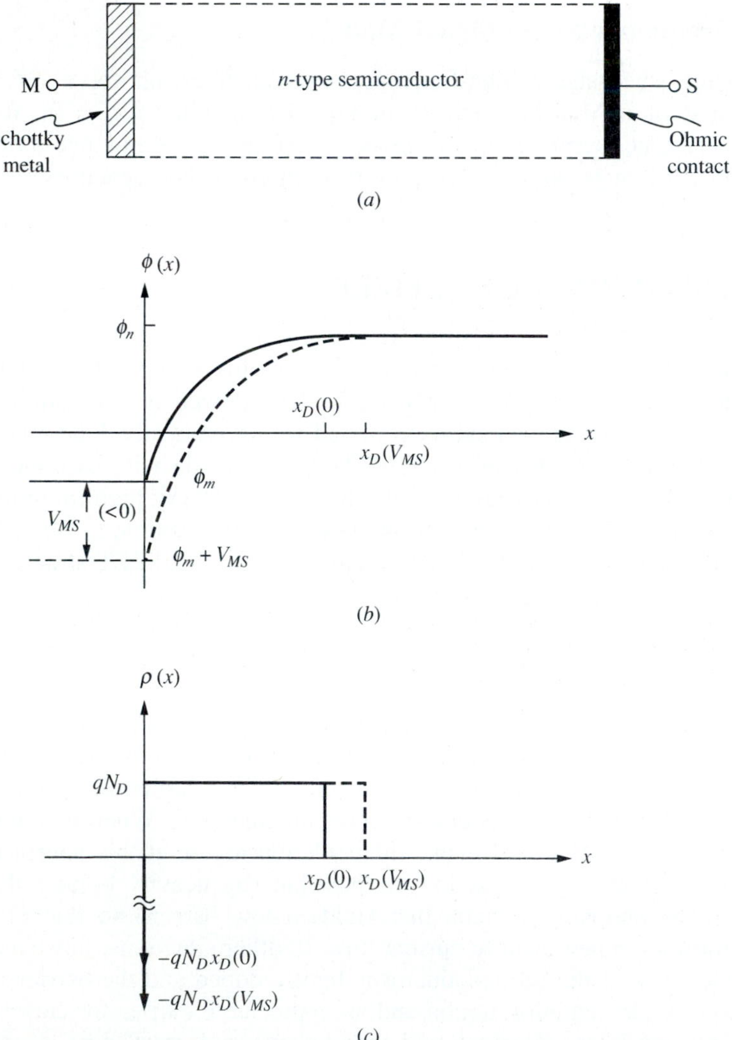

FIGURE 10.25
(*a*) Structure of a metal-semiconductor diode; (*b*) the corresponding electrostatic potential distribution; (*c*) the net charge distribution. (The solid line represents zero bias, and the dashed line represents an applied reverse bias $V_{MS} < 0$.)

the n-type material. It is given by

$$x_D \approx \sqrt{\frac{2\varepsilon_{\text{Si}}(\phi_b - v_{MS})}{qN_{Dn}}} \tag{10.75}$$

where N_{Dn} is the doping level in the semiconductor and ϕ_b is the built-in potential of the Schottky diode.

A Schottky diode like this can be used in place of the p-n junction in the gate of a JFET, as shown in Fig. 10.26. The resulting device is called either a Schottky-gate field effect transistor or, more commonly, a metal-semiconductor field effect transistor (MESFET). Except for the difference in the barrier height, this device is electrically identical to the JFET, certainly for purposes of the large- and small-signal modeling we have done; as such, we already have models for it.

As a practical matter, the MESFET has certain important advantages over the JFET and is a much more widely used device. It is very easy to fabricate and is particularly attractive for use on semiconductors other than silicon (e.g., gallium arsenide) in which it is technologically more difficult, inconvenient, or even impossible to make good p-n junctions. It can also be made very small, so devices with very short channels (i.e., small L) can easily be made in order to get very fast devices. The major disadvantage of the MESFET in some material systems is that it is difficult to find metals that yield sufficiently high barriers; thus in these situations the gate junction is too conductive when reverse-biased (and so is termed "leaky"). In general, however, MESFETs have been very successfully used with many semiconductors, and they are widely used in high-speed applications.

10.3.2 Velocity Saturation in MESFETs

In developing our large-signal FET models we have assumed that the velocity of the carriers in the channel can be written as the product of their mobility and the electric field. At the same time, however, we know from our discussion in

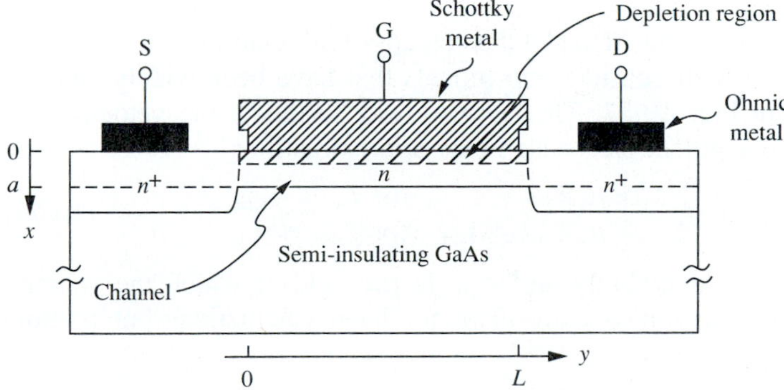

FIGURE 10.26
Cross-sectional drawing of a typical n-channel metal-semiconductor field effect transistor.

Chap. 3 that the assumption of a linear relationship between velocity and field is not valid at high fields. This is traditionally not a problem in silicon devices because velocity saturation does not occur in silicon until the electric field is well in excess of 10 kV/cm; if the gate length is 1 to 2 μm, this field is only reached for drain-to-source voltages of several volts, where the MOSFET is typically entering saturation anyway. In such a situation, accounting for velocity saturation has little impact on the characteristics.* For the semiconductors commonly used to make MESFETs, however, velocity saturation can occur at 3 kV/cm or less. This fact, coupled with the fact that gate lengths L in MESFETs can be as small as 0.25 μm or less, means that the critical field strength for velocity saturation in these devices can be exceeded at drain-to-source voltages of less than 0.1 V. Consequently, our assumption of a constant mobility is not valid over much of the normal operating range of these devices, so our model must be modified.

The starting point for our new model is the same as it was before, that is, Eq. (10.59), which relates the current in the channel to the product of the carrier concentration and the carriers' velocity, except that now instead of writing the velocity as $\mu_e \mathscr{E}_y$, we write it as $s_y(\mathscr{E}_y)$:

$$i_D = ZqN_{Dn}[a - x_D(y)]s_y[\mathscr{E}_y(y)] \tag{10.76a}$$

where $x_D(y)$ is now given by Eq. (10.75) with v_{MS} replaced with $[v_{GS} - v_{CS}(y)]$. The velocity s_y is a function of y because the electric field $\mathscr{E}_y$ is a function of y; the electric field is, as before, $-dv_{CS}/dy|_y$. Thus

$$i_D = ZqN_{Dn}\left\{a - \sqrt{\frac{2\varepsilon_{\text{Si}}[\phi_b - v_{GS} + v_{CS}(y)]}{qN_{Dn}}}\right\} s_y[\mathscr{E}_y(y)] \tag{10.76b}$$

or

$$i_D = ZqN_{Dn}a\left[1 - \sqrt{\frac{\phi_b - v_{GS} + v_{CS}(y)}{\phi_b - V_P}}\right] s_y[\mathscr{E}y(y)] \tag{10.76c}$$

with V_P defined in Eq. (10.62).

The key issue now is how to model the velocity-field relationship, which was shown in Fig. 3.2. We will consider two models that have been widely applied; both are illustrated in Fig. 10.27. The simplest way to model the velocity-field curve is to use a two-segment piecewise linear approximation:

$$s_y[\mathscr{E}_y(y)] = \begin{cases} \mu_e \mathscr{E}_y & \text{for } \mathscr{E}_y \le \mathscr{E}_{\text{crit}} \\ \mu_e \mathscr{E}_{\text{crit}} \equiv s_{\text{sat}} & \text{for } \mathscr{E}_{\text{crit}} \le \mathscr{E}_y \end{cases} \tag{10.77}$$

where μ_e is the low-field mobility and $\mathscr{E}_{\text{crit}}$ is the field at which the velocity saturates. A function like this is convenient for hand calculations but is more

*In MOSFETs with submicron gate lengths, however, velocity saturation can be more of an issue and should be taken into account. See Sec. 10.1.1*c* for a discussion of velocity saturation in MOSFETs.

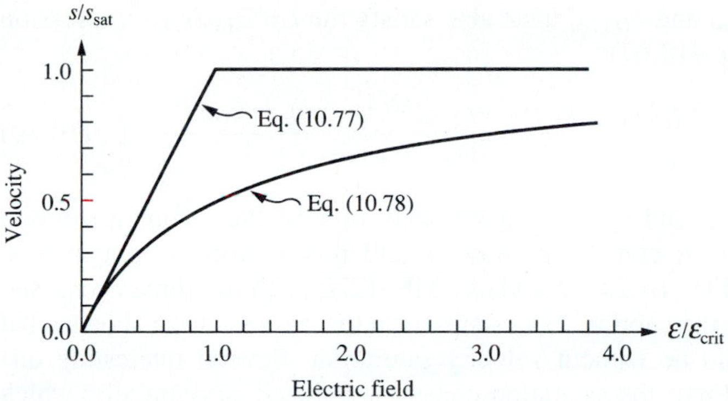

FIGURE 10.27
Plot of the two models given in Eqs. (10.77) and (10.78) for the velocity-field relationship of a typical semiconductor.

difficult to use with computer simulation, so a second commonly used model is one that fits a single analytical expression to the entire curve:

$$s_y[\mathscr{E}_y(y)] = \frac{\mu_e \mathscr{E}_y}{(1 + \mathscr{E}_y/\mathscr{E}_{\text{crit}})} \tag{10.78}$$

We used this model for velocity saturation in MOSFETs (Sec. 10.1.1*c*).

In both models s_y is $\mu_e \mathscr{E}_y$ when $\mathscr{E}_y$ is much less than $\mathscr{E}_{\text{crit}}$ and is $\mu_e \mathscr{E}_{\text{crit}}$ (which we define as s_{sat}) for $\mathscr{E}_y$ much greater than $\mathscr{E}_{\text{crit}}$. In between, the models are clearly quite different, yet both retain the essentials of velocity saturation. In treating the MESFET, we will use the piecewise linear model because it better matches the sharp saturation characteristics of high-mobility compound semiconductors. This model is also convenient to use because as long as the field in the channel is less than $\mathscr{E}_{\text{crit}}$, it is the same as our original model. Once the field exceeds $\mathscr{E}_{\text{crit}}$, the carrier velocity (and therefore the current) saturates, just as it does above pinchoff in the gradual channel approximation. However, now the critical drain-to-source voltage for the onset of saturation occurs not when the channel at the drain end becomes pinched off, but rather when the carriers at the drain end of the channel reach their saturation velocity. Referring to Eq. (10.76b), we can see that the saturation current $i_{D,\text{sat}}$ and drain-to-source voltage $v_{DS,\text{sat}}$ must be related as

$$i_{D,\text{sat}} = ZqN_{Dn}\left[a - \sqrt{\frac{2\varepsilon_{\text{Si}}(\phi_b - v_{GS} + v_{DS,\text{sat}})}{qN_{Dn}}}\right] s_{\text{sat}} \tag{10.79a}$$

Using our earlier definitions of G_0 [Eq. (10.66)] and V_P [Eq. (10.62)], this can be written as

$$i_{D,\text{sat}} = G_o\left[1 - \frac{(\phi_b - v_{GS} + v_{DS,\text{sat}})^{1/2}}{(\phi_b - V_P)^{1/2}}\right]\frac{s_{\text{sat}}L}{\mu_e} \tag{10.79b}$$

The values of $i_{D,\text{sat}}$ and $v_{DS,\text{sat}}$ must also satisfy the $i_D(v_{GS}, v_{DS})$ expression in the linear region, Eq. (10.67):

$$i_{D,\text{sat}} = G_o\left\{v_{DS,\text{sat}} - \frac{2}{3}\left(\frac{[(\phi_b - v_{GS} + v_{DS,\text{sat}})^{3/2} - (\phi_b - v_{GS})^{3/2}]}{(\phi_b - V_P)^{1/2}}\right)\right\} \tag{10.80}$$

The values of $i_{D,\text{sat}}$ and $v_{DS,\text{sat}}$ that we seek must be the common solution of these two equations. A convenient way to find this solution is graphically, which we illustrate in Fig. 10.28 for a GaAs MESFET, with the dimensions and parameters indicated in the caption. For comparison the dashed curve shows what the characteristics would be without velocity saturation. Several interesting differences are apparent. First, the saturation current is reduced substantially, which is not good. At the same time, however, the saturation occurs at a lower voltage and the curves are crisper, which is good. Since we cannot do much about the former difference, we might as well appreciate the latter.

It is difficult with only a graphical solution to get much design insight from this model and to see, for example, what we can do to modify $i_{D,\text{sat}}$ and $v_{DS,\text{sat}}$. To get a more analytical model, we next notice in Fig. 10.28 that velocity saturation occurs while the device is still well within the classical linear region (i.e., where the depletion region width changes very little along the length of the channel).

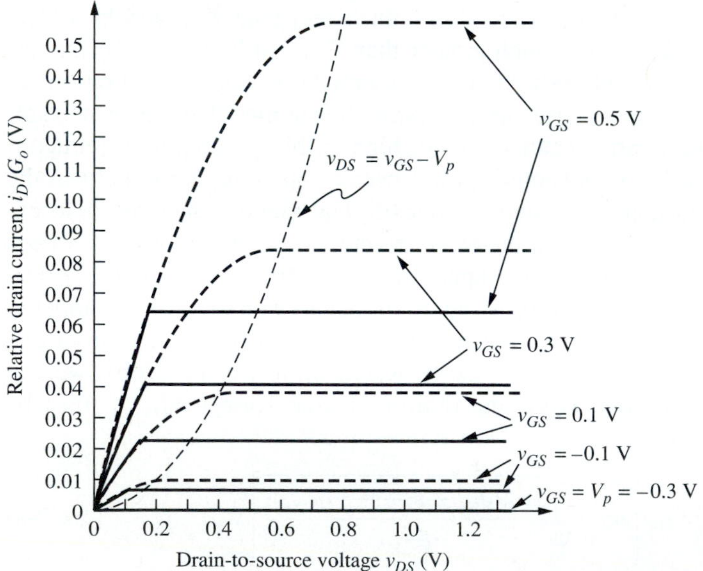

FIGURE 10.28
Output characteristics of a GaAs MESFET with $\phi_b = 0.9$ V, $a = 0.15\ \mu$m, $Z/L = 50$, $L = 0.5\ \mu$m, $\mu_e = 2500$ cm^2/V·s, $s_{\text{sat}} = 10^7$ cm/s, and $N_{Dn} = 6.7 \times 10^{16}$ cm^{-3}. The piecewise linear model of Eq. (10.77) is used for the velocity-field curve, and saturation is determined from the graphical solution of Eqs. (10.79) and (10.80).

Here the current is given approximately by the resistance of the channel times the drain-to-source voltage, that is,

$$i_D \approx q\mu_e N_{Dn}\frac{Z}{L}[a - x_{D_o}]v_{DS} \tag{10.81}$$

where

$$x_{D_o} \equiv \sqrt{\frac{2\varepsilon_{\text{Si}}(\phi_b - v_{GS})}{qN_{Dn}}} \tag{10.82}$$

This will be valid until $v_{DS}/L = \mathscr{E}_{\text{crit}}$, at which point the velocity saturates at s_{sat} and i_D saturates at

$$i_{D,\text{sat}} = qN_{Dn}Z(a - x_{D_o})s_{\text{sat}} \tag{10.83}$$

This last result shows us the importance of choosing a material with a large s_{sat}, along with a large μ_e and small $\mathscr{E}_{\text{crit}}$.

To compare the results of this model with our earlier models, it is convenient to write Eqs. (10.81) and (10.83) in terms of a and V_P using Eqs. (10.62) and (10.66). We find that we can then summarize our results as follows:

$$i_D = \begin{cases} G_o\left[1 - \dfrac{(\phi_b - v_{GS})^{1/2}}{(\phi_b - V_P)^{1/2}}\right]v_{DS} & \text{for } v_{DS} \leq \mathscr{E}_{\text{crit}}L \text{ and } v_{GS} \geq V_P \\ G_o\left[1 - \dfrac{(\phi_b - v_{GS})^{1/2}}{(\phi_b - V_P)^{1/2}}\right]\dfrac{s_{\text{sat}}L}{\mu_e} & \text{for } \mathscr{E}_{\text{crit}}L \leq v_{DS} \text{ and } v_{GS} \geq V_P \\ 0 & \text{for } v_{GS} \leq V_P \end{cases} \tag{10.84}$$

These expressions are plotted in Fig. 10.29 for the same device used in Fig. 10.28. In Fig. 10.29*a*, i_D/G_o is plotted, just as in Fig. 10.28. In Fig. 10.29*b*, i_D is plotted and G_o has been adjusted to yield the same peak current as when v_{GS} is 0.5 V. We adjust G_o [see Eq. (10.66)] by, for example, changing the value used for μ_e or the product aN_{Dn} to get a proper fit. If we do the latter, the values of a and N_{Dn} must then also be adjusted so that the product a^2N_{Dn} is unchanged in order to ensure that V_P will remain the same. In the present case, this means that to obtain the solid curves in Fig. 10.29*b* we had to assume that a is 0.2 mm and N_{Dn} is 5×10^{16} cm^{-3}.

This relatively simple model is seen to give very similar results to our earlier model, but we can now see several additional features. First, we see that the saturation voltage $v_{DS,\text{sat}}$ is independent of v_{GS} and $i_{D,\text{sat}}$, whereas when velocity saturation is not an issue it increases parabolically with $i_{D,\text{sat}}$. Second, since in this approximation $v_{DS,\text{sat}}$ is $\mathscr{E}_{\text{crit}}L$, to make $v_{DS,\text{sat}}$ small we need a short channel and low critical field. Third, we see that $i_{D,\text{sat}}$ is Ks_{sat}, so to make $v_{DS,\text{sat}}$ large we want s_{sat} and K large. The latter is made large by using a wide device, by making the product $N_{Dn}a$ as large as possible while still obtaining the desired V_P, and by keeping the gate leakage within acceptable bounds (which means that N_{Dn} cannot be too large). Finally, we note that the spacing of the constant v_{GS}

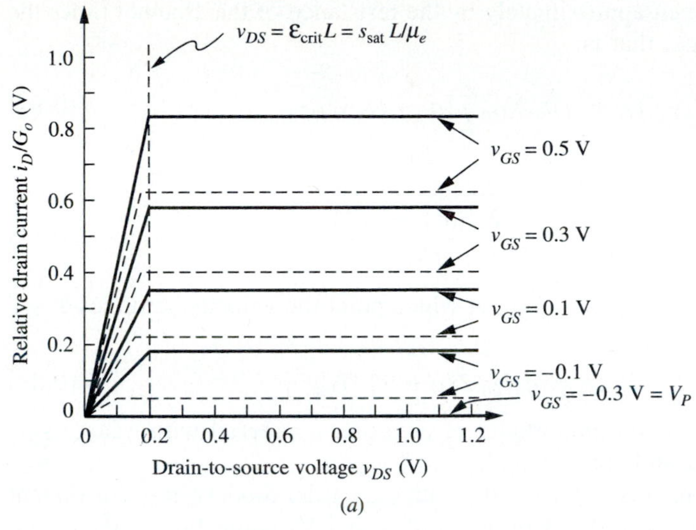

(*a*)

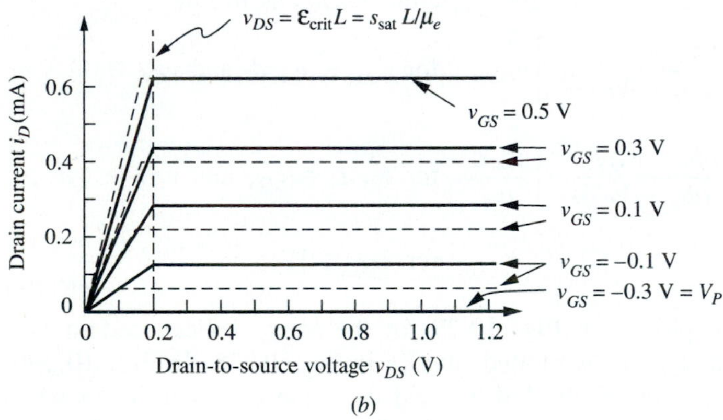

(*b*)

FIGURE 10.29
Output characteristics for the same MESFET as in Fig. 10.28, calculated using the approximation summarized in Eqs. 10.84: (*a*) plot of (i_D/G_o) versus v_{DS} (the dashed curves represent the solid curves in Fig. 10.28); (*b*) plot of i_D versus v_{DS} for G_o adjusted to yield the same peak current as when v_{GS} is 0.5 V.

curves is, in general, more uniform when velocity saturation is a factor. (Compare the solid and dashed curves in Fig. 10.28, for example.) Even after adjusting G_o to match the curves for $v_{GS} = 0.5$ V, the values of $i_{D,\text{sat}}$ still differ in the two models, but this difference is larger as v_{GS} approaches V_P. If we were to add curves for v_{GS} equal to 0.7 V and/or 0.8 V, for example, we would find closer agreement in those curves.

Before leaving velocity saturation, we should point out that we can also find an analytical expression for $i_D(v_{GS}, v_{DS})$ by using the second velocity-field model we introduced, Eq. (10.78). To do this, we substitute Eq. (10.78) for s_y into Eq. (10.76b) for i_D, solve for $\mathscr{E}_y$, replace $\mathscr{E}_y$ with $-dv_{CS}/dy$, and integrate from source to drain. We have chosen not to go through this exercise because the algebra is tedious and teaches us little, but you should realize that it is possible.

10.4 SUMMARY

In this chapter we have considered a second class of transistors, field effect transistors (FETs). These devices differ from bipolar junction transistors (BJTs) in that the potential barrier to current flow through the device is controlled indirectly by a field plate called the gate, rather than by direct contact to the barrier region. They also differ in that the output current is due to majority carrier drift in the channel, rather than due to minority carrier diffusion across the base. There are both *n*- and *p*-channel FETs, differing in the majority carrier type in the channel.

We have introduced three types of field effect transistors: the metal-oxide-semiconductor FET (MOSFET), the junction-gate FET (JFET), and the metal-semiconductor FET (MESFET). All have a characteristic gate voltage below which the channel does not conduct and the device is cut off; but with sufficient gate voltage the channel conducts and the device is either in the linear, or triode, region, which occurs at low output voltages, or is saturated, which occurs at larger output voltages and corresponds to a constant output, or drain, current independent of the drain-to-source voltage. If the channel is conducting when the gate voltage is zero, the device is said to be a depletion mode device; if it is not, the device is termed an enhancement mode device. We have used the gradual channel approximation model to describe the large-signal terminal characteristics of FETs. From the results of that modeling we have also obtained linear small-signal models. We have seen that an important characteristic of FETs is their very high input impedance.

PROBLEMS

10.1 Consider an *n*-channel MOSFET with $t_o = 5$ nm, $\varepsilon_o = 3 \times 10^{-13}$ f/cm^2, $L = 1\ \mu$m, and $\mu_e = 1200$ cm^2/V · s. Assume a bias level $(V_{GS} - V_T) = 2$ V and $v_{DS} > 2$ V.

(*a*) If we want I_D to be 1 mA for this bias condition, what must K be for this device? Recall that $i_D = K(v_{GS} - V_T)^2/2$ when $v_{DS} > (v_{GS} - V_T)$.

(*b*) What must W be for the device with the value of K you found in part a?

(*c*) What is the incremental transconductance g_m of this device at this bias point? Compare this to g_m of a bipolar transistor with $I_C = 1$ mA.

(*d*) Consider designing a MOSFET with $g_m = 40$ mS at a bias level $I_D = 1$ mA.

(i) What K value is required?

(ii) To achieve this K in the MOSFET structure described above, what W is required?

(iii) With this K, what is $(V_{GS} - V_T)$ when $I_D = 1$ mA? Compare this result to k_T and discuss.

10.2 Consider an n-channel silicon MOSFET like that pictured in Fig. 10.2 that has the following dimensions and properties:

$$t_o = 750\ \text{Å}$$
$$N_A = 1x10^{17}\ \text{cm}^{-3}$$
$$V_{FB} = -0.2\ \text{V}$$
$$\mu_e = 800\ \text{cm}^2/\text{V}\cdot\text{s}$$
$$L = 2\ \mu\text{m}$$
$$W = 30\ \mu\text{m}$$

(*a*) What is the threshold voltage V_T of this device when $v_{BS} = 0$?
(*b*) What is the value of the factor K in the large-signal model for $i_D(v_{GS}, v_{DS}, v_{BS})$ [see Eqs. (10.15)]?
(*c*) What is i_D when $v_{GS} = +2$ V, $v_{DS} = +5$ V, and $v_{BS} = 0$?

10.3 Consider a p-channel enhancement mode MOSFET with $V_T = -1$ V and $K = 2$ mA/V^2 connected as a diode as illustrated in Fig. P10.3.
(*a*) Calculate and graph i_D as a function of v_{DS} for $-5\ \text{V} \le v_{DS} \le 5$ V.
(*b*) Based on your results in part a, suggest a method of plotting i_D versus v_{DS} for such a connection that will yield (theoretically, at least) two straight lines intersecting at V_T.
(*c*) Suppose that the base and source terminals are now disconnected and that a positive supply V_{BS} is inserted. How would your plot in part a change qualitatively as $|V_{BS}|$ is increased?

10.4 Using the same design rules as in problem 8.9, lay out minimum-gate-length MOSFETs like those pictured in Figs. 10.11*a* and *b*. Assume that W is 10 μm. Compare the sizes of these two devices, especially the gate lengths L. Discuss the relative sizes of the gate-to-drain capacitance C_{gd} due to the overlap of the gate electrode and the drain diffusion in your two designs. Do the same comparison of your two designs with respect to the drain-to-substrate capacitance C_{db}, which arises from the depletion capacitance of the drain diffusion.

10.5 Suppose that you are an engineer with a company that has a MOSFET processing facility that can reliably produce features with dimensions as small as 1.5 μm and can reliably produce gate oxides as thin as 20 nm (200 Å). The process uses

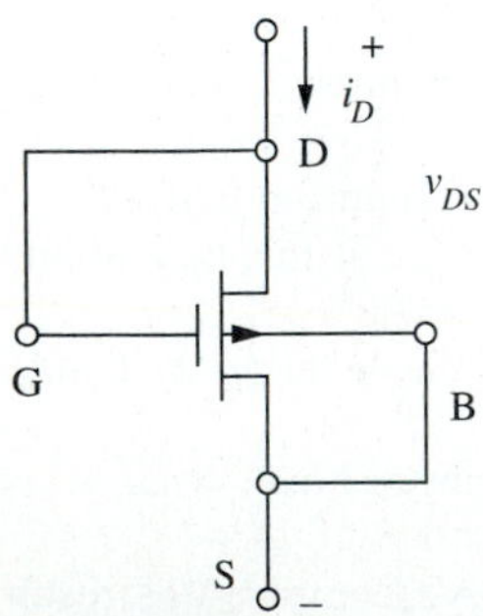

FIGURE P10.3

polycrystalline silicon doped with the same carrier type as the source and drain for the gate "metal"; the doping level of this gate material is typically 10^{19} cm^3. The electron mobility in the channel is 500 cm^2/V · s; the hole mobility is 150 cm^2/V · s.

Using these capabilities, specify W, L, t_o, and N_{Ap} for an n-channel enhancement mode MOSFET to obtain the following characteristics:

$$\text{Threshold voltage}: V_T = 0.5$$

$$K\text{-factor}: \frac{W}{L}\mu_e\frac{t_{\text{ox}}}{e_{\text{ox}}} = 2 \text{ mA/V}^2$$

Find the minimum gate capacitance possible given the above constraints.

10.6 You should have found that V_T for the device in problem 10.2 was such that the device is an enhancement mode FET. Often we want to selectively convert some of the FETs in an integrated circuit from enhancement mode to depletion mode. This is done by using a process called ion implantation to put positive or negative ions at the semiconductor oxide interface, which effectively changes Q_I and thereby V_{FB}. [See Sec. 9.5 and Eq. (9.33).] Suppose that you want to make the threshold of devices like this −2 V.

(*a*) How much does the flat-band voltage have to be changed, and what must its new value be?

(*b*) Does the charge introduced need to be positive or negative?

(*c*) What sheet density of ions (number of ions/cm^2) has to be introduced? (Assume that the ions are singly ionized.)

10.7 Calculate the body effect coefficient η [see Eq. (10.50)] for

(*a*) The MOSFET in problem 10.2

(*b*) The MOSFET you designed in problem 10.5

10.8 This problem concerns velocity saturation in MOSFETs.

(*a*) Assume a piecewise linear velocity field model as in Eq. (10.77). Using this model along with Eq. (10.4) and the approximation for the channel charge in Eq. (10.5′), find a relationship for $i_{D,\text{sat}}$ and $v_{DS,\text{sat}}$ that is the MOSFET analog of Eq. (10.79) for a MESFET. Equation (10.10) is a second relationship satisfied by $i_{D,\text{sat}}$ and $v_{DS,\text{sat}}$, so with these two relationships unique values may be found for $i_{D,\text{sat}}$ and $v_{DS,\text{sat}}$ for each value of v_{GS}.

(*b*) The critical field for velocity saturation in silicon is 2×10^4 V/cm. Assuming for purposes of estimation that the field in the channel is uniform (i.e., that $\mathcal{E} = v_{DS}/L$), at what v_{DS} will the field be 10^4 V/cm in devices with the following channel lengths?

(i) 1.0 μm

(ii) 0.25 μm

(iii) 0.1 μm

10.9 Redesign the channel height a and doping level N_{Dn} of the device in the example in Sec. 10.2.1 to achieve the same G_o but a pinchoff voltage V_p of −1.2 V. The same mask set is to be used to fabricate the device, so Z/L is unchanged.

10.10 (*a*) Calculate the small-signal transconductance g_m in saturation for the MESFET model incorporating velocity saturation summarized by Eq. (10.84) and compare your expression to that found when velocity saturation is not a factor, Eq. (10.70).

(*b*) Evaluate g_m using each of your expressions in part a for the device used in Fig. 10.28 and at the same v_{GS} values used in that figure (i.e., −0.3, −0.1, 0.1, 0.3, and 0.5 V).

10.11 Plot i_D versus v_{DS} curves for a gate-to-source voltage v_{GS} of 0.7 V like those in Figs. 10.28 and 10.29*b*. Note that you should plot i_D, not i_D/G_o.

CHAPTER 11

SINGLE-TRANSISTOR LINEAR AMPLIFIER STAGES

We now have models for bipolar and field effect transistors, and we understand how those models are based upon and related to the physical processes active within their respective devices. Next we will turn to applying transistors in useful circuits and to using our models to analyze, understand, and eventually design transistor circuits.

Transistor circuits can be divided into several groups; for each group a different type of analysis is appropriate. In Chaps. 11 through 14 we will consider transistor circuits designed to linearly multiply time-varying input signals by a constant factor, usually of magnitude much greater than 1. Such circuits are called *linear amplifiers*. The circuits we will discuss are designed so that the transistors in them are always biased in their forward active regions and can always be modeled using small-signal linear equivalent circuit models. These circuits are called *Class A* amplifiers and are what we will mean when we speak of "small-signal linear amplifiers."

Linear amplifier circuits can also be designed in which some of the transistors operate outside of their forward active regions and for which large-signal models must be used for some of the devices. We will not discuss these amplifiers, called *Class B* and *Class C* amplifiers, in any detail in this text.

Finally, there is a third group of transistor circuits that are highly nonlinear and for which large-signal models are used exclusively. These are *switching circuits* for use in digital logic, semiconductor memories, and various signal processing applications. We will discuss this group of circuits more in Chap. 15.

In this chapter we will begin with the all-important issue of establishing a stable bias point for a transistor. Then we will study simple circuits, each with a single transistor, that can be used as building blocks to assemble more complicated linear amplifier circuits. In Chap. 12, we will discuss additional linear amplifier building block circuits that use transistor pairs, and in Chap. 13 we will discuss assembling these building block circuits into complex multistage linear amplifiers.

11.1 BIASING TRANSISTORS

Our small-signal linear equivalent circuit models depend critically on the transistor bias point, so a major issue in designing a transistor amplifier is establishing a bias point in the forward active region for each of the transistors. Furthermore, because the transconductance g_m is in general the most important of the equivalent circuit parameters, we will generally give first priority to establishing a bias to also achieve a particular g_m. For a bipolar transistor this means that we bias to obtain a specific quiescent collector current because g_m is directly proportional to I_c, as we know from Eq. (8.53b), which is rewritten here:

$$g_m = \frac{q|I_c|}{kT} \tag{11.1}$$

For a field effect transistor in its forward active region (i.e., in saturation), the transconductance g_m can be viewed as being proportional to either the gate-to-source voltage V_{GS} or the drain current I_D, as we can see from Eqs. (10.42a) and (10.42*b*), which we rewrite here:

$$g_m = K|V_{GS} - V_T| \tag{11.2}$$

$$g_m = \sqrt{2K|I_D|} \tag{11.3}$$

The latter expression involves only one device variable, K, so it is preferred to the first, which involves both V_T and K. Thus we typically bias field effect transistors to achieve a specific value of I_D.

To summarize, the primary objectives of biasing are (1) to place the transistor in its forward active region and (2) to set g_m by establishing the quiescent value of the output current (i.e., I_C or I_D). We will look at biasing each type of transistor in turn below.

11.1.1 Bipolar Transistor Biasing

Our objective in biasing a bipolar transistor for small-signal linear circuit applications is to establish a specific value of quiescent collector current. Perhaps the simplest way to do this, conceptually at least, is to connect a current source to the collector terminal, as illustrated in Fig. 11.1*a* for an *npn* bipolar transistor.*

*We will tend to use *npn* transistors in all of our bipolar transistor circuits in this chapter because *npn*'s in general have higher gain and are faster than *pnp*'s; the modification of the circuits for *pnp* application is in most cases straightforward.

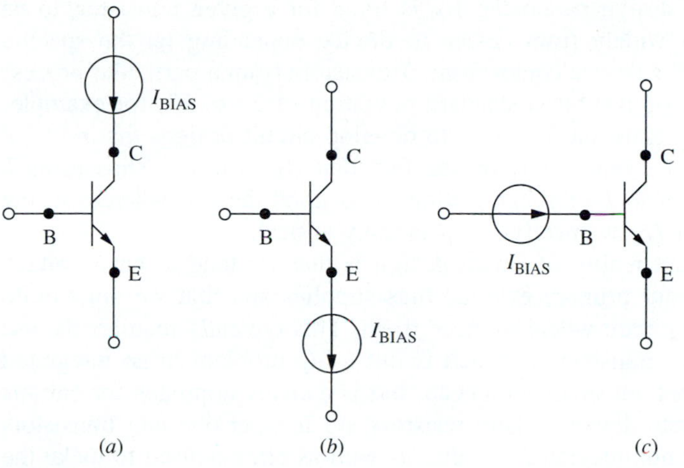

FIGURE 11.1
Use of a current source to establish a specific quiescent collector current. The current source is shown connected: (*a*) to the collector terminal; (*b*) to the emitter terminal (the only viable option of these three); (*c*) to the base terminal.

Unfortunately, the circuit in Fig. 11.1*a* turns out to be impossible to implement because it places too many constraints on the transistor. Specifically, there is no easy way to provide the base current without rendering the circuit useless. Thus, the circuit of Fig. 11.1*a* is not a viable bias scheme.*

Although we cannot set I_c directly with a current source, it is possible to put the current source in the emitter circuit, as illustrated in Fig. 11.1*b*. The emitter and collector currents are related as

$$I_C = I_E \frac{\beta_F}{(\beta_F + 1)} \tag{11.4}$$

so setting the value of I_E sets I_C. In fact, in a high-gain transistor (i.e., $\beta_F \gg 1$), the collector and emitter currents are essentially equal; that is,

$$I_C \approx I_E \tag{11.5}$$

Yet another biasing option is to apply the current source to the base terminal, as shown in Fig. 11.1*c*, and to use the relationship

$$I_C = \beta_F I_B \tag{11.6}$$

Doing this is theoretically possible, but it is not a wise choice as a practical matter. As a general rule of thumb, the current gain β_F of a bipolar transistor

*This does not mean that we will never put a current source in the collector circuit, because we can use a current source as a load, as we shall see in Sec. 11.2.

is not a very reliable design parameter. β_F is fixed for a given transistor, to be sure, but it can vary widely from device to device depending on the specific production run or lot the device comes from. Transistors from a particular process may have a mean β_F of 100 but a standard deviation of 25 to 50, for example. Thus experience teaches us that it is best to develop circuit designs that rely not on specific values of β_F but simply on the fact that β_F is large. Thus using a current source to establish I_C through setting I_E is good design, whereas trying to establish a value of I_C by specifying I_B is risky at best.

Another important reality of circuit design is that we tend to have voltage sources available for our primary external bias supplies and that we must build current sources in our circuit where we need them. This typically requires the use of active devices (i.e., transistors), which is not a big problem in an integrated circuit where transistors are small and cheap, but is a costly approach for circuits assembled from discrete devices where resistors are inexpensive and transistors are costly. Thus most nonintegrated circuits, as well as circuits used to make the current sources in integrated circuits, use *resistor biasing*, which we will discuss next.

A logical place to start when thinking about resistor biasing of a bipolar transistor is with the Ebers–Moll model (see Fig. 8.7). Looking at this model, you could reasonably assume that you want to establish a quiescent value of the base-emitter voltage V_{BE}, which would then fix I_E and thereby I_C (assuming that β_F is large). A way to do this using a voltage divider is illustrated in Fig. 11.2*a*. Again, however, practical considerations make this an unwise approach. The parameters involved, namely I_{ES} and α_F, are difficult to control from transistor to transistor, just as β_F is. Furthermore, because of the exponential nature of diode characteristics, I_E is too sensitive to V_{BE} even in an ideal transistor to make this a viable approach. A much better approach to biasing is to find schemes that are relatively insensitive to the precise value of V_{BE}.

Consider next the circuit of Fig. 11.2*b*, in which one of the bias resistors in the circuit of Fig. 11.2*a* has been eliminated. We know from our discussion of large-signal bipolar transistor equivalent circuit models that the base-emitter voltage is inevitably about 0.6 V. If the supply voltage is much larger than this, the base current will not vary much even if V_{BE} varies by ± 0.05 V or even ± 0.1 V. To examine this further we use the large-signal equivalent circuit model of Fig. 8.19*a*, to proceed with our bias point analyses. Since V_{BE} is essentially 0.6 V, we know that the base current is essentially

$$I_B \approx \frac{(V_{CC} - 0.6)}{R_B} \tag{11.7}$$

and thus

$$I_C \approx \beta_F \frac{(V_{CC} - 0.6)}{R_B} \tag{11.8}$$

These results are not particularly sensitive to the base-emitter voltage, as we anticipated, and in this sense this design is an improvement. However, we

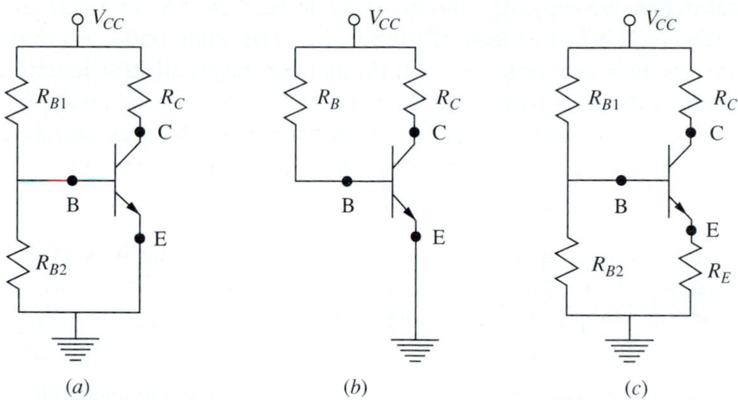

FIGURE 11.2
Three possible circuits for resistively biasing a bipolar transistor: (*a*) the base-emitter voltage is set by a voltage divider; (*b*) the base current is set; (*c*) the emitter current is set (the preferred option).

have already said that β_F is an unreliable design parameter and that we should not design circuits based on its specific value. Thus this is still not a good bias scheme.

A better approach is to return to the voltage divider of Fig. 11.2*a* and to add a resistor to the emitter terminal, as illustrated in Fig. 11.2*c*. Now the important voltage drop is that due to the emitter current and the value of the base current is unimportant, as long as it is small. To see this, notice first that the resistors R_{B1} and R_{B2} form a voltage divider that sets the voltage on the base terminal relative to ground. The idea is to make this voltage drop, which is approximately $I_E R_E + V_{BE}$, much greater than V_{BE} (≈ 0.6 V), so that any variation in V_{BE} will be reflected as only a small variation in I_E.

To proceed with our analysis we make several assumptions that are consistent with the governing assumption, namely that we are analyzing a well-designed circuit. First, we assume that the transistor is properly biased in its forward active region and thus that V_{BE} is approximately 0.6 V. Second, we assume that the transistor is a high-gain device and that the base current I_B is small compared to I_E and I_C. Finally, we assume that R_{B1} and R_{B2} have been chosen so that the current through them is much larger than the base current I_B. In this case, then, the bias current can be neglected and the voltage between the base and ground (i.e., the voltage drop across R_{B2}) is approximately $R_{B2}V_{CC}/(R_{B1}+R_{B2})$. We can thus write

$$\frac{R_{B2}V_{CC}}{(R_{B1}+R_{B2})} \approx I_E R_E + 0.6 \tag{11.9}$$

By using a bit of algebra and setting I_C equal to I_E, we get

$$I_C \approx \frac{R_{B2}V_{CC}/(R_{B1}+R_{B2}) - 0.6}{R_E} \tag{11.10}$$

As a practical matter we typically choose $I_E R_E$ to be 2 or 3 V, and R_{B1} and R_{B2} so that $V_{CC}/(R_{B1} + R_{B2})$ is at least 10 times I_B. The final point we must check is that the transistor is not saturated; that is, that the base-collector junction is not forward biased, at least not by more than 0.4 V. Since we now know I_C, we can easily calculate the voltage drop across the resistor R_C, and thus calculate the base-collector and/or collector-emitter voltage to confirm a proper bias.

Example

Question. Consider an *npn* bipolar transistor biased using the circuit illustrated in Fig. 11.2*c*. Assume for the transistor that β_F is 75 and $V_{BE,\text{on}}$ is 0.6 V. Assume also that V_{CC} is 9 V and R_C is 3 kΩ. Choose R_E, R_{B1}, and R_{B2} so that I_C is 1 mA.

Discussion. Since R_C is specified, the first step is to calculate the quiescent voltage on the collector, which then tells us the maximum voltage we can have at the emitter. The issue is not simply biasing the transistor in its forward active region, but also ensuring that the transistor will not saturate when it is amplifying an input signal. The quiescent voltage drop across R_C is 3 V, so the collector is at 6 V relative to ground; this restricts the positive output swing to 3 V. To achieve the same bound on the negative swing, the bias should be consistent with a collector voltage as low as 3 V. The upper limit on the emitter voltage is thus 2.8 V. If we conservatively choose the emitter bias to be 2.5 V, R_E must be 2.5 kΩ.

The quiescent voltage on the base terminal is 3.1 V (i.e., 2.5 + 0.6); this gives us one constraint on R_{B1} and R_{B2}, that is, $R_{B1}/(R_{B1} + R_{B2}) = 3.1/9$. The other constraint is set by requiring a quiescent current through R_{B1} and R_{B2} at least an order of magnitude larger than the base current of roughly 15 μA. Doing this we find that $(R_{B1} + R_{B2})$ must be less than 60 kΩ. We find that an R_{B1} of 21 kΩ and an R_{B2} of 39 kΩ are acceptable.

It is interesting to consider the sensitivity of this bias scheme to $V_{BE,\text{on}}$. If $V_{BE,\text{on}}$ varies from 0.5 to 0.7 V, which for this factor is a very large variation, I_C varies from 1.04 mA to 0.96 mA, or only 4%. As predicted, the bias point established by this circuit is relatively insensitive to the value of $V_{BE,\text{on}}$.

In this chapter we will tend to use the resistor-biasing scheme of Fig. 11.2*c* whenever we need a specific bipolar transistor circuit for purposes of illustration or discussion. This is a very common circuit, one you will see often. In Chap. 12, we will use current source biasing and will use the circuit of Fig. 11.1*b*. This is a very common circuit for use with integrated differential amplifiers.

11.1.2 Field-Effect Transistor Biasing

Current sources can be used to bias field effect transistors as well as bipolar transistors, and the FET equivalents to Figs. 11.1*a* and *b* should be obvious to you. Getting the necessary current sources, however, still requires active devices, and thus resistor biasing is also widely used.

Field effect transistors differ from bipolar transistors in several important ways that lead to additional techniques for resistor biasing. On the one hand, there is no gate current to be concerned with, so the gate potential can be set quite precisely using a voltage divider like we used to bias bipolar transistors. On the other hand, the gate-to-source voltage drop is not a simple 0.6 V but instead varies with bias point. Furthermore, the use of a voltage divider can significantly reduce the input resistance of a MOSFET amplifier stage.

Three possible ways of resistively biasing MOSFETs are illustrated in Figs. 11.3*a*, *b*, and *c*.* The circuit in Fig. 11.3*a* uses a voltage divider to set the voltage on the gate relative to ground in a fashion analogous to that used to bias the bipolar transistor in Fig. 11.2*c*. The idea is that if this voltage, which we call V_{REF}, is much larger than the threshold voltage V_T, the quiescent drain current will be relatively insensitive to V_T. We can see this by noting that $V_{GS} = V_{REF} - I_S R_S$; I_D equals I_S; and, in saturation, $I_D = K(V_{GS} - V_T)^2/2$. Combining these we arrive at a quadratic equation to solve for I_D:

$$V_{REF} = I_D R_S + \sqrt{\frac{2I_D}{K}} + V_T \tag{11.11}$$

Clearly the larger V_{REF} is, the less important small uncertainties in V_T are. The drawback of this circuit, as we shall see in Sec. 11.4.1, is that it compromises the

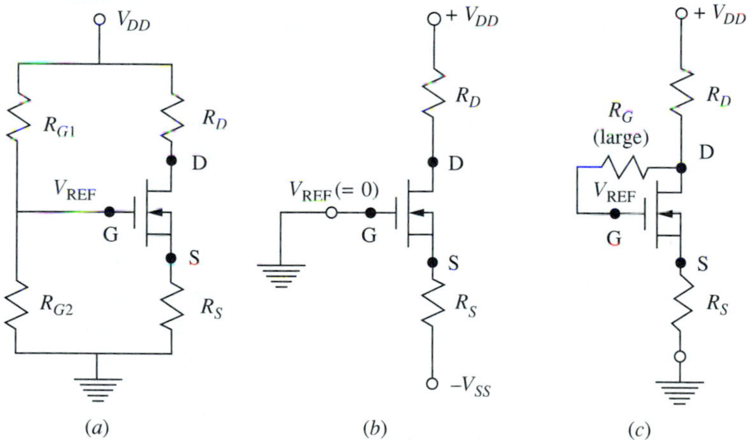

FIGURE 11.3
Three methods of resistively biasing an *n*-channel enhancement mode MOS field effect transistor: (*a*) a voltage divider is used to set a reference voltage on the gate terminal in a manner analogous to the bias in Fig. 11.2*c*; (*b*) two voltage sources are required, but the intrinsic high input resistance of field effect transistors is not compromised; (*c*) a large resistor is used between the drain and gate to automatically place the transistor in saturation.

---

*For purposes of illustration we will assume we are dealing with enhancement-mode, *n*-channel MOSFETs in our circuitry. You should be able to extend our discussions to other FETs without difficulty.

potentially very high input resistance of MOSFET amplifier stages. An alternative that does not use any resistors on the gate terminal but in general requires two bias supplies, one positive ($+V_{DD}$) and one negative ($-V_{SS}$) relative to ground, is shown in Fig. 11.3*b*. In this circuit, V_{SS} plays the role of V_{REF} in the first circuit.

The final step in the design, independent of which of the bias circuits in Figs. 11.3*a* and *b* is used, is to calculate the drain-to-source voltage V_{DS} and to verify that the MOSFET is indeed in its forward active region (i.e., in its saturation region).

The final bias circuit in Fig. 11.3 is one that is unique to enhancement-mode FETs. It makes use of the fact that if $V_{GS} = V_{DS}$, then the device is trivially in saturation, that is, V_{DS} is automatically greater than $(V_{GS} - V_T)$. No current flows into the gate terminal, so R_G can be made very large, which is important because its magnitude determines the input resistance of this stage. In this case the equation that relates I_D to the other circuit parameters is

$$V_{DD} = I_D(R_D + R_S) + \sqrt{\frac{2I_D}{K}} + V_T \tag{11.12}$$

This is also quadratic in I_D, but it is worth remembering that when we are designing a circuit we are not usually solving for I_D since that is specified as a design objective (i.e., is a "known"). We are more typically trying to determine suitable resistor, and possibly supply, values given a target value for I_D.

Example

Question. Consider an n-channel MOSFET biased using the circuit in Fig. 11.3*b*. Assume that the transistor is biased in the saturation region and that V_T is 0.9 V and K is 1 mA/V^2. Assume also that V_{DD} is 5 V, $-V_{SS}$ is -5 V, and R_D is 3 kΩ. Choose R_S to give a quiescent drain current of 1 mA.

Discussion. Assuming that the MOSFET is saturated, $V_{GS} - V_T$ must be 1.4 V, from Eq. (10.15b), and thus V_{GS} is 2.3 V. Since the gate is at ground potential, the source voltage must be -2.3 V, and the voltage drop across R_S must be 2.7 V; thus we select R_S to be 2.7 kΩ. The device will be biased in saturation as long as V_{DS} is greater than $V_{GS} - V_T$. Since the quiescent drain voltage is 2 V relative to ground, i.e. 5 V – (3 kΩ)(1 mA), V_{DS} is 4.3 V; the device is clearly biased in saturation.

The question of the maximum output voltage swing is an interesting one to consider. Clearly the output voltage can go as high as 5 V, so the positive swing is 3 V. The negative swing is determined by the value of v_{DS} that takes the MOSFET out of saturation. It is tempting to say that this occurs when v_{DS} is 1.4 V or when v_D is -0.9 V, yielding a maximum negative swing of 2.9 V, but this is not correct. The value of v_{GS} does not stay fixed; instead, it must increase to create the increase in i_D that reduces v_{DS}. In effect, $(v_{GS} - V_T)$ is increasing while v_{DS} is decreasing, so v_{DS} cannot decrease as much as it would if v_{GS} were fixed at 1.4 V. (We didn't have this problem with BJTs because v_{BE} changes very little. That is, in a BJT very small changes in v_{BE} can cause enormous changes in i_C. K would have to be much larger for the same thing to be true in this MOSFET example.)

To find out what the lower bound on v_{DS} is, we must know something about the circuit in which it will be used. If we assume that the source will be incrementally grounded in the circuit, then the source remains at −2.7 V. Thus, at the boundary of saturation where $v_{DS} = (v_{GS} - V_T)$, we have

$$v_{DS} = 5 - \frac{R_C K v_{DS}^2}{2} - (-2.3)$$

Upon solving this, we find that v_{DS} is 1.95 V and thus that the drain voltage relative to ground, $v_{DS} - 2.3$, is −0.35 V, corresponding to a negative voltage swing of 2.35 V. This is significantly less than our first (incorrect) estimate of 2.9 V.

Notice that the small-signal transconductance g_m of a field effect transistor always depends on device, as well as bias point, parameters (i.e., K and/or V_T, as well as I_D and/or V_{GS}). This is in contrast to the situation with bipolar transistors, where we could eliminate the dependence of g_m on β by making I_C largely independent of β_F. This makes it more difficult in practice to design linear amplifiers with field effect transistors for applications that require specific values of gain, which has limited their application in simple amplifier circuits. However, as MOSFET technology has advanced and K and V_T have become better controlled, more complicated circuits have become possible; now the use of MOSFETs in high-performance linear integrated circuits has become common. These circuits use current source biasing to reduce the dependence of g_m on V_T, but the sensitivity to K remains [see Eq. (11.3)].

11.2 THE CONCEPT OF MID-BAND

After completing the large-signal analysis and/or design of a linear amplifier circuit to determine the bias point, we will have to turn to an analysis of its small-signal linear operation about that bias point using our small-signal (i.e., incremental) equivalent circuit models. A question we must address first is what model to use.

Usually we will be interested in knowing the small-signal response because we have a time-varying signal that we wish to amplify. Thus we should assume that we must use a model which includes the capacitors we added to extend our initially quasistatic modeling to incorporate energy storage and so that we could treat time-varying signals. That is, we should use the models pictured in Figs. 8.24 and 10.13. This is a major complication.

The picture is further complicated when we realize that we will find that it is extremely useful to add additional capacitors to our circuits to introduce current paths for time-varying signals that do not exist for the bias currents. We very quickly find ourselves dealing with circuits containing many capacitors, in addition to all of the other resistors and dependent and independent sources; the analysis becomes overwhelming.

Fortunately, we will find that we can make major simplifications. To see how, let us look at a specific example to make sure that first the problem and then the solution are clear.

Consider the circuit shown in Fig. 11.4*a*. This is a bipolar amplifier that we will see a lot of in this text, but for now we just want to use it to illustrate some general points. The capacitors C_I, C_O, and C_E do not conduct non-time-varying

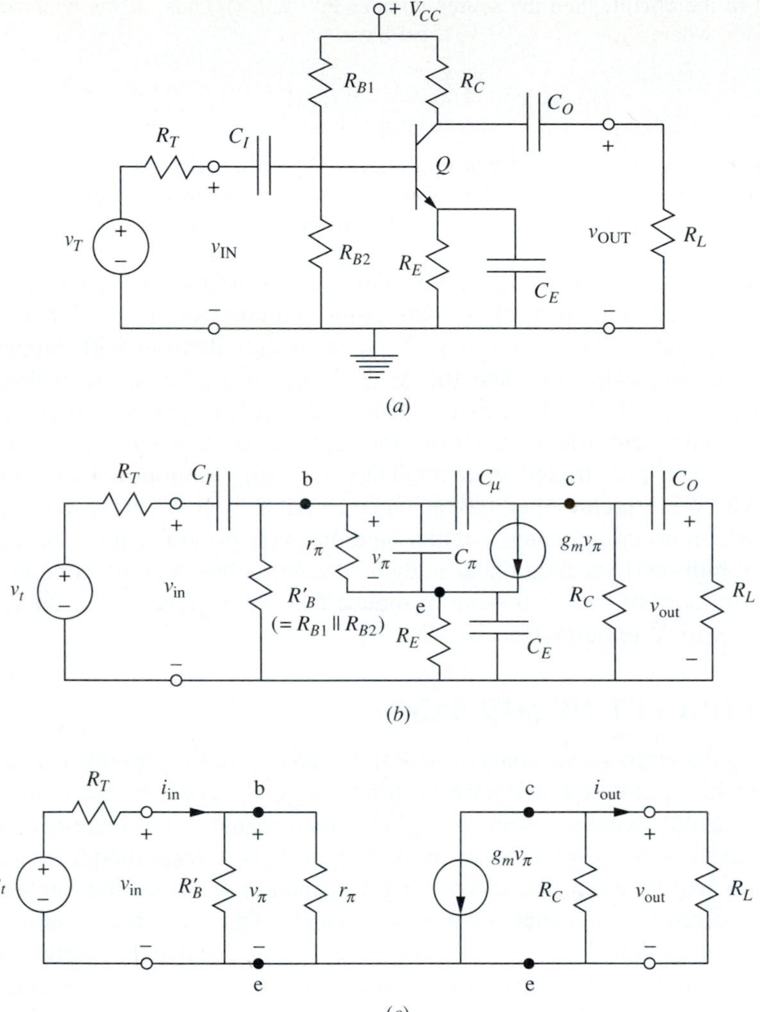

FIGURE 11.4
Resistively biased, capacitively coupled common-emitter bipolar transistor amplifier: (*a*) the complete circuit schematic; (*b*) the complete small-signal linear equivalent circuit; (*c*) the model for mid-band analysis.

(i.e., DC) currents, so for purposes of biasing the circuit is identical to the circuit in Fig. 11.2*c*. For small-signal linear operation about a bias point in the forward active region, the equivalent circuit becomes that illustrated in Fig. 11.4*b*. Here we have used the fact that the incremental signal on the power supply is zero (i.e., the V_{CC} terminal is incrementally grounded), and we have replaced the transistor with its hybrid-π equivalent circuit, Fig. 8.28*a*. Looking at Fig. 11.4*b*, we can count five capacitors. It is clear that unless we can do something dramatic we have a lot of work to do to analyze this circuit.

The key to simplifying the analysis of amplifier circuits like that of Fig. 11.4*b* is to note that the capacitors in the circuit vary widely in size and to recognize that the impedance of a capacitor varies inversely with frequency. The intrinsic device capacitors, C_π and C_μ, for example, are typically small and have relatively large impedances at the signal frequencies of interest. By "relatively large" we mean that the magnitude of the impedance presented by a given capacitor is so much larger than the equivalent resistance in parallel with it that it can be treated as an open circuit. At sufficiently high frequencies this can no longer be true, of course, but below some limiting frequency, which we call ω_{HI}, C_π and C_μ can be treated as open circuits and effectively neglected.

C_I, C_O, and C_E are elements whose values we choose, so they can be made as large or as small as we want. We said earlier that the reason for having these elements in the circuit is to provide additional current paths for the time-varying signals. This means that we want those capacitors to be large, so that their impedance is relatively low at the signal frequencies of interest. By "relatively low" we mean that the magnitude of the impedance of a capacitor is sufficiently lower than the equivalent resistance in series or parallel with it that the capacitor can be treated as a short circuit. There will in general be a frequency limit, which we will call ω_{LO}, above which the extrinsic capacitors like C_I, C_O, and C_E can be treated as short circuits.

The frequency range between ω_{LO} and ω_{HI} is called *the mid-band frequency range*. One of the objectives of linear amplifier design is to ensure that there is a mid-band range (i.e., that ω_{HI} is greater than ω_{LO}) and that the mid-band range encompasses the signal frequencies of interest. We will consider the problem of calculating ω_{LO} and ω_{HI} in Chap. 14. For now, we will assume that there is a mid-band range and that we are operating in it. In this case the circuit in Fig. 11.4*b* reduces to that shown in Fig. 11.4*c*. No capacitors remain. C_π and C_μ have been replaced by open circuits; and C_I, C_O, and C_E have been replaced by short circuits.

In summary, we will concentrate on analyzing the mid-band performance of linear amplifiers. In the mid-band range all of the capacitors are effectively either short or open circuits and do not appear in the analysis. The transistor models that we must use for mid-band analysis are the low-frequency incremental equivalent circuit models (i.e., those in Figs. 8.24 and 10.15).

11.3 SINGLE-BIPOLAR-TRANSISTOR AMPLIFIERS

As we look at various single-transistor amplifier stages, we will want to consider certain important performance characteristics as a way of evaluating their usefulness for various applications. The first such useful small-signal linear amplifier characteristic is the *mid-band voltage gain* A_v, which is defined as the ratio of the incremental output and input voltages (see Fig. 11.4*c*):

$$A_v \equiv \frac{v_{\text{out}}}{v_{\text{in}}} \tag{11.13}$$

In certain situations, it is useful to also introduce the concept of open-circuit voltage gain $A_{v,oc}$, which is defined as the value of A_v when R_L (see Fig. 11.4*c*) is infinite (i.e., with the output terminals open-circuited). The corresponding output voltage $v_{out,oc}$ is the Thevenin equivalent voltage seen when looking back in at the output terminals; clearly, $v_{out,oc} = A_{v,oc} v_{in}$.

We also define *mid-band current gain* A_i as

$$A_i \equiv \frac{i_{out}}{i_{in}} \tag{11.14}$$

Again, we can speak of a short-circuit current gain $A_{i,sc}$, which is the value of A_i when R_L is a short circuit. You will recognize the corresponding output current as the Norton equivalent current seen when looking back in at the output terminals; clearly, $A_{out,sc} = A_{i,sc} i_{in}$.

The *mid-band power gain* A_p is defined as

$$A_p \equiv \frac{p_{out}}{p_{in}} = \frac{v_{out} i_{out}}{v_{in} i_{in}} = A_v A_i \tag{11.15}$$

where p_{out} is $v_{out} i_{out}$ and p_{in} is $v_{in} i_{in}$. Equation (11.15) shows that the power gain A_p can also be written as the product of A_v and A_i.

Additional characteristics of interest are the input and output resistances. The *mid-band input resistance* R_{in} is defined as

$$R_{in} \equiv \frac{v_{in}}{i_{in}} \tag{11.16}$$

R_{in} is an important parameter because it provides us with a measure of how much the amplifier will load the input source. Referring to Fig. 11.4*c*, we see that v_{in} is related to v_t as

$$v_{in} = \frac{R_{in}}{R_T + R_{in}} v_t \tag{11.17}$$

Clearly, if we want the largest possible output signal v_{out} for a given source signal v_t, we also want the largest possible v_{in} for a given v_t. That is, we want R_{in} to be much larger than R_T, so v_{in} is essentially v_t. Input loading is an important factor to keep in mind as you study linear amplifiers. We will choose to think of the voltage gain as v_{out}/v_{in} rather than as v_{out}/v_t, so we must remember that our expressions may not reflect the negative impact of R_{in} and R_T seen in Eq. (11.17).

The *mid-band output resistance* R_{out} is defined as the resistance seen when looking back in at the output terminals with zero input signal. R_{out} is clearly also the Thevenin equivalent resistance of the amplifier seen when looking back in at the output terminals at mid-band.

We will now turn to the study of four single-transistor bipolar amplifier stages: the common-emitter, degenerate-emitter, common-base, and emitter-follower stages. After discussing these four stages here and similar field effect transistor stages in Sec. 11.4, we will conclude by comparing and contrasting all of these stages in Sec. 11.5.

11.3.1 Common-Emitter Stage

In the common-emitter stage an input voltage signal is applied to the base terminal of the transistor, the output voltage is taken from the collector terminal, and the emitter terminal is grounded (at mid-band frequencies). The output voltage is created by the collector current flowing through a device or circuit we call the *load*. This load can take several forms. We will first look at common-emitter stages in which a passive linear resistive network is connected to the collector as the load. Then we will look at circuits in which more complicated "active" devices, such as other transistors, are used as the load.

a) Linear resistor loads. We have already seen a resistively biased, capacitively coupled version of a common-emitter stage with a linear resistor load in Fig. 11.4*a*. To analyze the small-signal mid-band performance of this amplifier we use the circuit pictured in Fig. 11.4*c*. For convenience we redraw this common-emitter amplifier and its mid-band small signal linear equivalent circuit in Fig. 11.5. Notice that we have included the parasitic base series resistance r_x and the output resistance r_o in Fig. 11.5*b* because we do not know yet whether they can be neglected.

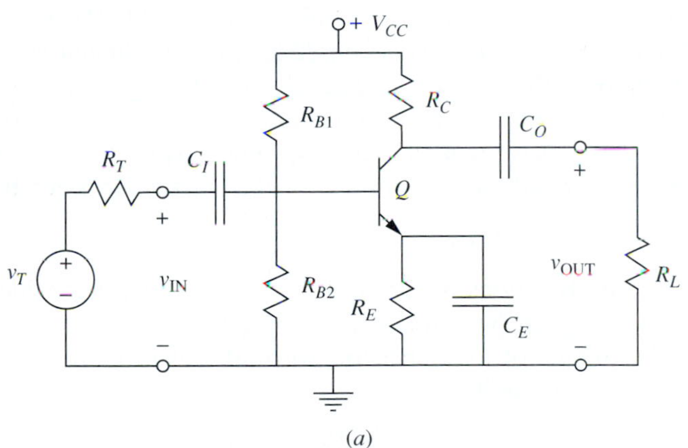

(*a*)

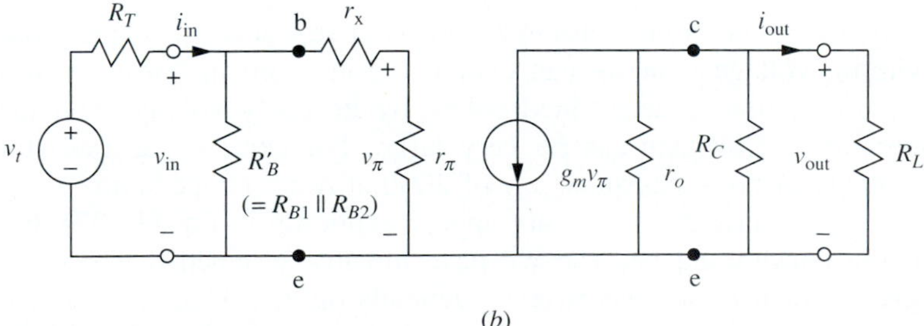

(*b*)

FIGURE 11.5
(*a*) Common-emitter bipolar transistor amplifier; (*b*) the small-signal linear equivalent circuit at mid-band, including r_x and r_o.

Looking first at the voltage gain, we see from Fig. 11.5*b* that v_{out} is given by

$$v_{out} = -g_m v_\pi R_L' \tag{11.18}$$

where R_L' is the equivalent of resistors r_o, R_C, and R_L in parallel; that is,

$$R_L' \equiv r_o \parallel R_C \parallel R_L \tag{11.19}$$

Next, we see that v_π can be related to v_{in} as

$$v_\pi = \frac{r_\pi}{r_\pi + r_x} v_{in} \tag{11.20a}$$

In a modern transistor r_x is typically 25 to 30 Ω; if β_f is 50 or more and I_C is on the order of 1 mA, r_π will be greater than 1 kΩ, so that to a good approximation we can write

$$v_\pi \approx v_{in} \tag{11.20b}$$

Substituting these results in Eq. (11.18) we arrive at the following expression for the voltage gain:

$$A_v = -g_m R_L' \tag{11.21}$$

A frequent objective of a circuit designer is to make A_v as large as possible, so let us now see how big we can make A_v. Looking at Eq. (11.21), we see that we want to make both g_m and R_L' as large as possible. Looking first at R_L', we see that it will essentially equal the smallest of r_o, R_C, and R_L. Assuming we have already chosen the transistor with the highest available r_o, the only quantities we can change are R_C and R_L. If we make R_C and R_L much larger than r_o, R_L' will be approximately r_o and A_v will be maximized for this particular transistor at

$$A_{v,\max} \approx -g_m r_o \tag{11.22}$$

Both g_m and r_o are functions of the bias point, so we next consider what bias point makes $A_{v,\max}$ largest. Recalling that g_m is qI_C/kT and r_o is $|V_A|/I_C$, where V_A is the Early voltage of the transistor, we find that in terms of the bias point, Eq. (11.22) can also be written as

$$A_{v,\max} \approx -\frac{q|V_A|}{kT} \tag{11.23}$$

Interestingly, the collector bias current I_C does not appear in this expression. Thus, the maximum voltage gain we can ever get from a given transistor in a common-emitter connection is determined solely by its Early voltage (and the operating temperature). This gain can be very large. For example, a transistor with an Early voltage of 50 V has an $A_{v,\max}$ of 2000 at room temperature.

The collector bias current I_C does not appear explicitly in Eq. (11.23), but it is lurking in the background because we have already assumed that R_C and R_L are much greater than r_o and because r_o depends on I_C. Thus if I_C is too small, r_o will be too large, and our assumption that it is less than R_C and R_L will no longer be valid. The implication is that we must make I_C greater than some minimum value, but there is also a problem in making it large. Specifically, if I_C is large, the quiescent voltage drop across R_C will be too large, and the transistor will be saturated. To see this, look back at Fig. 11.4*a* (you may also want to review the example on page 322). To keep the transistor biased in its forward active region, the voltage drop across R_C must be less than some value, call it $V_{C,\text{MAX}}$, and thus we must have

$$I_C R_C < V_{C,\text{MAX}} \tag{11.24a}$$

or

$$I_C < \frac{V_{C,\text{MAX}}}{R_C} \tag{11.24b}$$

This in turn places a restriction on r_o; that is, we have

$$r_o = \frac{|V_A|}{I_C} > \frac{|V_A|}{V_{C,\text{MAX}}} R_C \tag{11.25}$$

which says that to have R_C greater than r_o, we must have $V_{C,\text{MAX}}$ greater than $|V_A|$.

Now we have a problem. $V_{C,\text{MAX}}$ is determined by the power supply voltage V_{CC} and the desired output voltage swing, and it is typically at most a few tens of volts. At the same time, $|V_A|$ in a good transistor is several tens or even hundreds of volts. Typically then $|V_A|$ is at worst comparable to $V_{C,\text{MAX}}$, and frequently is much larger than $V_{C,\text{MAX}}$, so making R_C much greater than r_o is impossible!* We will see how to get around this problem by using nonlinear active loads in the next subsection, but for now where we are using linear resistors, we cannot have r_o much less than R_C and R_L, and we cannot get a gain as large as $A_{v,\max}$ in Eqs. (11.22) and (11.23).

If R_C and R_L are in fact restricted to be much less than r_o, as we have just seen they will be if we have a good transistor with a reasonable Early voltage, R_L' in Eq. (11.19) will be more nearly R_C in parallel with R_L than r_o, and our voltage gain expression is now approximately

$$A_v \approx \frac{g_m R_C R_L}{R_C + R_L} \tag{11.26}$$

or, using the bias dependence of g_m,

$$A_v \approx -\frac{qI_C R_L'}{kT} = -\frac{q}{kT}\frac{I_C R_L R_C}{R_L + R_C} \tag{11.27}$$

Again using our restriction on the $I_C R_C$ product [i.e., Eq. (11.24a)], we have

$$A_v < -\frac{q}{kT}\frac{V_{C,\text{MAX}} R_L}{(R_C + R_L)} \tag{11.28}$$

---

*"Impossible" is, of course, a bit strong; perhaps "impractical" is a better word. We can always find a poor transistor with a small Early voltage $|V_A|$ and small output resistance r_o, but $A_{v,\max}$ for this device will also be small [see Eq. (11.23)], so what's the point?

Clearly, to make A_v large we want to keep the product $I_C R_C$ as large as possible, but within this constraint we still have the freedom to make I_C small and R_C large, or vice versa. Looking at Eq. (11.27), we see that the best choice, if we want to increase A_v, is to reduce R_C. I_C will have to be increased correspondingly to keep the $I_C R_C$ product at its maximum value, of course, and this increases the power dissipation in the stage and reduces its input resistance (see below), both of which may be undesirable consequences. Notice also that once R_C is reduced to less than roughly a tenth of R_L, little is gained by reducing it further since the factor $R_L/(R_C + R_L)$ will already be just about as large as it can ever get (i.e., approximately 1).

Increasing the size of the bias supply V_{CC} is a way to increase the bound on the $I_C R_C$ product and thus is another way to increase A_v, but doing so also increases the power dissipation in the circuit and is not always an attractive or practical solution. A far better solution is to use an active load, as we shall see in the next subsection; the "cost" of doing this comes in terms of circuit complexity and device count rather than power or other performance parameters.

Returning to our characterization of the common-emitter amplifier stage, the easiest way to determine the mid-band current gain is to first think of the dependent current source as $\beta_F i_b$ rather than $g_m v_\pi$, and to notice that $-i_{\text{out}}$ is the fraction of this current flowing through R_L, or $\beta_F i_b R_C/(R_L + R_C)$, assuming r_o is so large that it can be neglected. Next notice that i_b is the fraction of i_{in} flowing through r_π, which is $i_{\text{in}} R'_B/(R'_B + r_\pi)$, assuming r_x can be neglected. (Here R'_B is the parallel combination of R_{B1} and R_{B2}.) By substituting this latter expression for i_b in the former expression for i_{out} and dividing by i_{in}, we arrive at

$$A_i = -\beta_F \frac{R_C}{(R_L + R_C)} \frac{R'_B}{(R'_B + r_\pi)} \tag{11.29}$$

Notice that A_i is always less than β_F, but in the limit of R_L much smaller than R_C and of R'_B much larger than r_π, A_i becomes very nearly β_F. Of course, making R_L very small means that the voltage gain is also very small, so clearly choices must be made in the design of the stage depending on the performance objectives.

The power gain A_p is the product of A_v and A_i. It is maximized when R'_B is much larger than r_π and when $R_C = R_L$, in which case

$$A_{p,\max} = \frac{\beta_F g_m R_C}{4} \tag{11.30a}$$

or, equivalently,

$$A_{p,\max} = \frac{q \beta_F I_C R_C}{4kT} \tag{11.30b}$$

Notice again the importance of the quiescent voltage drop across the collector resistor, $I_C R_C$.

The input resistance of this stage is R'_B in parallel with r_π, and the output resistance is R_C. In a typical common-emitter amplifier R'_B will be much larger than r_π, so R_{in} is essentially r_π and depends on the bias point as $\beta_F kT/qI_C$. As we have said earlier, this is typically on the order of a thousand ohms. Notice also that making I_C larger reduces R_{in}, as we mentioned above.

Example

Question. Assume that we have a common-emitter amplifier like that in Fig. 11.5*a*, biased with $I_C = 1$ mA, using the supply and resistor values from our earlier example; that is, $V_{CC} = 9$ V, $R_C = 3$ kΩ, $R_E = 2.5$ kΩ, $R_{B1} = 21$ kΩ, and $R_{B2} = 39$ kΩ. Assume also that R_L is 3 kΩ. What are the mid-band incremental voltage gain, current gain, power gain, and input resistance?

Discussion. The transconductance g_m for this bias point is 40 mS, and r_π is 1.88 kΩ. Applying our formulas we calculate that R_C' is 1.5 kΩ, so A_v is −60, A_i is −18.75, and A_p is 1125. The input resistance is 1.35 kΩ. These results will have more meaning to us after we discuss other amplifier stages in the next several sections.

To summarize the properties of the common-emitter stage with a linear resistor load, this stage can have significant amounts of both voltage and current gain. Its input resistance is typically r_π, which is often relatively low, and its output resistance is R_C.

b) Nonlinear and active loads. The voltage and power gains of the common-emitter amplifier are limited by the quiescent voltage drop across the collector resistor R_C caused by the quiescent collector current I_C flowing through it: the infamous $I_C R_C$ product, or $V_{C,\text{MAX}}$. For a given R_C, increasing I_C (to increase g_m, for example) reduces the magnitude of the permissible output voltage swing; and, as we have already pointed out, if the $I_C R_C$ product is made too large, the transistor will be saturated. Thus the $I_C R_C$ product can be only so large. As a practical matter, we find in many designs that $I_C R_C$ turns out to be on the order of $V_{CC}/2$ or $V_{CC}/3$.

A way around this dilemma is illustrated in Fig. 11.6. The idea (as shown in Fig. 11.6*a*) is to use a collector bias element in place of R_C that is nonlinear and for which the incremental resistance at the bias point, $dv_{AB}/di_D|_Q$, is much larger than the ratio of the quiescent terminal voltage and current, V_{AB}/I_D, as shown in Fig. 11.6*b*. If we define the incremental resistance of this nonlinear element at its bias point as r_c, that is,

$$r_c \equiv \left.\frac{dv_{AB}}{di_D}\right|_Q \tag{11.31}$$

then the incremental equivalent circuit of the amplifier is that illustrated in Fig. 11.6*c*. Now there is no bias-related restriction on the magnitude of r_c. If r_c and R_L are much greater than r_o, the voltage gain of the stage can indeed be the $A_{v,\text{max}}$ we defined earlier in Eq. (11.22), that is,

$$A_v = A_{v,\text{max}} = -g_m r_o \tag{11.32}$$

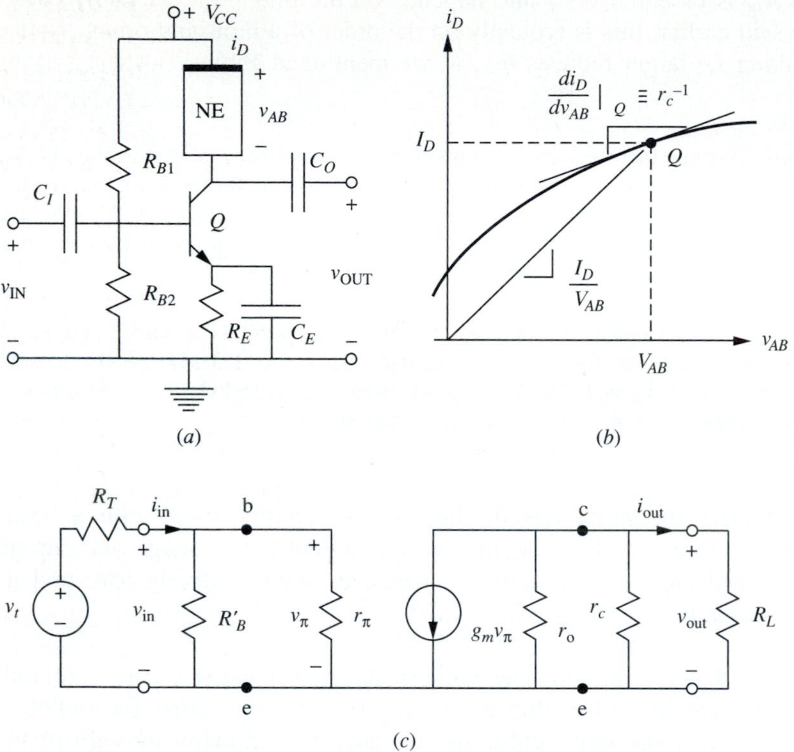

FIGURE 11.6
(*a*) Common-emitter circuit with a nonlinear element (NE) as a load; (*b*) the current-voltage characteristics sought for such a load; (*c*) the small-signal linear equivalent model for this circuit.

Since achieving this gain relies on R_L being very large, it is convenient at this point to recall that the definition of open-circuit voltage gain $A_{v,oc}$ is the gain of the stage with the output terminals open-circuited (i.e., with R_L infinite). Thus, what we want to be talking about is the open circuit voltage gain, and for the common-emitter stage in Fig. 11.6 we have

$$A_{v,oc} = -g_m \frac{r_o r_c}{r_o + r_c} \tag{11.33}$$

In the limit of $r_c \gg r_o$, this approaches $A_{v,max}$.

As far as finding a suitable nonlinear load is concerned, there are many nonlinear devices, some active and some passive, that have the property illustrated in Fig. 11.6*b* (and there are many, such as *p-n* diodes, that do not), but most nonlinear devices tend to be active. In fact, a near-ideal device for this application is a current source, and we can make excellent current sources using transistors. An example is shown in Fig. 11.7, where a bipolar transistor current source circuit is used to bias a bipolar common-emitter stage. (We will see additional examples involving FET amplifier stages later in Sec. 11.4.)

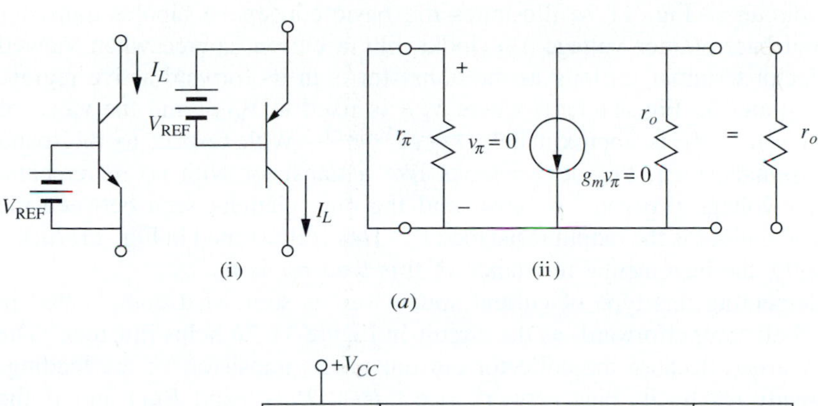

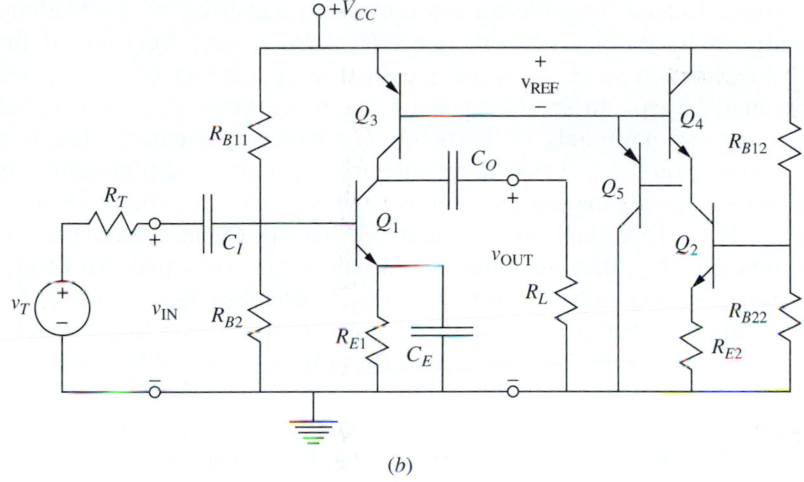

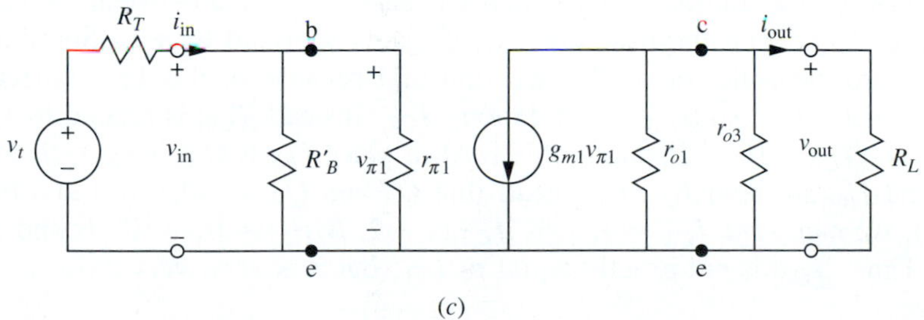

FIGURE 11.7
Use of *npn* and *pnp* bipolar transistors as loads: (*a*) the idea of a BJT as a current source, showing in (i) that fixing the base-emitter voltage of a high–β transistor at V_{REF} fixes its collector current at $I_L = I_{ES} e^{qV_{REF}/kT}$ and showing in (ii) that the corresponding incremental equivalent circuit reduces simply to r_o; (*b*) a common-emitter amplifier stage with a bipolar transistor current source replacing R_C in the collector circuit; (*c*) the corresponding mid-band small-signal linear equivalent circuit. Notice that a numerical subscript has been added to the equivalent circuit parameters to indicate to which transistor in the circuit they correspond.

The circuit in Fig. 11.7*a* illustrates the basic concept: a bipolar transistor with a fixed base-emitter voltage V_{BE} looks like a current source when viewed at the collector terminal, as long as the transistor is in its forward active region. This is illustrated in Fig. 11.7*a*(i) where V_{BE} is fixed at V_{REF}, and the value of the current source I_L is approximately $I_{ES}e^{qV_{\text{REF}}/kT}$. With respect to mid-band frequency signals, then, this device looks like a transistor with no incremental base-emitter voltage (i.e., v_{be} is zero), and the only element seen between the collector and emitter is the output resistance r_o. This is illustrated in Fig. 11.7*a*(ii). Consequently, the incremental resistance of this load r_c, is r_o.

Implementing this type of current souce load is somewhat complicated in practice, albeit straightforward, as the circuit in Figure 11.7*b* helps illustrate. The complexity arises because the collector current of the transistor we are loading, Q_1, is already set by its bias network (i.e., R_{B11}, R_{B21}, and R_{E1}) and if the value of the load current souce I_L is not identical to I_{C1}, either Q_1 or Q_3 will saturate. It would be easy to set I_L equal to I_{C1} if we knew I_{ES} for Q_3, but a circuit designer can never rely on knowing I_{ES} with any accuracy. The best we can do is to rely on the fact that in an integrated circuit we can comfortably assume that devices having the same size and shape will have essentially identical characteristics. Thus if we duplicate the network biasing Q_1 and use it to bias an identical transistor Q_2, then the collector current of Q_2 will equal that of Q_1. Then we can use I_{C2}, the collector current of Q_2, to establish V_{REF} by using I_{C2} to bias Q_4, a transistor that is identical to the current source load transistor Q_3. Doing this, V_{BE4} becomes the V_{REF} we seek, and with this value of V_{REF} we have $|I_{C3}| = |I_{C4}| \approx I_{C2} = I_{C1}$.

Notice that we did not say $|I_{C3}|$ and $|I_{C4}|$ equal I_{C2} and I_{C1}, but only that they are similar. The descrepency arises because we have to account for the base currents of Q_3 and Q_4. In the circuit in Fig. 11.7*b*, the base currents for Q_3 and Q_4 are supplied by the transistor Q_5, which has been connected between the base and collector of Q_4, and the base current of Q_5 is supplied by Q_2. Summing the currents into the collector of Q_2, we find that because of this base current, $|I_{C4}|$ is not exactly I_{C2}, so $|I_{C3}|$ is not exactly I_{C1}. Instead $|I_{C4}|$ is related to I_{C2} through $I_{C2} = |I_{C4}| + |I_{B5}|$. Pursuing this further, since I_{B5} is $(I_{B3} + I_{B4})/\beta_5$ and since I_{B3} and I_{B4} are both I_{C3}/β_3 (recall that Q_3 and Q_4 are identical and that $I_{C3} = I_{C4}$), we can write $I_{C1} = I_{C2} = |I_{C3}|(1 + 2/\beta_3\beta_5) \approx |I_{C3}|$ (if β_3 and β_5 are large). Thus, $|I_{C3}|$ is not exactly equal to I_{C1}, but it is very, very close if the βs are large.

An alternative to using Q_5 in this circuit is to simply short the base and collector of Q_4 together (you will find an illustration of this alternative applied to *npn*s in Fig. 12.16). When Q_5 is eliminated and the base and collector of Q_4 are shorted, Q_2 must supply the base currents of Q_3 and Q_4 directly, and we find that $I_{C1} = I_{C2} = |I_{C3}|(1 + 2/\beta_3)$. In this case, the difference between I_{C1} and $|I_{C3}|$ may be much more significant, and adding Q_5 is a wise design move.

Summarizing our discussion thus far, the practical implementation of a current source load is more complicated than one might have guessed looking at

Fig. 11.7*a*, but it can be done straightforwardly in an integrated circuit context where we can safely assume that the characteristics of devices will be matched. Turning now to the incremental analysis of this circuit, the transistor Q_3 is the current source, and the base-emitter voltage on Q_3 has a constant value established by Q_4. Thus the $g_{m3}v_{\pi 3}$ dependent generator in the hybrid-π model for Q_3 is zero, and the only element between the collector and emitter of the incremental model of Q_3 is the output resistance r_{o3}, as the sequence in Fig. 11.7*a* illustrates. The incremental equivalent circuit for the amplifier in Fig. 11.7*b* is therefore as shown in Fig. 11.7*c*. Thus, the load resistance r_c is now r_{o3}, and the open circuit voltage gain is

$$A_{v,\mathrm{oc}} = -g_{m1}\frac{r_{o1}r_{o3}}{r_{o1}+r_{o3}} \tag{11.34a}$$

which can also be written as

$$A_{v,\mathrm{oc}} = -\frac{g_{m1}}{g_{o1}+g_{o3}} \tag{11.34b}$$

By using the bias point dependences of g_m and g_o and noting that the magnitude of the quiescent collector current, $|I_C|$, is the same in Q_1 and Q_3, we find that Eq. (11.34a) can also be written as

$$A_{v,\mathrm{oc}} = -\frac{q}{kT}\frac{|V_{A1}||V_{A3}|}{|V_{A1}|+|V_{A3}|} \tag{11.34c}$$

Once again the importance of a large Early voltage, and thereby a large output resistance, is apparent.

A current source load like this is most commonly used with an emitter coupled pair, or differential amplifier, which we shall study in Chap. 12. The circuit in Fig. 11.7*b* is used in the 741 operational amplifier, for example (a schematic of the 741 circuit is given in Fig. 14.5). In this context, it is also called a current mirror, a subject we will discuss again in Sec. 13.3.

The incremental analysis of the amplifier in Fig. 11.7*b* is actually the easy part; the more troublesome aspect of the circuit is biasing it. As we discussed earlier, this circuit requires very close matching of the components to be successful: Q_2 must be identical to Q_1, Q_4 to Q_3, R_{B12} to R_{B22}, etc. Such close matching of components is possible only in integrated circuits where all of the devices are fabricated simultaneously. Even then, however, we must also stabilize the resulting high-gain amplifier in a feedback loop to keep the amplifier from saturating. This is so because the output of any very high-gain amplifier, such as the one we have just presented, will saturate unless the input is very small. At the same time, any imbalance in the circuit (including any imbalance in the components) will function effectively as a virtual input signal that can easily be large enough to saturate the output (i.e., saturate one or more of the transistors in the circuit). As a practical matter then, the only realistic way of using such a "beast" is to put it in a feedback loop.* This is exactly what you already do with an operational amplifier, for example, when you put a resistor between the output terminal and the negative input terminal. The price you pay is reduced overall gain, but what you buy is an amplifier that works and a gain you can rely on since it is set by passive, linear resistances.

11.3.2 Degenerate-Emitter Stage

The common-emitter amplifier stage is an extremely important one that is widely used, but it does have some shortcomings. In particular, its voltage gain is temperature-dependent, its current gain depends directly on β_F, and its input resistance is relatively low. A common solution for these problems is to leave some or all of the emitter bias resistor R_E in the small-signal circuit by not shorting it completely with C_E. The circuit, which is now said to have *emitter degeneracy*, is illustrated in Fig. 11.8*a*. The corresponding small-signal incremental equivalent circuit for mid-band analysis is presented in Fig. 11.8*b*.

The analysis of the circuit in Fig. 11.8*b* is facilitated if we recognize that the current through the resistor R_{E1} is $(g_m + g_\pi)v_\pi$. The input voltage v_{in} is thus equal to $v_\pi + R_{E1}(g_m + g_\pi)v_\pi$, and we can write v_π as

$$v_\pi = \frac{v_{\text{in}}}{1 + R_{E1}(g_m + g_\pi)} \tag{11.35}$$

The output voltage v_{out} is $-R'_L g_m v_\pi$, as it was in the common-emitter stage, so we can immediately write the voltage gain A_v as

$$A_v = -\frac{g_m R'_L}{1 + R_{E1}(g_m + g_\pi)} \tag{11.36a}$$

By multiplying the numerator and denominator of this expression by r_π and recognizing that the product $r_\pi g_m$ is β_F, we find that we can also write this as

$$A_v = -\frac{\beta_F R'_L}{r_\pi + (\beta_F + 1)R_{E1}} \tag{11.36b}$$

If β_F is large, as is typically the case, the r_π factor in the denominator will be negligible and Eq. (11.36b) for A_v can be simplified significantly to

$$A_v \approx -\frac{R'_L}{R_{E1}} \tag{11.36c}$$

We now see that A_v depends only on the ratio of resistor values. This is a useful result for an integrated circuit amplifier because it is often difficult to fabricate integrated circuit resistors to within 20 percent of their design value; however, the ratio of resistor values can easily be maintained to within a few percent of a

*This discussion can readily be quantified; this is done in Sec. 13.3. You may want to look ahead to that section and particularly to Fig. 13.17, which should help you visualize the concept of feedback stabilization.

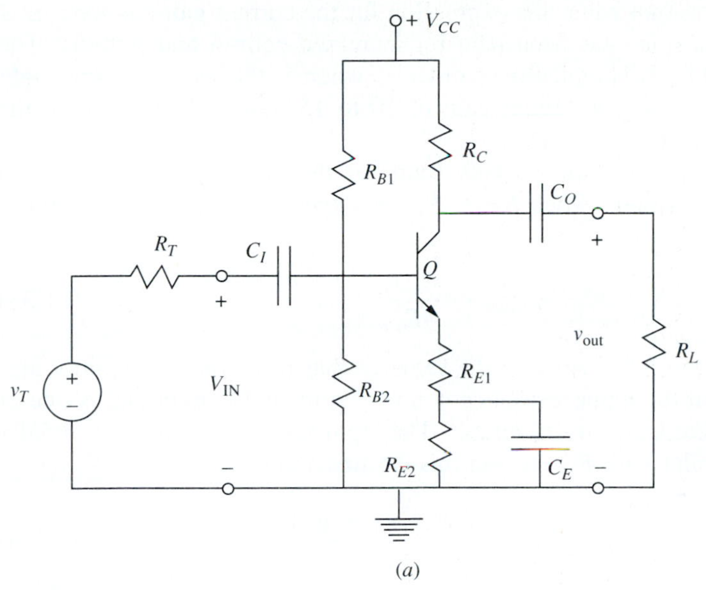

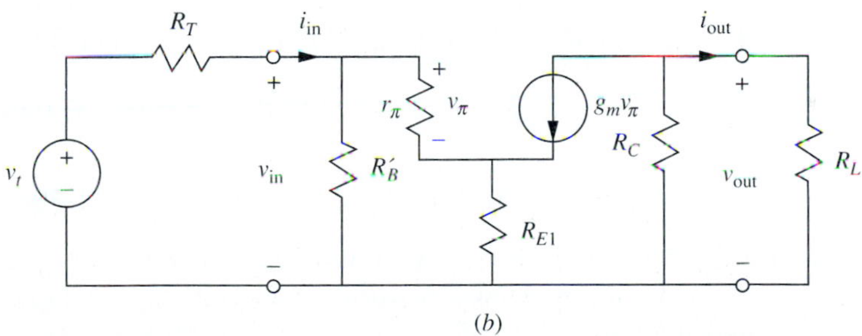

FIGURE 11.8
Degenerate-emitter stage: (*a*) the full circuit; (*b*) the small-signal linear equivalent circuit for mid-band analysis.

design value. The temperature dependence of A_v is, of course, also completely removed, assuming the temperatures of the two resistors stay the same.

Comparing Eq. (11.36c) with Eq. (11.20), we see that the magnitude of the gain is now smaller by a factor of essentially $1/g_m R_{E1}$, which can also be written as $r_\pi/\beta_F R_{E1}$. We said earlier that r_π is much smaller than $\beta_F R_{E1}$, so clearly this factor is much less than 1. This reduction in the magnitude of the voltage gain is one of the costs we must pay for the increased control that we have achieved over the value of the voltage gain.

The magnitude of the current gain is also reduced significantly from that of the common-emitter circuit. A little algebra shows that it is approximately

$$A_i \approx -\frac{R_C}{R_C + R_L} \cdot \left(\frac{R'_B}{R_{E1}}\right) \tag{11.37}$$

The parameter β does not enter this expression for the current gain, as long as β is large, but again a price has been paid for increased control and stability. The first factor in Eq. (11.37) is typically of order $\frac{1}{2}$, whereas the second factor might be as large as 30, yielding a current gain of 10 to 15, rather than β_F as in the common-emitter circuit.

The mid-band power gain is easily found as the product of Eqs. (11.36c) and (11.37). It is maximum when $R_C = R_L$, as expected, and is given approximately by

$$A_{p,\max} \approx \frac{R_L R'_B}{4R_{E1}^2} \tag{11.38}$$

The output resistance of this stage is the same as that of a common-emitter amplifier (i.e., R_C), but the input resistance is now significantly larger and is one of the important characteristics of this circuit. The input resistance is now essentially $(\beta + 1)R_{E1}$, in parallel with R'_B. To see this we first write

$$R_{\text{in}} = R'_B \parallel \frac{1 + R_{E1}(g_m + g_\pi)}{g_\pi} \tag{11.39a}$$

or, equivalently,

$$R_{\text{in}} \approx R'_B \parallel [(\beta_F + 1)R_{E1} + r_\pi] \tag{11.39b}$$

If we approximate $(\beta_F + 1)$ as β_F and neglect r_π relative to the other terms, this becomes

$$R_{\text{in}} \approx R'_B \parallel \beta_F R_{E1} \tag{11.39c}$$

Usually this is essentially R'_B because $\beta_F R_{E1}$ is very much the larger factor. In this case we would want to make the base bias resistors, R_{B1} and R_{B2}, as large as possible, keeping in mind the desirability of having the quiescent bias current through them be much larger than the quiescent transistor base current I_B.

Example

Question. Consider a circuit identical to the one in the preceding example except that the entire emitter resistor is no longer shorted incrementally to ground. Assume that the circuit now looks like that in Fig. 11.8*a* with $R_{E1} = 0.5$ kΩ and $R_{E2} = 2.0$ kΩ. What are A_v, A_i, A_p, and R_{in} in this circuit?

Discussion. The product $g_m R_{E1}$ is 20, which allows us to use Eq. (11.36c) for A_v. Doing this we find that A_v is -3. We also find that A_i is now -13.65 and A_p is $+41$. These gains are considerably smaller than the corresponding quantities for a common-emitter amplifier.

The input resistance is $[(\beta + 1)R_{E1} + r_\pi]$, which is 39.7 kΩ, in parallel with R'_B, which is 13.7 kΩ; the combination is 10.2 kΩ, which is clearly dominated by R'_B. A high input resistance is one of the attractive features of this stage.

The degenerate-emitter stage might seem like a good place to use a nonlinear active load as a way to recover the gain we lose from the presence of R_{E1}, but this is not often done. If emitter degeneracy is being used to increase the input resistance, then using it with an active load makes sense, but if it is being used to accurately set the gain (as is more common), an active load is counterproductive. This is because the effective resistance of a nonlinear active load is not a well-controlled parameter; therefore its value can be expected to vary widely from circuit to circuit. Consequently the advantage of using emitter degeneracy to precisely set the gain of the stage is lost.

We should point out that the use of emitter degeneracy is a form of feedback. An element such as R_{E1} (which appears in both the input and the output circuit) couples, or feeds back, some of the output signal to the input of the transistor in such a way that it controls the gain more precisely, albeit at a lower magnitude.

The degenerate-emitter amplifier stage may be summarized as follows: the use of a feedback resistor in the emitter yields a high input resistance and mid-band gains that depend only on the ratios of resistor values in the circuit and are independent of the transistor parameters.

11.3.3 Common-Base Stage

Sometimes we need an amplifier stage that has a very small input resistance, even smaller than that available from a common-emitter amplifier. This can be achieved by applying the input signal to the emitter of a bipolar transistor, taking the output off the collector, and incrementally grounding the base. This is illustrated for our standard resistively biased, capacitively coupled circuit topology in Fig. 11.9*a*. It is more common to draw this circuit, the common-base stage, as shown in Fig. 11.9*b*, which is exactly the same circuit as in Fig. 11.9*a* with the components positioned differently. The corresponding mid-band small-signal model is presented in Fig. 11.9*c*.

The mid-band input resistance of this circuit is R_E in parallel with r_e. The resistance r_e can be written as $(g_m + g_\pi)^{-1}$; writing it this way we can recognize that r_e is usually quite small, so that we have

$$R_{\text{in}} = R_E \parallel r_e \approx r_e = \frac{1}{g_m + g_\pi} = \frac{1}{g_m(1 + 1/\beta_F)} \tag{11.40a}$$

When β_F is large, we can neglect $1/\beta_F$ relative to 1 and this becomes

$$R_{\text{in}} \approx \frac{1}{g_m} = \frac{r_\pi}{\beta_F} \tag{11.40b}$$

This is much smaller (by a factor of β_F) than the input resistance of the common-emitter stage; it can be on the order of 25 to 50 Ω (see the example below).

The output resistance of the common base circuit is the same as that of the common-emitter and degenerate-emitter circuits. The magnitude of the voltage gain of this circuit is the same as that of the common-emitter circuit, but is now positive:

$$A_v = +g_m R_L' \tag{11.41}$$

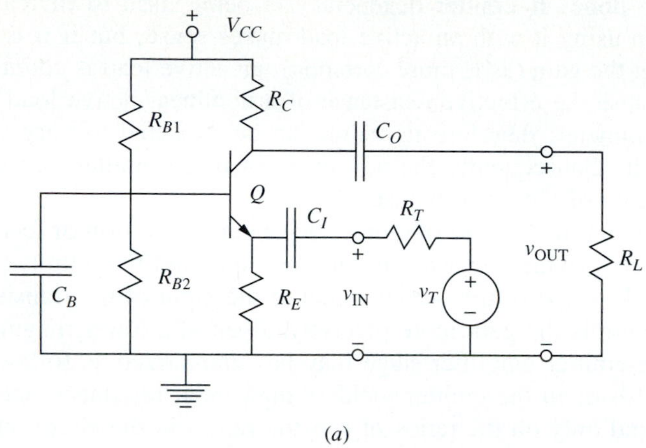

(a)

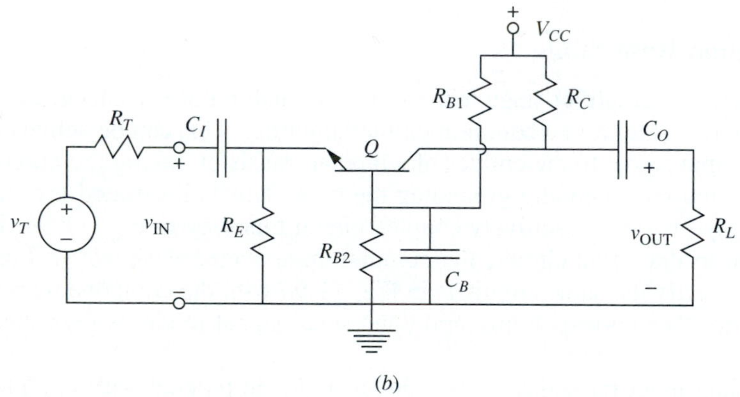

(b)

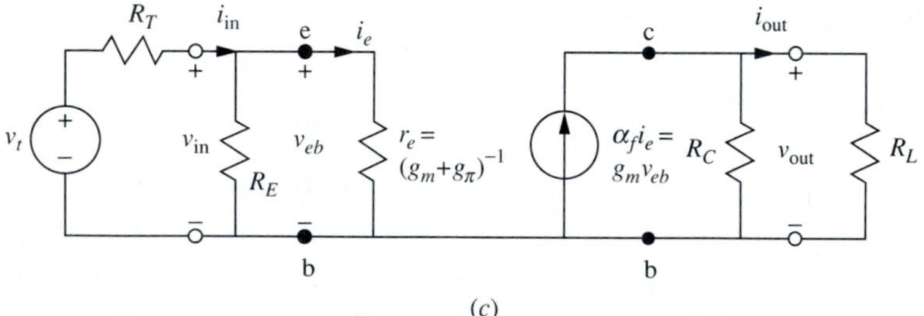

(c)

FIGURE 11.9
Common-base stage: (a) the full circuit drawn in the format used in earlier figures; (b) the full circuit in more standard common-base format; (c) the small-signal linear equivalent circuit for mid-band analysis.

The current gain is also positive but is now less than 1:

$$A_i \approx \frac{R_C}{R_C + R_L} \tag{11.42}$$

assuming that the product $R_E(g_m + g_\pi)$ is much greater than 1, as is typically the case. The power gain is still greater than 1, however, and the circuit is a very useful amplifier stage. The maximum power gain, which occurs when $R_C = R_L$, is approximately

$$A_p \approx \frac{g_m R_L}{4} \tag{11.43}$$

Example

Question. Consider a common-base stage biased using the same supply and resistor values used in the preceding examples. What are the mid-band voltage, current, and power gains of this stage, and what is the input resistance?

Discussion. Using Eqs. (11.41) through (11.43), we find that A_v is 60, A_i is 0.5, and A_p is 30. The input resistance R_{in} is 25 Ω, by far the lowest of any of the stages we have considered thus far.

In summary, the common-base circuit has a very low input resistance, high voltage gain, and no net current gain. It is a useful first stage in applications where a low input resistance is important.

11.3.4 Emitter-Follower Stage

All of the stages we have looked at thus far have had the same relatively large output resistance R_C. A stage with a low output resistance can be obtained by putting the input on the base, taking the output off the emitter, and making the collector common to both input and output (i.e., incrementally grounding it). This circuit is called the common-collector stage or the emitter-follower stage. It is illustrated in Fig. 11.10*a* using our standard resistor biasing and capacitor coupling. The mid-band equivalent circuit is illustrated in Fig. 11.10*b*.

The voltage gain of this current is given by

$$A_v = \frac{1}{1 + [1/(g_m + g_\pi)R_L']} \tag{11.44a}$$

where R_L' is now R_E in parallel with R_L. Since $(g_m + g_\pi)R_L'$ is typically much greater than 1, this expression for A_v reduces to approximately 1, that is,

$$A_v \approx 1 \tag{11.44b}$$

Note that A_v is in fact very slightly less than 1. Thus the output very closely matches, or follows, the input. Since the output is taken off the emitter, we arrive at the name emitter-follower.

Although the voltage gain is 1, the current gain is still appreciable for this stage. The expression is complicated because there are several current dividers in the circuit, but we find that we have approximately

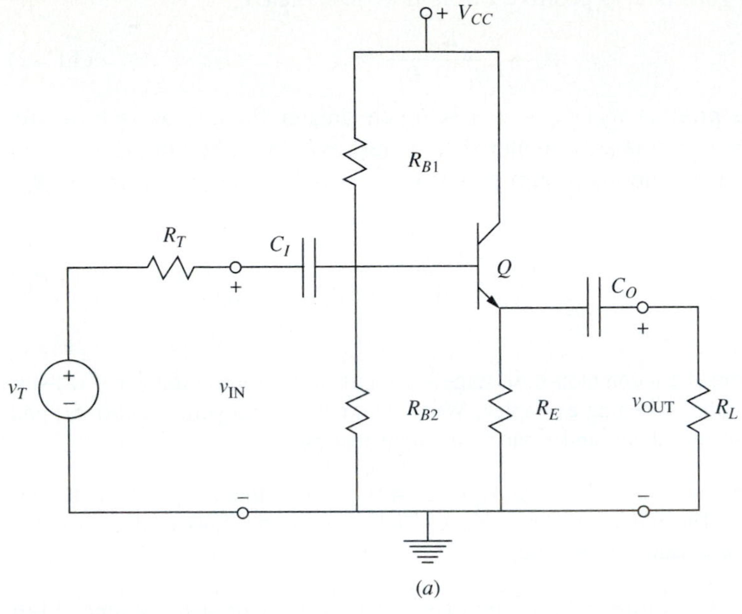

(a)

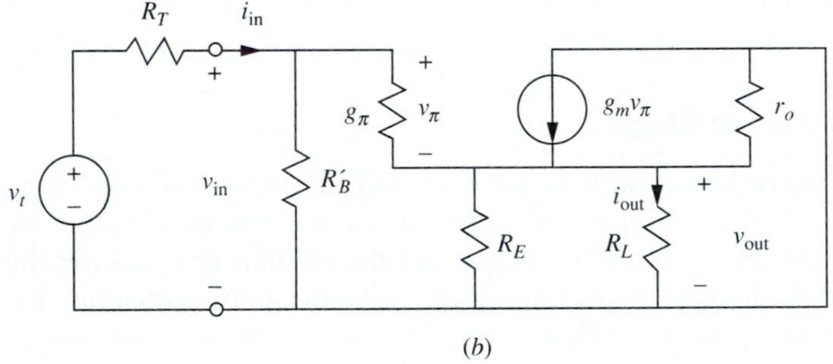

(b)

FIGURE 11.10
Emitter-follower stage: (a) the full circuit; (b) the small-signal linear equivalent circuit for mid-band analysis.

$$A_i \approx \frac{R_B'}{R_L} \tag{11.45}$$

Emitter-follower stages are designed to have a large input resistance (see below) and to be used with small load resistances, so A_i is typically large. Note, finally, that since the voltage gain is approximately 1, the current and power gains are essentially equal.

The input resistance of the emitter-follower stage is R_B' in parallel with $(\beta + 1)R_L'$, where R_L' is the parallel combination of R_E, R_L, and r_o; that is,

$$R_{\text{in}} \approx R_B' \parallel [(\beta + 1)R_L' + r_\pi] \tag{11.46}$$

This is clearly very much larger than R_L, and this stage very effectively buffers stages preceding it from small resistance loads, such as audio speakers, etc.

The output resistance of the emitter-follower stage is much lower than any of the other stages we have studied. Looking back in at the output terminals with v_t set to zero, we find

$$R_{\text{out}} = R_E \parallel \frac{(R_T \parallel R_B') + r_\pi}{\beta + 1} \parallel r_o \tag{11.47}$$

For typical bias levels, $[(R_T \parallel R_B') + r_\pi]/(\beta + 1)$ is by far the smallest of the three parallel resistances in Eq. (11.47), and we have, assuming β is much greater than 1,

$$R_{\text{out}} \approx \frac{(R_T \parallel R_B') + r_\pi}{\beta} \tag{11.48}$$

The output resistance is clearly much smaller than the output resistance of the input circuit (i.e., than R_T alone).

Example

Question. Consider an emitter-follower stage like that in Fig. 11.10*a* with $R_{B1} = 39\ \text{k}\Omega$, $R_{B2} = 21\ \text{k}\Omega$, $R_E = 2.5\ \text{k}\Omega$, $R_L = 1\ \text{k}\Omega$, and $R_T = 1\ \text{k}\Omega$. What are the linear small-signal mid-band voltage, current, and power gains; and what are the input and output resistances of this circuit?

Discussion. R_L' is 0.71 kΩ, so $(g_m + g_\pi)R_L'$ is approximately 29 and A_v is then 0.97 (i.e., essentially 1). The current and power gains are approximately 14. The input resistance is essentially R_B', and the output resistance is just under 40 Ω. This R_{out} is far smaller than in any of the preceding stages.

In summary, the emitter-follower is characterized by a large input resistance, small output resistance, unity voltage gain, and modest current and power gains.

11.4 SINGLE FIELD EFFECT TRANSISTOR AMPLIFIERS

We will continue to use n-channel, enhancement mode metal-oxide-semiconductor field effect transistors, or MOSFETs, for purposes of illustration as we now extend our discussion of single-transistor amplifiers to include field effect transistors. The results we obtain will, however, be applicable to all types of field effect transistors.

There are many similarities between the small-signal analysis and performance of bipolar and field effect transistor circuits, and we can use our knowledge of bipolar transistor circuits in our analysis to take certain shortcuts. The circuits we will consider—the common-source, degenerate-source, common-gate, and source-follower circuits—are the FET analogs to the common-emitter, degenerate-emitter, common-base, and emitter-follower bipolar circuits, respectively. The FET and bipolar circuits share many properties. You will notice, however, some important differences that arise from the fact that the input resistance of a field effect transistor is extremely large. A large input resistance is one of the attractive features of FETs.

11.4.1 Common-Source Stage

As we did when we discussed common-emitter amplifiers, we will divide our discussion of common-source amplifiers into two parts. The first deals with circuits that have only linear resistors as load elements in the drain circuit, and the second deals with the use of nonlinear, active elements as loads. We will see that using nonlinear active loads is much more important in FET amplifier design than it is in bipolar design and makes possible some very exciting circuits.

a) Linear-resistor load. A capacitively coupled, resistively biased common-source field effect transistor circuit is shown in Fig. 11.11*a*. In this circuit a voltage divider is used to set the gate-to-source bias, which then fixes the drain current as satisfying

$$I_D = \frac{K}{2}\left(\frac{R_{G2}V_{DD}}{R_{G1} + R_{G2}} - I_D R_S - V_T\right)^2 \tag{11.49}$$

The mid-band incremental equivalent circuit for the common-source amplifier of Fig. 11.11*a* is shown in Fig. 11.11*b*. The resistance R'_G is R_{G1} in parallel with R_{G2}. R'_L is the parallel combination of r_o, R_D, and R_L.*

Looking first at the mid-band voltage gain A_v, we see from Fig. 11.11*b* that v_{out} is $-g_m v_{gs} R'_L$ and that v_{gs} is v_{in}, so we immediately have

$$A_v = -g_m R'_L \tag{11.50}$$

This voltage gain has its maximum possible value for a given transistor when R_L and R_D are much larger than r_o, in which case

$$A_v = A_{v,\max} \equiv -g_m r_o = -\frac{g_m}{g_o} \tag{11.51a}$$

This quantity is very much dependent on the bias point because both g_m and r_o depend on the quiescent drain current. That is, g_m is $\sqrt{2K|I_D|}$ and r_o is $|V_A|/I_D$, where V_A is the Early voltage of the transistor. Thus

$$A_{v,\max} = -|V_A|\sqrt{\frac{2K}{|I_D|}} \tag{11.51b}$$

This expression tells us immediately that to make $A_{v,\max}$ large we want to keep the quiescent drain current small.

---

*Notice that the equivalent circuit in Fig. 11.11*b* is very similar topologically to the common-emitter mid-band incremental model in Fig. 11.5 and that many of the gain expressions are the same, as we shall see.

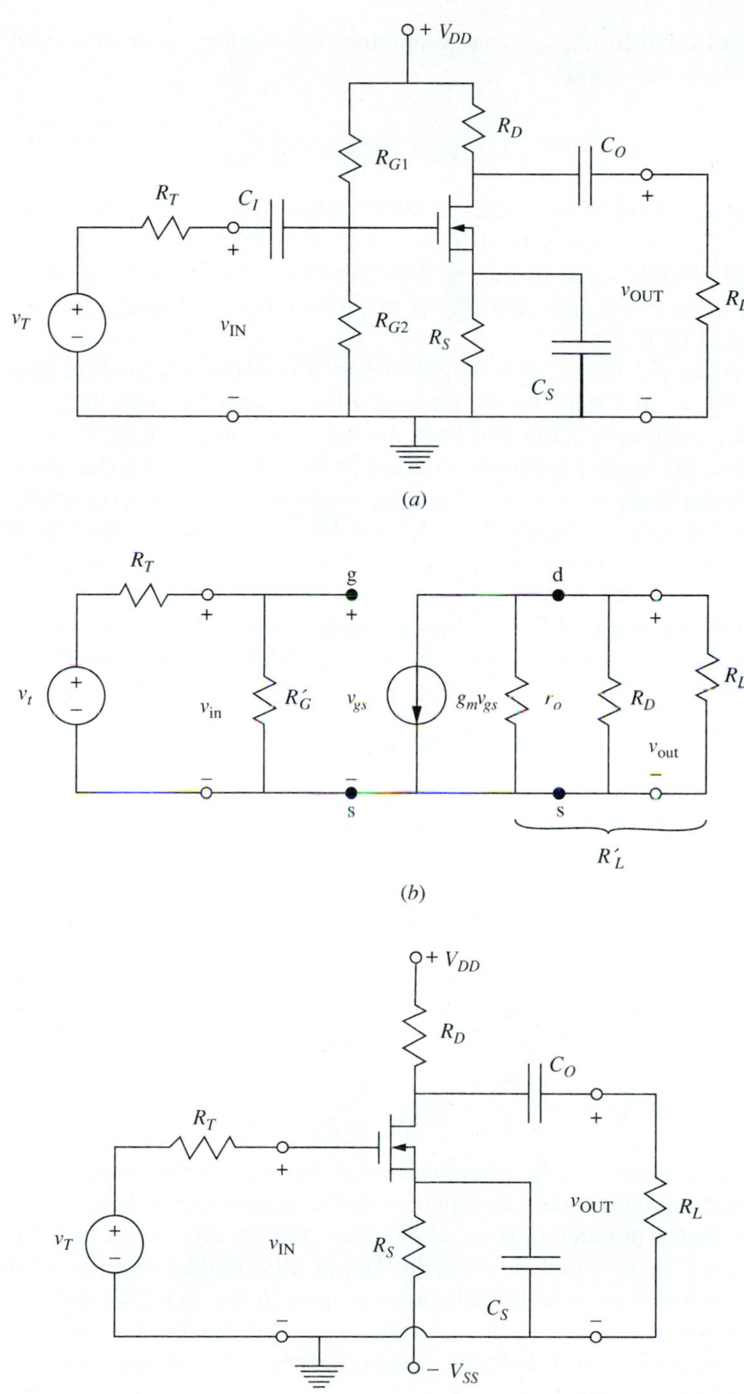

FIGURE 11.11
(*a*) Common-source amplifier circuit; (*b*) its mid-band small-signal linear equivalent circuit; (*c*) a second common-source amplifier circuit biased in such a way as to achieve an infinite mid-band input resistance (doing this requires the use of two bias supplies, V_{DD} and V_{SS}).

Another useful form for $A_{v,\max}$ can be obtained by writing I_D in saturation as $K(V_{GS} - V_T)^2/2$, which yields

$$A_{v,\max} = -\frac{2|V_A|}{|V_{GS} - V_T|} \tag{11.51c}$$

As a practical matter, it is difficult to bias an FET within several kT/q of V_T, so the factor $|V_{GS} - V_T|$ will typically be 4 to 5 kT/q. This fact, coupled with the fact that $|V_A|$ for MOSFETs tends to be less than for BJTs, results in $A_{v,\max}$ for a typical MOSFET being as much as an order of magnitude (i.e., 10 times) smaller than that of a typical BJT.

Unfortunately, as we discussed at length in Sec. 11.3.1*a*, we cannot realize a voltage gain of $A_{v,\max}$ in a stage biased through a linear output resistor because we cannot make R_D arbitrarily large and keep the transistor biased in its forward active region. Using the same arguments we used in Sec. 11.3.1*a*, we can show that to have R_D larger than r_o we must have the maximum voltage drop across R_D, which we can call $V_{D,\mathrm{MAX}}$, larger than $|V_A|$, and this is not a likely situation. It is only with active nonlinear loads, which we will discuss in the next subsection, that we can hope to approach $A_{v,\max}$.

In most situations where R_D is a linear resistor and the transistor has a reasonable Early voltage, r_o will be greater than R_D. In addition, r_o can frequently be neglected compared to R_D and R_L. In this case, the voltage gain becomes

$$A_v \approx -\frac{g_m R_L R_D}{R_D + R_L} \tag{11.52a}$$

To understand what freedom we have to make this factor large, it is helpful to write g_m in terms of its bias point dependence:

$$A_v = -\sqrt{2KI_D}\frac{R_L R_D}{R_D + R_L} \tag{11.52b}$$

As we have just said, the voltage drop $I_D R_D$ across resistor R_D can only be so large or the MOSFET will no longer be in saturation; this has important implications for the voltage gain in this case. Writing A_v to isolate this product, we have

$$A_v = -\sqrt{\frac{2K}{I_D}}I_D R_D \frac{R_L}{R_D + R_L} \tag{11.52c}$$

Written this way, we can see that the prescription for maximizing the voltage gain of a common-source stage is to use a transistor with the largest available value for K and to keep the $I_D R_D$ product as large as possible. Within this later constraint we also want to keep I_D as small as possible. Doing this implies that R_D must be made larger, which will eventually make the last term in Eq. (11.52c) smaller, but in a MOSFET circuit it is often the case that R_L is extremely large (it may even be infinite), and so R_D can usually be made quite big before it starts to have a detrimental effect on the gain.

Next consider the mid-band current gain A_i of this stage. The output current i_{out} is the fraction of $-g_m v_{gs}$ flowing through R_L, which, neglecting r_o, is $-g_m v_{gs} R_D/(R_L + R_D)$; and v_{gs} is $i_{in} R'_G$. Combining these and dividing by i_{in} yields

$$A_i = -\frac{g_m R'_G R_D}{R_D + R_L} \tag{11.53}$$

Finally, multiplying Eqs. (11.52c) and (11.53), we arrive at the mid-band power gain A_p:

$$A_p = \frac{g_m^2 R'_G R_L R_D^2}{(R_D + R_L)^2} \tag{11.54}$$

The input resistance to this stage is R'_G, and it is important to note that this factor can be much larger for an FET amplifier than is usually the case for a bipolar transistor amplifier. The intrinsic input resistance of a MOSFET is infinite, so the input resistance of the stage is finite only because of the bias resistors, R_{G1} and R_{G2}. Furthermore, since there is no quiescent gate current, we do not have the same type of limit on how large R_{G1} and R_{G2} can be as we do with base bias resistors in a bipolar circuit. The only limit is that we do have to supply charge to the gate capacitor through them, so they cannot truly be infinite; as a practical matter they might be several megaohms.

If we want a larger input resistance, we must use the bias scheme that was shown in Fig. 11.3*b*; a common-source amplifier biased in this way is illustrated in Fig. 11.11*c*. This circuit requires that we use a second bias supply voltage, but it achieves the maximum input resistance. It also eliminates the input coupling capacitor, which is also good. Before leaving this bias scheme, it is worthwhile to consider how to design it to achieve a particular I_D. At first glance this seems to be a bit messy because I_D is the solution to the quadratic

$$I_D = \frac{K}{2}(V_{SS} - I_D R_S - V_T)^2 \tag{11.55}$$

which we obtained by replacing V_{GS} in the expression for I_D of a MOSFET in saturation with $V_{SS} - I_D R_S$. Recall, however, that if you are designing a circuit to achieve a specific bias point, I_D is already known; what you need to calculate is either the value of the resistor R_S or the bias supply V_{SS}. Either of these is a relatively simple calculation given I_D.

Notice that A_i and A_p are infinite for the circuit in Fig. 11.11*c*, in which R'_G is infinite. This observation is a direct result of the infinite input resistance of FETs. In many FET circuits the mid-band current and power gain are infinite, as we have found here.

The output resistance of both of these circuits is R_D.

Example

Question. Consider a MOSFET, for which V_T is 0.9 V and K is 1 mA/V^2, used in the common-source circuit of Fig. 11.11*b* with V_{DD} = 5 V, V_{SS} = −5 V, R_D = 3 kΩ, R_S = 2.7 kΩ, and R_L = 3 kΩ. What is the mid-band linear small-signal voltage gain of this circuit?

Discussion. The bias circuit and device are the same as the ones we discussed in the example in Sec. 11.1.2, so we know that I_D is 1 mA. From Eq. (10.42b) we then find that g_m is 1.4 mS. Thus from Eq. (11.38), A_v is 2.1. This low value reflects the relatively small transconductance. The input resistance is infinite (and, thus, so too are the current and power gains); the output resistance of this stage is 3 kΩ.

b) Nonlinear and active loads. The use of FETs as active loads is very important in FET amplifier design because much more can be gained by using an active load in a FET amplifier than can be gained in a bipolar amplifier. This is true, as we shall see, in large part because the input resistance of an FET amplifier stage can be very large, often much larger than that of a bipolar amplifier gain stage, such as a common-emitter stage. A common-source stage like that in Fig. 11.11*b*, for example, ideally has an infinite input resistance, whereas the common-emitter stage in Fig. 11.4*a* has an input resistance of only a few kilo-ohms. We are typically interested in coupling several single-transistor amplifier stages together to form a multistage amplifier, as we shall see in Chap. 13; in this type of arrangement, the input resistance of one stage is the R_L of the preceding stage. In a bipolar circuit, R_{in} tends to be small (typically a few kilo-ohms) and making R_C large increases R_L' from something on the order of $R_{\text{in}}/2$ to roughly R_{in} (i.e., by a factor of 2) at best. With FET stages, on the other hand, R_{in} can be infinite and the net load resistance—R_L' in our previous discussions—is now entirely R_C. Using an active load to make R_C big is thus very attractive in this situation because increasing R_C by a factor of 10 or 100 will increase R_L' by the same factor. The payoff is much greater.*

In an integrated circuit based on n-channel enhancement mode MOSFETs, a logical first choice for an active load would be another enhancement mode MOSFET. A second choice would be an n-channel depletion mode MOSFET. Beyond that, we might consider using a p-channel MOSFET or even a *pnp* bipolar junction transistor, but these require much more complicated processing and have to be worth the trouble. To begin to understand which of these choices are worth the trouble, let us next consider what each of these possible FET loads looks like as a load. (We already know what the BJT looks like from the discussion in Sec. 11.3.1*b* and Fig. 11.7.)

Four possible MOSFET loads for an n-channel MOSFET amplifier stage are illustrated in Fig. 11.12*a* through *d*. The depletion mode device is already on, and its gate can simply be shorted to its source as in Fig. 11.12*c*. Enhancement mode devices, on the other hand, are normally off, and a voltage needs to be applied to their gates to turn them on so that they conduct and function as a finite load. The most desirable way to do this is to apply a bias between the gate

*The difference is not so dramatic if the following stage is a high input resistance stage like an emitter-follower stage, of course, but the advantage is still significant. We will discuss these issues more in Chap. 13.

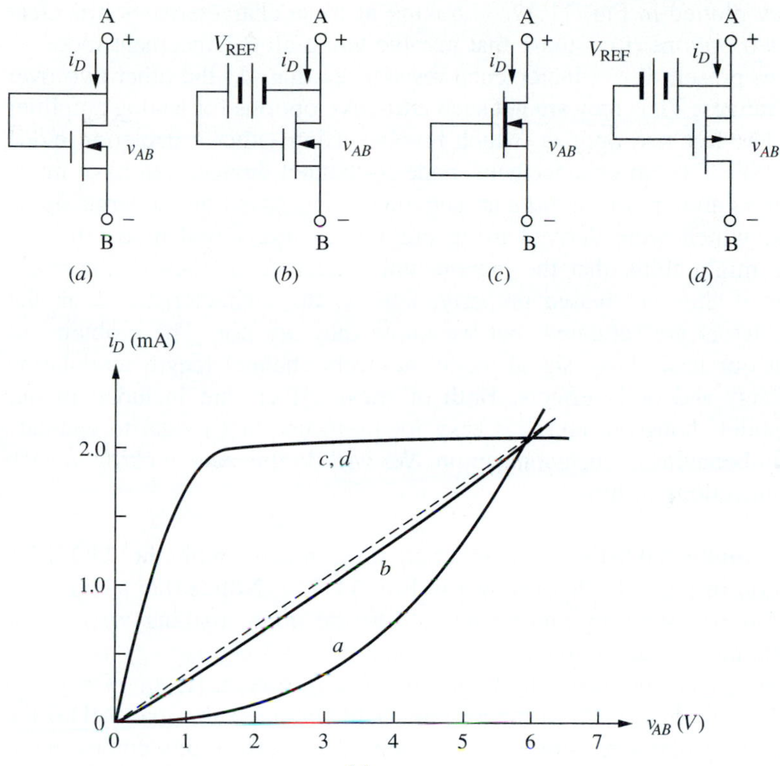

FIGURE 11.12
Four possible diode connections of MOSFETs that are useful as loads in an n-channel enhancement mode MOSFET amplifier circuit: (a) an enhancement mode n-channel MOSFET biased in saturation with $v_{GS} = v_{DS}$; (b) an enhancement mode n-channel MOSFET biased in its linear region; (c) a depletion mode n-channel MOSFET with $v_{GS} = 0$ V; (d) a p-channel enhancement mode MOSFET; (e) the large-signal diode characteristics of each connection. In plotting these characteristics it was assumed for circuit (a) that $K = 0.16$ mA/V^2 and $V_T = 1$ V; for (b) that $K = 28$ μA/V^2, $V_T = 1$ V, and $V_{REF} = 10$ V; for (c) that $K = 1$ mA/V^2 and $V_T = -2$ V; and for (d) that $K = 1$ mA/V^2, $V_T = -1$ V, and $V_{REF} = 3$ V. The characteristic of a linear resistor is shown as a dashed line for comparison.

and source, as is done for the p-channel MOSFET load in Fig. 11.12d; but doing this turns out to be impractical when using an n-channel MOSFET as a load with an n-channel amplifier MOSFET, so the bias must be applied between the drain and gate, as is seen in Figs. 11.12a and b.

There are several ways in which we can view these loads. One is to look at their large-signal characteristics in the connections shown. Realizing that the slope of the characteristic at any point is the incremental conductance of the load at that bias point, we see that the flatter the curve, the lower the conductance and the higher the resistance. The large-signal terminal characteristics of each of the connections are plotted in Fig. 11.12*e*. Looking at these characteristics it is clear that the first two options (i.e., those that involve using an enhancement mode n-channel device) present lower incremental resistances than do the other two over much of their ranges. Thus they are not such attractive options for analog amplifier applications. The last two options, which involve using either a depletion mode n-channel MOSFET or an enhancement mode p-channel device, can have much higher resistances and are much more attractive. In fact, based on the large-signal characteristics, which were derived using our basic large-signal model for the MOSFET, we might think that the incremental resistance of these connections can be infinite if they are biased properly; that is, the characteristics look flat when the transistors are saturated, but we know they are not. The problem, of course, is that our basic large-signal model neglects channel length modulation (the Early effect) and body effects. Both of these effects are included in our incremental model, however, and it is easy for us to use that model to evaluate the incremental behavior of each connection. We will do this now, looking at each of the four connections in turn.

Enhancement mode MOSFET. An inverter stage loaded with the MOSFET diode connection in Fig. 11.12*a* is shown in Fig. 11.13*a*. Notice that to turn this device "on" it is necessary to connect its gate to the drain, making v_{GSL} equal to v_{DSL}.* Thus the device is clearly always saturated as long as v_{DSL} is greater than V_{TL}, since v_{DSL} is automatically larger than $(v_{GSL} - V_{TL})$. [If $v_{DSL}(= v_{GSL})$ is less than V_{TL}, the device is no longer "on."] In this case the load MOSFET looks incrementally like a resistor of magnitude $1/g_{mL}$. How this comes about is illustrated in Fig. 11.13*b*. As shown in (i), the gate and drain are connected together; thus, as shown in (ii), $v_{gs} = v_{ds}$ and the dependent current generator $g_m v_{gs}$ can also be written as $g_m v_{ds}$. Electrically this is equivalent to having a conductance of magnitude g_m in parallel with g_o between the drain and source; this is shown in (iii). In most devices, g_m will be much larger than g_o and we arrive at our result: the load looks like a resistor of magnitude $1/g_{mL}$. In the present situation g_{mL} is $K_L(V_{DD} - V_{\text{OUT}} - V_{TL})$ since v_{GSL} is $(V_{DD} - V_{\text{OUT}})$; the incremental equivalent circuit is as shown in Fig. 11.13*c*. Unfortunately, however, this incremental load resistance is less than the static resistance V_{DSL}/I_{DL} by a factor of $(V_{DD} - V_{\text{OUT}} - V_{TL})/2(V_{DD} - V_{\text{OUT}})$. To see this we simply use the fact that V_{DSL} is $(V_{DD} - V_{\text{OUT}})$ and I_{DL} is $K_L(V_{DD} - V_{\text{OUT}} - V_{TL})^2/2$ and compare their ratio to $1/g_{mL}$. Since the active load resistance is lower, we are better off (at least in this case) using a linear resistor!

A partial solution to this problem is to connect the gate to a third supply, V_{GG}, as shown in Fig. 11.14*a*, and to force the load FET into its linear region. Now the load MOSFET again looks incrementally like g_{mL} in parallel with g_{oL}

---

*Note that an additional subscript has been added here to distinguish between the two FETs in this circuit. The upper FET (the one connected to V_{DD}) is the load device, and we use an "L" with it. We call the other FET the "driver" and use a "D" with it.

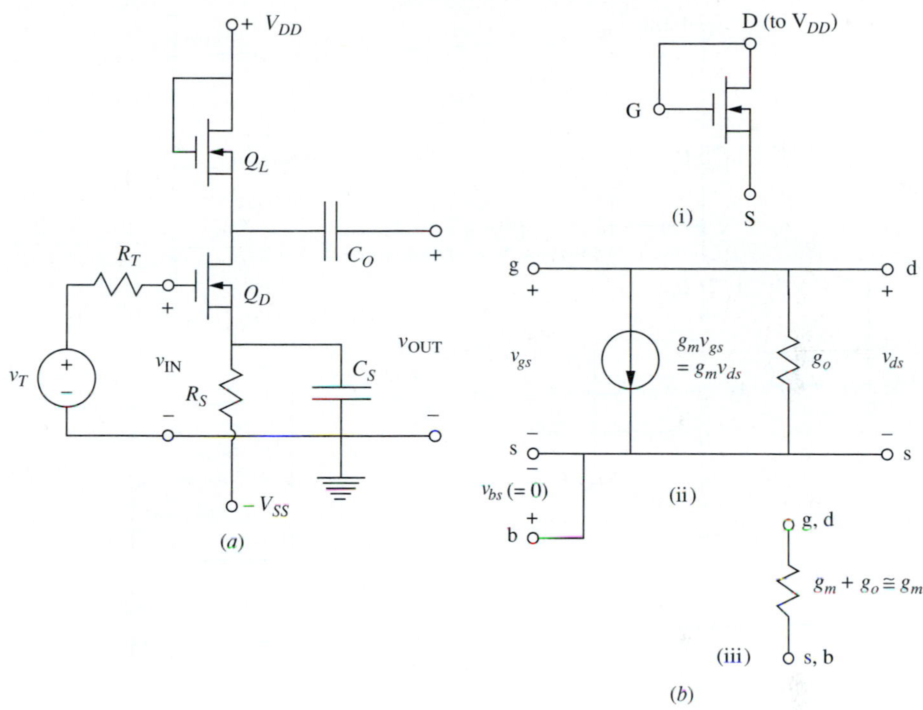

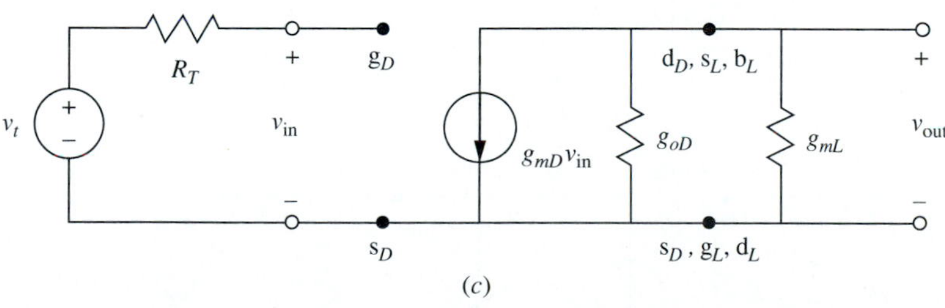

FIGURE 11.13
Use of a saturated enhancement mode MOSFET as the load in a common-source amplifier stage: (*a*) the complete stage; (*b*) (i) the load connection, (ii) the small-signal equivalent circuit, and (iii) the effective equivalent circuit forming the load; (*c*) the incremental equivalent circuit of the stage.

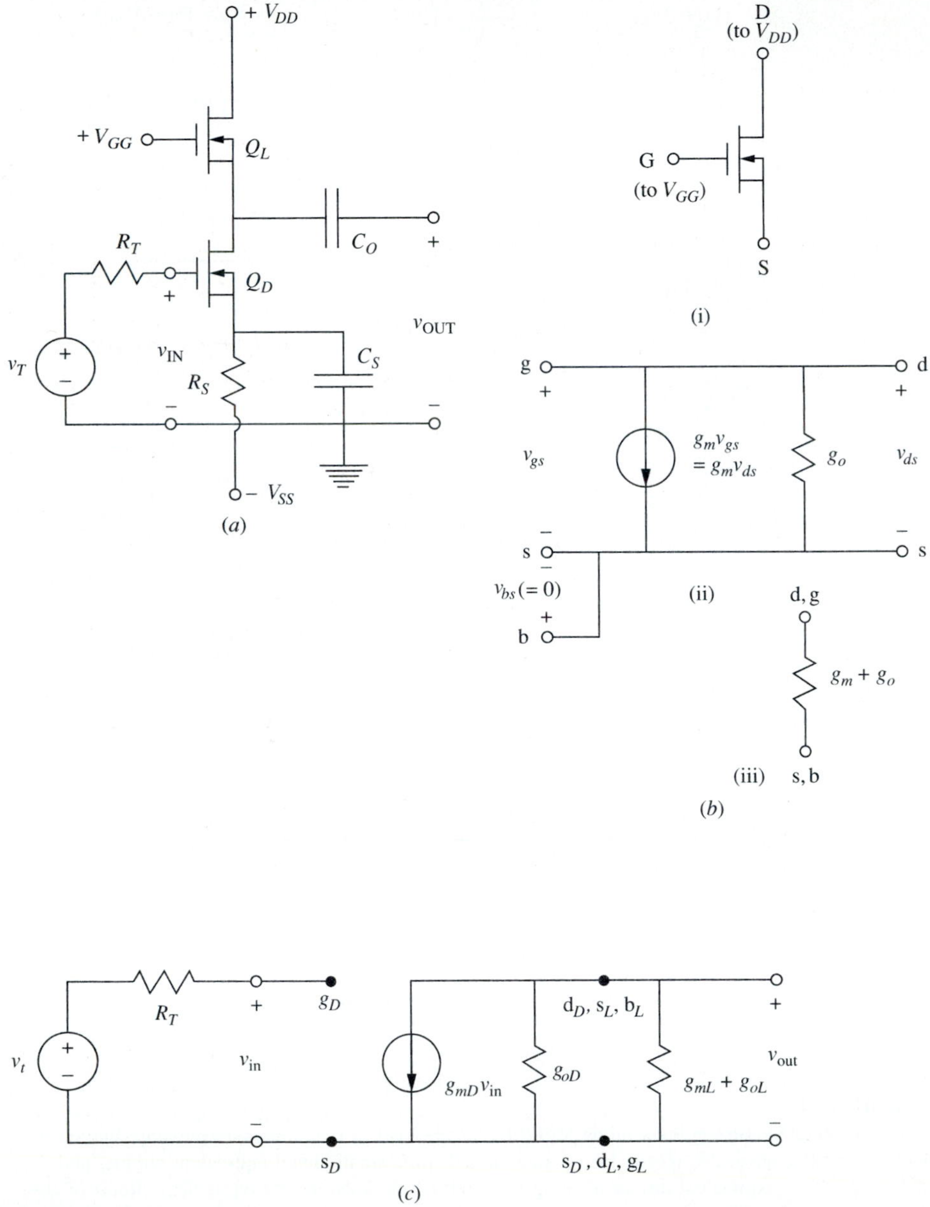

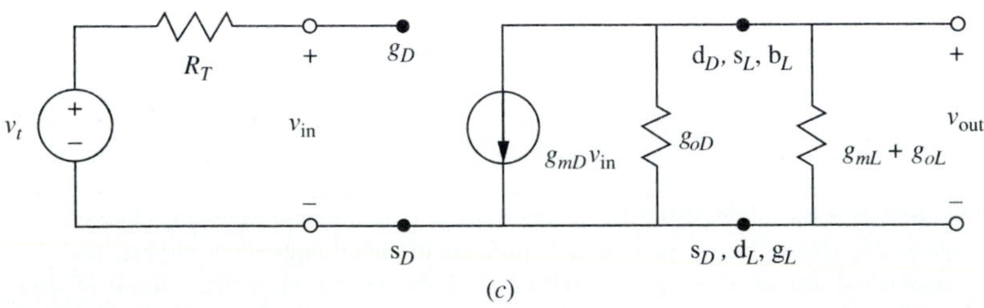

FIGURE 11.14
Use of an enhancement mode MOSFET strongly biased in its linear region as the load in a common-source amplifier stage: (*a*) the entire circuit; (*b*) (i) the load connection, (ii) the small-signal equivalent circuit, and (iii) the effective equivalent circuit forming the load; (*c*) the incremental equivalent circuit of the entire stage.

(as Fig. 11.14*b* shows), but now g_{mL} is smaller than before. This load looks very much like a linear resistor as V_{GG} is made very large. Nonetheless, an enhancement mode load is never any better than using a linear resistor. Having to provide another voltage supply is also a major complication—not so much because it has to supply much current (it is, after all, connected only to MOSFET gates) but rather because it has to be wired to all those gates. The only advantage that using this circuit might have over using a simple resistor load is that a MOSFET occupies less area in an integrated circuit layout than a resistor.

Depletion mode MOSFET (*n*-MOS). A far better active load is an *n*-channel depletion mode MOSFET. If we are making an integrated circuit, we presumably already have enhancement mode FETs in our process, and it turns out that simultaneously making depletion mode FETs is not particularly difficult or costly. The resulting circuit is shown in Fig. 11.15*a*, and the incremental equivalent circuits for the load device and the entire stage are shown in Figs. 11.15*b* and *c*, respectively.

There are several important new features in the circuit of Fig. 11.15*a* that you should note before proceeding. First, notice that it is biased using the scheme of Fig. 11.3*c*, in which a large resistance R_G is placed between the drain and gate of the driver transistor to ensure that it is biased in saturation and, equally important, that it is biased at a level of drain current set by the load, which is another saturated FET (i.e., a current source). (The depletion mode load MOSFET is saturated as long as $V_{DD} - v_{\text{OUT}}$ is greater than the magnitude of the threshold of the load MOSFET.) With two current sources in series, as we have here, we are asking for trouble unless the current in one depends on the current in the other in some way; the use of R_G to bias the driver so that it tracks the load is a very convenient solution to this problem. It is certainly much simpler than the arrangement that had to be used in the analogous bipolar circuit in Fig. 11.5. It is not without its cost, however, as you will explore in the problems in this chapter and Chap. 14. In our static analysis we can let R_G be arbitrarily large so that any problems disappear.

The second thing to notice about the circuit of Fig. 11.15*a* is that the substrate terminal of the load FET is not connected to the source as it was in Figs. 11.11 through 11.14; instead, it is grounded. This is more realistic because it represents the situation in an integrated circuit where all of the devices share a common substrate that is incrementally grounded. Thus the substrate generator g_{mbL} should be included as it is in Fig. 11.15*b*. Strictly speaking, we should also have done this in Figs 11.11 through 11.14, but doing so there would not have changed our results significantly. Now, the situation is very different. The incremental load resistance is now $1/(g_{mbL} + g_{oL})$, as Fig. 11.15*c* shows, and if the bias is such that the load FET is saturated, g_{mbL} will dominate this expression and the small-signal voltage gain of the stage will be approximately g_{mD}/g_{mbL}. This is much larger than we could achieve with a linear resistor load, but it is less than if v_{bsL} were zero and the substrate generator did not play a role.

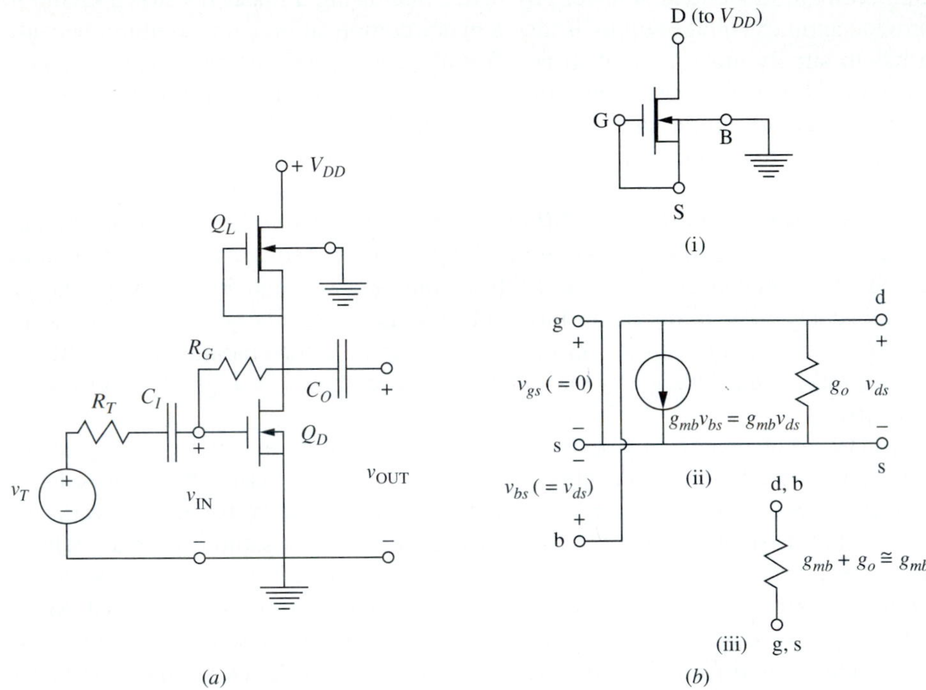

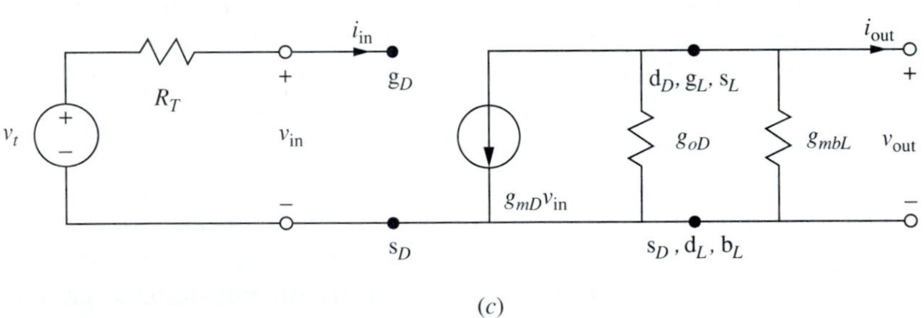

(c)

FIGURE 11.15
Use of a saturated depletion mode MOSFET as the load in a common-source amplifier stage: (*a*) the complete stage; (*b*) (i) the load connection, (ii) the small-signal equivalent circuit, and (iii) the effective equivalent circuit forming the load; (*c*) the incremental equivalent circuit of the entire stage. We assume that R_G can be made arbitrarily large and subsequently neglected in the incremental circuit.

It is instructive to look at the gain expression further by using our expressions for the model parameters in terms of the bias point. We have, assuming no loading from subsequent stages:

$$A_v \cong -\frac{g_{mD}}{g_{mbL}} \tag{11.56a}$$

In terms of the bias point, these conductances are

$$g_{mD} = \sqrt{2K_D I_{DD}} \tag{11.57a}$$

and

$$g_{mbL} \equiv \eta g_{mD} = \eta \sqrt{2K_L I_{DL}} \tag{11.57b}$$

Combining all of these results and noting also that I_{DL} and I_{DD} are equal, we have

$$A_v \cong -\frac{1}{\eta}\sqrt{\frac{K_D}{K_L}} \tag{11.56b}$$

Finally, recalling that K is $(W/L)\mu_e(\varepsilon_{\text{ox}}/t_{\text{ox}})$, we see that this can be written as

$$A_v \simeq -\frac{1}{\eta}\sqrt{\frac{W_D}{W_L}\frac{L_L}{L_D}} \tag{11.56c}$$

We see from this equation that the gain of this stage depends not on the bias current (as long as the MOSFETs are biased in saturation) but rather on the MOSFET dimensions and the factor η. With regard to the dimensions, it is clear that to get the largest possible voltage gain we want the driver device to be wide and short and the load device to be narrow and long.

Complementary MOSFET (CMOS). To eliminate the substrate generator and obtain the highest possible gain from a MOSFET amplifier stage, we need to be able to separate the substrates of the load and driver devices. A particularly elegant way to do this in an integrated circuit is to use a p-channel device for the load of an n-channel driver as is shown in Fig. 11.16*a*. For this to work, this circuit must be made perfectly symmetrical in the sense that Q_3 is identical to Q_4, Q_1 to Q_2, and R_{S1} to R_{S2}. Because this circuit involves both n- and p-channel devices, it is called a complementary MOS, or CMOS, circuit.

In CMOS circuits, the p-type substrate region of the n-channel device is isolated from the n-type substrate region of the p-channel device by the p-n junction at their interface as illustrated in Fig. 11.17. This junction is reverse-biased because, as the circuit illustrates, the p-type substrate of the n-channel device is connected to either ground or a negative voltage supply V_{SS}, and the n-type substrate of the n-channel device is connected to the positive voltage supply V_{DD}. The processing required to fabricate both n- and p-channel devices on the same silicon wafer is complicated, but the technology to do so has been thoroughly developed for digital integrated circuits, where CMOS technology also has major advantages over other technologies, as we shall see in Chap. 15. Thus, although the processing is more complicated, it is economical to use CMOS circuits in linear circuit design.

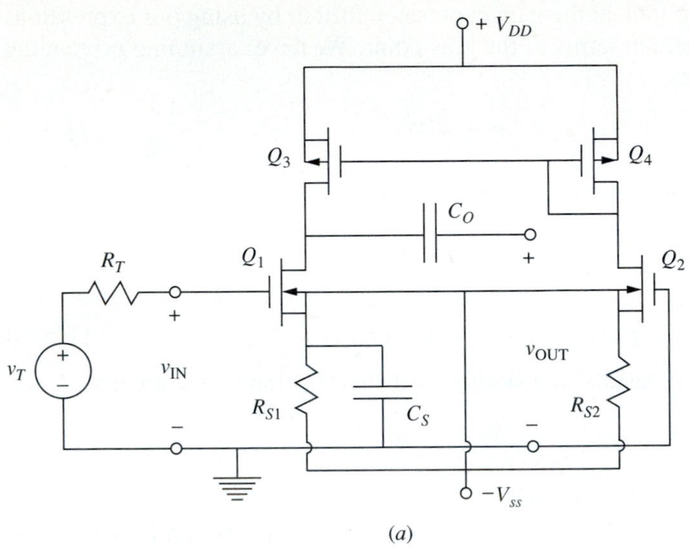

(*a*)

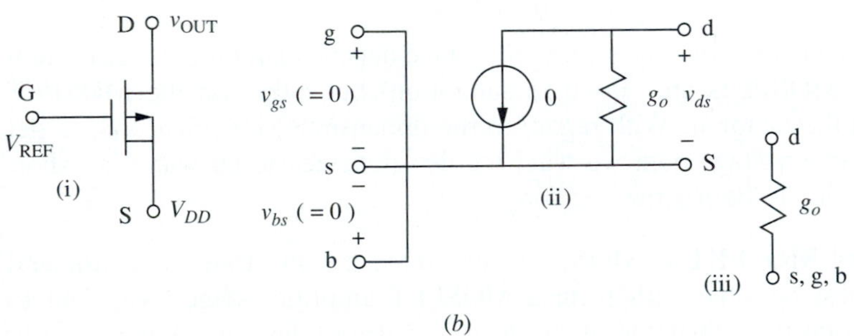

(*b*)

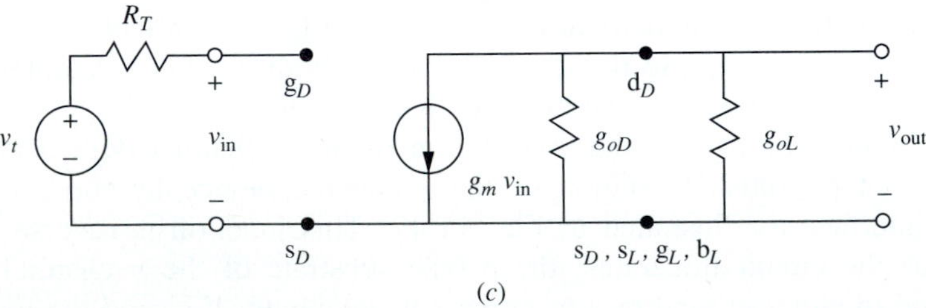

(*c*)

FIGURE 11.16
Use of a *p*-channel enhancement mode MOSFET biased in saturation as the load in a common-source amplifier stage with an *n*-channel driver—the basic complementary MOS (CMOS) amplifier stage: (*a*) the entire circuit; (*b*) (i) the load connection, (ii) the small-signal equivalent circuit, and (iii) the effective equivalent circuit forming the load; (*c*) the incremental equivalent circuit of the entire stage.

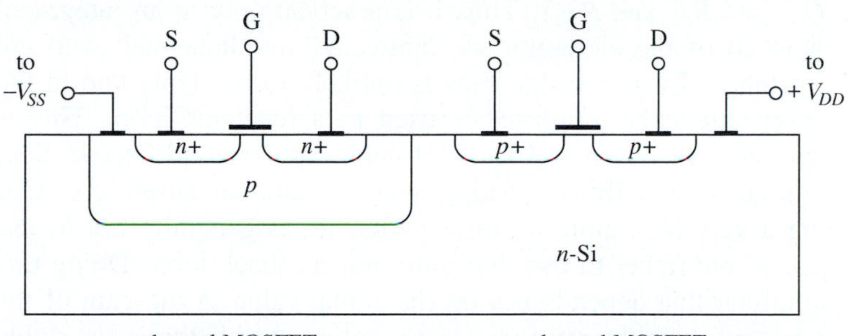

FIGURE 11.17
Cross-sectional drawing of a complementary MOS integrated circuit, illustrating how a p-type "substrate region" is formed in an otherwise n-type wafer and showing that there is a p-n junction formed between the n- and p-type regions. Other examples of CMOS structures are to be found in App. G.

The fact that the substrate and source of the load FET in the CMOS circuit are connected means that the load looks simply like the g_o of the load FET in parallel with the g_o of the driver device, as is illustrated in Fig. 11.16*c*. The load device is biased into saturation to maximize its output resistance using a scheme analogous to that used when a *pnp* bipolar transistor was used as a load for an *npn* common-emitter stage in Fig. 11.7*b*. As was the case there, this type of load is usually implemented in a differential amplifier context rather than a single-transistor amplifier context, and is then called a current mirror. (We will study differential amplifiers in Chap. 12 and current mirrors in Chap. 13.) CMOS amplifiers like this can have very high gains, as we shall see next, and are very important in integrated amplifier design.

Looking further at the gain of this stage, we have, assuming no loading from the following stage (i.e., R_L infinite),

$$A_v = \frac{g_m}{g_{oD} + g_{oL}} \tag{11.58a}$$

With this result we see that at last we are approaching the maximum possible common-source voltage gain $A_{v,\max}$ given in Eq. (11.51a).

Writing the output conductances in terms of the Early voltages and I_D, and writing the transconductance in terms of I_D, we can study the bias dependence of this gain. We have

$$A_v = \frac{\sqrt{2K_D I_D}}{I_D[(1/V_{AD}) + (1/V_{AL})]} = \sqrt{\frac{2K_D}{I_D}} \frac{V_{AD}V_{AL}}{V_{AD} + V_{AL}} \tag{11.58b}$$

Looking at this expression we see that there are very few design decisions that need to be made to make a high-gain CMOS amplifier. Clearly we want a large K_D and large Early voltages, and beyond that we simply want to make the drain current as small as practical.

A word of caution is in order at this point concerning the circuit in Fig. 11.16*a*. This circuit relies heavily on exact matching of the components (i.e., Q_1

and Q_2, Q_3 and Q_4, and R_{S1} and R_{S2}). Thus it is practical only in an integrated circuit context where all of the elements are fabricated simultaneously and are thus very closely matched. Even then the bias is unlikely to be stable and in the forward active region unless the amplifier is used in a feedback loop. This is the same type of problem we discussed for high-gain bipolar amplifiers in Sec. 11.3.1*b* and is familiar to you from working with operational amplifiers. Our objective in making a very high-gain amplifier, after all, is generally not to use all of that gain directly, but rather to use that gain in a feedback loop. Doing this we can make an amplifier that depends not on the actual value of the gain of the high-gain element but rather on the ratio of resistor values, and is thus very stable and highly predictable. We also can make many other circuits this way that are useful in signal processing applications (i.e., multipliers, adders, etc.), circuits you are familiar with from your work with generic operational amplifiers.

11.4.2 Degenerate-source

The sensitivity of an FET amplifier to the specific device characteristics and to the bias point can be reduced by using feedback, just as was possible with bipolar

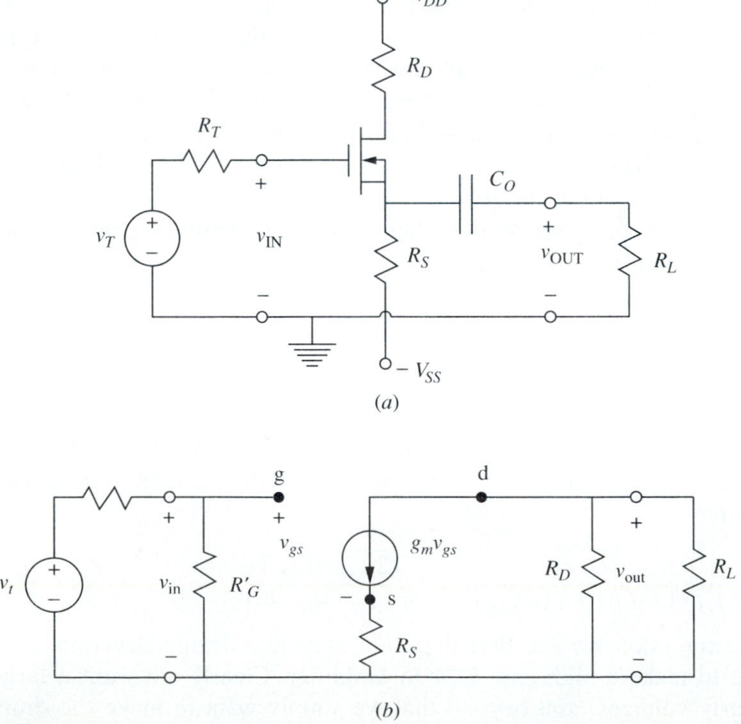

FIGURE 11.18
(*a*) Degenerate-source amplifier; (*b*) the mid-band small-signal linear equivalent circuit.

transistor amplifiers by using emitter degeneracy. Here the analogous solution is source degeneracy. A resistively biased degenerate-source FET amplifier circuit using two bias supplies is illustrated in Fig. 11.18*a*. The corresponding mid-band linear equivalent small-signal circuit is illustrated in Fig. 11.18*b*. Notice that we have included an R'_G in this equivalent circuit to allow for resistor divider biasing as in Fig. 11.11*a*; R'_G is, of course, infinite for the circuit in Fig. 11.18*a*.

Looking at the mid-band circuit, we see that the voltage gain is now given as

$$A_v = -\frac{g_m R'_L}{1 + g_m R_S} \tag{11.59a}$$

If $g_m R_S$ is much greater than 1, we have

$$A_v \approx -\frac{R'_L}{R_S} \tag{11.59b}$$

In practice, g_m is usually smaller in FET circuits than in bipolar transistor circuits, so this may not always be a good approximation.

The input and output resistances are R'_G and R_D, respectively, as they are in the common-source circuit. Notice that because the FET input resistance is already infinite, the presence of R_S does not increase R_{in}, whereas having a resistor in the emitter circuit of a bipolar transistor amplifier does increase its R_{in}.

11.4.3 Common-gate

On occasion it is useful to have a field effect transistor stage with a low input resistance; in such situations a common-gate topology can be used. An example is shown in Fig. 11.19*a*, and its mid-band small-signal linear equivalent circuit is shown in Fig. 11.19*b*.

Looking at this circuit we see that the mid-band input resistance R_{in} is given by

$$R_{\text{in}} = R_S \parallel \frac{1}{(\eta + 1)g_m} = \frac{R_S}{1 + (\eta + 1)g_m R_S} \tag{11.60}$$

(Remember that η is g_{mb}/g_m and is less than 1.) This is always less than R_S, and in the limit of the product $(\eta + 1)g_m R_S$ being much greater than 1, R_{in} approaches $1/(\eta + 1)g_m$, which will be much less than R_S. The output resistance R_{out} of the common-gate circuit is R_D, as it was in our two earlier FET circuits.

The mid-band voltage gain A_v of this stage is large, that is, $(\eta + 1)g_m R'_L$, where R'_L is the parallel combination of R_L and R_D; and the mid-band current gain A_i is given by

$$A_i = \frac{(\eta + 1)g_m R_S R_D}{[1 + (\eta + 1)g_m R_S](R_L + R_D)} \tag{11.61}$$

This is essentially 1. Strictly speaking, it is always less than 1, but it approaches 1 in the limit $g_m R_S \gg 1$ and $R_D \gg R_L$, which is typically the case.

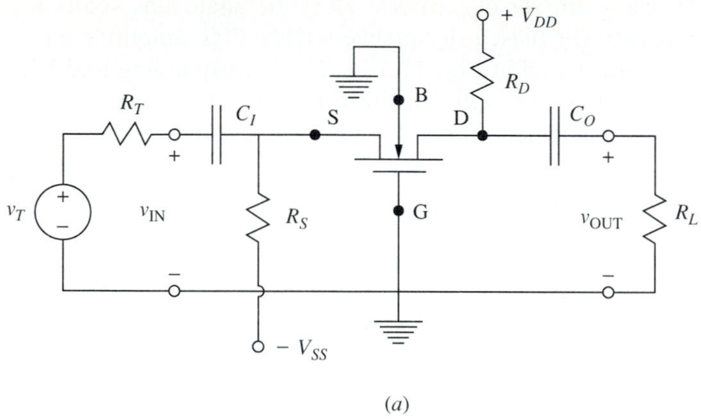

(*a*)

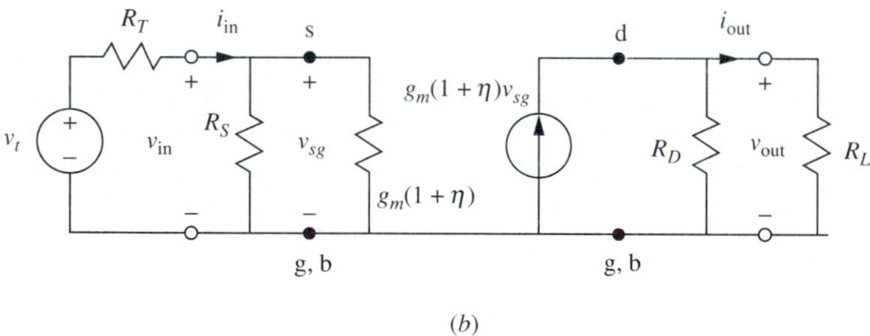

(*b*)

FIGURE 11.19
(*a*) Common-gate amplifier; (*b*) the mid-band small-signal linear equivalent circuit.

11.4.4 Source-follower

The final field effect transistor stage we consider in this chapter, the source-follower stage, has a large input resistance but a low output resistance. In that sense it is just like the emitter-follower circuit, and both are used in similar ways in multistage circuits. The circuit is shown in Fig. 11.20*a*. The mid-band voltage gain of this stage would ideally be 1, as it is for the emitter-follower. Notice, however, that the source is not grounded, so the substrate generator (back-gating effect) must be included; this places an important limitation on us. Looking at Fig. 11.20*b*, and noting that $v_{gs} = v_{\text{in}} - v_{\text{out}}$, we see that A_v is

$$A_v = \frac{1}{1 + (g_{mb} + G_S + G_L)/g_m} \tag{11.62a}$$

Using the relationship $g_{mb} = \eta g_m$, this becomes

$$A_v = \frac{1}{1 + \eta + (G_S + G_L)/g_m} \approx \frac{1}{1+\eta} \tag{11.62b}$$

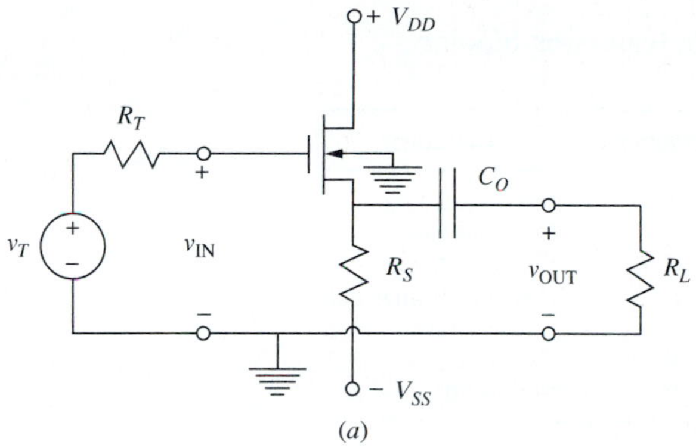

(a)

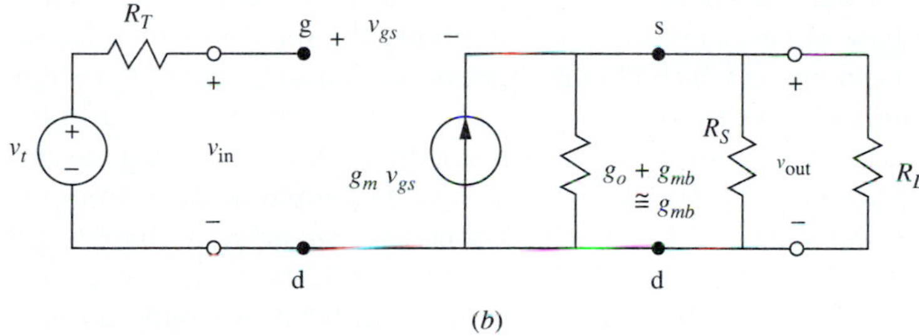

(b)

FIGURE 11.20
(a) Source-follower amplifier; (b) the mid-band linear equivalent circuit. Note that since $v_{bs} = v_{ds}$, the substrate generator factor g_{mb} enters in parallel with g_o. Notice also that $v_{gs} = v_{in} - v_{out}$.

We can expect R_L and R_S to be large, so that the factor $(G_S + G_L)/g_m$ is much less than 1, in which case the voltage gain is approximately $1/(1 + \eta)$. Recalling that η might be as large as a few tenths, it is easy to see the negative impact that the back-gating effect has on A_v. The back-gating effect can be eliminated by fabricating the n-channel MOSFET in a p-well (see Fig. 11.17, p. 359), so the back gate can be connected to the source and v_{BS} made zero.

The mid-band input resistance of this stage is infinite, but the output resistance R_{out} is small. A little consideration shows that R_{out} is given by

$$R_{out} = \frac{1}{g_m + g_{mb} + g_o + G_S} \approx \frac{1}{g_m(1 + \eta)} \tag{11.63}$$

11.5 SUMMARY

Before summarizing the results of our single-transistor amplifier discussion and proceeding on to more complicated circuits, it is interesting to ask whether we have missed any useful connections. If we concentrate for the sake of discussion on bipolar transistors, there are six possible connections because the input can be applied to any of the three terminals (base, emitter, or collector) and the output can be taken off either one of the other two. The six configurations are presented in Table 11.1.

TABLE 11.1
The six possible single-transistor bipolar amplifier stages.

Input	Output	Common	Comment
E	B	C	Not useful
E	C	B	Common-base
B	E	C	Emitter-follower
B	C	E	Common-emitter and degenerate-emitter
C	E	B	Not useful
C	B	E	Not useful

Although all of these connections are possible, as a practical matter taking the output off the base is never useful; nor is applying the input to the collector. This leaves the connections in which (1) the input is applied to the emitter and the output is taken from the collector (common-base), (2) the input is applied to the base and the output is taken from the collector (common-emitter and degenerate-emitter), and (3) the input is applied to the base and the output is taken from the emitter (emitter-follower). Notice that for the second case we actually studied two circuits, one in which the third terminal (the emitter in this case) was connected directly to ground (common-emitter) and one in which it went to ground through a feedback resistor (degenerate-emitter). The same choice of adding a resistor between the third terminal and ground exists for the other two cases as well, but neither of the circuits resulting from adding feedback like this are useful. In the common-base arrangement, adding such feedback is a bad idea because the objective in using this circuit is to get a low input resistance; putting a resistor between the base terminal and ground only increases the input resistance. In the emitter-follower arrangement, putting a resistor between the collector and ground does not change any of the mid-band characteristics of the stage and so gains us nothing. Thus we can rest assured that we have identified the complete set of useful single-transistor linear amplifier stages.

The characteristics of these stages are summarized in Table 11.2. Roughly speaking, the common-emitter and common-source stages combine large voltage and current gains, and have moderate-to-large input and output resistances. They have the highest power gain of any of the stages. Adding a resistor to the common terminal to create the degenerate-emitter and degenerate-source stages lowers the gains but at the same time makes them more independent of the device parameters and thus more stable and predictable. The input resistance is also increased.

The common-base and common-gate stages have good voltage gains but their current gains are always less than 1. Their most attractive feature is a low input resistance. The emitter-follower and source-follower stages, on the other hand, are of interest because they have very large input resistances and low output resistances. They have good current gains, but their voltage gains are typically a bit less than 1.

TABLE 11.2
Summary of the principal characteristics of the useful single-transistor amplifier stages. (Detailed expressions for each of these characteristics for each of the stages can be found in Secs. 11.3 and 11.4 of the text.)

Stage	A_v	A_i	A_p	R_{in}	R_{out}
Common-emitter Common-source	Large	Large	Large	Medium	Large
Degenerate-emitter Degenerate-source	Medium	Medium	Medium	Large	Large
Common-base Common-gate	Large	$\lesssim 1$	Medium	Small	Large
Emitter-follower Source-follower	$\lesssim 1$	Large	Medium	Large	Small

PROBLEMS

11.1 Consider the three bipolar transistor bias circuits in Figure 11.2 when V_{CC} is 5 V, R_C is 1 kΩ, and R_{B1} in Figs. 11.2*a* and 11.2*c* is 20 kΩ; assume for this transistor that $V_{BE,ON} = 0.6$ V and $\beta_F = 100$.

(*a*) Select values for R_{B2} or R_B, as appropriate, to result in a quiescent collector current I_C of 1 mA.

(*b*) Imagine that the transistor you used in part a is replaced by one for which $V_{BE,ON}$ is 0.7 V and β_F is 100. What is the value of I_C in each circuit now, assuming the same resistor values as in part a?

(*c*) Imagine next that the transistor in part a is replaced by one for which $V_{BE,ON}$ is 0.6 V and β_F is 75. Now what is the value of I_C in each circuit, assuming the same resistor values as in part a?

(*d*) Comment on your results in parts b and c. Which bias circuit is more stable (i.e., for which does I_C vary the least)?

11.2 (*a*) What is the open-circuit voltage gain (i.e., A_v when $R_L = \infty$) of the circuit in the examples on pages 322 and 333?

(*b*) Redesign the biasing for this circuit so that the input resistance is 2.5 kΩ. This will require that you change I_C; keep V_{CC} and R_C the same and allow the same output swing (i.e., ±3 V).

(*c*) What is the open-circuit voltage gain of your new circuit?

(*d*) If R_C in this circuit is replaced by a bipolar junction transistor current source, as illustrated in Figure 11.7, and the magnitude of the Early voltage of the *npn* transistor is 100 V and of the *pnp* is 50 V, what is the open-circuit voltage gain of the original circuit (i.e., when $I_C = 1$ mA)? What is the open-circuit voltage gain of the circuit when it is biased as in part b?

11.3 Consider the circuit illustrated in Fig. P11.3. The transistor in this circuit is an *n*-channel enhancement mode MOSFET for which K is 0.1 mA/V^2, V_T is 0.8 V, and $|V_A|$ is 10 V. The two supply voltages, V_{DD} and V_{SS}, are +5 V and −5 V, respectively.

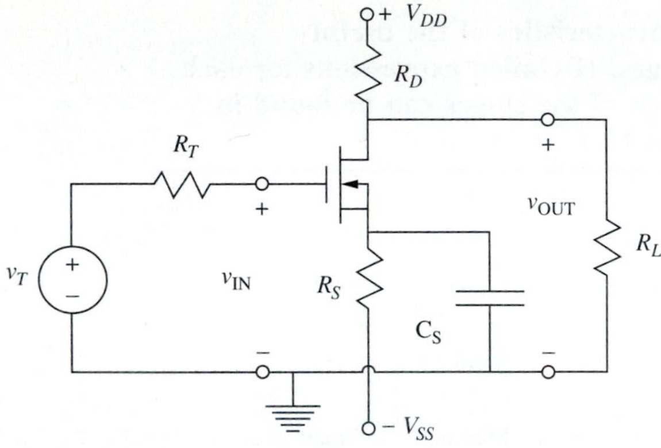

FIGURE P11.3

(*a*) Select R_S and R_D so that I_D is 0.2 mA, V_{IN} is 0 V, and V_{OUT} is 0 V.

(*b*) Draw a mid-band linear equivalent circuit for this amplifier valid for operation about the bias point you designed for in part a.

(*c*) Calculate the mid-band voltage gain A_v at the bias point in part a for the following load resistor values:

(i) $R_L = 1\ \text{k}\Omega$

(ii) $R_L = \infty$

(*d*) What is the small signal output resistance R_{out} of this stage for the bias point in part a?

11.4 Consider a common-source amplifier like those in Figure 11.11 but biased using the circuit in Figure 11.3*b*. Such an amplifier is shown in Fig. P11.4.

(*a*) Show that R_{in} is much less than R_G and that the reduction can be related to the mid-band voltage gain of this stage.

(*b*) Derive an expression for the mid-band incremental input resistance R_{in} of this circuit.

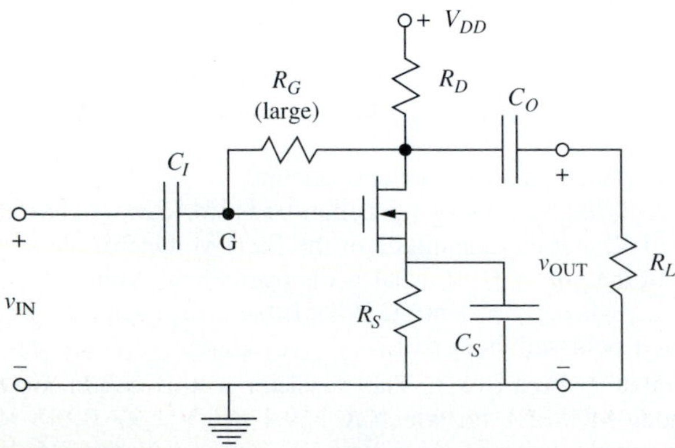

FIGURE P11.4

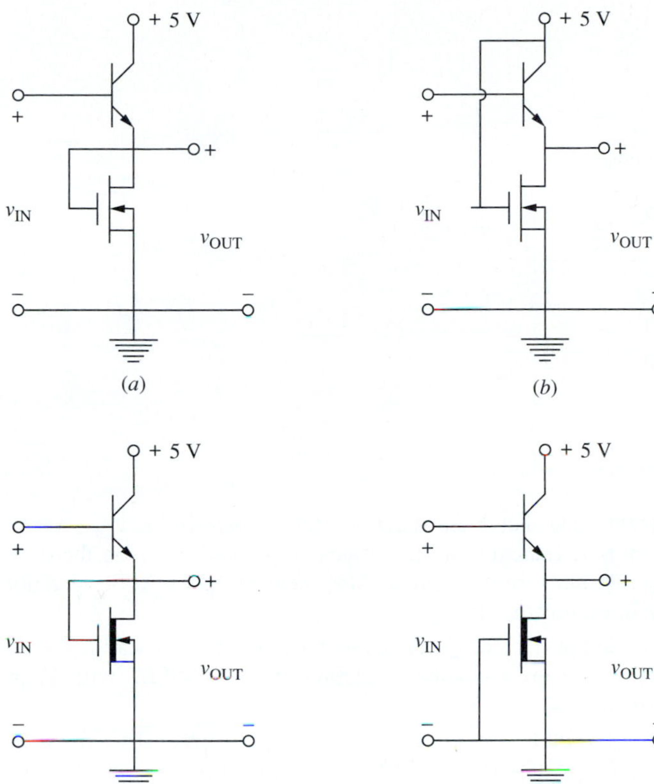

FIGURE P11.5

11.5 Consider the four emitter-follower circuits illustrated in Fig. P11.5, all of which have n-channel MOSFETs for loads. Notice that two of the circuits (A and B) have enhancement mode devices with $V_T = 1$ V as their loads, and that the other two (C and D) have depletion mode devices with $V_T = -1$ V for loads. K is 0.1 mA/V^2 for both the depletion and enhancement mode devices.

(a) For each of the four circuits, calculate the following parameters:

(i) $V_{IN,MIN}$: the minimum input voltage that will ensure that neither transistor is cut off.

(ii) $V_{OUT}(v_{IN} = V_{IN,MIN})$: the value of V_{OUT} for v_{IN} equal to the minimum v_{IN} found in (i).

(iii) $V_{OUT,MAX}$: the maximum value that the output voltage can have that will still ensure that the circuit will behave as a proper emitter-follower.

(iv) $V_{IN}(v_{OUT} = V_{OUT,MAX})$: the value of V_{IN} that results in the maximum v_{OUT} found in (iii).

(v) $I_{C,MAX}$: the maximum collector current for v_{IN} in the range between the values in (i) and (iv).

(vi) $g_c(v_{OUT} = V_{CC}/2)$: the incremental conductance of the MOSFET load transistor when the output voltage is 2.5 V. If the output can never have this value of a particular circuit, state this fact.

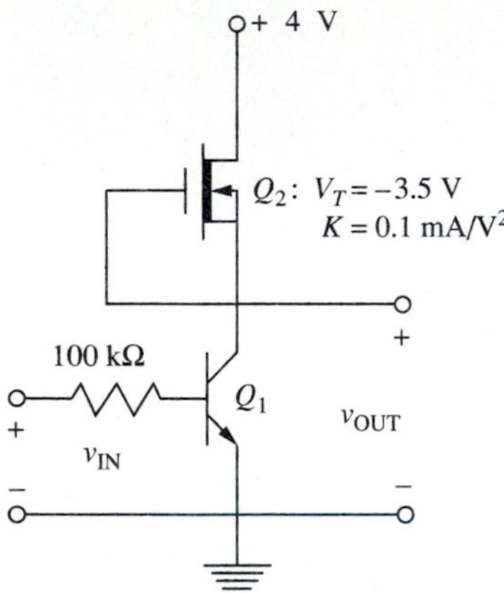

FIGURE P11.6

(*b*) For circuit D, calculate and sketch the static transfer characteristics, v_{OUT} versus v_{IN}, for $0 \leq v_{IN} \leq 6$ V. Indicate the key values of v_{IN} and v_{OUT} on the characteristic that separate the various regions. Also indicate the mode of operation of each transistor in each of the regions.

11.6 In the circuit illustrated in Fig. P11.6, Q_1 is an *npn* bipolar transistor with $\beta_F = 25$ and $v_{BE,\text{ON}} = 0.6$ V. Q_2 is an n-channel depletion mode MOSFET with $V_T = -3.5$ V, and $K = 0.1$ mA/V^2.

Notice that the MOSFET is connected so that v_{GS} is zero. Thus its drain current i_D is given by $KV_T^2/2$, which is about 0.6 mA, for $v_{DS} \geq -V_T$ (i.e., for $v_{DS} \geq 3.5$ V); and by $K(-V_T - v_{DS}/2)$, which equals $0.1(3.5 - v_{DS}/2)v_{DS}$ mA, for $0 \leq v_{DS} \leq 3.5$ V.

(*a*) (i) For what range of input voltages v_{IN} between 0 and 4 V will Q_1 be cut off?

(ii) What is v_{OUT} in this range?

(*b*) When Q_1 just begins to turn on and have nonzero base and collector currents, in what operating region is Q_2, and why?

(*c*) (i) What is v_{OUT} at the boundary between the linear and saturation regions of Q_2?

(ii) What would v_{IN} have to be to reach this point?

(*d*) (i) Draw a small-signal linear equivalent circuit for this circuit, valid for operation about the bias point $V_{IN} = 2.6$ V, $V_{OUT} = 2$ V. (*Note:* You should find for this operating point that Q_2 is biased in its linear region.)

(ii) Calculate the small–signal linear voltage gain $A_v \equiv v_{out}/v_{in}$ of this circuit for operation about this bias point.

(*e*) What would happen to v_{OUT} and to the transistor Q_1 if v_{IN} is increased beyond the value you found in (ii) of part c? Discuss briefly.

11.7 For the circuit in Fig. P11.7 we have the following:

$Q_1 := \beta_F = 150$; $v_{BE,\text{ON}} = 0.6$ V; $v_{CE,\text{SAT}} = 0.2$ V

Q_2: $K = 1$ mA/V^2; $V_T = 1$ V; $\eta = 10^{-2}$ (where $g_{mb} = \eta g_m$)

$R_1 = 9$ kΩ, $R_2 = 3$ kΩ

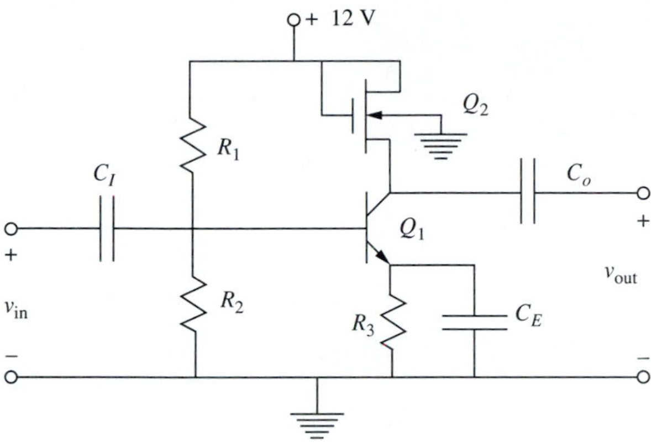

FIGURE P11.7

C_I, C_E, and C_O are all short circuits at the operating frequency.

(a) Select R_3 so that $I_{CQ} = 2$ mA.

(b) Calculate the quiescent value of the voltage on the collector of Q_1 relative to ground.

(c) Draw the mid-band incremental equivalent circuit for this amplifier stage. (*Note:* C_I, C_E, and C_O can be assumed to be short circuits for incremental operation.) Calculate the mid-band incremental voltage gain $A_v \equiv v_{out}/v_{in}$

(d) How far can the output voltage swing positive and negative before either Q_1 is saturated (negative swing) or Q_2 is driven out of saturation (positive swing)? Recall that saturation has different meanings in MOSFETs and BJTs.

11.8 In the circuit pictured in Fig. P11.8, V_T for both MOSFETs is 0.5 V and the K-factor for the lower device, K_D, is 0.2 mA/V^2. The supply voltage V_{DD} is 5 V. Calculate and plot v_{OUT} versus v_{IN} (i.e., the transfer characteristic) over the range $0 \le v_{IN} \le 5$ V for three values of K_L:

(a) $K_L = 0.01K_D$

(b) $K_L = 0.1K_D$

(c) $K_L = 1.0K_D$

(*Note:* You will find the discussion in Secs. 15.1.4 and 15.2.2*a* helpful in working this problem.)

11.9 Consider now a situation where the input voltage v_{IN} to the circuit in problem 11.8 is $V_{IN} + v_{IN}(t)$, where V_{IN} is 1 V and $v_{in}(t)$ is "small" and slowly varying with time. We can then in general write v_{OUT} as $V_{OUT} + v_{out}(t)$ and in turn write $v_{out}(t)$ as $A_v v_{in}(t)$. In this problem we are concerned with finding V_{OUT} and A_v.

(a) Use your results in problem 11.1 to find a numerical value for V_{OUT} for each of the three values of K_L when V_{IN} is 1 V. A_v can be found in several ways. Follow the two procedures described below in parts b and c to find A_v when K_L has each of the three values given in problem 11.8.

(b) A_v is dv_{OUT}/dv_{IN} evaluated at the bias point Q (i.e., $V_{IN} = 1$ V). Use your expressions or plots from problem 11.1 to find A_v from this fact.

(c) A_v is v_{out}/v_{in} in the circuit formed by replacing the devices in this circuit with their small-signal linear equivalent circuits valid for this bias point as illustrated

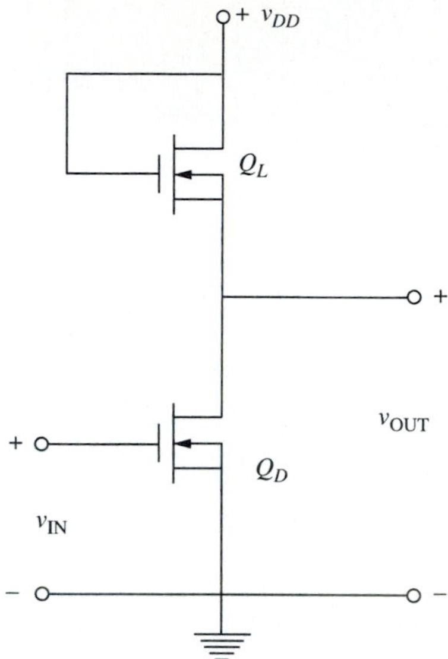

FIGURE P11.8

in Fig. P11.9*a*, which you should be able to convince yourself is equivalent to Fig. P11.9*b*.

(i) Evaluate g_{mD} and g_{mL} at this bias point for each of the circuits (i.e., for each K_L value).

(ii) Calculate v_{out}/v_{in} for each of the circuits, and compare your answers with those from part a. Assume that g_{oD} and g_{oL} are zero in saturation.

11.10 A measure of the maximum voltage gain achievable with a given transistor is its mid-band linear incremental voltage gain in a common-emitter or common-source configuration with an infinite load resistance (i.e., when it is incrementally open-circuited). We call this, not surprisingly, the mid-band open-circuit voltage gain A_{voc}.

(a) Show that A_{voc} is g_m/g_o for both BJTs and MOSFETs (assume $v_{bs} = 0$).

(b) Use our expressions for g_m and g_o in the forward active region in terms of the quiescent output current (I_C or I_D) and other device parameters to find an expression for A_{voc} in terms of these same quantities. Do this for a BJT and for a MOSFET.

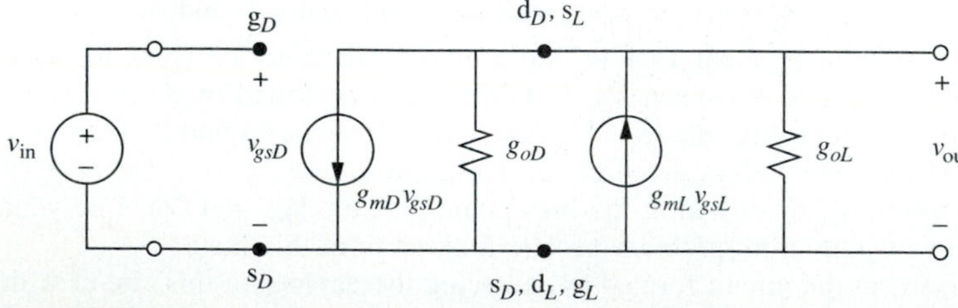

FIGURE P11.9a

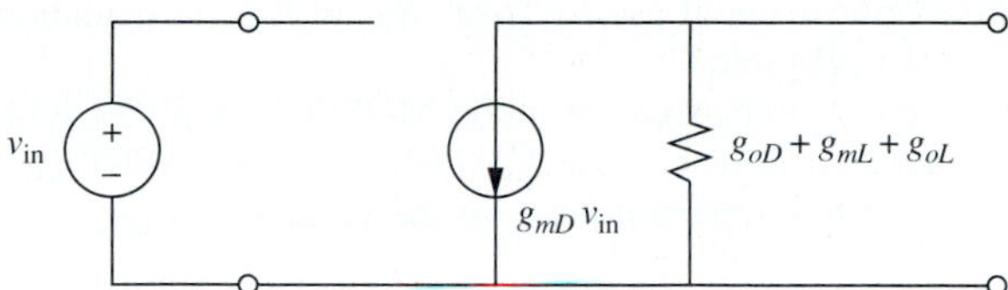

FIGURE P11.9b

(c) Calculate A_{voc} for a BJT assuming $V_A = 50$ V, $I_C = 0.1$ mA, $\beta = 100$, and $kT/q = 0.025$ V.

(d) Calculate A_{voc} for a MOSFET assuming $V_A = 50$ V, $I_D = 0.1$ mA, $K = 0.2$ mA/V^2, and $V_T = 0.5$ V.

(e) In parts c and d, how will A_{voc} change if the quiescent output current, I_C or I_D, is decreased?

11.11 Use the basic large-signal MOSFET model to derive expressions for the terminal characteristics of each of the four MOSFET loads illustrated in Figure 11.12. Show that your results yield the curves presented in that figure.

11.12 Consider the amplifier circuit illustrated in Fig. P11.12.

(a) Assuming R_G can be made arbitrarily large and can be neglected, derive an expression for the small-signal open-circuit voltage gain of this amplifier ($A_{v,oc} = v_{out}/v_{in}$ with no external load). State your result in terms of the quiescent collector/drain current and the Early voltages of Q_1 and Q_2. Suggest the optimum bias level.

(b) Now assume that R_G can no longer be made so large that it can be neglected. Derive an expression for $A_{v,oc}$ in this case and compare it to your result in part a.

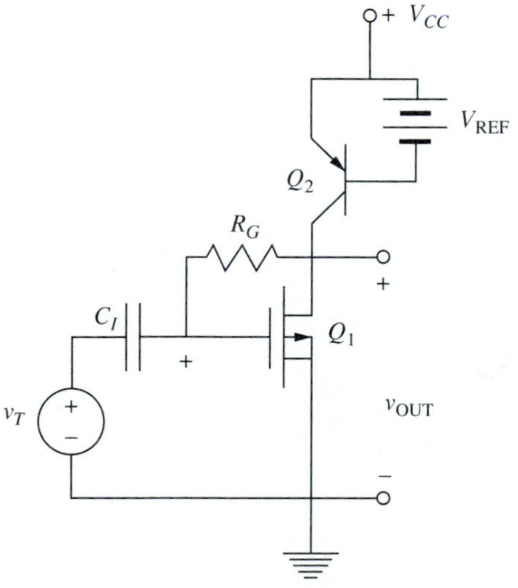

FIGURE P11.12

(c) Develop a design rule an engineer could use to "size" R_G in a given situation so that its impact on $A_{v,oc}$ is negligible.

(d) Design a circuit like this (i.e., an enhancement mode MOSFET amplifier with a *pnp* bipolar transistor load) that does not use R_G to bias the MOSFET Q_1. (*Hint:* One possibility is to use the approach taken in the circuits in Figs. 11.7 and 11.16.)

CHAPTER
12

DIFFERENTIAL AMPLIFIER STAGES

Thus far the amplifier circuits we have studied have had one input and one output. We now turn to a fundamentally different amplifier topology that has two inputs and two outputs. The outputs are related primarily to the difference between the two inputs, and consequently we call this type of amplifier a *difference*, or *differential*, amplifier. Because of its topology, it is also called an *emitter-coupled* pair when bipolar transistors are used as the active devices, or a *source-coupled* pair when FETs are used.

We will begin by looking at the basic differential amplifier stage. We will next consider the large-signal behavior of this circuit and then discuss its small-signal linear analysis. Finally, in Sec. 12.4, we will discuss the design of the current source circuits used to bias these amplifiers.

12.1 BASIC TOPOLOGY

The basic differential amplifier topology is illustrated in Fig. 12.1; the circuit in Fig. 12.1*a* is made with bipolar transistors, and the circuit of Fig. 12.1*b* uses MOSFETs. The qualitative behavior of both of these circuits is the same. The differential amplifier circuit is a perfectly symmetrical topology; both transistors are identical, as are each of the resistor pairs. Biasing is accomplished using a current source, and, because of the symmetry, half of the bias current flows through each transistor.

The operation of the circuits in Fig. 12.1 can be understood by first considering what happens when the two input voltages, v_{I1} and v_{I2}, are identical. Because of the symmetry of the circuit, there will clearly be no change in the current through the two transistors, Q, or through the output resistors, R_O, as

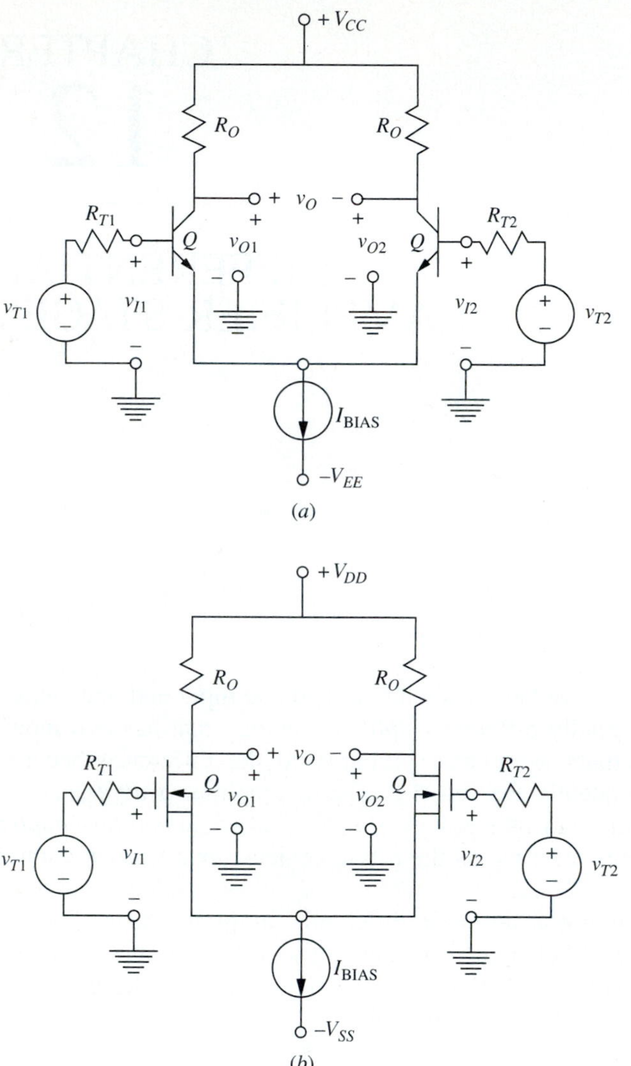

FIGURE 12.1
Basic differential amplifier topology: (*a*) circuit made using bipolar transistors as the active elements, also called an emitter-coupled pair; (*b*) the MOSFET version of the same circuit, also called a source-coupled pair.

v_{I1} and v_{I2} vary, as long as $v_{I1} = v_{I2}$. Thus there will also be no change in either of the two output voltages. They will stay fixed at $V_{CC} - R_O I_{\text{BIAS}}/2$ in the bipolar circuit and $V_{DD} - R_O I_{\text{BIAS}}$ in the MOSFET circuit.

If the two inputs are different, then the symmetry of the circuit is broken and the current I_{BIAS} no longer splits evenly between the two halves of the circuit. One of the output voltages will increase, and the other will decrease.

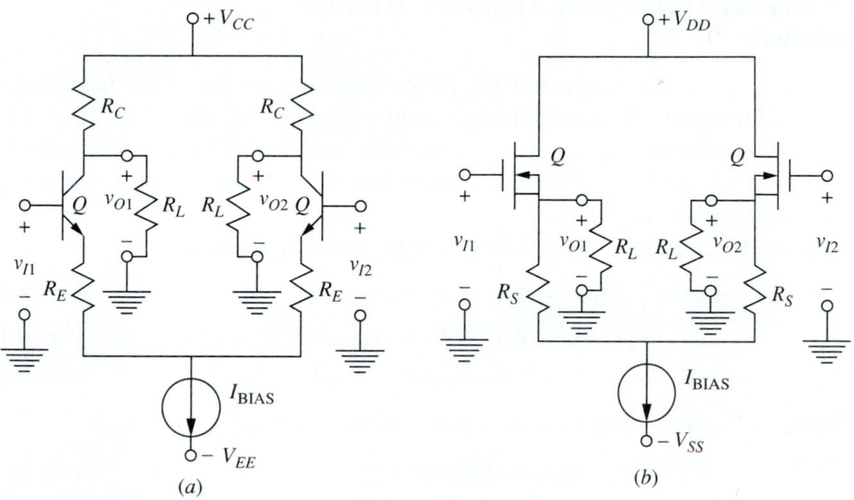

FIGURE 12.2
Two variations of the basic differential amplifier: (*a*) differential stage with emitter degeneracy; (*b*) differential source-follower.

Often we will take the difference between the two output voltages v_{O1} and v_{O2} as the output v_O. Clearly this difference will be zero if $v_{T1} = v_{T2}$ and nonzero only if $v_{T1} \neq v_{T2}$.

There are many variations of the basic differential amplifier. All are symmetrical, however, and all use current source biasing; most correspond to one of the various single-transistor stage configurations discussed in Chap. 11. For example, the circuits of Figs. 12.1*a* and *b* correspond to a common-emitter stage and a common-source stage, respectively. Differential amplifier stages analogous to a single-transistor stage with emitter degeneracy and a source-follower stage are shown in Figs. 12.2*a* and *b*, respectively. We will focus our analyses on the circuit of Figs. 12.1, but it should become clear to you as we go along that these analyses can readily be extended to other configurations, such as those of Fig. 12.2.

12.2 LARGE-SIGNAL ANALYSIS

To quantify our understanding of differential amplifier stages we will first consider a large-signal analysis of the bipolar stage of Fig. 12.1*a* using the Ebers–Moll model, and then we will do the same exercise for the MOSFET differential amplifier of Fig. 12.1*b*. In both cases, we will begin by considering a general pair of inputs that can have any values as long as the transistors Q_1 and Q_2 remain in their forward active region. After calculating the transfer characteristics (i.e., the output voltages as a function of the input voltages) for a general set of inputs, we will look at a way of defining a new set of inputs with important symmetry properties that will simplify the analysis of differential amplifier stages. We will call these the difference and common mode inputs.

12.2.1 Bipolar Differential Amplifier Transfer Characteristic

In Fig. 12.3, the transistors Q_1 and Q_2 in the amplifier of Fig. 12.1 have been replaced by their Ebers–Moll model equivalent circuits from Fig. 8.18. Our objective now is to calculate v_{O1} and v_{O2} and, later, v_O, which is $v_{O1} - v_{O2}$, each as a function of v_{I1} and v_{I2}. The relationship between v_O and v_I for a circuit is called its *transfer characteristic*.

Begin by writing the output voltages in terms of i_{F1} and i_{F2}:

$$v_{O1} = V_{CC} - R_C\alpha_F i_{F1} \tag{12.1a}$$

$$v_{O2} = V_{CC} - R_C\alpha_F i_{F2} \tag{12.1b}$$

$$v_O = -R_C\alpha_F(i_{F1} - i_{F2}) \tag{12.1c}$$

The currents i_{F1} and i_{F2} can now be written in terms of v_{BE1} and v_{BE2}:

$$i_{F1} \approx I_{ES}e^{qv_{BE1}/kT} \tag{12.2a}$$

$$i_{F2} \approx I_{ES}e^{qv_{BE2}/kT} \tag{12.2b}$$

where we have assumed that $v_{BE} \gg kT/q$, so the factor of 1 can be neglected. Using these expressions in Eqs. (12.1a) and (12.1b) yields

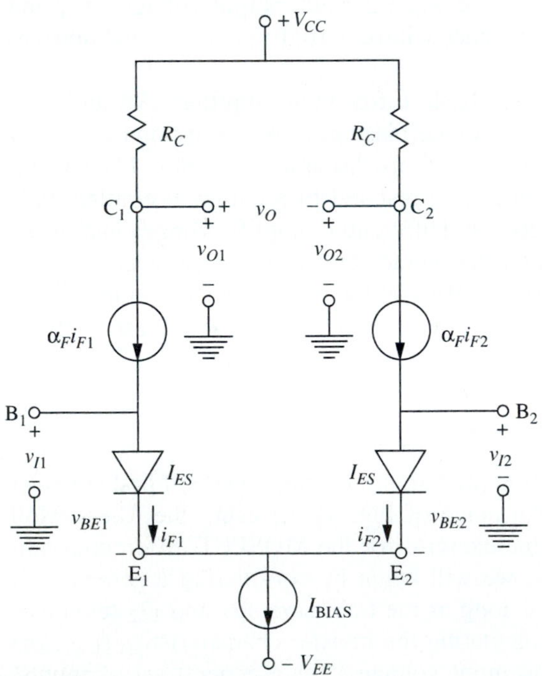

FIGURE 12.3
Differential amplifier of Fig. 12.1*a* with Ebers–Moll models for the *npn* bipolar transistors.

$$v_{O1} = V_{CC} - R_C \alpha_F I_{ES} e^{q v_{BE1}/kT} \tag{12.3a}$$

$$v_{O2} = V_{CC} - R_C \alpha_F I_{ES} e^{q v_{BE2}/kT} \tag{12.3b}$$

The next step is to sum the currents out of the common emitter node:

$$i_{F1} + i_{F2} = I_{\text{BIAS}} \tag{12.4}$$

Using Eqs. (12.2) in this yields

$$I_{\text{BIAS}} = I_{ES}\left(e^{q v_{BE1}/kT} + e^{q v_{BE2}/kT}\right) \tag{12.5}$$

This equation can be used to obtain expressions for v_{O1} and v_{O2} in terms of $v_{BE1} - v_{BE2}$. This is important because by summing the voltages around the loop through the two emitters and ground, we can also write

$$v_{I1} - v_{BE1} + v_{BE2} - v_{I2} = 0$$

or

$$v_{BE1} - v_{BE2} = v_{I1} - v_{I2} \tag{12.6}$$

This in turn lets us relate v_{O1} and v_{O2} to v_{I1} and v_{I2}, which is our goal.

Proceeding, we focus first on v_{BE1} and v_{O1}. A bit of algebraic manipulation of Eq. (12.5) yields

$$e^{q v_{BE1}/kT} = \frac{I_{\text{BIAS}}}{I_{ES}\left[1 + e^{-q(v_{BE1} - v_{BE2})/kT}\right]}$$

Inserting this into Eq. (12.3a) and using Eq. (12.6), we obtain

$$v_{O1} = V_{CC} - \frac{\alpha_F R_C I_{\text{BIAS}}}{\left[1 + e^{-q(v_{I1} - v_{I2})/kT}\right]} \tag{12.7a}$$

A similar examination of Eq. (12.3b) yields

$$v_{O2} = V_{CC} - \frac{\alpha_F R_C I_{\text{BIAS}}}{\left[1 + e^{q(v_{I1} - v_{I2})/kT}\right]} \tag{12.7b}$$

Finally, subtracting Eq. (12.7a) from Eq. (12.7b), we find, after a bit more algebraic manipulation, that v_O can be written as

$$v_O = -\alpha_F R_C I_{\text{BIAS}} \tanh \frac{q\,(v_{I1} - v_{I2})}{2kT} \tag{12.7c}$$

The important thing to notice about Eqs. (12.7) for the various output voltages is that all of these output voltages depend only on the difference between the input voltages. If v_{I1} is equal to v_{I2}, then v_{O1} and v_{O2} equal their quiescent values, $V_{CC} - R_C I_{\text{BIAS}}/2$, and v_O is zero. Change in the output occurs only if v_{I1} is not equal to v_{I2}, just as we argued qualitatively in Sec. 12.1.

It is instructive to plot Eq. (12.7c), the expression for v_O, as a function of $(v_{I1} - v_{I2})$, as is done in Fig. 12.4. The first thing to notice is that for $|(v_{I1} - v_{I2})| >> kT/q$, the output voltage saturates at $\pm\alpha_F R_C I_{\text{BIAS}}$, which says

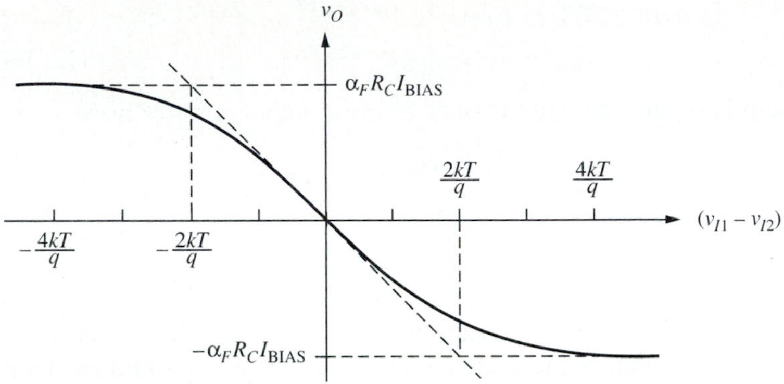

FIGURE 12.4
The large signal transfer characteristic of the circuit in Fig. 12.1*a* calculated using the model of Fig. 12.3.

that all of the current source current has been switched to flow totally through Q_1 when $(v_{I1} - v_{I2}) >> 0$, or through Q_2 when $(v_{I1} - v_{I2}) << 0$.

For $|(v_{I1} - v_{I2})|$ small, on the other hand, v_O varies linearly with $(v_{I1} - v_{I2})$, that is,

$$v_O = \frac{-R_C q \alpha_F I_{BIAS}}{2kT}(v_{I1} - v_{I2}) \tag{12.8a}$$

for $|(v_{I1} - v_{I2})| \lesssim kT/q$.

Notice that $q\alpha_F I_{BIAS}/2kT$ is the small-signal transconductance g_m of the transistors Q_1 and Q_2 for operation about the quiescent bias point $I_C = \alpha_F I_{BIAS}/2$. Thus Eq. (12.8a) can also be written as

$$v_O \approx -g_m R_C (v_{I1} - v_{I2}) \tag{12.8b}$$

for $|(v_{I1} - v_{I2})| \lesssim kT/q$. We will return to this point when we look at small-signal analysis of differential amplifiers.

12.2.2 MOSFET Differential Amplifier Transfer Characteristic

To calculate the transfer characteristic of the common-source MOSFET differential amplifier stage in Fig. 12.1*b*, we use our large-signal model of Sec. 10.1.1 to obtain the circuit of Fig. 12.5. Looking at this circuit we see, first, that the output voltage v_O is given by

$$v_O = -R_D(i_{D1} - i_{D2})$$

Assuming that both Q_1 and Q_2 are operating in saturation, we have

$$i_{D1} = \frac{K}{2}(v_{GS1} - V_T)^2 \tag{12.9a}$$

$$i_{D2} = \frac{K}{2}(v_{GS2} - V_T)^2 \tag{12.9b}$$

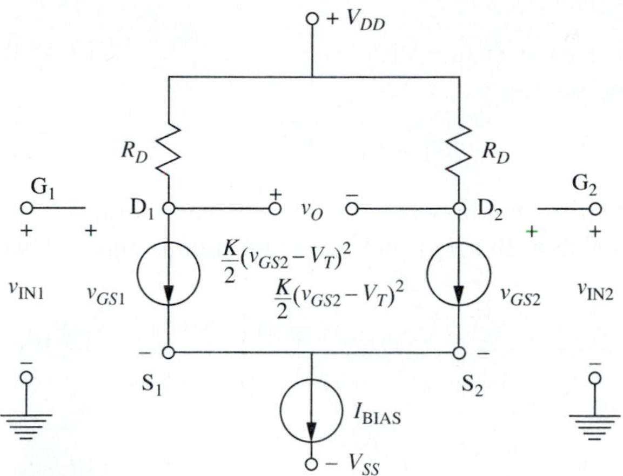

FIGURE 12.5
Differential amplifier of Fig. 12.1*b* with large-signal model of Sec. 10.1.1 inserted for the *n*-channel enhancement mode MOSFETs.

so we can write

$$v_O = -\frac{R_D K}{2}\left[(v_{GS1} - V_T)^2 - (v_{GS2} - V_T)^2\right] \quad (12.10)$$

Before going further it is important to understand why we can assume that both Q_1 and Q_2 have the same threshold voltage V_T in light of the fact that V_T depends on v_{BS}. In an integrated circuit, which is the context in which this circuit would be realized, both transistors share a common substrate, and their sources are already joined in the circuit, so clearly v_{BS} is the same for these two transistors. Thus we do not need to write V_{T1} and V_{T2}; there is only one V_T.

Returning to Eq.(12.10), we observe that it is of the form

$$v_O = -\frac{R_D K}{2}\left(a^2 - b^2\right) \quad (12.11a)$$

where a is $(v_{GS1} - V_T)$ and b is $(v_{GS2} - V_T)$. We can next write v_O in Eq. 12.11a as

$$v_O = -\frac{R_D K}{2}(a - b)(a + b) \quad (12.11b)$$

This is useful because the first factor, $(a - b)$, is related to the input voltages, v_{I1} and v_{I2}. To see this we first write

$$(a - b) = v_{GS1} - V_T - v_{GS2} + V_T = v_{GS1} - v_{GS2} \quad (12.12a)$$

Then, using Kirchhoff's voltage law and summing around the path that includes the two inputs and passes through the common source terminals, we have

$$-v_{I1} + v_{GS1} - v_{GS2} + v_{I2} = 0 \quad (12.12b)$$

Thus,

$$v_{GS1} - v_{GS2} = v_{I1} - v_{I2} \quad (12.12c)$$

and so we have

$$(a - b) = (v_{I1} - v_{I2}) \tag{12.12d}$$

The other factor, $(a + b)$, can be written as

$$(a + b) = \sqrt{2(a^2 + b^2) - (a - b)^2} \tag{12.13a}$$

(an obscure identity, but true). We already know $(a - b)$; an expression for $(a^2 + b^2)$ can be obtained by using the restriction that i_{D1} and i_{D2} must sum to I_{BIAS}. That is,

$$I_{\text{BIAS}} = \frac{K}{2}\left[(v_{GS1} - V_T)^2 + (v_{GS2} - V_T)^2\right] \tag{12.14a}$$

which, using our notation, has the form

$$I_{\text{BIAS}} = \frac{K}{2}\left(a^2 + b^2\right) \tag{12.14b}$$

So

$$\left(a^2 + b^2\right) = \frac{2I_{\text{BIAS}}}{K} \tag{12.14c}$$

and thus

$$(a + b) = \sqrt{\frac{4I_{\text{BIAS}}}{K} + (v_{I1} - v_{I2})^2} \tag{12.13b}$$

Combining Eq. (12.12d) and (12.13b) in Eq. (12.11b) yields our final result:

$$v_O = -\frac{R_D K}{2}(v_{I1} - v_{I2})\sqrt{\frac{4I_{\text{BIAS}}}{K} - (v_{I1} - v_{I2})^2} \tag{12.15}$$

We first note that v_O again depends only on the difference between the two input voltages, as we argued must be the case in Sec. 12.1. This large-signal transfer characteristic is plotted in Fig. 12.6. For v_{I1} much larger than v_{I2}, v_O saturates at $-R_D\, I_{\text{BIAS}}$, which corresponds to having all the bias current flow through Q_1

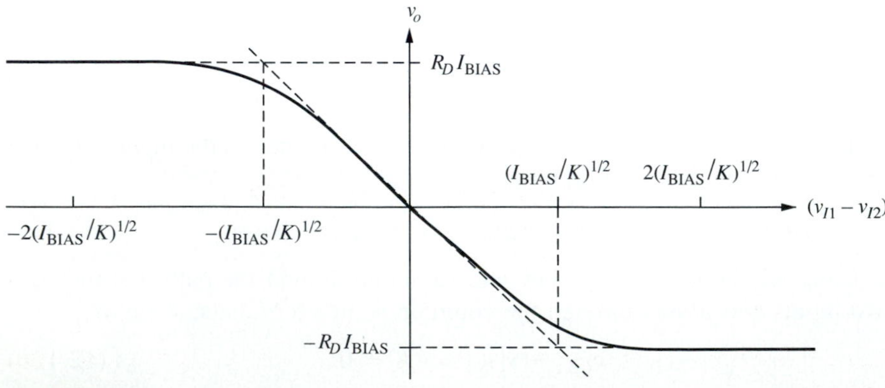

FIGURE 12.6
Large-signal transfer characteristic of the circuit in Fig. 12.1*b* as modeled in Fig. 12.5.

and none through Q_2. In the opposite extreme, when v_{I2} is much greater than v_{I1}, v_O saturates at $R_D\, I_{\text{BIAS}}$ because I_{BIAS} now flows entirely through Q_2.

For v_{IN1} similar to v_{IN2} so that $|(v_{I1} - v_{I2})|$ is small, v_O depends approximately linearly on this difference. That is,

$$v_O \approx -R_D \sqrt{I_{\text{BIAS}} K}\,(v_{I1} - v_{I2}) \tag{12.16a}$$

when $|(v_{I1} - v_{I2})| \ll (I_{\text{BIAS}}/K)^{1/2}$. Noting next that the drain current is $I_{\text{BIAS}}/2$ when the two input voltages are equal, and recalling Eq. 10.2b relating g_m to I_{DQ}, we see that $(I_{\text{BIAS}} K)^{1/2}$ is the small-signal transconductance of Q_1 and Q_2 at this bias point; thus we have

$$v_O \approx -g_m R_D\,(v_{I1} - v_{I2}) \tag{12.16b}$$

which is identical to the bipolar result, Eq. (12.8).

The transfer characteristic in Fig. 12.6 will have to be modified if the transistors go out of saturation and into their linear regions for $|(v_{I1} - v_{I2})|$ less than $(2I_{\text{BIAS}}/K)^{1/2}$. However, the transfer characteristic will still be symmetrical, will depend only on $(v_{I1} - v_{I2})$, and will have the same slope at the origin and the same maximum values for $|(v_{I1} - v_{I2})|$ large.

12.2.3 Difference and Common Mode Inputs

We have just seen, first qualitatively and then quantitatively, that the output voltage of a differential amplifier depends only on the difference between the two inputs. This observation leads us to define *difference mode input* and *common mode input voltages*, v_{ID} and v_{IC}, respectively, as

$$v_{ID} \equiv v_{I1} - v_{I2} \tag{12.17a}$$

$$v_{IC} \equiv \frac{(v_{I1} + v_{I2})}{2} \tag{12.17b}$$

We note that any arbitrary set of two inputs, v_{I1} and v_{I2}, can be written in terms of the difference mode input v_{ID} and the common mode input v_{IC} as follows:

$$v_{I1} = v_{IC} + \frac{v_{ID}}{2} \tag{12.18a}$$

$$v_{I2} = v_{IC} - \frac{v_{ID}}{2} \tag{12.18b}$$

Looking at the inputs in this manner, we can say that the output of a differential amplifier is independent of the common mode input signal v_{IC}. It depends only on the difference mode input signal v_{ID}.

The transfer characteristics, Eqs. (12.7) and (12.15) and Figs. 12.4 and 12.6, teach us that the magnitude of the difference mode input signal v_{ID} must be less than $2kT/q$ for a bipolar differential amplifier and less than $(I_{\text{BIAS}}/K)^{1/2}$ for a MOSFET differential amplifier, or the output voltage will saturate and become independent of v_{ID}. This usually is not a very useful situation, so we tend to operate with small v_{ID}.

There is also a restriction on how large the magnitude of the common voltage signal v_{IC} can be, but it is not found by looking at the transfer characteristic. Rather it arises because of the requirement that the transistors remain in their forward active regions. Looking at the bipolar circuit, Fig. 12.1*a* for example, we see that if the two input terminals become too positively biased, the transistors will saturate because their collector voltages are fixed at $V_{CC} - R_C I_{\text{BIAS}}/2$ relative to ground. Clearly we must have $v_{IC} < V_{CC} - R_C I_{\text{BIAS}}/2 + 0.4$ V, assuming $v_{CE,\text{SAT}} \approx 0.2$ V and $v_{BE,\text{ON}} \approx 0.6$ V. When the two input terminals are biased negatively, the limit on v_{IC} arises from the transistors making up the bias current source (i.e., providing I_{BIAS}). For v_{IC} sufficiently negative, one of these transistors will saturate (which one will be obvious when we discuss current source circuits in Sec. 12.5) and the current source circuit will no longer be operating properly.

The permissible range of common mode voltages is called the *common mode voltage swing* and is one of the performance parameters often quoted for a differential amplifier stage.

12.3 SMALL-SIGNAL LINEAR ANALYSIS

We will make great use of the concept of difference and common mode input signals in our small-signal analysis of differential amplifiers. The symmetry of these inputs and the symmetry and linearity of the circuit can be combined to yield very powerful analytical techniques. We will first discuss these techniques, called *half-circuit techniques*, in rather general, abstract terms. We will then apply them to calculate the small-signal linear gains and the input and output resistances of differential amplifiers.

12.3.1 Half-Circuit Techniques

Consider a symmetrical circuit with two input terminals and two output terminals like that shown in Fig. 12.7*a*. This circuit can be divided into two identical half-circuits connected by a number of links as shown in Fig. 12.7*b*.

If the same voltage v_{IC} is applied to the two inputs, as illustrated in Fig. 12.8, we can see right away by symmetry that the voltages on the two output terminals must be equal; that is,

$$v_{O1} = v_{O2} \equiv v_{OC} \qquad \text{when} \qquad v_{I1} = v_{I2} = v_{IC} \tag{12.19}$$

Furthermore, we can say on the basis of symmetry that there must be no current flowing in any of the links that join the two halves of the circuit. The argument is that because of the total symmetry in the circuit, there is no reason a current in any of the links should flow one way rather than the other. The only consistent condition is that the current is zero.

If there is no current flowing in any of the links, then they can be cut without affecting the circuit. Thus we can determine what v_{OC} will be, given v_{IC}, simply by breaking all of the links and solving half of the circuit. This is illustrated in

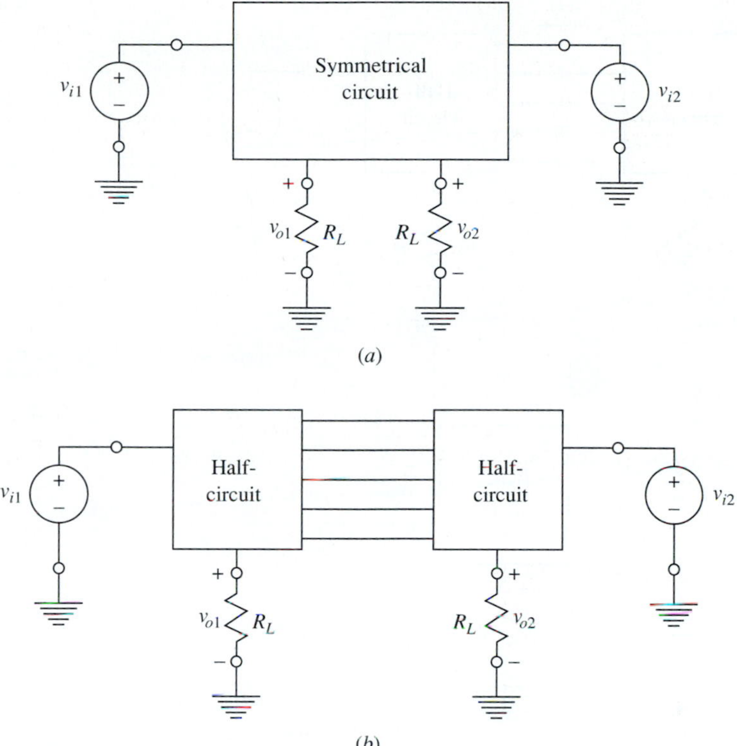

FIGURE 12.7
(*a*) Symmetrical circuit; (*b*) two identical half-circuits connected by a number of conducting links.

Fig. 12.8. This observation has practical significance because the newly created half-circuit for common mode inputs will in general be much simpler to solve than the original full circuit.

If equal but opposite voltages v_{ID} and $-v_{ID}$ are applied to the inputs v_{I1} and v_{I2}, respectively, we can in general realize a similar simplification of a symmetrical circuit only in the special situation where the circuit is linear and contains no independent sources. This sounds a bit restrictive until you realize that this is just the type of circuit we encounter when we do our small-signal analyses.

Consider, then, a symmetrical linear small-signal equivalent circuit with two inputs, two outputs, and no independent sources. With equal, but opposite voltages v_{id} and $-v_{id}$ applied to the inputs v_{i1} and v_{i2}, respectively, the outputs must, by symmetry, also be equal and opposite; that is,

$$v_{o1} = -v_{o2} \equiv v_{od} \qquad \text{when} \qquad v_{i1} = v_{i2} = v_{id} \tag{12.20}$$

To see mathematically why this must be true, realize that since the circuit is linear and has no independent sources, we must be able to write v_{o1} and v_{o2} as follows:

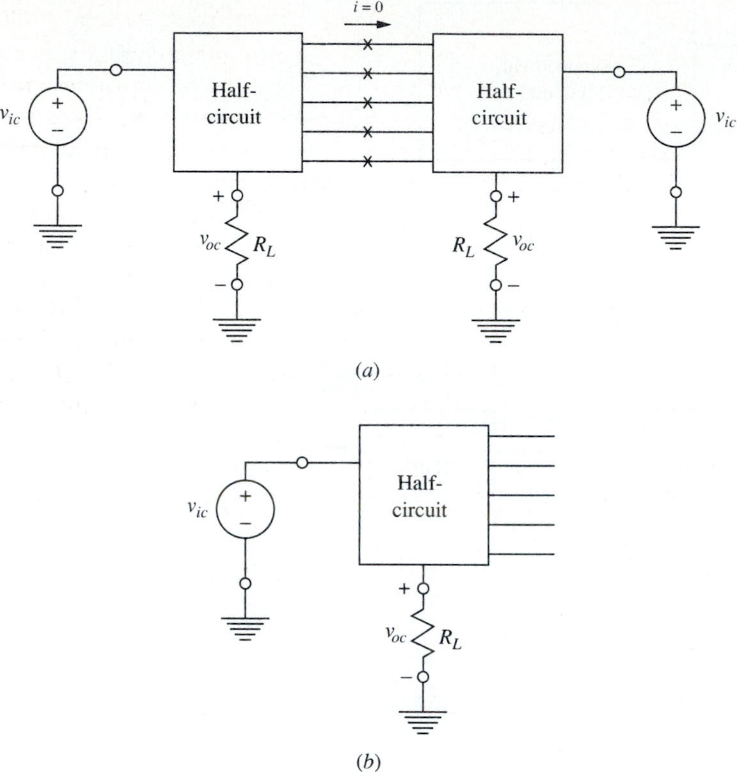

FIGURE 12.8
(*a*) Symmetrical circuit with common mode input signals applied;
(*b*) half-circuit equivalent.

$$v_{o1} = Av_{i1} + Bv_{i2} \tag{12.21a}$$

$$v_{o2} = Av_{i2} + Bv_{i1} \tag{12.21b}$$

Requiring the circuit to be linear means that the highest-order terms can at most be linear terms; requiring no independent sources means that there will be no constant term; and requiring the circuit to be symmetrical means that these expressions are symmetrical. Now, if $v_{i1} = -v_{i2} = v_{id}$, we have directly from Eqs. (12.21a) and (12.21b) that $v_{o1} = -v_{o2} = v_{od}$.

We can also say something about the voltage differences between any of the links between the two half-circuits. In particular, they must be zero, since they are zero in the absence of any input voltages and there is no reason they should increase or decrease when an input voltage to the right is increased a certain amount and that on the left is decreased by the same amount. The only consistent situation is that they remain at 0 V.

Mathematically, it must be true that the voltage, measured relative to some reference point (say, ground), at any point of symmetry in a symmetrical circuit depends in an identical way on both of the input signals. That is, if the point of symmetry in question is labeled "a", then we must have

$$v_a = Cv_{i1} + Cv_{i2} \tag{12.22a}$$

or simply

$$v_a = C(v_{i1} + v_{i2}) \tag{12.22b}$$

Thus, if $v_{i1} = -v_{i2}$, then clearly $v_a = 0$.

This result is the difference mode input equivalent to saying that the current in the links is zero with a common mode input. It has similar implications for the circuit. In particular, if all of the links stay at 0 V (i.e., ground potential) when $v_{i1} = -v_{i2}$, then they can all be connected together and grounded without affecting the circuit operation. Thus we can obtain v_{od} in terms of v_{id} by shorting all of the links to ground and solving for the voltages in one of the resulting half-circuits. This procedure is illustrated in Fig. 12.9. It is not hard to imagine that shorting all of the links together can simplify the analysis of the remaining new half-circuit immensely.

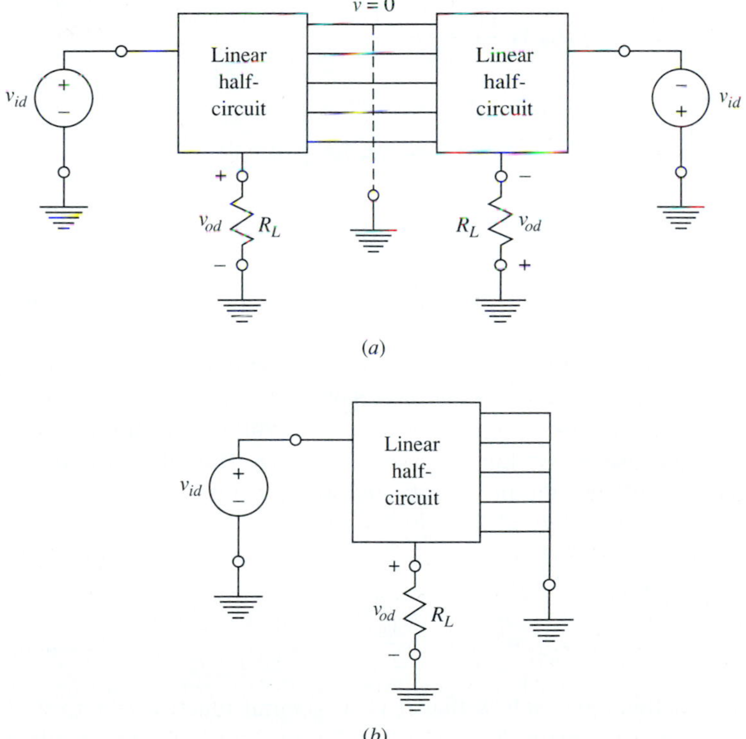

FIGURE 12.9
(*a*) Symmetrical linear circuit with difference mode input signals applied;
(*b*) Half-circuit equivalent.

These half-circuit observations are useful in several ways when we are analyzing differential amplifiers, which tend to be very symmetrical circuits. The first instance is for bias analysis. From a bias standpoint, the inputs are zero, which certainly means they are equal, or common mode, and this means that we can use our common mode half-circuit techniques to calculate the quiescent currents and voltages in the circuit. This is sometimes useful, and we already made use of it when we said that half of the bias current flows through each half of a differential pair.

The second application of half-circuit techniques in differential amplifier design is for small-signal linear equivalent circuit analysis. Here the impact of half-circuit techniques is much more significant because we can now also make use of superposition. That is, in general, two arbitrary inputs, v_{I1} and v_{I2}, can be written in terms of a common and a difference mode input, as we saw in Sec. 12.2.3. If we are dealing with linear circuits, we can find the output signals due to each of these inputs (i.e., the common and difference mode inputs) individually and we can use superposition to reconstruct the total response.

To do this type of analysis, we first define small-signal difference and common mode signals in terms of v_{i1} and v_{i2} :

$$v_{ic} \equiv \frac{(v_{i1} + v_{i2})}{2} \tag{12.23a}$$

$$v_{id} \equiv v_{i1} - v_{i2} \tag{12.23b}$$

Writing the inputs in terms of these quantities, we have simply

$$v_{i1} = v_{ic} + \frac{v_{id}}{2} \tag{12.24a}$$

$$v_{i2} = v_{ic} - \frac{v_{id}}{2} \tag{12.24b}$$

Thus we can first use half-circuit techniques to solve for the output voltages with $v_{i1} = v_{ic}$ and $v_{i2} = v_{ic}$. In this case, as we have said, we find $v_{o1} = v_{o2} \equiv v_{oc}$. Then we use half-circuit techniques to solve for the output voltages with $v_{i1} = v_{id}$ and $v_{i2} = -v_{id}$. In this case we obtain $v_{o1} = -v_{o2} \equiv v_{od}$. Having v_{od} and v_{oc} we superimpose these results to obtain the total output voltages

$$v_{o1} = v_{oc} + \frac{v_{od}}{2} \tag{12.25a}$$

$$v_{o2} = v_{oc} - \frac{v_{od}}{2} \tag{12.25b}$$

The advantage of this approach is that it is in general much easier to find v_{od} and v_{oc} given v_{id} and v_{ic} using half-circuit techniques than it is to calculate v_{o1} and v_{o2} given v_{i1} and v_{i2} using the entire circuit and without taking advantage of the symmetry of the problem. All of these points are best understood with a few examples, which we will turn to next.

12.3.2 Difference and Common Mode Voltage Gains

We know already that a differential amplifier responds differently to a difference mode input signal than it does to a common mode input signal. To quantify this difference we define two voltage gains, the difference mode voltage gain A_{vd} and the common mode voltage gain A_{vc} as follows:

$$A_{vd} \equiv \frac{v_{od}}{v_{id}} \tag{12.26}$$

$$A_{vc} \equiv \frac{v_{oc}}{v_{ic}} \tag{12.27}$$

If we know A_{vd} and A_{vc} for a circuit, its output voltages can be found for a given set of input voltages. Consider, for example, v_{o1}:

$$v_{o1} = v_{oc} + \frac{v_{od}}{2} \tag{12.28a}$$

From Eqs. (12.26) and (12.27) this becomes

$$v_{o1} = A_{vc}\, v_{ic} + A_{vd}\frac{v_{id}}{2} \tag{12.28b}$$

Then, using the definitions of v_{ic} and v_{id}, we find

$$v_{o1} = A_{vc}\frac{(v_{i1} + v_{i2})}{2} + A_{vd}\frac{(v_{i1} - v_{i2})}{2} \tag{12.28c}$$

or, rearranging,

$$v_{o1} = \left[\frac{(A_{vc} + A_{vd})}{2}\right] v_{i1} + \left[\frac{(A_{vc} - A_{vd})}{2}\right] v_{i2} \tag{12.28d}$$

Similarly we can find

$$v_{o2} = \left[\frac{(A_{vc} - A_{vd})}{2}\right] v_{i1} + \left[\frac{(A_{vc} + A_{vd})}{2}\right] v_{i2} \tag{12.29}$$

and finally

$$v_o = A_{vd}\,(v_{i1} - v_{i2}) \tag{12.30}$$

The careful reader will notice that we said earlier in our large-signal analyses that the output voltages do not depend on the common mode input signal [see Eqs.(12.7, for example)], yet Eq. (12.28b) involves v_{ic}. Thus unless A_{vc} is zero, the output voltages v_{o1} and v_{o2} do depend on v_{ic}. What is going on, as we shall quantify very shortly, is that our discussion in Sec. 12.2 assumed that the bias current is supplied by an ideal current source. If the current source is indeed ideal, then we will find that A_{vc} is identically zero, as is consistent with our earlier discussion. If, however, the current source is not ideal, but instead has a finite output resistance, then A_{vc} will be nonzero (albeit very, very small) and v_{o1} and v_{o2} will depend very slightly on v_{ic}. Notice, however, that v_o, which equals $(v_{o1} - v_{o2})$, never depends on v_{oc}, even if the current source is not ideal.

The above discussion can be quantified by introducing what is called the *common mode rejection ratio* (CMRR). CMRR is defined as the ratio of the output voltage v_{o1} that results from a difference mode input signal v_{id} to the output voltage that results from an identical common mode input signal v_{ic}. Referring to Eq. (12.28*b*), we have

$$\text{CMRR} \equiv \frac{A_{vd}}{2A_{vc}} \tag{12.31}$$

The idea is to make this quantity as large as possible.

Now we look at calculating A_{vc} and A_{vd} for some specific circuits as a way of illustrating the preceding discussions. As a first example, consider the bipolar circuit of Fig. 12.1*a*. For mid-band small-signal operation about the bias point $V_{I1} = V_{I2}$ and $I_C = I_{\text{BIAS}}/2$, the linear equivalent circuit is that shown in Fig. 12.10. Note that we have assumed that the bias current source has a finite output resistance R_I. R_I is presumably large. Notice also that in order to obtain a symmetrical circuit, it was necessary to draw the single resistor R_I as two resistors of value $2R_I$ in parallel.

In Fig 12.11*a* and 12.11*b* the half-circuit models for difference and common mode input signals, respectively, are drawn for the circuit of Fig. 12.10. We are left to analyze circuits that are very familiar to us from our work in Chap. 11 with single-transistor amplifier stages. We can write by inspection that

$$A_{vd} = -g_m R_L' \tag{12.32}$$

and

$$A_{vc} \approx -\frac{R_L'}{2R_I} \tag{12.33}$$

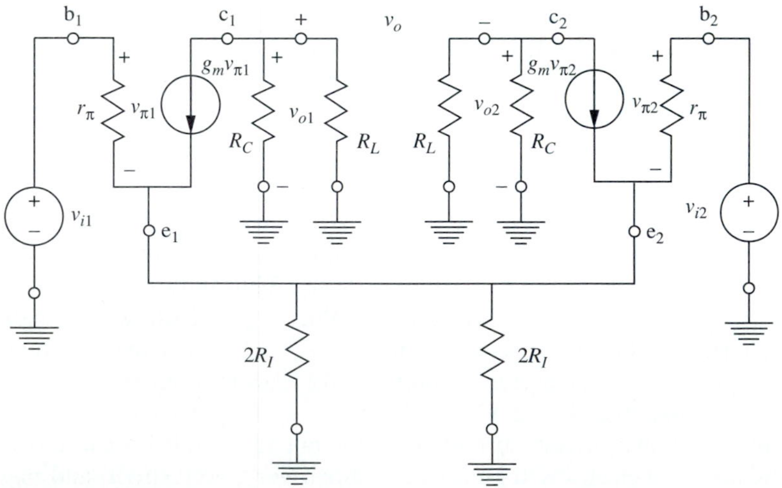

FIGURE 12.10
Small-signal mid-band linear equivalent circuit for the bipolar differential amplifier circuit of Fig. 12.1*a*.

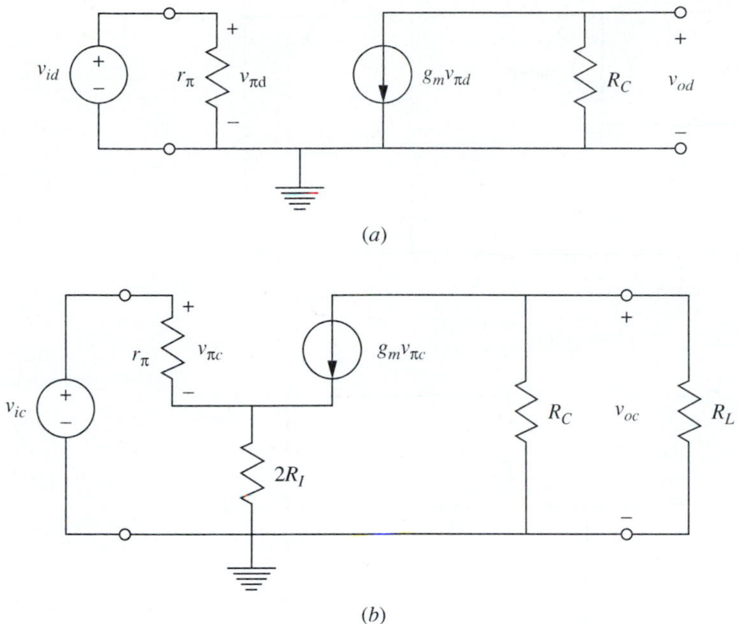

FIGURE 12.11
Half-circuit models of the circuit of Fig. 12.1*a* and 12.10: (*a*) for difference mode input signals; (*b*) for common mode input signals.

where R_L' is the parallel combination of R_L and R_C. Clearly, if R_I is very large, A_{vc} will be very small (i.e., $\ll 1$), whereas A_{vd} will be relatively large. The common mode rejection ratio is $g_m R_I$.

Next consider the two circuits of Fig. 12.2. Half-circuit models for difference mode input signals are drawn in Fig. 12.12. The similarity of these circuits to a single-transistor stage with a degenerate-emitter stage and to a source-follower stage are clear. Again the difference mode voltage gain can be written by inspection. For the circuit in Fig. 12.12*a* we have

$$A_{vd} \approx -\frac{R_L'}{R_E} \tag{12.34}$$

and for the circuit in Fig.12.12*b* we have

$$A_{vd} \approx 1 \tag{12.35}$$

You should be able to prove to yourself that the common mode voltage gain for the circuit in Fig. 12.12*a* is $-R_C/(R_E + 2R_I)$ and for Fig. 12.12*b* is approximately 1. Perhaps surprisingly, this last common voltage gain is large, as common mode voltage gains go, but this is of no practical consequence because this stage is always used after other differential stages that have very small common mode outputs. That is, there is no common mode signal left, so passing it unattenuated does not cause any problems.

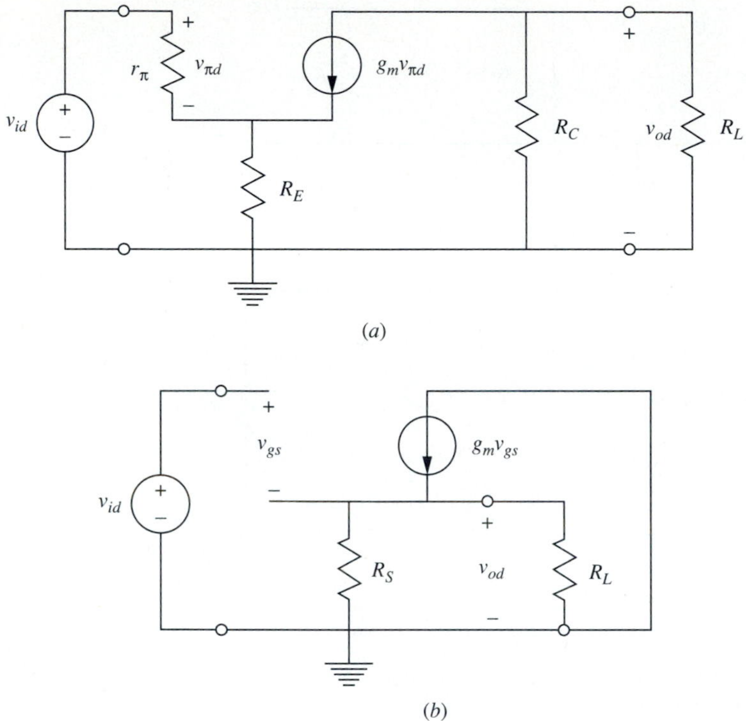

FIGURE 12.12
Half-circuit difference mode input models: (*a*) of the circuit in Fig. 12.2*a*; (*b*) of the circuit in Fig. 12.2*b*.

These few examples should offer you graphic proof that the half-circuit analysis technique greatly simplifies the problem of analyzing the small signal voltage gain performance of differential amplifiers. In the next sections we will expand our discussion to include current gains and input and output resistances and will see further evidence of the utility of the half-circuit technique.

12.3.3 Current Gains

We have thus far concentrated on voltage signals as the inputs and outputs to differential amplifiers. This is the way we usually think of differential amplifiers, but we could also have looked at current inputs and outputs. Our choice of voltages was based largely on convenience, as well as recognition of the fact that we usually think of the voltage drops caused by currents flowing through loads as our signals. Still, it is important to realize that an arbitrary set of input currents, i_{i1} and i_{i2}, can also be written in terms of a common mode input current i_{ic} and difference mode input current i_{id}; that is,

$$i_{i1} = i_{ic} + \frac{i_{id}}{2} \tag{12.36a}$$

$$i_{i2} = i_{ic} - \frac{i_{id}}{2} \tag{12.36b}$$

where the definitions of i_{ic} and i_{id} are analogous to, and consistent with, those for v_{ic} and v_{id}:

$$i_{ic} \equiv \frac{(i_{i1} + i_{i2})}{2} \tag{12.37a}$$

$$i_{id} \equiv i_{i1} - i_{i2} \tag{12.37b}$$

When the common mode input current i_{ic} is applied to both inputs, the output currents, i_{o1} and i_{o2}, are both i_{oc}. When the difference mode input current i_{id} is applied to input 1 and its negative is applied to input 2, the output currents are of equal magnitude, $|i_{od}|$, and of opposite signs (i.e., $i_{o1} = i_{od}$ and $i_{o2} = -i_{od}$). Using superposition, we find that the total output currents are then given by

$$i_{o1} = i_{oc} + \frac{i_{od}}{2} \tag{12.38a}$$

$$i_{o2} = i_{oc} - \frac{i_{od}}{2} \tag{12.38b}$$

We define a common mode current gain A_{ic} and difference mode current gain A_{id} as follows:

$$A_{ic} \equiv \frac{i_{oc}}{i_{ic}} \tag{12.39a}$$

$$A_{id} \equiv \frac{i_{od}}{i_{id}} \tag{12.39b}$$

Just as the common mode voltage gain will in general be very small for a well-designed differential amplifier, so too will the common mode current gain. The differential mode current gain will typically be extremely large.

12.3.4 Input and Output Resistances

The total input (and output) resistances of a differential amplifier can be defined just as they are for any circuit in terms of the total input (or output) current and voltage. However, it is far more useful when dealing with a differential amplifier to speak in terms of a difference mode and a common mode input resistance and a difference mode output resistance, since these are the quantities of importance in most applications of these amplifiers.

The difference mode input resistance R_{id} is defined as

$$R_{id} \equiv \frac{v_{id}}{i_{id}} \tag{12.40}$$

and the common mode input resistance R_{ic} is defined as

$$R_{ic} \equiv \frac{v_{ic}}{i_{ic}} \tag{12.41}$$

Half-circuit techniques can be used to calculate these quantities. Because the half-circuit models are analogous to those of the single-transistor amplifier stages discussed in Chap. 11, you are already familiar with them. For example, for the circuits of Figs. 12.11*a* and *b*, R_{id} is r_π and R_{ic} is $r_\pi + (\beta + 1)R_I/2$. The latter is essentially $\beta_{RI}/2$. Looking at these two results, we see that R_{ic} is clearly extremely large, whereas R_{id} is relatively much smaller.

Similarly, since the output is primarily due to the differential mode signal, it is almost exclusively the differential mode output resistance R_{od} that is of interest. This resistance is calculated using the difference mode half-circuit. The input is set equal to zero (i.e., shorted to ground), and the resistance seen looking back into the output terminals is calculated. This resistance is defined as R_{od}.

For the above definition, R_{od} is the output resistance for a single-ended output, that is, when either v_{o1} or v_{o2} (or i_{o1} or i_{o2}) is taken as the output. If the output is instead taken between both outputs (i.e., double-ended), then v_o will be $(v_{o1} - v_{o2})$, which is v_{od}, whereas i_o will still be $i_{od}/2$. Consequently the output resistance seen looking back from the two output terminals is $2v_{od}/i_{od}$, or $2R_{od}$.

12.4 OUTPUTS, CURRENT MIRRORS, AND ACTIVE LOADS

A differential amplifier offers a choice of output voltages, and this matter deserves a bit of discussion. We have identified three output signals, v_{o1}, v_{o2}, and v_o. In the jargon of the field, v_{o1} and v_{o2} are called *single-ended* outputs. For reasons that will become obvious soon, v_{o1} is called the *normal*, or *noninverting*, single-ended output and v_{o2} is called the *inverting* single-ended output. In the same vein, v_o is called the *double-ended* output. Notice that for the circuits we analyzed in Sec. 12.3.2 (i.e., those pictured in Figs. 12.2 and 12.10 through 12.12), we assumed that we were taking single-ended outputs.

We now want to show that these three signals are all related in a simple way if the common mode voltage gain is negligibly small, as it always is in a well-designed differential amplifier. To see this we refer to Eqs. (12.28d) and (12.29) for v_{o1} and v_{o2}, respectively. We assume that we are dealing with a well-designed circuit for which the common mode voltage gain is very small (i.e., $A_{vc} \approx 0$) to obtain first from Eq. (12.28d) that

$$v_{o1} \approx A_{vd}\frac{v_{id}}{2} \tag{12.42a}$$

which we can also write as

$$v_{o1} \approx A_{vd}\frac{(v_{i1} - v_{i2})}{2} \tag{12.42b}$$

Next we see from Eq. (12.29) that v_{o2} can be written as

$$v_{o2} \approx -A_{vd}\frac{v_{id}}{2} \tag{12.43a}$$

and thus

$$v_{o2} \approx -v_{o1} \tag{12.43b}$$

or

$$v_{o2} \approx -A_{vd}\frac{(v_{i1} - v_{i2})}{2} \tag{12.43c}$$

Finally, v_o is $v_{o1} - v_{o2}$, so we have

$$v_o \approx 2v_{o1} \tag{12.44a}$$

and thus

$$v_o \approx A_{vd}v_{id} \tag{12.44b}$$

or, equivalently,

$$v_o \approx A_{vd}(v_{i1} - v_{i2}) \tag{12.44c}$$

Comparison of Eqs. (12.42b), (12.43c), and (12.44c) shows that all three of the signals contain identical information; v_{o1} and v_{o2} are simply 180° out of phase, and the magnitude of v_o is twice that of v_{o1} and v_{o2}. You would logically choose v_o as the output signal, all else being equal, since it appears to be larger. It usually is, but a word of caution is in order because there is a rather subtle issue that comes into play here. To see what it is, let us assume that we are interested in applying the output to the same load R_L. In the situation where we are looking at the double-ended output, this load will be connected between the two output terminals. When we draw the differential mode half-circuit, this load will become a resistor of magnitude $R_L/2$ between the output node and ground (i.e., where R_L appeared in the circuits drawn in Figs. 12.11 and 12.12), which were drawn for a single-ended output. This may mean that A_{vd} is reduced, which is why we need to exercise caution. If we are dealing with an emitter- or source-follower stage, which is often the case when we are dealing with an output stage, A_{vd} will not be reduced significantly by this change and we do indeed gain a factor of two. If we are dealing with any of the other stages, however, A_{vd} will be reduced and we will not gain nearly this much.

Frequently, a grounded output is required, in which case v_o is not a useful output. In such situations either v_{o1} or v_{o2} must be taken as the output. This can result in gain reduced by a factor of two unless something is done. One thing that can be done to regain this factor of two is to convert the double-ended output v_o to a grounded singled-ended output using a current mirror. The current mirror circuit is illustrated in Fig. 12.13 along with a conventional common-emitter differential stage. In the conventional stage, the signal current i (which equals $g_m v_{id}/2$) results in an output v_{od} equal to $iR_LR_C/(R_L + R_C)$. In the current mirror circuit, the currents through the two *pnp* transistors used as collector "resistors" are constrained to be equal by tying the bases and emitters of these two transistors together. Since the currents through the differential pair increase and decrease by i (which equals $g_m v_{id}/2$), a current $2i$ is forced through the load, yielding an

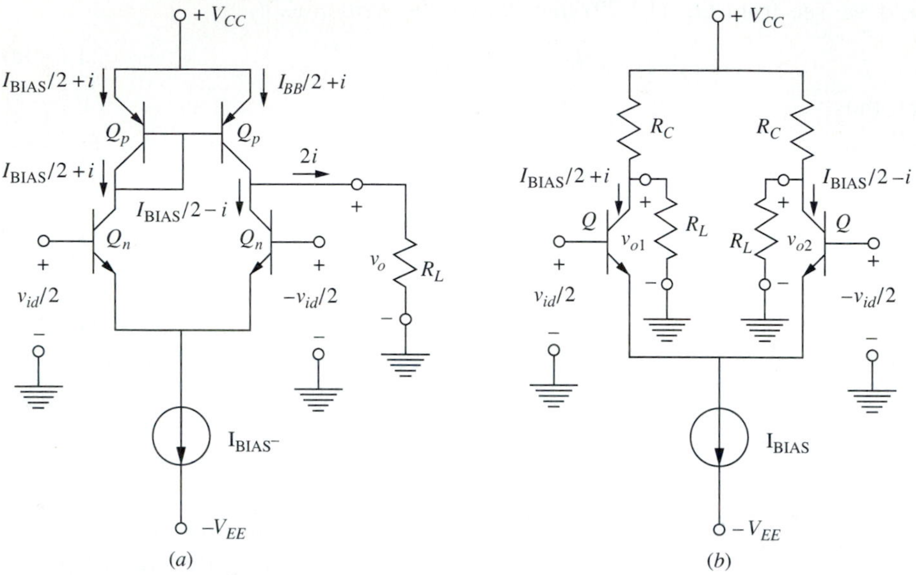

FIGURE 12.13
(*a*) Current mirror output stage; (*b*) a conventional single-sided output.

output v_o equal to $2iR_L$. The output voltage is now even more than twice as large as before since R_L is always larger than R_L in parallel with R_C.

If you recall our discussion of active loads in Chap. 11, you will recognize this last result as being a consequence of the fact that the current mirror also involves the use of active loads. Comparing the current mirror circuit of Fig. 12.13 with the circuit of Fig. 11.7*b* with a *pnp* active load, we see that they are the same basic idea. Significantly, however, in the present differential amplifier realization the load is even more active and doubles our gain. Physically what is going on is that we are applying a signal to both the *npn* transistor and to the *pnp* active load transistor, as we discussed above and as we will see again below.

As we know from our discussions in Chap. 11, the use of an active load gives us the possibility of using a very large load resistor and getting a very large gain. In such instances we need to investigate the role that the output conductances of our devices play in limiting the gain. To explore this, consider the small-signal linear equivalent circuits shown in Fig. 12.14, which correspond to the current mirror in Fig. 12.13*a*. Two circuits are shown, one for the left side and one for the right side of the mirror. The subscripts n and p refer to the npn and pnp transistors, respectively. Looking first at the left-side circuit, we see that $v_{\pi p}$, which we need in the right-side circuit, is

$$v_{\pi p} = -\frac{g_{mn}(v_{id}/2)}{(g_{on} + g_{mp} + g_{\pi p} + g_{op})} \approx -\frac{g_{mn}}{g_{mp}}\frac{v_{id}}{2} \tag{12.45}$$

where we have used the fact that g_{on}, g_{op}, and $g_{\pi p}$ are much smaller than g_{mp} to simplify the expression. We see right away that the $g_{mp}v_{\pi p}$ generator in the

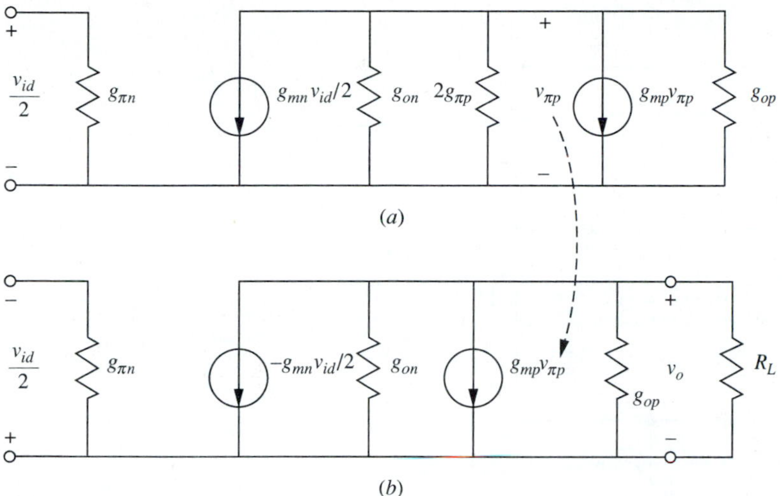

FIGURE 12.14
Small-signal linear equivalent circuits for analysis of the current mirror circuit in Fig. 12.13*a*: (*a*) for the left side of the circuit; (*b*) for the right side of the circuit.

right-side circuit is proportional to v_{id}; it is $-g_{mn}v_{id}/2$. Focusing now on the right-hand circuit, we see that we have

$$v_o = \frac{g_{mn}(v_{id}/2) - g_{mp}v_{\pi p}}{g_{on} + g_{op} + G_L} \approx \frac{g_{mn}v_{id}}{g_{on} + g_{op} + G_L} \tag{12.46}$$

Thus the differential mode voltage gain A_v is $g_{mn}/(g_{on} + g_{op} + G_L)$. If R_L is relatively small and G_L is much greater than g_{on} or g_{op}, this voltage gain is just $g_m R_L$. If R_L is large, the maximum gain will be limited by g_{on} and g_{op}; our familiar $g_m r_o$ (or g_m/g_o) factor shows up again.

It is important to realize that we can use a current mirror only if we are willing to accept a single-ended output, but that is often exactly what we want and is in general no problem.

12.5 CURRENT SOURCE DESIGNS

In our discussion of biasing single-transistor amplifier stages in Sec.11.1.1, we saw that the quiescent collector current in a transistor can be established independently of the output and load resistance, as long as the transistor is in its forward active region. We can say this another way: in the bipolar transistor, for example, the output portion of the large-signal model (i.e., the base-collector circuit in a common-base connection or the collector-emitter circuit in common-emitter connection) is simply a current source ($\alpha_F i_F$ or $\beta_F i_B$, respectively) that depends only on the input and not on the load. The same is true of the MOSFET; the output current in saturation is $K(v_{DS} - V_T)^2/2$, independent of the output v_{DS}. We now use this feature to get the current source I_{BIAS} that we need to bias our differential pair. We will look at a number of designs, both bipolar and MOSFET.

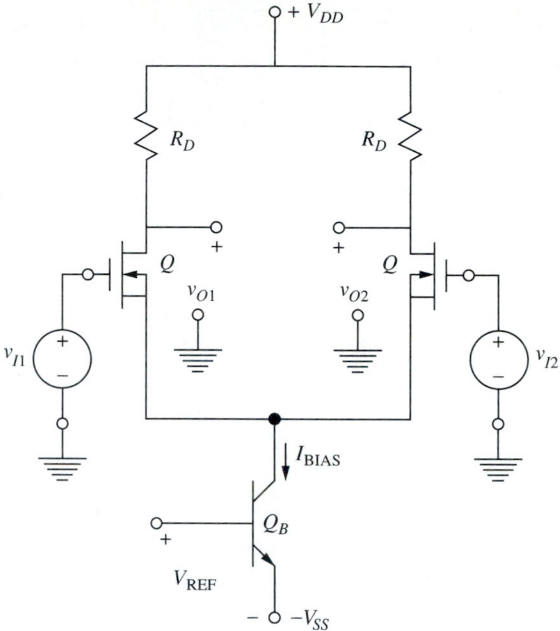

FIGURE 12.15
Use of an *npn* bipolar transistor to bias a differential amplifier.

12.5.1 Bipolar Current Sources

We use the common-emitter configuration to make a bipolar current source because it has high current gain; we connect the collector to the coupled emitters of the differential pair as illustrated in Fig. 12.15. The voltage reference set between the emitter and base terminals sets the collector current level, as long as the transistor Q_B is not saturated.

There are several common methods of setting the voltage reference on the base-emitter junction of this current source, just as there were when we were concerned with biasing bipolar single-transistor amplifier stages in Sec. 11.1.1. Four are illustrated in Fig. 12.16, and we will briefly discuss each below.

a) Resistive voltage divider. The resistive voltage divider is shown in Fig. 12.16*a*. Although this circuit is commonly used with single-transistor amplifiers made with discrete transistors, it is seldom used with integrated differential amplifiers because it can be readily improved upon. The improvements involve additional transistors that are expensive in discrete designs but have negligible impact on the cost of an integrated circuit.

b) Resistive voltage divider with temperature compensation. A major problem of simple resistive voltage divider biasing, Fig. 12.16*a*, is the variability and temperature sensitivity of the emitter-base voltage drop. The circuit of Fig. 12.16*b*

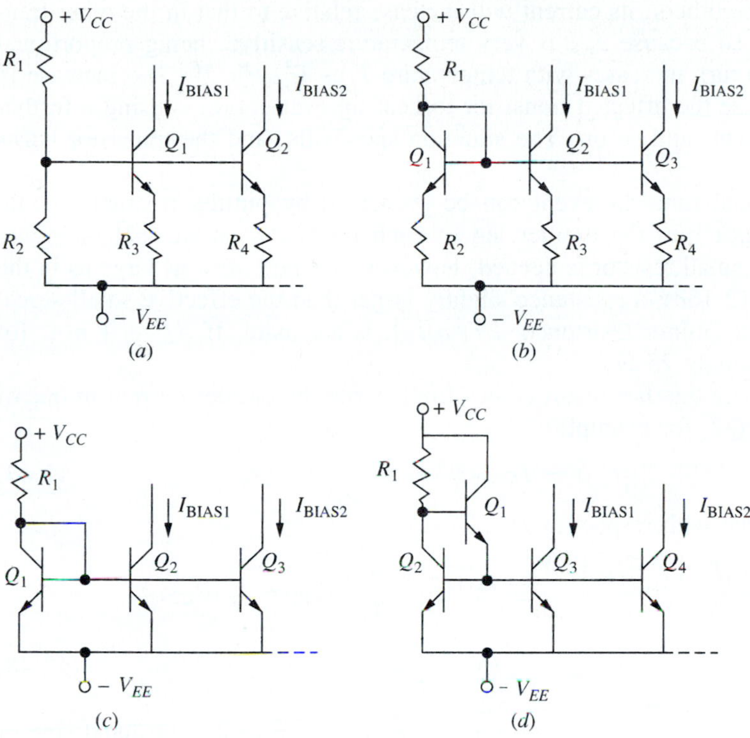

FIGURE 12.16
Several different bipolar current source designs: (*a*) resistive voltage divider; (*b*) resistive voltage divider with temperature compensation; (*c*) bias without emitter resistors; (*d*) base current compensation.

offers a ready solution by adding a matching junction to the voltage divider circuit. Adding another transistor is only a very minor complication in most integrated circuits and costs next to nothing. By using different-sized emitter resistors, different bias currents can be obtained.

c) Bias without emitter resistors. The problem with resistor biasing is that resistors consume a great deal of space on an integrated circuit and are to be avoided in general. A common solution is the circuit of Fig. 12.16*c*, in which the emitter resistors have been eliminated. To get different bias current levels, transistors with different emitter-base junction areas are used. For this scheme to work, however, the transistors must have identical values of J_{ES}, J_{CS}, a_F, and a_R. Although this is hard to achieve with discrete devices, such matching is routinely found in integrated circuits, and this scheme is very easy to implement.

There is a problem with this circuit, however, that has to do with its temperature stability. Since this scheme relies on identical transistors with identical values of v_{BE} having identical emitter currents, it also relies on all of the transistors having the same temperature. If one of the transistors should begin to warm up more than the others, its current will increase relative to that in the other transistors. This is so because J_{ES} is very temperature-sensitive, being proportional to n_i^2, which in turn increases with temperature T as $T^3 e^{-E_g/kT}$. The increase in current will cause the affected transistor to heat up even more, causing a further increase in current, and so on. The situation snowballs, and the transistor burns itself out.

This thermal runaway event can be prevented by putting a small amount of resistance back into the emitter leg of each transistor, as we had in Figure 12.16*b*. Only a small resistor is needed, however (nowhere near as large as in the scheme of Fig.12.16*b*): a resistance slightly larger than the effective small-signal equivalent linear emitter resistance, $kT/q|I_E|$, is adequate. If $|I_E|$ is 1 mA, for example, this is only 25 Ω.

To see where this last result comes from, write the emitter current in one of the transistors ($Q2$, for example):

$$|I_{E2}| = I_{ES2} e^{q(V_{\text{REF}} - I_{E2}R_{E2})/kT} \tag{12.47}$$

Then differentiate with respect to T:

$$\frac{d\,|I_{E2}|}{dT} = \frac{|I_{E2}|}{I_{ES2}}\frac{dI_{ES2}}{dT} - |I_{E2}|\frac{q}{kT^2}(V_{\text{REF}} - I_{E2}R_{E2}) + |I_{E2}|\frac{q}{kT}R_{E2}\frac{d\,|I_{E2}|}{dT} \tag{12.48}$$

Recognizing $q|I_{E2}|/kT$ as g_{e2} and moving the last term to the left-hand side of the equation, we have

$$\frac{d\,|I_{E2}|}{dT}(1 - g_{e2}R_{E2}) = |I_{E2}|\left[\frac{1}{I_{ES2}}\frac{dI_{ES2}}{dT} - \frac{q}{kT^2}(V_{\text{REF}} - I_{E2}R_{E2})\right] \tag{12.49}$$

Next, we look at dI_{ES2}/dT. The main temperature dependence of I_{ES2} is through the $e^{-Eg/kT}$ in n_i^2, and thus we have

$$\frac{1}{I_{ES2}}\frac{dI_{ES2}}{dT} \approx \frac{E_g}{kT^2} \tag{12.50}$$

and our equation for dI_{ES}/dT becomes

$$\frac{d\,|I_{E2}|}{dT} = \frac{|I_{E2}|}{(1 - g_{e2}R_{E2})}\frac{1}{kT^2}\left[E_g - q\,(V_{\text{REF}} - I_{E2}R_{E2})\right] \tag{12.51}$$

The last factor in this equation is always positive, so the only way to guarantee that $d|I_{E2}|/dT$ is negative is to make the term $(1 - g_{e2}R_{E2})$ negative. This occurs when R_{E2} is greater $1/g_{e2}$ (i.e., $KT/q|I_{E2}|$).

d) Base current compensation. A shortcoming of all of the circuits illustrated thus far is that they assume negligible base current. At times, such as when one reference transistor is used to establish the base-emitter voltages on many current sources, this is not a good assumption and a circuit such as that illustrated in

Fig. 12.16*d* is used. In this circuit an additional transistor Q_1 has been added to provide the base currents, and the imbalance is reduced by a factor of β_F.

e) Very low bias levels. The current sources in Fig. 12.16 would all require very large value resistors to yield bias currents in the microampere range; producing such large resistors is difficult in an integrated circuit. At the same time, it is sometimes desirable to have such low bias levels because this results in a large r_π and thus in a larger input resistance to a bipolar transistor stage. An interesting solution to this problem is the Widlar current source illustrated in Fig. 12.17. This circuit was invented by one of the early "gurus" of analog integrated circuit design, Robert J. Widlar, and is used, for example, in the 741 operational amplifier to bias the input stage.

To analyze the Widlar current source, we begin by calculating the current through the reference transistor, I_{REF}. Assuming that the transistors are identical, high-β devices and that $V_{BE,\text{ON}}$ is approximately 0.6 V, we have

$$I_{\text{REF}} \approx \frac{(V_{CC} + V_{EE} - 0.6\text{ V})}{R_1} \tag{12.52}$$

Next we move on to calculating I_{BIAS}, but we immediately note that if we assume $V_{BE,\text{ON}}$ is 0.6 V for both transistors, we will find that I_{BIAS} is zero, since summing voltages around the lower loop yields

$$V_{BE1} = V_{BE2} + R_2 I_{\text{BIAS}} \tag{12.53}$$

Clearly we must be more careful and cannot make this assumption at this stage of the calculation. Rather we must use the Ebers–Moll model. Assuming that both transistors are identical, have high gain, and are biased in their forward active region, we obtain

$$V_{BE1} \approx \frac{kT}{q} \ln \frac{I_{\text{REF}}}{I_{ES}} \tag{12.54}$$

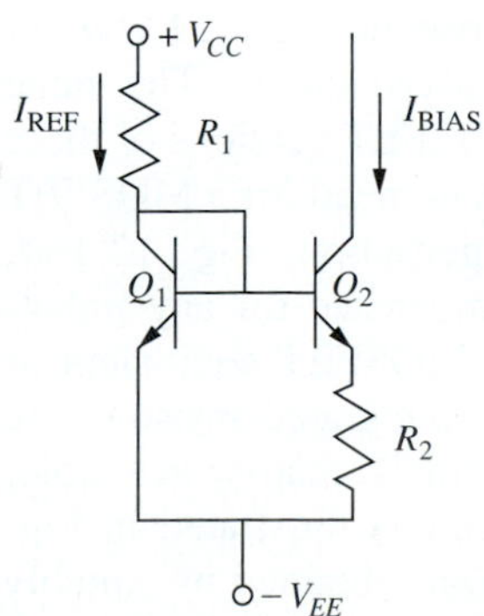

FIGURE 12.17
Widlar current source, a design used when relatively small bias currents are needed.

$$V_{BE2} \approx \frac{kT}{q} \ln \frac{I_{\text{BIAS}}}{I_{ES}} \tag{12.55}$$

Combining the last three equations gives us a transcendental equation for I_{BIAS}:

$$I_{\text{BIAS}} = \frac{kT}{qR_2} \ln \frac{I_{\text{REF}}}{I_{\text{BIAS}}} \tag{12.56a}$$

This looks messy at first, but remember that as a circuit designer you know the values of I_{BIAS} and I_{REF} you want to achieve and that what you need to calculate is the required value of R_2. Thus this equation should instead be written as it will be used:

$$R_2 = \frac{kT}{qI_{\text{BIAS}}} \ln \frac{I_{\text{REF}}}{I_{\text{BIAS}}} \tag{12.56b}$$

As a numerical example, assume we want I_{BIAS} to be 1.0 mA and choose I_{REF} to be 10 μA. We calculate $R_2 = 11.5$ kΩ. For comparison, a design like that of Fig. 12.16*c* or *d* would require an emitter resistor in excess of 200 kΩ, a prohibitively high value to realize on an integrated circuit.

f) Voltage compliance. The range of output voltages over which a current source can operate is called its *voltage compliance*; this is an important characteristic of any given current source design. In the designs in Figs. 12.16 and 12.17, the relevant voltage is that on the collector of the current source transistor, say Q_2, relative to the negative supply V_{EE}. The largest this voltage can be will be determined by the breakdown voltage of the transistor, in this case Q_2. The smallest it can be will be set by saturation of the same transistor; in designs without any emitter resistors, such as those in Figs. 12.16*c* and *d*, the output can go to within a few tenths of a volt of $-V_{EE}$. In the other designs, the output must be kept higher by an amount corresponding to the voltage drop across the relevant emitter resistor. This is a good argument for keeping the emitter resistor as small as practical in light of other considerations (see Sec.12.5.1*c* above).

12.5.2 MOSFET Current Sources

MOSFET current source topologies are analogous to those in Figs. 12.16*a*, *b*, and *c* (and you should be able to easily sketch and analyze them). The same comments concerning their relative merits apply to the MOSFET versions of these circuits as applied to the bipolar circuits. Note that there is no need for a MOSFET equivalent to the bipolar circuit with base current compensation, Fig. 12.16*d*, because there is no gate current and thus no need to compensate for any imbalance it would cause. In an integrated circuit context, the MOSFET equivalent of the circuit of Fig. 12.16*c* is the most attractive because integrated resistors are relatively large and space-consuming and transistors are small, readily available, and closely matched. This MOSFET current source circuit is illustrated in Fig. 12.18. As is shown in this figure, different current levels are obtained by suitably adjusting the width-to-length ratios of the MOSFET gate regions. In practice, the

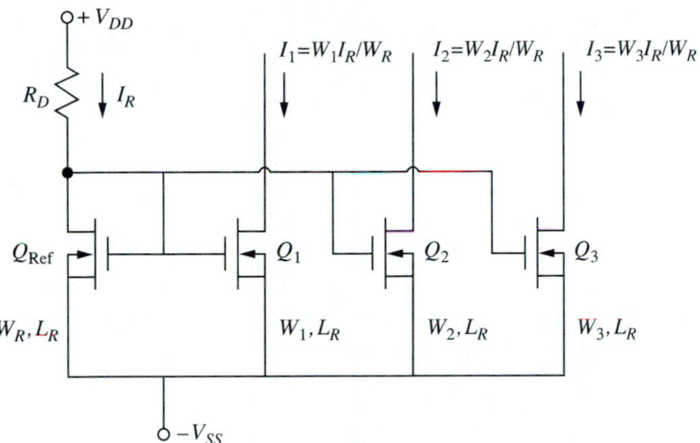

FIGURE 12.18
MOSFET current source design commonly used in integrated circuits.

gate length L is usually held fixed and the gate width W is varied from device to device.

The choice of whether to use a bipolar or a MOSFET current source in a given circuit usually depends on what type of integrated circuit—bipolar or MOS—is being built. That is, we often do not have a choice. In some cases, however, such as in discrete designs (which are extremely rare these days) or in processes yielding both BJTs and MOSFETs, we have an option and the need to choose does arise. In such situations, BJTs are preferred for several reasons. The most important is that a bipolar current source will have a larger voltage compliance; that is, it will tolerate a wider voltage swing on its output terminal without coming out of its forward active region: v_{CE} can be as small as 0.2 V, whereas v_{DS} has to be at least $(v_{GS} - V_T)$, which is typically a volt or more. This results in a larger voltage compliance and, consequently, a larger common mode voltage range. Another reason to prefer BJT current sources is that BJTs tend to have larger output resistances than MOSFETs and thus look more nearly like ideal current sources. MOSFETs do have one advantage; they do not have a gate current and thus there is no need to compensate for the imbalance caused by the nonzero base current in a BJT.

The problem of the lower output resistance of MOSFETs can be serious when we have to use a MOSFET current source, so ways have been developed to improve upon this aspect of the basic MOSFET current source shown in Fig. 12.18. An example is shown in Fig. 12.19*a*, in which a second layer of transistors has been added, yielding a cascode-like* connection with significantly enhanced output resistance. The analysis of this circuit is relatively straightforward. The

*The cascode connection is introduced in Sec. 13.2.2. Knowing what it is at this time is not essential to your understanding of this current source.

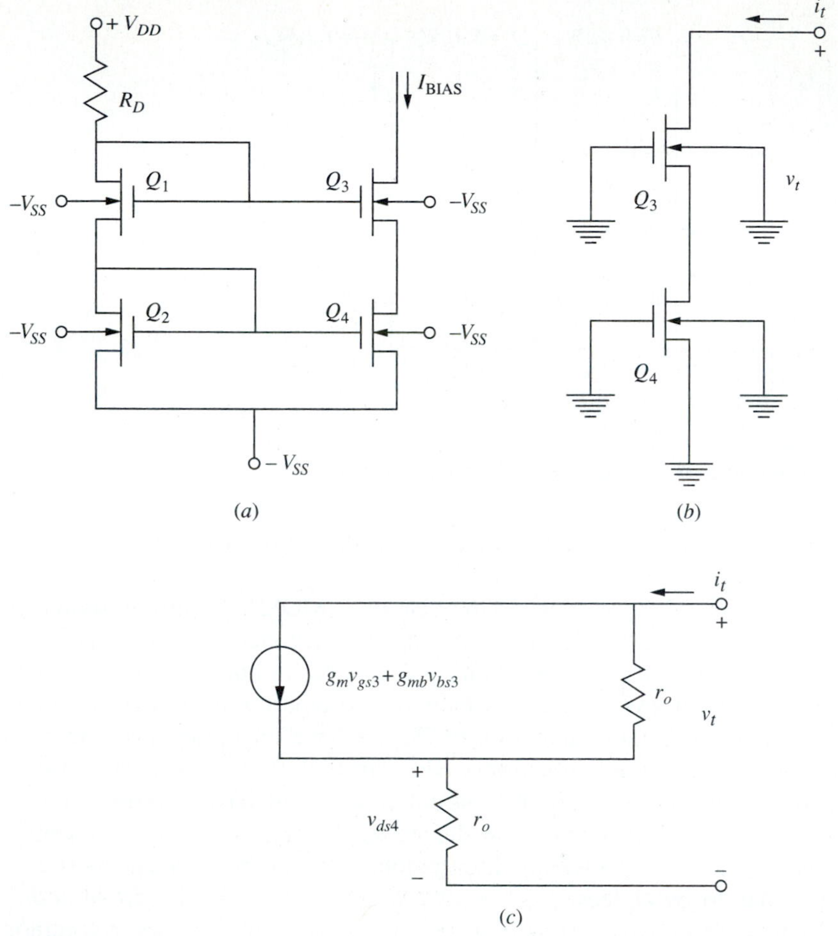

FIGURE 12.19
(*a*) MOSFET current source design that overcomes the problem of the relatively low output resistance often encountered in MOSFETs. (*b*) The input resistance test circuit; (*c*) The resulting incremental equivalent circuit.

incremental output resistance is measured by setting all independent voltage sources to zero, except for a test voltage v_t applied to the output terminals, and by determining the current i_t. If you refer to the input resistance test circuit in Fig. 12.19*b* and its incremental equivalent circuit in Fig. 12.19*c* when you perform the analysis of this circuit, you will find that the output resistance is given by

$$R_{\text{out}} = r_o[2 + r_o(g_m + g_{mb})] \tag{12.57a}$$

(In arriving at this result we have assumed that the output resistances of all of the transistors in the circuit are the same.) Using the fact that we can also write g_{mb} as ηg_m, we have

$$R_{\text{out}} = r_o[2 + r_o g_m(1 + \eta)] \tag{12.57b}$$

This is to be compared with an output resistance for the circuit of Fig. 12.18 of simply r_o. The output resistance is thus increased by a factor of more than $r_o g_m$, which as we discussed in Sec. 11.4.1*a*, can be quite significant. Recalling Eq. (11.51), this factor can be written as $2|V_A/(V_{GS} - V_T)|$; thus if $|V_A|$ is on the order of 30 V and the numerator is 1.5 V, this will be a factor of 40. If we can be comfortable biasing even closer to V_T, a choice that depends on our process control, we can make it even larger.

Notice that adding a second layer of transistors means that this circuit has a lower voltage compliance than the circuit in Fig. 12.18. By the same token, it also reduces the common mode voltage swing of any stage biased using this scheme, so this is not necessarily a good circuit for use on an input stage. On later stages common mode voltage swing is no longer a concern, as will become clear in the next chapter.

12.6 SUMMARY

In this chapter, as in most of this text, there is something basic and general you should learn, and there are numerous smaller and more specific things you should learn—the forest and the trees, as it were. In this case the "forest" is the concept of symmetry and the power of invoking symmetry to simplify an analysis. The "trees" are the specifics and properties of differential amplifier and current source circuits.

Symmetry is a very powerful tool that is used to advantage in many disciplines. In this chapter we have used symmetry to argue that certain nodes in a symmetrical linear circuit with differential mode inputs must be at zero potential and thus are incremental grounds. We have also argued that the current in links that connect the two halves of a symmetrical circuit with common mode inputs must be zero and that these links thus are functionally open circuits. Finally, we have argued on the basis of symmetry that corresponding signals on either side of a symmetrical circuit are either of equal magnitude and sign or of equal magnitude but opposite sign, respectively, for common mode or difference mode inputs. The net result has been a tremendous simplification of our problem. Identifying certain nodes as grounded and/or certain links as open simplifies the circuit. Furthermore, recognizing that the answers for one half of a circuit trivially gives us those for the other half cuts our remaining work in half, all because we stopped to think about the problem before we attacked it.

The specific conclusions we have reached in this chapter about differential amplifiers are also very important. We have seen that these circuits are ideally perfectly symmetrical and that they are typically biased using current sources. They have two input signals, and the output can be taken in several ways (i.e., either from the two separate output terminals or as the difference between the signals on these two terminals). We have shown that it is possible to decompose any arbitrary pair of inputs into a common mode input and a difference mode input, and we have seen that a differential amplifier responds primarily only to difference mode inputs (it responds quite well, in fact, and the differential input voltage of an emitter-coupled pair must be less than kT/q to maintain linear operation). Common mode inputs, on the other hand, have almost no effect on the output of the differential amplifier, as long as they are not so positive or negative that they drive the circuit out of its linear active region. It is safe to say that this sensitivity to differential mode inputs and insensitivity to common mode inputs is the most important practical feature of differential amplifiers.

To aid our analysis, we have used symmetry to introduce the concept of half-circuit models and thereby greatly simplify our analyses. With this step, we have found that our circuit models became identical to those we had analyzed in our study of single-transistor linear amplifier stages, circuits with which we are already quite familiar.

Finally, we have studied several designs for current source circuits, which are used to bias differential amplifiers. The circuits we have looked at range from the very simple and rather sensitive (to device and temperature variations), to the more complex and more robust. These circuits, in fact, represent a very nice set with which to begin to understand some of the issues a circuit designer working with real physical devices must consider; and they are worth reviewing in this light. There are many circuits that can do a particular job, but not all designs are good designs. In rare cases, circuit designs with improved performance and insensitivity to device and environmental variations can be implemented at very modest cost in terms of realizing them as an integrated circuit (the format we usually encounter in modern design). However, many designs—which for the most part we do not discuss—are impractical to implement.

PROBLEMS

12.1 All of the transistors in the differential amplifier circuit illustrated in Fig. P12.1 are identical with $\beta_f = 100$, $v_{BE,\text{ON}} = 0.7$ V, and $v_{CE,\text{SAT}} = 0.2$ V.

(*a*) What are the quiescent collector currents in these transistors when $v_{I1} = v_{I2} = 0$?

(*b*) What is the largest positive value of pure common mode voltage that can be applied to the input terminals without driving the transistors into saturation?

(*c*) What is the largest negative value of pure common mode voltage that can be applied to the input terminals without driving the transistors into cutoff?

(*d*) What is the differential mode voltage gain of this circuit?

(*e*) What is the differential mode input resistance of this circuit?

12.2 In the circuit in Fig. P12.2*a*, all the transistors are identical with $\beta = 500$, $v_{BE,\text{ON}} = 0.6$ V, and r_x (the base resistance other than r_π) $= 0$. Use reasonable approximations in your solution.

(*a*) Specify the values of I_1 and R_1 necessary to achieve an operating point of $I_{CQ} = 1$ mA for each transistor and zero offset on the output (i.e., $v_{\text{OUT}} = 0$ when $v_{\text{IN}} = 0$).

(*b*) Determine the open-circuit ($R_L \to \infty$) mid-band voltage gain of the circuit.

(*c*) Determine the mid-band voltage gain when $R_L = 1$ kΩ.

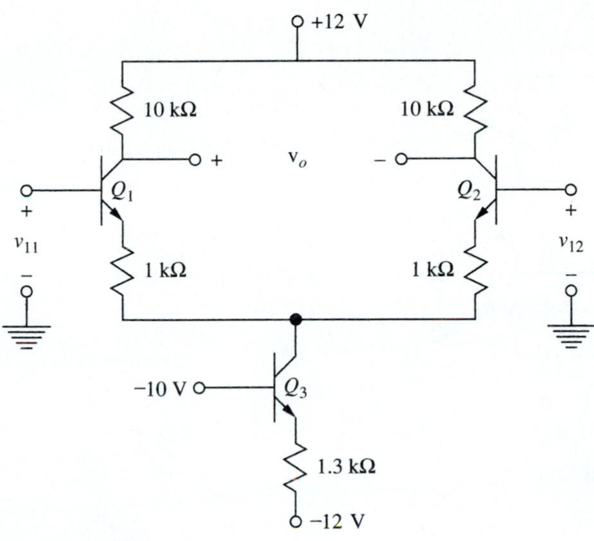

FIGURE P12.1

(*d*) If the current source I_1 is to be realized through the circuit in Fig. P12.2*b*, determine the appropriate value for R_2.

12.3 The circuit parameters for the circuit in Fig. P12.3 are as follows:

$$I = 2 \text{ mA}$$
$$kT/q = 0.025 \text{ V}$$
$$R_L = 2 \text{ k}\Omega$$
$$R_E = 1 \text{ k}\Omega$$
$$R_O = 10^6 \ \Omega$$
$$V = 6 \text{ V}$$

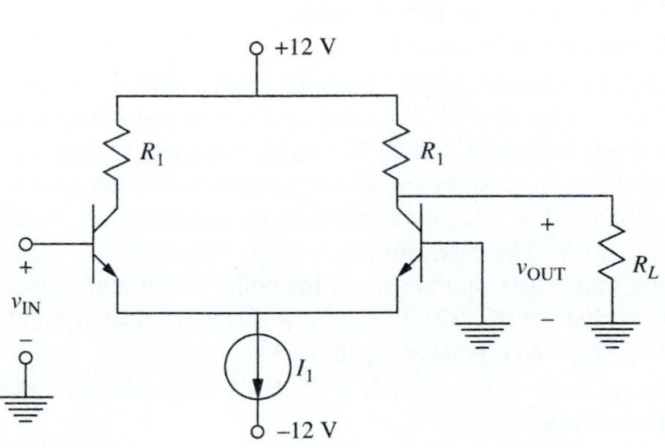

FIGURE P12.2*a*

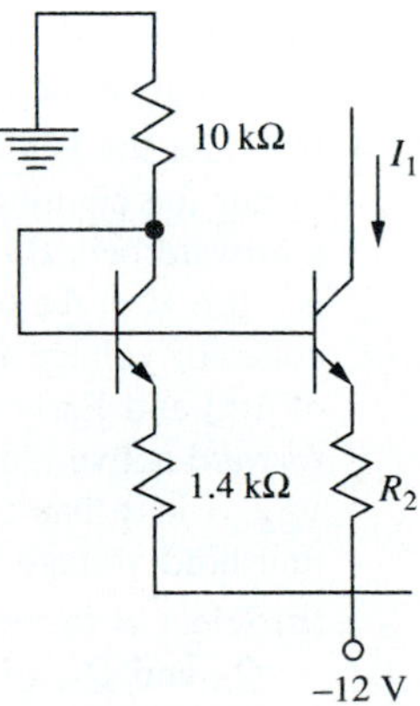

FIGURE P12.2*b*

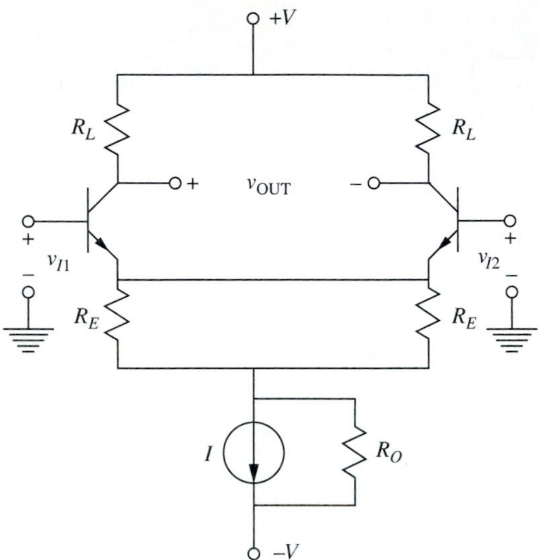

FIGURE P12.3

The hybrid-π parameters are as follows:

$$\begin{aligned} r_b &= 0 \\ C_\pi &= 2 \text{ pf} \\ C_\pi &= 3 \text{ pf} \\ g_m &= qI_C/kT \\ g_\pi &= g_m/\beta \\ \beta &= 100 \end{aligned}$$

(*a*) For the circuit illustrated above, draw the small-signal incremental half-circuit models valid for (i) differential mode input, and (ii) common mode input.
(*b*) Calculate the mid-band differential mode voltage gain.
(*c*) Calculate the mid-band common mode voltage gain.

12.4 Consider the BiMOS differential amplifier circuit illustrated in Fig. P12.4. (BiMOS means the circuit contains both bipolar and MOS devices.) The *pnp* transistors have a forward beta β_F of 50 and Early voltage V_A of 20 V. The base-emitter voltage V_{BE} is -0.6 V in the forward active region, and the transistors saturate when the emitter-collector voltage V_{EC} is less than 0.2 V. The *npn* transistors have a forward beta β_F of 100 and Early voltage of -60 V. The base-emitter voltage V_{BE} is 0.6 V in the forward active region, and the transistors saturate when the collector-emitter voltage V_{CE} is less than 0.2 V. The *n*-channel MOSFETs have a K-factor of 100 μA/V^2, threshold voltage V_T of 1.0 V, and Early voltage V_A of 10 V.

(*a*) Select R to yield a quiescent collector current in Q_6 of 0.1 mA. (Assume that Q_5 and Q_6 are identical transistors.)
(*b*) With R as in part a and with $v_{IN1} = v_{IN2} = 0$, what is the gate-to-source voltage V_{GS} on Q_3?
(*c*) What is the maximum possible common mode input voltage for which the transistors will be operating in their forward active regions?

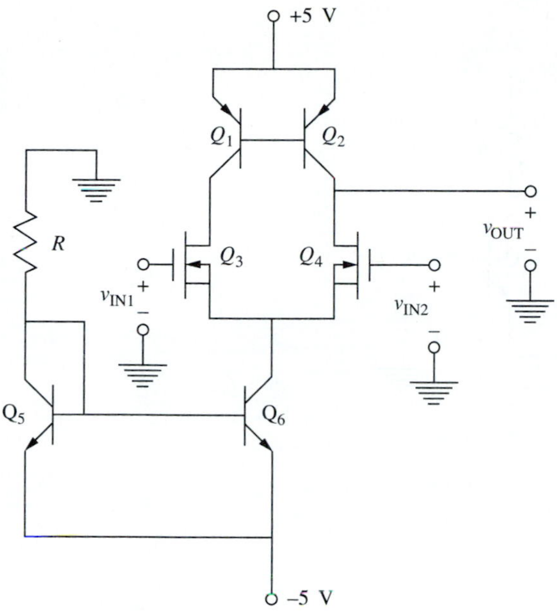

FIGURE P12.4

(*d*) What is the mid-band small-signal output resistance of this amplifier?

(*e*) The mid-band small-signal open-circuit voltage gain of this stage, $A_{v,\text{oc}}$, is a function of I_{C6}, the quiescent collector current of Q_6. Does $A_{v,\text{oc}}$ increase, decrease, or remain essentially unchanged if I_{C6} is increased? Support your answer by explicitly stating the functional proportionality between $A_{v,\text{oc}}$ and I_{C6}.

12.5 The emitter-coupled amplifier shown in Fig. P12.5*a* contains identical transistors Q_1 and Q_2, which have the following characteristics:

$$V_{BE,\text{ON}} = 0.6 \text{ V}$$
$$V_{CE,\text{SAT}} = 0.2 \text{ V}$$
$$\beta_F = 200$$

The amplifier is driven by the ideal incremental voltage sources v_{i1} and v_{i2}.

Notice that this amplifier is resistively biased, not current source biased.

(*a*) With $R_1 = 1 \text{ k}\Omega$, and $R_2 = 1.2 \text{ k}\Omega$, verify that with $v_{I1} = v_{I2} = 0$ the transistors are operating in their forward active region.

(*b*) With $R_2 = 1.2 \text{ k}\Omega$ and $v_{I1} = v_{I2} = 0$, how large can R_1 be before the transistors cease to operate in their forward active region?

The circuit is modified as shown in Fig. P12.5*b* by connecting a resistor R_3 between the two output terminals.

(*c*) With $R_1 = 1 \text{ k}\Omega$ and $R_2 = 2 \text{ k}\Omega$, the amplifier is driven by a pure difference mode incremental signal $v_{i1} = -v_{i2} = v_{id}/2$. Evaluate the incremental voltage gain v_{o2}/v_{id}. Give your answer first in literal (symbolic) form and then in numerical form.

(*d*) Repeat part c when the amplifier is driven by a pure common mode incremental signal $v_{ic} = v_{i1} = v_{i2}$ (i.e., find v_{o2}/v_{iC}).

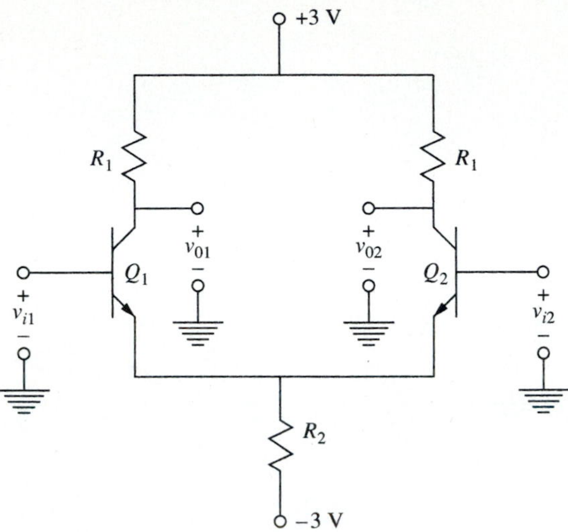

FIGURE P12.5*a*

12.6 Consider the design of a series of three MOSFET current sources providing 0.1, 0.2, and 0.3 mA, respectively. The circuit is shown in Fig. P12.6.

Each MOSFET has the same gate length L, which is 1 μm, but they may have different widths W. All have the same threshold voltage V_T, which is 1.0 V. For the reference transistor Q_R, W is 200 μm and K is 0.12 mA/V^2.

(*a*) Select a value for the quiescent drain current of Q_R and values for W_1, W_2, and W_3. Assume that you want to minimize the size of devices in this current source.

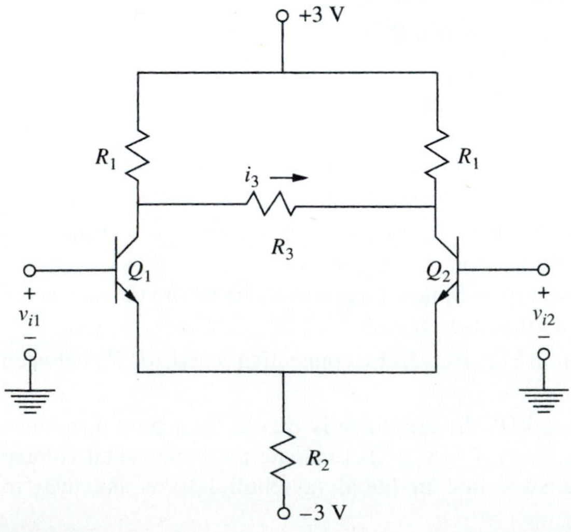

FIGURE P12.5*b*

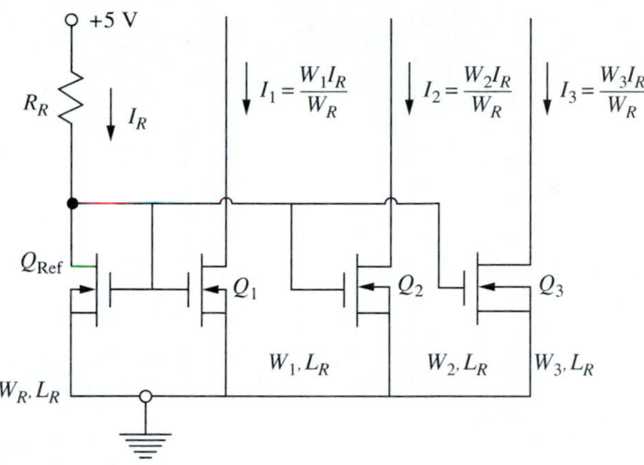

FIGURE P12.6

(*b*) What value should R_R have to get the quiescent drain current you designed in part a?

(*c*) Assuming that the Early voltage V_A of Q_R is 20 V, what is V_A for Q_1, Q_2, and Q_3? (*Note:* You will have to reason for yourself how V_A should vary with W.)

(*d*) Using your results in part c, calculate the mid-band incremental linear output resistance of each of the three current sources. Notice that this is just $1/g_o$ for the relevant transistor, that is, of Q_1, Q_2, and Q_3, respectively.

12.7 This question concerns the design of the differential amplifier circuit pictured Fig. P12.7*a*. The box labeled "Output stage" will be described in more detail later; for parts a through c you may assume that it has infinite input resistance. The transistors

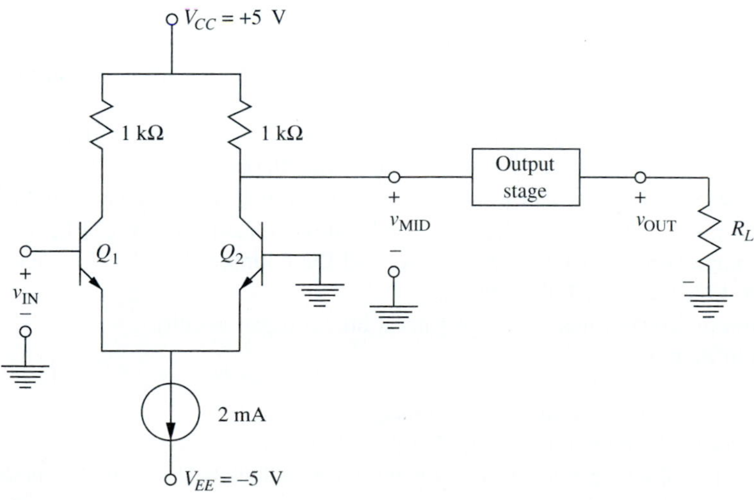

FIGURE P12.7*a*

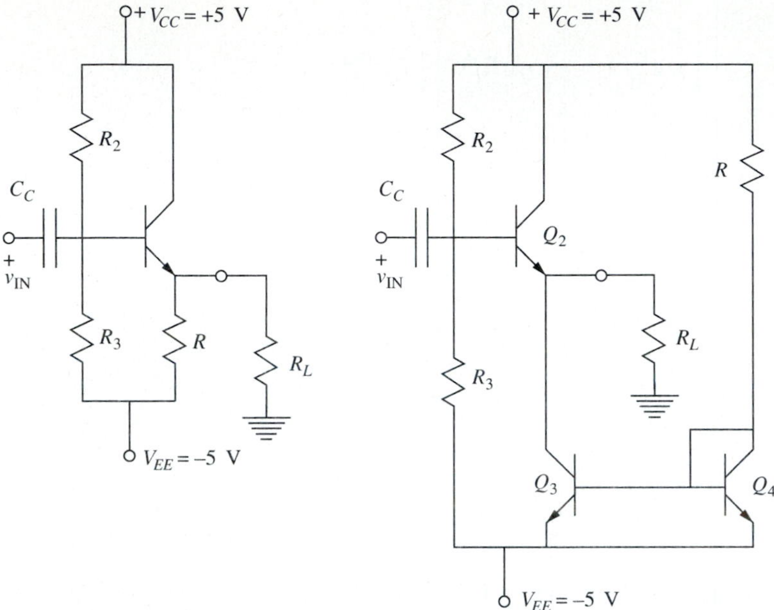

FIGURE P12.7*b*

are *npn* bipolar transistors with $\beta = 100$; in their hybrid-π models r_x is zero and g_o is given by I_C/V_A, where $V_A = 50$ V.

(*a*) Draw a small-signal linear equivalent circuit for the input stage suitable for calculating $v_{\text{mid}}/v_{\text{in}}$. Clearly label the values of r_π, g_π, g_o, etc.

(*b*) Derive an expression for the mid-band incremental voltage gain of the first stage, $v_{\text{mid}}/v_{\text{in}}$.

(*c*) What is the maximum common mode input voltage v_C that can be applied to this amplifier without affecting its operation?

Next consider the two possible topologies of the output stage box illustrated in Fig. P12.7*b*.

(*d*) Suppose that you want each of these output stages to be capable of delivering ± 2 V to a 1-kΩ load. What is the maximum value the resistor R can have, and what is the corresponding quiescent collector current in Q_2, I_{C2}, in each circuit?

12.8 Consider the four input device/active load combinations illustrated in Fig. P12.8. If I_{BIAS} can range between 10 μA and 1 mA, find the optimum bias level for each combination to achieve the following:

(*a*) Maximum differential mode voltage gain at output (open circuit)
(*b*) Maximum input resistance
(*c*) Maximum output resistance
(*d*) Largest positive common mode input voltage limit
(*e*) Largest negative common mode input voltage limit

12.9 For each of the following input signal voltage pairs, calculate the common mode and difference mode voltages.

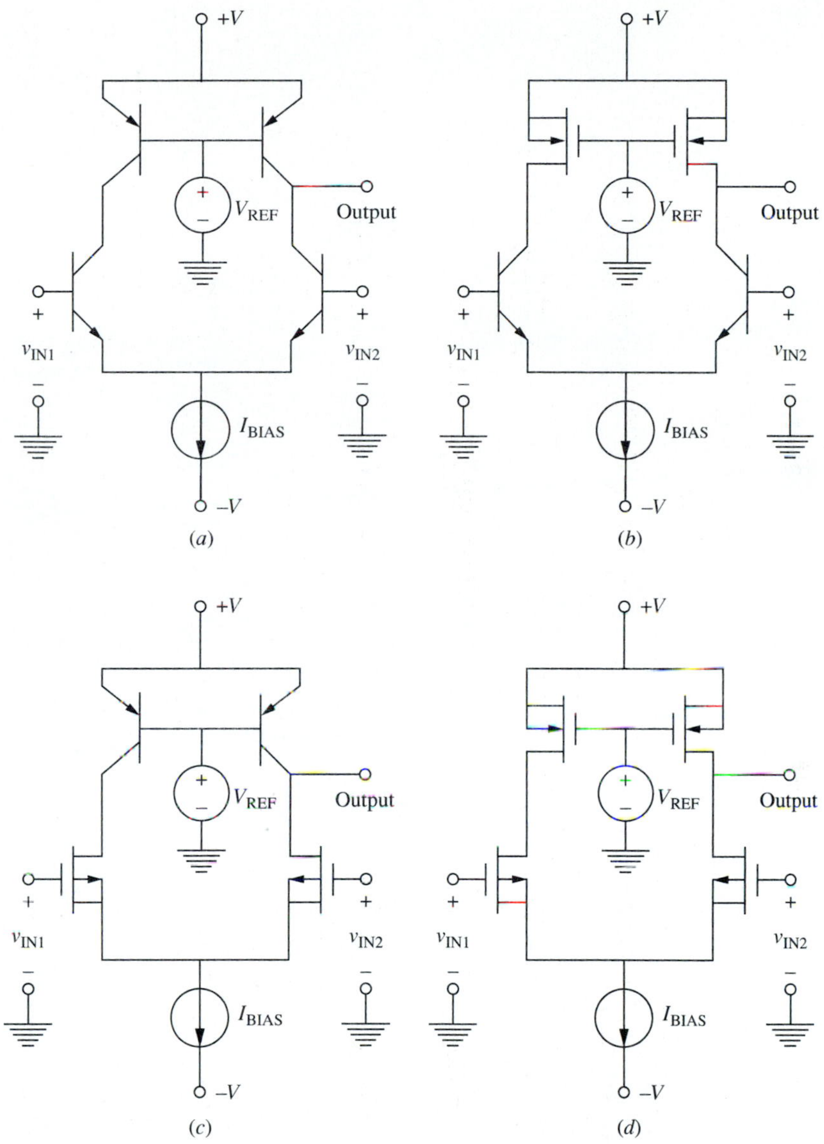

FIGURE P12.8

(*a*) $v_{IN1} = 6$ V, $v_{IN2} = 3$ V
(*b*) $v_{IN1} = 5 \sin \omega t$ V, $v_{IN2} = 0$
(*c*) $v_{IN1} = (r \sin \omega t + 3 \sin \omega_2 t)$ V
$v_{IN2} = 3 \sin \omega_2 t$ V
(*d*) $v_{IN1} = 5 \cos(\omega t + \theta)$ V
$v_{IN2} = 5 \cos \omega t$ V

CHAPTER 13

MULTISTAGE AMPLIFIERS

The single-transistor circuits discussed in Chap. 11 and the differential amplifier circuits discussed in Chap. 12 can be used as building blocks to assemble more complex amplifier circuits. Through the careful selection and combination of building-block circuits, or "stages," it is possible to design circuits that have levels of gains and combinations of input and output resistances unattainable from single stages. These *multistage* circuits will be our subject in this chapter.

An important consideration in the design of multistage amplifiers is how the individual stages interact and influence the characteristics of their neighbors. As we shall see, the output of any given stage will be the input to the succeeding stage, and the input resistance of any given stage will be the load seen by the stage preceding it. It is essential that individual stages be selected and combined with these interactions taken into account.

Another important consideration, and perhaps the most difficult challenge encountered when combining two or more transistors into a complex circuit like a multistage amplifier, is to simultaneously bias all of the transistors in the circuit in their forward active region without compromising the performance of any of the individual stages. Each of the approaches to multistage amplifiers we will study in this chapter handles this problem in a different way.

We will begin in the next section by considering an old, relatively primitive, yet powerful approach to combining multiple stages: the capacitively coupled cascade. Then we will look at more sophisticated directly coupled stages, and finally we will discuss differential amplifiers, an important class of multistage amplifiers built up primarily of differential-pair stages.

13.1 CAPACITIVELY COUPLED CASCADE

The simplest solution to the problem of combining and biasing several transistor stages is to couple them using capacitors. The capacitors are open circuits to the bias voltages and currents, so the biases on the individual stages are unaffected by combining the stages in this way. At the same time, if the capacitors are large enough, they will look like short circuits to the time-varying signals to be amplified, as you will recall from our discussion of the concept of mid-band frequencies in Sec. 11.2. Coupling stages one after another is termed *cascading*, and doing so via capacitors like this creates what is called a *capacitively coupled cascade*.

An example of two common-emitter stages coupled capacitively is shown in Fig. 13.1*a*. The capacitor C_C is used to couple the output of the first stage to the input of the second; clearly the bias points are not changed by coupling them in this way.

The mid-band small-signal linear equivalent circuit for the circuit in Fig. 13.1*a* is drawn in Fig. 13.1*b*. Again we are interested in the voltage, current, and power gains of this circuit, as well as its input and output resistances.

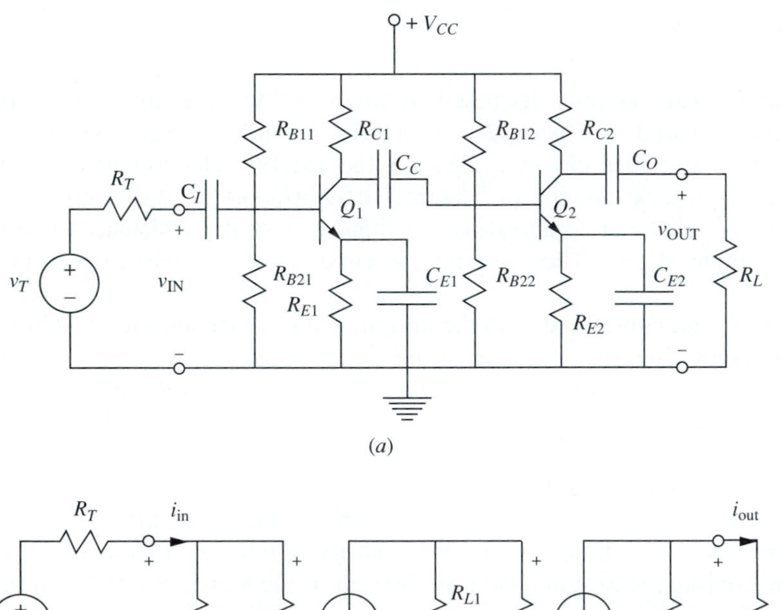

FIGURE 13.1
(*a*) Two common-emitter stages coupled capacitively via C_C; (*b*) the corresponding mid-band small-signal linear equivalent circuit (R_{B1} is the parallel combination of R_{B11} and R_{B21}, and R_{L1} is the parallel combination of R_{C1}, R_{B12}, and R_{B22}).

A little thought shows us that the voltage gain A_v is just the product of the voltage gains of the individual stages. To see this, define the voltage gains of the first stage, A_{v1}, and of the second stage, A_{v2}, as follows:

$$A_{v1} \equiv \frac{v_{out1}}{v_{in}} \tag{13.1a}$$

$$A_{v2} \equiv \frac{v_{out}}{v_{in2}} \tag{13.1b}$$

Since v_{in2} is identical to v_{out1}, we have immediately that

$$A_{v1}A_{v2} = \frac{v_{out}}{v_{in}} \equiv A_v \tag{13.2}$$

The issue now is to calculate the voltage gain of each stage. Looking at the first stage, we see that the load on this stage is the parallel combination of the stage-one collector resistor, the stage-two base bias resistors, and $r_{\pi 2}$ (i.e., $R_{C1}\|R_{B12}\|R_{B22}\|r_{\pi 2}$). A_{v1} is thus given by

$$A_{v1} = -g_{m1}\left(R_{C1}\,\|R_{B12}\,\|R_{B22}\,\|r_{\pi 2}\right) \tag{13.3a}$$

Because $r_{\pi 2}$ will typically be the smallest of these resistors, it is frequently true that this reduces to

$$A_{v1} \approx -g_{m1}r_{\pi 2} \tag{13.3b}$$

For the second stage we have

$$A_{v2} = -g_{m2}R'_{L2} \tag{13.4}$$

where, as before, R'_{L2} is defined as the parallel equivalent of R_{C2} and R_L.

The total mid-band voltage gain is thus approximately

$$A_v \approx g_{m1}g_{m2}r_{\pi 2}R'_{L2} \tag{13.5a}$$

Recognizing the product $r_{\pi 2}\ g_{m2}$ as β_{F2} we can write A_v as

$$A_v \approx g_{m1}\beta_{F2}R'_{L2} \tag{13.5b}$$

Writing the voltage gain in this way, we see immediately that the magnitude of the gain of this two-stage cascade is β_{F2} times as large as that of a similar single-stage amplifier.

The current and power gains are also the products of the gains of the individual stages and can be calculated just as easily. The input and output resistances of this cascade are the same as the input and output resistances of the first and second stage, respectively.

Cascading two common-emitter stages gives us more gain than we can achieve with a single stage, as we have seen; this is a common reason for going to a multistage design. Another reason for combining multiple stages is to obtain independent control over the input and output resistances and the gain. It is often desirable, for example, to have an amplifier with a very low output resistance. This can be accomplished by using an emitter-follower as the last stage. The input resistance of a follower stage is large, so it also does not reduce the voltage gain of the preceding stages. It is an excellent final, or "output," stage.

It may also be desirable to have a high input resistance in an amplifier, in which case a degenerate-emitter or degenerate-source stage can be used as the first stage. If, on the other hand, a low input resistance is needed, a common-base or common-gate stage should be used as the input stage.

Example

Question. Consider the capacitively coupled three-stage bipolar amplifier with a common-base input stage, a common-emitter gain stage, and an emitter-follower output stage shown in Fig. 13.2*a*. Assume that this circuit is designed to be used in an application where its input resistance is matched to that of the source; also assume that R_T is 50 Ω. Derive approximate expressions for the mid-band voltage gain and the mid-band input and output resistance for this amplifier. The transistors have current gains β_F of 80.

Discussion. Based on what we know about the individual stages used to assemble this amplifier, we anticipate that it will have low input and output resistances and

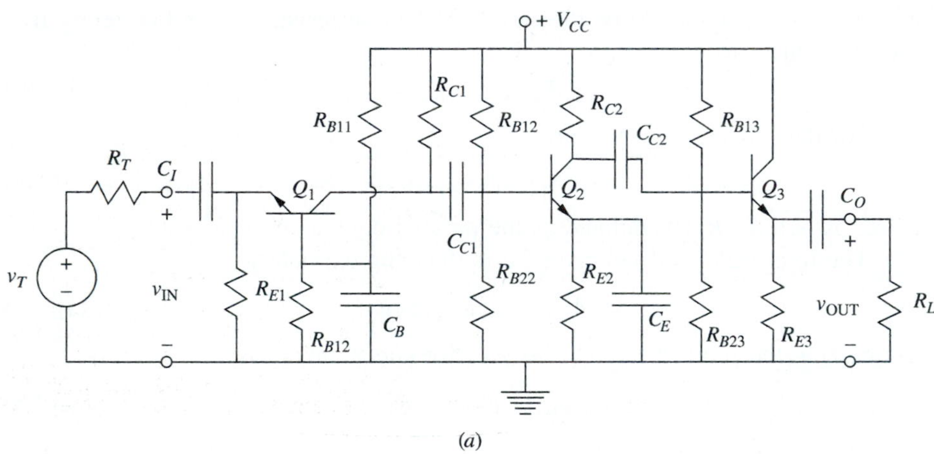

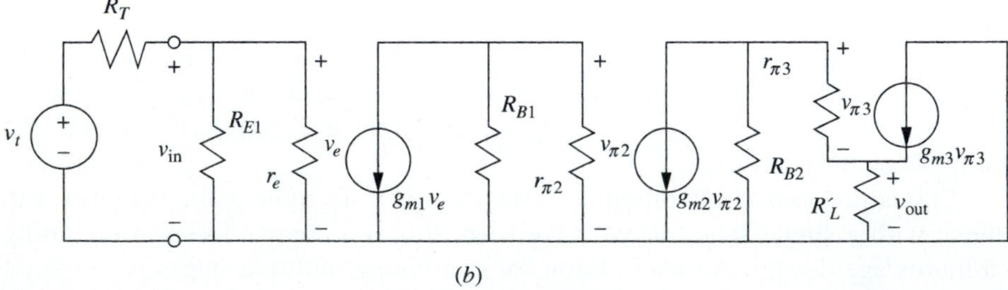

FIGURE 13.2
(*a*) Three-stage capacitively coupled amplifier having a low-input-resistance common-base first stage, a high-gain common-emitter second stage, and a low-output-resistance emitter-follower final stage; (*b*) the mid-band incremental equivalent model.

a large mid-band voltage gain. To see if this is indeed the case, we first determine the mid-band small signal equivalent circuit; this is shown in Fig. 13.2*b*. In this circuit we have defined R_{B1} as $R_{C1}\|R_{B12}\|R_{B22}$ and R_{B2} as $R_{C2}\|R_{B13}\|R_{B23}$. Base bias resistors are typically 10 to 100 times as large as collector resistors, so we expect that R_{B1} is approximately equal to R_{C1} and R_{B2} is approximately R_{C2}.

The input and output resistances are the easiest to calculate. The input resistance is $R_{E1}\|r_{e1}$; since R_{E1} is typically several kΩ, the only way this will be as small as 50 Ω is if r_{e1} is the dominant term. That is, we want $r_{e1} << R_{E1}$ so that

$$R_{\text{in}} \approx r_{e1} = 50\ \Omega \tag{13.6}$$

From Eq. (8.62), r_{e1} is approximately kT/qI_{C1}, so to have an R_{in} of 50 Ω we need a bias level I_{C1} of 2 mA.

This circuit indeed has a small input resistance. It is so small in fact that we should ask if our model is adequate and, in particular, if there are parasitic elements we have neglected that we should include. In this case it is the base resistance r_x we may want to consider. It is of the same magnitude as r_{e1} (i.e., 25 to 50 Ω), and it is positioned between the intrinsic base terminal and ground. Fortunately, however, in this position r_x looks from the input like an even smaller resistor that is, $(1-\alpha)r_x$; and thus it has essentially no effect on R_{in} (you should take the time to convince yourself of this).

The output resistance [see Eq. (11.48)] is R_{E3} in parallel with $(r_{\pi 3} + R_{B2})$ divided by $(\beta_F + 1)$; that is,

$$R_{\text{out}} = R_{E3} \left\| \frac{(r_{\pi 3} + R_{B2})}{(\beta_F + 1)} \right. \tag{13.7a}$$

Since all of these resistors are of comparable magnitude, the latter factor will clearly dominate. Thus we have

$$R_{\text{out}} \approx \frac{(r_{\pi 3} + R_{C2})}{\beta_F} \tag{13.7b}$$

where we have also made use of the facts that all of the transistor values of β_F in this circuit are identical and much greater than 1 and that R_{B1} is approximately R_{C2}. The value of $r_{\pi 3}$ is typically several kilo-ohms, and we expect R_{C2} to be several kilo-ohms as well. Thus R_{out} will be 100 Ω or less, which is indeed low as output resistances go, as we expected it would be.

Turning next to the voltage gain, we can easily write an exact expression for A_v, but this will be unnecessarily complicated. It is easier to assume we have a well-designed circuit and to develop an approximate solution that might allow us more insight. (We should, of course, check our assumptions once we finish.)

We expect, for example, that the voltage gain of the emitter-follower stage is approximately 1. Thus we have

$$v_{\text{out}} \approx -g_{m2} v_{\pi 2} R_{B2} \tag{13.8}$$

We also have

$$v_{\pi 2} = g_{m1} v_e \frac{R_{B1} r_{\pi 2}}{(R_{B1} + r_{\pi 2})} \tag{13.9}$$

and

$$v_e \approx v_{\text{in}} \frac{r_{e1}}{(r_{e1} + R_T)} \tag{13.10}$$

Combining these three expressions to obtain the overall mid-band voltage gain, we find

$$A_v \approx -\frac{g_{m1} g_{m2} r_{e1} R_{B1} R_{B2} r_{\pi 2}}{(R_{B1} + r_{\pi 2})(r_{e1} + R_T)} \tag{13.11a}$$

At this point we have an expression, but we still don't know much about the voltage gain. To see what this expression says, we begin by pointing out that the product $g_{m2} r_{\pi 2}$ is β_F. We could similarly note that the product $g_{m1} r_{e1}$ is approximately 1, but rather than use this relationship we instead note that a low-resistance input like that of this circuit is typically used, as it is here, to achieve matching to a source; that is, $R_{\text{in}}(\approx r_{e1}) = R_T$. Thus the factor $r_{e1}/(r_{e1} + R_T)$ can be expected to be on the order of $\frac{1}{2}$.It certainly won't be any smaller than this, and the largest it can be is 1; in this example we have been told to select r_{e1} so that it is exactly $\frac{1}{2}$. Simialrly, the factor $R_{B1}/(R_{B1} + r_{\pi 2})$ will also be on the order of $\frac{1}{2}$ since R_{B1} and $r_{\pi 2}$ will be of the same order of magnitude (i.e., several kilo-ohms).

Using all of these observations in our expression for the gain, we obtain

$$A_v \approx -\frac{\beta_F g_{m1} R_{B2}}{4} \tag{13.11b}$$

This starts to look like something we can appreciate. It looks almost like $\beta_F/4$ times the gain of a single common-emitter gain stage, $-g_m R_L$, except, of course, that the transconductance and load correspond to different stages. Notice that g_{m1} is directly related to R_{in}, so its maximum value is already constrained by the input resistance specified in this example. Similarly, R_{B2} plays a major role in determining R_{out}, so if there had been a constraint on R_{out} in this example, the size of R_{B2}, and thus the magnitude of the maximum voltage gain, would have been largely predetermined.

Another way to look at the voltage gain is in terms of performance measures such as input and output resistances and maximum voltage swings. To do this, note first that in a common-base stage, g_{m1} equals $1/r_{e1}$, and in this circuit this is essentially $1/R_{\text{in}}$. Then note that R_{B2} is approximately R_{C2}, which can be written as $\Delta v_{\text{out}}/I_{C2}$, where Δv_{out} is the magnitude of the maximum positive output voltage swing; this is limited by the bias on the collector of Q_2. Using these equivalents in Eq. 13.11b, we arrive at

$$A_v \approx -\frac{\beta_F}{4} \frac{\Delta v_{\text{out}}}{I_{C2} R_{\text{in}}} \tag{13.11c}$$

Again we see that our only real design option is to reduce I_{C2}. Of course, as we do this, we must also increase R_{C2} to keep the voltage drop across it at Δv_{out} or more, and as we increase R_{C2}, our approximation that R_{B2} is effectively just R_{C2} starts to suffer. One way or another, there is a limit to how small we can make I_{C2}, and thus on how large A_v can be.

Notice, finally, that the input stage contributes significantly to the overall voltage gain, along with the so-called gain stage. There is nothing wrong with this, of course, and the more benefit we can get from the individual stages, the better. Strictly speaking, perhaps, we should call the first stage an input-gain stage in this case, but this is not usually done.

Capacitively coupled cascades are easy to design but use many passive elements (i.e., capacitors and resistors). Although this is not a significant problem for circuits made by soldering individual ("discrete") components together, it is a major problem for integrated circuits. Putting large capacitors in an integrated circuit is difficult because they would occupy large areas of the silicon chip. As such, capacitively coupled circuits cannot be economically integrated. They are simply not practical, so alternatives must be found. Another shortcoming of capacitively coupled circuits is that they have a limited mid-band frequency range. In particular, they are not useful at low frequencies unless very large coupling capacitors are used, which becomes prohibitive, even for circuits made of discrete components. The solution is to go to direct coupling (i.e., coupling without the use of capacitors). We will examine doing this in the next two sections, beginning in Sec. 13.2 with direct-coupled single-transistor stages and ending in Sec. 13.3 with direct-coupled differential pairs.

13.2 DIRECT-COUPLED AMPLIFIERS

If the bias levels on two successive capacitively coupled stages are selected so that the quiescent voltage across the coupling capacitor is zero, then the capacitor can be removed and the two terminals connected without disturbing the bias of either stage. The two stages are then said to be *direct-coupled*. It is clear that we have less freedom in selecting the biases on the individual stages of a direct-coupled multistage amplifier because the bias levels must match in this way, but this may be a small price to pay to eliminate the coupling capacitors. It also turns out, as we shall see shortly, that we can also often eliminate a significant number of resistors through direct coupling, which is also important, especially in an integrated circuit.

The input and output coupling capacitors can also be eliminated if two supply voltages are used. We have already seen two supplies being used to bias a MOSFET in Sec. 11.1.2, and two supplies can similarly be used with bipolar amplifiers. Then, if the biasing is designed so that the quiescent voltage on the input and output terminals is 0 V, the input and output can be directly coupled to the signal source and load, respectively. We will see an example of this next in Sec. 13.2.1.

We will look at directly coupling specific combinations of single-transistor stages in the rest of this section. We will find that there are limits to how far we can go with this scheme and that we must work hard to eliminate all of the bias capacitors. In Sec. 13.3 we will see how differential pairs let us overcome these final limitations.

13.2.1 Direct-Coupled Cascade

Imagine that in the amplifier in Fig. 13.1 the bias is such that the voltage on the collector of the first transistor and that on the base of the second transistor are identical, and thus there is no voltage drop across the coupling capacitor C_C. This capacitor can then be removed, leaving us with the circuit of Fig. 13.3*a*. When

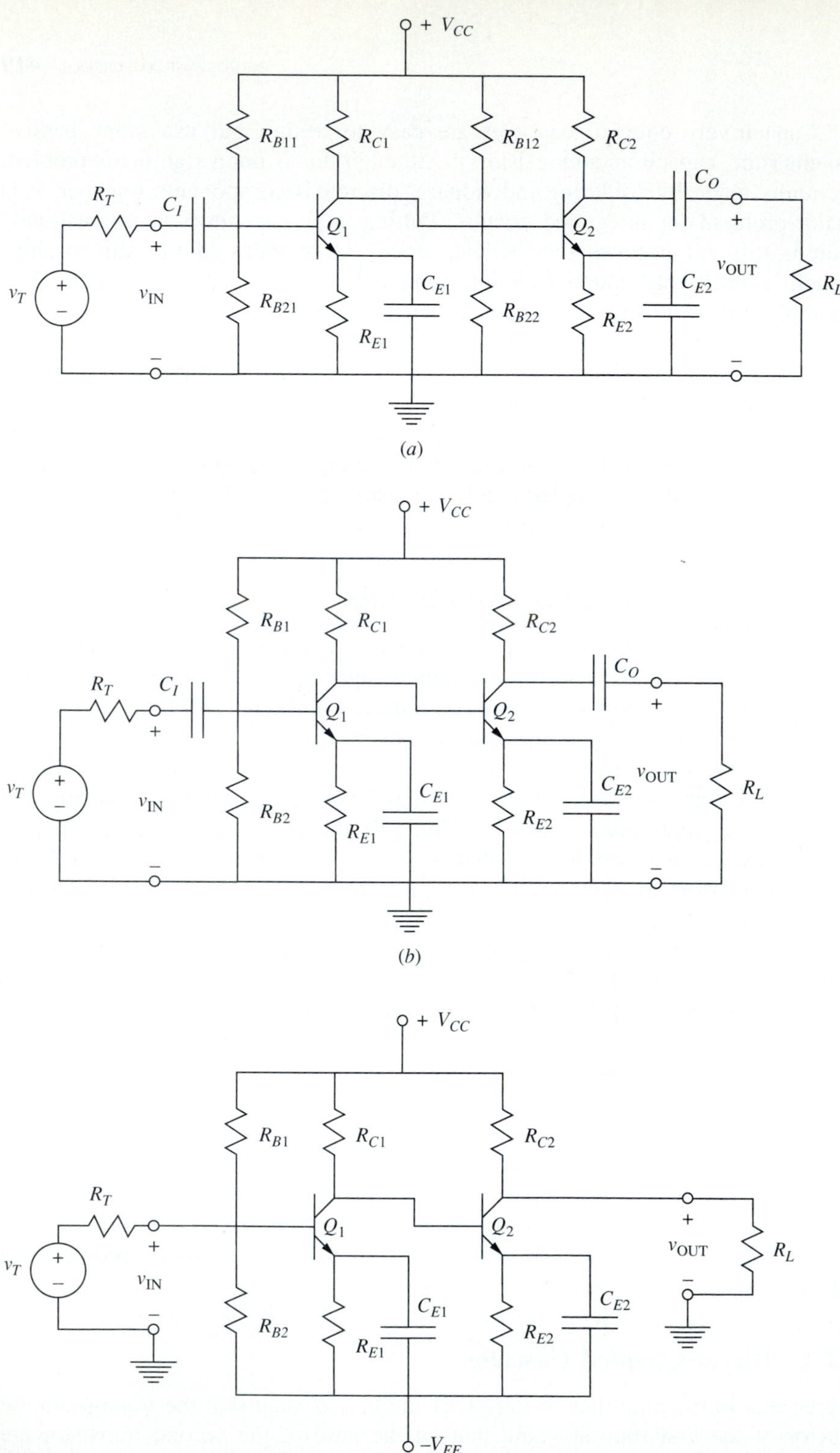

+ V_{CC}
R_{B11}
R_{C1}
R_{B12}
R_{C2}
R_T
C_I
Q_1
Q_2
C_O
+
v_T
v_{IN}
R_{B21}
R_{E1}
C_{E1}
R_{B22}
R_{E2}
C_{E2}
v_{OUT}
R_L
−
(a)
+ V_{CC}
R_{B1}
R_{C1}
R_{C2}
R_T
C_I
Q_1
Q_2
C_O
v_T
v_{IN}
R_{B2}
R_{E1}
C_{E1}
R_{E2}
C_{E2}
v_{OUT}
R_L
(b)
+ V_{CC}
R_{B1}
R_{C1}
R_{C2}
R_T
Q_1
Q_2
v_T
v_{IN}
v_{OUT}
R_L
R_{B2}
R_{E1}
C_{E1}
R_{E2}
C_{E2}
$-V_{EE}$
(c)

FIGURE 13.3

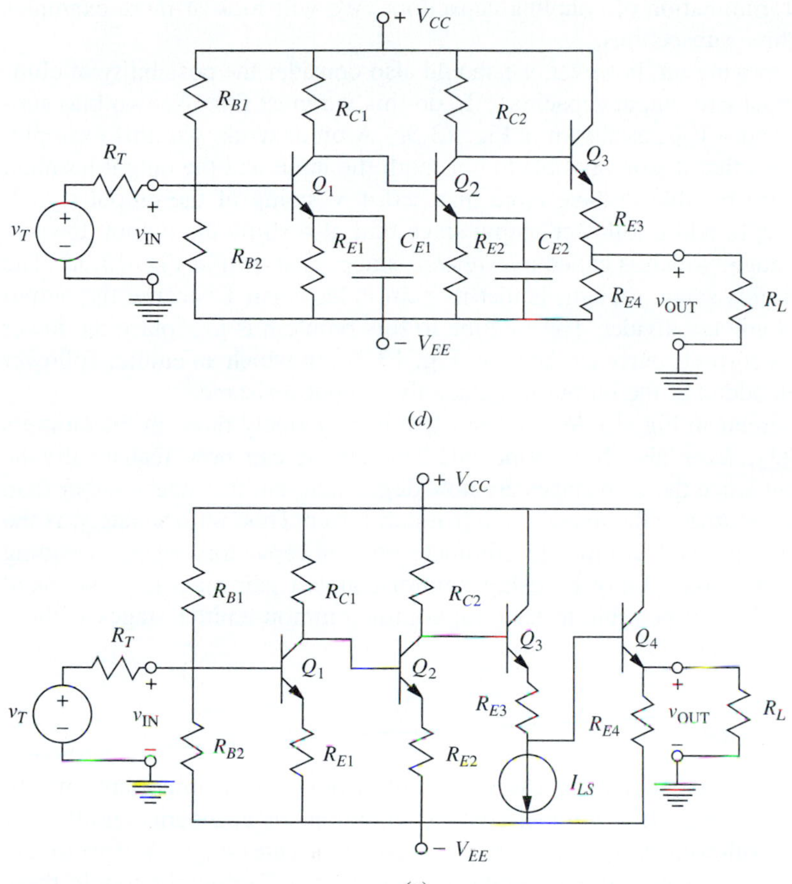

FIGURE 13.3 (*Continued*)
Direct-coupled versions of the amplifier in Fig. 13.1: (*a*) the coupling capacitor has been removed; (*b*) the redundant resistors have also been removed; (*c*) two sources have been used to also permit direct coupling of the input and output; (*d*) the circuit of (*c*) has been modified with a level-shift stage placed after gain stages to achieve a quiescent output voltage V_{OUT} of 0 V; (*e*) the circuit has been further modified by using a current source to bias the level-shift stage, so that the gain of this stage is unity, by adding an emitter-follower output stage and by eliminating the emitter capacitors.

you look at this circuit it should be clear to you that the base bias resistors R_{B12} and R_{B22} are also superfluous and can be removed without changing the bias point of either transistor. Doing this yields the circuit of Fig. 13.3*b*. This circuit is an example of a direct-coupled cascade of two common-emitter stages.

Other combinations of single-transistor stages can also be direct-coupled and cascaded in this same fashion with similar reductions in the number of biasing resistors and elimination of coupling capacitors. We will look at more examples in the next three subsections.

Before moving on, however, we should also consider the possibility of eliminating the input and output capacitors. To do this we must first use two bias supplies, $+V_{CC}$ and $-V_{EE}$, as shown in Fig. 13.3*c*. A bit of work with this example, however, shows that it is impossible to bias both the input and the output terminal to 0 V and still be able to have more than ±0.4 V swing of the output signal. The solution is to add a follower output stage that also shifts the output down to 0 V. Such a stage, which is called a *level-shift* stage, is shown in Fig. 13.3*d*. The problem with this stage, though, is that its gain is less than 1 because the output is taken off a voltage divider. The solution to this problem is to replace the lower resistor with a current source as shown in Fig. 13.3*e*, in which an emitter-follower has also been added at the output to reduce the output resistance.

In the circuit in Fig. 13.3*e*, the last capacitors, namely those in the emitters of Q_1 and Q_3, have also been removed. The circuit can now realistically be integrated, but since the gain stages are now degenerate-emitter stages rather than common-emitter stages, the overall gain is much lower. This, unfortunately, is the price that must be paid in order to eliminate emitter capacitors when cascading single-transistor stages. Only by using emitter-coupled pair stages, as we shall do in Sec. 13.3, is it possible to have high-gain common-emitter stages without using emitter capacitors.

13.2.2 Cascode

The *cascode* is a direct-coupled cascade combination that is important enough to have its own name. It is a direct-coupled common- or degenerate-emitter (or -source) stage followed by a common-base (or common-gate) stage. A capacitively coupled bipolar version of this is shown in Fig. 13.4*a*. To directly couple these two stages we connect the emitter of the second stage to the collector of the first, as in Fig. 13.4*b*, so that the same collector current flows through both transistors. We also obtain the base biases from a single three-resistor voltage-divider chain. In this way we eliminate three resistors and the coupling capacitor between the two stages. We cannot eliminate any more of the capacitors, however, even if we use two bias supplies. The more common way of drawing the bipolar cascode is shown in Fig. 13.4*c*.

This combination of stages might seem a bit strange to you at first because using a low-input-resistance common-base circuit as the load on a degenerate-emitter or common-emitter stage ensures that the voltage gain of the first stage will be very low. The first stage will, however, still have a current gain of β_F; since the common-base stage will provide a voltage gain of $g_m R'_L$, the combination of the two stages turns out (see below) to have roughly the same overall mid-band characteristics as the first stage alone, so nothing is lost. In fact, a great deal is actually gained, but this does not become clear until one analyzes the high-frequency performance of the cascode, as we shall do in Chap. 14. What we

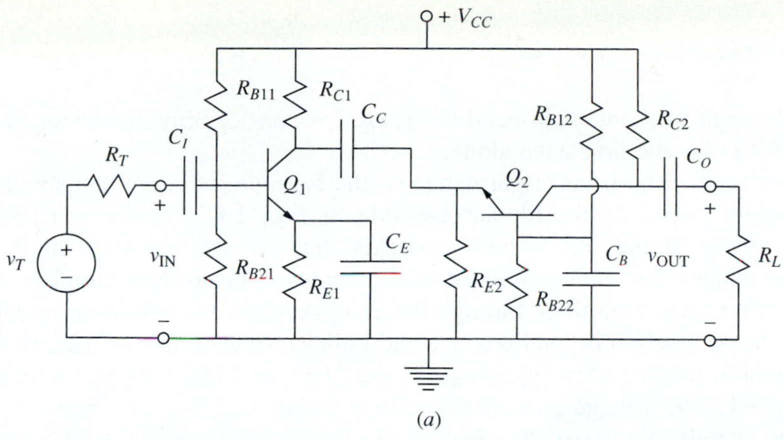

(a)

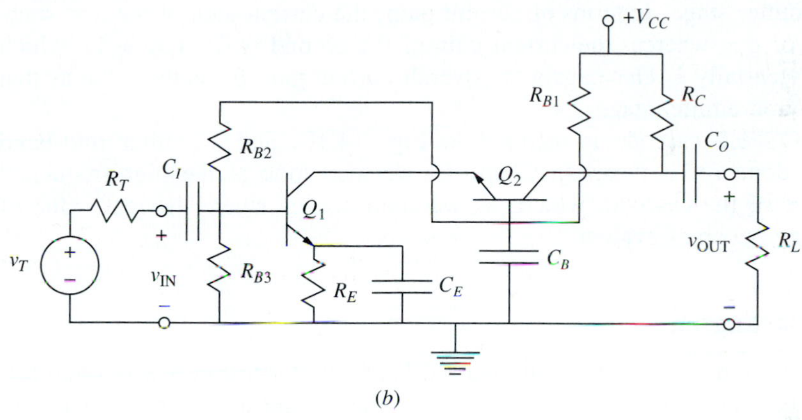

(b)

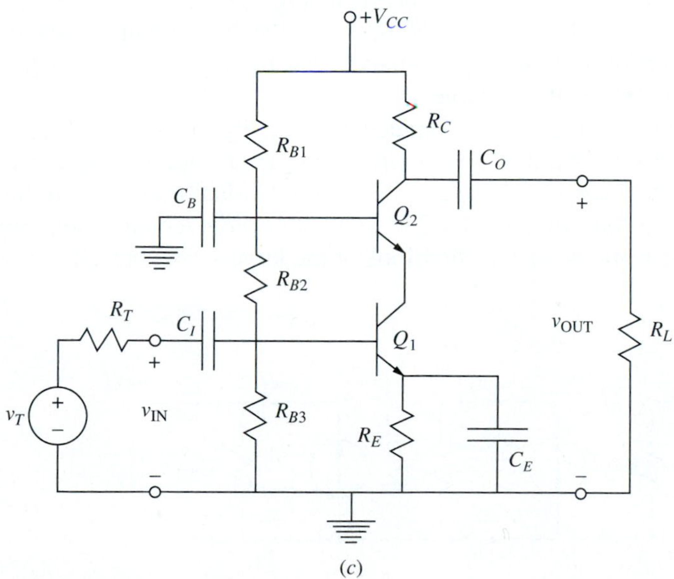

(c)

FIGURE 13.4
Cascode configuration: (a) a capacitively coupled common-emitter and common-base pair; (b) the cascode, a direct-coupled common-emitter and common-base pair; (c) the cascode circuit of (b) redrawn in the form typically used to draw the cascode.

find is that the high-frequency mid-band limit, ω_{HI}, is considerably higher for the cascode than it is for the first stage alone.

To examine the mid-band performance of the cascode, we draw the small-signal equivalent circuit of the bipolar cascode in Fig. 13.5. Notice that the small-signal model of Fig. 8.25*b* has been used for Q_2, the transistor in the common-base stage. This is not essential to the analysis, but it does simplify it considerably. (You may want to go through the analysis using the hybrid-π model for Q_2 to see for yourself; it is good practice and builds character, too.) Notice that the voltage gain of the first stage, $v_{eb2}/v_{\pi 1}$, is $-g_m/g_e$, or $-(\beta_F+1)/\beta_F$, which is essentially -1. The voltage gain of the second stage, v_{out}/v_{eb2}, is, however, $g_m R_{L'}$, so the overall gain is $-g_m R_{L'}$, just as it is in a similarly biased and loaded common-emitter stage. In terms of current gain, the current gain of the first stage is g_m/g_π, or β_F, whereas the current gain of the second is $\beta_F/(\beta_F+1)$, which is α_F, or essentially 1. Once again the overall current gain β_F is the same as that of the common-emitter stage.

A MOSFET cascode is pictured in Fig. 14.10, and a similar mid-band analysis is done for it there. In Chap. 14 we also look at the high-frequency performance of the cascode, which, as we shall see, is where the real value of this topology becomes evident.

13.2.3 Darlington

A very common direct-coupled combination is an emitter-follower first stage followed by a common-emitter or a degenerate-emitter second stage. The capacitively coupled version of such a combination is shown in Fig. 13.6*a*, and the direct-coupled version is shown in Fig. 13.6*b*. Notice that the high input resistance sought from the emitter-follower stage is enhanced by biasing it at a very low collector current, which makes its r_π large.

The composite of two transistors connected as in Fig. 13.6*b* is called a *Darlington pair*. It looks a great deal like a single transistor with a current gain β' that is essentially the product of the βs of the two individual transistors in the pair, with an emitter-base "on" voltage of 1.2 V, and with a large incremental input resistance. To see these features we will first look at the large-signal behavior of a

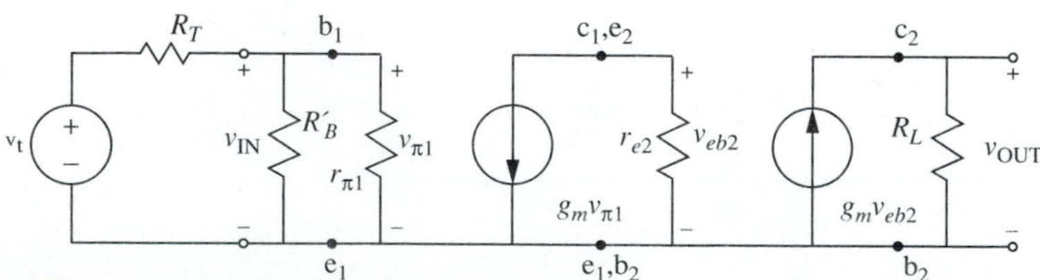

FIGURE 13.5
Mid-band incremental equivalent circuit for the bipolar cascode pictured in Fig. 13.4*c*.

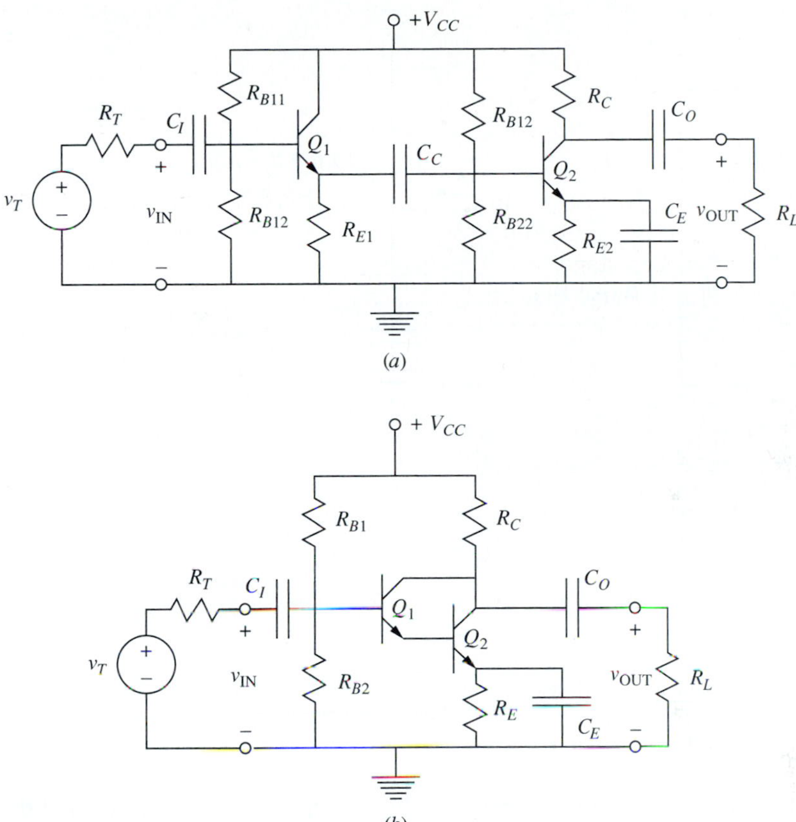

FIGURE 13.6
(a) Capacitively coupled emitter-follower stage and common-emitter stage; (b) the direct-coupled version (the last combination of two transistors is called a Darlington pair).

Darlington pair and then look at a mid-band small-signal linear equivalent circuit model. To examine the large-signal behavior, consider the large-signal equivalent circuit in Fig. 13.7a, which we obtain by simply replacing the two transistors of the pair by their forward-active-region large-signal models. This model can be simplified to that illustrated in Fig. 13.7b by a suitable choice of element values. To begin with, $V_{BE,\mathrm{ON}}$ of the composite device must clearly be 1.2 V. Next notice that the base current of the second transistor, i_{B2}, is $(\beta_1+1)i_{B1}$. Thus the collector current i'_C of the composite structure is $\beta_1 i_{B1} + \beta_2(\beta_1+1)i_{B1}$, and the equivalent current gain β' is given by

$$\beta' = \beta_1\beta_2 + \beta_1 + \beta_2 \tag{13.12}$$

which is approximately $\beta_1\beta_2$ if β_1 and β_2 are large.

To consider the small-signal linear circuit behavior of a Darlington pair, assume that both members of the pair are biased in their forward active region

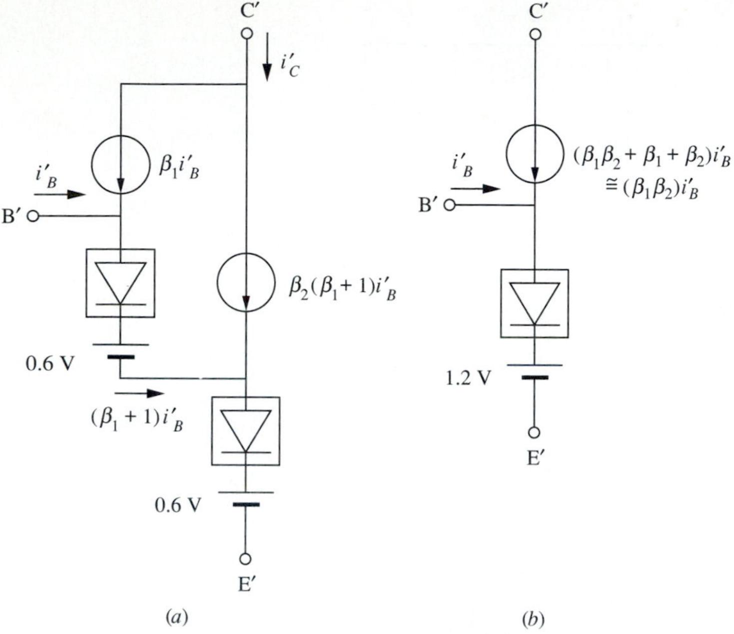

FIGURE 13.7
Large-signal circuit models for a Darlington pair based in its forward active region: (*a*) the circuit obtained by modeling the two individual transistors using hybrid-ϕ-like model for the composite Darlington transistor.

and draw the equivalent circuit illustrated in Fig. 13.8*a*, where we have used the mid-band hybrid-π models for the two transistors. We want to find an equivalent circuit for the composite device like that shown in Fig. 13.8*b*. Focusing first on Fig. 13.8*a*, we note that since I_{B2} is $(\beta_1+1)I_{B1}$ (see above and Fig. 13.7*a*), $r_{\pi 2}$ is equal to $r_{\pi 1}/(\beta_1+1)$. This has two consequences. First, because the base signal current i_{b2} of Q_2 is $(\beta_1+1)i_{b1}$, where i_{b1} is the base signal current of Q_1, the two voltage drops $v_{\pi 1}$ and $v_{\pi 2}$ (which are, respectively, $r_{\pi 1}i_{b1}$ and $r_{\pi 2}i_{b2}$) turn out to be the same (i.e., $v_{b'e'}/2$). Second, the input resistance of the composite device is $r_{\pi 1}+(\beta_1+1)r_{\pi 2}$, and because $r_{\pi 2}$ is $r_{\pi 1}/(\beta_1+1)$, this sum is simply $2r_{\pi 1}$. Thus in Fig. 13.8*b* we have

$$r_{\text{in}} \equiv r'_\pi = 2r_{\pi 1} \tag{13.13}$$

$$v_{b'e'} \equiv v'_\pi = 2v_{\pi 1} \tag{13.14}$$

Proceeding, we short-circuit the output and note that the collector current i'_c of the composite device is the sum of the two individual transistors' collector currents, i_{c1} and i_{c2}, so we must have

$$i'_c = g_{m1}v_{\pi 1} + g_{m2}v_{\pi 2} \tag{13.15a}$$

which, using the fact that $v_{\pi 1}$ and $v_{\pi 2}$ are equal, is

$$i'_c = (g_{m1} + g_{m2})\,v_{\pi 1} \tag{13.15b}$$

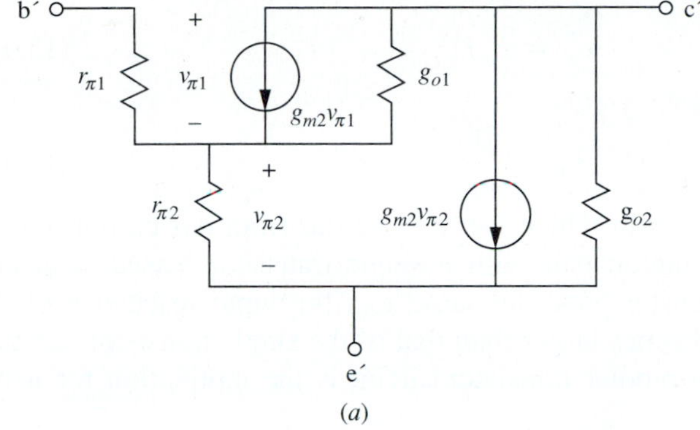

(*a*)

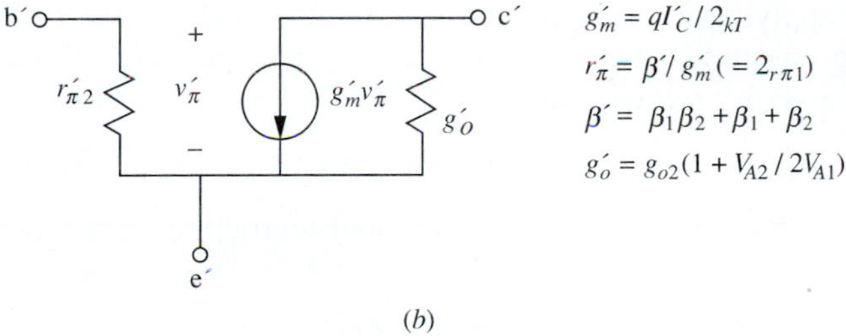

(*b*)

FIGURE 13.8
Small-signal mid-band linear equivalent circuit models for a Darlington pair: (*a*) the circuit obtained by modeling the two individual transistors using hybrid-π models; (*b*) a hybrid-π-like model for the composite Darlington transistor.

or

$$i'_c = (g_{m1} + g_{m2}) \frac{v_{e'b'}}{2} \tag{13.15c}$$

We define the factor $(g_{m1} + g_{m2})/2$ as g'_m. Then clearly

$$g'_m = \frac{q(I_{C1} + I_{C2})}{2kT} \tag{13.16a}$$

which in terms of the quiescent collector current I'_C of the composite device is

$$g'_m = \frac{qI'_C}{2kT} \tag{13.16b}$$

This is a relationship with which we are familiar, except that there is now a factor of 2 in the denominator. This factor comes from the fact that we now have two transistors and the input voltage is split equally between them.

The only factor for which we do not yet have a practical expression is r'_π. There are various ways to obtain the expression we seek, but a convenient one is to note that we must have

$$g'_m v'_\pi = \beta' i'_b \tag{13.17}$$

and also that

$$v'_\pi = r'_\pi i'_b \tag{13.18}$$

Combining these two equations yields

$$r'_\pi = \frac{\beta'}{g'_m} \tag{13.19}$$

which is another relationship with which we are familiar from our earlier work.

If we compare a Darlington pair with a single transistor biased such that the Darlington and the transistor have the same g_m, the input resistance of the Darlington pair is roughly β times larger than that of the single transistor. Getting a large input resistance in a bipolar transistor circuit is the motivation for using the Darlington connection.

Next we consider the output resistance of the Darlington connection. Imagine setting $v_{b'e'}$ to zero and applying a test voltage v_t between c' and e'. We want to calculate the resulting current i_t that flows into c'; r'_o will be v_t/i_t. First, summing the currents at node c', we will have

$$i_t = g_{o1}v_t + g_{m2}v_{\pi 2} + (v_t - v_{\pi 2})\, g_{o1} + g_{m1}v_{\pi 1} \tag{13.20a}$$

Noting that since $v_{b'e'}$ is zero, we have $v_{\pi 1} = -v_{\pi 2}$, and regrouping terms, we can write this as

$$i_t = (g_{o1} + g_{o2})\, v_t + (g_{m2} - g_{m1} - g_{o1})\, v_{\pi 2} \tag{13.20b}$$

Next, summing currents at the node between $r_{\pi 1}$ and $r_{\pi 2}$ (i.e., at the emitter of Q_1), we find

$$(g_{\pi 1} + g_{m1})\, v_{\pi 1} + g_{o1}\,(v_t - v_{\pi 2}) - g_{\pi 2}v_{\pi 2} = 0 \tag{13.21a}$$

which, again using $v_{\pi 1} = -v_{\pi 2}$ and regrouping, becomes

$$v_{\pi 2} = \frac{g_{o1}v_t}{g_{m1} + g_{\pi 1} + g_{\pi 2}} \tag{13.21b}$$

This can now be combined with Eq. (13.20b) to obtain

$$\frac{i_t}{v_t} = g'_o = g_{o2} + g_{o1} + \frac{(g_{m2} - g_{m1} - g_{o1})\, g_{o1}}{g_{m1} + g_{\pi 2} + g_{\pi 1} + g_{o1}} \tag{13.22a}$$

Looking first at the last term in this expression, the sum in parentheses in the numerator is essentially g_{m2} because g_{m2} is by far the largest term (assuming a reasonable output resistance). In the denominator, $g_{\pi 1}$ is clearly much less than g_{m1}, and g_{o1} should also be negligible. At the same time, $g_{\pi 2}$ and g_{m1} are essentially equal and are β_2 times smaller than g_{m2}. The denominator is thus effectively $2g_{m2}/\beta_2$, and the entire last term in Eq. (13.22a) is approximately $\beta_2 g_{o1}/2$, so we have

$$g'_o \approx g_{o2} + \frac{\beta_2 g_{o1}}{2} \tag{13.22b}$$

Finally, recalling that g_{o1} can be written in terms of the Early voltage and bias point as $I_{C1}/|V_{A1}|$, that g_{o2} can be written as $I_{C2}/|V_{A2}|$, and that $\beta_2 I_{C1}$ is approximately I_{C2}, we find that Eq. (13.22b) can also be written as

$$g'_o \approx g_{o2}\left(1 + \frac{|V_{A2}|}{2|V_{A1}|}\right) \tag{13.22c}$$

If the Early voltages of Q_1 and Q_2 are equal we have simply that

$$g'_o \approx 1.5g_{o2} \tag{13.22d}$$

The bottom line is that the output conductance is larger and the output resistance is smaller, and this is not good. Fortunately, there is an easy fix to this problem. By leaving the collector of Q_1 connected to the power supply line as it was originally in Fig. 13.6*a* and as shown in Fig. 13.9, rather than connecting it to the collector of Q_2 as in Fig. 13.6*b*, we recover our original output conductance; that is, g'_o becomes g_{o2}. You should be able to see this by referring to Fig. 13.8*a*: The collector of Q_1 will now be incrementally grounded, so when we short the input and apply our test voltage, we have $v_{\pi 1} = v_{\pi 2} = 0$ and $i_t = g_{o2}v_t$. Our conclusions about r'_{in} and g'_m are, for all practical purposes, unchanged in this new connection.

Before leaving the Darlington we should make two final points. First, because the first transistor in the pair, Q_1, is biased at a very low current level, the β of this transistor may be lower than that of Q_2 because of beta fall-off due to space-charge layer recombination (see Sec. 8.1.7*d* and Fig. 8.14). Second, although you have no way of knowing it yet, the high-frequency behavior of the Darlington connection is poorer than that of a single transistor (we discuss high-frequency performance in Chap. 14). A solution to both of these problems can be found by reinserting a resistor R_{E1} between the emitter of the first transistor and ground and by connecting the collector of the first transistor Q_1 to the power supply as we did in the previous paragraph. Both of these changes are illustrated

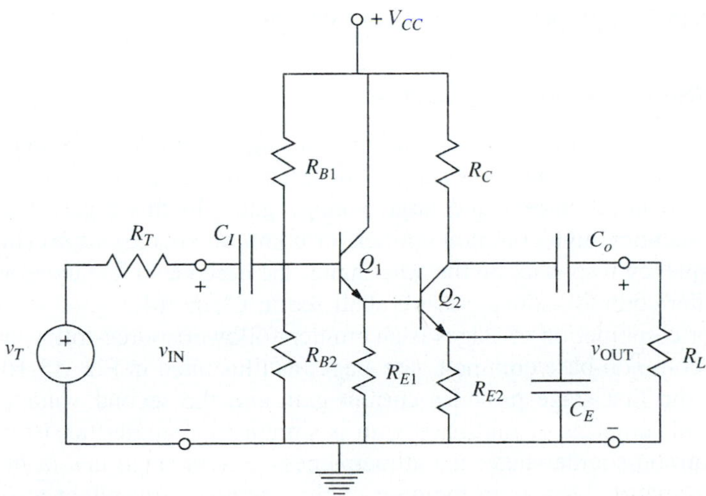

FIGURE 13.9
Improved Darlington connection, which is superior to the classical Darlington pair illustrated in Fig. 13.6*b* in terms of its output resistance, transconductance, and dynamic response.

in Fig. 13.9 (which you will notice starts to look a lot like our original connection in Fig. 13.6*a*).

We have already discussed the impact that tying the collector of Q_1 to the supply has on the output conductance, and in Chap. 14 we will discuss its effect on the high-frequency performance. Turning then to the resistor R_{E1}, adding this resistor means that the bias level of Q_1, the first transistor, can be increased. This in turn means that Q_1 is less likely to be biased where its current gain is low and, more importantly, that there will be more current available to charge and discharge the capacitive charge stores associated with the base of Q_2; the pair will have much better high-frequency performance. We will analyze this and quantify the impact of R_{E1} in Chap. 14, Sec. 14.2.7.

Another important plus of adding the resistor R_{E1} is that the transconductance of the stage is increased. Simply put, because the input resistance of the first transistor is reduced, a greater fraction of the input signal appears at the input of the second transistor. Now $v_{\pi2}$ is greater than $v_{\pi1}$, so more of the signal is applied to the base Q_2, the transistor with the higher transconductance. The cost of adding this resistor is that the input resistance of the stage will be reduced somewhat. We have

$$r_{\text{in}} = r_{\pi1} + (\beta_1 + 1)\left(r_{\pi2} \| R_{E1}\right) \tag{13.23}$$

Because R_{E1} is usually much smaller than $r_{\pi2}$ and because $r_{\pi1}$ will now be much smaller than previously and, if R_{E1} is doing its job, much less than $(\beta_1 + 1)r_{\pi2}$, this is approximately

$$r_{\text{in}} \approx (\beta_1 + 1)\, r_{\pi2} \tag{13.24}$$

This input resistance is roughly a factor of only two smaller than before, so it will still be very large.

Clearly the circuit topology in Fig. 13.9 represents a superior way to use the Darlington concept in high-performance circuit design.

13.2.4 Emitter/Source-Coupled Cascode

In the cascode circuit we saw that the combination of a stage with a large voltage gain and unity current gain, following a stage with large current gain but unity voltage gain, had both large current and large voltage gain. In this regard the combination looked identical to a common-emitter (or common-source) stage. (In terms of its high-frequency response, on the other hand, the cascode is far superior to the common-emitter/common-source, as we shall see in Chap. 14.)

Another similar combination of stages is an emitter-follower/source-follower stage followed by a common-base/common-gate stage, as illustrated in Fig. 13.10 using BJTs. Again, the first stage provides current gain and the second voltage gain. The overall result in terms of mid-band gain is similar to a single-transistor common-emitter/common-source stage; the attractiveness of this stage lies in its high-frequency performance, just as in the case of the cascode. You might also expect the BJT version of this combination to have a very large input impedance because of the common-emitter input, but as we shall see, this is not necessarily the case.

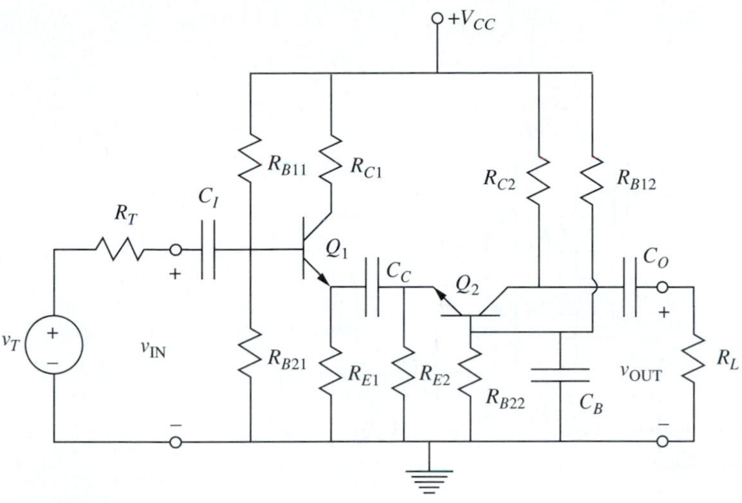

FIGURE 13.10
Capacitively coupled amplifier composed of an emitter-follower stage followed by a common-base stage.

There are several ways to realize a direct-coupled version of this pairing. One is shown in Fig. 13.11*a*. This circuit, which is called the emitter-coupled cascode, uses a *pnp* transistor for the second stage, and the two transistors then end up in series. The two diodes, D_1 and D_2, establish the bias point of Q_1 and Q_2, and how this is done merits a bit of discussion. D_1 is formed by connecting together the base and collector of a transistor that is identical to Q_1, and D_2 is formed in the same way from a transistor identical to Q_2 (an example of a transistor connected as a diode in this way can be found in Fig. 16.3*c*). These two diodes therefore have the same saturation currents, I_{S1} and I_{S2}, respectively, as the base–emitter junctions of the corresponding transistors (i.e., I_{ES1} and I_{ES2}). Thus when the diodes and transistors are connected together as they are in this circuit, the magnitude of the emitter currents, I_{E1} and I_{E2}, will be the same as the magnitude of the current through the two diodes; this current is approximately $(V_{CC} - 1.2)/(R_{B1} + R_{B2})$. This is another example of a situation we often encounter where we can use a break-point model in certain parts of an analysis, but must use exponential diode models for other parts (other examples arose in Chap. 12 when we discussed the design of current sources). Here we are able to assume that the voltage drop across a forward-biased silicon junction is approximately 0.6 V for purposes of estimating the current through the diodes, whereas for purposes of biasing the transistors we have to remember that this is only an approximation and that the diode currents really depend exponentially on the junction voltages. Thus if we are careful to match the saturation currents and applied junction voltages of the devices, we can easily establish the desired bias levels. It is also important to recognize that we are not required to have the same quiescent current through the diodes and transistors; if the junction areas in the diodes differ from those of the

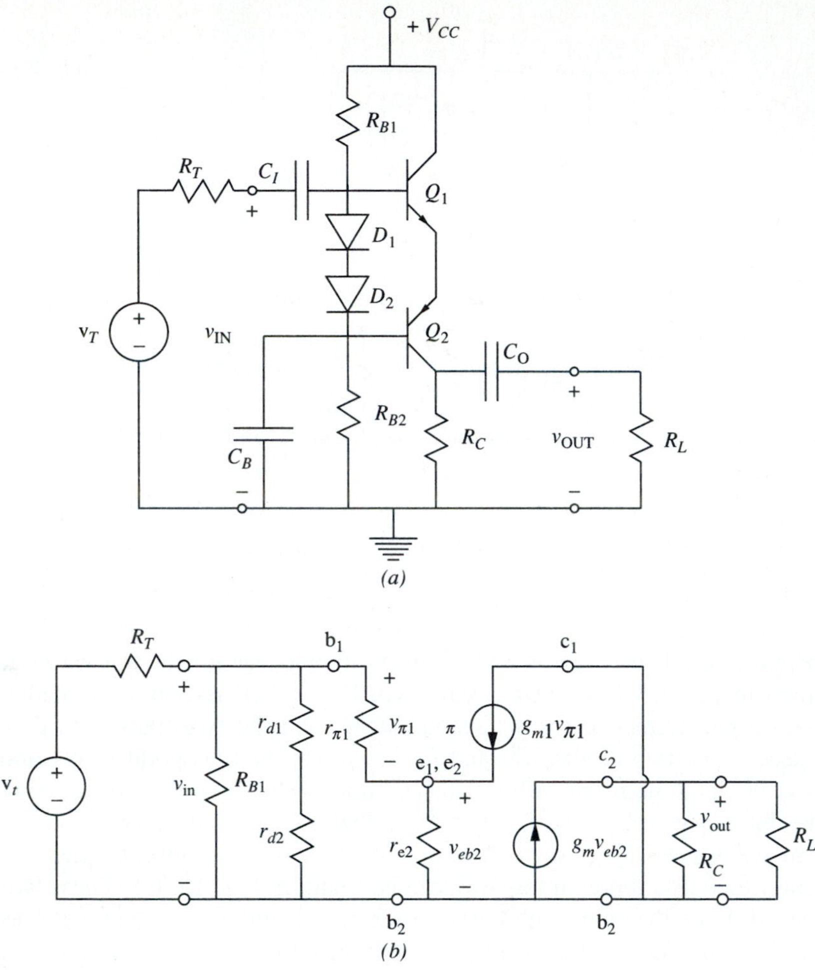

FIGURE 13.11
(*a*) Emitter-coupled cascode, a direct-coupled version of the circuit in Fig. 13.10 that uses an *npn* transistor in the emitter-follower stage and a *pnp* in the common-base stage; (*b*) the incremental equivalent circuit.

transistors, the currents will differ by the same ratio, since it is really the junction saturation current densities we are matching.

The incremental equivalent circuit is shown in Fig. 13.11*b*. There are several important observations we can make about this circuit. First, the input resistance is only $r_{\pi 1} + (\beta_{F1} + 1)r_{e2}$, which is much less than you might have expected. The problem is that the resistance in the emitter circuit of the emitter-follower stage is only the input resistance of the common-base stage, which is small. It appears at the input multiplied by $(\beta_{F1} + 1)$, but that still only increases it to $r_{\pi 1}$. The input resistance of this stage is thus approximately $2r_{\pi 1}$, or only twice that of a comparably biased common-emitter stage.

The other thing to note is that the mid-band voltage gain of this amplifier is given by

$$A_v = \frac{\beta_{F1} + 1}{\beta_{F1} + \beta_{F2} + 2} g_{m2} R_L \tag{13.25}$$

There is no minus sign, and the stage is noninverting. Also, the factor $(\beta_{F1} + 1)/(\beta_{F1} + \beta_{F2} + 2)$ is on the order of 0.5. It is usually a bit larger than 0.5 because the current gain of the *npn*, β_{F1}, can be expected to be two to three times larger than that of the *pnp*, β_{F2}, but it is always less than 1; thus the magnitude of the mid-band voltage gain is always somewhat lower than that of a comparably biased common-emitter stage. This is the price that must be paid for the superior high-frequency performance of this stage.

A differential amplifier version of the emitter-coupled cascode is used as the input stage of the 741 operational amplifier. We will briefly consider this integrated circuit and see a schematic for it in Sec. 13.3.

Another direct-coupled version of this combination of stages can be realized using all the same types of active devices (e.g., *npn* BJTs), as illustrated in Fig. 13.12*a*. The interesting thing about this circuit is that it is essentially one we have already spent an entire chapter on (Chap. 12) without pointing out that it could be viewed as a direct-coupled pair. That is, the emitter-coupled pair can be thought of as having its origins in a direct-coupled cascade of an emitter-follower followed by a common-base stage, as shown in Fig. 13.12*a*. Using a current source to bias both transistors and a little imagination to see the symmetry and the possibilities of having two inputs and a differential output, we have the emitter-coupled pair of Fig. 13.12*b*, and of Chap. 12.

13.2.5 Complementary Output

The use of an emitter-follower output stage on a multistage amplifier, as was done in the circuit illustrated in Fig. 13.3*e*, makes good sense because it has a high input resistance, even when the load resistance is small, so it does not degrade the performance of the preceding stage by "loading" it with a low resistance to ground. It also has a voltage gain of essentially 1, so it doesn't reduce the overall gain appreciably; and it has a relatively low output resistance, so it can be connected to a low-resistance load without significant loss of signal.

At the same time, however, the emitter-follower does have limitations when used as an output stage in an amplifier like that pictured in Fig. 13.3*e*, and it can be improved upon by adding to it a second, complementary stage. To see why this is so, consider the limitations on $|v_{\text{out}}|$ in the circuit of Fig. 13.3*e*. The first place to look is in the last gain stage, Q_2. To maximize $|v_{\text{out}}|$, the collector of Q_2 should be biased midway between the maximum voltage it can reach, which is V_{CC}, and the minimum voltage it can have, which will be roughly 0 V, assuming V_{IN} is 0 V and Q_1 is biased near saturation. With Q_2 biased in this way, $|v_{\text{out}}|_{\max}$ will be $V_{CC}/2$, unless it is limited even more severely by the level-shift or output stages.

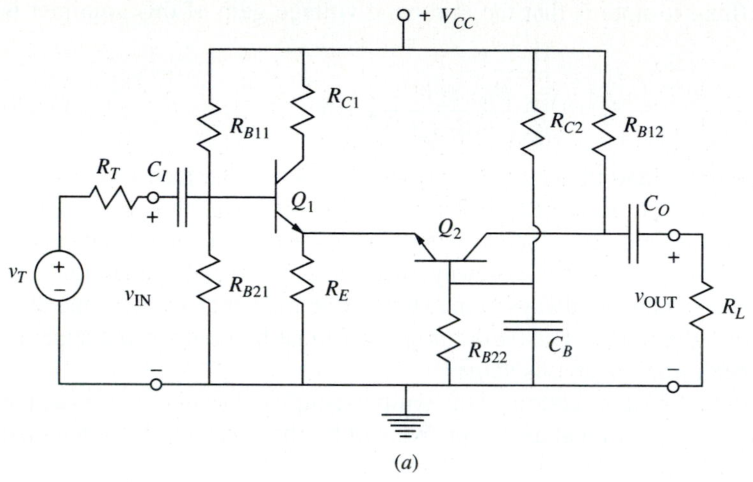

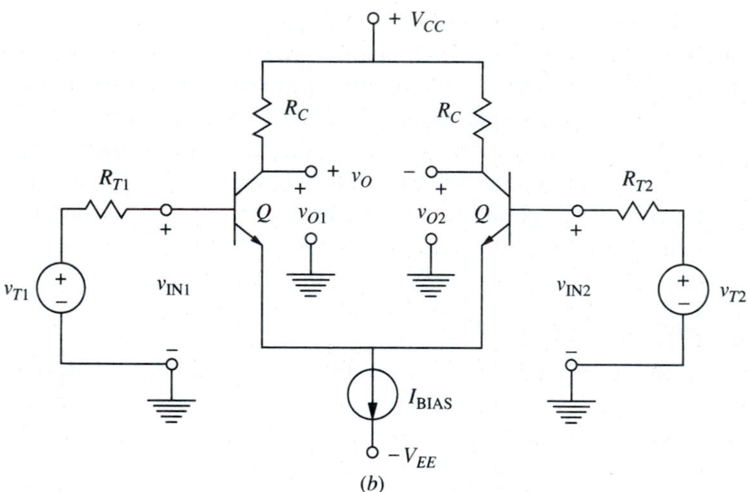

FIGURE 13.12
(*a*) Direct-coupled cascade of the circuit in Fig. 13.10, an emitter-follower stage followed by a common-base stage, that uses all *npn* transistors;
(*b*) the emitter-coupled pair.

In the positive direction, v_{out} can be increased (by driving more current through the load R_L and through R_{E4}) until the collector of Q_2 is at V_{CC} without any problem. At this point v_{out} will be $+V_{CC}/2$, so the last two stages do not limit the positive excursion of v_{out}.

In the negative direction, v_{out} will be its most negative when the transistor Q_4 is nearly cut off and when the only current flowing through R_{E4} is that coming from ground through R_L and through R_{E4}, to $-V_{EE}$. Of course, the larger this current through R_L is, the more negative v_{out} will be, but this depends on R_{E4}.

That is, the current in question is $V_{EE}/(R_{E4}+R_L)$, and thus the minimum v_{out} is $-R_L V_{EE}/(R_{E4}+R_L)$. To get the full $\pm V_{CC}/2$ range that we said Q_2 allowed us, we must have this be $-V_{CC}/2$. If, as is typically the case, $V_{CC} = V_{EE}$, this says that we must have $R_{E4} \leq R_L$.

Making R_{E4} this small may not seem like a big deal until we look at the implications of doing so for the quiescent power dissipation and the efficiency of this output stage. With $R_{E4} = R_L$, and assuming $V_{\text{OUT}} = 0$, the quiescent collector current in Q_4 is V_{EE}/R_L. The quiescent power dissipation in the output stage is therefore equal to $(V_{CC}-V_{EE})^2/R_{E4}$, or with $V_{CC} = V_{EE}$, $4V_{CC}{}^2/R_L$. For comparison, the maximum power that will be delivered to the load is $(|v_{\text{out}}|_{\max})^2/R_L$, or $V_{CC}^2/4R_L$ if, as we have said, $|v_{\text{out}}|_{\max}$ is $V_{CC}/2$. Thus with this circuit the quiescent power dissipation is an alarming 16 times greater than the peak signal power delivered to the load! A more realistic comparison would actually be to assume a sinusoidal signal and to look at the average power delivered to the load; on this basis the efficiency is even worse!

To see a possible solution to this problem, recall that in the positive excursion we simply turned the output transistor Q_4 "on" more strongly, and its quiescent collector current was not an issue; it could have been as low as we wanted and we still could have gotten our desired positive swing. What is needed is another stage in parallel with the first that does the same thing for the negative swing. Such a stage is a *pnp* emitter-follower; an output stage with a directly coupled pair of emitter-followers, one *npn*, and the other *pnp*, is illustrated in Fig. 13.13*a*. Notice that each of these stages requires a different amount of level-shifting and that this difference is conveniently provided by two forward-biased *p-n* diodes. Notice also that now both stages can be biased at low quiescent current levels because when v_{out} is positive, Q_4 is turned on more strongly and supplies, or "pushes," the needed current to R_L from V_{CC}, whereas when v_{out} is negative, Q_4 turns off but Q_5 turns on more strongly and draws, or "pulls," the necessary current through R_L to $-V_{EE}$. Because the stage operates with low quiescent current levels, the quiescent power dissipation is low. The value of bias current that is set in a given circuit will depend in large part on the output resistance sought.

A little consideration of the circuit in Fig. 13.13*a* will show you that R_{E4} and R_{E5} can be eliminated and that the two output transistors can be connected in series as shown in Fig. 13.13*b*. This direct-coupled complementary pair (i.e., an *npn* and a *pnp*) is called a *complementary*, or a *push-pull*, output stage.

The two diodes used to provide the necessary 1.2-V level shift between the bases of Q_4 and Q_5 are often obtained by using the base-emitter junctions of two transistors identical to Q_4 and Q_5 with their base-collector junctions shorted. This provides precisely the right voltage drop and in fact ensures that the magnitude of the quiescent collector currents in Q_4 and Q_5 will be I_{LS} (see the discussion of the circuit in Fig. 13.11*a* for a detailed explanation of this point).

Now the maximum negative excursion on v_{out} is determined either by saturation of Q_5 or by the circuit used to realize the current source I_{LS}. That is, the

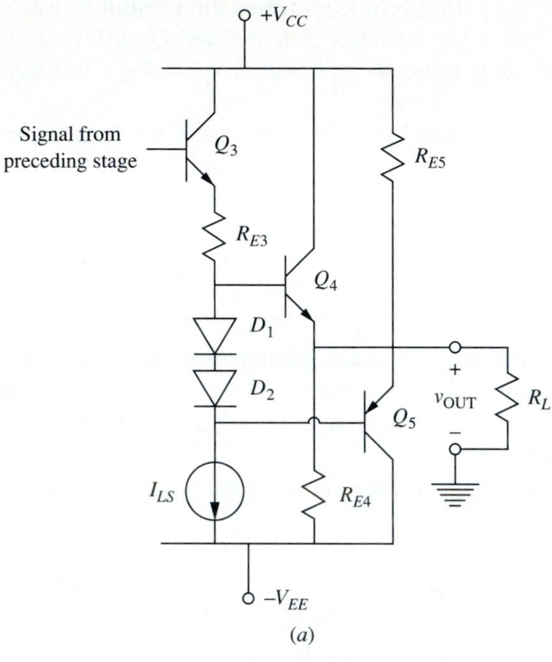

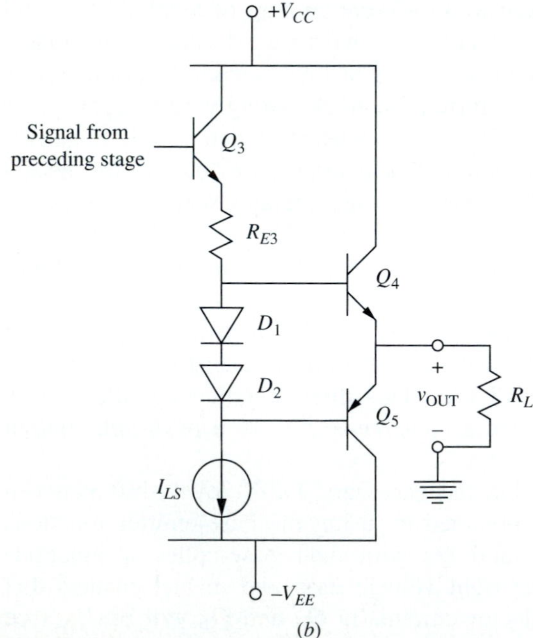

FIGURE 13.13
(*a*) Output of the amplifier of Fig. 13.3*e* modified by the addition of a *pnp* emitter-follower; (*b*) simplified version of this same complementary output pair, called a complementary output stage.

node connected to the base of Q_5 is very likely tied to the collector of a transistor in the current source that will saturate if v_{out} is too negative.

13.3 MULTISTAGE DIFFERENTIAL AMPLIFIERS

Because they are insensitive to common mode input voltages, emitter-coupled pair, or differential, stages are extremely easy to couple directly, in marked contrast to what we have found for single-transistor stages. As long as the quiescent output voltage of a stage falls within the common-mode input voltage range of the following stage, the two stages can be directly coupled; it is as simple as that.

An example of a multistage differential amplifier made of the differential-pair-stage equivalents of the single-transistor stages used in the circuit in Fig. 13.3*e* is shown in Fig. 13.14. Note that the gain stages are slightly different in these two circuits because in Fig. 13.3*e* we had to use degenerate-emitter stages to eliminate the final capacitors, the emitter capacitors. Now, however, with differential-pair stages we can achieve common-emitter performance without having to use emitter capacitors, and thus we can again use higher-gain common-emitter gain stages.

Although this amplifier is now a perfectly reasonable circuit, it is unlikely that it would be built exactly like this because there are numerous improvements that can still be made to it. Some are well beyond what we should be concerned with in an introductory text such as this, but others make use of tricks, known in the trade as "tools," that we already know.

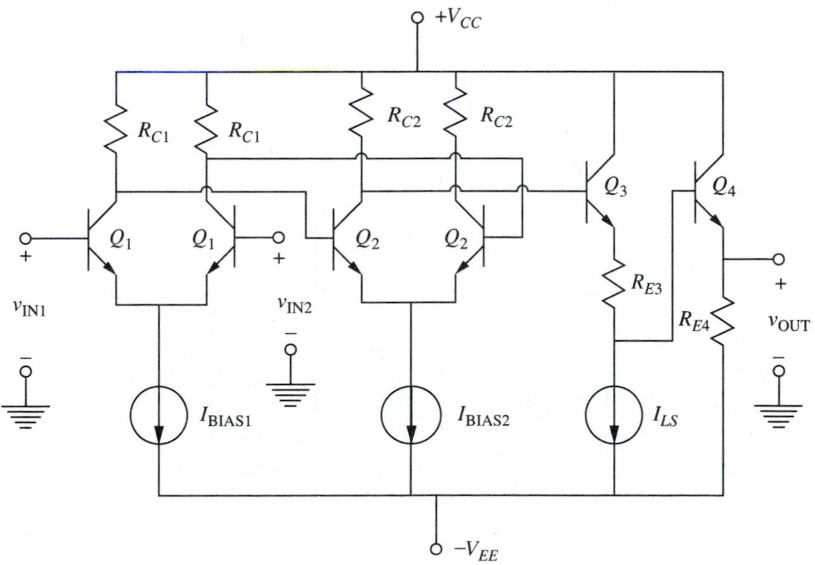

FIGURE 13.14
Differential amplifier version of the multistage amplifier with two common-emitter gain stages discussed in Sec. 13.2 and illustrated in Fig. 13.3*e*.

First, we can increase the input resistance, which is always a desirable goal in a differential amplifier, by replacing Q_1 with either a Darlington pair or a MOSFET.

Second, we can reduce the quiescent power dissipation and increase the efficiency by using a push-pull output stage.

Third, it is often the case that we want a single-ended rather than a differential output. In this case we could leave out the left-hand member of the second differential pair.

Finally, we know that we can significantly increase our gain if we use a current mirror on a gain stage to convert to a single-ended output. In the first place, we get a much larger gain by using an active load, and, second, using the current mirror adds another factor of two to the gain.

An additional benefit of using a current mirror is that we can improve the output voltage swing and further increase the gain when putting the current mirror in the first stage by using a *pnp* common-emitter gain stage with a current source load as the second stage. The amplifier resulting from all of these improvements is shown in Fig. 13.15.

The increase in input resistance, the increase in the voltage gain, and the reduction in the quiescent power dissipation achieved by these changes should

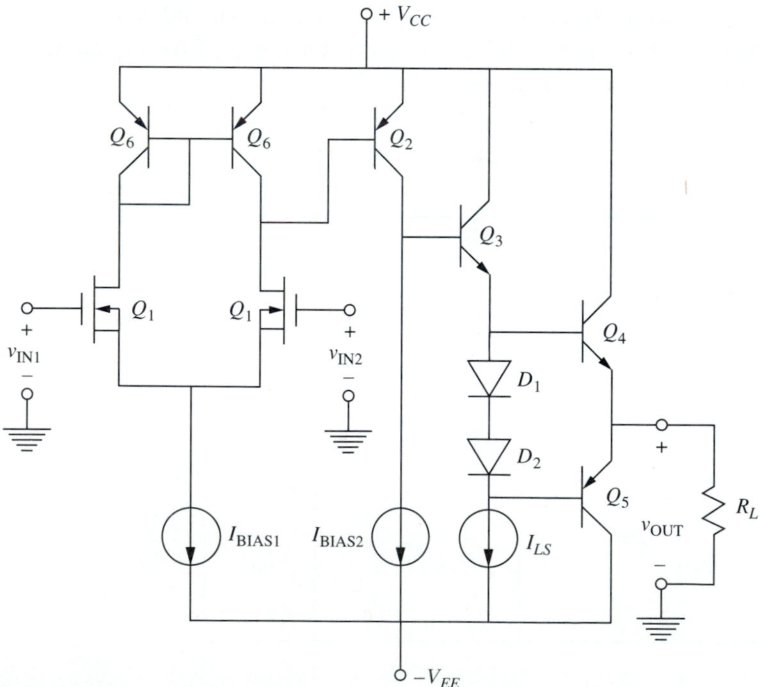

FIGURE 13.15

Differential amplifier of Fig. 13.14 modified by making Q_1 a MOSFET, adding a current mirror to the first stage, making the second stage a *pnp* common-emitter stage with a current source load, and using a push-pull output stage.

be clear to you in light of our earlier discussions in this chapter, but the issue of the increased output voltage swing merits some discussion. Now the collector of Q_2 can be as positive as $V_{CC} + 0.2$ V before it saturates, so v_{out} can be as large as $(V_{CC} + 0.2 - 0.6 - 0.6)$, or $(V_{CC} - 1$ V). In the negative direction, the collector of Q_2 can go negative until the current source I_{BIAS2} saturates. Before this happens, however, the current source I_{LS} will probably saturate, but clearly we should be able to make v_{OUT} as negative as $(V_{CC} - 1)$, and achieve $|v_{\text{out}}|_{\text{max}} = (V_{CC} - 1)$, which is a considerable improvement over the situation in the circuit of Fig.13.14 (see the discussion in the following section).

To "improve" this circuit further, we would want to consider such issues as its dynamic performance, its temperature stability, its manufacturability, etc. First and foremost, however, we would have to know what this circuit was being designed to do. In retrospect this is an obvious consideration, and hopefully you have been concerned by the fact that this issue has not been raised previously in this discussion. It is not our goal to address specific applications in this text, however, and we will leave the issue of further improvements upon this circuit to another text.

Before moving on to a look in the next section at the design of a multistage differential amplifier to meet specific performance objectives, it is interesting to look at a commercial integrated circuit, the 741 operational amplifier. The 741 represented a significant advance in integrated linear amplifier design when it was first introduced and is now recognized as a classic.

The circuit schematic of the 741 is complicated and can be overwhelming unless you first know what to look for in it. Thus, although you can find the full circuit in Fig. 14.5*a*, it is perhaps best if you first focus your attention on the simplified schematic in Fig. 13.16*a*. An even better starting point might be the block diagram in Fig. 13.16*b*, which highlights the basic elements of the circuit. Referring to this figure, we see that the first, or input, stage is an emitter-coupled cascode (see Sec. 13.2.4) biased at a low collector current level to obtain a high input resistance. It has a current mirror load. The second stage is a Darlington common-emitter stage (see Sec. 13.2.3) with a current source load, and the output stage is a push-pull combination (see Sec. 13.2.5).

The 741 circuit is actually very similar to the circuit in Figure 13.15. However, the 741 predates the development of BiCMOS processes that now allow MOSFETs and BJTs to be combined on an integrated circuit chip as we did in Fig. 13.15, so it uses the emitter-coupled cascode instead of a MOSFET for the input stage. The emitter-coupled cascode has excellent high-frequency properties, as we shall study in Chap. 14, and it will have a large input resistance if it is biased at a low level of collector current. To get a low bias level, a Widlar current source, like that shown in Fig. 12.17, is used. (This source is I_1 in Fig. 13.16*a*; it is also used to set I_2 to the proper value.)

The second stage of the 741 differs from that of the circuit in Fig. 13.15 in two important ways. First, it uses a Darlington pair in place of a single transistor to increase the input resistance of this stage and thereby decrease its loading of the first stage. Second, it is based on *npn*, rather than *pnp*, BJTs. This is done because an *npn* is faster than a *pnp* and in general has higher β values. The former feature

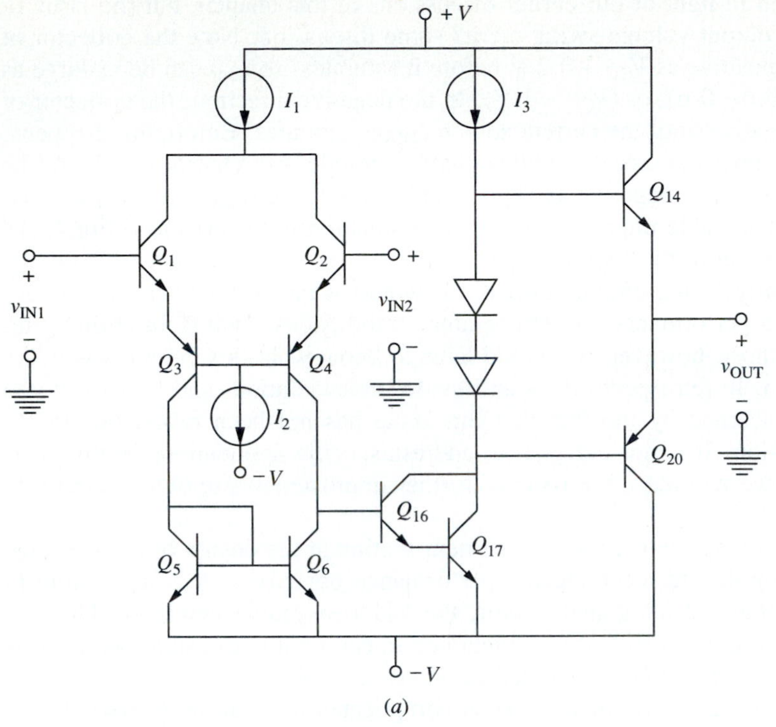

(a)

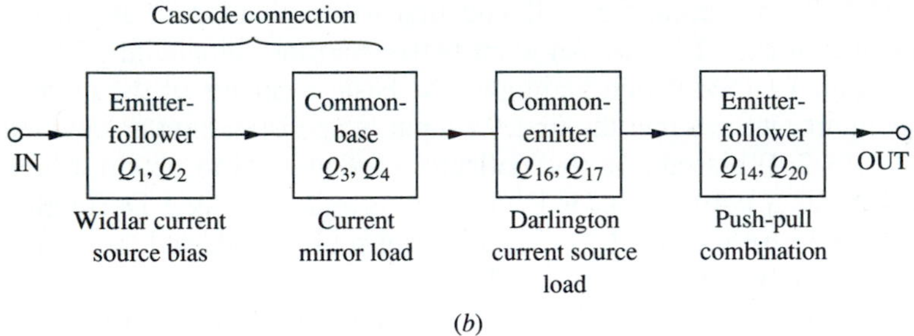

(b)

FIGURE 13.16
741 operational amplifier: (*a*) a simplified schematic; (*b*) a block diagram.

results in a circuit with better high-frequency performance, whereas the latter means that the input resistance will be higher for a given collector bias point.

A final important difference between the 741 and the circuit in Fig. 13.15 is that the 741 does not have a level-shift stage and the quiescent output voltage must be found through other considerations. A little thought will show you that if I_3 is an ideal current source and Q_{16} and Q_{17} have infinite output resistances ($g_o = 0$), then the voltage on the bases of Q_{14} and Q_{20} can take on a wide range of values just so long as neither Q_{16}, Q_{17}, nor the transistors in the current source I_3 saturate. Since I_3 is not ideal and it, along with Q_{16} and Q_{17}, has a finite output resistance, the voltage will settle at a value determined by the relative sizes of these output resistances because they essentially form a voltage divider. This is not a very fortunate design result because it is very difficult (probably impossible) to rely on matching output resistances to make a design work; they have too much uncertainty associated with them. So the quiescent value of v_{OUT} in this circuit is not indeterminate (it will certainly have some value), but it is certainly undesignable.

Actually, the same problem exists in the circuit of Fig. 13.15. As soon as we loaded Q_2 with a current source we lost control over the voltage on the base of Q_3.

The solution to this problem lies in the way that high-gain differential amplifiers like the circuits in Fig. 13.15 and 13.16 are used. They are always used in a feedback connection in which some of the output signal is coupled back to the negative input terminal. In this connection the circuit adjusts itself to have a very small quiescent output voltage. That is, a positive voltage results in an input that pushes the output negative, and vice versa. As soon as such a high-gain amplifier is put into such a feedback circuit, its quiescent output settles at zero.

To quantify this discussion, imagine that we have a very high-gain linear amplifier that has a nonzero quiescent output voltage V_0; that is, the output is V_0 even though there is zero voltage applied to the input. The input and output voltages of this amplifier will then be related as

$$v_{OUT} = A_v v_{IN} + V_0 \tag{13.26}$$

where we assume the voltage gain A_v is very large and negative. V_0 is often called the *quiescent output offset voltage*. This amplifier is illustrated in Fig. 13.17*a*.

Next consider placing this amplifier in a simple feedback circuit like that in Fig. 13.17*b*. To show that the magnitude of the output offset voltage is dramatically reduced by doing this, we can calculate v_{OUT} in this circuit. Summing currents at the input node, we have

$$(v_S - v_{IN})G_1 - v_{IN}G_{IN} + (v_{OUT} - v_{IN})G_2 = 0 \tag{13.27}$$

(Notice that we write this expression using conductances rather than resistances because it is much more convenient to write node equations this way.) Writing v_{IN} as $(v_{OUT} - V_0)/A_v$ and doing a bit of algebraic manipulation, we find

$$v_{OUT} = \frac{A_v G_1 v_S - (G_1 + G_2 + G_{IN})V_0}{A_v G_2 - (G_1 + G_2 + G_{IN})} \tag{13.28}$$

If A_v is very large, the factor $A_v G_2$ will be dominant in the denominator, and if the input resistance is very large, G_{IN} will be negligible relative to G_1 and G_2. For these conditions the above expression reduces to

$$v_{OUT} \approx \frac{G_1}{G_2} v_S - \frac{G_1 + G_2}{G_2} \frac{V_0}{A_v} \tag{13.29a}$$

or, in terms of resistances,

$$v_{OUT} \approx \frac{R_2}{R_1} v_S - \frac{R_1 + R_2}{R_1} \frac{V_0}{A_v} \tag{13.29b}$$

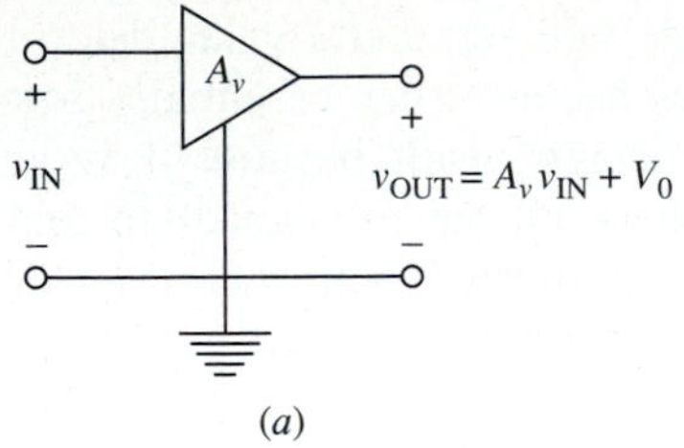

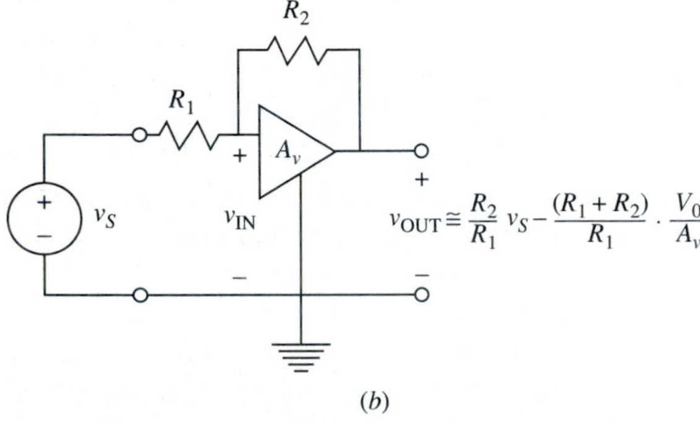

FIGURE 13.17
High-gain linear amplifier with a nonzero quiescent output offset voltage V_0: (*a*) isolated and without any feedback elements; (*b*) connected in a simple feedback circuit.

Either way, the first term in this expression should be familiar to you as the gain of this feedback connection. The second term involving V_0 confirms the reduction in the offset voltage that we argued earlier would occur. The offset is reduced by a factor roughly equal to the ratio of the open-loop voltage gain A_v to the feedback stabilized gain R_2/R_1; this ratio can be very large indeed. If, for example, the open-loop voltage gain is greater than 10,000 and the stabilized gain is 20, the offset is reduced by a factor of over 500.

As we stated earlier, the actual 741 schematic shown in Fig. 14.5*a* looks more complicated than what is shown in Fig. 13.16*a*. You may now want to look at Fig. 14.15*a* and identify the basic building-block components shown in Fig. 13.16. (The transistor numbering is the same in these two figures.) Beyond the basic elements, you should also notice the 50-kΩ resistors added between the bases of Q_5, Q_6, and Q_{17} and ground; these resistors help make the circuit faster by providing a path to discharge the bases of these BJTs.* The exact value of these resistors is not particularly important; they just need to be large. To save space they are actually realized as depletion mode junction field effect transistors with their gate shorted to their source. JFETs made for this purpose are called *pinch resistors*.

*This benefit is discussed and analyzed in Sec. 14.2.7.

Note also the 25- and 50-Ω resistors in the emitter leads of Q_{17}, Q_{19}, Q_{20}; these are included to combat thermal runaway (see Sec. 12.5.1*c*). Finally, notice that an additional provision has been made to adjust the quiescent output voltage with an external resistor attached to the terminals labeled "offset null"; this is used if the scheme described in the preceding paragraph is not satisfactory. Do not be too concerned about the other "extra" elements in the circuit. You may be able to figure out the roles of some of them, but the subtleties of others are well beyond us at this point. The important thing is to see the essential elements.

13.4 A DESIGN EXERCISE: A BASIC *npn* OP-AMP

Perhaps the best way, possibly the only way, to appreciate and truly learn many of the points we have made concerning transistor circuits in the last several chapters is to design an amplifier to meet certain performance specifications. Ideally you will have the opportunity to do this soon in your career. In anticipation of this, and to help you further exercise the analytical skills you have developed in studying this text, we will now consider a design example. Specifically we will consider the choice of resistor values in the operational amplifier (op-amp) circuit illustrated in Fig. 13.14, which has been redrawn in Fig. 13.18*a* with the full current-source circuits included, to meet the following seven performance goals (unless otherwise specified, all refer to mid-band frequencies):

Differential mode voltage gain: as high as possible
Common mode input voltage swing: as large as possible
Differential mode input resistance: ≥ 10K ohms
Output voltage swing into a 1-kΩ load: approximately 2 V
Differential mode output resistance: ≤ 50 Ω.
Quiescent level of output voltage: approximately 0 V
Total quiescent power dissipation: as small as possible

We will assume that all of the transistors are identical, with β_F equal to 100 for I_{CQ} between 100 nA and 10 mA, and that we must bias the transistors within this range. We will also assume that the resistors must be greater than 50 Ω and less than 15 kΩ, unless we choose to short- or open-circuit them, and that the voltage supplies are +10 V and −10 V.

Furthermore, we will assume for the purposes of this design that the large-signal behavior of the transistors is adequately modeled by a model like that of Fig. 8.19*b* with $V_{BE,\text{ON}} = 0.6$ V, and $V_{BC,\text{SAT}} = 0.4$ V; and that the small-signal behavior is suitably modeled by the hybrid-π model of Fig. 8.24*a* with $r_x = 25\ \Omega$ and $g_o = I_C/V_A$, where V_A is 50 V.

13.4.1 The Parts

To proceed with our design we must first make certain that we understand how each one of the performance goals depends on the circuit parameters (i.e., on

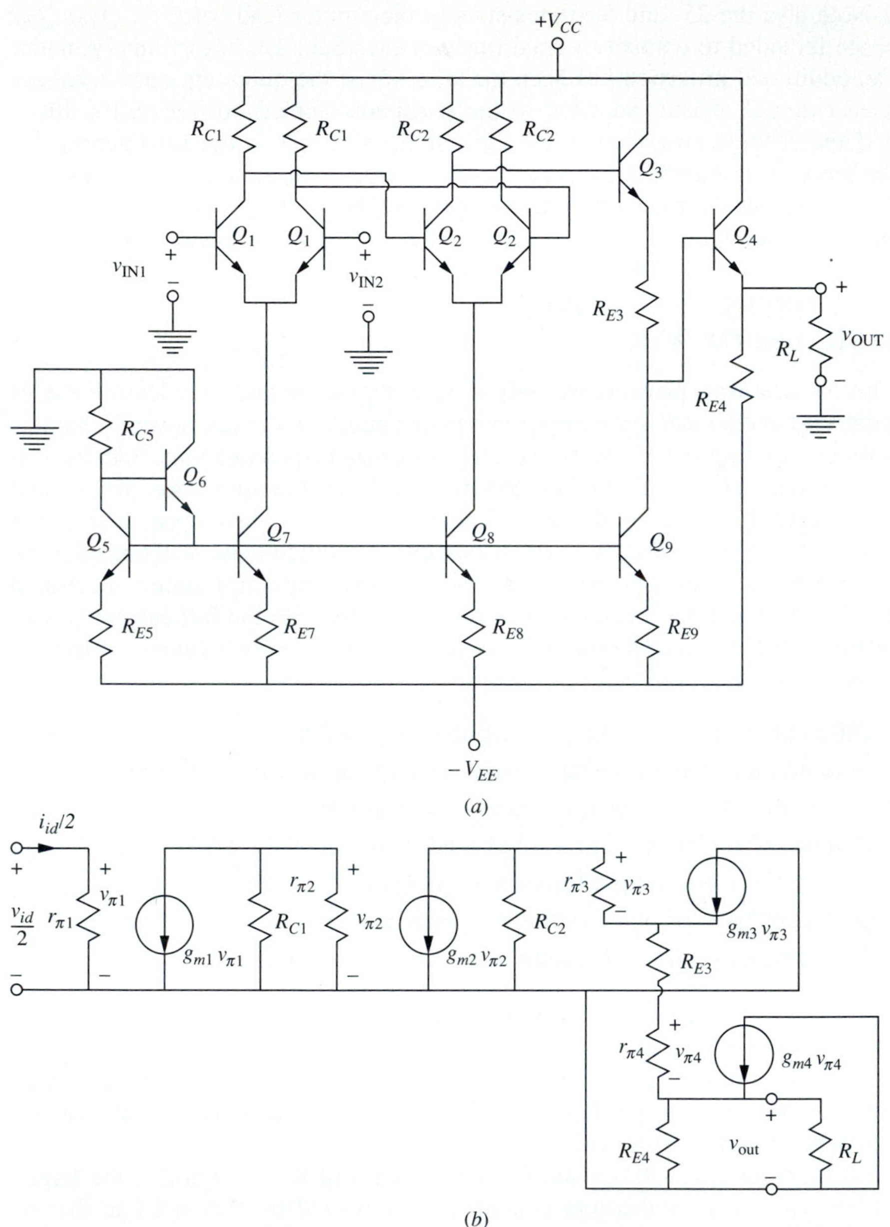

FIGURE 13.18
(a) Differential amplifier of Fig. 13.14 redrawn with the full current-source circuits shown; (b) the mid-band small-signal linear differential mode equivalent half-circuit model for this amplifier.

the resistor values and transistor bias points). Then we need to look at how the goals are interrelated and at how changing the circuit to improve one performance characteristic affects the circuit's performance in other areas. Finally, we can attempt to find an operating point where all the goals are met. The process can be complex, and successful design usually requires a combination of systematic analysis and intuitive deduction. If you expect all of the answers to come just from equations, the process will take a very long time. So, we will start out fairly systematically, all the while trying to develop insight into the overall problem, so that by the time we must choose the values in our final design we have a good "feel" for the circuit.

a) Differential mode voltage gain A_{vd}. To find the differential mode voltage gain A_{vd}, we first draw the small-signal half-circuit model for the amplifier, as shown in Fig. 13.18b. The voltage gain of the last two stages will be essentially 1, and the equivalent resistance in parallel with R_{C2} is very large, so v_{out} is approximately $-g_{m2}\, v_{\pi 2}\, R_{C2}$, which gives us

$$v_{\text{out}} \approx \frac{1}{2} g_{m2} R_{C2} g_{m1} v_{id} \frac{R_{C1} r_{\pi 2}}{(R_{C1} + r_{\pi 2})} \tag{13.30}$$

and

$$A_{vd} \approx \frac{1}{2} g_{m1} R_{C1} g_{m2} R_{C2} \frac{r_{\pi 2}}{(R_{C1} + r_{\pi 2})} \tag{13.31}$$

b) Common mode input voltage swing $\pm v_{IC}$. The inputs can increase in common until Q_1 saturates and can decrease until Q_6 saturates. Thus if we want v_{IC} to be, for example, ±6 V, we must bias Q_1 so that its collector is at approximately 5.6 V or more. Similarly the reference voltage on the base of Q_6 must be −6.2 V —that is,(−6 V − 0.6 V + 0.4 V)—or less. This value is 3.8 V above the negative supply, so a negative common mode excursion of 6 V would not appear to cause any difficulty in this circuit.

It is important to note that the positive excursion also places a limitation on the gain. In our example of v_{IC} being +6 V, for which the collector of Q_1 must be at 5.6 V or more above ground, the gain is restricted because the voltage drop across R_{C1} must correspondingly be 4.4 V (i.e., $V_{CC} - 5.6$ V), or less. Thus we have the constraint that

$$R_{C1} I_{C1} \leq 4.4 \text{ V} \tag{13.32a}$$

or

$$g_m R_{C1} \leq 4.4 \frac{q}{kT} = 176 \tag{13.32b}$$

In arriving at these expressions we have neglected the base current into Q_2, which also flows through R_{C1}, but this is adequate for the first time through and is standard practice. We will refine things later on.

Before proceeding, remember that the range on V_{IC} is not specified in our design structure but rather is something we want to maximize. We used ±6 V as an example above simply to have a concrete number to work with.

c) Differential mode input resistance r_{id}. The differential mode input resistance of this circuit is simply $r_{\pi 1}$, which is $\beta kT/qI_{C1}$. This specification thus places another constraint on I_{C1}, that is,

$$I_{C1} \leq \frac{\beta kT}{q r_{id}} \tag{13.33}$$

Making r_{id} greater than $10k$ thus restricts I_{C1} to 0.25 mA or less.

d) Output voltage swing $|v_{od}|_{\max}$. The voltage on the collector of Q_2 changes directly with v_{od}, so one of the limitations on $|v_{od}|_{\max}$ is the allowable swing of this collector voltage. It can increase to 10 V (i.e., V_{CC}), and it can decrease until Q_2 saturates, a point determined by the bias on Q_1. The former consideration constrains the voltage drop across R_{C2} to be greater than 2 V (i.e., $|v_{od}|_{\max}$) and thus restricts $g_{m2}R_{C2}$:

$$g_{m2}R_{C2} \geq q\left|v_{od}\right|_{\max}/kT = 80 \tag{13.34}$$

Another possible limitation on the negative excursion of v_{od} is placed by R_{E4}, as we discussed in Sec. 13.2.5. We must have

$$-V_{CC}R_L/(R_L + R_{E4}) \leq -\left|v_{od}\right|_{\max} \tag{13.35}$$

In our case, with $V_{CC} = 10$ V, $R_L = 1$ kΩ, and $|v_{od}|_{\max} = 2$ V, we must have $R_{E4} \leq 4$ kΩ.

e) Differential mode output resistance r_{od}. The differential mode output resistance of this circuit can be deduced from the incremental half-circuit in Fig. 13.18*b* to be given by

$$r_{od} = R_{E4} \left\| \frac{r_{\pi 4} + R_{E3} + [(r_{\pi 3} + R_{C2})/\beta]}{\beta} \right. \tag{13.36}$$

The term $(r_\pi^3 + R_{C2})/\beta^2$ is probably very small, so for design purposes our main concerns should be $(r_{\pi 4} + R_{E3})/\beta$ and R_{E4}. We have said that we need R_{E4} to be less than 4 kΩ, and we will probably make it exactly 4 kΩ to minimize the quiescent power dissipation. With R_{E4} so large, the only way we can have r_{od} less than 50 Ω is if we have $(r_{\pi 4} + R_{E3})$ less than 5 kΩ. Furthermore, if R_{E4} is 4 kΩ, and V_{OUT} is 0 V, then I_{C4} will have to be 2.5 mA, which says that $r_{\pi 4}$ is 1 kΩ. Having $(r_{\pi 4} + R_{E3})$ less than 5 kΩ and $r_{\pi 4}$ equal to 1 kΩ means in turn that we must have R_{E3} less than 4 kΩ. Again, we will want to try to keep R_{E3} as large as possible to minimize I_{LS} and the quiescent power consumption, so we will probably make it exactly 4 kΩ.

f) Quiescent output voltage V_{OUT}. V_{OUT} is the voltage level on the collector of Q_2 less two 0.6-V base-emitter drops and the voltage drop across R_{E3}. Thus, given R_{E3} and taking into consideration the value of r_{od}, we can adjust I_{LS} to make V_{OUT} zero once we select the bias of Q_2.

g) Quiescent power dissipation. Summing the quiescent power dissipated in all of the elements to determine the total quiescent power consumption is a hopeless, and fortunately unnecessary, exercise. The efficient way to calculate the power consumption is to focus on calculating the power supplied by the sources, which is simply the sum of the bias currents times the supply voltage. Thus, looking at Fig. 13.18a, we have

$$\begin{aligned} P &= (V_{CC} + V_{EE})(I_{C4} + I_{C7} + I_{C8} + I_{C9}) \\ &\quad + V_{EE}\left[I_{C5} + \frac{1}{\beta}(I_{C5} + I_{C7} + I_{C8} + I_{C9})\right] \end{aligned} \tag{13.37}$$

The supply voltages are, of course, fixed, so our design latitude lies in reducing the bias currents. We have found restrictions on most of them already but will in general want to keep them small.

13.4.2 The Whole

Now that we have had a first look at the factors affecting the individual performance parameters in our circuit, we need to look at how they interact and the compromises we face. There is no right order in which to do this, nor even a best order, so we just have to start someplace and see what happens. We have to be prepared to iterate several times and backtrack when we get into trouble meeting specifications, but hopefully we will eventually be able to focus in on an optimum design.

We will look first at r_{id} because it is a fairly clean specification. Fixing r_{id} exactly at 10 kΩ means that I_{C1} must be 0.25 mA. We could try to make r_{id} even smaller, which would reduce the power, but we also know that I_{C1}, or at least the product $I_{C1}R_{C1}$, enters into the gain and the common mode voltage swing, so let's wait to see what conclusions these other constraints lead us to.

The next hard constraint is that the amplifier must be able to supply ±2 V to a 1-kΩ load. This implies that the collector of Q_2 must be able to swing at least ±2 V, which says that it must be able to go to as low as 6 V (i.e., $V_{CC} - 4$ V). This in turn says that the base of Q_2 and thus the collector on Q_1 must be biased at, at most, 6.4 V above ground, so $I_C R_{C1}$ must be $\leq$ 3.6 V. Making it larger increases A_{vd} [see Eq. (13.31)], but making it smaller increases $|v_{IC}|_{\max}$; we clearly have to compromise on these two specifications.

There is yet another factor to consider here. The largest resistor we can have in the circuit is 15 kΩ, so there is in fact an upper bound on $I_C R_{C1}$ since we have $I_{C1} \leq 0.25$ mA and $R_{C1} \leq 15$ kΩ. In particular, we must have $I_{C1}R_{C1} \geq 3.75$ V. Fortunately this is not inconsistent with the lower bound of 3.6 V set by $|v_{\text{out}}|$, but it certainly narrows our options. To proceed, let's assume gain is more important to us and set $I_{C1}R_{C1}$ equal to 3.75 V, with R_{C1} at 15 kΩ and I_{C1} at 0.25 mA. Our positive common mode voltage swing will thus be limited to +6.65 V; call it 6.6 V.

Since we have now set the bias on the collector of Q_1 at 6.25 V, the collector on Q_2 can go as low as 5.85 and the voltage drop across I_{C2}, which also enters

A_{vd}, can be increased from 2 V to 2.15 V. A safer design would use 2.1 V, or perhaps even a bit lower; we will use 2.1 V, and thus the quiescent voltage at the collector of Q_2 is 7.9 V above ground.

With the bias on Q_2 set, we can look at making the quiescent output voltage V_{OUT} zero. Doing so requires a voltage drop of 6.7 V across R_{E3}. If possible we would like to make R_{E3} as large as possible to minimize I_{LS}, so let's try 15 kΩ for R_{E3}. Thus I_{LS} must be approximately 0.45 mA. R_{E3} also enters r_{od}, however, so we had best look at this parameter next.

We found an expression for r_{od} in Eq. (13.36) and argued that we would have to keep $(r_{\pi 4} + R_{E3})$ below 5 kΩ. Clearly we cannot make R_{E3} equal to 15 kΩ, but let's see what we can do. We already have a constraint on $r_{\pi 4}$ that was set by $|v_{out}|_{max}$. R_{E4} has to be less than 4 kΩ, and thus I_{C4} will be greater than 2.5 mA, at which bias level $r_{\pi 4}$ is 1 kΩ. This implies, as we have said earlier, that we must have $R_{E3} \leq 4$ kΩ, and fixing R_{E3} at 4 kΩ leads to an I_{LS} of 1.7 mA. Notice, however, that increasing I_{C4} would reduce $r_{\pi 4}$ and allow us to make R_{E3} larger and I_{LS} smaller. For minimum power, however, we want the sum $I_{LS} + I_{C4}$ to be a minimum; so it is worth asking whether we gain or lose by increasing I_{C4} and decreasing I_{LS} in this way, and if we win, what is the optimum situation. Going through this exercise we find that the optimum I_{C4} is actually less than our current bias point, so it is best to leave I_{C4} at 2.5 mA.

Looking back, we see that we have actually been able to meet all of the fixed specifications. We can now see how we are doing on the gain, common mode swing, and power. We turn first to the voltage gain since it involves the one thing we don't have yet, the bias current on the second stage. Our expression for A_{vd} was given by Eq. (13.31), which we repeat here with g_m replaced by qI_C/kT:

$$A_{vd} = \frac{1}{2}\frac{qI_{C1}R_{C1}}{kT}\frac{qI_{C2}R_{C2}}{kT}\frac{r_{\pi 2}}{(R_{C1} + r_{\pi 2})} \tag{13.38}$$

The first two factors are already set at 150 and 84, respectively, since the products $I_{C1}R_{C1}$ and $I_{C2}R_{C2}$ are set at 3.75 V and 2.1 V, respectively. The factor $r_{\pi 2}/(R_{C1} + r_{\pi 2})$ is still open to design. Looking at it we see that since R_{C1} is already fixed, this term is maximized by making $r_{\pi 2}$ as large as possible. This we do by minimizing I_{C2}, which, since the product $I_{C2}R_{C2}$ is 2.1 V, can be done by picking the maximum value for R_{C2}, or 15 kΩ. Doing this yields $I_{C2} = 0.14$ mA, $r_{\pi 2} = 18$ kΩ, and the factor $r_{\pi 2}/(R_{C1} + r_{\pi 2}) \approx 0.55$. A_{vd} is thus 3465.

The differential voltage gain is actually somewhat less than this figure because we have made several approximations we might want to reconsider. First, we have ignored the fact that the gain of the last two stages is somewhat less than 1, but this is a minor correction. Second, and more importantly, we have ignored the base currents, but since Q_2 is biased at a low level and Q_3 at a high level, the base current on Q_3, which flows through R_{C2}, is important. Specifically, if $I_{C3} (\approx I_{LS})$ is 1.7 mA, I_{B3} is 0.017 mA. With $R_{C2} = 15$ kΩ and the voltage drop across it being 2.1 V, the current through it, which we have been saying is I_{C2}, is 0.14 mA. Clearly 0.017 mA, or over 10 percent of this current, is I_{B3}, so the portion going to Q_2 (i.e., I_{C2}) is only 0.123 mA. Thus the product $I_{C2}R_{C2}$ is really only about 1.85 V rather than 2.1 V, and A_{vd} is thus only 3050.

We should similarly adjust I_{LS} to account for the base current of Q_4, which is also biased at a large quiescent value. I_{B4} is 0.025 mA, so I_{LS} should really be 1.675 mA rather than 1.7 mA; this is not a big deal, perhaps, but it does lead to a difference in the voltage drop across R_{E3} of 0.1 V.

Next we need to design the current sources, determine the allowable common mode voltage swing, and calculate the power dissipation. The maximum common mode voltage is limited by the voltage on the collector of Q_1 to +6.6 V, as we said earlier. The minimum common mode voltage is limited by the saturation of Q_7 and thus depends on the details of the current source design, specifically on the value of the reference voltage V_{REF} set by Q_5 on the bases of Q_7, Q_8, and Q_9; the lower V_{REF} is, the more negative the common mode voltage can be. Otherwise, this voltage does not affect the amplifier performance significantly; it has only a minor impact on the power dissipation since the base currents of Q_7, Q_8, and Q_9 flow through R_{C5}, and thus we would like to keep the voltage drop across R_{C5} small. Assuming for the sake of argument that we want a symmetrical common mode voltage swing (i.e., ± 6.6 V), we can set V_{REF} at -6.8 V, or 3.2 V above $-V_{EE}$, which is a reasonable value. With this V_{REF}, we can next choose R_{E6}, R_{E7}, and R_{E8}. Our design values for I_{C7}, I_{C8}, and I_{C9} are 0.5, 0.246, and 1.7 mA, respectively, so we find that R_{E7} must be 5.2 kΩ, R_{E8} must be 10.6 kΩ, and R_{E9} must be 1.53 kΩ.

The final parameter we must select is the quiescent collector current in Q_5. Power considerations would tell us to make this as small as possible by making R_{C5} equal to 15 kΩ. The corresponding current through R_{C5} is 0.41 mA (since $V_{REF} = -6.8$ V). This is, strictly speaking, not I_{C5}, however, because it also includes the base current to Q_6. This current equals the sum of the base currents of Q_5, Q_7, Q_8, and Q_9, which turns out to be roughly 40 μA, divided by β. Thus I_{B6} is only 0.4 μA and can be neglected relative to I_{C5}. Thus I_{C5} is 0.41 mA, and R_{E5} must be 6.3 kΩ.

The design is now complete, and we can at last calculate the power dissipation. Summing the power dissipation using Eq. (13.37), we find it is approximately 103 mW, just over 80 percent of which (84 mW) occurs in the output stages, Q_3 and Q_4.

13.5 BEYOND BASIC: DESIGN WITH BiCMOS

Looking back over our design in the preceding section, it is striking how important the output specifications were. In addition to requiring very high bias levels on the output stages, in this particular design they affected the design all of the way back to the input, where they even limited the maximum common mode voltage. The input resistance specification placed still further constraints on the design. In all of these aspects the improved amplifier design in Fig. 13.15 is far superior to the amplifier we have just analyzed and designed in Sec. 13.4. To help us explore further why this is so, and to see

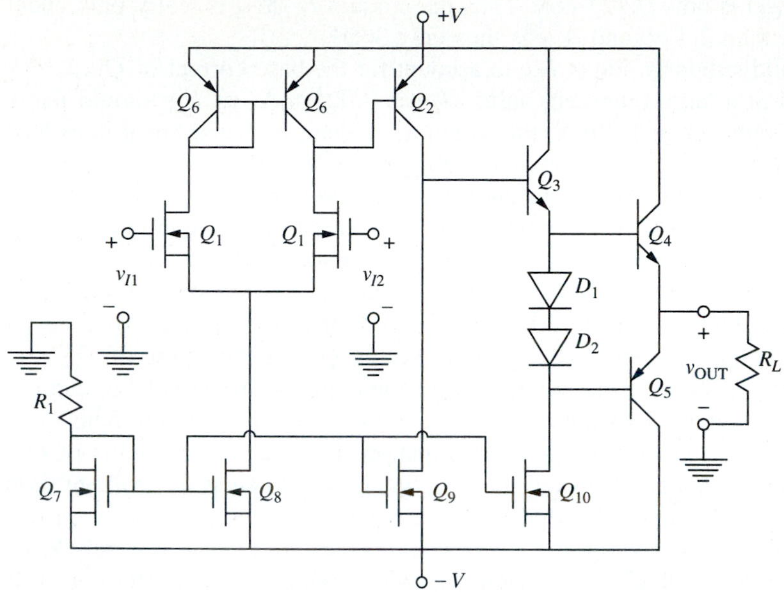

FIGURE 13.19
Circuit of Fig. 13.15 redrawn with the current-source circuits shown explicitly.

ways of making the improved design even better, the amplifier of Fig. 13.15 is shown again in Fig. 13.19, including the full current-source circuits as well.

An important difference between the amplifier in Fig. 13.18 and that in Fig. 13.19 is that the former uses only passive resistor loads and has only *npn* transistors, whereas the latter uses active loads, a larger variety of active device types, and almost no resistors. In fact, it uses both *npn* and *pnp* bipolar transistors and *n*-channel MOSFETs and has only one resistor. Such a circuit is said to use a BiMOS, or BiCMOS, technology.* It is more difficult to fabricate an integrated circuit with so many different transistor types on it, but doing so provides circuit designers with more options and flexibility and lets them extract much higher performance from designs.

You may want to explore the design of the amplifier of Fig. 13.19 to meet the same design goals we set in Sec. 13.4 for the amplifier of Fig. 13.18. You will find that the interplay of the stages is now rather different and that a different set of constraints is active, but the same general approach to the design can be used.† We will not do such a complete and detailed design again here; instead we will focus on just one aspect of the circuit's performance, the differential voltage gain.

*Strictly speaking, adding the "C" to BiMOS should only be done if both *n*- and *p*-channel MOSFETs are used, but this rule is frequently ignored.

†Assume that for the MOSFET $V_T = 1$ V and $K = 0.1$ mA/V^2, and assume V_A is 15 V for the MOSFET and 50 V and 10 V for the *npn* and *pnp* BJTs, respectively. Assume further that β is 100 for the *npn* BJTs, and 40 for the *pnps*.

The differential mode voltage gain of the first stage of this amplifier is proportional to g_{m1} times the load resistance, which is the parallel combination of r_{o1}, the output resistance of Q_1; r_{o6}, the output resistance of Q_6; and $r_{\pi 2}$, the input resistance of Q_2. This is in turn simply g_{m1} divided by the sum of g_{o1}, g_{o6}, and $g_{\pi 2}$. Writing this out, we have

$$A_{vd1} = \frac{g_{m1}}{g_{o1} + g_{o6} + g_{\pi 2}} \tag{13.39a}$$

Since g_{o1} and g_{o6} are likely to be much smaller than $g_{\pi 2}$, this is essentially g_{m1} divided by $g_{\pi 2}$:

$$A_{vd1} \approx \frac{g_{m1}}{g_{\pi 2}} \tag{13.39b}$$

Inserting the bias point dependences of g_{m1} and $g_{\pi 2}$, we then have

$$A_{vd1} \approx \sqrt{2KI_{D1}}\frac{\beta_2 kT}{qI_{C2}} \tag{13.39c}$$

The voltage gain of the second stage is $-g_{m2}$ times the load resistance seen by this stage, which is somewhat complicated. We have

$$A_{vd2} \approx -g_{m2} \cdot r_{o9} \| r_{o2} \| \{r_{\pi 3} + \beta_3 [\beta_4 R_L + r_{\pi 4} \| (2r_d + r_{\pi 5})]\} \tag{13.40a}$$

The resistance in parallel with r_{o9} and r_{o2} will be dominated by the $\beta_3\beta_4R_L$ factor if our transistors have reasonable β-values and the load resistor R_L is not too small; $\beta_3\beta_4R_L$ is in turn likely to be much larger than the parallel combination of r_{o9} and r_{o2} (at least, we want this to be the case in our design), so we have

$$A_{vd2} \approx -g_{m2}(r_{o9} \| r_{o2}) = -\frac{g_{m2}}{g_{o9} + g_{o2}} \tag{13.40b}$$

which, in terms of the bias point dependences, is

$$A_{vd2} \approx -\frac{q\,|V_{A9} \| V_{A2}|}{kT(|V_{A9}| + |V_{A2}|)} \tag{13.40c}$$

It is significant that this gain is solely dependent on device parameters. The only way to increase it is to make the devices better (e.g., to increase $|V_A|$).

Combining Eqs. (13.39c) and (13.40c), we find that the total voltage gain of the gain stages is

$$A_{vd} \approx -\sqrt{2KI_{D1}}\frac{\beta_2}{I_{C2}}\frac{|V_{A9}|\,|V_{A2}|}{(|V_{A9}| + |V_{A2}|)} \tag{13.41}$$

This result tells us that we want to bias the first stage (Q_1) at as large a quiescent drain current as possible. The limit will be set by the common mode input voltage swing and by any power dissipation restrictions. Equation (13.41) also tells us that we want to bias the second stage (Q_2) at as small as possible a level (so that $r_{\pi 2}$ is large); how low we can go will be set by the decrease in β at low collector current levels (recall Sec. 8.1.7*d*). Notice also, however, that as I_{D1} is increased and I_{D2} is decreased, the contrast between $r_{\pi 2}$ and r_{o1} and r_{o6} becomes smaller and the assumption we made to go from Eq. (13.39a) to (13.39b) becomes weaker. Also, as we make I_{C2} smaller, r_{o2} and r_{o9} increase and it becomes more and more likely that we can no longer assume that $\beta_3\beta_4R_L$ is much larger than the parallel combination of r_{o2} and r_{o9}.

The input resistance of Q_2 clearly plays a major role in limiting the gain of this stage, and it would be nice to be able to reduce the loading that the second stage of this amplifier places on the first. We will look very briefly at two ways we can try to achieve this objective. The first is to replace Q_2 with a Darlington connection as is done in the 741 (see Fig. 13.16). The second is to replace Q_2 with a *p*-channel MOSFET; to do this successfully the *pnp* current mirror must also be replaced with a *p*-MOS current mirror. We will look at these two options in turn in the following two subsections.

13.5.1 Darlington Second Stage

Replacing Q_2 with a Darlington pair, as shown in Fig. 13.20*a*, significantly increases the input resistance of the second stage, but it can also lead to a nonzero output voltage when there is no input voltage; this so-called *null offset problem* must be addressed. To see why this is so, consider that, for the original circuit, a circuit designer can balance the first stage by ensuring that the base-emitter voltages on Q_6 and Q_2 are identical. This can be done by sizing Q_6 and Q_2 so that they have the same quiescent emitter current densities. This means that $V_{BE6} = V_{BE2}$, which in turn means that the voltages on the collectors of both transistors Q_6 are the same (i.e., that the first stage is balanced). In the circuit of Fig. 13.20*a*, on the other hand, the collector-emitter voltage of the left-hand Q_6 is V_{BE6}, whereas that of the right-hand Q_6 is $V_{BE2'}$ plus V_{BE2}, which is roughly 0.6 V higher than the collector-emitter voltage of the right-hand Q_6. The first stage is clearly no longer balanced, and this imbalance is indistinguishable from an input signal when the amplifier is connected in a feedback circuit like that illustrated in Fig. 13.17. To overcome this problem an additional diode forward voltage drop (i.e., roughly 0.6 V) must be added in series with the emitter of Q_6. Three possible ways of doing this are shown in Figs. 13.20*b*, *c*, and *d*. In Fig. 13.20*b*, diodes (made from transistors) are placed in the emitter leads of each of the two transistors Q_6. This is a reasonable thing to do, but we can do even better if a second current mirror circuit is used.

One example of using a second current mirror is shown in Fig. 13.20*c*. In this circuit, a diode is placed in the voltage circuit of the left-hand Q_6 and its base-emitter voltage is mirrored to the transistor Q_6' of the right-hand member of the pair. The beauty of this circuit is that the incremental resistance seen when looking in at the collector of the right-hand Q_6 is now $r_{o6} + r_{o6'}$, or twice as much as before. To the extent that this resistance plays a role in limiting the stage gain, this is good; in practice, however, the gain is probably still limited by the input resistance of the Darlington, and this advantage is modest. The problem with this circuit is that yet another base current must be supplied by the left-hand transistor cascode, and this is an imbalance in the circuit that will manifest itself as an offset. We can often live with this imbalance, but it is possible to reduce it significantly using the second current mirror connection shown in Fig. 13.20*d*.

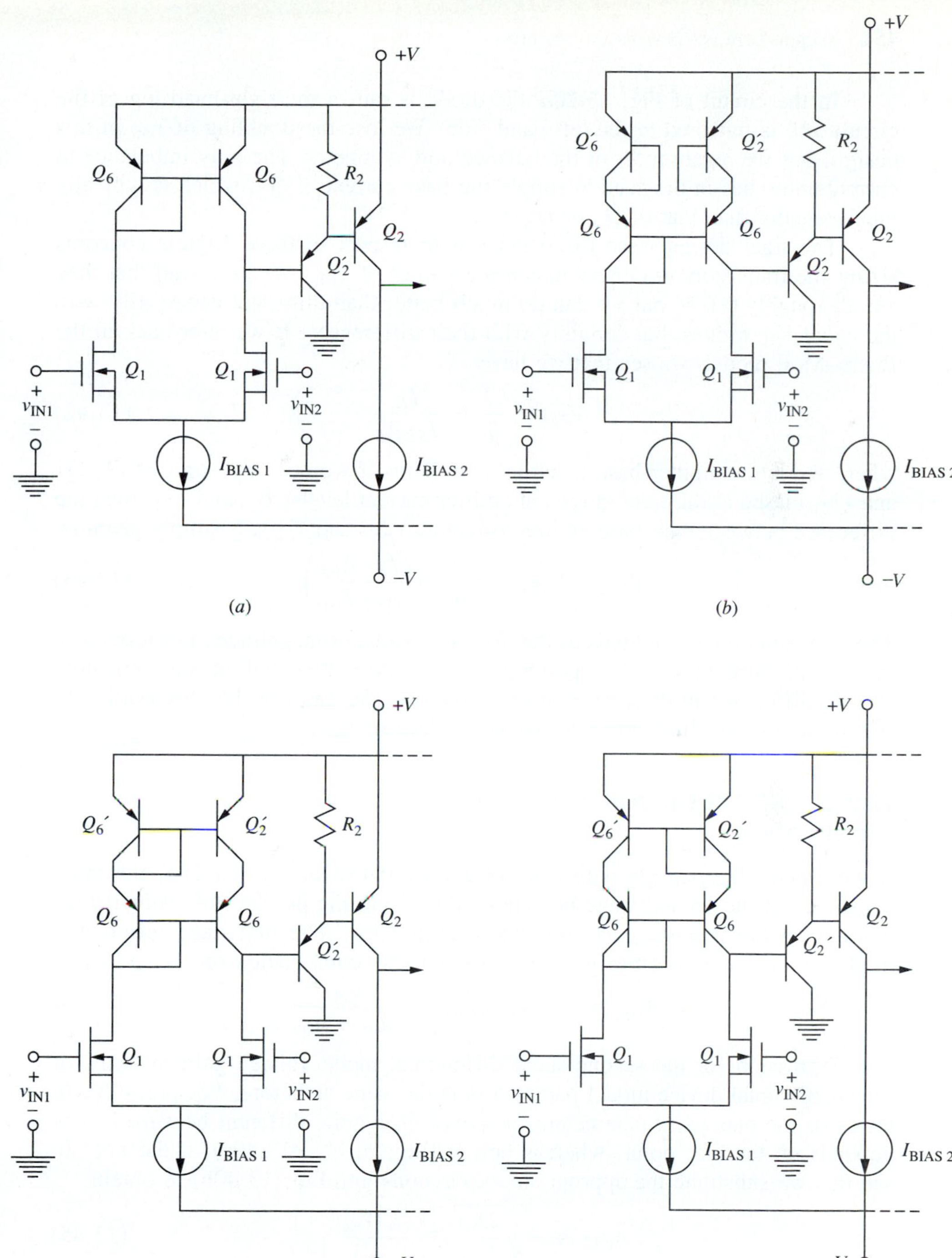

FIGURE 13.20
Circuits incorporating a Darlington second stage to reduce the loading between the first and second stages: Simply adding a Darlington as in (*a*) creates offset problems that can be corrected by adding diodes as in (*b*) or, a better choice, by adding a second current mirror as in (*c*) and (*d*). Of these, (*c*) has higher output resistance, but (*d*) is better balanced.

In the circuit of Fig. 13.20d the diode is put in the right-hand leg of the circuit and is mirrored to the left-hand side. We lose the doubling of r_{o6} in this design, but we regain most of the balance and symmetry. The only imbalance in currents now lies in the need to supply the base current of Q_2', which is typically much smaller than that of Q_6 or Q_6'.*

The final design issue to consider with respect to these circuits concerns sizing the transistors to closely match the values of V_{BE}. We have said that they are all roughly 0.6 V, but we can do much better than this—not necessarily with the exact V_{BE} values, but certainly with their differences. If we refer back to the Ebers–Moll model, we see that we have

$$V_{BE} \approx \frac{kT}{q} \ln \frac{I_E}{J_{SE} A_E} \tag{13.42}$$

where A_E is the emitter-base junction area. Thus if we have two transistors, Q_1 and Q_2, biased at different quiescent emitter current levels, I_{E1} and I_{E2}, then the difference between their base-emitter voltages, V_{BE1} and V_{BE2}, is simply given by

$$V_{BE2} - V_{BE1} = \frac{kT}{q} \ln\left(\frac{I_{E2}}{A_{E2}} \frac{A_{E1}}{I_{E1}}\right) \tag{13.43}$$

This very important result tells us that for every order of magnitude of difference in the emitter current densities in two bipolar transistors, there will be approximately 60 mV difference in their base-emitter voltages. We can use this observation to size the transistors in a circuit to balance values of V_{BE}.

13.5.2 *p*-MOS Current Mirror and Second Stage

If we replace the *pnp* Q_2 with a MOSFET as shown in Fig. 13.21a, the input resistance of the second stage becomes infinite and the problem of second-stage loading on the first stage is completely eliminated. The first-stage differential mode voltage gain becomes g_{m1} times the parallel combination of r_{o1} and r_{o6}:

$$A_{vd1} \approx g_{m1}\left(r_{o1} \| r_{o6}\right) = \frac{g_{m1}}{g_{o1} + g_{o6}} \tag{13.44}$$

The expression for the second-stage differential mode voltage gain in terms of the small-signal device model parameters is the same as before, Eq. (13.40b). In terms of the bias point parameters, however, it is quite different because it now depends on the bias point, whereas before [i.e., in Eq. (13.40c)] it did not. To see this we substitute the appropriate expressions into Eq. (13.40b) to obtain

$$A_{vd2} \approx -\sqrt{\frac{2K_2}{I_{D2}}} \frac{|V_{A9}|\,|V_{A2}|}{|V_{A9}| + |V_{A2}|} \tag{13.45}$$

*Note that another possibility is to place a resistor in series with the emitters of the Q_6 transistors. This is done in the 741 circuit found in Fig. 14.5. Notice, however, that the circuit of Fig. 14.5 also has provision for an external offset adjustment.

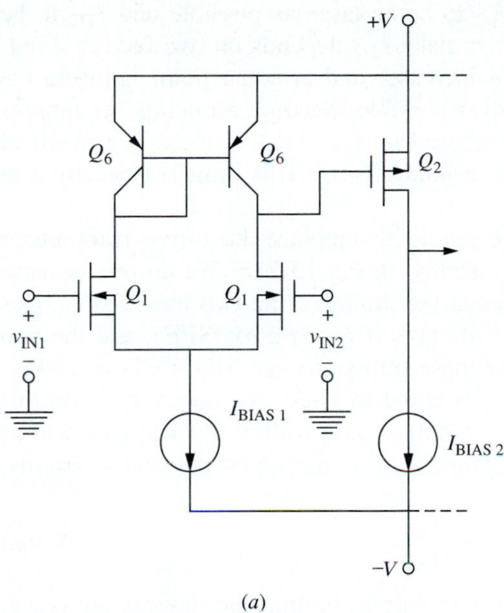

(a)

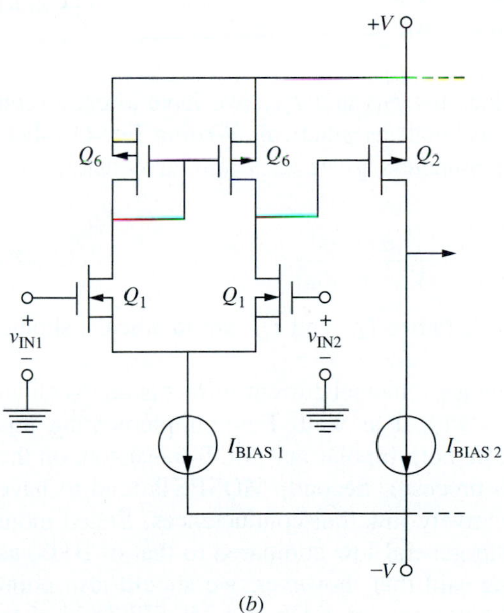

(b)

FIGURE 13.21
Circuit of Figure 13.19 modified to have a p-channel MOSFET second stage: (a) circuit with the *pnp* Q_2 simply replaced with a MOSFET; (b) circuit that uses p-channel MOSFETs for both Q_2 and the current mirror.

from which it is clear that we want K_2 to be as large as possible and I_{D2} to be as small as practical. How small we can make I_{D2} depends on two factors. First, as we make I_{D2} smaller, r_{o2} and r_{o9} increase, and at some point ignoring the other factors in Eq. (13.40a) is no longer possible. Second, reducing I_{D2} implies reducing $(V_{GS2} - V_{T2})$, and, as we discussed in Sec. 11.4.1, there is a practical lower limit on $(V_{GS} - V_T)$ set by subthreshold effects. This limit is typically 3 to 4 kT/q.

Having made Q_2 a MOSFET, we should also replace the *pnp* current mirror with a *p*-channel current mirror, as illustrated in Fig.13.21*b*. We do this because we want to keep the quiescent voltages at the drains of the two transistors Q_6 as similar as possible, and this a formidable task if Q_2 is a MOSFET and the two Q_6 transistors are BJTs. Even if all of these transistors are MOSFETs as in Fig. 13.21*b*, we still must ensure that V_{GS2} is equal to V_{GS6}. An easy way to do this is to make Q_2 and Q_6 identical except for their gate widths W. The gate widths are then designed to be in the same proportion as the quiescent drain currents, that is,

$$\frac{W_6}{W_2} = \frac{I_{D6}}{I_{D2}} \tag{13.46a}$$

so the drain current densities per unit gate length through the devices are equal; that is,

$$\frac{I_{D2}}{W_2} = \frac{I_{D6}}{W_6} \tag{13.46b}$$

This ensures that V_{GS2} and V_{GS6} are equal.

With regard to the optimum values for I_{D2} and I_{D6}, we have already seen from Eq. (13.45) that I_{D2} should be as small as practical. Writing Eq. (13.44a) for A_{vd1} in terms of the bias point parameters gives us a similar constraint on I_{D6}. We have

$$A_{vd1} \approx -\sqrt{\frac{2K_1}{I_{D1}}} \frac{|V_{A1}|\,|V_{A6}|}{|V_{A1}| + |V_{A6}|} \tag{13.44$'$}$$

which tells us that I_{D1}, and therefore I_{D6} (since I_{D1} and I_{D6} are identical), should also be as small as practical.

Making Q_2 a MOSFET and using a *p*-channel current mirror is an excellent design choice, but there are problems with it as well. First, implementing this approach requires being able to fabricate both bipolar and MOS transistors on the same chip (i.e., it requires a BIMOS process). Second, MOSFETs tend to have relatively small early voltages and relatively low transconductances. Stated more concisely, the $A_{v,\max}$ of MOSFETs is in general low compared to that of BJTs, as we discussed in Sec. 11.4.1*b*. Having said that, however, we should also point out that the performance differential between *pnp* BJTs and MOSFETs is often less than between *npn*'s and MOSFETs because technologies are often focused on optimizing the performance of *npn*'s (possibly at the expense of *pnp* performance). It is also true that MOSFET performance is continually being improved. The bottom line is that MOS current mirrors are an excellent design choice and are widely used.

13.6 SUMMARY

In this chapter we have considered the problem of connecting basic amplifier stages to form multistage amplifiers that have combinations and levels of input and output resistances, as well as gains, not achievable from single stages. We have seen that to combine stages successfully we must pay careful attention to how the stages we are joining interact with regard both to their respective bias conditions and to their small-signal performances. We have studied several approaches that have been developed to address these issues and to simplify the problem of joining, or "cascading," stages.

The simplest way of overcoming the biasing problem is to couple stages with large capacitors that pass the signals through the cascade while keeping the stages isolated for biasing purposes. We call these designs capacitively coupled cascades.

Although convenient conceptually and for discrete designs, the use of capacitors to couple and bias stages is not at all attractive for integrated circuits, where large-value capacitors are difficult to realize. Thus in design for integration, direct coupling without resorting to capacitors is preferred. We have seen that direct coupling of more than two or three gain stages is difficult, however, and that a level-shift stage, as well as output buffer stages, must be added to make a useful direct-coupled amplifier. We have also seen that there are several direct-coupled dual-stage amplifiers that are so useful and important that they can be considered standard building-block stages themselves. In particular, we have introduced the cascode, the Darlington, the emitter-coupled pair, and the push-pull output stage.

We have shown that because of their rejection of common mode input signals, differential pair stages are relatively easy to cascade. And, finally, we have considered at length the analysis and improvement of multistage differential amplifiers and have seen in several specific examples how to design circuits to meet certain performance goals.

PROBLEMS

13.1 In the bipolar transistor circuit shown in Fig. P13.1 the two *npn* transistors are identical and have $\beta_F = 100$ and $V_{BE,\text{ON}} = 0.6$ V. Calculate the following quantities:

(*a*) The quiescent collector and base currents in Q_1 and Q_2.

(*b*) The quiescent power dissipation in the circuit. *Hint:* Sum the currents supplied by the voltage source and multiply by its value (i.e., 6 V).

(*c*) The mid-band linear incremental voltage gain $v_{\text{out}}/v_{\text{in}}$.

(*d*) The mid-band linear incremental input resistance seen at the terminals where v_{in} is indicated.

(*e*) The mid-band linear incremental output resistance seen at the terminals where v_{out} is indicated (i.e., in parallel with the 1-kΩ load resistance).

13.2 (*a*) In the amplifier shown in Fig. P13.2*a* the transistor Q_1 is used as a diode in a biasing circuit for transistor Q_2. The two silicon transistors have identical current gain β_F, but the emitter-base area of Q_2 is twice that of Q_1. For this circuit we have $\beta_F = 200$ and $V_{BE,\text{ON}} = 0.7$ V.

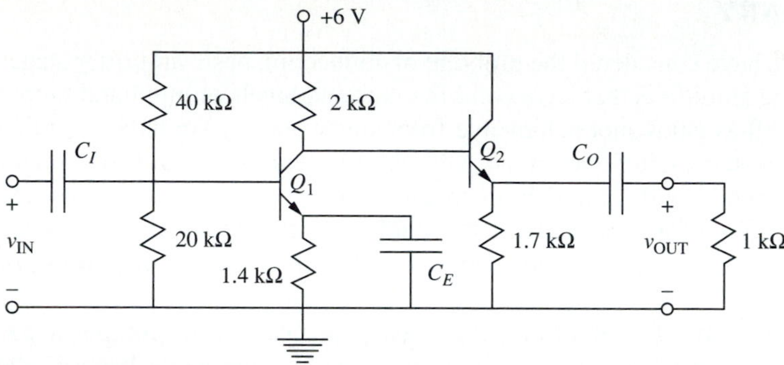

FIGURE P13.1

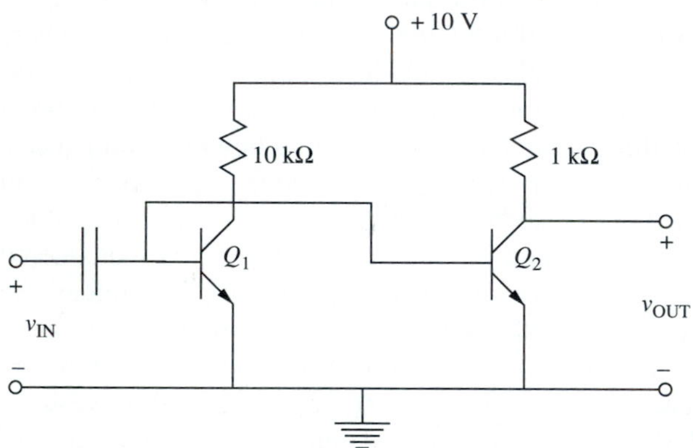

FIGURE P13.2*a*

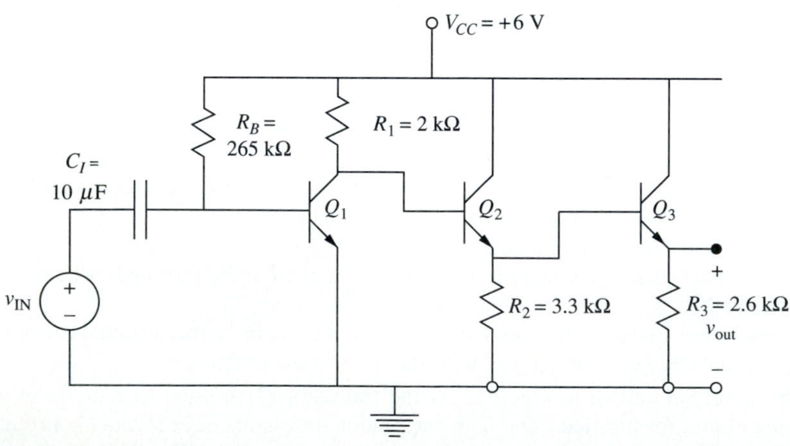

FIGURE P13.2*b*

(i) Find the approximate dc voltage at the collector of Q_2.
(ii) Calculate the mid-band voltage gain of this circuit.
(iii) Calculate the mid-band output resistance of this circuit.

(*b*) The amplifier shown in Fig. P13.2*b* consists of a common-emitter stage (transistor Q_1) followed by a cascade connection of two emitter-followers (Q_2, Q_3), that is, a Darlington connection. The transistors are identical with $\beta = 50$ and $V_{BE,ON} = 0.7$ V.
(i) Find the quiescent currents in each of the load resistors R_1, R_2, R_3 shown in the circuit.
(ii) Calculate the mid-band gain of this circuit.
(iii) Calculate the mid-band output resistance of this circuit.

(*c*) Compare your answers in (iii) of parts a and b. The first circuit has common-emitter output stages, whereas the second circuit has two common-collector output stages.

13.3 Consider the emitter-follower/common-base cascade illustrated in Fig. 13.10.
(*a*) Draw a mid-band linear equivalent circuit for this amplifier using the hybrid–π model for Q_1 and the common-base model (see Fig. 8.25*b*) for Q_2. Assume that both transistors are identical and are identically biased (i.e., $I_{C1} = I_{C2}$).
(*b*) Calculate the input resistance seen between the base of Q_1 and ground. Express your answer in terms of $r_{\pi 1}$ (in the model for Q_2) and R_E.
(*c*) Calculate the mid-band linear small-signal voltage gain $A_v (\equiv v_{\text{out}}/v_{\text{in}})$ of this circuit, paying careful attention to the sign as well as to the magnitude.
(*d*) Compare and contrast your result in part c:
(i) to a common-emitter amplifier
(ii) to a cascade
(*e*) Redraw your circuit in part a, adding the intrinsic capacitances (i.e., the C_π and C_μ terms).
(*f*) In the 741 operational amplifier the common-base stage uses a *pnp* rather than an *npn* transistor. What impact would this difference have on
(i) the incremental circuit you drew in part a?
(ii) the input resistance found in part b?
(iii) the voltage gain found in part c?

13.4 First consider the circuit in Fig. P13.4*a*.

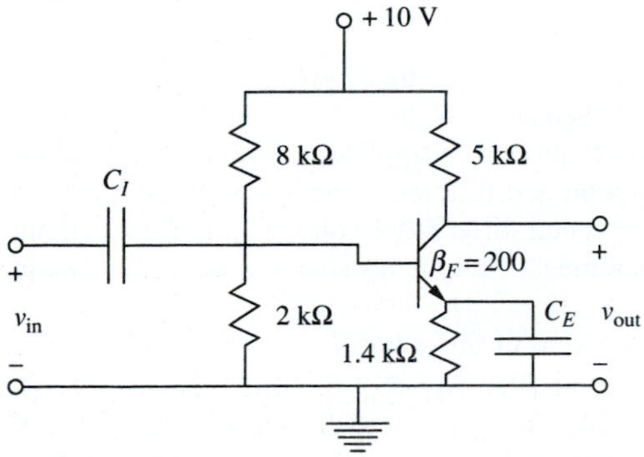

FIGURE P13.4*a*

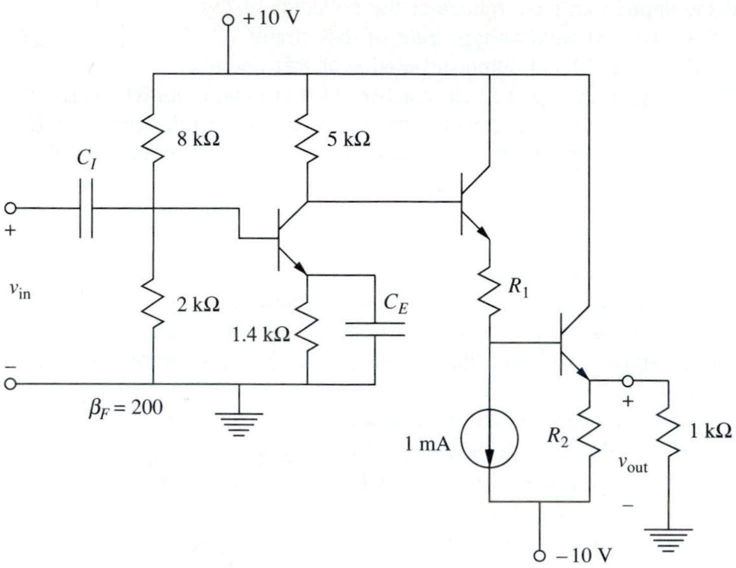

FIGURE P13.4*b*

(*a*) What is the quiescent collector current I_{CQ} in this circuit?
(*b*) What is the quiescent value of the output voltage V_{OUT}?
(*c*) What is the incremental voltage gain $A_v = v_{out}/v_{in}$ of this circuit?

Next consider the circuit in Fig. P13.4*b*.

(*d*) Select R_1 so that the quiescent value of the output voltage is 0 V.
(*e*) Select R_2 so that this amplifier can deliver ±3 mA to a 1-kΩ load (i.e., so that the output voltage can swing ±3 V.)
(*f*) Calculate the output resistance of this amplifier (i.e., looking in at the output terminal).
(*g*) What is the quiescent power dissipation in this amplifier?

13.5 This question concerns the differential amplifier circuit illustrated in Fig. P13.5. All of the transistors in this circuit are identical and may be modeled with $\beta_F = 100$, $v_{BE,ON} = 0.6$ V, and $v_{CE,SAT} = 0.2$ V.

(*a*) Assume both inputs are grounded. Select R_2 so that $I_C(Q_1) = 1$ mA.
(*b*) Assume both inputs are grounded. Select R_1 so that $V_{OUT} = 0$ V.
(*c*) Assume that a v_{IN} of 1 V (relative to ground) is applied to Input 1 and that Input 2 is grounded. What are the common and difference mode input voltages?
(*d*) What is the mid-band linear incremental differential voltage gain of this circuit?
(*e*) What is the mid-band linear incremental output resistance seen when looking back from the load resistor?
(*f*) What is the quiescent power dissipation in this circuit?

13.6 This question concerns the circuit illustrated in Fig. P13.6. In this circuit, Q_1 and Q_2 are identical transistors with $\beta = 200$. $V_{BE,ON} = 0.6$ V and $V_{CE,SAT} = 0.2$ V. Three of the register values are specified as $R_1 = 1.4$ kΩ, $R_2 = 6$ kΩ, and $R_3 = 21$ kΩ. The voltage at point a, relative to ground, is 3 V.

(*a*) (i) What is the quiescent collector current of transistor Q_1?
(ii) What is R_4?

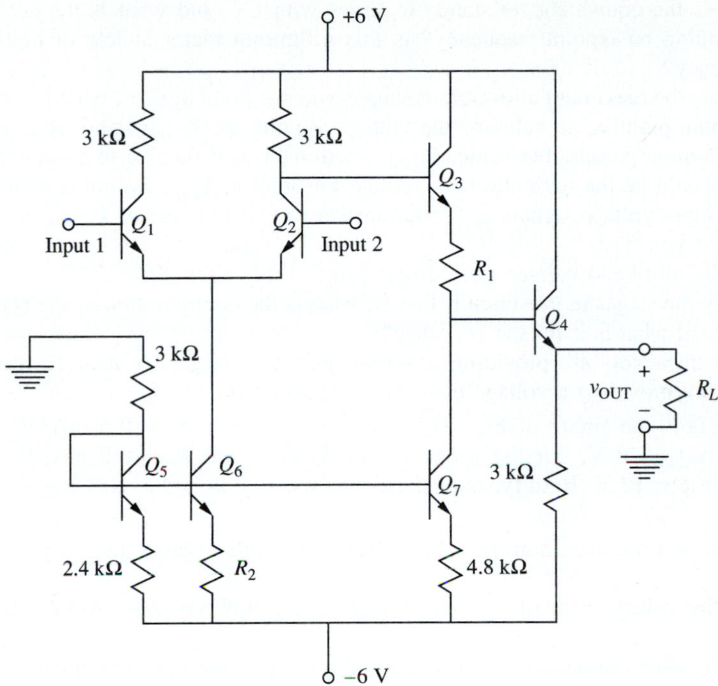

FIGURE P13.5

(iii) What must R_5 be to make the quiescent collector current of Q_2 equal to 2 mA?

(iv) What is the quiescent power dissipation in this circuit?

(v) What is the input resistance of this amplifier in mid-band?

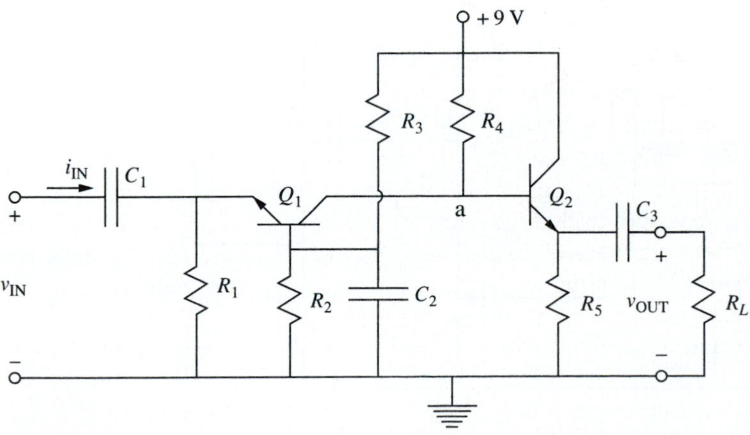

FIGURE P13.6

(ii) What is the equivalent resistance in series with C_3, and what is the corresponding breakpoint frequency? Is this a limiting factor at low or high frequency?

(*c*) (i) What are the maximum allowable voltage swings at point a, (i.e., what is the maximum permissible value of the voltage at point a), $V_{a,\max}$, and what is the minimum permissible value, $V_{a,\min}$ (both measured relative to ground)?

(ii) What would be the optimum bias voltage for point a, V_{aQ}, assuming sinusoidal input voltage signals v_{in}? Your answer can be in terms of $V_{a,\max}$ and $V_{a,\min}$ if you wish.

(*d*) What are the mid-band voltage and current gains of this circuit?

(i) Identify the stages in this circuit, that is, what is the configuration of the Q_1 stage, and what is it for the Q_2 stage?

(ii) Which transistors are providing a current gain that is greater than 1, and which are providing a voltage gain that is greater than 1?

13.7 The n-MOSFETs in the circuit of Fig. P13.7 have $V_T = +1$ V, $K = 0.5$ mA/V^2, $\eta = 0.2$, and $|V_A| = 20$ V. For the p-MOSFETs, $V_T = -1$ V, $K = 0.2$ mA/V^2, $\eta = 0.1$, and $|V_A| = 10$ V. Both types of transistors must be biased so that $|v_{GS} = V_T| \geq 0.25$ V.

(*a*) Select R_1 to get the maximum possible differential mode voltage gain at point A.

(*b*) Calculate the voltage gain of the output stage (i.e., between point A and the output).

(*c*) Calculate the output resistance of this circuit. Discuss the consequences of having the substrate of the output transistor grounded.

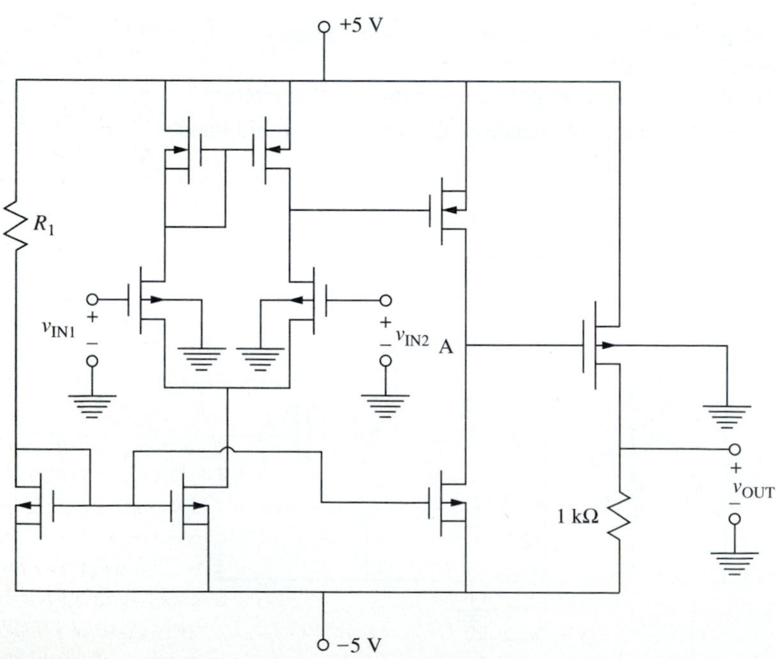

FIGURE P13.7

(*d*) Dimension the *p*-MOSFETs in the first and second stages to minimize the output offset voltage.
(*e*) Calculate the common mode voltage gain of this circuit at point A. Discuss.
(*f*) Suggest additions to the circuit that might improve its performance.

13.8 Consider the two cascode current mirrors shown in Fig. P13.8.
(*a*) Calculate and compare the incremental output resistances of each of these designs.
(*b*) Calculate and compare the output voltage imbalances in the two circuits.

13.9 In this circuit the *npn* transistors have $\beta = 100$ for $10\ \mu\text{A} \leq I_C \leq 10$ mA and $|V_A| = 50$ V. For the *pnp*'s, $\beta = 50$ for $50\ \mu A \leq I_C \leq 5$ mA and $|V_A| = 20$ V. For the *p*-channel MOSFETs, K is 0.1 mA/V^2, V_T is -1 V, $|V_A|$ is 10 V, and the minimum $|v_{GS} - V_T|$ is 0.2 V. The resistor R_2 is 10 kΩ, and in this problem R_3 is infinite.
(*a*) To maximize the first-stage gain, should the bias level of Q_2 be as large or as small as possible, or does it matter?
(*b*) To maximize the first-stage gain, should the bias level of Q_3 be as large or as small as possible, or does it matter?
(*c*) To maximize the second-stage gain, how should the bias level of Q_3 be set (i.e., large, small, either)?
(*d*) Specify the quiescent collector currents of Q_2, Q_3, and Q_4 to get the maximum possible differential mode voltage gain to point A.
(*e*) What role does the bias level of Q_4 play in determining the overall amplifier gain?

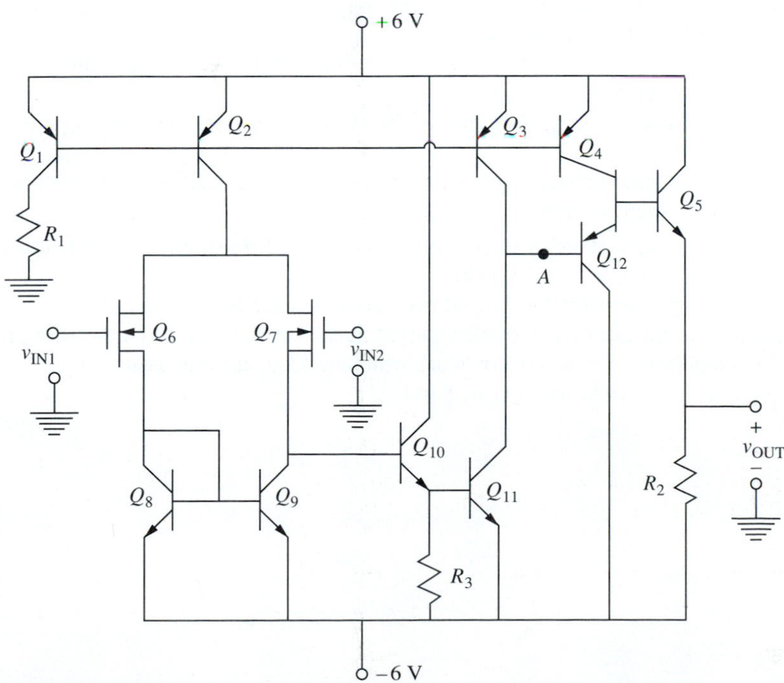

FIGURE P13.8

(*f*) (i) What is the output resistance r_o of this amplifier as you have designed it in part d?
(ii) What role does the bias level of Q_4 play in r_o?
(iii) What role does the bias level of Q_3 play in r_o, and how would a design constraint on r_o have changed your answer in part d?

13.10 Consider the circuit of problem 13.9 when R_2 is 50 kΩ.

(*a*) What effect does this change have on the first-stage gain if you leave the bias level of Q_3 the same as in your design in problem 13.9?

(*b*) Can the bias level of Q_3 be changed to increase the first-stage gain, and what effect will such a change have on the second-stage gain?

(*c*) What effect does changing the bias level of Q_3 have on the output resistance of this amplifier?

13.11 This problem concerns the imbalance in the first stage of the circuit in problem 13.9 caused by the Darlington load. (If you did not work problem 13.9, work this problem assuming I_{C2} is 0.1 mA and I_{C3} is 1 mA.)

(*a*) Assuming all of the *npn*'s are identical-size devices, what is the difference in the voltages at the collectors of Q_8 and Q_9?

(*b*) Suppose that you can make some of the transistors in this circuit larger. The gate widths can be made as much as 10 times wider, and the emitter-base areas can be made up to 20 times larger. The current operating ranges of the devices scale in direct proportion to these changes. Can you use this design freedom to reduce the voltage difference in part a? (Maintain the same bias levels.)

Consider next modifying the circuit by using a cascode current mirror like that in Fig. 13.20*d*.

(*c*) What is the voltage difference between the collectors of Q_8 and Q_9 now, assuming all devices are identical?

(*d*) Can you scale the devices now and reduce this voltage difference, and if you can, what should be done?

(*e*) What impact does making R_3 equal to 50 kΩ have on your answers in parts c and d?

(*f*) What is the common mode input voltage range of this circuit with and without the cascode current mirror?

13.12 (*a*) Redesign the output stage of the circuit of problem 13.9 using a complementary pair stage like that in Fig. 13.13*b*.

(*b*) Derive an expression for the output resistance of your new design.

(*c*) Compare the quiescent power dissipation levels in the old and new designs of this amplifier. (If you did not work problem 13.9, do this assuming I_{C2} is 0.1 mA, I_{C3} is 1 mA, and Q_4 is 1 mA.)

CHAPTER
14

HIGH-FREQUENCY ANALYSIS OF LINEAR AMPLIFIERS

Now that we have studied the biasing and mid-band analysis of various linear amplifier configurations and are starting to understand some of the issues of amplifier design, we will turn in this chapter to considerations of amplifier operation at high frequencies. One of the general problems facing device, circuit, and system designers is how to get ever-higher performance at ever-higher frequencies from their designs. In preparation for doing this ourselves, we will consider here several aspects of high-frequency analysis of linear amplifiers. First, we consider techniques for determining the bounds of the mid-band frequency range for an arbitrary amplifier design. Then we look at the high-frequency behavior of some specific building-block circuits in an attempt to gain insight into how we should expect various common amplifier configurations to perform. Finally, we conclude by looking at figures of merit through which the inherent, intrinsic high-frequency potential of devices can be evaluated independent of any additional constraints placed upon them by the circuits in which they are being used.

14.1 DETERMINING THE BOUNDS OF THE MID-BAND RANGE

In Sec. 11.2 we introduced the concept of the mid-band frequency range of an amplifier; we said that the mid-band range was bounded on the low-frequency side by a limit we called ω_{LO} and on the high side by ω_{HI}. Below ω_{LO}, the various capacitors we have added to the circuit for coupling stages and for bypassing resistors are no longer effectively short circuits. The gain is smaller at frequencies below ω_{LO} than it is in the mid-band range. Above ω_{HI}, the capacitors intrinsic to the transistors themselves begin to shunt significant amounts of signal current around the active region of the device and the gain is again lower than it is in the mid-band range. Our task now is to determine what ω_{LO} and ω_{HI} are for a given circuit.

The methods we will describe, the methods of open- and short-circuit time constants, are based on rigorous linear circuit analyses that we will not attempt to duplicate here and that we only mention by way of providing assurance that these methods are well-founded theoretically. They are approximations, as we shall point out as we go along, and give only approximate bounds. Thus, like much we have learned, they require modeling skill to implement efficiently.

We begin by considering ω_{HI}. We then do an example and briefly look at ω_{LO}.

14.1.1 Method of Open-Circuit Time Constants

To determine ω_{HI}, we need to know at what frequency one or more of the various intrinsic capacitors—C_π and C_μ in the case of a bipolar transistor, C_{gd} and C_{gs} in the case of an FET—start to shunt appreciable current past the resistors in parallel with them. It can be shown that we can obtain a conservative estimate for ω_{HI} by looking at each of the intrinsic capacitors individually, calculating the resistance in parallel with them under the assumption that all of the other intrinsic capacitors are still perfect open circuits, and then taking ω_{HI} as a weighted sum of the various *RC* products thus calculated.

Specifically, the procedure for this method is as follows:

1. Pick one intrinsic capacitor, call it C_i, and assume all of the others are perfect open circuits.
2. Determine the resistance, call it R_i, in parallel with C_i with all of the independent sources set equal to zero and with all of the other intrinsic capacitors treated as open circuits.
3. Calculate ω_i, defined as $(R_i C_i)^{-1}$.
4. Repeat steps 1 through 3 for all of the intrinsic capacitors.
5. When ω_i has been calculated for all of the relevant capacitors, calculate ω_{HI}^*, which is defined as follows:

$$\omega_{HI}^* \equiv \left[\sum_i (\omega_i)^{-1}\right]^{-1} \tag{14.1a}$$

which is also

$$\omega_{HI}^* \equiv \left[\sum_i R_i C_i\right]^{-1} \tag{14.1b}$$

Linear circuit analysis tells us that the actual mid-band high-frequency breakpoint ω_{HI} of the amplifier in question will always be greater than or equal to ω_{HI}^*. That is,

$$\omega_{\mathrm{HI}} \geq \omega_{\mathrm{HI}}^* \tag{14.2}$$

This technique of estimating ω_{HI} is called the *method of open-circuit time constants*.

Notice that summing the individual breakpoint frequencies as in Eq. (14.1) gives the most weight to the ω_i with the smallest values. It also results in an ω_{HI}^* that is lower than any of the individual ω_i.

Example

Question. Consider an amplifier containing six capacitors limiting high-frequency performance. The open-circuit breakpoint frequencies ω_i corresponding to these six capacitors are 1, 5, 10, 30, 50, and 100 MHz. Estimate ω_{HI} for this circuit.

Discussion. Applying Eq. (14.1a), we calculate that ω_{HI}^* is $(1/1 + 1/5 + 1/10 + 1/30 + 1/50 + 1/100)^{-1} = (1.363)^{-1} = 0.73$ MHz. Clearly the lowest open-circuit breakpoint frequency, 1 MHz, dominates this result, and the poles at 5 and 10 MHz also play important roles, together reducing ω_{HI}^* to 0.77 MHz. The final three poles only decrease ω_{HI}^* roughly 5% more.

Interestingly, it can be shown that ω_{HI}, the true breakpoint frequency, can always be written as a sum like that in Eq. (14.1). Our method of estimating ω_{HI} based on Eq. (14.1) is approximate, however, because the procedure used to calculate the individual ω_i terms is approximate. A little thought shows that this fact is not surprising since clearly not all of the other capacitors are open circuits at the breakpoints of many of the capacitors, especially those for which ω_i is much greater than ω_{HI}^*. You could consider improving on the method outlined above by modifying the procedure of calculating ω_{HI}^* by, for example, recalculating all of the ω_i except the smallest and starting with the second smallest by assuming that all of the capacitors yielding smaller ω_i values are short circuits. This sort of refinement is seldom called for, however. The fact that the present method gives a conservative (i.e., low) bound for ω_{HI} means it provides a safe "quick and dirty" estimate that is usually adequate. If a more precise number is required, it would be more reasonable to do a computer analysis using any of a number of available simulation programs.

14.1.2 Method of Short-Circuit Time Constants

There is a technique analogous to that used in the preceding subsection to find ω_{HI}^* that can be used to estimate the low-frequency breakpoint ω_{LO} of the mid-band gain of an amplifier. This technique, called the *method of short-circuit time* *constants*, focuses on the extrinsic capacitors used to couple inputs, outputs, and adjacent stages and to shunt biasing resistors. It proceeds as follows:

1. Pick one extrinsic capacitor, call it C_j, and assume all of the others are perfect short circuits.
2. Determine the resistance, call it R_j, in parallel with C_j with all of the independent sources set equal to zero and with all of the other extrinsic capacitors treated as short circuits.
3. Calculate ω_j, defined as $(R_j C_j)^{-1}$.
4. Repeat steps 1 through 3 for all of the intrinsic capacitors.
5. When ω_j has been calculated for all of the relevant capacitors, calculate ω_{LO}^*, which is defined as follows:

$$\omega_{\mathrm{LO}}^* \equiv \sum_J \omega_j \tag{14.3a}$$

which is also

$$\omega_{\mathrm{LO}}^* \equiv \left[\sum_J (R_j C_j)^{-1}\right] \tag{14.3b}$$

The actual mid-band frequency breakpoint ω_{LO} of the amplifier in question will always be less than or equal to ω_{LO}^*. That is,

$$\omega_{\mathrm{LO}} \le \omega_{\mathrm{LO}}^*$$

Note that this time the sum of the individual breakpoint frequencies in Eq. (14.3) favors the largest of the ω_j and results in an ω_{LO}^* that is larger than any of the individual ω_j terms. The same comments can be made here as were made in the discussion of ω_{HI} with respect to the accuracy of this technique. Suffice it to say that it is a very useful back-of-the-envelope method for estimating ω_{LO}.

14.2 EXAMINATION OF SPECIFIC CIRCUIT TOPOLOGIES

The methods outlined in Sec. 14.1 are useful for quantifying the mid-band range. But it is also important that as a circuit designer, you have an intuitive feel for which capacitors will limit the high-frequency performance of a circuit. To this end we will now look at several of our standard building-block stages to develop some general rules of thumb that can guide our consideration of more complicated circuits.

14.2.1 Common-Emitter/Source

The first circuit we will consider is the common-emitter amplifier shown in Fig. 14.1*a*. The small-signal linear equivalent circuit for this amplifier including the intrinsic parasitic capacitances C_π and C_μ, is presented in Fig. 14.1*b*. Notice

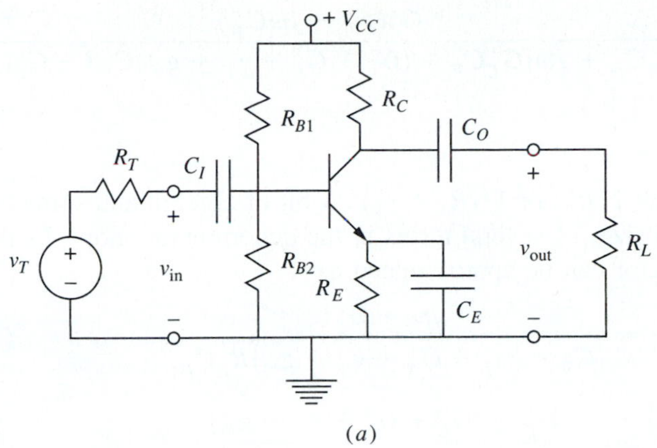

(*a*)

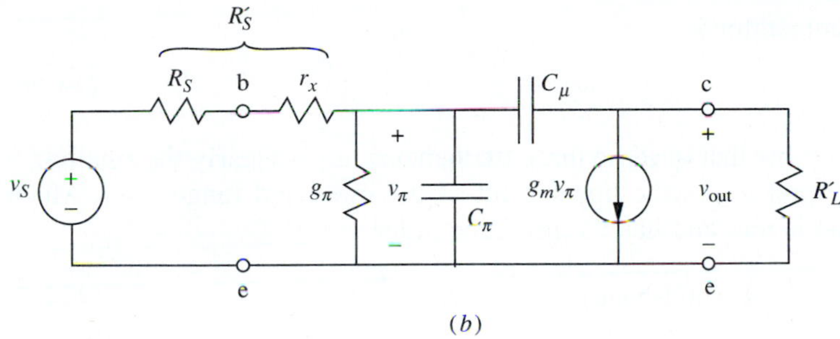

(*b*)

FIGURE 14.1
(*a*) Common-emitter amplifier like that first introduced in Sec. 11.3.1;
(*b*) the small-signal linear equivalent circuit, including the instrinsic parasitic capacitances C_π and C_μ.

that in the equivalent circuit we have introduced several new elements that are defined as follows:

$$R_S \equiv R_{B1} \parallel R_{B2} \parallel R_T \tag{14.4a}$$

$$R_L' \equiv R_L \parallel R_C \parallel r_o \tag{14.4b}$$

$$v_S \equiv v_T \frac{(R_{B1} \parallel R_{B2})}{(R_T + R_{B1} \parallel R_{B2})} \tag{14.4c}$$

Notice also that we include the base resistance r_x in the incremental model because it may be comparable to R_S; the size of r_x relative to R_S is what is important in determining the breakpoint frequency. Previously, in determining voltage gain, it was the size of r_x relative to r_π that was important. We will write the sum of R_S and r_x as R_S'.

Assuming a small-signal sinusoidal input signal, we can calculate the complex voltage gain $A_v(j\omega) \equiv v_{out}(j\omega)/v_s(j\omega)$. Doing so we obtain

$$A_v(j\omega) = -\frac{G_s'(g_m - j\omega C_\mu)}{(j\omega)^2 C_\pi C_\mu + j\omega[G_L' C_\pi + (G_L' + G_S' + g_\pi + g_m)C_\mu] + G_L'(g_\pi + G_S')} \tag{14.5}$$

where G_S' is defined as $1/R_S'$, or $1/(R_S + r_x)$. A bit of algebra and some consideration of the relative sizes of several terms in the denominator shows us that the roots of the denominator can be approximated as*

$$\omega_1 \approx \frac{(g_\pi + G_S')}{[C_\pi + (G_L' + G_S' + g_\pi + g_m)R_L' C_\mu]} \tag{14.6a}$$

$$\omega_2 \approx \frac{G_L'}{C_\mu} + \frac{(G_L' + G_S' + g_\pi + g_m)}{C_\pi} \tag{14.6b}$$

The root of the numerator is

$$\omega_3 = \frac{g_m}{C_\mu} \tag{14.6c}$$

We can also show that of these three frequencies, ω_1 is clearly the smallest.† Thus we can interpret ω_1 as the upper limit of the mid-band range, ω_{HI}. Much below ω_1, $A_v(j\omega)$ is real and has its mid-band value

$$A_v\,(\text{mid-band}) = -g_m R_L' \frac{G_S'}{(g_\pi + G_S')} \tag{14.7}$$

At $\omega = \omega_1$, $A_v(j\omega)$ has a phase of 45° and its magnitude is 0.707 of its mid-band value; for $\omega > \omega_1$, $|A_v(j\omega)|$ decreases as $1/\omega$.

This is all fine, but it is just a lot of mathematics. You probably aren't getting much general insight from the discussion thus far. To correct this situation we need to look first at our expression for ω_1, Eq. (14.6a), and then at our circuit, Fig. 14.1*b*.

Looking at our expression for ω_1, we see that ω_1 is the characteristic frequency of the parallel combination of two conductances, g_π and G_S', and two capacitors, C_π and C_μ', where we define C_μ' as $(G_L' + G_S' + g_\pi + g_m)R_L' \cdot C_\mu$. If g_m is much greater than G_S', as it typically is, ‡ and since g_m is β_F times larger

---

*In arriving at these roots, we can make use of the fact that if we have the quadratic equation $ax^2 + bx + c = 0$ and if a, b, and c are such that $b^2/ac \gg 1$, then the roots can be approximated as b/a and c/b. [Try it yourself; just multiply out $(x - b/a)(x - c/b)$.] A little simple algebra (no more tricks) will show you that in the present situation, b^2 is ac plus many other terms and thus their ratio is easily much greater than 1. In Eq. (14.6a) and (14.6b), we have taken ω_1 to be the root c/b and ω_2 to be the root b/a.

†Referring to the preceding footnote, if we have $b^2/ac \gg 1$, then we clearly have b/a (which is ω_2) much greater than c/b (which is ω_1). Comparing Eqs. (14.6b) and (14.6c) shows us that ω_3 is also larger than ω_1 since the numerator of Eq. (14.6c) is larger and its denominator is smaller. Thus we clearly have $\omega_1 < \omega_2, \omega_3$.

‡Recall that G_S' includes r_x. Thus the largest G_S' can be is $1/r_x$, which is comparable to g_m. Typically G_S' is much smaller than this, which is why we say we can neglect it.

than g_π, then the factor multiplying C_μ is approximately $(1+g_m R_L')$. Recognizing $g_m R_L'$ as the magnitude of the mid-band voltage gain of the transistor, v_{out}/v_π, we understand that this is a large factor and that C_μ somehow now looks much larger in terms of its effect on the circuit breakpoint than it physically is. Since a larger capacitor implies a lower breakpoint frequency, this is a significant (often detrimental) effect. We will explore this further in Sec. 14.2.2 after we look at the common-source stage next.

The situation with the common-source stage is very similar to that with the common-emitter. The small-signal linear equivalent circuit for a common-source stage like that in Fig. 11.11c on page 347, including the parasitic capacitances C_{gs} and C_{gd}, is shown in Fig. 14.2. We have not included the source-to-substrate or drain-to-substrate capacitances since they are small and are an unnecessary complication at this point in our investigation.

The topology in Fig. 14.2 is identical to the common-emitter equivalent circuit in Fig. 14.1b with r_π infinite and r_x zero. These are two rather important differences, as we shall see. The latter says that the R_S' we had earlier (here it is just R_T) can now actually be zero (it could only be as small as r_x in a BJT circuit), and the former leads to problems when R_T is very large (i.e., with a current source drive).

To find the time constants we calculate the small-signal complex voltage gain for sinusoidal input and get an expression analogous to Eq. (14.5). We find

$$A_v(j\omega) = -\frac{G_T(g_m - j\omega C_{gd})}{(j\omega)^2 C_{gs}C_{gd} + j\omega\left[G_L' C_{gs} + (G_L' + G_T + g_m)C_{gd}\right] + G_L G_T} \tag{14.8}$$

We solve for the roots in the same way we did in the case of Eq.(14.5) and find that the roots of the denominator are

$$\omega_1 \approx \frac{G_T}{C_{gs} + \left[1 + (G_T + g_m)R_L'\right]C_{gd}} \tag{14.9a}$$

$$\omega_2 \approx \frac{G_L'}{C_{gd}} + \frac{\left(G_L' + G_T + g_m\right)}{C_{gs}} \tag{14.9b}$$

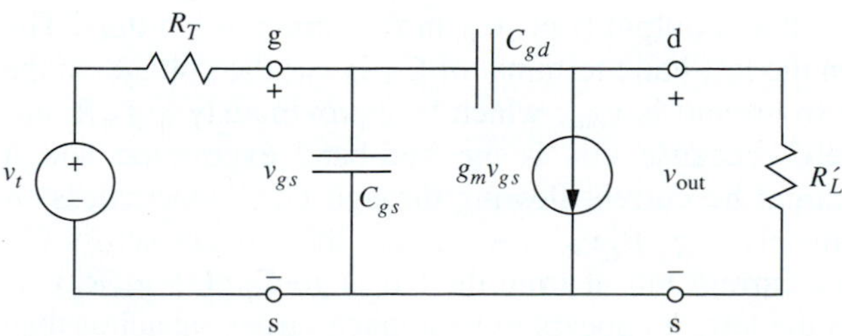

FIGURE 14.2
Incremental equivalent circuit for the common-source amplifier of Fig. 11.11c, including C_{gs} and C_{gd}.

The root of the numerator is

$$\omega_3 = \frac{g_m}{C_{gd}} \tag{14.9c}$$

The lowest frequency is again ω_1, which is effectively $\omega_{\rm HI}$ for the common-source stage. Looking at Eq. (14.9a), the first thing to notice is that the capacitor bridging the input and output, C_{gd} in this circuit, again appears multiplied by a large factor, $(G_T + g_m)R_L'$. G_T will often be smaller than g_m, so the factor $(G_T + g_m)R_L'$ is approximately $g_m R_L'$, which is again the magnitude of the mid-band voltage gain just as it was in the common-emitter stage. We will discuss this phenomenon extensively in Sec. 14.2.2.

The signal-source resistance R_T plays an important role in this stage. Notice that for very large R_T (or small G_T), which corresponds most nearly to a current source input, we find that $\omega_1(\approx \omega_{\rm HI})$ is very small and that the mid-band range is pushed to very low frequencies. This is, consequently, not an attractive input situation if a frequency-independent response is sought. (See Sec. 14.3.2 for further discussion.)

Notice, finally, that if G_T is very large and the input approximates an ideal voltage source, then ω_1 approaches $1/R_L'C_{gd}$. This drive condition yields the largest $\omega_{\rm HI}$ and widest mid-band region.

In all cases, C_{gd} plays an important role in setting $\omega_{\rm HI}$. It is thus worth realizing that C_{gd} can be zero in an ideal MOSFET and in reality can be made very small using a self-aligned gate technology, as described at the end of Sec. 10.1. This is in contrast to the situation in a BJT, where C_μ is unavoidable because the base-collector junction is an intrinsic part of a bipolar transistor. In general for a MOSFET, C_{gs} is much larger than C_{gd}. Whether C_{gs} or C_{gd} dominates ω_1 [see Eq. (14.9a)], however, depends on the size of C_{gd} relative to C_{gs} and on the size of the Miller effect (see next section).

14.2.2 The Miller Effect

The magnification of C_μ and C_{gd} that we have seen in the common-emitter and common-source circuits is called the *Miller effect* and was first described for vacuum tube circuits. It is easiest to understand by looking at one of the circuits, say the common-emitter stage in Fig. 14.1*b*, and focusing on the voltage across the capacitor that couples the input and output (i.e., C_μ in the common-emitter). The voltage relative to ground on the left-hand terminal of C_μ is v_π; the voltage on the right-hand terminal relative to ground is $v_{\rm out}$, which is approximately $-g_m R_L' v_\pi$. We must say "approximately" because this is the mid-band expression and it ignores the fact that there might be current flowing through C_μ. Nonetheless, if we say that $v_{\rm out}$ is approximately $-g_m R_L' v_\pi$, we see that the voltage across C_μ is $(1 + g_m R_L' v_\pi)$ and that the current into it from the left is $j\omega C_\mu(1 + g_m R_L')v_\pi$. Thus, looking into C_μ from the left, it appears to be a much larger capacitor than it really is. It looks like a capacitor C_μ^* whose value is $(1 + g_m R_L')C_\mu$.

The above discussion can be generalized to any capacitor that sits astride a stage with gain; Fig. 14.3 illustrates this point. In Fig. 14.3*a*, a capacitor C_M

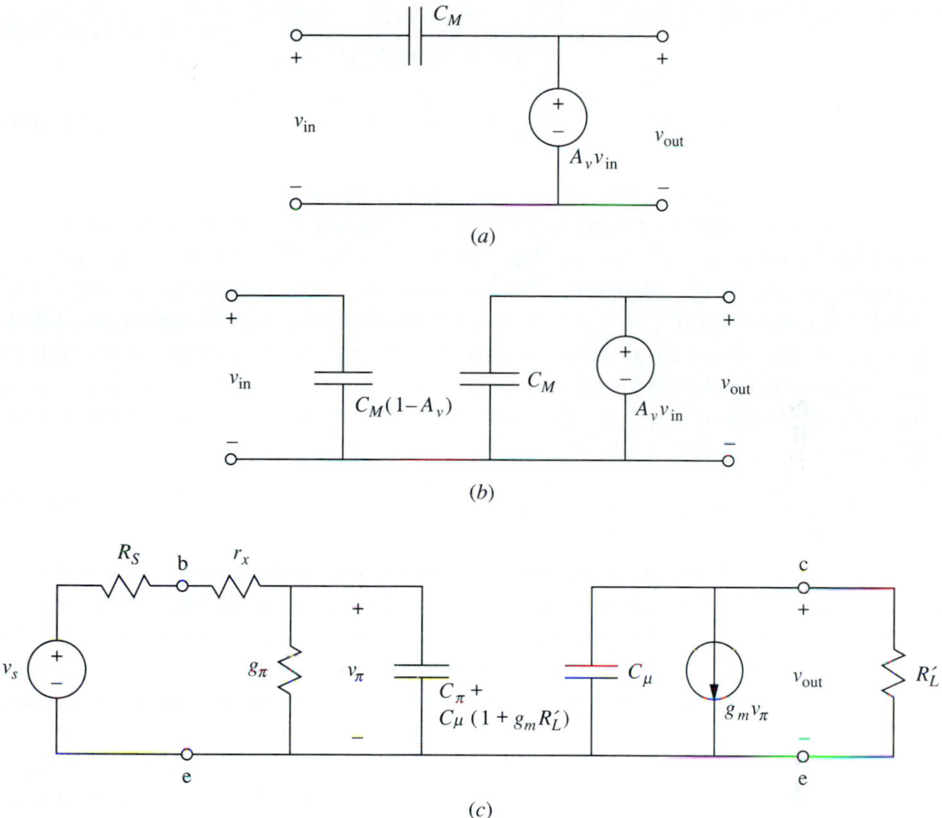

FIGURE 14.3
(*a*) Amplifier stage with a capacitor C_M bridging the input and output terminals; (*b*) the circuit of (*a*) with the bridging capacitor replaced by the equivalent capacitances seen from the left and from the right; (*c*) the incremental equivalent circuit for the common-emitter amplifier of Fig. 14.1*b* after it has been simplified by taking the Miller effect into account.

is shown bridging the input and output terminals of a stage with a voltage gain A_v. The voltage across the capacitor is clearly $v_1(1 - A_v)$, so from the left it looks like a capacitor of magnitude $(1 - A_v)C_M$, as illustrated in Fig. 14.3*b*. From the right it looks essentially unchanged, as Fig. 14.3*b* also illustrates.

In addition to vividly illustrating the implications of the Miller effect, the circuit in Fig. 14.3*b* is much easier to analyze than the circuit of Fig. 14.3*a* because it separates naturally into easily analyzed segments. With C_M bridging the input and output as in Fig. 14.3*a*, the circuit has to be analyzed as a whole and the exercise quickly becomes counterproductive.

The equivalent circuit in Fig. 14.1*b* has been modified in Fig. 14.3*c* using the Miller effect result. The voltage gain has been taken to be $-g_m R_L'$, which is its mid-band value. If we apply the open-circuit time constant technique to this circuit we find two frequencies:

$$\omega_a = \frac{(g_\pi + G_S')}{[C_\pi + (1 + g_m R_L')C_\mu]} \tag{14.10a}$$

$$\omega_b = \frac{1}{R_L' C_\mu} \tag{14.10b}$$

Clearly, ω_a is much less than ω_b, so ω_{HI}^* is essentially ω_a.

It is now interesting (and important) to compare this result with our earlier estimate of ω_{HI}, namely ω_1 in Eq. (14.6a). Doing this we see that the two expressions are nearly identical. They differ only in the denominator where Eq. (14.6a) has the sum $(G_S' + g_\pi + g_m)$ in place of simply g_m. However, we know that g_m is β_F times larger than g_π, so clearly g_π can be neglected relative to g_m. Furthermore, the factor G_S' is typically much smaller than g_m. In such cases our two estimates of ω_{HI} [i.e., Eqs. (14.6a) and (14.10a)], are equivalent and we can say

$$\omega_{HI}\,(\text{common-emitter}) \approx \frac{(g_\pi + G_S')}{(C_\pi + g_m R_L' C_\mu)} \tag{14.11}$$

As an aside before summarizing our discussion, notice that we have not tried to compare the other breakpoint frequency we found using the Miller approximation and the open-circuit time constant method (i.e., ω_b) with ω_1 in Eq. (14.6b) because the open-circuit time constant method is not valid for such a comparison. Its purpose is only to estimate the lowest breakpoint frequency; it is not a valid way to calculate any of the other breakpoint frequencies.

To summarize, we have learned that a capacitor in the Miller position (i.e., bridging the input and output of an amplifier with a large negative voltage gain A_v) has a detrimental impact on the high-frequency response of the circuit far greater than we would normally expect based on its value alone. In the Miller position the capacitor's apparent size is approximately $|A_v|$ times greater. This effect, which is important because this can so significantly reduce the ω_{HI} of an amplifier, is particularly important in high-gain common-emitter and common-source amplifiers.

Normally the Miller capacitor effect is viewed as a problem because it reduces ω_{HI}; it is thus something to be avoided. There are some situations, however, in which a large capacitor is actually needed in a circuit and where the Miller effect can be used to advantage. An interesting example is found in the 741 operational amplifier integrated circuit. In the 741 circuit, the parasitic bipolar transistor capacitors (i.e., the C_π and C_μ capacitors) create relatively closely spaced high-frequency poles; the situation is illustrated by the dashed curves in Figs. 14.4*a* and *b*. Above ω_{HI} the magnitude of the gain decreases and additional phase shift (90°) is introduced by each pole. If the magnitude of the gain is still greater than 1 well above the second pole, where the phase shift is 180° or more, as it is in the situation illustrated by the dashed curves in Fig. 14.4, there can be positive feedback between the output and the input and the circuit can oscillate, which is not a good situation. Operational amplifiers like the 741 are especially susceptible to this problem because they have such large low-frequency gains. The magnitude

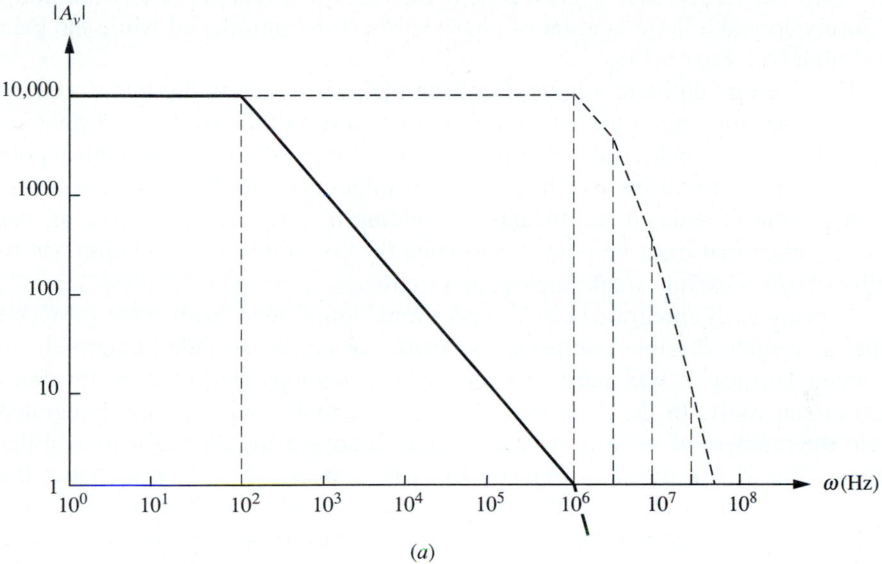

(a)

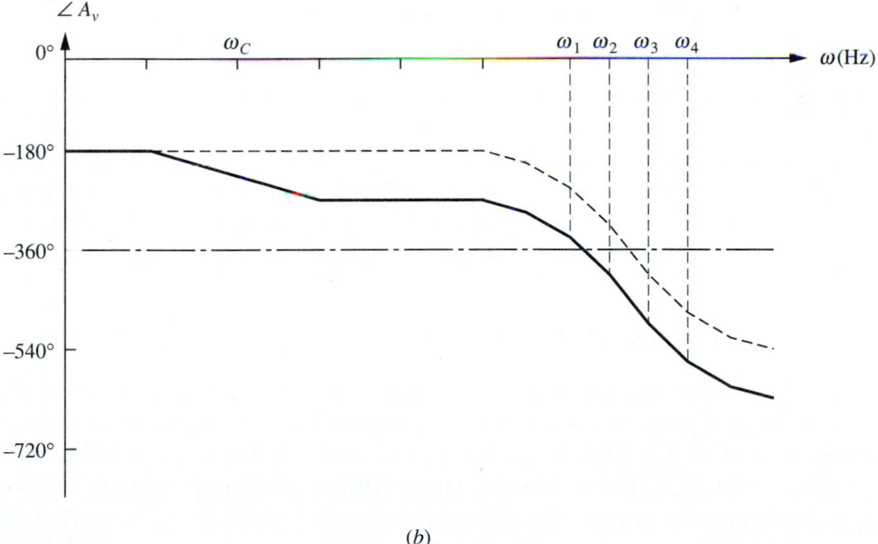

(b)

FIGURE 14.4
Bode plots of the voltage gain of a typical operational amplifier without (dashed curves) and with (solid curves) compensation: (*a*) the magnitude; (*b*) the phase.

of the gain has to decrease a great deal before it is less than 1, and if the poles are closely spaced a large amount of phase shift can be introduced while the gain is still high (see Fig. 14.4).

To solve this problem a lower-frequency pole is intentionally introduced by adding a capacitor, called a *compensating capacitor*, to the circuit. The pole ω_c is made far enough below the next higher pole that by the time the higher pole is reached the gain will be less than 1, as the solid curves in Fig. 14.4 illustrate. Of course, ω_{HI} is reduced significantly by adding a compensating capacitor, but this is the price that must be paid to eliminate the possibility of oscillation and to thereby obtain a useful, stable high-gain amplifier.

In many early integrated-circuit operational amplifiers, leads were provided so that a separate discrete compensating capacitor could be added externally to the circuit because it was hard to make a large enough capacitor on the integrated circuit itself. In the 741, the capacitor is actually made on the integrated circuit; the problem of making it large enough is solved by placing it in a Miller position. This is illustrated in Fig. 14.5*a*, which shows the 741 schematic; the capacitor in question is C_1, and it bridges transistor Q_{16}. Using this trick, the actual capacitance needed is only 30 pF, as opposed to the several nanofarads that would be needed otherwise. Even then, however, this much smaller capacitor still takes almost 10% of the chip area and is much larger than any of the resistors or transistors in the circuit, as the photomicrograph in Fig. 14.5*b* clearly illustrates.

14.2.3 Degenerate-Emitter/Source

Adding degeneracy to a common-emitter or common-source stage changes the Miller effect only in that since the voltage gain of this stage is smaller, so too is the apparent increase in the size of the bridging capacitor, C_μ or C_{gd}. Thus ω_{HI} is larger for the degenerate-emitter and degenerate-source stages, but what is gained in a wider mid-band frequency range is lost in lower gain. The product of the two, called the *gain-bandwidth product*, is essentially unchanged.

14.2.4 Emitter/Source-Follower

The capacitor connecting the input and output sides of the transistor (i.e., C_μ in the case of a bipolar transistor and C_{gd} in the case of an FET) also plays an important role in the high-frequency performance of the emitter-follower or source-follower circuits, but it does not suffer Miller effect amplification in these circuits. Since in these circuits the collector and drain terminals are incrementally grounded, this capacitor appears directly across the input to the stage. This is illustrated for the emitter-follower in Fig. 14.6. In Fig. 14.6*a* the small-signal equivalent circuit is drawn for an emitter-follower amplifier with C_π and C_μ included. In Fig. 14.4*b* the circuit is redrawn to emphasize the point that C_μ appears across the input. (We again use the bipolar transistor circuit for the sake of discussion; a similar discussion can be presented for FET circuits.)

Recalling that R'_L looks like $(\beta_F + 1)R'_L$ when viewed from the input terminals of an emitter-follower amplifier, we realize that the open-circuit time constant

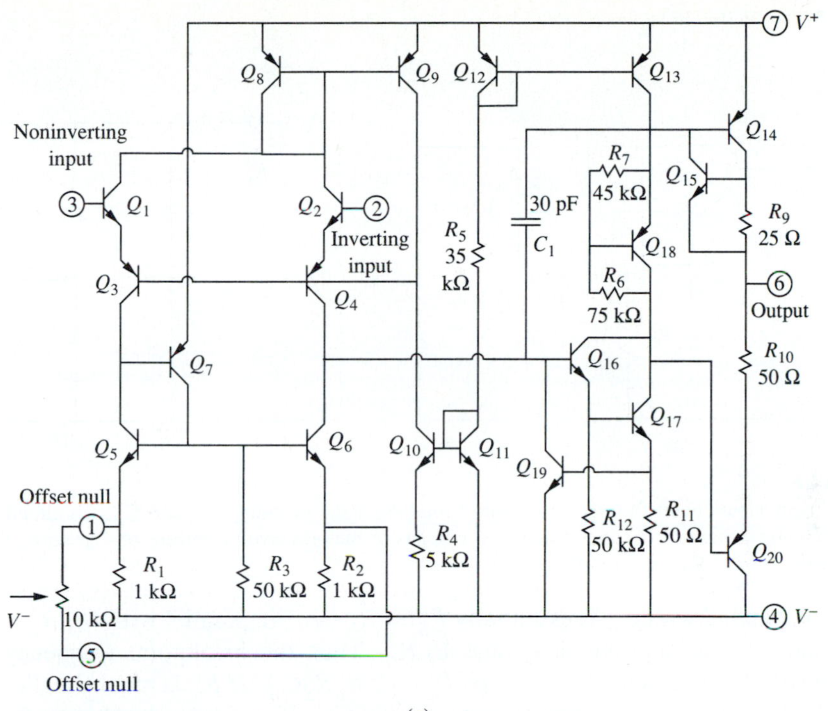

(*a*)

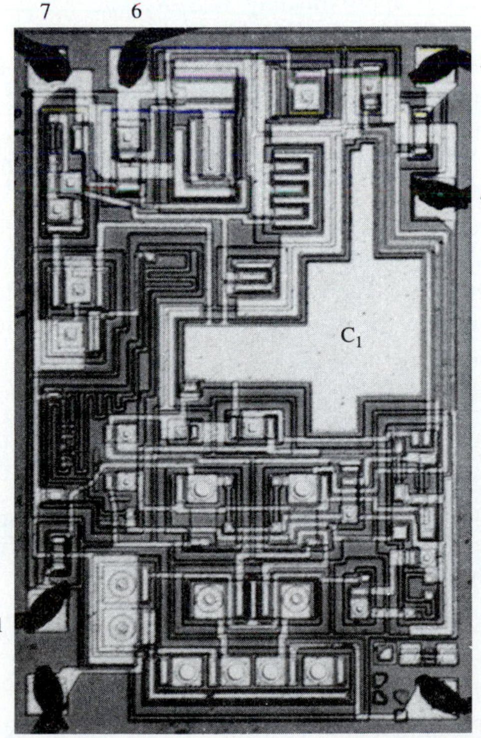

(*b*)

FIGURE 14.5
741 operational amplifier, showing the use of the Miller effect to monolithically integrate a compensating capacitor: (*a*) the circuit schematic, in which you should notice C_1 bridging Q_{16}; (*b*) a photomicrograph of the integrated-circuit chip with the terminals 1 through 7, and the capacitor C_1 labeled. (Photograph courtesy of P. Martin, T. McClure, and R. Perilli of M.I.T.; chip provided by J. Chernoff and D. Coan of Analog Devices.)

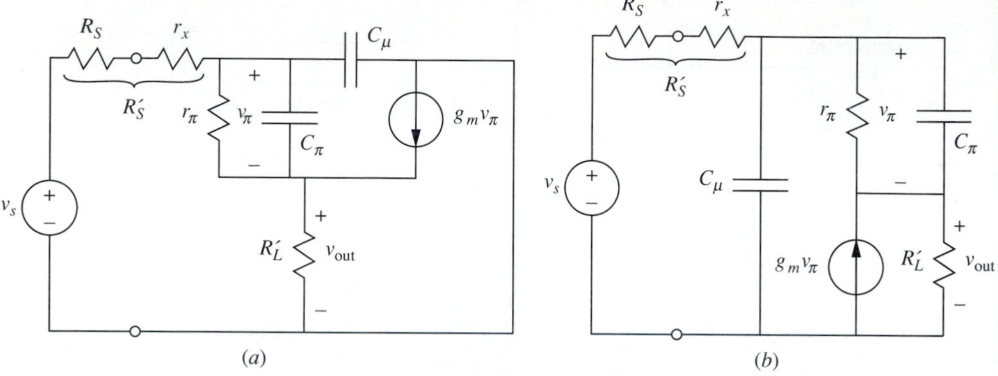

FIGURE 14.6
Incremental equivalent circuit for a generic emitter-follower stage including C_π and C_μ: (*a*) circuit drawn in the normal manner; (*b*) circuit drawn to emphasize the effective placement of C_μ across the input terminals.

resistance in parallel with C_μ is essentially $R_S'(\equiv R_S + r_x)$ in parallel with $(\beta_F R_L' + r_\pi)$, the latter being approximately just $\beta_F R_L'$. Thus the breakpoint frequency associated with C_μ is essentially $(R_S' + \beta_F R_L')/\beta_F R_L' R_S' C_\mu$. If R_S' is much smaller than $\beta_F R_L'$, this frequency is approximately $1/R_S' C_\mu$. If, on the other hand, R_S' is much larger than $\beta_F R_L'$, this frequency is approximately $1/\beta_F R_L' C_\mu$.

The open-circuit time constant resistance in parallel with C_π is more complicated, but you should be able to show that it is essentially $(R_S' + R_L')r_\pi/(\beta_F R_L' + R_S')$. Looking at this result we see that in the limit of large $\beta_F R_L'$ and moderate R_S', it approaches r_π/β_F and the breakpoint frequency is approximately $\beta_F/C_\pi r_\pi$, or g_m/C_π; in the limit of very large R_S', it approaches r_π and the breakpoint frequency is β_F times smaller.

The question now is, how do we compare all of these frequencies to see what limits the response of this stage, and, more fundamentally, how does this stage compare with the common-emitter stage? The way to proceed is to first note that in most situations, R_S will be small and the two relevant time constants are $R_S' C_\mu$ and C_π/g_m; consequently we have

$$\omega_{\text{HI}}\,(\text{emitter-follower}) \approx \frac{1}{R_S' C_\mu + \left(\dfrac{C_\pi}{g_m}\right)} = \frac{g_m}{C_\pi + g_m R_S' C_\mu} \tag{14.12a}$$

Comparing this to ω_{HI} for a common-emitter, Eq. (14.11), we see that ω_{HI} for the emitter-follower is much higher because $g_m << g_\pi$ and $R_S' >> R_L'$. In situations where R_S' is very large, we have

$$\omega_{\text{HI}}\,(\text{emitter-follower}) \approx \frac{1}{\beta R_L' C_\mu + \left(\dfrac{C_\pi}{g_\pi}\right)} = \frac{g_\pi}{(C_\pi + g_m R_L' C_\mu)} \tag{14.12b}$$

This breakpoint is closer to that of the common-emitter, (Eq. 14.11), and in fact looks to be a bit lower until you also realize that if we are looking at a multistage amplifier to see, for example, which is the limiting stage, we would find that R_L'

for the common-emitter stage is much larger than R_L' for the emitter-follower. Thus the advantage of the emitter-follower is much greater than a superficial comparison of Eqs. (14.11) and (14.12b) would indicate. We can conclude that the emitter-follower stage is in general much faster than the common-emitter stage.

The source-follower stage, pictured in Fig. 14.7, is also straightforward to analyze and leads us to similar conclusions. Doing an open-circuit time constant analysis we see that the resistance in parallel with C_{gd} is R_T and that in parallel with C_{gs} is $(R_L' + R_T)/(1 + g_m R_L)'$. The latter resistance is smaller, but C_{gs} is larger than C_{gd}, so it is hard to say in general which is the larger time constant (and thus lower breakpoint frequency). We must combine them to estimate ω_{HI} as

$$\omega_{\mathrm{HI}}\,(\text{source-follower}) \geq \frac{1}{R_T C_{gd} + \left[(R_L' + R_T)/1 + g_m R_L'\right] C_{gs}} \tag{14.13a}$$

Multiplying the numerator and denominator by $(1 + g_m R_L')G_T$ we get a form we can compare with our common-source result, Eq. (14.9a):

$$\omega_{\mathrm{HI}}\,(\text{source-follower}) \geq \frac{\left(1 + g_m R_L'\right) G_T}{\left(1 + R_L' G_T\right) C_{gs} + \left(1 + g_m R_L'\right) C_{gd}} \tag{14.13b}$$

Clearly this is a higher frequency, by a factor of at least $(1 + g_m R_L')$, and we can conclude that the source-follower stage is in general much faster than the common-source stage.

14.2.5 Common-Base/Gate

The common-base/gate stage is particularly easy to analyze because there are no capacitors in feedback positions (i.e., coupling the input and output), as can be seen by examining Fig. 14.8. We can readily apply the open-circuit time constant method to this circuit and calculate the time constants associated with C_π and C_μ as

$$\omega_\pi = \frac{\left(g_e + G_S'\right)}{C_\pi} \approx \frac{g_m}{C_\pi} \tag{14.14a}$$

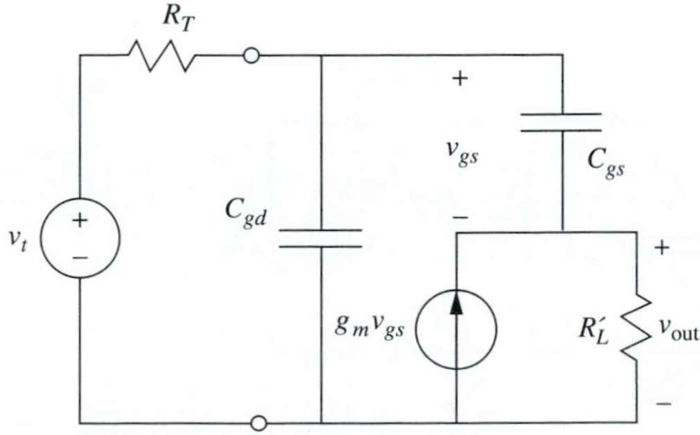

FIGURE 14.7
Incremental equivalent circuit for a source-follower stage including C_{gs} and C_{gd}.

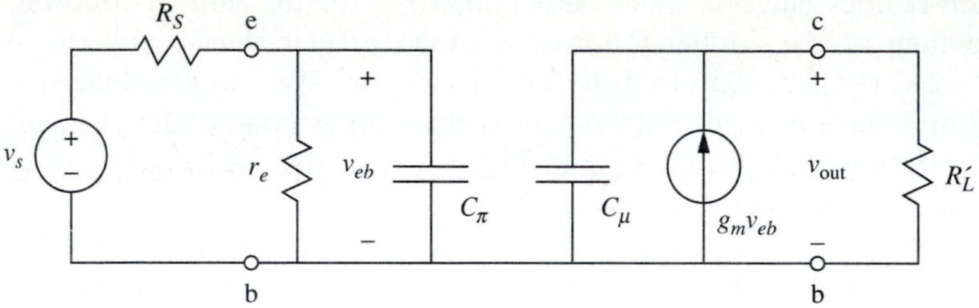

FIGURE 14.8
Incremental equivalent circuit for a generic common-base stage including C_π and C_μ.

$$\omega_\mu = \frac{1}{R_L' C_\mu} \tag{14.14b}$$

Notice that in the second expression for ω_π we have used the fact that g_e is approximately g_m and have neglected G_S relative to g_m (see the last footnote on page 470 for a justification of this). Combining these two frequencies, we have

$$\omega_{\text{HI}}(\text{common-base}) \geq \frac{1}{R_L' C_\mu + (C_\pi / g_m)} = \frac{g_m}{(C_\pi + g_m R_L' C_\mu)} \qquad 14.15(a)$$

Comparing this to the common-emitter result, Eq. (14.11), we see that this ω_{HI} is β_F times larger, since $g_m = \beta_F g_\pi$. That is,

$$\omega_{\text{HI}}\,(\text{common-base}) \approx \beta_F \omega_{\text{HI}}\,(\text{common-emitter}) \tag{14.15b}$$

The incremental equivalent circuit for a common-gate stage with the substrate grounded is illustrated in Fig. 14.9. We can see by inspection that the conductance in parallel with C_{gs} is $(1 + \eta)g_m + G_T$ and that the resistance in parallel with C_{gd} is R_L'. Thus we have

$$\omega_{\text{HI}}\,(\text{common-gate}) \geq \frac{1}{R_L' C_{gd}} + \frac{g_m + G_T}{C_{gs}} = \frac{g_m + G_T}{C_{gs} + (g_m + G_T) R_L' C_{gd}} \tag{14.16}$$

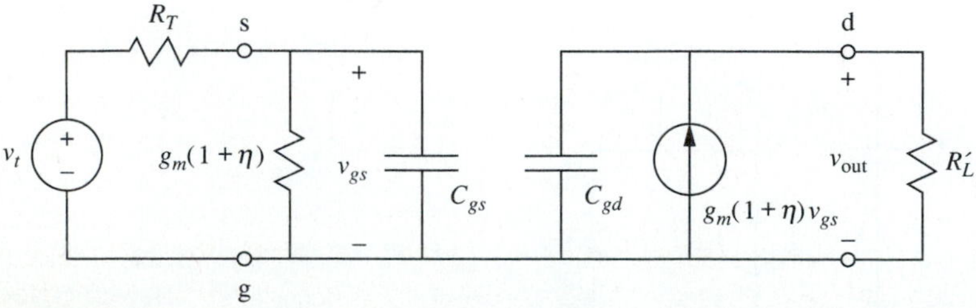

FIGURE 14.9
Incremental equivalent circuit for a common-gate stage with a grounded substrate including C_{gs} and C_{gd}.

Comparing this to the common-source result, Eq. (14.9a), we see that it is larger by a factor of $(1 + g_m/G_T)$, which can often be substantial since, as we have said, G_T is often much less than g_m.

Comparing the common-base/gate, common-emitter/source, degenerate-emitter/source, and emitter/source-follower stages, we see that the common-base/gate stage and the emitter/source-follower stage have the best high-frequency response.

14.2.6 Cascode

We are now in a position to appreciate the logic behind the cascode configuration we first considered in Sec. 13.2.2. In the cascode the first stage is a common-emitter or common-source stage that has only a small voltage gain, but we now see that this also means there will be a very small Miller effect on this stage and the magnitude of the stage's high-frequency breakpoint will be increased. The second stage, which provides the cascode's voltage gain, is a common-base or common-gate stage that has an inherently large high-frequency breakpoint. Thus the composite cascode amplifier has high gain up to a considerably higher frequency than would a simple common-emitter or common-source stage.

To quantify these points, consider the MOSFET cascode in Fig. 14.10*a* and its small-signal equivalent circuits in Figs. 14.10*b* (mid-band) and 14.10*c* (mid- and high-frequencies). Referring first to the mid-band circuit, we can see that $g'_{m2}v_{gs2}$ is equal to $g_{m1}v_{gs1}$, so the two dependent current sources turn out to be equal.* Thus the first-stage voltage gain v_{sg2}/v_{gs1} (note the order of the subscripts) is $-g_{m1}/g'_{m2}$, which is also $-(K_1/K_2)^{1/2}$ divided by $(1+\eta)$ since Q_2 and Q_1 have equal quiescent drain currents. The second-stage voltage gain v_{out}/v_{sg2} is $-g'_{m2}R_D$, and thus the cascode voltage gain v_{out}/v_{gs1}, is $-g_{m1}R_D$, which is the same as the gain of a common-source stage biased and loaded similarly. We, of course, essentially knew this result already from Sec. 13.2.2.

Looking now at the high-frequency model, Fig. 14.10*c*, we see that the Miller effect on the first stage for which A_v is only -1, assuming $K_1 = K_2$, is to double C_{gd1}. In contrast, in a common-source stage the Miller effect would effectively increase C_{gd} as seen from the input by a factor of g_mR_D, which is undoubtedly much greater than 2.

Looking back at our analysis of the bipolar cascode in Sec. 13.2.2, we see that the first-stage voltage gain there was also -1, so again the Miller effect multiplication factor on the C_μ of the first stage is only 2.

If you have been alert you will have noticed that the magnitude of the voltage gain of the first stage of the MOSFET cascode can actually be less than 1 if K_2 is larger than K_1, and we can easily make this the case by making Q_2 wider than Q_1 (i.e., $W_2 > W_1$). Making K_2 bigger than K_1 does not change the overall gain, but it does reduce the Miller effect even further. In the bipolar cascode the first-stage voltage gain is -1 independent of the transistor β_F-valves, (assuming

*Notice that we have defined g'_{m2} to be $(1 + \eta)g_{m2}$

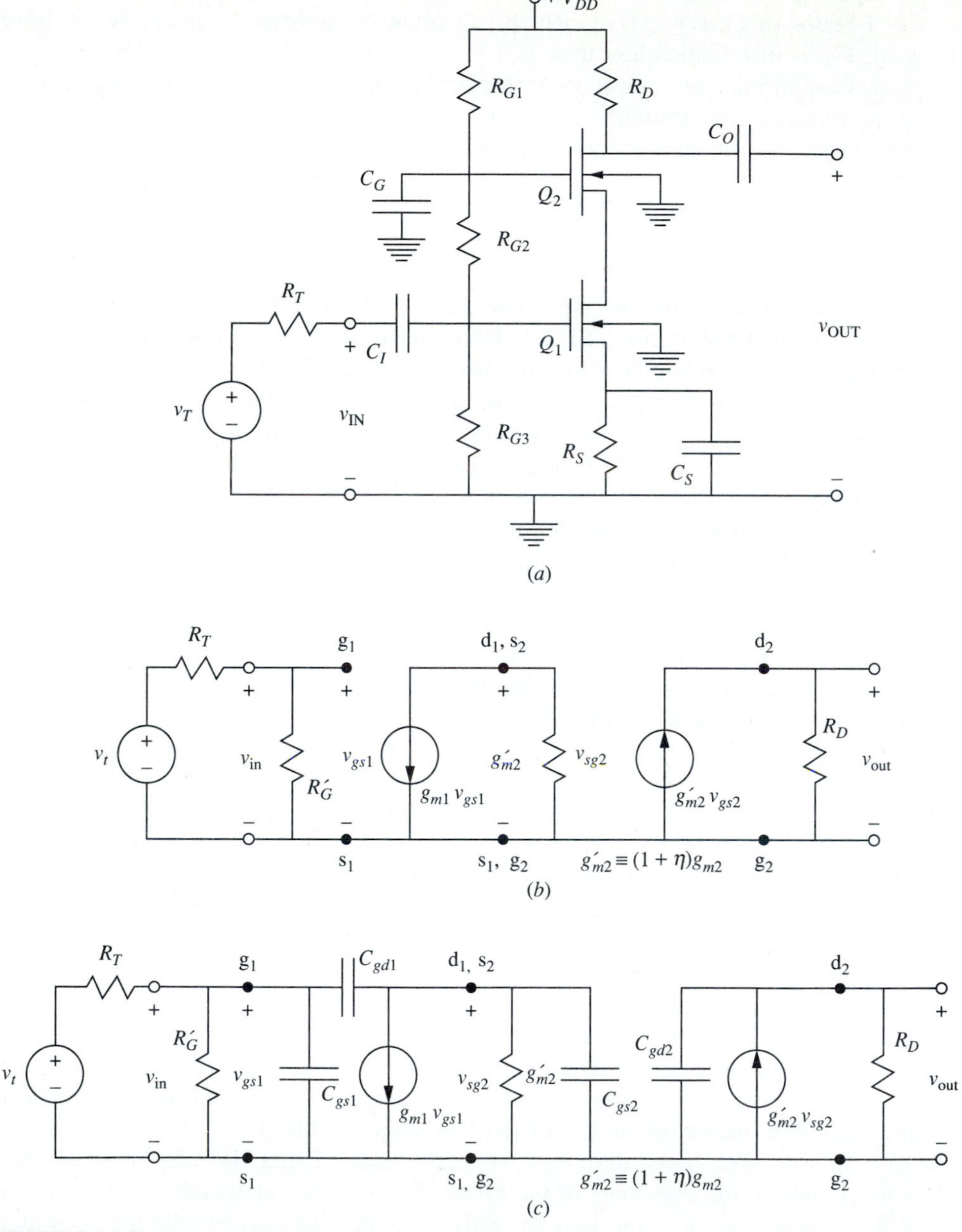

FIGURE 14.10
MOSFET cascode: (*a*) the circuit schematic; (*b*) the mid-band small-signal equivalent circuit; (*c*) the small-signal equivalent circuit useful at mid and high frequencies and, in particular, for determining the upper mid-band bound.

they are large, of course), so we cannot use a similar trick to reduce the Miller effect multiplier below 2 in the bipolar cascode.

14.2.7 Darlington Pair

The traditional Darlington pair that we studied in Sec. 13.2.3 and was pictured in Fig. 13.6*b* is usually used in a common-emitter stage and thus suffers from the Miller effect typical of the common-emitter topology. The situation is worse with a Darlington than with a single transistor, however, because of the large input resistance of the Darlington pair and the fact that the Darlington pair is usually driven from a relatively high-output-resistance stage. These large resistances are in parallel with the Miller effect-multiplied C_μ of the first transistor, $C_{\mu 1}$; the resulting RC time constant is relatively much larger, and $\omega_{\rm HI}$ is relatively much lower than for a single-transistor common-emitter stage.

The high-frequency performance of the Darlington connection can be improved by connecting the collector of the first transistor Q_1 to the power supply and by adding an emitter resistor R_{E1} to the first transistor; these changes were illustrated in Fig. 13.9. To see why these changes increase $\omega_{\rm HI}$, refer to Fig. 14.11, which compares the small-signal linear equivalent circuits for the

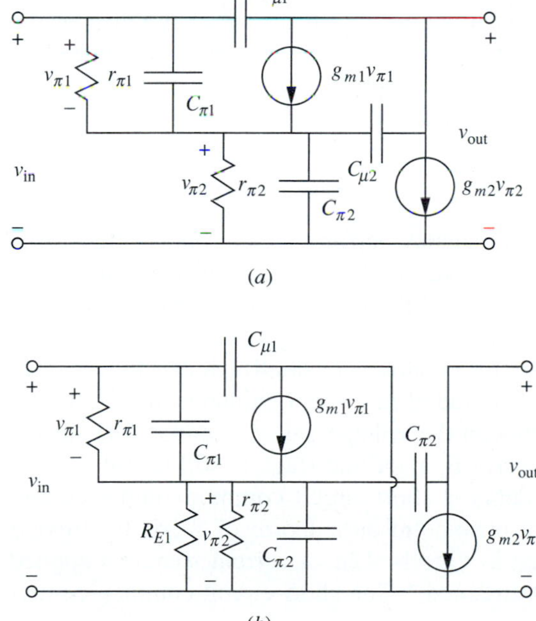

FIGURE 14.11
Small-signal high-frequency linear equivalent circuits for two different versions of the Darlington pair: (*a*) the equivalent circuit of the basic Darlington shown in Fig. 13.6*b*; (*b*) the equivalent circuit of the improved Darlington connection shown in Fig. 13.9.

"traditional" and the "improved" Darlington connections. In the improved connection, shown in Fig. 14.11*b*, the first stage is an emitter-follower and there is minimal Miller multiplication of $C_{\mu 1}$. At the same time, $r_{\pi 1}$ is much lower in this connection because of the presence of R_{E1}, which increases the quiescent collector current
of Q_1, I_{C1}; thus the RC time constant associated with $C_{\mu 1}$ is much smaller and the pole frequency ω_j is much higher here than in the traditional Darlington. The only appreciable Miller effect in the improved configuration is that associated with $C_{\mu 2}$. The resistance seen by the Miller-multiplied $C_{\mu 2}$ is the parallel combination of $r_{\pi 2}, R_{E1}$, and $(r_{\pi 1} + R_S)/\beta$, where R_S is the equivalent source resistance (see Eq. 14.4a). Since $r_{\pi 1}$ is now much smaller than before, the later factor typically dominates the resistance and the RC time constant associated with $C_{\mu 2}$ is much smaller than in the traditional Darlington connection.

14.3 INTRINSIC HIGH-FREQUENCY LIMITS OF TRANSISTORS

We have seen in the preceding sections that both the transistor and the circuit configuration in which it is used affect the high-frequency breakpoint of an amplifier. Device designers often want figures of merit for their devices that are independent of any particular circuit and are somehow intrinsic to the device. It is the challenge of the circuit designer to find a circuit topology that can extract as much of the intrinsic performance capability as possible.

In this section we will consider intrinsic high-frequency figures of merit for bipolar transistors first and then for field effect transistors.

14.3.1 Bipolar Transistors

The first figures of merit for the high-frequency performance of bipolar transistors will concern the common-emitter configuration. Recalling our discussion in Sec. 14.2.2, we saw that the Miller effect reduced the high-frequency breakpoint. The Miller effect can be reduced and ω_{HI} increased by making R_L as small as possible and by making R_S as large as possible (i.e., making G_S small). Both actions reduce the voltage gain of the circuit, however, and at first seem uninteresting. However, a bit more thought shows us that although the voltage gain is reduced, the current gain of the stage stays large (i.e., nearly β_F) and the stage is still useful.

Such observations lead us to define a short-circuit common-emitter current gain and to take its high-frequency breakpoint as a figure of merit for bipolar transistors. The concept is illustrated in Fig. 14.12*a*; a current source is applied to the input, and the output is short-circuited.* The short-circuit common-emitter current gain $\beta(j\omega)$ is defined as

$$\beta(j\omega) \equiv \frac{i_c(j\omega)}{i_b(j\omega)} \tag{14.17}$$

*Notice that r_x is not included in Fig. 14.12*a* because the input is a current source (i.e., R_S is infinite) and r_x plays no role in the circuit performance.

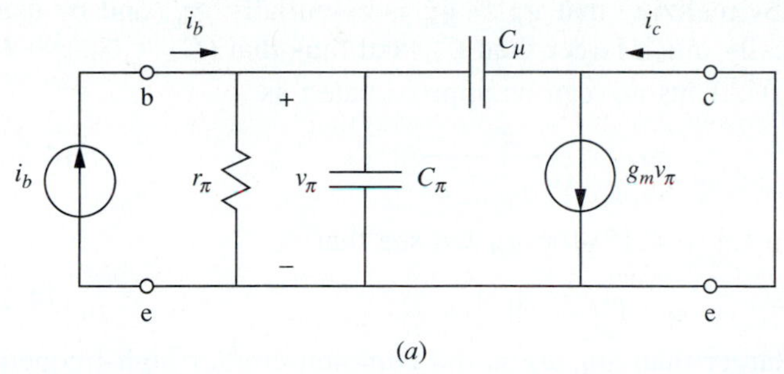

(*a*)

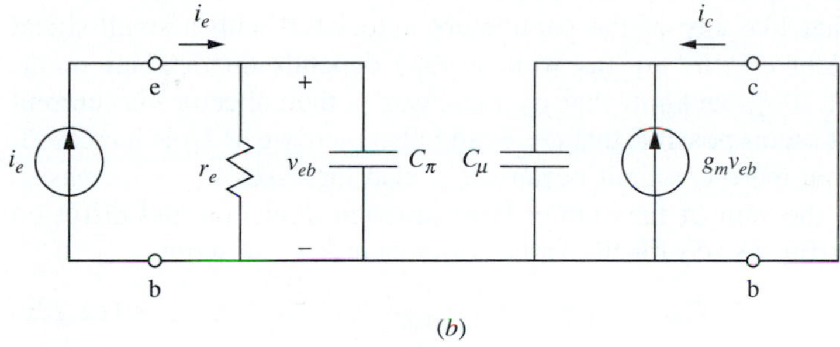

(*b*)

FIGURE 14.12
Small-signal linear equivalent circuits: (*a*) appropriate for calculating the short-circuit common-emitter current gain; (*b*) appropriate for calculating the short-circuit common-base current gain.

Referring to Fig. 14.12, we find that $\beta(j\omega)$ can be written as

$$\beta(j\omega) = \frac{(g_m - j\omega C_\mu)}{[g_\pi + j\omega(C_\pi + C_\mu)]} \tag{14.18}$$

At low frequencies, $\beta(j\omega)$ reduces to g_m/g_π, or β_F. The high-frequency breakpoint is clearly at $g_\pi/(C_\pi + C_\mu)$. We define this breakpoint as ω_β. Thus

$$\omega_\beta = \frac{g_\pi}{(C_\pi + C_\mu)} \tag{14.19}$$

It can be argued that the transistor is useful above ω_β because the magnitude of the short-circuit current gain is still greater than 1. We thus define another frequency figure of merit ω_T, which is the frequency at which the magnitude of $\beta(j\omega)$ is 1. Examination of Eq. (14.18) shows us that

$$\omega_T = \left[\frac{g_m^2 - g_\pi^2}{(C_\pi + C_\mu)^2 - C_\mu^2}\right]^{1/2} \tag{14.20a}$$

This can be simplified by realizing that $g_m^2 - g_\pi^2$ is essentially g_m^2, and by using the fact that C_π is typically much larger than C_μ and thus that $(C_\pi + C_\mu)^2 - C_\mu^2$ is essentially $(C_\pi + C_\mu)^2$. Thus ω_T can be approximated as

$$\omega_T \approx \frac{g_m}{(C_\pi + C_\mu)} \tag{14.20b}$$

Comparing this result to Eq. (14.15) for ω_β we see that

$$\omega_T \approx \beta_F \omega_\beta \tag{14.21}$$

Because it is so much larger than ω_β, ω_T is the common-emitter high-frequency figure of merit usually quoted for bipolar transistors.

Notice next that like any of the parameters associated with a small-signal incremental equivalent circuit, ω_T (as well as ω_β) depends on the bias point. Referring to Eq. (14.20b), we know that g_m increases as the collector bias current I_C is increased, so it seems possible that ω_T would also increase as I_C is increased. It will, to a point, but there is a limit because C_π also increases as I_C increases. In particular, C_π is the sum of the emitter-base junction depletion and diffusion capacitances. Using Eq. (8.65) for the latter component we can write

$$C_\pi = g_m \tau_b + C_{\text{e-b,depl}} \tag{14.22a}$$

where g_m is $q|I_C|/kT$ and τ_b is $(w_B^*)^2/D_{\min,B}$. Clearly as I_C is made larger and larger, the depletion capacitance contribution to C_π will become unimportant and C_π can be approximated as

$$C_\pi \approx g_m \tau_b \quad \text{for } I_C \text{ large} \tag{14.22b}$$

At such a large bias level, the base-collector junction depletion capacitance C_μ can also be neglected and ω_T approaches the limit

$$\omega_T \approx \frac{1}{\tau_b} \quad \text{for } I_C \text{ large} \tag{14.23}$$

We know from Sec. 14.2 that the common-base stage has a higher high-frequency response than the common-emitter stage, so it is natural that we next consider the high-frequency breakpoint of the short-circuit common-base current gain $\alpha(j\omega)$. The idea is illustrated in Fig. 14.12*b*. We define $\alpha(j\omega)$ as follows:

$$\alpha(j\omega) \equiv -\frac{i_c(j\omega)}{i_e(j\omega)} \tag{14.24}$$

Referring to Fig. 14.12*b*, we see that

$$\alpha(j\omega) = \frac{g_m}{(g_\pi + g_m + j\omega\, C_\pi)} \tag{14.25}$$

At low frequencies this is clearly α_F and the high-frequency breakpoint, which we will define as ω_α, is

$$\omega_\alpha = \frac{(g_\pi + g_m)}{C_\pi} \tag{14.26a}$$

or, assuming β_F is much greater than 1,

$$\omega_\alpha \approx \frac{g_m}{C_\pi} \tag{14.26b}$$

In the limit of large collector current bias levels, ω_α approaches the same bound as did ω_β; that is, we have

$$\omega_\alpha \approx \frac{1}{\tau_b} \quad \text{for } I_C \text{ large} \tag{14.27}$$

Comparing Eqs. (14.19), (14.20b), and (14.26a), we see that we have the following relationship between the various figures of merit we have identified:

$$\omega_\alpha > \omega_T >> \omega_\beta \tag{14.28}$$

We should also note that since τ_b varies inversely with $D_{\min,B}$, *npn* transistors will be faster than *pnp* transistors. It is furthermore clear that it is very desirable to make w_B as small as possible to further reduce τ_b.

At this point it is appropriate to finally look back at our assumption of quasistatic conditions for purposes of obtaining solutions to the flow problems we set up in the quasineutral regions of our transistors. Can we simultaneously have a quasistatic problem and high-frequency operation? Since "quasistatic" and "high-frequency" are not absolutes but must always be considered in an appropriate context, the answer can certainly be yes, but this is something that must be checked.

To proceed, we note that both ω_α and ω_T approach, but are always less than, $(\tau_b)^{-1}$, where τ_b can be interpreted as the average time it takes a minority carrier to transit the base. The argument then is that if the minority carriers can get across the base fast enough to adjust the quasistatic minority carrier profiles quickly enough for them to keep up with the signal voltages, then the structure looks static (i.e., it is quasistatic). Clearly, we are very close to the limit where this is no longer true, but not quite.

14.3.2 Field Effect Transistors

In a manner analogous to the one in which we obtained intrinsic high-frequency figures of merit for a bipolar transistor by calculating the device's short-circuit current gain, we evaluate field effect transistors. In particular, we calculate the common-source short-circuit current gain $\beta(j\omega)$ and define an ω_T that is the frequency at which the magnitude of $\beta(j\omega)$ is 1.

The appropriate small-signal equivalent circuit for determining $\beta(j\omega)$ when v_{bs} is zero is shown in Fig. 14.13. The capacitance C'_{gs} in this figure is defined to be $C_{gs} + C_{gb}$. A bit of algebra leads us to

$$\beta(j\omega) = \frac{(g_m - j\omega C_{gd})}{j\omega\left(C'_{gs} + C_{gd}\right)} \tag{14.29}$$

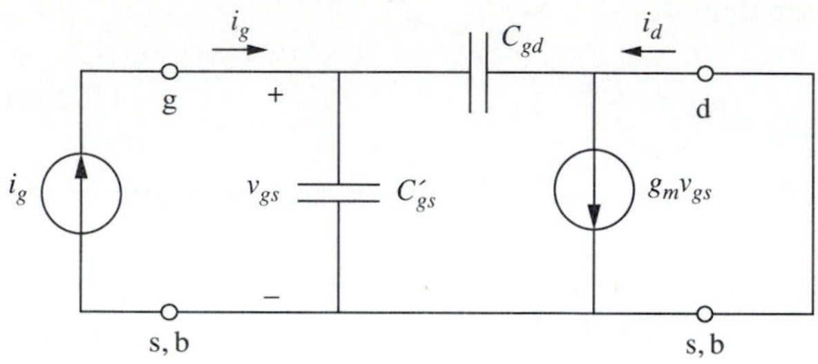

FIGURE 14.13
Small-signal linear equivalent circuit used to calculate the short-circuit common-source current gain of a field effect transistor in saturation. The incremental substrate-to-source voltage v_{bs} has been assured to be zero.

This expression has a rather different frequency dependence than did the short-circuit common-emitter current gain, Eq. (14.18), in that its maximum magnitude occurs at $\omega = 0$. Its magnitude decreases with increasing ω until ω is greater than the zero of the numerator, which occurs when ω is g_m/C_{gd}. By then, however, the magnitude of $\beta(j\omega)$ is much less than 1 because it approaches $C_{gd}/(C'_{gs}+C_{gd})$ and typically C'_{gs} is much larger than C_{gd}.

The frequency at which the magnitude of $\beta(j\omega)$ is 1, which we call ω_T for a field effect transistor, is

$$\omega_T = \left[\frac{g_m^2}{\left(C'_{gs}+C_{gd}\right)^2 - C_{gd}^2}\right]^{1/2} \tag{14.30a}$$

In practice C'_{gs} is typically much larger than C_{gd}, and in such cases ω_T can be approximated as follows:

$$\omega_T \approx \frac{g_m}{C'_{gs}} \tag{14.30b}$$

We didn't need to model the FET gate capacitances (C_{gs}, C_{gd}, and C_{gb}) in detail when we first introduced them in Chap. 10, but now it is useful to obtain more detailed expressions for them. To calculate these capacitances we first need to find an expression for the gate charge q_G as a function of v_{GS}, v_{DS}, and v_{BS}. The capacitances we seek will then be the derivatives of q_G with respect to the appropriate voltages, evaluated at the quiescent operating point. We will do these calculations now for a MOSFET, first because that is a very important device, but also because the mathematics for a MOSFET is more tractable than for a JFET or MESFET; nonetheless, the conclusions we will ultimately reach on the importance of the transit time are relevant to all FETs.

We will use the gradual channel approximation and ignore body effects when we need to use a specific MOSFET model, and we will restrict ourselves to gate biases above threshold so that the MOSFET is not cut off. We can then say that the gate charge q_G will be equal to the sum of the gate charge at threshold, Q_{GT}, plus the negative of the channel charge q_N; that is,

$$q_G = Q_{GT} - q_N \tag{14.31}$$

The gate charge at threshold, Q_{GT}, consists of any gate charge at flat-band, Q_{GFB}, plus the negative of the depletion region charge at threshold, $WLQ_D^*(0, v_{BS})$, where Q_D^* is given by Eq. (10.13):

$$Q_D^*(0, v_{BS}) = -\sqrt{2\epsilon_{si} q N_A(|2\phi_p| - v_{BS})} \tag{10.13}$$

Above threshold this charge does not change with v_{GS} or v_{DS} (it does change with v_{BS}, however). We have

$$Q_{GT} = Q_{GFB} - WLQ_D^* \tag{14.32}$$

The channel charge q_N is the integral of the channel sheet charge density $q_N^*(y)$ over the area of the gate:

$$q_N = W \int_0^L q_N^*(y)\,dy \tag{14.33}$$

where $q_N^*(y)$ is given by

$$q_N^*(y) = -C_{OX}^*[v_{GS} - v_{CS}(y) - V_T(v_{BS})] \tag{14.34}$$

This latter expression is Eq. (10.5′) after the definition of V_T in Eq. (10.12a) has been used to simplify it (we dropped the subscript S, also) and ε_o/t_o has been replaced with C_{OX}^*.

To do the integral in Eq. (14.33) we need to know $v_{CS}(y)$. To find this we return to Eq. (10.4b), which we rewrite here:

$$i_D = -W\mu_e q_N^*(y)\frac{dv_{CS}}{dy} \tag{14.35}$$

We substitute Eq. (14.34) for $q_N^*(y)$ to obtain

$$i_D = W\mu_e C_{OX}^*(v_{GS} - v_{CS} - V_T)\frac{dv_{CS}}{dy} \tag{14.36}$$

This is the same expression we integrated to calculate the terminal characteristics in Chap. 10, but now instead of integrating from 0 to L and from 0 to v_{DS}, we integrate from 0 to y and from 0 to $v_{CS}(y)$ [with $v_{CS}(y)$ being the quantity we want].

We proceed as follows. Rewrite Eq. (14.36) as

$$\int_0^y i_D\,dy = \int_0^{v_{CS}(y)} W\mu_e C_{OX}^*(v_{GS} - v_{CS} - V_T)\,dv_{CS} \tag{14.37}$$

and integrate to obtain

$$i_D y = W \mu_e C_{OX}^* \left[(v_{GS} - V_T) v_{CS} - \frac{v_{CS}^2}{2} \right] \tag{14.38}$$

Solving this quadratic for v_{CS}, we find

$$v_{CS}(y) = (v_{GS} - V_T) - \sqrt{(v_{GS} - V_T)^2 - \frac{2 i_D y}{Z \mu_e C_{OX}^*}} \tag{14.39}$$

Using this in Eq. (14.34) we have

$$q_N^*(y) = -C_{OX}^* \sqrt{(v_{GS} - V_T)^2 - \frac{2 i_D y}{Z \mu_e C_{OX}^*}} \tag{14.40}$$

We are at last in a position to do the integral in Eq. (14.33). Doing the integral and substituting the resulting expression for q_N into Eq. (14.31), we obtain the equation we seek for q_G:

$$q_G = Q_{GT} - \frac{2}{3} \frac{\mu_e (W C_{OX}^*)^2}{2 i_D} \left\{ \left[(v_{GS} - V_T)^2 - \frac{2 i_D L}{C_{OX}^* \mu_e W} \right]^{\frac{3}{2}} - (v_{GS} - V_T)^3 \right\} \tag{14.41}$$

At this point it is easiest to look at independently evaluating this equation for biases in the saturation region and in the linear region.

In saturation, i_D is $\mu_e W (v_{GS} - V_T)^2 / 2L$, so the first term in brackets in Eq. (14.41) is zero and q_G becomes simply

$$q_G\,(\text{saturation}) = Q_{GT} + \frac{2}{3} W L C_{OX}^* (v_{GS} - V_T) \tag{14.42}$$

Calculating the gate capacitances, we find, assuming that Q_{GT} and V_T are constants,

$$C_{gs} \equiv \frac{\partial q_G}{\partial v_{GS}} \Big|_Q = \frac{2}{3} W L C_{OX}^* = \frac{2}{3} C_G \quad \text{in saturation} \tag{14.43}$$

where we have defined C_G to be $W L C_{OX}^*$ and

$$C_{ds} \equiv \frac{\partial q_G}{\partial v_{DS}} \Big|_Q = 0 \quad \text{in saturation} \tag{14.44}$$

We had said earlier that C_{ds} should ideally be zero in saturation, and Eq. 14.44 just confirms that conclusion. Also, we see that C_{gs} is proportional to C_{OX}^* and to the gate area WL as we had anticipated. The curious feature is the factor of 2/3 but it should not be too surprising since the inversion layer charge is not uniform and neither is the gate charge. The charge store is thus less than that on a parallel-plate capacitor, and so is the capacitance.

In the linear region, i_D is more complicated. Substituting our expression for it into Eq. (14.41) we find, after a bit of algebra,

$$q_G\,(\text{linear}) = Q_{GT} + \frac{2}{3} C_G \frac{(v_{GS} - V_T)^3 - (v_{GD} - V_T)^3}{v_{GS}^2 - 2 V_T (v_{GS} - v_{GD}) - v_{GD}^2} \tag{14.45}$$

Notice that we have written this expression as dependent on v_{GS} and v_{GD}, rather than v_{GS} and v_{DS}, because we find C_{gd} by differentiating with respect to v_{GD}. Taking the derivatives, assuming Q_T and V_T are constants, we find

$$C_{gs} = \frac{2}{3}C_G\left\{\frac{3(V_{GS}-V_T)^2}{[\text{term}]} + \frac{\left[(V_{GD}-V_T)^3-(V_{GS}-V_T)^3\right](2V_{GS}-2V_T)}{[\text{term}]^2}\right\} \tag{14.46}$$

and

$$C_{gd} = \frac{2}{3}C_G\left\{\frac{3(V_{GD}-V_T)^2}{[\text{term}]} + \frac{\left[(V_{GD}-V_T)^3-(V_{GS}-V_T)^3\right](2V_{GS}-2V_T)}{[\text{term}]^2}\right\} \tag{14.47}$$

Where [term] in the denominator denotes $[V_{GS}^2 - 2V_T(V_{GS} - V_{GD}) - V_{GD}^2]$.

These expressions do show us that everything is still proportional to C_G, but beyond that they are more "inciteful" than insightful. Fortunately we can learn more by looking at them in two limits: first, for bias points near the saturation point (i.e., $V_{DS} \approx V_{GS} - V_T$) and, second, for bias points near the origin (i.e., $V_{DS} \approx 0$).

Near saturation we find

$$C_{gs} \approx \frac{2}{3}C_G \qquad \text{when } V_{DS} \approx V_{GS} - V_T \tag{14.48}$$

$$C_{gd} \approx 0 \qquad \text{when } V_{DS} \approx V_{GS} - V_T \tag{14.49}$$

This is consistent with what we know must be the case in saturation, that is, Eqs. (14.43) and (14.44).

For small V_{DS}, multiple applications of L'Hôpital's rule lead us to the following conclusion:

$$C_{gs} = \frac{1}{2}C_G \quad \text{when } V_{DS} \approx 0 \tag{14.50}$$

$$C_{gd} = \frac{1}{2}C_G \quad \text{when } V_{DS} \approx 0 \tag{14.51}$$

Again this result makes sense. It tells us that when both ends of the channel are at the same potential, the structure is uniform and symmetrical and so we see the full oxide capacitance, now split equally between the source and drain.

Between these two limits, C_{gs} will increase from $C_G/2$ to $2C_G/3$ as V_{DS} increases from 0 to $V_{GS} - V_T$, whereas C_{ds} will decrease from $C_G/2$ to zero.

Finally, before returning to Eq. (14.30b) and ω_T, we should say a few words about C_{gb}. We have not bothered to calculate it because we made v_{bs} zero and, equivalently, we assumed that V_T and Q_{GT} were constants. If v_{bs} is not zero, then we not only should calculate C_{gb}, but we should also notice that C_{gs} and C_{gd} now include additional terms because of the variations of V_T and Q_{GT} with

v_{BS} and thus with v_{GS} since we will want to write v_{BS} as $v_{GS} - v_{GB}$.* We have all the expressions we need to do this but will not pursue it further here.

Returning to ω_T in Eq. (14.30b), we see that in saturation, which is where we need to know C_{gs}, the gate-to-source capacitance is not a function of the bias current. At the same time, the transconductance g_m increases as the square root of I_D [see Eq. (10.42b)]. Thus we see that ω_T varies with the bias point and increases as I_D is increased; specifically, it increases as the square root of I_D.

The term ω_T can also be interpreted as the inverse of a transit time, just as it was in a bipolar transistor. In this case the relevant transit time is the time required for a carrier in the channel to travel from the source end of the channel to the drain end. To see this recall that the transconductance in saturation can be written in terms of $(V_{GS} - V_T)$ as [see Eq. (10.42a) for g_m and Eq. (10.11a) for K]:

$$g_m = \frac{W}{L}\mu_e \frac{\varepsilon_o}{t_o}(V_{GS} - V_T) \tag{14.52}$$

Combining this expression and Eq. (14.43) for C_{gs} in saturation into Eq. (14.30b) for ω_T, we have

$$\omega_T = \frac{3\mu_e(V_{GS} - V_T)}{2L^2} \tag{14.53}$$

Now, the voltage drop along the channel in saturation is $(V_{GS} - V_T)$, so the average electric field is $(V_{GS} - V_T)/L$, and the corresponding carrier velocity is $\mu_e(V_{GS} - V_T)/L$. The transit time τ_{tr} of carriers traveling from the drain to the source can thus be estimated by dividing the drain-to-source distance L by this velocity, which yields

$$\tau_{tr} \approx \frac{L^2}{\mu_e(V_{GS} - V_T)} \tag{14.54}$$

Comparing this result with ω_T in Eq. (14.53), we see that ω_T is proportional to, and for all practical purposes equal to, $(\tau_{tr})^{-1}$.

Equation (14.53) is very instructive. It tells us that we gain big by reducing the channel length L. It also tells us we gain by having a high carrier mobility in the channel (i.e., n-channel is better than p-channel). And, it tells us that it is advantageous to bias the gate well above threshold. There are limits to making $(V_{GS} - V_T)$ large, however. In particular, the gate oxide may break down and, more fundamentally, the carrier velocity may saturate, putting a lower bound on the transit time. That is, if the saturation velocity is s_{sat}, the minimum transit time will be L/s_{sat} and ω_T will be limited to less than roughly s_{sat}/L. Clearly we still want to make L small, but now the increase in ω_T with decreasing L will be only

---

*We can show that the C_{gs} we calculate assuming V_T and Q_{GT} are constants is equal to the sum $(C_{gs} + C_{gb})$ we would calculate if we did not make this assumption. That is, our result is in fact rigorously true when v_{bs} is zero.

linear rather than quadratic. We also want the highest possible s_{sat}, although in practice variations in s_{sat} from material to material are modest.

14.4 SUMMARY

There are many computer programs available for analyzing circuit performance over wide frequency ranges. These circuits are widely used by circuit designers and engineers, but in this chapter we have concentrated on developing simplified methods of analysis that hopefully promote intuitive insight into what elements limit the performance of various circuit configurations, especially at high frequencies. We have seen, for example, that the inverse of the sum of the open-circuit time constants associated with each of the parasitic capacitors in a circuit yields a good estimate of ω_{HI}, the high-frequency boundary of the mid-band range. We have also pointed out that this sum is dominated by the largest of these time constants. Furthermore, we have seen that a capacitor in the Miller position (i.e., bridging from the input to the output of a stage) will appear magnified by the magnitude of the voltage gain of the stage at the input and is likely to play a major role in limiting ω_{HI}.

Looking at specific stages, we have found that the common-base/gate and emitter/source-follower stages do not suffer from the Miller effect and offer the best high-frequency performance, whereas the high-voltage-gain common-emitter/source stage offers the worst. We have also seen how the cascode configuration combines the common-emitter/source and common-base/gate stages to simultaneously achieve the high gain of the former and the large bandwidth of the latter.

Finally, we have considered the intrinsic high-frequency limitations of both bipolar transistors and MOSFETs. We have seen that both perform best at high bias current levels and that both are ultimately limited by the transit time of carriers through the active region of the device (i.e., from the emitter to the collector in a BJT and from the source to the drain in a MOSFET). This observation teaches us that devices in which electrons comprise the main signal current will be faster than those relying on holes, and it illustrates the value of reducing transistor base widths and gate lengths.

PROBLEMS

14.1 Refer to the *p-n* diode in problem 7.6.

(*a*) Calculate the following small-signal model parameters for two bias points, $V_{AB} = 0.25$ V and $V_{AB} = 0.5$ V.

(i) Small-signal conductance g_d

(ii) Small-signal depletion capacitance C_{dp}

(iii) Small-signal diffusion capacitance C_{df}

(*b*) Sketch Bode plots of the magnitude and phase of the small-signal admittance of this diode for the two bias points in part a. Be careful to label the breakpoint frequencies.

(*c*) The quasistatic approximation is quite good as long as things change slowly relative to the time it takes carriers to move through the device, the so-called transit time t_{tr}.

(i) Find an expression for the transit time for holes crossing the n-side of this diode by approximating t_{tr} as the total number of excess holes on the n-side [i.e., the integral of $p'(x)$ from 0 to w_n] divided by the total hole flux [i.e., $F_h = J_h/q = D_h p'(0) W_n$]. Your answer should look like the expression after Eq. (7.44′) on page 156 assuming x_n is negligible, an assumption we usually make.

(ii) Calculate t_{tr} for this diode.

(iii) Indicate $1/t_{tr}(\equiv \omega_{tr})$ on your Bode plots in part b, and comment on the validity of the quasistatic approximation at the two bias points in part a.

14.2 (*a*) Draw the mid-band incremental linear equivalent circuit of the capacitively coupled emitter-follower stage illustrated in Fig. 11.10*a*. Your circuit should include C_I and C_O.

(*b*) Assuming a sinusoidal input signal $v_t(t) = V_t \sin \omega t$, find a literal expression for the transfer function $V_{out}(j\omega)/V_t(j\omega)$.

(*c*) Find numerical values for the poles of the transfer function, assuming C_I = 1.5 μF, C_O = 25 μF, R_T = 4 kΩ, R_E = 3.4 kΩ, R_L = 50 Ω, $R_{B1} = R_{B2}$ = 40 kΩ, β_f = 200, and $|V_A|$ = 100 V.

(*d*) Use the method of short-circuit time constants (i) to find the short-circuit time constant associated with each transistor C_I and C_O, and (ii) to estimate ω_{LO}.

(*e*) Compare the time constants you have calculated in part d with the poles you found in part c; discuss the similarities and differences.

14.3 In our analysis of the common-base/gate circuit in Sec. 14.2.5, we ignored the parasitic base resistance. This problem explores this issue further.

(*a*) Use the method of open-circuit time constants to find a numerical value for the high-frequency cutoff ω_{HI} of the common-base amplifier shown in Fig. P14.3 when

$$C_\pi = 20 \text{ pF}, \quad R_S = 1 \text{ k}\Omega$$
$$C_\mu = 0.5 \text{ pF}, \quad R_L = 2 \text{ k}\Omega$$
$$r_x = 0, \quad \beta_F = 200$$

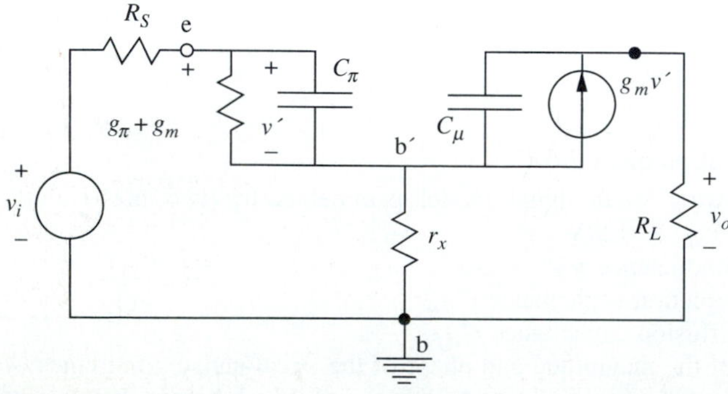

FIGURE P14.3

(*b*) Assume now that $r_x \neq 0$ and find expressions for the open-circuit time constants associated with C_μ and C_π.
(*c*) Find a numerical value for the high-frequency cutoff when $r_x = 200\ \Omega$.

14.4 How large is the Miller effect multiplier in a logic inverter? That is, approximately how much larger is the gate-to-drain, or base-to-collector, capacitive charge storage in an inverter stage, as the input is changed from v_{LO} to v_{HI} and the output switches from v_{HI} to v_{LO}, because of the Miller effect?

14.5 The discussion in Sec. 14.2.7 provides explanation of the superior high-frequency performance of the "improved" Darlington connection (see Fig. 13.9), but leaves a lot of detail to the reader. In this problem you are encouraged to fill in some of that detail.

(*a*) Your understanding of a circuit is often influenced by how it is drawn. One way of configuring the small-signal high-frequency linear equivalent circuit for the improved Darlington is shown in Fig. 14.11*b*. Redraw this equivalent circuit, repositioning the $g_{m1}v_{\pi 1}$ dependent current source in parallel with R_{E1} and repositioning $C_{\mu 1}$ in parallel with v_{in}.
(*b*) The discussion in Sec. 14.2.7 notes that $r_{\pi 1}$ is smaller in the improved connection than in the basic connection. How do $C_{\pi 1}$ and $C_{\mu 1}$ differ in the two connections?
(*c*) Estimate the high-frequency breakpoint ω_{HI} for the two circuits in Fig. 14.11, assuming that they are both connected to a 1-kΩ load and that their inputs are connected to a current source with an equivalent output resistance of 100 kΩ. Both transistors have $\beta = 200$, and Q_2 is biased at 1 mA. Assume that the base transit time is 10 ps, that C_μ is 1 pF independent of bias, and that R_E is 10 kΩ.
(*d*) Based on your calculations in part c, which capacitor in each connection dominates the high-frequency performance?
(*e*) The equivalent circuits in Fig. 14.11 do not include r_{o1} and r_{o2}. Justify or criticize this omission.

14.6 Look back at the transistor described in problem 8.1. This vertical structure is used in an integrated *npn* transistor that has a base-emitter junction that is 10 μm by 100 μm (10^{-5} cm^2) and a base-collector junction that is 20 μm by 125 μm (2.5×10^{-5} cm^2).

(*a*) Calculate the base transit time τ_b in this structure.
(*b*) Calculate ω_T for this transistor when $I_C = 1$ mA and $V_{CE} = 10$ V.
(*c*) Repeat part b with (i) $I_C = 0.1$ mA, and (ii) $I_C = 10$ mA.
(*d*) Comment on your results in parts b and c above, and compare them with $1/\tau_b$ from part a.

14.7 A common way for manufacturers to provide information on the small-signal high-frequency characteristics of their transistors is by quoting typical and minimum (or maximum) values for the current-gain bandwidth product (f_T), the collector-base capacitance (C_{cb}), and the emitter-base capacitance (C_{eb}) under specified measurement conditions. For example, the following information might be given:

(*a*) Describe a procedure for obtaining C_π in the high-frequency hybrid-π model from this information, and calculate a value for it.
(*b*) Do the same as in part a for C_μ.
(*c*) Calculate the base transit time, τ_b for this transistor.

14.8 In this problem we want to analyze the high-frequency performance of the emitter-follower/common-base combination illustrated in Fig. 13.10; we call this circuit an emitter-coupled cascode.

(*a*) Draw an incremental equivalent circuit for this amplifier that includes the C_π and C_μ terms of Q_1 and Q_2.

(*b*) Estimate the open-circuit time constant associated with each C_π and C_μ, and indicate which if any can be expected to dominate ω_{HI}.

(*c*) The topology of the circuit you drew in part a is very similar to the corresponding circuit for the improved Darlington connection (illustrated in Fig. 14.11*b*), but the sizes of the elements and the location of $C_{\mu 2}$ are quite different. Compare the high-frequency models, and comment on the differences in terms of their impact on the high-frequency performance of the stages.

14.9 Active loads add capacitance as well as resistance at the output of an amplifier circuit. Determine the high-frequency incremental equivalent circuits, including parasitic capacitances, for each of the following, and give an expression for the capacitance in terms of the relevant small-signal transistor model signal parameters.

(*a*) The BJT load in Fig. 11.7*a*.

(*b*) The saturated enhancement mode MOSFET in Fig. 11.12*a*.

(*c*) The linear enhancement mode MOSFET in Fig. 11.12*b*.

(*d*) The depletion mode MOSFET in Fig. 11.12*c*.

(*e*) The complementary MOSFET in Fig. 11.12*d*.

14.10 We use half-circuit analysis techniques to simplify the analysis of symmetrical differential amplifier circuits. Consider now the implications of using a half-circuit to estimate the high-frequency breakpoint of a differential amplifier.

(*a*) How would the ω_{HI} of a fully symmetrical differential amplifier be related to the ω_{HI} you would calculate for the difference mode half-circuit of this amplifier?

(*b*) Clearly you would estimate a different ω_{HI} if you used a common mode rather than a difference mode half-circuit. What does this mean?

14.11 A certain n-channel MOSFET has a channel length of 2 microns, a gate oxide thickness of 40 nm, and a channel mobility for electrons of 600 $cm^2/V \cdot s$. The threshold voltage is 1 V.

(*a*) What is the transit time of the electrons through this channel when V_{GS} is 3 V?

(*b*) What is ω_T for this transistor at the same bias?

(*c*) How do your answers in parts a and b change if the channel length is reduced to 1 μm and the gate oxide thickness is reduced to 30 nm? Assume that when the gate oxide thickness is reduced, the mobility also decreases to 400 $cm^2/V \cdot s$.

(*d*) Calculate the minimum transit times for these two channels assuming s_{sat} is 10^7 cm/s. Calculate also what value of gate-to-source voltage V_{GS} this transit time would correspond to if velocity saturation is not a factor (or if the saturation model of Eq. (10.77) is used); that is, find V_{GS} in $(V_{GS} - V_T) = Ls_{sat}/\mu_e$.

(*e*) What limits us from biasing any MOSFETs to the point that the carrier velocity is saturated in the channel?

14.12 Several times in Chap. 11 we biased a MOSFET using a resistor R_G between the drain and gate terminals of the MOSFET. Examples can be found in Fig. 11.15*a* and in problem 11.12. We saw then that making R_G very large was important to achieving high gain and high input resistance, but we said nothing about what doing this does to the frequency response of the circuit. Using the circuit of problem 11.12, determine the impact of a finite R_G on the ω_{HI} of this stage.

14.13 For the circuit in problem 12.3 do the following:

(*a*) Calculate the high-frequency breakpoint of the differential mode gain. Assume ideal voltage source inputs (i.e., zero source resistance).

(*b*) Calculate the low-frequency breakpoint of the differential mode gain.

(*c*) Is the high-frequency breakpoint of the common mode gain higher or lower than the differential mode gain breakpoint? Explain your answer.

CHAPTER 15

DIGITAL BUILDING-BLOCK CIRCUITS

With this chapter we begin consideration of the application of bipolar and field effect transistors as switches to perform digital logic operations and to store digital information. These "digital" applications use the large-signal characteristics of transistors and take advantage of the fact that they are very nonlinear elements. They are thus quite different than those applications explored in Chaps. 11 through 14, which made use of the incremental linearity of transistors and dealt with their use in circuits designed to linearly amplify small time-varying signals.

When we speak of working in the digital world, we are dealing with information in the form of integer numbers. This is in contrast to information in the form of signals that can have magnitudes falling anywhere on a continuously varying scale, as we use when we speak of dealing in the analog world. Thus, rather than processing information in the form of a time-varying signal $v_I(t)$ of arbitrary (within bounds) amplitude, we want to process information (it may be the same information) in the form of a series of numbers $v_I[nT]$ that represent the amplitude of the signal $v_I(t)$ at successive times nT spanning the period in which we are interested. If the amplitude is recorded with enough precision and enough frequency, the time-varying, continuous analog signal $v_I(t)$ and the collection of digital values $v_I[nT]$ will contain essentially the same information and are equally "good" representations of the signal.

It has proven most useful in the electronic processing of digital information to use a binary system rather than a decimal, octal, or other number system. The choice of a number system has absolutely no impact on the precision of a number being represented, of course, but the binary system maps very nicely onto the on/off states of a switch. It is also simple enough to be comprehensible and useful to human designers like you and me. Thus we will look specifically at digital circuits that work with binary signals and that thus use a number system with only two digits. We call these two digits *zero* (0) and *one* (1), or, equivalently, *LO* and *HI*.

In the following sections we will first consider how transistors can be used as switches to perform digital (in particular, binary) logic functions. Then we will look at specific realizations of logic circuits made, first, with MOSFETs, and, then, with bipolar transistors. Finally, we will look at how transistor switches can be used to store binary information, and we will discuss representative memory cell designs.

15.1 GENERIC BINARY LOGIC CIRCUITS

The basic building block for circuits that manipulate and store binary information is the *inverter*. We will thus first look at this circuit in a very general form in this section and then study specific MOSFET and BJT realizations in Secs. 15.2 and 15.3.

15.1.1 Generic Inverter

An inverter is a circuit that has a high, or large, output signal when the input signal is low, or small, and a small output signal when the input signal is large. This relationship is illustrated in Figs. 15.1*a* and *b*.

The inverter is the basic building block for logic gates and memory cells; complex logic circuits are composed of many inverter-based stages interacting with each other. Thus the output of one stage serves as the input to another simi-

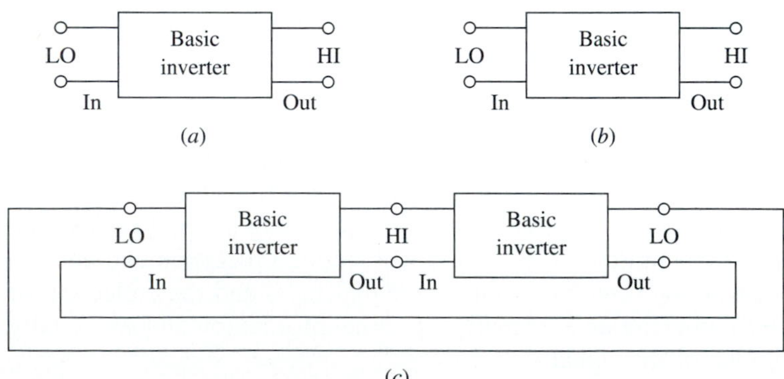

FIGURE 15.1
Input/output relationship of a generic inverter stage: (*a*) with a low, or 0, input; (*b*) with a high, or 1 input; (*c*) illustration of the self-consistency of the high and low input and output signals.

lar stage, and when we speak of a high input, we mean an input signal identical to the high output of an identical inverter stage with a low input. Similarly, when we speak of a low input, we mean an input signal identical to the low output of an identical inverter with a high input. It all sounds very circular, and it is, because that is exactly what we want and require. This relationship is illustrated in Fig. 15.1*c*.

The input and output signals can be either voltages or currents, and both types of inverters exist. As a practical matter, however, the majority of inverters are voltage-based and tend to look a great deal like common-emitter/source linear amplifier stages. In general, as is illustrated in Fig. 15.2*a*, they consist of one transistor, which acts like a switch and is called the *driver device*, and another element that we call a *load*. The basic idea is that with the input low, the switch is open, no current flows through the load, and the output voltage is high. With the input high, the switch closes, current flows through the load, and the output voltage is low. The switch, or driver, device is a transistor that does not conduct unless it is turned on by an input signal. Thus the driver can be either an enhancement mode FET, as we shall see in Sec. 15.2 and as Fig. 15.2*c* illustrates, or a bipolar junction transistor, as we shall see in Sec. 15.3 and as shown in Fig. 15.2*b*. A depletion mode FET, on the other hand, is not an attractive choice as a driver.

15.1.2 Realizing Logic Functions with Inverters

We represent, or define, a logic operation by a *truth table*, which is a chart that specifies the output for each of a complete set of inputs. As an example, the truth table of an inverter is shown in Fig. 15.3 along with a generic inverter stage.

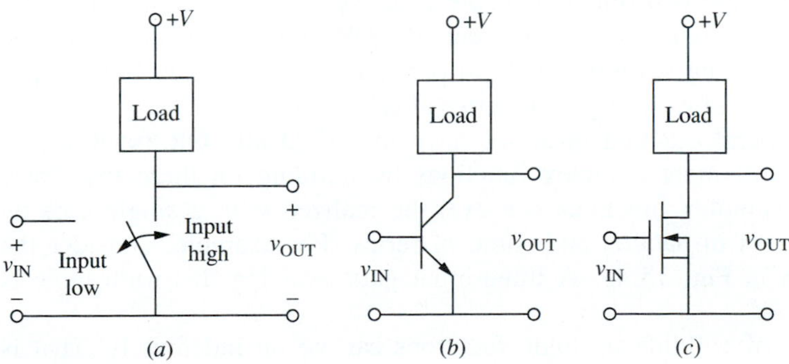

FIGURE 15.2
(*a*) Use of a generalized switch and load to achieve the inverter function; (*b*) specific transistor inverter using a bipolar junction transistor switch, or driver; (*c*) specific transistor inverter using an enhancement mode MOSFET driver.

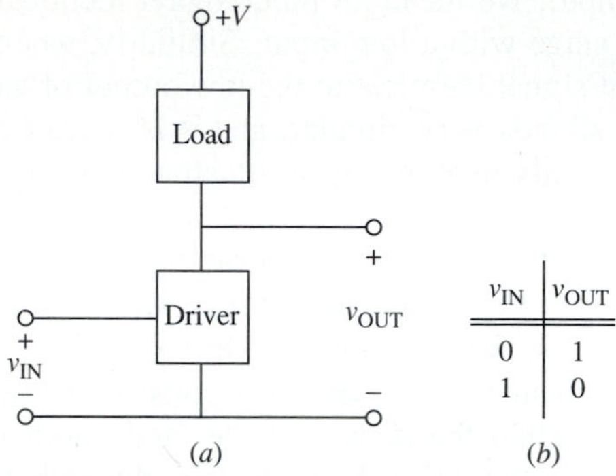

v_{IN}	v_{OUT}
0	1
1	0

FIGURE 15.3
(*a*) Generic inverter stage; (*b*) its truth table.

The basic inverter stage can be extended to perform more complicated logic operations by combining several different inputs via several coupled driver devices.

As a first example, consider the AND function and its inverse, the NAND function. The logic AND is a function for which the output is a 1 only if all of the inputs are 1; it is 0 otherwise. For NAND, the output is 0 only if all of the inputs are 1; it is 1 otherwise. The corresponding truth table is presented in Fig. 15.4*a*. We can realize the NAND by putting several drivers (one for each input) in series as illustrated in Fig. 15.4*b* for a two-input gate. The output V_C in Fig. 15.4*b* represents the NAND output. Putting an inverter on the output yields the AND of the inputs. The output V_D in Fig. 15.4*b* represents the AND output.

Another important group of logic operations is the OR function and its inverse, the NOR function. The logic OR is a function for which the output is a 1 if any of the inputs is a 1; for the NOR the output is 0 if any inputs are 1. The truth table for these two functions is presented in Fig. 15.4*c*. The output V_C represents the NOR output, and V_D represents the OR output. We can realize the NOR function by putting several drivers in parallel as illustrated in Fig. 15.4*d*. Again, OR is obtained by putting an inverter after a NOR gate.

Finally, we point out that once we have the AND and OR functions, it is possible to realize more complex functions by building on these two basic functions. Some complex functions can even be realized with a single gate by placing some drivers in parallel and some in series. For example, consider the truth table shown in Fig. 15.4*e*. A three-input gate realizing this truth table is shown in Fig. 15.4*f*.

The process of building up logic functions can go on indefinitely. That is not our purpose in this text, but the central role played by the basic inverter stage should be very clear to you. We will focus in Secs. 15.2 and 15.3 on inverter design, but in doing so we will in fact be laying the groundwork for the design of arbitrarily complex logic circuits.

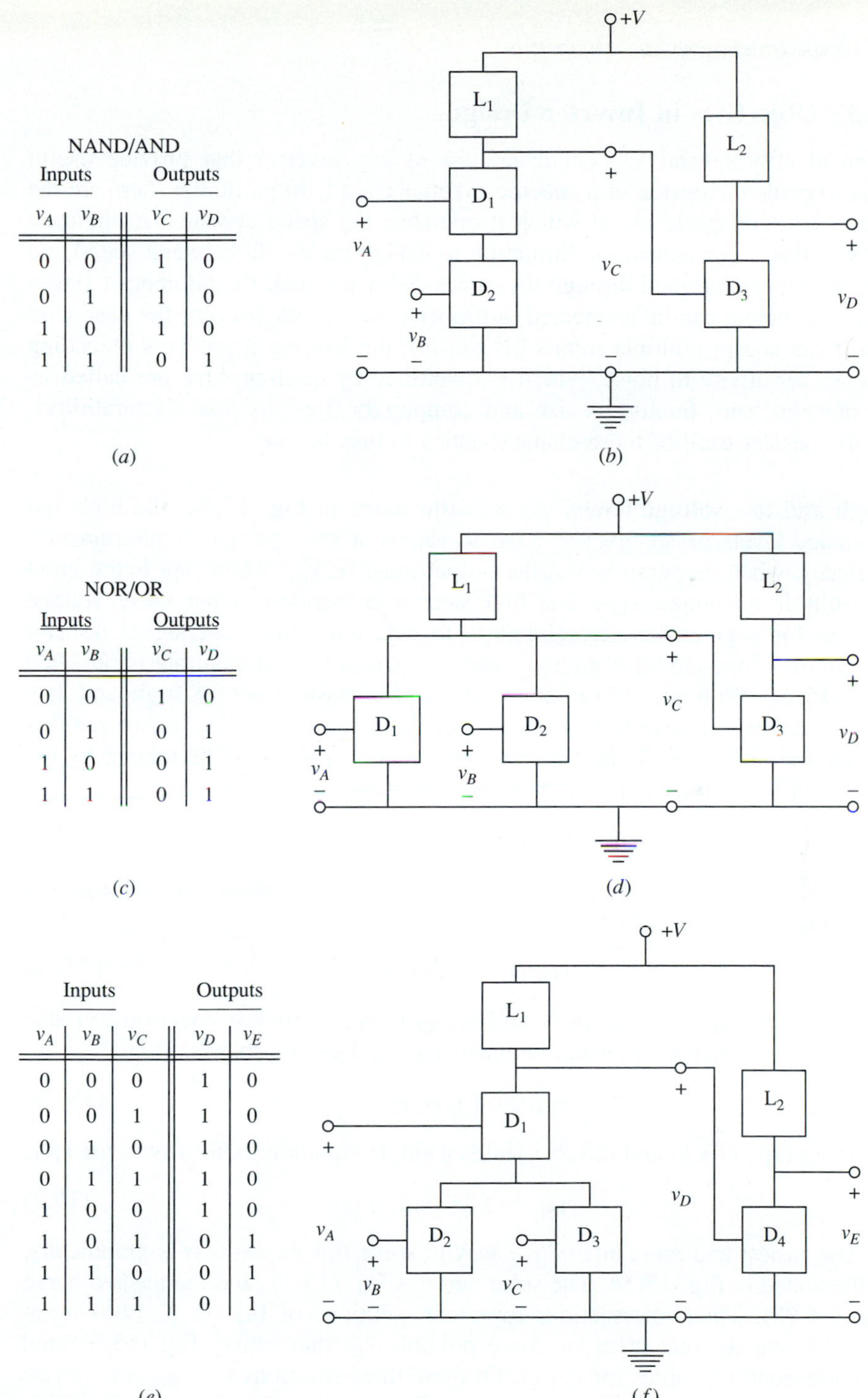

NAND/AND

Inputs		Outputs	
v_A	v_B	v_C	v_D
0	0	1	0
0	1	1	0
1	0	1	0
1	1	0	1

(*a*)

(*b*)

NOR/OR

Inputs		Outputs	
v_A	v_B	v_C	v_D
0	0	1	0
0	1	0	1
1	0	0	1
1	1	0	1

(*c*)

(*d*)

Inputs			Outputs	
v_A	v_B	v_C	v_D	v_E
0	0	0	1	0
0	0	1	1	0
0	1	0	1	0
0	1	1	1	0
1	0	0	1	0
1	0	1	0	1
1	1	0	0	1
1	1	1	0	1

(*e*)

(*f*)

FIGURE 15.4
Logic operations based on expansion of an inverter stage: (*a*) the truth table of the AND and NAND functions; (*b*) the circuit realization of (*a*); (*c*) the truth table of the OR and NOR functions; (*d*) the realization of (*c*); (*e*) a multioperation truth table; (*f*) the circuit realization of (*e*).

15.1.3 Objectives in Inverter Design

We can identify several key characteristics of any inverter that provide useful criteria to guide the design of a specific inverter circuit. In particular there are the high and low voltage levels at which it operates; the speed at which it operates; the power that it consumes; the limitation to design trade-offs between speed and power, which is quantified through the power-delay product; the number of stages to which its output can be connected, a property we call its *fan-out;* the ease with which it can accept multiple inputs (its *fan-in*); the loading it presents preceding stages; its sensitivity to noise, which is quantified by quoting what are called its *noise margins*; and, finally, its size and complexity (i.e., its manufacturability). We will consider each of these characteristics in turn below.

a) High and low voltage levels. As was illustrated in Fig. 15.1*c*, the high and low voltage levels of an inverter have to satisfy a very particular relationship. Specifically, when the input is V_{LO} the output must be V_{HI}, where V_{HI} is the input that results in an output V_{LO}. The first step in determining what these voltage levels are for a given inverter circuit is to determine the large-signal transfer characteristic of the circuit (i.e., v_{OUT} versus v_{IN}). A typical example is sketched in Fig. 15.5*a*. With this information, the self-consistent set of high and low voltages we seek can readily be determined. Referring to Fig. 15.1*c*, we see that the input and output of the first inverter, v_{IN1} and v_{OUT1}, must be related by the inverter transfer characteristic through the first stage:

$$v_{OUT1} = f(v_{IN1}) \tag{15.1}$$

At the same time, v_{IN2} and v_{OUT2} must be related in the same way through the second stage:

$$v_{OUT2} = f(v_{IN2}) \tag{15.2a}$$

However, since v_{IN2} is v_{OUT1} and v_{OUT2} is v_{IN1}, this last equation can also be viewed as another relationship between v_{IN1} and v_{OUT1}; that is,

$$v_{IN1} = f(v_{OUT1}) \tag{15.2b}$$

Combining Eqs. (15.1) and (15.2b) yields a single equation to be solved for v_{IN1}:

$$v_{IN1} = f[f(v_{IN1})] \tag{15.3}$$

The easiest and most instructive way to solve this expression is graphically, as is illustrated in Fig. 15.5*b*. The solid curve is Eq. (15.1), and the dashed curve is Eq. (15.2b). Their intersections represent solutions of Eq. 15.3. Looking at Fig. 15.5*b*, we see that there are three possible v_{IN} that satisfy Eq. (15.3) (and three corresponding values for v_{OUT}). Of these three solutions for v_{IN1}, the lowest corresponds to V_{LO}, and the highest to V_{HI}. The middle value V_{TR} is not a stable solution. (The "TR" stands for "trigger," a name that will become clear when we discuss noise margins below.)

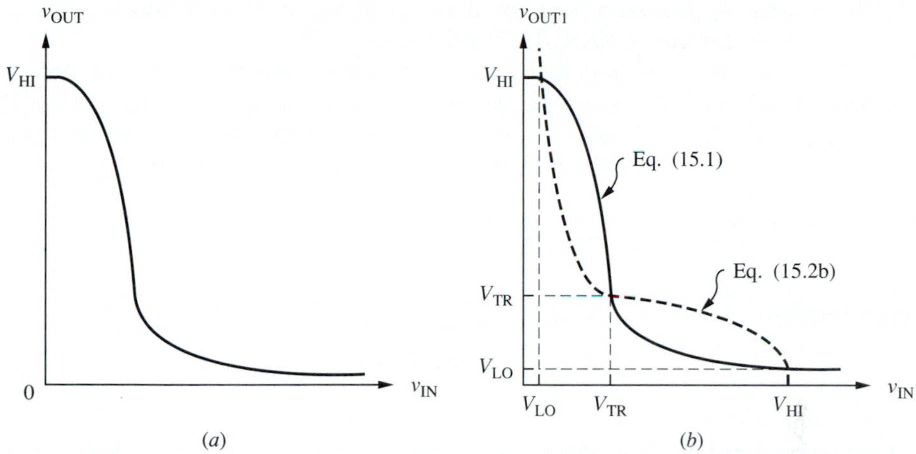

FIGURE 15.5
(*a*) Transfer characteristic for a typical inverter stage; (*b*) graphical solution of Eq. (15.3) for a connection as in Fig. 15.1*c*.

b) Switching Speed. The *switching speed* of an inverter is the time it takes for the output to change from one state to another for a step change in the input. Clearly there are actually two switching times of interest, corresponding, respectively, to the input going from HI to LO and to the input going from LO to HI. In general these times will be different, in some cases quite different.

The switching times of an inverter are determined by the difference in the amounts of energy stored in the inverter elements in each of its two states. We know from our discussion of *p-n* junctions and MOS capacitors, for example, that there are numerous capacitive charge stores in any device and that the amount of charge stored in a device changes as the terminal voltage and state of the device change. Thus as a transistor is switched from off to on or on to off, these charge stores have to be either filled or emptied; we say *charged* or *discharged*. The time it takes to accomplish this charging and/or discharging determines in large part how quickly an inverter will switch from one state to the other (i.e., its switching speed).

The on-to-off switching time is determined predominantly by the load because the switch transistor is off and the output is changing from its low value to its high value. Any "charging up" of the output node must occur through the load device. If the dynamic load on this node can be modeled as a linear capacitor C_L and the current supplied to this node through the load is i_L, we have

$$i_L = C_L \frac{dv_{OUT}}{dt} \tag{15.4a}$$

or rearranging,

$$\frac{dv_{OUT}}{dt} = \frac{i_L}{C_L} \tag{15.4b}$$

In general, i_L will be a function of v_{OUT}, as we shall see when we look at specific inverter designs in Secs. 15.2 and 15.3.

The off-to-on switching time is determined by the switching, or driver, transistor, which must discharge the output node as it swings from v_{HI} to v_{LO}. It conducts this discharge current as well as the load current, and thus we have the following expression relating the driver drain current and the output voltage:

$$i_{DD} = i_L - C_L \frac{dv_{\text{OUT}}}{dt} \tag{15.5a}$$

which yields

$$\frac{dv_{\text{OUT}}}{dt} = -\frac{(i_{DD} - i_L)}{C_L} \tag{15.5b}$$

In this expression both i_{DD} and i_L are functions of v_{OUT}, and in general i_{DD} is much larger than i_L. In many inverters this transient is significantly faster than the on-to-off transient.

As we stated before writing Eq. (15.4a), the above equations are valid only if we can assume that the charge store can be modeled as an ideal linear capacitor, but the basic conclusions we have reached about the importance of the load current in charging the output note and of the difference between the driver and load currents in discharging it are quite general. So too is the idea that the rate at which the node charges (or discharges) will be directly proportional to the net current into (or out of) the node and inversely proportional to the amount of charge stored there. We will study all of these issues in much more detail in Chap. 16, which is devoted to analyzing switching transients and speed.

c) Power consumption. The power consumed by an inverter stage depends on its logic state, so we speak in terms of the average power an inverter consumes if it is, on average, in each state half of the time. Furthermore, an inverter will consume additional power each time it changes state because in doing so energy must be put into or taken out of the charge stores in the devices. Thus there is also a component of the average power consumption that depends on how frequently the inverter is being switched, that is, on the clock frequency. Putting these components together we have the following expression:

$$P_{\text{AVE}} = \frac{1}{2}P_{\text{ON}} + \frac{1}{2}P_{\text{OFF}} + f_{\text{CLOCK}}E_{\text{CYCLE}} \tag{15.6}$$

where P_{ON} and P_{OFF} are the average powers dissipated in the "on" and "off" states of the inverter, respectively, f_{CLOCK} is the clock frequency, and E_{CYCLE} is the energy dissipated each cycle in switching. The factors of $\frac{1}{2}$ in the first two terms assume that the inverter is on half of the time and off half of the time, as we have said, and that the switching time is a small fraction of the total cycle time.

If this is not true, these factors should be adjusted accordingly. Also, multiplying E_{CYCLE} by f_{CLOCK}, rather than by a fraction of f_{CLOCK}, assumes that the inverter switches every cycle, which is clearly a worst-case assumption for an average gate.

d) Power-delay product. A little thought about the switching speed and power consumption discussion in the preceding two subsections will show you that both quantities vary in the same way with some design variables, such as the load current, and in opposite ways with others, such as the size of the charge store. In general we want to increase the speed of a circuit and decrease its power consumption, and because of the interdependence of these factors it is convenient to define a third quanitity that clearly shows us what our design options are (i.e., what we can do to improve performance in both respects and when we have to compromise). The parameter that is commonly used for this purpose is the *power-delay* product. By "delay" we mean the minimum length of a complete logic cycle (i.e., the sum of the switching transients for the low-to-high and the high-to-low transitions). Clearly designing for maximum speed is equivalent to designing for minimum delay.

Forming the product of the average power consumption during a cycle and the minimum delay gives us a quantity we call the power-delay product. The power-delay product has the units of energy and is a useful parameter for understanding inverter design trade-offs.

e) Fan-in and fan-out. The fan-in of an inverter stage is the number of inputs it has. A simple inverter, of course, has only one input signal, but since we are looking at inverters as the basis of mulitple-input logic gates, as we did in Fig. 15.4, we will want to consider in each case how we can add multiple inputs for both NAND and NOR functions to a basic inverter stage and what effects these inputs have on the inverter performance.

The fan-out of an inverter stage is the number of similar stages that can be connected to its output and still allow the circuit to remain functional and to maintain useful high and low output levels. The fan-out thus depends in large part on how much input current the following stages require and how much output the inverter stage can supply. The switching speed of a stage will also be affected by the number of stages connected to its output, and this may place another restriction on the fan-out.

In practice fan-ins and fan-outs of 3 or 4 are usually adequate for an inverter design. A minimum of 2 is needed to do anything useful, and more than 4 is seldom required.

f) Noise margins. It is desirable from power considerations to keep the voltage levels in an inverter as low as possible. Considering what limits us in this regard, we typically find that the minimum power supply voltage is determined by the stability of the inverter states. There are random voltage and current fluctuations in any electrical system, and this "noise" can inadvertently cause a chain of inverters (i.e., a series of gates) to change states if a fluctuation is large enough. The measure of how large a fluctuation must be to switch a given inverter out of a particular state is that state's *noise margin*.

We can find the noise margins of an inverter from its transfer characteristic. Referring to Fig. 15.5*b*, recall that there is a third solution for v_{IN} and v_{OUT} that we said was unstable and that fell between the two solutions we selected as determining V_{LO} and V_{HI}. This third solution, $v_{IN} = v_{OUT} = V_{TR}$, is unstable because any slight fluctuation of v_{IN} away from this value V_{TR} causes the circuit to switch to one of the other two solutions (which one depends on the sign of the fluctuation). This is important because if we now consider ourselves to be at one of the two stable solution points and a voltage fluctuation occurs that is large enough to push us momentarily past the unstable point V_{TR}, the inverter will inadvertently switch states.

When we have several inverters connected in a chain, the fluctuations can be amplified through the chain if the magnitude of the incremental voltage gain exceeds 1. Thus even though the initial fluctuation is not large enough to push us past V_{TR}, it may become large enough to switch a later stage; thus the critical margins are the voltage differences between V_{LO} and V_{HI} and the nearest points on the transfer characteristic at which the magnitude of the slope (i.e., the gain) exceeds 1. These points are labeled V_{1L} and V_{1H} on Fig. 15.6. We define the low and high state noise margins, NM_{LO} and NM_{HI}, as $(V_{1L} - V_{LO})$ and $(V_{HI} - V_{1H})$, respectively. That is

$$NM_{LO} = (V_{1L} - V_{LO}) \tag{15.7a}$$

and

$$NM_{HI} = (V_{HI} - V_{1H}) \tag{15.7b}$$

It should be clear that we want the two noise margins to be equal and as large as possible. Optimally, then, we want to design our inverter to have as sharp and steep a transfer characteristic as possible, and to have the steep portion centered midway between V_{HI} and V_{LO}. This latter feature is consistent with designing V_{TR} to be approximately $(V_{HI} + V_{LO})/2$.

g) Manufacturability. As important as all of the performance considerations we have just outlined are concerns about building integrated circuits based on a given inverter design. We call this *manufacturability.* It is affected by such factors as the complexity of the circuit and of the process required to fabricate it, the size of the building-block circuits and the number of building-block units required to realize the logic functions of interest, and the tolerance of the design to process variations. We will not attempt to give an exhaustive treatment of these issues here, but we will comment on them from time to time, and it is important that you be sensitive to them.

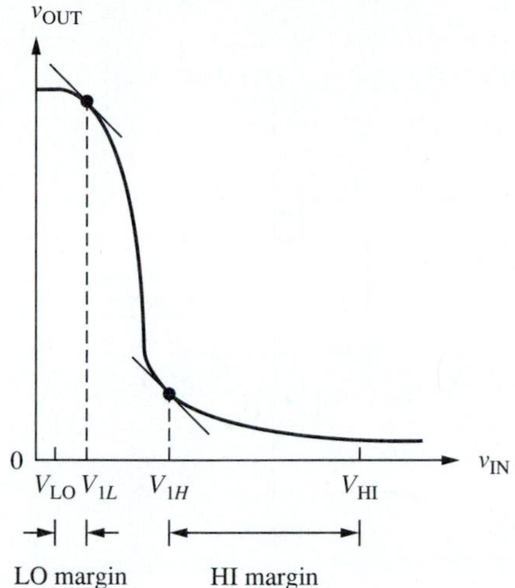

FIGURE 15.6
Transfer characteristics for a typical inverter stage with the points of unity incremental voltage gain, V_{1L} and V_{1H}, identified and with the high and low noise margins, NM_{HI} and NM_{LO}, respectively, indicated.

15.1.4 Determining the Transfer Characteristic

It is clear from the preceding discussion of inverter design objectives that the transfer characteristic of an inverter is one of its key features. Consequently, understanding how to determine it for a given inverter and how to then design a particular inverter to achieve a desirable transfer characteristic are important.

In general, the transfer characteristic can be determined by summing the currents into the node at the top of the driver. The current from the voltage source through the load device and the current out the output terminal into the following gate(s) are typically functions of v_{OUT} alone, whereas the current through the driver is a function of v_{IN} and possibly v_{OUT}. Kirchhoff's current law applied to this node thus yields the desired relationship between v_{IN} and v_{OUT}.

If we have analytical expressions for terminal characteristics of the driver and load devices, we can determine the transfer characteristic analytically. We will see numerous examples of this in the following sections. Alternatively, it is often convenient and/or instructive to determine the transfer characteristic graphically. To do this, we can plot a family of curves relating the driver current to v_{OUT}, with v_{IN} as the stepped variable. On the same graph, the difference between the load current and the current into the following stage is plotted on the same axes; this curve is called the *load line*. The intersection of the load line and the driver

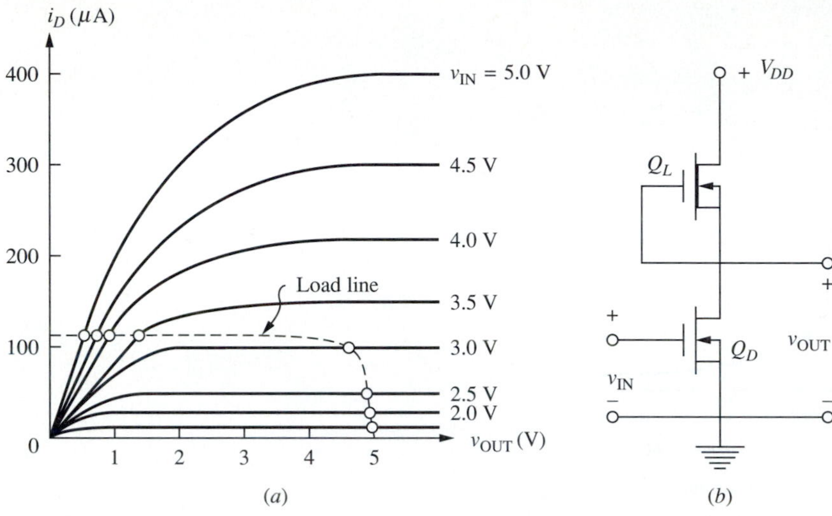

FIGURE 15.7
(*a*) Graphical determination of the static transfer characteristic of the inverter illustrated in (*b*). The actual transfer characteristic can be found in Fig. 15.11.

curve at a given V_{IN} yields the corresponding V_{OUT}. This procedure is illustrated in Fig. 15.7 for an inverter we will study in Sec. 15.2.3.

15.2 MOSFET LOGIC

The MOSFET has proven to be *the* device par excellence for integrated circuit logic because of its relative simplicity (compared to bipolar transistors), small size, and low power demands (in large part because of its infinite input resistance); only in the area of speed does MOSFET logic circuitry fall short of bipolar logic circuitry. In this section we will look at several MOSFET logic families. They are all basically common-source circuits and differ only in the nature of their load devices.

The examples we will use to illustrate the different MOSFET logic families will all use n-channel enhancement mode MOSFETs as driver devices because they are faster than p-channel devices. Historically, however, the first commercial MOSFET logic used p-channel MOSFETs because it is more difficult to fabricate enhancement mode n-channel MOSFETs than enhancement mode p-channel devices. The problem lies in a naturally occurring positive-surface state charge density at the Si–SiO_2 interface (see Sec. 9.5, page 257). Before it was learned how to control, minimize, and, ultimately, counterbalance the effects of this charge, n-channel devices tended to be solely depletion mode devices. We need not be overly concerned with these problems, of course, since they were solved before most of us were born, but they are nonetheless worth keeping in mind because they help explain the role that the various logic families we will study played in the evolution of the currently dominant technologies. We will thus make reference to this history at several points in the following sections.

15.2.1 Resistor Load

The simplest MOSFET inverter is an enhancement mode driver with a resistor load, as is illustrated in Fig. 15.8*a*. To analyze this circuit, we first write the expression for the load current as a function of the output voltage v_{OUT}. This relationship is important to us because of the roles it plays, first, in the switching transient and, second, in the transfer characteristic. We will discuss the switching transient a bit later; for now we focus on the transfer characteristic. In this inverter we have

$$i_L = \frac{(V_{DD} - v_{OUT})}{R_L} \tag{15.8}$$

The general procedure we follow to find the static transfer characteristic is to equate this expression for the load current to that for the driver drain current and to solve the resulting equation for v_{OUT} in terms of v_{IN}. The expression for the driver drain current depends on the state of the MOSFET driver, which in turn depends on the relative magnitudes of the input and output voltages, v_{IN} and v_{OUT}. That is, if v_{IN}, which is identically v_{GS}, is less than V_T, the driver is off and i_D is zero. If v_{IN} is greater than V_T and if v_{OUT}, which is also v_{DS}, is greater than $(v_{IN} - V_T)$, then i_D is $K(v_{IN} - V_T)^2/2$. If, on the other hand, v_{OUT} is less than $(v_{IN} - V_T)$, then i_D is $K(V_{IN} - V_T - v_{OUT}/2)v_{OUT}$. Thus we can identify three regions in the static transfer characteristic and write an expression for v_{OUT} in terms of v_{IN} for each:

Region I: $(v_{IN} - V_T) \leq 0$ [Q_D cut off]

$$i_D = 0 \tag{15.9a}$$

$$\therefore v_{OUT} = V_{DD} \tag{15.9b}$$

Region II: $0 \leq (v_{IN} - V_T) \leq v_{OUT}$ [Q_D saturated]

$$i_D = \frac{(V_{DD} - v_{OUT})}{R_L} = \frac{K}{2}(v_{IN} - V_T)^2 \tag{15.10a}$$

$$\therefore v_{OUT} = V_{DD} - \frac{R_L K}{2}(v_{IN} - V_T)^2 \tag{15.10b}$$

Region III: $0 \leq (v_{IN} - V_T) \leq v_{OUT}$ [Q_D linear]

$$i_D = \frac{(V_{DD} - v_{OUT})}{R_L} = K(v_{IN} - V_T - v_{OUT})v_{OUT} \tag{15.11a}$$

$$\therefore v_{OUT} = (v_{IN} - V_T) + \frac{1}{R_L K} - \left\{\left[(v_{IN} - V_T) + \frac{1}{R_L K}\right]^2 - \frac{2V_{DD}}{R_L K}\right\}^{\frac{1}{2}}$$

$$\approx \frac{V_{DD}}{[R_L K(v_{IN} - V_T) + 1]} \tag{15.11b}$$

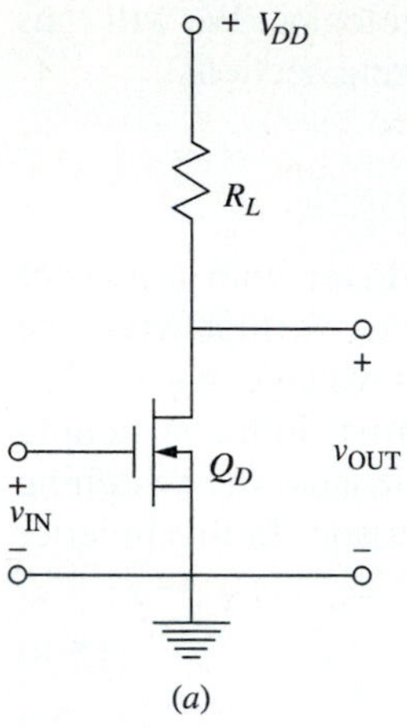

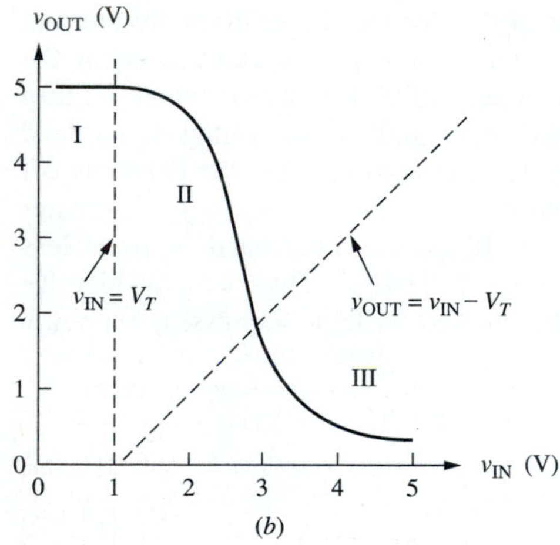

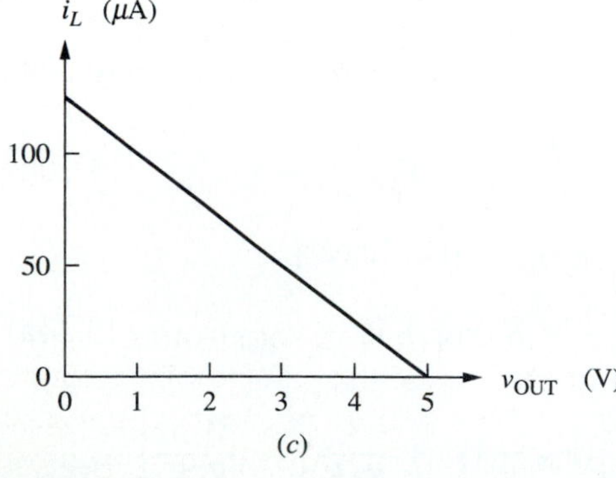

FIGURE 15.8
(*a*) MOSFET inverter stage with an *n*-channel enhancement mode driver and a resistor load; (*b*) the static transfer characteristic assuming $V_{DD} = 5$ V, $V_T = 1$ V, and $R_{LK} = 2\ \text{V}^{-1}$; (*c*) the current characteristic of the load.

These characteristics are plotted in Fig. 15.8*b* for a representative set of parameters: $V_{DD} = 5$ V, $V_T = 1$ V, and $R_L K = 2$ V^{-1}. These values give a reasonable transfer characteristic with V_{LO} approximately 0.6 V [obtained from solving Eq. (15.11b) with $V_{IN} = V_{DD}$, i.e., V_{HI}] and V_{HI} equal to 5 V [from Eq. (15.9b)]. It is highly desirable that V_{LO} be less than V_T so that the driver device is cut off when the input is low. The circuit designer, in general, has to choose R_L and K to achieve this result. We will not concern ourselves further with refining the design of this type of inverter stage because resistor loads are of little commercial interest. Instead, we will turn our attention to alternate loads.

Before leaving the resistor load, however, there are several additional points we should make. First, note that the on-to-off switching transient is simply an exponential with a time constant $R_L C_L$, assuming that the dynamic load is a linear capacitor of value C_L. That is, we have

$$i_L = C_L \frac{dv_{OUT}}{dt} = \frac{(V_{DD} - v_{OUT})}{R_L} \tag{15.8$'$}$$

Assuming that the inverter switches at $t = 0$ and that $v_{OUT} = v_{LO}$ for $t \le 0$, we find that v_{OUT} is given as

$$v_{OUT} = V_{DD} - (V_{DD} - v_{LO})\, e^{-t/R_L C_L} \qquad \text{for } t \ge 0 \tag{15.12}$$

We will use this result as a point of reference when we discuss other loads below and when we discuss switching transients in detail in Chap. 16.

Second, notice that since i_D is zero when the inverter is in its "off" state, P_{OFF} is also zero. This is the primary motivation for insisting that V_{LO} be less than the threshold voltage of the driver device.

And finally, because all of the stages we will look at in this section use the same type of switch (or driver) device, they share the same fan-in and fan-out features; it is thus appropriate to discuss these features now before proceeding to look at the other possible loads. First, the input to each stage is a MOSFET gate, so there is no static loading of the output of the preceding stages. The limit on fan-out will thus be determined by dynamic considerations, the topic of Chap. 16. Second, to obtain multiple inputs, we add driver devices in series as shown in Fig. 15.4*a* for NAND operations or in parallel as in Fig. 15.4*c* for NOR operations.* As we have seen, an important design parameter is the driver K-factor, and when we have multiple driver devices we want to size them so that taken together they yield the target K-value. When the drivers (say there are n of them) are in a series, this means we want to have the sum of the gate lengths, nL, divided by the gate width W (which we assume is the same for all of the n drivers) be equal to the target W/L ratio. Since we usually design devices with the minimum gate length we can fabricate, this means that each input device should have a

*The situation is a bit more complicated for CMOS, as we will discuss in Sec. 15.2.4.

gate width of nW (i.e., $nW/nL = W/L$). When the drivers are in parallel, the situation is more complicated because having any combination of drivers on will switch the state of the inverter and it is impossible to have the same effective K-factor for all possible inputs. That is, if only one input is high, the effective driver gate width is W; if two are high it is $2W$, etc. Fortunately, the performance of a MOSFET inverter stage in general improves as the K-factor of the driver is increased, so if in our design we assume one high input, things will only improve with more high inputs. Thus with multiple parallel drivers, we design them each to have the target W/L ratio.

15.2.2 Enhancement Mode Loads

A major problem with using a resistor as a load is that the required resistors occupy a large area. In the above example, for instance, the $R_L K$ product was 2 V^{-1}, and if we assume a typical K value of 50 to 100 $\mu\text{A/V}^2$, we find a resistor value of 20 to 40 kΩ! Such large values are achievable from thin resistive films deposited and patterned on the Si wafer surface, but rather than develop such a technology, most manufacturers have looked instead at using another MOSFET as a load. The MOSFETs that are most readily available for this purpose are enhancement mode MOSFETs like those used for the driver. They will have the same threshold but can have different K values since changing K involves only changing the W/L ratio.

We will study two ways to use an enhancement mode load: with the gate and drain connected so that the load MOSFET is saturated, and with the gate tied to a separate supply so that the load MOSFET is always in its linear regime. We consider each in turn below.

a) Saturated load. The simplest way to use an enhancement mode MOSFET as a load is to connect its gate and drain as illustrated in Fig. 15.9*a*. Connected in this way, v_{DS} is always greater than $(v_{GS} - V_T)$ for the load MOSFET, so it is always either saturated or cut off. Thus the load current in terms of v_{OUT} is $K_L(V_{DD} - v_{\text{OUT}} - V_T)^2/2$, where K_L refers to the load device, as long as v_{OUT} is less than $(V_{DD} - V_T)$; i_L is 0 otherwise.

Once again the correct expression for the drain current of the driver device depends on the relative sizes of v_{IN} and v_{OUT}, and again we have three regions:

Region I: $(v_{\text{IN}} - V_T) \leq 0$ [Q_D cut off]

$$i_D = 0 \tag{15.13a}$$

$$\therefore v_{\text{OUT}} = V_{DD} - V_T \tag{15.13b}$$

Region II: $0 \leq (v_{\text{IN}} - V_T) \leq v_{\text{OUT}}$ [Q_D saturated]

$$i_D = \frac{K_L}{2}(V_{DD} - v_{\text{OUT}} - V_T)^2 = \frac{K_D}{2}(v_{\text{IN}} - V_T)^2 \tag{15.14a}$$

$$\therefore v_{\text{OUT}} = V_{DD} - V_T - \sqrt{\frac{K_D}{K_L}}(v_{\text{IN}} - V_T) \tag{15.14b}$$

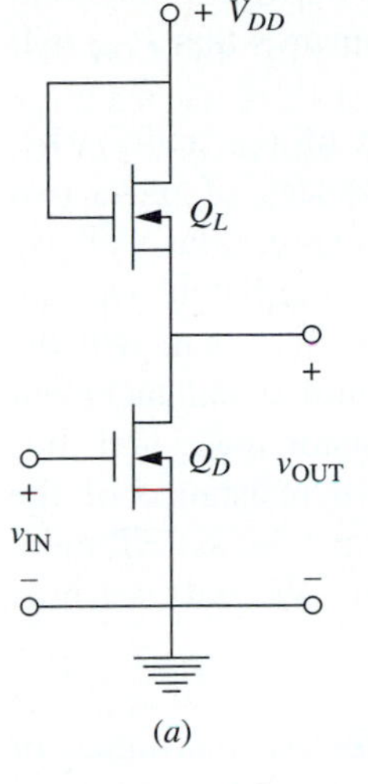

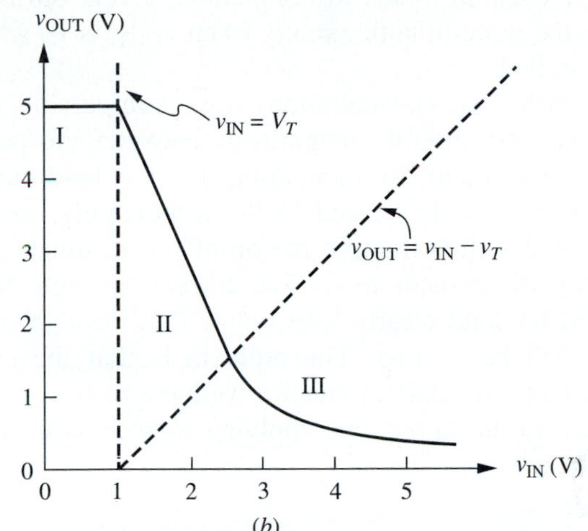

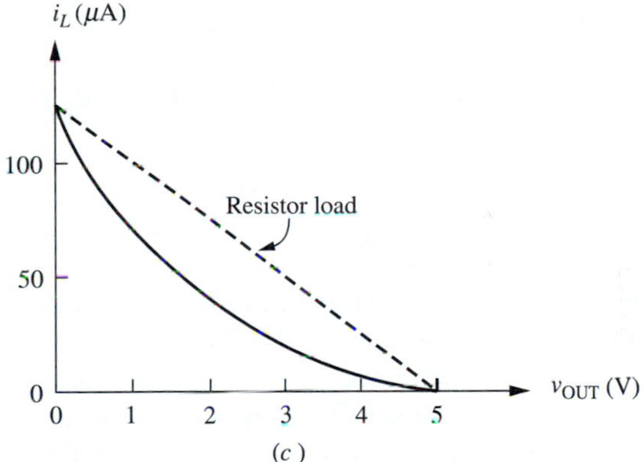

FIGURE 15.9
(*a*) MOSFET inverter stage with an n-channel enhancement mode driver and a saturated n-channel enhancement mode load; (*b*) the static transfer characteristic, assuming $V_{DD} = 6$ V, $V_T = 1$ V, $K_D = 50\ \mu\text{A/V}^2$, and $K_L = 10\ \mu\text{A/V}^2$; (*c*) the current characteristic of the load.

Region III: $0 \leq v_{OUT} \leq (v_{IN} - V_T)$ $\quad [Q_D$ linear$]$

$$i_D = \frac{K_L}{2}(V_{DD} - v_{OUT} - V_T)^2 = K_D\left(v_{IN} - V_T - \frac{v_{OUT}}{2}\right)v_{OUT} \tag{15.15a}$$

$$\therefore v_{OUT} : \text{quadratic function of } v_{IN}; \text{ concave up} \tag{15.15b}$$

This static transfer characteristic is plotted in Fig. 15.9*b* assuming $V_{DD} = 6$ V, $V_T = 1$ V, $K_L = 10\ \mu\text{A/V}^2$, and $K_D = 50\ \mu\text{A/V}^2$. With these parameters v_{HI} is the same as in our resistor load example (i.e., 5 V), so both inverters have to charge their dynamic loads to comparable levels during the on-to-off transient. Also, i_L is the same in both circuits when $v_{OUT} = 0$, which ensures that P_{ON} will be similar in both.

With these two considerations [i.e., comparable values of v_{HI} and $i_L(0)$], we can make meaningful comparisons between the performances of these two inverters. In particular, by comparing the two load current expressions that we have plotted in Figs. 15.8*c* and 15.9*c*, respectively, we can immediately see that this circuit will switch through the on-off cycle much more slowly than will the inverter with the resistor load. The current through the saturated enhancement mode MOSFET load clearly falls below that through the resistor load, and thus dv_{OUT}/dt will be smaller. The problem is that the effective resistance of the load is too large; to make it smaller we have to turn on the load MOSFET more strongly, and to do so requires applying more bias to the gate. We will see how to do this next.

b) Linear load. The "fix" for the problem of the high effective resistance of the saturated load is to apply a bias V_{GG} to the gate of the load MOSFET, as illustrated in Fig. 15.10*a*. The load current is now

$$i_L = K_L\left[V_{GG} - V_T - \frac{(V_{DD} - v_{OUT})}{2}\right](V_{DD} - v_{OUT}) \tag{15.16a}$$

which in the limit of very large V_{GG} approaches

$$i_L \approx K_L(V_{GG} - V_T)(V_{DD} - v_{OUT}) \tag{15.16b}$$

Comparing this last expression to Eq. (15.7), you can see that they have identical forms and that the heavily biased MOSFET load looks like a linear resistor.

The transfer characteristic of this inverter circuit with $V_{DD} = 5$ V, $V_{GG} = 15$ V, $V_T = 1$ V, $K_D = 50\ \mu\text{A/V}^2$, and $K_L = 2\ \mu\text{A/V}^2$ is shown in Fig. 15.10*b*; the load current is plotted versus v_{OUT} in Fig. 15.10*c*.

As a practical matter, adding a second voltage source V_{GG} to the circuit is a bothersome complication, but not, as you might first guess, because it consumes significant additional power. This source actually supplies very little power because it is tied only to MOSFET gates and thus provides no quiescent current. The problem with adding V_{GG} is that it must be wired to every logic gate in the circuit, which makes the entire integrated circuit larger than it would be otherwise and complicates the layout. Nonetheless, these circuits were used for a number of years, using *p*-channel MOSFETs, before the technology was developed to make *n*-channel MOSFETs and the inverter stages we will discuss next.

15.2.3 Depletion Mode Load: *n*-MOS

When we use an enhancement mode load we have to apply a large gate bias to get a switching speed that approaches that of a comparable inverter with a resistor load, but what we would really like to do is to switch even faster. To do this we need a load through which the current does not decrease as the output

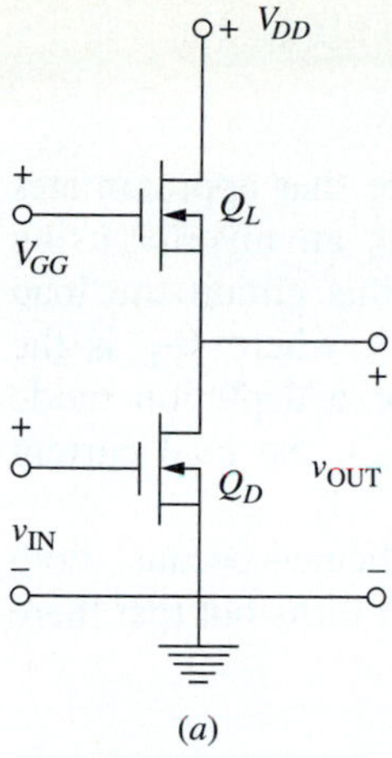

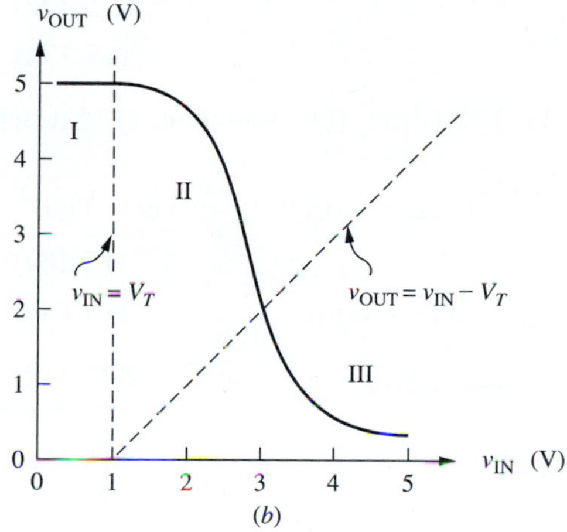

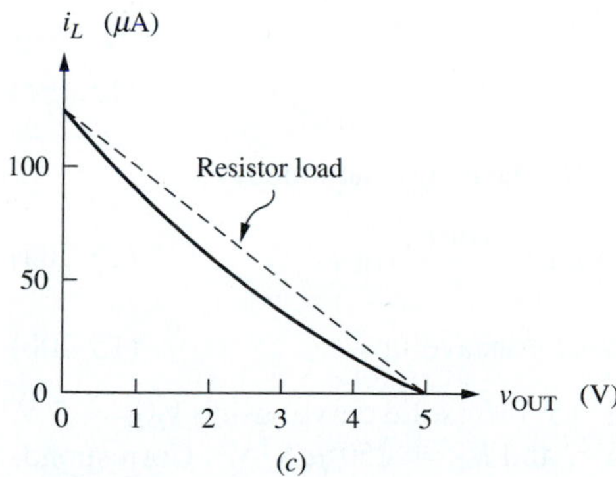

FIGURE 15.10
(*a*) MOSFET inverter stage with an *n*-channel enhancement mode driver and a linear *n*-channel enhancement mode load; (*b*) the static transfer characteristic assuming $V_{DD} = 5$ V, $V_{GG} = 15$ V, $V_T = 1$ V, $K_D = 50\ \mu\text{A/V}^2$, and $K_L = 2\ \mu\text{A/V}^2$; (*c*) the current characteristic of the load.

voltage v_{OUT} increases until v_{OUT} has reached v_{HI}. A device that approximates this behavior is a depletion mode MOSFET with $v_{GS} = 0$; an inverter using such a MOSFET as a load is shown in Fig. 15.11*a*. For this circuit the load current i_L is $K_L V_{TL}^2/2$ when v_{OUT} is less than $(V_{DD} + V_{TL})$, where V_{TL} is the threshold of the load device. (Note that V_{TL} is negative for a depletion mode *n*-channel MOSFET.) When v_{OUT} is greater than $(V_{DD} + V_{TL})$, the load current i_L is $K_L[-V_{TL} - (V_{DD} - v_{OUT})/2](V_{DD} - v_{OUT})$.

The transfer characteristic of this inverter is more complicated because both the load and driver devices can have several different states. It turns out that there are four regions of the characteristic:

Region I: $(v_{IN} - V_{TD}) \leq 0$ $\quad [Q_D$ cut off, Q_L linear$]$

$$i_D = 0 \tag{15.17a}$$

$$v_{OUT} = V_{DD} \tag{15.17b}$$

Region II: $0 \leq (v_{IN} - V_{TD}) \leq (V_{DD}) + V_{TL}) \leq v_{OUT}$ $\quad [Q_D$ saturated, Q_L linear$]$

$$i_D = K_L\left[-V_{TL} - \frac{(V_{DD} - V_{OUT})}{2}\right](V_{DD} - v_{OUT}) = \frac{K_D}{2}(v_{IN} - V_{TD})^2 \tag{15.18a}$$

v_{OUT}: quadratic function of v_{IN}; concave down (15.18b)

Region III: $0 \leq (v_{IN} - V_{TD}) \leq V_{OUT} \leq +(V_{DD} + V_{TL})$ $\quad [Q_D$ and Q_L saturated$]$

$$i_D = \frac{K_L}{2}V_{TL}^2 = \frac{K_D}{2}(V_{IN} - V_{TD})^2 \tag{15.19a}$$

v_{OUT}: any value from $\sqrt{\dfrac{K_L}{K_D}}|V_{TL}|$ to $(V_{DD} + V_{TL})$ (15.19b)

$$v_{IN} = V_{TD} + \sqrt{\frac{K_L}{K_D}}|V_{TL}| \tag{15.19c}$$

Region IV: $0 \leq v_{OUT} \leq (v_{IN} - V_{TD})$ $\quad [Q_D$ near, Q_L saturated$]$

$$i_D = \frac{K_L}{2}V_{TL}^2 = K_D\left(v_{OUT} - v_{TD} - \frac{v_{OUT}}{2}\right)v_{OUT} \tag{15.20a}$$

v_{OUT}: quadratic function of v_{IN}; concave up (15.20b)

This transfer characteristic is plotted in Fig. 15.11*b* (solid curve) using $V_{DD} = 5$ V, $V_{TD} = 1$ V, $V_{TL} = -1$ V, $K_D = 50\ \mu\text{A/V}^2$, and $K_L = 250\ \mu\text{A/V}^2$. Correspondingly, V_{HI} is 5 V, V_{LO} is approximately 0.7 V, and V_{TR} is approximately 3.2 V. Notice from Eq. (15.19c) that the input voltage at which the curve is vertical in region III (which is also the value of V_{TR}) is determined by the threshold voltages and the ratio of K_L to K_D. We can use this dependence to optimize the noise margins in this logic family.

Region III in this characteristic deserves a bit more discussion. It is vertical according to our simple large-signal model, but in reality it has a finite slant due

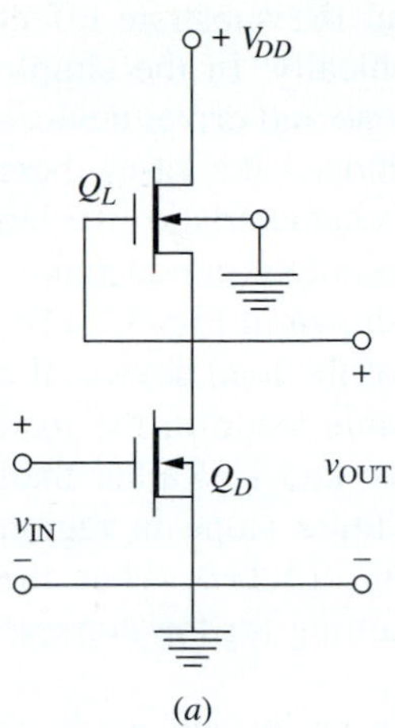

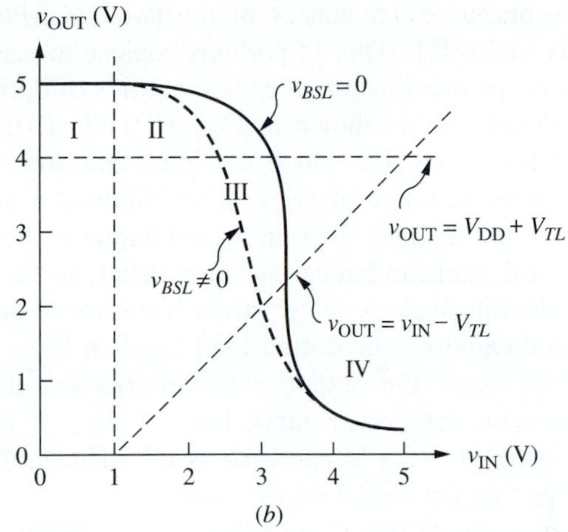

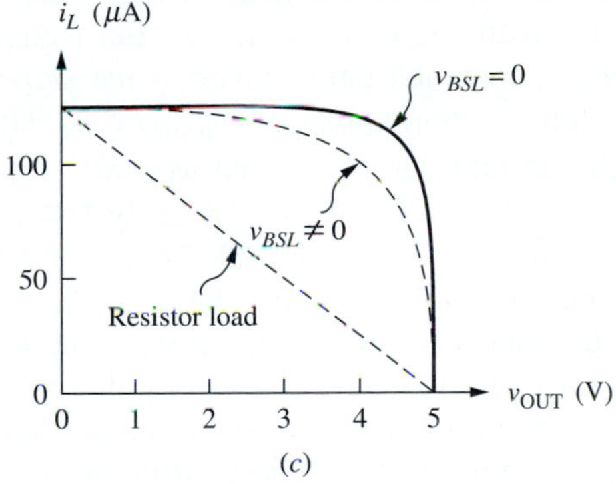

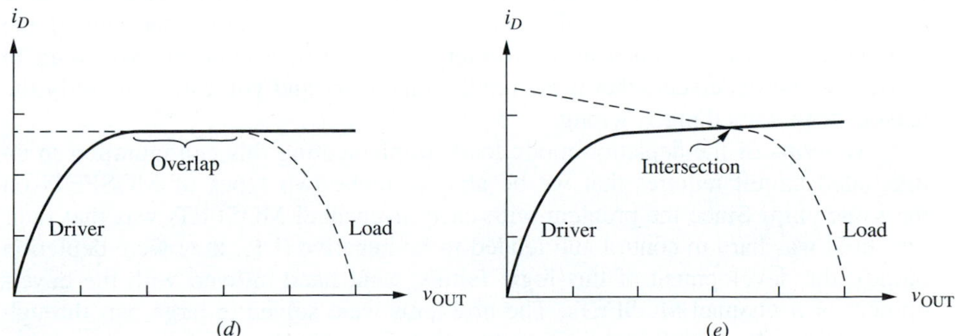

FIGURE 15.11
(*a*) MOSFET inverter stage with an *n*-channel enhancement mode driver and an *n*-channel depletion mode load; (*b*) the static transfer characteristic assuming $V_{DD} = 5$ V, $V_{TD} = 1$ V, $V_{TL} = -1$ V, $K_D = 50\ \mu\text{A/V}^2$, and $K_L = 250\ \mu\text{A/V}^2$; (*c*) the current characteristic of the load; (*d* and *e*) graphical illustration of the construction of the transfer characteristic in the vicinity of the steepest portion for $v_{BSL} = 0$ and $v_{BSL} \neq 0\ (= v_{OUT})$, respectively.

to the finite output conductances of the two MOSFETs and the substrate effect on the load MOSFET. This is perhaps easiest to see graphically. In the simple model we assume that the output characteristics of both the load and driver devices are flat in saturation, as shown in Fig. 15.11*d*. If this is indeed the case, there will be a value of v_{IN} for which the load line and driver characteristic overlap over a considerable range of v_{OUT}. The effect of a nonzero output conductance, however, is to put a slight slope in these characteristics, as shown in Fig. 15.11*e*, so they can still intersect but can never overlap. In the case of the load device, the changing substrate bias as v_{OUT} varies leads to an appreciable slope in the load line, as is indicated by the dotted load lines in Figs. 15.11*c* and *e*. Rather than being vertical, then, the output characteristic will have a finite slope in region III, as shown by the dotted curve labeled $v_{BSL} \neq 0$ in Fig. 15.11*b*. Thus the dotted lines in Figs. 15.17*b* and *c* show the effects of accounting for the nonzero substrate bias v_{BS} $(= v_{\text{OUT}})$ on the load.

We can evaluate this slope using our small-signal models; in fact, we have done so already in Sec. 11.4.1*b*, although we didn't think in such terms there. In Chap. 11, we consider the incremental gain of this same circuit biased at points in regions II and III of this transfer characteristic. Referring back to that discussion we see that the incremental gain, which is the slope, in region III is $-g_{mD}/(g_{oL} + g_{oD} + g_{mbL})$, or approximately $-g_{mD}/g_{mbL}$ since g_{oL} and g_{oD} should be very small. This in turn can be written as $-K_D^{1/2}/\eta K_L^{1/2}$, and in this form we can estimate it. We have $(K_D/K_L)^{1/2}$ roughly 0.4 in the example of Fig. 15.11*b*, so if we assume η is, for example, 0.1, we find a slope of 4. This is a lot less than infinity, and we clearly have to refine our large-signal model to account for the dependence of V_T on v_{BS} if we want to do more accurate modeling of this inverter stage. There is no need to do so for our present purposes, but it is important that you be aware that our simple model has limitations. You should in general be suspicious of any model when it predicts something is either zero or infinity. Another equally important lesson from this discussion is that the incremental and large-signal models must be consistent and must yield the same results. It is OK for one model to predict something the other does not if the relevant effect was included in the former and not in the latter, but you want to recognize and understand that if the predictions differ and you cannot identify the reason, then something is wrong.

In terms of the depletion mode load, implementing this configuration in an integrated circuit requires that we be able to make two types of MOSFETs on the same chip. Since the problem with early *n*-channel MOSFETs was that their threshold was hard to control and tended to be negative (i.e., they were depletion mode), the development of this logic family went hand-in-hand with the development of *n*-channel MOSFETs. The problems were solved in large part through the use of polycrystalline silicon gates (see Fig. 10.10*b*) and the use of ion implantation to control the threshold voltages by adjusting the effective interface charge density Q_{SS}. There was already a big incentive to use *n*-channel rather than *p*-channel MOSFETs since the electron mobility is significantly higher than the hole mobility. This means that, all else being equal, *n*-channel devices have higher gain and are intrinsically faster. Thus since ion implantation was required to make n-channel logic work, there was little technological cost in implanting some devices to make their thresholds positive and leaving the others with negative thresholds. Since previous technologies had used p-channel MOSFETs, this "new" n-channel, depletion-mode-load, silicon-gate MOSFET logic technology was called simply n-MOS, for short.

The big win in n-MOS then is improved speed for comparable power, both because n-channel MOSFETs are used and because the load current stays high until v_{OUT} is very near V_{HI} $(= V_{DD})$, as shown in Fig. 15.11c. Therefore dv_{OUT}/dt stays large over most of the on-to-off transient. With this load we have at last done better than we could with a simple, albeit large, resistor. In the next subsection we see how we can do even better.

15.2.4 Complementary Load: CMOS

A way to improve on the depletion mode load in terms of speed and power, which are the performance factors we tend to focus on since they are the ones that differ from load to load, is to increase the load current above its "on" value I_{ON} during the on-to-off switching transient. This sounds a bit tricky to do at first, but it turns out to be very easy if you use a p-channel enhancement mode MOSFET as the load and connect its gate to that of the driver and thus also to v_{IN}, as illustrated in Fig. 15.12a. Now when v_{IN} is v_{HI} and what we have been calling the driver is "on," the load MOSFET is off, so I_{ON} is zero. Thus P_{ON} is zero, and since P_{OFF} is also zero, power is dissipated in this inverter only during switching.

During the on-off switching cycle the driver is turned off, but the load is turned on and its load characteristic looks exactly like that of the depletion mode load. By sizing the devices so that $K_L = K_D$ and $V_{TL} = -V_{TD}$, the two switching transients, on-to-off and off-to-on, can be made equally fast. It becomes a bit academic to distinguish between the driver and the load devices in such a symmetric situation.

The static transfer characteristic now has five regions; deriving it is thus tedious but still very straightforward. For completeness we will enumerate this multitude of regions here, but your attention is called especially to regions III and V (we will discuss these two regions somewhat later below):

Region I: $(v_{\text{IN}} - V_{TN}) \le 0 \le v_{\text{OUT}}$ $[Q_n$ cut off$]$

$(v_{\text{IN}} - V_{DD} - V_{TP}) \le (v_{\text{OUT}} - V_{DD}) \le 0$ $[Q_p$ linear$]$

$$i_D = 0 \tag{15.21a}$$

$$v_{\text{OUT}} = V_{DD} \tag{15.21b}$$

Region II: $0 \le (v_{\text{IN}} - V_{TN}) \le v_{\text{OUT}}$ $[Q_n$ saturated$]$

$(v_{\text{IN}} - V_{DD} - V_{TP}) \le (v_{\text{OUT}} - V_{DD}) \le 0$ $[Q_p$ linear$]$

$$i_D = \frac{K_N}{2}(v_{\text{IN}} - V_{TN})^2 \tag{15.22a}$$

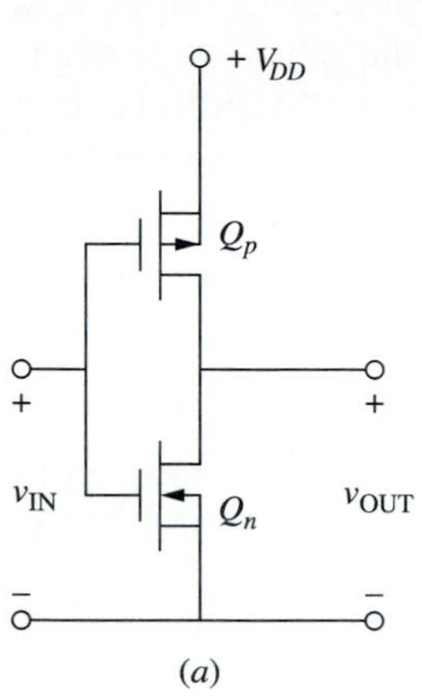

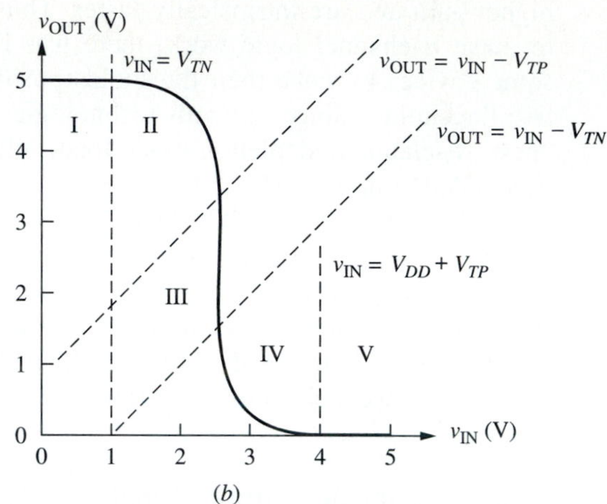

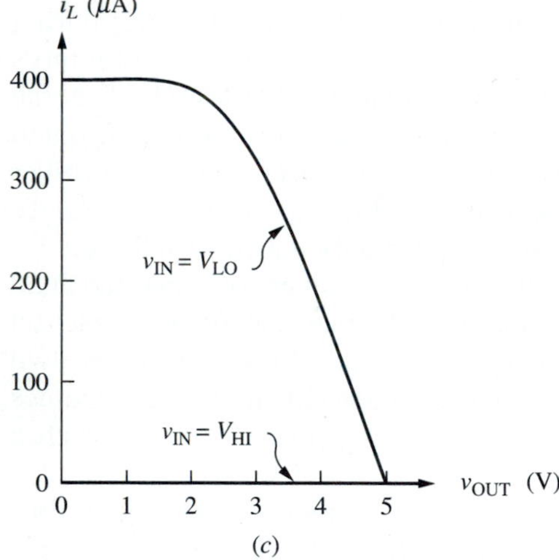

FIGURE 15.12
(*a*) MOSFET inverter stage with an *n*-channel enhancement mode driver and a *p*-channel enhancement mode load (this inverter with its complementary pair of MOSFETs is called CMOS); (*b*) the static transfer characteristic assuming $V_{DD} = 5$ V, $V_{TN} = 1$ V, $V_{TP} = -1$ V, and $K_N = K_P = 50\ \mu\text{A/V}^2$. (*c*) the current supplied to the following stage through Q_P as a function of v_{OUT} for two values of v_{IN}.

$$= K_P\left[v_{IN} - v_{DD} - V_{TP} - \frac{(v_{OUT} - V_{DD})}{2}\right](v_{OUT} - V_{DD})$$

v_{OUT} : quadratic function of v_{IN}; concave down (15.22b)

Region III: $0 \leq (v_{IN} - V_{TN}) \leq v_{OUT}$ [Q_n saturated]

$(v_{OUT} - V_{DD}) \leq (v_{IN} - V_{DD} - V_{TP}) \leq 0$ [Q_p saturated]

$$i_D = \frac{K_N}{2}(v_{IN} - V_{TN})^2 = \frac{K_N}{2}(v_{IN} - V_{DD} - V_{TP})^2 \tag{15.23a}$$

$$v_{IN} = \frac{\sqrt{K_P}(V_{DD} - V_{TP}) + \sqrt{K_N}V_{TN}}{\sqrt{K_P} + \sqrt{K_N}} \tag{15.23b}$$

$(= V_{DD}/2$ if $V_{TP} = -V_{TN}$ and $K_p = K_N)$

v_{OUT} : any value between $(v_{IN} - V_{TN})$ and $(v_{IN} - V_{TP})$ (15.23c)

Region IV: $0 \leq v_{OUT}(v_{IN} - V_{TN})$ [Q_n linear]

$(v_{OUT} - V_{DD}) \leq (v_{IN} - V_{DD} - V_{TP}) \leq 0$ [Q_p saturated]

$$i_D = K_N\left(v_{IN} - V_{TN} - \frac{v_{OUT}}{2}\right)v_{OUT} = \frac{K_P}{2}(v_{IN} - V_{DD} - V_{TP})^2 \tag{15.24a}$$

v_{OUT} : quadratic function of v_{IN}; concave up (15.24b)

Region V: $0 \leq v_{OUT} \leq (v_{IN} - V_{TN})$ [Q_n linear]

$(v_{OUT} - V_{DD}) \leq 0 \leq (v_{IN} - V_{DD} - V_{TP})$ [Q_p cut off]

$$i_D = 0 \tag{15.25a}$$

$$v_{OUT} = 0 \tag{15.25b}$$

The transfer characteristic is illustrated in Fig. 15.12*b* for a CMOS gate for which $V_{DD} = 5$ V, $V_{TN} = 1$ V, $V_{TP} = -1$ V, and $K_N = K_P = 50\ \mu A/V^2$. For this gate V_{LO} is 0 V, V_{HI} is 5 V, V_{TR} is 2.5 V, and the curve is very steep, characteristics you will recognize (based on our discussion in Sec. 15.1.3) as extremely attractive for a good noise margin. Notice, however, that achieving such a symmetrical transfer characteristic requires that we have K_N and K_P equal and that the threshold voltages have the same magnitude.

Region V is of interest because there, as well as in region I, one of the MOSFETs is cut off, so V_{LO} goes all the way to zero just as V_{HI} increases to V_{DD}. That is, the voltage swings through the entire available range.

Region III is of interest because the simple large models predict that it will be vertical. As was the case with the depletion mode load, however, we know that it isn't truly vertical because of the finite output conductance of any real MOSFETs. (There is no substrate effect in this inverter because we can short both substrates to the respective source.) Doing a small-signal analysis of this inverter for a bias point in region III yields a voltage gain of $-2_{gm}/(g_{oN} + g_{oP})$. This is also the slope of the transfer characteristic in this region, and although it is not infinite, it clearly is indeed very large, unlike what we found to be true for the depletion mode load inverter. The secret is being able to keep the substrate bias v_{BS} from changing with v_{OUT}; in this family it is zero on both devices.

To make multiple-input gates in this inverter family we have to add both driver and load devices. To make an n-input NAND gate, for example, we put n n-channel MOSFETs in parallel, as in Fig. 15.4*d*, and n p-channel MOSFETs in series. To make NOR gates the n-MOSFETs are in series and the p-MOSFETs in parallel. In all cases the gates of the n- and p-channel devices are connected in pairs for each input.

This inverter family is called *CMOS*, for *complementary-MOS*; the term complementary comes from the use of both n- and p-channel enhancement mode devices. Simultaneously producing both n- and p-channel MOSFETs on the same silicon substrate (an example is pictured in Fig. 11.17 and the process is discussed in Appendix G) requires much more additional processing but is well worth the effort in many situations. The main reason is that the static power is zero in CMOS and power is dissipated only during switching. Referring to Eq. (15.6), we find that for CMOS we have

$$P_{\text{ave}} = f_{\text{CLOCK}} E_{\text{CYCLE}} = f_{\text{CLOCK}} C_L V_{DD}^2 \tag{15.26}$$

where to obtain the last expression we have assumed that the charge store on the output node can be modeled as an ideal linear capacitor C_L. The power-delay product is thus simply $C_L V_{DD}^2$, a result that shows clearly the advantage of reducing the power supply voltage.

CMOS is, like n-MOS, a potentially very fast technology; both have been used in very fast MOS logic circuits. At the same time, however, the fact that the static power dissipation in CMOS circuits is negligible has led to their application in many relatively slow circuits. Many devices that do not require blinding speed, such as simple pocket calculators and wristwatches, use CMOS for its low power requirements.

15.3 BIPOLAR INVERTERS

The bipolar junction transistor is distinctly different from the MOSFET, and these differences have led, as we shall see, to different solutions to the challenges of inverter design. On the one hand, BJTs operate at higher current levels than MOSFETs, which has made it possible to design bipolar inverter families that operate at speeds well beyond what has been achieved with MOSFETs. At the same time, however, BJTs do not have an infinite input resistance like a MOSFET, and their operation can involve large charge stores. These "problems" tend to complicate BJT inverter design and lead to relatively more complex inverter circuits than those used with MOSFETs. Consequently bipolar logic tends to be applied where high speed is essential and worth the cost in complexity and power that must be paid to use BJTs. It is also being used increasingly in combination with MOSFETs, using one of a number of BiMOS processes designed to integrate MOS and bipolar devices on the same integrated-circuit chip. In these circuits each device can be used where it functions best: the MOSFETs for the bulk of the computation and memory, and the bipolar to provide the high currents necessary to interface with the off-chip world.

In the following subsections we will take a first look at bipolar transistor inverter designs. We begin with a simple bipolar inverter built around resistors and a single transistor switch. After analyzing this circuit and considering its limitations, we study its evolution into higher-performance transistor-transistor logic, TTL. Finally, we look briefly at still more advanced bipolar logic families.

15.3.1 The Simple Bipolar Inverter

The simplest bipolar inverter you might imagine is a single BJT used as a switch and a resistor load like the circuit illustrated in Fig. 15.13*a*. This circuit is analogous to the MOSFET inverter with a resistor load pictured in Fig. 15.8. A little thought about this circuit, however, shows that it will draw an excessive amount of current from the stage preceding it. That is, there is very little to limit the current when the input is high. This loading clearly also affects the "high" voltage level, limiting it to on the order of 0.6 V. Although logic operations could be performed using such an inverter, the voltage swings and noise margins are very low and get worse with increasing fan-out. Furthermore, the power requirements are excessive, and the circuit is simply not attractive. We immediately see that the low input resistance of a BJT necessitates a more complicated response.

To limit the input current a simple "fix" is to add a resistor in series with the base, as illustrated in Fig. 15.13*b*. This circuit now is much less power-

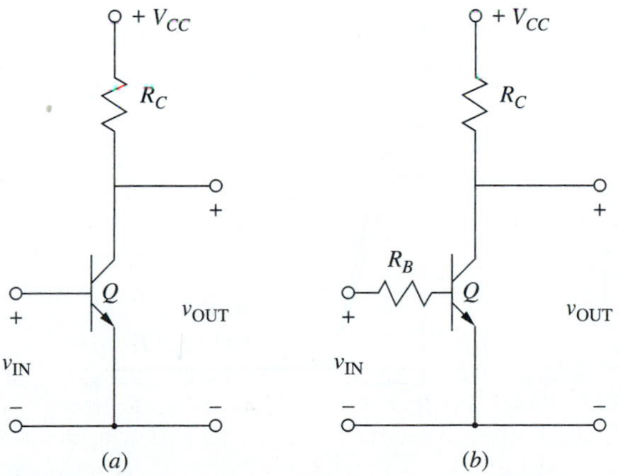

FIGURE 15.13
Simple bipolar inverters: (*a*) a single BJT used as a switch with a resistor load; (*b*) the same circuit with a resistor added to the base circuit to limit the loading on the preceding stage and to increase the output voltage swing. (The latter circuit is the basic building block for resistor-transistor logic, RTL.)

hungry and has reasonable high and low voltage levels. To calculate the transfer characteristic we need to take into account the loading from the succeeding stage since it does draw current through the load, unlike the situation in a MOSFET inverter. Thus we want to calculate v_{OUT} versus v_{IN} for the circuit as modeled in Fig. 15.14*a*, where we have used the simplified piecewise-linear breakpoint model instead of the full Ebers–Moll model. Notice that we have assumed that the output is fanning out to n similar stages, so the effective resistance seen at the output is R_B/n.

The breakpoints of the various diodes in Fig. 15.14*a* define regions in the transfer characteristics, and we can write expressions relating v_{OUT} and v_{IN} in each. For example, when v_{IN} is less than 0.6 V the transistor is off and v_{OUT} is constant and equal to $[0.6 + (V_{CC} - 0.6)R_B/(R_B + nR_C)]$. For v_{IN} greater than 0.6 V, i_B is $(v_{IN} - 0.6)/R_B$. The value of v_{OUT} will then be given by $[R_B V_{CC} + 0.6\, R_C(\beta_F + n) - \beta_F R_C v_{IN}]/(R_B + nR_C)$, so long as it is greater than 0.6 V. When v_{OUT} drops below 0.6 V the transistors in the following stages turn off and v_{OUT} becomes $[V_{CC} - \beta_F(v_{IN} - 0.6)R_C/R_B]$ and continues to drop until it reaches 0.2 V, at which point it remains constant at this value. In this region, of course, the transistor is in saturation. These transfer characteristics are plotted in Fig. 15.14*b* for an inverter for which $V_{CC} = 5$ V, $R_B = 10$ kΩ, $R_C = 1$ kΩ, and $\beta_F = 50$, and for fan-outs of 1 and 4.

This simple *resistor-transistor logic* (RTL) inverter stage has limitations that led designers to look for alternatives. First, it uses large-value resistors, which

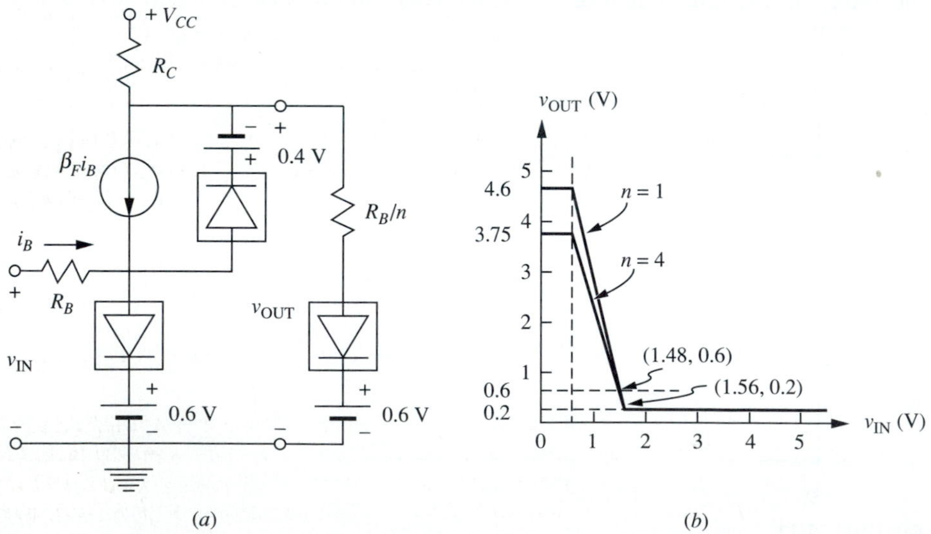

FIGURE 15.14
(*a*) Resistor-transistor logic circuit of Fig. 15.13*b* modeled using the breakpoint diode approximation to the Ebers–Moll model; (*b*) the static transfer characteristic calculated with this model and $V_{DD} = 5$ V, $R_B = 10$ kΩ, $R_C = 1$ kΩ, and $\beta_F = 50$ (characteristics are shown for fan-outs of 1 and 4).

are always a concern with integrated circuits. Second, it is sensitive to fan-out and fan-in of the following stages (though we didn't look at fan-in here).* Finally, this circuit is slowed by the fact that the transistor gets driven into saturation. To switch the transistor off, this excess charge must be removed through R_B, and the *RC* time constant associated with this path can be large. One solution to this problem has been to replace the current-limiting resistors in the base (i.e., the R_B resistors) with other elements, in particular diodes and transistors. We shall consider this course of action next.

15.3.2 Transistor-Transistor Logic: TTL

The main problem with the very simple bipolar inverter pictured in Fig. 15.13*a* is that it draws a large current from the preceding stage and pins the output voltage at a low value. Adding a base resistor solves these problems but is not a totally satisfactory solution, as we have just seen. Another approach is to supply the current from the main power supply and within the stage itself, and then to use the input to send it into the base when v_{IN} is high or shunt it to ground when v_{IN} is low. The concept is illustrated in Fig. 15.15*a*. A problem with this idea, however, is that it still pins the input at a very low upper bound (i.e., approximately 0.6 V) since the input is still not buffered from the base of the switch transistor.

A way to provide the needed buffering is to use a diode at the input, as illustrated in Fig. 15.15*b*. Now when the input is "high," the input diode is reverse-biased and there is no loading of the preceding stage. When the input is low, the current source is no longer shunted to ground but is held 0.6 V above ground by the forward drop of the input diode. This is not low enough to turn the transistor off, however, so a second diode must be added in series with the switch transistor base to ensure that the switch transistor is indeed not turned on.

In practice, we do not need to go to the complication of using a true current source in this stage, but can more easily use a resistor as shown in Fig. 15.15*c*. This inverter forms the basis for what is called *diode-transistor logic*, (DTL) and was widely used for discrete component logic.

The problem with the DTL inverter in Fig. 15.15*c* appears when we try to turn off the switching transistor, bringing it out of saturation and into cutoff. To do this, the excess charge in the base and collector regions of the device has to be removed, and in this circuit this charge cannot be pulled out of the base because the diode connected to the base node blocks current flow out of the base. The solution is to replace the back-to-back diodes pictured in Fig. 15.15*c* with an *npn* transistor as shown in Fig. 15.15*d*. When the input is high the circuit behaves pretty much as it did before. It now does load the preceding stages a little bit

*This statement assumes that multiple-input gates are formed by adding more input resistors connected in parallel to the base of a single switching transistor, as opposed to by adding additional switching transistors as was done in Fig. 15.4.

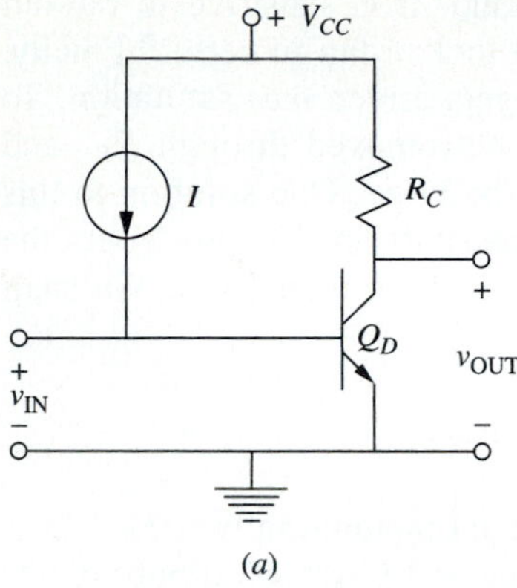

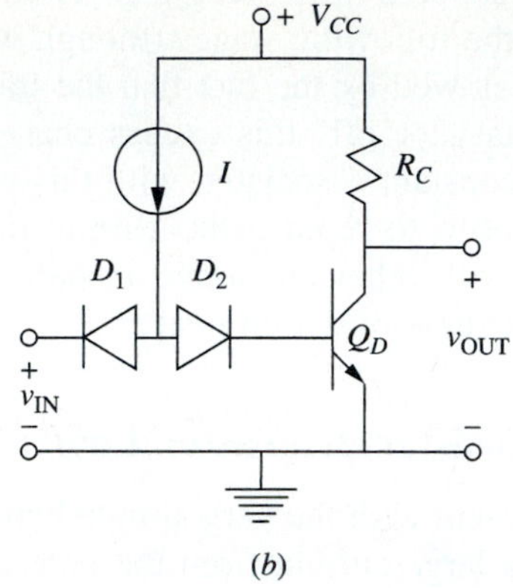

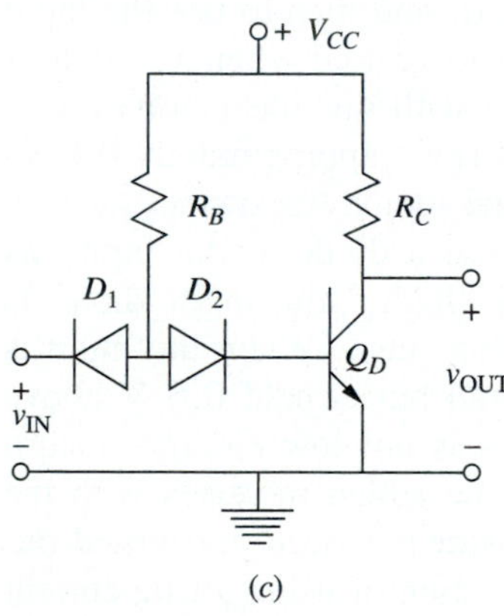

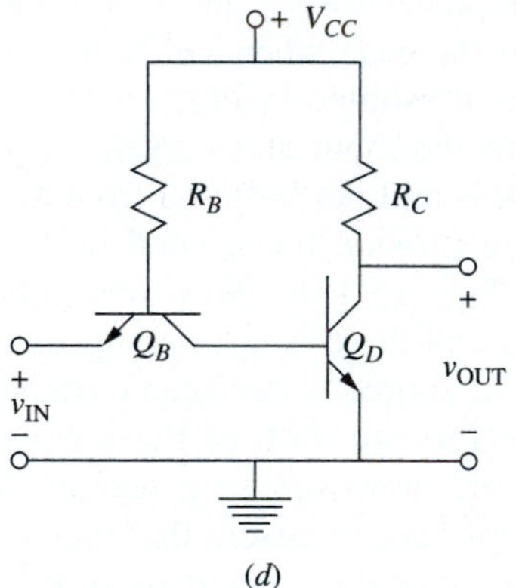

FIGURE 15.15
(*a*) Simple bipolar inverter with an integral current source to reduce the input loading but with inadequate isolation or buffering at the input to achieve a large voltage level swing; (*b*) the circuit of (*a*) modified by adding diodes to isolate the input terminal from the base-emitter junction and thereby achieve the sought-after reduced loading and to allow for a larger input voltage swing; (*c*) the circuit of (*b*) with the current source replaced by a resistor; (*d*) the circuit of (*c*) with a transistor replacing the back-to-back diodes.

because the transistor Q_B is in its reverse active region and β_R is not zero, but this is a small effect. The real change occurs during the switching cycle when $v_{\rm IN}$ suddenly becomes low. Q_B is then operating in its forward active region and actually draws current out of the base of Q_D; this results in a much shorter on-off switching time.

The inverter concept pictured in Fig. 15.15*d* is the basis for transistor-transistor logic (TTL). Numerous refinements and tweaks in this basic structure have been developed over the years, and there are actually many flavors of TTL optimized for particular applications: low-power/low-speed, high-power/high-speed, etc. We will focus our attention on the two-input TTL gate illustrated in Fig. 15.16*a*.

To help you understand this circuit a similar DTL gate is shown in Fig. 15.16*b*. Looking first at the DTL circuit and comparing it to the DTL inverter in Fig. 15.15*c*, we see that an additional diode has been added in series with the base terminal of Q_D to increase the noise margin for a low input; that is, now Q_D will not begin to turn on until the input exceeds 1.2 V rather than 0.6 V.

Returning to the TTL gate in Fig. 15.16*a* we see that the added diode in Fig. 15.16*b* becomes another transistor Q_D in a Darlington connection with Q_S in the TTL gate. This additional transistor helps buffer the input and increases the noise margin. It does block Q_B from pulling the stored charge out of the base of Q_S (Q_B now pulls charge out of Q_D), but the resistor R_E can be small enough that Q_S can discharge quickly through it to ground during the on-off switching cycle.

Another new feature of this TTL gate is the use of the transistor Q_L in the output circuit. This output combination, Q_L and Q_S, is called a "totem-pole" connection; it functions similarly to a push-pull output stage (see Sec. 13.2.5) and is analogous to the use of a depletion mode load in *n*-MOS or a *p*-channel load in CMOS. When the output switches from low to high, the current needed to charge up the output node (i.e., mainly the input capacitances of the following stages) is supplied through Q_L, rather than R_C as before. Q_L supplies a larger, constant current, much like the depletion mode in the *n*-MOS, for example, and this reduces the on-off switching time. When the output switches from high to low, the load is discharged through Q_S.

Finally, note that the circuit in Fig. 15.16*a* is a two-input gate rather than a simple inverter. What is interesting is that multiple inputs are achieved by adding emitters to Q_B. Pulling any one emitter low turns Q_B on and results in a high output; thus logically this is a NAND gate. Structurally adding another emitter involves simply enlarging the area of the base region and placing the added emitter within it. It involves no additional processing.

Another thing we can do without additional processing is to add diodes to the circuit that keep the transistors in the gate from going into saturation. This change has a major impact on the switching speeds because it eliminates the largest charge stores. To prevent saturation we do what is called *clamping*: very simply, a diode with a low turn-on voltage and small diffusion capacitance is placed in parallel

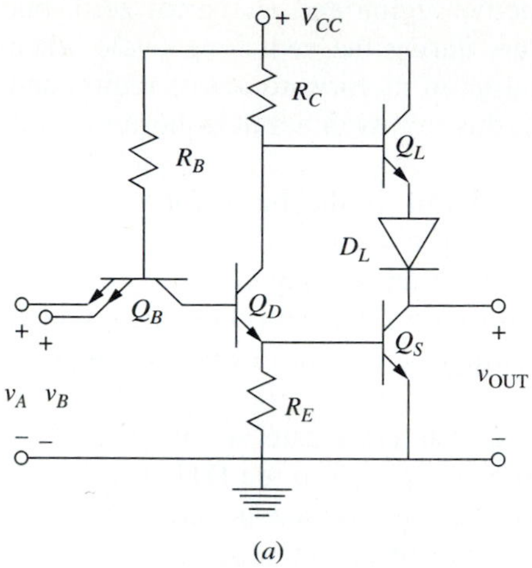

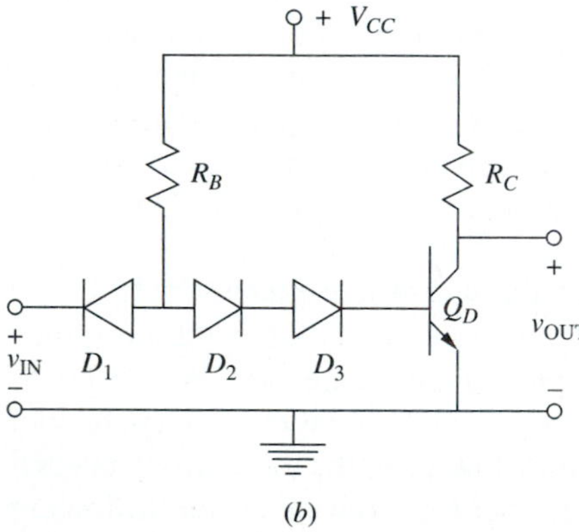

FIGURE 15.16
(*a*) Two-input TTL NAND/AND gate with a second stage of input buffering and a totem-pole output stage; (*b*) similar DTL stage to indicate the role of the additional diode drop at the input in increasing the turn-on and trigger voltages.

with the base-collector junction. When that junction is reverse-biased, as it is in the forward active region or cutoff, the reverse-biased clamping diode has no impact on the operation of the gate. When the base-collector junction is forward-biased, however, the clamping diode turns on and diverts the current away from the transistor junction. Very little, if any, flows across the base-collector junction, and there is no excess charge stored in the transistor. If the clamping diode has much less excess charge storage at a given current level than would the transistor, we gain a large speed advantage.

Fortunately it is very easy to make a diode that meets the two criteria we have set for the clamping diode (i.e., low turn-on voltage and small charge storage) simply by making metal contact on the lightly doped collector region. Recall from our discussion of contacts to n- and p-type silicon in Sec. 6.4 that we said it was necessary to heavily dope the n-region next to the contact in order to get a good ohmic contact. If we do not do this, we get a contact with a nonlinear current-voltage characteristic, and if the n-region is lightly doped, as it is in the typical collector, the characteristic is actually that of a very good diode. Furthermore this diode has a relatively low turn-on voltage, and when it is forward-biased all of the current flow is comprised of carriers flowing from the semiconductor to the metal (i.e., there is negligible minority carrier injection into the semiconductor). Such a diode, called a Schottky diode, is an ideal clamp and is easily implemented. The concept of a Schottky clamp and its realization are illustrated in Fig. E.6 in Appendix E. (Appendix E discusses metal-semiconductor diodes in detail; you do not need to read it in order to understand the Schottky clamp and Fig. E.6, but you may find it interesting.)

With the introduction of the Schottky clamp and TTL circuits that do not saturate, it has even been feasible in some designs to return to diode-transistor logic for some portions of more complex gates. As you should recall, our main argument for TTL over DTL was that in DTL we could not pull charge out of the base of the saturated switch transistor. With the need to do so eliminated, this drawback of DTL disappears as well.

15.3.3 Emitter-Coupled Logic: ECL

Another very successful way to use bipolar transistors for binary logic is to build upon the transfer characteristic of the emitter-coupled pair. This characteristic, which we calculated in Sec. 12.2.1 and displayed in Fig. 12.4, certainly has the right shape and is in fact very sharp, being only a few kT/q wide. More significantly, it turns out to be possible, as we shall see, to design logic inverters based on the emitter-coupled pair in which the transistors do not saturate and thus are very fast. Furthermore, we can obtain both an output and its inverse from the same gate. This logic type is called *emitter-coupled logic*, or ECL.

An illustrative ECL inverter is shown in Fig. 15.17. The input is applied to one of the transistors, Q_1, of the emitter-coupled pair, and a reference voltage V_{REF} is applied to the base of the other, Q_2. V_{REF} is typically chosen to be midway between V_{LO} and V_{HI}; that is,

$$V_{REF} = \frac{(V_{HI} + V_{LO})}{2} \tag{15.27}$$

The output is taken via an emitter-follower, Q_3, from either the collector of Q_1 if the inverted output is desired or Q_2 if the noninverted output is sought.

To understand the operation and design of this inverter, consider first applying V_{LO} to the input, in which case Q_1 is to be off and Q_2 should be on.

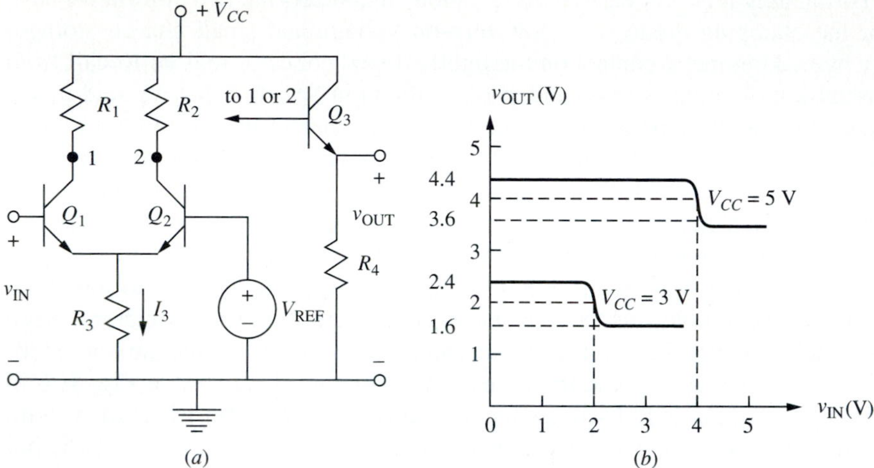

FIGURE 15.17
(*a*) Basic emitter-coupled logic inverter (the circuitry supplying the reference voltage V_{REF} to the base of Q_2 is not shown); (*b*) the transfer characteristics of this inverter for values of V_{CC} of 3 and 5 V and a logic swing of 0.8 V.

Assuming that this is indeed the case, we see that node 1 is at V_{CC} and that v_{OUT} is $V_{CC} - 0.6$ V. This output voltage must be V_{HI}, so we have

$$V_{HI} = V_{CC} - 0.6 \tag{15.28}$$

We can also find an expression for the voltage on node 2, which must be $V_{LO} + 0.6$ V. The current through R_3, which we label i_3, is $(V_{REF} - 0.6)/R_3$, so the voltage on node 2 is also $V_{CC} - R_2(V_{REF} - 0.6)/R_3$. Equating these two expressions gives us an expression for the ratio R_2/R_3, that is,

$$\frac{R_2}{R_3} = \frac{(V_{CC} - V_{LO} - 0.6)}{(V_{REF} - 0.6)} \tag{15.29a}$$

which, using Eqs. (15.27) and (15.28), can also be written as

$$\frac{R_2}{R_3} = \frac{2\,(V_{HI} - V_{LO})}{(V_{HI} + V_{LO} - 1.2)} \tag{15.29b}$$

Next consider applying V_{HI} to the input, which should turn Q_1 on and Q_2 off. With Q_1 on, the voltage on node 1 should be $V_{LO} + 0.6$. We can also write the voltage on this node as $V_{CC} - R_1 i_3$, where i_3 is not $(V_{HI} - 0.6)/R_3$. Combining these expressions we find that

$$V_{LO} + 0.6 = V_{CC} - \frac{R_1}{R_3}(V_{HI} - 0.6) \tag{15.30a}$$

Using Eq. (15.28) and rearranging terms, this becomes

$$\frac{R_1}{R_3} = \frac{(V_{HI} - V_{LO})}{(V_{HI} - 0.6)} \tag{15.30b}$$

To complete our compilation of design equations, we finally note that bounds are placed on the voltage swing ($V_{HI} - V_{LO}$). For example, we do not want Q_1 to be saturated when v_{IN} is V_{HI} and Q_1 is on, so we must have the voltage on node 1, which is then $V_{LO} + 0.6$ V, no less than $V_{HI} - 0.4$ V. Thus we must have

$$V_{HI} - (V_{LO} + 0.6) \leq 0.4 \tag{15.31a}$$

which tells us that

$$(V_{HI} - V_{LO}) \leq 1.0 \tag{15.31b}$$

Similarly, we assume that Q_1 is off when v_{IN} is V_{LO} and that Q_2 is off when v_{IN} is V_{HI}. If we assume that Q_1 and Q_2 will be off when their emitter-base voltages are less than 0.4 V, we find that V_{REF} must fall within the following bounds:

$$V_{LO} + 0.2 \leq V_{REF} \leq V_{HI} - 0.2 \tag{15.32}$$

Combining this result with Eq. (15.27) gives us a lower bound on the voltage swing, namely

$$(V_{HI} - V_{LO}) \leq 0.4 \tag{15.33}$$

Combining this result with Eq. (15.31b), we find that ($V_{HI} - V_{LO}$) is bounded as follows:

$$0.4 \leq (V_{HI} - V_{LO}) \leq 1.0 \tag{15.34}$$

It makes sense to choose the swing to be on the high side, and a typical value is 0.8 V. Once we make this choice and decide on the value of the supply voltage V_{CC}, we can use Eqs. (15.28) through (15.30) to calculate the resistor values and determine the voltages.

Example

Question. Suppose that we have $V_{CC} = 5$ V and $V_{HI} - V_{LO} = 0.8$ V. What will V_{HI}, V_{LO}, and V_{REF} be, and what values should R_1, R_2, and R_3 have? How do these values change if $V_{CC} = 3$ V?

Discussion. Calculating the voltages, we find $V_{LO} = 3.6$ V, $V_{HI} = 4.4$ V, and $V_{REF} = 4.0$ V. From Eqs. (15.29b) and (15.30b), for the resistor ratios we find that $R_1/R_3 = 0.21$ and $R_2/R_3 = 0.235$. Thus if R_3 is 1 kΩ, for example, R_1 must be 210 Ω, and R_2 must be 235 Ω.

With $V_{CC} = 3$ V, we find $V_{LO} = 1.6$ V, $V_{HI} = 2.4$ V, and $V_{REF} = 2.0$ V. The resistor ratios are now $R_1/R_3 = 0.445$ and $R_2/R_3 = 0.57$. With $R_3 = 1$ kΩ, we find $R_1 = 445$ Ω and $R_2 = 570$ Ω. We thus see that we can still design an inverter that gives the same magnitude of voltage swing with a lower voltage supply; this is important because it will reduce the power dissipation significantly.

The transfer characteristics of the ECL gate we have just analyzed for the conditions corresponding to the above example are plotted in Fig. 15.17*b*. Plots for supply voltages V_{CC}, of both 3 and 5 V are presented. In making these sketches (and they are just that—sketches) it was assumed that the emitter-base diodes start to conduct at a forward bias of 0.4 V and are completely on at a forward voltage of 0.6 V. The voltage swing in ECL is considerably smaller than it has been for the other logic gates we have investigated, but the transfer characteristic is also sharper. For this reason, and because this is largely a current-controlled gate, the noise stability of ECL is actually very good in spite of its relatively small voltage noise margins.

To create a multiple-input ECL gate, we can place additional input transistors in parallel with Q_1, in the spirit of Fig. 15.4*d*. Since we can get both the inverted and noninverted outputs from a single stage, such a gate can simultaneously provide both the NOR and OR of the inputs. To achieve the NAND and AND functions in ECL we have to duplicate the entire emitter-coupled pair for each input and connect their outputs together at the input to Q_3, which then in effect performs the logic operation.

In an actual ECL gate, V_{REF} will be obtained from the main voltage supply V_{CC} through a resistive voltage divider and buffer transistor. A single such reference circuit may be used to supply a V_{REF} signal to several gates on a single chip or in an integrated circuit. Typically, a −5.2-V supply is used to power ECL gates. Using a negative supply simply means that the terminal marked V_{CC} in Fig. 15.17 is actually grounded; the grounded terminal in this figure is connected to the negative supply.

Because it realizes nonsaturating bipolar logic in a relatively simple and extremely fast circuit configuration, ECL has become the dominant bipolar logic family. It has been realized in compound semiconductors such as gallium arsenide, as well as in silicon, and is the benchmark against which competing high-speed technologies are measured.

15.4 MEMORY CELLS

The *memory cell* is the basic building block for a semiconductor memory in much the same way that an inverter is the basic building block for semiconductor logic. Memory cells can themselves also be built up from inverters, as we shall see below, but because they are such a specialized and important element, many memory cell designs have been developed and optimized for their own sake, often largely independently of inverter designs (independently, that is, except for issues relating to the problems of interfacing between logic and memory). In the following two subsections we will first look at memory cells that derive directly from inverter concepts and represent what is called static, but volatile, memory. We will also look briefly at cells that qualify as nonvolatile static memory cells. Finally, we will look at dynamic memory cells; these cells do not derive directly from inverter designs but are, of course, fabricated on the same chip with inverter-based logic circuitry and thus are fabricated simultaneously with the inverters and using the same process technology.

In general, any memory cell is designed to be used in a two-dimensional array of cells arranged in rows and columns. Thus, in addition to how a cell stores information, an equally important part of any cell design is the way in which that cell is selected from or identified in the array for purposes of either writing information (i.e., a 1 or a 0) into it or reading information out of it. The objective is to have a design in which a signal applied to one row of the array and another signal applied to one column of the array will access the cell at the intersection of the chosen row and column and will not affect any other cell in the array. We shall see examples of how this is done as we look at specific cells shortly.

Because memory cells are employed in large arrays, two obvious objectives in their design are (1) making them as small as possible and (2) reducing the power dissipation in each cell to a minimum. We will want to keep these objectives in mind as we look at different approaches to memory in the following subsections.

15.4.1 Static Memory Cells

By *static memory* we mean a memory that retains its information indefinitely, but by indefinitely we don't mean forever; we distinguish between two types of static memory: *volatile* and *nonvolatile*. Volatile memory loses its information if the power supply is removed; the information in a sense evaporates. Nonvolatile memory does not lose its information when it is unpowered. We will discuss examples of each in turn.

a) Volatile static memory cells. The ring connection of two inverters in Fig. 15.1*c* constitutes a memory cell called a *flip-flop*. Such a ring, or flip-flop, has two states: the first inverter on and the second off, or the first inverter off and the second on. The flip-flop will stay in whichever condition it is placed indefinitely, which is why we can call it *static*, unless the power supply is removed, which is why it is also volatile.

An example of an *n*-MOS flip-flop is shown in Fig. 15.18*a*, and an entire *n*-MOS static memory cell including the addressing MOSFETs is shown in Fig. 15.18*b*. The operation of the basic flip-flop should be obvious to you based on our discussions in Sec. 15.2.3. The flip-flop is addressed and accessed through additional enhancement mode MOSFETs used in essentially a common-gate mode to either sense, or "read," the state of the flip-flop or to actually change the state of the flip-flop, if necessary, when writing information into the memory cell.

The row-select line is normally maintained at a voltage below the enhancement mode MOSFET threshold V_{Te}, so Q_5 and Q_6 are not on when the appropriate row-select line is not activated. To access a row, the row-select line voltage is raised to V_{DD}, turning Q_5 and Q_6 on. The column read/write select lines, when not activated, are maintained at a standby voltage V_{REST}, intermediate between V_{HI} and V_{LO}. V_{REST} is selected, and Q_5 and Q_6 are sized so that their conductance is small enough that turning them on in this condition does not affect the state of the flip-flop. Thus if, for example, Q_1 is on and Q_2 is off, closing Q_5 must not

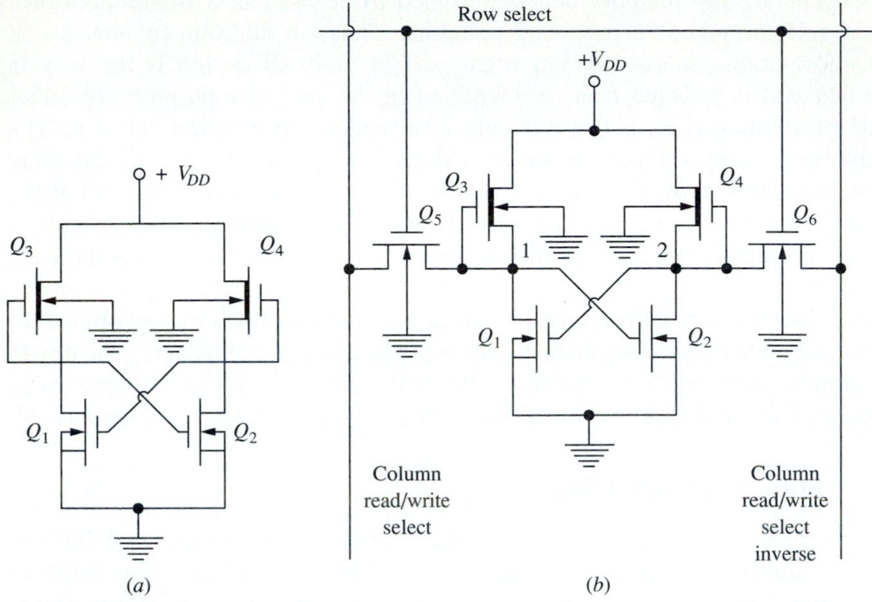

FIGURE 15.18
(*a*) *n*-MOS flip-flop; (*b*) an *n*-MOS static memory cell built around a flip-flop and including row and column read and write access circuitry.

cause node 1 to rise above V_{Te} and closing Q_6 must not cause node 2 to drop below V_{Te}. The latter will not occur because node 2 will clearly fall somewhere between V_{REST} and V_{DD} (both of which will be greater than V_{Te}) assuming that Q_2 stays off, but node 1 can rise above V_{Te} if too much current flows into this node through Q_5. For this reason, the *K*-factor of Q_5 (and Q_6) must be smaller than that of Q_1 and Q_2, and V_{REST} cannot be too high. (We will find additional constraints on these quantities below.)

To read the state of a particular cell in the selected row, the appropriate column lines are disconnected from V_{REST} and are allowed to assume the voltages of the corresponding nodes 1 and 2 of the cell. By sensing the voltage difference between the two lines, we can determine whether node 1 or 2 is higher, and thus whether a zero or a one is stored in the cell.

To write data into the flip-flop, one of the column lines is lowered to ground while the other is maintained at V_{REST}. For the sake of discussion, suppose the column line connected to Q_5 is grounded. The intent is that this will force node 1 below V_{Te}, turning Q_2 off, which in turn will turn Q_1 on. When the column line is returned to V_{REST}, the flip-flop remains in the selected state. For this sequence to work, however, the conductance of Q_5 must be sufficient that the voltage on node 1 drops below V_{Te}; this requirement places another restriction on the *K*-factor of Q_5 (and Q_6) and on V_{REST}. We will not go through the mathematics required to determine a self-consistent set of *K*-factors and value for V_{REST}, but doing so involves only a straightforward, albeit tedious, application of our large-signal MOSFET model and considerable algebra.

b) Nonvolatile static memory cells. It has not proven practical to date to produce nonvolatile memory cells into which data can be written rapidly. That is, it has not been possible to find a method of storing information in a semiconductor memory cell in which the state can be changed easily and quickly if so desired and that will also retain its state information if power is lost (i.e., a cell that is nonvolatile). The best that has been achieved with nonvolatile cells is to create cells whose state can be changed relatively slowly and with considerable effort, so they are best used in situations where they are for the most part only read and seldom if ever written (i.e., changed). It turns out, however, that there is a considerable demand for such *read-mostly* memory cells, and even for *read-only* memory cells (i.e., cells that are never changed and are only read). Furthermore, such read-only cells can be extremely simple and very small, so they can be built into relatively large arrays.

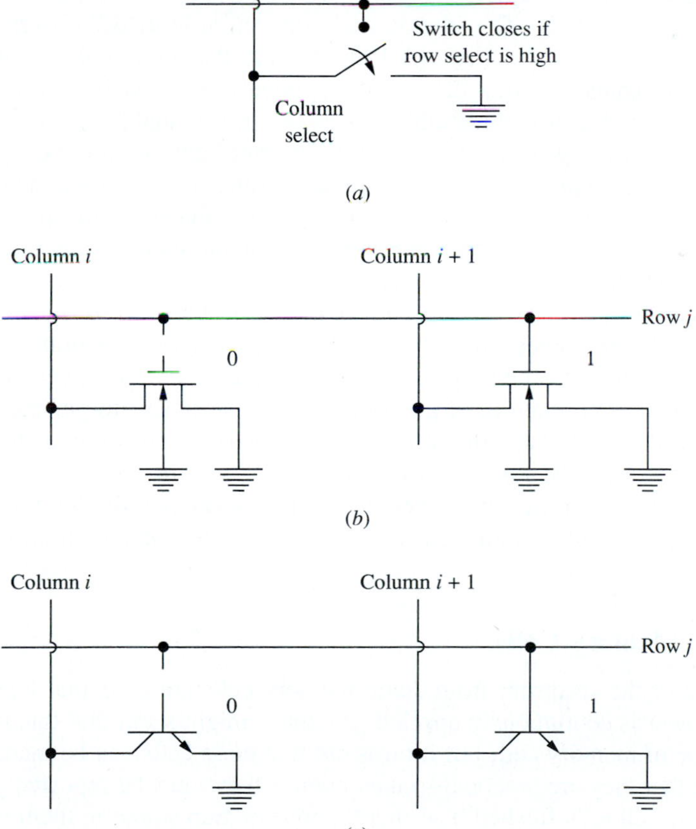

FIGURE 15.19
Static, nonvolatile read-only and read-mostly memory cells: (*a*) the basic memory cell concept; (*b*) its implementation in MOS technology; (*c*) its implementation in bipolar technology. In (*b*) and (*c*) the device on the left represents storage of a 0, the one on the right storage of a 1.

Nonvolatile memory cells tend to all be based on a relatively simple concept: A transistor switch is placed where each column and row line cross. It is connected in such a fashion that if the row is activated the switch either closes or remains open, depending on whether there is a 0 or 1 at that location, thereby either connecting the column line to ground or leaving it isolated from ground. This idea is illustrated in Fig. 15.19*a*.

The easiest way to ensure that a given switch will not close when a row line is activated is not to form the connection between the control electrode and the row line, as illustrated on the left side of Figs. 15.19*b* and 15.19*c*, for MOSFET and bipolar versions, respectively, of such a read-only memory (ROM) cell. Clearly, the information in this type of memory cell must be written in at the time of manufacture.

With MOSFETs it has proven to be possible in some structures to alter the threshold electrically or optically. These devices can be used to make memories of this type that can be changed, albeit not easily, and that thus are suitable for read-mostly memories, or RMMs. The idea is that connection is made to every gate in an array like that shown in Fig. 15.19*b*, but the threshold voltage of some of the devices is changed so that the voltage applied to the row line is not sufficient to turn them on. The low-threshold devices do turn on and connect the corresponding column lines to ground, but the high-threshold devices do not.

There are several techniques that have been successfully used to implement this type of read-mostly memory. Most involve changing the threshold by somehow placing charge either directly in the gate dielectric or on another electrode placed between the gate electrode and the channel. Doing this typically involves applying a very large voltage to the device and momentarily breaking down the dielectric so that the charge moves through it and into the desired position. To erase the memory (i.e., to set all of the cells back to zero), the cells can be illuminated with high-energy ultraviolet light. This light is sufficient to generate hole-electron pairs in the gate insulator, turning it temporarily into a conductor (this is in fact photoconductivity, just like we studied in Sec. 3.3), allowing the stored charge to leak off. There are also memory cell technologies of this type in which the stored charge can be removed by applying a sufficiently high erase bias to the cell.

15.4.2 Dynamic Memory Cells

At the other extreme of the spectrum from static memory cells are cells that lose their state even if power is continuously applied. At first it might seem that this is not a very useful type of memory cell, but it turns out that these cells can be made so compact and fast that they are practical to use, even if they must be repeatedly read and rewritten (we call it "refreshed") so that the information stored in them is not lost. The space gained by being able to make the cells much smaller is considerably more than that which is lost because of the peripheral circuitry needed to refresh the cells. Furthermore, since the cells are much smaller, the rows and columns can be much shorter, making access faster. Alternatively, a memory can have more rows and columns (i.e., can store more information) before it becomes too large.

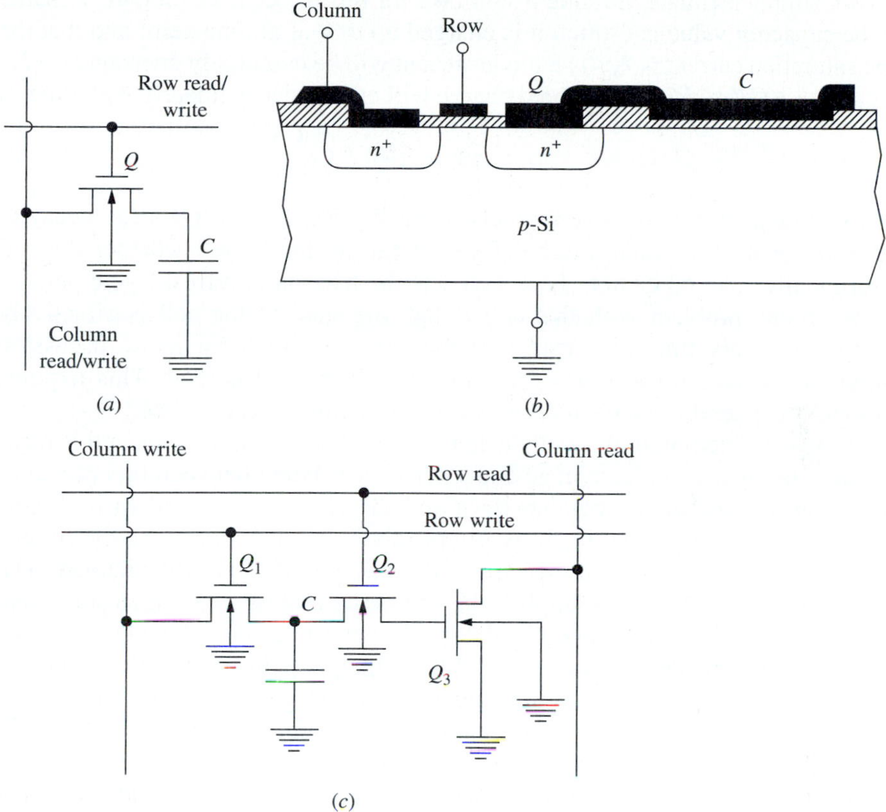

FIGURE 15.20
Dynamic random-access memory cells: (*a*) the circuit schematic of a single transistor cell; (*b*) a possible implementation shown in cross section; (*c*) the schematic of a three-transistor cell (the additional transistors in this latter cell provide amplification of the stored charge, making it easier to sense the state of the cell.)

The simplest dynamic memory cell consists of a single transistor (usually a MOSFET) and a capacitor, as pictured in Fig. 15.20*a*. An integrated implementation of this cell is shown in cross section in Fig. 15.20*b*. The idea is that a 1 is written into the cell by raising the appropriate row and column lines high, turning the transistor on and charging up the capacitor. When the lines are returned to their low state, the capacitor remains charged. To read a cell, the appropriate row line is raised, again turning the transistor on, and the presence or absence of charge on the capacitor is determined by sensing whether or not charge has flowed onto the appropriate column line.

There are clearly some problems with this scheme that have to be addressed. First, there is the matter of how the charge is stored. The capacitor, however it is formed, is connected to the drain n^+-region of the MOSFET, and thus there is a reverse-biased *p-n* junction diode between the capacitor and ground. Consequently, the capacitor will eventually discharge to ground through this diode. We can very simply estimate the time it will take for this to occur as follows: Assume that the capacitor value is C, that it is charged up to V_{DD} at time zero, and that the diode saturation current is I_S. The diode current will be essentially constant at $-I_S$; this current is $C\,dv/dt$, so the stored charge will clearly decay linearly with time as

$$Q(t) = CV_{DD} - I_S t \qquad \text{for } t < \frac{CV_{DD}}{I_S} \tag{15.35}$$

and it will be zero in CV_{DD}/I_S seconds. Typically we say that $Q(t)$ can decay to 50 percent of its maximum value before we can no longer tell whether the cell was originally charged or not. This then sets the maximum refresh cycle period.

A second problem with this cell is that the state of the cell is effectively reset to zero every time it is read (see the next paragraph for more discussion of this), so the data must be rewritten every time the cell is read. This requires additional peripheral circuitry and increases the memory access time.

A final problem with this cell design is that when the state of the cell is read, the charge originally on the storage capacitor is distributed between this capacitor and the capacitance of the column lines and the circuitry attached to it. If this represents a large capacitive load, as it typically does, the corresponding voltage change may be very small and difficult to detect, even if C is fully charged. The solution to this problem is to amplify the charge by adding more transistors, and thereby gain, to the cell. A three-transistor cell that implements this idea is shown in Fig. 15.20*c*. This design does not eliminate the problem of the cell's volatility and the need to regularly refresh it, but because the cell has gain, less charge can be sensed and the refresh period can be made considerably longer. It is still necessary, however, to rewrite the cell after reading it.

The one- and three-transistor dynamic memory cells we have just seen are widely used to realize fast random-access memories (RAMs) on digital integrated circuits because of their simplicity, small size, and speed. They are very important elements in modern system design.

15.5 SUMMARY

In this chapter we have studied basic building-block circuits for binary logic and memory. For logic, the basic building block is the inverter. We have shown that an important feature of any inverter is its transfer characteristic, and we have identified several key parameters of inverters that provide criteria for comparing and optimizing inverter designs, including the high and low voltage levels, the switching speed, the fan-in and fan-out capability, the power dissipation, and the noise margins. We have studied MOS and bipolar versions of inverters. As a general rule, we have found that MOS inverters can be relatively simple because of the high input resistance of the MOSFET. Bipolar inverters, for their part, tend to be larger and more complicated than MOS inverters, involve higher current levels, and dissipate more power, but they are also faster.

For memory, the basic building block is the memory cell. We have looked at static memory cells, both volatile and nonvolatile, and at dynamic memory cells. In our brief introduction, we have seen that MOS memory cells can be realized with even a single transistor and can be used to realize large-scale, high-density random-access memory.

PROBLEMS

15.1 Design an MOS logic circuit using depletion mode loads to have the truth table given in Table P15.1.

This function is called the *majority logic* function.

15.2 An important parameter in any MOSFET inverter design is the ratio of K_L to K_D.

(*a*) Investigate the effect of varying this ratio on the transfer characteristics of the n-MOS inverter in Fig. 15.11 by sketching the characteristics for $K_L = 50, 100, 250$, and $50\ \mu A/V^2$. Use the other device parameters as given in the caption of the figure. In your sketch do accurate plots in regions I and III and sketches in regions II and IV. Ignore the body effect (i.e., assume $\eta = 0$).

(*b*) From your results in part a, suggest an optimum K_L/K_D for the best noise margin.

15.3 Answer the questions posed in problem 15.2 for the CMOS inverter in Fig. 15.12 (i.e., assuming $K_N = 50\ \mu A/V^2$) and for $K_P = 50, 100, 250$, and $500\ \mu A/V^2$.

15.4 This question, and the following one, concern the design of the K-factors of the individual driver FETs in a multiple-input NOR gate.

(*a*) Draw the circuit schematic of a two-input n-MOS NOR gate.

(*b*) Sketch the transfer characteristic of this gate assuming one input is zero; that is, plot v_C versus v_A with $v_B = 0$ (the notation refers to Fig. 15.4*d*). Assume $V_{DD} = 5$ V, $V_{TD} = 1$ V, $V_{TL} = -1$ V, $K_D = 50\ \mu A/V^2$, and $K_L = 200\ \mu A/V^2$.

(*c*) Repeat part b with $v_B = v_A$. Do your sketch on the same set of axes you used in part b.

(*d*) Repeat parts b and c assuming $K_D = 25\ \mu A/V^2$.

(*e*) From your results in parts b through d, suggest a strategy for sizing K_D in multiple-input n-MOS NOR gates.

15.5 Answer the questions posed in problem 15.4 for multiple-input n-MOS NAND gates (refer to Fig. 15.4*b*).

15.6 You are assigned the task of laying out the gates of the driver devices in the n-MOS equivalent of the logic gates in Fig. 15.4, and you are told that you have the following constraints and design objectives:

Table P15.1

INPUTS		OUTPUTS	
A	*B*	*C*	*D*
0	0	0	0
1	0	0	0
0	1	0	0
0	0	1	0
1	1	0	1
1	0	1	1
0	1	1	1
1	1	1	1

The minimum gate length L is 1 μm.

The minimum gate width W is 2 μm.

The effective driver K-factor K_D is to be 50 $\mu A/V^2$ when all the driver devices in a given stage are on.

The K-factor of a minimum-geometry device (i.e., with $W = 2$ μm and $L = 1$ μm) is 20 $\mu A/V^2$.

The total gate area is to be kept to a minimum.

(*a*) Specify the gate dimensions of D_1, D_2, and D_3 in the AND gate in Fig. 15.4*b*.
(*b*) Do the same for D_1, D_2, and D_3 in the OR gate in Fig. 15.4*d*.
(*c*) Do the same for D_1, D_2, D_3, and D_4 in the LOGIC gate in Fig. 15.4*f*.

15.7 The layout rules given in Fig. 15.4 for multiple-input gates don't quite work with CMOS since both the n-channel and p-channel MOSFETs in a CMOS inverter are turned on and off (i.e., act as switches and also as loads). Recognizing the complementary nature of the n- and p-channel devices and the complementary nature of the NOR and NAND functions, draw the circuit schematic of the following CMOS gates.

(*a*) two-input NAND gate
(*b*) two-input NOR gate
(*c*) three-input gate having truth table in Fig. 15.4*e*.

15.8 With an eye toward reducing the power dissipation in his CMOS product line, your employer asks you to assess the impact on the static transfer characteristics and noise margins of reducing the power supply from 5 V to 3 V.

(*a*) Calculate and plot the transfer characteristic of the CMOS inverter in Fig. 15.12 when $V_{DD} = 3$ V. Nothing else is changed.
(*b*) It should be clear to you from your result in part a that it will be desirable to reduce the magnitudes of the threshold voltages of the n- and p-channel MOSFETs in these inverters. Recalculate the transfer characteristics assuming, first, that $V_{TN} \equiv |V_{TP}| = 0.75$ V, and, then, that $V_{TN} = |V_{TP}| = 0.5$ V.
(*c*) A logic gate requiring a 3-V supply can be powered by three 1.1-V batteries. However, once operation of three batteries is achieved, the logical next step is to try to use two and perhaps even one battery to do the job. Comment on the constraints that doing this places on the threshold voltages and on what happens to the noise margins.

15.9 In the circuit pictured in Fig. P15.9, the transistor Q_1 has $\beta = 25$ and the Ebers–Moll model parameters, I_{ES} and I_{CS}, are 10^{-13} Å and 5×10^{-12} Å, respectively. Frequently, the full Ebers–Moll model is not necessary and $v_{BE,\text{on}} = 0.6$ V and $v_{CE,\text{sat}} = 0.2$ V are adequate approximations.

(*a*) With the input open-circuited and no load attached to the output (i.e., with the output also open-circuited), what are the following quantities? You may assume $v_{BE,\text{on}} = 0.6$ and should first confirm that Q_1 is biased in its forward active region.
(i) The collector current I_C
(ii) The output voltage V_O
(iii) The voltage at the input terminal V_I

(*b*) To answer this question assume $v_{BE,\text{on}} = 0.6$ V and $v_{CE,\text{sat}} = 0.2$ V. Assume also that the output terminal remains open-circuited as in part a.
(i) When $v_{\text{IN}} = 0$ V, in which region is the transistor Q_1 biased (cutoff, forward active, or saturation) and why? What is v_{OUT} in this situation (i.e., when $v_{\text{IN}} = 0$ V)?

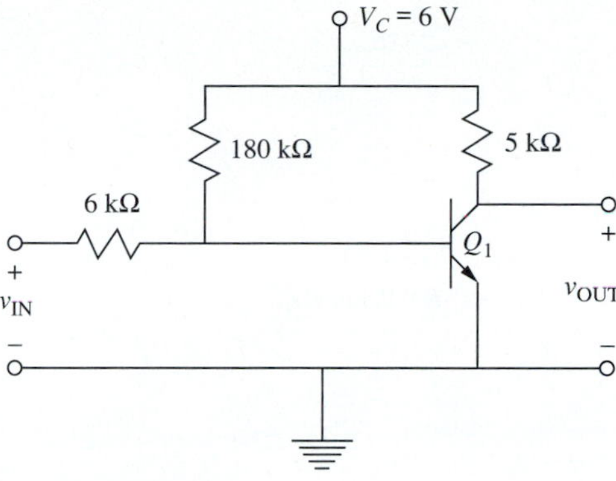

FIGURE P15.9

(ii) When $v_{IN} = 6$ V, in which region is the transistor Q_1 biased (cutoff, forward active, or saturation) and why? What is v_{OUT} in this situation?

15.10 Consider the circuit in Fig. P15.10*a* containing two identical transistors, Q_1 and Q_2. You may model these transistors using $\beta_F = 50$, $v_{BE,ON} = 0.6$ V, and $v_{CE,SAT} = 0.2$ V.

(*a*) With $v_{IN} = 0$ V, Q_1 is cut off and Q_2 is saturated. What are v_{MID} and v_{OUT}?

(*b*) Estimate how large v_{IN} can be before v_{MID} and v_{OUT} change from their values in part a.

(*c*) To reduce power dissipation, it is desirable to make R_B as large as possible. What is the maximum value of R_B that will keep Q_2 saturated when Q_1 is off?

(*d*) What is the total power dissipation in this circuit when $v_{IN} = 0$, Q_1 is off, and Q_2 is saturated if $R_B = 15$ kΩ and $R_L = 5$ kΩ?

Now consider a similar circuit fabricated using two identical enhancement mode MOSFETs as shown in Fig. P15.10*b*.

(*e*) For what range of v_{IN} between 0 and 6 V will Q_1 be off?

(*f*) When Q_1 is off, in which region is Q_2 biased and what is v_{OUT}?

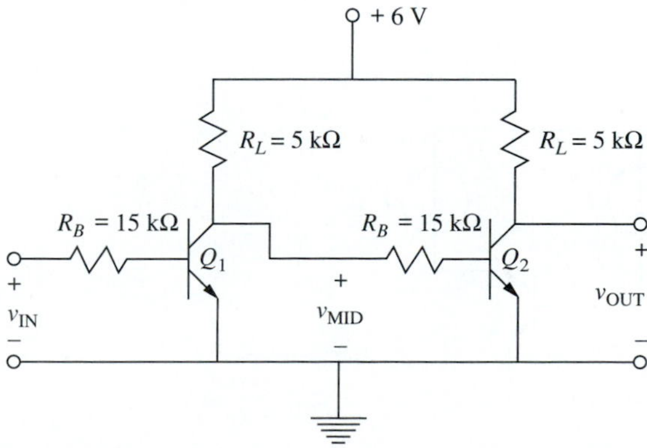

FIGURE P15.10*a*

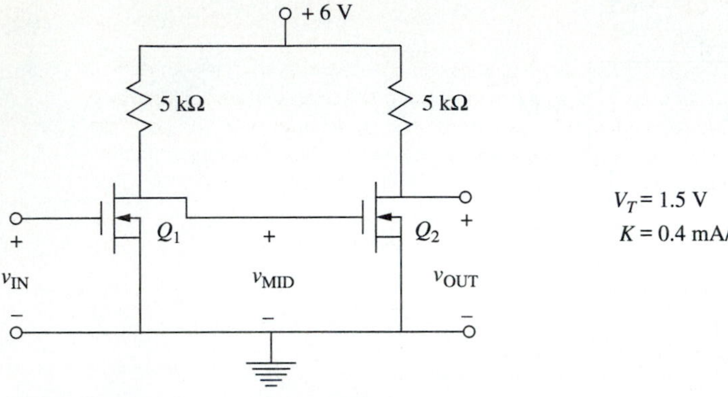

FIGURE P15.10*b*

15.11 The inverter chain pictured in Fig. P15.11 is made with silicon *npn* bipolar transistors having the following parameters: $N_E = 10N_B = 100N_C$; $w_E = w_B = 0.2w_C$; and $\beta = 20$. The value of the current source is 0.1 mA.

(*a*) Sketch and dimension the transfer characteristic, v_{OUT} versus v_{IN}, for one inverter stage.

(*b*) What are the "high" and "low" logic levels of this inverter?

15.12 Draw the circuit schematics for the following emitter-coupled logic (ECL) gates:

(*a*) two-input NOR

(*b*) two-input OR

(*c*) two-input NAND

Your NAND circuit should show you why designers avoid the NAND and AND functions when working with ECL.

15.13 The logic levels and transfer characteristic of an emitter-coupled logic gate depend only on the ratio of the resistor values in the circuit.

(*a*) Why is this a desirable situation?

(*b*) As an ECL designer, how do you choose the values of the resistors R_1, R_2, and R_3 in Fig. 15.17? That is, what is the optimal value for R_1? Be sure

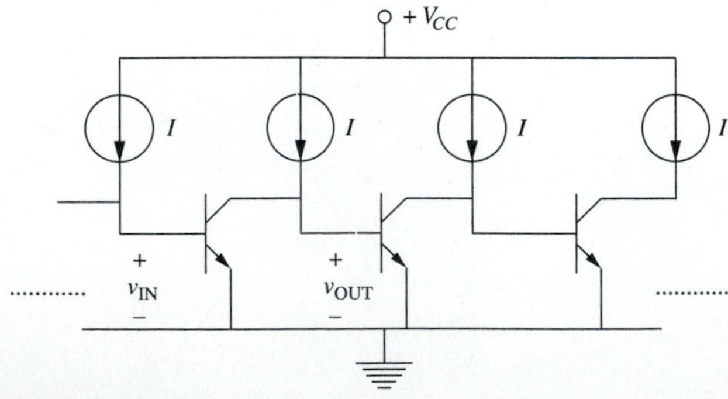

FIGURE P15.11

to state what "optimal" means to you and why optimal is not equivalent to unique.

(*c*) On what basis would a designer select R_4 in Fig. 15.17? (Your answer to this question may be different before and after you read Chap. 16.)

(*d*) What is the power dissipation in each of the ECL gates designed in the example in Sec. 15.33 on page 533, that is, in the 5-V and 3-V designs?

CHAPTER 16

SWITCHING TRANSIENTS IN DEVICES AND CIRCUITS

In this chapter we will address the question of how quickly devices and simple inverters can be switched from one steady-state condition to another and what design options we have available to make them switch faster. How quickly, for example, will a bipolar transistor turn on if we suddenly increase its base-emitter voltage from zero to a value in the forward active region? Or to a value in saturation? And what can be done with the device structure to minimize this turn-on delay? How quickly, for example, will the output of a CMOS NOR gate become high after one of its inputs has been changed from high to low? And what performance penalties do we suffer in terms of power, noise margin, or other factors when we redesign the gate to make it faster? How quickly can we read data into or out of a particular cell in a memory? And how does the access time scale with the size of the memory?

The issues in this chapter are the large-signal, time-domain equivalents for inverter building-block stages of the small-signal, sinusoidal steady-state issues we addressed for linear amplifier stages in Chap. 14.

When we speak of switching transients, as we do in the title of this chapter, we imply an interest in how the terminal voltages and currents evolve while the state of a device or circuit is changing, as well as an interest in knowing how long it takes the change to occur. Predicting the actual current and voltage waveforms during a switching transient is often difficult to do using hand calculations, however, because we are dealing with nonlinear devices and large signals. Detailed waveform analysis is usually best done by computer, and excellent transient analysis programs are available for this purpose. Consequently, we focus our efforts here on developing an intuitive feel for the switching process and, for the most part, on simply estimating the duration of the transient.

We begin with the general problem of estimating the duration of switching transients in nonlinear circuits, and we will develop several simplified methods for doing so. Then we will look at the behavior of individual devices when we suddenly switch their inputs. Finally, we will look at using the insight we have gained on devices to analyze some representative digital circuits.

16.1 GENERAL TECHNIQUES

As we have seen earlier, there is stored charge associated with the operation of any electronic device, and it is this stored charge that determines the switching transient. That is, changing the state of a device or circuit involves changing the amount of charge stored in that device or circuit, and this takes time.

The time rate of change of the charge store associated with any circuit node is determined by the net current into that node. If we have a node A with an associated charge store q_{A} and with N currents $i_{\mathrm{A}n}$ flowing into it, then

$$\frac{dq_{\mathrm{A}}}{dt} = \sum_{n=1}^{N} i_{\mathrm{A}n} \equiv i_{\mathrm{A}} \tag{16.1}$$

Notice that we have written the total net current into the node as i_{A}.

Writing the charge q_{A} and the currents $i_{\mathrm{A}n}$ as functions of the node voltages in the circuit (v_{A}, v_{B}, v_{C}, etc.) and doing this for each node (A, B, C, etc.) gives us a set of coupled differential equations that can be solved for the transient node voltage signals [$v_{\mathrm{A}}(t)$,$v_{\mathrm{B}}(t)$, $v_{\mathrm{C}}(t)$, etc.] that we seek.

To see how this works in a familiar situation, consider a circuit containing an ideal linear capacitor. Both nodes, A and B, of a linear capacitor have charges associated with them that are linearly related to the size of the capacitor and the voltage difference between the two terminals. We write for an ideal linear capacitor C that

$$q_{\mathrm{A}} = C v_{\mathrm{AB}} \tag{16.2a}$$

$$q_{\mathrm{B}} = C v_{\mathrm{BA}} (= -q_{\mathrm{A}}) \tag{16.2b}$$

Summing the currents into node A, for example, we have

$$i_{\mathrm{A}} = \sum_{n=1}^{N} i_{\mathrm{A}n} = \frac{dq_{\mathrm{A}}}{dt} = C\frac{dv_{\mathrm{AB}}}{dt} \tag{16.3a}$$

Now, to continue this exercise, assume that this capacitor is connected to a circuit that contains only linear resistors and sources (and no other capacitors). This circuit can therefore be represented by its Thevenin equivalent circuit, and we have $i_{\mathrm{A}} = (V_S - v_{\mathrm{AB}})/R_S$, where V_S and R_S are the Thevenin equivalent voltage and resistance, respectively, of the circuit connected to the capacitor. Using this in Eq. (16.3a), we arrive at the familiar result

$$R_S C \frac{dv_{AB}}{dt} = V_S - v_{AB} \tag{16.3b}$$

This relationship is linear, and we know all about solving linear differential equations. We also know how to solve problems like this involving circuits that contain several linear capacitors.

So far so good, but the charge stored in a nonlinear electronic device is typically a nonlinear function of the terminal voltages. Thus the stored charge associated with a node is in general not linearly related to the voltage on that terminal, and if the voltage changes, the change in the amount of stored charge is in general a complicated nonlinear function of the change in voltage. That is, unlike the situation in an ideal linear capacitor, we *cannot* write the change in the amount of stored charge as some constant C times the change in voltage; that is

$$\Delta q_A \equiv q_A\big|_{V_{AB}=V_F} - q_A\big|_{V_{AB}=V_I} \neq C\,(V_F - V_I) \tag{16.4a}$$

when C is a constant independent of v_{AB}. In the above equation, V_F represents the voltage after the change and V_I is the voltage before. Often it is convenient to write the above expression more compactly as

$$\Delta q_A \neq C\,\Delta v_{AB} \tag{16.4b}$$

We have seen earlier in nonlinear problems that for small-signal variations about a quiescent bias point, it is useful to define a capacitance C that is a function of the quiescent voltage V_{AB},

$$C(V_{AB}) \equiv \frac{dq_A}{dv_{AB}}\bigg|_{v_{AB}=V_{AB}} \tag{16.5}$$

but for large-signal variations, which we are currently discussing, this is not useful. We must deal with the nonlinearity in a different way.

To address this new problem we will begin by making two assumptions. First, we assume that we are more interested in the duration of a switching transient than in its detailed shape. Second, we assume that the transient is dominated by the charging of only one element and thus that we need only be concerned with the charging of one node. Label this node as A, and proceed as follows: From quiescent (dc) analyses we determine the initial and final voltages on node A. Then we calculate the corresponding initial and final charge stores and from their difference calculate the net change in the charge on the node, Δq_A. We also estimate the average net current into the node, $\bar{I}_A$. Finally, as a first-order approximation, we estimate the switching time (i.e., the duration of the transient τ_T) as

$$\tau_T \approx \frac{\Delta q_A}{\bar{I}_A} \tag{16.6}$$

where Δq_A is the net change in the charge on the mode and $\bar{I}_A$ is the average net current into node A during the transient.

This method of estimating τ_T is fast and easy, and it is used in a wide variety of situations, as we shall see. It is most accurate, however, in cases where the net current into the node, i_A, is approximately constant over the major portion of the transient. In cases where the current varies continuously during the transient, it may be wise to also consider an alternative approach. For example, it may be possible to model the charge store as a linear capacitor during the transient. This is most reasonable if over the entire range between V_I and V_F the capacitance of the charge store, dq_A/dv_{AB}, is comparable to the ratio of Δq_A to Δv_{AB}. If the capacitance is close to this ratio over most of the range, then we can approximate the charge store as a linear capacitor with value C_A, where

$$C_A \equiv \frac{\Delta q_A}{\Delta v_{AB}} \tag{16.7}$$

With this approximation we can write

$$\frac{dq_A}{dv_{AB}} \approx C_A \qquad \text{for } V_I \leq v_{AB} \leq V_F \tag{16.8}$$

and thus

$$\frac{dv_{AB}}{dt} \approx \frac{i_A}{C_A} \qquad \text{for } V_I \leq v_{AB} \leq V_F \tag{16.9}$$

Writing i_A in terms of v_{AB} yields a first-order differential equation for $v_{AB}(t)$, which we can solve subject to the boundary condition that $v_{AB}(0) = V_I$. Assuming that we can solve the differential equation (and this is not obvious because the equation may very well be nonlinear), this procedure gives us an expression for the waveform itself during the transient, as well as an estimate for the switching time τ_T. [The time τ_T is t such that $v_{AB}(t) = V_F$.]

To summarize, we have seen that calculating the switching transients in circuits with elements that contain nonlinear charge stores is in general a formidable task, but we have also seen that in certain situations tractable approximations can be formulated. In particular, when the current is approximately constant during the transient, then the switching time is given approximately by the change in stored charge divided by the average current [i.e., by Eq. (16.6)]. When the node capacitance is approximately constant during the transient, then the switching transient can be approximated as the solution to a first-order differential equation [i.e., Eq. (16.9)]. In the following sections we will look at applications of these techniques to several specific examples, beginning with devices and then looking at several inverter circuits.

16.2 TURNING DEVICES ON AND OFF

We have studied two broad classes of transistors (i.e., bipolar and field effect), and each has its own distinct charge stores that play dominant roles in switching. We will look first at bipolar junction devices, beginning with the diode and then turning to the BJT. We will then look at field effect devices, taking the MOSFET as the most important representative. We will finish with a look at a surprising "new" (to us) field effect device, the isolated MOS capacitor.

16.2.1 Bipolar Junction Devices

In this section we consider devices in which a forward-biased *p-n* junction plays a major role. The examples we choose are the *p-n* junction diode and the bipolar junction transistor. As we know, there are two charge stores associated with any *p-n* junction: the junction depletion region and the excess carrier populations. When changing the voltage across a *p-n* junction, charge must be added to or removed from both of these stores; this is what limits how fast a diode or transistor can be turned on or off.

a) *p-n* **diodes.** Consider the diode circuit shown in Fig. 16.1, which contains batteries, resistors, a three-position switch, and a diode. The switch is connected so that when it is down, the diode is unexcited (i.e., is in thermal equilibrium). When the switch is in its middle position, the diode is forward-biased; when the switch is in its upper position, the diode is reverse-biased.

Imagine, first, that after being in the lower, off position for a long time, the switch is put (at $t = 0$) in the middle, forward-bias position. How long does it take the circuit to reach steady state? To answer this question, a good starting point is to consider the initial and final states. Initially the diode voltage and current are zero and the charge stored in the diode is that in the zero-biased depletion region.

At $t = 0^+$, just after the switch is closed, the diode voltage remains zero (because the voltage across a charge store cannot change instantaneously) and the current jumps to V_S/R_S. Eventually, at times much greater than 0, the diode voltage stabilizes at a value on the order of $V_{\rm ON}$ and the diode current i_D is approximately $(V_S - V_{\rm ON})/R_S$. If V_S is much greater than $V_{\rm ON}$, then i_D is essentially constant during the transient, i_A will be approximately V_S/R_S, and we can hope to use Eq. (16.6) to estimate τ_T.

To apply Eq. (16.6), we need to estimate $\Delta q_{\rm A}$. The main charge store in a forward-biased *p-n* diode is in the excess carrier profiles. To calculate this charge we refer back to our discussion of diffusion capacitance in Sec. 7.3.4 and, specifically, to Eq. (7.41). A typical integrated-circuit diode, for example, will be a short-base, n^+-p device, in which case we have

$$Q_{\rm DF}(V_{\rm AB}) \approx Aq\frac{n_i^2}{N_{Ap}}\left(e^{qV_{\rm AB}/kT} - 1\right)\frac{w_p^*}{2} \tag{16.10a}$$

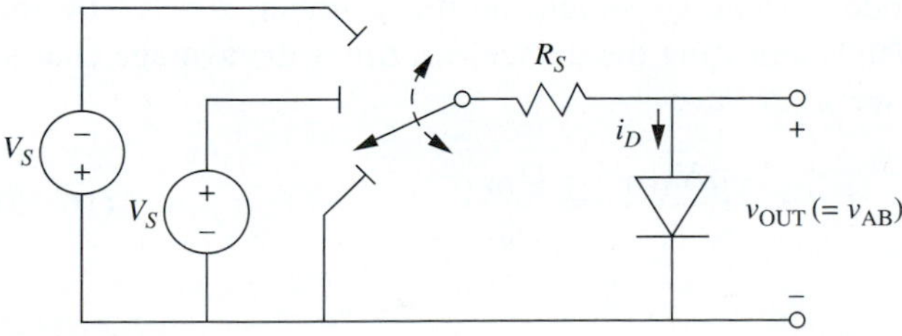

FIGURE 16.1
Simple diode circuit containing batteries, resistors, a three-position switch, and a diode.

where A is the area of the junction, N_{Ap} is the doping level on the p-side, and w_p^* is the effective width of the p-side.* We use our quiescent notation to emphasize that we are dealing with transient switching between steady-state endpoints. This charge can also be written in terms of the diode current $I_D(V_{AB})$, which is approximately

$$I_D(V_{AB}) \approx Aqn_i^2 \frac{D_e}{N_{Ap}w_p^*}\left(e^{qV_{AB}/kT} - 1\right) \tag{16.11}$$

Inserting Eq. (16.11) into Eq. (16.10a) yields

$$Q_{DF}(V_{AB}) = \frac{w_p^{*2}}{2D_e} I_D(V_{AB}) \tag{16.10b}$$

Applying Eq. (16.4a) to find Δq_A we have

$$\Delta q_A = Q_{DF}(V_{ON}) - Q_{DF}(0) \approx \frac{(w_p^*)^2}{2D_e} I_D(V_{ON}) \tag{16.12a}$$

where $I_D(V_{ON})$ is $(V_S - V_{ON})/R_S$. Assuming that V_S is large, so that $I_D(V_{ON})$ can be approximated as V_S/R_S, we then have

$$\Delta q_A \approx \frac{(w_p^*)^2}{2D_e} \frac{V_S}{R_S} \tag{16.12b}$$

Returning to Eq. (16.6), and recognizing that $\bar{I}_A$ is V_S/R_S, we have immediately

$$\tau_T \approx \frac{(w_p^*)^2}{2D_e} \tag{16.13}$$

This factor, $(w_p^*)^2/2D_e$, is often called the transit time τ_{tr} of the diode because it can be looked upon as the average time it takes an electron to transit the p-side of the device. To see this we note that the total number of electrons on the p-side of the diode when it is forward-biased is given approximately by

$$N_{TOT} \approx -\frac{Q_{DF}}{q} \tag{16.14}$$

We then argue that the diode current I_D should be this number divided by the average time an electron spends transiting the device, τ_{tr}, times the average charge on an electron, $-q$. Thus we must have

$$I_D \approx -\frac{qN_{TOT}}{\tau_{tr}} = \frac{Q_{DF}}{\tau_{tr}} \tag{16.15}$$

*Note that Eq. (7.41) refers to a p^+-n diode, rather than an n^+-p diode, so Eq. (16.10a) has been modified accordingly.

Substituting this expression for I_D into Eq. (16.12) yields

$$\tau_{tr} \approx \frac{(w_p^*)^2}{2D_e} \tag{16.16}$$

In summary, we see that the diode turns on immediately in the sense that it conducts current in the forward direction as soon as the switch is closed, but there is a delay on the order of a minority carrier transit time τ_{tr} before the excess carrier profiles are established and the diode reaches steady state. Notice also that the duration of the turn-on transient is independent of the final diode current. (You should think about that.)

Imagine now that the switch has been in the middle, forward-bias position for a long time and is suddenly moved at $t = 0$ to the upper, reverse-bias position. In the final, steady state we know that the diode current will be negative and very small (that is, the diode current will be the reverse bias value, $-I_s$,which is approximately $-q_A n_i^2 D_e / N_{Ap} w_p^*$) and that the diode voltage will be $-V_S$.

At $t = 0^-$, however, just before the switch is moved, the diode voltage is approximately V_{ON} and it cannot change discontinuously when the switch is thrown. Thus at $t = 0^+$ the diode voltage must also be V_{ON}, and the diode current at $t = 0^+$ must be $-(V_T + V_{ON})/R_S$, which is negative and large. But does this make sense? Can the diode be conducting in the reverse direction?

A little thought and some consideration of the excess carrier profiles will show you that the diode can indeed conduct in the reverse direction, at least for a brief time after it has been switched from forward to reverse bias. The key point to realize is that the reason a diode does not conduct in the reverse direction in the steady state is that there are so few minority carriers on either side of the junction in the steady state that they cannot sustain a significant reverse current. Right after a *p-n* junction has been forward-biased, however, there are plenty of minority carriers, and a large reverse current can flow until they are removed. The diagrams in Fig. 16.2 might help you see this. The situation at $t = 0^-$ is shown in Fig. 16.2*a* for our short-base, n^+-*p* diode. The situation at $t = 0^+$ and for several times $t > 0$ is shown in Fig. 16.2*b*.

Looking at Fig. 16.2*b*, we see that the excess carrier profile can support an electron diffusion current of V_S/R_S until the voltage across the diode, and thus $n'(0^+)$, is zero. Beyond that point, $n'(0^+)$ decreases to $-n_{po} (= -n_i{}^2/N_{Dp})$, the diode starts to become reverse-biased, and the current falls toward zero. The two-step nature of the transient is illustrated in Fig. 16.2*c*.

During the initial portion of the transient, some electrons flow back across the junction and others continue to flow to the ohmic contact, where they recombine. These two currents are roughly the same and equal in magnitude to V_S/R_S, so the current discharging the charge store during this portion of the transient is approximately $2V_S/R_S$, or twice the current during charging. Looking further at the distributions in Fig. 16.2*b*, we see (and you can show rigorously) that by the time $n'(0^+)$ is zero, two-thirds of the total excess carriers have been removed. Thus we can estimate that τ_1, the duration of the first portion of the transient, is one-third of the turn-on delay (two-thirds of the total removed twice as fast); thus

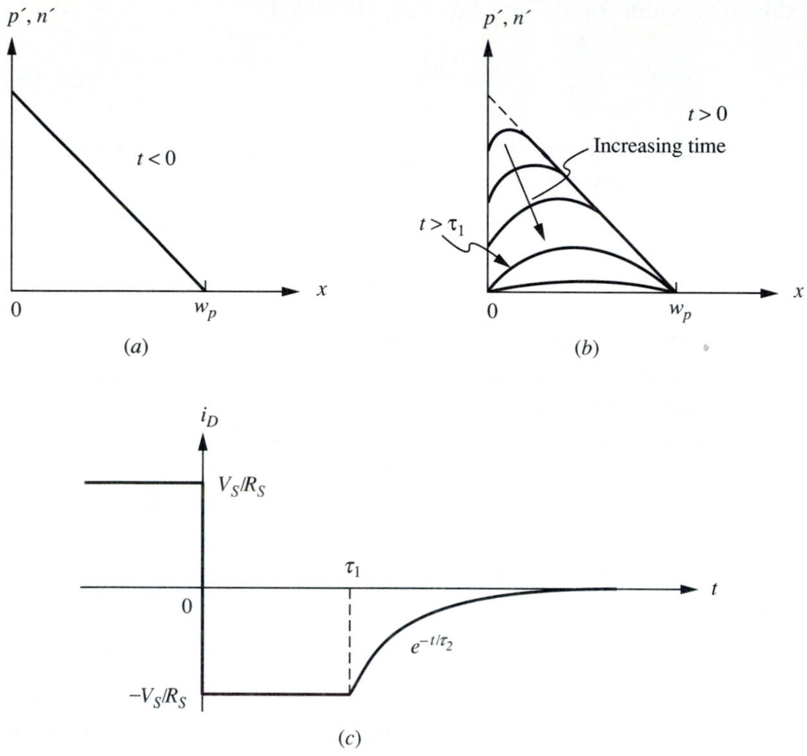

FIGURE 16.2
(*a*) Excess carrier profile in a forward-biased n^+-p diode; (*b*) excess carrier profile at several times shortly after the same diode has been reverse-biased using the circuit of Fig. 16.1; (*c*) the corresponding current transient.

$$\tau_1 \approx \frac{\tau_{tr}}{3} = \frac{w_p^2}{6D_e} \tag{16.17}$$

The second portion of the transient is more complex. It involves the removal and/or recombination of the remaining excess charge as well as the charging of the reverse-bias depletion region. Assuming that the former is still the dominant charge store, we can argue that the dynamics of the excess charge store will continue to dominate the transient and that one-half of the excess carriers will diffuse to the contact and recombine and one-half will diffuse to the now reverse-biased junction and contribute to the current transient. The plane at $x = w/2$ becomes a plane of symmetry for $t > \tau_1$, and we can anticipate that the time constant τ_2 for the remaining transient is the transit time of a diode of width $w_p/2$; that is,

$$\tau_2 \approx \frac{1}{2D_e}\left(\frac{w_p}{2}\right)^2 = \frac{\tau_{tr}}{4} \tag{16.18}$$

Perhaps the most important lesson to be gained from this discussion is the realization that a forward-biased *p-n* junction diode cannot be turned off immediately and that the excess carrier charge store plays the dominant role in determining the transient. This knowledge, in turn, helps us to design a faster-switching diode. For example, it is clear that an n^+-p diode will be faster than a p^+-n diode because D_e is larger than D_h. Also, it is clear that the narrower we make the *p*-region, the better.

When a *p-n* diode is needed in a bipolar integrated circuit, an *npn* transistor is usually used. This is done (1) because *npn* transistors are the device for which the fabrication process has been optimized and they are readily available, and (2) because *npn* transistors make excellent diodes. To see how and why, consider the several possible connections of a BJT as a diode shown in Fig. 16.3. A little thought should show you that the emitter-base diode will be faster than the Base-collector diode because it is an n^+-p diode and because w_B is typically much less than w_C. Assuming then that we choose the emitter-base diode, there is still a question as to what we do with the base-collector diode. Clearly we do not want to connect the collector to the emitter as shown in Fig. 16.3*a* because then the slow base-collector diode would dominate the switching transient, but should the collector be left unconnected as in Fig. 16.3*b* or be shorted to the base as in Fig. 16.3*c*? It is an instructive exercise to convince yourself that the latter is by far the better choice. (See also Problem 16.1.) Interestingly, the full transistor is needed to get the best diode.

b. Bipolar transistors. The first issue to address as we now consider turning BJTs on and off is how we reconcile the methodology we presented earlier, which subtly implied we were dealing with only a pair of terminals and a single charge store, with a three-terminal device with multiple charge stores like a transistor. The answer is that although transistors have three terminals, the charging and discharging of the dominant charge stores occur primarily through only one pair of terminals and that our methodology works just fine. This will become clear as we proceed with our analysis.

Consider, then, using the same voltage source, resistor, and switch we used to turn our diode on and off to now turn an *npn* BJT on and off. The connection

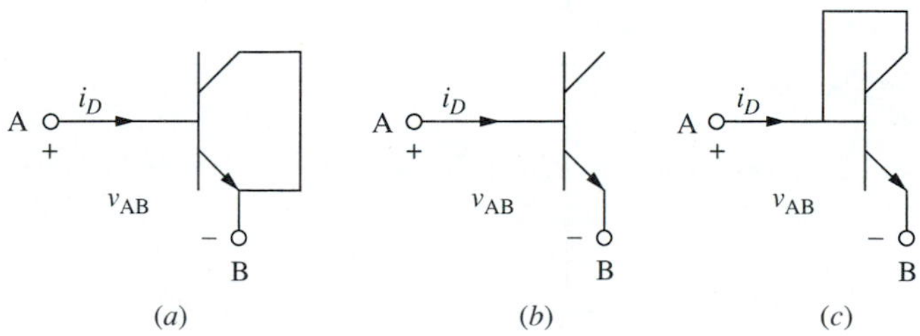

FIGURE 16.3
Three possible interconnections of an *npn* BJT as a diode: (*a*) emitter and collector junctions in parallel; (*b*) collector terminal open-circuited; (*c*) base-collector junction shorted.

is illustrated in Fig. 16.4. When the switch is in the lower position, the device is off, with no bias on the base-emitter junction. When the switch is in the middle position, the base-emitter junction is forward-biased and the BJT will be turned on. When the switch is all the way up, the BJT will be turned off, with the base-emitter junction reverse-biased. The question again is how quickly does all this happen?

Assume that the switch is initially in the lower position and at $t = 0$ is moved to the middle position. The steady-state base current will be approximately $(V_S - V_{ON})/R_S$, and the steady-state collector current will be β_F times larger, or $\beta_F(V_S - V_{ON})/R_S$. Assuming that when on, the transistor is in its forward active region and is not saturated (we will consider saturation shortly), then the main charge store that has to be built up during the turn-on transient is that in the base. This is illustrated in Fig. 16.5*a*. There is also charge stored in the depletion regions associated with each junction, which we are not including in our analysis. The assumption is that a modern, integrated digital BJT is designed to minimize the junction capacitances and, more importantly, is operated at sufficiently high current densities that the excess carrier charge stores are dominant.

Recalling our diode discussion, particularly Eq. (16.12a), we realize that the excess charge store in the base, Q_B, can be written as

$$\Delta q_A = Q_B = \frac{I_C w_B^2}{2D_e} = \frac{\beta_F I_B w_B^2}{2D_e} \tag{16.19}$$

The holes in this store are supplied through the base current; the electrons are supplied through the emitter.

Assuming that V_S is much greater than V_{ON}, the base current will be essentially constant, at its steady-state value I_B, which we have said is approximately $(V_S - V_{ON})/R_S$ over the entire turn-on transient; thus we can use Eq. (16.6) to estimate the turn-on switching time to be

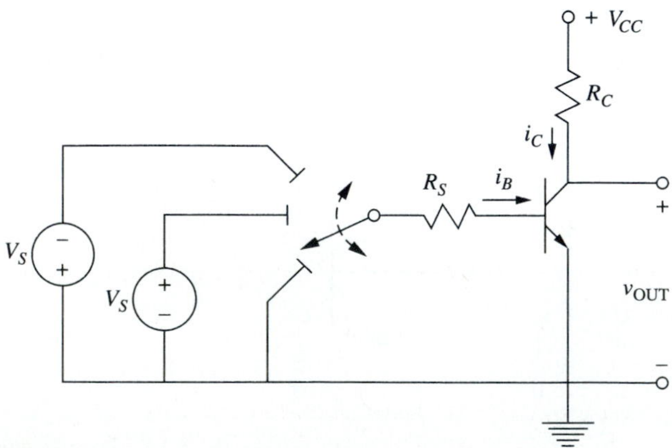

FIGURE 16.4
Simple bipolar transistor circuit to illustrate the switching transients encountered when turning a BJT on and off.

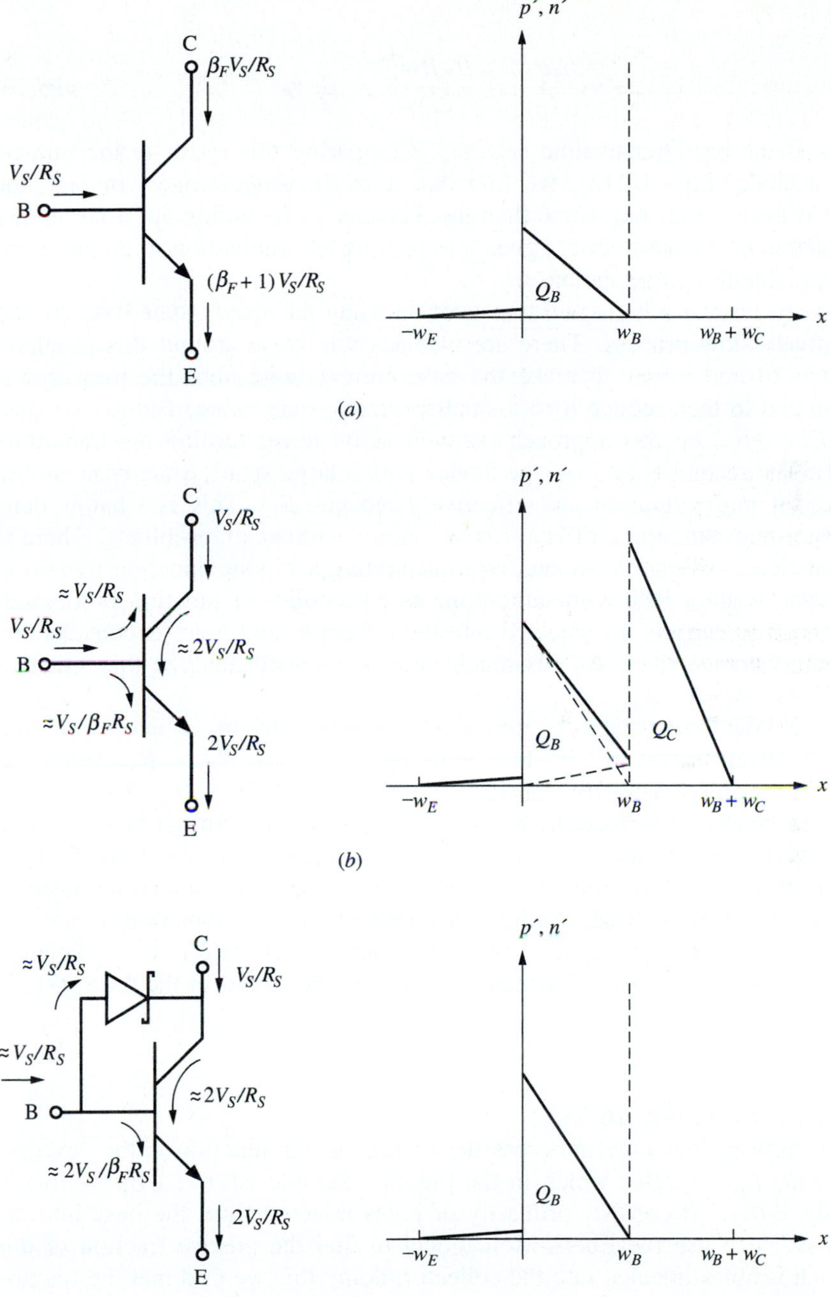

FIGURE 16.5

Excess charge stores within an *npn* bipolar transistor: (*a*) biased in the forward active region with a base current V_S/R_S; (*b*) biased into saturation with equal base and collector currents of V_S/R_S [the values of V_S and R_S are of course different from (*a*)]; (*c*) the same charge stores illustrated for an *n pn* bipolar transistor biased as in (*b*) but with a Schottky diode clamp on the base-collector junction. In the graphs $w_E = w_B = w_C$, $\mu_e = 3\mu_h$, and $N_{DE} = 10N_{AB} = 100N_{DE}$.

$$\tau_T \approx \frac{\Delta q_A}{I_B} = \frac{\beta_F B w_B^2}{2D_e} = \beta_F \tau_B \tag{16.20}$$

where τ_B is the base transit time $w_B^2/2D_e$. Comparing this result to the turn-on time of a diode, Eq. (16.13), we find that it is β_F times longer! In fact, the situation is even somewhat worse than this because as i_C builds up, a larger and larger fraction of the base current goes into feeding recombination in the base and less is available to charge the base.

Clearly, turning a high-gain transistor on using the steady-state base current is a relatively slow process. There are two possible ways around this problem. The first is to find a way to make the base current large until the transistor is turned on and to then reduce it to a smaller, steady-state value. Emitter-coupled logic (ECL) relies on this approach (as well as on never turning the transistors fully off). The second is to drive the device with a large steady-state base current that forces it into saturation and effectively reduces β_F. This is what is done in transistor-transistor logic (TTL),* but it is not without its problems. There is additional charge storage associated with saturating a bipolar junction transistor. In particular, when a BJT is in saturation, its base-collector junction is forward-biased, minority carriers are injected into the collector, and there is considerably more charge storage (i.e., Δq_A is much larger). We will analyze this situation next.

To see how long it takes to turn a BJT on when driving it into saturation, let us look at our circuit in Fig. 16.4 with $V_{CC} = V_S$ and $R_C = R_S$. When the switch is in the on position, the transistor saturates with $I_B \approx V_S/R_S$, $I_C \approx V_S/R_S$, and $I_E \approx -2V_S/R_S$. The forward bias current crossing the emitter-base junction is thus $2V_S/R_S$ and consists mainly of electrons injected into the base. A little work with the Ebers–Moll model shows us that the current of electrons injected from the emitter into the base, assuming negligible base recombination, is actually $(2 - \alpha_R)[\alpha_F/(1 - \alpha_F\alpha_R)](V_S/R_S)$, but this reduces to $2V_S/R_S$ if we assume α_F is nearly 1, and α_R is small. Consequently, the charge stored in the base, Q_B, is

$$Q_B \approx \frac{2V_S}{R_S}\frac{w_B^2}{2D_e} \tag{16.21}$$

This is illustrated in Fig. 16.5*b*.

The forward bias current across the base-collector junction is the "excess" base current, $I_B - I_C/\beta_F$, which in the present example is $(1 - 1/\beta_F)V_S/R_S$, or essentially V_S/R_S;† it consists primarily of holes injected from the base into the collector. We can use the Ebers–Moll model to find the precise fraction of this current that is holes injected into the collector; doing this we find that the fraction

---

*See Sec. 16.3.2*a* for further discussion of TTL transients.

†This is not simply I_C but is instead equal to $(-I_E - I_C)$. The fact that in this case it happens to also equal I_C is simply a consequence of the fact that our biases are such that $|I_C| = 2|I_E|$, so $-I_E - I_C = I_C$.

is $(2\alpha_F - 1)(1 - \alpha_R)/(1 - \alpha_F\alpha_R)$, which is approximately 1 when α_F is close to 1 and α_R is small. Thus the charge store in the collector, Q_C, is

$$Q_C \approx \frac{V_S}{R_S}\frac{w_C^2}{2D_h} \tag{16.22}$$

Fig. 16.5*b* illustrates this also.

All of this stored charge, Q_B and Q_C, is supplied by the base current, so in the notation of Eq. (16.6) we have

$$\Delta q_A = Q_B + Q_C \tag{16.23}$$

$$\bar{I}_A = \frac{V_S}{R_S} \tag{16.24}$$

Combining these last four equations in Eq. (16.6) yields

$$\tau_T = 2\frac{w_B^2}{2D_e} + \frac{w_C^2}{2D_h} \tag{16.25a}$$

which is twice the base transit time τ_B plus the collector transit time τ_C; that is,

$$\tau_T = 2\tau_B + \tau_C \tag{16.25b}$$

This result again is independent of the magnitude of the base current; it does depend quantitatively on the fact that we assumed that the transistor is in a circuit with $V_{CC} = V_S$ and $R_C = R_S$ so that in saturation $I_C = I_B$, but the basic elements are the same whatever the bias condition and level of saturation.

Now it is time to step back and see what driving the transistor into saturation has gotten us or has cost us. We certainly have reduced the time it takes to charge the base from $\beta_F\tau_B$ to $2\tau_B$, but we have added the collector transit time, which can be substantial. The factor D_h in the denominator is roughly $D_e/3$, so even if $w_C \approx w_B$, then τ_C is approximately $3\tau_B$ and thus τ_T is approximately $5\tau_B$. More realistically, w_C will be 3 to 4 times w_B, so τ is 10 to 16 times τ_C and τ_T is more likely to be 30 or more times τ_B. We don't seem to have gained much.

The ultimate solution to this dilemma is to shunt the base-collector junction with a diode that has a smaller turn-on voltage and less charge storage associated with it. Then when the base-collector terminals become forward-biased, the current flows through this shunting diode and not across the base-collector junction. A metal-semiconductor, or Schottky diode, is the perfect choice for this shunting diode because it has a relatively small turn-on voltage and no excess charge store; Schottky clamps are widely used in TTL to eliminate Q_C (see App. E). In such cases, the excess current input at the base (i.e., $V_S/R_S - I_C/\beta_F = V_S/\beta_F$) flows through the Schottky diode and into the collector terminal in the steady state, and the total collector current is V_S/R_S plus this amount, or essentially $2V_S/R_S$. Correspondingly, minority carrier injection occurs only at the emitter-base junction, and the associated charge store Q_B is that due to an emitter current of $2V_S/R_S$ as illustrated in Fig. 16.5*c*. Q_B is again given by Eq. (16.21), and this charge is again supplied by the base current, which (initially at least) is V_S/R_S. We say "initially at least" because as the transistor tries to saturate, some of this current is shunted through the Schottky diode and is no longer available to charge up Q_B in the base. Ignoring this complication, we find that τ_T is approximately $2\tau_B$. Thus we have been able to eliminate τ_C, and τ_T is the smallest we have seen so far.

Next consider the problem of turning a BJT off. All of the excess charge must be removed before the device will turn off and the collector current will drop to zero. In our circuit in Fig. 16.4, suppose we suddenly move the switch from the middle position to the up position. At first a negative base current of approximate magnitude V_S/R_S flows, removing holes from the base and, if the device is saturated, from the collector. More dramatically, because of all of the excess carriers in the device, the collector current will continue to flow and will be essentially unchanged until the excess populations at the junctions fall to zero, as was much the case in the *p-n* diode. Only then will the collector current begin to decrease. This behavior is illustrated in Fig. 16.6.

First consider the situation when the transistor is not saturated. In this case the negative base current $-V_S/R_S$ flows, removing holes from the base. At the same time, however, the much larger collector current will continue to flow, also removing charge from the base. As we have said, the collector current will remain at its initial level, which in this case is $\beta_F V_S/R_S$, until the excess population at the base-emitter junction drops to zero. When this happens, roughly two-thirds of the excess charge will have been removed. The time it takes for this to occur is $2Q_B/3I_C$, or $2\tau_B/3$. (Notice that this is considerably less time than the time, $\beta_F \tau_B$, it took for the base current to charge up the base.) After this time, the collec-

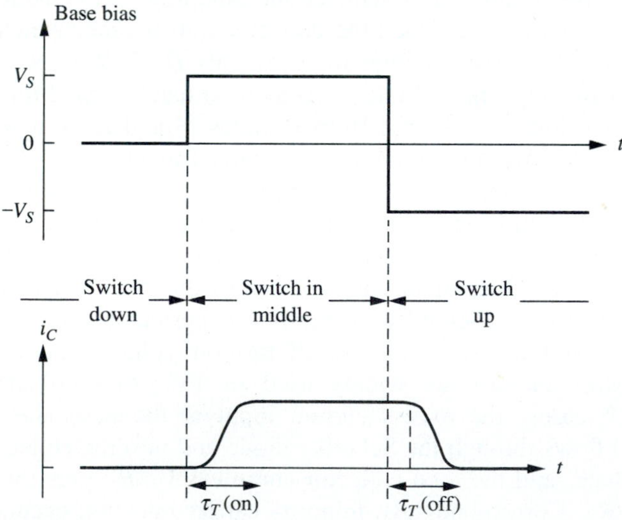

FIGURE 16.6
Qualitative sketch of the collector current as an *npn* bipolar transistor is switched from an unbiased state to a forward-biased state and then is switched off with a reverse bias applied to the base-emitter junction.

tor current decreases to zero and the transistor starts to really turn off. Beyond this point the remaining collector current will continue to be the main mechanism discharging Q_B, but the rate of discharge will be reduced and the transient will have a long tail.

If the transistor had been turned on so strongly that it was saturated, as in Fig. 16.5*b*, then the collector current will continue to flow until both Q_B and Q_C are removed. Now, however, we have a larger base current (i.e., V_S/R_S in our example) aiding the collector current in removing the stored charge. Using the same arguments as above, we conclude that since we have a total current of $2V_S/R_S$ discharging a charge store of $Q_B + Q_C$, with Q_B and Q_C given by Eqs. (16.21) and (16.22), respectively, the current will remain constant for roughly $(2\tau_B + \tau_C)/3$ and will then decay to zero, this time with a somewhat shorter tail.

Finally, if the base-collector junction had been clamped with a Schottky diode, there would be no Q_C to remove and we would need to remove only Q_B, just as was the case with a transistor initially biased in its forward active region. An important difference, however, is that we now have a relatively much larger base current helping the collector current discharge Q_B, just as we did with the transistor driven into saturation. Since the magnitude of this I_B is comparable to that of I_C (e.g., both are V_S/R_S in our example), the rate of discharge will be doubled and I_C will remain constant only half as long (i.e., for only a time of roughly $\tau_B/3$) and will then fall to zero more quickly. The overall turn-off transient may well be less than τ_B.

Note that in all of these cases, if more current can be drawn out of the base, the transient can be reduced correspondingly. We will see how this observation is used to increase the speed of bipolar logic circuits when we study TTL in Sec. 16.3.2.

16.2.2 Field Effect Devices

The dominant charge store in a field effect device is that associated with the gate electrode; it is the gate current that supplies this charge and determines the switching time. This is true of all field effect devices, but we will focus on the MOSFET because it is by far the most important FET; our treatment can be easily extended to other types of FETs. In the second part of this section, we will also look at a "new" device, the isolated MOS capacitor, and will learn how a modern video camera sees.

a) MOSFETs. A MOSFET is turned on or off by charging or discharging its gate, and this is done with the gate current. We normally do not think of the gate current of a MOSFET because in the steady state i_G is zero, but when the voltage on the gate is changing, the gate current is the whole story and is definitely not zero.

The variation of the gate charge with the gate voltage depends on the condition of the channel. Below threshold, the gate "capacitor" looks like a linear parallel-plate capacitor C_{OX} in series with a nonlinear depletion region charge store and the charge on the gate is a nonlinear function of v_{GS}. To the extent that there is a physical overlap between the gate metal and the drain region (e.g., the n^+-region in an n-channel device), there will also be a parallel charge store that is linearly dependent on the gate-to-drain voltage v_{GD}, but this should be very small in a modern self-aligned MOSFET.*

Above threshold the charge on the gate, q_G, can be written as [see Sec. 14.3.2, Eq. (14.42)]

$$q_G = Q_{\mathrm{TH}} + \frac{2}{3} W L C^*_{\mathrm{OX}} (v_{GS} - V_T) \tag{16.26}$$

when the MOSFET is in saturation and as

$$q_G = Q_{\mathrm{TH}} + \frac{2}{3} W L C^*_{\mathrm{OX}} \frac{(v_{GS} - V_T)^3 - (v_{GD} - V_T)^3}{v_{GD}{}^2 - 2V_T(v_{GD} - v_{GS}) - v_{GS}{}^2} \tag{16.27}$$

when the MOSFET is in the linear, or triode, region. Q_{TH} in Eqs. (16.26) and (16.27) is the gate charge at threshold. In deriving these expressions we have assumed that v_{BS} is zero and that variations in the depletion region charge along the channel are negligible. Notice also that we have written Eq. (16.27) in terms of v_{GS} and v_{GD}, rather than v_{GS} and v_{DS}, because we are thinking in terms of the charge on the gate and thus want to consider the voltage on the gate relative to the other terminals.

Looking first at Eq. (16.26), we see that when the MOSFET is in saturation, the gate charge store looks like an ideal parallel-plate capacitor $2C_G/3$, where C_G is WLC^*_{OX}, and that the charge increases linearly with the gate voltage in excess of threshold [i.e., with $(v_{GS} - V_T)$]. This is a very important and convenient result.

If the MOSFET is not saturated (i.e., if it is in its linear or triode region), the gate charge is a more complex function of both v_{GS} and v_{GD}. Closer examination of the capacitance between the gate and source, dq_G/dv_{GS}, and between the gate and drain, dq_G/dv_{GD}, showed us in Chap. 14 [see Eqs. (14.48) to (14.51) in Sec. 14.3.2] that when v_{DS} is small, the gate charge varies as $(C_G/2)v_{GD}$ and as $(C_G/2)v_{GS}$; whereas when v_{DS} is near saturation (i.e., $v_{DS} \approx v_{GS} - V_T$ and thus $v_{GD} \approx V_T$), the gate charge varies as $(2C_G/3)\, v_{GS}$ and does not vary appreciably with v_{GD}.

The capacitance of the gate is clearly a nonlinear function of the gate voltage when a MOSFET is in its linear region. Nonetheless, a convenient, worst-case approximation is to assume that the capacitance is linear and constant, just as it is in saturation, and to say that when the MOSFET is in the linear region

$$q_G \approx Q_{\mathrm{TH}} + \frac{2}{3} C_G (v_{GS} - V_T) + \frac{1}{3} C_G (v_{GD} - V_T) \tag{16.28}$$

Being able to model a charge store as linearly dependent on the terminal voltages is a major simplification and allows us to use Eq. (16.9) to determine

---

*In devices that are not self-aligned and in which there is appreciable gate-drain overlap capacitance, we model this portion of the gate charge store with a linear capacitor $C_{GD,\mathrm{ex}}$ (the "ex" standing for extrinsic). This element can be an important factor limiting switching speed, and its impact is doubled by the Miller effect since the drain voltage goes from V_{HI} to V_{LO}, while the gate voltage goes from V_{LO} to V_{HI} (or vice versa); the magnitude of the gate-to-drain voltage change is thus $2(V_{\mathrm{HI}} - V_{\mathrm{LO}})$.

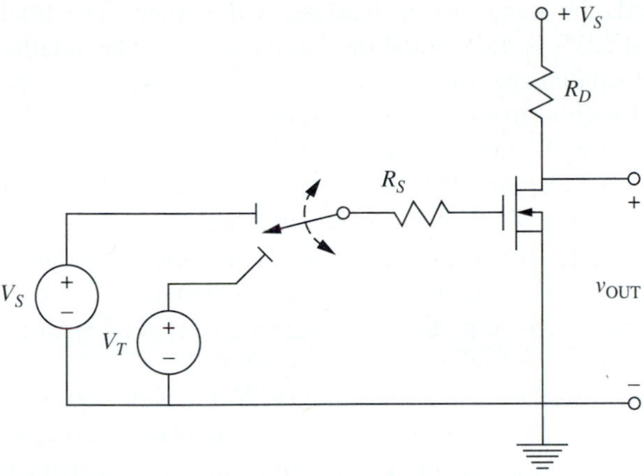

FIGURE 16.7
Simple circuit used to illustrate the switching transients encountered in turning a MOSFET on and off.

the switching transient [along with Eq. (16.6) if the charging current is constant]. To see how this works consider the circuit shown in Fig. 16.7.

With the switch in the lowest position the MOSFET is biased just at threshold and is essentially off and $v_{OUT} \approx V_S$. Using this starting point lets us ignore the transient involved with charging the gate to threshold; this should be a negligible delay in a well-designed circuit, so ignoring it is reasonable.

Next assume we move the switch to the middle position at $t = 0$. The transistor will be in saturation initially with $v_{GS} = V_T$ and $v_{OUT} = V_S$. The gate charge varies linearly with v_{GS} according to Eq. (16.26), so the charging occurs with an RC time constant of $2R_SC_G/3$ and v_{GS} varies with time as

$$v_{GS}(t) = V_T + (V_S - V_T)\left(1 - e^{-3t/2R_SC_G}\right) \tag{16.29}$$

Simultaneously, v_{OUT} increases since v_{OUT} is $(V_S - i_DR_D)$, where $i_D(t)$ is $K[v_{GS}(t) - V_T]^2/2$.

This transient continues until $v_{OUT} = (v_{GS} - V_T)$, at which time the device enters its linear region and the capacitance of the gate increases and the rate of charging decreases somewhat. The largest this capacitance becomes is C_G, however, or only 33 percent higher, so the error in assuming the same transient for $v_{GS}(t)$ is modest.* Alternatively, we could use C_G rather than two-thirds C_G for the entire transient; this is often what is done.

*These numbers ignore the Miller effect, but its impact on the intrinsic portion of the gate-to-drain charge store is small since it is active only over the final portion of the transient when the device is in the linear region. This is not true of the gate-to-drain extrinsic overlap capacitance, however, which is active independent of the region in which the device is biased (see the footnote on page 562).

Whatever fraction is used, the lesson to be learned is the same: The total gate oxide capacitance $C_G \equiv WLC^*_{ox}$ is the critical device parameter. The smaller the gate area $(= WL)$ and the smaller the value of $C^*_{ox}(= \varepsilon_o/x_o)$, the faster the MOSFET can be turned on through a given source resistance R_S.

Another important lesson to be learned about MOSFET switching is that, in contrast to the situation with BJTs, the smaller the value of R_S and/or the larger the gate charging current, the faster a MOSFET can be switched.

The turn-off transient is pretty much the same as the turn-on transient in reverse. The gate charge must be discharged to turn the MOSFET off, and if the switch is returned to this initial position, the discharge will proceed with an exponential decay having a time constant of approximately $R_S C_G$.

We will have a good deal more to say about MOSFET transients in Sec. 16.3.1 when we look at various MOSFET inverters, and you may want to proceed directly there. You will find the next section interesting, too, however, so read it eventually.

b) Isolated MOS capacitors and charge-coupled devices. All of the MOS structures we have considered thus far have included adjacent, heavily doped regions that can readily supply the inversion layer carriers. An interesting situation arises if we do not have these regions but instead simply have an isolated MOS capacitor like that illustrated in Fig. 16.8. Now if we suddenly apply a voltage greater than V_T between the gate and the substrate, an inversion layer cannot form quickly since there are very few minority carriers (electrons in the case of Fig. 16.8) in the substrate. Instead what happens initially is that all of the charge induced in the semiconductor is in the form of ionized acceptors in a depletion region that is now wider than the X_{DT} we defined in Chap. 9. The steady-state depletion region width is still X_{DT}, but initially the structure is not in its steady-state condition. The corresponding net charge, electric field, and electrostatic potential distributions are shown in Figs. 16.9*a, b,* and *c*. Going through the type of depletion approximation

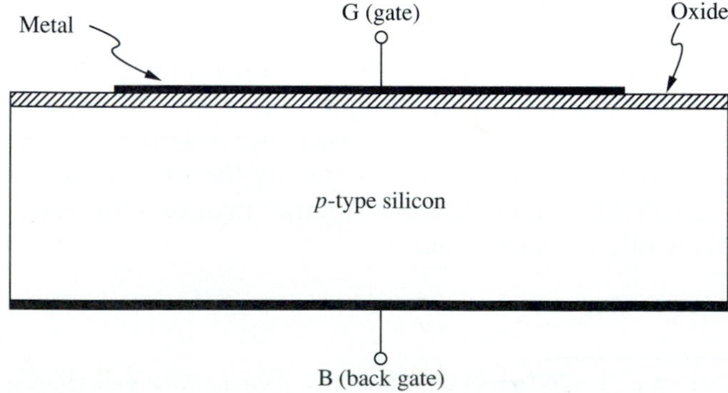

FIGURE 16.8
Cross-sectional drawing of an isolated MOS capacitor fabricated on a *p*-type silicon substrate.

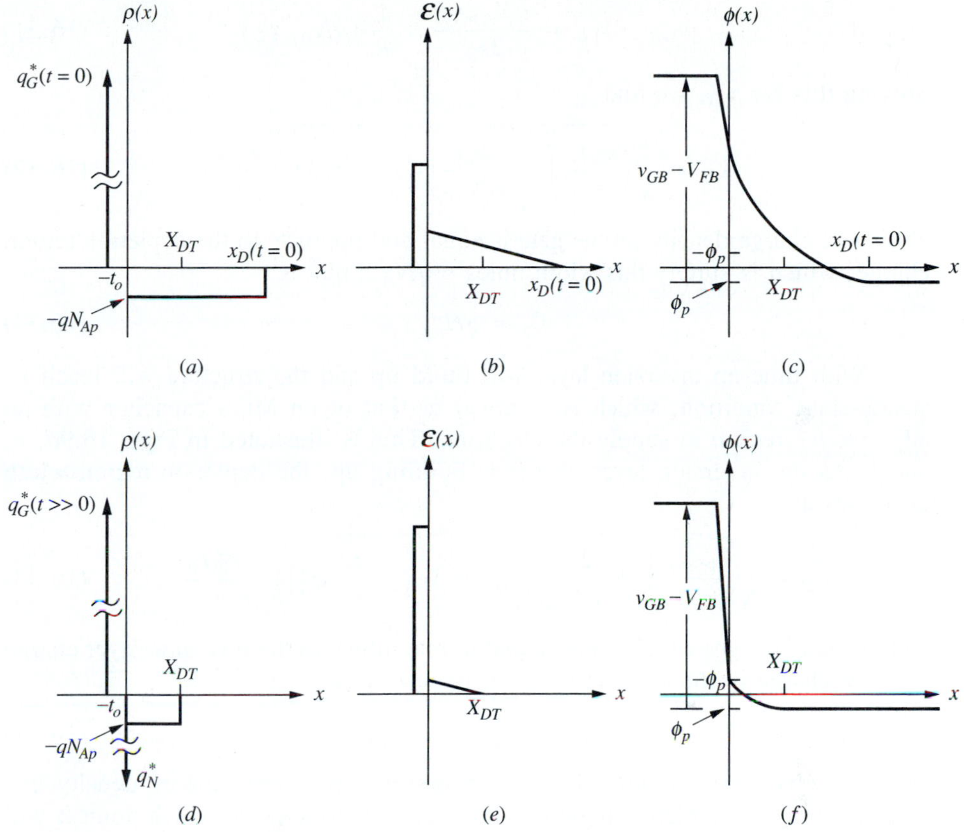

FIGURE 16.9
(*a*, *b*, *c*) The net charge, electric field, and electrostatic potential profiles, respectively, through an isolated MOS capacitor immediately after the application of a bias voltage v_{GB} that exceeds the threshold V_T; (*d*, *e*, and *f*) the same quantities at a much later time.

calculations we did in Chap. 9 to relate the charge and voltage in such structures, we find that the depletion region width x_D is the solution to the quadratic equation obtained by adding the change in electrostatic potential across the oxide and in the semiconductor (i.e., across the depletion region) and setting this sum equal to the voltage on the gate in excess of the flat-band voltage:

$$v_{GB} - V_{\text{FB}} = \frac{qN_{Ap}x_D^2}{2\varepsilon_{\text{Si}}} + \frac{t_o}{\varepsilon_o}(qN_{Ap}x_D + |q_N^*|) \tag{16.30}$$

The first term on the right-hand side of the equation is the voltage drop in the semiconductor, and the second is the drop across the oxide. Initially, of course, the inversion layer charge q_N^* is zero, so the relationship right after application of v_{GB} is

$$v_{GB} - V_{FB} = \frac{qN_{Ap}x_D^2}{2\varepsilon_{Si}} + \frac{t_o}{\varepsilon_o}(qN_{Ap}x_D) \tag{16.31}$$

Solving this for x_D, we find

$$x_D = \sqrt{\left(\frac{\varepsilon_{Si}t_o}{\varepsilon_o}\right)^2 + \frac{2\varepsilon_{Si}}{qN_{AP}}(V_{GB} - V_{FB})} - \frac{\varepsilon_{Si}t_o}{\varepsilon_o} \tag{16.32}$$

The sheet charge density on the gate is equal and opposite to the depletion region charge, which is simply this width times $-qN_{Ap}$; that is,

$$q_G^* = qN_{Ap}x_D \tag{16.33}$$

With time an inversion layer will build up and the structure will reach its steady-state condition, which is identical to that of an MOS capacitor with an adjacent n^+-region to supply the electrons. This is illustrated in Figs. 16.9*d, e,* and *f.* As the inversion layer charge is building up, the depletion region width decreases as

$$x_D = \sqrt{\left(\frac{\varepsilon_{Si}t_o}{\varepsilon_o}\right)^2 + \frac{2\varepsilon_{Si}}{qN_{Ap}}\left(v_{GB} - V_{FB} - \frac{t_o}{\varepsilon_o}|q_N^*|\right)} - \frac{\varepsilon_{Si}t_o}{\varepsilon_o} \tag{16.34}$$

and the gate charge, which is now equal in magnitude to the inversion layer charge plus the charge in the depletion region, increases as

$$q_G^* = |q_N^*| + qN_{Ap}x_D \tag{16.35}$$

with x_D given by Eq. (16.34). The inversion layer sheet charge density can increase until the depletion region width decreases to x_{DT}, at which point it will be $-(v_{GB} - V_T)\varepsilon_o/t_o$. That is, $|q_N^*|$ has the following bounds:

$$0 \le |q_N^*| \le (v_{GB} - V_T)\frac{\varepsilon_o}{t_o} \tag{16.36}$$

The key question is where do the electrons in the inversion layer of an isolated MOS capacitor come from? The answer is from several possible places. One such place is from the substrate bulk. Minority carriers from the bulk can diffuse to the edge of the depletion region and be swept to the oxide-silicon interface, where they accumulate in the inversion region. This is analogous to the reverse-bias current in a *p-n* diode and has a magnitude

$$i_1 = qA\frac{n_i^2}{N_{A_p}}\frac{D_e}{L_e} \tag{16.37}$$

A second source of electrons is generation in the depletion region, and a third source is generation at the oxide-semiconductor interface. We separate these two generation sources because the minority carrier lifetime is typically shorter, and thus the generation is somewhat higher, at the interface than in the bulk. In a modern device, however, neither of these generation mechanisms is as important as the first mechanism (i.e., diffusion from the bulk).

To estimate how long it takes to reach equilibrium, suppose we apply a bias 1 V in excess of threshold to an isolated MOS capacitor with $t_o = 40$ nm, $N_{Ap} = 10^{16}$ cm^{-3}, $D_e = 40$ cm^2, and $L_e = 2 \times 10^{-2}$ cm. The Δq_A is $AC_{ox}^*(v_{GS} - V_T)$, which is 9×10^{-7} C/cm^2. The charging current $\bar{I}_A$ is i_1, which turns out to be 2.7×10^{-12} A/cm^2. Thus, using Eq. (16.6), we find that τ_T is 3×10^5 s, or roughly 100 hours!*

Looking at this result (i.e., that it takes a relatively long time for an inversion layer to accumulate under an isolated MOS gate), device researchers soon realized that this structure could form the basis of a very sensitive light detector. Light incident in or near the depletion region will generate hole-electron pairs, and the electrons will collect in the inversion layer, building it up relatively quickly. The more intense the light, the faster the inversion layer builds up.

What is needed next is a method for sensing how much charge is in the inversion layer of a given isolated MOS capacitor. There are several ways to do this, but the most interesting and significant methods involve first moving the charge to another MOS capacitor structure or, better yet, through a series of "isolated" MOS capacitors. The process of moving the charge is illustrated in Fig. 16.10.

Suppose that the left-most MOS capacitor in Figure 16.10 is biased above threshold with a holding voltage V_{Ho} and is illuminated briefly so that an inversion layer forms under it. If an even larger transfer voltage V_{Tr} is applied to the adjacent MOS capacitor to its right and if the two structures are sufficiently close together, the inversion layer charge of the first structure will be drawn under the second. If the bias on the first electrode is then reduced to zero and the bias on the second electrode is reduced to V_{Ho}, the optically injected charge will have been moved one step to the right. If the process is now repeated with the next electrode, the charge can be moved one more step to the right. This process can be repeated over and over, moving the charge to the right through the chain of electrodes.

Strings of MOS capacitors designed to pass charges along like this are called *charge-coupled devices*, or CCDs. The individual MOS capacitors are often designed so that the charge sits to one side; they are connected in two sets that are biased alternately to move the charge along. Fig. 16.11*a* shows an example where each capacitor is a composite of two gates, each with a different threshold.

Two-dimensional arrays of CCDs can clearly also be formed that, when exposed to an image, translate the image into an array of variously charged inversion layers, as shown in Fig. 16.11*b*. By shifting the charge to the right, into another vertical CCD, which in turn shifts it downward, the image can be "scanned" out as a sequence of charge packets, each of which corresponds to one point, or pixel, of the image. The total amount of charge in each packet represents the intensity of the image at the corresponding pixel location. Notice that since the vertical

*It is interesting to note that some early researchers did not realize that the carriers in a MOSFET inversion layer could come from the source and drain regions, and thus after doing calculations like this they concluded (incorrectly) that MOSFETs would be hopelessly slow.

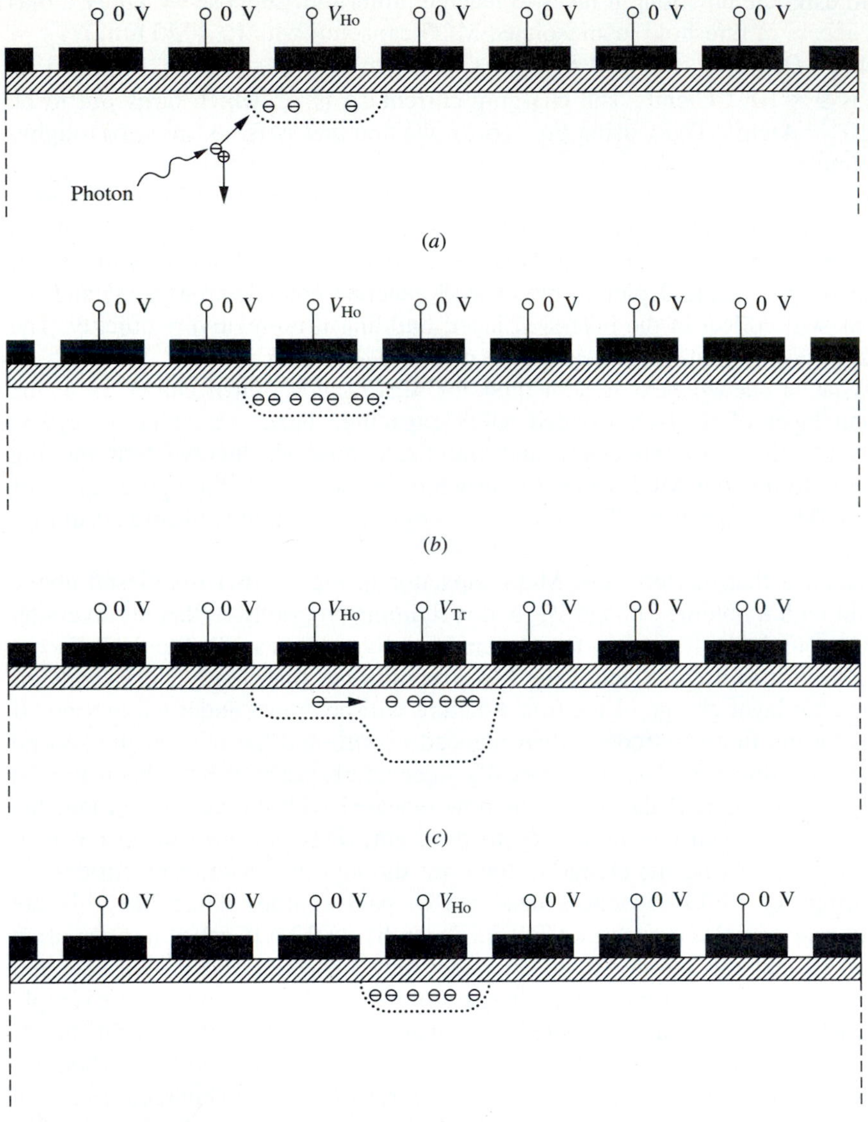

FIGURE 16.10
Process of moving the charge in the inversion layer from one MOS capacitor to the next: (*a*) optical injection of a packet of charge under an MOS capacitor biased with a holding voltage V_{Ho}; (*b*) the initially biased electrode shown with its charge packet; (*c*) the larger transfer voltage V_{Tr} applied to an adjacent electrode, to which the charge is attracted; (*d*) the bias on the first electrode reduced to zero and that on the second electrode reduced to the holding voltage V_{Ho}, completing the transfer cycle. The dotted lines indicate the maximum extent of the depletion region and give some indication of the attraction of the electrode for charge.

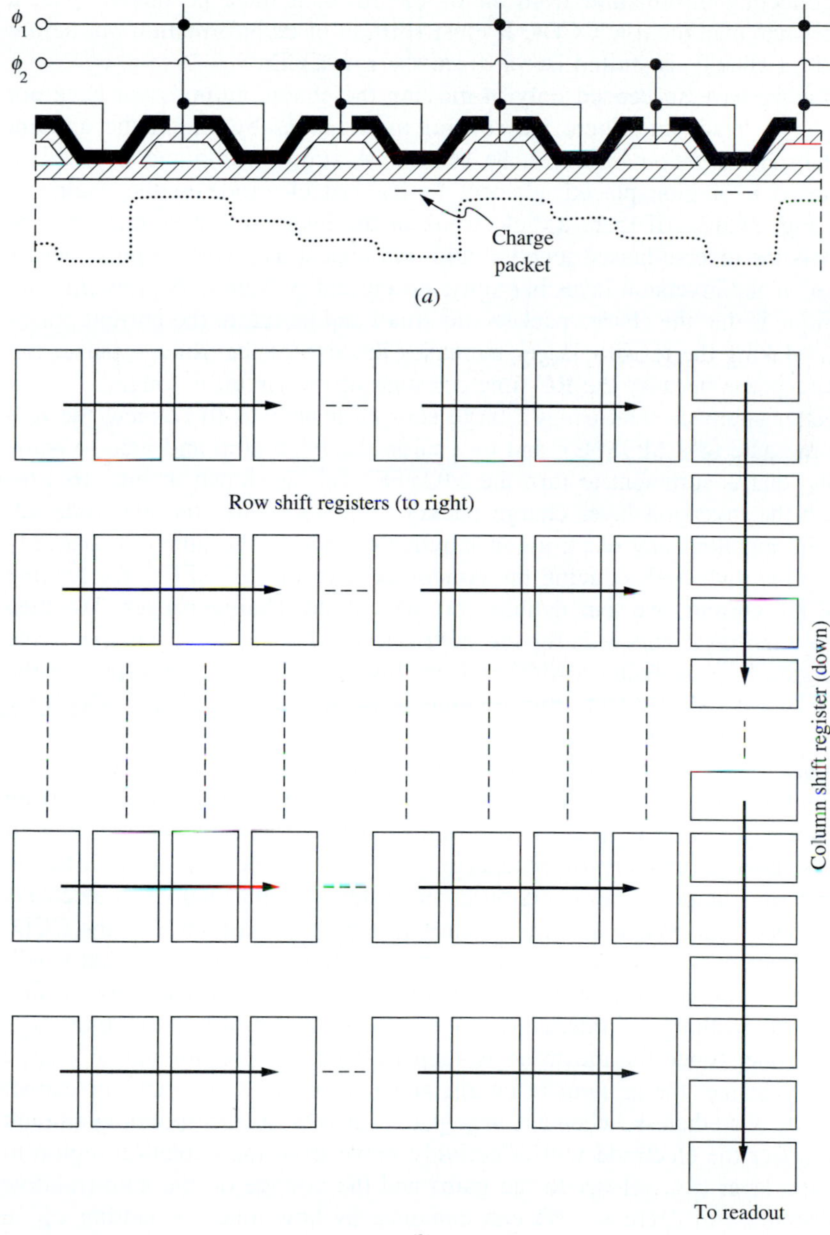

FIGURE 16.11
Charge-coupled devices: (*a*) a linear two-phase CCD shift register; (*b*) the layout of a two-dimensional CCD array of the type that might be used in an image sensor.

CCD is collecting information from all of the rows, it must be operating at a much faster rate than the row CCDs. It must shift all of its information out before another set of charges is shifted into it from the row CCDs.

So far we have succeeded only in moving the charge around, but have not yet sensed, or "read," it. There are several mechanisms by which the amount of charge in an inversion layer can be sensed. A simple technique is to use a reverse-biased n^+-region placed adjacent to the last electrode in the chain, as shown in Fig. 16.12*a*. If there are electrons in the inversion layer, they will be swept across the reverse-biased junction and will appear as a voltage pulse across the resistor; if the inversion layer is empty, no current will flow. A problem with this technique is that the charge packets are small and therefore the current pulses are small. Making the resistor larger increases the size of the voltage pulse, but slows the response because the RC time constant of the circuit is longer.

A better approach than using a large sensing resistor is to connect the n^+-region to the gate of a MOSFET and precharge the n^+-region and gate to some voltage V_{PC} that is sufficient to turn the MOSFET on, as shown in Fig. 16.12*b*. Then when the inversion layer charge packet is moved under the electrode adjacent to the junction, any electrons in it will flow across the junction, partially discharging the node and reducing the conductivity of the MOSFET. By sensing the MOSFET current, we can deduce the size of the charge packet. We then re-precharge the node and wait for the next packet. This method has the virtue of having gain because using a MOSFET in this way amplifies the effect of the charge packet. For best results this scheme is usually used with the MOSFET as part of a high-gain differential amplifier stage, and the whole package is then called a *sense amplifier*. Similar circuits are used to read MOS memories.

A final important observation is that the charge need not be removed from the inversion layer, as it is in the two schemes just described, to be detected. It can be read nondestructively by precharging a "sense" electrode to a sufficient voltage that any charge in the inversion layer of the adjacent final CCD electrode will be attracted to it. When a charge packet arrives at the last stage of the CCD, it will be attracted to the sense electrode and will change its voltage. That it will have this effect may not at first be obvious to you, but to see what happens, first realize that the precharging process places a certain amount of sheet charge, Q_G^*, on the electrode. Since the electrode is then isolated and the amount of charge on it cannot change, the amount of charge under it in the semiconductor cannot change either. Nonetheless, when a charge packet arrives, a corresponding amount of charge under the electrode will effectively move from the depletion region to the inversion layer (i.e., closer to the gate) and the voltage on the gate (relative to the substrate) will decrease. We can calculate by how much by setting q_G^* in Eq. (16.35) equal to Q_{G}^* and solving for v_{GB}. The change in voltage, Δv_{GB}, is the difference between v_{GB} with q_N^* equal to the charge in the charge packet and V_{GB} with q_N^* equal to zero; we find

$$\Delta v_{GB} = -\frac{2Q_G^*|q_N^*| - |q_N^*|^2}{2\varepsilon_{\text{Si}} q N_{Ap}} \tag{16.38}$$

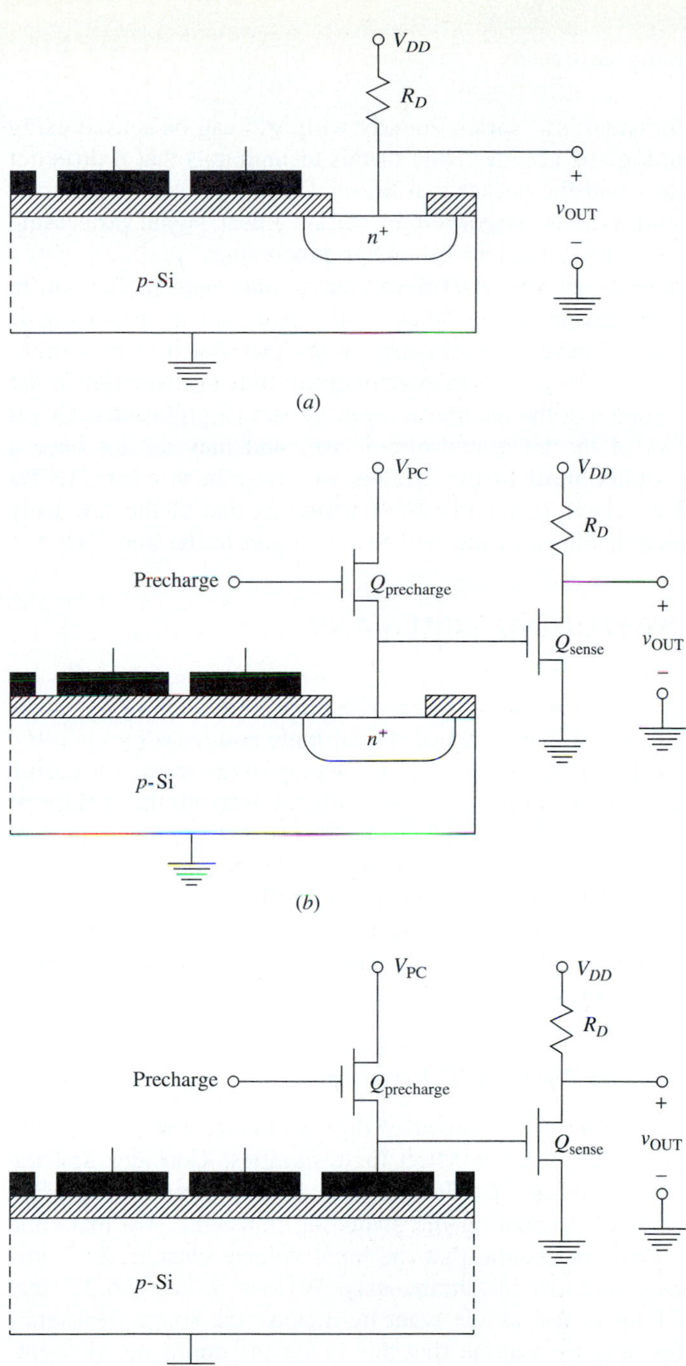

FIGURE 16.12
Three methods of sensing a charge packet in a CCD shift register: (*a*) a reverse-biased *p-n* junction diode in series with a resistor; (*b*) a reverse-biased *p-n* junction connected to a precharged MOSFET gate; (*c*) a precharged electrode connected to a MOSFET gate. The latter method does not destroy the charge packet, whereas the first two are destructive processes.

This decrease, which for small $|q_N^*|$ varies linearly with $|q_N^*|$ can be sensed using a MOSFET as shown in Fig. 16.12*c*. A virtue of this technique is that it does not destroy the charge packet, and the packet can be moved into another CCD train if so desired. This feature is most important in certain linear signal processing applications of CCDs; it is less important for image processing.

Charge-coupled devices are very useful structures, and their application in solid state video cameras, analog delay lines, and linear signal processing is widespread. They rely, as we have seen, entirely on the fact that it takes a high-quality MOS structure a very long time to reach equilibrium in inversion in the absence of any external source of the inversion layer carriers. Significantly, CCDs are very much a product of the integrated-circuit age, and they do not have a discrete-device analog, unlike most of the circuits we study in this text. CCDs were invented in 1972 and have frequently been touted as one of the few truly new device families since the dawn of the silicon revolution in the mid '60s.*

16.3 INVERTER SWITCHING TIMES AND GATE DELAYS

The problems of turning devices on and off and of estimating switching transients takes on practical significance in the world of digital logic and memory circuitry, where high computation speeds and short memory access times are major design objectives. As with many topics in this text, we can barely scratch the surface of this vast area, but we should be able to get at the essence of several important issues. We will first look at MOSFET logic and how the various inverters we considered earlier compare. Then we will consider how TTL and CCL logic gate designs address the issue of speed. Finally we will look at issues that arise as we try to make devices and circuits smaller, in particular how MOSFET designs evolve through the process called *scaling*.

16.3.1 CMOS and Other MOSFET Inverters

We will begin our consideration of the speed of digital circuits with CMOS and then compare this logic family to other MOS logic families. Consider first the CMOS inverter circuit shown in Fig. 16.13*a*. We will take this circuit to represent a typical gate for purposes of calculating the switching transients. We make the following assumptions: First we assume that the input voltage changes from low to high, and vice versa, essentially instantaneously. We saw in Sec. 16.2.2 that we can turn a MOSFET on as fast as we want by making the source resistance sufficiently small, so for now we assume that this is not the dominant transient. Instead, we assume that the dominant switching transient is that associated with

*Quantum effect devices, which are not discussed in this text, would be another truly new device family.

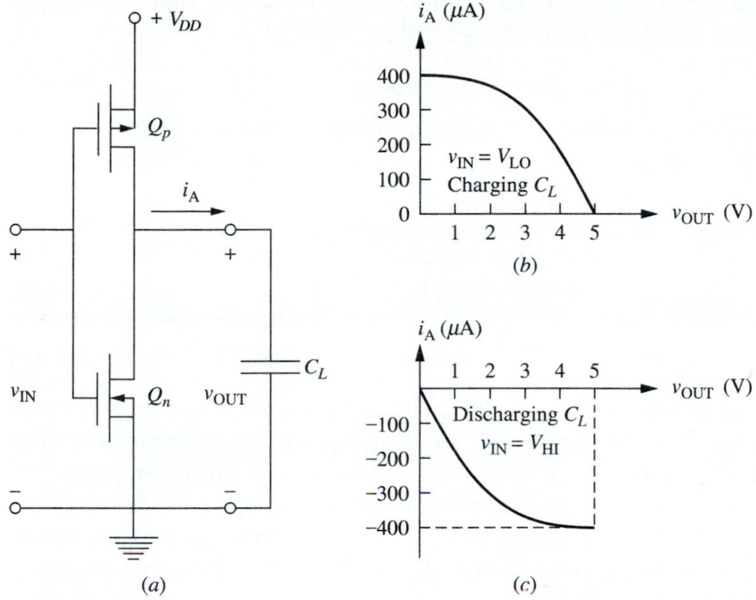

FIGURE 16.13
(*a*) CMOS inverter stage; (*b*) a plot of the current available for charging the output node as a function of the output voltage v_{OUT}; (*c*) a plot of the current available for discharging the output node as a function of v_{OUT}. The curves correspond to an inverter for which $V_{DD} = 5$ V, $V_{Tp} = -1$ V, $V_{Tn} = 1$ V, and $K_n = K_p = 50\ \mu A/V^2$.

charging and discharging the load, which we take to be an ideal capacitor C_L. C_L represents the loading presented by the inputs of the logic gates connected to the output node of the stage. Thus it is the fan-out of the stage times two-thirds the gate capacitance $C_G(= WLC_{ox}^*)$, plus any parasitic capacitance C_p associated with the interconnecting loads. Assuming that the parasitic capacitance is small,* C_L will be dominated by and proportional to C_G; that is,

$$C_L = nC_G + C_P \approx nC_G \tag{16.39}$$

where n is typically taken to be 3 or 4. We will analyze a symmetrical CMOS gate with $V_{Tn} = |V_{Tp}|$ and $K_n = K_p$. Assuming that C_{ox}^* is the same for both devices, and that $\mu_e = 2\mu_h$ and $L_n = L_p$, the condition that $K_n = K_p$ implies that we must have $W_p = 2W_n$.

Consider first the transient when the input goes from high to low. With the input high, the n-channel FET is on, the p-channel FET is off, and the output is zero, so C_L is in its discharged state. When the input goes low, the n-channel

*It is not always a good assumption that C_p will be small; see Sec. 16.3.3 for more discussion of this topic.

FET turns off and the p-channel device turns on. In the steady state, the output voltage will be V_{DD} and C_L will be charged; thus

$$\Delta q_A = C_L V_{DD} \tag{16.40}$$

The charging current will be the drain current through the p-channel device when v_{GS} is $-V_{DD}$; that is,

$$i_A = \begin{cases} \dfrac{K_p}{2}(-V_{DD} - V_{Tp})^2 = \dfrac{K_p}{2}(V_{DD} - |V_{Tp}|)^2 & \text{for } v_{\text{out}} \le -V_{Tp} \\ K_P\left[-V_{DD} - V_{Tp} - \dfrac{(v_{\text{out}} - V_{DD})}{2}\right](v_{\text{out}} - V_{DD}) & \text{for } v_{\text{out}} \ge -V_{Tp} \end{cases} \tag{16.41}$$

The meaning of all of this is best seen by plotting i_A versus v_{OUT}, as is done in Fig. 16.13*b*. We see from this figure that the charging current remains large until v_{OUT} is well over 3 V, after which it falls off approximately linearly to zero.

We have enough information to apply Eq. (16.9) and solve for the transient directly, but this is, frankly, too much work. For a first-order calculation, we do just as well to approximate i_A as a constant, $K_p(V_{DD} - |V_{Tp}|)^2/2$, during the entire transient and use Eq. (16.6). Doing this we find

$$\tau_{\text{LO}\to\text{HI}} \approx \frac{2C_L V_{DD}}{K_p(V_{DD} - |V_{Tp}|)^2} \tag{16.42}$$

The transient when the input goes from low to high is very symmetrical. The n-channel device is now on, and the p-channel device is off, so the C_L is discharged by the drain current of the n-channel device. This current is plotted as a function of v_{OUT} in Fig. 16.13*c*. Again the prudent engineering choice is to approximate this current as constant over the transient at $K_n(V_{DD} - V_{Tn})^2/2$, yielding

$$\tau_{\text{HI}\to\text{LO}} \approx \frac{2C_L V_{DD}}{K_n(V_{DD} - V_{Tn})^2} = \tau_{\text{LO}\to\text{HI}} \tag{16.43}$$

Equations (16.42) and (16.43) provide reasonable estimates of how quickly this CMOS inverter will switch, but even more importantly they also tell us how to design a faster inverter. That is, they teach us what the key parametric dependences are and where to direct our design efforts. Consider, for example, Eq. (16.43). We deduced earlier that C_L was essentially nC_G and that in a CMOS gate C_G is the sum of the gate capacitances of the n- and p-channel MOSFETs. Thus

$$C_G = n(W_n L_n + W_p L_p)C_{\text{ox}}^* \tag{16.44a}$$

Since W_p is $2W_n$, this becomes

$$C_G = 3nW_n L_{\min} C_{\text{ox}}^* \tag{16.44b}$$

Using this in Eq. (16.42) yields

$$\tau_{\text{LO}\to\text{HI}} = \tau_{\text{HI}\to\text{LO}} \approx \frac{6nW_n L_{\min}^2 C_{\text{ox}}^* V_{DD}}{W_n \mu_e C_{\text{ox}}^*(V_{DD} - V_{Tn})^2} = \frac{6nL_{\min}^2 V_{DD}}{\mu_e(V_{DD} - V_{Tn})^2} \tag{16.45}$$

Significantly, we see that the oxide capacitance and device width drop out of the picture. At the same time, the minimum gate length $L_{\min}$ enters quadratically, and we gain significantly if we can improve our technology and make $L_{\min}$ smaller. We also gain by keeping the threshold voltage near zero.

It would also seem that we should increase V_{DD}, since τ varies roughly as $(V_{DD})^{-1}$, but we have to be careful about such a conclusion. We must realize that increasing V_{DD} and reducing $L_{\min}$ impacts other important circuit characteristics, such as the power dissipation. For CMOS, the average power dissipation is given by Eq. (15.6) with P_{ON} and P_{OFF} equal to zero, and E_{CYCLE} is given by $C_L V_{DD}^2$; thus

$$P_{\mathrm{AVE}} = f C_L V_{DD}^2 = f 3n W_n L_{\min} C_{\mathrm{ox}}^* V_{DD}^2 \tag{16.46}$$

The power-delay product PDP, which we defined in Sec. 15.1.3 to be P_{ave}/f, is thus

$$\mathrm{PDP} = 3n W_n L_{\min} C_{\mathrm{ox}}^* V_{DD}^2 \tag{16.47}$$

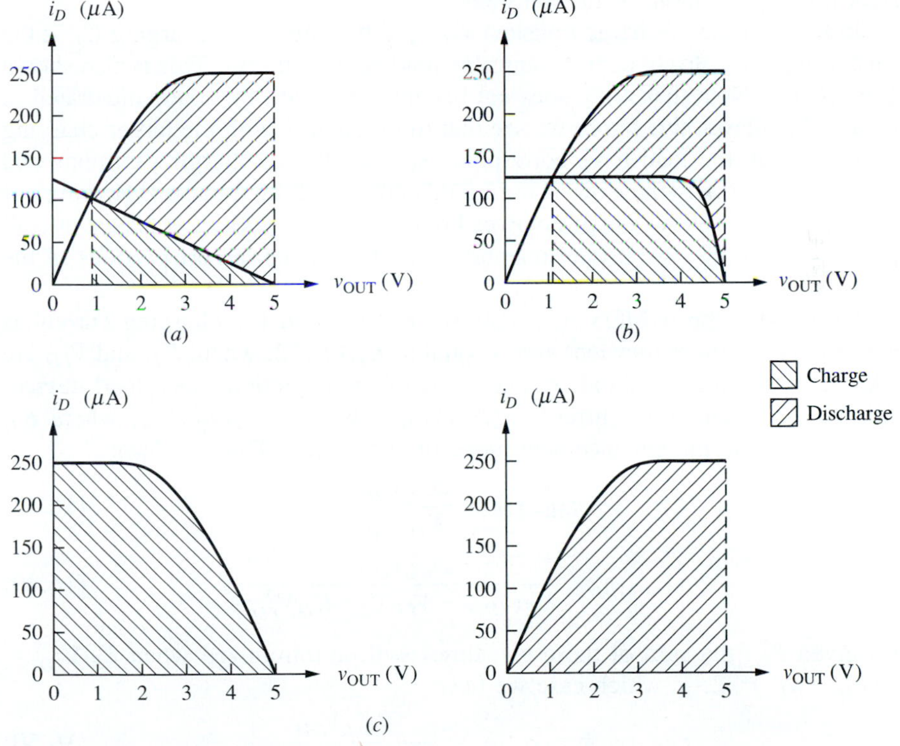

FIGURE 16.14
Currents available from the various MOS inverter stages to charge and discharge a load: (*a*) a resistor load or an enhancement mode load biased in its linear region; (*b*) a depletion mode load (i.e., *n*-MOS); (*c*) CMOS. In all cases the *n*-channel enhancement mode device is assumed to have $K = 40\ \mu\mathrm{A/V^2}$ and $V_T = 1.5$ V. The resistor load is 40 kΩ. The *n*-MOS depletion mode load has $K = 250\ \mu\mathrm{A/V^2}$ and $V_T = -1$ V, and the CMOS *p*-channel device has $K = 40\ \mu\mathrm{A/V^2}$ and $V_T = -1.5$ V.

Now we can see that it is important to reduce W_n and C^*_{ox}, along with L_{min}, and that although increasing V_{DD} may reduce the switching time, the power goes up faster than the delay comes down. The better direction to go is toward reducing V_{DD}. We will have more to say about these issues in Sec. 16.3.3.

CMOS is the lowest-power MOS logic because it dissipates power only during switching, but it is not necessarily the fastest because C_L is relatively large (i.e., we have to turn on two MOSFETs per inverter, one with twice the gate area of the other). In Chap. 15 we discussed four other MOSFET logic families, each of which used a different load device; we had resistor load, saturated enhancement mode load, linear enhancement mode load, and depletion mode load (n-MOS). In terms of the $\tau_{LO\to HI}$ transient, C_L will be charged by the drain current of the load device, so the larger this current is, the shorter the transient. This current is plotted versus v_{OUT} for several of the loads in Fig. 16.14, assuming the same static power dissipation in each inverter. (We also assume that each circuit uses the same driver, so that C_L is the same for each.) The depletion mode load (i.e., n-MOS) has the shortest transient of those shown because it maintains the charging current higher over more of the transient.

In terms of the discharge transient $\tau_{HI\to LO}$, the current discharging C_L is the drain current of the driver device minus the load device current. This is also shown in Fig. 16.14. (Note that v_{OUT} does not become zero with the loads illustrated in parts *a* and *b*.) From this figure we see that those circuits with the larger charging currents through the load have correspondingly smaller discharging currents and that n-MOS is actually the slowest during this portion of the transient. However, if we consider a full cycle, which involves both transients, n-MOS is fastest overall because with it both currents are maintained high over the largest portions of the transients.

To quantify the n-MOS transients we assume that the charging current is constant over the entire transient and is equal to $K_D V_{TD}^2/2$, where K_D and V_{TD} are the K-factor and the threshold, respectively, of the depletion mode load device. Similarly, the discharging current is $[K_E(V_{DD} - V_{TE})^2 - K_D V_{TD}^2]/2$, where K_E and V_{TE} pertain to the enhancement mode driver device. Thus we have

$$\tau_{HI\to LO} = \frac{2C_L V_{DD}}{K_D V_{TD}^2} \tag{16.48}$$

$$\tau_{LO\to HI} = \frac{2C_L V_{DD}}{K_E(V_{DD} - V_{TE})^2 - K_D V_{TD}^2} \tag{16.49}$$

For a given K_E, the sum of these two times will be minimized when $K_D V_{TD}^2 = K_E(V_{DD} - V_{TE})^2/2$, in which case we have

$$\tau_{HI\to LO} = \tau_{LO\to HI} = \frac{4C_L V_{DD}}{K_E(V_{DD} - V_{TE})^2} \tag{16.50}$$

C_L will be approximately $nW_E L_E C^*_{ox}$, and K_E is $\mu_e W_E C^*_{ox}/L_E$, so with $L_E = L_{min}$ this becomes

$$\tau_{LO\to HI} = \tau_{LO\to HI} = \frac{4nL_{min}^2 V_{DD}}{\mu_e(V_{DD} - V_{TE})^2} \tag{16.51}$$

Comparing this result to Eq. (16.45), we see that the n-MOS is somewhat faster. However, it is important to also realize that n-MOS's advantage is not large, and that this advantage will be reduced if the parasitic interconnect capacitance is significant because the currents are larger in CMOS, all else being equal.

A final observation concerning n-MOS is that the switching power is also less than in CMOS, again because C_L is smaller, so when operating at top speed, n-MOS will dissipate less power. Unfortunately, many gates in a complex logic circuit or a static memory do not switch rapidly but instead sit and wait. In that case the real advantage is in having a low static power dissipation, for which CMOS is far superior.

16.3.2 TTL and ECL Gates

The excess carrier charge stores in a bipolar transistor are intrinsic to the operation of this device and are directly proportional to the junction currents. As we saw in Sec. 16.2.1*b*, the charging and discharging rates of these stores are not changed by increasing the operating current levels of a given device. At the same time, however, there are parasitic charge stores associated with any logic gate circuit, and the delays involved with charging and discharging these stores will definitely decrease as the operating currents are increased. The idea then in operating bipolar logic to achieve the shortest switching transients is to operate at a high enough high current level that the intrinsic switching delays due to the excess charge stores are the dominant delays. There is no point in increasing the currents beyond the level where this occurs because the switching delays cannot be reduced further.

As the currents are increased the power dissipation will also increase. Initially, as the switching delays are decreasing, this is just the classic trade-off between speed and power. Ultimately, however, the switching delay saturates at some minimum bound, the *intrinsic switching delay*, and further increases in current just lead to more power dissipation without a corresponding increase in speed.*

The two bipolar logic families we discussed in Chap. 15, transistor-transistor logic (TTL) and emitter-coupled logic (ECL), each take a different approach to the problem of achieving switching speeds limited only by intrinsic time constants. We will take a brief qualitative look at each now.

a) TTL. A basic transistor-transistor gate, which we discussed in Sec. 15.3.2, is illustrated in Fig. 16.15. The first thing to recall is that TTL is a saturating logic family, meaning that some of the bipolar transistors in the circuit, specifically Q_D and Q_S, are in saturation when the input is high. We saw earlier that with a

*There is no corresponding delay saturation in MOSFETs; a MOSFET always switches faster with a larger input current. The problem with MOSFETs is getting large currents from them, which is why we try to make them smaller. The problems involved with this are discussed in Sec. 16.3.3.

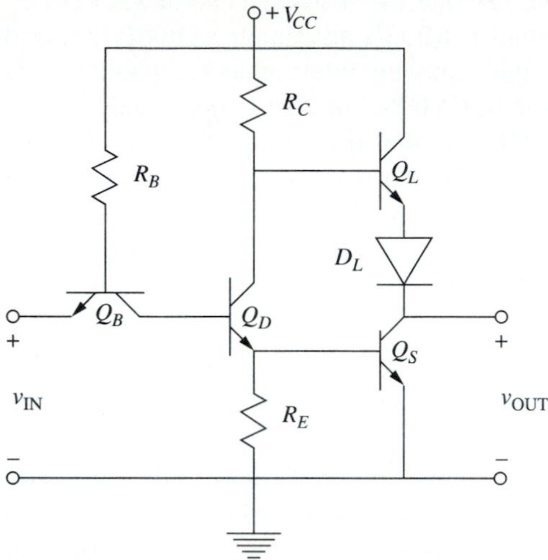

FIGURE 16.15
Transistor-transistor logic inverter stage similar to that discussed in Sec. 15.3.2 and illustrated in Fig. 15.16.

constant base current we can turn a BJT on and drive it into saturation faster than we can bias it into the forward active region. The transient is even faster if we put a Schottky diode in parallel with the critical base-collector junctions (i.e., by using Schottky clamps), and this is common practice in TTL.

Looking at the TTL gate, we see that large base currents are supplied to turn on and saturate Q_D and Q_S when the inputs are high. The turn-on transient will thus be relatively fast.

To turn a TTL gate off, the excess charge stored in the bases of Q_D and Q_S has to be removed. Q_B plays an important role in this because it becomes active and can actually pull a larger current out of the base of Q_D than the original charging current. Once Q_D is off and its collector current has become small, Q_S will begin to turn off. There is no device actively removing charge from the base of Q_S, but it can discharge through R_E. Furthermore, as the collector current continues to flow it will itself discharge the excess carrier charge store in the base. The key step, clearly, is turning Q_D off so that the process of discharging Q_S can begin, and Q_B does this very effectively.

The transistor Q_L is important in providing drive to charge any parasitic charge stores associated with the output node. As we mentioned in Chap. 15, this active element is much more effective than a collector resistor in providing the necessary charging current. In the other half of the transient, when the output node must be discharged, Q_S is active and will quickly draw charge off the output node.

Summarizing TTL, we see that it is a so-called saturating logic that uses Schottky clamping to keep the key transistors from actually saturating and uses several active transistors (i.e., Q_B, Q_L, and Q_S) to charge and discharge key charge stores in the gate.

b) ECL. A basic emitter-coupled logic gate, which we first discussed in Sec. 15.3.3, is illustrated in Fig. 16.16*a*. Unlike TTL, ECL is a nonsaturating logic family; during switching the transistors in the circuit are changed between bias points in cutoff and the forward active region. This is illustrated in Figs. 16.16*b*

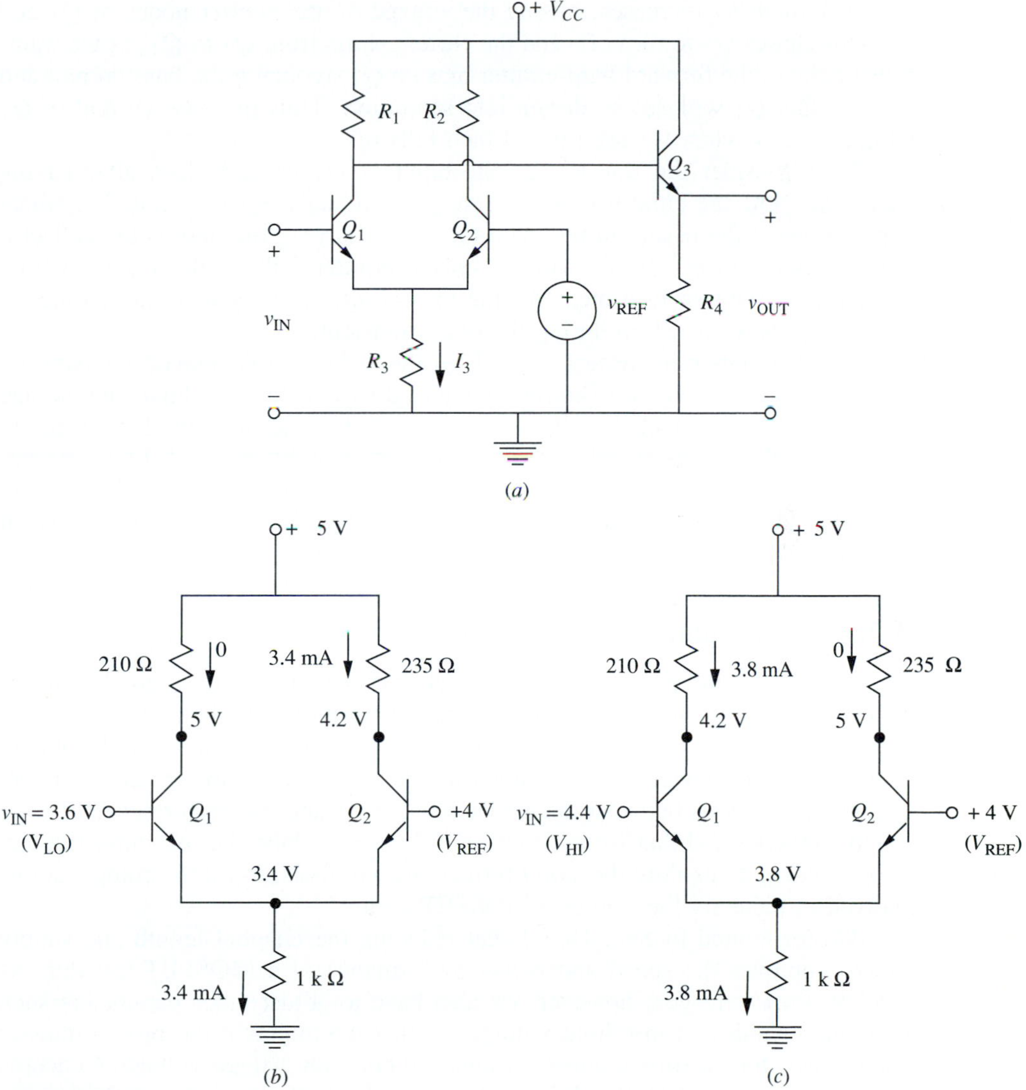

FIGURE 16.16
(*a*) Emitter-coupled logic inverter stage similar to that discussed in Sec. 15.3.3 and illustrated in Fig. 15.17; (*b*) the voltage and current levels in a representative stage when the input is low; (*c*) the voltage and current levels when the input is high.

and c, in which the voltage and current levels are indicated on a representative ECL gate (the one used in the example on page 533) with the input, respectively, low and high.

Figures 16.16b and c can also help us understand the switching transients in an ECL gate. Imagine first that the input, after having been low, is suddenly changed to high (i.e., 4.4 V). Since the emitter of Q_1 is initially at 3.4 V, the bias on the base-emitter junction is actually quite large and a relatively large base current will flow, helping to turn on Q_1 quickly. As Q_1 turns on, however, the current through R_3 increases, raising the voltage on the emitter nodes of Q_1 and Q_2. This causes Q_2 to turn off, and the current shifts from Q_2 to Q_1, as we want. It also reduces the forward base-emitter bias on Q_1, reducing the base current and ensuring that Q_1 will not be driven into saturation. Thus the base current of Q_1 is high initially when we need it and then falls off.

Next consider the transient as the input of Q_1 is made low, after having been high. Now the emitter-base bias on Q_1 is actually negative initially, which helps discharge the base, but the main factor discharging the base is the collector current. As Q_1 turns off, the voltage on the emitter falls as the voltage across R_3 decreases. This in turn increases the bias on Q_2, turning it on more quickly, much as Q_1 was turned on during the other transient.

Another important aspect of ECL is the reduced role played by parasitic charge stores in the circuit. The role is reduced by two factors. First, the voltage swings in ECL are much less than in the other logic families we have studied. The sizes of the charge stores are correspondingly smaller. Second, ECL operates at relatively high current levels, meaning that there is more current available to charge and discharge the parasitic charge stores. The downside of ECL is that it dissipates a lot of power, but it is the fastest logic family.

16.3.3 Device and Circuit Scaling

It is clear from our preceding discussions that making devices smaller makes them and the switching circuits that incorporate them faster. Thus it is a general objective of device and circuit designers as well as process engineers to be able to reduce the size of devices. At the same time, however, we recognize that there are complex interactions between the device parameters and the performance of even a simple inverter and that we must be careful to understand the full impact of any changes made. To explore this point further, we will look now at the complications involved in reducing the size of a MOSFET circuit.

We mentioned in Sec. 16.3.1 that reducing the channel length and supply voltage improves the speed and power performance of a MOSFET inverter. As we make these changes, however, we also have to adjust other parameters such as the gate width and threshold voltage, so that we maintain the proper transfer characteristic for maximum noise margins and optimum trigger voltage. Concerns such as this have led to the development of rules to follow when reducing the dimensions and operating levels of a logic family. This process is called *scaling*, and the rules are called scaling rules. The use of the verb *scale* in this context implies that it is necessary to somehow shrink the inverter dimensions and its operating parameters in unison to ensure proper operation.

To explore this issue a bit more, imagine that we have made advances in our processing technology and we are now able to reduce the gate length of our MOSFETs by a factor s from L to L/s, where $s > 1$. We call s our *scaling factor*. If we reduce L, we should also reduce the gate width W by the same factor to W/s, so that K and our transfer characteristics stay the same. If these two dimensions are all that we change, none of the device terminal characteristics change, but the power and switching delay both decrease [see Eqs. (16.45) and (16.46)]. It sounds like a big win all around.

There are subtleties that arise, however, that complicate this picture. Very importantly, as we reduce the lateral dimensions of a MOSFET we find that we must also reduce the vertical dimensions to keep the device operating as much as possible in the gradual channel approximation regime (i.e., in such a way that the drift fields and currents in the channel are predominantly parallel to the gate—y-directed in our convention). This may sound like a strange constraint because, although we have seen that the gradual channel approximation is a very convenient model, it is hard to justify restricting a device's structure just for our convenience! Of course, we can't justify such constraints on this basis; the real reason we try to design a device to operate in this regime is because that is where we find we obtain the optimal device characteristics. That is, we find in practice that unless we scale a device's dimensions vertically, as well as horizontally, the device characteristics are severely degraded. Specifically, we find that the output conductance g_o increases and that it may even be impossible to turn the device off (i.e., to close the switch, as it were). Thus the reason we also scale vertically is to get good output characteristics.

To scale vertically by a scaling factor s, we must increase the substrate doping as s^2 to decrease the depletion region width as $1/s$, and we must scale the oxide thickness by $1/s$, which increases C_{ox}^* by s. The net effect on K of these changes is to increase it by s, which means the currents in the circuit will be larger by a factor of s if we operate at the same voltages.

Changes in both the oxide thickness and the substrate doping level combine to reduce the magnitude of several terms in the threshold voltage V_T by $1/s$, although other terms are unaffected. Through processing, we can choose to compensate for these changes to keep V_T unchanged or we can scale V_T by $1/s$. Our decision depends on what we do with the supply voltage V_{DD}.

If we scale both the power supply and threshold voltages by a factor of $1/s$, the drain currents in the circuit will also scale as $1/s$ because they are proportional to these voltages squared, a factor that scales as $1/s^2$, and to K, which scales as s. For a fixed operating frequency f, the gate delay will then scale by $1/s$ [see Eq. (16.45)], and the dynamic power dissipation per gate will scale as $1/s^3$. The tendency will be to increase f proportionally to the decrease in gate delay, however, since we always want things to go faster, and if we scale f by s the dynamic power dissipation per gate will scale as $1/s^2$, since it is proportional to f. These effects are summarized in Table 16.1.

Table 16.1

		Scaling factors for operating voltage scaling factor of 1/s		**Scaling factors for operating voltage scaling factor of 1**	
Drain current		$1/s$		1	
Gate delay		$1/s$		s	
		Frequency scaling factor		**Frequency scaling factor**	
		1	s	1	s
Dynamic power	Per gate	$1/s^3$	$1/s^2$	$1/s$	1
	Per cm^2	$1/s$	1	s	s^2
Statics power	Per gate	$1/s^2$	$1/s^2$	s	s
	Per cm^2	1	1	s^3	s^3
		Metal and field oxide thickness scaling factor		**Metal and field oxide thickness scaling factor**	
		$1/s$	1	$1/s$	1
Current density in metal		s	1	s^3	s^2
Charging time	Scaled length	$1/s$	$1/s^2$	$1/s^2$	$1/s^3$
	Fixed length	1	$1/s$	$1/s$	$1/s^2$

The static power dissipation per gate in n-MOS and the other MOSFET families in which it is relevant scales as $1/s^2$ also. This comes about because the static power is proportional to the product of V_{DD} and I_{ON}, both of which scale as $1/s$.

Notice, finally, that the area occupied by a given circuit will scale as $1/s^2$ if we scale all of the lateral dimensions by $1/s$, and thus the power dissipation per square centimeter in an integrated circuit will stay constant since power and area both scale by $1/s^2$. This is fortunate because if the power did not go down at least as fast as the area of the circuit, the power density would increase and limit how tightly circuits could be packed on an integrated-circuit chip. With a constant power dissipation density, the number of circuits that can be placed on a given size chip scales (increases) as s^2, a very significant factor.

Clearly it is desirable to scale the supply voltage, V_{DD}, but we must also be aware of the realities and restrictions of the marketplace. Many circuits are designed to replace existing circuits already in use in systems, and many others are designed to be compatible with existing integrated-circuit product lines. In both cases, the power supply voltages are fixed and the designer does not have the freedom to change them. On the other hand, the practical incentives to develop new generations of circuits and systems that operate on lower supply voltages is clearly strong, and "standard" supply levels have decreased over the years from 12 V to 9 V to 5 V to, more recently, 3 V. Scattered circuits biased from 2-V and even 1-V supplies are even found. (The 1-V increments seen at the lower voltage levels correspond to the nominal voltage available from most dry battery cells.)

Also in scaling voltages, we must be aware of the realities of circuit operation in a real, noisy environment. If we scale the voltages as $1/s$, then the high and low voltage levels and the noise margins will all be scaled by $1/s$. If we scale far enough (i.e., make s large enough), the noise margins will become impractically small and the circuit will no longer operate reliably. There is thus a very real limit to how far we can scale a given design.

If for whatever reason we cannot reduce the voltages in a circuit as we scale the dimensions, we run the risk of exceeding breakdown fields at certain critical points, especially in the gate regions. Electric field is voltage divided by length, and thus if the voltages are unchanged and dimensions are scaled by $1/s$, the field strengths will scale as s. Only by also scaling voltages by $1/s$ can we keep the electric field strengths from increasing dangerously.

Another consequence of not scaling the voltage is that the dissipated power density increases dramatically. The currents now scale as s, rather than as $1/s$, and if the frequency is increased as s, the dynamic power density increases as s^2! Clearly we cannot increase the packing density very much at this rate before we get into trouble with excessive heating.

Finally, consider what is happening in the thin film interconnects (i.e., wires) in an integrated circuit and with the parasitic elements as we scale. The currents are scaled as $1/s$, as we have said. Because we assume that we scale both the thickness and the width of the interconnect lines, the conductor cross-sectional area is scaled as $1/s^2$. The current densities in these conductors thus scale as s (i.e., they increase). This can lead to serious reliability problems because the metal can actually be moved at very high current densities, a phenomenon called *electromigration*, and this is to be avoided. Consequently, the thicknesses of the metal films used as interconnects on an integrated circuit are usually not scaled, so the cross-sectional area of the leads scales more nearly as $1/s$ and the current density stays constant.

Parasitic lead capacitances should scale roughly as $1/s$, because lateral areas scale as $1/s^2$ and capacitances per unit area scale as s (the vertical thickness scales as $1/s$). Lead resistances will scale as 1 if the metal thickness is not scaled and as s if it is. In the former case, any relevant RC time constants scale as $1/s$, a desirable result, whereas in the latter case they are unchanged.

The impact of scaling on the time required to charge a parasitic capacitance with a current-source-like input will depend on whether or not the voltages are scaled. To see this we begin with Eq. (16.6) and rewrite Δq_{A} as $C_{\text{A}}\Delta v_{\text{AB}}$, where C_{A} is the parasitic capacitance; this yields

$$\tau_T = \frac{C_{\text{A}}\Delta v_{\text{AB}}}{\bar{I}_{\text{A}}} \tag{16.52}$$

Writing the transient time in this way, we can see that if the voltages as well as dimensions are scaled, then τ_T will decrease as $1/s$ because $C_{A,}\Delta v_{AB}$, and $\bar{I}_A$ all scale as $1/s$. If the voltages are not scaled, then τ_T decreases even more quickly (i.e., as $1/s^2$) since the charging current $\bar{I}_A$ is now larger by a factor of s, whereas C_A is smaller by $1/s$ and Δv_{AB} is unchanged.

The preceding discussion assumes that the capacitances scale as $1/s$ because we have assumed that all of the dimensions are scaled as $1/s$. We have seen in the case of metal interconnects, however, that there are good reasons not to scale all of the vertical dimensions in an integrated circuit; that is, we are better off keeping the metal lines thicker. The same is true of the dielectric layers other than the dielectric under the MOSFET gate. If we do not scale the dielectric layers in the so-called field regions (i.e., in the regions outside of the gate regions) but instead keep them thick, then the parasitic capacitances associated with them will scale as $1/s^2$ rather than simply as $1/s$ and the delay times associated with charging or discharging these parasitic charge stores will be correspondingly smaller, scaling as $1/s^2$ if the voltages are scaled and as $1/s^3$ if they are not.

Any RC time constants associated with metal leads also decrease if the field dielectric is not scaled; in fact, they decrease by as much as $1/s^2$ if both the metal and field dielectric are kept thick (i.e., are not scaled).

This all sounds pretty good, but there is one important further consideration. As we scale circuits and increase their density we are not content only to make smaller versions of the same circuits; instead we tend to want to make larger and larger circuits. An obvious example is a memory array. We don't want smaller 1-Mbit chips; we want to replace our 1-Mbit chips with 4-Mbit chips that fit the same package. The result is that the length of critical path interconnect lines often does not decrease at all, (i.e., it scales as 1 rather than as $1/s$). The corresponding parasitic capacitances then scale only as $1/s$, assuming the field dielectric is kept thick (not scaled), and the transient associated with charging the parasitic capacitance of a line with a current source [e.g., Eq. (16.52)] scales as $1/s$ (i.e., decreases).

The overall picture we have presented of the problem of scaling a MOSFET inverter circuit is summarized in Table 16.1. To summarize its message and our discussion in a general way, we can say that we have seen that making devices smaller is important to making circuits faster and to reducing power dissipation, but we have also seen that any changes must be made in concert. We have seen that certain parameters, such as the thickness of the interconnect metal and of the field dielectric, are best left unchanged, whereas other parameters, such as the power supply voltages and the size of the chip, may be dictated by other considerations.

There are several other interesting things to note specifically in looking at Table 16.1. First, it is clear from the right-hand columns that not scaling the voltages actually makes a circuit faster, as we have noted before, but it also results in rapid increases in the power densities. This is particularly true of the static power and is another strong argument for CMOS. Not scaling the voltages also has a major negative impact on the current densities in the metal lines, even if the metal thickness is not scaled. It is clear from the table that we must eventually face the need to scale operating voltages to keep the power and current densities under control. It is also clear that we must not scale the metal and field oxide thickness if we want to increase the operating frequency of the circuit. This requires that the charging time (the last line in Table 16.1, assuming that we also want to keep the chip size large and pack more circuitry onto it) scale at least as $1/s$, and this occurs only in the second column for a situation in which the voltage is also being scaled, as we have urged we should try to do. Finally, we should point out that we have assumed that all dimensions and voltages are being scaled by the same amount. Although it is desirable to scale the dimensions by the same factor, a different factor could be used for the voltages as a compromise between the demands of increasing the operating speed, keeping the power and current densities under control, and fitting in with existing voltage level standards and convention.

16.4 SUMMARY

In this chapter we have considered the problem of estimating the large-signal switching times of nonlinear semiconductor devices. We have seen that charge stores, which are also often nonlinear, in devices and circuits are the primary limitations to how quickly the state of a device or circuit can be changed.

We have looked at the general problem of switching and have identified two situations in which it is possible to obtain reasonable, perhaps even analytical, solutions. One such situation occurs when the current charging or discharging a charge store can be approximated by a constant value over the duration of the transient. In that case the transient time is approximately just the total charge store divided by the current [Eq. (16.6)]. The second situation we identified occurs when the charge store can be approximated as a fixed-value linear capacitor over the duration of the transient. In this case, the time derivative of the voltage is directly proportional to the current [Eq. (16.9)] and the transient waveform is found by integrating the current.

We have also looked at the specific problems of turning devices on and off and have turned to using this information to estimate the switching times of digital circuits. We have seen that bipolar junction devices, specifically *p-n* diodes and BJTs, have intrinsic diffusive charge stores that are directly proportional to terminal currents. This then places a lower limit on the switching time that is essentially independent of the operating current level, assuming that we are at current levels sufficiently large that the parasitic charge stores are negligible. MOSFETs, on the other hand, can be turned on or off arbitrarily quickly if a large enough current is supplied to charge or discharge the gate (until, of course, the switching times approach the transit time of carriers through the channel); the real problem is getting enough current from a MOSFET to switch the following device quickly. In this light, we have looked at the implications of making devices smaller and the options we face in doing so. We have used MOSFET logic as the vehicle to examine scaling rules and have shown that it is desirable to scale the device dimensions and the operating voltages as much as possible while keeping the metal and field oxide thicknesses unchanged. This allows us to realize the attractive goals of increasing the operating frequency, maintaining the same chip size, and not melting the circuit.

PROBLEMS

16.1 Three possible connections of a bipolar transistor as a diode were illustrated in Fig. 16.3. To quantify the differences in the switching behaviors of those connections, consider using a transistor with $w_E = 2w_B = 0.2w_C = 1\,\mu\text{m}, N_{DE} = 5N_{AB}, N_{AB} = 5N_{DC}$, and $N_{AB} = 5 \times 10^{16}\ \text{cm}^{-3}$. Assume that the minority carrier lifetimes are infinite and that $D_e = 3D_h = 30\ \text{cm}^2/\text{V}\cdot\text{s}$ throughout the device.

(a) Sketch the excess minority carrier populations in the transistor for each of the connections, assuming a moderate forward bias, (i.e., $V_D >> kT/q$). Notice that in the connection of Fig. 16.3*b* the base-collector junction actually becomes forward-biased.

(b) Estimate the duration of the first portion of the switching transient, τ_1, and the time constant in the second portion, τ_2 (refer to Figure 16.2) in the connection of Fig. 16.13*a*.

(c) Repeat part b for the connection of Fig. 16.3*c*.

(d) Now consider the connection in Fig. 16.3*b*.

(i) What happens to the excess carriers stored in the collector region as the transistor is turned off; that is, how does the excess dissipate?

(ii) Based on your understanding of (i), how would you expect the turn-off transient in this connection to compare to those of the connections Figs. 16.3*b* and *c*?

16.2 You are asked to estimate the switching speed of the chain of bipolar inverters described in problem 15.11. Follow the steps outlined below:

(a) Sketch the excess minority carrier charge distribution in one transistor of the inverter chain when that transistor is on and its output is low. Label the vertical axis (i.e., p' and n') in terms of the current-source value I and the device parameters specified in the problem statement (algebraic expressions are expected).

(b) Estimate the time for a transistor in this inverter to turn on when its input voltage is suddenly changed from V_{LO} to V_{HI}; give your answer in terms of the current I and the parameters given.

(c) Estimate how many times faster or slower the same transistor turns off when the output of the preceding stage switches suddenly from high to low (i.e., from V_{HI} to V_{LO}).

16.3 In Sec. 16.2.1*a*, we considered turning a diode on (and off) when it was connected through a resistor to a voltage source. Now consider turning a diode on with a current source, as illustrated in Fig. P16.3.

Assume that you have a silicon p^+-n diode with $w_p = w_n = 10\ \mu\text{m}, D_e = 40\ \text{cm}^2/\text{s}, D_h = 15\ \text{cm}^2/\text{s}, N_{Ap} = 5 \times 10^{18}\text{cm}^{-3}, N_{Dn} = 5 \times 10^{16}\ \text{cm}^{-3}$, and $\tau_{\min} = \infty$. The cross-sectional area of the device is $10^{-4}\ \text{cm}^2$, and I_T is 1 mA.

(a) Draw the excess carrier population distributions in this device for $t >> 0$.

(b) Calculate the turn-on transient time of this device assuming the dominant charge store is that in the excess carrier populations.

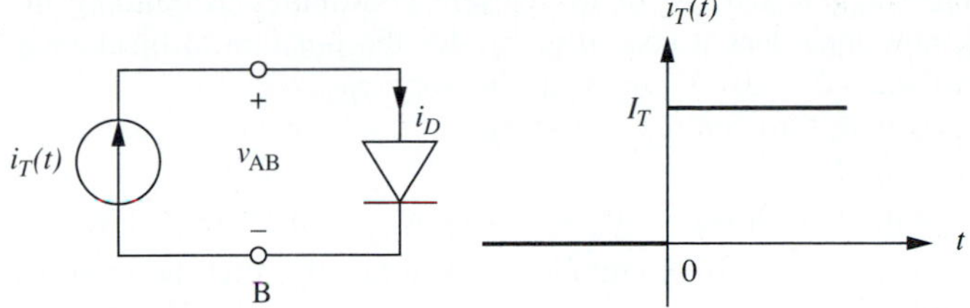

FIGURE P16.3
(*a*) Emitter-coupled logic inverter stage similar to that discussed in Sec. 15.3.3 and illustrated in Fig. 15.17; (*b*) the voltage and current levels in a representative stage when the input is low; (*c*) the voltage and current levels when the input is high.

(*c*) What is v_{AB} for $t >> 0$?
(*d*) Sketch (qualitatively) the excess carrier population profile in this device at several times during the transient to illustrate how it will evolve with time.
(*e*) Your sketches for part d should show $p'(0^+)$ increasing with time. What will be the approximate function dependence of $p'(0^+)$ on time?
(*f*) How do you expect v_{AB} to depend on time for $t \geq 0$?
(*g*) Calculate the change in charge stored in the junction depletion regions, and estimate how much time supplying this charge adds to the transient.

16.4 Problem 16.3 concerned turning a diode on with a current source. In this problem we consider turning the same diode off with a current source. The circuit is the same as in problem 16.3 ,but now consider the current waveform shown in Fig. P16.4. After the current changes sign at $t = 0$, reverse current I_T flows through the diode. Initially this current primarily removes charge from the diffusion charge store (i.e., excess carriers). After v_{AB} reaches zero and becomes negative, this current charges the junction depletion region. This continues until v_{AB} is sufficiently negative that the junction breaks down, at which point the transient is complete.

(*a*) Estimate the time at which $v_{AB} = 0$; call this τ_{R1}.

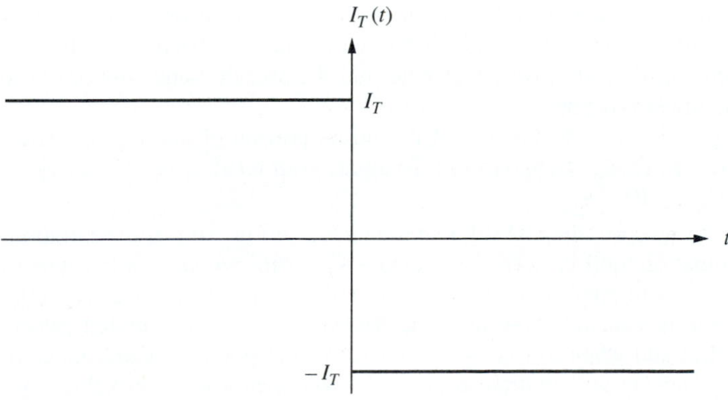

FIGURE P16.4

(*b*) Assuming that once v_{AB} is zero all of the current contributes to building the depletion region, how long does it take after τ_{R1} for the junction to breakdown if the breakdown field is 3×10^5 V/cm? Call this time τ_{R2}.

(*c*) How does v_{AB} vary with time for $\tau_{R1} \leq \tau \leq \tau_{R2}$?

(*d*) What is v_{AB} at $t = \tau_{R2}$?

16.5 Consider an abrupt *p-n* diode with $w_n = w_p = 2\ \mu\text{m}, N_{Ap} = 10^{17}\ \text{cm}^{-3}, N_{Dn} = 5 \times 10^{18}\ \text{cm}^{-3}$, and $\mu e = 4\mu_h = 1600\ \text{cm}^2/\text{V}\cdot\text{s}$. Assume also that the minority carrier lifetime is infinite.

(*a*) What is the ratio of hole to electron current across this junction? Are you justified in neglecting one of these current components?

(*b*) What is τ_{tr} for this device? [See Eq. (16.16).]

(*c*) How does τ_{tr} change if w_n and w_p are reduced to 0.5 μm?

(*d*) If the original diode had been symmetrically doped with $N_{Dn} = N_{Ap} = 10^{17}\ \text{cm}^{-3}$, what would τ_T in Eq. (16.13) be? To answer this, first derive the general expression for τ_T in a symmetrically doped diode. State your result, and then evaluate it for this specific device.

(*e*) What is the ratio of hole to electron current in the diode of part d? Comment on this result in light of your answer in part d.

16.6 (*a*) Calculate the emitter, base, and collector transit times for the transistor structure described in problem 8.1.

(*b*) Calculate the same quantities you did in part a for a *pnp* transistor in which the magnitudes of the doping levels in the emitter, base, and collector are identical to those in the *npn* device.

(*c*) Comment on the relative speed of *npn* and *pnp* bipolar junction transistors. Consider both turn-on and turn-off transients.

16.7 (*a*) The analysis of the transients when driving a transistor into and out of saturation in Sec. 16.2.1*b* assumed that R_S and R_C in Fig. 16.4 were equal. Establish the duration of the turn-on transient if you instead have $R_S = 5R_C$. (Continue to use $V_S = V_{CC}$.)

(*b*) Discuss the effect of changing R_S from R_C to $5R_C$ on the turn-off transient, that is, when the switch in Fig. 16.4 is changed from the middle to the upper position.

16.8 (*a*) In the discussion of the turn-on transient of a MOSFET in Sec. 16.2.2*a*, the gate was precharged to a voltage V_T and the MOSFET was always on. Consider now how the turn-on transient would differ if this had not been done, that is, if the V_T source in Fig. 16.7 were not there and the switch made connection to ground in the lower position.

(*b*) Derive an expression for the duration of the initial portion of the transient (i.e., the time for v_{GS} to change from 0 to V_T). Evaluate your result if $V_S = 5$ V, $V_T = 1$ V, and $R_S C_G = 10^{-8}$ s.

16.9 Immediately after turning on, the MOSFET in the circuit in Fig. 16.7 is in saturation, and it stays in saturation until $v_{\text{OUT}}(t) = v_{GS}(t) - V_T$. Until we know what type of capacitive loading is connected to the output terminal we cannot calculate $v_{\text{OUT}}(t)$, so it is not possible to calculate how long the MOSFET remains saturated [where Eq. (16.29) is valid] and when it becomes linear (at which point the capacitance of the gate increases and the gate-to-drain capacitance assumes a nonzero value). We can, however, set bounds on this v_{GS} and thus bound the duration of the saturated portion of the transient.

(*a*) The minimum bound will occur if there is no capacitive loading of the output, in which case $v_{OUT}(t)$ responds instantly to $v_{GS}(t)$. Derive an expression for the value of v_{GS} at which $v_{OUT} = v_{GS} - V_T$, and use your result to find an expression for the minimum length of the time the transistor can be in saturation. Evaluate your result assuming $V_S = 5$ V, $V_T = 1$ V, and $R_D K = 2\ \mathrm{V}^{-1}$.

(*b*) The maximum bound on the transient will occur when there is so much capacitive loading that $V_{out}(t)$ doesn't change during the transient (i.e., remains at V_S). If this is the case, at what value of v_{GS} does the transistor go out of saturation? Can you suggest an algorithm for defining the duration of the transient in this situation? Use your answer to calculate a time.

16.10 Consider a DRAM cell like that illustrated in Fig. 15.20.

(*a*) Estimate the storage time of a cell with the following parameters:

Diode current	As in Fig. 7.8
n^t-p junction area	5 μm × 5 μm
Capacitor area	10 μm × 10 μm
Oxide thickness	30 nm
Supply voltage V_{DD}	5 V
MOS thresholds V_T	1 V

(*b*) The time you found in part a should have been rather substantial, and actual RAM storage times are much shorter because of additional leakage paths. One such path corresponds to excess diode current around the perimeter of the junction at the oxide interface. How will your answer change if there is an additional current of 10^{-10} A per centimeter of perimeter?

(*c*) Another source of leakage is subthreshold conduction, which is current flow between the source and drain of a MOSFET that occurs even though the device is cutoff. (We modeled this as R_{SD} in Fig. 10.9.) Suppose that this current is 10^{-8} A per centimeter of gate width and that the gate is 5 μm wide. What is the storage time now?

16.11 A determining factor in the speed of a charge-coupled device is the time required to transfer the charge from one gate to the next, as shown in Fig. 16.10*c*. We can get a rough estimate of how long this is by assuming that the electrons in the charge packet move by drift and that the drift field is the voltage difference between the electrodes, $V_{Tr} - V_{Ho}$, divided by the distance between the midpoints of two adjacent electrodes.

(*a*) Use the estimated time presented above to obtain an expression for the packet transfer time in terms of the device dimensions, terminal voltages, and carrier mobility.

(*b*) Evaluate your answer in part a when the electrodes are 5 μm wide, the gap between electrodes is 0.1 μm, $V_{Tr} - V_{Ho}$ is 2 V, and the electron mobility in the channel is 200 μm^2/V. Use reasonable values for any other parameters you need.

16.12 A certain CMOS process has a minimum gate length and width of 1.5 μm and runs off a 5-V supply with 1-V threshold voltages. The electron mobility in the channel is 300 cm^2/V · s; the oxide thickness is 5 nm.

(a) Assuming $K_n = K_p$ and taking n to be 4, calculate the switching time for CMOS inverters made using this process.

(b) Calculate the power delay product PDP for this same technology.

(c) Consider now scaling this process by a factor of 5/3. Initially assume the supply and threshold voltages remain unchanged. Then scale them by a factor of 5/3 also. Calculate the switching time and PDP for these two situations. Assume that the mobility remains the same as the oxide thickness is reduced, but be aware that in practice it may actually decrease somewhat.

16.13 In this question you will consider the effects of parasitic interconnect capacitance on the switching speeds of CMOS and n-MOS logic. To model the effects of this parasitic capapacitance, assume that the interconnect lines are L_{min} wide and of average length mL_{min}, where m is a number much greater than 1, also assume that the thickness of the oxide under the lines is such that their capacitance per unit area is aC^*_{ox}, where a is a fraction much less than 1.

(a) Derive an expression analogous to Eq. (16.45) for the switching transients in CMOS when the interconnect loading is accounted for through the model just described.

(b) Do the same as in part a for an n-MOS invertor.

(c) Assuming the multiplicative factors m and a are the same for CMOS and n-MOS, for what values of m and a does CMOS become faster than n-MOS. Assume $W_n = L_{\text{min}}$.

(d) Calculate the switching speed for CMOS and n-MOS inverters fabricated by the process described in Problem 16.12 when the average length of interconnect that each inverter drives is 60 μm (i.e., $m = 40$) and when the thickness of the oxide under the interconnect lines is 600 nm (i.e., $a = 0.05$).

APPENDIX

SOME REPRESENTATIVE PROPERTIES OF COMMON SEMICONDUCTORS

It is best to begin listings like the ones in this appendix with a word of caution. Only representative values can be given for many of the quantities listed. Some properties, like mobility, vary widely with specimen purity and quality; the numbers quoted in these cases are for typical moderately doped "good" material. Other properties, like the intrinsic carrier concentration, are hard to measure accurately and there is still disagreement in the literature; in these cases we quote the most widely accepted values.

Table A.1 focuses on silicon, germanium, and gallium arsenide. These semiconductors are the most widely used; silicon is by far the most important commercially.

Table A.1.
Room temperature properties of silicon, germanium, and gallium arsenide

	Si	Ge	GaAs
ΔE_g(eV)	1.124	0.67	1.42
$n_i\,(\text{cm}^{-3})$	1.08×10^{10}	2.4×10^{13}	9×10^{6}
$\mu_e\,(\text{cm}^2/\text{V}\cdot\text{s})$	1500	3900	8500
$\mu_h\,(\text{cm}^2/\text{V}\cdot\text{s})$	600	1900	400
$\varepsilon_r\,(\varepsilon/\varepsilon_0)$	11.7	15.8	13.1

Table A.2 lists some typical values for representative properties of a number of common elemental and compound semiconductors at room temperature. Looking at this table in light of the periodic table, you should notice certain trends in the properties. For example, you should see that the energy gap tends to decrease as you move down the columns of the periodic table and tends to increase as you move along the rows out from column VI. Thus the energy gap of InAs is smaller than that of InP, and that of InSb is even smaller. Similarly the energy gap of InAs is less than that of GaAs, which in turn is less than AlAs. Moving out along a row, the energy gap of GaAs is larger than that of Ge, while that of ZnSe is even larger. If you go even further out to the I-VII's (e.g., NaCl) you find that the energy gaps are so large that the materials are insulators. An opposite trend is seen in the lattice constants and to some extent in the mobilities. Other properties also show the tendency to reflect the chemistry of their constituents, and a knowledge of the periodic table can be valuable to the electronic materials engineer or scientist.

Table A.2

Properties at room temperature (300 K) of some representative elemental and compound semiconductors.

	Lattice		Energy Gap		Mobilities	
	Period (↔)	**Type**	**Size (ΔE_g)**	**Type**	$\mu_e(\mathrm{cm}^2/\mathrm{V}\cdot\mathrm{s})$	$\mu_h(\mathrm{cm}^2/\mathrm{V}\cdot\mathrm{s})$
C	3.57	d	5.5	d	2000	2100
Si	5.43	d	1.124	i	1500	500
Ge	5.64	d	0.67	i	3900	1900
a-Sn	6.49	d	≈ 0.08	d	2500	2400
AlP	5.46	z	2.43	i	80	
AlAs	5.66	z	2.17	i	1000	180
AlSb	6.13	z	1.58	i	200	420
GaP	5.4	z	2.26	i	300	150
GaAs	5.65	z	1.42	d	8500	400
GaSb	6.09	z	0.72	d	4600	850
InP	5.86	z	1.35	d	4000	600
InAs	6.05	z	0.36	d	33,000	200
InSb	6.47	z	0.17	d	80,000	1700
ZnS	5.42	z	3.68	d	165	5
ZnSe	5.67	z	2.70	d	500	30
ZnTe	6.10	z	2.26	d	340	50
CdS		w	2.42	d	250	
CdSe		w	1.73	d	650	
CdTe	6.48	z	1.56	d	1050	100

The abbreviations used are, in the lattice type column: d—diamond, z—zinc blende, w—wurtzite (hexagonal); and in the energy gap type column: d—direct, i—indirect.

APPENDIX B

SEEING HOLES AND ELECTRONS

There are two basic experiments that can be performed on a semiconductor sample to determine whether it is n-type or p-type, that is, whether it contains an excess of donors or an excess of acceptors. The first experiment, called the *hot point probe measurement*, is a simple test that can very quickly tell us whether a sample is n- or p-type. The second experiment, the *Hall effect measurement*, is more complex to implement than the hot point probe experiment, but it can tell us both the majority carrier type and concentration. By measuring the conductivity at the same time, we can also determine the majority carrier mobility. We will consider each experiment in turn.

B.1 HOT POINT PROBE MEASUREMENT

In the hot point probe measurement, two electrodes are used, one of which is heated to between 100°C and 150°C. The heated electrode (for example, the tip of a small soldering iron) is connected to the negative input terminal of a sensitive DC ammeter. The unheated electrode is connected to the positive terminal. The two probes are then touched against the semiconductor sample to be tested, and the reading of the ammeter is monitored. This situation is illustrated in Fig. B.1. A positive current indicates a p-type sample, a negative current an n-type.

What is happening in the hot point probe experiment is that a temperature gradient is being created in the sample; the carriers tend to move down the gradient (i.e., from hot to cold). If the majority of the carriers are holes, there is a positive current within the sample that flows from the hot region to the cold electrode through the ammeter to the hot electrode. A positive current is registered on the ammeter. If the majority carriers are electrons, the flux of carriers is in the same

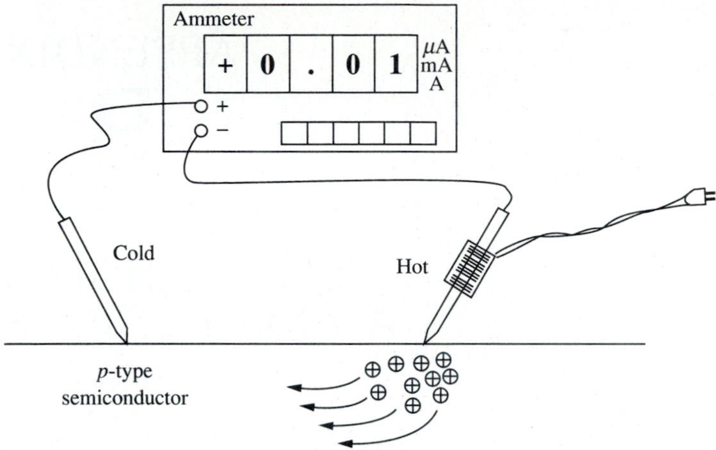

FIGURE B.1
Illustration of the hot point probe experiment being performed on a p-type semiconductor sample.

direction, but since they are negatively charged, the current is in the opposite direction.

The motion of carriers in a temperature gradient is called the *thermoelectric effect;* it is also called the *Thompson effect*. It can be used to convert thermal energy to electrical energy and has been used in applications where other electrical power sources are impractical and/or where there is a good source of heat. Some satellites use thermoelectric power supplies heated by nuclear reactors, and small generators heated by oil burners have been developed for use in polar regions. These cells are designed to have many p- and n-regions connected electrically in series and thermally in parallel, as pictured in Fig. B.2.

Interestingly, this device can also be operated in reverse. A current forced through a thermoelectric cell will cause one side to become hot and the other to become cold. This effect is called the *Peltier effect*. A device designed specifically to operate in this mode is called a Peltier, or thermoelectric, cooler.

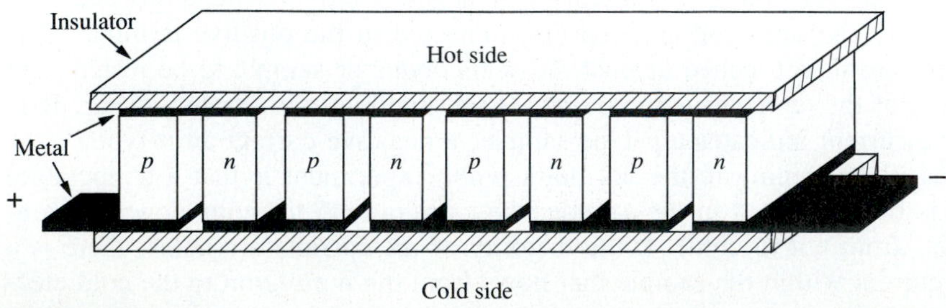

FIGURE B.2
Thermoelectric generator or cooler.

B.2 HALL EFFECT MEASUREMENT

The Hall effect measurement is performed on a bar-shaped sample with large area electrical contacts on each end and two small-area contacts in its middle on opposite sides of the sample. Two other small area contacts are usually also applied to one side of the sample; these are not part of the Hall effect measurement but are used to make a simultaneous conductivity measurement, as will be explained below. A magnetic field is applied normal to the top of the sample, as illustrated in Fig. B.3.

A current I is sent through the bar from end to end, and a voltage is measured between the two small contacts opposite each other near the middle of the bar. This voltage, labeled V_H in Fig. B.3, is the *Hall voltage*. It is inversely proportional to the equilibrium majority carrier concentration, as we shall see next.

Imagine that our sample is p-type and has an equilibrium hole concentration p_o. If a current I is flowing in the bar, then the net average velocity in the x-direction of each of the holes is

$$\bar{v}_x = \frac{I}{q p_o w t} \tag{B.1}$$

Because of the magnetic field, each of the holes will experience a force $q\boldsymbol{v} \times \boldsymbol{B}$ in the negative y-direction,

$$F_y^{\text{mag}} = -q v_x B = -\frac{IB}{p_o w t} \tag{B.2}$$

and the moving holes will be deflected toward the near side of the bar in Fig. B.3.

As the charge carriers are deflected to one side of the bar they will create an electric field $\mathscr{E}_y$, that will eventually be strong enough to balance the force due to the magnetic field. The force due to the electric field is

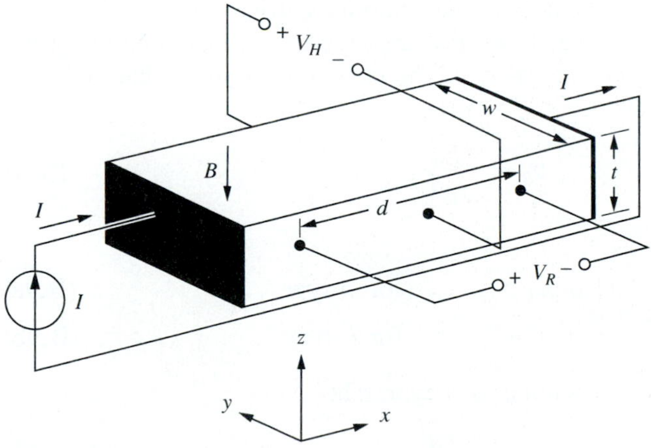

FIGURE B.3
Experimental setup of the Hall effect measurement.

$$F_y^{\text{elect}} = q\mathscr{E}_y = \frac{qV_H}{w} \tag{B.3}$$

In the steady state, these two forces will balance each other and the total force in the y-direction is zero.

$$F_y^{\text{tot}} = \frac{qV_H}{w} - \frac{IB}{p_o wt} = 0 \tag{B.4}$$

Solving this equation for V_H, we can relate V_H to $I, B, t,$ and p_o:

$$V_H = \frac{IB}{qp_o t} \tag{B.5}$$

If the majority carriers had been electrons, they would have been moving in the negative x-direction:

$$v_x = \frac{I}{(-q)n_o wt}$$

and the force due to the magnetic field again would have deflected them to the near side of the bar:

$$F_y = -(-q)\, v_x\, B = -\frac{IB}{n_o wt} \tag{B.6}$$

The electric field in this case is thus in the opposite direction, and the Hall voltage is negative:

$$V_H = -\frac{IB}{qn_o t} \tag{B.7}$$

We see that the sign of the Hall voltage tells us the majority carrier type and, furthermore, that we can calculate the majority carrier concentration from the magnitude of the Hall voltage. If we also measure the voltage drop along the bar (i.e., V_R in Fig. B.3), we can calculate the conductivity of the bar and then the carrier mobility. We have

$$V_R = \frac{Id}{\sigma_o wt} \tag{B.8}$$

and

$$\sigma_o = \begin{cases} q\,\mu_h p_o & \text{for } p\text{-type} \quad \text{(B.9a)} \\ q\,\mu_e n_o & \text{for } n\text{-type} \quad \text{(B.9b)} \end{cases}$$

Combining these we find if the sample is n-type that

$$\mu_e = \frac{Id}{V_R wtqn_o} \tag{B.10}$$

If the sample is p-type we find

$$\mu_h = \frac{Id}{V_R w t q p_o} \tag{B.11}$$

We can write both Eq. (B.10) and Eq. (B.11) in terms of V_H as

$$\mu_e = \frac{|V_H|\, d}{V_R B w} \qquad \text{for } n\text{-type} \tag{B.12a}$$

$$\mu_h = \frac{|V_H|\, d}{V_R B w} \qquad \text{for } p\text{-type} \tag{B.12b}$$

The Hall effect measurement is a standard materials characterization technique. Next to conductivity it is perhaps the most commonly used electrical measurement for analyzing semiconductor crystals.

APPENDIX C

SOME IMPORTANT CONCEPTS OF SOLID-STATE PHYSICS

In our modeling and discussions in this text, we have not needed to introduce quantum mechanical models for the energy states and transport properties of electrons in semiconductors. We have, in fact, rigorously avoided doing so, and we have been able to understand and model everything we needed to without such advanced physics. Nonetheless, the use of quantum mechanical terminology in discussing semiconductor device physics is common practice. It is consequently important that you become familiar with certain concepts of modern quantum physics if you are to go further in the study of semiconductor physics and if you are to read the technical and professional device literature. Of particular importance are the concepts of *energy bands* and *effective mass*, which are the subjects of this appendix. The discussions in this appendix can only give you the briefest introduction to these subjects. Nonetheless they will get you started and will hopefully whet your appetite and motivate you to take additional quantum and solid-state physics courses.

C.1 ENERGY BANDS

One of the critical steps in the progression of our present understanding of atoms and solids was the development of the atomic orbital model by Neils Bohr in 1913. This model states that electrons orbiting about an atomic nucleus can have only certain specific energies and that they occupy well-defined, discrete energy levels. For example, in the simplest of atoms, the hydrogen atom, this model tells us that these specific energies E_n are given by

$$E_n = -\frac{13.6}{n^2} \text{ eV} \tag{C.1}$$

Here n is an index ranging from 1 to infinity that defines the different energy levels, and the zero reference for electron energy has been taken to correspond to a situation where the electron is at rest infinitely far away from the nucleus (a proton in the case of the hydrogen atom), which is also at rest.

In this model every energy level represents a possible location, or *state*, for two electrons, one we identify as having spin $+\frac{1}{2}$, and the other spin $-\frac{1}{2}$. *Spin* is another index, like n, that describes a characteristic (in this case, a rotational characteristic) of electrons.

For atoms more complicated than the hydrogen atom, the distribution of energy levels and their calculation is more complex, but the basic model of well–defined, discrete energy levels is maintained. These discrete energy levels are identified by a series of indices, such as n and spin, that are called *quantum numbers*.

When atoms are combined to form molecules, the components of the individual atoms (i.e., electrons, protons, and neutrons) interact and the energy levels of the individual atoms are modified; they evolve into the energy levels of the molecule. The total number of possible states is unchanged, but their energies are shifted from their original values. For example, when a hydrogen molecule is formed from two hydrogen atoms, the $n = 1$ levels of the two isolated hydrogen atoms become two closely spaced levels near -13.6 eV in the hydrogen molecule. This evolution is illustrated in Fig. C.1. Although not shown in this figure, the other energy levels split similarly. Note, however, that the energy levels with higher n values, which correspond to electrons in orbitals with larger radii, split more because the electrons in these larger "outer" orbitals interact more with the

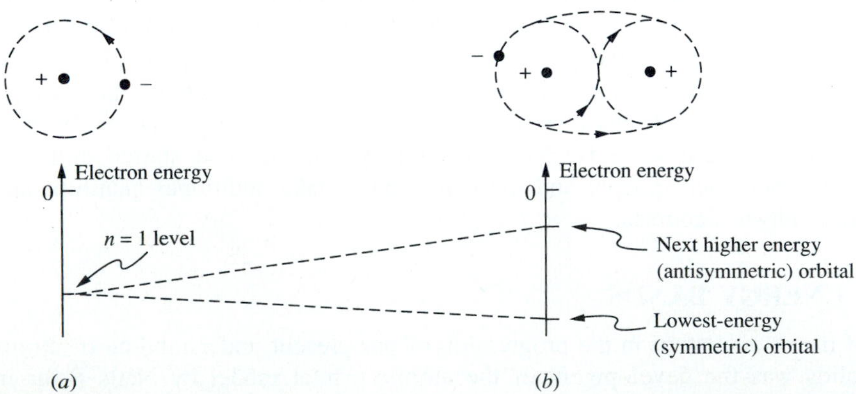

FIGURE C.1
Schematic comparison of the energy levels of a hydrogen atom and a hydrogen molecule, illustrating the modification of the atomic energy levels by the formation of a molecule.

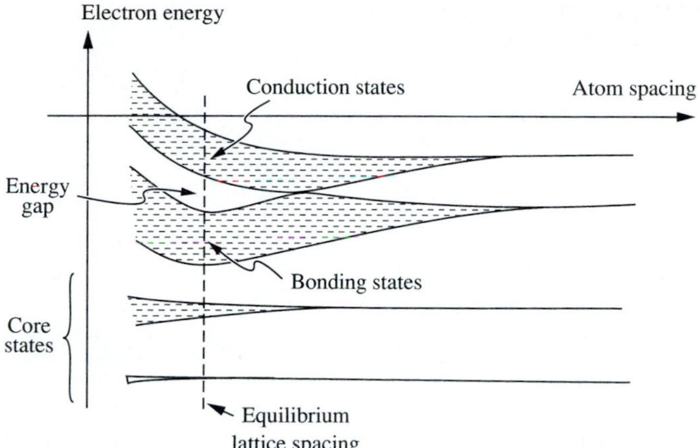

FIGURE C.2
Representation of the evolution of the discrete atomic energy levels of isolated atoms into the tightly spaced bands of energy levels in a solid.

electrons of the neighboring atom than do the electrons in the smaller "inner" orbitals.

When many atoms come together to form a solid, the energy levels of the individual atoms coalesce into bands of closely spaced energy levels, as is illustrated in Fig. C.2. The electrons in low-lying energy levels, corresponding to orbitals nearer to the atomic nuclei, do not interact much, and these levels form a relatively narrow band. The higher-energy electrons—those in larger radii ("outer" orbitals)—interact more, resulting in the spreading of their energy levels into a wider band. Some of the higher bands spread so much that they overlap other bands, and some of the overlapping bands mix so much that the identities of the original atomic levels from which they evolved is completely obscured.

In summary, the picture of energy levels in a solid looks quite different from that of an atom and consists of a series of energy bands, each band containing many closely spread energy levels that electrons can occupy, two to a level, one with spin "up" and one with spin "down."

A common way of presenting information on the distribution of electron energy levels in a solid is to plot the density of levels as a function of energy. We plot what is termed the *density of states* $\rho(E)$ versus the electron energy E, as illustrated in Fig. C.3. The units of $\rho(E)$ are number of states per $\mathrm{eV} \cdot \mathrm{cm}^3$.

Knowing the density of states function $\rho(E)$ gives us a model for where electrons can be, but it doesn't tell us where they actually are. To determine where the electrons are, we have to model how the electrons in the solid are distributed among the possible states. For this it is necessary to turn to statistical mechanics and to develop a model for the probability of finding an electron in a particular energy level. When this is done we find that the probability distribution appropriate to electrons is something called the *Fermi distribution function* $f(E)$, given by

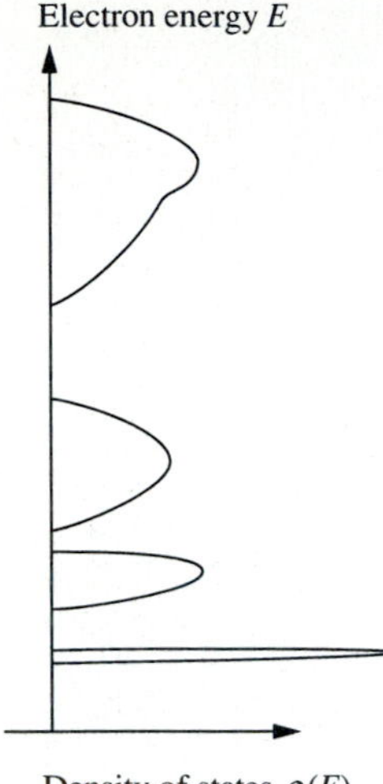

FIGURE C.3
Representative plot of the density of states for electrons as a function of the electron energy in a typical crystalline solid such as silicon.

$$f(E) = \frac{1}{\left[1 + e^{(E-E_f)/kT}\right]} \tag{C.2}$$

where the parameter E_f is called the *Fermi energy*. We will discuss how E_f is determined shortly, but it is first instructive to look at some of the general properties of the Fermi distribution function. This function is plotted for several values of kT in Fig. C.4. We note that the function $f(E)$ is nearly 1 for $E \ll E_f$ and is nearly 0 for $E \gg E_f$; it is exactly $\frac{1}{2}$ for E exactly equal to E_f.

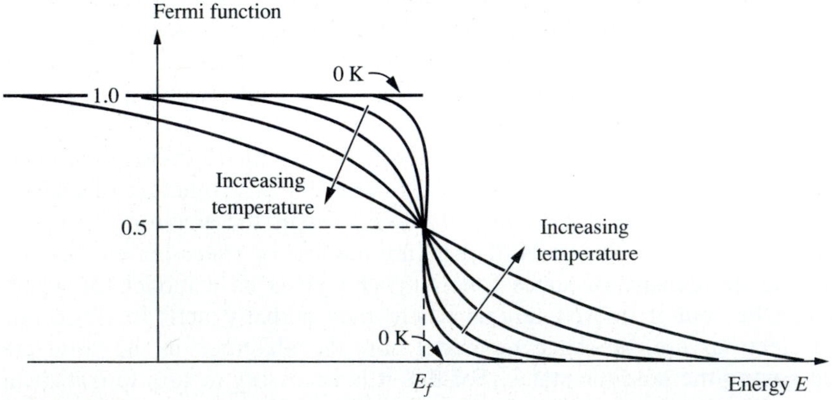

FIGURE C.4
Plot of the Fermi distribution function versus the electron energy for several temperatures to illustrate the general shape of this function as well as its evolution as the temperature is increased.

More quantitatively, when E is several kT less than E_f, $f(E)$ can be approximated as

$$f(E) \approx 1 - e^{(E-E_f)/kT} \qquad \text{for } (E - E_f) << -kT \tag{C.3a}$$

and when E is several kT greater than E_f, $f(E)$ is approximately

$$f(E) \approx e^{(E-E_f)/kT} \qquad \text{for } (E - E_f) >> kT \tag{C.4}$$

These expressions should have a familiar look, especially if we write the first in terms of the probability of not finding an electron in a state well below E_f. This is simply $1 - f(E)$, which is

$$1 - f(E) \approx e^{-(E-E_f/kT)} \qquad \text{for } (E - E_f) << -kT \tag{C.3b}$$

Written this way, Eqs. (C.3b) and (C.4) bear a striking similarity to Eq. (6.7) and (6.8), and we shall have more to say about this shortly.

Note, finally, the very high symmetry of $f(E)$ about the point $(E_f, 0.5)$. It is easy to show that

$$f(E_f + E_0) = 1 - f(E_f - E_0) \tag{C.5}$$

which says simply that the probability of finding an electron at an energy E_0 above E_f equals the probability of not finding it at an energy E_0 below E_f.

The density of electrons with energies between E and $E + dE$ in a material with a density of states function $\rho(E)$ is given by the product of $\rho(E)$ and the probability function $f(E)$, that is,

$$n(E)\,dE = f(E)\,\rho(E)\,dE \tag{C.6}$$

The term $n(E)$ has units of number of electrons per $\text{eV} \cdot \text{cm}^3$.

Up to this point in our discussion the Fermi energy E_f is still unspecified, but we are now in a position to determine what it is. We determine E_f by insisting that the sum of $n(E)dE$ over all E is n_{TOT}, the total number of electrons per unit volume (i.e., the density of atoms times the number of electrons per atom), in the semiconductor we are modeling:

$$n_{\text{TOT}} = \int_{-\infty}^{\infty} f(E)\,\rho(E)\,dE \tag{C.7}$$

Since the only unknown that enters into Eq. (C.7) is E_f, the above equation effectively specifies the value of E_f.

Physically we can think of the Fermi energy E_f as the energy value to which the available electron energy levels in a solid are, on average, filled. Referring to Fig. C.4, we see that there is little probability of finding an electron in a state much above E_f, whereas there is a virtual certainty of finding electrons in all of the states well below E_f. The probabilities we refer to here are, of course, all dependent on temperature because all energy differences are referenced to kT in our expressions and because the lower the temperature, the more abrupt is the step in $f(E)$ (see Fig. C.4). In the extreme of absolute zero temperature, 0 K, $f(E)$ is identically 1 for E below E_f and 0 above E_f, so all of the states below E_f are filled and all of the states above E_f are empty. At higher temperatures, electrons from some of the levels below E_f acquire enough energy from the lattice to occupy energy levels above E_f.

In a semiconductor the Fermi level typically falls between two bands of energy levels. The lower band, called the *valence* band, corresponds to the energies of electrons in the bonding orbitals, or states, of the crystal (i.e., in the covalent bonds in silicon). The upper band, the *conduction* band, corresponds to the energies of electrons that can move throughout the crystal lattice. The upper edge of the valence band is called the *valence band energy* E_v; the lower edge of the conduction band is called the *conduction band energy* E_c. The difference between these two energies is called the *energy gap* ΔE_g. These quantities are illustrated in Fig. C.5, which diagrams the density of states function of a representative semiconductor in the vicinity of the energy gap. Also indicated on this figure are representative donor and acceptor energies. Notice that $\rho(E)$ decreases to zero at the band edges and increases going away from the edge and "into" the band. This variation is often approximated as being parabolic for purposes of performing calculations with $\rho(E)$.

We are now actually in a position to calculate the Fermi energy and carrier concentration using our new models and to compare the results with our discussion in Chap. 2. Before doing this, however, it is a useful first exercise to reason through what the Fermi energy is qualitatively in several representative situations.

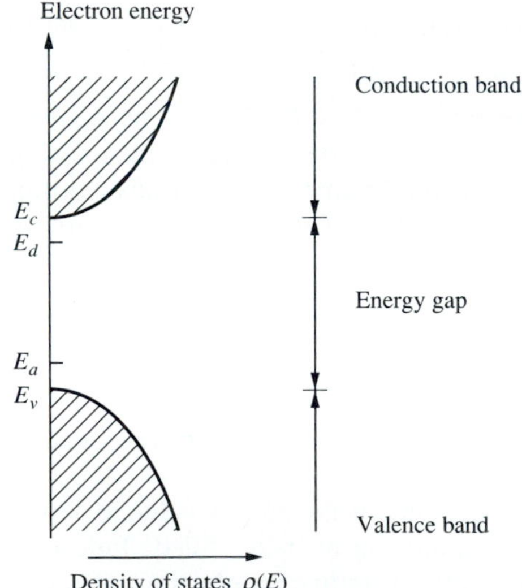

FIGURE C.5
Density of states for a typical semiconductor in the vicinity of the energy gap. The conduction band edge energy E_c and valence band energy E_v are both illustrated, as are the positions of typical donor and acceptor energies, E_d and E_a, respectively.

In doing so it is often helpful to first find E_f near 0 K and then to see what it is at higher temperatures. Consider first an intrinsic semiconductor. In an intrinsic semiconductor at 0 K, all of the valence band states are occupied and all of the conduction band states are empty. Thus E_f clearly falls somewhere between E_v and E_c. We can reason that it must be near the middle of the energy gap [i.e., near $(E_v + E_c)/2$] because of the symmetry of $f(E)$ evident in Fig. C.4 and pointed out in Eq. (C.5). Above 0 K the intrinsic population of electrons in the conduction band equals the population of empty states in the valence band, which means that the probability of finding electrons above E_c must be the same as the probability of not finding them below E_v. Thus we must have E_f roughly halfway between E_v and E_c at all temperatures in an intrinsic sample. We call this energy Ei, and this behavior is illustrated in Fig. C.6 by the curve labeled A. Note that the horizontal axis in this plot is $1/T$.

Next consider a sample with N_d donor states with energies clustered about E_d. At 0 K all of the donor states are occupied and there are no conduction electrons, so E_f must fall somewhere between E_d and E_c, as the curve labeled B in Fig. C.6 illustrates. At higher temperatures, E_f must decrease until at room temperature it is several kT below E_d. Nonetheless, it remains much nearer to the donor level E_d than to the valence band edge E_v. If you think a bit more about this picture you may be terribly bothered by the fact that the donor states are expected to be largely unoccupied (i.e., ionized) while the higher conduction band states are occupied by N_d electrons, even though the probability of these conduction band states being occupied is lower than it is for the donor states. The solution to this puzzle lies in the numbers: there are far, far more conduction band states than donor states (in samples for which this approximation—full ionization of donor states at room temperature—is valid), so the product of the density of

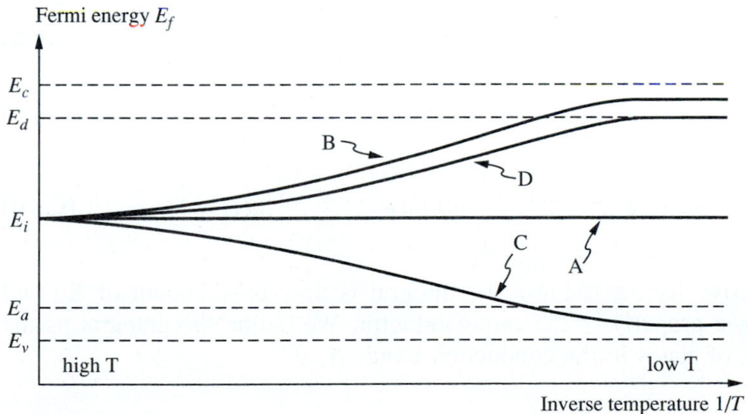

FIGURE C.6
Values of the Fermi energy E_f as a function of inverse temperature $1/T$ in four different situations. Curve A represents intrinsic material, $N_d = N_a = 0$; Curve B represents n-type material, $N_d \neq 0$, $N_a = 0$; Curve C represents p-type material, $N_d = 0$, $N_a \neq 0$; and Curve D represents compensated material that is net n-type, $N_d \neq 0$, $N_a \neq 0$, $N_d - N_a > 0$.

states times the probability is still N_d even though the probability of any one state being occupied is very small. At very large temperatures, well above room temperature, the Fermi level moves down well into the energy gap and the sample again looks intrinsic (recall Fig. 2.9; the curve in this figure was calculated using precisely the models we are describing in this appendix). This is also illustrated by the curve labeled B in Fig. C.6.

Similar arguments can be used to determine E_f in a sample containing N_a acceptors and also in samples containing both donors and acceptors. You may want to try it yourself and to compare your results with the curves labeled C and D in Fig. C.6.

Next we turn to the issue of relating the discussion in this appendix to the models we developed in Chap. 6 in which we related the thermal equilibrium carrier populations to the electrostatic potential ϕ [i.e., Eqs. (6.7) and (6.8), which we repeat here]:

$$n_o = n_i e^{q\phi/kT} \tag{6.7}$$

$$p_o = n_i e^{-q\phi/kT} \tag{6.8}$$

Using our present model we can calculate the total number of conduction electrons, n_o, by integrating $n(E)\,dE$ over all E greater than E_c. Using Eq. (C.7) we have

$$n_o = \int_{E_c}^{\infty} f(E)\,\rho(E)\,dE \tag{C.8}$$

Assuming that $E_c - E_f$ is greater than several kT, we can use Eq. (C.4) for $f(E)$ and write

$$n_o \approx \int_{E_c}^{\infty} \rho(E)\,e^{-(E-E_f)/kT}\,dE \tag{C.9}$$

which we can rewrite as

$$n_o = e^{-(E_c-E_f)/kT} \int_{E_c}^{\infty} \rho(E)\,e^{-(E-E_c)/kT}\,dE \tag{C.10}$$

This is an attractive format because the integral is now independent of E_f and thus is an intrinsic property of the semiconductor. We define this integral as the effective density of states in the conduction band, $N_c(T)$:

$$N_c(T) \equiv \int_{E_c}^{\infty} \rho(E)\,e^{-(E-E_c)/kT}\,dE \tag{C.11}$$

We thus write

$$n_o = N_c(T)\,e^{-(E_c-E_f)/kT} \tag{C.12}$$

Using similar reasoning we can define an effective density of states in the valence band, $N_v(T)$. This time, however, we are concerned with the number of states below E_v that are unoccupied. Thus we have

$$p_o = \int_{-\infty}^{E_v} \rho(E)\,[1 - f(E)]\,dE \tag{C.13}$$

Assuming that $E_f - E_v$ is positive and greater than several kT, we use Eq.(C.3) to arrive at

$$p_o = N_v(T)\, e^{-(E_f - E_v)/kT} \tag{C.14}$$

where the effective density of states in the valence band, $N_v(T)$, is given by

$$N_v(T) = \int_{-\infty}^{E_v} \rho(E)\, e^{-(E_v - E)/kT}\, dE \tag{C.15}$$

In Eq. (6.7) and (6.8), n_o and p_o are expressed in terms of the intrinsic carrier concentration n_i rather than E_f, so it is logical to next turn to finding an expression for n_i. In an intrinsic sample, $n_i = n_o = p_o$; thus if we call E_f in intrinsic material E_i, we have

$$n_i = N_c(T)\, e^{-(E_c - E_i)/kT} = N_v(T)\, e^{-(E_i - E_v)/kT} \tag{C.16}$$

Solving this equation for E_i, we have

$$e^{E_i/kT} = \sqrt{\frac{N_v(T)}{N_c(T)}}\, e^{(E_c + E_v)/2kT} \tag{C.17a}$$

or

$$E_i = \frac{(E_c + E_v)}{2} + \frac{[\ln(N_v/N_c)]}{2} \tag{C.17b}$$

Using the first expression in Eq. (C.17), we find

$$n_i(T) = \sqrt{N_c(T)\, N_v(T)}\, e^{-(E_c - E_v)/2kT} \tag{C.18}$$

Notice that $n_i(T)$ depends only on intrinsic material parameters and temperature; it does not depend on the doping levels, just as we argued must be the case in Chap. 2.

Notice also from Eqs. (C.12) and (C.14) that the $n_o p_o$ product is n_1^2. This is reassuring, but you should realize that the relative simplicity of these two equations and this result depend on E_f being well within the energy gap, far away from either band edge (i.e., $E_v \ll E_f \ll E_c$, where "$\ll$" indicates several kT). If the semiconductor under question is so heavily doped, either n-type or p-type, that this is no longer the case, then the $n_o p_o$ product will no longer be simply n_1^2. Recalling our discussions in Chap. 2, we had in fact indicated that this would be the case, but we were unable to quantify that argument. Now we are in a position to do so. Clearly when the net donor (or acceptor) concentration gets to within a factor of 10 of the effective density of states in the conduction (or valence) band, we should anticipate problems with the simple model.

Finally, you should compare Eq. (C.18) with Eq. (2.29a), keeping in mind that $E_c - E_v$ is ΔE_g. If we had developed a sufficiently detailed model for $\rho(E)$ we would have also found that $N_c(T)$ and $N_v(T)$ each vary as $T^{3/2}$.

We next rewrite Eqs. (C.12) and (C.14) using Eq. (C.18) for n_i. Doing this yields

$$n_o = n_i e^{[E_f - (E_c+E_v)/2 + (\ln N_c/N_v)/2]/kT} \quad \text{(C.19a)}$$

$$p_o = n_i e^{-[E_f - (E_c+E_v)/2 + (\ln N_c/N_v)/2]/kT} \quad \text{(C.19b)}$$

We have already identified the quantity $(E_c + E_v)/2 + (\ln N_c/N_v)/2$ as the Fermi level in intrinsic material, E_i, so we in fact have

$$n_o = n_i e^{(E_f - E_i)/kT} \quad \text{(C.20a)}$$

$$p_o = n_i e^{-(E_f - E_i)/kT} \quad \text{(C.20b)}$$

Comparing these expressions to Eqs. (6.7) and (6.8), we see that the electrostatic potential in a semiconductor, ϕ, is equivalent to the difference between the Fermi level and its value in intrinsic material (with a suitable factor of q included to convert from potential to energy), that is,

$$\phi = \frac{(E_f - E_i)}{q} \quad \text{(C.21)}$$

Thus far we have obtained expressions for the equilibrium carrier concentrations in a uniformly doped semiconductor given the Fermi energy [Eqs. (C.12) and (C.14) or Eqs. (C.20a) and (C.20b)], but except for the case of intrinsic material, we do not yet know how to find the Fermi energy given the dopant concentrations. We are, however, now in a position to do just that. In fact, we can calculate the thermal equilibrium Fermi energy and carrier concentrations in a uniformly doped semiconductor if we know the doping concentration and dopant energies, even at low temperatures where all of the dopants are not ionized and at very high temperatures where there is an appreciable intrinsic concentration.

The starting point for such a calculation is Eq. (2.8), which we rewrite here as

$$p_o + N_d^+ - n_o - N_a^- = 0 \quad \text{(C.22)}$$

Eqs. (C.20a) and (C.20b) provide us with expressions for p_o and n_o in terms of the unknown E_f. We simply need to write N_d^+ and N_a^- in terms of E_f and we will have one equation we can solve for E_f.

The Fermi function for dopant atoms is slightly different than the Fermi function for bulk levels, and the number of occupied donor states, or $(N_d - N_d^+)$, is given by

$$N_d - N_d^+ = \frac{N_d}{\left[1 + g_d e^{(E_d - E_f)/kT}\right]} \quad \text{(C.23a)}$$

where the new factor g_d takes on values ranging from 0.5 to 2 depending on the nature of the donor. (This factor is often ignored since doing so contributes an error on the order of only kT to the final result.) Similarly, the number of occupied (ionized) acceptors is

$$\bar{N}_a = \frac{N_a}{\left[1 + g_a e^{(E_d - E_f)/kT}\right]} \tag{C.23b}$$

where the factor g_a is on the order of 1 and is also often ignored.

Combining these two equations in Eq. (C.22) with our equations for n_0 and p_0 gives us the expression we need to solve to find E_f:

$$n_i e^{(E_f - E_i)/kT} + N_d \left\{ 1 - \frac{1}{\left[1 + g_d e^{(E_d - E_f)/kT}\right]} \right\}$$
$$- n_i e^{(E_f - E_i)/kT} - \frac{N_a}{\left[1 + g_a e^{(E_a - E_f)/kT}\right]} = 0 \tag{C.24}$$

In any given situation this expression can be simplified greatly by approximating the Fermi function terms as we did in Eqs. (C.3) and (C.4). Often, an analytical expression can even be obtained. In any event, we can solve for E_f either numerically or analytically, and if we have E_f we can also calculate n_0, p_0, N_d^+, and N_a^-.

Thus far we have restricted our discussion in this appendix to thermal equilibrium and uniformly doped semiconductors. Strictly speaking, the Fermi distribution applies only in thermal equilibrium, which explains our insistence on equilibrium, but there is no reason we cannot treat nonuniformly doped samples in thermal equilibrium. In doing this, the most important thing to realize is that even though the doping varies spatially and therefore there are built-in fields and variations in the electrostatic potential, the Fermi energy must be constant and independent of position. That is,

$$\frac{\partial E_f}{\partial x} = 0$$

To understand that this must be the case, recall the origin of E_f: the Fermi distribution function tells us the probability of finding an electron with a given energy. In thermal equilibrium the probability of finding an electron at energy E_1 at site x_A must be the same as that of finding an electron at the same energy E_1 at x_B. If not, the carriers at x_B would tend to move to x_A, or vice versa, a situation that is inconsistent with thermal equilibrium. Thus, E_f must be independent of position in thermal equilibrium.

To proceed, we rewrite Eq. (C.21) in thermal equilibrium using this fact:

$$q\phi(x) = E_f - E_i(x) \text{ in the thermal equilibrium} \tag{C.21$'$}$$

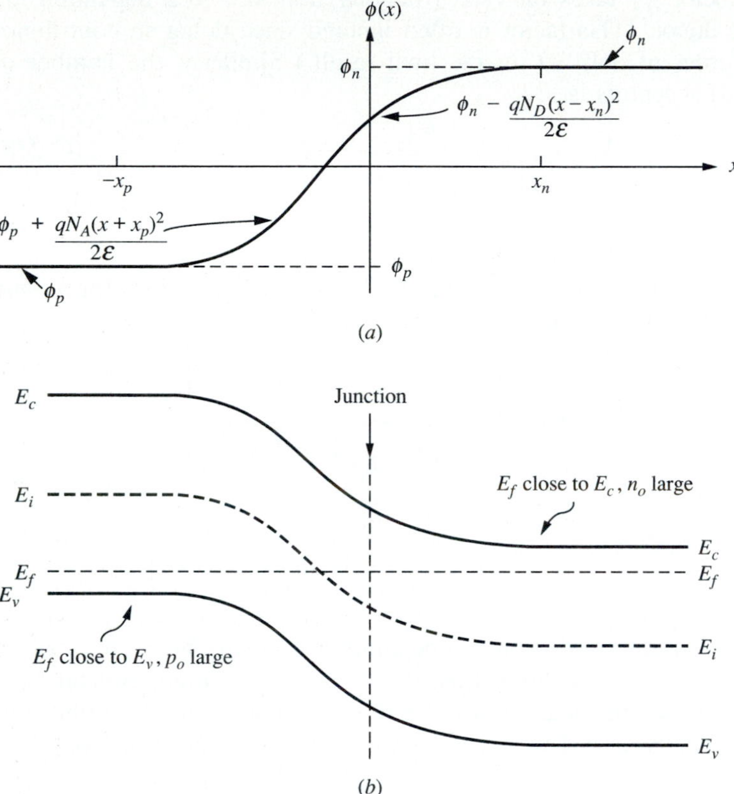

FIGURE C.7
(*a*) Plot of the electrostatic potential through a *p-n* junction in thermal equilibrium; (*b*) the corresponding plot of the energy band profile through the same junction.

We next recall that we already know how to determine $\phi(x)$ in nonuniform situations, such as in a *p-n* junction, and thus we know $E_i(x)$. It is useful to rewrite Eq. (C.21) in this light.

$$E_i(x) = E_f + (-q)\phi(x) \tag{C.21''}$$

In rewriting Eq. (C.21′) we have also tried to bring out the idea that at any position x, the energy level picture of the semiconductor under consideration is shifted up and/or down, relative to a reference level, by the electrostatic potential energy of the electrons at that point, $(-q)\phi(x)$. To emphasize this result, we present both the electrostatic potential profile and the energy level profile through a *p-n* junction in Fig. C.7. The electrostatic potential picture, Fig. C.7*a*, is just repeated from Fig. 6.5*c*. In the corresponding energy level plot, Fig. C.7*b*, we have plotted not only $E_i(x)$ but the band-edge energies $E_c(x)$ and $E_v(x)$ as well. These energies track $E_i(x)$ exactly, so they do not provide new information in

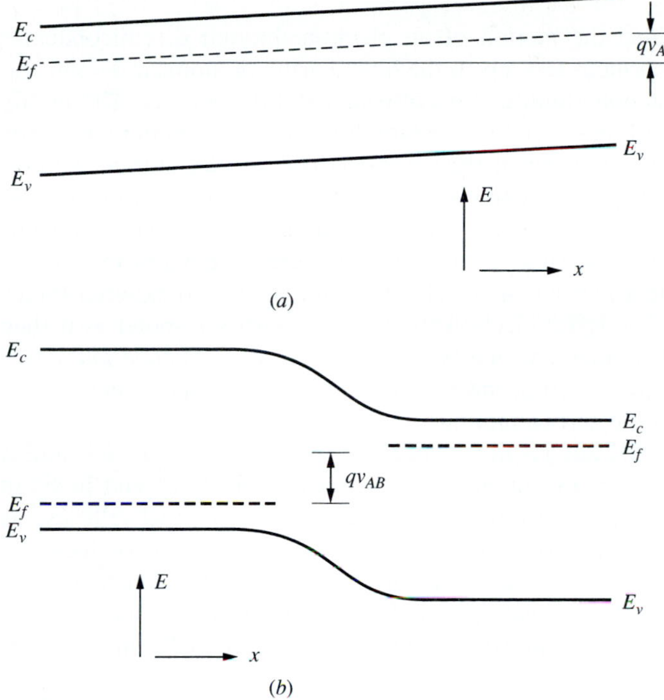

FIGURE C.8
Energy level profile in two semiconductor device structures under mild applied biases: (*a*) a uniformly doped bar; (*b*) a *p-n* junction.

that sense, but since the hole and electron populations depend on the proximity of the band edges to the Fermi energy, you can more easily get an idea of how the carrier populations vary spatially when E_c and E_v are included in the figure. Plots like those in Fig. C.7*b* are widely used by device engineers.

We said earlier that the Fermi function is, strictly speaking, valid only in thermal equilibrium. Nonetheless it can be extended to quasiequilibrium situations if we are careful. Doing so is well beyond our mission in this text, however, and we want to consider only small excursions away from equilibrium here before stopping. When we externally impose a potential difference between two positions, x_{A} and x_{B}, in a sample, what we are doing is creating a difference of $-qv_{\mathrm{AB}}$ in the Fermi energies at those two positions; that is,

$$E_f(x_{\mathrm{A}}) - E_f(x_{\mathrm{B}}) = qv_{\mathrm{AB}} \tag{C.25}$$

With this observation you can now begin to extend band profile pictures like that in Fig. C.7 to situations with an applied bias. Two examples, a uniformly doped bar of semiconductor (i.e., a resistor) and a forward-biased *p-n* junction, are shown in Figs. C.8*a* and *b*, respectively.

C.2 EFFECTIVE MASS THEORY

The problem of describing the motion of an electron through a semiconductor seems at first to be an enormous task given the high density of atoms in a solid and the apparently numerous opportunities for collisions and deflections. The highly ordered, periodic nature of the crystal lattice simplifies the problem tremendously, however. In particular, we find that if the crystal is perfect and infinite with all of the atoms fixed in their proper positions, then the conduction electrons can be modeled as particles that move through the lattice without suffering any collisions or deflections. They move essentially as though they were traveling in free space. The only difference is that rather than accelerating in response to external forces as though they had the free space electron mass, the electrons respond as if they had a different mass. This mass, which we call the *electron effective mass* m_e^*, is usually less than the free electron mass, and contains all of the effects of the perfect crystal lattice on the carrier motion.

The model that yields this result is called the *effective mass model*, and it is the theoretical basis for all of our intuitive pictures of electrons and holes in semiconductors. In the case of electrons, the effective mass model tells us, as we have just said, that we can model conduction electrons in a semiconductor as particles in free space with a mass m_e^* and a net charge $-q$. We call these new particles electrons also, but we must be careful to remember that they are not really electrons but rather are some sort of quasiparticle that looks and behaves much like an electron.

In the effective mass picture, defects in the perfect lattice structure introduce objects in the path of the electrons with which they can collide. For example, an impurity atom occupying the site in a silicon crystal that would normally be occupied by a silicon atom would be modeled as a sphere fixed in free space. An electron traveling through the crystal can collide with or be deflected by this object. This idea is illustrated in Fig. C.9.

The concept of a hole is another very important result of the effective mass model. According to this model, an unoccupied state in the valence band (i.e., an unoccupied covalent bond in the lattice) can also be modeled as a particle traveling in free space. This particle has a positive mass, now called the *hole effective mass* m_h^*, and it has a positive charge $+q$. As was the case with electrons, holes, too, can collide with and be deflected by defects in the crystal.

The vibrations of the lattice atoms about their equilibrium positions, which are always happening at finite temperature, are also "defects" in the perfectly periodic lattice, and they can also deflect or scatter electrons and holes moving through a crystal. These lattice vibrations can themselves be modeled as objects, called phonons, with which the charge carriers interact (i.e., collide and scatter). The number of phonons increases as the temperature increases, so the holes and electrons suffer more collisions with phonons at higher temperatures. This leads to a decrease in the mobility of the carriers at higher temperatures, as we discussed in Sec. 3.1.3.

In summary, the effective mass model is one of the most amazing results of solid-state physics, but we seldom even think about it in most of our dealings with

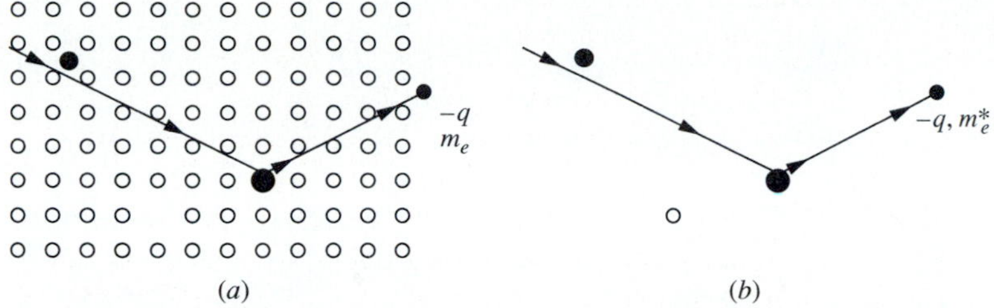

FIGURE C.9
Two possible pictures of an electron moving through a crystal lattice: (*a*) the classical picture of a conventional electron in a periodic grid of obstacles (the lattice atoms) containing an occasional additional obstacle (defects); (*b*) the effective mass picture of an electron with a different mass, m_e^*, moving in free space and encountering occasional obstacles.

semiconductors and devices. That conduction electrons and mobile holes exist in a semiconductor is just taken for granted, and yet holes and electrons are also models. It is perhaps a testimonial to the importance of the effective mass model that we rarely even question the appropriateness of using it in our dealings with semiconductors and device structures. It is unlikely that you can fully appreciate this at this stage in your career, but the more you learn about solid-state physics and semiconductor devices, the more you will be impressed by the ubiquitousness of this model and the amazing breadth of structures and situations in which it is useful.

APPENDIX D

QUANTIFYING THE TENDENCY TO QUASINEUTRALITY

One way to begin to develop an intuitive feel for the strength of quasineutrality and to associate temporal and spatial dimensions with this phenomenon is to look at the excess *majority* carrier population. The population of majority carriers is very large compared to that of the minority carriers (assuming low-level injection), and this population can readily adjust itself as necessary to try to neutralize any charge imbalances. As we discussed in Chap.5, any deviation from charge neutrality will create an electric field, which will in turn cause a drift flux of majority charge carriers in such a direction as to restore neutrality.

To quantify this argument, we focus on the excess majority carrier holes in a uniformly doped p-type semiconductor under low-level excitation. We begin by rewriting Eqs. (5.16), (5.18), and (5.19) here as

$$J_h = \sigma_o \mathcal{E} - qD_h \frac{\partial p'}{\partial x} \tag{D.1}$$

$$\frac{\partial p'}{\partial t} = g_l - \frac{n'}{\tau_e} - \frac{1}{q}\frac{\partial J_h}{\partial x} \tag{D.2}$$

$$\varepsilon \frac{\partial \mathcal{E}}{\partial x} = q\left(p' - n'\right) \tag{D.3}$$

Combining these we obtain

$$\frac{\partial p'}{\partial t} = g_l - \frac{n'}{\tau_e} - \frac{\sigma_o}{\varepsilon}\left(p' - n'\right) + D_h \frac{\partial^2 p'}{\partial x^2} \tag{D.4}$$

We define the dielectric relaxation time τ_D as

$$\tau_D \equiv \frac{\varepsilon}{\sigma_o} \tag{D.5}$$

We can rearrange Eq. (D.4), collecting the terms involving p' on one side, to obtain

$$\frac{\partial p'}{\partial t} - D_h \frac{\partial^2 p'}{\partial x^2} + \frac{p'}{\tau_D} = g_l + n'\left(\frac{1}{\tau_D} - \frac{1}{\tau_e}\right) \tag{D.6}$$

This way of writing this equation suggests that we can view the excess minority carrier population, along with any external generation process g_l, as a driving function for the majority carrier population. This is another way of stating that the majority carrier population adjusts itself to counteract deviations from neutrality. Equation (D.6) says that p' tracks n' and gives us the information we need to quantify how well it tracks. To do this we look at the homogeneous solutions to Equation (D.6) in two special cases, uniform time-varying excitation and nonuniform static excitation.

D.1 UNIFORM TIME-VARYING EXCITATION: τ_D

If there is no spatial variation of g_l or n', then the gradient term must be zero and the homogeneous equation is

$$\frac{dp'}{dt} + \frac{p'}{\tau_D} = O \tag{D.7}$$

The homogeneous solution is therefore

$$p'(t) = Ae^{-t/\tau_D} \tag{D.8}$$

which tells us that p' tracks driving functions temporally on a time scale comparable to τ_D. If $n'(t)$ varies with time more slowly than this, $p'(t)$ will follow it closely and quasineutrality will hold (i.e. will be a good assumption). This is illustrated in Fig.D.1a, where the response of p' to a temporal step change in n' is shown.

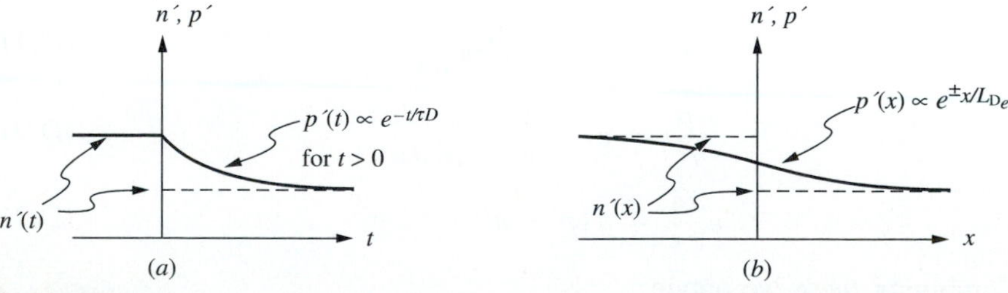

FIGURE D.1
Variations of the excess majority carrier concentration $p'(x)$ (solid curve) in response to a hypothetical temporal or spatial step change, respectively, in the minority carrier concentration n$'(x)$ (dashed curve): (a) temporal; (b) spatial.

D.2 NON-UNIFORM STATIC EXCITATION: L_{De}

If there is no variation of g_l and n' with time, then the homogeneous equation of interest is

$$\frac{d^2p'}{dx^2} - \frac{p'}{D_e\tau_D} = 0 \tag{D.9}$$

The homogeneous solution is

$$p'(x) = Be^{x/L_{\text{De}}} + Ce^{-x/L_{\text{De}}} \tag{D.10}$$

where we have defined the extrinsic Debye length L_{De} as $\sqrt{D_e\tau_D}$. This result teaches us that p' will track its driving functions spatially on a distance scale comparable to L_{De}. If $n'(x)$ varies appreciably only over distances larger than this, $p'(x)$ will follow it closely and again the assumption of quasineutrality with hold. Figure D.1*b* illustrates this concept.

To summarize the discussion of this appendix, we have found that two characteristic parameters, the extrinisic Debye length L_{De} and the dielectric relaxation time τ_D provide us with reference meters by which we can judge whether quasineutrality is likely to be a good assumption in uniformly doped samples in which the excitations and/or excess carrier populations vary either spatially or temporally. This result can be looked at in several ways. On the one hand, we can say that if not much happens on a time period of τ_D or if things vary little over a distance L_{De}, then quasineutrality is probably a good assumption. Alternatively, we can say that if things do change more rapidly than this, then we should expect quasineutrality to be restored within a few τ_D after a rapid temporal change and within several L_{De} on either side of a rapid spatial change.

APPENDIX E

METAL-SEMICONDUCTOR CONTACTS AND DEVICES

Metals are generally put on semiconductors with the intent to form either low-resistance ohmic contacts or high-quality, highly rectifying diodes. However, when an arbitrary combination of metal and semiconductor is placed in contact the result is more typically an electrical union with a current-voltage characteristic that is rather nonlinear but not highly rectifying and certainly not ohmic. Thus, like most things in life, the interface between a metal and a semiconductor is not simple, and careful engineering is required to ensure that the desired result is obtained when a metal-semiconductor junction is formed. In this appendix we will take a beginning look at the metal-semiconductor junction, its variety of electrical properties, and the engineering of its characteristics to obtain either strong rectification or low-resistance linearity.

E.1 THE METAL-SEMICONDUCTOR JUNCTION IN THERMAL EQUILIBRIUM

In Chap. 6, when we first discussed putting electrical contacts on semiconductors (see Sec. 6.4), we stated that there is in general a difference in electrostatic potential between a metal and a semiconductor. This potential difference is usually such that a depletion region is formed in the semiconductor adjacent to the metal. Simultaneously, a thin layer of charge is induced on the adjacent surface of the metal; this charge is positive if the metal is on a *p*-type semiconductor (in which the depletion region is negatively charged) and negative if it is on an n-type semiconductor (with positive depletion region charge).

We argue that the layer of charge in the metal is extremely thin because there is a very large density of mobile carriers and fixed ions in a metal (i.e., one of each per atom, or roughly 10^{22} cm^{-3}). Thus a small readjustment of the carriers over only a few tens of angstroms in the metal can easily yield the net charge needed to balance the semiconductor charge. The charged layer in the metal is always much thinner than the depletion region in the semiconductor, and we usually model it as a sheet of charge on the surface of the metal, that is, as a spatial impulse of charge in the direction normal to the surface at the metal-semiconductor interface.

We model the charge in the semiconductor near a metal-semiconductor interface using the depletion approximation; that is, by assuming that the mobile carriers are fully depleted from a region x_d wide and that deeper into the material quasineutrality holds. The resulting net charge distribution is illustrated in Fig. E.1*a* and *b* for metals on n- and p-type semiconductors, respectively.

Proceeding as we did in the depletion approximation model for a p-n junction in thermal equilibrium, we integrate the net charge density once to get the electrical field distribution. For a structure made on an n-type semiconductor, the net charge density is $+qN_d$ between 0 and x_d, there is an impulse of charge with intensity $-qN_d x_d$ at the metal surface, and there is zero net charge elsewhere. Thus we find that the electric field is

$$\mathscr{E}(x) = -\frac{qN_D}{\varepsilon_s}(x - x_d) \tag{E.1}$$

for $0 \le x \le x_d$, and zero elsewhere. This result and the corresponding result for a p-type sample, are plotted in Fig. E.1*c* and *d*, respectively. Note that the peak field intensity occurs at the interface.

We next integrate the electric field to get the electrostatic potential profile. Noting that $\phi(x)$ is ϕ_m in the metal (i.e., for $x \le 0$) and ϕ_n in the quasineutral region of an n-type semiconductor (i.e., for $x_d \le x$), we obtain

$$\phi(x) = \begin{cases} \phi_m & \text{for } x \le 0 \\ \phi_n - \dfrac{qN_D}{2\varepsilon_s}(x - x_d)^2 & \text{for } 0 \le x \le x_d \\ \phi_n & \text{for } x_d \le x \end{cases} \tag{E.2}$$

This result and the corresponding result for a p-type semiconductor are plotted in Fig. E.1*e* and *f*. Note in these illustrations of the field and potential that the electric field peaks at the interface and that the change in the potential occurs entirely within the semiconductor. The structure looks very much like a p^{++}-n or an n^{++}-p junction, with the metal playing the role of the heavily doped semiconductor. (As we shall see, however, there are important differences in other aspects of the device operation.)

To complete our model we need to find the depletion region width x_d in terms of the total change in the electrostatic potential occurring inside the semiconductor. If we call this change the *built-in potential* and label it $\Delta\phi_o$, then

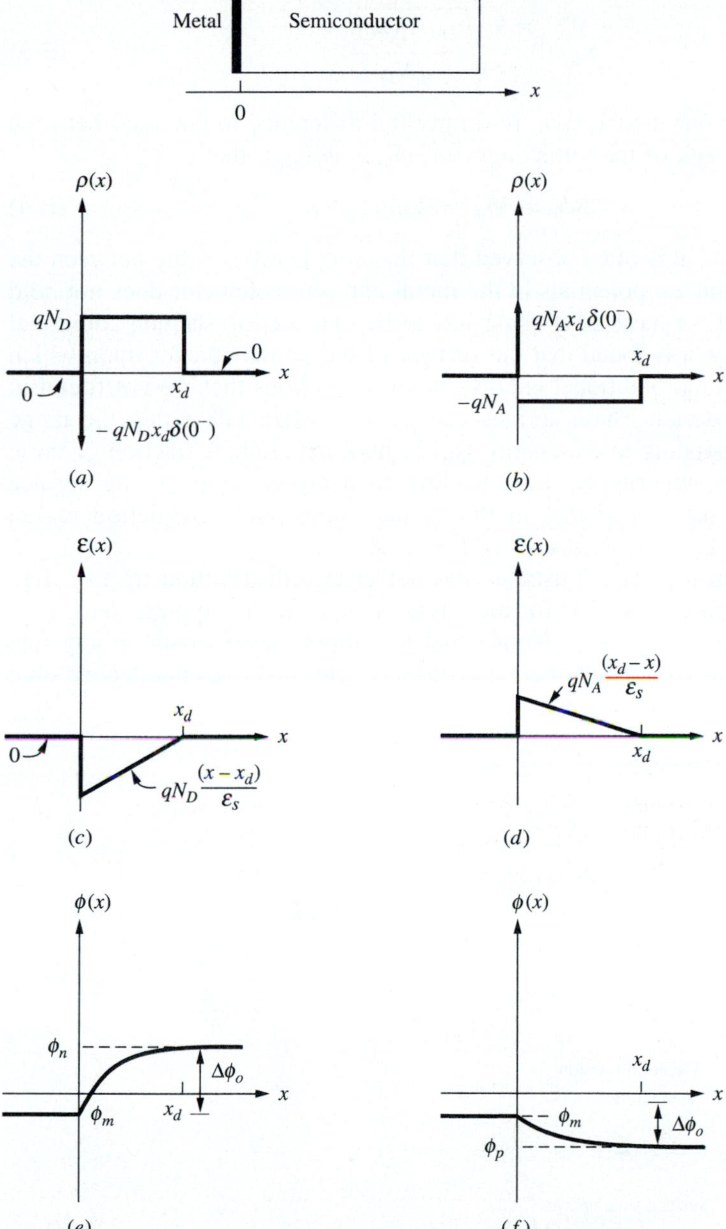

FIGURE E.1
Net charge distribution, electric field profile, and electrostatic potential profile for a metal-semiconductor junction formed on an n-type semiconductor—(a), (c), and (e), respectively—and on a p-type semiconductor—(b), (d), and (f), respectively—modeled using the depletion approximation.

we have

$$x_d(0) \approx \sqrt{\frac{2\varepsilon_s\,|\Delta\phi_o|}{qN_D}} \tag{E.3}$$

According to our model, $\Delta\phi_o$ is simply the difference in potential between the metal and the bulk of the semiconductor, $\phi_m - \phi_{n(\text{or}\,p)}$, that is,

$$\Delta\phi_o = \phi_m - \phi_{n(\text{or } p)} \tag{E.4}$$

In practice, however, it is often observed that this simple relationship between the built-in potential and the potentials in the metal and semiconductor does not hold and that the model we have been using has to be extended to include additional effects. Specifically, it is found that the surface of the semiconductor upon which the metal is placed has additional energy sites for electrons that are not found in the bulk of the material. These surface energy sites often fall within the range of energies corresponding to the energy gap in bulk material. A fraction of these states are filled by majority carriers, leading to a dipole layer on the surface comprised of the sheet of charge in the surface states and a depletion region extending into the bulk, as illustrated in Fig. E.2.

The sketch in Fig. E.2 illustrates the net charge distribution up to a free semiconductor surface at $x = 0$ for an n-type sample with a typical density of surface states in the energy gap. Notice that this dipole layer exists on any free semiconductor surface on which there are surface states and does not depend on a

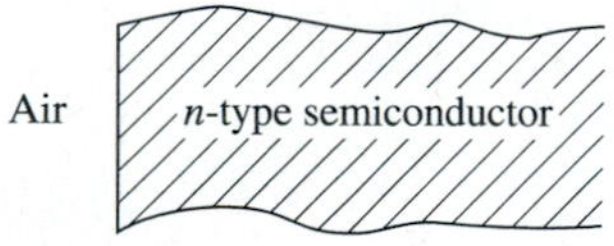

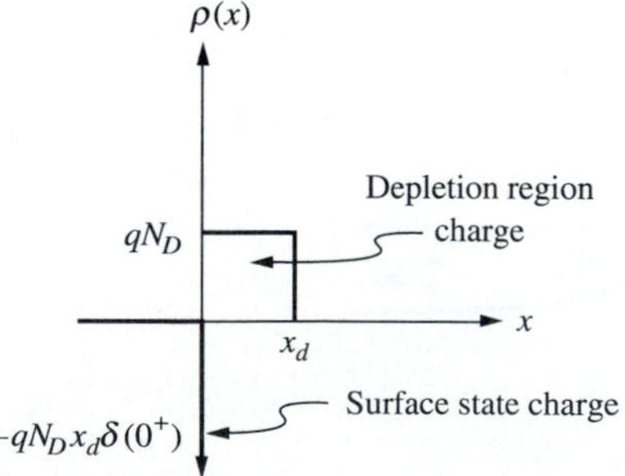

FIGURE E.2
Net charge distribution in the vicinity of the free surface of an n-type semiconductor sample with a typical density of surface states.

metal being present. If there were no surface states, there would be no depletion of the surface (i.e., the net charge would be zero up to the surface).

When a metal is put on this surface, the electrostatic potential profile and net charge distribution change to reflect both the difference in the electrostatic potential between the metal and the bulk of the semiconductor (as before) and now also the surface states on the semiconductor surface. Typical profiles are illustrated in Fig. E.3, which presents the same information as was presented earlier in Fig. E.1, but now for a situation in which there are also surface states. For this figure we see that the electric field and charge profiles in the semiconductor look pretty much the same as they did before, although at the interface there is an additional impulse of charge just inside the semiconductor (recall that the original impulse was just inside the metal) and there is now an impulse in the electric field. The potential profile in the semiconductor also has the same shape, but now there is a step change in potential at the interface between the semiconductor and the metal. Equation (E.2) describing $\phi(x)$ must be modified as follows:

$$\phi(x) = \begin{cases} \phi_m & \text{for } x \leq 0 \\ \phi_i & \text{at } x = 0^+ \\ \phi_n - \dfrac{qN_d}{2\varepsilon_s}(x - x_d)^2 & \text{for } 0^+ < x \leq x_d \\ \phi_n & \text{for } x_d \leq x \end{cases} \tag{E.2$'$}$$

Thus the built-in potential in the semiconductor, $\Delta\phi_o$, is no longer given by Eq. (E.4); the step change, $\phi_m - \phi_i$, caused by the charge doublet at the interface has to be subtracted; thus

$$\Delta\phi_o = \phi_i - \phi_{n(\text{or } p)} \tag{E.4$'$}$$

We can presumably extend our model to incorporate surface states and calculate the step change in the potential at the interface, but as a practical matter the problem of modeling the surface states and the interface in detail and relating the potential step to fundamental materials parameters has proven to be very difficult. A satisfactory, general model for the interface has yet to be developed. In practice, therefore, the built-in potential $\Delta\phi_o$ between a given metal and semiconductor is more often determined experimentally than theoretically. That is, we don't calculate it, we measure it.

To summarize our model for an unbiased metal-semiconductor (m-s) junction, there is a dipole layer at an m-s junction formed by sheets of charge at the metal-semiconductor interface and a depletion region extending into the semiconductor surface.* The strength of the dipole and width of the depletion region

*This is usually the situation, but in a few rare cases there is an accumulation layer on the semiconductor, too. For these cases, the m-s junction behaves like an ohmic contact and none of the discussion in Sec. E.2 and E.3 is relevant.

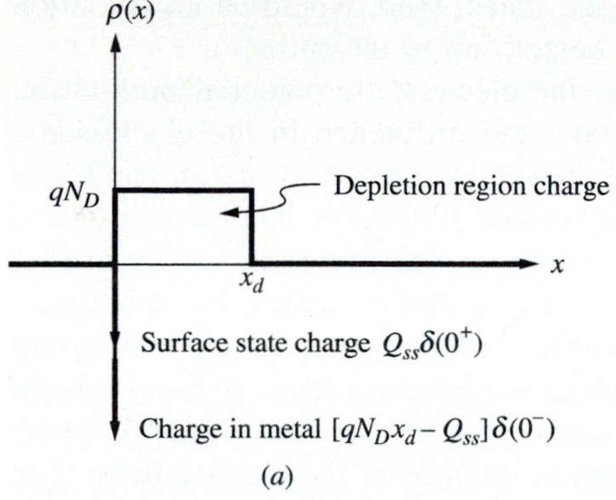

(a)

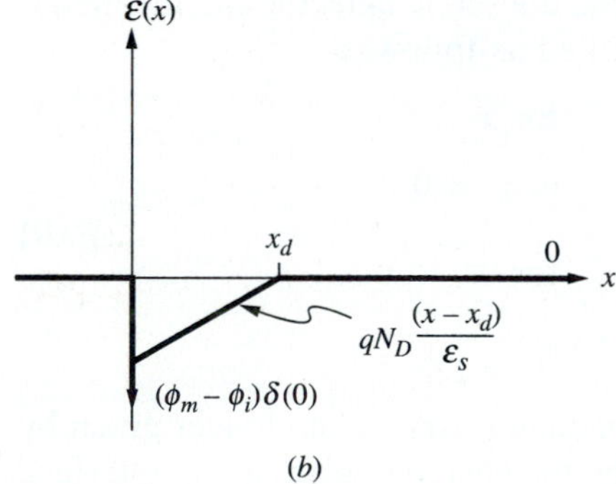

(b)

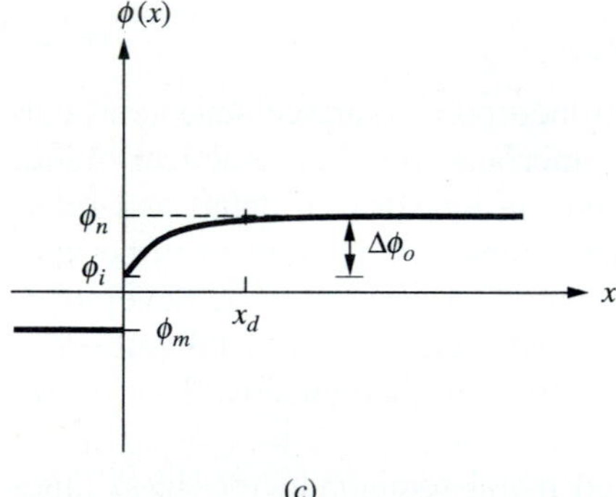

(c)

FIGURE E.3
Net charge distribution, electric field profile, and electrostatic potential profile for a metal-semiconductor junction formed on an *n*-type semiconductor [(*a*), (*b*), and (*c*), respectively], modeled using the depletion approximation and assuming the existence of surface states.

x_d depend on the built-in potential $\Delta\phi_o$, at the m-s junction through Eq. (E.3). The built-in potential is related to the electrostatic potential difference between the metal and the semiconductor and to the surface state density and distribution on the semiconductor surface. It is in general determined empirically for a given combination of metal, semiconductor, and fabrication process.

E.2 REVERSE BIASED METAL-SEMICONDUCTOR JUNCTIONS

When we form a metal-semiconductor junction on a moderately doped semiconductor and the built-in potential is on the order of 0.5 V or more, that junction will behave electrically much like a *p-n* junction; that is, it will conduct relatively well for one polarity of bias (forward bias) and will block the current flow in the other polarity of bias (reverse bias). Assuming for now that we have such a junction and that we reverse-bias it by an amount v_{ms}, the main change to occur is that the electrostatic potential drop in the semiconductor will increase from $\Delta\phi_o$ to $\Delta\phi_o - v_{ms}$ and the depletion region width will increase to

$$x_d(v_{ms}) \cong \sqrt{\frac{2\varepsilon_s\left|\Delta\phi_o - v_{ms}\right|}{qN_d}} \tag{E.5}$$

This observation provides us with a means to measure $\Delta\phi_o$. As we saw with a *p-n* junction, the small signal depletion capacitance of a reverse-biased junction is given by

$$C_{dp} = \frac{\varepsilon_s A}{w} \tag{E.6}$$

which in this case becomes

$$C_{dp}(V_{MS}) = A\sqrt{\frac{\varepsilon_s qN_d}{2\left|\Delta\phi_o - V_{MS}\right|}} \tag{E.7}$$

because w is essentially x_d. Rewriting this as

$$\frac{1}{C_{dp}^2} = \frac{2(\Delta\phi_o - V_{MS})}{\varepsilon_s qN_d A^2} \tag{E.8}$$

gives us the result we want. We see clearly that if we measure C_{dp} as a function of V_{MS} and plot $(1/C_{dp})^2$ against V_{MS}, we should get a straight line whose intercept on the horizontal axis is $\Delta\phi_o$. Furthermore, from the slope of the line we can also determine the doping level in the semiconductor. Such a plot is called a C-V plot, and this procedure, illustrated in Fig. E.4, is an extremely common technique used to measure the doping level in semiconductor samples and is one of the primary ways of determining $\Delta\phi_o$.

E.3. FORWARD BIAS AND CURRENTS

As we start the discussion of current flow across m-s junctions, a word of explanation is in order. Without developing models for the carrier populations and for

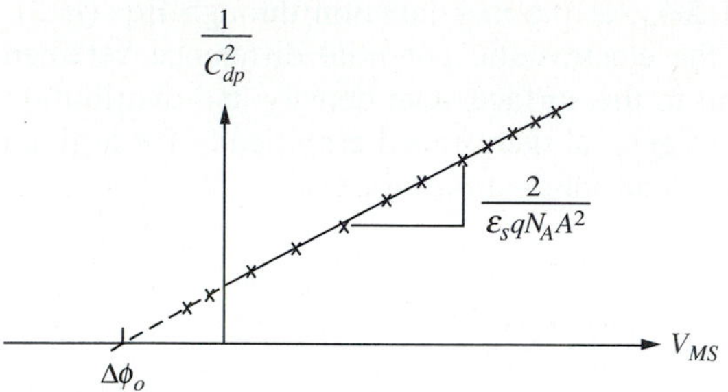

FIGURE E.4
Illustration of how a typical C-V plot might appear. The slope of the remaining straight line is inversely proportional to the doping concentration of the semiconductor.

carrier flow in metals, we cannot be particularly quantitative; consequently the qualitative discussion to follow asks you to accept more facts on faith than do other parts of this text. Nonetheless, based on your knowledge of *p-n* junctions, you should be able to understand the discussion and, hopefully, be comfortable with the results presented.

The first point to appreciate is that an m-s junction with a large built-in potential and wide depletion region, like those pictured in Fig. E.1 and E.3, does behave electrically like a diode. When the bias is such that the built-in potential is lowered, then majority carriers in the semiconductor readily flow into the metal. There is no corresponding increase in the flow of charge carriers from the metal to the semiconductor, however, because it turns out that the barrier to carrier flow from the metal into the semiconductor is not affected significantly by the bias. This is one place where we need more detailed models for a metal to really explain what is going on, but you can perhaps understand this a little by realizing that essentially all of the potential drop is in the semiconductor and that the picture in the metal changes very little with bias. Thus in an m-s diode, the current that flows in forward bias consists almost exclusively of majority carriers moving from the semiconductor into the metal. In reverse bias there are very few minority carriers in the semiconductor to flow into the metal; the barrier in the metal changes very little, and few carriers flow from the metal into the semiconductor. The barrier at an m-s junction thus blocks carrier flow in reverse bias just as it does in a *p-n* junction.

The second point to appreciate is that unlike the situation in a *p-n* junction, the flow of carriers into the metal across an m-s junction is not limited by minority carrier diffusion, the controlling process in a *p-n* junction. Instead the current is limited by how readily the majority carriers in the semiconductor drift and diffuse across the space-charge layer (a process that happened so quickly in a *p-n* junction compared to minority carrier diffusion that we neglected it) and by how fast the carriers move into the metal (a process called *thermionic emission*). Since these processes do not limit the carrier motion as much as diffusion, the carrier and charge fluxes (i.e., the current densities) are larger across an m-s junction than across a *p-n* junction (assuming the same applied bias and similar doping levels). This difference in current densities between m-s and *p-n* junctions is made even greater by the fact that the potential barrier the carriers must surmount (i.e., the built-in potential) is lower in an m-s junction than in a *p-n* junction.

Quantitatively, the current across an m-s junction varies exponentially with the applied bias just as it does for a *p-n* junction. Thus we have, assuming for purposes of discussion an *n*-type semiconductor,

$$i_D = I_S(v_{AB})\left[e^{qv_{AB}/kT} - 1\right] \tag{E.9}$$

This relationship is plotted for a representative device in Fig.E.5. The exponential behavior is a consequence of the fact that the number of carriers with enough energy to surmount the potential energy barrier varies exponentially with the height of the barrier (normalized to *kT*), just as was the case in a *p-n* junction, and of the fact that the barrier height $(\Delta\phi_o - v_{AB})$ varies linearly with the applied voltage v_{AB}.

We cannot model the saturation current I_S without having modeled the metal in more detail, so we will limit ourselves here to general comments about it. As we have already stated, I_S for an m-s junction is typically larger than the saturation current in a comparable *p-n* diode.* This difference can amount to many orders

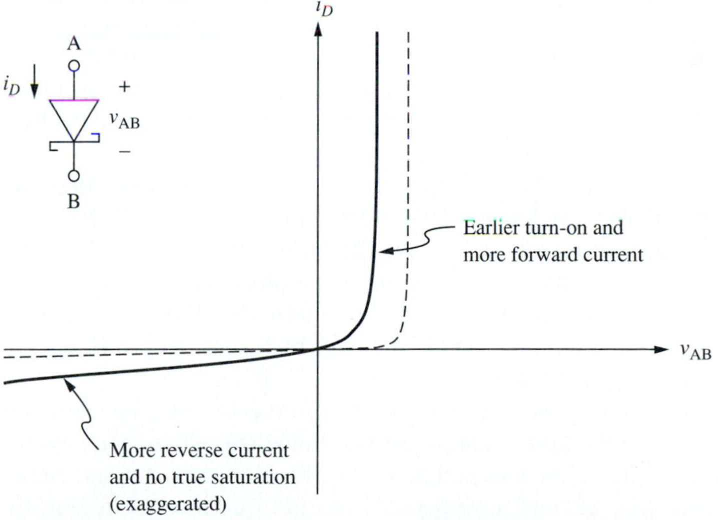

FIGURE E.5
Current-voltage relationship for a representative metal-semiconductor diode (solid curve) plotted on the same axes as a comparable *p-n* junction diode (dashed curve). Notice the larger forward and reverse currents in the m-s diode and the lack of true current saturation in the reverse characteristic.

*By "comparable" we mean that it has similar doping levels on the more lightly doped side of the junction.

of magnitude, which translates to several tenths of a volt on the voltage scale, as illustrated in Fig. E.5. Also, there is a weak dependence of I_S on the applied bias in an m-s junction. This factor is not noticeable in forward bias, where the exponential factor dominates, but it is evident in reverse bias as the absence of a true saturation of the reverse current, as illustrated in Fig. E.5. This feature is more of a curiosity than anything of any practical consequence, however.

Summarizing the key differences between m-s and *p-n* junctions, the most prominent feature is that an m-s junction has a larger forward current at a given forward bias than does a comparable *p-n* diode. Furthermore, this current is comprised almost entirely of majority carriers from the semiconductor; there is typically negligible injection of excess minority carriers into the semiconductor from the metal. Both of these features (i.e., the larger forward current and the lack of minority carrier injection) are used to advantage in many of the applications of m-s junction as diodes (see Sec. E.4).

E.4 SCHOTTKY DIODES

Historically, rectifying metal-semiconductor junctions have been called Schottky diodes, after W. Schottky, the researcher who first correctly modeled the current-voltage characteristics of these devices (previous models had predicted the opposite polarity for the rectification). More recently, the trend has been to call them simply metal-semiconductor, or m-s, diodes. As a rule of thumb, an m-s junction with a barrier greater than 0.5 V and a depletion region at least 0.1 μm wide will show useful rectification at room temperature (i.e., will have terminal characteristics like those shown in Fig. E.5) and will be modeled well by Eq. (E.9).

Such m-s diodes find a number of applications. One of the most common is in the gate of a metal-semiconductor field effect transistor, or MESFET (see Sec. 10.3). In this application the m-s diode has the virtues that it is much easier to fabricate than a *p-n* junction and that it can be made physically much smaller than a *p-n* junction. It has also made it possible to fabricate FETs (and diodes, for that matter) in wide-bandgap semiconductors in which it is very difficult or even impossible to make a *p-n* junction.

The MESFET application uses the m-s diode in reverse bias, but another important application uses this diode's unique forward characteristics. That application is in collector clamping. The idea is that when a bipolar transistor saturates, a large number of minority carriers are injected into the quasineutral region of the collector and the transistor cannot be switched out of saturation until these carriers are removed (see Chap. 16). This slows saturating logic circuits such as transistor-transistor logic (TTL) dramatically. One solution is to put an m-s diode in parallel with the base-collector diode. In the forward active region, when the base-collector junction is reverse-biased, so too is the m-s diode and nothing is changed by the diode's presence. In saturation, however, when the collector-base junction is forward biased, the m-s junction with its much larger current is the one that conducts; the collector-base *p-n* junction never really turns on and so doesn't conduct. Consequently, there are no minority carriers injected into the collector

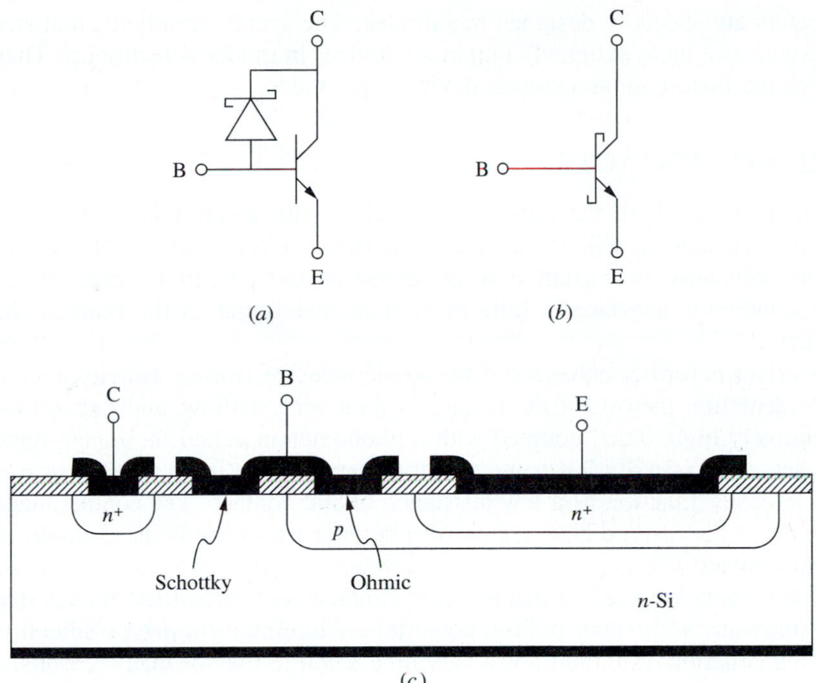

FIGURE E.6
(*a*) Schematic representation of a Schottky clamped bipolar transistor; (*b*) the normal circuit symbol used to represent this device; (*c*) the cross-section of a typical realization of this device on a silicon substrate.

and the transistor can be switched out of saturation very quickly. The m-s junction itself switches very quickly because there is no minority carrier charge storage associated with it either, as we discussed in Sec. E.3. That is, the current through an m-s diode consists of carriers flowing into the metal. TTL logic that uses this concept is called *Schottky-clamped TTL*. A Schottky-clamped bipolar transistor, shown schematically in Figs. E.6 *a* and *b*, is easily fabricated in silicon because aluminum deposited on the lightly doped *n*-type collector region forms a good m-s diode. The device cross section in Fig. E.6*c* illustrates how this might be implemented in practice. Note that the metal is patterned so as to simultaneously make an ohmic contact to the base and a rectifying contact to the collector. The same metal is patterned to make ohmic contact to the collector elsewhere on the device via the heavily doped n^+-region.

Other applications of m-s diodes also make use of the fact that there is no minority carrier injection associated with them and that they can therefore operate extremely quickly. This, coupled with the fact that they can be patterned in very small dimensions, has resulted in their wide use as high-frequency rectifiers. Very small–diameter m-s diodes are used in radio astronomy, for example, to rectify signals at hundreds and even thousands of gigahertz. Similarly, the fastest photodetectors are specially designed m-s diodes. The speed, simplicity, and size of m-s diodes make them extremely important devices in modern electronics. They are some of the fastest semiconductor devices ever made.

E.5 OHMIC CONTACTS

In m-s junctions in which the built-in potential is only a few tenths of a volt, the saturation current I_s will be so large that there is very little useful rectification. The resistance to current flow presented by the potential barrier at the metal-semiconductor interface is little more than that found in the bulk of the semiconductor.

This effect is further enhanced if the semiconductor is more heavily doped. What little depletion there is at the surface is then very shallow, and the surface field is relatively high. This, coupled with a phenomenon called the image force potential, serves to actually lower the potential barrier even further. Such an m-s junction can easily function as a low-resistance ohmic contact. The contact made by aluminum to the p-type base region of a bipolar transistor is an example of this type of contact.

In many cases we need to make ohmic contacts and cannot use metals that form m-s junctions with small built-in potentials. Aluminum on n-type silicon is just one such situation. Aluminum is a very nice metal to use for many reasons—it is a good conductor, it is inexpensive, it is easily etched and patterned, it is fairly inert, and it adheres well to silicon and to silicon dioxide—but it yields a large built-in potential on n-type silicon. To overcome this problem, we must very heavily dope the silicon under the aluminum when we want an ohmic contact with aluminum to n-type silicon. This results in a depletion region at the metal-semiconductor interface that is very, very narrow, and two things happen. First, because of image force lowering, the height of the potential barrier is reduced somewhat. Second, and more importantly, we find that the carriers can *tunnel* right through the very thin barrier. Tunneling is a quantum mechanical phenomenon that describes the fact that there is a finite probability that a particle can penetrate any potential energy barrier. If the barrier is thin enough and/or low enough, the probability of penetration can be very high and, in the case of an m-s junction, there will be negligible resistance to current flow and the contact will look ohmic. This is the way ohmic contact is made to the collector and emitter regions of an npn silicon BJT.

For many semiconductors it is common practice to make ohmic contacts by depositing on the surface an alloy that contains a suitable dopant, say zinc in the case of p-type GaAs, along with the primary contact metal, say gold. The structure is then heated to diffuse some of the dopant into the semiconductor to produce a very heavily doped region under the metal. As we have just said, the corresponding depletion region at the m-s interface is very narrow in such a situation and can easily be tunneled by the charge carriers. The result is a low-resistance "alloyed" ohmic contact.

APPENDIX F

LARGE- AND SMALL-SIGNAL VALUES OF β

In our models for bipolar junction transistors, two different common-emitter forward current gains β have been introduced. There is the large-signal current gain, which is given an uppercase F subscript and is defined as

$$\beta_F = \frac{I_C}{I_B} \tag{F.1}$$

and there is the small-signal, or incremental, current gain, which is given a lowercase f subscript and is defined as

$$\beta_f = \frac{\partial i_c}{\partial i_b} \tag{F.2}$$

In the operating regions where a given bipolar transistor is accurately modeled by the Ebers–Moll model, these two β are identically equal and we need not be concerned about distinguishing between them. In other regions of operation such as those corresponding to very low and very high collector current operation, for example, effects not included in the Ebers–Moll model tend to become important; these effects can lead to significant differences in these two expressions for β. Seeing how this is treated in practice can give us some useful lessons in modeling.

Since the effects that we have neglected in the Ebers–Moll model—such as excess recombination in the emitter-base junction, series resistance in the base, and base-width modulation—arise initially as small effects, we are usually able to ignore them in our large-signal modeling much longer than we can in our small-signal analyses. A picture that might help you visualize this is to think first of a region of operation in which the Ebers–Moll model is adequate for both large-

and small-signal operation; this region, which strictly speaking is the only place we would try to use the Ebers–Moll model, is depicted schematically in Fig. F.1 as region A. It is a natural desire, however, to want to use our models over as wide a range as possible, and if we can stretch things a bit, as it were, so much the better. As we consider using the Ebers–Moll model outside of this strictly valid region, we tend to find that the first parameters to "feel" this change (i.e., to be affected by the inadequacy of the model) are the incremental parameters (e.g., β_f) whereas the large-scale parameters, such as β_F, are initially much less affected. This should intuitively seem very reasonable. If you are initially on a large flat plateau and begin to move off this plateau, the first thing you will sense in doing so will be the downward (or upward) slope of the edge. You will sense this slope long before you have actually moved down (or up) much at all on an absolute scale.

There is thus typically a boundary region around the central "ideal" region (see Fig. F.1) where, in the case of a bipolar junction transistor, the Ebers–Moll model is useful and reasonably accurate for large-signal calculations even if it neglects certain effects, while at the same time the presence of these effects must be acknowledged and included in the small-signal model. Eventually we find ourselves in an operating region where the effects we neglected initially are so important that they cannot be ignored in the large-signal model either, but until that point we use the Ebers–Moll model for large-signal modeling and we need to adjust only the incremental model by, for example, replacing β_F with β_f, adding r_x to the base lead, putting g_o across the output, inserting C_π and C_μ, etc.

When you are faced with a problem in which the large-signal and small-signal β terms differ, you can usually decide which β to use in a particular situation fairly easily. There is at least one situation, however, that may be more confusing but can also be very instructive to consider in more detail: the relationship between g_π and g_m in the hybrid-π model.

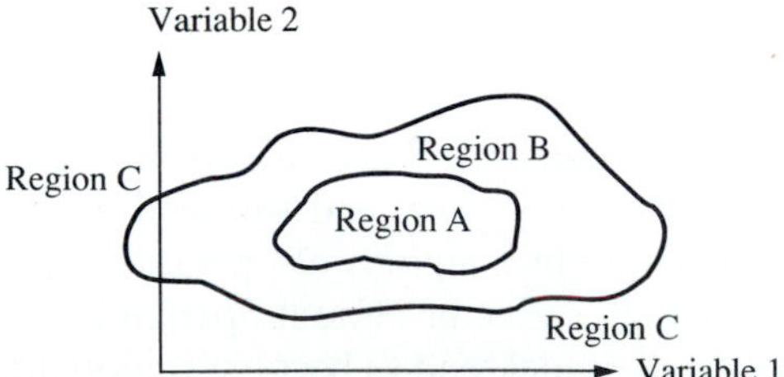

FIGURE F.1
Illustration of the operating variable space for a model depicting regions A, where large-signal and small-signal models based on the same description hold; B, where the large-signal model is adequate but where additional effects need to be incorporated into the small-signal model; and C, where both models must acknowledge the presence of effects not considered in the original model.

We specified in Sec. 8.2.2*a* that g_m is the more fundamental of these quantities and is given by $q|I_C|/kT$. We also said that the incremental input conductance g_π is to be determined from g_m as g_m/β_f, where the small-signal β is to be used. This last point seems perfectly reasonable, but you might just as well consider it equally reasonable to start with the base-emitter diode and say that the incremental input conductance g_π is $q|I_B|/kT$, which, since $I_B = I_C/\beta_F$, says now that g_π is g_m/β_F. This is not what we said above. Which is it, β_f or β_F?

The answer is β_f, but to understand why, we need to look at what is going on physically. We will consider the case of small currents, where base-emitter recombination becomes important. The Ebers–Moll model neglects the excess recombination component of the emitter-base junction current; to include this current in our model we will add a new element in parallel with the emitter-base junction, as illustrated in Fig. F.2. Since we are discussing the issue in the context of the hybrid-π model, a common-emitter configuration, we will focus on the large-signal model in Fig. F.2*b*, which is the more convenient one for analyses of common-emitter topologies. In both Fig. 2*a* and *b*, a nonlinear element representing the excess junction current has been inserted across the emitter and base terminals and in parallel with the ideal exponential base-emitter junction diode (this element is the same in both representations). Notice in Fig. F.2*b* that we have used B_F rather than β_F for the current gain of the Ebers–Moll transistor to avoid introducing yet another current gain labeled β. When excess recombination (i.e., the shunting element) can be neglected, all of these current gains (B_F,β_F, and β_f) are identical; in general, though, all three are different.

We next find an incremental equivalent circuit for the model in Fig. F.2*b*; this is illustrated in Fig. F.2*c*. The new elements in this model have the following definitions: The conductance of the nonlinear element representing the excess currents is simply

$$g_{bn} = \left.\frac{\partial i_{BN}}{\partial v_{BE}}\right|_Q \tag{F.3}$$

We will not specify it further. The conductance of the exponential diode is

$$g_{bi} \equiv \frac{qI_{BI}}{kT} \tag{F.4}$$

and since both derive from the Ebers–Moll model, the transconductance g_m must be related to g_{bi} as follows:

$$g_m = B_F g_{bi} \tag{F.5a}$$

Using Eq. (F.4), we find that this becomes

$$g_m = \frac{qB_F I_{BI}}{kT} \tag{F.5b}$$

which, referring to Fig. F.2*b*, can be written as

$$g_m = \frac{qI_C}{kT} \tag{F.5c}$$

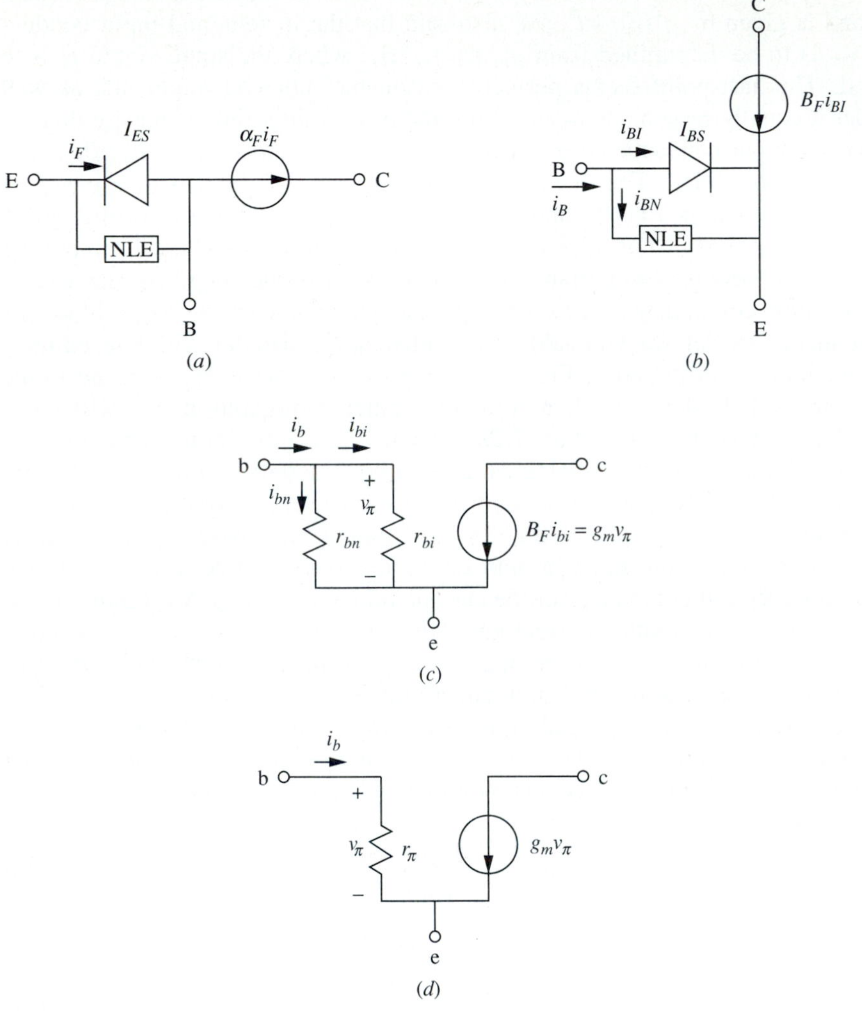

FIGURE F.2
(*a* and *b*) Common-base and common-emitter large signal Ebers–Moll bipolar transistor models, respectively, with a nonlinear element (NLE) added to represent excess low-level recombination at the emitter-base junction; (*c*) an incremental equivalent circuit for the large-signal model in (*b*); (*d*) the mid-band hybrid-π model.

since I_C is $B_F I_{BI}$. So our first result is that g_m is still given by the same expression, qI_C/kT, even in the presence of excess junction recombination.

Now we turn to the input conductance, which we call g_π in the hybrid-π model, Fig. F.2*d*. Now the input conductance is g_{bn} in parallel with g_{bi}, so $g_\pi = g_{bn} \parallel g_{bi}$. This expression does not help us much, however, since we don't know anything about g_{bn}. In fact, we would like to avoid altogether having to develop a model for the nonlinear shunting element, if at all possible.

To be able to proceed, we first note that g_π can also be written as $\partial i_b/\partial v_\pi$. Since β_f is $\partial i_c/\partial i_b$ and g_m is $\partial i_c/\partial v_\pi$, we should be able to relate g_π to g_m, which we know, and β_f, which we can easily measure using the sum rule of differential equations. Specifically, then, we start with

$$g_\pi = \frac{\partial i_b}{\partial v_\pi}$$

Viewing i_b as a function of i_c and v_{ce}, we can write this as

$$g_\pi = \frac{\partial i_b}{\partial i_c}\frac{\partial i_c}{\partial v_\pi} + \frac{\partial i_b}{v_{ce}}\frac{\partial v_{ce}}{\partial v_\pi} \tag{F.6}$$

However, the last term is negligible since the current i_b does not depend on the collector-emitter voltage. Thus after recognizing β_f and g_m in Eq. (F.6), we have

$$g_\pi = \frac{g_m}{\beta_f} \tag{F.7}$$

It is clearly β_f that enters here, as we said earlier was the case.

We have skirted the issue of modeling or otherwise specifying the characteristics of the shunting element in our schematics. You realize, of course, that it is present through β_f in our model at this stage. We can measure β_f, and we can determine what g_{bi} is, so it is actually possible to extract g_{bn} from data, but this is not usually done. Instead, we normally study deviations from ideality in the base emitter junction through large-signal plots of log I_C and log I_B versus V_{BE}. Such a plot, called a *Gummel plot*, is a very powerful and widely used analytical tool for studying low-level junction currents in transistors.

APPENDIX G

INTEGRATED-CIRCUIT FABRICATION

Manufacturing the microelectronic devices and integrated circuits studied in this text involves a fascinating mix of many disciplines of science and engineering. We will have room for only a brief exposure in this appendix, but even then you should start to see both the power and beauty of the vast array of fabrication technologies that have been developed to produce semiconductor electronics. These technologies drive the microelectronics revolution that has been proceeding unabated since the 1960s and has continued to evolve at a hectic pace. Some of you may well want to make this area a major focus of your career.

In this appendix we will first look from a general perspective at the variety of technologies used to fabricate devices and circuits. After this overview of the device engineer's technological toolbox, we will look step-by-step at the processing sequences followed to realize several representative integrated circuits. Specifically, we will look at the fabrication of junction isolated bipolar ICs, at n-MOS, at CMOS and BiCMOS, and at refractory-metal-gate MESFET logic.

G.1 ELEMENTS OF SEMICONDUCTOR PROCESSING

There are certain process technologies that are intrinsic to all semiconductor fabrication. These include crystal growth, doping, encapsulation, microlithography, metallization, and etching and cleaning. We will look at each in turn in this section.

G.1.1 Crystal Growth

Most microelectronic processing begins with a single crystal semiconductor disk called a *wafer*. This wafer is the foundation upon which the device or circuit is built and as such is called the *substrate*. Wafers are cut from long cylindrical crystals called *boules* using special high-speed saws with very thin blades to minimize kerf loss. They are then polished on one side, first mechanically and then chemically, to yield a flat, damage-free surface. The wafers are made only as thick as necessary for them to have sufficient mechanical strength that they do not break during processing; making them thicker only wastes valuable material. As a consequence, GaAs wafers are thicker than the same-diameter Si wafers, because GaAs is more brittle. A typical wafer of either material is on the order of half a millimeter thick (e.g., 0.4 to 0.6 mm, or 400 to 600 μm). A boule and a wafer cut from a boule are illustrated in Fig. G.1*a* and *b*, respectively.

The "bulk" crystal growth technology used to produce boules of silicon and other semiconductors (Ge, GaAs, GaP, InP, etc.) has developed over the years to the point that it is possible to produce bulk single crystals of exceptional purity (less than 10^{12} unintentional electrically active impurities per cm^3), perfection (less than 10 defects per cm^2 on any cross section), and size (up to 30 cm in diameter and 1 m in length). The standard wafer diameter used in processing tends to increase with each generation of technological improvements and equipment because the economics of the business favors larger wafers. At present, most Si processing is done using 6 in. or 8 in. wafers, whereas GaAs and InP process lines use 3 in. or 4 in. wafers.

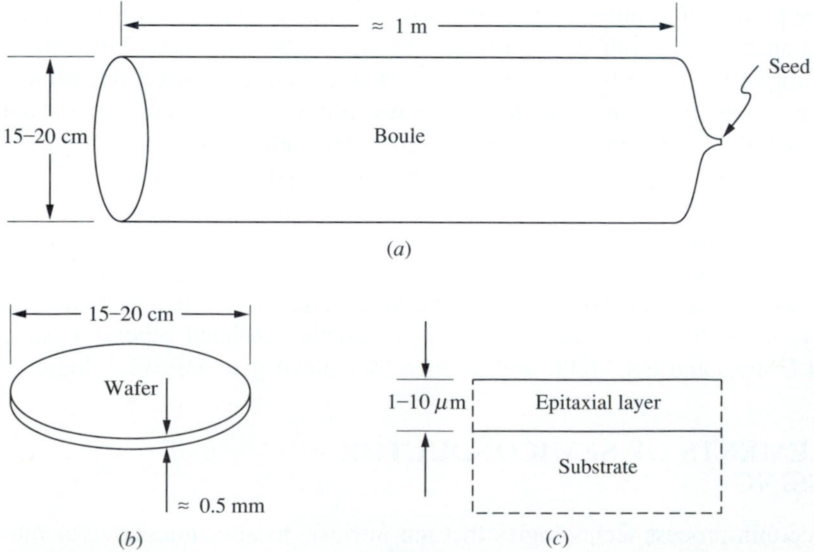

FIGURE G.1
(*a*) Single crystal boule; (*b*) a single wafer cut from a boule like the one shown in (*a*); (*c*) cross-sectional sketch near the upper surface of a wafer upon which a thin epitaxial layer has been grown.

Almost as important as the growth and preparation of bulk crystals for substrates is the growth of thin crystalline layers on these substrates. In this process, which is called *epitaxy*, the wafer surface provides the template, or *seed,* for continued crystal growth. The growth is usually relatively thin (it is measured in microns) and usually differs from the substrate in terms of its doping level and perhaps even composition (in which case it would be called *heteroepitaxy*); an example is shown in Fig. G.1*c*. The epitaxial layer need not be uniform in doping or composition, of course, and many advanced research devices incorporate doping and/or composition profiles that are controlled with atomic-layer precision.

Most silicon epitaxy is done in a growth chamber, or *reactor*, in which the silicon wafers are heated to a temperature in the vicinity of 1000° C and exposed to a gas stream containing silicon tetrahydride (silane) and hydrogen. The silane decomposes near the heated substrate, depositing silicon on it; that is,

$$SiH_4 \xrightarrow{\Delta} Si\downarrow + 2H_2\uparrow \tag{G.1}$$

If the deposition occurs slowly enough and the temperature is high enough that the depositing silicon atoms can move about and find their energetically favored crystal lattice sites, the layer that is formed will be a single crystalline continuation of the substrate. This process is called *chemical vapor deposition* (CVD) or *gas-phase epitaxy.* A typical reactor used for this type of growth is illustrated in Fig. G.2.

Epitaxy can also be accomplished through solidification from a solution (liquid-phase epitaxy, LPE) or by direct condensation from a beam of atoms and/or molecules in a vacuum (molecular-beam epitaxy, MBE). LPE is widely used, for example, to produce gallium phosphide light-emitting diodes and gallium arsenide–based and indium phosphide–based laser diodes. MBE is used for many high-speed gallium arsenide field effect transistors and some laser diodes.

Epitaxial structures that incorporate layers with different compositions (but essentially the same lattice constant) are called *heterostructures*. III-V semiconductor devices have traditionally made wide use of heterostructures grown by LPE, MBE, and/or CVD. Most silicon integrated circuits using epitaxial layers

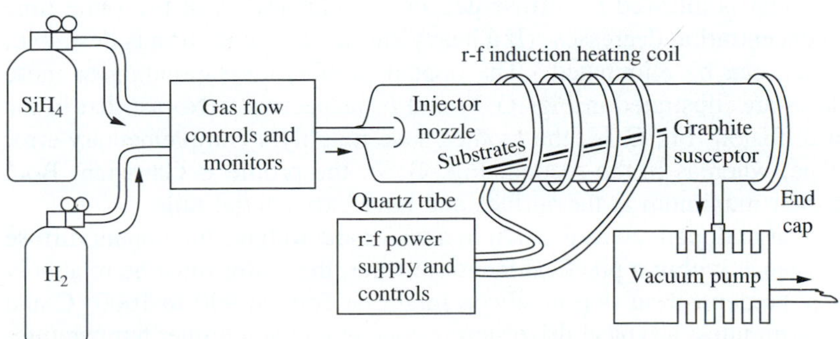

FIGURE G.2
Representative chemical vapor deposition system for epitaxial growth of silicon.

simply use silicon epilayers, but heterostructures involving alloys of silicon and germanium also exist. Heterostructures that mix different families of semiconductors (elemental, III-V, II-VI, etc.) as well as insulators and metals have proven very difficult to realize, and perfecting them remains a research dream.

G.1.2 Doping

Doping is the introduction of dopants into a semiconductor in a controlled manner. There are three common ways in which this is done: during crystal growth, by solid-state diffusion, and through ion implantation.

Bulk crystals are doped as they are grown by adding a controlled amount of dopant to the molten semiconductor as the crystal is being formed. A great deal of attention must be paid to ensuring that the doping is uniform across the diameter of a boule and from end to end. Variations of only a few percent can be tolerated. Doping during epitaxy is also accomplished by adding controlled amounts of dopants to the source solution, gas stream, or molecular beam. In the case of silicon CVD, for example, this might involve the addition of dopant hydrides such as diborane, phosphine, or arsine to the silane and hydrogen mixture. Again the control of the doping level and its uniformity across a wafer is a key processing issue.

Doping by solid-state diffusion involves establishing an elevated concentration of the desired dopant around a wafer (which is being held at a high temperature) and letting the dopant diffuse into the surface. By controlling the concentration of dopant in the ambient atmosphere, the temperature of the wafer, and the time of exposure, the amount of dopant introduced and its profile can be controlled.

A typical diffusion doping process involves two stages. In the first stage, called *predeposition*, a shallow doping profile having a very high surface concentration is created. The surface concentration after this step may be too high to be useful in a device, but it turns out that such high surface concentrations can at least be reproducibly established since they represent "saturation" levels. Thus this represents a very practical way of controlling the total amount of dopant introduced, even if it isn't all located exactly where we want it. In the second stage, called the *drive*, the exterior source of dopant is removed and the dopant left in the wafer after the first step is allowed to diffuse deeper into the wafer; at the same time the surface concentration decreases. (If a heavy surface concentration is desirable, the second step can be eliminated.) The dopant profiles corresponding to these two procedures are illustrated in Figs.G.3*a* and *b*, respectively. Notice that in the first type of diffusion, Fig.G.3*a*, the profiles have roughly a complementary error function shape, whereas in the second, Fig. G.3*b*, the profile is Gaussian. Both profiles are their maximum at the surface and have exponential tails.

To get a large dopant concentration in a wafer and to have the dopant diffuse in a useful distance within a practical length of time, the wafer must be relatively hot. A typical predeposition step in silicon might be done at 900 to 1000° C and last for tens of minutes; a typical drive step is done at an even higher temperature, say 1100° C, for upwards of an hour or more. The resulting junction depth will be measured in microns (i.e., 1 to 10 μm).

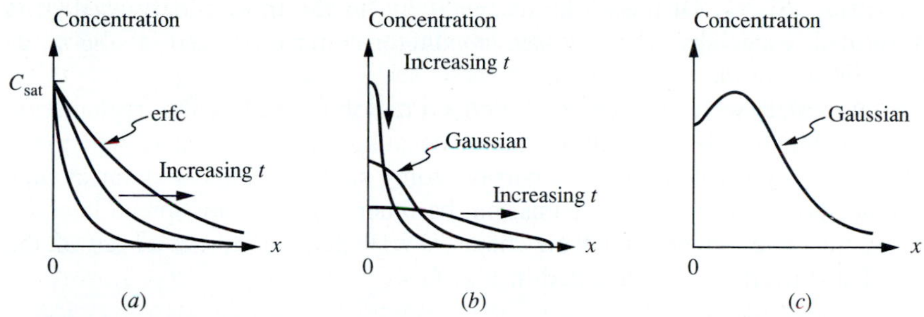

FIGURE G.3
Doping profiles created by diffusion and ion implantation: (*a*) a constant surface concentration diffusion profile like that used for predepositoin; (*b*) a constant total dopant diffusion profile; and (*c*) a typical ion implanted dopant profile.

The second post-growth doping process, ion implantation, begins by first stripping electrons off the desired dopant atoms to produce ions. A broad beam of these ions is accelerated through a large potential difference, say 100 kV, and is directed at the wafer surface. The impinging high-energy ions penetrate the wafer surface a fraction of a micron or more, depending on the accelerating voltage and the particular ion and semiconductor being implanted. The resulting profile is roughly Gaussian with the peak occurring in from the surface, as illustrated in Fig. G.3*c*. A major attraction of ion implantation is the amount of control that can be achieved over this profile, particularly at low doping levels and for relatively shallow junction depths.

A problem with ion implantation is that it creates a great deal of damage in the crystal. The atoms in the crystal lattice are, after all, what stop the impinging ions, and many of the lattice atoms are literally knocked out of position. To repair this damage and to encourage the implanted dopant atoms to occupy lattice sites themselves, a wafer is usually *annealed* (i.e., held at an elevated temperature for a period of time). The time and temperature of this annealing process are chosen to be long and high enough to promote the desired healing but not so long and high as to lead to appreciable diffusion of the implanted atoms.

In contrast to doping during bulk or epitaxial crystal growth, solid-state diffusion and ion implantation offer ways of selectively doping a semiconductor wafer in patterned areas or regions. This is particularly easy to do with ion implantation because it can be done simply by putting a polymer or metal film that is a few microns thick on the wafer surface and patterning it using the microlithography techniques we will discuss in the next section. The film, which blocks the impinging ions during the implantation sequence, is then removed before the postimplant anneal.

Doing a patterned diffusion is somewhat more difficult since diffusion occurs at such a high temperature. The layer that is used to block the dopant must be able to withstand these temperatures, must be an effective diffusion barrier, and must be easily patterned before diffusion and easily removed, if necessary, after. Two excellent choices for barrier materials are silicon dioxide, SiO_2, and silicon nitride, Si_3N_4. Of these, the former is by far the most widely used. It is easily formed, especially when the semiconductor being processed is silicon, as we shall discuss in the next section.

An important difference between a doped region formed by ion implantation and one formed by diffusion comes about because diffused dopants will move laterally under a patterned diffusion barrier, going sideways almost as far as they go into the surface. Implanted dopants, on the other hand, do not spread laterally to any appreciable extent, and their shape is well defined by the edges of the pattern. This difference is illustrated in Fig. G.4.

G.1.3 Encapsulation

Encapsulation refers to the formation of a protective layer on a wafer surface. Such a layer might be used to protect the wafer from dopants during diffusion or ion implantation, to protect and insulate the wafer from metal lines formed to connect the devices in a monolithic integrated circuit (and to insulate these metal lines from one another), to protect the exposed edges of *p-n* junctions formed in the wafer from shorting due to contamination, and/or to simply shield the wafer from its environment.

It is particularly easy to form such an encapsulating layer on a silicon wafer by simply placing it in an oxidizing ambient at an elevated temperature. A tough, durable, and contiguous film of amorphous silicon dioxide, SiO_2, forms over the entire surface. SiO_2 is an excellent insulator and dielectric, and it is also impervious to most acids and solvents. At the same time, it is easily etched by hydrofluoric acid, HF, a dangerous but relatively easily handled acid that in dilute form will only very slowly attack most plastics and organic polymers. This is significant because although the SiO_2 film that forms on the silicon surface is durable, it can be easily removed selectively using a combination of HF and a polymer film that has been patterned as desired to protect certain regions. This patterning process will be described in the next subsection on microlithography.

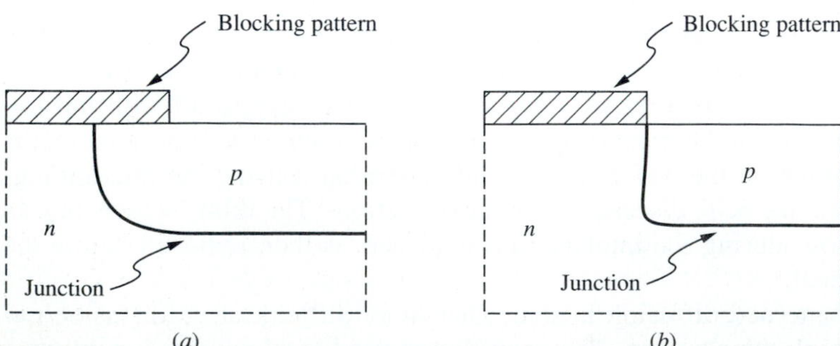

FIGURE G.4
Vertical doping profiles at the edges of a patterned *p*-doped region created in an *n*-type wafer: (*a*) by diffusion; (*b*) by ion implantation. Note that the position of the junction is used to indicate the extent of the doping profile.

The SiO_2 film, which is typically a few thousand angstroms thick, is transparent, although it appears to the observer to be colored because of optical interference. Different thicknesses display different colors. The situation is analogous to what is seen when there is a thin film of oil on a puddle of water. The result is very colorful in both cases.

Silicon dioxide forms on silicon when either oxygen or OH^- ions diffuse through any SiO_2 already on the surface and react with Si at the SiO_2-Si interface. Thus as oxidation proceeds, the original silicon surface is consumed and a new, clean SiO_2-Si interface is continually re-formed.

In addition to being a good insulator and a good protective layer, SiO_2 is also a good diffusion barrier for many common *n*- and *p*-type dopants, as we mentioned in the earlier subsection on doping. The use of SiO_2 to block the diffusion of dopants is one of the most important uses of SiO_2 in microelectronic device and integrated-circuit processing.

Silicon and silicon dioxide form a rather unique combination of materials. No other semiconductor forms a comparable durable, chemical-resistant, insulating film in this fashion, nor is there another film like it that forms on silicon. Silicon nitride, Si_3N_4, is another excellent encapsulant material, for example, yet it is very difficult to nitridize silicon, and it is not possible to form thick Si_3N_4 layers on silicon in the same way that SiO_2 layers can be formed. The problem is that neither silicon nor nitrogen diffuse through Si_3N_4, so the reaction quickly stops after a thin layer forms. The only way to form a thick Si_3N_4 layer on silicon is by chemical vapor deposition, employing a reaction such as

$$3SiH_4 + 4NH_3 \xrightarrow{\Delta} Si_3N_4 \downarrow + 12H_2 \tag{G.2}$$

The reason it might be interesting to have silicon nitride available to use in a silicon process is that Si_3N_4 is a diffusion barrier to oxygen also. Thus it can be used to block oxidation in selected regions on a silicon wafer.

Silicon dioxide and silicon nitride are also widely used in the processing of semiconductors other than silicon, and chemical vapor deposition is often used to form them. The reaction of Eq.(G.2) is used to produce Si_3N_4 films, and SiO_2 is obtained in a similar manner using a reaction such as

$$SiH_4 + 2O_2 \xrightarrow{\Delta} SiO_2 \downarrow + 2H_2O\uparrow \tag{G.3}$$

Alternatively, it is also possible to create films of SiO_2, Si_3N_4, and other inorganic encapsulants (e.g., Al_2O_3), by a process called *sputter deposition*. The sample to be coated and a disk of the desired encapsulant material are placed facing each other in an evacuated vacuum chamber. The surface of the disk is then bombarded with high-energy argon ions, knocking some of its molecules off. If things are positioned correctly, these freed molecules will deposit on the sample surface, building up the desired encapsulating film. A major problem with sputter deposition is that the ions present can create damage on the semiconductor surface, which can be detrimental to device performance.

SiO_2 and Si_3N_4 are both materials that can withstand elevated temperatures, and they thus can be present during high temperature processing steps (i.e., diffusion, oxidation, annealing, etc.). There are other useful films (mostly organic in nature) that cannot withstand high temperatures and thus must be used only at later stages of processing (i.e., after the last high-temperature step). These materials (polyimide is a common example) are often used to build up a relatively thick encapsulating cover over a wafer and to separate multiple layers of interconnect metals. These layers can easily be several microns thick, whereas the SiO_2 and Si_3N_4 layers mentioned earlier tend to be only a few tenths of a micron thick.

G.1.4 Microlithography

The patterning that has been mentioned in previous sections is accomplished by applying a light-sensitive organic polymer to the surface of the wafer, thereby converting it into, if you will, a photographic plate. This organic substance, called resist or, if it is light-sensitive, *photoresist*, is applied as a liquid to the top surface of a spinning wafer so that it forms a uniform thin film roughly a micron thick over the entire surface. (The exact thickness depends on the viscosity of the liquid and the rate of rotation.) After the coated wafer is heated briefly to dry and set the film, it is ready to be exposed in the desired pattern. Some photoresists, called *positive* resists, are depolymerized by light so that regions are exposed to illumination will be removed when the resist is subsequently developed. Other resists, *negative* resists, are polymerized by light, and it is the unexposed areas that are removed during developing. In either case, the developed wafer is left with certain regions protected by a photoresist film, and other regions bare. Consequently, by using suitable etchants, pre-existing metallic and/or dielectric layers on the wafer surface, or even some of the semiconductor itself, can be etched away in the open areas. Once the desired etching has been accomplished, the photoresist layer can itself be selectively removed using organic solvents, which do not affect the underlying structures. As an example of this type of processing, the use of this technique to etch an opening in a silicon dioxide layer on a silicon wafer is illustrated in Fig. G.5.

The exposure of a desired pattern in photoresist on a wafer and the alignment of that pattern to a pre-existing pattern already on the wafer surface can be accomplished in several ways. Most commonly, a glass plate, called a *mask*, that contains the desired pattern is first prepared. A typical mask is illustrated in Fig. G.6. Making such a mask is itself a major challenge because the pattern on it may contain upwards of a million rectangles, many with submicron widths and spacings, and it must be perfect.

An important point to realize in looking at the mask in Fig. G.6 is that each wafer processed will contain many circuits. These circuits will eventually be cut apart, but they are kept together and processed simultaneously as long as possible, typically until the time comes to package them individually. This ability to process many circuits at once and thus to share the cost of processing an individual wafer among many chips significantly reduces the cost per chip and is a major factor in the economics of the integrated-circuit industry. Equally important is the possibility at many stages of the processing to process many wafers simultaneously. As we shall see shortly, this is not possible in photolithography, but

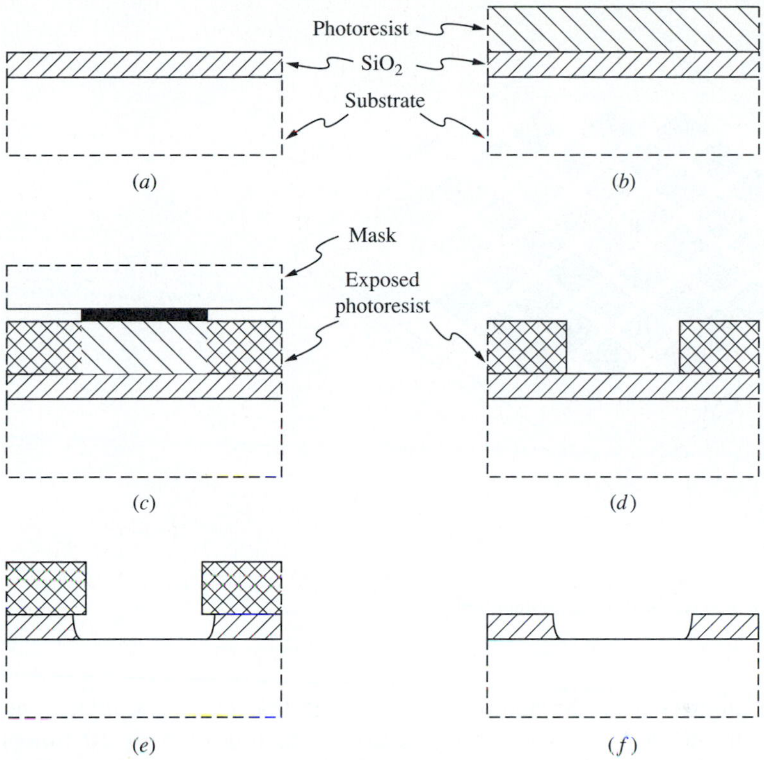

FIGURE G.5
Etching an opening in a SiO_2 film on a Si surface photolithographically: (*a*) the oxidized silicon wafer; (*b*) the same wafer coated with photoresist; (*c*) exposure of the photoresist to the mask pattern; (*d*) after development of the resist; (*e*) after etching; (*f*) after removal of the resist.

other processes such as diffusion and chemical vapor deposition can be performed on batches of 25 to 50 wafers at a time.

The pattern on a mask is transferred onto a photoresist-coated wafer on an instrument called a *mask aligner*. An aligner first lets its operator align the pattern on a mask with any pattern already on the wafer, and then it exposes the resist to light. In some aligners, called *contact aligners*, the mask and wafer are brought into actual contact and pressed together during the exposure cycle. If the two can be brought into perfect contact, this technique will replicate extremely small patterns. In practice, perfect contact is difficult to achieve, so this technique is primarily used where feature sizes exceed 1 μm. Contact printing is also very hard on both wafers and masks. A gentler alternative is to simply bring the mask and wafer into close proximity and do the exposure using a highly columnated light beam. More common than such proximity aligners, however, are *projection aligners*, which actually project the image on the mask through a lens and onto the wafer

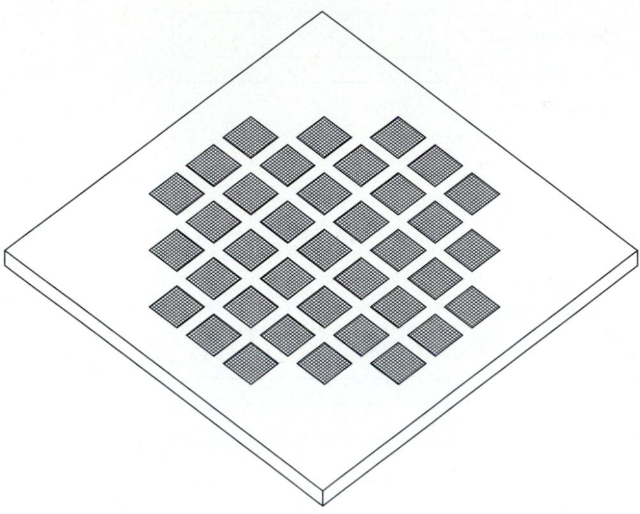

FIGURE G.6
Perspective view of a mask used in photolithography.

surface. These aligners have the additional advantage that the mask image can be larger than the ultimate device size (typically by factors of 5 or 10 times) because the projection need not be one-to-one; furthermore, the mask needs to contain only one of the patterns to be repeated over the wafer surface because a projection aligner can itself easily do mulitiple exposures, stepping and repeating the pattern across the wafer at this stage of the processing. This allows a certain degree of flexibility in the processing as well, since patterns can be different in the various cells if that is desired.

As modern integrated circuits and microelectronic devices have been pushed to smaller and smaller dimensions, the limits of optical lithography techniques imposed by the wavelength of light have led to the extension of optical systems to vacuum ultraviolet operation and, more fundamentally, to the development of still other lithography techniques. The two most successful such techniques use, respectively, x-rays and electrons to expose a pattern in resist.

X-ray lithography is conceptually identical to optical proximity lithography and differs mechanically only in such details as the nature of the mask (a thin membrane rather than a piece of glass), the composition of the resist (one sensitive to x-rays rather than light), and the radiation source (a syncrotron or other intense x-ray source rather than a lamp). The x-rays used have a wavelength on the order of a few angstroms, however, rather than a few thousand angstroms, so the resolution potential of x-ray lithography is correspondingly orders of magnitude greater than that of optical lithography.

Electron-beam (e-beam) lithography involves an entirely different approach. In this technique, a fine beam of electrons is used to write the desired pattern directly into the resist. The image is re-created on every wafer, so this process is relatively slow, but by the same token, every device or circuit can be individually tailored (i.e., customized) if that is of interest. In practice what is often done is that a mixture is used of optical lithography for the large portions of the pattern and e-beam lithography for the critical small-dimension elements. Since the latter typically represents but a tiny fraction of the total pattern, this approach can result in dramatic savings in processing time and expense with no loss in product performance. E-beam lithography is also often used to generate mask patterns for X-ray lithography and for vacuum ultraviolet optical lithography.

G.1.5 Metallization

Contact is made where necessary to the various doped regions in a wafer, and the various devices on the wafer are interconnected electrically, by etching openings through any dielectric layers that cover the wafer, depositing a thin metallic film on the wafer surface, and then etching the metal into the desired wiring pattern. Alternatively, after the contact holes have been etched through the dielectric, resist can be put on the wafer and patterned so as to remove it where metal is desired; a metallic film is then deposited over the wafer, and the resist is removed. If care has been taken to produce a thick resist pattern with vertical, or even retrograde, sidewalls so that the metal film is discontinuous over the edges of the pattern, the resist will lift the metal off with it as it is removed. This procedure, called *lift-off*, is particularly useful with metals such as gold that are troublesome to etch and when very fine metal patterns are sought. These two procedures for producing metal contacts and interconnect patterns are illustrated in Fig. G.7.

Vacuum deposition techniques are most commonly used to coat a wafer with a metallic film. The simplest such technique is called *thermal evaporation*. In this technique, the wafer to be coated is placed in a vacuum chamber, which can be evacuated to a pressure below 10^{-6} torr, along with a source of the metal of interest, which is itself in a vessel in which it can be heated to boiling. The idea is that when the metal is brought to boiling, atoms gain enough thermal energy to leave the metal and travel in the vacuum until they collide with a cold surface and condense. If the wafer is positioned so that an appreciable number of these escaping atoms condense on its surface, the desired metallic thin film is obtained. If we want a metallic film that is an alloy and/or is comprised of several layers of different metals, multiple source vessels can be provided inside the vacuum chamber.

Certain metals have extremely low vapor pressures and do not evaporate except at extremely high temperatures, so simple thermal evaporation of the metals is impractical because no vessel can contain them. Sometimes, such metals can be *electron-beam evaporated*. In this technique an intense electron beam is directed at the surface of a pellet of metal, producing a very localized, extremely hot molten puddle of the metal in the large pellet. The metal serves as its own vessel and thus is not contaminated in the process.

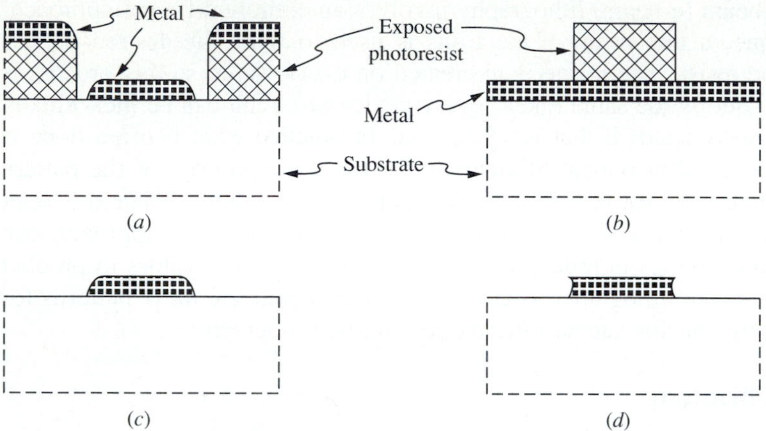

FIGURE G.7
Two methods of patterning metal films: (*a* and *c*) the lift-off process; (*b* and *d*) the use of photoresist as an etch mask. In (*a*), the photoresist has been spun-on, exposed, and developed and metal has been deposited over the wafer; in (*c*) the photoresist has been removed, lifting off the metal. In (*b*) the metal has been deposited over the wafer and photoresist has been spun-on, exposed, and developed; in (*d*) the metal has been etched and the photoresist removed.

Metal films can also be formed by *sputter deposition* and by *chemical vapor deposition*, processes described in the section on encapsulation. As important as how the metal film is deposited, however, is what metals are used. To be useful, an interconnect metal system has to satisfy several criteria: it should have a low resistance, must adhere well to and make good ohmic contact with the semiconductor, must adhere well to the dielectric coating, should be mechanically and chemically robust and stable, should be easily patternable, and must be economical to process. The solution to this puzzle on a silicon wafer, for example, might simply be to use aluminum, or it may involve using a multilayer Pt/Ti/Pt/Au stack, for which the materials science involved is very sophisticated.

G.1.6 Etching and Cleaning

Frequently in the preceding sections we have mentioned the need to remove material from the wafer surface. We have implied that it would be etched or dissolved away in a chemical solution. This is indeed true in many cases, and again careful engineering is required to make the process work. In particular, we always need solutions that are compatible with the material to be processed and selective to the particular layer being removed. An acid used with a resist pattern to etch openings through a dielectric layer, for example, should not etch the underlying semiconductor, nor should it attack the resist.

Not surprisingly, the etching and cleaning that is done using liquid solutions is called *wet chemical* processing, and wet processes play a major role in semiconductor fabrication. At the same time, however, so-called *dry* processing techniques are being used for an increasingly large fraction of the processing. Dry processing refers to the use of gases, rather than liquids, in processing and is felt to be easier to control and less susceptible to the introduction of contaminants than wet processing.

An important dry processing technique is *plasma etching*. In this process the wafer being processed is immersed in a plasma created by exciting and ionizing a low-pressure reactant gas such as $SiCl_4$ or O_2 with a radio-frequency (r-f) source. The r-f excitation supplies the energy to drive the etching or cleaning reaction, and the chemistry is engineered so that the reactor products are gaseous and can be readily pumped out of the processing chamber. An oxygen plasma is often used to remove resist films, for example, in a process called *ashing*, an obvious reference to the fact that the resist is essentially burned off.

One feature of plasma etching is that it tends to be isotropic, meaning that the etching proceeds on all exposed surfaces much as wet etching does. If, on the other hand, a wafer is placed in a low-pressure plasma reactor between two parallel electrodes that are biased so as to attract ions to the wafer surface, the etching will tend to occur only in the direction normal to the wafer surface and a very anisotropic profile with little or no lateral spread will result. This is a very desirable result in many situations, especially when we are dealing with very small pattern dimensions; this process, called *reactive ion etching*, or RIE, is an important fabrication tool.

G.2 EXAMPLES OF INTEGRATED CIRCUIT PROCESSES

The first electronic circuits (ICs) used bipolar junction transistors as the active devices, and thus it is appropriate that we begin our discussion of integrated circuit technologies with bipolar ICs. We will then consider several MOSFET IC technologies (nMOS and CMOS), and after that look at a BiMOS process that can produce integrated circuits containing both MOS and bipolar transistors. Finally we will walk through a process used to create gallium arsenide MESFET integrated circuits.

In any integrated circuit, many devices—transistors, diodes, resistors, etc.—must be fabricated simultaneously on the same piece of semiconductor and then must be electrically interconnected in a controlled fashion to create the desired circuit. A fundamental issue in any technology is how these many devices can be fabricated on the same semiconductor substrate and still be electrically decoupled (until they are intentionally "wired" together to form the desired circuit). As we shall see, a key element in achieving this isolation is the reverse-biased *p-n* junction. Incrementally a reverse-biased *p-n* junction looks like a capacitor in parallel with a large value resistor. The incremental resistance R is in fact very large in a typical silicon or gallium arsenide *p-n* junction, and if the junction is lightly doped (on at least one side), the incremental capacitance C will be relatively small so that the resistor–capacitor combination is effectively an open circuit up to frequencies well beyond $1/RC$. Another way to achieve isolation is to interpose an insulating layer (or layers) between the devices, but this is often relatively difficult to do. Such dielectric isolation tends to be used only in situations where *p-n* junction isolation is not sufficient isolation, i.e., for circuits that must work at very high frequencies, and/or in situations where dielectric isolation is easy to implement. We will see examples of both techniques in the following discussions.

Before looking at specific processing sequences, it is interesting to note that in the following discussions the processes are presented in terms of a long series of steps and appear to be quite involved. The situation is in fact even more complicated than it seems because often times each "step" in these descriptions involves handling the semiconductor wafers many times and doing many different operations on them. A detailed, truly step-by-step description of each process would run many pages, and the amount of work and number of operations involved in converting a semiconductor wafer into finished integrated circuits is truly impressive. The only way that such a complex process can be executed economically is if advantage is taken of batch processing and of the economies of scale. Each semiconductor wafer has to contain as many individual circuits as possible, and whenever possible many wafers must be processed simultaneously. Only at the very end when the circuits are mounted and bonded in their individual packages are they handled one at a time. In this way, the cost of making each circuit can be kept withing reasonable bounds.

Finally, note that in each sequence we will assume that an appropriate set of masks have been prepared, and we will refer to them in order as Mask #1, Mask #2, etc. One of the important features of any process is how many masking steps are required, and in general an effort is made to keep this number as low as possible because each mask step implies more processing and more opportunities for errors to be made and for defects to be introduced, thereby reducing the overall yield, i.e., the fraction of working circuits left when the processing is complete.

We now turn to looking at seven specific processes. Any given company will have its own version of one or more of these processes, and those versions will undoubtably differ in detail from the sequences given here. Thus while the essential features of each class of processes are embodied in the examples given here, you should not be disturbed if you encounter processes that differ in detail. Rather you can take it as a challenge to determine the reasons behind the differences.

G.2.1 *p-n* Junction Isolated Bipolar IC Technology

The majority of the earliest commercial integrated circuits, dating from the 1960s, were bipolar integrated circuits that relied upon *p-n* junction isolation, and the same basic technology is still widely used in analog bipolar integrated circuits. As you read through the description of a basic *p-n* junction isolated bipolar IC process below, you will want to refer to Fig. G.8 which shows an *npn* bipolar transistor in perspective top view and in cross section at selected points during the processing.

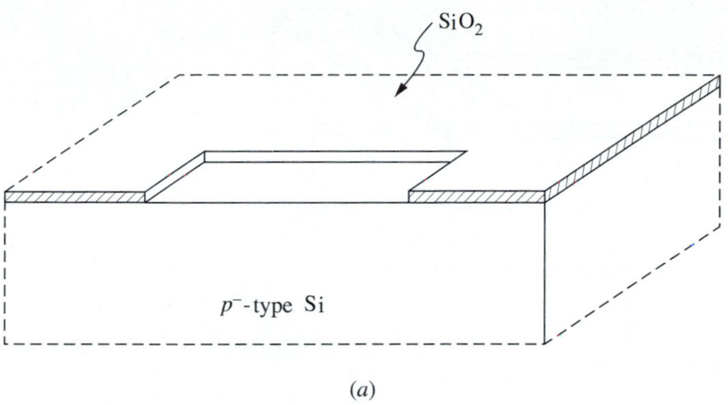

(*a*)

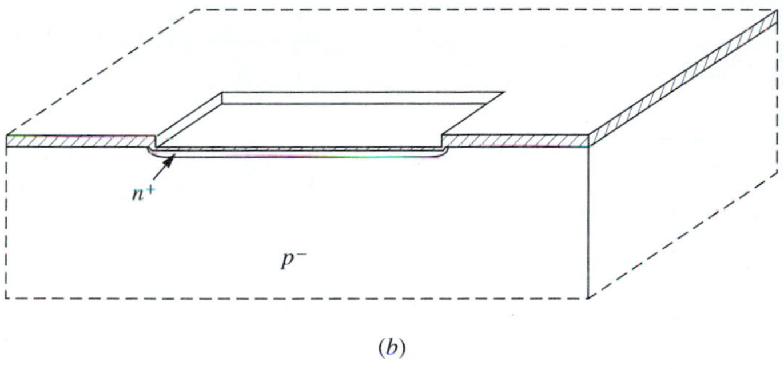

(*b*)

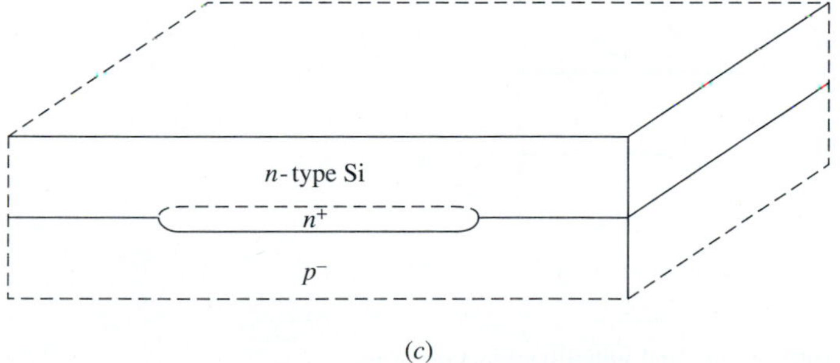

(*c*)

FIGURE G.8 a, b, c
Selected stages in the fabrication of an *npn* bipolar transistor in a *p-n* junction-isolated bipolar integrated circuit: (*a*) The oxidized *p*-type starting wafer with openings cut for the buried collector regions. (*b*) After doping of the buried collector regions and regrowth of an oxide over them. (*c*) After the deposition of an *n*-type epitaxial layer on the original substrate. Note that the *n*-type dopant from the buried regions diffuses slowly into the epitaxial layer, as well as into the substrate.

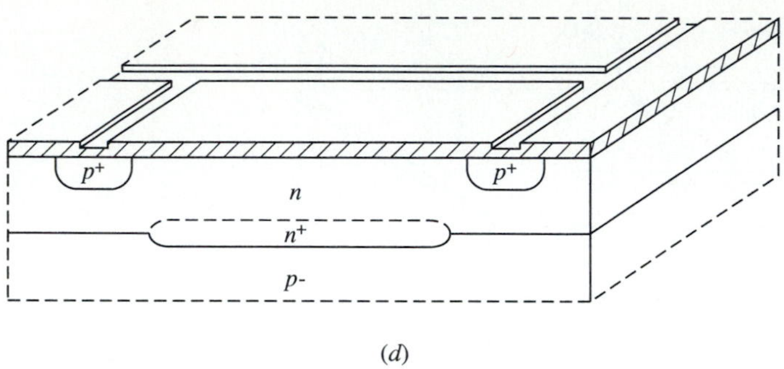

(*d*)

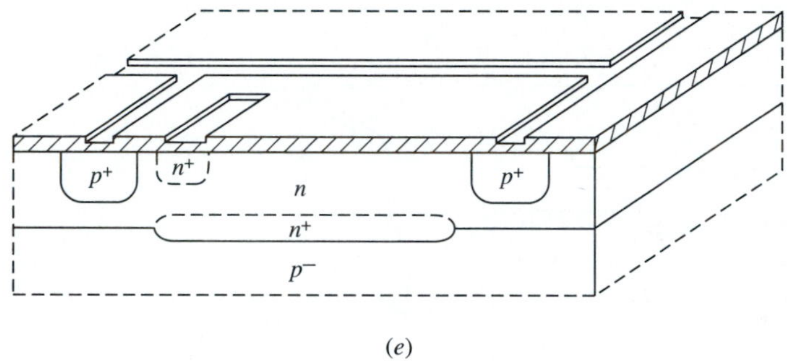

(*e*)

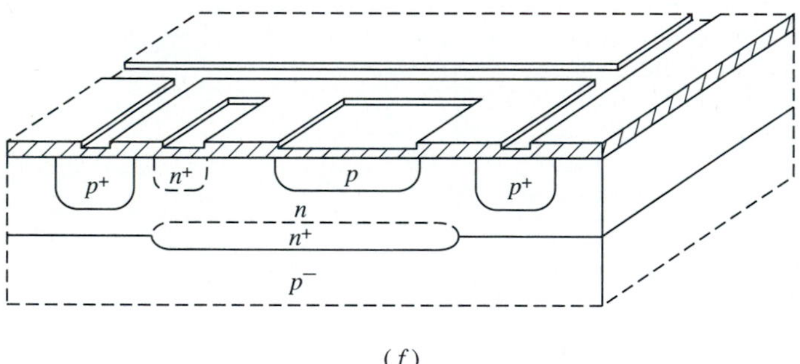

(*f*)

FIGURE G.8 d, e, f
(*d*) After definition of the isolation vias and initial introduction of the p-type dopant. This dopant will continue to diffuse during subsequent processing and will ultimately penetrate to the substrate. (*e*) After introduction of the n-type collector plug dopant and partial diffusion of the dopant into the collector region. (*f*) After definition and doping of the base region. Note that the p-type isolation and n-type collector plug dopants continue to penetrate further and further into the epitaxial layer with continued high temperature processing.

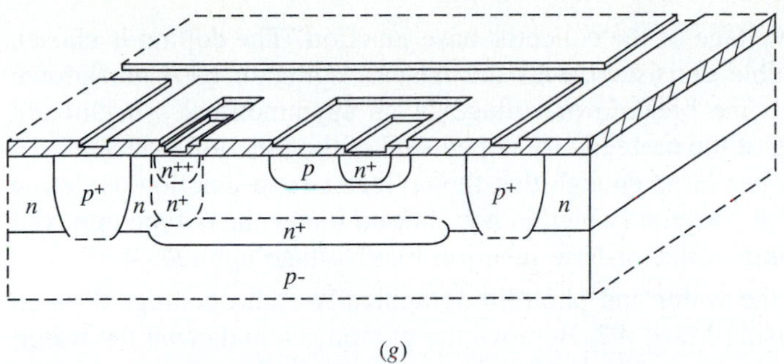

(g)

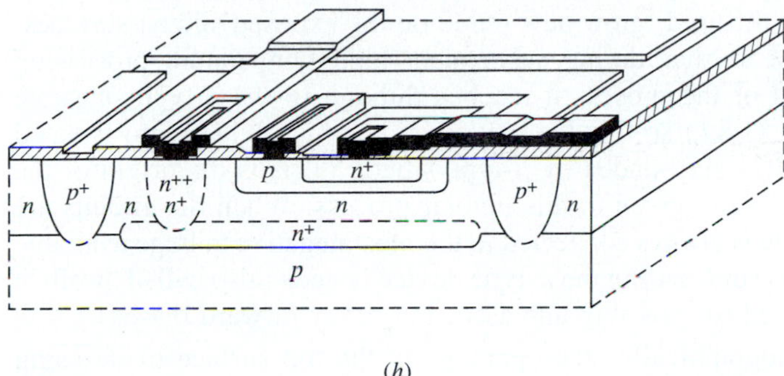

(h)

FIGURE G.8 g, h
(g) After formation of the n^+ emitter and collector contact regions.
(h) The completed device after the contact areas have been opened and the first layer of metal has been deposited and patterned. After this point additional layers of dielectric and metal interconnect lines may be added as needed based on the complexity of the integrated circuit being fabricated.

Starting wafer. p-type silicon, lightly doped, thoroughly cleaned.

Step 1. Cover the wafer completely with silicon dioxide by oxidizing it in an oxygen-containing ambient at elevated temperatures.

Step 2. Etch openings through the oxide layer on the top surface of the wafer by doing photolithography using Mask #1, followed by wet chemical etching in a hydrofluoric acid-based solution. Remove the photoresist and clean the wafer (see Fig. G.8a).

Step 3. Dope (by solid state diffusion) the exposed Si areas heavily n-type with antimony (a slowly diffusing dopant) and grow more oxide on the wafer (see Fig. G.8b). These heavily doped n-regions, i.e., n^+-regions, serve to reduce the resistance in series with the collector lead (as will become more clear later) and are called "buried collector" regions.

Step 4. Remove all of the oxide from the wafer and grow an n-type Si epitaxial layer on the top surface (see Fig. G.8c). This n-region is the collector region of the *npn* transistors in the circuit. Its doping level and thickness depend on the target breakdown voltage of the collector-base junction. The doping is chosen to be as high as possible consistent with the desired collector-base breakdown voltage (remember that the breakdown voltage of an asymmetrical *p-n* junction decreases as the doping of the more lightly doped side of the junction is increased). The thickness is made just large enough that the collector-base junction depletion region just reaches the n^+-region (which is now buried under the n-type epitaxial layer) with the maximum collector-base junction bias voltage applied.

Step 5. Oxidize the wafer and photolithographically etch openings through the top surface oxide using Mask #2. Remove the photoresist and clean the wafer.

Step 6. Dope the exposed regions heavily p-type with boron and diffuse the dopant into the surface part way through the n-type epitaxial layer (see Fig G.8*d*). As the dopant is being diffused, grow new oxide on the exposed silicon surfaces. The boron will diffuse further during subsequent high temperature processing steps, until by the end of the process it reaches through to the p-type substrate (dashed profile in Fig. G.8*d*) so that the n-type epilayer is divided into isolated n-type islands completely surrounded by p-type silicon. This is the origin of the name "*p-n* junction isolated" given to this bipolar process. When the circuits are used the p-type substrate is always connected to the most negative voltage available so that the *p-n* junctions surrounding the n-type device islands (also called "wells") are always reverse biased (or possibly unbiased, but never forward biased).

Step 7. Photolithographically etch openings in the top surface oxide using Mask #3. Remove the photoresist and clean the wafer.

Step 8. Dope the exposed regions heavily n-type with phosphorus, a relatively fast diffusing dopant, and diffuse the dopant into the surface part way through the n-type epitaxial layer. Regrow oxide on the exposed areas (see Fig. G.8*e*). The phosphorus will diffuse further during subsequent high temperature processing steps, until by the end of the process it reaches through to the n^+ buried collector region and provides a low resistance path from the top surface of the wafer to the active portion of the collector. This diffusion is often called a "collector plug" structure. *Note:* Boron and phosphorus diffuse about an order of magnitude faster than does antimony, so the buried collector region will not diffuse far out into the epitaxial layer, even though the p-type isolation regions and n-type plug are diffused entirely through the epilayer. The success of this process depends very much on having dopants available with such different diffusion rates.

Step 9. Photolithographically etch openings in the top surface oxide using Mask #4. Remove the photoresist and clean the wafer.

Step 10. Dope the exposed regions p-type with boron and diffuse the dopant into the surface to form the base regions of the npn transistors. Reoxidize the exposed areas (see Fig. G.8*f*). Note that the base region "nests" within the collector region, which in turn requires that the collector region be large enough to accommodate both the base and the contact to the buried collector without having any of these elements short together or to the p-type isolation regions. *Note:* This same diffusion can be used in other isolated n-regions to form diffused resistors like the one in Problem 3.4, and to form the emitter and collector regions of lateral *pnp* transistors like the one in Problem 8.6. It can also be used as the gate region of an n-channel JFET like the one pictured in Fig. 10.18, or the channel region of a similar p-channel JFET.

Step 11. Photolithographically etch openings in the top surface oxide using Mask #5. Remove the photoresist and clean the wafer.

Step 12. Dope the exposed regions heavily n-type with phosphorus and diffuse the dopant into the surface to form the emitter regions of the *npn* transistors, and to further reduce the resistance of the plug regions. Reoxidize the exposed areas (see Fig. G.8*g*). Notice that the emitter region must be "nested" within the base region, which requires that the base region must be considerably larger than the emitter region since it must contain both the emitter, with suitable tolerances around the edges for possible errors in alignment of the mask patterns during exposure, and the base contact(s). The emitter, in turn, must be sufficiently large that it will be easy subsequently to make electrical contact to it. *Note:* This same diffusion is used any place low resistance contact must be made to the n-type epitaxial material, such as to the base of a lateral *pnp* transistor or to the well region around a diffused resistor.

Step 13. Photolithographically etch openings in the top surface oxide using Mask #6. Remove the photoresist and clean the wafer.

Step 14. Vacuum-deposit (i.e., evaporate) a layer of aluminum over the entire wafer surface.

Step 15. Photolithograhically pattern the aluminum layer using a weak acid solution and Mask #7. Remove the photoresist, clean the wafer, and heat the wafer to approximately 450°C in an inert atmosphere for a few minutes to "form" the contact (see Fig. G.8*h*). During the "forming" process the aluminum reacts with any silicon dioxide with which it is in contact. Where the patterned aluminum crosses the silicon dioxide layer covering the wafer this increases the adhesion of the aluminum to the oxide. Where the aluminum is in contact with silicon this chemically reduces any trace of oxide at the interface and helps form a clean, intimate contact between the aluminum and the silicon. If the underlying silicon is doped p-type or heavily n-type, such an aluminum-silicon contact that will be low resistance and ohmic. If the underlying silicon is lightly n-type, the contact will be a rectifying Schottky barrier (see Appendix E).

Step 16. Deposit a layer (or layers) of silicon dioxide and/or silicon nitride over the entire surface of the wafer. If more than one layer of metal interconnection is required in this circuit, photolithographically define openings in this new dielectric layer, remove the photoresist and clean the wafer, deposit metal over the entire surface, and pattern the metal using the next mask. Repeat as needed (usually two or three layers of interconnect are adequate). The step always ends with the wafer being coated with a dielectric layer and openings being etched through it to expose relatively large metal pads (typically 50 to 100 microns square) to which electrical contact will be made between the integrated circuitry on the chips and the "outside world," i.e., the package or the mounting substrate or multichip module.

Step 17 and beyond. Electrically "probe" the circuit, i.e., make electrical contact to the bonding pads using adjustable needle "probes," and test its electrical performance. Mark the non-functioning circuits with a dye. Cut the wafer into individual integrated circuit chips, mount each functioning chip in its individual package, bond thin gold wires between the contact pads on the chip and the corresponding contact leads in the package, seal the package, retest and qualify it, and ship it to a vendor or customer.

In describing this sequence we have focused our attention on the *npn* bipolar transistor, but it is important to realize that many other devices can be made at the same time in the same sequence of steps. This is significant because most integrated circuits can benefit from incorporating *pnp* bipolar transistors, as well as *npn's,* and any integrated circuit will require passive devices (i.e., resistors, capacitors, diodes, etc.), as well as active devices. Thus while the process was designed with top priority being given to optimizing the performance of the *npn* transistors, it is very important that other devices are available as well, and that those devices be similarly high performance. In the case of the junction isolated bipolar process, an extensive complement of other devices is available. In Step 10, for example, the *p*-type base diffusion can be used to make resistors and lateral *pnp* transistors. The base, collector (without a buried n^+-region), and substrate together form another *pnp* structure, known as a "substrate *pnp*." Capacitors can be fabricated in several ways. Any junction can be used, of course, but the depletion capacitance of a junction is voltage dependent and often has a large series resistance. A better capacitor is a metal-dielectric-metal capacitor formed using two of the metal interconnect layers, or a metal-oxide-semiconductor capacitor formed between the first layer of metal and an n^+-region created along with the *npn* emitters. Diodes are best made from transistors (see Problems 8.10 and 8.11). The only common passive device that is not available is a high performance inductor, an intrinsically three-dimensional device that has defied integration in the two-dimensional world of integrated circuits.*

G.2.2 Dielectrically Isolated Bipolar Technologies

The junction isolated process described in the preceeding subsection has several shortcomings, most having to do with its performance at high frequences. In particular, the degree of isolation weakens at high frequency as the capacitive impedance becomes smaller and smaller. Of particular concern in this regard are the lateral junctions between the p^+-moat regions and the *n*-type islands (or wells) because the capacitance per unit area of these side junctions is much larger than that of the horizontal junctions between the islands and the substrate.

Techniques have been developed in which all of the *p-n* junction isolation is replaced by dielectric isolation, but these processes are relatively costly and

*This is overstating the case just a bit in the sense that spiral inductors have been produced successfully on very high frequency monolithic microwave integrated circuits (MMICs), but as a rule of thumb it is true that inductors should be avoided whenever possible in IC design.

are only used in very specialized situations. A more commonly encountered compromise is one in which only the p^+-moat regions are replaced with dielectric isolation. As we shall see shortly, doing this also reduces the area of the horizontal junctions formed between the *n*-regions and the substrate by eliminating some of the need to nest the emitter diffusion region and base contact within the base region, and the base region and collector contact within the collector region, as was necessary in a *p*-*n* junction isolated circuit. This reduction in area further reduces the impact of the capacitance of the remaining horizontal *p*-*n* junctions between the collector and substrate.

The major changes made in the processing when dielectric isolation* is used show up in the isolation step, and the remaining processing follows pretty much the same sequence. The mask patterns, and the actual devices, however, look quite different because, as we have mentioned, there is no longer the need to nest the various structures. We will not go through such a detailed description of this process as we did in the case of *p*-*n* junction isolation, but will merely indicate where the key differences are, and show how the resulting devices look. Refer to Fig. G.9 as you go through this description.

Starting wafer and Steps 1 through 5. The same as for *p*-*n* junction isolation, except that in Step 5 the surface is not oxidized; instead a layer of silicon nitride is deposited on it and this silicon nitride layer is patterned photolithographically using Mask #2. (This is the second mask in the set of masks for this process; it is not the same mask as Mask #2 in the mask set used for the *p*-*n* junction isolation process.)

Step 6. Using an isotropic silicon etchant,† etch the patterned wafer surface forming grooves that penetrate about a third of the way through the epitaxial layer (see Fig. G.9*a*). Then oxidize the wafer. The silicon nitride layer will keep the silicon covered by it from oxidizing and only the silicon exposed in the grooves will oxidize. The oxide that forms is about 60 percent thicker than the silicon consumed by the oxidation process, so the grooves will eventually fill with oxide. At the same time, since silicon is consumed as the oxidation proceeds, the groove will also eventually penetrate all the way through the epitaxial layer down to either the *p*-type substrate and/or to the n^+ buried collector layer, depending on what is directly under the groove. This is shown in Fig. G.9*b*. After groove oxidation is complete, the silicon nitride is removed and the entire exposed wafer surface is reoxidized.

*By current convention this process is called dielectric isolation even though there is some *p*-*n* junction isolation used in the structure. Strictly speaking, this term should be reserved for the processes in which complete dielectric isolation is used and the process being described here should be called partial dielectric isolation, but this later terminology is more cumbersome and doesn't sound quite as nice.

†An isotropic etchant is one that does not etch preferencially in certain crystal directions, but rather etches uniformly in all directions. There are dielectric isolation processes that use anisotropic etchants that etch much more slowly in the ⟨111⟩-direction; brief mention is made of these techniques near the end of this subsection.

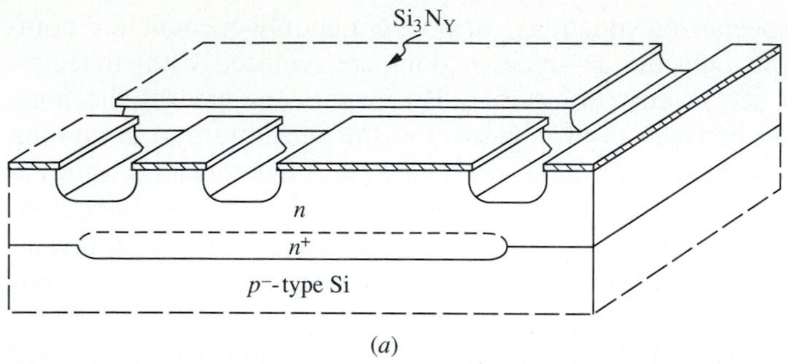

(*a*)

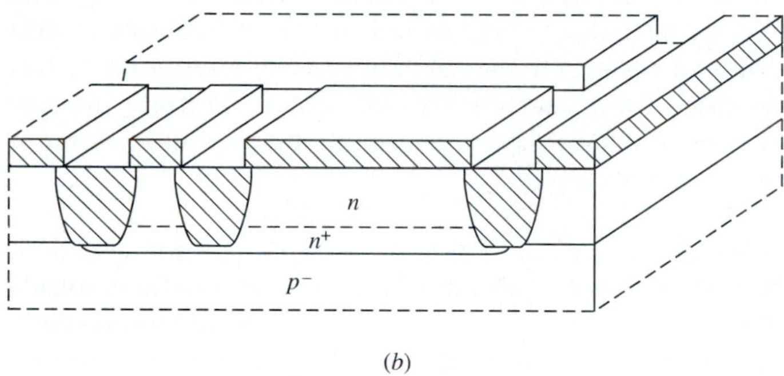

(*b*)

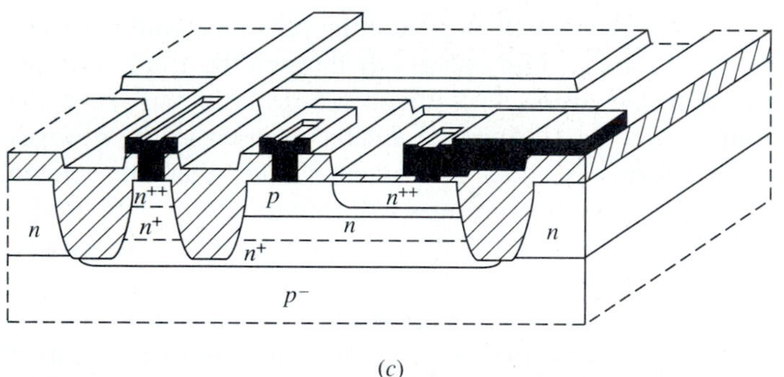

(*c*)

FIGURE G.9
Selected stages in the processing of an *npn* bipolar transistor in a dielectrically isolated integrated circuit: (*a*) The wafer after definition of the isolation vias by patterning a surface silicon nitride layer and using that pattern to selectively etch approximately one third of the way through the epitaxial layer. Note that a via is also etched within the device itself between what will turn out to be the collector contact region and the active device region. (*b*) After oxidation of the nitride masked wafer to fill in the vias with a native silicon dioxide. Note that as the oxide forms the underlying silicon is consumed so that when the process is complete the oxide penetrates through the epitaxial layer. The buried collector region provides continuity between the collector contact region and the actual transistor region. (*c*) A completed transistor.

Step 7 and beyond. Beyond Step 6 the processing proceeds following essentially the same steps as in the *p-n* junction isolation process, except that the need for much of the nesting of patterns no longer exists. The various doped regions can now extend all of the way out to the oxided groove without shorting out any junctions. A completed device is pictured in Fig. G.9*c*.

The points to emphasize again about the dielectric isolation process is that it allows the device designer to both eliminate the sidewall *p-n* junctions and substantially reduce the area of the bottom *p-n* junction. The net result is that the collector-to-substrate capacitance is significantly reduced, and the speed of the circuits is greatly enhanced.

There are numerous variations on the basic dielectric isolation process outlined above. One worth mentioning is one that relies on an anisotropic silicon etchant, rather than an isotropic etchant (see the footnote on page 657). If the mask pattern is oriented properly with respect to the crystal lattice, v-grooves will be formed by the etchant; an example is illustrated in Fig. G.10*a*. The nice thing about these grooves is, first, that their depth can be controlled by the width of the opening etched through the nitride layer on the wafer surface, and, second, that the groove does not have to be completely filled in with oxide because the sides of the groove are slanted. An important reason the groove formed by an isotropic etchant has to be filled in with oxide is that the edges of an isotropically etched groove are quite steep and the metal film deposited in step may be too thin, or possibly even discontinuous, going over the edges. With v-grooves this problem is significantly reduced, as illustrated in Fig. G.10*b*. A relatively thin oxide is adequate, so the processing time can be reduced. On the other hand, there are many other advantages in keeping the wafer surface as flat as possible (we term it "planar") during the entire process, and planarity is much more closely approximated in the process we described initially in which an isotropic etchant is used.

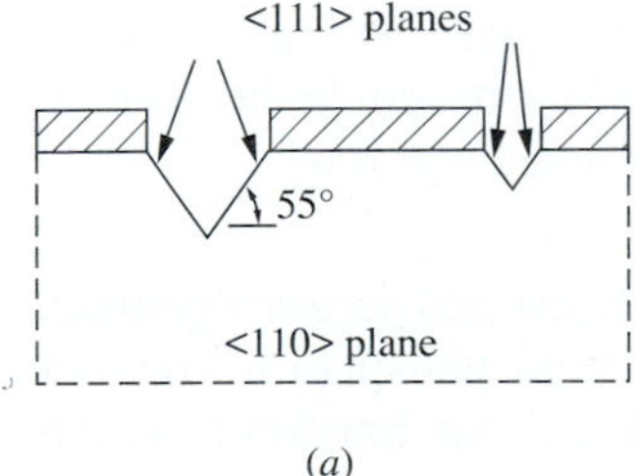

(*a*)

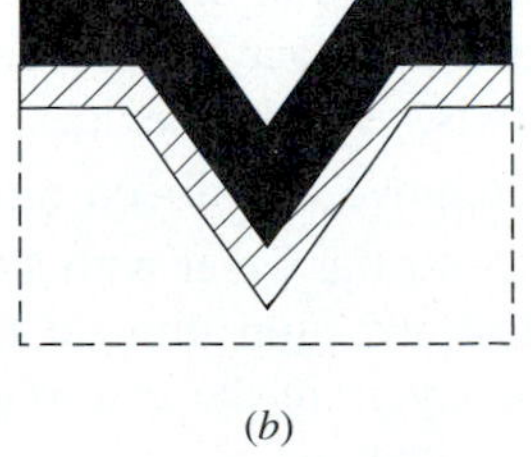

(*b*)

FIGURE G.10
The key features of a dielectric isolation process based on use of an anisotropic silicon etch: (*a*) The v-groove shape of channels etched parallel to the ⟨110⟩ direction in a ⟨100⟩-oriented silicon wafer using an etchant that etches slowly on ⟨111⟩ planes. (*b*) The profile of an evaporated metal line crossing a v-groove illustrating the ease with which contiguous coverage is achieved if the sides of the groove slope gradually.

G.2.3 Silicon-Gate nMOS Processing

The processing required to produce basic MOSFET integrated circuits is relatively less complex than that encountered with bipolar ICs in large part because MOSFETs are easier to isolate, and because they involve less complicated doping profiles. Historically, the first MOSFETs were p-channel devices made using a so-called metal gate technology, and looked similar to the device pictured in Fig. 10.16a. This technology borrowed directly on the processes developed to fabricate junction isolated bipolar circuits and was actually a simpler process, but the resulting MOSFETs were relatively large and, most importantly, had very large gate-to-drain capacitances due to the large overlap between the gate dielectric and metal patterns, and the drain diffusion. The process also only worked well with p-channel devices (which, as we know, are slower than n-channel devices). Consequently, a great deal of effort was put into developing higher performance n-channel self-aligned-gate technologies, the most successful of which uses polycrystalline silicon as the gate "metal." The following discussion details the steps used in such a process; you should refer to Fig. G.11 as you read through it.

Starting wafer. p-type silicon, lightly doped, thoroughly cleaned.

Step 1. Grow a thin oxide on the wafer and then deposit a thicker layer of silicon nitride over the entire top surface of the wafer.

Step 2. Etch openings in the silicon nitride layer photolithographically using Mask #1. Remove the photoresist and clean the wafer.

Step 3. Dope the exposed silicon areas p-type with boron either by ion implantation (the preferred method) or solid state diffusion.

Step 4. Oxidize the wafer. The silicon nitride will prevent oxidation in the areas protected by it, while a thick oxide (1 micron or more) is grown in the exposed areas (see Fig. G.11a). This thick oxide is called the "field oxide" and is formed everywhere except where devices will be fabricated. Its thickness, and the increased p-doping level produced under it by Step 3 insure that the oxide-silicon interface under it, i.e., in the "field" region between the devices, will not become inverted. If this interface did invert, leakage paths or shorts could be formed between otherwise isolated devices, making the circuit non-functional.

Step 5. Remove the silicon nitride.

Step 6. Cover the wafer with a thick layer of photoresist and pattern openings in it using Mask #2. Ion implant the exposed silicon with phosphorus creating shallow n-type layers in the gate regions of the depletion-mode transistors in the circuit. (The photoresist pattern and field oxide keep the ions from doping the regions they cover; see Fig. G.11b.) If properly designed, this shallow implant will result in n-channel depletion-mode devices in these regions which have the desired negative threshold value. Remove the photoresist and clean the wafer. *Note:* In some processes an additional step will be added before or after this step in which the channel regions of the enhancement-mode devices are implanted, this time with boron, to adjust their thresholds as well.

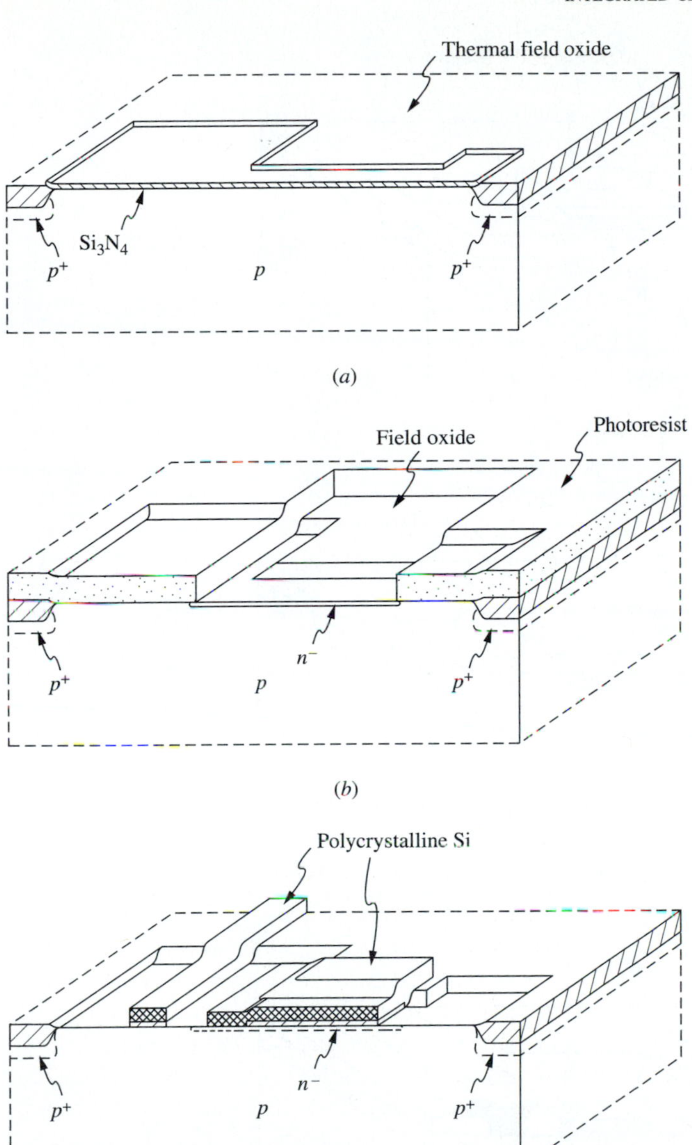

FIGURE G.11 a, b, c
An illustration of several stages in the processing of a silicon-gate nMOS depletion-mode load inverter stage: (*a*) The *p*-type substrate after deposition and patterning of a silicon nitride layer defining the active device regions, and after the growth of a thick native silicon dioxide film in the field regions. Note how the oxide grows laterally under the nitride mask leading to what is called a bird's peak profile at the edges. (*b*) After formation of the *n*-channel layer for the depletion-mode *n*-channel MOSFETs. (*c*) After deposition and patterning of the *n*-type polycrystalline silicon (poly-Si) gate material. Note that the enhancement-mode device (the one on the left) has a relatively short, wide gate, while the depletion-mode device (the one on the right) has a much longer, narrower gate. Note also that the *n*-type poly-Si also makes contact directly to the silicon between the two devices. The region where it makes contact will eventually serve as both the drain of the enhancement-mode device and the source of the depletion-mode device, as is seen in the next frame, and as needed to form the depletion-mode load nMOS inverter circuit (see Fig. 15.11).

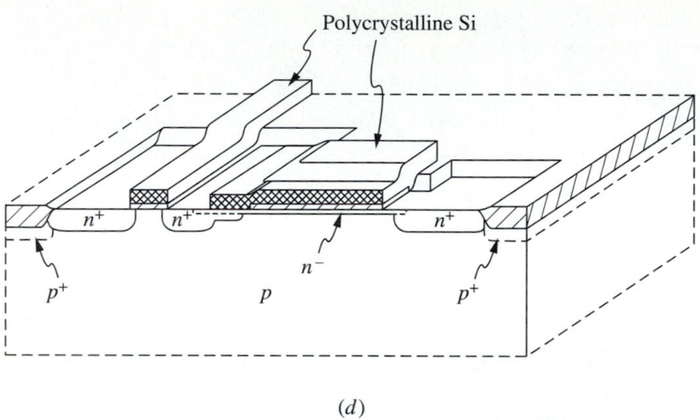

(*d*)

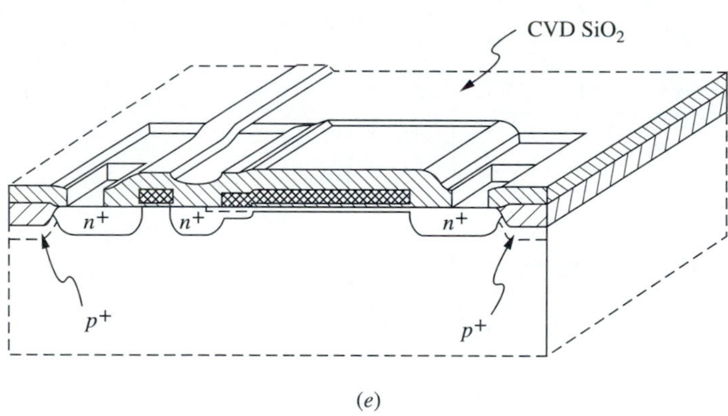

(*e*)

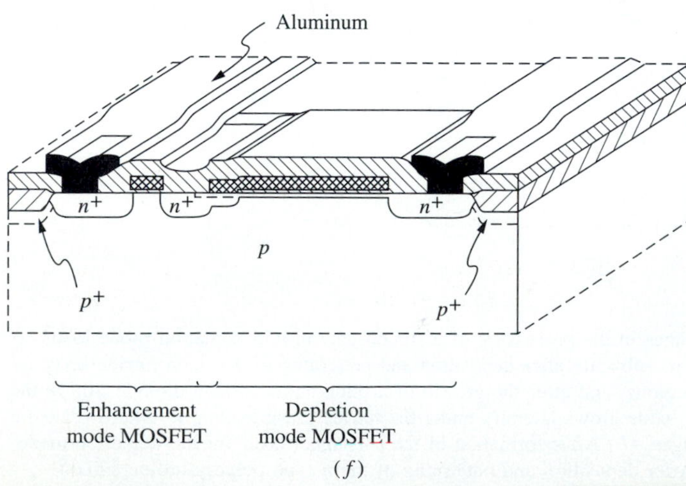

(*f*)

FIGURE G.11 d, e, f
(*d*) After formation of the n^+ source and drain regions of the MOSFETs. (*e*) After deposition of a thick oxide layer by chemical vapor deposition and formation of the contact openings, or "vias." (*f*) A completed inverter stage.

Step 7. Grow a thin oxide layer on the exposed silicon surfaces. This oxide will be the gate oxide so its thickness is critical and is determined by the target gate oxide thickness (typically a few hundred Angstroms or less).

Step 8. Photolithographically etch openings in the gate oxide where contact is desired between the polycrystalline silicon (to be deposited later) and the silicon using Mask #3. Remove the photoresist and clean the wafer.

Step 9. Deposit a film of n-type polycrystalline silicon over the entire top wafer surface. This material's primary purpose is to serve as the gate "metal"; it is also used as an interconnect metal in some regions where having a relatively high resistance wire is not a problem.

Step 10. Photolithographically etch-pattern the polycrystalline silicon film using Mask #4 (see Fig. G.11*c*). This is a relatively important step because it determines the channel length and thus must be carefully controlled. Remove the photoresist and clean the wafer.

Step 11. Form the source and drain regions by ion implanting arsenic into the top surface of the wafer. The field oxide and the polycrystalline silicon gate patterns will protect the regions that should not be implanted (see Fig. G.11*d*). Using the gate itself as the mask defining the edges of the source and drain regions guarantees that the structures will be precisely aligned—the so-called self-alignment feature of this process. This is illustrated in Fig. G.11*d*. After implantation the wafer can be annealed for a brief period at elevated temperature to remove damage introduced during the implantation process. Using arsenic as the implant species means that there will be less lateral diffusion of the source and drain regions under the gate during this step than if the faster diffusing dopant phosphorus had been used.

Step 12. Deposit a layer of silicon dioxide over the entire surface using a chemical vapor deposition (CVD) technique. This provides an insulating layer that is compatible with the underlying structure, yet does not require going to high temperatures which might cause further lateral diffusion of the source and drain regions under the gate.

Step 13. Etch contact openings through the last oxide layer and down to the source, drain, and gate regions using Mask #5. Remove the photoresist and clean the wafer (see Fig. G.11*e*).

Step 14. Vacuum-deposit (i.e., evaporate) a layer of aluminum over the entire wafer surface.

Step 15. Photolithographically pattern the aluminum layer using a weak acid solution and Mask #6. Remove the photoresist, clean the wafer, and heat the wafer to approximately 450°C in an inert atmosphere for a few minutes to "form" the contact.* The devices are essentially complete at this stage; they are illustrated in Fig. G.11*f*.

---

*The process of forming a contact was introduced in Step 15 of the *p-n* junction isolated bipolar process.

Step 16 and beyond. Upper levels of metal interconnects and dielectric insulating layers are added and the devices are tested and packaged following the same procedures described for the *p-n* junction isolated bipolar process earlier in this Appendix (see Steps 16 and 17 of that process).

Before leaving our discussion of the nMOS process it is interesting to compare it to the junction isolated bipolar process. As presented, the number of mask levels was very similar (seven for the bipolar process through Step 15, versus six for the nMOS process), but the bipolar process was actually considerably more complicated. It involved the use of more doped regions with ohmic contacts being made to both *n*- and *p*-type regions, and more importantly it involved the use of epitaxy. The processing advantage of the nMOS process, coupled with the lower power dissipation levels achieved by MOS logic circuits compared to bipolar logic circuits, were primary factors in the tremendous impact MOS circuitry has had in the digital logic and memory fields. The relatively lower power levels meant that it was feasible to put many thousands of logic gates and/or memory cells on a single integrated circuit chip, and the relatively simpler processing meant that it was possible to accomplish the task.

G.2.4 A Silicon-Gate CMOS Process

The highest-performance MOSFET circuits require both *n*- and *p*-channel devices, and fabricating both types of device on the same substrate involves a more complex processing sequence. The increased complexity is well worth the trouble, however, because of the greatly reduced power dissipation of CMOS logic circuits, the higher gain of CMOS analog circuitry, and the high speed of CMOS in both analog and digital applications.

The process described below is called an "*n*-well" process for reasons that will become clear. The process is illustrated in Fig. G.12.

Starting wafer. *p*-type silicon, lightly doped, thoroughly cleaned.

Step 1. Oxidize the wafer.

Step 2. Etch openings through the oxide on the top surface of the wafer photolithographically using Mask #1. Remove the photoresist and clean the wafer.

Step 3. Heavily dope the exposed surface area *n*-type by ion implantation and then diffuse the *n*-type dopant into the wafer at high temperature. This step forms the *n*-type wells (see Fig. G.12*a*), which is where the *p*-channel devices will be fabricated. The oxide functions as the implantation mask.

Step 4. Remove the oxide from the wafer and regrow a thin oxide over the entire surface. Then deposit a thicker film of silicon nitride over the top wafer surface.

Step 5. Etch-pattern the silicon nitride using Mask #2. Remove the photoresist and clean the wafer. This step defines the active device areas (see Fig. G.12*b*).

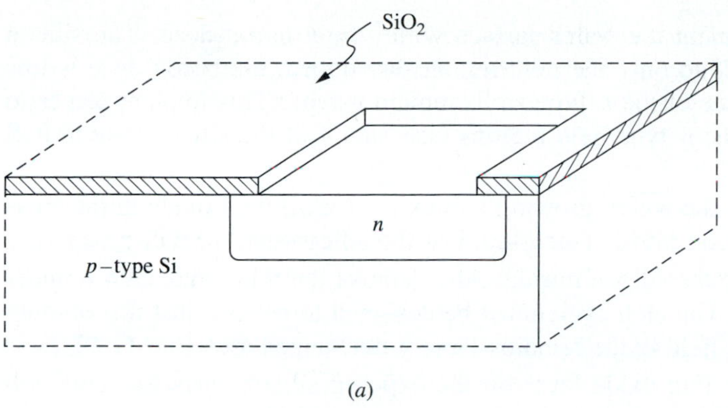

(*a*)

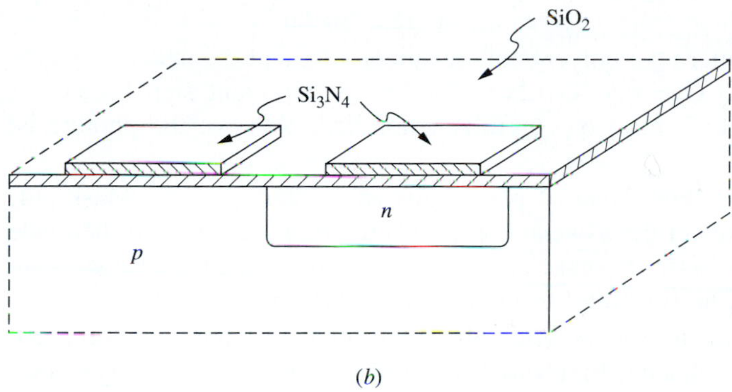

(*b*)

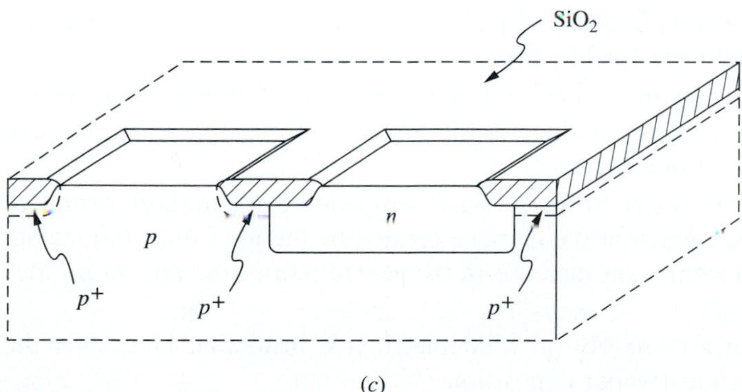

(*c*)

FIGURE G.12 a, b, c
Selected stages in the processing of a CMOS inverter stage using an n-well (or n-tub) silicon gate process: (*a*) The starting p-type wafer after formation of the n-wells where the p-channel MOSFETs will be fabricated. (*b*) After deposition and patterning of the silicon nitride regions defining the active device areas and the field region. (*c*) After p-doping of the field regions and growth of the field oxide.

Step 6. Ion implant the wafer surface with a light boron dose. The silicon nitride acts as a mask so only the field regions are doped; the boron dose is low enough that the surface of the n-type wells remain n-type. This implant serves to inhibit inversion of the p-type field regions (see Step 4 of the silicon-gate nMOS process description).

Step 7. Oxidize the wafer, growing a thick ($\approx 1\ \mu$m) field oxide in the areas not covered with silicon nitride (see Step 5 of the silicon-gate nMOS process).

Step 8. Remove the silicon nitride. Also remove the thin oxide grown under the nitride in Step 4. The etch cycle must be designed to remove just this amount of oxide so the thick field oxide remains largely unchanged (see Fig. G.12*c*).

Step 9. Grow a thin oxide layer on the exposed silicon surfaces. This will be the gate oxide so its thickness must be precisely controlled.

Step 10. Deposit n-doped polycrystalling silicon over the entire wafer surface. This polycrystalline silicon serves as the gate "metal."

Step 11. Etch pattern the polycrystalline silicon film and the underlying gate oxide using Mask #3 (see Fig. G.12*d*). This is an important step because it defines the gate length; it must be carefully controlled. Remove the photoresist and clean the wafer.

Step 12. Apply a thick layer of photoresist and pattern it using Mask #4. This pattern should protect the n-wells except where ohmic contact will be made to them. *Note:* It is necessary to make ohmic contact to the wells because we want to be able to connect the substrates to the p-channel MOSFETs to their sources.

Step 13. Ion-implant a heavy dose of arsenic producing the n^+ source and drain regions of the n-channel FET's and n^+ contact regions in the n-type (see Fig. G.12*e*). Remove the photoresist and clean the wafer.

Step 14. Apply another thick layer of photoresist and pattern it using Mask #5. This pattern is the complement of Mask #4, so only the n-wells are exposed (but not the n^+ contact implanted in them).

Step 15. Ion-implant the wafer with a heavy dose of boron to create the source and drain regions of the p-channel MOSFET's (see Fig. G.12*f*). Remove the photoresist and clean the wafer.

Step 16. Raise the wafer to an elevated temperature for a short period of time, sufficient to repair much of the damage created by the ion implantations but so much as to cause a significant increase in the penetration of the dopant profiles into the surface.

Step 17. Deposit a relatively thick silcon dioxide insulating layer over the entire wafer using chemical vapor deposition.

Step 18. Use Mask #6 to photolithographically etch openings through the oxide layer where contacts will be made to the sources and drains, and to the n-wells. Remove the photoresist and clean the wafer.

Step 19. Vacuum deposit a layer of aluminum over the entire wafer surface.

Step 20. Photolithographically pattern the aluminum using Mask #7. Remove the photoresist, clean the wafer, and form the contacts. The devices are essentially complete at this stage (see Fig. G.12*g*).

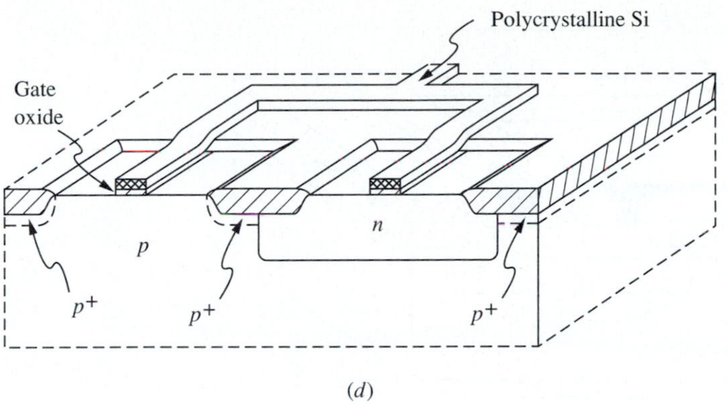

(d)

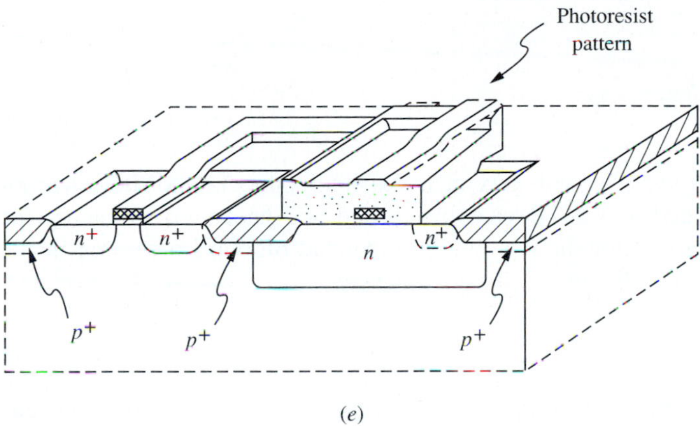

(e)

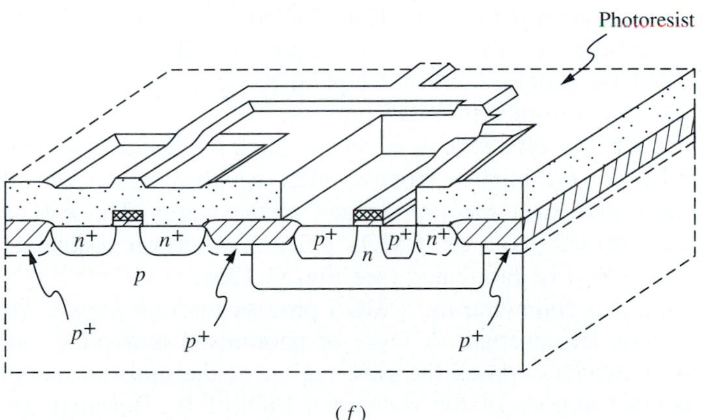

(f)

FIGURE G.12 d, e, f
(*d*) After deposition and patterning of the polycrystalline silicon gate regions. Note that the pattern also interconnects the gates of the two devices as required by the CMOS inverter circuit (see Fig. 15.12). (*e*) With the photoresist pattern protecting the *p*-channel devices in place and after implementation of the *n*-channel MOSFET source and drain regions, and of the contact region to the *p*-channel MOSFET substrate region. (*f*) After implementation of the *p*-channel MOSFET source and drain regions, shown with the photoresist mask still in place.

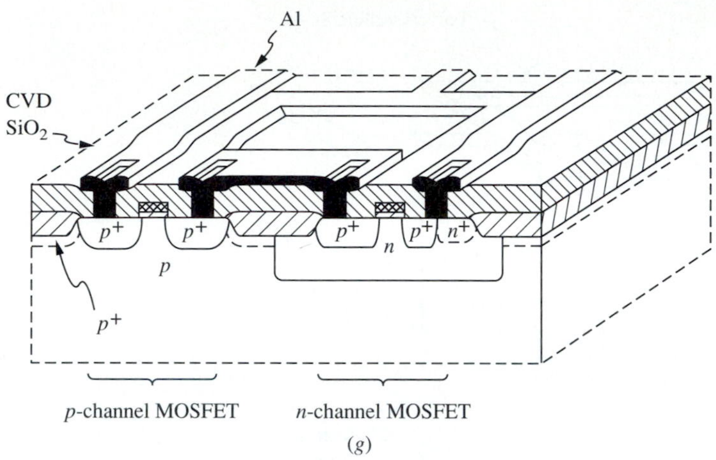

FIGURE G.12 g
(*g*) A completed CMOS inverter stage.

Step 21 and beyond. Upper levels of metal interconnects and dielectric insulating layers are added and the devices are tested and packaged following the same procedures described for the *p-n* junction isolated bipolar process earlier in this Appendix (see Steps 16 and 17 of that process).

G.2.5 BiCMOS

The ultimate silicon technology in terms of flexibility is one that gives the circuit designer access to both *n*- and *p*-channel MOSFETs and both *npn* and *pnp* bipolar transistors. Process sequences that do this are called BiMOS or BiCMOS processes, and many have been developed. The example we will consider here is a mix of elements from the junction isolated bipolar process and the Si-gate CMOS process. It is called a twin-tub BiCMOS process.

The process begins with a *p*-type silicon wafer in which n^+ buried collector regions are first formed as in the bipolar process, after which a lightly doped *p*-type epitaxial layer is grown over the top surface of the wafer. The *n*-type tubs (i.e., wells) are then formed, as in the CMOS process, wherever *p*-channel MOSFETs and *npn* bipolars will be fabricated (see Fig. G.13*a*).

The processing continues following the CMOS process through Step 8. At this point several new steps are inserted. A layer of photoresist is applied and patterned using Mask #3, which exposes the base region of the *npn* transistors and the channel and contact regions of the *n*-channel MOSFETs. Boron is ion implanted into the exposed regions using two implant cycles. The dose and energy of the first implant cycle are chosen to give the desired *npn* base region depth and doping level. The second is a more shallow implant chosen to adjust the doping near the surface to yield the desired *n*-channel MOSFET threshold voltage.

The photoresist is then removed, the wafer is cleaned, and the processing continues with Step 9 of the CMOS process, in which the thin gate oxide is

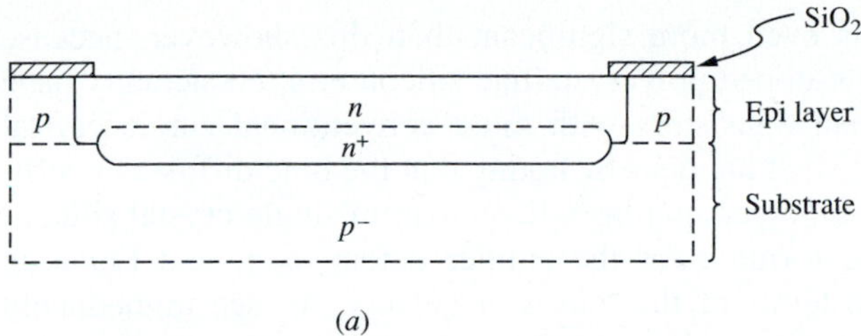

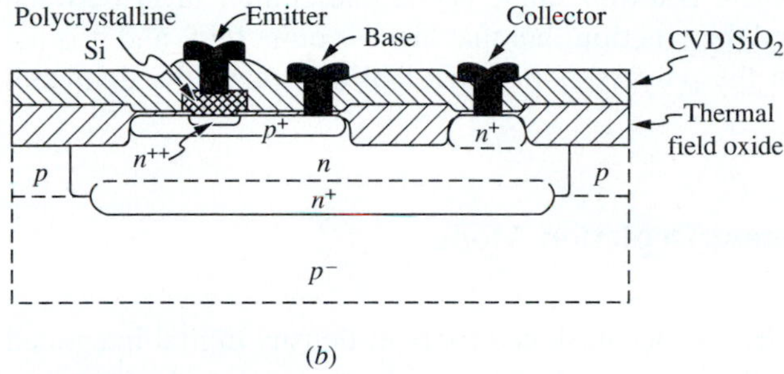

FIGURE G.13
Cross-sections at two stages in the fabrication of an *npn* bipolar transistor in a twin-tub BiCMOS process, in which bipolar and MOS transistors are fabricated simultaneously: (*a*) After formation of the n^+ buried collector regions, growth of the *p*-type epitaxial layer for the *n*-channel MOSFETs (not shown in this figure; see Fig. G.12*a*), and implantation of the *n*-type wells (tubs) for then *npn* bipolar transistors (and the *p*-channel MOSFETs, which are not shown in this figure; see Fig. G.12*a*). The substrate is a *p*-type silicon wafer; (*b*) the completed *npn* bipolar transistor structure.

grown. After this step, another new step is added in which openings are photolithographically cut (using Mask #4) through the gate oxide where *npn* emitters are to be formed. Then the CMOS process is picked up again at Step 10 and followed through to the end. The mask used to pattern the polycrystalline material (it is now Mask #5) is now designed so that polycrystalline silicon remains in the openings cut through the gate oxide, as well as in the gate regions. The polycrystalline silicon that is in contact with the single crystal silicon through these openings will form the emitters of the *npn* transistors, as we will discuss in the next paragraph. The masks are also designed to shield the bipolar transistors during implantation of the sources and drains of both the *n*-channel and *p*-channel MOSFETs. The final bipolar transistor structure is shown in Fig. G.13*b*.

A novel feature of this process is that the *npn* transistor emitters are formed where the *n*-doped polycrystalline silicon makes contact with the *p*-type base regions. There is a slight diffusion of phosphorus from the heavily doped polycrystalline silicon which converts a thin layer of the crystalline silicon underneath it to heavily *n*-type, thereby forming the n^+-*p*-*n* structure we need. The role of the polycrystalline silicon is even more significant than this, however, because *npn* transistors with heavily *n*-doped polycrystalline silicon emitters actually have higher current gains (β) than transistors with more conventional single crystal emitters. We can understand what happens by noting that the hole diffusion coefficient (D_h) is much smaller in polycrystalline silicon than in single crystal silicon. Recalling Equation 8.7, the formula for the emitter defect (δ_E), and Equation 8.17a, the formula for β in terms of the transistor defects, we see immediately that making D_h smaller makes δ_E smaller and β larger. The situation is somewhat more complicated because there is a thin single crystalline emitter layer between the polycrystalline region and the junction, but that layer is quite thin, and it is the hole diffusion coefficient in the polycrystalline material that plays the dominant role.

G.2.6 GaAs Enhancement/Depletion Mode Digital Logic Process

The process we will discuss here is one designed for high-density digital integrated circuit applications. A variety of processes have also been developed to produce GaAs microwave analog integrated circuits; these processes often involve the use of epitaxial layers, tend to be more complicated, and are not intended for large scale integration; i.e. they are used for small and medium scale integrated circuits. The digital logic process that follows is used for large scale or very large scale integrated circuits (LSI or VLSI), as were the silicon processes described earlier.

Starting wafer. GaAs, undoped semi-insulating, thoroughly cleaned.

Step 1. Deposit a silicon dioxide film over entire wafer surface.

Step 2. Etch openings through the oxide photolithography using Mask #1. The FETs will be fabricated in these open areas. Remove the photoresist and clean the wafer.

Step 3. Use ion implantation to dope the exposed GaAs areas *n*-type with silicon (see Fig. G.14*a*). The depth and dosage of this implant is selected to yield the desired enhancement-mode device channel profile.

Step 4. Apply more photoresist and pattern it using Mask #2. This pattern protects the enhancement-mode device channel, leaving only the depletion mode FET channel regions exposed.

Step 5. Ion-implant the *n*-type wafer with Si. The depth and dose of the implant are selected to yield the desired depletion-mode device channel profile (see Fig. G.14*b*).

Step 6. Remove the photoresist and clean the wafers. Deposit the gate metal over the wafer top surface. A refractory metal such as tungsten or tantalum silicide, that will not be effected by any subsequent high temperature processing (e.g., Step 9 below), is used for the gate metal.

Step 7. Photolithographically pattern the gate metal using Mask #3 and a dry etch process. Remove the photoresist and clean the wafer (see Fig. G.14*c*).

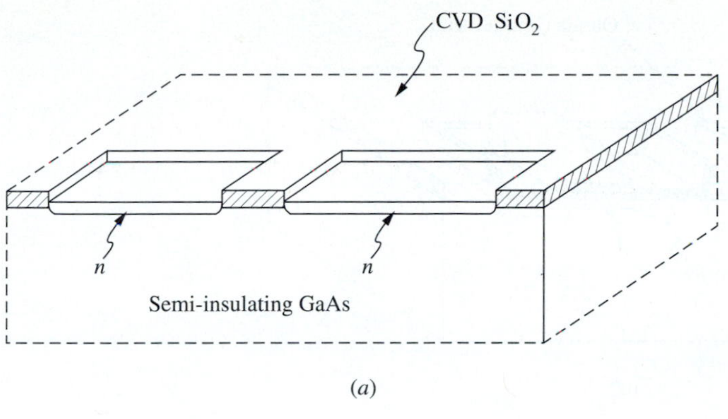

(*a*)

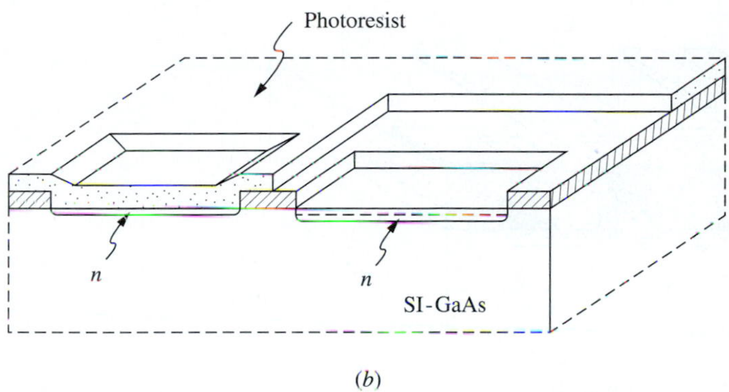

(*b*)

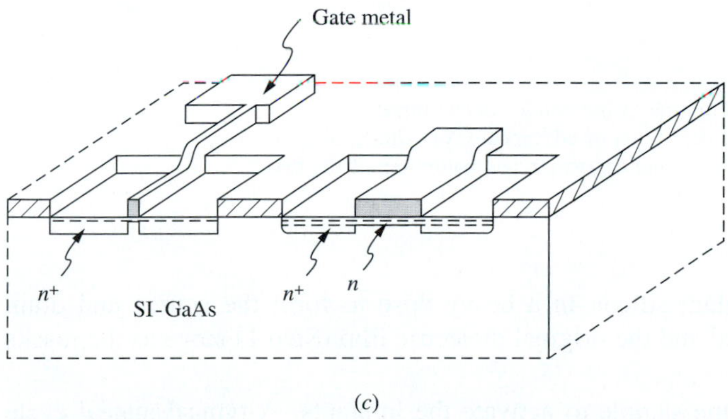

(*c*)

FIGURE G.14 a, b, c
Selected stages in the fabrication of enhancement and depletion mode gallium arsenide MESFETs by a digital integrated circuit process: (*a*) The semi-insulating GaAs starting wafer after deposition and patterning of a CVD silicon dioxide masking layer, and after subsequent ion implantation of silicon to define the active device areas; (*b*) after implantation of additional silicon in the active areas of the depletion-mode MESFETs to adjust the channel doping profile, and thereby adjust the device threshold; (*c*) after deposition and definition of the gate metal, and subsequent high-dose ion implantation of silicon to form the source and drain contact areas.

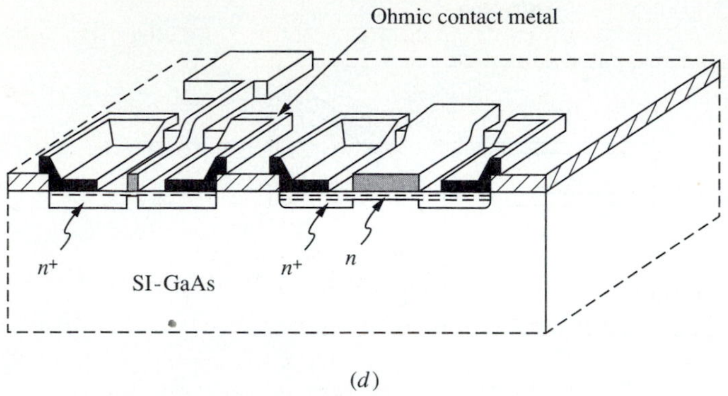

(d)

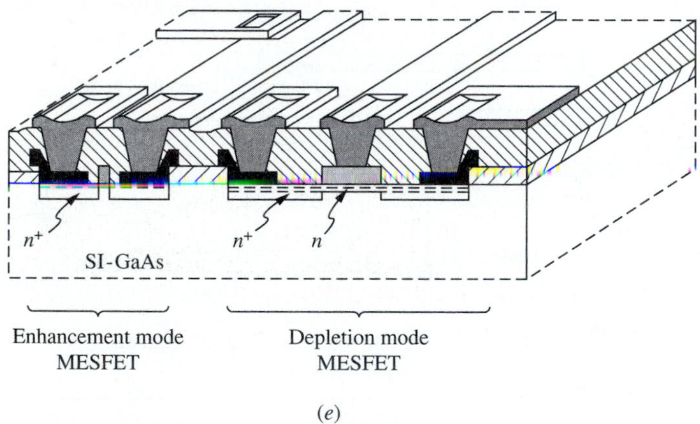

(e)

FIGURE G.14 d, e
(*d*) After deposition and definition of the ohmic contact metal;
(*e*) completed devices after deposition of additional CVD silicon dioxide layer, definition of contact vias, and deposition and patterning of the first metal interconnect layer.

Step 8. Ion implant silicon in a heavy dose to form the source and drain regions. The gate metal and the original dielectric film (Step 1) serve as the masks (see Fig. G.14*c*).

Step 9. Anneal the sample to activate the implants. A typical anneal cycle is 30 min at 850°C, with 5-min heat-up and cool-down periods.

Step 10. Coat the wafers with photoresist and pattern using Mask #4, which opens areas for the source and drain ohmic contact metal. Deposit the ohmic contact metal over the wafer and pattern by lift-off, i.e., by subsequently removing the photoresist and thereby also removing the metal over it (see Fig. G.14*d*). To be successful this requires that the metal be deposited using a technique that only coats the top surfaces of the photoresist pattern and not the edges. Clean the wafers.

Step 11. Sinter (i.e., form) the source and drain ohmic contacts. (See Step 5 in the junction isolated bipolar process.)

Step 12. Deposit silicon dioxide or silicon nitride over the entire wafer surface.

Step 13. Photolithographically open (using Mask #5) holes through this dielectric layer to expose the source and drain ohmic contact metal and the gate metal.

Step 14. Deposit the first layer of interconnect metal (Al).

Step 15. Photolithographically pattern the first interconnect metal layer using Mask #6 (see Fig. G.14*e*).

Step 16 and beyond. The processing of the upper levels of metal interconnect and dielectric insulation, and the final testing and packaging follow exactly the same steps as in the junction isolated bipolar process (see Steps 16 and beyond in that process description).

This process relies heavily on techniques and procedures developed originally for use with silicon so it is not surprising that it looks very similar to a silicon process. There are significant differences, however. In particular, there is no use of a native oxide such as SiO_2 on silicon, and all doping is done by ion implantation; solid state diffusion is not used. Furthermore, the circuit is built on an undoped, semi-insulating substrate, so isolation problems are greatly reduced. The availability of semi-insulating substrates is an important advantage when trying to achieve very high-frequency operation.

INDEX